P9-EDX-386

ALSO BY LES BROWN

Televi$ion: The Business Behind the Box

Electric Media

The New York Times Encyclopedia of Television

Keeping Your Eye on Television

Fast Forward: The New Television and American Society

Les Brown's

Encyclopedia of Television

3RD EDITION

LES BROWN'S

Encyclopedia of Television

3RD EDITION

 Gale Research Inc. • DETROIT • LONDON

Les Brown

Neil R. Schlager, *Project Coordinator*

Mary Beth Trimper, *Production Manager*
Mary Winterhalter, *Production Assistant*

Arthur Chartow, *Art Director*
Yolanda Y. Latham, *Keyliner*
Kathleen A. Mouzakis, *Page Design*

Technical photos on cover taken by Robert J. Huffman
on location at WTVS-Channel 56 studios in Detroit, MI.

Special acknowledgment is due to
Christa Brelin, Christine B. Jeryan, and Jeffrey Muhr
for their editorial assistance,
and to the Research and Permissions
departments of Gale Research Inc. for their help

This book is printed on acid-free paper that meets the minimum
requirements of American National Standard for Information
Sciences—
Permanence Paper for Printed Library Materials, ANSI Z39.48-1984. 

Library of Congress Cataloging-in-Publication Data

Brown, Les, 1928-
[Encyclopedia of television]
Les Brown's encyclopedia of television. – 3rd ed.
p. cm.
Includes bibliographical references and index.
ISBN 0-8103-8871-5 : $39.95
1. Television broadcasting–Encyclopedias. I. Title. II. Title:
Encyclopedia of television.
PN1992.18.B7 1992
791.45'03–dc20 91-48157
CIP

Printed in the United States of America

Pulished in the United States by Gale Research Inc.
Published simultaneously in the United Kingdom
by Gale Research International Limited
(An affiliated company of Gale Research Inc.)

For the baby—our first grandchild—
who will be born to Jessica and Brent at about the time
this book arrives.

CONTRIBUTORS

Foreword: Ron Miller
Public television: James Day
Law and regulation: Andrew Schwartzman
Television technology: Peter Caranicas
Ratings and business: Jack Loftus
Programs: Catherine Williams
News and documentary: Morton Silverstein
Cable television: John Flinn
International television: Paul Nicholson
Canada: Carrie Hunter
Companies: Al Jaffe
Sports: Warren Boorom
Writers, producers and directors: Bob Knight

Copy coordinator and head researcher: Devonne Johnson
Planning coordinator and contributor: Michael Burgi
General contributor: Rich Katz
Researcher: Claudia Hirsch

Ron Miller is a nationally syndicated TV critic for the *San Jose Mercury News.*

James Day is professor emeritus of Brooklyn College and former president of public television stations WNET New York and KQED San Francisco. For several years he conducted a public television interview show, *Day At Night.*

Andrew Schwartzman, an expert in communications law, has been executive director of the Media Access Project, a public interest law firm in Washington, D.C., since 1978.

Peter Caranicas, former editor of *Videography* and *Millimeter* magazines, is currently editor of the technical trade journal, *Backstage/Shoot.*

Jack Loftus is a former television editor of *Variety,* executive editor of *Channels Magazine* and founding editor of the newsletter *Market Shares.* He is currently a vice president of Nielsen Media Research Inc.

Catherine Williams is a former Canadian journalist who is program director for the Center for Communication.

Morton Silverstein is a noted producer of news documentaries who has worked for NBC, CBS and public television.

John Flinn is former editor of *Channels Magazine* and currently managing editor of *Cablevision* magazine.

Paul Nicholson is executive editor of *Television Business International,* which is published in London.

Carrie Hunter, a former Canadian journalist, was the founder of the Banff International Television Festival and its managing director for 12 years.

Al Jaffe is former editor of *TV/Radio Age,* a position he held for 22 years.

Warren Boorom is a television consultant after a long career as vice president of sales for ABC-TV. For several years he has organized the sports seminars for the Internaional Radio and Television Society.

Bob Knight was a television reporter and reviewer for *Variety* for 22 years and its resident expert on programming.

Michael Burgi is a reporter for *Multichannel News* and a former assistant editor of *Channels Magazine.*

Rich Katz is a reporter for *Cablevision* magazine and a former assistant editor of *Channels Magazine.*

The author is profoundly indebted to the Center for Communication in New York; its managing director, Irina Posner; and her associates, Marilyn Jessup, Pauline Freedman, and Jodi Goalstone, all of whom lent considerable moral and material support. The

Center not only served as the base of operations for this encyclopedia but was an invaluable information resource. Three of the Center's interns were also helpful: Gurdon J. Blackwell, Anne Green, and Elana Mintz.

The author is also grateful for varied informational contributions from Dawson Nail of *Communications Daily,* Rita Silverstein of *Entertainment Weekly,* Kevin Pearce of *Countryside,* William Sloan of the Museum of Modern Art's Film and Video Library, Michael J. Berlin of Boston University, Ray Weiss, formerly of NBC News, and Jay McMullen, formerly of CBS News.

Much appreciated also was the gracious cooperation of Peggy Hubble and Katherine McQuay of NBC; Sherry Rollins and Jeff Cusson of ABC; Roy Brunett, Tom Goodman, Ed Devlin, and Ann Morfogen of CBS; and Alyssa Levy, Juli Mortz and Lisa Dallos of CNN.

Finally, but far from least, the author thanks his dear wife, Jean, for as always sustaining him through it all.

CONTENTS

HIGHLIGHTS OF THIS EDITION

The third edition of *Les Brown's Encyclopedia of Television*, like its predecessors, is a one-stop source for information on the television industry. Unlike other sources that concentrate on a single aspect of the field—usually either biographical or programming information—*Les Brown's Encyclopedia* provides comprehensive coverage of all facets of the TV industry, both on screen and behind the scenes.

NEW FEATURES

The third edition of *Les Brown's Encyclopedia of Television* is significantly expanded and updated, reflecting the enormous changes that occurred in the television industry in the past decade. This edition contains several new features, including:

- A general subject index
- 900 new entries
- Extensive revision of entries from the second edition
- An expanded Bibliography
- New and updated tables in the Appendix

SCOPE

With the 900 entries appearing for the first time in this edition, *Les Brown's Encyclopedia of Television* now includes almost 3,000 entries on notable people, programs, and companies as well as legal, regulatory, and technological issues. Its scope is historic, ranging from the birth of the industry to the present. Also, the *Encyclopedia*'s coverage extends beyond the U.S. television industry to the rest of the world, providing information on major markets in North and South America, Europe, Asia, Africa, and Australia.

FOREWORD

In the 10 years since the last edition *Les Brown's Encyclopedia of Television,* it has become increasingly clear that such a reference work isn't just a guide to the medium, but is also a road map tracing pathways of American culture in the second half of the 20th century.

Most living Americans have grown up in the TV age, so thumbing through the pages of the *Encyclopedia of Television* is like leafing through a high school yearbook filled with familiar names and places. Now that we derive much of our information about the world from television it stands to reason that we remember most of the people and events of our time the way we saw them first—as images on TV.

That idea struck me as I watched former President Richard Nixon celebrate his 79th birthday on TV—not by blowing out candles on a birthday cake, but by plugging his latest book on CNN's *Larry King Live.* One of the most controversial figures in American political history was busy recasting his image to that of distinguished elder statesman, once again with the help of the medium that chronicled his rise to national prominence in the 1950s and fall from grace in the 1970s. Indeed, he's a man virtually defined by the TV images he has left in the collective memory of most Americans.

Wanted or not, we've locked those memories away: the young, earnestly sincere Nixon of the "Checkers" speech; the nervous, perspiring Nixon of the Kennedy-Nixon debates; the grim, besieged president of the Watergate years, trying to save himself with direct TV appeals to the public; the broken, emotion-choked Nixon waving farewell to the White House staff in 1974 as he left office in disgrace; maybe even a stray memory of a sublimely ridiculous Nixon saying "Sock it to me!" on *Rowan and Martin's Laugh-In.*

That's the nature of television: It keeps on keeping on through endless reruns until the persistent images finally are absorbed into our collective memory banks. Only in recent years have we begun to appreciate the emotional hold our TV memories can have on us. When TV comedy queen Lucille Ball died in 1989, the enormous outpouring of national grief was the kind normally reserved for heads of state. The nearly 40 years Lucy had spent in our living rooms had left America's memory banks overflowing with affection.

The persistence of TV images and their capacity for forming national attitudes is awe-inspiring. After TV cameras caught Gerald Ford stumbling in public, those video clips were seen so often that one of the most athletic of U.S. presidents is now mostly remembered as the clumsiest. General Norman Schwarzkopf's forceful presence at TV news briefings is the principal reason he is remembered as the symbol of American resolve in the Persian Gulf War.

There's great promise for enriching our culture as we learn how to make TV images more evocative, but equally great potential for misusing the phenomenal persistence of TV memories. Lately, shrewd merchandisers have been finding ways to milk these memories for profit. It began with TV recycling TV: those nostalgic "reunion" movies at ratings sweeps times. Now it's a full-blown trend for movie theaters. When Paramount releases, in the same month, a new *Star Trek* film and a big budget movie based on *The Addams Family,* the studio is pushing buttons that tap our collective memory. It knows that millions of movie-goers are predisposed to like these movies because they're so fond of the perpetually recycled TV shows that spawned them.

Our culture won't suffer permanent damage from another *Brady Bunch* TV reunion or an *Addams Family II* at the movies. But as we enter an era of computerized technology that threatens to make TV an even more pervasive part of our lives than it is now, it's fretful to imagine that somebody might be hatching some diabolical new plan to manipulate our stored memories.

The real challenge for the 1990s may be to persuade the powers behind the medium to be more creative—and responsible—while concocting our future TV memories. After all, these memories are likely to be with us well into the 21st century.

Ron Miller

INTRODUCTION

Between editions of this encyclopedia the 1980s happened. For television the 1980s were a turbulent time, like no decade before, with wild expansion and manic consolidation, propelled first by technology and deregulation, and then by Reaganomics, leveraged buyouts, globalization, and swashbuckling empire-builders. Looking back now from the 1990s, which are well underway, it is clear that the television we grew up on is gone forever, and that something quite new is evolving.

The living-room set that today can receive somewhere between 30 and 70 channels may well be the same appliance that for so many years brought in only three networks, PBS, and one or two independent stations. On its face, the revolution has meant only more television, more pictures with sound on the home screen. But the immutable set belies what has occurred behind the picture tube these last 10 years—the stormy changes in the structure and economy of the industry and, perhaps more importantly, in its value system. Moreover, the enduring old set belies the cultural change that has taken place in the living room itself, a change in our expectations of television and the way we watch it, in the different kinds of images and language we accept from the tube, and in our concession to the idea of paying for some kinds of television service. For all that is to be enjoyed from having a multitude of choices on the screen, we may yet think back fondly to a time when watching television from a limited program menu provided us a shared national experience.

The 1980s were a watershed. Cable, in its rapid spread to 60 percent of U.S. homes, produced a rainstorm from space of some 50 satellite-distributed networks, including a number of pay channels. It also inspired the building of new UHF stations around the country, which, as it happened, led to the creation of the Fox network, the first successful challenger to ABC, CBS and NBC. VCRs, meanwhile, changed the life-styles of young people on Saturday nights, and the remote-control tuner altered the way most people watch television. All the new television options, in making ever larger claims on the audience, have devastated the economy of the three major networks that once had ruled the airwaves. In 1991, when for the first time all three lost money, it became clear that the established practices of the networks were seriously out of date.

In the mid-1980s, on another front, a seductive Wall Street instrument, the junk bond, helped change who owned television. In the giddy business climate that made a virtue of debt—and fostered hostile takeovers and leveraged buyouts (along with friendly mergers)—the whole television industry, cable included, was suddenly on sale. The activity of buying media companies was sped on by deregulation, which among other things permitted a promiscuous trading of television licenses, making station properties more attractive than ever to speculators. As for financing, junk bonds provided the easy means. Timing also contributed to the frenzy, since the spree occurred just when the television pioneers who had built the great networks and station groups were retiring, dying off, or preparing to "cash out." The changing of the guard was fairly complete in the 1980s; the new television had a whole new cast of characters, most of whom were indifferent to the medium's professional traditions and viewed broadcasting as essentially a business, like any other.

A number of venerable institutions vanished in the turmoil of the decade: RCA, Metromedia, Teleprompter, Storer, Taft, RKO General, Golden West, Field, and even NBC Radio, the original American network. In mid-decade, all three of the big networks changed hands and had to adapt to austere new corporate cultures. Meanwhile, such entrepreneurial high-rollers as Ted Turner and Rupert Murdoch ranged over the new landscape, changing almost at their whim, in a scant few years, the industry that William S. Paley, Gen. David Sarnoff, and Leonard Goldenson had helped build over the previous 50. Meanwhile, Hollywood, a name as American as America itself, came increasingly under the ownership of foreign companies, mainly Japanese.

Despite the collapse of the business boom in 1990, the television revolution rolls on, as it must, because technology does not stop for a breath. Before the end of this decade, cable will have a channel capacity of 150 or more, whether by means of digital compression or fiber optics. Compression technology will also increase the capacity of satellites, making the delivery of signals covering the country substantially cheaper. These certainties alone are a recipe for radical change. But also, predictably, some form of high-definition television will be accepted by the Federal Communications Commission and vigorously marketed by manufacturers in the mid-1990s; and the convergence of television and computer technologies will continue to bring forth intriguing forms of interactive television that go well beyond pay-per-view—possibly making possible, in this decade, television-on-demand, programming that can be ordered electronically from a catalog, obviating the need for video rental shops. Direct-to-home broadcasting by satellite, known as DBS, has been England's alternative to cable and has active proponents in the U.S. who mean to test it in the 1990s.

Far from a distinctly American experience, the TV revolution is a worldwide phenomenon that, in fact, promises to draw the U.S. industry, previously insular, into the international television sphere. Satellites, showing no respect for national boundaries, are tying the world together. Commercial television, much like the American kind, is epidemic in Western Europe, which until the late 1980s was largely served by state-run public television systems. The proliferation of new commercial channels in Europe, Latin America, and the Pacific Rim has been a boon to American program distributors, since the new channels have relied heavily on U.S. movies and hit television series to fill out their initial schedules. But most foreign networks do best in the ratings with indigenous programs, and the new commercial broadcasters have begun producing—and frequently coproducing in international partnerships—programs of mass-audience appeal. Many of the coproductions involve the U.S. cable networks, which have taken the lead in international television commerce. Increasingly, the major U.S. networks will be forced by their economic circumstances to join in.

The foreign influence on American television is already being felt. Rupert Murdoch's style of tabloid journalism, honed in Australia, has for better or worse inspired the leading program trend of the early 1990s, the exploitative news magazines descended from *A Current Affair. America's Funniest Home Videos,* a big hit on ABC in 1990, was a concept borrowed from the Japanese, while Fox's *America's Most Wanted* was a format that came from England by way of Germany. Over time, with the foreign ownership of such studios as Columbia, MCA, 20th Century-Fox (though Murdoch has become an American citizen), MGM, and MTM, along with a Japanese involvement in Warner Bros., the U.S. television industry that was once American to the core—operating in what had been the world's most self-sufficient television market—is bound to adopt a more worldly view of programming.

The ever-widening dimensions of television increase the scope of this encyclopedia. When it was originally published in 1977 as *The New York Times Encyclopedia of Television,* the work had the luxury of focusing on a stable, prosperous, and fairly orderly television system operating under a set of rules to fulfill the public interest mandate of the Communications Act of 1934. Stations and networks were limited in number by available technology, and by and large they continued what radio began in the 1930s and 1940s in devising entertainment programming for the largest possible audience. By the second edition, published in 1982 under the current title, cable was becoming a force to reckon with, and a raft of new technologies and satellite networks entering the marketplace foreshadowed the revolution. That book is now thoroughly revised, with 900 new entries added, all reflecting the changes wrought by the tempests of the 1980s.

Television is made of so many people and parts that a book such as this, while aspiring to be all-encompassing, could not hope to be so or the writing would never end. For the most part, the selection of entries was made by me, based on my experience in covering television as a journalist since 1953, but I was guided also by a team of experts assembled for this project, many of them former colleagues who have specialized in particular aspects of television. The advisory group, which reviewed with me all the candidates for entries to ensure that nothing vital was left out, also included two former television executives, a producer of news documentaries, and a veteran communications lawyer. The same team contributed to the research and the writing in their areas of expertise, using both primary and secondary sources, principally the trade publications for which several of the journalists work.

In selecting the entries, the overriding criterion in any of the categories was reference value. That was easy enough to determine in matters of law and regulation, technology, history, networks, cable, executives, production companies, producers, writers, foreign systems, news, and sports, but somewhat more difficult in areas of performers and programs. In the main, the performers selected were those who had had starring roles in at least two hit series or for whom television had been a springboard for a larger career. Programs were selected for inclusion on the basis of their great popularity or because they were controversial, innovative, somehow influential, or in some way historically significant.

It is possible, and maybe even necessary, to refer today to the Television That Was, the Television That Is, and a Television That Probably Will Be. These ages of the medium, along with the people, practices, and programs peculiar to each, are part of the mosaic of this book. Past, present, and future (represented by arrived technology) mingle here in an alphabetical system, not too unlike the way old and new programs habitually mingle on the multichannel television screen.

This edition of the encyclopedia is not simply a continuation of the last, because the continuity is so tenuous. There is still a CBS, for example, but it is not the CBS that was. Nor is television the medium we once knew.

Les Brown
December, 1991

ACKNOWLEDGMENTS

Following is a list of the copyright holders who have granted permission to reprint photographs in this book. Every effort has been made to trace copyright, but if omissions have been made, please contact the publisher.

ABC News—Roone Arledge, David Brinkley, Daniel Burke, Sam Donaldson, Hugh Downs, Leonard Goldenson, Herbert Granath, Robert Iger, Peter Jennings, Ted Koppel, Al Michaels, Thomas S. Murphy, Brent Musburger, Diane Sawyer, John Sias, Brandon Stoddard, Richard Wald, Barbara Walters. Photos used courtesy of ABC News. **Act III Productions**—*All in the Family* (Carroll O'Connor, Jean Stapleton), *Designing Women* (cast photo), *Good Times* (Esther Rolle, Jimmie Walker). Photos used courtesy of Act III Productions. **The Estate of Lucille Ball**—Lucille Ball photo used courtesy of Lucie Arnaz. **BBC Lionheart/MGM**—John Reith, *EastEnders, The Singing Detective* photos used courtesy of BBC Lionheart/MGM. **Black Star Productions**—*Eyes on the Prize*/Birmingham, Alabama riots. © Charles Moore. Photo used courtesy of Black Star Productions. **John Blair Communications, Inc.**—James H. Rosenfield photo used courtesy of John Blair Communications, Inc. **Buena Vista Television**—Siskel & Ebert, Richard H. Frank, *Live with Regis and Kathie Lee* (cast photo). All photos used courtesy of Buena Vista Television. **Capital Cities/ABC, Inc.**—*All My Children* © 1991 Capital Cities/ABC, Inc./Cathy Blaivas; *The Day After* © 1991 Capital Cities/ABC, Inc./Dean Williams; *Dynasty* © Capital Cities/ABC, Inc./Chic Donchin; *Moonlighting* © 1991 Capital Cities/ABC/Bob D'Amico; *Roseanne* © 1991 Capital Cities/ABC, Inc./Lynn Goldsmith; *thirtysomething* © Capital Cities/ABC, Inc./Jim Shea; *Winds of War* © 1991 Capital Cities/ABC, Inc./Jim Globus; *The Fugitive* © 1991 Capital Cities/ABC, Inc.; Jacques Cousteau and Lawrence Welk photos © 1991 Capital Cities/ABC. All photos used courtesy of Capital Cities/ABC, Inc. **Children's Television Workshop**—Big Bird and Snuffleupagus (*Sesame Street*) photo used courtesy of Children's Television Workshop. **Chrysalis Visual Programming Limited**—Max Headroom photo. © 1988 Chrysalis Visual Programming Limited. All rights reserved. Used courtesy of Chrysalis Visual Programming Limited. **CBS**—Alistair Cooke photo used courtesy of Alistair Cooke. Ed Bradley, Connie Chung, Walter

Cronkite, Greg Gumbel, Don Hewitt, Andrew Heyward, Charles Kuralt, John Madden, Eric Ober, Charles Osgood, Dan Rather, Andy Rooney, Morley Safer, Bob Simon, Lesley Stahl, Howard Stringer, Pat Summerall, Laurence Tisch, Mike Wallace photos used courtesy of CBS. **CNN**—Larry King, Bernard Shaw, Ted Turner, CNN logo all used courtesy of CNN. **Columbia University Seminars on Media and Society**—Fred W. Friendly photo used courtesy of Fred W. Friendly. **Family Communications, Inc.**—Fred Rogers photo used courtesy of Family Communications, Inc. **FCC (Federal Communications Commission)**—James Quello, Al Sikes photos used courtesy of FCC. **Richard Fulton, Inc.**—Edwin Newman photo used courtesy of Richard Fulton, Inc. **Granada Television**—*Coronation Street* (cast photo), David Plowright photos used courtesy of Granada Television. **Group W Productions**—Larry Fraiberg, Donald H. McGannon, Burt Staniar, Teenage Mutant Ninja Turtles, Derk Zimmerman. All photos used courtesy of Group W Productions. **Henson Productions, Inc.**—Jim Henson, *Fraggle Rock.* © Jim Henson Productions, Inc. Photos used courtesy of Henson Productions, Inc. **HBO**—Edward R. Murrow photo used courtesy of HBO. **King World Productions**—Michael King, Roger King (together); Alex Trebek (*Jeopardy!*); Pat Sajak, Vanna White (*Wheel of Fortune*). Photos used courtesy of King World Productions. **David Kramer & Associates**—Carol Burnett photo used courtesy of Carol Burnett. **London Weekend TV**—*Upstairs, Downstairs* (cast photo) used courtesy of London Weekend TV. **Lorimar Productions**—*Dallas* (cast photo) used courtesy of Lorimar Productions and cast members where appropriate. **MacNeil-Lehrer NewsHour**—Robert MacNeil and Jim Lehrer photo used courtesy of *MacNeil-Lehrer NewsHour.* **MCA Inc.**—Milton Berle, Morton Downey, Jr., *Leave It to Beaver* (cast photo), *Murder She Wrote* (Angela Lansbury), *Wagon Train* (cast photo). © Universal Pictures, a Division of Universal City Studios, Inc. Photos used courtesy of MCA Publishing Rights, a Division of MCA Inc. **MTM Enterprises, Inc.**—Mary Tyler Moore, *Lou Grant* (cast photo) used courtesy of MTM Enterprises, Inc. **MTV Networks**—Tom Freston, Geraldine Laybourne photos used courtesy of MTV Networks. **Multimedia Entertainment**—Sally Jessy Raphael photo used courtesy of Multimedia Entertainment. **NBC**—Phil Donahue photo used courtesy of Phil Donahue. Marv Albert, Lucille Ball and Bob Hope, Tom Brokaw, Johnny Carson, Bob Costas, Linda Ellerbee, Michael Gartner, Alfred Hitchcock, David Letterman, Warren Littlefield, Lorne Michaels, Robert "Shad" Northshield, Tom Rogers, Willard Scott, Maria Shriver, O. J. Simpson, John Cameron Swayze, Brandon Tartikoff, Grant Tinker, Robert Wright. *ALF, The Burning Bed* (Farrah Fawcett, Paul LeMat), *Cheers, The Cosby Show, Diff'rent Strokes, The Golden Girls, Hill Street Blues* (Daniel Travanti, Michael Conrad), *Meet the Press* (Bill Monroe, Golda Meir), *Miami Vice* (Philip Michael Thomas, Don Johnson), *Mr. Peepers* (Wally Cox, Pat Benoit), *Saturday Night Live, Taxi* (Judd Hirsch, Danny DeVito). Photos used courtesy of The National Broadcasting Company, Inc. **New World TV**—*Tour of Duty* (cast photo) used courtesy of New World Television. **Orion Television Entertainment**— *Green Acres* (Eddie Albert, Eva Gabor) photo used courtesy of Orion Television Entertainment. **Paramount Pictures Corporation**—Kerry McCluggage photo used courtesy of Kerry McCluggage. William Shatner photo used courtesy of William Shatner. **Python**

Productions Ltd.—*Monthy Python* (cast photo) used courtesy of Python Productions Ltd. **Aaron Spelling Productions**—Jules Haimovitz, Aaron Spelling photos used courtesy of Aaron Spelling Productions. **Tribune Entertainment Company**—Geraldo Rivera photo used courtesy of Tribune Entertainment Company. **20th Century-Fox Television**—Alan Alda photo used courtesy of Alan Alda; Rupert Murdoch photo used courtesy of Howard J. Rubenstein Associates, Inc.; Tracey Ullman photo used courtesy of Dennis Davidson Associates, Inc.; *M*A*S*H* (cast photo) used courtesy of 20th Century-Fox Television and individual cast members. **USA Network**—Kay Koplovitz photo used courtesy of USA Network. **Warner Bros. Television**—*Murphy Brown* (cast photo), *Night Court* (cast photo). © 1987, 1989 Warner Bros. Inc. All rights reserved. Photos used courtesy of Warner Bros. Television. **Worldvision Enterprises**—Marlo Thomas photo used courtesy of Marlo Thomas.

LES BROWN'S

Encyclopedia of Television

3RD EDITION

AAAA, OR THE 4-A'S (AMERICAN ASSOCIATION OF ADVERTISING AGENCIES) ▶ national organization for ad agencies founded in 1917 to improve agency business and advance the cause of advertising as a whole. Today it has a membership of 385 agencies, all of which must adhere to the 4-A codes for agency service and standards and practices.

AA RATING (AVERAGE AUDIENCE) ▶ a measure of the size of a program's audience; it is expressed as the percentage of all TV households in the survey area tuned to a telecast in the average minute. Thus, an AA rating of 24.2 means that an average of 24.2% of all TV households in the survey area were viewing at any point in the program.

Because the universe is constant—all TV households in the survey area, whether it be the national market or a local one—an AA rating can be translated directly into the number of households that were tuned in. Advertisers usually refer to the AA rating to determine how many people watched their commercials.

The TA (Total Audience) rating differs from the AA in that it represents the total number of *different* homes that watched all or part of a telecast for six minutes or longer. Unlike an AA rating, the TA is not an average but rather is a measure of the cumulative audience—that is, all those who watched some of the program, even if they tuned out.

A comparison of the TA and AA ratings for any given telecast usually indicates how well it was liked. When there is no great disparity between the two rating indices (the TA will always be somewhat larger), it may be concluded that viewers who tuned in enjoyed the program because they remained with it. A wide difference, however suggests that the program did not satisfy viewer expectations.

AARON, JOHN A. (d. 1972) ▶ co-producer with Jesse Zoussmer of Edward R. Murrow's *Person To Person* (1953-60). Earlier he had been a journalist with CBS.

ABC ▶ youngest of the major networks and for most of its formative years the weak sister of the three, although its fortunes began to change in 1976 with a new management team that brought in a rash of hit programs in prime time. ABC used the revenues from prime-time hit series to make major advancements in daytime, news and especially sports. ABC successfully launched NFL football on Monday nights and raised the level of special events coverage with its broadcasts of the Olympic Games.

In January 1986 Capital Cities Communications, a low-profile but well-managed media company, bought ABC for $3.5 billion. Between 1985 and 1986, control of all three networks changed hands (NBC to General

Electric, CBS to the Tisch family and ABC to Cap Cities), but only ABC remained under the control of broadcasters. Before the decade ended, ABC dominated morning programming with *Good Morning America,* Peter Jennings was the No. 1 evening news anchor, and *Nightline* with Ted Koppel was uniquely suited to give the network an edge in covering world events; ABC and CBS were nearly tied for daytime leadership in the ratings, and prime time was a tossup.

For most of the early days of its history, ABC perennially ran last and was forced continually to find new ways to compete. These efforts on several occasions created dramatic changes in television: it was ABC that brought the major Hollywood film studios into TV production, causing all television to jettison live programs for film (later videotape); and it was ABC that opened prime time to participating advertising in the 1960s, signaling the end of program sponsorships.

Even while enjoying extraordinary success, ABC broke new ground in the medium in February 1977 with the unusual scheduling tactic for *Roots,* the 12-hour serialization of the novel by Alex Haley that attracted one of the largest single-night audiences in the history of television (the final episode of *Roots* was eclipsed only by the final episode of *M*A*S*H* in 1983 and the "Who Killed J. R.?" episode of *Dallas* in 1980). By airing the full adaptation over eight consecutive nights, ABC demonstrated that the practice of playing a series in weekly installments was only a tradition and not a television commandment etched in stone.

ABC is the offspring of two government-ordered divestitures, the breakup of NBC's two-network system of radio in 1943 and the divorcement of Paramount Pictures from its theaters division, creating United Paramount Theaters. The newly liberated theater chain and the young network merged in 1953 and proceeded to build up the TV network, scrambling with the equally weak DuMont network for affiliates from the relatively few stations not linked with CBS and NBC. DuMont eventually folded.

The history of ABC has been the history of a struggle for economic survival against the two powerful and well-entrenched networks. ABC was the lone captive of network television's poverty cycle. Having fewer stations than its rivals and fewer powerhouse shows to bring over from radio, it drew smaller audiences and was perpetually on the lean end of what was then called "a 2 1/2 network economy."

ABC survived in those early times on expedient moves and the exploitation of fads. Unable to sign stars, it turned instead to the major film studios for products and made a significant impact in 1955 with shows from Walt Disney and Warner Bros. It also developed an unwanted tradition of bringing in shows that had great appeal one season and very little a season or two later (*Batman,* for instance), the result of aiming them at teenagers, whose tastes are notoriously fickle.

ABC was saved finally by the prime-time access rule, which confined the networks to three hours of programming in the peak hours, forcing them to cut back their schedules by 30 minutes a night in 1971. This enabled ABC to slough off seven failures, shore up its finances and build its evenings around its most dependable programs. Within five years, ABC rocketed into first place.

HISTORY—Edward J. Noble, the maker of Life Savers Candy, created ABC in 1943 when he purchased radio's Blue Network, which NBC was forced to shed. Ten years later, the network entered into a $25 million merger with United Paramount Theaters, whose president, Leonard Goldenson, became president of the new company, AB-PT. (In the late 1960s, the corporate name was changed to American Broadcasting Companies.) Noble became chairman of the finance committee and Robert E. Kintner remained president of the broadcast division.

Goldenson's deal with Disney—his motion picture background paying off—gave the network its first big lift. The first show, *Disneyland* (which later became *The Wonderful World of Disney* when Kintner joined NBC and lured it away), was a substantial hit; and the second, *The Mickey Mouse Club,* created a sensation with children in the early evening.

But ABC's attempt to keep up with its rivals in entertainment as well as news proved costly, and throughout most of the decade of the 1960s the network lost money. The network's financial problems were exacerbated by the need to equip for color in 1965, just after CBS joined NBC as an all-color network.

The enormously expensive conversion to color prompted ABC to sell off some of its properties and its investment in Disneyland, and the hard-pressed company in 1965 agreed to a merger with the giant international conglomerate, ITT. The FCC approved the merger by a 4-3 vote in December 1966, but the Justice Dept. objected. While the merger was bouncing back and forth between government agencies, ITT loaned ABC $25 million to help it through its critical cash shortage. When the FCC again approved the merger, and the Justice Dept. announced its intention to appeal, ITT bowed out and the merger was called off in January 1968.

This made ABC ripe for attempted takeovers. Reclusive billionaire Howard Hughes offered $50 million in 1968 for working control of ABC and was rebuffed. Goldenson was also able to thwart a move for control by industrialist Norton Simon. ABC reorganized the management of its broadcast operations, naming Elton H. Rule president of the network, and raising financing through a convertible bond issue. (The next investor to make an unwanted run at ABC was Loews chairman Laurence Tisch—who later bought CBS—who bought up to 5% of ABC's stock in 1981. Goldenson demanded Tisch sell, and he did.)

Throughout the difficult period, ABC continued to improve its competitive standing in a single program area: sports, with Monday Night Football, *Wide World of Sports* and the Olympics. The aggressive and imaginative leadership of Roone Arledge, president of ABC Sports, was largely the reason; another was the logistical genius of Julius Barnathan, head of engineering and operations who designed and arranged most of the coverage, including the Olympics.

Although ABC had made considerable inroads with its prime-time movies, the 1974 season was a flop. Goldenson and Rule immediately elevated the network's cagiest programmer and strategist, Frederick Pierce, to president of ABC Television. He reversed the network's downward trend and the following year hired away from CBS its program chief, Fred Silverman (who would later go on to run NBC). Together, Silverman and Pierce improved ABC's ratings in the fall of 1975 and then made mid-season changes that shot the network ahead of its rivals.

Pierce also had in his stable of programmers Brandon Stoddard, who joined ABC in 1970 and became president of ABC Motion Pictures in 1979. Under his direction, ABC brought *Roots, The Thorn Birds* and *The Winds of War* to the screen, three of the highest-rated miniseries in the history of television. Pierce was also able to see potential in specialized programming on cable, buying a controlling interest in ESPN soon after its launch in 1979.

By 1984, however, ABC had slipped into third place in the prime-time standings, the overall network economy had turned sour, Pierce had succeeded Rule as president of ABC, and Goldenson was worried. ABC—like CBS and its founding chairman, William S. Paley—was preparing for a time without Goldenson. Pierce was the heir-apparent, but not to Goldenson. Although Pierce deserved credit for much of the network's program success, he had also presided over a bloated staff and spiraling costs. As chronicled in Ken Auletta's book *Three Blind Mice,* by the time Pierce woke up to reality, it was too late. Goldenson had concluded that Pierce was not the right man to lead the company through the minefields of Wall Street and ABC's growing vulnerability to outside takeover.

At that time Thomas S. Murphy, chairman and CEO of Cap Cities Communications, entered the picture. Murphy and his No. 2 in charge of day-to-day operations, Daniel B. Burke, had built their company from a single UHF station in Albany, N.Y., into a formidable media company with revenues of just under $1 billion (about one-quarter those of ABC). It owned seven TV stations, 12 radio outlets, 10 newspapers, 36 specialty magazines, dozens of assorted weeklies and shopping guides and more than 40 cable TV systems. Cap Cities stock, worth under $20 a share in 1974, was valued at $200 a share by the time Murphy and Goldenson sat down to talk in 1984. In addition to being a natural fit—both were broadcasting companies, and Murphy and Goldenson knew and liked each other—a factor favoring a merger was the FCC. The government was easing up on its regulations governing network-station ownership, and de-regulation was the mandate from the Reagan White House. Yet Cap Cities was not Goldenson's first choice. He first approached IBM but was turned down. Once Goldenson and Murphy began talking, it was clear that ABC could not afford to buy Cap Cities, because the stock price was too high. But with ABC stock valued (and clearly underperforming) at under $45 a share, Cap Cities could swallow a company three times its size for an agreed upon price (including warrants) of about $121 a share.

Borrowing the money was not the problem. Holding on to a company saddled with $3.5 billion of debt and vulnerable to an unfriendly takeover was the challenge. To save the deal, Murphy turned to his longtime friend Warren E. Buffett, one of the country's richest men and a Cap Cities stockholder. Buffett put down more than $500 million of his own money, good for 18% of the new company, enough to keep Cap Cities/ABC in friendly hands. The deal was announced in March 1985 and made official on Jan. 3, 1986.

The clash of cultures and management style was immediate. Pierce was asked by Murphy to stay on but in a diminished role as president of the network. Pierce resigned and was immediately replaced by John B. Sias. Sias, who headed Cap Cities' publishing operations, had no television programming experience, but he had a more important asset: he was on the Murphy-Burke team—and they ran a "lean, mean machine," the antithesis of what ABC had become. Cost-cutting led to massive layoffs, as Murphy, Burke and Sias piloted the new company through one of the deepest recessions in the history of television.

ABC CLOSE-UP! ▶ series of news documentaries on ABC that began in 1960 under the sponsorship of Bell & Howell and were produced by an independent company, Bob Drew Associates. The early works were noted for Drew's cinema verite style, evidenced in such works as *Yanki No!* and Nicholas Webster's *Walk in My Shoes.*

When Bell & Howell's association with the series ended, production moved in-house at ABC News, initially under the stewardship of John Secondari and then passing, successively, to Tom Wolfe, Av Westin in 1973, Marlene Sanders in 1976, and Pam Hill in 1978. Among the timely hours produced by the various units were *Gun Control: Pro & Con, The CIA, Crashes: The Illusion of Safety,* and *Prime Time: The Decision-Makers.*

After 1978, under Pam Hill, the series grew bolder, more venturesome, and more controversial. Notable examples were *The Politics of Torture,* examining U.S. support of repressive regimes in Third World countries in the light of Carter Administration human rights rhetoric; *Terror in the Promised Land,* a documentary on Palestinian terrorists and their mystique of martyrdom; *Arson: Fire for Hire!,* a Brit Hume opus on the fastest-growing crime in the U.S.; *Youth Terror: The View from Behind the Gun,* a cinema verite film, with no written narration, on youth crime, produced and directed by Helen Whitney; and *The Shooting of Big Man: Anatomy of a Criminal Case,* a two-hour examination of an entire criminal case, much of it shot in the courtroom, produced and directed by Eric Saltzman, a trial attorney associated with Harvard University, with the cooperation of Charles Nesson, a professor and assistant dean of Harvard Law School.

Hill left to join CNN in 1989, as the *Close-Up!* unit began to be phased out at ABC after the network's purchase by Capital Cities.

ABC STAGE 67 ▶ hour-long weekly anthology series created in the fall of 1966 for experimentation with new forms of programming and new talent. Little came of the venture, however, since its offerings received only moderate critical approval and generally unimpressive ratings. The series opened with an original film drama featuring Alan Arkin, *The Love Song of Barney Kempinski,* and over its course presented programs with such titles as *The Kennedy Wit, The Bob Dylan Show, The Anthony Newley Show, Rogers & Hart Today, Noon Wine, The Many Worlds of Mike Nichols, The Legend of Marilyn Monroe* and *An Essay on the American Jew.* Hubbell Robinson, the former head of programs for CBS who had been responsible for *Playhouse 90,* was executive producer of the series.

ABC VIDEO ENTERPRISES ▶ a unit created by ABC in 1979 to explore opportunities in the new fields of television spawned by technology. Its results have been exceptional. It was Video Enterprises that got ABC successfully into cable, where the other networks failed. Its early venture into a part-time network called ARTS (Alpha Repertory Television Service) led, after a merger with the Entertainment Channel, into the Arts & Entertainment Network (A&E), one of the staples of basic cable. Another early ABC channel called Daytime, in partnership with Hearst Corp., evolved into the successful Lifetime channel, another of the staples. An investment in a third cable channel, ESPN, the 24-hour sports network, turned out to be a bonanza when ESPN grew to become one of the hottest and highest-rated of the basic-cable networks. The three have given ABC a foothold in the cable field that the rival networks can only envy.

When Capital Cities bought ABC in 1986, the three cable networks amounted to throw-ins. But as it developed, they were just coming into their own and starting to be profitable when the main network Capital Cities bought had started its economic decline. The cable networks turned out to be a huge unexpected bonus for Cap Cities. ABC now owns 80% of ESPN, 38% of A&E, and 33% of Lifetime. Moreover, through ESPN, Video Enterprises has become an investor in similar sports channels abroad, such as the European Sports Network and the Japan Sports Channel.

Video Enterprises is also ABC's international arm, whose activities—like those of its counterparts at the other networks—center on the sale of ABC program properties abroad. But like few other American companies, Enterprises has concentrated on establishing tight business and production relationships in other countries and as a result has become a participant in Europe's commercial television revolution. Enterprises has bought an interest in Telemunchen, a prominent German production and distribution company; Tesauro, a film and production company in Spain; and Hamster Productions, a leading French independent production company. These production partnerships may benefit the ABC network in time, as the U.S. becomes more involved in international coproductions. Also, they position ABC on the European side against quotas that may be adopted for American programming.

Herb Granath has headed ABC Video Enterprises from the start.

ABC-OWNED TELEVISION STATIONS ▶ group of stations that, by virtue of common ownership, represent the nucleus of the ABC network's affiliate lineup. Making up the group are four of the original five stations founded by the American Broadcasting Co. and four that were added in 1986 when Capital Cities bought ABC. The eight stations, four of which are in the nation's largest markets, come close to reaching 25% of the population, which is the FCC's penetration limit for TV groups.

The five ABC stations before the merger, all founded in 1948, were generally prosperous and supported by the ABC network through the two decades during which it operated in the red. They became the most profitable station group in the country during the late 1970s, when the ABC network finally became the equal of its rivals and later forged ahead of them. With the need to divest of several stations when Cap Cities arrived with its own group, the original Detroit station, WXYZ-TV, became one of the outlets sold off.

Known now as the CapCities/ABC Stations, they are WABC-TV New York, KABC-TV Los Angeles, WLS-TV Chicago, KGO-TV San Francisco, WPVI-TV Philadelphia, KTRK-TV Houston, WTVD Raleigh-Durham, and KFSN-TV Fresno. The group is divided into two by geographical zones. Lawrence J. Pollock is president of the four stations in the East, and Kenneth M. Johnson is president of those in the West.

ABEL, ELIE ▶ NBC diplomatic correspondent during the 1960s who resigned in 1970 to become Dean of the Columbia University Graduate School of Journalism. He gave up the post in 1979 to become Norman Chandler Professor of Communications at Stanford University.

During the period Abel served as head of NBC's London bureau (1965-67), his book, *The Missile Crisis*, was published. Later he collaborated on separate books with Marvin Kalb and Averell Harriman. Abel had a long career as a print journalist before joining NBC, working variously as a national and foreign correspondent for the *Montreal Gazette, The New York Times* and the *Detroit News.*

ABOVE THE LINE/BELOW THE LINE ▶ terms for the general types of television production costs. On the budgeting sheet, a line separates the constants and the variables. Technical expenses are listed below the line and generally are determined by union requirements, so that they are virtually fixed costs; creative expenses are written above the line and may range widely according to terms made with writers, directors and producers.

For most network television programs of a specified length, the below-the-line costs are standard. They involve the basic technical staff, camera unit, electrical unit, music, wardrobe, makeup, props, set design, special effects, editing, laboratory processing, transportation, and the cost of film stock.

The venturesome area is above the line. A script property may involve the payment of literary rights or may be a modest original purchased at Writers Guild scale. The director may be famous and highly expensive or a journeyman who works for the going rate. The program may have a small cast with few salaries or a large cast with many. The difference between a superstar and a relatively unknown actor can amount to $200,000 or more per program, or even a percentage of the profits. The producer may be extravagant or resourceful with regard to his concept of the production and his administrative style. Location and night shooting are extra, as are elaborate special effects.

For a typical half-hour television program of modest pretensions, the above-the-line costs will exceed the below-the-line by around 25 per cent.

The costs for promotion, program testing and the rental of facilities are listed separately as a third general category.

ABRAHAMS, MORT ▶ TV producer in the 1950s and 1960s. He was executive producer of *Producers Showcase* on NBC (1956) and *Suspicion* (1958). His producing credits included *Target, The Corrupters* and *Route 66.*

ABRAMS, FLOYD ▶ probably the most prominent lawyer specializing in First Amendment issues. A partner in the New York law firm of Cahill, Gordon & Reindel, he was co-counsel in the Pentagon Papers case, and represented NBC in its decade-long defense against entertainer Wayne Newton. Although a jury had awarded Newton $5.2 million damages because of 1980-81 newscasts linking the Las Vegas showroom star to organized crime, appeals courts ultimately vacated the award. Abrams also represented Meredith Corporation's WTVH Syracuse, N.Y., in *Syracuse Peace Council* litigation, which led to the invalidation of the Fairness Doctrine. He was less successful representing the three major networks in a challenge to the 1971 Communications Act amendments giving federal candidates "reasonable access" to buy airtime.

ACADEMY AWARDS TELECAST ▶ also known as *The Oscar Show,* biggest of the TV awards shows and annually one of the medium's most potent special events, nearly always ranking among the top-rated shows of the year, despite the late hour of the broadcast in the East, usually 10 or 10:30 pm.

The first national telecast of the Oscar ceremonies was provided by NBC on March 19, 1953, although the awards had been covered on local Los Angeles stations in years before, as well as on network radio. NBC continued to televise the event through 1960, when ABC acquired the rights. After 10 years on ABC, the Oscars went back to NBC for five (1971-75) and then returned to ABC.

The Oscars have had the appeal of suspense, glamour, the unpredictability of live TV and a procession of stars whose dress or deportment might be the stuff of gossip. Although the TV Emmy Awards would seem to have comparable attraction, in fact those ceremonies have been less an event in audience terms and on the whole less successful as programs. Largely this is because the quality and variety of TV programs make for an excess of categories, which tends to dilute the suspense, even when not causing confusion.

While the Oscar presentations have undergone changes year by year, the performer most closely associated with the ceremonies has been Bob Hope, who has been emcee more than 15 times, including the years before TV coverage, when the awards were broadcast on radio. The comedian served as host for five consecutive telecasts (1958-62) and sporadically thereafter.

ACADEMY OF TELEVISION ARTS & SCIENCES ▶ see National Academy of Television Arts & Sciences (NATAS).

ACE AWARDS ▶ annual awards conferred by the National Cable Television Association (NCTA) in recognition of outstanding achievement in original programs for cable television. Initiated in 1979, the awards reflected a recognition in the cable industry that the medium's future depended on the variety of new, specialized programming made possible by cable technology, rather than on the traditional retransmission of broadcast signals. The awards were made both to national cable-TV program suppliers and to local cable systems for innovative programming, including that on public access channels.

ACE, GOODMAN (d. 1982) ▶ one of the radio era's most successful comedy writers. He made the transition to television in 1952, working first for Milton Berle and later for the Perry Como and Sid Caesar shows. That he was adaptable to the vastly differing styles of Berle and Como—one brash and slapstick, the other relaxed and low-key—was the essence of Ace's success. He did little TV writing after the 1950s.

ACKERMAN, HARRY ▶ head of production for Screen Gems from 1958 through the 1960s and previously a program executive for CBS. At Screen Gems he was executive producer of *Bewitched, Hazel, Temperature's Rising, The Paul Lynde Show* and numerous others. He was also head of Ackerman Productions and v.p. of Capitol Pictures until 1973.

ACQUISITIONS AND MERGERS OF THE 1980s ▶ leading factors in the corporate upheavals and industry turmoil that characterized the decade and altered the television landscape forever.

In the 1980s the entire business world was caught up in the excitement of takeovers and leveraged buyouts (LBOs), with all manner of companies suddenly finding themselves "in play." At the same time, the television business became more attractive than ever to big-time investors and financial speculators because it had become largely deregulated. The Federal

Communications Commission during the Reagan Administration had lifted the yoke of "public trustee" from license holders of television stations, and it had abolished scores of government regulations that had been adopted over 50 years earlier to allow broadcasting to operate under the rules of the market.

The general mania to acquire companies on borrowed money, in hostile fashion or otherwise, was fed by confidence that economic growth would go on indefinitely and that financing with high-risk junk bonds made perfect sense because everyone was doing it. For inspiration there were the examples of leveraged buyouts that made instant millionaires, and in some cases billionaires, of canny investors.

Where television was concerned, there were special factors that stimulated station trading: the repeal of the anti-trafficking rule that had required buyers of stations to hold a license at least three years before attempting to sell it; the liberalizing of the ownership provision that allowed group broadcasters to have as many as 12 each of TV, FM and AM stations, when previously the limit was 7-7-7; and the continually rising prices for commercial time, despite the continuing loss of audience share by the networks and their affiliates.

While there was considerable acquisition activity in the first half of the decade, it went into high gear in 1985, the year the 12-12-12 rule took effect. What was to come was foreshadowed at the start of the year when Sen. Jesse Helms, the ultra-conservative Republican from North Carolina, made a stab at conquering CBS. In a heavy mailing, he urged conservatives to buy up CBS stock and use their holdings to suppress what he maintained was the "liberal bias" of CBS News. At almost the same time, Atlanta entrepreneur Ted Turner, then considered a thoroughgoing conservative and possibly in league with Helms, made a move on CBS. Neither of these efforts was successful, but they caused CBS to take on debt in buying back its own stock to fend off a possible takeover. Some of the debt was paid down by the selling of KMOX-TV St. Louis, the smallest of the network's owned stations. This was the cue for Laurence Tisch, billionaire trader in companies, to enter the picture.

At the end of January in 1985 Taft Broadcasting became the first group to reach the 12-station TV ceiling with the acquisition of Gulf Broadcasting, including its seven radio properties and other assets, for $755 million. With the five Gulf TV stations added to Taft's seven, the company covered only 11.2% of the national market, well under the FCC coverage limit. Taft was to undergo further changes in the next few years.

The big jolt to the television industry came in March of the year, when Capital Cities Communications acquired ABC, a curious case of a small fish consuming one much larger. The takeover price of $3.5 billion was an extraordinary bargain, and it turned out to be the most successful broadcast merger of the decade. It required substantial divestiture of stations because of the duopoly and cross-ownership regulations and because the combined TV station group covered more than 28% of U.S. TV households, well over the limit.

During the same month, an internal battle erupted at Storer Communications, one of the country's most prominent TV groups. A dissident faction led by Coniston Partners proposed to liquidate Storer's seven TV stations and its 1.5 million-subscriber cable MSO. While the public company was considered undervalued, it had been losing money for three years. A fight ensued over the technicality of whether a change of ownership had occurred, which brought the FCC into the fray. In April the commission came down on the side of the dissidents. That brought Kohlberg, Kravis, Roberts & Co. onto the scene in the guise of "white knight."

KKR was the most accomplished practitioner of the leveraged buyout, by which companies are purchased on borrowed money—often high-interest junk bonds—and the debt paid off from the normal cash flow. KKR was not primarily a broadcast-oriented firm, but it had a pleasant taste of station trading when it bought KTLA Los Angeles from Gene Autry for $245 million in 1982 and three years later sold it to the Tribune Company for $510 million. KKR in 1984 took over Wometco Enterprises, including its six TV stations, and sold some of them off. With Storer, KKR's bid of more than $2 billion was accepted.

While this was going on, Multimedia Inc., a communications company with five TV stations, found itself in a battle after the group of families that controlled it made known their intention to take the company private. This was contested first by Wesray, an investment firm and LBO specialist led by former Treasury Secretary William E. Simon and his partner Ray Chambers. Then Lorimar entered, flush with network TV successes, and then Jack Kent Cooke, the real estate and sports tycoon who had bought 9.7% of the company. But Multimedia's owners, the four families who had put the company together in the late 1960s—the Sisks, Jolleys, Furmans and Peaces—were not selling. Nevertheless, they had to scrap their original LBO and revise their goals.

In May 1985 the Metromedia TV station group was preparing to sell to 20th Century-Fox, jointly owned then by the Australian media giant, Rupert Murdoch, and Denver oil man Marvin Davis (later bought out by Murdoch). The seller was John W. Kluge, Metromedia chairman, who 11 months earlier had succeeded in taking the company private in an LBO valued at $1.45 billion. The sale to Fox was for $2.1 billion and involved seven stations, with one, WCVB-TV Boston, sold off in turn to the Hearst Group for $450 million. This group of independent stations, all in the top 10 markets, became the basis of the fourth national network, Fox, which began on a limited scale the following year.

The summer of 1985 brought Coca Cola to the table, with swift acquisitions in Hollywood, including Columbia Pictures, Merv Griffin Productions and Embassy Communications, which had been owned by sitcom producer Norman Lear and his partner, the former talent agent Jerrold Perenchio. Lear and Perenchio then staged a hostile takeover attempt of the Detroit-based Evening News Assn., offering to buy the 435,000 shares at $1,000 per. The company, which owned *The Detroit News* and other newspapers, also owned TV stations in Washington, Tucson, Oklahoma City, Mobile and Austin. The pair later raised their bid to $1,250, but after the proposed acquisition ended up in court and before the FCC, the Evening News Assn. wound up with the Gannett Co. for $1,583 a share. Later that year, Lear started a new media company that assembled a UHF station group called Act III Broadcasting.

Coca Cola did not last long in Hollywood. Once it discovered that marketing movies was nothing like marketing soft drinks, and far more treacherous as a business, it divested itself of Columbia and beat a retreat.

Ted Turner, meanwhile, announced that he had an agreement to acquire MGM/UA for $1.5 billion. Turner was interested primarily in the film library and immediately sold off the other parts. The historic Culver City film lot was sold to Lorimar Telepictures, and the company name and famed roaring lion logo sold back to Kirk Kerkorian, the previous owner of the company. But Turner was still left with a crushing debt and eventually was bailed out by a number of large cable operators, in exchange for equity and seats on the board of Turner's company. In the fall of 1991, Turner Broadcasting bought Hanna-Barbera Productions, with its huge animation library, from Great American Communications for $320 million. In this, Turner had a 50% partner, Apollo Investment Fund.

Laurence Tisch, chairman and chief executive of Loews Inc., started buying CBS's stock in July 1985 and by mid-November had accumulated 11.7%. Soon after, he had 24.9% (just under the 25% that under FCC definition would constitute a change of ownership, requiring a divesture of radio stations in the same markets as the CBS television o&os) and became chief executive officer of CBS.

Early in November, the disturbing question of what to do about RKO arose at the FCC. The group of stations owned by RKO General, a subsidiary of GenCorp (previously the General Tire and Rubber Co.), was beset with applicants for the licenses that would have to be surrendered because of the company's misconduct in a number of episodes over the years. The company's final sin was in making false representations to the FCC. What brought the question to the fore was Group W's bid for the Los Angeles station KHJ-TV, which was blocked by a long-standing challenge for the license by a company called Fidelity Television Inc. Group W offered $313 million, which included a hefty payoff of $95 million to Fidelity, but after an involved series of events the deal fell through. Instead the station wound up as a property of the Disney Co. in 1986.

Capping 1985 was the General Electric purchase of RCA, which included NBC. Thus, in the span of a single year all three major networks were essentially taken over and the groundwork laid for the fourth network. The RCA sale was announced on Dec. 11 and completed the following year. Each of the networks, with a new corporate culture, was to change radically.

The merger activity continued in 1986. Wesray, having failed to capture Multimedia, started things off by backing the management buyout at Outlet Communications. Outlet had been owned by the Rockefeller Group, which bought it in 1984 but then reportedly became disenchanted with its earning strength. A year after the Rockefellers bought it they attempted to sell Outlet to the Pritzker family in Chicago, but a deal failed to develop. With the Wesray deal, the investment company owned three-quarters of Outlet, and the Outlet management, headed by Bruce G. Sundlun (later governor of Rhode Island), got the other quarter. But to pay down debt, the new owners of Outlet sold three of the seven TV stations. In getting $625 million for the Outlet group, the Rockefellers, according to some estimates, cleared around $200 million. After the sale, in early 1987, Outlet went public again, although Wesray and the management kept 70% for themselves.

In late February of 1986 the keystone of the dismantled RKO General broadcast empire, WOR-TV New York, went to MCA Inc. with a winning bid of $387 million. MCA actually had a partner, Cox Enterprises, at the time the bid was accepted, but Cox backed away just before the signing and MCA proceeded on its own. (When MCA was purchased by the Japanese company Matsushita in 1991, it had to divest itself of the station, renamed WWOR; it spun the station off in a separate company called Pinelands Broadcasting).

In mid-May of 1986 KKR, which was in the business of buying and then turning over properties rather than running them, got an agreement in principle from Lorimar Telepictures to acquire the six Storer stations plus the Wometco Miami station for a total $1.85 billion. Lorimar and Telepictures were a newly minted merger, having knitted themselves together only three months before. But in trying to swing the financing for the station purchases, the company discovered that it had overreached, and the deal was called off in November.

A 55% interest in the Storer stations finally ended up with the busy entrepreneur George Gillett, who was involved in sports, newspapers, banks and oil. Gillett already owned a dozen stations, many of them in small markets, and the addition of the six put him well over the FCC ceiling of 12. Gillett got around the rule by putting some of the stations in trust for his children, as Busse Broadcasting Corp. But two years later, some of his biggest stations were on the block, as his accumulated debts and a slowdown in advertising bore down on him. KKR also suffered in this.

Another family-owned TV group that got caught up in the turmoil of the 1980s was Pulitzer Broadcasting, consisting of seven TV stations and two radio ones. The ownership was a relatively concentrated group of 20, all heirs of Joseph Pulitzer, one of America's foremost publishers in his day. They split on the issue of whether to sell the company, with a minority favoring the sale. A buyer was in the wings, Alfred Taubman, investor and real estate developer. In the spring of 1986 Taubman had laid out $10 million for an option to buy 20% of the company for $90 million. He had offered $500 million for the Pulitzer Publishing Co. and later increased the bid to $625 million, while family members sued and counter-sued each other. Late in the year the heirs settled the battle, with the company buying out the minority family members and making a public offering of 1.4 million shares. Despite the offering, nearly all the voting power in the company remained with Joseph Pulitzer, Jr., Michael Pulitzer and their cousin David E. Moore.

The Taft group that had bought Gulf Broadcasting in early 1985 made another move toward the end of 1986, selling off all its non-network affiliates to the TVX Broadcasting Group. The five stations went for $240 million, which was disappointing to Taft but indicative of the waning of the go-go years. Since TVX already owned nine stations, the acquisition of five meant two would have to be sold. The sale of the stations was prompted by a sharp decline in earnings for the first quarter of fiscal 1985 (ending Sept. 30), not unexpected after the company took on $680 million in debt after the Gulf purchase. But what made it serious was that Taft's big independent stations in Texas were suffering from the soft oil economy.

Auguring further changes in the company's picture was the departure from Taft Broadcasting in early 1987 of vice chairman Dudley Taft, who took one of the stations with him, WGHP-TV Greensboro, N.C. The station was in the same market as a former Wometco cable system that had been bought in a joint venture by Taft, the Robert M. Bass group, and some of the Wometco management. This was part of the $625 million purchase of Wometco Cable TV from a group of institutional investors headed by KKR.

While Taft would have had to get rid of the Greensboro station anyway because of the FCC cross-ownership rules, Dudley Taft's claiming of it stirred up a conflict among the financiers of the group. The Bass group owned 24.9% of Taft Broadcasting—another fraction of a point and the question of control could be raised with the FCC. At the same time, Carl Lindner's American Financial Corp. had increased its stake in Taft to 15.6% and had gotten an okay from the FCC to increase to 24.9%. AFC also had a 5% stake in Scripps Howard Broadcasting and owned 10% of Aaron Spelling Productions.

The split in ownership made for a most unstable company. The conflicts were resolved in a complex arrangement in April 1987 that gave Lindner the stations and the entertainment group (Taft Entertainment, a production company that included the Hanna-Barbera and Ruby-Spears animation houses and Worldvision Enterprises, a major distributor of syndicated programs). The Bass group, in turn, wound up with Wometco Cable and part of Taft Cable Partners, a joint venture with the giant cable owner, TCI. Dudley Taft got the company name, Taft Broadcasting, and the promise of loans from the Lindner group. Under Lindner, the broadcast stations and entertainment group became Great American Communications Co. In October 1991 it sold off Hanna-Barbera to Turner Broadcasting System in a joint venture with Apollo Investment Fund for $320 million.

In August 1988 Lindner and Aaron Spelling merged Worldvision and Aaron Spelling Productions under a separate holding company, linking one of Hollywood's most prolific producers with a leading independent distributor.

One of the more successful takeovers was that of Viacom International by Sumner Redstone, head of National Amusements, a 400-screen theater chain. Viacom, a station owner, cable operator, and program producer and distributor, was seen by Redstone as a hedge against the decline in the movie theater business. The company was experiencing a management LBO initiated in September 1986. Redstone had acquired 19.6% of Viacom and made a tender offer in February 1987. After both sides increased their bids, the Viacom board signed an agreement with Redstone in March that put a value of $3.4 billion on the company.

One of the early signs of trouble in TV paradise was Grant Broadcasting's filing for bankruptcy protection under Chapter 11 in December 1986. Grant had independent TV stations in Chicago (actually Joliet, Ill.), Philadelphia and Miami. Among the big creditors of the two-year old company, which had invested heavily in programming, were the program syndicators, with 10 major distributors owed $25 million. Highly leveraged, Grant was financed primarily with $85 million in bonds paying 14.5% and 17.25% interest, plus $20 million in bank loans. The bonds were placed by Drexel Burnham Lambert, which itself invested $5.6 million in the company. A month later, Drexel's first equity investment in a TV property, an Indianapolis station, also filed under Chapter 11.

The industry was stunned by Grant's failure, because of Milt Grant's reputation as a successful operator and owner of independent stations. He had made a quick fortune in selling two Texas independents to Gulf Broadcasting, but found himself over-extended in the new company. The Grant stations eventually ended up as Combined Broadcasting Co. 18 months later.

By 1988 it was clear that the boom in TV station prices was over. At the year's end, an estimated 40 VHF stations were on the block and a good many more UHF stations. The heavy debts were proving difficult to pay off, and owners were looking for ways out. By 1989, the junk bond market was in serious trouble.

The TV program market was also affected negatively by the excesses of the decade. Lorimar Telepictures had reached the top of the mountain in 1985 when it felt capable of pulling off a $1.85 billion station deal, but by the end of 1987 its financial seams were coming loose. In March 1988 preliminary merger discussions began with Warner Communications. Despite a cash bid of $760 million from financier Marvin Davis, a definitive agreement was reached for Warner to acquire Lorimar Telepictures in a tax-free exchange of stock. After some stockholder snags, a revised deal was approved at the end of 1988, and a huge producer-distributor emerged.

Impressive as this merger was, it was dwarfed by the next development, the announcement of a merger between Warner and Time Inc. Plans for the combination were revealed in March 1989, only a few months after the Lorimar union was clinched. If nothing else, the joining of the media giants would result in an entity that could turn out more TV programming than any other company on the planet. The merger also would make for a company that contained the largest magazine publisher and largest record company in the U.S., the second largest cable operator and owner of the largest pay-cable network, the largest company in the direct marketing of books, and arguably the largest international distributor of TV programs in the world.

Barriers to the deal quickly arose. The first was posed by Warner's dissident stockholder, Herbert Siegel, chairman-president of Chris-Craft. Siegel's company had the largest block of stock in Warner as a result of a stock swap by the companies in 1984, when Warner chairman Steve Ross was trying to protect his company against a possible takeover attempt by

Rupert Murdoch. The issue with Siegel was eventually settled, but a bigger threat to the merger came from Martin Davis, chairman of Paramount Communications (and not to be confused with Marvin Davis, the financier). Paramount Communications was the new name for Gulf & Western, signaling a strategy that would concentrate on building up Paramount's entertainment and information businesses. Davis offered $175 a share for Time, all cash and worth $10.7 billion. Later this was raised to $200 a share.

There was little doubt on Wall Street that Time shareholders would approve the price, if asked. But a battery of lawyers from the two corporations argued that company directors did not have to abide by a majority vote of the stockholders and that a vote was not required. In July 1989, the Delaware Supreme Court upheld that view. The result was a takeover of Warner by Time, which cost the merged company $13 billion and a huge debt. By early 1990 all the loose ends were tied and the deal was complete.

As the decade was coming to a close, a major shift in studio ownership occurred in Hollywood. Sony's purchase of Columbia Pictures in September 1989 for $3.4 billion served notice—as had Murdoch's buy of 20th Century-Fox in mid-decade—of the Hollywood industry's vulnerability to cash-rich foreign companies. Sony had bought CBS Records in 1988 for $2 billion. Following the Columbia Pictures acquisition, it laid out an additional $200 million for Guber-Peters Entertainment Co. to recruit Peter Guber and Jon Peters to run Columbia, and additional millions were spent to free Guber and Peters from their Warner Bros. contract.

A third major studio to be taken over by a foreign buyer was MGM/UA, major pieces of which had remained under the control of Kirk Kerkorian after Ted Turner bought the company for its film library. In December 1989 Turner returned with an offer of $1 billion for MGM's TV and film production facilities and for the 1,000-title United Artists library, but he was turned down. Earlier that year, two other efforts to buy what remained of MGM/UA came up—a $1.5 billion offer from Australia's Qintex and a $1.4 billion bid by Rupert Murdoch.

Finally, in March 1990 Kerkorian signed what was called a definitive agreement with Giancarlo Parretti, an Italian financier, under the terms of which Parretti's Pathe Communications would acquire the famed studio for $1.3 billion. To nail down Parretti's intentions and financial capabilities, some $275 million in escrow payments were required. At one point during the search for financing, there was a possibility of Time Warner making a bridge loan to Parretti in return for distribution rights, but this fell through. Money to meet the scheduled payments continued to be a problem for Parretti and after a few months he lost control of the company he had bought to his backers.

A fourth major Hollywood studio, MCA Inc., came under foreign ownership in November 1990 when it was purchased by Japan's Matsushita Electric Industrial Co. for $6.13 billion. WWOR-TV New York, the only station owned by MCA, had to be spun off because of restrictions against foreign ownership of broadcast outlets, and this was valued at an additional $460 million. MCA's long-term debt of $1.13 billion was assumed by Matsushita. Universal Pictures had thus also become foreign-owned.

As the 1990s began, a chastened television industry was busy restructuring debt. George Gillett's GHI station group was in bankruptcy proceedings under Chapter 11. Murdoch's News Corp. began slimming down by selling off magazine properties. Time Warner, in attempting to reduce its debt, separated its entertainment divisions into a new limited partnership in the fall of 1991 to accept an investment of $1 billion from two Japanese concerns, the Toshiba Corporation and C. Itoh & Co., the country's largest trading house. The venture, called Time Warner Entertainment, encompassed Time Warner's movie, recording, television and cable businesses, including HBO, but not the publishing group. With their investment, the Japanese companies came to own 12.5% of TWE. That brought to five the total of major Hollywood studios owned entirely or in part by foreign interests, with only Paramount and Disney still wholly American.

Domestically, with borrowing from banks more difficult, the acquisitions mania subsided in the early 1990s. Still, there was activity. ABRY Communications took a major position in Norman Lear's Act III Broadcasting, consisting of eight UHF stations. Paramount Communications completed a takeover of the TVX stations from Salomon Bros. CBS bought Midwest Communications' WCCO-TV Minneapolis for its sixth owned-TV station. But the wild days were clearly over. Following are some additional acquisitions and mergers that took place in the go-go years of the LBO era:

In 1986 Lionheart Television International, distributor of British TV fare in the U.S., was bought by BBC Enterprises from Western World Television and Public Media.

In 1986 Prism Entertainment acquired a major interest in Fox Lorber Associates. Later Fox Lorber bought back control and in 1991 sold an equity position to a Japanese concern, Gaga.

Primetime Entertainment, which specialized in international TV co-production and packaging, was taken over by Southbrook Entertainment in 1986.

In 1986 John Blair and Co., the only publicly owned station representative firm, was taken over by Reliance Capital Group, after Blair over-extended itself by acquiring printing and marketing operations. The next year it was acquired by a group of investors led by James H. Rosenfield, a former top executive of CBS. JHR Acquisition Co. paid an estimated $100 million for the rep firm, which was renamed Blair Communications and included a program development and distribution arm, Blair Entertainment. Major investors included Saratoga Partners, a limited partnership managed by Dillon Read & Co., and Washington National Investment Co., an affiliate of Sifcorp. Reliance kept the Spanish-language TV stations that had been owned by Blair, however, and made them the nucleus of the Telemundo Hispanic network.

In 1987 Hallmark Cards Inc. bought the nine stations of the Spanish International Network for $265 million and established Univision as a new Hispanic network to compete with Telemundo. In 1991, through its Crown Media subsidiary, Hallmark bought Cencom Cable for around $1 billion.

In 1988 TVS, the ITV programming contractor for southeast England, bought Hollywood's MTM Enterprises for $320 million. The company had been a successful network program producer under Grant Tinker in the 1970s but fared poorly under TVS ownership, and the purchase led to the downfall of the company's chief executive, James Gatward. In 1991 TVS lost its franchise in the British license auction.

In January 1990 Britain's Thames Television, which had the broadcast franchise for London on weekdays but lost it in 1991, acquired Reeves Communications.

Australian-based Qintex Entertainment, which made a $1.5 billion bid for MGM/UA Communications in 1989 but was forced to file for bankruptcy in October of that year, had a year earlier acquired Hollywood's Hal Roach Studios, which included Robert Halmi Inc.

In 1991 Sony Pictures Entertainment bought most of the domestic production assets of New World Television, subsidiary of New World Entertainment. With these assets, Sony's intent was to bring back TriStar Television, which had been merged with Columbia Pictures Television in 1989, and thus offer a second brand name to TV program buyers. NWT brought Sony four prime-time network series, two off-network series and several projects in development.

In 1991 Turner Broadcasting System acquired Hanna Barbera Productions from Great American Communications. The deal involved more than 3,000 half hours of animated productions and included such characters as the Flinstones, the Jetsons, Yogi Bear and Scooby Doo.

Katz Communications, biggest of the station rep firms, was acquired in 1990 by a large group of top and middle management from the company's Employment Stock Ownership Plan.

In 1991 Providence Journal Broadcasting Corp., which publishes the *Providence Journal-Bulletin* and owns TV stations in Louisville, Charlotte, Tucson and Albuquerque, acquired five King Broadcasting TV stations and King's cable systems. The King stations in Seattle, Portland, Spokane, Honolulu and Boise tripled the coverage of the Providence Journal group.

ACROSS THE BOARD ▶ term for the scheduling of a program or commercial at the same hour every day of the week, usually the five weekdays.

ACTION FOR CHILDREN'S TELEVISION (ACT) ▶ a national citizens group formed in 1968 by four women in Newton, Mass., which from the beginning has been extraordinarily effective in pressuring the television industry for reforms in children's programming and advertising. Largely through ACT's early efforts in calling attention to the violence and commercialism in Saturday morning children's programming, the networks shifted to more wholesome shows. In response to an ACT petition, the FCC adopted rules limiting commercial time from up to 14 minutes per hour to 10 1/2 minutes per hour on weekends and 12 minutes per hour on weekends. Regular prime-time programming has an average of less than 8 minutes of commercials per hour.

ACT produced literature, games and consumer kits designed to discourage heavy television viewing of inferior shows and to alert parents and children to healthier kinds of food than those advertised on television.

Today ACT has 20,000 members nationwide. Peggy Charren has been president from its inception.

ACTION NEWS ▶ a style of local newscasting in the 1970s that placed a heavy emphasis on newsfilm and on the "realism" of the newsroom: newsmen in shirtsleeves and reporters typing in the background. Some also featured an ombudsman or problem-solving service for viewers. "Action News" formats usually involved joshing among the reporters and informal exchanges that strived for humor. Although it was not TV's noblest contribution to journalism, the style was popular and won audiences for stations.

AD HOC NETWORKS ▶ temporary hook-ups of stations, nationally or regionally, for a single specific purpose, usually the distribution of a sports event or entertainment program in behalf of a sponsor. Such occasional networks enlist affiliates of ABC, CBS and NBC as well as independent stations, the lineup differing for each event. Network affiliates are usually won by the inherent appeal of the event and by the fact that ad hoc networks either barter the shows or pay a higher rate of compensation than the commercial networks, usually 40% or more of ratecard for the time period. Among the leading ad hoc networks were Operation Prime Time, the Mobil Network and SFM's Family Network.

***ADAM 12*▶** half-hour, low-key police series on NBC (1968-75) about the day-to-day activities of two Los Angeles Police Department officers who ride a patrol car identified as Adam-12. It featured Martin Milner as Pete Malloy and Kent McCord as Jim Reed and was produced by Jack Webb's Mark VII Productions and Universal TV.

***ADAMS CHRONICLES, THE* ▶** ambitious historical drama series on PBS produced by WNET New York for the Bicentennial; it not only won critical praise but drew the largest audiences ever for a PBS series. In addition, the series inspired a college-credit extension course designed by Coast Community College District in Costa Mesa, Calif., and offered by around 400 colleges around the country.

A series of 13 one-hour programs on four generations of the family descended from John and Abigail Adams, *Chronicles* covered American history, from the viewpoint of the Adamses, from 1750 to 1900. It premiered on PBS Jan. 20, 1976, and was repeated that fall. The series was produced with meticulous attention to historical and cultural detail, using as its source The Adams Papers, letters, diaries and journals written by members of the Adams family and preserved by the Massachusetts Historical Society. Various scholars quarreled with the historical accuracy of the series, but the producers maintained that, while it was never intended as objective history, it was faithful to The Adams Papers.

The program was conceived and produced by Virginia Kassel through WNET New York, which aspired to create a dramatic series equal in scale and quality to those imported from the BBC. The project raised $5.2 million in grants from the National Endowment for the Humanities, the Andrew Mellon Foundation and the Atlantic Richfield Co. George Grizzard and Kathryn Walker starred as John and Abigail Adams.

ADAMS, DAVID C. ▶ former key corporate figure at NBC, member of its board of directors since 1958, chairman from 1972-74, and vice chairman thereafter, until his retirement in the spring of 1979. Disdaining public prominence, Adams preferred to serve in the background as high councillor and grey eminence, with titles such as vice chairman or executive v.p. His judgment was brought to bear on a wide range of NBC management matters and general industry problems, as well as in formulating NBC's position when it was called to testify before congressional committees or the FCC.

A lawyer, he came to NBC in 1947 from the staff of the FCC. Working initially in the legal area, he shortly moved into the corporate sphere and in 1956 became executive v.p. for corporate relations. Except for a year's leave of absence in 1968, he was involved in NBC policy decisions for 23 years.

***ADDAMS FAMILY, THE* ▶** live-action situation comedy based on the macabre cartoon characters of Charles Addams. It had a moderately successful run on ABC (1964-66). Produced by Filmways, it featured Carolyn Jones as Morticia, John Astin as Gomez and Jackie Coogan as Uncle Fester.

ADDRESSABILITY ▶ ability to control viewer access to particular programs or channels. Cable systems use addressable technology for pay-per-view programs that are only delivered in unscrambled form to those who have agreed to pay for them. The technology is facilitated by addressable converters, devices installed by cable operators that allow for direct communication between the cable head-end and individual TV sets in subscriber homes. In addition to activating the appropriate channel on demand for pay-per-view programs, addressable converters permit the remote-control unscrambling of premium channels.

ADELSON, MERV ▶ co-founder with Lee Rich of Lorimar Television, which became the leading supplier of prime-time programming to the networks throughout the 1980s. After a rapid series of corporate acquisitions and mergers, resulting ultimately in Lorimar becoming a unit of Time Warner, Adelson went off on his own to start an investment consultancy, East West Capital Associates, with Time Warner as a principal client. He also is a member of the media giant's board of directors.

After making a fortune in real estate development, Adelson joined with Rich, a former advertising executive who had worked closely with the networks, to form Lorimar Productions in 1968. Lorimar hit the jackpot with *Dallas* and scored again with *Knots Landing,* in addition to other successful series and miniseries. In 1985 it merged with Telepictures Corp., a company that gave Lorimar strength in distribution to ancillary markets. Four years later, when Warner Communications acquired Lorimar-Telepictures, Adelson relinquished all operating control, taking a settlement that included cash, stock and a seat on the Warner board. His Warner stock increased substantially in value the following year, when Warner merged with Time Inc.

Adelson is the estranged husband of Barbara Walters.

ADI (AREA OF DOMINANT INFLUENCE) ▶ a means by which a television station's market is defined for ratings and sales purposes. Each ADI market consists of all counties in which the home market stations receive a preponderance of their viewing. Each county in the U.S. belongs only to one ADI, so that the total of all ADI's represents the total number of TV households in the country.

The system of ADI allocations was introduced in 1966 by Arbitron, one of the rating services, and the concept has become standard. ADI rankings and population data (households, TV households, persons, penetration of cable TV, multi-set households, etc.) are revised every year to reflect population shifts. The A.C. Nielsen Co.'s equivalent of the ADI is the DMA (Designated Market Area).

The largest ADI's in the 1990-91 report are, in order, New York, Los Angeles, Philadelphia, San Francisco (the Bay area), Boston, Dallas-Ft. Worth, Detroit, Washington, D.C., Houston, and Cleveland. Together, the ten cover slightly more than one-third of the potential viewing population in the United States.

ADJACENCIES ▶ short periods of commercial time that come before or after a program rather than in the breaks within the show.

ADMINISTRATIVE LAW JUDGE ▶ previously known as hearing examiner, a member of the FCC staff responsible for conducting hearings for mutually exclusive license applications involving a problem at renewal time. After hearing testimony from parties of interest, usually with the aid of counsel, and on considering the evidence submitted,the ALJ issues an Initial Decision, which is reviewed by the agency's Review Board, and then by the full membership of the Commisssion.

ADVANCED TELEVISION (ATV) ▶ term encompassing all forms of television technology that offer better images than those available through the established NTSC, PAL and SECAM standards in their unaltered forms. HDTV (high-definition television), EDTV (extended- or enhanced-definition television) and IDTV (improved-definition television) are all forms of ATV.

ADVANCED TELEVISION SYSTEMS COMMITTEE (ATSC) ▶ organization formed in 1982 by the Joint Committee on Inter-Society Coordination (JCIC) to coordinate and develop voluntary national technical standards for advanced television (ATV) systems. ATSC is divided into two technology groups: one develops and recommends voluntary technical standards for TV program distribution using advanced technology, the other does the same for TV program production. ATSC member companies and organizations represent the motion picture and television industries. Members of the JCIC—the Electronics Industries Association (EIA), the Institute of Electrical and Electronics Engineers (IEEE), the National Association of

Broadcasters (NAB), the National Cable Television Association (NCTA) and the Society of Motion Picture and Television Engineers (SMPTE)—are charter members of ATSC.

ADVANCED TELEVISION TEST CENTER (ATTC) ▶ industry-supported laboratory mandated by the FCC to test broadcast ATV systems and recommend one for approval in the U.S.

ADVENTURES OF OZZIE AND HARRIET, THE ▶ long-running family situation comedy on ABC (1952-66) whose principals were actually a family, that of Ozzie Nelson, a former bandleader, and Harriet Hilliard, a former band singer. Their two sons, Ricky and David, grew up on the TV series and eventually were joined by their wives. When the series ended, the sons were launched on show business careers of their own.

ADVENTURES OF RIN TIN TIN, THE ▶ ABC series (1954-57) based on the movies of the canine hero, produced by Screen Gems and featuring Rin Tin Tin, Lee Aaker as Rusty, Jim Brown as Lieutenant Ripley Masters and Joe Sawyer as Sergeant Biff O'Hara. The series was re-run on ABC (1959-61) and then on CBS (1962-64). Tinted in sepia with new wraparounds, it was revised for syndication in 1976 and bartered by SFM Media Services.

ADVENTURES OF ROBIN HOOD, THE ▶ one of the first British series to play successfully on American TV. Starring Richard Greene, it was produced by Sapphire Films Ltd. in England and was carried by CBS (1955-58).

ADVERTISER BOYCOTTS ▶ see "Hit" Lists.

ADVOCATES, THE ▶ essentially a debate series, produced for PBS on an alternating basis by KCET Los Angeles and WGBH Boston, from 1969-73. The series sprung amid criticism from the Nixon Administration that TV, in general, was coloring the issues with a liberal bias and that public TV was not giving adequate voice to conservative views. A creature of those pressures, *The Advocates* allowed both sides of a public issue to be argued in courtroom fashion, live, by expert representatives. The series was produced on grants from the Ford Foundation. It was revived by WGBH in 1978 for another season.

AFFILIATE ▶ a privately owned broadcast station aligned with a network by contract. In exchange for airing the network's programs and commercials on an exclusive basis in its market, the affiliate receives a guaranteed, prearranged fee from the network (known as station compensation). In addition, the affiliate is allotted segments of the commercial adjacencies for its own ad sales; these spots command premium rates because they occur in the usually high-rated flow of the network feed. A network achieves national distribution through its affiliate infrastructure, while the affiliate benefits from receiving popular new programming that normally attracts large audiences. Moreover, the affiliate's annual expense for programming is far lower than that of any nonaffiliated station because the network supplies around 60% of its daily schedule. In general, network affiliates fetch a much higher price when trading hands than independents in the same TV market.

AFRICA ▶ four-hour documentary by ABC News examining Africa in the modern world, to which the network devoted a full evening in 1967 as the opening night event of the fall season. The longest single program produced for U.S. TV at the time, it had been more than a year in production with six film crews assigned to the project. Although lavishly promoted, and despite the popular appeal of Gregory Peck, who narrated, it drew modest ratings.

James Fleming was executive producer and Blaine Littell, who had covered Africa as a correspondent, was the project producer. Others who figured prominently in the production were Eliot Elisofon, Richard Siemanowski, Leon Gluckmas, Edward Magruder Jones and William Peters. Alex North composed the original score. The program was later syndicated by Worldvision as four one-hour specials.

AFTERSCHOOL SPECIALS ▶ occasional series on ABC of quality productions for 8- to 14-year-old children. Begun in 1972 with eight telecasts, seven new dramas and seven repeats were broadcast each subsequent season. The stories are built around the problems of youngsters in which the resolution is brought about by the actions of children rather than intervening adults. Themes include divorce, first love, parent-child relationships, physical handicaps and children's rights.

AGB TELEVISION RESEARCH ▶ a publicly held British company that attempted, unsuccessfully, to compete against A.C. Nielsen in the mid-1980s with a national television ratings service. The company claimed to have lost more than

$100 million during its four-year venture in the U.S.

AGB was first to introduce the people meter—an electronic metering device attached to a TV set to measure usage as well as demographic data—initially in Europe and Asia during the 1970s. In 1984 it tested people meters in Boston before launching a nation-wide U.S. service based on the device in 1987. Nielsen met the challenge by rolling out a similar service that year, and the battle of the people meters began. AGB signed up CBS and a few advertising agencies but failed to gain financial backing from ABC or NBC. AGB subsequently pulled out of the U.S., though it continues to expand its people meter service in other countries.

In 1990 AGB was bought by Pergamon, a conglomerate owned by British media baron Robert Maxwell, and immediately it announced another run against Nielsen in the U.S. By late 1991 AGB had not re-entered the U.S. market. Maxwell died in that year.

AGNEW'S ATTACK ON TV NEWS ▶ a televised speech by Vice President Spiro T. Agnew (Nov. 13, 1969) before a Republican party conference in Des Moines, Iowa, which became the opening shot in the Nixon Administration's continuing assault on the credibility and integrity of network news. Agnew, who up to that point was scarcely known to the public, became thereafter the leading White House critic of the media.

The networks actually were responsible for the wide circulation the Des Moines speech received. In the belief that they would be ventilating an important issue that concerned them, the three networks—in carrying the speech live—in effect force-fed it to the viewers. And the fact that Agnew was addressing a partisan group that applauded everything he said undoubtedly heightened his effectiveness with the TV audience.

"The purpose of my remarks tonight is to focus your attention on this little group of men who not only enjoy a right of instant rebuttal to every presidential address, but, more importantly, wield a free hand in selecting, presenting and interpreting the great issues of our nation," Agnew said.

"Is it not fair and relevant to question concentration (of power) in the hands of a tiny, enclosed fraternity of privileged men elected by no one and enjoying a monopoly sanctioned and licensed by government?"

"The views of the majority of this fraternity do not—and I repeat, not—represent the views of America."

The address, written by one of President Nixon's speech writers, Patrick J. Buchanan, conveyed strong hints that the networks were controlled by an Eastern establishment with a decidedly liberal bias, a theme which was to become a motif in Agnew's later speeches, as well as those of Buchanan and Clay T. Whitehead, director of the Office of Telecommunications Policy.

The Des Moines speech also denounced the networks' practice of following a President's speech with instant analysis by newsmen, without taking into account the fact that newspaper pundits also write their analyses immediately after such a speech, although those do not appear until the following morning. The networks did not follow Agnew's speech with an analysis, and not long afterwards CBS chairman William S. Paley banned instant analysis on his network, although he restored the practice later.

AGRAMA, FRANK ▶ international television producer who began as a child TV actor in his native Egypt and as an adult began making movies, variously in California, Lebanon, and Rome. In the 1980s he moved back to California and concentrated on television, establishing Harmony Gold as a production and distribution company. In 1990 he shut down the distribution business to concentrate on production. Among his credits are *Shaka Zulu, Robotech,* and *Around the World In 80 Days.*

AGRONSKY, MARTIN ▶ former TV newsman who worked between commercial and public television. After a network career with NBC, ABC and CBS, spanning the period 1952-69, he became an anchorman and commentator for the Post-Newsweek Stations, based at WTOP-TV in Washington, and simultaneously for PTV's Eastern Educational Network. His principal programs were *Agronsky and Company, Evening Edition,* and *Agronsky At Large.*

Agronsky joined NBC in 1952 as a foreign correspondent and later became a Washington correspondent for ABC, performing his most distinguished work in covering the activities of Sen. Joseph McCarthy. He rejoined NBC in 1956 and covered the Eichmann trial in Jerusalem (he had once been a reporter for the *Palestine Post* in that city) in 1961, among other assignments. In 1965 he went to CBS and produced several noted documentaries (including *Justice Black and the Constitution*) before becoming Paris bureau chief (1968-69).

Agronsky & Company, a series featuring Washington correspondents from the right, left and center heatedly discussing topical issues, had an 18-year run on WTOP (now WUSA-TV) until Agronsky retired in January 1988. It was replaced, in similar format, by *Inside Washington,* hosted by Gordon Peterson.

AILES, ROGER ▶ independent newsfilm and television producer who put his talents to work for Richard Nixon, Ronald Reagan, and George Bush as a political consultant on their presidential campaigns. His most conspicuous political successes were with Reagan in 1984 and Bush in 1988. He was also Nixon's TV advisor for the 1968 campaign. Before working for Nixon, Ailes was producer of *The Mike Douglas Show* in Philadelphia (1965-67) and an executive producer at Westinghouse Broadcasting Corp. (1967-68). In 1969 he started Ailes Communications Inc.

Ailes' TV career continued in the 1970s when he became executive v.p. of Joseph Coors's TV News Inc. (1975-76) and later a consultant with CBS-TV (since 1978). Ailes produced and directed such TV specials as *The Last Frontier* (1974), *Fellini: Wizards, Clowns and Honest Liars* (1977), and *Television and the Presidency* (1984). Additionally, Ailes produced the Broadway musical *Mother Earth* (1972) and the play *Hot L Baltimore* (1973-76).

Ailes became executive producer of the *Rush Limbaugh Show,* a syndicated latenight talk show hosted by Limbaugh, an arch-conservative who formerly worked in radio, which was to launch in 1992.

AIM (ACCURACY IN MEDIA) ▶ a Washington-based citizens organization founded in 1969 that watches over print and broadcast media for instances of what it judges to be biased, slanted or unbalanced reporting. The organization, which could be characterized as politically conservative, reports its specific complaints to the FCC and the broadcaster (or publisher) involved, and to the public as well, through its newsletter, the *AIM Report.* Its charges of one-sidedness and journalistic unfairness in NBC's documentary, *Pensions: The Broken Promise* (aired on Sept. 12, 1972), were upheld by the FCC. In 1974, however, the Court of Appeals for the District of Columbia reversed the FCC's decision to avoid inhibiting investigative journalism. AIM claims between 20,000 and 30,000 members. Reid Irvine has headed the organization since its inception. Joe Goulden, a longtime investigative journalist, joined the staff in 1989 as Irvine's heir-apparent.

***AIRWOLF* ▶** action-adventure series in which the protagonists use a heavily armed, high-tech attack helicopter to battle evil. The show, which premiered on CBS in 1984, was one of two dramatic series built around helicopters that year, the other being *Blue Thunder.* The series starred Jan-Michael Vincent and featured Ernest Borgnine, Alex Cord, Belinda Bauer and David Hemmings. Executive producers were Bernard Kowalski and Donald Bellisario, who also directed and wrote some of the episodes.

CBS canceled *Airwolf* in 1986, but the series moved to the USA cable network the following year, with new episodes and a new cast in a more economical production. The new cast was headed by Barry Van Dyke and Michele Scarabelli.

ALABAMA ETV LICENSES ▶ case in which the FCC denied the renewal of Alabama's eight public TV licenses but then permitted the licensee to reapply for them.

The licenses of the Alabama Educational Television Commission (AETC), an agency of the state of Alabama, were denied renewal in 1975 when the FCC determined that the stations followed a racially discriminatory policy in their overall programming practices. Citing "pervasive neglect" of Alabama's black population, the commission maintained that the stations failed to meet adequately the needs of the public they were licensed to serve. The FCC's opinion was based on AETC's conduct during the 1967-70 license term, during which the licensee rejected most of the black-oriented programming available to it and failed to give blacks adequate representation on the air or in the production or planning operations at the stations. The commission said that while it recognized the vital service of educational TV, it would not condone AETC's dereliction and deficiency simply because it was engaged in public broadcasting.

However, the commission noted that improvements had occurred since 1970 and that there was a pressing need for public television in Alabama. It ruled, therefore, that the public interest would be served by granting AETC interim authority to continue operating the eight stations.

ALBERT, EDDIE ▶ character actor who made a highly successful switch from movies to television. He starred in the sitcom *Green Acres* (1965-71), playing a citified lawyer who moves to the country. He played a private detective in *Switch* (1975-78) and a scoundrel on *Falcon Crest* (1987). In 1988 he was featured in the TV mini-series *War And Remembrance.*

ALBERT, MARV ▶ sports broadcaster for some three decades, half of which have been devoted to handling the NFL play-by-play for NBC Sports. Albert is identified in the New York area as the voice of the New York Knicks and Rangers. He began his professional career in 1963, assisting Marty Glickman on Knicks and Rangers broadcasts, duties he continues currently on the Madison Square Garden cable network. Albert is famous for yelling "Yesss!" when a player sinks a basket. For NBC, he is teamed with Dick Enberg for NBA play-by-play duties and is the host/play-by-play man for the NBC's coverage of the NHL All-Star Game—the only hockey game to appear on broadcast TV. Albert earned praise for his boxing work with analyst Dr. Ferdie Pacheco during the network's coverage of the controversial boxing competition at the 1988 Summer Olympics in Seoul.

Marv Albert

ALDA, ALAN ▶ star of the smash comedy series, *M*A*S*H* (1972-83), who also wrote and directed some episodes of that series. The popularity of the series gained him the highest Q-rating for popularity with viewers during much of the 1980s and made him one of the richest actors in television. His earnings from the syndication of the series reportedly came to $30 million.

Alan Alda

Alda won four Emmies for his role as the wry, war-weary combat surgeon, Hawkeye Pierce. Alda's crisp delivery of wisecracks became a hallmark, and he developed into one of television's most distinctive actors.

He directed and appeared in the TV production of the play *6 Rms Riv Vu* (1974), and he was creator and co-executive producer of *We'll Get By,* a situation comedy that had a brief run on CBS (1975). Most of his work after *M*A*S*H* was in movies.

In his youth he worked with such improvisational theater groups as Second City and Compass, where he honed his talent for social and political satire. This prepared him for his entry into television as a regular in *That Was the Week That Was.*

ALEXANDER, DAVID ▶ director whose credits range from *U.S. Steel Hour, Climax* and *Studio One* in the 1950s to episodes of *Marcus Welby, M.D., Emergency, F. Troop, My Favorite Martian, Gunsmoke, Please Don't Eat the Daisies* and other comedy and action series in the 1960s and 1970s.

ALEXANDER, JANE ▶ widely acclaimed stage actress who made her TV debut as Eleanor Roosevelt in *Eleanor and Franklin* (1976) and then co-starred in the sequel, *The White House Years* (1977). She later appeared in the powerful drama special, *Playing for Time,* the CBS mini-series *Blood and Orchids* (1986), and *Malice in Wonderland* (1985).

ALEXANDERSON, ERNST F. W. (d. 1975) ▶ engineer of the General Electric Co. (U.S.) whose invention of the alternator made possible long-distance radio communications and who presented the first home and theater demonstrations of television. The first home reception of television took place in 1927 in his home in Schenectady, N.Y., and the theater demonstration was held the following year in the same city. Both demonstrations used perforated scanning discs and high-frequency neon lamps to originate and reproduce the picture. In the theater demonstration the picture was flashed on a seven-foot screen.

The loveable title character of the NBC series *ALF*

ALF ▶ successful NBC sitcom (1986-90) with both child and adult appeal that revolved around a wisecracking, overeating alien life form (hence the title) from the planet Melmac who settles in with a suburban family. Paul Fusco, ALF's creator, did the voice and puppetwork for the show. Max Wright and Anne Schedeen played Willie and Kate Tanner, the parents of the household in which ALF hid from the government, and Andrea Elson and Benji Gregory played their children, Lynn and Brian.

Beyond its appeal to kids, the show possessed a satirical edge that targeted politics and pop culture. Ironically, ALF the character became very much a part of pop culture, producing a merchandising bonanza. The series was also sold in 50 countries around the world by producer Lorimar Television. *ALF*'s executive producers were Bernie Brillstein and Tom Patchett.

ALFRED HITCHCOCK PRESENTS ▶ popular series of mystery and suspense stories hosted by Alfred Hitchcock, famed producer of classic suspense movies. Hitchcock's wry delivery and his sardonic closing speech were important assets to the series, which ran from 1955 to 1962 in half-hour form and three additional seasons in a one-hour version, *The Alfred Hitchcock Hour*. Produced by Shamley Productions, the half-hour series began on CBS (1955-59) and switched to NBC (1960-62). Similarly, the hour version began on CBS in the fall of 1962 and moved to NBC in 1964. The USA Network began carrying reruns of the series in the 1980s and had new episodes created exclusively for it in 1987 and 1988.

ALICE ▶ half-hour videotaped situation comedy on CBS (1976-85) loosely based on the film *Alice Doesn't Live Here Anymore,* concerning a widow waiting tables in a diner to support her young son. Linda Lavin was featured in the title role, with Vic Tayback as the owner of Mel's Diner and Beth Howland, Polly Holliday, Diane Ladd and Celia Weston as waitresses Vera, Flo, Belle and Jolene. The series was produced by Warner TV, with Bob Carroll Jr. and Madelyn Davis as executive producers. It became a hit in a Sunday night parlay with *All in the Family* and regularly made the top 10 as a mainstay of the strong Sunday lineup at CBS.

Carroll O'Connor and Jean Stapleton as Archie and Edith Bunker in *All in the Family*

ALL IN THE FAMILY ▶ a landmark series that changed the nature of situation comedies, opening them to realistic characters, mature themes and frank dialogue. Written by Norman Lear and produced by Yorkin-Lear Productions, the series was introduced on CBS in January 1971 as a second season entry and did poorly in the ratings at the outset. Rare among TV programs, it developed its great popularity during the summer reruns.

Based on an immensely popular and controversial British series, *Till Death Us Do Part,* created by Johnny Speight for a limited run on

BBC-TV, *Family* was built upon the clashes of a working-class bigot, Archie Bunker, with his neighbors and his liberal son-in-law. (Bunker's British counterpart was named Alf Garnett.) Bunker became so well established as representative of an American type that his name bid fair to enter the language.

The half-hour series was developed by ABC, but when that network rejected two versions of the pilot, Lear took it to CBS and landed a berth. Fortuitously, CBS at the time was actively searching for programs relevant to contemporary life and to the liberal-conservative rift in American attitudes.

The series made stars of its principals—Carroll O'Connor as Archie, Jean Stapleton as his wife Edith, Sally Struthers as their daughter Gloria and Rob Reiner as their live-in son-in-law Mike Stivic—none of whom was well known before *Family* began. It also spun off two other successful series, *Maude* and *The Jeffersons.*

Reiner and Struthers quit the series after the 1977-78 season to pursue other ventures, but it maintained its popularity without them. When Stapleton also withdrew as a regular a year later, the concept of the series was altered and the basic setting changed to a bar. It opened the 1979-80 season with a new title, *Archie Bunker's Place,* and continued strong in the popular CBS Sunday lineup. CBS programmed selected reruns of the show during prime time in June 1991 to run in tandem with a new Lear entry, *Sunday Dinner.* The ploy succeeded in gaining attention for the new comedy, but it was not renewed after its eight-week run.

ALL MY CHILDREN ▶ see Soap Operas.

ALL-CHANNEL LAW ▶ passed by Congress in 1962, legislation designed to help faltering UHF broadcasting by giving the FCC the power to require that all television sets shipped in interstate commerce be "capable of adequately receiving" all 82 channels—the 70 UHF channels as well as the 12 VHF channels.

The FCC implemented the law by setting minimum standards for UHF tuners and requiring that they be included in all receivers manufactured after April 30, 1964. Since that time the FCC has added new rules designed to make UHF channels as easy to tune as VHF. As the result of the law, more than 90% of all television-equipped homes now have sets with UHF tuners.

ALLEN, FRED (d. 1956) ▶ one of radio's leading comedians who made the switch to TV in 1950, although he disapproved of the new medium and continually railed against it. A satirist and social commentator who had become a darling of the intellectuals, Allen made his first TV appearances in the *Colgate Comedy Theater* as one of the stars in the rotation. He became emcee of *Judge for Yourself* (1953-54), starred in *Fred Allen's Sketchbook* in 1954 and became a member of the *What's My Line?* panel in 1955, serving until his death on March 7, 1956. He was never to recapture the glory of his radio days, and his own show, *Sketchbook,* was knocked off the air by competition with one of the big giveaway shows of the time. He made guest appearances on numerous shows, and his last special effort for NBC was to narrate "The Jazz Age" for the *Project 20* series. It aired nine months after his death.

ALLEN, MEL ▶ sportscaster prominent from the late 1930s to the early 1970s, whose authoritative style and polished delivery won him network assignments for major baseball and football events. The regular commentator for the N.Y. Yankees games for three decades, he was also announcer for most of the annual All-Star games during that period, as well as for many of the football bowl games. He was also commentator for the Fox Movietone Newsreel (1946-64) and host of *Jackpot Bowling* (1959). In the 1970s, he narrated the syndicated *This Week in Major League Baseball.*

ALLEN, STEVE ▶ multi-talented TV personality who hosted several successful shows, including the first *Tonight Show* on NBC and a Sunday evening variety series that was competitive with *The Ed Sullivan Show* for a few seasons. He was also a pianist, composer, recording artist, fiction writer and political activist.

The Steve Allen Show began as a late-night program in New York on July 27, 1953, and went on the NBC network in September 1954 as *The Tonight Show.* Aired on weeknights for 90 minutes, it was a potpourri of music, comedy, interviews and inventive sketches with the resident cast, many of whom went on to become stars—Andy Williams, Eydie Gorme, Steve Lawrence, Don Knotts and Bill Dana, among them.

Simultaneously, Allen served as a panelist on *What's My Line* on CBS from 1953-55 and starred in spectaculars for Max Liebman. He left *Tonight* in January 1957 after having begun the Sunday evening *Steve Allen Show,* a jazz-accented variety hour pitted against *Ed Sulli-*

van on CBS. It featured his wife, Jayne Meadows.

He later did several syndicated programs, including a popular talk show for Westinghouse Broadcasting and a series for PBS in 1977, *Meeting of Minds.*

A new prime-time venture on NBC in 1980, *The Steve Allen Comedy Hour,* was short-lived. Allen went on to appear on *The Comedy Zone* (CBS), *Life's Most Embarrassing Moments* (ABC), and a music and comedy series for the Disney Channel. In 1986 he was named to the Television Hall of Fame.

'ALLO 'ALLO ▶ BBC-produced sitcom set in France during World War II, about a French restaurant owner who offers his establishment to the British as a place of refuge while they battle the Germans. Syndicated by Tribune Entertainment in the U.S., the show drew modest ratings when it aired in the States in 1987. Featured were Gordon Kaye, Carmen Silvers, Vickie Michelle, Kristen Cooke, Francesca Gonshaw, Richard Marner, Richard Gibson, Kim Hartman and Rose Hill. David Croft produced and directed, and wrote some of the episodes.

ALTERNATIVE TELEVISION ▶ cultural movement of the early days of small-format video recording that emerged outside the formal broadcast system. It grew up around portapak equipment following its introduction into the consumer market by Japanese manufacturers in 1970. The field embraced student groups, individual techno-artists, community video centers and a range of collectives and groups dedicated to innovative television. Some of them functioned as the video equivalents of the underground press.

Nam June Paik, a Korean-born artist who had been experimenting with abstract images on television since 1963, is generally credited with having fathered the alternative television movement when he exhibited, at the Cafe Au Go Go in Greenwich Village in 1970, scenes shot from a taxi with his newly purchased portapak gear.

The portapak units, initially costing around $2,000 for a complete system, were built around lightweight hand-held cameras that recorded on 1/2 inch tape. An attractive feature of the videotaping unit was its playback capability, which allowed the operator to review immediately what was shot. Portapak technology thus permitted one person to achieve a video result which in studio television involves a clutch of professionals, from director to lighting engineer.

Usually without expectation of remuneration for their efforts and with few outlets for their work beyond public access channels on cable television or varied forms of video theaters, several schools of alternative television began to grow, some devoted to service video (serving the communications needs of communities too small for broadcast TV to serve, such as ethnic ghettos, schools, banks and industries); some to explorations of optical effects; some to producing nonfiction programs, such as documentaries; and some to perfecting "street video" as an art form.

A leader in the documentary field was TVTV (Top Value Television), a San Francisco-based group whose candid two-part report on the way the media covered the 1972 political conventions was carried by the Group W television stations and several cable systems. This was followed by the sale to public television of two more documentaries, *Adland,* on the advertising industry, and *Lord of the World,* on the 16-year-old guru Mahara-ji in his 1973 appearance at the Houston Astrodome. Both were well-received by the critics.

The development of the Time-Base Corrector (TBC) by Consolidated Video Systems in 1973, chiefly for the expensive minicameras that had begun to come into use in commercial television for newsgathering, made it possible for alternative television productions to infiltrate broadcast television.

Alternative television groups took such names as Raindance, the Videofreex, the Ant Farm, Alternate Media, People's Video Theatre and Global Village. The hundreds of groups operating in various parts of the U.S., with hundreds more throughout the world, gave rise to networks-by-mail, video festivals and exhibitions, and a periodical, *Radical Software.*

AMAHL AND THE NIGHT VISITORS ▶ Gian Carlo Menotti opera on a Christmas theme, the first opera to be written expressly for TV; it premiered in a two-hour production by the NBC Opera Company on Christmas Eve, 1951, and was a seasonal offering for many years afterwards. The 1953 production, presented in the *Hallmark Hall of Fame* series, was the first sponsored show to be televised in color. Samuel Chotzinoff produced the early telecasts of the opera.

The role of Amahl, the crippled shepherd boy, was performed the first year by Chet Allen and in many of the subsequent productions by Bill McIver. Rosemary Kuhlmann performed the role of the boy's mother in the original and the later productions.

In 1978, NBC offered a new filmed production of the opera with Teresa Stratas as the mother and Robert Sapolsky as Amahl, and with Giorgio Tozzi, Nico Castel and Willard White as the Three Kings.

AMATEAU, ROD ▶ producer-director, very active in the 1950s, best known for creative supervision of *The Burns and Allen Show.* More recently, he was line producer for NBC's ambitious 1979 series, *Supertrain.* He segued from that fiasco to supervising producer of *Dukes of Hazzard,* a ratings hit on CBS.

AMATEUR NEWS VIDEOS ▶ video footage taken by ordinary citizens of events and occurrences that prove newsworthy. Increasingly, they are being used in local and national newscasts and often in the weekly tabloid shows; frequently, they are purchased. The availability of amateur news footage grew in the late 1980s with the proliferation of personal video cameras, which now number in the millions. Coincidentally, comical amateur videos also became the basis of two highly rated prime-time series on ABC, *America's Funniest Home Videos* and *America's Funniest People.*

News organizations all over the country, including CNN, have been tapping into this new well of video stringers, some setting up toll-free hotlines for amateurs who may have recorded episodes of police brutality, fires, explosions or natural disasters. Some journalists are concerned about the trend because of the possibility of events being staged or because some of the footage may be bogus—a notable example being the widely used footage of the explosion at Chernobyl, which later was found to have been an explosion elsewhere in Europe.

The most important and famous bit of amateur news footage was that taken by Abraham Zapruder, a Dallas resident who was filming the presidential motorcade on Nov. 22, 1963 and captured the assassination of President Kennedy. This was before the era of camcorders, however; Zapruder used an 8mm Bell & Howell movie camera.

Amateur videos as a source of news came into prominence with footage recorded in 1987 of the Tompkins Square riots in New York City, which graphically revealed a police rampage when a demonstration turned violent in the East Village section of Manhattan. Virtually every newscast in New York carried the disturbing images. In 1991 the amateur recording of the now famous brutal beating of Rodney King by Los Angeles police aired nationally as well as locally. The scandal reverberated in police departments everywhere and led to self-examination and reforms.

As video submissions from amateurs increase around the country, stations have had to consider policies and create contracts to settle on fees and rights to the footage.

***AMEN* ▶** NBC Saturday night sitcom (1986-91) revolving around a Philadelphia church and its black deacon (Sherman Hemsley) and reverend (Clifton Davis). The series was a successful follow-up for Hemsley to his long-running hit, *The Jeffersons.* NBC has paired it with *227,* another half-hour sitcom with black principals. The show's executive producers included Ed. Weinberger, Arthur Julian, Lloyd David, James Stein and Robert Illes. It was produced by Carson Productions.

***AMERICA (ALISTAIR COOKE'S AMERICA)* ▶** 13-hour series produced by the BBC as a sort of personal essay by journalist Alistair Cooke on the history of the United States. NBC televised it simultaneously with the BBC in 1972; then it went to PBS in 1974 in a different form—26 half-hour episodes underwritten by Xerox.

Cooke, an Englishman who became a U.S. citizen, called the series a "personal interpretation" of American history and was its writer as well as narrator. The shows, which won numerous honors, traced the country's growth from Indian times to the present. Michael Gill was producer, and Time-Life Films co-financed the production with the BBC.

***AMERICA AFTER DARK* ▶** an attempt by NBC at a new concept in late-night television, that of surveying live the key population centers for coverage of the social and celebrity functions. The nightly program, which began in January 1957 in the 11:30 p.m. time slot, was poorly received and lasted only seven months.

Columnists Hy Gardner, Earl Wilson and Bob Considine covered the New York segments, while Paul Coates went on for the West Coast and Irv Kupcinet for Chicago. Jack Lescoulie served as moderator. The program gave way to the vastly more successful *Tonight* show, with Jack Paar.

***AMERICA ALIVE!* ▶** NBC daytime magazine program (1978) that switched around the country for interviews and features to convey a sense of covering life-styles in America on a daily basis. Jack Linkletter was host and Bruce Jenner, Janet Langhart and Pat Mitchell traveling co-hosts. The series began in July 1978 and was dropped by the end of the year because of lean ratings. Woody Fraser, who had left ABC's *Good Morning, America* to take on the project, was executive producer.

AMERICA 2NIGHT ▶ syndicated series via the Norman Lear shop satirizing the crassness of television talk shows. It ran one season (1977-78), growing out of a summer entry, *Fernwood 2-Night,* which in turn was a spin-off of *Mary Hartman, Mary Hartman.*

When *Mary Hartman,* as a comic soap opera, could not sustain the grind of five shows a week, Lear's T.A.T. Productions came up with the idea of *Fernwood 2-Night*—a fictional local TV talk show using some of the cast and the mythical locale of *Mary Hartman*—as a summer replacement. The concept was broadened to a national talk show with *America 2Night.* While it had a loyal and appreciative following, the audience was by TV standards a small one. Martin Mull played the talk-show host, Barth Gimble, Fred Willard portrayed his sidekick, Jerry Hubard, and Frank De Vol was Happy Kyne, bandleader of the Mirthmakers.

AMERICAN ASSASSINS, THE ▶ 1975 documentary series by CBS that was remarkable not only for its content but also for the manner in which it was scheduled. The four one-hour programs aired on four consecutive nights in prime time. The programs examined in detail the wave of assassinations and attempted assassinations in the 1960s, drawing from the Warren Commission findings and the wealth of books and other written material on the subject, in addition to the series' own investigations. The effort won a Peabody, among other awards. Leslie Midgley was executive producer, Bernard Birnbaum the producer, and Dan Rather the correspondent.

AMERICAN BANDSTAND ▶ a TV disk jockey show that originated on a local station, WFIL-TV, in Philadelphia in the mid-1950s and made a national figure of host Dick Clark when it went on the ABC network in 1957. The program was televised daily in the afternoons and soon added a Saturday evening version, helping to introduce such rock stars of the era as Chubby Checker, Paul Anka and Frankie Avalon. In 1963, it was cut back to the Saturday edition, which ran for nearly three decades. Meanwhile, Clark himself branched into program-packaging, producing, and other TV ventures.

AMERICAN EXPERIENCE, THE ▶ a series of one-hour documentaries produced weekly for public TV, highlighting pivotal events and people who helped shape the destiny of America. Each program, varied in format and theme, tells its own story. Since its debut in 1988, independently produced shows have profiled, among others, Lindbergh, LBJ, Duke Ellington, Nixon, J. Edgar Hoover and Ida B. Wells; examined the meaning to the American experience of events like World War I, the economic crash of 1929, Pearl Harbor, and the 1906 San Francisco earthquake; and recalled America's nostalgic past in visits to Coney Island, Barnum's circus, and the Great Air Race of 1924.

The series, produced by Judy Crichton—who came to *The American Experience* after five years with ABC's *Closeup* and another seven years with *CBS Reports*—is a coproduction of the Boston, New York and Los Angeles public TV stations and is underwritten by Aetna and the Corporation for Public Broadcasting.

AMERICAN FAMILY, AN ▶ a PBS documentary series (1973) on the affluent William C. Loud family of Santa Barbara, Calif., which some critics considered a brilliant television venture and others a grotesque use of the medium. Producer Craig Gilbert and his cameras in effect moved in with the family from May 1971 to the following New Year's Eve to record the life-style, values and relationships of Bill and Pat Loud and their five children, Lance, Kevin, Grant, Delilah and Michele. The cinema verite portrait that resulted was provocative because it captured highly personal moments in their lives, including the break-up of the parents and the eldest son's flamboyant involvement in the New York homosexual scene.

When the series aired, the Louds went on talk shows and gave newspaper interviews contending that the 12-part documentary presented a distorted picture, emphasizing the bad moments in their lives rather than the good. Meanwhile, the press and public debated whether the film was valid as a revelation of American family life or was merely a form of peeping tomism with exhibitionists. The series originated as a project of NET and was completed when that organization was absorbed by WNET New York.

AMERICAN FEDERATION OF MUSICIANS (AFM) ▶ large and powerful union established in 1896 (AFL-CIO) with 725 chapters in the U.S. and Canada. It currently claims more than 450 local unions with a total membership of approximately 200,000. Its TV contracts involve few individual stations and are mainly with networks and group owners. During the radio era, AFM fought a famous battle to prohibit stations from using prerecorded music but lost when a federal court, in 1940, ruled that a musician's rights to recorded music ended with the sale of the record.

AMERICAN FEDERATION OF TELEVISION AND RADIO ARTISTS (AFTRA) ▶ broadcast performers union (AFL-CIO) founded in August 1937 as AFRA (radio artists). It added the "T" in 1952 after a merger with the Television Authority. The Television Authority had been formed by the American Guild of Variety Artists, Actors' Equity, Chorus Equity and the American Guild of Music Artists to represent their membership in the new electronic medium.

With AFTRA representing performers in live TV and Screen Actors Guild those in filmed TV programs, a jurisdictional dispute developed with the advent of video tape. SAG contended it was a new form of film, and AFTRA insisted the intent of tape was to preserve a live performance. AFTRA prevailed, but the two unions have been discussing the possibility of a merger ever since.

AFTRA staged a 13-day strike against the networks in March 1967, chiefly over a contract for new employees at the network-owned stations, and in the fall of that year the union briefly honored the picket lines of a technical union, NABET. In 1980 a strike by AFTRA and SAG, running from mid-July to October, halted much television production and caused delays in the new season premieres. The issue was the actors' stake in the new electronic media.

The federation is made up of 30 local chapters and claims more than 70,000 members. Bruce A. York became its chief executive in November 1990.

***AMERICAN MASTERS* ▶** the umbrella title of an occasionally scheduled public TV series of biographical documentaries, each paying tribute to an American who has achieved distinction in the arts or entertainment. The series has presented multipart profiles of comedians Charlie Chaplin, Buster Keaton and Harold Lloyd and single shows saluting musicians, artists, actors, composers, writers and movie directors. Ironically, many of the shows saluting American artists were produced by British TV. Susan Lacy is executive producer of the series, which has been seen on PBS since 1986.

AMERICAN MOVIE CLASSICS (AMC) ▶ 24-hour basic-cable network specializing in vintage films from the 1930s through the 1970s. Uniquely, it carries no advertising but is supported entirely by carriage fees charged to cable operators.

Launched in 1984 by Cablevision Systems' Rainbow Programming Enterprises, the channel today reaches about 30 million homes. The network began experimenting in the late 1980s with thematic scheduling of movies and the use of celebrity guest hosts such as Anthony Quinn and Douglas Fairbanks, Jr. The channel's regular host is actor Bob Dorian. Original programming includes movie trivia, panel shows and documentaries on movie stars of the past. Josh Sapan is president of AMC, and Kate McEnroe is vice president and general manager.

Because it is advertising-free and operates on a single revenue stream, AMC is one of the more expensive services to operators.

***AMERICAN PLAYHOUSE* ▶** long-running PBS series that represents public TV's commitment to serious drama. On a limited budget, *American Playhouse* has managed since 1982 to provide PBS with an annual offering of plays, literary adaptations, feature films and original works. Deft management has permitted the series to stretch its production dollars with coproduction arrangements and the presale of cable and theatrical rights, though a substantial portion of its support still comes from public TV's own funds, the National Endowment for the Arts, and underwriting from the Chubb Group of Insurance Companies.

David M. Davis, president and CEO of the producing organization, Public Television Playhouse Inc., created the series shortly after leaving the Ford Foundation. With help from CPB and PBS, he formed a production consortium of four public stations (with WNET New York as lead station) and brought in Lindsay Law as executive producer. Under Law's guidance, *American Playhouse* has presented in addition to original works such major plays as Eugene O'Neill's *Long Day's Journey Into Night,* Thornton Wilder's *The Skin of Our Teeth,* and Arthur Miller's *All My Sons,* along with literary adaptations such as Katherine Anne Porter's

Noon Wine and James Baldwin's *Go Tell It On The Mountain.* Its feature films include *Smooth Talk, Stand and Deliver, The Thin Blue Line,* and *Metropolitan,* and its original television plays, primarily by American writers, include *Concealed Enemies, The Shady Hill Kidnapping,* and *Oppenheimer.*

AMERICAN SHORT STORY ▶ public television anthology of short-story adaptations, which made its debut in 1977 with nine films and then received funding for eight more productions airing in the spring of 1980. Among its distinctions, the series was the first major work for American public TV to be purchased by the BBC.

The short-story series was produced by Robert Geller, a former high school English teacher, through his company, Learning In Focus, Inc. The series was presented on PBS by the South Carolina ETV Network and WGBH Boston.

The critical success of the series won Geller an opportunity to produce for NBC *Too Far To Go,* a two-hour adaptation of a series of stories by John Updike. The program aired in March of 1979, and it too was a critical success. Since then, Geller has been producing dramas for *American Playhouse.*

AMERICAN WOMEN IN RADIO AND TELEVISION (AWRT) ▶ nonprofit professional organization of women working in broadcasting and allied fields. Its purpose has been to encourage cooperation between, and to enhance the role of, females in the industry. Its national and regional conferences are forums for the discussion of industry issues.

Established in 1951, AWRT now has more than 50 chapters in the U.S. and some 2,500 members. In addition, there are campus groups assisted by the chapters known as College Women in Broadcasting. An AWRT educational foundation formed in 1960 finances broadcast industry forums, career clinics, international study tours and closed-circuit programs for hospitalized children.

AMERICA'S FUNNIEST HOME VIDEOS ▶ half-hour series on ABC (1990—) that started as a mid-season replacement and surprisingly became the smash hit of an otherwise hit-barren season. The show, which borrowed its concept from a Japanese hit and even used some of the footage from Japan in the early episodes, owes its existence to the proliferation of personal video cameras. Hosted by comedian-actor Bob Saget (*Full House*), the show solicits clips of unusual and humorous video footage from ordinary people across the country and organizes them in a rapid-fire presentation. At the end of each program, the studio audience picks a prize-winner, deemed the funniest of the week's clips.

The program's popularity spawned a spin-off series, *America's Funniest People,* which is scheduled in tandem with *Home Videos* to comprise a high-rated hour in ABC's Sunday evening lineup. That spin-off's premise is similar to the original, but hosted by Saget's co-star on *Full House,* David Coulier, along with Arleen Sorkin. Both programs are produced by Vin DiBona Productions in association with ABC Productions.

AMERICA'S MOST WANTED ▶ reality-based series on the Fox Network that with NBC's *Unsolved Mysteries* helped spawn a new genre in American television—one in which the viewers help police solve cases. The show took its inspiration from a British series, which in turn had borrowed the idea from a German show. When it began in 1988 the show blossomed into one of fledgling Fox Network's first hits. The series recreates crimes whose suspected perpetrators have disappeared, and it presents pictures of them in enlisting viewers to call in with any information that might lead to their capture. In the first few years of the show, scores of criminals were apprehended on leads from viewers, and the program's role in the capture is frequently credited in the press.

Host of the series is John Walsh, whose son was kidnapped and murdered in 1981. Using verite-style reporting and recreations, the show not only gave rise to imitators in syndication but also on cable shows aiming to aid the police locally.

America's Most Wanted is produced by STF Productions, Fox's in-house production unit. Its executive producers are Lance Heflin and Michael Linder.

AMERIKA ▶ futuristic epic mini-series that was televised on ABC in 14 1/2 ponderous hours for seven consecutive nights in February 1987. It proved one of the most expensive and colossal flops in television history. Its controversial premise—a Soviet takeover of the United States in the 1990s—created a mild furor at the time and led to a flurry of pro and con newspaper editorials and political cartoons. The show was directed and written by David Wrye, who was also the executive producer.

The $40 million mini-series, which starred Robert Urich, Christine Lahti, Sam Neill and Kris Kristofferson as the one-time presidential candidate who emerges from a labor camp to lead a dissident uprising, was universally panned and drew comparisons to *Heavens Gate,* the Hollywood disaster epic, which ironically also starred Kristofferson.

AMOS 'N' ANDY ▶ TV version of the enormously popular radio series, produced and carried by CBS (1951-53). It ceased production not for lack of audience but because black organizations such as the NAACP objected to it for depicting blacks in a demeaning and stereotyped manner. When Blatz Beer yielded to the organizations' campaigns and withdrew its sponsorship, CBS took the show off the network, but the reruns continued to be syndicated by CBS Films until 1966. During the civil rights movement, CBS responded to protests by removing the show from both domestic and overseas sale and making it unavailable for any purpose. The series featured Alvin Childress and Spencer Williams, with Tim Moore in the focal role of "Kingfish."

AMPEX ▶ company founded near San Francisco in 1944 by electrical engineer Alexander M. Poniatoff as a supplier to the U.S. war effort that grew into one of the world's largest manufacturers of television broadcast products. With the coming of peace, Ampex focused on magnetic technology. Backed by entertainer Bing Crosby in the late 1940s, Ampex was one of the early developers of audio tape recording. In 1956 the company introduced the world's first practical videotape recorder (VTR) at the National Association of Broadcasters convention in Chicago—a development that made a huge impact on the television industry, allowing it to progress beyond the presentation of live programming and canned movies.

In addition to several generations of VTRs that the company has developed over the years, Ampex has launched products in the areas of electronic video editing, the playback of TV commercials, stills storage and electronic art systems. In 1981 the company launched its ADO (Ampex digital optics), an electronic effects system widely adopted by networks, stations and teleproduction facilities worldwide.

AMPTP (ALLIANCE OF MOTION PICTURE AND TELEVISION PRODUCERS) ▶ trade association representing about 70 production companies. As the collective bargaining arm of the Motion Picture Association of America (MPAA), it handles contract negotiation and labor relations in television for the member companies. It also conducts training, apprenticeship and technical research programs.

ANALOG ▶ transmitted signal that is continuously variable, unlike digital signals, which are made up of discrete pulses. While current television signals are analog, those in the not too-distant future are likely to be digital.

ANCHOR ▶ the main presenter of news in a television newscast; in effect, the host and star who holds the fore. The term is so widely used it seems to have been born with television, but actually it was coined in 1952 by Sig Mickelson, then president of CBS News. At the political conventions that year, Mickelson needed a word to describe Walter Cronkite's role as the central figure of the broadcast who would receive reports from all the scattered correspondents on the scene and cue the cutaways. For lack of a better word, Mickelson noted that Cronkite anchored or held down the CBS ship before the cameras and relayed the news from the field. The term, which originated for the coverage of live news events, soon was applied to network and local newscasts. Today many local newscasts have dual anchors, male and female, who deliver the stories, though the stories are usually gotten or written by others.

ANCIER, GARTH ▶ a program executive with one of the most densely packed resumes in the business, at least for someone in his early thirties. In 1983, at 25, he was named NBC's vice president of current comedy programs, at a time when the network was assembling a lineup of hits that included *The Cosby Show* and *Family Ties.* In early 1986 he left NBC, where he was a protege of programming chief Brandon Tartikoff, and took a gamble on an extremely uncertain start-up: Fox Broadcasting Company, which was assembling a fourth network under Fox chairman Barry Diller. Ancier was named president of programming the next year, and his department developed the young network's first hits, including *Married...with Children, 21 Jump Street* and *The Tracey Ullman Show,* along with, of course, its fair share of flops.

By early 1989, however, with the Fox schedule shy of hits and internal politics at Fox creating pressure, Ancier left the network and soon after joined Disney as president of network television production. He left Disney toward the end of 1990. In mid-1991 Ancier rejoined Fox in an unusual capacity, as an untitled executive working on program development and production for the network.

ANCILLARY MARKETS ▶ secondary avenues for revenues after a program's primary run. A series or TV movie produced for a U.S. network may be sold simultaneously to television systems abroad. When the network license expires, the reruns may be offered to cable networks or sold to local stations in domestic syndication. For certain programs, the sale of home video rights can be very lucrative, and there is as well a school market for programs of particular cultural or educational value. Because most prime-time series cost more to produce than the networks pay for firstrun rights, the shows derive their essential profits from the ancillary markets.

ANDREWS, EAMONN ▶ a leading British TV personality who since 1968 has been a dominant on-camera figure for Thames Television. He has been one of the co-hosts of the Thames *Today* show, which is televised in the evening, and also host of *This Is Your Life* (a program quite different in the U.K. from its U.S. counterpart). Before signing on with Thames, he had been a BBC performer, hosting the British edition of *What's My Line?*, which ran for 12 years, and doubling as a sportscaster on BBC Radio. An Irishman, he broke into radio in Dublin as a boxing commentator at the age of 16.

***ANDY GRIFFITH SHOW, THE* ▶** a countrified situation comedy concerning a small town sheriff and his friends. A Monday night fixture on CBS for nearly a decade (1960-68), it featured Don Knotts as Deputy Barney Fife, Ronny Howard as Andy's son Opie and Frances Bavier as Andy's aunt, Bee Taylor. When Griffith left the series, it continued in its CBS time period as *Mayberry R.F.D.*, with Ken Berry in the principal role as a small town councilman. It fell, finally, not to poor ratings but to the CBS decision to undo what had become the network's rural image. The syndicated reruns of the Andy Griffith version carried the title *Andy of Mayberry*. The series was by Mayberry Productions.

***ANDY WILLIAMS SHOW, THE* ▶** title of four different music-variety series starring one of the leading popular singers of the 1960s. Longest-running of the four was Williams's first NBC variety hour (1962-67), which featured The New Christy Minstrels and a singing group of young boys, The Osmond Brothers. It was by Barnaby Productions. Two years later NBC mounted a new series for Williams with a different supporting cast that lasted two seasons, until 1971.

A 1959 *Andy Williams Show* was a summertime venture for CBS. In 1976 Williams began a new half-hour variety series for prime-access syndication, produced by Pierre Cossette.

ANGLIA TELEVISION ▶ commercial licensee for the East of England region, based in Norwich and founded in 1961. Survival Anglia, Ltd., its production subsidiary, made its mark globally with the *Survival* series of nature and animal shows.

ANIK ▶ early domestic satellite, launched by Canada in November 1972 and used for transcontinental Canadian television links and for TV and telephone links with remote Arctic settlements.

***ANN SOTHERN SHOW, THE* ▶** moderately successful CBS situation comedy (1958-61) which was part of a parade of shows in the 1950s that absorbed movie actors into TV. Actually, Sothern had made the transition earlier with *Private Secretary* (1952-54), whose reruns went into syndication under the title *Susie*. In both series she played opposite Don Porter. The first series cast her as a secretary in a talent agency, the second as an assistant manager at a New York hotel. In 1965 Sothern performed the voice of the car in the short-lived fantasy comedy *My Mother, The Car*.

***ANNE OF GREEN GABLES* ▶** successful Canadian mini-series (1988) based on the Canadian children's book of that title by Lucy Maud Montgomery. Produced by Sullivan Films in Toronto, it starred Colleen Dewhurst, Richard Farnsworth and Megan Follows. The four-hour show was produced, directed and co-written by Kevin Sullivan. A follow-up mini-series, *Anne of Green Gables: The Sequel*, appeared two years later. Both mini-series sold well around the world, playing in more than 80 countries. (A two-hour theatrical version played in Japan and Israel for a year.). The mini-series also yielded a weekly series spin-off, *Road to Avonlea*, which airs in the U.S. on the Disney Channel.

ANNENBERG, WALTER H. ▶ former head of a media empire largely concentrated in Philadelphia and eastern Pennsylvania. It was dismantled after his appointment as President Nixon's Envoy to the Court of St. James. Annenberg's broadcast group, Triangle Stations, was broken up in 1970, with a total of nine stations sold to Capital Cities and the remainder to former employees under the banner of Gateway Communications. Earlier he had divested himself of his two newspapers, the *Philadelphia Inquirer* and the *Philadelphia Daily News.* In 1988 he sold the remaining Triangle publications, including *TV Guide,* to Rupert Murdoch's News Corp. for $3 billion.

Annenberg was also founder and president of the Annenberg schools of communications at the University of Pennsylvania and the University of Southern California, and he contributed to the communications program at Temple University. In 1977 he proposed to establish a multimillion-dollar communications facility and school at the Metropolitan Museum of Art in New York, but he withdrew the offer when it proved controversial with the Museum's board.

In 1981 Annenberg announced a grant to public TV of $150 million—$10 million for each of 15 years—for the development of television courses to be used in higher education. The funds, administered by the Corporation for Public Broadcasting, aided in the development of such PBS series as *The Brain, Race to Save the Planet,* and *Ethics in America.* Nine years into the 15-year project, however, Annenberg canceled the remaining portion of the grant, citing tax reasons growing out of the sale of his publications. Public television's shock at the loss was somewhat assuaged by the announcement in June 1991 of a new Annenberg grant of precisely the same amount and duration as the canceled portion of the original grant—$60 million for six years. But the new grant had a different purpose and a younger audience: TV courses to improve the teaching and learning of science and math in grades kindergarten through twelve.

ANOTHER WORLD ▶ see Soap Operas.

ANTENNA FARM ▶ a location set aside for all or most of the television transmitting antennae in a community or area. The use of antenna farms is considered preferable to locating antennas in various different areas because it reduces air traffic hazards and usually makes possible better home television reception by permitting all receiving antennae to be oriented in the same direction.

ANTHOLOGY ▶ nonepisodic program series constituting an omnibus of different programs that are related only by genre. The studio drama series of the 1950s—*U.S. Steel Hour, Philco Playhouse,* etc.—are notable examples, as in another sphere is ABC's *Wide World of Sports.* Often a host is used to provide a sense of weekly continuity, as with *Alfred Hitchcock Presents, Boris Karloff's "Thriller," Dick Powell's Zane Grey Theater* and Rod Serling's *Twilight Zone.* The longest-running anthology in prime time was NBC's *Wonderful World of Disney.*

The so-called "golden age" of TV drama ended and anthologies in general went into a decline in the early 1960s, when network programmers determined that TV's heavy viewers—the habit viewers—were more likely to embrace episodic shows with familiar elements than series whose casts changed every week. Through most of the 1960s the networks usually avoided the anthology series as a high-risk item except in one form, theatrical movies.

Audience criteria changed around 1970, however, sparking the return of the anthology. The advertising industry's preoccupation with demographics sent the networks in quest of viewers in the 18-49 age range; this ruled out the habit viewer, who was perceived as either very young or over 50. The 18-49 group was the movie-going group, and the networks catered to it with made-for-TV movies that, of course, were merely telefilm anthologies going by the names of *World Premiere* and *Movie of the Week.* Other anthologies such as *Police Story* and the news-magazine *60 Minutes* soon after established themselves in prime time.

ANTI-BLACKOUT LAW ▶ legislation enacted in 1972 prohibiting local TV blackouts of major professional sports events if they are sold out 72 hours ahead of game time. The law, as initially passed, was contingent on a three-year trial basis, the result of public disaffection at being denied telecasts of sold-out home games. The blackouts occurred, according to team spokespersons, because owners feared that the availability of home games on TV would discourage ticket sales. Annual studies by the FCC, however, have proved otherwise, prompting Congress to consider legislation to make the original law permanent.

ANTIOPE ▶ videotext system developed in the 1970s by the French communications industry under government leadership. That same development work also led to France's nationwide Minitel personal computer service that had 6 million subscribers by 1990.

APPELL, DON ▶ director-writer whose credits include *Apple's Way, Love Story, Love, American Style, Arnie* and *Run For Your Life,* among scores of other shows.

***APPOINTMENT WITH DESTINY* ▶** series of specials by the Wolper Organization using documentary techniques in dramatic reenactments of historical events. Six were televised by CBS between 1971 and 1973 and a seventh, *They've Killed President Lincoln,* by NBC.

The CBS group included *The Crucifixion of Jesus,* narrated by John Huston; *Surrender at Appomattox,* narrated by Hal Holbrook; *Showdown at the O.K. Corral,* narrated by Lorne Greene; *The Plot to Murder Hitler,* narrated by James Mason; *The Last Days of John Dillinger,* narrated by Rod Serling; and *Peary's Race to the North Pole,* narrated by Greene. The Lincoln episode was narrated by Richard Basehart. Nicholas Webster and Robert Guenette separately produced and directed various episodes.

APS (AMERICAN PROGRAM SERVICES) ▶ an association of public television stations joined to provide program services to its members through acquisition, coventures and coproductions to supplement the programming of PBS. Formerly the Interregional Program Service (IPS).

ARBITRON RATINGS CO. ▶ the television and radio ratings service owned by Control Data Corp. It is the prime competitor to the A.C. Nielsen Co. in gathering TV audience data at the local level.

In the late 1980s and early 1990s, with the local television market economy ailing, many stations could afford only one ratings service. This "single service" trend produced heated competition between Arbitron and Nielsen. In 1988 nearly 570 commercial stations subscribed to both services. By 1991 the number had shrunk to 345. About 275 commercial stations were exclusive to Nielsen in 1991, compared to 195 for Arbitron. Nielsen had set-tuning meters in 25 local markets against 13 for Arbitron.

The Arbitron Television Market Report provides individual surveys of TV viewing, with demographic breakdown, in more than 200 marketing areas defined as Areas of Dominant Influence (ADI). The Arbitrons—as the rating reports are called—also offer estimates of the number of TV households, homes subscribing to cable TV, owning VCRs, and other information of the kind. The Arbitron ADI's are nearly identical to Nielsen's DMA's.

***ARCHIE BUNKER'S PLACE* ▶** Carroll O'Connor vehicle on CBS (1979-83) which represented the remains of *All in the Family* after the three other principals, Jean Stapleton, Sally Struthers and Rob Reiner, left the cast. The newer series featured Bunker (O'Connor), a widower, tending a neighborhood saloon with his business partner Murray Klein (Martin Balsam), and raising his young niece Stephanie Mills (Danielle Brisebois). Bunker without his family proved nearly as popular as before and helped maintain the CBS dominance of Sunday night. Via Tandem Productions and Ugo Productions, with Joseph Gannon as producer, the series featured Allan Melvin, Denise Miller, Steven Hendrickson, Jason Wingreen, Barbara Meek, Bill Quinn, Anne Meara, and Abraham Alvarez.

ARDEN, EVE (d. 1990) ▶ comedy actress who appeared in more than 60 movies but is best remembered for her portrayal of the title character in an early TV sitcom, *Our Miss Brooks.* The series began in radio in 1948 and shifted to television in 1952, where it ran for four years on CBS and many years after in reruns. Arden's hallmark was the sharp, deflating wisecrack, which she delivered with devastating timing. In the 1960s she co-starred with Kaye Ballard in *Mothers-In-Law,* a short-lived NBC sitcom. Among her TV movies were *The Dream Merchants, A Guide for the Married Woman, In Name Only* and the 1983 version of *Alice in Wonderland.*

ARGENTINA ▶ country with 9.7 million television households (against a total population of 32 million people) served by five TV networks, four of which are privately owned and the other, Argentina Televisora Color (ATC), state-run. Until the administration of the Peronist Party's Carlos Menem, which began in 1989, there were three state channels. Two were privatized the following year. All, including ATC, compete with each other for advertising and all are based in Buenos Aires. Cable penetration is around 8%, most of it in Buenos Aires.

ARLEDGE, ROONE ▶ president of ABC News since 1977 and previously president of both the News and Sports divisions. He has been a leading figure in TV sports since the 1960s when, as v.p. for ABC Sports, he moved aggressively to acquire rights to top events, developed omnibus programs such as *Wide World of Sports* and *The American Sportsman* and stimulated innovations in live production. He was named president of ABC Sports in 1968 and shortly afterwards successfully negotiated for the Monday night *NFL Football* series, giving an important lift to the network's prime-time schedule.

Roone Arledge

His promotion to head of News, at a time when ABC was prospering on the entertainment front, was alarming to many in the industry since Arledge had no background in journalism. It was feared that in his zeal to improve the network's news circulation, Arledge would let high news standards fall to showmanship and electronic razzle-dazzle. To a certain degree he did, at first, as with the pilot for the news magazine *20/20* and with his multiple anchor format to enliven the evening newscast. But despite some early lapses, ABC News maintained respectability and gained in stature in Arledge's administration, and by the second year the ratings for the evening newscast, *World News Tonight,* had for the first time caught up with those for NBC's *Nightly News* and on several occasions surpassed them. By 1981, ABC News had become a full-fledged competitor to the other networks, and equally respected.

Arledge outbid his rivals for Olympic events in 1968, 1972 and 1976 and won honors for ABC with distinguished coverage. By using the Atlantic satellite he arranged live coverage of numerous international sporting events, including heavyweight title fights, the U.S.-Russia Track Meet from Kiev, the Le Mans endurance race in 1965, the Irish Sweepstakes and the World Figure Skating Championships.

His skill in producing elaborate live sports events brought him into the show business realm in the mid-1970s as producer of live specials with Frank Sinatra and Barbra Streisand, and later as executive producer of the variety series *Saturday Night Live with Howard Cosell.* None, however, scored impressively in the ratings.

Arledge's impact on news, when he assumed charge in 1977, was as profound as his impact on sports. His talent raids netted David Brinkley from NBC and Diane Sawyer from CBS, among others, and at one point he came close to wooing away Dan Rather from CBS. In the process he drove up salaries for top network TV journalists.

Perhaps Arledge's most important contribution to ABC was his eventual selection of Peter Jennings to anchor the *World News Tonight* newscast from New York. This came after a number of attempts at creating a different sort of newscast. Arledge had inherited a dual-anchor team of Harry Reasoner and Barbara Walters. Reasoner, who had left CBS to become sole anchor of *World News Tonight,* made it evident that he resented Walters and in time returned to CBS News and *60 Minutes.* For a short time, Arledge experimented with a tri-anchor system of Max Robinson in Chicago, Peter Jennings in London, and Frank Reynolds in Washington (occasionally, Walters filled in from New York). It wasn't until Arledge settled on the single-anchor format with Jennings in 1983 that ABC began to have a real shot at becoming the leader in network news. The introduction of *Nightline* with Ted Koppel put ABC over the top. Arledge was always seeking broader scale concepts, and the *Nightline* format, with Koppel shifting from one guest to the other and from one location to another via satellite, proved to be a winner. Arledge also had another winner in *20/20* when he teamed Hugh Downs with Walters.

But Arledge could not continue to oversee two dynamic divisions, news and sports, indefinitely. The new management at Cap Cities/ABC determined in 1986 that with ABC Sports losing money, the division needed a full-time president. Arledge was succeeded at ABC Sports by Dennis Swanson, former general manager of WLS-TV, the ABC-owned station in Chicago. Arledge did, however, produce the 1988 Olympics from Calgary.

Arledge joined ABC in 1960 in a production capacity after six years at NBC, during which time he produced news and special events broadcasts and the series *Hi Mom.* He created *Wide World of Sports* in 1961 and, with that, started ABC Sports on its period of rapid growth.

ARMY-McCARTHY HEARINGS ▶ an historic congressional proceeding which began April 22, 1954; it marked the end of Sen. Joseph McCarthy's career as a ruthless hunter of communists and subversives in government, largely because it was televised. The hearings spanned two months and occupied a total of 35 broadcast days. ABC, which had a meager daytime schedule at the time, carried the hearings in full, as did the fading DuMont Network. CBS and NBC carried excerpts.

As he had on Edward R. Murrow's *See It Now* programs weeks before the hearings began, Sen. McCarthy projected the image of a callous and opportunistic villain to millions in the viewing audience. Largely as a result of the hearings, the Senate voted 67 to 22 to condemn McCarthy for his tactics and irresponsible charges, and conventional wisdom insists that it was this television exposure that turned public opinion against the Wisconsin senator and was his real undoing.

ARNAZ, DESI (d. 1986) ▶ co-star of the *I Love Lucy* series and subsequently producer and occasional director of *Lucy* and *The Lucille Ball Show* while he was married to the comedienne. He also headed their Desilu Studios prior to its sale to Paramount TV. Before embarking on a TV career, Arnaz, a Cuban, had been leader of a Latin band.

ARNESS, JAMES ▶ star of *Gunsmoke* (1955-75) on CBS, through which he became one of TV's best-known and highest-paid actors, while the character he portrayed, Marshal Matt Dillon, became a national folk hero. A relatively obscure screen actor, he won the role because he bore a resemblance to John Wayne, who had been envisioned for the part. Arness eventually became part-owner of the series. He later starred in a two-hour series, *How the West Was Won* (1976-79), which was aired by ABC on Monday nights in place of the NFL games when the football season ended.

Arness returned to a new NBC series in 1981-82, *McClain's Law,* with Eric Bercovili as executive producer. But it was one of that season's many casualties.

ARNETT, PETER ▶ tough veteran journalist working for CNN who became famous for his coverage of the Persian Gulf war. Working under censorship control by Iraqi authorities, Arnett was the only American journalist reporting live from Baghdad for most of the war. He remained there for the duration of hostilities and scored a coup in an exclusive interview with Saddam Hussein. However, he also came under fire by some in the U.S. who felt Arnett was being used by the enemy and that the interview provided Hussein the opportunity to disseminate his propaganda to the world.

A native of New Zealand, Arnett covered the Vietnam War for the Associated Press from 1962 until the fall of Saigon in 1975, winning a Pulitzer Prize in 1966 for international reporting. He left the AP to join CNN in 1981, serving as Moscow and Washington bureau chief, respectively.

ARNOLD, DANNY ▶ comedy writer-producer whose series credits include *Barney Miller* (which he created with Theodore Flicker and of which he was executive producer until 1982) and *My World and Welcome to It.*

He began as a film editor, worked briefly as a standup comedian and actor in films with Dean Martin and Jerry Lewis and, in 1956, became a writer for the *Tennessee Ernie Ford Show* and later the *Rosemary Clooney Show.* He was producer and story editor for *The Real McCoys* (1962), and producer of *Bewitched* (1963-67) and of *That Girl* (1967-69). Arnold was executive producer for *Stat,* a sitcom centered on a hospital emergency room, which was a 1990-91 entry and was canceled that season. He formed his own company, Four D Productions, in 1974; the company is named for his wife, his two sons and himself, all of whose names begin with the letter *D.*

ARREST AND TRIAL ▶ 90-minute series introduced by ABC (1963-64), which was two shows in one: a 45-minute police show involving the capture of a suspect, followed by a 45-minute courtroom drama on the prosecution of the case. The joining of two popular modes of melodrama did not catch the public fancy, however, and the series lasted only one season. Ben Gazzara starred in the "Arrest" segment as police detective Nick Anderson, and Chuck Connors played criminal lawyer John Egan in the "Trial" portion. The series was by Universal TV.

ARSENIO HALL SHOW, THE ▶ late-night syndicated talk show hosted by black actor-comedian Arsenio Hall, which established itself nicely in 1989 as an alternative to the *Tonight Show* with its appeal to a younger audience.

Hall's previous talk show experience was as sidekick to Alan Thicke on the ill-fated *Thicke of the Night.* Later he replaced Joan Rivers on *The Late Show,* Fox's failed bid into the late-night genre. Paramount Domestic Television, which produces and distributes Hall's show, had to break the comedian's contract with Fox to get him, after executives noticed him during his acting work on the Paramount film *Coming to America.*

The show debuted in 1989 and broke some new ground in the genre with Hall's selection of guests, particularly musical, which reflected more contemporary black tastes. The show also employs music video-style camerawork for its musical segments and has eschewed the traditional desk & sofa set-up, opting for a more intimate chair instead of desk.

Arsenio Hall with guest Jesse Jackson on *The Arsenio Hall Show*

ARTHUR, BEATRICE ▶ comedy actress who plays the role of the ever pragmatic Dorothy on NBC's *The Golden Girls.* She began her television career in 1971 as Maude, the liberal foil to Archie Bunker in CBS's *All in the Family.* The character made such a strong impression that it spawned a spin-off series, *Maude,* in which Arthur starred for six seasons. She also co-starred in the made-for-TV movie, *One More Time.*

***ARTHUR MURRAY DANCE PARTY, THE* ▶** prime-time ballroom dance show which ran through the 1950s variously on four networks. It featured the head of the famous dance-instruction chain but actually starred his wife, Kathryn Murray, as hostess. The series, which involved skits, demonstrations of dance steps, and dance contests among celebrities began on the DuMont Network in 1950 and the following year switched to ABC. Later it went to NBC, CBS and back to NBC. Murray died in 1991.

ARTS & ENTERTAINMENT NETWORK (A&E) ▶ 24-hour basic-cable network aimed at an audience similar to that for public TV in offering British comedies and dramas, performing arts programs and documentaries. But in striving to reach the largest possible audience among the 42 million homes that receive it, A&E includes a considerable amount of light entertainment in its schedule, such as the series with stand-up comedians, *Evening at the Improv.* Among the national cable services, A&E has consistently ranked well below the leaders in audience ratings.

Launched in 1984 as a merger of ABC-owned Alpha Repertory Television Service (ARTS) and RCA-owned The Entertainment Channel, A&E is jointly owned by the Hearst Corporation, Capital Cities/ABC and NBC. The channel's contractual relationship with the BBC for programming pre-dates the merger and has resulted in a siphoning off of British programs that previously would have gone to PBS.

***AS THE WORLD TURNS* ▶** see Soap Operas.

ASCAP (AMERICAN SOCIETY OF COMPOSERS, AUTHORS AND PUBLISHERS) ▶ founded in 1914, the oldest of the U.S. music licensing organizations. As a nonprofit membership society, it collects copyright fees from users of music and distributes the royalty payments to writers and publishers. Radio and TV stations and networks are permitted to use ASCAP music under a blanket annual license fee; ASCAP then surveys the air plays to determine what each song has earned in royalties.

ASCAP's ability to control absolutely the copyright fees for music during the 1930s so concerned the broadcast industry that it created the National Association of Broadcasters to fight the anticipated increases in licensing fees. In 1939 the broadcast industry created a new music licensing organization as a counter-force, BMI (Broadcast Music, Inc.), which was controlled by broadcasters. Lacking the big-name established song writers, BMI endeavored to sign up young new composers; many were drawn to BMI because its formulas for royalty payments were more generous to writers of current hits than were those of ASCAP, oriented as it was then to the established writers.

In 1941, when broadcasters would not agree to ASCAP's demands for higher royalty payments, all ASCAP music was barred from the air—the current popular hits as well as the standards by Berlin, Kern, Porter, Gershwin, and others. Radio stations were left to play public-domain and BMI music until the matter was settled, but in holding out ASCAP actually helped BMI to grow stronger. ASCAP's new rival developed initially in the peripheral country music, jazz and rhythm & blues fields, and BMI came to full flower with the emergence of rock in the mid-1950s. Today ASCAP claims 45,000 members. Morton Gould is president.

ASCENT OF MAN, THE ▶ outstanding 13-hour series on the history of the ideas of humankind from prehistoric times to the present, prepared and presented by the late Dr. Jacob Bronowski. A co-production of the BBC and Time-Life Films, it had its U.S. premiere on PBS Jan. 7, 1975 on underwriting from Mobil Oil.

Dr. Bronowski, a noted scholar and leader in the movement of Scientific Humanism, proved an engaging TV performer, warm and infectiously enthusiastic; these appealing personal qualities made the difference in a remarkable mustering of knowledge and a television triumph. More than informative, the series was inspirational because of Bronowski's concern not with the historical discoveries themselves—"the great moments of human invention"—but with what they revealed of humankind.

Bronowski died of a heart attack in California, where he was a fellow at the Salk Institute, shortly before the series aired on PBS. But he had already assisted in the design of the college-credit courses that were to be based on the programs, courses which marked a breakthrough in the use of television for off-campus education.

ASCERTAINMENT PRIMER ▶ a spelling out by the FCC of requirements and procedures to assist stations in their ascertainment activities, issued on Dec. 19, 1969 as *Primer on Ascertainment of Community Needs.* It was amended and clarified by a Report and Order of Feb. 23, 1971; in 1981 it was discarded for radio by President Carter's chairman Charles Ferris, and in 1984 it was discarded for television by President Reagan's chairman Mark Fowler.

The primer, whose leading proponents on the commission were Robert Taylor Bartley and Kenneth Cox, made ascertainment of the needs and interests of a licensee's market an ongoing procedure rather than one performed only at license-renewal time. With the primer, the FCC hoped to create a formal mechanism by which to put all broadcasters in continual touch with all significant elements of the communities they were licensed to serve. Following the guidelines prescribed, each station was required to show what it ascertained of community needs and how it responded to those needs on the air. The primer called for key station personnel, including management, to meet on a regular basis with community leaders and to conduct surveys of the general population.

The commission's ascertainment procedures came in stages, beginning with its 1960 Programming Policy Statement, which expressed the agency's interest in licensees making a concerted effort to seek out the community issues that would lead to programming. In 1968, the FCC Public Notice *Ascertainment of Community Needs by Broadcast Applicants* asserted that long residency in an area was not necessarily an indication of familiarity with the programming needs of the community, and that a survey of needs was mandatory. The primer that resulted was hatched in part by the Federal Communications Bar Association (FCBA).

ASHER, WILLIAM ▶ producer-director whose credits include the *Fibber McGee & Molly* TV series and *The Shirley Temple Show* in the late 1960s, as well as *Bewitched, Temperature's Rising* and the *Paul Lynde Show.*

ASHLEY, TED ▶ noted talent agent who became chairman of Warner Bros. in 1969 when Kinney Services Inc. acquired the motion picture company; in 1975, he gave up the day-to-day operational responsibilities to Frank Wells and became active on a part-time basis as co-chairman.

A force in show business since the early 1950s, Ashley was an agent for William Morris for six years before starting his own agency at about the time commercial TV was beginning to grow. His agency expanded through acquisitions, becoming known as the Ashley Famous Agency, and was instrumental in packaging and selling to the networks around 100 series, including *The Carol Burnett Show, The Doris Day Show* and *Mission: Impossible.* Ashley represented such artists as Tennessee Williams, Arthur Miller, Perry Como, Burt Lancaster, Rex Harrison and Ingrid Bergman.

The agency was acquired by Kinney in 1967, and Ashley became a director and member of the executive committee. Two years later, when Kinney acquired Warner Bros., it sold off the talent agency to avoid the conflict of interests in both representing talent and producing, but it retained Ashley and named him head of the motion picture subsidiary of what became Warner Communications Inc.

ASI (AUDIENCE STUDIES, INC.) ▶ program testing system in Hollywood that was used by NBC, ABC and the production studios to determine whether a program would be popular and whether the storylines and cast members had appeal. CBS rarely used ASI because it operated its own testing system, "Little Annie." ASI testing was conducted in a plush Sunset Strip theater, Preview House, with a seating capacity of 400, to which the randomly accumulated participants were invited free. Each filled out forms to provide a breakdown of the group by age, sex, education and income and was asked to operate a dial at his or her seat to indicate when something in the program was pleasing or displeasing. The dial had degrees for either reaction. To set a norm for each night's audience, a Mister Magoo cartoon was run before the program. Oscilloscopes in the control room produced graphs of the audience reactions as expressed in dial-turning, and this information was collated with data from questionnaires and personal interviews. Although ASI had been owned by Screen Gems in the 1960s, other studios and the networks used it and trusted its results.

ASNER, EDWARD ▶ television star and president of Screen Actors Guild (1981), who became controversial as a liberal political activist during the Reagan Administration. An issue developed over whether the causes he championed—the Equal Rights Amendment, opposition to American involvement in El Salvador, opposition to nuclear arms—were perceived by the public as the point of view of his television persona, the sympathetic crusading newspaper editor, Lou Grant. Thus it became a journalistic issue, not unlike the issue of patent medicine endorsements by actors portraying doctors on television. Asner argued that actors on the right were able to endorse political causes with impunity, while liberals taking a position were considered out of line.

Asner became a star, and winner of numerous Emmy awards, through his role as the hard-boiled but sentimental boss of the newsroom in *The Mary Tyler Moore Show* (1970-77). When that sitcom folded, Asner's character, Lou Grant, was kept alive in a new CBS series by that title under the same production auspices, MTM Productions. There were two switches, however: in the new series, Grant became head of a newspaper's newsroom instead of a television station's and in the one-hour format he became a dramatic rather than a comic character. For all Asner's popularity, *Lou Grant* was a slow starter and didn't establish itself firmly as a hit until its third season on the air. It became one of the most respected shows in television and was acknowledged as being generally accurate in its portrayal of newspaper life.

As a television character, Lou Grant grew into a classic—not a leading man, but an everyman—a beefy, blustering, blundering, middle-aged, all-around fellow working in rolled-up shirtsleeves. The good, decent boss: gruff but underneath it all, humane.

During the actors' strike of 1980, Asner, for all his success and wealth, became a leading activist and spokesman for the workers' cause. A year later he was elected president of SAG, the post that started Ronald Reagan on his political career. Asner was at political odds with Reagan, and he was outspoken in opposing Administration policies that did not concern actors or the union directly. These activities made him a controversial figure in 1982. Asner resigned as SAG president in 1985 but is still active in social and political issues.

Asner was a serious actor on the stage before going into television. He made his mark first with Chicago's Playwrights Theatre Company and later appeared off-Broadway as Mr. Peachum in *The Threepenny Opera.* On television, in addition to his *Lou Grant* roles, he played Capt. Davies in *Roots* in 1977 and in the same year starred in the drama, *The Gathering.* He also was featured in the 1980 motion picture *Fort Apache, the Bronx* and starred in the 1981 teleplay, *A Small Killing.* In 1985 Asner starred in a new series, *Off the Rack,* and in 1991 was added to the cast of *The Trials of Rosie O'Neill.*

ASPECT RATIO ▶ referring to a TV screen's dimensions, its width in relation to its height. Conventional TV tubes have a 4:3 ratio. High-definition television (HDTV) requires a wider tube with an aspect ratio of about 5:3.

ASPEN INSTITUTE PROGRAM ON COMMUNICATIONS AND SOCIETY ▶ project of the Aspen Institute for Humanistic Studies to propose policies and action on major issues relating to the communications media. The institute's initial areas of priority have been government and the media, public broadcasting, television and social behavior and the humanistic uses of cable and the new technologies. Begun in 1971 with Douglass Cater as director, the program has consisted of seminars and conferences and has produced a number of books, policy papers and special reports. Michael Rice became director of the communication project in 1978 and continued until he died in 1987. He was succeeded by Charles Firestone.

It was at the instigation of the Aspen Institute that the FCC late in 1975 reinterpreted the Equal Time Law, classifying debates between political candidates and their press conferences as exempt from equal time considerations if they are covered by TV and radio as external, on-the-spot news events. Thus the institute helped to make possible the 1976 presidential and vice-presidential debates.

The focus for the 1990s is on four subject areas: communications policy, communications for social benefit, communications and education, and communications for global understanding.

ASTAIRE, FRED (d. 1984) ▶ incomparable dancer who achieved stardom in movies during the 1930s and contributed three dazzling TV specials almost a quarter-century later. His first, *An Evening With Fred Astaire,* was an artful blockbuster in 1958, winning a passel of Emmy Awards. Barrie Chase was his dancing partner, Hermes Pan the choreographer and Bud Yorkin the producer, with the Jonah Jones Quartet also featured. Astaire encored the following year with *Another Evening With Fred Astaire* and in 1960 offered *Astaire Time.*

Aside from the specials, he hosted *Alcoa Premiere* in 1962, a drama anthology that went into syndication as *Fred Astaire Presents.* He also had a featured role for one season (1969-70) in the ABC series, *It Takes a Thief.*

ASTRA ▶ Europe's first commercial broadcasting satellite which, when it launched under Luxembourg auspices in December 1988, transformed the television landscape in the Old World for all time. A medium-powered satellite, known as ASTRA 1A, it transmits 16 channels of television across much of Europe, mostly in the English and German languages. The signals are either taken down by cable or by private dish antennas as small as 60 cm at the base of the beam. ASTRA is an impudent satellite that has shown no respect for the sovereignty of national borders; its footprint comes down over much of western Europe.

Among the first prospectors in pan-European television by means of ASTRA was Scansat, which sent a channel from London, with advertising, to the Scandinavian countries that largely had barred all forms of commercial television on their native systems. Rupert Murdoch's venture into direct-to-home broadcasting with Sky Channel (known now as BSkyB) utilizes five transponders on ASTRA. The satellite also carries ScreenSport and two commercial German networks, RTL Plus and Sat 1 (Sat Eins), which have been very successful.

The satellite is operated by Societe Europeene des Satellites (SES), which holds a franchise from the Luxembourg government to use the country's allocated orbital space to provide satellites from multi-channel and multi-national services. A second satellite, ASTRA 1B, went aloft in 1991, with ASTRA 1C planned for launch in 1993.

***AT MOTHER'S REQUEST* ▶** four-hour mini-series, adapted from Jonathan Coleman's book of that title, about a New York socialite who in 1978 persuaded her son to kill his grandfather (her father) for his inheritance. It starred Stefanie Powers and Frances Sternhagen and aired on CBS Jan. 4 and 6, 1985, in two-hour segments. Gabriel Katzka and Bob Markell produced. Others in the cast were E. G. Marshall, John Wood, Corey Parker, Ray Baker and Penny Fuller.

Curiously, in March of the same year, another mini-series based on the same subject—this one six hours in length and shown on three consecutive nights (March 22-24)—was presented by NBC. It was based on Shana Alexander's book, *Nutcracker: Money, Madness, Murder,* with Lee Remick starring.

***A-TEAM, THE* ▶** popular NBC action series (1983-87) with an almost cartoon-like penchant for extreme violence with little death or injury, from Stephen J. Cannell Productions. Starring George Peppard as John "Hannibal" Smith, the leader of a renegade squad of Vietnam vets using their crack military skills to help out anyone up against bad guys, the team also included Dirk Benedict as Templeton "Face" Peck, Dwight Schultz as H. M. "Howlin' Mad" Murdock, and Mr. T, whose career was boosted by the show, as B. A. Barracus.

Cannell produced for Universal Television.

ATLANTIS FILMS ▶ one of Canada's most successful independent film and television companies, engaged both in the production of its own TV projects and in arranging financing and joint ventures for outside producers.

The Toronto-based company began in 1977 when three Queens University students, Michael MacMillan, Seaton McLean and Janice Platt, began making documentaries. A year later they were in Toronto making industrial and government films. In 1983 they won an Oscar in the live-action short film category for *Boys and Girls.* Today the company has more than 300 different programs in its library, many of them coproductions with U.S. and European companies. Michael MacMillan is president of Atlantis.

ATLASS, H. LESLIE (d. 1960) ▶ a pioneer in radio and TV who founded the WBBM stations that became the powerful and lucrative CBS base in Chicago. Atlass had been owner of WBBM Radio until it was purchased by CBS in 1933. He was then named v.p. in charge of the network's central division and in the early 1950s acquired a TV station for CBS, which became WBBM-TV. He then became v.p. and general manager of the Chicago TV, AM and FM stations and was a forceful figure in the company until he reached the mandatory retirement age in 1959. At WBBM Atlass groomed numerous executives who rose to high positions at CBS.

ATS-6 (APPLICATIONS TECHNOLOGY SATELLITE 6) ▶ an experimental NASA satellite launched in May 1974 with the largest antenna yet devised for space and powerful enough to transmit directional signals to small and inexpensive ground receivers, making it a prototype for direct-broadcast satellites. ATS-6, in its first year, was used for communications experiments, among them health and education transmissions to Appalachia, Alaska and the Rocky Mountain region. In 1975 the satellite was repositioned for use by the Government of India for an instructional television experiment. In late 1976, it was moved back to the Western hemisphere.

AUBREY, JAMES T. ▶ president of CBS-TV from December 1959 to February 1965. His administration was probably the most competitively successful in TV history but was marked by hints of scandal. A cum laude graduate of Princeton, Aubrey was a champion of unsophisticated entertainment programs of strong rural appeal (*Mister Ed, The Andy Griffith Show, The Beverly Hillbillies, Petticoat Junction*) and a leading exponent of the "habit" theory of television, which holds that most people want the same series in the same time periods every week, without interruption by specials. In the years before demographic ratings, when reaching the greatest numbers of viewers was the objective, his approach proved sound and his programming prowess made him the most powerful—albeit most arrogant—of network presidents.

His business style—which included an ability to tell a star of long standing, simply and coldly, "You're through."—earned him the nicknames of "Jungle Jim" and "The Smiling Cobra." Still, he was held in awe for his ability to win the ratings race decisively and for his assertions of power. Rumors began to circulate about his allegedly bizarre personal life; about his acceptance of an apartment in Manhattan and private limousine from Filmways, a studio supplying programs to CBS; and mainly about his strange business association with Keefe Brasselle, an actor of modest achievement who professed a connection with the underworld.

Brasselle's company, Richelieu Productions, with no record of achievement in television, suddenly landed three major shows on CBS in the 1964 season, all without benefit of a pilot—*The Reporter, The Baileys of Balboa* and *The Cara Williams Show,* the latter expected to be the successor to the Lucille Ball show. The arrangement with Brasselle raised suspicions within CBS as well as at the FCC, and both conducted investigations. All three Richelieu programs were failures, and the CBS rating lead shrunk for the first time in Aubrey's presidency. Over a weekend, in late February 1965, Aubrey was fired and was replaced at the network by John A. Schneider, who had been v.p. and general manager of WCBS-TV, the flagship station. Aubrey went into independent production, then became president of MGM for a time. In recent years he returned to TV as an independent producer, mostly of made-for-TV movies, and had a series sale as well—*Shannon,* on CBS in the 1981-82 season.

Aubrey started with CBS in 1948 as a salesman for KNX Radio and KNXT Los Angeles, later becoming general manager of the television station and of what was then the CBS Pacific Network. In 1956 he became manager of network programs for CBS-TV in Hollywood, then skipped to ABC in New York as a v.p. in charge of programs and talent. There he introduced a number of hit shows, *77 Sunset Strip, The Rifleman, The Real McCoys, Hawaiian Eye,* demonstrating that the wave of the future in TV was the Hollywood film series and not the New York game- or variety-show. CBS rehired him in 1958 as v.p. of creative services, having apparently decided then that he was to be the next president. Within a year he had the job.

AUDIENCE COMPOSITION ▶ a breakdown of the viewership of any program by such demographic categories as age, sex, education and income. Such profiles, which are provided by the ratings services, govern the rates charged for commercial spots in the programs. An audience predominating in young adults, for example, will command higher advertising rates than one of similar size with a large proportion of middle-aged or elderly viewers.

AUDIENCE FLOW ▶ the movement of the audience between programs and stations during successive time periods. By scheduling programs consecutively that appeal to similar audiences, the networks and local stations attempt to achieve a flow of audience to minimize the tuning away to other channels. Program schedules are devised with a mind to audience flow, because programmers have found that when two contiguous shows appeal to different kinds of viewers, neither will do well.

AUDILOG ▶ Nielsen's television viewing diary used for both national and local market (NSI) estimates of audience size and demographics. Households agreeing to keep a diary for Nielsen fill out how long the set was on, to which program or channel the viewing was given, and which household members were watching. For national ratings, the diaries are kept during designated weeks on a continuing basis. For NSI, the local market viewing data is gathered from three to eight times annually (depending on the size of the market). NSI households keep a diary only for one week, and they are selected at random from telephone listings.

Diaries are used by the ratings services to find out who in the household was viewing. These data are collated with those from metered households, because the meter can only record how long each TV set was on and to which channel it was tuned.

AUDIMETER ▶ a metering device patented by the A.C. Nielsen Co. that is attached to television sets in sample households to record minute-by-minute viewing. The device was acquired by Nielsen in the late 1930s and was first used to measure national radio audiences in 1942. Within the standard Audimeter, now called a set-tuning meter, a slowly revolving cartridge of film recorded the set-on, set-off information and the channel tuned. The results, from approximately 1,200 Audimeter households for the national sample, were tabulated and projected for the Nielsen weekly and bi-weekly television reports.

Starting with the 1973 season, Nielsen put into national operation the Storage Instantaneous Audimeter (SIA), an electronic information storage and retrieval system capable of monitoring TV sets in the sample household. Once a day, usually late at night, a central office computer dials the household units and retrieves the stored viewing information. Unlike the standard Audimeter, which required the removal and mailing of the cartridge by members of the sample household, the automatic process requires no such work.

In 1987 Nielsen introduced the People Meter to measure national television viewing. The People Meter has two parts: one, similar to the SIA, measures standard household tuning information; the second uses buttons to measure who is watching television. Each member of the sample household is assigned a button to push when watching TV. Nielsen has installed People Meters in approximately 4,000 households to measure nationwide viewing but still uses SIAs to measure local viewing in 26 major U.S. markets.

AURTHUR, ROBERT ALAN (d. 1978) ▶ a prolific writer during the "golden age" of live TV drama, best known for his *A Man Is Ten Feet Tall.* He later doubled as an executive producer of drama specials, such as *What Makes Sammy Run?* for NBC's *Sunday Showcase* in 1959. During the 1960s and 1970s he worked mainly in motion pictures.

AUSTRALIA ▶ a country with only 5 million television households that became a presence in the English-speaking world during the 1980s with a number of exceptional mini-series, typified by *A Town Called Alice* and *The Shiralee.* Even more successful among its exports is a daily soap opera, *Neighbours,* that became the rage in Britain.

Australia experienced both boom and bust in the 1980s. It had a terrific growth period in the early half of the decade, and the Australian industry was justifiably assertive in the world market with programs that were distinctive and of a high order. But just as suddenly, in the late 1980s the country became a disaster area after the purchase of its three commercial networks by swashbuckling entrepreneurs. Not only did Christopher Skase, Alan Bond and Frank Lowy probably overpay for the Seven, Nine and Ten Networks, respectively, they immediately joined in a reckless bidding war for stars and imported programming (mainly from the U.S.), driving up prices well beyond reasonable levels for a country Australia's size.

Hit additionally by the economic recession of the late 1980s, all three buyers lost their networks in short order, while suffering huge financial losses. Since then, the chastened commercial system has entered into a period of tenuous recovery, with the possibility that one of the three networks might not survive.

Paradoxically, the network that early in the decade seemed to have the most severe problems—the venerable public network, ABC (Australian Broadcasting Corp.), established in 1956—has emerged as the last bastion of stability. It alone has been in position to invest millions in commissioning domestic productions. The ABC's chief strengths have been in news, current affairs and science programming, although it has been successful also with mini-series based on history.

A fifth Australian network, founded in 1978, is the Special Broadcasting Service, which was created by the government to serve the country's multicultural society. The network carries a range of programs in some 40 different languages. The station is funded by a combination of government grants and commercial sponsors.

Australia has no cable penetration whatsoever, but the country's principal satellite company, Aussat, has the ability to license a direct-to-home satellite service. A pay service is also expected to be operational some time in the 1990s.

AUSTRIA ▶ one of the few countries in Western Europe to remain a holdout against privately owned television systems. The country of 2.8 million TV households continues to be served by two public television channels provided by the state-run monopoly, Osterreicher Rundfunk und Fernsehen (ORF). They are supported chiefly by receiver license fees and program underwriting, in the manner of U.S. public television.

However, the 500,000 Austrian households with cable are able to receive commercial television from Germany, whose main private networks, Sat 1 and RTL Plus, beam into Austria from satellite.

***AUTOBIOGRAPHY OF MISS JANE PITTMAN, THE* ▶** two-hour dramatic film on CBS (premiere: Jan. 31, 1974) tracing the life of a black woman in the South from slavery to the civil rights movement of the 1960s. A poignant made-for-TV movie, it won nine Emmy Awards and at once seemed destined for annual repeats (which so far have not occurred). The fictional film proved a triumphant vehicle for actress Cicely Tyson, affording a role in which she advanced from young womanhood to old age. It climaxes with a powerful scene in which the ancient woman makes a protest by drinking from a water fountain marked "Whites Only."

The film was written by Tracy Keenan Wynn, based on a novel by Ernest J. Gaines. Robert W. Christiansen and Rick Rosenberg were the producers for Tomorrow Entertainment, and John Korty was the director. Featured were Odetta, Josephine Premice, Ted Airhart, Richard Dysart, Roy Poole and Valerie O'Dell.

AUTRY, GENE ▶ singing cowboy of the movies and early western star of TV who became a station tycoon as majority owner and chairman-president of Golden West Broadcasters, a West Coast group whose flagship was KTLA-TV Los Angeles. Through his Flying A Productions, he produced *The Gene Autry Show* (1947-54), with Pat Buttram as his sidekick, which enjoyed particular popularity with children. In 1966, at KTLA, he produced the syndicated series *Gene Autry's Melody Ranch.* But the era of the singing cowboy had already ended with the arrival of the more sophisticated westerns, such as *Cheyenne, Gunsmoke* and *Rawhide.*

Autry sold KTLA in 1982, and the station was later acquired by the Tribune Company.

AVAILABILITIES (AVAILS) ▶ unsold time in the active commercial inventory of a station, network or cable channel.

***AVENGERS, THE* ▶** secret agent series produced in England by Associated British Pathe, which played on ABC in interrupted runs from March 1966 to September 1969. Of the 83 films made, 57 were in color. Patrick Macnee starred as Steed, the stylish independent sleuth. His original female partner, with a talent for karate, was Honor Blackman as Cathy Gale; she was succeeded by Diana Rigg as Emma Peel and then by Linda Thorson as Tara King.

In marketing terms, at least, *The Avengers* was probably the most successful British-flag series, sold in approximately 120 world markets. After a hiatus of several years, producers Brian Clemens and Albert Fennell briefly reactivated the show, with Macnee again in the lead, and with financing by a French syndicator. Reruns of the series were appearing on A&E as recently as 1991.

AYKROYD, DAN ▶ one of the notable alumni of *Saturday Night Live* (1975-79) who fashioned a film career on the popularity he gained from the irreverent NBC show. In one of his strongest turns on *SNL,* he teamed up with the late John Belushi as a rock act called the Blues Brothers; in 1980 that routine became the basis for a comedy movie, *The Blues Brothers.* Aykroyd was also featured in *Ghostbusters* (1984) and *Driving Miss Daisy* (1989), among a number of lesser box-office films.

AYLESWORTH, MERLIN HALL (d. 1952) ▶ nicknamed "Deac," first president of NBC, joining on Nov. 15, 1926, after having been managing director of the National Electric Light Association. Initially, he concentrated on promoting the sale of radio sets for NBC's parent, RCA, but toward the end of his nine-year term he was a dominant figure in the entertainment and advertising fields and had played a key role in the development of the Radio City complex and the Radio City Music Hall. He left the network on Dec. 31, 1935 to become chairman of RKO-Radio Pictures, which RCA had acquired several years earlier, and in 1938 he became publisher of the *New York World-Telegram.*

AZCARRAGA, EMILIO, Sr. (d. 1973) ▶ co-founder (with Romulo O'Farrill) of Telesistema Mexicana and head of that television monopoly in Mexico for two decades, until his death. Azcarraga, who earlier had dabbled in radio after working as a representative for RCA Records, built his fortune in TV and expanded his business interests with cable television, automobile sales, hotels and the ownership of a soccer team.

Azcarraga's system controlled four channels in Mexico City, one of which served as a national commercial network, and other stations in Monterrey, Guadalajara and Tijuana. He also established Televisa, a production company for the stations, which has sold its programs throughout Latin America and to the Spanish-language networks in the U.S.

Azcarraga was succeeded by his son, Emilio, Jr.

B

BAA BAA BLACK SHEEP ▶ hour-long NBC action-adventure series (1976) based on the World War II exploits of Marine Corps Major Gregory (Pappy) Boyington and his crew of nonconformist fighter pilots. After its second week on the air, the series drew a formal complaint from CBS for allegedly violating the "family viewing time" code in glorifying characters who engage in brawling, drinking, wenching and violence. NBC explained that the series had not initially been conceived for "family time" (before 9 p.m.) and that subsequent episodes had been cleaned up to meet the code standard. CBS withdrew the complaint but the publicity it generated helped to build an audience for the NBC show, although the ratings later flagged.

Produced by Universal TV, with Stephen J. Cannell as executive producer, the series featured Robert Conrad as Boyington. It was canceled after one season but then was given a second chance as a mid-season replacement in 1977-78 with a new title, *Black Sheep Squadron,* and in a 9 p.m. time period. Again it failed, against tough competition from ABC's *Charlie's Angels.*

BABBIN, JACQUELINE ▶ New York-based producer-writer specializing in drama. Her first major credits were as an adapter of plays and novels for the David Susskind productions in the "golden age" of TV drama. In 1962 she produced the *DuPont Show of the Week* and in the 1970s a series of dramas for ABC's *Wide World of Entertainment.* In 1975 she became producer of the weekly CBS series *Beacon Hill,* and in 1976 she produced the three-hour *Sybil* for NBC's *The Big Event.*

After working in network programming on the west coast for a number of years, she gave up her job as vice president at ABC in early 1982 to return to New York as producer of Agnes Nixon's *All My Children* daytime serial. Babbin left the show in 1986. Later she worked on *Loving* (1990-91).

BACHELOR FATHER ▶ successful situation comedy about an eligible bachelor raising his teenage niece. It premiered on CBS in September 1957, then moved to NBC (1958-60) and finally to ABC (1961-62). By Bachelor Productions, it starred John Forsythe as attorney Bentley Gregg and featured Noreen Corcoran as his niece, Kelly Gregg, and Sammee Tong as the butler, Peter Tong.

BACK, GEORGE ▶ veteran syndication executive and chairman of All American Television. He was one of the pioneers of barter syndication, which involves reserving time in syndicated programs for the sale of national spots—a practice that has overtaken the syndication industry. All American TV distributes such shows as *USA Update, America's Top Ten With*

Casey Kasem, Beyond 2000, and *The Howard Stern Show,* among others. It also sells barter spots for other clients, including *Stuntmasters,* which is distributed by Blair Entertainment.

Back, one of the few syndicators with a Ph.D. degree, which he earned in the late 1970s, began in the program syndication business in 1967 as head of the Chicago office of ABC Films. He left in 1970 for Group W Productions, where he remained for seven years. It was while selling Group W's *Mike Douglas Show* that he introduced the practice of claiming spots for national sale in lieu of raising the price to local stations at renewal time. The practice was controversial at the time, but it soon spread in the industry to the point where many shows are distributed entirely on a barter basis.

For two years after his Group W stint, Back was chief executive of the Hughes TV Network. In 1980 he became the first executive director of the National Assn. of Television Program Executives (NATPE), a leading trade association. He left in 1982 to start up All American TV.

BACKE, JOHN D. ▶ former president of CBS Inc. whose term began in October 1976 upon chairman William S. Paley's sudden dismissal of Arthur R. Taylor, who had been Paley's heir-apparent since 1972. He received the additional title of chief executive officer in May 1977. But he was ousted suddenly by Paley in the Spring of 1980 and was succeeded by Thomas Wyman. The following year he joined Tomorrow Entertainment, an independent production company, as president, where he remained until 1984. He then went on to become CEO of Backe Group Inc. and owner of WDKY-TV in Kentucky since 1986.

Backe's background was in publications. He joined CBS in 1973 as corporate vice president of the CBS Publishing Group (Holt, Rinehart and Winston, W.B. Saunders, Popular Library and magazines such as *Field and Stream, Road and Track* and *Popular Tennis*). Just before his promotion to corporate president, he helped to engineer, with Taylor, the acquisition of Fawcett Publications.

Earlier, Backe was president and chief executive of General Learning Corp., a joint venture of General Electric and Time Inc., rising to that position after heading its textbook publishing subsidiary, Silver Burdett Co.

BACK-END ▶ all sources of income for a program beyond that for which it was originally created. For a network show or series these might include syndication, foreign sales and home video, as well as publications based on the property and product licensing. Successful animated programs tend to do exceedingly well in the back-end. *The Simpsons* and *Teenage Mutant Ninja Turtles* were two that hit the jackpot.

See also Ancillary Markets.

***BACKSTAIRS AT THE WHITE HOUSE* ▶** well-received nine-hour NBC mini-series in 1979 presenting a docu-drama view into the private lives of America's first families from the Tafts to the Eisenhowers. The story of the domestic lives of the presidents was told from the perspective of two generations of black maids who between them worked at the White House for more than 50 years. In the background were such major events as World Wars I and II and the Great Depression.

The production was based on material from the 1961 best-selling memoir, *My Thirty Years at the White House,* by Lillian Rogers Parks and Frances Spatz Leighton. The husband and wife team of Gwen Bagni and Paul Dubov adapted the story for television. Ed Friendly produced and Michael O'Herlihy directed. The cast included Leslie Uggams, Olivia Cole, Cloris Leachman, George Kennedy, Robert Vaughn, Harry Morgan, Paul Winfield, Robert Hooks, Louis Gossett, Jr. and Ed Flanders.

BAERWALD, SUSAN ▶ a former vice president for mini-series at NBC who went on to become an independent producer in the form. Those she has produced since leaving the network include *Blind Faith, Jackie Collins: Lucky/Chances* and *Cruel Doubt.*

BAILEY, JACK (d. 1979) ▶ veteran game-show emcee, best known for *Truth or Consequences* and *Queen for a Day.* Earlier he had been an announcer for network radio programs.

***BAILEYS OF BALBOA, THE* ▶** CBS situation comedy (1964) whose flop contributed to ending James Aubrey's reign as president of the network. Produced by Richelieu Productions, it featured Paul Ford, John Dehner, Sterling Holloway and Judy Carne.

BAIRD, JOHN LOGIE (d. 1946) ▶ Scottish inventor who developed the first television system in full-scale use. He demonstrated a mechanically scanned television system which showed objects in outline in 1924, recognizable faces in 1925. In 1928 he transmitted a television signal from England that was received in the U.S. The BBC adopted Baird's mechanical system in 1936 for regular transmissions, but it was replaced the next year by the Marconi Company's all-electronic system using a cathode-ray tube.

In 1939 Baird demonstrated color television using a picture tube, and shortly before his death he had completed research on a stereoscopic television system. In the 1920s Baird demonstrated the first videodisc (using a standard wax phonograph record) and the first projection television system.

BAKER, WILLIAM F. ▶ president and CEO of New York public television station WNET since May 1987, succeeding John Jay Iselin. The station is one of the most influential in the public TV system. Before arriving at WNET Baker worked in commercial broadcasting, serving simultaneously as president of Group W Television and chairman of Group W Satellite Communications. At Group W he was involved in the launch of several cable networks, among them the Disney Channel, the Discovery Channel, and the Travel Channel. He joined Group W from Scripps Howard Broadcasting in 1978 and a year later was promoted to head of all television operations, including the station group and the company's production and syndication subsidiary. In 1981 he added oversight of the satellite unit. Baker began working in broadcasting while still a student at Case Western Reserve University in Cleveland, where he earned a Ph.D.

BALL, LUCILLE (d. 1989) ▶ probably TV's biggest star, familiar to viewers throughout the world through her classic situation comedy *I Love Lucy,* and the subsequent *Lucy* series that ran almost continuously on CBS from 1951 until her retirement from weekly television (ratings still high) in the fall of 1974. She created such a vast library of episodes that it was typical, in the 1970s, for the *Lucy* reruns to have four or five different airings over the course of a day in large markets like New York. On a network laden with stars in the 1960s, Ball remained the heart of the CBS schedule, her show the one "sure thing" in the lineup.

Her TV run had a brief hiatus in 1960 after her divorce from her husband and partner Desi Arnaz. She emerged from the divorce as president of their production company, Desilu, which had grown into one of the large independents, supplying a number of shows to the networks. She doubled as an executive and star when she resumed weekly television with *The Lucy Show* in 1962, until Paramount purchased the company in 1967.

Although she had previous stage and film credits, Ball was scarcely known to most of the TV audience when *I Love Lucy* premiered on Oct. 15, 1951. Arnaz, a Cuban band leader whom she had married in 1940, had only a slight reputation in U.S. show business. But the zany series was an instant hit and rose quickly to become the most popular show on TV. Ball portrayed a beautiful, well-meaning schemer who seemingly never lived a day without becoming involved in an outlandish predicament. The situations gave full range to her talents for sight comedy, but remarkably—through all the absurd disguises and broad physical antics—she was able to preserve a lady-like persona.

There were strong contributions from William Frawley and Vivian Vance, who portrayed Fred and Ethel Mertz, neighbors and close friends of Lucy and Ricky Ricardo, the leads.

When Ball became pregnant in 1952, producer Jess Oppenheim decided that television's Lucy would become pregnant too. The dual event, Ball's real-life delivery of Desi Arnaz Jr., and the arrival of the baby on the program, Ricky, Jr., was nationally awaited, and the birth episode achieved an enormous rating.

I Love Lucy ended its run on June 24, 1957, when the stars decided to concentrate on specials. In November 1957 they began a one-hour monthly telecast, *The Lucille Ball-Desi Arnaz Show,* a comedy hour with guest stars. The series ended with their divorce, and Ball left TV to star in the Broadway musical *Wildcat,* which was both a hit and a personal triumph for her.

She returned to TV with a weekly series, *The Lucy Show* (1962-68), featuring Vivian Vance and Gale Gordon. The following year the series was changed to include her children Desi Jr. and Lucie Arnaz, and given the title *Here's Lucy* (1968-74). Gordon remained as a principal, and Desi, Jr., left the series after three seasons.

All three Lucy sitcoms played Mondays at 9 p.m., giving CBS dominance of the night through virtually every season Ball was with the network.

In 1979 she was recruited by NBC president Fred Silverman—with whom she had worked at CBS—to develop comedy series and talent for the network through her own new production company, and also to star in comedy specials. This resulted in little more than publicity, however, although two unsuccessful pilots were made, neither starring Ball. In 1986, she starred in the short-lived *Life with Lucy* series on ABC. Her last show was a made-for-TV movie, *The Stone Pillow,* in which she portrayed a homeless woman.

Lucille Ball

BALMUTH PETITION ▶ a futile attempt by Hollywood craft unions in the early 1970s to persuade the FCC to adopt rules limiting the volume of network reruns in prime time to 25% a year from more than 40%. Such a restriction, the petition argued, would stimulate creativity, boost employment, give the viewer a wider choice of fare and curtail the networks' ability to use prime time as they pleased for their greatest economic gain.

The original petition was filed in 1972 by Bernard A. Balmuth, a film editor, and was staunchly supported by the Screen Actors Guild, the Writers Guild of America—West, and the Hollywood Film Council, representing 28 labor organizations, in addition to others. In July 1976, while acknowledging that many people felt strongly about the saturation of reruns, the FCC rejected the plea in a 7-0 decision. It reasoned that the government had no right to control such matters and that the issue was better resolved by market forces.

In denying the petition, the FCC reasoned also that the limiting of reruns would increase network production costs, reduce their profits and probably result in cheaper programming overall. The commission added that to engage in regulatory action for the purpose of improving employment was not within its province. It said, finally, that it lacked the authority to regulate the type and quality of programming unless a substantial public benefit was certain.

***BANACEK* ▶** NBC series (1972) about an investigator dealing in the recovery of lost or stolen property, which rotated as part of the *Wednesday Mystery Movie.* George Peppard starred in the 16 episodes produced by Universal TV.

BANDWIDTH ▶ a section of the frequency spectrum needed to transmit visually, aurally or both. The bandwidth of the average television channel is 6 million cycles per second (6 MHZ).

***BANKS AND THE POOR* ▶** controversial public TV documentary in 1970 critical of money-lending institutions and which held the banking industry to blame for perpetuating slum conditions. The program, which was produced by Mort Silverstein, ended with a crawl that listed 98 members of Congress who were either shareholders or directors of banks, while "The Battle Hymn of the Republic" ironically played on the soundtrack.

Such theatrical flourishes made the film vulnerable to journalistic criticism. But the documentary caused nervousness among the PBS stations because the congressmen named on the crawl (including Sen. John O. Pastore, chairman of the Senate Communications Subcommittee) would be voting on the next federal appropriation for public TV. Many of the stations, besides, had board members who were bankers. Several stations postponed the showing and a few declined to show it at all. PBS acted against its own policy by inviting representatives of the banking industry for prescreenings.

The hour was produced by NET for the *Realities* series, which was canceled after that season.

BANNER, BOB ▶ independent producer-director, whose credits include *The Dinah Shore Chevy Show* in the mid-1950s, *The Garry Moore Show* in the late 1950s and *Candid Camera* (as executive producer) in the mid-1960s. Early in his career he was director for NBC of *Garroway at Large* and *Omnibus.* His independent company, Bob Banner Associates, has concentrated primarily on music-variety specials, such as *Carnegie Hall Salutes Jack Benny, Julie and Carol* *at Carnegie Hall, Here's Peggy Fleming, The Kraft Music Hall* and the John Davidson shows, with occasional ventures into made-for-TV movies. More recently, his company produced Perry Como's seasonal special for ABC, and *Solid Gold,* which he also directed for Operation Prime Time syndication until the show was canceled in 1988. He also directed the syndicated variety contest, *Star Search.*

Recently, he, Gary Pudney and others consolidated their independent production activity in the newly created Paradigm Entertainment.

BANZHAF CASE ▶ (*John F. Banzhaf III v. FCC* [405 F2d 1082 (1968)]) the Fairness Doctrine applied to the broadcast of cigarette commercials. In December 1966, John Banzhaf, a New York lawyer acting as a private citizen, requested free time from WCBS-TV New York to answer its cigarette commercials under the Fairness Doctrine. When the station rejected the request, Banzhaf filed a complaint with the FCC. The commission ruled, six months later, that a station presenting such advertisements had the duty of informing the public of the hazards of smoking because the promotion of smoking was proved not to be in the public interest. Banzhaf's bid for counter-commercial time approximately equal to that for cigarette ads was rejected, however; instead, the FCC proposed a 3 to 1 ratio.

A number of appeals were instituted. The NAB filed for review in the Court of Appeals in Richmond, Va. Banzhaf filed for review in the District Court of Appeals claiming that while the commission awarded significant time he had not been afforded equal time. The tobacco and broadcasting industries' argument was that by passing the Cigarette Labeling Act of 1965, the Congress meant to forbid any additional regulation addressed to the problem of danger to health.

The two cases were joined in the District Court of Appeals in Washington, and in 1968 the court upheld the commission's ruling. The court rejected the intent of Congress's argument and also concluded that cigarette advertisements were not constitutionally protected speech. The court did not accept Banzhaf's equal time claim nor the cigarette manufacturers' claim for rebuttal time to answer antismoking messages.

The cigarette companies appealed, but certiorari was denied by the Supreme Court. Antismoking commercials became familiar on TV until cigarette advertising was barred from broadcast media by the Public Health Cigarette Smoking Act of 1969, which went into effect in January 1971. The constitutionality of the law was upheld in 1971 by a special three-judge court in *Capitol Broadcasting v. Mitchell* [333 F Supp. 582 (1971)] with a strong dissent from Judge J. Skelly Wright.

BAR (BROADCAST ADVERTISERS REPORTS) ▶ company engaged in monitoring commercials televised on networks and stations; its syndicated reports are used by advertisers and agencies as proof-of-performance for their commercials and by stations to keep abreast of advertising purchased at competing stations.

BAR monitors 351 stations in 75 TV markets by means of off-air tape recordings. The markets covered represent around 80% of the ADI households and 85% of spot TV dollar expenditures. Sixteen major markets are monitored on an everyday basis. The remaining 59 are monitored randomly for one week each month.

In monitoring the networks, BAR is able to keep a running score on the estimated revenues for each.

***BARBARA McNAIR SHOW, THE* ▶** half-hour music-variety series produced in Canada for U.S. syndication in the prime time-access periods (1969-71). Winters-Rosen Productions taped 52 programs, but the series was not widely accepted by stations.

***BARBARA STANWYCK THEATRE, THE* ▶** 30-minute anthology series on NBC (1960-61) with Barbara Stanwyck as hostess and frequent star. It was by E.S.W. Enterprises.

BARBER, RED (WALTER L.) ▶ one of the most popular and respected sportscasters in the medium whose career spanned the period 1934-66. Chiefly associated with baseball, he was dismissed by the Yankees management after a dozen years as the team's play-by-play announcer for reporting that home attendance was low and then directing the TV cameras to scan the empty seats. The incident raised the issue of whether TV sportscasters employed by teams should be identified as hired boosters or be allowed to pose as objective journalists. Barber did the play-by-play for the Cincinnati Reds (1934-39), then became the "voice" of the Brooklyn Dodgers (1939-54) and then of the Yankees (1954-66).

His refined Mississippi accent contributed to his distinctive style, and he popularized such Southern expressions as "catbird seat" (sitting high up in an advantageous position) and "rhubarb" (an argument on the playing field). After his dismissal he wrote, freelanced occasionally in broadcasting and went into retirement around 1970. In the late 1980s he began a weekly five-minute commentary on National Public Radio and reached an affectionate new audience.

BAREFOOT IN THE PARK ▶ NBC situation comedy (1970) drawn from the Neil Simon play of that title but with an all-black cast. The series fared poorly and ran less than half a season. Featured were Scoey Mitchlll and Tracy Reed as Paul and Corie Bratter, along with Thelma Carpenter and Nipsey Russell. It was by Paramount TV.

BARETTA ▶ ABC series about an unorthodox undercover police detective portrayed by Robert Blake. The series had an unusual history. It began in 1973 as *Toma,* a series with Tony Musante based on the adventures of a real-life cop who relied on his wits and imaginative disguises, but ended after one season when Musante became disenchanted with the role. Because the ratings were promising, it was revived in January 1975 with Blake as Tony Baretta, and although the title was changed the show was given the Friday night slot originally held by *Toma.* For several weeks the series fared poorly, but when ABC switched it to Wednesdays the ratings began to soar. *Baretta* went on to demolish *Cannon* on CBS and to become a mainstay of the ABC lineup. It was canceled in the spring of 1978. Among the regulars in the series were Dana Elcar as Lieutenant Shiller and Tom Ewell as the apartment attendant Billy Truman. Bernard L. Kowalski was executive producer and Jo Swerling Jr. producer for The Public Arts, Roy Huggins Productions and Universal TV.

BARKER, BOB ▶ TV emcee who hosted Ralph Edwards's *Truth or Consequences,* first on NBC and then in syndication, for 18 seasons (1956-74). In 1972 he also took on *The New Price Is Right* on CBS and then the syndicated nighttime version of that show. In 1966 he became the emcee for both the *Miss Universe* and the *Miss USA* beauty pageants; in 1967 he began hosting the Indianapolis 500 Parade; and in 1969 he began announcing the Rose Bowl Parade on CBS. All these he did for many years. Through his own production company, he has also produced the *Pillsbury Bake-Off* specials.

BARNABY JONES ▶ hour-long private-eye series that held its own nicely in a variety of time periods on CBS from 1973-80. Starring Buddy Ebsen, who overcame the typecasting of his previous hit series, *The Beverly Hillbillies,* it featured Lee Meriwether as Betty Jones and Mark Shera as Jebediah Jones, and was produced by Quinn Martin Productions.

BARNATHAN, JULIUS ▶ for three decades a key ABC executive, whose quick intelligence and adeptness at solving problems gained him the most diverse appointments of any official at that network. At various points he has been head of research, head of affiliate relations, head of the owned TV stations, general manager of the network and head of engineering and broadcast operations.

In the latter capacity, he has been responsible for the planning, designing and acquiring of broadcast facilities and equipment for all areas of the company, radio as well as TV, and for directing the technical operations for major special events coverage, from political conventions to the Olympic Games.

Barnathan was named v.p. for engineering in 1965 to supervise the equipping of the network and owned stations for color TV. For the three previous years he had been v.p. and general manager of ABC-TV, and for a brief period earlier was president of the ABC o&os. From 1959-62 he was v.p. for affiliated TV stations. He began with ABC in 1954 as supervisor of ratings and swiftly won promotions in the research department until, in 1959, he became v.p. in charge. In 1976 he received the title of president of engineering and operations. Following the acquisition of ABC by Capital Cities, in April 1989 he was named senior v.p. of Capital Cities/ABC in charge of technology and strategic planning. He retired at the end of 1991 but continues his relationship with the company as a consultant.

BARNEY MILLER ▶ ABC half-hour comedy centering on an ethnic-rich squad room of New York precinct detectives. After an unsteady start in January 1975, the series developed into a hit and ran until 1982. Hal Linden starred in the title role, with Barbara Barrie as his wife Elizabeth. Featured as other detectives in the squad were Abe Vigoda as Phil Fish, Max Gail as Stan (Wojo) Wojehowicz, Gregory Sierra as Chano Amengual, Jack Soo as Nick Yemana, Ron Glass as Ron Harris, Steve Landesberg as Arthur Dietrich and Ron Carey as Carl Levitt. The series was created by Danny Arnold and Theodore Flicker, with Arnold as executive producer for Four D Productions. Producers were Chris Hayward and Arne Sultan, and Norm Pitlik directed most of the episodes. In 1977 Vigoda's character was spun off into a new ABC situation comedy, *Fish,* but the show was unsuccessful.

BARNOUW, ERIK ▶ leading broadcasting historian, author of the three-volume *History of Broadcasting in the United States* and chief of the Motion Picture, Broadcasting and Recorded Sound Division of the Library of Congress (1978-81). From 1946 to 1973, he taught courses in film and television and chaired the film division at Columbia University's School of Arts. During much of that period he was also active in the broadcast industry, chiefly as a writer, and at one time headed the Writers Guild of America (1957-59). He also produced and wrote several films for National Educational Television.

His books include *Mass Communication* (1956); the trilogy comprising the *History of Broadcasting: A Tower in Babel* (1966), *The Golden Web* (1968) and *The Image Empire* (1970); as well as *Tube of Plenty* (1975) and *The Sponsor* (1978).

***BARON, THE* ▶** British action-adventure series slotted by ABC as a midseason replacement in January 1966 with unimpressive results. Based on mystery stories by John Creasey, it starred Steve Forrest as American John Mannering and was by ATV.

BARRETT, RONA ▶ Hollywood gossip columnist carrying on, via TV, the tradition of Hedda Hopper and Louella Parsons. In the late 1960s she began doing two-minute reports for ABC o&os to use in their newscasts, and in 1969 she started a daily syndicated TV "column" distributed by Metromedia. In 1976 she became a regular contributor to ABC's *Good Morning, America* and later that year hosted the prime time ABC special *Rona Barrett Looks At the Oscars.*

NBC hired her away in 1981 to team her with Tom Snyder on *Tomorrow,* but the two quarreled over turf and the match was never consummated. Barrett wound up with a short-lived prime-time series of her own, *Television Inside and Out,* in the winter of 1981.

BARRIS, CHUCK ▶ game-show packager whose long list of entries began with *The Dating Game, The Newlywed Game* and *Operation Entertainment* for ABC, the network with which he had previously been associated as a program executive. His Chuck Barris Productions was also responsible for *The Game Game* and others in that perishable daytime genre, and it provided the financial backing for the Blye-Bearde production of the syndicated *Bobby Vinton Show* (1975). Barris cast himself as host of the daytime NBC series *The Gong Show* in 1976.

During 1979, Barris had five syndicated programs in production: *The Gong Show, Three's a Crowd, The $1.98 Beauty Show, The Newlywed Game* and *The Dating Game.* A year or so later most of them were gone.

BARRON, ARTHUR ▶ freelance producer, director and writer generally associated with documentaries, although in latter years his work extended to movies and some TV drama. Between 1975 and 1977, Barron produced two episodes of the *Six American Families* series for Group W, adaptations of short stories by Henry James and Ambrose Bierce for the PBS *American Short Story* series and a theatrical movie for Warner Bros., called *Brothers.*

While on the staff of CBS News in the 1960s Barron was responsible for such documentaries as *Sixteen in Webster Groves, Webster Groves Revisited* and *The Berkeley Rebels.* He also had worked for NBC News and Metromedia. As a freelancer, he produced, wrote and directed *Birth and Death, Factory* and *An Essay on Loneliness* for PBS. His credits in the sphere of TV drama include *The Child Is Father of the Man* for CBS and *It Must Be Love 'Cause I Feel So Dumb,* an ABC *Afterschool Special.*

BARRY, JACK (d. 1984) ▶ prominent game-show producer and host in the 1950s who was forced to drop out of television for more than a decade after being implicated in the quiz-show scandals of 1958. Barry and his partner Jack Enright had been the producers of *21,* one of the programs that congressional witnesses had said was rigged. Later, their application for radio station licenses was challenged on the ground of character, but the FCC ruled those objections invalid. Having served his term of penance, Barry was admitted back into television as a game show producer in 1970 and made his comeback with such successful shows as *The Joker's Wild* and *Break the Bank.* Among the earlier programs he had produced and appeared on were *Winky Dink, Tic Tac Dough* and *Juvenile Jury.*

BARRY, PHILIP, JR. ▶ executive producer, chiefly of made-for-TV movies. Son of the famous playwright, he began his television career in the early days of the medium working on such prestigious drama series as *Goodyear Television Playhouse.* In the early 1970s he served for CBS as executive producer of its made-for-TV movies and then moved on to Tomorrow Entertainment in a similar capacity.

BARTELME, JOE (d. 1991) ▶ veteran NBC News executive who in May 1979 became executive producer of *Today.* He had been v.p. of NBC News, responsible for all regularly scheduled news programs, which included *Today* as well as the *Nightly News.* Previously (1974-77), he was v.p. of news for the NBC o&os and before that the network's West Coast news director. He came to NBC in 1971 after having been news director for WCCO-TV in Minneapolis.

BARTER ▶ a form of advertising sale in which the advertiser gives a program or program matter to a station or network in exchange for commercial spots. The number of spots and the time periods in which they are played are subject to negotiation. While barter was common in the early years of television, such as when the companies that manufacture bowling equipment produced bowling shows with built-in plugs and offered them to stations gratis, the practice fell into disrepute for many years.

It was revived on a large scale in 1971 when the prime time-access rule went into effect and many stations hesitated to invest in programming. Here advertisers seeking bargains in choice viewing hours provided stations with reasonably attractive programs containing two or three minutes of their commercials. The stations' profits came from the sale of up to three additional minutes in those half-hour programs.

Colgate-Palmolive bartered *Police Surgeon* in this manner for several seasons, and Chevrolet did the same with such series as *Stand Up and Cheer, The Golddiggers, The Jonathan Winters Show* and *The Henry Mancini Show.*

Some advertising agencies bartered programs for more than a single client and thus became involved in the production of TV programs again. Other advertisers bartered program matter, such as syndicated news or feature pieces, in exchange for commercial time.

Some advertisers preferred to barter on a time-bank principle, giving programs to stations in exchange for credit so that they were owed commercial time to dispose of as and whenever they chose.

By the 1980s practically everything in syndication was sold on a barter basis, and many of the most desirable shows were offered for cash-plus-barter. The reruns of *The Cosby Show* were syndicated at the highest cash price ever; still, the terms included a single barter segment per program, which was sold nationally by the syndicator, Viacom. Barter tends to be a godsend for small-market stations which are spared having to put up cash for programming, but it sometimes presents a problem for stations in the largest markets which are loath to give up spots that sell at high rates.

Certain American distributors have been trying to introduce the barter concept to European markets but have met with resistance, in part because it seems to represent a relinquishing of program control to advertisers. Most of the new European commercial networks do not view themselves primarily as advertising media, and in some countries—the U.K., for example—strict prohibitions exist against advertisers participating in program decisions.

BARTLESVILLE TEST ▶ an early pay-TV experiment begun in the fall of 1957 in which a Bartlesville, Okla. theater owner sent movies by wire to subscribing homes for a monthly fee. It ended the following spring, deemed a failure.

BARTLEY, ROBERT T. (d. 1988) ▶ FCC commissioner who served three terms (1952-72). He was concerned particularly with media monopolies and the concentration of control, and he had cast a dissenting vote in the proposed ABC-ITT merger essentially on the ground that a vast international conglomerate with its impersonal approach to business could have little sense of local community needs. He was the FCC's leading advocate of ascertainment rules for license renewals. A democrat from Texas and generally considered a liberal, he had been administrative assistant to Speaker of the House Sam Rayburn. He was also an executive with the old Yankee Network and for five years a staff member of NAB.

BARUCH, RALPH M. ▶ one-time major figure in both the cable TV and syndication industries as president and chief executive officer of Viacom International Inc., a company that in 1979 began expanding also into broadcast station ownership and network program production. Baruch was one of the CBS executives who was spun out of the company when CBS spun off Viacom in June 1971, after the FCC ordered the networks out of syndication and cable ownership.

BASEBALL ▶ a huge ratings-getter in October at World Series time, and earlier for the divisional playoffs and the All-Star game, but otherwise not the national draw during the course of the season that professional football has been. Indeed, it was television that reduced baseball from national pastime to probably the number two sport in America, amplifying as it does the relative slowness of the game and the length of the season. Locally and regionally, however, baseball has been a powerful TV attraction, especially for teams that are both colorful and pennant contenders.

But despite baseball's history as a sport of predominantly local interest, CBS raised licensing of network rights to extraordinary heights in December 1988 when it negotiated a four-year exclusive network deal for $1.08 billion. This had to do with a CBS strategy adopted that year, when it had sunk into third place in the prime-time competition, of projecting itself as the network providing the "major events." Where baseball is concerned, the major event is the World Series in October. In securing the network baseball rights, CBS stole away NBC's distinction as the baseball network, which dated to 1947.

The previous contract, which ended after the 1989 World Series, was a six-year pact divided between NBC and ABC, each getting a Game-of-the-Week package and alternating year by year in the coverage of the World Series, the playoffs and the All Star game. NBC reportedly paid $525 million and ABC $575 for the six-year term, and both did no better than break even. ABC was believed to have lost a few million.

CBS's billion-dollar contract was exclusive only where the other broadcast networks were concerned. Major League Baseball plucked an additional $400 million from cable's ESPN for a package of around 190 regular season games a year, over four years. The two contracts work out to $362 million a year, which is divided equally among the local clubs and represents roughly one-fourth of their income. It raised each club's take from national TV rights from $7 million to $14 million for each year of the contract. This, of course, does not include what the clubs receive for local TV and radio rights and from regional pay cable.

As with most other major sports, the economics of professional baseball has become tied to television economics. When baseball stars are performing on the field they are television stars, and the astronomical amounts paid by the clubs for their services are made possible by the ever-increasing rights-fees from the TV networks, cable networks, local stations and regional sports channels on cable. CBS's baseball contract has put a new valuation on televised sports generally and raised expectations of higher network rights fees for all other popular sports.

Another significant contract signed in December 1988 was that between the New York Yankees and the Madison Square Garden cable channel, MSG, for rights to televise a substantial number of regular season games. Under the 12-year contract, which started in the 1991 season, the Yankees are to receive $500 million, or more than $41 million a season. This amount for a single team, from cable rights alone, exceeds the combined payrolls of the three lowest-ranked teams in 1990.

The teams in the largest television markets have a distinct economic advantage over those from the smaller ones, an imbalance that eventually could create a competitive imbalance among the teams. One year the Boston Red Sox's player payroll was larger than the total revenues for the Seattle Mariners. Red Sox income from the local media alone was greater than the Chicago White Sox player payroll.

Agents were quick to negotiate huge new contracts for the players based on the newest windfall from television. Boston's star pitcher, Roger Clemens, established a new high in salary levels with a contract for $5 million a year.

But many who follow the business of baseball believe the big money from national television has peaked with the CBS and ESPN deals. Both are expected to lose considerable amounts of money from their baseball commitments, especially since the advertising market for sports went uncharacteristically soft in the early 1990s. In fact, CBS is believed to have lost $170 million in the first year of its baseball coverage. Its losses were made worse by a one-sided World Series that lasted only 4 games. The network fared better in 1991, especially with a World Series that more than fulfilled the network's "big event" strategy. It was a gem of a series that ran the full seven games and was decided in the 10th inning of the final game, with Minnesota beating Atlanta 1-0. The series was lush with interesting angles, even for the lay public: it was played between two Cinderella teams that had finished last in their divisions the previous year, and it was a contest of North vs. South. The press attention was extraordinary and was reflected in the ratings, which were among the highest ever for a World Series. Three extra-inning games added substantially to CBS's revenues. Still, the dream sports event did not keep CBS from losing money in the second year of its baseball contract.

The next contract may not be as large, and this may pose a crisis for Major League Baseball, particularly as it enters a new expansion phase. The only untapped new revenue source appears to be pay-per-view, but any attempt to sell games that historically have been available free to television consumers is sure to meet with congressional intervention.

BASIC CABLE ▶ the assortment of program services and superstations that cable systems offer under the regular subscription fee. Mostly these are channels such as CNN, USA, Nickelodeon and ESPN, which carry advertising, and C-SPAN, the non-commercial public affairs channel. Every cable system makes its own selection of program services for the basic package, leaving room for the various premium channels—HBO, Showtime, Disney and the regional sports networks—for which the subscribers pay extra. The basic-cable services, sometimes spoken of as cable networks, survive on a dual revenue stream: the sale of advertising and the payment by the systems of a small share of the subscriber fees.

BASKETBALL ▶ see College Basketball; Professional Basketball (the NBA).

BAST, WILLIAM ▶ screenwriter and TV scripter, working for periods of time in Britain, whose credits include *The Man in the Iron Mask* for NBC and *The Legend of Lizzie Borden* for ABC, in addition to episodes of various weekly series. A close friend of the late actor James Dean, whom he had met at college, Bast wrote the TV special, *James Dean: Portrait of a Friend,* which aired on NBC in 1976. In the U.K., he wrote and adapted several plays for the BBC and a number for Granada TV, the best known of which was probably *The Myth Makers.*

***BAT MASTERSON* ▶** western series on NBC (1958-60) about a fashion-plate marshal who wears a derby and carries a cane. It starred Gene Barry and was produced by United Artists TV.

***BATMAN* ▶** popular ABC prime-time series (1966-68) that, in spoof style, was a live-action representation of the famous comic book creations of Bob Kane. Batman (Bruce Wayne) was played by Adam West and Robin (Dick Grayson) by Burt Ward. When ratings began to slip, Yvonne Craig was introduced in the third season as Batgirl. Recurring villains were portrayed by such guest stars as Burgess Meredith as the Penguin, Vincent Price as Egghead, Cesar Romero as the Joker, Frank Gorshin as the Riddler and Eartha Kitt, Lee Meriwether and Julie Newmar as Catwoman. Other regulars included Alan Napier as Wayne's butler Alfred Pennyworth, Madge Blake as Aunt Harriet, Neil Hamilton as Commissioner Gordon and Stafford Repp as Chief O'Hara. Among notable gimmicks of style was the superimposition over the fight scenes of comic book words like "Pow" and "Bam." Via Greenway Productions and 20th Century-Fox TV, the half-hour series continues in syndication.

BATON BROADCASTING ▶ one of Canada's largest private broadcasting companies, with 18 stations in Ontario and Saskatchewan. Some of its stations are affiliates of CTV and some of CBC. Chairman and CEO is Douglas Bassett, Jr.

***BATTLE OF NEWBURGH, THE* ▶** social documentary produced in 1962 in the NBC *White Paper* series that stirred the country. The film, produced by Arthur Zegart and Al Wasserman, reported on City Manager Joseph Mitchell's attempt to rid Newburgh, N.Y., a small Hudson River community, of what he called "welfare cheats." Mitchell decided, contrary to New York law, that he would decide who did and did not qualify for aid. In covering cases of families denied aid, the documentary refuted Mitchell's allegations that some families cheated. After the broadcast, Mitchell charged that NBC paid off the families in poverty to appear on camera. NBC denied the accusation and stood by the broadcast. The film has become a classic of the social documentary genre.

***BATTLESTAR GALACTICA* ▶** high-budgeted ABC science-fiction series (1978-79) that attempted, without success, to trade on the popularity of the movie *Star Wars.* The special effects and costumes of the Universal hour-long series resembled those of the 20th Century-Fox movie, and John Dykstra, who managed the motion pictures special effects, was employed to do the same for *Galactica* and to be producer.

The series, a space-age mutation of the traditional Western, concerning a group of homeless pioneers making their way in a caravan of space vessels to find a new frontier, made a soaring start in the ratings but soon went into a decline and eventually became earthbound when CBS moved *All in the Family* against it.

Lorne Greene starred as Adama, commander of the fleet, with Richard Hatch featured as Apollo, Dirk Benedict as Starbuck, Herb Jefferson Jr. as Boomer, Maren Jensen as Athena, Noah Hathaway as Boxey and Terry Carter as Tigh. Glen Larson, whose company produced the series in association with Universal, was executive producer. Leslie Stevens had the title of supervising producer.

BAXTER, MEREDITH ▶ familiar television actress who played the mother on the enormously popular *Family Ties* (1982-89). She also played the older sister on *Family* (1976-80). Prior to that, she starred in *Bridget Loves Bernie* (1972-73), a series about a mixed religion marriage, which was mildly controversial at the time and lasted one season.

She has also acted in several films and appears frequently in made-for-TV movies.

BAXTERS, THE **▶** unusual 1979 syndicated series combining the entertainment elements of situation comedy with local public-affairs discussion. This odd mix was achieved by a format that provided for a 12-minute prepackaged dramatic scene followed by a locally produced segment in which viewers commented on the issues raised by the fictional material. The program was developed as a local series by Hubert Jessup at WCVB-TV Boston and went into syndication when it caught the fancy of Norman Lear, the noted Hollywood producer of social comedy.

Lear's T.A.T. Communications Co. created the provocative opening sitcom sequences, leaving it to the stations themselves to produce, each in its own way, the group discussion segments. The fictional scenes focused on a middle-class family named Baxter and contained standard sitcom ingredients developed around such themes as the effects of inflation, the problems of the elderly, responsibility for birth control and a variety of marital and family stresses. Featured in the regular cast were Larry Keith and Anita Gillette as Fred and Nancy Baxter, Terri Lynn Wood and Derin Altay as their daughters, Rachel and Naomi, and Chris Petersen as son Jonah. Lear was executive producer and Fern Field the producer. It was via T.A.T. in association with Boston Broadcasters Inc.

BAZELON, DAVID L. ▶ former chief judge of the U.S. Court of Appeals for the District of Columbia Circuit from 1962 to 1979, in which capacity he was a force in striking down numerous regulations and decisions of the FCC. Heading the court most active in the judicial review of FCC actions, Judge Bazelon, a liberal with a strong sense of the public interest in broadcast matters, served as a counterbalance to the commission's tendency to accommodate the industry it is supposed to regulate. He figured prominently in negating the FCC's renewal of the WLBT license and in denying the commission's policy statement on license renewals; in speeches he was openly critical of the quality of broadcasting and of broadcast regulation in the U.S. In later years, he won the affection of broadcasters for his opposition to the Fairness Doctrine, although he maintained that stiff enforcement of limits of the size of media holdings was still necessary.

He was appointed to the court in 1949, having been nominated by President Truman, and became Chief Judge through seniority 13 years later. He retired as Chief Judge in 1979. Technically remaining on the Court as Senior Judge, he ceased active service in 1984.

BBC (BRITISH BROADCASTING CORPORATION) ▶ since 1927 the public broadcasting entity operating in the United Kingdom of England, Scotland, Wales, Northern Ireland, the Channel Islands and the Isle of Man in the Irish Sea. BBC was the first to operate a regularly scheduled television service, starting in 1936, though operations were suspended in September 1939 for the duration of World War II.

The BBC is not state-owned, as is widely believed, but operates independent of government control under a Royal charter (first granted in 1927) and a license from the secretary of state for home affairs as stipulated by the terms of the wireless telegraphy acts of the U.K.

Financial support for the corporation derives mainly from an annual tax called a license fee, payable by all who maintain a radio or TV receiver—the equivalent of $136 for color TV. These fees are collected for the company by the post office. The company, whose radio and television services have never carried paid advertising (unlike some broadcast systems that are state owned), also receives revenue from the activities of its commercial arm, BBC Enterprises, which includes the publishing of books derived from, or related to, its broadcast output, e.g., *Alistair Cooke's America,* Dr. Jacob Bronowski's *The Ascent of Man,* and Nigel Calder's *Violent Universe.*

In 1932, the BBC added an external services division, subsidized by the government, dominantly for the world-wide dissemination of news but also including programs of music, drama and discussion. This offshore radio service currently beams daily in 39 languages, in addition to an English service that operates around the clock.

In 1991, the BBC began World Service Television, broadcasting in English across the European continent and into Eastern Europe via satellite. Some of its broadcasts are carried by terrestrial TV stations. In November of the year, BBC initiated 24-hour World Service telecasts to Asia through a joint venture with a private satellite network, Star TV, based in Hong Kong. This became a unique commercial venture for the BBC, since the channel carries advertising. The BBC has also made it clear that this would be the prototype for a worldwide news channel to challenge CNN's dominance in the field.

Domestically, the BBC operates two television channels (BBC-1 and BBC-2), as well as four national radio channels and local radio stations in London and 19 other key cities. British television (including the independent advertiser-supported stations; commercial television in the U.K. started in 1956) uses the German-developed 625-line PAL color system.

Organizationally, BBC is headed by a board of governors appointed by the Queen, on the advice of her ministers, for five-year terms. The permanent staff, which currently numbers approximately 24,000, is headed by a director-general as the chief executive officer of the company.

The unique constitutional position of the BBC, broadly unaltered since the first Royal charter was granted, was determined largely by the policy and operational practices adopted by its predecessor, the British Broadcasting Company, which inaugurated regular radio service in Britain in 1922. That original company was formed, at the invitation of the postmaster general, by the principal manufacturers of radio receivers, and their only brief was to provide a service "to the reasonable satisfaction" of the postmaster general.

To run the service for them, the manufacturers recruited the late J.C.W. Reith (later to become a peer of the realm), a strict Scottish Calvinist who believed in *noblesse oblige.* He was to become the first director-general of the successor broadcast corporation in 1927, and the single most influential figure in the development of public broadcasting in Britain.

In the first years of British radio, starting in 1922, the postmaster general was the ultimate arbiter of what was suitable for the nation to hear. The fledgling company had no charter from the crown, and no statutory sanction from Parliament. Reith, in command of the service, believed the new medium had a great capacity for public service. He saw it providing not only entertainment, but also information and enlightenment.

In 1925, evidently pleased with the way broadcasting had evolved under Reith's stewardship, the government appointed a blue ribbon committee under Lord Crawford whose assignment was to frame the guidelines for the future structure of broadcasting in Britain. In time, the committee came up with the recommendation that the nation's broadcasting service should henceforth be operated by an independent public corporation "acting as trustee for the national interest." And so the present-day BBC was born.

Over the years the BBC was to become a national institution, an instrument for uniting the British people in times of stress, and for transmitting the ideas and values that collectively make up the British way of life. By intent or otherwise, the BBC became a national arbiter of taste and standards. Admittedly by design, there was even an attempt over many years to impose standards of language that came to be known as "BBC English." The attempt was clearly doomed to failure, and the corporation today appears to have retreated from the position that all voices with access to its microphones should speak as one in oval tones. Contrarily, these days the richness and diversity of British dialects and accents is acknowledged and encouraged.

Besides its broadcasting functions, the BBC has a number of subsidiary roles in British life. It is an archivist, Britain's voice to the world and a patron of the arts. The corporation maintains the acclaimed BBC Symphony, which regularly performs in public concert at home and abroad with some of the world's leading conductors and soloists. It is also a significant force in education, producing more than 3,000 hours of classroom programming for radio and television each year. It also transmits the Open University, an adult education school that awards recognized diplomas and degrees.

In the breadth and variety of its program output, both for radio and television, the BBC is probably unrivaled. Its drama output alone, both in anthology and serial form, totals hundreds of hours annually for TV, and many of these productions are seen around the world. Under new U.K. rules, however, 25% of its productions must be commissioned from independent British producers.

The BBC's charter comes up for review in 1996.

BBC ENTERPRISES ▶ commercial arm of the British Broadcasting Corporation responsible for exploiting BBC products in domestic and global markets and for seeking new sources of revenues for the noncommercial networks. Profits from the Enterprises division are returned to the corporation to help finance new programs. Enterprise's activities include the creation and sale of magazines and books based on BBC programs, product licensing, the sale of audio and video recordings, and the sale of programs abroad. BBC Enterprises also publishes the listings magazine, *The Radio Times,* and operates an American syndication subsidiary, BBC Lionheart, based in New York, which handles sales of BBC programs in North America and arranges coproductions. BBC Enterprises is headed by James Arnold-Baker. BBC Lionheart is headed by Sarah Frank.

BEACON HILL **▶** ambitious CBS dramatic serial (1975) about the intertwined lives of a wealthy Irish-American family and their staff of servants in Boston just after World War I. Aspiring to the critical success of *Upstairs, Downstairs,* the British series from which it borrowed its form and concept, *Beacon Hill* failed to win either acclaim or a large enough audience to last more than three months. Produced in New York by the Robert Stigwood Organization, with Beryl Vertue as executive producer and Jacqueline Babbin as producer, it featured Stephen Elliott and Nancy Marchand as household heads Benjamin and Mary Lassiter, and David Dukes, Kathryn Walker, Maeve McGuire, DeAnn Mears and Kitty Winn as the Lassiter children. As Mr. and Mrs. Hacker, George Rose and Beatrice Straight headed the staff of servants, who included Paul Rudd as chauffeur Brian Mallory. Fielder Cook was director.

BEARDE, CHRIS ▶ see Blye, Allan and Bearde, Chris.

BEAT THE CLOCK **▶** see Game Shows.

BEAUTY AND THE BEAST **▶** crime drama-cum-romance that took its premise from the classic fable. While the hour-long CBS show had a spotty run, being brought back from hiatus more than once during its tenure (1987-1990), it developed somewhat of a cult following.

The stories centered around a beautiful attorney, Catherine Chandler (played by Linda Hamilton), who devotes her life to battling crime after being rescued by a man with animal features and traits, Vincent (played by Ron Perlman), who lives in the subterranean depths of New York's subways and sewers. *Beauty and the Beast* maintained a platonic romance between its two central characters until one of the last episodes.

It was produced by Republic Pictures Television and created by Ron Koslow, who was executive producer along with Paul Junger Witt, Tony Thomas and Stephen Kurzfeld.

Linda Hamilton as Catherine Chandler in *Beauty and the Beast*

BECKER, ARNOLD ▶ v.p. of national television research for CBS-TV since 1977 and for many years a key advisor to the network's programmers. He joined CBS in 1959, after holding research posts with Lennen & Newell Advertising and ABC-TV, and steadily advanced in the research department ranks. When CBS moved its program unit to the West Coast in 1977, Becker was transferred with it. His father, the late I. S. (Zac) Becker, had been v.p. of business affairs for the CBS Radio network during the 1950s.

BECTON, HENRY P., JR. ▶ a national leader in public TV by virtue of his post as president and general manager of Boston's WGBH, one of the system's foremost local stations and a principal producer of its national programming. Becton came to WGBH in 1970 as a producer, rose to vice president and general manager eight years later, and was elected president in 1984. He serves on the executive committee of the PBS board.

BELGIUM ▶ one of Europe's most complex TV markets. With only 3.6 million television homes, the country funds two separate public broadcasters: RTBF for the French-speaking part of the country and BRT for the Flemish. Both operate two channels, and both face considerable competition from recently launched commercial channels as well as signals spilling over from neighboring France and Holland. Belgium has Europe's highest cable penetration at 92%.

The two public broadcasters share the same building, though they have completely separate administrations, film crews, facilities and even entrances to the building. Flemish-language BRT is not permitted to carry commercials, leaving the spot advertising market wide open to the commercial channel, VTM. In the French-speaking area, RTBF competes with commercial RTL-TV1 (owned by Luxembourg's CLT) as well as with the French station La Cinq. France's Canal Plus has also introduced a version of its successful pay-TV movie service for the French-speaking Belgians. The long-established pay-TV movie channel FilmNet also has a strong base in Belgium.

***BELL TELEPHONE HOUR* ▶** weekly series of light-classical and Broadway show music that was a Friday night fixture for most of its nine seasons on NBC (one year it shifted to Tuesday nights and another to Sunday, and it began on TV playing alternate weeks with a Bell-sponsored science show).

The hour-long program, which ran from 1959-68, was the television extension of a radio series that had run for 19 years under Bell System sponsorship. The orchestra, regularly conducted by Donald Voorhees, billed itself as the Bell Telephone Orchestra. Voorhees composed the familiar theme music, which was titled "The Bell Waltz." The music occasionally featured jazz and other pop forms, but never rock. The guest performers each week included many of the top names in their music fields, from Bing Crosby to Pablo Casals.

Bell wanted to continue the series even when the ratings began to decline, but NBC, needing to protect its numbers in the ratings race, nudged it off the air.

BELLISARIO, DONALD ▶ creator and executive producer of *Magnum, P.I.,* one of the few hits of the 1981-82 season which ran until 1988. He went on to create his own production company, Belisarius Productions, through which he created and produced *Quantum Leap* for NBC, which began in 1989. Previously he was writer and producer of the *Black Sheep Squadron* series.

BELSON, JERRY ▶ comedy writer whose long string of credits includes *The Dick Van Dyke Show.* With Garry Marshall he adapted Neil Simon's play *The Odd Couple* as a TV series and served with Marshall as co-executive producer of the early episodes. He later went on to write its revival, *The New Odd Couple,* which survived only a one season run (1982-83). He also wrote Fox-TV's cutting-edge comedy series, *The Tracey Ullman Show* (1987-90), for which (with James L. Brooks, Heide Perlman and Ken Estin) he served as co-creator and co-executive producer.

BEM CASE ▶ (*Business Executives' Move for Vietnam Peace v. FCC/Post-Newsweek Stations v. Business Executives' Move for Vietnam Peace* [412 U.S. 94 (1973)])—legal test on rights of broadcasters to deny the sale of time for the discussion of controversial issues. The Supreme Court in 1973 determined that broadcasters had such a right.

In June 1969 BEM, an ad hoc organization of 2,700 business executives opposed to the U.S. involvement in the Vietnam War, was thwarted by station policy in its attempt to buy a series of one-minute antiwar spots on WTOP-TV Washington. Like many other stations and the three TV networks, WTOP refused to sell air time for editorial advertising. BEM then filed a complaint with the FCC claiming that its First Amendment rights were violated by the licensee's policy.

The FCC upheld the broadcaster, deeming it unnecessary for a station to sell editorial advertising if a broadcaster was fulfilling its duty under the Fairness Doctrine by adequately covering all sides of the Vietnam debate.

But the D.C. Court of Appeals, joining the case with that of the Democratic National Committee (which sought to buy time on CBS to reply to President Nixon's policies on the war), ruled in 1971 that a flat ban on paid public issue announcements was in violation of the First Amendment. The case was remanded to the FCC to develop reasonable procedures and regulations determining how to implement editorial advertisements on the air. Essentially, the court found that broadcasters could not retain total editorial control.

The case was appealed to the Supreme Court, which in five complex and multifaceted opinions, reversed the Court of Appeals.

BEN CASEY ▶ very popular, hour-long medical series in the early 1960s whose appeal centered on the refreshingly different antihero personality of the title character, a surly and haunted but gifted surgeon. It played on ABC from 1961-66. Vince Edwards, who was propelled to stardom by the series, oddly was unable to carry his popularity from that show to others. Featured were Sam Jaffe as neurosurgeon David Zorba, Bettye Ackerman as anesthesiologist Maggie Graham, Jeanne Bates as Nurse Wills, Nick Dennis as orderly Nick Kanavaras and, for a time, Franchot Tone as neurosurgeon Dr. Freeland.

BENDICK, ROBERT ▶ producer of *Wide, Wide World* and the Dave Garroway *Today* show in the late 1950s and, earlier, a program and special events executive with CBS. Trained as a documentary cameraman, he became one of the producers of *This Is Cinerama* and a director of *Cinerama Holiday.*

BENDIX, WILLIAM (d. 1964) ▶ character actor best known in TV for his portrayal of Chester Riley, the bumbling father of the popular situation comedy *The Life of Riley* (1953-58). He performed a wide range of dramatic roles, however, including one in the western series *Overland Trail* (1960).

BENJAMIN, BURTON (d. 1988) ▶ one of the backstage stars of television journalism in a varied and distinguished career at CBS News that began in 1957 and embraced hard news, documentaries and management. In latter years he was the *eminence gris* at CBS News, the pure journalist who adhered strictly to the high standards of the profession. Because he was so straight-arrow, he was chosen by the president of CBS News to conduct an unprecedented in-house inquiry into charges that an aired CBS documentary, which alleged a serious deception by General Westmoreland during the Vietnam War, was essentially rigged to make its point.

The investigation took six months and resulted in the now famous 59-page Benjamin Report, which found the documentary guilty on 11 counts of violating the CBS News guidelines and codes. For its honesty as an in-house probe into journalistic practices, the Benjamin Report reflected favorably on CBS.

Benjamin feared he would be remembered for the report and not for his other achievements at CBS News. He was executive producer of *The Twentieth Century,* an occasional documentary series that ran nine years, and for a time was executive producer of *CBS Reports.* As senior executive producer for CBS News he produced such specials as *Mr. Justice Douglas* (1972), *The Rockefellers* (1973) and *Solzhenitsyn* (1974). From 1975-78 he was executive producer of *The CBS Evening News with Walter Cronkite* and then was named vice president and director of news for the division.

He came to CBS in 1957 from a background with the *Cleveland News,* UPI, NEA and RKO-Pathe.

BENJAMIN FRANKLIN ▶ four-part series of 90-minute dramatic specials highlighting the life of Franklin. Offered by CBS (1974-76) for the Bicentennial, each episode had a different writer and a different actor playing Franklin. The role was taken variously by Eddie Albert, Lloyd Bridges, Richard Widmark and Melvyn Douglas. The executive producer was Lewis Freedman, the producers Glenn Jordan and George Lefferts and the director Jordan.

BENJAMIN, ROBERT S. (d. 1979) ▶ lawyer and film company executive who was a charter member of the Corporation for Public Broadcasting and became its chairman in 1975. In 1977, after serving nine years as a director, he resigned and was elected chairman emeritus of CPB. He was also chairman of United Artists Pictures Corp. and a partner in the law firm of Phillips, Nizer, Benjamin & Krim.

BENNETT, HARVE ▶ series producer associated with Universal TV who was executive producer of *The Six Million Dollar Man, The Invisible*

Man and the *Rich Man, Poor Man* mini-series. Bennett had been an ABC program v.p. in Hollywood during the 1960s, leaving in 1968 to become coproducer of *Mod Squad* for Thomas-Spelling Productions. During his childhood, he was one of the prodigies on radio's *Quiz Kids* and was known then as Harve Fischman.

Robert Bennett

BENNETT, ROBERT ▶ owner of Trans Atlantic Entertainment, an international production and distribution company, who was a leading broadcasting figure throughout the 1970s and 1980s. Bennett was best known as the principal architect of Boston station WCVB-TV's development when its license changed hands in 1971 and for its exemplary local programming.

Bennett started his career in 1952 as a sales rep for Metromedia, later becoming v.p. of sales in Los Angeles and eventually general manager of WTTG Washington and then New York's WNEW.

When the Boston *Herald-Traveler* lost the WCVB-TV license to BBI Communications, Bennett was hired as general manager and obliged to fulfill the programming promises made to the FCC. His work there earned a Peabody award for station performance and several Emmys. When Metromedia Broadcasting purchased WCVB in 1981, he was president of the station as well as senior v.p. of Metromedia Inc. Bennett tried to take Metromedia into national program syndication with such series as *Thicke of the Night* and *Onstage America* but didn't have much success.

In 1986 Bennett left Metromedia when it was sold to Rupert Murdoch's News Corp and formed Bob Bennett Productions, dealing mostly with sports-related programming. With two partners in 1989, Bennett bought the New World Entertainment library and formed Trans Atlantic Pictures, which he renamed Trans Atlantic Entertainment when he bought out his partners.

Bennett also was the founding president of the National Academy of Television Arts and Sciences (NATAS).

***BENNY HILL* ▶** popular British series of slapstick and sometimes bawdy comedy sketches that was successfully repackaged for the American market, where it continues to be distributed in syndication. All the skits, sight gags, drag routines and blackouts are built around the star, Benny Hill, a deft comedian of English music hall tradition whose demeanor shifts readily from angelic to mischievous to lecherous. He is assisted by a resident cast of comedy players headed by Jackie Wright, Henry McGee and Bob Todd and by a bevy of sexy women in brief costume.

The original series by Thames Television began production in 1969, and the edited-down, half-hour U.S. version came onto the market ten years later via D.L. Taffner Ltd. Many of the American stations scheduled it late at night because *Hill*'s material tends to be racy; it won a following there.

BENNY, JACK (d. 1974) ▶ one of the great radio comedians who made the transition to television in the 1950s and had a weekly series on CBS-TV from 1950 to 1965. With a kind of continuing sketch comedy, in which he represented himself as an aging and somewhat pompous bachelor who was an outstanding tightwad, Benny held forth in radio and TV for more than 40 years. Through most of it he carried the same troupe of supporting players, which included his wife, Mary Livingstone, announcer Don Wilson, singer Dennis Day, band leader Phil Harris and character comedians Eddie (Rochester) Anderson and Mel Blanc, all of whom served him as foils.

Benny was not a joke-telling or slapstick comedian. A peer described him aptly as "not one who said funny *things* but one who said things *funny.*" The character he created was always the source of the humor, the butt of insults, made funnier by Benny's catalog of mannerisms and responses—a martyr-like stare, with hand against chin; facial expressions of disbelief or frustration; and the utterances, "Well!," "Hmm" and "Now cut that out!" These became comedy motifs savored in their weekly repetition by huge audiences. Fellow comedians admired Benny's expert timing and his ability to mine laughter from glowering silence.

Familiar trappings of the Benny shows were the antiquated car, a Maxwell, and the violin on which he regularly essayed an inept version of "Love in Bloom." He made famous the birthday on which he annually turned 39, and he maintained a mock feud with the dry-witted comic Fred Allen, through which they cross-plugged each other's programs.

Benny's radio series began in 1932 on NBC, and from 1934 through 1936 it led the popularity polls; after that it was seldom out of the top 10. CBS hired Benny away in 1948, and he continued on radio until 1955. In the meantime, Benny and his cast made sporadic television appearances and eventually were able to transfer the basic elements of their radio success to the new medium. When his radio series ended, Benny increased his television work from occasional programs to a bi-weekly series and finally to a weekly.

After 1965, his television performances were limited to a few specials each year. His last, *Jack Benny's Second Farewell,* was on Jan. 24, 1974. He died of cancer of the pancreas, at 80, the following December.

BENTON, NELSON (d. 1988) ▶ CBS News correspondent for 20 years. He covered such major stories as the civil rights movement and the Vietnam War.

BERCOVICI, ERIC ▶ veteran writer, often in collaboration with Jerry Ludwig, specializing in writing TV series pilots and made-for-TV movies. He came into prominence as producer and adapter of James Clavell's *Shogun,* the hit mini-series. Later, he created two series for NBC, *McClain's Law* and *Chicago Story,* and was executive producer of both.

BERG, GERTRUDE (d. 1966) ▶ character actress identified with her role as Molly Goldberg, the matriarch of a Jewish family in the Bronx, in the situation comedy *The Goldbergs* (1949, revived in 1956). Berg created the series and also wrote for it.

BERGEN, EDGAR (d. 1978) ▶ ventriloquist whose most famous creation was his dummy, Charlie McCarthy. Their popular radio series led to movies and frequent appearances on TV variety shows. In the 1950s they hosted the daytime quiz show *Do You Trust Your Wife?,* which later became *Who Do You Trust?* (with Johnny Carson as host).

BERGER, MARILYN ▶ broadcast journalist with ABC News since 1982, after stints with NBC and PBS. She is married to Don Hewitt, executive producer of the CBS show *60 Minutes.*

BERGER, ROBERT (BUZZ) ▶ producer noted for modern historical dramas whose credits include such specials as *Holocaust, The Missiles of October, Pueblo* and *Skokie,* all winners of important awards. He also did a series of three profiles for HBO in the form of made-for-TV movies: *Sakharov, Murrow,* and *Mandela.*

Long associated with famed East Coast producer Herbert Brodkin in Plautus Productions and Titus Productions, Berger formed his own company, Plautus II, when Brodkin died in 1991. Brodkin hired him in 1962 to work on his new TV series, *The Nurses,* as casting director and executive assistant. Later he was promoted to producer of *The Nurses.* He worked with Brodkin on virtually all of his programs and was executive producer or producer of most of them.

Not all were modern historical dramas. Berger proposed the suspense novel *Switch* for television, for instance, and it played on CBS under the title *Doubletake.* That was followed by three sequels featuring the fictive police detective Janek, played by Richard Crenna. Berger was also executive producer of such TV movies as *Welcome Home, Bobby, Johnny Bull,* and *Stones For Ibarra.*

BERGMAN, JULES (d. 1988) ▶ ABC News science editor beginning in 1961 who covered all U.S. manned spaceflights and many of the key developments in fields ranging from medicine to aeronautics. His documentary credits included the six-part series *What About Tomorrow* (1973), *Closeup on Fire* (1973), *Closeup on Crashes: The Illusion of Safety* (1974), *Earthquake* (1972) and *SST: Super Sound and Fury.* He joined ABC News as a newswriter in 1952 after brief stints with *Time* magazine and CBS.

BERGMANN, TED ▶ managing director of the DuMont Television Network (1953-56), after which he entered the advertising industry. He worked previously for NBC in the international division and joined DuMont in 1947 as a sales executive.

BERLE, MILTON ▶ a practitioner of broad and noisy comedy who, through his popularity from 1948 to 1956, earned the sobriquet of "Mr. Television." His program, beginning in a time when TV was a luxury enjoyed chiefly by the wealthier families, helped to spur the sale of television sets to working-class homes. Always presented on Tuesday nights on NBC, his *Texaco Star Theater,* as it was originally called, underwent several changes of title and sponsorship over its eight-year run.

Although a champion of buffoonery and lavish production, Berle was later to surprise viewers with his adeptness at serious drama when he began accepting occasional roles in TV plays. At the height of his popularity, he became known affectionately as "Uncle Miltie" and was chided by other comedians as "The Thief of Badgags." Such was his popularity that NBC offered him a contract through 1981, under which he was paid after his series ended.

In the 1960s there was an unsuccessful attempt to revive his comedy series. Under a modification of the contract, he was able to host a prime-time bowling series for ABC, which was also unsuccessful.

Milton Berle, "Mr. Television"

BERLIN WALL ▶ icon of the Cold War and, as such, a natural for television, especially at the historic end on Nov. 9, 1989, when the wall that separated East from West Berlin began coming down.

It was erected as a barrier between East and West by the Soviets on Aug. 13, 1961. Network news cameras were there in 1963 when President John F. Kennedy declared "Ich bin ein Berliner." NBC News went under the Wall in 1962 when Reuven Frank and Piers Anderton filmed a remarkable documentary, *The Tunnel,* which showed how a secret route 15 feet below the wall allowed 59 men, women, and children to escape to the West. Eighteen years later, when the Wall itself came down, NBC News anchor Tom Brokaw was at the scene holding a chunk of the wall, beating all his rivals to the site just when it was the focus of television viewing worldwide. ABC's Peter Jennings and CBS's Dan Rather were dispatched to Berlin only after their evening broadcasts.

The fall of the Berlin Wall, which signified the end of Communist domination in Eastern Europe, became an event that television itself helped make possible. As observers have noted: the real pressure for change in East Germany and elsewhere was generated largely by images seen on western television—western lifestyles, products, and free press. The contrast to the frequently austere daily lives of those in the East had to be stunning. Once again, television had not only recorded history but been a participant in its making, helping produce what turned out be an unforgettable fade-out shot—Berliners hoisting aloft pieces of the Wall—a metaphor of a political system that now may be in permanent ruin. "Something there is," said Dan Rather, quoting Robert Frost, "that doesn't love a wall".

Silvio Berlusconi

BERLUSCONI, SILVIO ▶ Italy's powerful television tycoon, who is also a force in the European industry. He is the chairman of Fininvest, a huge media conglomerate privately owned by Berlusconi that houses his many broadcasting, publishing and related business interests.

Berlusconi became a pioneer of commercial television in Europe almost by accident. As a young man with a law degree he began making his fortune in real estate, creating new housing developments. At one of them, Milano 2 on the outskirts of Milan, he created a closed-circuit internal television service for the tenants that later became the basis for TeleMilano in 1975.

When the government deregulated television that year, allowing commercial stations to be established everywhere, Berlusconi was well prepared to move into the field, and he moved swiftly. TeleMilano became national network Canale 5 in 1980, and soon after Berlusconi acquired sufficient stations to operate two additional networks, Retequattro and Italia 1. He has also been the motivating force behind Italy's three-channel pay-TV service, Telepiu, launched in 1991, in which he has a 10% interest. His company, Reteitalia, is one of the leading production and distribution companies in Europe.

Berlusconi also has a host of publishing, retailing, insurance and real estate interests and owns the AC Milan soccer club. He also owns a production facility in Spain and has an equity position in that country's Tele 5, and he owns a substantial share of the French national network, La Cinq.

BERNSTEIN, LEONARD (d. 1990) ▶ conductor and composer who introduced millions of children to classical music through the *Young People's Concert* series on CBS. His extraordinary ability to explain the complexities of symphonic music to the uninitiated, and his highly theatrical style in conducting, served to make the series one of the most popular cultural offerings on TV. Bernstein became music director of the New York Philharmonic in 1958 with the reputation of "wunderkind." The Philharmonic had been doing *Young People's Concerts* since 1922, but it was Bernstein who put them on TV. He left the orchestra in 1969 but continued to conduct the educational concerts on CBS until 1972, after which the TV baton passed to Michael Tilson Thomas.

***BEST SELLERS* ▶** umbrella title for a weekly NBC series (1976-77) of dramatization of best-selling novels, each book serialized over several weeks. The program was inspired by the success of ABC's mini-series *Rich Man, Poor Man,* a TV adaptation of a novel by Irwin Shaw. First of the *Best Sellers* was Taylor Caldwell's *Captains and the Kings,* whose cast included Richard Jordan, Barbara Parkins, Charles Durning, David Huffman and Jenny Sullivan. Others were Anton Myrer's *Once an Eagle,* with Sam Elliott, Cliff Potts, Darleen Carr, Amy Irving and Glenn Ford; Norman Bognar's *Seventh Avenue,* with Steven Keats, Kristoffer Tabori, Jane Seymour, Dori Brenner, Alan King, Eli Wallach and Jack Gilford; and Robert Ludlum's *The Rhinemann Exchange,* with Stephen Collins and Lauren Hutton.

The series was produced by Universal TV, with Charles Engel as executive in charge. Executive producers of the serials included Roy Huggins, William Sackheim and David Victor.

BETAMAX ▶ first home video system to be successfully launched in the U.S. Developed and marketed by Sony, Betamax used cassettes containing half-inch-wide tape. It was introduced in 1975 as an expensive console incorporating a recorder, TV set and wood cabinetry and was soon thereafter brought out as a stand-alone VCR. For several years Betamax machines co-existed alongside recorders of the VHS format, introduced by Matsushita the year after Betamax appeared, but VHS gradually prevailed thanks to its longer recording time, and Betamax became extinct.

BETTAG, TOM ▶ executive producer of ABC News' *Nightline* since May 1991. Prior to joining ABC News, he spent 22 years at CBS News, where he was executive producer of *The CBS Evening News with Dan Rather* (1986-91). Prior to that, he was a senior political producer for CBS and a producer for *60 Minutes.*

He joined CBS News in 1969 as an assignment editor based in Washington, D.C. In 1977, as a Fulbright Scholar, he took a leave of absence from CBS News to travel to Japan to study its television networks. He began his career as a reporter for the *Grand Rapids Press* and *Saginaw News* in Michigan in 1965.

BETZ, CARL (d. 1978) ▶ actor who figured in two hit series, as the husband in *The Donna Reed Show* (1958-66) and as star of *Judd For the Defense* (1967-69).

***BEVERLY HILLBILLIES, THE* ▶** situation comedy about kindly country bumpkins, the Clampetts, who move to posh Beverly Hills after striking oil. A smash hit when it premiered on CBS in 1962, it ran through 1971 despite abuses heaped on it by the critics. Created and produced by Paul Henning for Filmways, it starred Buddy Ebsen as Jed Clampett, Irene Ryan as Granny, Donna Douglas as Jed's daughter Elly May and Max Baer Jr. as Jed's nephew Jethro Bodine, and it featured Raymond Bailey as banker Milburn Drysdale and Nancy Kulp as Drysdale's assistant, Jane Hathaway. Reruns were stripped daytime on CBS, 1968-72.

***BEWITCHED* ▶** highly successful ABC fantasy situation comedy (1964-72) about an ordinary fellow, Darin Stevens, married to a beautiful witch, Samantha. It starred Elizabeth Montgomery and Dick York (who left after the fifth season to be replaced by Dick Sargent). Other regulars were Agnes Moorehead as Samantha's mother Endora, David White as Darin's boss Larry Tate and Alice Pearce (and, later, Sandra Gould) as neighbor Gladys Kravitz. It was by Screen Gems.

BEWKES, JEFF ▶ president and chief operating officer of Home Box Office Inc., promoted to that post in 1991 by chairman Michael Fuchs when E. Thayer Bigelow was given a new post by parent Time Warner. Bewkes had been with the company for 12 years, working up through affiliate relations and finally to executive v.p. and chief financial officer. He is known as a deal-maker, having worked to facilitate the merger between HBO's and Viacom's competing comedy channels that resulted in the basic network, Comedy Central. He also watched over HBO's investments in other cable programmers, such as E! and Black Entertainment Television.

***BICENTENNIAL MINUTES* ▶** series of one-minute programs broadcast every evening in prime time on CBS from July 4, 1974 through the end of 1976 as a Bicentennial salute. Each minute offered a vignette of an occurrence 200 years earlier on that date, related to the birth of the U.S.; each also featured a different well-known personality. Among those who appeared on the *Minutes* were Charlton Heston, Deborah Kerr, Rise Stevens, Beverly Sills, Kirk Douglas, Alfred Hitchcock, Zsa Zsa Gabor and Walter Cronkite, in addition to senators, generals and scientists. Lewis Freedman was succeeded by Bob Markell as executive producer. Shell Oil sponsored.

BICYCLING ▶ term for the distribution of film or videotape programs to stations by means other than electronic interconnection, such as by air freight or mail. In earlier times, episodes of syndicated programs arrived at stations in cans, with instructions to ship them to a station in another market after use.

BIERBAUER, CHARLES J. ▶ senior White House correspondent for Cable News Network and anchor of CNN's *Newsmaker Saturday.* Bierbauer has covered the 1984 and 1988 presidential campaigns for CNN and seven superpower summits, including all five Reagan-Gorbachev meetings. He began covering the White House during President Reagan's first term.

His first assignment for CNN was in 1981 as defense correspondent, based in the Washington bureau. Prior to that, he was ABC News bureau chief/correspondent in Moscow and Bonn from 1978 to 1981, and with Westinghouse Broadcasting for nine years as foreign news editor in London, bureau chief in Bonn and East European correspondent in Vienna. Bierbauer also was a correspondent for the *Chicago Daily News* and reporter for the Associated Press.

***BIG BLUE MARBLE, THE* ▶** Emmy- and Peabody-award-winning children's magazine series devoted to the life-styles of children around the world. Each half-hour included seven- to ten-minute portraits of children, a regular "Dear Pen Pal" feature that arranged correspondence between American children and English-speaking youngsters in other countries, and five-part serialized dramas related to the general theme of international understanding.

Designed to run without commercial interruption, the series was underwritten by ITT as a public service. It premiered in September of 1974 and was carried on 180 commercial and public stations in the U.S. and in 60 countries and areas abroad. It was created by Alphaventure and produced by that company from 1974 to 1978. In 1978 the program became a Blue Marble Co. Production, ending in 1983.

***BIG EVENT, THE* ▶** NBC's attempt in the fall of 1976 to carve out a weekly two- or three-hour block on Sunday nights for varied blockbuster special programs as the keystone of its commitment to "event television" (i.e., unique and momentous specials). The effort had uneven results but was continued the following season and then dropped.

Alvin Cooperman had been brought back to the network to concentrate exclusively on securing properties for the time period, but he was dismissed before the season ended. The opening program, *The Big Party,* was conceived as a salute to the start of various show business and sports seasons through the device of switching live among three parties arranged by NBC in New York. The program fizzled as entertainment, a fact which was reflected in the ratings. *The Big Event* rallied from that embarrassment with the showing of the movie *Gone With the Wind;* the presentation of *The Moneychangers,* an adaptation of a best-selling novel; and a star-laden four-hour extravaganza celebrating NBC's 50th anniversary in broadcasting. But overall, the timeslot failed to deliver on its grandiose billing.

BIG MARCH, THE ▶ CBS News special report on highlights of the civil rights rally known as the March On Washington of Aug. 28, 1963, at the Lincoln Memorial. The hour special that night included Dr. Martin Luther King Jr. delivering his famous "I Have a Dream" speech.

BIG TOP, THE ▶ CBS circus show which debuted in 1950, with Jack Sterling as ringmaster. Ed McMahon, who later became Johnny Carson's announcer and sidekick, played one of the clowns.

BIG TOWN ▶ NBC series (1950-56) based on a successful radio series about the crusading reporter/editor of *The Illustrated Press.* Mark Stevens played the lead, Steve Wilson, the final two seasons and Patrick McVey the first four. The role of Lorelei Kilbourne, the society reporter, was played by a number of actresses, among them Julie Stevens, Jane Nigh and Beverly Tyler. The series was produced by Gross-Krasne Inc. and in syndication went by such titles as *Heart of the City, City Assignment, Headline Story* and *Byline—Steve Wilson.*

BIG VALLEY, THE ▶ hour-long saga of a family living in the heartland of California in the 1870s that starred Barbara Stanwyck as Victoria Barkley, strong-willed widow and leader of her powerful family of four sons and a daughter. Co-starring Richard Long as Jarrod, Peter Breck as Nick, Lee Majors as Heath, Charles Briles (for a season) as Eugene and Linda Evans as Audra, the series premiered on ABC Sept. 16, 1965, and ran until 1969, when it was put into syndication by its producer, Four Star Productions.

BIGELOW, E. THAYER ▶ veteran executive who worked his way up the video side of Time Inc., becoming president of HBO in 1988 and three years later chief executive of Time Warner Cable Programming Inc., a newly formed unit of the newly merged company.

Bigelow joined Time Inc. in 1967, and when the company purchased Manhattan Cable from Chuck Dolan in 1973 Bigelow was assigned to it as v.p. and treasurer. Later he became president of the unit (1976-79) and then moved to the Time-Life Films subsidiary. After several years in corporate financial posts, Bigelow in early 1988 was named president of American Television and Communications (ATC), Time's cable systems group, the nation's second largest multiple-systems operator. Some four months later he was named to head HBO. The frequent moves reflect Bigelow's reputation in the company as a financial problem-solver.

BILBY, KENNETH W. ▶ v.p. of public relations for NBC (1954-60) who moved up to the parent company RCA, first as v.p. of public affairs and then as an executive v.p. He retired from RCA in 1979 but returned in 1981 to help the new chairman, Thornton Bradshaw, through a transition period.

Early in his career he was a foreign correspondent for the *New York Herald-Tribune.*

BILLBOARD ▶ a slide at the start or end of a show noting the principal advertisers in the telecast and offered as a bonus to the sponsors. Billboards are most often seen today in sporting events and public television programs.

BINDER, STEVE ▶ director associated with comedy shows, including *The Danny Kaye Show* and *Steve Allen Comedy Hour* for CBS, Allen's syndicated show for Westinghouse and network specials with Jack Paar, Liza Minnelli, Bob Newhart, Petula Clark and Lucille Ball. In recent years, he doubled as a producer with his own production company.

BING CROSBY SHOW, THE ▶ domestic situation comedy on ABC (1964) starring Crosby as architect Bing Collins and featuring Beverly Garland as his wife Ellie, Dianne Sherry and Carol Faylen as their daughters, Janice and Joyce, and Frank McHugh as Willie Walters. It was produced by Bing Crosby Productions.

BIOGRAPHY OF A BOOKIE JOINT ▶ extraordinary CBS documentary by investigative reporter Jay McMullen on the operations of an illegal Boston betting parlor that posed as a key-maker's shop; it aired Nov. 30, 1961 and brought about the resignation of Boston's police commissioner. Working with Palmer Williams, McMullen spent several months filming the entrance to the key shop from a room across the street, catching numerous visits by police officers. The documentary also contained footage of the bookie joint in operation, photographed by McMullen with a concealed 8mm camera.

BIONDI, FRANK ▶ television executive widely respected for his business acumen, program savvy and general intelligence. In 1987 he became president and CEO of Viacom International, a media company whose holdings include cable networks and systems, TV and radio stations, and program production and syndication operations. Before being hired by Viacom, he was head of Coca-Cola Television (formerly Columbia Pictures Industries).

Prior to that he was chairman and CEO of Home Box Office Inc. (1983-85), having joined HBO in 1978 as director of entertainment program planning. With Michael Fuchs, who has since succeeded him as HBO chairman, Biondi guided the network's programming and marketing strategies.

A graduate of Harvard Business School, Biondi set out on a career in finance by working at Shearson Lehman Hutton and Prudential Bache. Later he started his own financial consulting firm, through which he became involved with the Children's Television Workshop, his entree to television.

BIONIC WOMAN, THE ▶ successful spin-off of ABC's *Six Million Dollar Man* introduced in January 1976 with Lindsay Wagner in the role of Jaime Somers, a reconstituted woman with superhuman powers. Featuring Richard Anderson as Oscar Goldman, Martin E. Brooks as Dr. Rudy Wells, Martha Scott as Helen and Ford Rainey as Jim, it was by Harve Bennett Productions and Universal TV, with Bennett as executive producer.

Although it ranked in the Nielsen Top 10, the series was dropped by ABC for the 1977 fall schedule, but it was immediately picked up by NBC. Its run ended in 1978.

BIRT, JOHN ▶ director general-designate of the BBC (British Broadcasting Corporation), named to the post in July 1991 but unable to assume it until the contract of Michael Checkland expired in 1993. Checkland had brought Birt into the BBC in 1987 from London Weekend Television, one of the commercial broadcast companies. His brief was to overhaul BBC's journalism operations and make a single department of news and current affairs, a task he executed efficiently if sometimes controversially. In marked contrast to Checkland (an accountant who came up on the business side), Birt has had extensive experience producing for television, initially for BBC and then for 21 years with two commercial companies, Granada TV and London Weekend.

BIXBY, BILL ▶ TV actor who starred in three hit series, *My Favorite Martian* (1963-66), *The Courtship of Eddie's Father* (1969-72), for which he received an Emmy nomination, and *The Incredible Hulk* (1978-82). He revived the role of David Banner in a few *Incredible Hulk* movies-of-the-week that ran on NBC in the late 1980s. Since the late 1980s he has done a considerable amount of directing, primarily on sitcom pilots.

BLACK ENTERTAINMENT TELEVISION (BET) ▶ one of the early basic-cable networks and the first to target a black audience. Founded in 1980 by black entrepreneur Robert L. Johnson, BET received an infusion of capital in exchange for equity from Tele-Communications Inc., Great American Broadcasting and HBO. It currently reaches about 25 million cable subscribers. Though it carries movies and public affairs programming of interest to blacks, BET's programming relies heavily on music videos ranging from gospel to rap.

BLACK PERSPECTIVE ON THE NEWS ▶ weekly public affairs series on PBS that began in 1973 and covered current events from a black point of view or national issues of specific interest to blacks. Originating at WHYY, the Wilmington-Philadelphia PTV station, the series was produced by Acel Moore of the Philadelphia *Inquirer* and Reginald Bryant, who was also host-moderator.

BLACK SHEEP SQUADRON ▶ see *Baa Baa Black Sheep.*

BLACK WEEK ▶ one of four weeks during the year (a fifth week occurs every fifth year) when Nielsen's household and persons audience estimates were not reported in the definitive rating report, known as the Pocketpiece. The ratings, in effect, took a rest. This was the practice until 1987, when the People Meter supplanted the Audimeter as the essential audience-measuring technology.

Prior to 1970, the black weeks were periods when no audience data were gathered, and a programming tradition grew up around them. As unrated weeks—and therefore non-competitive for the networks—they became the most suitable time for documentaries, cultural programs and public affairs offerings that stood to receive low ratings under normal conditions. The networks also made a practice of scheduling reruns during black weeks since there was no point in wasting firstrun episodes of series in a time when Nielsen was not counting the audience.

For practical purposes, the black weeks vanished when the overnight and weekly services began. Although the audience is now being counted during these four weeks by the

Pocketpiece, the programming tradition of black weeks remain. There is still a tendency at the networks to concentrate programs of low rating potential in those periods.

Black weeks were adopted by Nielsen to enable the company to review its internal tabulations and to create vacation time for its field staff.

BLACKLIST ▶ a shameful industry practice during the McCarthy Era in the early 1950s, when performers and writers suspected of being communist sympathizers were denied employment in the broadcast media. In the hysteria of the times, organizations like Aware Inc., which published *Red Channels*, and newspaper columnists like Walter Winchell and Jack O'Brian dedicated themselves to rooting out the people in show business who might use the mass media to propagandize for the enemy. They provided the names that served as the blacklist.

At first the networks resisted such pressures, but when the sponsors of their programs were threatened with consumer boycotts if they used talent that was suspect, the whole system caved in. Advertisers wanted nothing to do with anyone who was thought to be subversive, even if there was no proof. Fearful of losing their sources of revenue, the networks complied, as did the packagers of programs. The blacklist was never publicly posted but existed in the inner sanctums of each company. Even after the witch hunts ended, the effect of the blacklist remained. Well into the 1960s, performers who had been listed continued to be barred by one or another network from doing guest shots.

BLAIR, FRANK ▶ newscaster for NBC's *Today* show who was with the program from its premiere in January 1952 until his retirement in 1975. For the first two years Blair was *Today's* Washington correspondent; then he moved to New York to read the four daily news summaries. Blair retired to Charleston, S.C., where he had begun his broadcast career in 1935 at radio station WCSC.

BLANC, MEL (d. 1989) ▶ known in Hollywood as the "man of a thousand voices" for his extraordinary range with cartoon characters. For Warner Brothers' *Looney Tunes and Merrie Melodies* he created the voices for Porky Pig, Bugs Bunny, Daffy Duck, Elmer Fudd, Tweety Bird, Sylvester the Cat, Pepe Le Pew and Yosemite Sam. Though originating in movie shorts, all had television careers in ABC's prime-time *The Bugs Bunny Show* (1960-62), in which Blanc did all the voices. Later the series continued on Saturday mornings. For Hanna-Barbera in the late 1960s, Blanc created the voices for Barney Rubble and Dino the Dinosaur in the TV animated sitcom, *The Flintstones*. He also worked in television as a featured character on *The Jack Benny Show*.

BLEIER, EDWARD ▶ president of a Time Warner division responsible for domestic pay TV, animation and network features. Beginning in 1976 he was the executive v.p. of Warner Bros. TV and head of its New York office. He joined the company in 1969 after 14 years as an ABC executive variously in sales, programming, planning and public relations. In the 1950s he worked in sales and programming for several New York stations and for the DuMont Network.

***BLIND AMBITION* ▶** eight-hour dramatic serial based on the personal accounts of John W. Dean III and his wife, Maureen, of their years in the Nixon Administration and the effects of Watergate upon their lives. It was presented on CBS on four consecutive nights from 9 to 11 p.m., May 20 to May 23, 1979, and drew excellent ratings.

In the Time-Life Television production, Martin Sheen portrayed Dean, Theresa Russell his wife and Rip Torn President Nixon. Others in the cast were Michael Callan as Charles Colson, Lonny Chapman as L. Patrick Gray, William Daniels as G. Gordon Liddy, Fred Grandy as Donald Segretti, Graham Jarvis as John Ehrlichman, Lawrence Pressman as H.R. Haldeman, John Randolph as John Mitchell, William Schallert as Herbert Kalmbach, James Sloyan as Ron Ziegler and William Windom as Richard Kleindienst.

Written by Stanley R. Greenberg from material in two books—*Blind Ambition* by John Dean and *Mo* by Maureen Dean—the program was produced and directed by George Schaefer, with Renee Valente as coproducer and David Susskind as executive producer.

BLINN, WILLIAM ▶ prolific writer and producer whose notable scripts range from *Brian's Song* and an episode of *Roots* to the pilot scripts for *S.W.A.T.* He was coproducer of *The New Land, The Rookies* for two years, and the NBC series *Fame* in 1982.

Blinn created the popular action series *Starsky and Hutch*, which ran from 1975-1979, and produced *Our House*, which ran from 1986-88.

In 1990 he produced two TV movies for NBC, *Polly* and *Polly: Comin' Home,* through his own company, Echo Cove Productions, in conjunction with Walt Disney Productions.

BLOCK PROGRAMMING ▶ the bunching of shows similar in type into a number of consecutive time periods for the purpose of serving a single audience over the span. A children's block may run as long as six hours, a sports block may consume an afternoon or an evening. Protracted periods may also be blocked out for news, game shows, soap operas or public affairs.

Program blocks differ from *ghettos* in that they are created affirmatively and represent a technique for maintaining audience, while ghettos connote a dumping ground for programs not likely to attain large audiences.

BLOCK, RICHARD C. ▶ veteran broadcaster who pioneered UHF broadcasting in the 1950s and 1960s and since then has headed Block Communications Group, a Santa Monica consulting firm he founded in 1975. He left the firm for a two-year period (1983-85) to become executive vice president of Metromedia Television.

In 1958 he coaxed the Kaiser Corp. into building independent UHF stations in seven of the top ten markets and was president of the group until 1975. UHF stations were difficult to receive then, requiring special tuners and antennas. Block was instrumental in achieving the legislation requiring TV sets to be built with all-channel tuning. When Kaiser gave up on UHF in 1975, the group was sold to the Marshall Field family and became Field Broadcasting. Later the stations were sold off.

Block's consultancy has both domestic and international clients, including major distributors, studios and trade associations.

BLONDIE **▶** situation comedy on CBS (1968-69) that was an attempt by the network to resurrect the successful radio and movie series that had starred Penny Singleton and Arthur Lake. The TV version starred Pat Harty as Blondie Bumstead, Will Hutchins as husband Dagwood, and Jim and Henny Backus as J. C. and Cora Dithers. It was not successful. Based on the popular comic strip by Chic Young, it was produced by King Features and Kayro Productions.

BLUE BOOK ▶ a controversial FCC report issued in 1946 with the formal title of *Public Service Responsibility of Broadcast Licensees,* which set forth program criteria for license renewals. Although its supporters on the commission considered it nothing more than the enunciation of minimum standards for broadcasting in the public interest, the document was immediately attacked by broadcasters and some members of Congress as an instrument of censorship representing an attempt by the FCC to control programming. The combination of these attacks and public indifference to the issue rendered the Blue Book ineffective. But it was never rescinded and presumably could be made to apply to TV licensees today if the commission saw fit.

The Blue Book came by its nickname from the blue paper cover on the mimeographed report. In essence it maintained that though the licensee had the primary responsibility to determine its own programming, the FCC had a duty to consider a station's program service in determining whether it was operating in the public interest. The basic criteria to be applied in license renewal decisions concerned (1) a station's commitment to sustaining (noncommercial) programs in the interest of a balanced program structure; (2) its use of local talent; (3) the presentation of programs dealing with important public issues; and (4) discretion in the amount of advertising carried.

Heightening the controversy over the report was the fact that its author, Dr. Charles Siepmann, was an Englishman who had been with the BBC. He came to the U.S. at the behest of FCC chairman Paul A. Porter specifically to direct a study and draw up proposed criteria by which the FCC might evaluate program service. Porter was acting in response to congressional criticism of the FCC for its low requirements from broadcasters that made license renewals almost automatic. Not long after the Blue Book was issued, Siepmann published a hard-cover book, *Radio's Second Chance,* which echoed the FCC report and articulated the rationale for standards. Dr. Siepmann's book gave broadcasters the opportunity to charge him with opportunism.

Ironically, the much respected chairman Porter had left the FCC before the Blue Book was released. It fell to Charles R. Denny Jr., the young new chairman, to defend the report. But its real champion was Commissioner Clifford J. Durr, a liberal from Alabama who was vilified by the industry for his vigorous support of the document.

Although the Blue Book was of little practical use, its criticisms of broadcast practices prompted the industry to tighten its own codes somewhat along the lines prescribed.

BLUE KNIGHT, THE ▶ initially a four-hour mini-series on NBC (1973) and then a weekly series on CBS (1976-77). At both networks it was based on the best-selling novel by Joseph Wambaugh. The limited series starred William Holden and Lee Remick and was a straight adaptation of the book, airing on four consecutive nights (Nov. 13-16, 1973); it was rerun in the spring of 1975 on consecutive nights as two two-hour programs. The CBS series was built around Wambaugh's character Bumper Morgan, portrayed by George Kennedy. Both series were by Lorimar, with Lee Rich as executive producer.

BLYE, ALLAN and BEARDE, CHRIS ▶ successful team of comedy writer-producers whose credits include the *Andy Williams Show, Ray Stevens Show, Sonny & Cher Comedy Hour, Sonny Comedy Revue* and the first season of *That's My Mama.* The partnership dissolved in 1975, and Blye teamed up with Bob Einstein to form Blye-Einstein Productions.

BMI (BROADCAST MUSIC, INC.) ▶ music licensing organization created by the broadcast industry in 1939 as a weapon against ASCAP, the licensing society that enjoyed a monopoly and that was, at the time, threatening to raise the blanket license fees paid by stations for the use of copyrighted music. Because ASCAP's formula for the payment of royalties tended to favor established songwriters and penalize the newer composers, BMI was able to build rapidly a rival group of new publishers and writers. By the time the negotiations with ASCAP were resolved in 1941, BMI was firmly established. It grew to be the largest of the music licensing organizations, with nearly 45,000 writer and publisher affiliates and 850,000 licensed works as of the mid-1970s.

Giving impetus to BMI's catalog was the denial to broadcasters of ASCAP music for several months when they resisted ASCAP's demands for an increase in fees (stations had been paying 2 1/8% of their gross revenues from time sales for their music licenses up to that time). During that period, only public-domain and BMI music was heard on the air.

The emergence of BMI changed the nature and the flavor of popular music in the U.S. since it provided for royalty payments to be made to every kind of songwriter, even those composing specialized music restricted to a locale or ethnic group. Under the ASCAP system before 1941, broadcast royalties were not paid for recorded music, and the monies were distributed solely on the basis of live performance during evening hours on the country's four radio networks. Since payments to writers of country music and rhythm and blues were therefore scant, those fields had remained in the background of pop music for lack of economic encouragement. BMI devised a system that would cover recorded as well as live music, and all air performances, whether national, regional or local.

This change in broadcast royalty procedures stimulated activity in regional and ethnic music, and much of it found its way into the mainstream. These new influences were synthesized into rock and roll in the 1950s.

As do ASCAP and SESAC, the other two licensing societies, BMI issues a license to stations for the use of its music and collects fees based on station income. Stations are required to keep logs of the music they play; to determine how the money is to be distributed to songwriters, BMI projects the number of air performances for each song from a representative sample of the logs. In television, producers maintain cue sheets listing all music performed in a program for the licensing societies.

BMI operates as a nonprofit society, and its board of directors is made up exclusively of broadcasters.

BMS ▶ symbol used in Nielsen rating reports for programs with too small an audience to be rated. The letters stand for "below minimum standards" and often, but not necessarily, refer to a rating below 0.5. The actual BMS level varies by market and time period and is determined by Nielsen according to the sample size in the survey area.

BOBBY GOLDSBORO SHOW, THE ▶ syndicated country music-variety series in the mid-1970s notably successful in areas where country music has greatest acceptance. Bill Hobin, Jane Dowden and Reginald Dunlap produced for Show Biz Inc., with Bill Graham as executive producer.

BOCHCO, STEVEN ▶ writer-producer whose landmark successes with the innovative *Hill Street Blues* (1981-87) and *L.A. Law* (1986—) have made him one of Hollywood's preeminent creators of dramatic series. The formats for the two series were similar in that they both had ensemble casts, began each episode with an all-cast meeting (the partners' meeting in *L.A.*

Law; the morning roll call in *Hill Street*), often dealt with difficult issues, and occasionally carried the storylines over from one week to the next. These two winning shows led Bochco to sign a precedent-setting contract with ABC, calling for ten series pilots over six years. Out of that contract emerged *Doogie Howser, M.D.* (1989—), *Hooperman* (1987-89), and *Cop Rock* (1990), an extremely expensive musical police series that flopped almost immediately.

Earlier in his career, Bochco created *Sarge* (1971-72) and collaborated on the pilot for *The Six Million Dollar Man* (1974). He also produced the series *Griff* (1973-1974) and *Delvecchio* (1976-77) and served as executive producer of *Paris* (1979-80), a series starring James Earl Jones. Another series, the grittily realistic (though not police-related) *The Bay City Blues,* aired in 1983 and was canceled after three weeks.

BOCK, LOTHAR ▶ impresario from West Germany who served as go-between with the Soviet negotiating team in gaining for NBC the exclusive U.S. rights for the 1980 Moscow Olympics. Bock, who had had a number of previous theatrical and TV dealings with the Soviets, initially had been engaged by CBS to help land the Olympics plum. When CBS decided to drop out of the bidding early in 1977, Bock, who had already worked out most of the arrangements for an $85 million deal, immediately offered his services to NBC and promptly wrapped up the prize. For his efforts, he was paid a commission of $1 million and also received commitments from NBC for TV specials over a period of years.

BOGART, PAUL ▶ noted director for such prestigious drama anthologies as *Armstrong Circle Theatre* during the early years of TV. During the 1960s he divided his time between films and occasional TV drama specials. In the 1970s he directed a number of productions in public TV's *Hollywood Television Theatre* series and such commercial specials as *The House Without a Christmas Tree.* He became director of *All in the Family* for the 1975-76 season.

***BOLD ONES, THE* ▶** umbrella title for several rotating adventure series on NBC (1969-72) produced by Universal TV. From season to season, some rotating elements were dropped and others added. Included were *The Doctors,* with E.G. Marshall, David Hartman and John Saxon; *The Lawyers,* with Joseph Campanella, Burl Ives and James Farentino; *The Senator,* with Hal Holbrook; *Protectors,* with Leslie Nielsen and Hari Rhodes; and *Sarge,* with George Kennedy.

***BOLD AND THE BEAUTIFUL, THE* ▶** see Soap Operas.

BOLEN, LIN ▶ onetime v.p. of daytime programs for NBC (1972-76), the highest position held by a woman at any TV network up to that time. She left to establish her own independent production company with certain exclusive ties to NBC. Her first series, *W.E.B.,* an episodic melodrama set at a mythical TV network, was a flop in 1978.

As daytime chief Bolen added dazzle and larger cash prizes to the network's game shows and broke the 30-minute tradition of soap operas in expanding such serials as *Another World* and *Days of Our Lives* to an hour's length. In early 1982, she joined Fred Silverman's independent InterMedia Entertainment as head of creative affairs.

***BONANZA* ▶** a great Sunday night hit on NBC for most of 14 years (1959-73) that many critics considered to be a western soap opera, dealing as it did with the concerns and adventures of a widower and his sons on the prosperous Ponderosa ranch. Dozens of competing shows were overwhelmed by its popularity, as the fictional Cartwrights became part of Americana. Lorne Greene portrayed the patriarch (Ben Cartwright) and Michael Landon, Dan Blocker and Pernell Roberts his sons (Little Joe, Hoss and Adam). Roberts left the cast after six seasons, and Blocker died in the 13th year. Other regulars were David Canary (as "Candy" Canaday), Mitch Vogel (Jamie Hunter), Tim Matheson (Griff King) and Victor Sen Yung (Hop Sing). Produced by David Dortort for NBC Productions, it began as an advertising vehicle for Chevrolet.

BOND, ALAN ▶ Australian media tycoon whose star fell with two severe setbacks in the late 1980s, made worse by the Black Monday stock market crash in October 1987. In a span of two or three years, Bond went from being one of the most formidable figures on the international scene to virtual obscurity in the field.

A transplanted Britisher who made a fortune in real estate in Perth, Australia, Bond pulled off a huge coup in a 1986 media venture. He bought Thorn EMI's Screen Entertainment division, and five days later sold it to the Cannon Group for an $80.6 million profit. In 1987 Bond Media bought Australia's

Nine Network from Kerry Packer for an astounding $877 million, and then bought into TVB in Hong Kong and took a 22.5% position in the U.K.'s emerging DBS system, British Satellite Broadcasting (BSB). Everything went downhill from there.

Bond had purchased the Nine Network at around the time Australia's other two commercial networks changed hands, the Seven Network going to Christopher Skase and the Ten Network to Northern Star Holdings, headed by Frank Lowy. The three immediately began competing for position and plunged into a bidding war for American programs, driving prices to unrealistic heights. At a time when all three had assumed huge debt service, they severely impaired the cash flow by paying exorbitantly for programs and stockpiling them. On top of that, BSB was having technical problems with the "squarial"—the small square-shaped home antenna that could be hung out a window and was thought to be a key to the venture's success—allowing Rupert Murdoch's competing Sky Channel to establish itself before BSB could get started. BSB was clearly doomed and in the end was absorbed by Sky.

Bond Media was forced to sell off some of its better assets to meet debt payments on the Nine Network, and eventually it lost the network in 1990 because it was unable to pay the final $173 million to secure the acquisition. Kerry Packer, who had owned the network for 33 years before selling it to Bond, regained it after four years at almost no cost after realizing a tremendous profit from the sale.

BONDS, BILL ▶ opinionated and often controversial news anchor for Detroit ABC station WXYZ. In 1991 he joined a select club of local anchors popular enough to earn over $1 million a year. Long the dominant newsperson in the Detroit market, Bonds has gained a loyal following for his outspokenness on the air. Often he expresses his views with a vehemence verging on rage (once during a newscast he challenged Detroit's mayor to a boxing match). His 5 p.m. newscast typically beats its rivals in audience share.

Bonds joined WXYZ in 1964 but left in 1968 in an unsuccessful attempt to establish himself in Los Angeles. Four years later he went to New York—again he was disappointed—before returning to Detroit to stay. Bonds was off the air for a time in the late 1980s to combat alcohol addiction but returned in 1989. Soon after, he negotiated a contract that will permit him to remain with the station as a commentator or consultant when he retires from anchoring the newscast.

BONUS SPOTS ▶ commercial time given to advertisers at no cost to make up for a shortfall in projected ratings or demographics. Sometimes they are offered as an inducement for a larger purchase of air time.

BOOSTER ▶ an unattended, low-powered TV rebroadcasting station that picks up the signal of a conventional station and amplifies and rebroadcasts it; the booster is generally used to fill in gaps within a station's assigned coverage area.

BORDER WAR ▶ TV conflict between the U.S. and Canada during the 1970s growing out of Canada's attempts to curtail the penetration of American TV so that its native TV systems might have better opportunity to develop and thereby serve to strengthen a Canadian national identity.

The popularity of U.S. TV was reflected in the fact that more than 40% of Canadian households subscribed to cable TV chiefly to receive the American networks. Meanwhile, U.S. border stations were beaming directly into Canada, fragmenting the audiences for its stations and drawing off an estimated $20 million a year in advertising revenues. The stations of Buffalo, N.Y., blanketing the Toronto market, were estimated to be earning $9 million a year from Canadian audiences, while WVOS-TV in Bellingham, Wash., beaming into Vancouver, alone earned close to $8 million a year from serving Canada.

Under the chairmanship of Pierre Juneau in the early 1970s, the CRTC took steps to inhibit the U.S. spillover, the major one being its order to cable systems to delete commercials from the U.S. programs they carried. U.S. stations protested, calling the interception of their signals without the commercials tantamount to piracy, and asked the U.S. State Department to intervene.

Also upsetting to U.S. broadcasters is the amendment to the Income Tax Act (known as Bill C-58) that bars deductions for Canadian companies for advertising purchased out of the country, specifically advertising purchased in U.S. media directed at Canadian audiences. The purpose was to keep Canadian ad dollars in Canada for the support of the country's own media.

In retaliation the Buffalo stations threatened to jam their own signals to keep them from entering Canada. Senators and the Secretary of State, as well as the chairman of the FCC, have met with Canadian officials at various points in efforts to resolve the problem.

BORN INNOCENT ▶ made-for-TV movie which, when it aired on NBC in 1974, triggered the congressional concern that brought on the industry's adoption of "family viewing time" in 1975. The two-hour film, which featured Linda Blair as a 14-year-old in a juvenile detention home, contained a violent sexual scene in which the girl is raped with a broomhandle by other female inmates. Since the film was scheduled at 8 p.m. it had a large audience of juveniles, and the network received protests from its own affiliated stations as well as from the public.

Making matters worse, soon thereafter a young child in California was raped by other children in a manner resembling that in the film; the child's parents sued the network and lost the case. Three congressional committees subsequently demanded that the FCC take action to protect children from the excesses of sex and violence on television. Prohibited by the Communications Act from engaging in any form of censorship, the FCC held meetings with the heads of the networks to suggest ways in which the industry might, on its own, take corrective steps. CBS later proposed to create a "family viewing" hour at 8 p.m., and the other networks followed.

Despite the graphic controversial scene, *Born Innocent* won commendations from critics. It was produced by Tomorrow Entertainment, with Rick Rosenberg and Robert Christiansen as executive producers.

The film was rerun by NBC the following season but at a later hour, with some editing of the rape scene and with advisories for parental guidance.

BOSLEY, TOM ▶ portly character actor who has enjoyed a three-decade career on television, having had a 10-year role as Howard Cunningham in *Happy Days* and another long run as the sheriff in *Murder, She Wrote,* which began in 1984. In 1989 he began starring as the title character in another series, *The Father Dowling Mysteries.* For six years he also narrated the syndicated *That's Hollywood* (1976-82).

He began as a stage actor and in 1959 won a Tony for *Fiorello!* In the 1960s he crossed over into television, initially as a regular on *That Was the Week That Was.* After that he made numerous appearances on variety shows until he was cast in *Happy Days.*

BOURGHOLTZER, FRANK ▶ NBC News correspondent beginning in 1946. He became head of the Los Angeles bureau in 1969 after having been the network's bureau chief in Paris (1953-55), Bonn (1955-56), Vienna (1957-58) and Moscow (1961-63), with returns to Paris and Moscow in the 1960s. At intervals, he was also a Washington correspondent for NBC.

BOUYGUES, FRANCIS ▶ French business tycoon who heads France's leading commercial TV channel, TF1, having beaten back in 1991 a play for control by British media baron Robert Maxwell, who also has a stake in the channel. Bouygues, who heads a construction empire, was part of the group awarded the channel when TF1 was privatized in 1987. It was then the main public TV channel, and when the state turned it over to the big money TF1 simply carried along as the dominant station it had been. Bouygues and the station have managed to stand off challenges by other commercial operators, such as Silvio Berlusconi's La Cinq, which have conducted raids on the station's talent.

BOWLING ▶ a televised sport that has been the province of a single promoter, Eddie Elias, an Akron attorney and sports entrepreneur, since 1958. That was the year he started the Professional Bowlers Assn. of America (PBA) with 33 champion bowlers as charter members. Today there are more than 3,400 members who compete for more than $6 million annual on the national tour.

ABC began its *Pro Bowler's Tour* series in 1961, and it claims today to be the longest continuing live sports series on network television. During most of those years, Chris Schenkel has done the telecasts. Television has been the PBA's life-blood from the beginning. In addition to ABC, such other networks as NBC, CBS, ESPN, HBO and USA have carried the finals of the various tournaments.

BOXING ▶ a prime-time staple of the 1950s with regular telecasts on Wednesdays and Fridays, which all but disappeared from the medium after 1960. A chief reason was that the matches promoted for television were arranged for exigencies of the medium and therefore were not as consequential as those arranged for the normal progress of a fighter; too often, also, they were of poor quality.

Among the leading boxing announcers of the period were Jack Drees, Jimmy Powers, Russ Hodges and Don Dunphy. Dr. Joyce Brothers, a winner of *The $64,000 Question* for her knowledge of the sport, occasionally contributed her observations.

In 1976, Barry Frank, then the new v.p. of CBS Sports, made arrangements to revive the sport on TV on an occasional basis, Saturday afternoons or Friday evenings. He maintained that CBS would carry only boxing events that were independently promoted and not matches conceived for TV exhibition.

ABC then invested $1.5 million for a weekly elimination tournament, the United States Boxing Championship, put together for television by Don King Productions and designed to develop American champions capable of challenging for world titles. The tournament began in January 1977 but was suspended the following April amid charges of kickbacks, falsified ring ratings for the fighters, phony won-lost records and other irregularities. ABC Sports met the scandal by appointing Michael Armstrong, former counsel to the Knapp Commission which had helped to expose police corruption in New York City in 1972, to direct its investigation of the tournament. Meanwhile, both ABC and CBS had begun to sign the most promising boxers to exclusive contracts for TV coverage of their bouts.

Of the three networks, ABC has remained the most active in covering boxing events, mostly on weekends. But during the 1980s boxing became almost strictly the domain of cable. HBO and USA pursued and won the rights to a number of big-name matches, while ESPN, the all-sports network, includes boxing specials among its staple fare. MSG (Madison Square Garden Network), along with several of the regional networks, have carried the Golden Gloves Tournament, along with other amateur fights.

But virtually all the big and highly publicized professional title bouts today are carried live on cable's pay-per-view channels, where the box-office exceeds what any network could normally pay for rights. The two Mike Tyson matches with Razor Ruddick aired on pay-per-view in 1991. The Evander Holyfield-George Foreman match for the heavyweight title in 1991 racked up more than $50 million in pay-per-view billings. Often reruns of the fights air in their entirety on other cable networks several days after the pay-per-view coverage.

Sugar Ray Leonard, Tyson, and Foreman have become color announcers for many of the bouts carried on cable.

BOZO ▶ clown character around whom numerous successful children's shows have been built by local stations since 1959. Larry Harmon, who developed and marketed the property, created a library of cartoon films featuring Bozo and also franchised the character as a live local program host. Those who portrayed the local Bozo had to be trained by Harmon, and the programs were required to feature the Bozo film shorts. In 1966 Bozo was on more than 70 stations, half of them carrying a program furnished by Harmon, the other half building their own shows around the live clown. At WGN-TV Chicago, the locally produced *Bozo's Circus* was a daily one-hour extravaganza of circus acts and was consistently popular with children.

BPME (BROADCAST PROMOTION AND MARKETING EXECUTIVES) ▶ association of industry professionals working in the fields of advertising, promotion and public relations, whose essential purpose is to raise the stature of those facets of the business and advance their role. Its broad membership base of some 1,700 represents networks, stations, cable, radio, syndication and independent practitioners, some from foreign organizations. The organization's annual convention offers a variety of professional workshops on trends and practices, and confers awards for creative excellence in station and program promotions. Originally called BPA (Broadcasters Promotion Assn.), it changed its name in the mid-1980s, when marketing became the operative word for what every company needed to excel at. BPA was founded in 1955 by a group of TV and radio promotion managers, with initial underwriting from *Advertising Age.* Today the organization is supported by its membership.

BRADLEY, ED ▶ CBS News correspondent and co-editor of *60 Minutes,* having joined the top-rated magazine series in 1981. Some of his best-known pieces have included "In the Belly of the Beast," a report on convicted murderer and author Jack Henry Abbott, and an affecting profile of singer Lena Horne.

Prior to *60 Minutes,* Bradley was a correspondent for *CBS Reports,* with such broadcasts as "The Boat People" and the two-hour special, "Blacks in America: With All Deliberate Speed?"

Ed Bradley

Bradley began his career as a reporter for WDAS Radio in Philadelphia in 1963. He joined CBS News as a stringer in the Paris bureau in 1971, was assigned a year later to the Saigon bureau, and in 1973 was wounded while on assignment in Cambodia. In 1975 he returned to Indochina, covering the fall of Cambodia and Vietnam.

The cast of the classic ABC series *The Brady Bunch*

BRADY BUNCH, THE ▶ comedy series about a young widow and widower merging their families in a second marriage. It enjoyed a good run on ABC (1969-74), with Robert Reed and Florence Henderson as the parents (Mike and Carol Brady) and Ann B. Davis as housekeeper Alice Nelson. The Brady kids were Maureen McCormick (Marcia), Eve Plumb (Jan), Susan Olsen (Cindy), Barry Williams (Greg), Christopher Knight (Peter) and Mike Lookinland (Bobby). It was via Paramount TV.

Late in 1976 the cast was reassembled for a variety show special on ABC. It was so well received that ABC installed *The Brady Bunch Hour* in a regular Monday night slot in March 1977 for a number of weeks.

BRAIN, THE ▶ an 8-part public TV science series that struggled onto the air in 1984 after five years of funding problems, resolved in the end by a grant from Ciba-Geigy. The $8 million project, exploring various aspects of the human brain and coproduced by WNET New York with television companies in Britain, France, Japan and Israel, was developed by George Page—who also narrated—and science editor Richard Hutton.

BRAND, JOSHUA and FALSEY, JOHN ▶ writing team that attracted attention by creating the honest and grimly humorous *St. Elsewhere* (1982-88) for NBC. They also created an hour-long family drama for NBC, *A Year in the Life,* in the 1987-88 season. Later CBS picked up their imaginative, off-beat creation *Northern Exposure* (1990—), an hour-long comedy-drama portraying the trials of a medical school graduate from New York City who must pay off his government tuition grants by serving as Cicely, Alaska's only doctor. In the 1991-92 season Brand and Falsey returned to NBC with *I'll Fly Away,* a family drama set in a small town in the American south at the beginning of the civil rights movement. The team's company is called Falahey-Austin Street Productions.

BRANDED ▶ briefly popular Western series on NBC (1964-66) about an Army officer, Jason McCord, discharged as a coward but dedicated to proving that he is not. It starred Chuck Connors and was by Goodson-Todman Productions.

BRASSELLE, KEEFE (d. 1981) ▶ one-time movie actor who made a stir in 1964 as an independent producer of series for CBS through his production company Richelieu. All three series failed. Brasselle, who had been a friend of then CBS-TV president James T. Aubrey, wrote a bitter and poorly disguised novel about the experience, *The CanniBalS.*

BRAUN, ZEV ▶ film and television producer who after producing a number of TV movies scored with a moderately successful series on CBS, *Tour of Duty* (1987-90), set in Vietnam during the war. His credits include such TV movies as *Stillwatch, The Father Clements Story* (1987) and *A Seduction in Travis County* (1991), as well as the mini-series *Murder Ordained* (1987). Braun also produced two sitcoms, *Murphy's Law* (1988-89) and *Bagdad Cafe* (1990).

BRAVO ▶ basic-cable network specializing in cultural programming such as foreign movies and performing arts specials. One of the several cable networks owned by Rainbow Programming Enterprises, Bravo was launched in 1980 as a pay service airing only in the evenings. While it is now considered part of basic cable on some systems—those in the New York City area, for example—it is offered as a bonus basic service carrying a small extra charge. This may account for its meager subscriber count, which stands today at about 5 million. One of its programming keystones is *The South Bank Show,* a British arts series featuring biographical profiles. Bravo's performing arts programs range from classical to rock.

BRAZIL ▶ Latin America's largest and most populous country with 154 million people and 22 million television households. Though the country supports six major networks, one of them—TV Globo—so dominates the market that it properly claims to be the fourth largest network in the world, after ABC, CBS and NBC.

TV Globo (or Rede Globo, as it is known in the native Portuguese) is owned by Roberto Marinho, one of the world's most powerful media barons, who also owns the country's leading newspaper, *O Globo,* and a radio network. With 53 affiliated television stations, TV Globo has been known on occasion to achieve national audience shares in excess of 90%. The network is one of Latin America's principal producers and world distributors of telenovelas (serials that run a year or longer and are represented as TV novels). Its revenues from international program sales average around $15 million annually.

Brazil's other powerful private network, TV Manchete, is owned by the publisher of four national magazines, including *Manchete,* and the Manchete radio network. Heading this media empire is Adolpho Bloch. The country's other private TV networks are TV Gaucha, TV Bandeirantes, and Sistema Brasileiro de Televisao (SBT). All provide an entertainment-based schedule but are required by the government to include news, educational and religious programming.

The state-operated network, TVE (also known as Funteve), concentrates on informational and cultural programming and does not carry commercials. It has stations in 10 of Brazil's 23 states. All of the networks achieve national distribution through the use of the Brasilsat and Intelsat satellites.

BRC (BROADCAST RESEARCH COUNCIL) ▶ organization of professionals in broadcast audience measurement and research. It represents all parts of the industry concerned with the examination and improvement of techniques in the field. The organization was formed after the congressional investigation of TV ratings in the 1960s. The BRC "approved" symbol is carried on all data reports passed by the group.

***BREAK THE BANK* ▶** see Game Shows.

BRESNAN, WILLIAM J. ▶ former chairman of Group W Cable who left in 1983 to start his own cable operating company, Bresnan Communications, based in White Plains, N.Y. Bresnan had been president of Teleprompter Cable when it was sold to Group W and had agreed to stay on for two years to facilitate the transition.

Bresnan entered the cable field as an engineer in 1958 and worked for a number of small systems until he was hired in 1965 as chief engineer of American Cablevision Co. in Los Angeles. Three years later the company merged with H&B American Corp. and Bresnan was named president of the cable-TV subsidiary, H&B Cablevision Co. When H&B was acquired by Teleprompter in 1970, Bresnan became western v.p. and rose eventually to president. Throughout his career, he was active in numerous capacities with NCTA, including a stint as board chairman (1972-73).

***BRIAN'S SONG* ▶** poignant and popular ABC TV movie (premiere: Nov. 11, 1971) based on the real-life relationship between Brian Piccolo and Gale Sayers, professional football players and roommates with the Chicago Bears. The drama centers on the illness that eventually takes Piccolo's life and is heightened by the fact that one roommate is white, the other black. Written by William Blinn and produced by Paul Junger Witt for Screen Gems, it featured James Caan, Billy Dee Williams, Jack Warden, Shelley Fabares and Judy Pace, with some football stars playing themselves.

***BRIDESHEAD REVISITED* ▶** opulent 11-episode adaptation of Evelyn Waugh's novel of that title, which drew critical praise and enjoyed an intense following on American public television during its initial run early in 1982. Produced by Granada Television International of England, on the largest production budget ever for a British commercial series—$13 million—it was a smash in its native country in two runs prior to its American debut. The 11 episodes are of uneven lengths and consist of 12 1/2 hours of film.

John Mortimer wrote the adaptation of the Waugh novel, concerning an Oxford student who gets drawn into the extravagant, careless way of life of the young nobility in the years between the wars. The serial was filmed entirely on location in England, Venice, Malta and the island of Gozo. Brideshead Castle was represented by Castle Howard in Yorkshire.

Heading the cast were Jeremy Irons as Charles Ryder, Anthony Andrews as Sebastian Flyte and Diana Quick as Sebastian's sister Julia. Laurence Olivier and Claire Bloom as Lord and Lady Marchmain, along with John Gielgud, Stephane Audran, Mona Washbourne and John Le Mesurier, received guest star credit.

Derek Granger was producer and Charles Sturridge director. Michael Lindsay-Hogg, sharing the directing credit, had been the original director but withdrew for other commitments when a strike halted the production for several months in its early stages. Original music was composed by Geoffrey Burgon. WNET New York and NDR West Germany produced in association with Granada Television. The series aired in the U.S. as part of Exxon's *Great Performances* series.

BRIDGET LOVES BERNIE ▶ situation comedy about Irish-Jewish newlyweds. Adapting the *Abie's Irish Rose* premise to modern times, it ran one season on CBS (1972) and featured Meredith Baxter as Bridget Theresa Mary Coleen Fitzgerald, David Birney as Bernie Steinberg, David Doyle and Audra Lindley as Bridget's parents, Walter and Amy Fitzgerald, and Harold J. Stone and Bibi Osterwald as Bernie's parents, Sam and Sophie Steinberg. Screen Gems produced, in association with Douglas S. Cramer Co. and Thornhill Productions.

BRIDGING ▶ a programming maneuver to cripple a competing show by starting 30 minutes earlier, thus gaining the advantage of being in progress when the other begins. An hour-long program scheduled at 8:30 thus would *bridge* the opening of a 9 o'clock show on another channel, presumably keeping an audience that might have been inclined to watch the competing show.

BRIGHTER DAY, THE ▶ see Soap Operas.

David Brinkley

BRINKLEY, DAVID ▶ leading NBC News figure for more than two decades, who left for ABC News in 1981 after being shunted out of the main newscasts. At ABC, where he represented a prize catch, he was given a Sunday morning news program, *This Week.*

Brinkley shot into prominence in 1956 when he was teamed with Chet Huntley for the political conventions and later for the evening news. Ever the consummate journalist, however, Brinkley adhered to professional standards despite the commercial opportunities afforded by his public acclaim and recognition. Wit and a dry, sardonic delivery were the hallmarks of his style, and his baritone intonations and distinctive phrasing were imitated by dozens of reporters at NBC.

While the *Huntley-Brinkley Report* was at its height in the 1960s, Brinkley ventured into the documentary field with a distinguished series, *David Brinkley's Journal.* When Huntley retired in 1970, Brinkley was teamed with other network correspondents for a time. In 1971 he gave up the anchor position to become a commentator for what was then called the *NBC Nightly News* and to work on news specials. During 1976 he co-anchored the political conventions with John Chancellor and proved as appealing to viewers as he had been 20 years before. Following the conventions, he became co-anchor with Chancellor of the *Nightly News.*

BRITAIN'S BROADCASTING COMMISSIONS ▶ the history of broadcasting in Great Britain has been punctuated and shaped by a series of ad hoc committees appointed by the government of the day. There have been seven such bodies in all, and their brief has been to formulate national policy with respect to the structure and performance of broadcasting in the U.K.

Some of these committees, such as the one headed by Lord Crawford in 1925, have been more significant than others. The Crawford committee, convened in the days when radio in Britain was still a private enterprise, laid the foundations for the royally chartered British Broadcasting Corp. in 1927.

The first of these blue ribbon committees was created in 1923 and chaired by Sir Frederick Sykes. It produced some rudimentary ideas about public service radio that were to be more fully developed two years later by the Crawford committee.

Subsequent committees were headed by Lord Selsdon (1934), Lord Ullswater (1935), Lord Beveridge (1949), Sir Harry Pilkington (1960), and Lord Annan (1974). The most recent committee, invoked in the mid-1980s, was headed by Professor Alan Peacock.

Spadework by the Selsdon panel led to Britain incepting, in 1936, the world's first high-definition television service on a regular basis. The daily service was interrupted by the outbreak of war in 1939, resuming in mid-1946.

The advent of a commercial television medium in competition with the BBC was "seeded" by proposals of the Beveridge committee. These were subsequently endorsed by two government white papers, and in 1954 an act of Parliament created the Independent Television Authority (ITA) as the instrument that would assign and administer commercial station licenses. The first of these independent stations began operating in 1955.

One of the more famous committees was the one headed by Sir Harry Pilkington. It proposed more air time and more channels, described British broadcasting as a potent national asset and gave the broadcast establishment a vote of approval. None of its specific recommendations was acted on, however, although the Pilkington Report was said to have prompted the shake-up in British Commercial TV that created new licensees and struck down some of the regional broadcasters.

In the late 1970s a commission was constituted under Lord Annan to help the government determine what policy changes might be needed in the 1980s and beyond. Its brief was of the most fundamental kind—to study the technological changes brought by cable, satellites and home video and make proposals for possible structural changes in the British industry.

A decade later, the Thatcher government created a new commission under the direction of Prof. Alan Peacock that concerned itself primarily with looking into alternative ways of funding the BBC. Rather than place the continuing burden for BBC's support on TV households paying license fees, the government asked the Peacock commission to examine how the BBC might pay its own way in a new television era. The commission looked into the feasibility of creating a BBC pay-television service and considered also the option of advertising support. The commission's report was submitted to the Thatcher government toward the end of the 1980s.

BRITISH SKY BROADCASTING (BSkyB) ▶ Rupert Murdoch's satellite-to-home broadcast service in the U.K. that has slowly been catching on, after absorbing the competing British Satellite Broadcasting (BSB) in 1990.

Until the merger, the competition between the two direct-broadcast satellite (DBS) services was bizarre because they elected to use totally different methods of transmission. Selling the DBS concept was difficult enough, since it meant viewers would have to pay a fee to receive the channels, but the odds against the success of either were raised because consumers were put in the position of having to bet on a technology. If one system won and the other was eliminated, then consumers who chose the loser would find themselves with equipment as obsolete as the Sony Betamax VCR. Had both services used the same kind of satellite transmission, the competition would have been more spirited, and DBS would undoubtedly have had a quicker acceptance.

Murdoch's Sky Channel, carried on the medium-powered Astra satellite, was first to launch, in the late 1980s, with four channels that were offered as additions to the country's four terrestrial networks and received by a parabolic dish antenna about twice the size of a large pizza. BSB, whose investors included a number of the large regional broadcasters in Britain, decided to be the more sophisticated service. Using the Marco Polo high-powered satellite, its five channels were to be received by a small dish antenna that could actually be hung out a window instead of mounted on a rooftop or perched on a terrace. That receiving dish, called the "squarial" because of its shape, was the key to the marketing strategy. However, there were continual snags in the technology, and each delay in the launch of BSB strengthened Murdoch's position, even though his Sky was losing millions of pounds every month.

When BSB finally began its service early in 1990, after an enormous development and start-up investment, it was clearly too late to be entering the market. Sky was by then too well entrenched, and the best strategy to stem losses was to merge. Though it was called a merger, it was in fact a takeover by Sky. The resulting BSkyB became a six-channel service on the Astra satellite, with two channels devoted to movies, and others to news on a 24-hour basis, general entertainment, sports, and comedy. At the time of the merger, the two services were losing a combined $16 million a week. A year later that had been reduced to $2.5 million, with the prospect of break-even in view.

BROADBAND ▶ term applicable to cable and fiber optics for their ability to carry a sizeable number of channels, each with a larger bandwidth than conventional broadcast channels. This can matter with certain forms of high-definition television (HDTV) that require a bandwidth that cable can provide but broadcast stations cannot.

BROADCAST JOURNALISM ▶ see News.

BROADCAST REFORM MOVEMENT ▶ an effort by citizens groups and public interest organizations to counterbalance the economic drive of broadcasters by working actively to safeguard the public's rights in TV and radio. With broadcasting the common focus of the various groups, although they represented diverse special interests, a movement began to form in the late 1960s to keep watch on individual stations negligent of their responsibilities to the total community and also to influence regulatory policies to achieve an equitable and properly responsive broadcast system. Among the motivating concerns of the groups were excessive violence on TV, insensitivity toward children in programming and advertising, lack of access to broadcasting for minorities, discriminatory hiring practices and concentration of control of the mass media.

The movement foundered under the pressure of Reagan-era deregulation, as an overtly hostile FCC and increasingly conservative appeals court judges took away the legal tools that the movement had used with varying degrees of success.

The movement received its greatest impetus from a 1969 landmark case in which the U.S. Court of Appeals ordered the revocation of the license for WLBT-TV in Jackson, Miss., for discriminating against the interests of the black community, which constituted 45% of its potential viewing population. The case established the right of citizens' groups to participate in license renewal proceedings. The Office of Communication of the United Church of Christ had joined with two black civil rights leaders from Jackson to file a petition to deny against WLBT. When the court upheld the validity of the petition, the grassroots participation movement had the legal tool that would foster its growth.

Around the country, stations entertained dialogues with dissatisfied groups in preference to facing possible petitions to deny. In Lansing, Michigan, the Citizens for Better Broadcasting, a local group, succeeded in persuading WJIM-TV to remove reruns of *Wild, Wild West* from its afterschool time slot and in general to improve its service to children. A petition to deny was the wedge for negotiations and was withdrawn when the grievance was settled.

The National Organization for Women (NOW) used the license lever to pry agreements from KCST San Diego and WXYZ Detroit to hire quotas of women, provide serious women's programming and accept women's advisory councils. Action for Children's Television (ACT) petitioned the FCC to adopt regulations for children's television. Hearings on the petition elicited around 100,000 letters from concerned parents around the country. The networks, in response to efforts by broadcast reform groups, reduced violence-oriented programs on Saturday mornings, created children's programs with pro-social messages, cut back the number of commercials carried in children's programming, altered their hiring practices to include more members of minority groups, gave ethnic identities to protagonists in entertainment programs and accelerated the promotion of women and blacks to managerial posts.

In the wake of deregulation, individual license renewal challenges became increasingly rare, although the movement scored a major symbolic victory against WBUZ, a Fredonia, N.Y., radio station whose license was stripped in 1991 when its owner was found to have discriminated in hiring based on race. For the most part, the groups devoted their attention to major policy proceedings and placed increased attention on working to obtain legislative pressure for reforms. The Children's Television Act of 1990 was a particularly important accomplishment, ending some 15 years of effort by ACT and its allies.

BROADCASTING ▶ according to the FCC definition, radio communication designed for reception by the general public. Television is a form of radio, involving synchronous transmissions that are both visual and aural. The television transmitter may be regarded as two separate units, one visual signals by AM (Amplitude Modulation), the other sound by FM (Frequency Modulation).

***BROADWAY OPEN HOUSE* ▶** first late-night series by a network, essayed by NBC in the summer of 1950, which featured variety acts and the broad, brash comedy of Jerry Lester, with Dagmar as his sexy, dumb sidekick. It ended its run as a weeknight entry in August 1951.

BRODKIN, HERBERT (d. 1991) ▶ producer of quality drama, one of the few based in New York who had remained active in television since the early years of the medium. In the 1950s he produced for *Studio One, Motorola Hour Playhouse 90* and other showcases, his credits including such plays as *Judgment at Nuremberg* and *Child of Our Times.* Later, he produced such series as *The Defenders, The Nurses, Shane* and *Coronet Blue.* A drama he produced for CBS in the 1960s, *The People Next Door,* was subsequently made into a theatrical movie, which Brodkin also produced. His principal work in the 1970s was for *ABC Theatre* and included the documentary-dramas *Pueblo* and *The Missiles of October* and the biographical dramas *F. Scott Fitzgerald and the Last of the Belles* and *F. Scott Fitzgerald in Hollywood.* In 1978 he produced the highly successful mini-series *Holocaust;* in 1981, *Skokie* for CBS; in 1984, *Sakharov* for HBO; in 1985, *Doubletake,* a four-hour mini-series for CBS; in 1986, *Welcome Home, Bobby* for CBS and *Night of Courage* for ABC; in 1987, *Mandela* for HBO; in 1988, *Stones for Ibarra* for *Hallmark Hall of Fame;* in 1989, the CBS mini-series *Internal Affairs;* and in 1990, *Murder in Black and White* for CBS and *Murder Times Seven.*

Brodkin came to television from the theater in the early 1950s, initially as a designer. After being elevated to producer at CBS and working on the numerous live anthology series that flourished in that decade, he formed his own company, Plautus Productions, to make filmed programs. When Plautus was purchased by Paramount in 1965, Brodkin continued as an independent in forming Titus Productions, with Robert (Buzz) Berger was his executive assistant. Berger later became his partner. Titus was acquired by Taft Broadcasting in 1981 but continued to operate as before.

Tom Brokaw

BROKAW, TOM ▶ one of TV's most prominent journalists as anchor of NBC's *Nightly News* since April 1982. Initially he co-anchored with Roger Mudd but soon after won the solo spot. The two succeeded John Chancellor. Brokaw's exposure with the network was expanded in 1991 with the prime-time investigative news series *Expose.*

Brokaw became a leading candidate for the anchor post after six distinguished years as host of NBC's *Today.* He joined the morning program as Barbara Walters's replacement in August 1976 when she was hired away by ABC News. Brokaw had been NBC's White House correspondent for three years and in addition was anchorman of the NBC Saturday night newscast. Brokaw continued to be given some top news assignments while hosting *Today,* and he was rated NBC's leading candidate for an anchor position on the *Nightly News* when one became available. He became a network correspondent in 1973 after having anchored the 11 o'clock news for NBC's Los Angeles station, KNBC.

BROKERING TIME ▶ the practice of selling air time, usually to entrepreneurs who create programs and keep the revenues from the advertising they sell. Prevalent in the early years when television was not such an easy sale to advertisers, it remains a fairly widespread practice among foreign-language or ethnic-oriented stations. Despite legal questions, FCC deregulators signalled increasing tolerance starting in late 1990 for the sale of large blocks of time. Marginal UHF stations increasingly began to sell such blocks to stations in nearby markets, which then began simulcasting newscasts and other programming. By 1991 a number of licensees were entering into contracts to "lease" their entire program schedules.

BROOKHAVEN CABLE TV V. KELLY ▶ [*aff'd* 573 F.2d 765 (2nd Cit. 1978) *cert denied* 47 U.S.L.W. 3005 (U.S. July 11, 1978) 77-1845] case in which the U.S. Court of Appeals for the Second Circuit upheld the FCC's authority to preempt state and local regulation of pay-cable television rates. At issue were rules issued by the New York State Commission on Cable Television requiring municipal authorities to regulate the rates charged subscribers for pay-cable channels despite a clearly stated FCC policy that such rates should remain unregulated.

Brookhaven Cable TV brought the action against New York Cable Commission chairman Robert F. Kelly and the four other state commissioners after the commission ordered local authorities in 1976 to include regulation of pay-cable rates in all new cable-television franchises and to require cable companies to submit notice of their current rates within two months. Brookhaven challenged the order under the supremacy clause of the Constitution, arguing that the FCC's policy that pay-cable rates should remain unregulated took precedence over state regulations. Although the complaint also sought a judgment under the First, Fourteenth and Fifteenth Amendments as well, a federal district court granted summary judgment only on the supremacy clause arguments, and the Court of Appeals upheld the ruling solely on that basis.

The court found that the FCC's preemption of pay-cable price regulation was "reasonably ancillary" to its responsibilities for regulation of television broadcasting under the Communications Act of 1934, in line with *United States v. Southwestern Cable Co.* (1968). The court found that "a policy of permitting development free of price restraints at every level is reasonably ancillary to the objective of increasing program diversity" and is therefore within the FCC's authority.

BROOKS, JAMES L. ▶ producer, writer and director for film and television, whose brilliant career began at the top of the television industry, as producer-writer of *The Mary Tyler Moore Show* (1970-1977) with his then partner, Allan Burns. The two also created *Friends and Lovers* (1974-75) and *Rhoda* (1974-78). Brooks signed an exclusive contract with ABC in 1977, working through Paramount TV. This pact led to the creation, with associates, of *Taxi,* which ran on ABC from 1979-82 and continued on NBC from 1982-83. Then came *The Associates* (1979), Brooks' only serious flop. He also was responsible for *Lou Grant* (1977-82), an hour-long dramatic series that spun off from *The Mary Tyler Moore Show.*

In the 1980s Brooks concentrated primarily on three motion pictures, all of which were highly acclaimed: *Terms of Endearment* (1983), *Broadcast News* (1987) and *Big* (1988). In 1987 Brooks signed on with Fox TV as co-creator, executive producer and executive consultant on *The Tracey Ullman Show,* a precedent-setting comedy series starring the British comedienne. That series was canceled in 1990 but an animated spin-off series, *The Simpsons,* was developed for the Fox Network, with Brooks as executive producer. *The Simpsons,* created by cartoonist Matt Groening, became a huge hit. Brooks signed another contract with ABC to provide six series, the first of which, *Sibs,* premiered in the 1991-92 season.

BROOKS, MEL ▶ comedy writer, producer and occasional performer who first attracted attention as a member of the writing stable for *Your Show of Shows.* He later was co-creator (with Buck Henry) of the hit series *Get Smart.* In 1975, while enjoying success as a movie producer, he became executive producer and co-creator of the ABC series *When Things Were Rotten,* which ran a scant four months in 1975. In 1989 he was executive producer of *The Nutt House* on NBC, a quick flop.

BROOKSHIER, TOM ▶ sportscaster who joined CBS and its owned station in Philadelphia, WCAU-TV, following his retirement as a star defensive back for the Philadelphia Eagles. Since 1964 he has been an analyst for CBS in its pro football telecasts, also covers boxing and serves as host of *CBS Sports Spectacular.* For several years he hosted two syndicated series, *This Is the NFL* and *Sports Illustrated.*

BROTHERS ▶ a ground-breaking sitcom, the first to deal straightforwardly with the subject of homosexuality; one of the three central characters, who are brothers, is gay. The show, which aired on the cable's Showtime network, began its healthy 115-episode run in July 1984. It starred Robert Walden, Brandon Maggart and Paul Regina, and featured Philip Charles MacKenzie, Donald Maltby, Hallie Todd, and Robin Riker. Executive producers were Greg Antonacci and Gary Nardino.

BROTHERS, JOYCE ▶ quiz-show contestant of the 1950s who briefly became a national celebrity through winning the top prizes on both *The $64,000 Question* and *The $64,000 Challenge.* An attractive blonde, she was at the time a clinical psychologist and the newly wed wife of a doctor, but her field on the quiz shows was boxing. After her dual triumph in 1957, she was signed by NBC to co-host *Sports Showcase* and then did radio pieces for *Emphasis* and *Monitor.* Later she conducted syndicated TV programs as a psychologist, variously called *Dr. Joyce Brothers, Consult Dr. Brothers, Tell Me, Dr. Brothers* and *Ask Dr. Brothers.*

BROWN, JAMES ▶ CBS Sports commentator, primarily working college and professional basketball games. Brown joined the network in 1984 as an analyst and play-by-play announcer for NCAA and NBA basketball. He co-hosted the NCAA Division I Men's Basketball Championship from 1984-1990 and hosted weekday, midday coverage of the Olympic Winter Games. Brown was briefly with WJLA-TV Jacksonville in 1984, then with WUSA-TV Washington, D.C., from 1984-89.

BROWN, TYRONE ▶ brilliant young FCC commissioner, appointed in November 1977 at the age of 35 to replace Benjamin L. Hooks in what had looked to become the permanent black seat on the commission. Brown was the FCC's second black member, Hooks the first. A lawyer, Brown had worked previously as v.p. for legal affairs for the Post-Newsweek Stations, as staff director of the Senate Intergovernmental Relations Subcommittee and as law clerk to former Chief Justice Earl Warren. He was appointed to a Democratic seat on the FCC and became part of the liberal minority, with chairman Ferris and commissioner Fogarty. He left the FCC to return to law practice in 1981 after the defeat of President Carter. Later, in partnership with Robert Johnson of Black Entertainment Television and others, Brown helped win the District of Columbia cable TV franchise and served briefly as CEO of the franchise.

BROWNING, KIRK ▶ veteran director of cultural programming. With NBC he directed the *Bell Telephone Hour* and productions of the NBC Opera. In public television he helped develop the techniques for live telecasts from concert halls that were unobtrusive to the paying customers. These techniques made possible *Live from Lincoln Center,* for which he directed the New York City Opera's telecast of *Don Carlo, Handel's Messiah,* and the Beverly Sills farewell gala. He also directed the drama *Big Blonde* for PBS's *Great Performances.*

BTS (BROADCAST TELEVISION SYSTEMS) ▶ multinational developer and manufacturer of professional television equipment, jointly owned by the Netherlands' Philips and Germany's Bosch and formed in 1986 through the merger of their broadcast equipment divisions.

BUCHANAN, PATRICK J. ▶ hard-line conservative and former speechwriter for President Nixon, credited with writing Vice President Agnew's famous attack on network news, delivered in Des Moines in November 1969. Buchanan, who was also in charge of Mr. Nixon's morning news summary and was responsible for monitoring the media's coverage of the White House, personally kept up the public assaults on what he considered to be the liberal bias of TV journalism. A former newspaperman, he became a media watch columnist for *TV Guide* when the Nixon Administration ended and wrote a syndicated column for *The New York Times*'s special features subsidiary. In the late 1980s he became a regular on CNN's *Crossfire* as the "voice from the Right."

BUCK, JACK ▶ announcer for CBS Sports who continues to be the voice of the St. Louis Cardinals and sports director of KMOX Radio in St. Louis, a post he's held for 36 years. During his tenure at KMOX, Buck has also worked many big sports events for various TV and radio networks, covering the 1965 and 1976 baseball All-Star Games, serving as play-by-play announcer for CBS Radio Networks, covering professional football for all three TV networks, and serving with Hank Stramm as the CBS Radio Network's primary NFL broadcast team since 1978. In 1976 Buck handled various play-by-play responsibilities for NBC and hosted that network's *Grandstand.* He joined CBS Sports in 1990 as play-by-play announcer for the TV network's Major League Baseball schedule, working the National League Championship Series and World Series in 1990 and 1991. On CBS-TV, Buck is teamed with analyst Tim McCarver. Prior to arriving in St. Louis in 1954, he called baseball games in Columbus, Ohio, and Rochester, N.Y. In 1987 Buck was inducted into baseball's Hall of Fame as the recipient of its prestigious Ford C. Fisk Award for broadcast excellence.

BURCH, DEAN (d. 1991) ▶ former director general of Intelsat, appointed in 1987 in the wake of scandals involving kickbacks in high echelons. Burch was credited with restoring the organization's credibility and good name. But he is best known for having been chairman of the FCC (1969-74) and an advisor to several republican presidents.

At the FCC he was an activist chairman, and after some disconcerting early incidents in which he seemed to be politicizing the office, he won the respect of broadcasters and citizens groups alike for his even-handed policies and personal fairness. He came to exemplify what the head of a federal agency should be and was considered by many the best FCC chairman in modern times.

The radical decisions made by the agency during his administration belied the fact that Burch was a political conservative—he was formerly an aide to Sen. Barry Goldwater (R-Ariz.) and then his campaign manager for the 1964 presidential race.

It was not Burch's way to push controversial issues onto the backburner or to postpone the voting on items that he knew would leave him in the minority. Thus, the prime-time access rule came into being and the WHDH license was denied to the Boston *Herald-Traveler,* two of the most momentous developments in the industry in years. Burch's chairmanship was marked also by periodic clashes with his ideological opposite number, the gadfly commissioner, Nicholas Johnson, although their disagreements were as often over style as over ideologies.

Burch alarmed many during his first weeks on the commission when he openly praised Vice President Agnew's attack on liberal bias of network journalism and followed by remarking to the industry, "Physician, heal thyself!" He also personally made calls to the networks to question certain news decisions. But he quickly ceased those activities, recognizing their impropriety and First Amendment implications, and began to apply himself vigorously to the work of the commission.

During the Watergate episode, memoranda surfaced from the early years of the Nixon Administration suggesting that Burch would exercise control over news programming. But Burch said he had never discussed such matters with the White House and that even if he had he would never abide the idea of government interference in news.

Under Burch the FCC approved the full-scale release of cable TV for expansion into the major cities, gave the long delayed go-ahead to over-the-air pay TV (STV), tentatively adopted the one-to-a-market rule for ownership of media in new situations, levied a license fee on broadcasters to help defray the commission's expenses and reaffirmed the Fairness Doctrine after a long inquiry and study.

Also notable was a decision that the congressional opponents to administration policies were entitled to free air time to respond to prime-time speeches by presidents, in the interest of keeping the executive branch from attaining excessive power through TV.

In February 1974 Burch left the commission to become counselor to the president, with cabinet rank. He served in that capacity ten months, staying on when Nixon resigned to assist President Ford through the transition period. At the end of the year, Burch left government service to join the Washington firm of Pierson, Ball and Dowd, which specialized in communications law. He left the law firm in 1987 to put out the fires at Intelsat.

BURDEN OF PROOF (FAIRNESS ISSUE) ▶ (Allen C. Phelps/21 FCC 2d 12 [1969]) FCC determination that the initial burden in the fairness area rests with the complainant. The case involved a charge that WTOP Washington presented only liberal positions on several issues, but the complainant otherwise made no showing on his general allegation. The FCC, in dismissing the complaint, listed among the elements necessary for a prima facie Fairness Doctrine complaint a reasonable basis for the complainant's conclusion that the licensee failed in its overall programming to present a reasonable opportunity for opposing views. While this decision was never directly appealed, it was cited with approval by the Supreme Court in the BEM Case.

BURDETTE, WINSTON ▶ veteran CBS News correspondent who joined the network in 1941 while on free-lance assignments in Europe during the outbreak of World War II. Although he later worked briefly for CBS in New York, Washington and London, most of his career was spent on the European continent, with Rome as his base. From the Rome bureau, which he joined in 1956, Burdette covered events in Europe, Africa and Asia.

BURKE, DANIEL B. ▶ president of Cap Cities/ABC since the merger of the two companies in 1986, who succeeded chairman Thomas Murphy as CEO in 1990. Burke, nicknamed "the Cardinal" because of his strict standards and withering stare, had been No. 2 to Murphy at Cap Cities since 1972, running the business day to day while Murphy concentrated on strategy. Soon after the Cap Cities $3.5 billion acquisition of ABC, Burke engineered a radical downsizing of the new company, cutting costs, perks and waste, and along the way eliminating thousands of jobs. While the cutbacks were painful, a leaner ABC was considered necessary for the new economics of network television.

Daniel B. Burke

BURKE, DAVID W. ▶ president of CBS News from 1988-1990, and for 10 years before that No. 2 to ABC News president Roone Arledge. Despite a strong background in national and New York Democratic politics (Lyndon Johnson administration, administrative aide to Sen. Edward Kennedy, secretary to N.Y. Gov. Hugh Carey), during his tenure at ABC Burke was known as a fierce guardian of the integrity of broadcast news and its independence from corporate interference.

Burke became a vocal critic of ABC's new owner, Capital Cities, after its 1986 acquisition of the network, and in 1988 he was lured to CBS. He was the first president of CBS News not to be drawn from the company's own ranks. There, Burke found himself immersed even more deeply in company politics and staff cutbacks, and he had to cope with the low morale engendered by the new administration of Larry Tisch. Burke was forced out in 1990 and left broadcasting to become chief administrative officer of the Dreyfus Corp.

While he was a top executive at ABC News, Burke contributed strongly to its emergence as a leader in network journalism. He is also credited with strengthening its domestic and overseas bureaus (later cut back by Cap Cities), contributing to the success of *20/20* and *Nightline,* and helping to hire David Brinkley from NBC and Diane Sawyer from CBS.

***BURNING BED, THE* ▶** searing social drama in the form of a two-hour TV movie that was distinguished also by a powerful performance from Farrah Fawcett. She played a battered wife who is charged with her husband's murder after he had abused her physically and mentally for several years. The movie, which first aired on NBC on Oct. 10, 1984, raised national interest in the issue of battered women. Because she had been known previously in glamour roles, Fawcett surprised critics with her deft, realistic performance. Paul LeMat played the brutish husband, Richard Masur her attorney. Others in the cast were Grace Zabriskie, Penelope Milford, Gary Grubbs, James Callahan and Virgil Frye. The screenplay by Rose Leiman Goldemberg was based on a book by Faith McNulty. Robert Greenwald directed. It was a Tisch-Avnet production.

Farrah Fawcett and Paul LeMat in the NBC movie *The Burning Bed*

***BURNS AND ALLEN SHOW, THE* ▶** see *The George Burns and Gracie Allen Show.*

BURNS, KEN ▶ documentary filmmaker whose 12-hour, five-night series *The Civil War,* which aired in 1990, became PBS's most successful prime-time show to date. The show scored a 9.0 rating in Nielsen's 24 major metered markets, and PBS jumped on its success by rerunning it and selling a videocassette collection.

Burns was nominated for an Academy Award in 1981 for *Brooklyn Bridge,* the first film he ever did. In 1985 he received both Oscar and Emmy nominations for his documentary on the Statue of Liberty, celebrating that landmark's 100th birthday. A piece on Senator Huey Long followed before he started work on *The Civil War.*

For that project, Burns researched for more than five years, compiling thousands of pictures, organizing $3.5 million in grant money and lining up such well-known actors as Jason Robards, Sam Waterston and Morgan Freeman to read the first-person letters unearthed in his research.

In 1991 Burns followed up his success with the two-hour *Songs of the Civil War.* He planned to continue producing for PBS, with a project on the origins of broadcasting called *Empire of the Air* and one on the history of baseball in the works.

BURR, RAYMOND ▶ actor who starred in two series that were mammoth hits, *Perry Mason* (1957-66) and *Ironside* (1967-75). Earlier, he was featured in numerous TV dramas. In March 1977 he essayed another series, *Kingston: Confidential,* on NBC, but it was short-lived. After that he confined his work to TV movies and mini-series, including *Seventy Nine Park Ave.* and *Centennial,* and several movie-length revivals of *Perry Mason.*

BURRUD, BILL (d. 1991) ▶ prolific producer and host of syndicated outdoor, travel and animal series. His Hollywood-based Bill Burrud Productions turned out such skeins as *Animal World, Safari to Adventure* and *World of the Sea,* along with dozens more over two decades.

***BUS STOP* ▶** ABC series (1961-62) loosely based on the William Inge play of the title, one of whose episodes led to the downfall of a network president. The hour-long dramatic series dealt with strangers passing through a small western community, the focus of which was a bus stop luncheonette run by Grace Sherwood, played by Marilyn Maxwell. In the fateful episode "Told by an Idiot," which was based on a novel by Tom Wicker, the pop singer Fabian portrayed a psychopath whose sadistic excesses in the show raised a storm of public protest that led to one of the several congressional investigations into television violence. Oliver Treyz, then president of ABC, was fired shortly after the congressional inquiry in what many believe was a corporate action to place the responsibility for the episode upon him. The series, by 20th Century-Fox TV, otherwise was of no distinction. Besides Maxwell, it featured Rhodes Reason as Sheriff Will Mayberry, Richard Anderson as District Attorney Glenn Wagner, Joan Freeman as waitress Emma Gahringer and guest performers.

BUTLER, DAWS (d. 1988) ▶ the voice of such cartoon characters as Yogi Bear, Huckleberry Hound and Quick Draw McGraw.

***BUTTERFIELD THEATERS v. FCC* ▶** (237 F2d 552 (D.C. Circ. 1956) case involving a license applicant that substantially modified its license proposals after winning the license in a comparative hearing.

Three applicants sought a license to construct and operate a TV station in Flint, Mich.: WJR, Butterfield and Trebit. After a comparative hearing, the FCC found WJR best qualified, basing its decision on a number of factors, including the proposed location of the WJR transmitter, the WJR programming proposals and its proposed studio construction. Butterfield and Trebit asked the FCC to rehear the argument but the commission declined. Ten days later WJR filed a petition to alter its application.

In its modification petition, WJR proposed to move its transmitter farther away from the city and to a lower altitude than it had originally proposed, affiliate with a network other than the one initially mentioned, offer different kinds of local live programming than it had promised at first and purchase a one-story building for studios at a cost of $125,000 instead of constructing a two-story building at a cost of $776,000. On the basis of this petition, Trebit and Butterfield again sought to reopen the hearing. Again the commission refused, and the losing parties appealed.

The D.C. Court of Appeals held that the commission had erred by not reopening the hearing. The court stated that the FCC unquestionably had the power to call a rehearing and that it was an abuse of discretion not to do so. The changes proposed by WJR were directed at the very reasons it had been given preference in the first place. An alteration of these proposals mandated a review of the commission to determine if WJR's application was still superior to those of the competing applicants.

On remand the FCC determined that the new transmitter site was as good as the initial one and that it was as good as those proposed by Trebit and Butterfield. The FCC additionally found that the changes for programming were not substantial, and that the less expensive studio building did not affect the preference given to WJR in that category. Finally, the commission decided that the proposed modification did not reflect adversely upon WJR's character and fitness as a licensee. Therefore, the commission affirmed its original decision to award the license to WJR.

BUTTONS, RED ▶ a former burlesque comedian who had a brief fling at TV stardom with a half-hour comedy variety series on CBS (1952-54), *The Red Buttons Show,* and then became a dramatic actor in serious roles.

BUXTON, FRANK ▶ producer-director and writer, whose credits include *The Odd Couple; Love, American Style; The Bob Newhart Show; Hot Dog* and *Children's Letters to God.*

BYINGTON, SPRING (d. 1971) ▶ comedy actress in movies who became a TV star in 1954 with her situation comedy *December Bride.* It ran five seasons on CBS and the reruns remained popular in syndication.

C

CAA (CREATIVE ARTISTS AGENCY) ▶ mightiest of the show-business talent agencies, largely because of the extraordinary influence and deal-making skills of its chairman, Michael Ovitz. With a roster of around 700 clients, including many of the top box-office stars and leading directors and writers in Hollywood, CAA has the ability to assemble powerhouse talent "packages" for movies, TV series and mini-series.

The agency was created in 1975 by five young agents who left the then-dominant William Morris Agency. CAA grew rapidly, overtaking both the Morris office and Marvin Josephson's International Creative Management (ICM) agency. ICM is now second in rank, and William Morris third. The field also includes a number of so-called boutique talent agencies, of which Triad is the most prominent.

In the early 1990s, Ovitz extended his activities beyond talent representation and packaging into a larger deal-making sphere. He helped engineer both Sony's $3.4 billion purchase of Columbia Pictures Entertainment and Matsushita's $6.6 billion acquisition of MCA Inc., deals that changed the face of Hollywood. Reportedly, his commissions were $8 million and $40 million, respectively.

CABLE COMMUNICATIONS POLICY ACT OF 1984 ▶ package of amendments to the Communications Act that turned the tables on broadcasters long accustomed to using the FCC to stifle cable's growth. It liberated the cable industry from its regulatory shackles just as the wiring of the nation's cities began in earnest. Widely regarded as one of the most successful legislative accomplishments attained by any industry group, the 1984 law resulted from the confluence of several factors, including a Republican administration and Senate, public disdain for federal regulation, and a textbook lobbying effort by the National Cable Television Association (NCTA).

The cable industry especially benefitted from an extremely effective hometown ally in the House (Telecommunications Subcommittee chairman Tim Wirth, who later became a Senator), who delighted Colorado-based companies such as Jones Intercable, Tele-Communications Inc., and American Television & Communications by out-maneuvering more regulatory-oriented Democratic colleagues.

The new law eliminated unwanted regulation (most especially on pricing), substituted lax federal regulation on programming and other service duties for more rigorous local strictures, and imposed regulation to keep out competition, particularly from telephone companies.

CABLE CONVERTER ▶ unit installed in the home that allows a cable system to bring in a multitude of channels, today anywhere from 30 to 70. Without the converter and with a straight hook-up to cable, a television set could receive only 12 channels—the number on the VHF dial.

CABLE FRANCHISE ▶ authorization to a cable-TV company by the issuing authority, usually municipalities or other local governments, defining conditions under which it may construct, operate and maintain a cable service. The agreed-upon contract amounts to a license to operate and ensures due process and public involvement. Because of the localized nature of cable TV, the franchising authority has the principal responsibility for the regulation of the service. The license establishes construction timetables, technical standards, extension of services, rates, channel utilization not expressly forbidden by the FCC, consumer services, channel leasing and access channels.

CABLE LABS ▶ nonprofit research and development consortium of cable television system operators founded in 1988 to plan and fund technical research and to transfer results of that research to the industry. Cable Labs' potentially most significant work is in the areas of video compression, coax and fiber network design, and advanced television technology. In the latter area it is working both with the ATTC and with consumer electronics manufacturers to ensure compatibility of any future high-definition TV (HDTV) system with cable operations.

CABLE NETWORKS ▶ program services distributed by satellite to cable systems, either nationally or regionally. Unlike the established terrestrial networks that play to the broadest possible audience, most cable networks offer a specialized service targeted to a specific interest or to a particular demographic group in the audience. These specially focused networks brought into use the term *narrowcasting* to distinguish them from *broadcasting*.

There are three categories of national cable networks—those like HBO, Showtime and Disney that are pay channels (the cable industry prefers calling them premium channels), which survive on subscriptions alone and do not sell advertising; advertising-supported channels like USA and the Discovery Channel; and nonprofit public affairs channels, like C-SPAN 1 and 2.

As more and more new cable networks are created, the cable systems begin to resemble a magazine rack, with a range of niche programming. There are channels devoted exclusively to news, movies, sports, business, children's fare, family programming, religious programming, rock music, women's interest programming, comedy, court cases, Hispanic programming, black-interest programming, soft documentaries, weather, travel and science-fiction. Most of these channels draw ratings that would be disastrous for a broadcast network or station, usually at the level of 1.0 and often lower. But they survive, and in fact thrive, because they have a dual revenue stream. In addition to the sale of advertising, they receive a share of the cable operator's subscription fees. The larger, more popular services may get upwards of 25 cents per subscriber; others desperate for a place in the scheme may charge as little as 1 cent per subscriber. Most cable networks are in the range between. Because the audiences for these networks are so targeted, they tend to get advertising from companies wanting to reach their segment of the audience specifically.

Critical to the success of these networks is the regular availability of programming at costs commensurate with their economic structure. They cannot compete with the major networks in what they can pay for programming, but several cable channels can afford to outbid public television for foreign programming, and others have been able to get off-network reruns ahead of the syndication market.

The cable networks have been a chief agent in the erosion of network audiences during the 1980s. Collectively they claim at least 20 percent of the viewing in a typical day, and as they prosper and can afford to pay more for programming they stand to cut into the big networks even more over time. New networks are constantly in the wings, but access to the medium has grown difficult and is essentially controlled by the major cable operators, who are characterized as the gatekeepers. In cutting themselves in for ownership in the services they allow to get on, the cable networks are following practices of the major television networks before 1970 that eventually led to regulations that restricted their control of the program market. The following are among the better known cable networks:

ARTS & ENTERTAINMENT NETWORK (A&E)—devoted to comedy, drama, documentary and performing arts programming, much of it from the BBC. It is owned jointly by Hearst Corp. and Capital Cities/ABC and is advertising-supported.

BLACK ENTERTAINMENT TELEVISION (BET)—ad-supported service for black audiences, which was founded in 1979 by Bob Johnson. Its ownership includes Tele-Communications Inc. and HBO.

BRAVO—originally a pay-cable channel that began conversion to a basic service in 1986, it provides arts fare and foreign films. It is owned by Cablevision Systems' Rainbow Programming Enterprises.

C-SPAN (CABLE-SATELLITE PUBLIC AFFAIRS NETWORK)—non-commercial network providing live coverage of the House of Representatives sessions, other newsworthy forums and special news features. Founded in 1979 by Brian Lamb, it is supported by cable systems.

CINEMAX—companion network to HBO, a movie channel with a different selection of films, offered as HBO's second-tier pay service.

CNN (CABLE NEWS NETWORK)—24-hour all-news network founded in 1980 by Ted Turner and operated from Atlanta. It immediately became one of the basic services offered by all new cable systems. Advertising supported, it is owned by Turner Broadcasting Systems.

COURTROOM TELEVISION NETWORK (COURT TV)—devoted to live coverage of actual court trials, with analyses. Founded in 1991 and jointly owned by American Lawyer Media, Cablevision Systems, NBC and Time Warner, it is ad-supported.

THE DISCOVERY CHANNEL—all-documentary channel with emphasis on nature, science-technology, history, and human adventure. Launched by John Hendricks in 1985, the channel is now owned by TCI.

THE DISNEY CHANNEL—pay-cable service for family viewing drawing much of its programming from the Walt Disney library. The network is owned by The Disney Company.

ESPN (ENTERTAINMENT AND SPORTS PROGRAMMING NETWORK)—24-hour service devoted entirely to sports coverage and sports-related programming. It was founded in 1979 and is now owned by Capital Cities/ABC and Hearst.

THE FAMILY CHANNEL—features family-oriented programming and is advertising-supported. Founded as a religious programming network by Pat Robertson in 1977, it changed its name in 1988 as it moved away from its religious roots.

GALAVISION—pay-cable network formed in 1979 by Spanish International Network featuring movies, variety, and sports programs for Spanish-speaking subscribers.

HBO (HOME BOX OFFICE)—far the most profitable of the pay-cable services. Founded by Time Inc. in the early 1970s, it triggered the boom in cable and ushered in the other satellite networks. In 1991, HBO had over 17 million subscribers.

HOME SHOPPING NETWORK—24-hour shopping service featuring merchandise that viewers can order by calling a toll-free number. It was launched in 1985 by two Florida entrepreneurs, Roy Speer and Lowell (Bud) Paxton.

THE MOVIE CHANNEL—the only pay service devoted exclusively to movies. Created in 1979 and owned by Viacom, it had just over 3 million subscribers in 1991.

MTV (MUSIC TELEVISION)—ad-supported service devoted entirely to pop music, which started in August 1981 and quickly became a solid hit with youthful viewers. It is another of the Viacom networks.

NICKELODEON—commercial network of children's programming founded by Warner-Amex in 1979 and now owned by Viacom. It is well regarded for its efforts and a responsible approach to advertising.

SHOWTIME—pay-cable network directly competitive with HBO, created in 1978 by Viacom. Offering entertainment specials as well as movies, the network had more than seven million subscribers by 1991.

TNT (TURNER NETWORK TELEVISION)—entertainment network owned by Turner Broadcasting System that was started in 1988 and now reaches more than 54 million homes with its mix of classic MGM films, major sporting events, and made-for-cable movies.

USA NETWORK—broad-based entertainment network programmed much like a traditional broadcast network or independent TV station. Begun in the late 1970s, it is owned now by Paramount and MCA and reaches some 58 million subscribers.

THE WEATHER CHANNEL—launched in 1982, it now reaches more than 49 million subscribers with a 24-hour service of local, regional and national weather reports.

CABLE PENETRATION ▶ the proportion of cable-subscribing homes relative to all households in a city, region or country. This is expressed in percentages. By the end of 1991, cable penetration in the U.S. was around 60%, in Canada over 70% and in the United Kingdom less than 5%. In New York, the largest American market, cable penetration was almost 57%, while in the Boston area it was close to 70%.

CABLE TELEVISION ▶ technology of transmitting program signals by coaxial cable, whose broadband capacity makes possible a vast number of channels in a variety of modes. Because cable TV not only retransmits ordinary broadcast signals to improve their reception but also makes possible a multitude of specialized and localized services, it is the technology most threatening to conventional broadcasting with its spectrum scarcity and mass-appeal standards.

After several false starts in its quarter-century of development, cable caught fire in the mid-1970s chiefly for the appeal to consumers of pay-cable channels that deliver movies to the home, uncut and without commercials. The spur to the expansion of cable in the cities was the conversion of Home Box Office (HBO) into an instant national network when it began distributing its programming by satellite in 1975. Its wide acceptance was a signal to entrepreneurs of a monumental cultural change: the willingness of people to pay for television.

A rainstorm of other cable networks quickly followed, some offering pay services, some advertiser-supported programming. But the importance of the development was that cable at last had something to sell in the major cities—something more than better television reception. By the 1980s, cable was in demand everywhere in the U.S., and virtually every large city was either being wired for cable or in the thick of the franchising process. Most cities were demanding large-capacity systems with two-way capability.

By 1982 there were more than 4,700 cable systems in operation with more than 23 million subscribers, or close to 30% of all television households. Cable thus became a medium taken seriously by advertisers, and the satellites systems became saturated with cable networks.

While over-the-air television is restricted by mileage separation standards to no more than seven VHF stations in a market and by economics to a sprinkling of UHFs, cable immediately lends itself to anywhere from 30 to 70 channels, and with the new technology of digital video compression can expand to 150 channels or more, without rebuilding. And when cable is supplanted by the lightwave technology of fiber optics, as is expected, the capacity easily increases to an almost infinite number of channels. Moreover, sophisticated interactive systems are in the wings that permit two-way communications. In these systems, the TV viewer may send digital responses to the origination point of the transmission. This is useful for polling, adult education, playing games, ordering merchandise and home security services. But mainly it will be used for programming-on-demand, making cable an electronic video rental store.

Cable communications may be offered in the broadcast mode, reaching all subscribers at once, or point-to-point, as in the interconnection of a medical center to an outlying clinic. Its multiplicity of channels opens television to common carrier use and in theory provides long-sought access to the medium for minorities, independent producers and private parties who have felt shut out of conventional TV.

But cable TV must be purchased, its subscribers charged a monthly fee ranging from $15 to $20 for the basic service, while over-the-air TV is delivered free. The reluctance toward paying for TV when free service already enters the home—service that is sufficient for most people—and the great cost of constructing cable systems were among the reasons for the relatively slight penetration of cable in the U.S. its first quarter century. Aside from these factors, the growth of cable had been hampered by the lack of a broad and enlightened national policy. Cable TV struggled against the complexities of regulation at three tiers of government—federal, state and municipal—and against the political pressures exerted by the vested interests that were most wary of cable: commercial broadcasting and the telephone companies.

The FCC, which finally assumed regulatory jurisdiction over cable TV in 1966 at the urging of Congress, is also the agency regulating the broadcast and telephone industries. Its policies for cable have mainly been forged in attempts to be even-handed with all three industries.

Cable's beginnings were humble. In the late 1940s, when it was known as CATV, it was nothing more formidable than a master antenna system for communities with little or no TV reception. Signals picked off the air by an antenna situated on high ground were carried to homes by cable systems concentrated in small-town America.

Not until the 1960s did the realization dawn that cable might ultimately serve as more than a retransmission system—that it might function as an independent medium in its own right. The original systems used unsophisticated cable that could carry only a few channels, mostly devoted to picking up nearby broadcast signals. But during the late 1950s and early 1960s, technical improvements made it possible for systems to carry as many as 12 channels of programming. As a result, cable operators began to seek new sources of programming to fill their new channels, turning to origination of their own local programs and, more extensively, to broadcast television signals from distant cities. Suddenly, cable television was transformed from a reception-improving system into a medium that could offer subscribers more program choices than were available off the air even in areas with a full complement of broadcast stations.

The transformation launched the industry into a new wave of growth between 1960 and 1965. Some of the original "Mom & Pop" cable systems were absorbed into larger companies, which became known as MSOs (multiple system operators). The greater revenues of these companies and their ability to attract heftier financing enabled them to actively seek new franchises in communities spread across the country and to build larger and more sophisticated systems. Cable began to infiltrate suburban areas around some major cities—areas of *good* local television reception.

Not only did cable TV attract venture capital, it also excited interest among futurists, city-planners, social scientists and arts promoters because it promised a cornucopia of educational, cultural and social services. Foreseeably, on bi-directional systems, those services were likely to include schooling, banking and shopping by TV, fire and burglar alarm protection (the TV set in effect watches the house), automated meter reading, facsimile print-outs of newspapers and even the delivery of mail. But more immediately, the channel capacity of the prevailing one-way systems made possible separate channels for use by local government, school systems and business institutions, stations for the elderly conveying health-care information, neighborhood stations, ethnic stations, free-speech public access stations, closed channels for data transmission and channels carrying pay television.

In the practical world, however, cable TV proliferated on the strength of the entertainment channels it provided. Canada, for example, has experienced greater cable penetration than any country in the world—by 1991, more than 75% of the country was hooked up—and the single reason for cable's rapid growth there was that it brought in the over-the-air signals of U.S. stations.

Cable began to spread rapidly in the U.S. in the 1960s, not for its promise of new communications services, but for its ability to import distant TV signals and to equalize VHF and UHF (making them equally accessible on the tuner). Communities that were unable to receive ABC and had no local independent stations (desirable for their movies and sports programming) were prime markets for cable. During the 1960s the industry burgeoned from the 70-odd cable systems of the previous decade to more than 800 systems, and it enlisted more than one million subscribers. The MSOs then moved upon the big cities, but just as that frontier was opening the FCC effectively froze the development of urban cable with stiff regulations on the importation of distant signals while it pondered rules for cable in the top 100 markets.

The rules were promulgated finally in the 1972 Report and Order, but developments in the meantime had dampened the enthusiasm of cable entrepreneurs and lending institutions for wiring the cities. The MSOs that had begun building big-city cable systems before the freeze found striking differences between urban and small-town cable, and several were in a financial struggle as a result. The two Manhattan cable systems, which had expected to produce a bonanza, were each running up operating losses of $3 million a year. Along with unforeseen construction costs and impediments created by the telephone company, they encountered landlords seeking payoffs for entry to their property, neighbors of subscribers stealing the service by tapping into the feeder line, thefts of the converters, acts of vandalism and innumerable parking tickets during service calls.

But even more significant was the indifference of most New Yorkers to the offer of cable service, even with the inducement of a channel presenting Madison Square Garden events, including professional hockey and basketball.

By 1974 it was clear that basic cable would not suffice for the cities and that a special mass-appeal service was needed. That role fell to pay cable, which was developing nicely in California and in a three-state area on the Atlantic coast. It was reasoned that urban residents would subscribe to cable for the opportunity to receive major box office events—chiefly movies and sports—despite the fact that they would be faced with two fees, one for cable service and another for the pay channel. A selling point was that the pay-cable movies were presented numerous times, so that they might be watched at the subscriber's convenience, and without editing or interruption for commercials.

At that point, the cable industry appealed to the FCC to ease its restrictions on pay cable, and it was joined in the effort by representatives of the motion picture industry who saw in cable a potentially lucrative new market for their products. Among other restrictions, the existing FCC rules had prohibited cable from using new movies after they were more than two years out of theatrical release, which caused many to be lost to them entirely.

The request unleashed the broadcast industry's heaviest propaganda barrage against cable. With a war chest of around $1 million, the NAB—backed by campaigns of the networks—lobbied before the public, warning that if the pay-cable rules were eased the new medium would siphon away commercial TV's most popular programs, and people would be made to pay for what they now received free. The industry bore down heavily on the theme that the poor, the children and the elderly would suffer most. Typical was a CBS ad with a cartoon of a little boy saying, "Daddy, can I have a dollar to buy *Gunsmoke?*" The FCC's modified rules for pay cable issued in 1975 satisfied neither the broadcast nor the cable industries, and both appealed the commission's action in court. In March 1977 the D.C. Court of Appeals held that the rules were unconstitutional and ordered them vacated; the Supreme Court upheld the ruling.

Meanwhile, an eastern pay-cable distributor, Home Box Office, which presented a daily channel of fare for a monthly fee, arranged to disseminate its programming to all parts of the country by domestic satellite. Agreements from several major companies, including Teleprompter, to put HBO on their local systems gave birth to the first national pay-cable network.

The introduction of satellite transmission and its growth between 1975 and 1979 marked a new stage of development for cable TV. One of the key impediments to the growth of original cable programming throughout the 1970s had been the lack of a low-cost national distribution system. Since 1975, however, a variety of new program services have been developed for satellite transmission, ranging from the Cable-Satellite Public Affairs Network, which offers gavel-to-gavel coverage of the House of Representatives from Washington, to Nickelodeon, a full channel of original children's programming.

Cable has raised a swarm of problems. The wire leading into the home will tell what people are watching, opening a Pandora's box on the right of privacy. Copyright questions arise with the importation of signals. The common carrier virtues of the medium—giving people the uncensored right to broadcast for whomever may be watching—has the negative side of bringing offensive material into homes, which is sure to create enemies for cable. On the other hand, if cable is not permitted to be a common carrier, the owners of the systems stand to become more powerful than any media barons ever dreamed of becoming.

Cable enthusiasts have called the medium a better mousetrap and the most significant development in communications since the telephone. Nicholas Johnson, the former FCC commissioner, said that broadcasting is unto cable what the garden hose is to Niagara Falls. The landmark Sloan Commission Report on Cable Communications (1971) hailed the medium as "the television of abundance" and concluded that the encouragement of cable TV's growth would be in the public interest.

CABLECASTING ▶ televised programming originating on cable channels, including locally originated programs produced by the cable system or public access groups, programs on leased channels, and satellite-transmitted national programming made specially for cable TV. The term distinguishes this programming from a cable system's retransmission of broadcast signals.

CABLE-TELEVISION REGULATION ▶ more complex than that for conventional television because it is accomplished on the municipal level as well as the federal, and in some cases even on the state level.

Municipalities are involved because they, logically, are best qualified to award franchises to serve the specific needs of their communities and because they govern the use of the streets and ways required for building cable systems. Local governments, through their power to grant franchises, thus are in a position to determine who may enter the cable business.

Federal regulation began effectively in 1966, under pressure from local broadcast stations and regulators concerned with issues of copyright, technical standards and the protection of over-the-air television. Until Congress passed the Cable Communications Policy Act of 1984, the FCC's jurisdiction over cable rested entirely on the agency's assertion (upheld by the Supreme Court's 1968 *Southwestern Cable* decision) that the medium is "ancillary" to over-the-air broadcasting.

Despite liberalization in 1972, the FCC maintained various limitations that tended to protect broadcasters. These included "must carry" requirements for many local signals, prohibitions against "signal importation" of more attractive distant stations, and program origination capability (struck down by the Supreme Court in the 1979 *Midwest Video* case). "Program exclusivity" (or "syndex") rules mandating blackout of distant stations' carriage of programs available on local stations (including sports) were lifted in 1980 but reimposed in watered-down form in 1988.

The original rationale for state regulation was that it provided balance to the FCC's traditional overprotection of broadcasters, but passage of the 1984 amendments circumscribed the power of, and need for, these bodies.

CAESAR, SID ▶ sketch comedian, pantomimic and satirist who reigned as one of TV's stars from 1949 to 1954, chiefly on *Your Show of Shows,* a 90-minute Saturday night series on NBC. A comic of uncommon versatility and ingenuity, he had a special appeal to the literate viewer and may have been, like studio drama, a casualty of the proliferation of TV receivers into the lower income, lesser educated homes during the mid-1950s.

If Caesar was celebrated for his comic range and inventiveness, he was faulted for overworking his funniest concepts until they palled. While he was at his height his female co-star was Imogene Coca. The popularity of both performers declined when their partnership ended. Coca was succeeded on Caesar's shows by Nanette Fabray, Janet Blair and Gisele MacKenzie. Also regularly featured with Caesar were Carl Reiner, Howard Morris and Marguerite Piazza.

An attempt to reunite Caesar and Coca in 1958 was unsuccessful, and Caesar's TV appearances since then have been chiefly guest shots.

***CAGNEY & LACEY* ▶** critically and popularly successful CBS buddy crime drama series with a twist—the two buddies were female detectives. The roles were played by Tyne Daly and Sharon Gless (who replaced Meg Foster early on, after Foster replaced Loretta Swit from the show's pilot movie).

The pilot movie aired on CBS in 1981, and the series began appearing sporadically through most of 1982. It was canceled by CBS in 1983 but was brought back the next year when CBS received a flood of mail supporting the show. Revived, it ran until 1988.

Exploring the working and personal lives of the two detectives, the show touched on abuse, rape, alcoholism and a host of other social ills, winning a number of Emmy awards for its stars and executive producer, Barney Rosenzweig. It was also the first network television success for the then-fledgling independent studio, Orion Television.

CAIN, BOB ▶ Atlanta co-anchor (with Norma Quarles in New York) of CNN's *Daybreak* and *Morning News* programs. He also co-anchors CNN's *The Week in Review.* He has anchored various segments of the network's 24-hour news programming since joining CNN in 1980. Prior to that, he was an NBC News radio correspondent for 10 years. He started his career in 1952 at KSWI Radio in Council Bluffs, Iowa, and from there worked at several TV and radio stations around the country as a newscaster and reporter.

CALL SIGNS (CALL LETTERS) ▶ distinctive combinations of letters by which stations are identified, normally consisting of four letters (followed by -TV), although stations descended from the earliest radio operations may retain three. By international agreement, the broadcast stations of a nation are identified by the first letter, or the first two letters in some cases, of their assigned call signal. Under the agreement, the U.S. was apportioned call letters beginning with K or W. (Canadian stations begin their call signs with C and those of Mexico with X).

In the U.S. most stations east of the Mississippi River were required from early times to begin their call signs with W, those west of the Mississippi with K. (KDKA Pittsburgh is one of several exceptions, its calls having been grandfathered because they were assigned before the system went into effect.) Some call signs contain the initials of people (WPLG for Philip L.Graham), some code initials for the ownership group (WCBS, WNBC, WABC) and some stand for a slogan (WGN, World's Greatest Newspaper—it was founded by the *Chicago Tribune*). Other call signs are selected because they spell out words for easy identification, e.g., KAKE, KISS, KEEN, WAVY. Until deregulation in the 1980s, call signs were authorized by the FCC; previously, they could be changed with FCC approval if they did not duplicate another or did not create confusion with a similar-sounding call in the service area. In 1983, though, the FCC removed itself from the process of approving call letter changes, permitting licensees to adopt at will any unused four letter "W" or "K" combination. It was left to the courts to address problems such as use of similar call signs in the same market.

The suffix "TV" is required with TV stations that share call letters with jointly owned radio stations; in other instances stations may opt to use the "TV" suffix at their discretion.

CAMCORDER ▶ single-unit video camera and recorder. Before the emergence of camcorders in the late 1980s, VTRs and cameras were separate units connected by a cable. Lighterweight, smaller-format systems in the professional market brought increased portability to ENG operations and, in the consumer market, spurred the emergence of millions of additional home video enthusiasts who tape outside the home. Professional camcorders are usually of the Betacam, MII or S-VHS formats; consumer camcorders are usually of the VHS or 8mm video formats.

CAMEL NEWS CARAVAN **▶** NBC's 15-minute early evening newscast presented by John Cameron Swayze that ran from 1948 to 1956, when it was replaced by *The Huntley-Brinkley Report.* Swayze, dapper and suave, became known for the lines used in every program: "A good good-evening to you," "hopscotching the globe" and "glad we could be together." The program, sponsored by Camel cigarettes, competed with CBS's *Douglas Edwards with the News.*

The termination of the *Camel News Caravan* marked a turning point in TV journalism. After it came the network policies dissociating advertisers from the news product and the practice of using working reporters as newscasters.

CAMERA THREE **▶** half-hour CBS cultural series on Sunday mornings (1956-79) that maintained a high standard of quality on a spartan budget from its beginning as a local show on WCBS-TV New York in 1953. It became a network series in 1956 and soon won the admiration of critics for its innovative and imaginative presentations. Devoted to all the arts—dance, poetry, opera, theater, cinema—the series was a showcase for numerous performers who were later to become celebrated, among them Beverly Sills, Twyla Tharp and scores of actors. Under its original producer-director Robert Herridge, who helped shape the series when it had to be presented live, the show leaned heavily to drama and poetry readings, and it undertook such ambitious projects as a six-part adaptation of Dostoevski's *Crime and Punishment.* In latter years, its executive producer was John Musilli.

It was canceled by CBS early in 1979, along with the long-running religious series *Lamp Unto My Feet* and *Look Up and Live,* to make way for the new 90-minute newscast, *CBS News Sunday Morning.* Ironically, it was the only CBS program to win a Peabody Award in 1978.

Camera Three became a prime-time PBS series, underwritten by Arco, in the fall of 1979. Musilli and writer Stephan Chodorov formed their own company, Camera Three Productions, to produce new segments, while CBS made available tapes of the old programs without charge. But the program had only a brief run on PBS.

CAMPBELL, NORMAN ▶ noted Canadian director and producer of specials for the CBC, mostly in areas of musicals and light cultural productions. Working occasionally in the U.S., he directed *The Gershwin Years* for CBS and *The Golddiggers in London* for NBC. His productions of the ballets *Sleeping Beauty, Cinderella* and *Romeo and Juliet* for the CBC were aired internationally.

CANADA ▶ a country with a unique and complex television system, which evolved from Canada's unusual geography, its proximity to the U.S. and its bilingualism.

Although Canada inhabits a huge land mass, its population is less than 26 million, less than one-tenth that of the U.S. Approximately 90% of its people live within 100 miles of the United States in a 3000-mile band along the southern border stretching from coast to coast. The other 10% live in relative isolation. The country is separated, besides, into two quite distinct cultures: that of Quebec, which is French-speaking and comprises around one-fourth the population, and that of all the other provinces, which are largely anglophone and sometimes indistinguishable from the U.S. Moreover, in the last few decades, the country has experienced an influx from Europe, India, Hong Kong, Japan, and the Caribbean. Government immigration policy has traditionally encouraged multi-culturalism for its newcomers, as opposed to the American melting-pot concept, which has further fragmented the country's sparse population.

Canada was linked by railroad in 1885, but today the government looks to television to unify the country culturally and promote national identity. The problem, however, is that American programs overwhelm most Canadian productions in the ratings. Canadian broadcasters buy virtually everything that airs on the U.S. networks. With Canada's fragile cultural identity threatened by the domination of American media, the Canadian government, in an effort to stem the tide, has built up a wall of protectionist law. One measure has been the efforts of the Canadian Radio-Television and Telecommunications Commission (CRTC)—Canada's counterpart to the FCC—requiring all broadcasters to carry 60% Canadian content during daytime hours and 50% in prime time.

The country's total population barely equals that of America's northeast corridor, but anglo Canada alone has an extraordinary amount of television service: a national public network, the CBC (Canadian Broadcasting Corporation); a national commercial network, CTV; and several other networks that cover specific regions, such as Global, CanWest, WIC and Baton Broadcasting. In addition, there are multiple local television stations in virtually every city and successful independents like CITY-TV in Toronto, along with educational networks in four of the provinces.

Moreover, Canada is surpassed only by Belgium as the most cabled country in the world, with 75% of its television households wired (Belgium has 92%). Of the 8.5 million cable homes, some 7.3 million are able to receive an average of 35 channels. There are abundant pay and specialty networks not unlike those of the U.S.

Canada and the U.S. are each other's largest trading partners, but when it comes to television, the trading has traditionally been one-way. Over the years, U.S. TV stations close to the border have treated Canada as part of their viewing market and sold advertisers their reach across the border. This created friction between the two countries and led Canada to retaliate with such measures as disallowing tax deductions to Canadian companies advertising in U.S. media to reach their own domestic audience. When the Canadian networks or stations buy American shows that come into the country anyway via cable, they are permitted to knock out the commercials on the ABC, CBS or NBC cable channels and substitute their own.

Because it has not been able to compete with the U.S. in the production of dramatic programs, in part because of their great expense, Canadian television has concentrated a great deal of its resources in news, current affairs and documentaries, and has excelled in these areas. Some of its programs have inspired American adaptations. *This Hour Has Seven Days,* for example, was thought to be a progenitor of *60 Minutes.*

On top of its other problems that rise from its proximity to the U.S., the Canadian industry has suffered a continuous talent drain over the years. Journalists, actors, writers and directors who want to succeed in television beyond what Canada affords leave the country for New York or Los Angeles. The American industry is heavily populated with Canadian expatriates. Among the many are Peter Jennings, Morley Safer, Reuven Frank, Arthur Kent, and Henry Champ in the news field, producers such as Lorne Michaels, and such performers as Michael J. Fox, Dan Aykroyd, William Shatner, Paul Shaffer, Alan Thicke, John Candy, Mike Myers, Michael Ontkean, Sheila McVicar, Catherine O'Hara, Rick Moranis, David Steinberg, Christopher Plummer, Martin Short, Dave Thomas and the late Lorne Greene and Colleen Dewhurst.

Despite its struggles in television, Canada manages admirably to support an independent production community, largely through such government funding agencies as Telefilm Canada, the National Film Board and the Canada Council, in addition to provincial departments that offer grants and subsidies. Among the more successful anglophone producers are Alantis, Alliance, Sunrise, Nelvana, Primedia, and Sullivan Films. Nearly all engage extensively in international coproduction, because that is virtually the only way sufficient budgets can be raised in the country for ambitious productions. Canadians, from necessity, became adept at negotiating coproduction arrangements before the practice was significant to the rest of the television world.

Coproduction is encouraged by the Canadian government, which, through the Department of Communications, has become actively involved in forming treaties with other countries. More than 22 countries have signed coproduction treaties with Canada. These are significant in that programs made with treaty countries, even if dominantly produced abroad, qualify as domestic content for purposes of Canada's quota system.

QUEBEC—the French-speaking province is the other Canada and, although small in size, it has far fewer of the problems that beset anglophone Canada. Tightly bound in a single province, with a language of its own and a well-developed national culture, it is unthreatened by invasions of American programs. Its own programs do best in the ratings. More than 70% of the television watched in Quebec is Canadian in origin (in contrast, less than 20% of the TV actually watched in English Canada is Canadian in origin). This gives Quebec a thriving production industry, one that has a greater involvement with France when it comes to ambitious production than with the rest of Canada.

Quebec's television broadcasters, which include a separately programmed French-language CBC network known as Radio Canada, are less concerned with unifying the country than with enjoying the distinct culture that is theirs. The long-established private network, TVA, is the Quebec equivalent of Anglo Canada's CTV; the newer commercial network, Television Quatre Saisons, is committed to working with independent Quebec producers.

Cable channels also have French and English counterparts. When Moses Znaimer of CITY-TV in Toronto created MuchMusic for cable, he later added a similar music video channel for Quebec known as MusiquePlus. There are also separate sports channels for French and English Canada.

CABLE—Canada's largest cable companies are Rogers Cable Systems, Videotron, Maclean Hunter Cable TV, Shaw Cablesystems, COGECO Telecom, Cablecasting Ltd., CUC, CF Cable TV, Moffat Communications, Northern Cable Holdings, Fundy Cable, Classic Communications, Cable Atlantic, Halifax Cable and Telecable Laurentian. Following are the Canadian cable channels:

Super Channel: Pay service providing movies and general interest programming based in Edmonton and available west of the Ontario-Manitoba border.

First Choice: Toronto-based pay service available east of the Manitoba-Ontario border.

Super Ecran: Montreal-based pay service for the province of Quebec.

Family Channel: Basic service offering programming suitable for all-family viewing.

Canal Famille: Service for all-family viewing in Quebec.

YTV (Youth Channel): Channel serving children and teenagers.

Cathay International TV: Multilingual general interest service to the province of British Columbia and the Yukon Territories.

Chinavision Canada: Service of Chinese language news, entertainment, information and education.

Telelatino Network: Service providing programming in the Italian and Spanish languages.

CBC Newsworld: All-news channel airing 24 hours a day, the Canadian equivalent of CNN.

Weather Now/Meteomedia: Bilingual weather service with local, regional, national and international weather reports.

MuchMusic: Channel devoted to rock music videos in stereophonic sound, with music-related news and occasional concerts.

MusiquePlus: The Quebec equivalent of MuchMusic, in French.

TSN (The Sports Network): Channel devoted to sports from North America and Europe, 24 hours a day.

RDS: The French-language equivalent of TSN.

Vision TV: Religious channel, a national multi-faith service.

Canadian Home Shopping Network: A non-programming service using still video and operating 24 hours a day nationally.

CANADIAN FILM AND TELEVISION PRODUCTION ASSOCIATION (CFTPA) ▶ a national, non-profit association of over 350 independent companies, including producers, distributors, facility and service suppliers, and entrepreneurs from all sectors of the feature film, television entertainment, corporate video and TV commercial production industry.

CFTPA promotes the interests of its memberships by lobbying on government policy matters and co-production agreements, negotiating labor agreements for independent producers, sponsoring conferences and workshops, and presenting special achievement awards. It maintains close ties with the national independent production associations of other countries.

CANADIAN RADIO-TELEVISION AND TELECOMMUNICATIONS COMMISSION (CRTC) ▶ Canada's equivalent to the FCC, an independent agency that regulates and supervises telecommunications, broadcasting, cable, and pay TV. Established in 1968 by the Canadian Broadcasting Act, it amends or renews licenses, monitors the performance of licensees and establishes regulations and policies of broadcasting. The CRTC also ensures that at least 60% of radio and television daytime programming (50% in the evening) is Canadian in content.

Under CRTC regulations, cable networks such as MuchMusic, The Sports Network, The Weather Network, YTV, le Canal Famille and TV5 are required to televise a specific quota of Canadian programming. Canadian pay-TV companies such as First Choice, Superchannel, The Family Channel, and Super Ecran are required by the CRTC to spend a minimum of 20% of their revenue on Canadian programs.

The CRTC also acts as a watchdog on such issues as sex-role stereotyping, cultural-minority rights, violence, and programs and advertising directed at children.

The commission has 19 members who are appointed by the Governor in Council. Nine full-time members form the executive committee and 10 part-time members are appointed on a regional basis.

CANAL PLUS ▶ France's over-the-air pay channel, launched in 1984, and the most successful pay channel in the world after HBO. One of the engines of the commercial television revolution in Europe, Canal Plus has established versions of its French formula in Spain, Belgium and North Africa and has become partnered in Germany's pay channel. Moreover, it has created subsidiaries to engage in international program production and distribution. In less than a decade, the company has become a force to reckon with in the international industry.

Canal Plus is one of the great success stories of Europe's television boom. It had net profits of $160 million in 1990 on revenues of $1.2 billion, a cash reserve of $400 million and virtually no debt. Led by the politically astute Andre Rousselet, the channel has built its reputation on quality entertainment and innovative programming, along with a heavy reliance on recent movie releases and national league soccer.

***CANDID CAMERA* ▶** unusual CBS series (1960-67) that sought to reveal human foibles by using a hidden camera to catch the reactions of ordinary people to unusual situations. The situations were devised by Allen Funt, producer and creator of the series who also participated in the humorous deceptions, his ordinary looks and con-artist gifts making him perfect for the role. It was revived briefly in the early 1970s in a new format and then was produced in half-hour form for syndication as *The New Candid Camera.* A new round of production for syndication began in 1979.

The show originated on radio in 1947 as *Candid Microphone* and became so popular that it spawned a series of movie shorts using film cameras in place of concealed mikes. The TV version began in 1948 with the title, *Candid Mike,* changed the following year to *Candid Camera.* It played sporadically until 1960, when it became a regular series on CBS. For several years it ranked in the Nielsen Top 10.

During that run, which lasted until 1967, Funt had a succession of co-hosts, among them Arthur Godfrey, Durward Kirby and Bess Myerson. CBS carried the series as a daytime strip in 1967. It was by Bob Banner Associates and Allen A. Funt Productions. In 1991 the series was revived yet again in syndication with Dom DeLuise as host.

CANNELL, STEPHEN J. ▶ writer and producer who was one of TV's top hit-makers in the 1980s, specializing in action-adventure. He polished his reputation on *The Rockford Files,* then became executive producer of *Baa Baa Blacksheep* and its successor, *Black Sheep Squadron.* Later, with his own production company, he created and produced *Tenspeed and Brown Shoe* and *The Greatest American Hero* for ABC. Although neither succeeded in the ratings, they led to an exclusive agreement with ABC to produce one series a year.

Since then, Cannell has produced a succession of popular series, including *Hunter, Wiseguy,* and *21 Jump Street.* In 1991 he began hosting CBS's late-night series, *Scene of the Crime,* while also serving as executive producer of ABC's *The Commish* and CBS' *Palace Guard.*

In the late 1980s Cannell moved his production company from Hollywood to Vancouver.

***CANNON* ▶** hour-long private-eye series on CBS (1971-76) whose hero was distinctively overweight and middle-aged. William Conrad, who portrayed Frank Cannon, made a comeback as an actor with the series. In the radio era, he had originated the role of Marshal Dillon in *Gunsmoke* but was unable to continue when that series moved to TV because he was the wrong physical type. He became a producer-director in TV and films until Quinn Martin chose him for the role in *Cannon.*

CANTOR, EDDIE (d. 1964) ▶ radio entertainer who made the transition to television in 1950 as one of the rotating stars on *The Colgate Comedy Hour* on NBC. He remained with the show through four seasons despite suffering a heart attack after a performance during the second year.

A former Ziegfeld star, he became nationally famous on radio and in movies as a singer and funnyman. Cantor made an early television appearance, in March 1944, on the *Philco Relay Program,* which was beamed locally in New York by NBC. After the Colgate series he appeared frequently on TV as a guest and as the subject of tributes.

CAPICE, PHILIP ▶ independent Hollywood producer associated with Lorimar Television, and executive producer of such Lorimar series as *Eight Is Enough, Dallas* and *Married: First Year.* A former CBS-TV program executive, he served as president of Lorimar for a year (1978-79), giving up the post voluntarily to return to production with his own company, Raven's Claws Productions, which has exclusive ties to Lorimar.

CAPITAL CITIES COMMUNICATIONS ▶ large and prosperous broadcast group owner that, though much smaller than ABC Inc., succeeded in acquiring the network and its related units in January 1986 for $3.5 billion. In merging the stations of both companies into a single group, Cap Cities was forced to sell off some of its own.

The company, which is known now as Capital Cities/ABC, has been noted for the astuteness and high moral character of its top executives, Thomas S. Murphy, Daniel Burke, Joseph Dougherty, John B. Fairchild and John B. Sias, and for its efficient management style, widely characterized as "lean and mean" ("mean" in the old sense of stingy, or fiscally prudent). Murphy remains chairman of the company but has turned over the responsibilities of chief executive to Burke, his longtime colleague and president of Cap Cities/ABC. Sias is president of ABC Television. Dougherty and Fairchild have retired.

The company was founded in 1954 by Frank M. Smith, Lowell Thomas, Ellen B. Elliott and Alger B. Chapman with a single station in Albany, N.Y. Murphy joined the company that year and in 1964 became its chairman, leading Cap Cities to steady growth with station acquisitions, including several in 1971 from Walter Annenberg's Triangle group. Until the ABC acquisition, Cap Cities' stations had been affiliated with either ABC or CBS.

***CAPITOL* ▶** see Soap Operas.

***CAPTAIN KANGAROO* ▶** a pillar of preschooler programming from its debut on CBS, Oct. 3, 1955, running more than 24 years without substantial change on weekdays in the 8 a.m. hour. For most of those years it was the only daily program for children on the networks.

The program was cut back to 30 minutes in the fall of 1981 in favor of the news program, *Morning,* which it preceded in the schedule. A few months later, Kangaroo was shifted to 6:30 A.M. to allow *Morning* to expand to two hours, that it might be fully competitive with *Today* and *Good Morning America.* The shift was costly to *Kangaroo,* since a number of key affiliates refused to clear the new time period. The show was canceled in 1984 but held the distinction of being the longest-running children's program.

Hosted from its inception by Bob Keeshan, a low-key performer with a straightforward manner, the programs presented a form of situation comedy for the very young, involving other live performers, animals and puppets. In that, it represented a departure from children's programming that attempted to seduce an audience through loudness, silliness and animated cartoons.

Captain Kangaroo, as portrayed by Keeshan, was an avuncular, heavyset and easily gulled master of a bachelor household, identified by his uniform, cap and ample grey mustache. Seeming formless, the programs made use of music, dance and conversation and dealt both with fantasy and aspects of daily living.

A long-time producer of the show, David Connell, left in 1968 to produce *Sesame Street* for public television and took with him knowledge gained from *Captain Kangaroo* in communicating with young children effectively.

***CAPTAIN VIDEO* ▶** early space-adventure series featuring the far-out weaponry and costumes reminiscent of Flash Gordon. Captain Video was played by Al Hodge. The series premiered on the DuMont Network in 1949. It ended in 1955 with the demise of the network.

CAPTIONING ▶ superimposing subtitles on TV programs at the bottom of the screen for the benefit of an estimated 13.4 million persons in the U.S. who are deaf or have hearing impairments. Broadcasters generally have resisted using "open" captions—lettering visible to all—because they tend to annoy viewers with normal hearing. But in the early 1970s PBS began experimenting with electronic systems developed for "closed" captions—those that come into view only on specially equipped sets—and in 1976 received approval from the FCC for full-scale use of the system.

ABC, NBC and PBS all agreed to begin offering closed-caption programs in 1980 on a limited basis, using the same technology. CBS declined to go along, saying it was holding out for the development of a more sophisticated device that could also be used for teletext services. NBC dropped out in 1982.

The PBS system involves the use of Line 21 on the TV screen, the first nonvisual line above the picture, for the transmission of the captions, which are dropped onto the screen by the special decoder. In four years of experimentation with prototype decoders placed at various sites accessible to the hearing-impaired, PBS captioned such programs *Upstairs, Downstairs* and *The Adams Chronicles.* They were unnoticed by viewers without the special unit.

Meanwhile, appeals from associations for the hearing-impaired have resulted in some use of open captions or in the use of inserts on the screen carrying a sign-language interpreter. These found their widest use in local five-minute morning newscasts.

WGBH, Boston's public TV station, took a major step in captioning in the early 1970s by securing the right from ABC to repeat the network's evening newscast at midnight with bottom-of-the-screen open captions. The agreement also permitted the commercials to be deleted.

The captioned newscast then was sent out over the Eastern Educational Network, but the PBS stations in those markets were free to carry it only if they received permission from the local ABC affiliate.

***CAR 54, WHERE ARE YOU?* ▶** half-hour comedy series about a team of inept police officers who share a patrol car. Shot in New York, it featured Joe E. Ross as Gunther Toody and Fred Gwynne as Francis Muldoon and was produced by Nat Hiken for Euopolis Productions. It aired on NBC (1961-63).

CARLIN "SEVEN DIRTY WORDS" DECISION ▶ case in which the D.C. Court of Appeals reversed the FCC on its ruling that indecent language ("dirty words") be barred from the air during the hours when children were likely to be in the audience. The Supreme Court then reversed the Appeals Court decision and upheld the FCC's right to suppress foul language. The Supreme Court's ruling was widely considered a severe blow to the First Amendment rights of broadcasters.

The FCC's action had come in response to a single citizen's complaint about a broadcast on WBAI-FM, a listener-supported station in New York, which had featured a recording of a comedy monologue by George Carlin. In the monologue Carlin discussed "seven dirty words you can never say on television"; the words are "shit," "piss," "fuck," "cunt," "cocksucker," "mother-fucker," and "tits." The program aired on the afternoon of Oct. 30, 1973, and the complainant said his young son had heard the broadcast.

Citing its authority under the obscenity-indecency statute, the FCC held that the seven words used by Carlin were indecent and said that language describing "sexual or excretory activities and organs," used in a way that is offensive under community standards, could not be broadcast. The commission said the words might be aired late at night but only on condition that the context in which they were used have serious artistic, scientific or political value. WBAI then appealed on constitutional grounds.

In March 1977 the Court of Appeals ruled 2 to 1 that the FCC violated Section 326 of the Communication Act, the provision prohibiting the commission from censoring by interfering with the licensee's discretion. Judge Edward A. Tamm, who wrote the opinion, said also the FCC's position on the WBAI indecency question was "overbroad and vague" and that its attempt to channel the allegedly offensive material into the late evening still constituted censorship.

In a 5 to 4 decision in July 1978, the Supreme Court supported the FCC's position in ruling that the First Amendment does not bar the government from prohibiting broadcasts of words that are "patently offensive," although they may fall short of the Constitutional definition of obscenity. FCC chairman Charles D. Ferris assured the broadcast industry that he would not use the power given him by the Court to bar the use of bad language if it were used legitimately, as in news documentaries.

Ferris's successor, Mark D. Fowler, adhered to the same enforcement policy but, on his last day in office in April 1987, announced a tougher policy. Fowler's willingness to take credit for this new standard helped incoming chairman Dennis Patrick weather the political storm that followed.

CARLIN, STEVE ▶ game-show producer who, in the mid-1950s, mounted *The $64,000 Question* and *The $64,000 Challenge.* He revived *Question* for syndication in the 1976 season.

CARNEGIE COMMISSION REPORT ▶ the publication of a study by a 15-member commission whose recommendations led to the Public Broadcasting Act of 1967 and caused educational television to become public television. The report, *Public Television: A Program for Action,* was the product of a two-year investigation of ETV begun in 1965 by a distinguished panel headed by Dr. James R. Killian, Jr., chairman of the corporation of MIT. The commission was funded by the Carnegie Corp.

Recommended was a system that would be devoted in the broadest sense to public service and cultural enrichment and that would have a national sweep while being essentially local-oriented. Central to the recommendations was the proposed creation of a corporation to serve the system (the Corporation for Public Broadcasting) and increased appropriations by all levels of government to support it. The report estimated that $270 million per year would be needed to maintain a strong national system, and it suggested an excise tax on the manufacture of TV sets to help in the funding. The Carnegie Report remained the gospel for public TV. A second Carnegie Commission, formed in 1977, examined the eleven-year history of public television and recommended a revamping of the system.

Other members of the original commission were James B. Conant, former president of Harvard University; Lee A. DuBridge, president of the California Institute of Technology; Ralph Ellison, author; John S. Hayes, Ambassador to Switzerland; David D. Henry, president of the University of Illinois; Ovetta Culp Hobby, chairman of the Houston Post Co.; J.C. Kellam, president of Texas Broadcasting Corp.; Edwin H. Land, president of Polaroid Corp.; Joseph H. McConnell, president of Reynolds Metal Co.; Franklin Patterson, president of Hampshire College; Terry Sanford, former Governor of North Carolina; Robert Saudek, TV producer; Rudolf Serkin, concert pianist; and Leonard Woodcock, v.p. of United Automobile Workers of America.

CARNEGIE II ▶ short for the Carnegie Commission on the Future of Public Broadcasting, whose report issued in January 1979 called the system created by the first Carnegie Commission a failure and proceeded to make recommendations for a legislated restructuring of the public broadcasting apparatus. To head off any such legislation, the Corporation for Public Broadcasting and PBS both took steps to reorganize themselves somewhat along the lines charted by Carnegie II.

Headed by Dr. William J. McGill, then president of Columbia University, the 17-member commission also called for a commitment by the federal government to a larger, better-insulated and better-financed noncommercial system than the existing one. It put the proper level of total support for public TV and radio at $1.2 billion annually, of which the federal government's share should be $590 million by the mid-1980s. It recommended that some of this money come from a spectrum-use fee imposed on commercial broadcasters and other users of the public airwaves.

The commission's report, the product of an 18-month examination and evaluation of public broadcasting, urged that the CPB be eliminated and replaced by the Public Telecommunications Trust, as an organization serving as fiduciary agent for the system with no involvement whatever in programming. It proposed the creation of the Program Services Endowment, which would be a semi-autonomous division of the trust, to control a budget of $190 million a year that would be used almost exclusively for the development and financing of national programming.

Carnegie II was established in June 1977 on a $1 million grant from the Carnegie Corporation of New York. Its report was published as a paperback by Bantam Books under the title *The Public Trust.* The commission's members, in addition to McGill, were Stephen K. Bailey, Red Burns, Henry Cauthen, Peggy Charren, Wilbur Davenport, Virginia Duncan, Eli N. Evans, John Gardner, Alex Haley, Walter Heller, Josie Johnson, Kenneth Mason, Bill Moyers, Kathleen Nolan, Leonard Reinsch and Tomas Rivera.

CARNEY, ART ▶ versatile actor who enjoyed great popularity as Jackie Gleason's sidekick Ed

Norton, the sewer-worker, in *The Honeymooners.* Carney was able to surmount a legendary identification with that role and to perform serious roles in the drama showcases of the 1950s. He played the lead in a TV production of *Harvey* and was host in a production of *Peter and the Wolf.* He went on to star in movies and Broadway shows, yet for all his success he never starred in a TV series of his own, although he was a regular in NBC's *Snoop Sisters,* which starred Helen Hayes.

Carol Burnett with Jim Nabors in a scene from *The Carol Burnett Show*

CAROL BURNETT SHOW, THE ▶ durable comedy-variety series on CBS in which Carol Burnett established her preeminence in the vaudeville style of comedy. Premiering in the fall of 1967, the program held up steadily in the ratings and enjoyed a harvest of Emmy Awards. Major support came from comedian Harvey Korman. Other regulars were Lyle Waggoner, Vicki Lawrence and the Ernest Flatt Dancers, with sketch comedian Tim Conway joining in the 1975 season. Executive producer was the star's husband, Joe Hamilton, and the producer was Ed Simmons. It was via Punkin Productions.

Korman left the show in 1977, and his place in the regular cast was taken by Dick Van Dyke. The show was terminated in 1978 and the reruns successfully syndicated, edited down to a 30-minute form. In 1991 the title and basic format were reactivated for an hour-long CBS series, produced by Burnett's Kalola Productions and Touchstone TV.

CARON, GLENN GORDON ▶ producer-writer who was executive producer of *Moonlighting* throughout its four-year run. His own company, Picturemaker Productions, produced the series with ABC and then entered into an exclusive development deal with the network. His previous credits as producer-writer include stints with such series as *Breaking Away, Remington Steele* and *Taxi.*

CARR, MARTIN (d. 1987) ▶ producer of muckraking documentaries for CBS News (1963-69) and NBC News (1969-74). Earlier he produced cultural documentaries and children's public affairs shows for CBS. Among his notable works were *Migrant* for NBC (1970) and *Hunger in America* for CBS (1968). He also produced and directed *Five Faces of Tokyo, Search for Ulysses* and *Gauguin in Tahiti,* among other films.

CARRASCOLENDAS ▶ bilingual (Spanish-English) children's series for PBS produced for the system by KRLN-TV San Antonio-Austin, Texas, on funds from the U.S. Office of Education. It premiered in 1972 with Aida Barrera as executive producer and Raoul Gonzales as story editor.

CARROLL, CARROLL (d. 1991) ▶ writer of comedy material dating to radio days when he wrote for Bing Crosby, Burns and Allen, Eddie Cantor, Rudy Vallee and Milton Berle, among others. In the employ of J. Walter Thompson on the West Coast, he was head writer of numerous shows sponsored by the ad agency. He made the transition into television with Bob Crosby's daytime show for CBS and later worked on programs for NBC. He then took to ghost writing autobiographies for such TV personalities as Ed McMahon, Henny Youngman, Mike Douglas and Liberace. In retirement, he wrote a weekly column of witty commentary on TV commercials for *Variety,* "And Now a Word From..." (1967-85). His own autobiography was entitled *None of Your Business.*

CARRUTHERS, BILL ▶ producer-director with credits in *The Newlywed Game, The Dating Game, Operation Entertainment* and others; he was executive producer of *The Johnny Cash Show* on ABC in 1970. In 1976 he became TV adviser to President Ford.

CARSEY-WERNER CO., THE ▶ production company that has enjoyed extraordinary success in the sitcom field with *The Cosby Show, Roseanne, A Different World,* and *Davis Rules.* The company was formed in the 1980s by Marcy Carsey and Tom Werner, both former ABC program executives, and has specialized in finding sitcom concepts to suit the talents of exceptional stand-up comedians. Their approach worked with Bill Cosby, Roseanne Barr (Arnold), and Jonathan Winters, but it failed with Jackie Mason in *Chicken Soup.* It also failed with the 1990 sitcom, *Grand.*

The company, which has become a trio with Caryn Mandabach as president, has reaped some of the benefits of *Cosby*'s enormous success in syndication. The show's revenues from the sale of reruns to local stations were in the hundreds of millions of dollars.

Johnny Carson

CARSON, JOHNNY ▶ perennially boyish comedian whose major TV assignments were all outside prime time, a fact that didn't prevent him from becoming one of the medium's most popular personalities and consistently its highest paid talent. By the 1970s NBC was paying Carson more than $2 million a year to continue as host of *The Tonight Show,* a job he began in 1962. With each contract period the network made greater concessions to him for vacation time, in addition to money.

Most of Carson's earlier shows were daytime series in the 1950s, principally standard quiz programs such as *Who Do You Trust?* and *Earn Your Vacation.* His qualifications for *Tonight* were demonstrated, however, in a daytime *Johnny Carson Show,* which began in 1955.

Witty, urbane and cool, Carson proved an even more effective host of the late-night show than his predecessor, Jack Paar. A chief strength was his opening monologue; another, from a ratings standpoint, his penchant for slightly off-color material. Carson came to represent on TV the clean-cut Midwesterner with a bad-boy streak, just mild enough to make him endearing. He carefully avoided intellectual pretensions and usually drew his guests from show business.

In the spring of 1979 Carson elevated the crises NBC was facing on a number of program fronts by announcing that he intended to leave before the termination of his contract in 1981. The news made the front pages across the country and was covered in the network newscasts and on *60 Minutes.* The episode served to illuminate Carson's importance to NBC as a major source of income both to the network and to its affiliated stations. It was estimated that his nightly program produced 17% of the network's total revenues. He stayed on as host for another decade, before announcing that he would retire in the spring of 1992, rounding out 30 years. NBC immediately named comedian and substitute host Jay Leno to succeed him.

CART MACHINES ▶ tape-cartridge systems used to play TV commercials in station and network operations. Early cart machines built by Ampex and RCA bore quadruplex-format cartridges and were considered cumbersome to run. Later cart machines launched by such companies as Sony, Panasonic and Ampex in the late 1980s are computerized and far more versatile. They hold hundreds of cassettes of any cassette-based video format and contain literally thousands of spots, on-air transitions, or actual shows, and can be programmed days in advance to play them back in any order and combination. Stations have used them to automate their operations.

CARTER, HODDING III ▶ a regular participant on ABC News's *This Week with David Brinkley* and president of MainStreet, a Washington, D.C.-based television production company. From 1981-84 he was anchor and chief correspondent for the PBS series, *Inside Story,* a weekly half-hour critique of press and media performance. Subsequently, he was editor and chief correspondent of *Capitol Journal,* a weekly PBS series on Congress.

Carter began his journalism career in 1957 on his family's newspaper, the *Delta Democrat Times,* in Greenville, Miss., eventually becoming editor and associate publisher. Later he became closely involved in Democratic Party affairs and served as Assistant Secretary of State for Public Affairs and State Department spokesman during the Carter Administration.

CARTER MOUNTAIN DECISION ▶ (Carter Mountain Transmission Corp./32 FCC 459 [1962]/Off'd 321 F2d [D.C. Cir. 1963], cert. den./375 U.S. 951 [1963])—case in which the FCC refused to authorize a CATV system that would import distant signals to a rural area where the sole existing television station would, as a result, be driven out of business. The D.C.

Court of Appeals affirmed the commission's decision.

The Carter Mountain Transmission Corp. applied to the FCC for a permit to construct a microwave radio communication system to transmit signals received from TV stations in distant cities to CATV systems in Riverton, Lander and Thermopolis, Wyo. The only television station in the area, KWRB-TV in Riverton, protested, saying that the importation of distant stations would cause its demise.

After examining the evidence the FCC concluded that KWRB's protest had substance and that the importation of distant signals would leave the residents of the three towns without a local TV station. The commission decided that it was better to have a single local TV station than several distant ones that would only be available to subscribers. When the FCC denied Carter's application, Carter appealed.

The Court of Appeals held that the FCC had the power to deny the application and that the denial did not amount to censorship. The Supreme Court refused to hear the case.

CARTER, THOMAS ▶ much-in-demand director of pilots for dramatic series, because his track record with shows accepted by the networks has been exceptional. His successes include the pilot for *Midnight Caller,* the two-hour pilot for *Miami Vice,* the mini-series *A Year in the Life* and the series *Hill Street Blues.* He started out as an actor on *The White Shadow* and directed a few episodes of that CBS series, but he found he preferred directing and soon had a hit streak. Later he became a producer as well. His Thomas Carter Co. produced *Equal Justice,* an hour-long series that aired in the spring of 1990 and again in the spring of 1991, both times to mediocre ratings.

CARTER-FORD DEBATES ▶ a series of televised confrontations in 1976 between the major-party presidential candidates—the incumbent President Gerald R. Ford and his Democratic challenger, Gov. Jimmy Carter—modeled somewhat on the Kennedy-Nixon "Great Debates" of 1960 and staged under auspices of the League of Women Voters. While the Nixon-Kennedy debates required a special act of Congress suspending the Equal Time Law just for that campaign, the Carter-Ford debates were born under a new interpretation by the FCC of the equal time requirements.

Just before the election year opened, the FCC determined that political debates could be exempt from equal time if the confrontations were arranged by independent organizations and the debates held outside the television studios. If two candidates agreed to meet to debate the issues before a live audience, the rationale went, it would be appropriate for television to cover the occurrence as a legitimate news event. The FCC stipulated, however, that television would have to cover the event live and in its entirety—no delayed telecasts and no presentation of excerpts.

With Jim Karayn spearheading the effort, the League of Women Voters offered to become the organization sponsoring the debates. The networks, which were still seeking another suspension of the Equal Time Law, had to give up trying when the candidates accepted the League's proposal. All three commercial networks and PBS carried the debates simultaneously and among them reached 90 percent of the households (per Nielsen TA ratings) with the four telecasts. Three of the four involved Ford and Carter; the third was between the vice presidential candidates, Robert Dole and Walter Mondale.

The first debate, airing on Thursday, Sept. 23, from Philadelphia, ran two hours rather than the scheduled 90 minutes because of a protracted audio outage caused by the failure of a simple electronic part. ABC provided the pool coverage. The telecast had a total audience of 51.6 million households. According to Nielsen, the average duration of tune-in was 88 minutes.

The second debate, on Wednesday, Oct. 6, from San Francisco, ran 90 minutes and had a total audience of 46.5 million households. The fourth, on Oct. 22 from Williamsburg, Va., also ran 90 minutes and drew 42.5 million households. The third, between the vice presidential candidates, aired on Friday, Oct. 15, from Houston and was produced for the pool by PBS. It had a total audience of 35.6 million households and ran 75 minutes.

While the debates were generally considered to have been a draw, the eventual election of Carter was probably foretold in the ratings for the paid political programs each candidate bought on all three networks on election eve. Carter and Ford purchased alternate half hours from 8 to 11 p.m., playing the same program once on each of the networks at different hours. Carter had a gross rating of 34.2 for his three telecasts and Ford 25.3. In each hour, regardless of the competition from other networks, Carter beat Ford.

CARTER-MONDALE DECISION ▶ case that affirmed the right of "reasonable access" to television by candidates for federal offices and established that broadcasters may not decide for candidates when their campaign periods shall begin.

In the fall of 1979, the Carter-Mondale committee was turned down by all three networks when it sought to buy 30 minutes of prime time for a special program to kick-off the President's reelection campaign. The networks, which were in the midst of their own autumnal ratings campaigns, argued that the request was unreasonable, since political campaigns normally begin during the year in which the elections are held and not an entire year before.

The question of "reasonableness" was key, because Congress in 1971 had amended the Communications Act to prevent broadcasters from restricting access to candidates. The amendment gave the FCC authority to revoke the license of a broadcaster who would deny a "reasonable" request for access from a candidate for a federal office.

When the FCC ruled that the Carter-Mondale request was reasonable and that the candidates' needs were paramount to those of the broadcasters', the case went to the Court of Appeals for the District of Columbia, which concurred with the commission. Later the Supreme Court upheld the FCC ruling and the 1971 amendment—Section 312 (a) (7)—which states that the statutory right of access properly balances the First Amendment rights of federal candidates, the public and broadcasters.

***CASE AGAINST MILO RADULOVICH, THE* ▶** one of the famous Edward R. Murrow documentaries in the *See It Now* series. It aired on CBS Oct. 20, 1953, preceding by almost six months Murrow's devastating half-hour *Report on McCarthy.* McCarthyism was actually the theme of this 30-minute program, which focused on the case of an Air Force Reserve officer forced as a security risk to resign his commission because of anonymous charges that his father and sister harbored pro-Communist sympathies. Murrow's editorial stand was bold and controversial, and his defense of Lt. Radulovich against guilt-by-association reasoning led the Air Force to reverse itself and reinstate him as an officer. The program, produced by Murrow and Fred W. Friendly, was a prelude to the expose on McCarthy.

CATES, GILBERT ▶ veteran producer-director who has become dean of the UCLA School of Theatre, Film and Television, having worked in all three fields. In recent years he directed the 1990 and 1991 Academy Award telecasts, winning a pair of Emmys for the former, and an ABC drama special, *Call Me Anna.* In the 1970s he was producer of Arthur Miller's *After the Fall* on NBC and *To All My Friends On Shore* and *I Never Sang for My Father* on CBS. Earlier he was producer-director of NBC's *International Showtime* (1962-65) and the Timex-sponsored *All-Star Circus.* He is a former president of the Directors Guild of America.

CATES, JOSEPH ▶ director specializing in music-variety whose credits include specials with Anne Bancroft, Gene Kelly, Victor Borge, Ethel Merman and Yves Montand. He was associated with his brother, Gil Cates, in *International Showtime,* which had a three-year run on NBC in the early 1960s. On Broadway, he produced *Joe Egg, What Makes Sammy Run?* and *Spoon River.* In recent years he has been involved in country music TV specials originating in Nashville, and in the late 1980s he succeeded Alexander Cohen as producer of the annual Tony Awards telecasts.

CATHODE-RAY TUBE (CRT) ▶ an electron tube designed for graphic display, of which the television picture tube is one type. Invented in 1897 by Karl Ferdinand Braun of the University of Strasbourg, the CRT was in the 1920s converted by Philo T. Farnsworth and Vladimir K. Zworykin, working independently, into a device to display television pictures.

A black-and-white picture tube has three principal components: an electron gun, a deflection system and a phosphor-coated screen. A stream of electrons flows from the gun to the screen and is deflected from left to right and from top to bottom. The beam activates one tiny spot of phosphor at a time, causing it to glow, but the persistence of the phosphor makes the entire screen appear to glow. The intensity of the electron beam determines the brightness with which the appropriate phosphor spot glows.

The color picture tube has three electron guns, or three "barrels" in a single gun—one for each of color television's three primary colors (red, blue and green). A "shadow mask" (also called aperture mask) is located between the electron gun and the screen. The shadow mask is perforated with tiny round holes and the screen is coated with triads of phosphor dots which glow red, blue and green activated by the electron beam. The positioning of the mask with respect to the electron guns and phosphor screen is such that the beam from the "red" gun lands only on red phosphor dots, the beam from the "green" gun only on green phosphor, the beam from the "blue" gun only on blue phosphor.

A variation of the color picture tube is called the "slot-mask" type, which has alternate red, blue and green phosphor stripes on the faceplate and a mask with vertical slits or slots. The principle of operation is the same as that of conventional color tubes.

CATHOLICS ▶ adaptation by Brian Moore of his own short novel for *CBS Playhouse 90* (Nov. 29, 1973) concerning the conflict between an aging abbot and a young American priest with new ideas. It starred Trevor Howard and Martin Sheen and was filmed in Ireland. Sidney Glazier was executive producer, Barry Levinson producer (Lewis Freedman producer for CBS) and Jack Gold director. The program was repeated on the network Aug. 1, 1975.

CATV ▶ acronym for Community Antenna Television, the early name for cable TV when it provided essentially an antenna service for households with poor TV reception or those in under-serviced markets needing additional stations. The term "CATV" is still in use, interchangeably with cable TV, although the latter better suggests the range of sophisticated communications services afforded by the broadband technology, including pay cable.

As a community antenna for retransmission of broadcast stations, CATV draws TV signals off the air from an advantageous location, amplifies them and distributes them by a wire-thin coaxial cable to TV sets. A single cable may carry up to 70 channels, although 36 is typical today. In rural areas the cable is strung over telephone poles; in cities the trunk cable is laid in underground telephone ducts.

When the incoming cable is attached directly to the antenna input of the TV set, which is the simplest method, the normal dial is used for channel selection. This, however, limits the subscriber to the 12 VHF channels on the dial. In order to receive the full channel-carrying capacity of the cable, tunable converters must be attached to television sets to replace the limited tuners.

CAUCUS FOR PRODUCERS, WRITERS AND DIRECTORS ▶ an organization of members of the Hollywood creative community formed in 1975 to give those who create TV programs and motion pictures a voice in industry issues that are beyond the scope and concern of the guilds. The essential aims of the Caucus are to protect the standards and integrity of the creative work of its members and to allow producers, writers and directors to assume a more direct responsibility to the viewing public in network programming and films.

CAUTHEN, HENRY J. ▶ president of South Carolina ETV since 1985 and a leader in educational television and radio. In the late 1950s he conceived and engineered SCETV's extensive statewide networks of closed- and open-circuit television and radio, the nation's largest. As a member of the Carnegie Commission on the Future of Public Television, in addition to the boards of PBS, SECA and APTS, and with presidential appointments also to the National Council on the Arts and the board of CPB, Cauthen has been one of the most influential figures in shaping the policies and programming of public television.

CAVETT, DICK ▶ urbane comedian and talk show host who, although praised by many critics as witty and intellectual, failed to establish a competitive program on ABC-TV in a number of tries from 1968 through 1974. He was more successful on PBS with his nightly interview series which ran from 1977 to 1982.

A onetime comedy writer for Jack Paar and others, Cavett made his debut as a program host on March 4, 1968 with a 90-minute daytime talk show on ABC entitled *This Morning*, which soon was changed to *The Dick Cavett Show*. It won an Emmy Award but was terminated for low ratings on Jan. 24, 1969. In the summer of that year Cavett conducted a prime-time series on ABC three nights a week and, on Dec. 29, was given the network's late-night program, previously hosted by Joey Bishop. The program ran five nights a week, opposite *Tonight* with Johnny Carson on NBC and *The Merv Griffin Show* on CBS. Cavett won another Emmy but ran third in the competition.

In December 1972 his nightly series was cut back to one week in four, where it alternated with a week of Jack Paar (in his return to the late-night arena) and two weeks of varied programming. Two years later, when ABC adopted *Wide World of Entertainment* as its late-night entry, Cavett was again cut back, this time to two programs a month (alternate Thursdays). He won a third Emmy. But when it appeared that ABC might not renew his contract, late in 1974, he signed with CBS for specials and other projects, and also did occasional programs for PBS, including *V.D. Blues* and *Feelin' Good.*

No permanent program for Cavett developed at CBS, and in the fall of 1977 he began a nightly interview series for PBS, produced by WNET New York. The program became one of the bread-and-butter entries of public television until the stations voted it out of the lineup in 1982. In 1991 he began a regular series on CNBC, the cable network.

A native of Nebraska, Cavett worked initially in summer stock in the east and became a comedy writer when Paar accepted his material for his opening monologues. He later wrote for Merv Griffin, Jerry Lewis and Johnny Carson, before developing the nightclub act that led to his career in TV.

C-BAND ▶ wide-beam signal from a satellite that requires an earth station 12 feet or more in diameter for clear pick-up. C-band signals are generally used by cable operators and broadcasters. In contrast, the narrow ku-band signals from high-powered satellites can be received by dishes as small as a foot square and are used for DBS.

CBC (CANADIAN BROADCASTING CORPORATION) ▶ Canada's public broadcasting service, which operates TV and radio networks in both English and French on an infrastructure of CBC-owned stations. Because CBC must service the entire vast country, including the sparsely populated northern regions, its programs are distributed through six time zones. The TV service grew out of CBC Radio, which was established in 1936.

The CBC's mandate is to provide a national broadcast service which is predominantly Canadian in content and character, and covers a wide range of interests for all age groups. Under what Americans consider to be a quota system, it is required to limit acquired foreign programs to 40% of its overall schedule and 50% in prime time. However, in recent years CBC has set itself a Canadian content goal of 90%. It is financed mainly by public funds, which are voted annually by the Canadian Parliament.

CBC's budget for 1990 was $1.21 billion, of which $849 million was a parliamentary appropriation and $360 million earned revenue, mostly from ad sales. On its face, the amount would seem more than sufficient for public broadcasting in a nation of only 26 million people. But it gets diluted in the need to distribute CBC signals to every corner of the second largest national land mass in the world (after what used to be the Soviet Union). Moreover, the CBC must provide two national television networks, one for its anglophone population and another for francophones. In addition, it operates two national cable channels: one, like C-SPAN, carrying the proceedings of the House of Commons live; the other, CBC Newsworld, a full-time all-news service like CNN, launched in 1989.

Meanwhile, it must compete for advertising with commercial networks, both national and regional, and for distinction with several provincial public television stations, such as TV Ontario and Access. And finally, it operates in a country that, largely through cable, is inundated with American TV programs.

Because of its financial limitations, CBC Television, like its radio counterpart, has tended to accent news, documentaries and current affairs. In these spheres, it is one of the most trusted and respected broadcasters in the world.

CBC's chairman is Patrick Watson, a distinguished journalist and filmmaker. Its president is Gerard Veillieux, a veteran public servant.

CBS ▶ a network once so obsessed with being first and best that it liked to describe itself as "The Tiffany Network." The company's fastidiousness with graphics, decor and good form were qualities that carried over to the picture on the screen. Under the influence of its founding chairman, William S. Paley, and president, Frank Stanton, CBS was the leading network in the ratings through virtually all of the years of three-network competition until ABC's ascendancy in 1976.

A few years before Paley's death in 1990, control of CBS shifted to the Loews Corp., owned by Laurence A. Tisch and family, and the company went through an agonizing restructuring not unlike those of ABC and NBC when they were sold: all CBS non-broadcast assets were sold, thousands of employees were fired, and the once proud Tiffany Network found itself struggling for survival in a rapidly changing television environment. The Big Three networks, which feasted on lush profits when TV viewing choices were few, could no longer sustain that growth by 1990, when at least 60% of U.S. households subscribed to cable TV, better than 70% had a VCR and the average home could receive at least 30 channels.

The biggest of the Big Three—in profits as well as in the public mind—CBS was for many years the runaway leader in such lucrative areas as daytime and Saturday mornings, as well as in prime time and news. Its string of television gems included *Playhouse 90, Studio One, I Love Lucy, The Honeymooners, The Defenders, East Side, West Side, The Dick Van Dyke Show, All in the Family, The Mary Tyler Moore Show, Kojak, See It Now, The Autobiography of Miss Jane Pittman, CBS Reports, M*A*S*H* and *60 Minutes.*

CBS's supremacy began with the raids by Paley in the late 1940s on NBC's biggest attractions: Jack Benny, Red Skelton, Amos 'n' Andy, and Edgar Bergen & Charlie McCarthy. It proceeded from there to the building and maintenance of a regular star roster unmatched by the rival networks, including Lucille Ball, Jackie Gleason, Arthur Godfrey, Garry Moore, Ed Sullivan, Jim Arness, Danny Kaye, Red Skelton and Andy Griffith. CBS also spawned the most distinguished journalist in broadcasting, Edward R. Murrow, and the one most trusted by the public in the 1970s, Walter Cronkite.

Contributing to the TV network's success in the early years was the effort to secure the Channel 2 position for the owned stations and, wherever possible, with affiliates. Controlling the first spot on the dial proved especially advantageous because the Channel 2 signal carried farther than that of the other channels.

Previously known as the Columbia Broadcasting System, the company changed its name in 1974 to CBS Inc. to reflect its diversification in other fields, such as publishing, musical instrument manufacturing, toys and recordings, fields it later abandoned.

HISTORY—CBS began in 1927 as United Independent Broadcasters, founded by a small group headed by Arthur Judson, a talent agent and packager who determined to set up his own radio network when he was unable to do business with NBC. But the company was under-financed and before going on the air took in a partner, the Columbia Phonograph and Records Co. The network finally went into operation on Sept. 18, 1927, as the Columbia Phonograph Broadcasting System, providing 10 hours a week of service to 16 affiliates, with Judson's company supplying the programs.

Discouraged by mounting losses, Columbia Phonograph withdrew, and the controlling interest was purchased by Jerome Louchheim, a wealthy Philadelphia builder and friend of Ike and Leon Levy, owners of Philadelphia station WCAU, the first affiliate of the network. The Levys also bought shares. Louchheim changed the name to the Columbia Broadcasting System, but just as the network was beginning to make progress with advertisers he was sidelined by a hip injury.

It was then that William S. Paley entered the picture. An advertiser on the network (for his father's company, Congress Cigar Co., whose most popular brand was La Palina) and brother-in-law of Leon Levy, Paley purchased control of CBS on Jan. 8, 1929, for less than $400,000 and moved to New York to operate the company.

The network then had 22 affiliates and 16 employees. Largely through devising a contract offering more favorable terms to affiliates, Paley succeeded in expanding the network, and by 1932 CBS realized a profit of more than $3 million, notwithstanding the Great Depression. In 1939 CBS bought up one of its original owners, the Columbia Phonograph and Records Co., and built Columbia Records into a leader in the field.

Frank Stanton, who was to exert an influence on CBS second only to that of Paley, joined the company as a researcher in 1934 and became its president in 1946. As CBS prospered, it acquired radio stations of its own in major cities and later built their TV counterparts, which were to become hugely profitable.

Beginning in the mid-1960s, CBS began preparing for a future without Paley. Initially, the plan was to merge with a larger company, and when brokers advised that the management cadre was too old for CBS to be attractive for an acquisition, CBS embarked on a youth program. But shortly after the heads of the divisions were replaced by younger men, the plan was changed. CBS decided instead to diversify in a way that would make broadcasting only one facet of a conglomerate rather than a small company's primary business.

To accomplish the growth and to prepare for the succession, CBS hired away Charles T. Ireland from ITT as its new president in 1972. But Ireland died of a heart attack a few months later, and in July 1972 CBS tapped Arthur R. Taylor, a 37-year-old executive of the International Paper Co., to be Stanton's successor, heir-apparent to Paley and engineer of the acquisitions. Taylor was successful, and CBS quickly moved into publishing, musical instruments, toys and for a brief time, cable television. CBS Records was the top music company in the world.

Paley fired Taylor in 1976 and replaced him with John D. Backe, head of the publishing division. Backe was forced out in 1980, and Thomas H. Wyman, an executive at Pillsbury Co., was named president. By then, the CBS board of directors was becoming impatient with Paley's insatiable appetite for shredding presidents. Capitalizing on this discontent, Wyman won a majority of the board to his side, and in 1983 ousted Paley from control.

By 1985, however, Wyman found himself sitting on a powder keg. NBC, under the direction of Grant Tinker, had surged past CBS into first place in the prime-time ratings. CBS's chief news anchor, Dan Rather, was certainly no Walter Cronkite, and CBS News was falling behind ABC and NBC. With the exception of CBS Records, the company's diversification efforts—especially in publishing and toys—were not panning out. But most important, the bottom was falling out of the broadcasting side of the company. Television revenues were way down, the overall advertising economy was weakening, and growing competition from advertiser-supported cable networks was applying even more pressure.

On Wall Street and along network row (the three networks were then all headquartered within several blocks of each other on Sixth Avenue in New York City), speculation was rampant. Rumors spread of LBOs and junk-bond buyouts. NBC's then parent, RCA, was rumored to be talking to MCA about a merger. ABC was talking to IBM. Then in January 1985, arch-conservative Sen. Jesse A. Helms (R-NC) launched a crusade to take over CBS, inviting investors to "become Dan Rather's boss." CBS never took the threat seriously, but the company suddenly found itself "in play," and for the next year and a half CBS was under siege.

In April 1985 Ted Turner announced a $5.4 billion junk-bond bid for CBS. Turner, who had taken a small UHF television station in Atlanta, WTBS, and transformed it into a satellite-distributed superstation and successfully launched CNN, had CBS on the run. Desperate for a white knight, the network sought out GE, Gannett and the Loews Corp., owned by the Tisch family. By the summer of 1985, CBS had embraced Laurence Tisch, who by then owned 11% of the company's stock. By the following fall Tisch had upped his investment to a shade under 25%, had more than twice the stock as CBS's second largest stockholder—Bill Paley—and refused to sign a "standstill" agreement.

The CBS board was concerned that by inviting Tisch to become a major investor to help fend off the attack from Turner, they had unwittingly handed over control of the company for considerably less money than an outside bidder. There was fear the board may have violated its fiduciary responsibilities to the stockholders and subjected themselves to legal challenge.

With 25% of the stock in his pocket, Tisch was invited to join the CBS board. He did so, pledging his full support for Wyman and vowing to keep the company "independent." In his book *Three Blind Mice,* Ken Auletta chronicles the takeover of CBS by Tisch, his falling out with Wyman, Wyman's last-minute, desperate attempt to sell the company to Coca-Cola, Paley's decision to throw his support behind Tisch, Wyman's departure from CBS and Tisch's takeover of the day-to-day control of the company.

By late 1985, still reeling from the Turner takeover attempt, CBS exercised a $1 billion stock buyback plan, and began to sell assets to service the debt. The diversification plan that began in the 1960s and 1970s was scrapped, as CBS bailed out of film production and sold its interest in toys, its one-third interest in Tri-Star, its publishing jewel, Holt, Rinehart & Winston, and its St. Louis station, KMOX-TV. In addition, Tisch sold CBS Records to Sony for $2 billion. Later, CBS bought KCIX-TV in Miami, and in 1991 reached agreement to buy Midwest Communications, including WCCO-TV in Minneapolis-St. Paul. Paley died in 1990.

CBS STUDIO CENTER ▶ film lot of CBS, formerly the Republic Pictures lot before CBS purchased it in February 1967 for $9.5 million. It occupies 70 acres in Los Angeles, contains 17 sound stages and is used primarily for the production of TV series, whether or not they are on CBS.

CBS-OWNED TELEVISION STATIONS ▶ the six TV stations owned by CBS that make up the nucleus of its national network. The division was created in 1958 when the management of the CBS o&os was separated from the management of the TV network. The TV stations are WCBS New York, KNXT Los Angeles, WBBM Chicago, WCAU Philadelphia, KCIX Miami and WCCO Minneapolis-St. Paul.

CCD (CHARGE-COUPLED DEVICE) ▶ electrical signal-transferring chip with image-sensing capabilities that performs the same function in a video camera as an image orthicon tube. Because of their advantages—lower cost, lighter weight, sensitivity to lower light, no smearing or lag, and no damage by exposure to too much light—CCD cameras now dominate the broadcast marketplace.

CD (COMPACT DISC) ▶ laser-based playback technology that grew out of videodisc development efforts of the 1970s. Although laser-based videodiscs found a niche market in program playback for home video, the system upon which they are based came to dominate home audio playback in the late 1980s, as CDs all but supplanted vinyl phonograph records thanks to their resistance to use and wear and to their superior sound quality. In the 1990s CDs also began to find applications in computer-based home learning and entertainment systems.

CD-I (COMPACT DISC-INTERACTIVE) ▶ extension of CD-ROM technology that allows users simultaneous access to more than one function of the disc. For instance, they can display text while music is playing.

CD-ROM (COMPACT DISC-READ ONLY MEMORY) ▶ mixed media information and entertainment system that plays five-inch CDs similar to those of audio playback systems. The information stored on these discs is accessible via personal computer combined with a CD-ROM disc drive that can also be hooked up to a home TV set and stereo system. CD-ROMs can contain text, data, still images, motion video, and audio in any combination. The user cannot alter the information on the disc but can access it in an interactive manner via menus presented by the program.

CEASE AND DESIST ORDER ▶ an order by the FCC to a station or person to refrain from actions found to be in violation of the Communications Act, the United States Code of the conditions of the license that had been granted. Authorized by Section 312 of the Communications Act of 1934, a Cease and Desist order implies serious federal penalties for noncompliance.

CEEFAX ▶ data transmission system developed by the BBC which, with a decoder attachment, allows the viewer to select news bulletins, stock quotations, sports results and other reading matter, which may be called forth on the screen by pushing buttons. A similar system, Oracle, was developed at about the same time by Britain's Independent Broadcasting Authority. The two systems were activated in 1974. Ceefax is now used by millions of people in Great Britain and the technology has spread to other European countries.

The systems utilize two unused lines (at the very top of the screen) out of the 625-line PAL television picture in the U.K. By pushing buttons on the decoder, the viewer can choose from around 100 pages of printed news and information that he or she may wish to have appear on the screen.

See also Frame-Grabber.

CENTER FOR COMMUNICATION ▶ independent nonprofit organization based in New York that aims at being a bridge to the professional world for college students planning careers in the various fields of media. Founded in 1980 by Dr. Frank Stanton, former vice-chairman of CBS, and Robert Batscha, president of the Museum of Television and Radio, the Center produces 40 seminars a year with top media professionals, in addition to international forums and other special conferences. Irina Posner is executive director.

***CENTENNIAL* ▶** 26-hour adaptation of James A. Michener's best-selling novel of that title, presented on NBC in the fall of 1978 mainly in Sunday-night time periods. With moderate success in the ratings, it spanned half a season and held the distinction of being the longest movie—actually mini-series—ever made.

An epic on the evolution of the Old West, it was filmed in various American locations by Universal TV. The large cast included Robert Conrad as Pasquinel, Richard Chamberlain as McKeag, Raymond Burr as Bockweiss, Sally Kellerman as Lise, Clint Walker as Joe Bean, Barbara Carerra as Clay Basket, Chad Everett as Maxwell Mercy, Michael Ansara, Stephanie Zimbalist and Donald Pleasence. John Wilder was executive producer and wrote the screenplay's first five hours. Virgil Vogel directed.

CENTRAL INDEPENDENT TELEVISION ▶ one of Britain's richest regional TV franchises, licensed to the Midlands region and established in 1982 as successor to Lord Lew Grade's Associated Television (ATV) after the franchise shakeup the previous year. Based in Birmingham, it has been one of the major program producers for the ITV Network (now called Channel 3) and one of England's most successful exporters of TV programs. The company owns a large production studio, the FilmFair animation house, and a motion pictures subsidiary, Central Films.

Among Central's original shareholders were Carlton Communications, D.C. Thompson & Co., and the late Robert Maxwell's Pergamon Holdings Ltd. In the 1991 British franchise auctions, Carlton won the license to operate the London weekday station previously owned by Thames Television. Central's managing director is Leslie Hill.

CHAMBERLAIN, RICHARD ▶ TV and film actor who has made a career of starring in high-budgeted mini-series. After playing the lead in the *Dr. Kildare* series (1961-66), he mostly confined his work to such mini-series as *Shogun* (1980), *The Thorn Birds* (1983), *Wallenberg: A Hero's Story* (1985), *Dream West* (1986) and *The Bourne Identity* (1988). He also starred in the short-lived CBS series *Island Son* (1989-90) and the TV movie *Night of the Hunter* (1991).

CHAMBERLIN, WARD B., JR. ▶ vice chairman of Washington's WETA-TV-AM (1990-1991), after serving as president of the station for the previous 15 years. On retiring in December 1991, he set up a consultancy with offices at PBS headquarters. An attorney, Chamberlin left corporate life in 1968 to assist Frank Pace in the initial organization and operation of the Corporation for Public Broadcasting. As CPB's vice president, he played a key role in the restructuring of public television and the formation of PBS. He subsequently served as executive vice president of WNET, New York, and as senior vice president of PBS.

John Chancellor

CHANCELLOR, JOHN ▶ senior commentator for NBC News, appearing on NBC *Nightly News* with Tom Brokaw. After eleven years in the role of anchor, Chancellor stepped down in the spring of 1982, succeeded by the team of Tom Brokaw and Roger Mudd, and took on the commentator role.

In his half century at NBC News, Chancellor gained prominence as a correspondent, reporting from more than 50 countries and as many battlefronts; as host of the *Today* show; and as one of NBC's "four horsemen," aggressively covering the floor action of the political conventions of the 1960s (the other three were Edwin Newman, Sander Vanocur and Frank McGee).

Chancellor headed the Voice of America from 1965-67, returning to NBC as a Washington-based national affairs correspondent. He joined NBC News at WMAQ-TV Chicago in 1950, after having been a reporter for the *Chicago Sun-Times.* He is co-author of the book *The News Business.*

CHANDLER, ROBERT ▶ longtime CBS News executive (1963-85) who later produced several independent documentaries, among them *Learning In America* and *Schools That Work,* a two-hour special for MacNeil/Lehrer Productions that aired on PBS in 1990.

At CBS News he was v.p. and director of public affairs broadcasts from 1977 to the year he left, with overall responsibility for such programs as *60 Minutes, CBS Reports,* news specials, and children's news and religious news broadcasts. For two years previously, he was v.p. of administration and assistant to the president of CBS News.

Chandler joined CBS News in 1963 as head of information services, following a brief stint with MGM Television and a considerably longer one with *Variety* as a TV-radio reporter. During his years at CBS he produced special events and documentaries and was a supervisor of the network's election units.

CHANNEL ▶ in the U.S., six megacycles of spectrum space in the television bands which provide a single path for a station's transmissions. TV channels are designated by number from two to 83. However, on behalf of other users the FCC has whittled away at the broadcasters' claim to channels at the upper and lower ends of the UHF range. Thus in many parts of the U.S. channels 21 through 50 are reserved for broadcasters, while many channels numbered 14 through 20 and 51 through 83 are allocated to land-mobile and other uses.

CHANNEL AMERICA ▶ aspiring terrestrial television network launched in October 1988, initially with an affiliate lineup of low-power stations, subsequently augmented with some full-power stations and local cable channels. Offering a full-week 24-hour program service, Channel America claimed by late 1991 an audience reach of some 20 million households through 110 affiliates plus home satellite dishes. For the use of their airtime, the affiliates receive six minutes an hour for local commercials while the network takes six for national spots. The programming is standard television fare: vintage movies and series, game shows, talk shows and sports.

Founder of the channel was David Post, who previously was active in the field of cellular phones. In the spring of 1991, Elvin Feltner, a Florida-based owner of television stations and the large Krypton film library, acquired a 35% interest in exchange for programming and several million dollars in guaranteed advertising purchases through companies he controlled. Feltner became chairman of Channel America, and Post assumed the title of vice chairman.

CHANNEL CAPACITY ▶ the number of channels a given cable system is technologically able to provide, depending usually on when the system was built. Some of the earlier systems can handle up to 30 channels, while the more recent installations, and older systems that have been rebuilt, provide as many as 70. The new digital compression technology, when adopted, can expand capacity fivefold to eightfold; thus, by the end of the 1990s, cable systems should be able to provide upwards of 150 channels. And when systems are rebuilt with fiber optic technology, as all will be eventually, channel capacity could expand to the thousands.

CHANNEL 4 ▶ Britain's unique commissioning channel, which went on air in 1982 with a charter to serve minority interests and provide alternative programming to that of the BBC and ITV channels. The channel has proved a godsend to Britain's independent producers and has had numerous national and international successes, mainly with commissioned movies such as *My Beautiful Laundrette* and *A Room With a View.* Although Channel Four is a commercial operation, it is regarded around the world as a possible model for public television systems.

When the channel was conceived, however, few gave it a chance of surviving because it was to be supported by the commercial ITV companies, which were responsible for selling advertising time on the new network. The idea, advanced by the British government from recommendations made by an independent commission studying the country's television needs, was thought to be naive and unrealistic. There seemed little chance of advertising flowing to a minority-interest channel in sufficient quantity to support it. But the channel has proved successful both in fulfilling its charter and as an advertising medium.

Under the original arrangement the ITV companies sell the Channel Four airtime and pay for the network's upkeep by a levy on their revenues. Under the new U.K. rules, which become effective in 1993, Channel Four will be responsible for its own advertising sales in competition with ITV's Channel 3.

The architect of Channel Four's success was its original managing director, Jeremy Isaacs, whose strategy was to buy popular American series to draw viewers to the channel where they might then be exposed to original British programs. Many of the program series gave voice to minority political viewpoints or visibility to immigrant cultures. Isaacs left Channel Four in 1989 to head Covent Garden and was succeeded by Michael Grade, who had been chief programmer for BBC after a stint with Embassy Television in the U.S.

CHANNEL ONE ▶ 44-50 Megacycles, deleted from VHF allocations by the FCC in 1948 and assigned to land-mobile and two-way radio service.

CHARACTER GENERATOR ▶ a studio device for electronically projecting text upon the screen.

CHARLES-BURROWS-CHARLES ▶ production team that came out of the *Taxi* series and hit it even bigger with *Cheers.* It consists of writers-producers Les and Glen Charles and director-producer James Burrows. Burrows also directed the pilots for *Wings* and *Flesh 'N' Blood.*

***CHARLIE BROWN* SPECIALS ▶** perennial CBS animated specials, principally for children, featuring characters of Charles M. Schultz's popular comic strip, *Peanuts.* Drawing high ratings from the start, the programs seem to gain viewers with repetition. Most are tied to holidays or to the seasons. The specials are via Lee Mendelson-Bill Melendez Productions, in cooperation with United Features Syndicate, with Mendelson as executive producer, Melendez in charge of animation, and Schultz the writer.

Of all the specials produced up to 1977, the first and most frequently played was *A Charlie Brown Christmas,* which had its debut on Dec.

9, 1965, and has been shown annually ever since. It won both Emmy and Peabody Awards. Others that are aired almost annually are *It's the Great Pumpkin, Charlie Brown* (original air date, Oct. 27, 1966); *A Charlie Brown Thanksgiving* (OAD Nov. 20, 1973); and *You're In Love, Charlie Brown* (OAD Nov. 12, 1967).

The other titles include *It Was a Short Summer, Charlie Brown; Play It Again, Charlie Brown; You're Not Elected Charlie Brown; There's No Time for Love, Charlie Brown; It's the Easter Beagle, Charlie Brown; Be My Valentine, Charlie Brown; It's Arbor Day, Charlie Brown; You're a Good Sport, Charlie Brown; Charlie Brown's All Stars; It's a Mystery, Charlie Brown;* and the mini-series *This Is America, Charlie Brown.*

Two 90-minute theatrical movies, *A Boy Named Charlie Brown* and *Snoopy, Come Home,* also were telecast as specials. CBS also mounted a special on Jan. 9, 1975, to mark the 25th anniversary of the comic strip.

The voice of Charlie Brown has variously been played by Todd Barbee, Chad Webber and Peter Robbins; the voice of Lucy by Robin Kohn, Pamelyn Ferdin, Sally Dryer and Tracy Stratford; and that of Linus by Stephen Shea and Chris Shea.

CHARLIE'S ANGELS ▶ ABC crime series introduced in September 1976 concerning three young female private detectives working for the fictive Charlie Townsend, whose voice (read by John Forsythe) is heard but who is never seen. The series was a runaway hit when it began. It featured Kate Jackson as Sabrina Duncan, Farrah Fawcett as Jill Munroe and Jaclyn Smith as Kelly Garrett; David Doyle played their colleague, John Bosley. A Spelling-Goldberg production, it was produced by Rick Husky.

Within months of the show's premiere, Farrah Fawcett (then Farrah Fawcett-Majors) was a household word, a new glamour queen featured on scores of magazine covers. She left the program before the second season's episodes went into production and was replaced by Cheryl Ladd, who played Jill's sister Kris. In 1979 Kate Jackson's contract was not renewed. She was replaced by Shelley Hack, a model who had been prominent in Revlon's "Charlie" perfume commercials, who played Tiffany Welles. Hack, in turn, was replaced by Tanya Roberts (as Julie Rogers) in 1980. The series itself was canceled after the 1980-81 season.

CHARNIN, MARTIN ▶ producer-director responsible for *Annie, the Woman in the Life of a Man,* a tour-de-force for Anne Bancroft that aired on CBS in 1970; *George M!,* with Joel Grey, on NBC in 1971; *Dames at Sea* (1971); *'SWonderful, 'SMarvelous, 'SGershwin,* on NBC in 1972; and *Get Happy,* with Jack Lemmon, on NBC in 1973.

CHARREN, PEGGY ▶ president of Action for Children's Television (ACT) and one of its founders. She was its moving force as it grew from a small group of Boston-area parents in 1968 to a forceful national organization effecting changes in children's programming and commercials. Largely through Charren's energies, ACT became a major component of the broadcast reform movement, receiving most of its support from foundations and national membership. As ACT's representative, she testified before congressional committees and the regulatory agencies whenever issues concerning children's television arose.

CHASE, CHEVY ▶ comedian who attained TV stardom in 1975 on NBC's *Saturday Night Live,* the 90-minute "underground" comedy show airing at 11:30 p.m., and left the following year to pursue a broader career. As a member of the program's repertory company and one of its several writers, Chase caught the public fancy with his regular spot, a satirical newscast, and with his impressions of a clumsy President Ford.

CHASEMAN, JOEL ▶ former president of the Post-Newsweek Stations (1973-90) and previously president of Group W Television. During his years with the Group W organization, beginning in 1957, he had been variously national program manager for the radio stations; v. p. and general manager of the newly formed syndication division; executive producer of the syndicated *Steve Allen Show;* and v.p. and general manager of WINS New York, a station he converted into an all-news service in 1965. He became president of the radio division and eventually of the television division, shortly before being hired away by Post-Newsweek.

CHAYEFSKY, PADDY (d. 1981) ▶ one of TV's foremost dramatists in the "Golden Age" of television in the 1950s, responsible for such classics of the medium as *Marty, The Bachelor Party* and *Middle of the Night,* all of which were later made into movies. Others by the Bronx-born playwright were *The Catered Affair, Printer's Measure* and *Holiday Song.* When TV drama gave way to filmed melodramas and quiz shows, Chayefsky turned to writing motion pictures. In 1976 his devastating satire of the TV industry, *Network,* was one of the big box office films of the year.

CHECKBOOK JOURNALISM ▶ the competitive practice of paying for exclusive news stories or interviews. It is considered dangerous by most journalists because it can restrict the flow of news, pervert the newsgathering process and ultimately undermine public confidence in journalism.

Although the networks profess to have policies against outbidding each other for news exclusives, CBS News has paid for interviews with H. R. Haldeman, G. Gordon Liddy, and Sirhan B. Sirhan. In each case, CBS News justified its action by claiming to have purchased "electronic memoirs," but Richard S. Salant, then president of the division, conceded at the height of the controversy over payment of $100,000 to Haldeman for a two-part interview that it is difficult to draw the line between news and memoir and called the decision a mistake. Nevertheless, months later CBS lost $10,000 to a bogus informer who claimed to know the whereabouts of the body of James Hoffa.

CHECKERBOARDING ▶ the prevailing method of scheduling programs in prime time, with a different show in each time slot every night. The alternative form is stripping, with the same series airing in the same time period every day, which is the prevailing form for all other dayparts but prime time.

The effect of checkerboarding is that one episode of a series is aired each week. This allows for flexibility in canceling shows or shifting them to other nights where they might find a more felicitous time slot. Checkerboarding has rarely worked in daytime where viewing habits tend to become fixed.

***CHECKERS SPEECH* ▶** the historic political telecast in which Sen. Richard M. Nixon, on Sept. 23, 1952, used the airways to defend himself in a scandal that threatened his candidacy for the vice-presidency on the ticket headed by Gen. Dwight D. Eisenhower. It came to be known as the *Checkers Speech* because of the candidate's emotional digression into a tale of how his children came to possess a dog they loved named Checkers. The speech turned public opinion in Nixon's favor and, many believe, preserved his political career.

In mid-campaign, Nixon was charged with having accepted from wealthy friends an $18,000 slush fund for his personal use, the suggestion being that the money was given in return for political favors. When Eisenhower reacted by saying he would seek the presidency only with a running mate who was "clean," there were strong recommendations by Republican leaders that Nixon withdraw. But Eisenhower accepted the view of other party members that Nixon be permitted to present his case to the public.

On $75,000 raised by the party, time was purchased on CBS-TV, NBC-TV and the Mutual radio network for Nixon's speech. He dealt with the charge at once, denying that any part of the $18,000 went to him for personal use but insisted instead that it was given and used for campaign purposes. Seated nearby and occasionally sharing the screen was his wife Pat, whose composure and forbearance was demonstrated that night and was to become legendary during the Nixon presidency, some two decades later.

Having issued his denial, Nixon then discussed his childhood, his early poverty, his Quaker mother and his courtship of Pat. To close, he made a confession, as follows:

"One thing I should probably tell you, because if I don't they'll probably be saying this about me, too. We did get something—a gift—after the election. A man down in Texas heard Pat on the radio mention the fact that our two daughters would like to have a dog. And believe it or not, the day before we left on this campaign trip we got a message from Union Station saying they had a package for us. We went down to get it. You know what it was? It was a little cocker spaniel in a crate that he had sent all the way from Texas. Black and white spotted. And our little girl—(Tricia, the six-year-old)—named it Checkers. And you know, the kids love that dog, and I just want to say this right now, that regardless of what they say about it, we're going to keep it."

In its time the speech was a winner, and it remains a television classic.

CHECKLAND, MICHAEL ▶ director general of the British Broadcasting Corp. since 1987, considered an unusual appointment at the time since Checkland's background was in accounting.

He joined the BBC as an accountant in 1964, and by 1971 had worked his way up to chief accountant for BBC Television. In 1977 he was promoted to controller of planning and resource management for television, and in July 1985 was named deputy director general. Checkland's successor as director general, John Birt, was designated in 1991, two years before the expiration of Checkland's contract, making Checkland a lame-duck chief executive until 1993.

CHEERS ▶ one of the great sitcom hits of the 1980s, with an excellent ensemble cast and consistently intelligent comedy writing. After an uncertain start it caught fire and became one of the dominant prime-time series, often the top-rated show of the week in the Nielsens. Moreover, it has held down the same Thursday night time slot on NBC since it began in 1982. The Boston bar that is the model for the show's set has become one of the top tourist attractions in that city.

Ted Danson and Kirstie Alley of the popular NBC series *Cheers*

The show's success has boosted a few careers, notably those of Ted Danson, who plays the womanizing bartender/owner Sam Malone, and Shelley Long, who played Diane Chambers, an intelligent dreamer who waits tables at the bar and continues an on-again, off-again romance with Sam. When Long left the series she was replaced by Kirstie Alley in the role of Rebecca Howe. The supporting actors, all deft at delivering comedy lines, include Rhea Perlman as Carla, John Ratzenberger as Cliff, George Wendt as Norm, Woody Harrelson as Woody, Kelsey Grammar as Frasier, and Bebe Neuwirth as Lilith.

Glen and Les Charles and James Burrows produce the show for Paramount Television.

CHER ▶ pop singer of the recording team of Sonny & Cher who became a CBS star in the 1970s. She was noted for her wry quips, bold wardrobe and rock-generation insouciance. With her partner and husband, Sonny Bono, she launched the successful *Sonny & Cher Hour* in 1971. Divorce snuffed out the program in 1974, however. ABC then signed Bono for a Sunday night series, *The Sonny Comedy Revue,* but it flopped and was quickly canceled in the fall of 1974. At mid-season, Cher (Cherilyn Sarkisian) returned to CBS as a solo in a Sunday night slot and scored so well in her new series, *Cher,* that she became one of the most publicized talents in the CBS stable. When the series began to falter in the first half of the 1975-76 season, she was teamed once again with Bono, and the series, retitled *The Sonny and Cher Hour,* regained its old footing for a while. But it skidded again and was canceled in 1977.

Cher has made a number of motion pictures and won an Oscar for *Moonstruck* in 1988.

CHERCOVER, MURRAY ▶ former president of CTV, the Canadian private national network, and now an independent producer. His tenure as president may have been the longest ever at a network anywhere, dating from 1966, when CTV effectively began as a full-fledged national cooperative, to 1990. Previously, when CTV began operations in 1961 with eight independent affiliated stations, Chercover was chairman of the program committee. He is credited with building the network to one that now covers 97% of English-speaking Canadian households, making it a commercial success, and being the first in Canada to initiate and develop international coproductions on a regular basis.

Among his distinctions, Chercover reversed the television talent flow from Canada to the U.S.; he was raised in New York. He continues to serve the CTV board as a program consultant.

CHERMAK, CY ▶ series producer. He was executive producer of *Ironside* (except for its last season), "The Doctors" element of *The Bold Ones,* the "Amy Prentiss" element of the *Sunday Mystery Movie* and *Barbary Coast.* He took over as producer of *Kolchak—The Night Stalker* midway in the 1974-75 season. He took over as executive producer of *CHiPs* during its first year.

CHERTOK, JACK ▶ producer of TV series in the 1950s and 1960s through his own Jack Chertok Productions, notably *The Lone Ranger, Sky King, Private Secretary, My Favorite Martian* and *My Living Doll.* Earlier in his career, as head of short subjects for MGM, he produced the Robert Benchley and Pete Smith series and *The Passing Parade.*

CHESTER, GIRAUD ▶ executive v.p. of Goodson-Todman Productions since 1964 and previously a program executive for NBC, ABC and Ted Bates Advertising. Earning a Ph.D. from the University of Wisconsin, he first taught speech at Cornell University and Queens College, then joined NBC's program department in 1954, working with Pat Weaver. He became ABC's v.p. of daytime programming (1958-62) after a stint with the Bates agency and returned to NBC as v.p. in charge of program administration. He nourished his academic interests with several books, including the textbook *Television and Radio* (1963).

***CHEYENNE* ▶** a classic TV western with historical significance in the medium. It was the show that started the stampede of "adult" oaters in prime time during the late 1950s, and as one of the first shows produced for TV by Warner Bros. it helped pave the way for the other major studios to enter television. *Cheyenne,* which featured Clint Walker as frontier scout Cheyenne Bodie, had an eight-year run on ABC (1955-62).

CHICAGO SCHOOL ▶ appellation for the style, ingenuity and resourcefulness that characterized the network television programs emanating from Chicago in the early years of commercial TV. Having been an originating center for radio, principally with soap opera, Chicago quite naturally became a hub of television production when the new medium began, and it contributed to the national scene such programs as *Garroway-at-Large,* with Dave Garroway; *Kukla, Fran and Ollie; Studs' Place,* with Studs Terkel; *Zoo Parade,* with Marlin Perkins; *Super Circus,* with Mary Hartline and Claude Kirshner; *Ding Dong School,* with Dr. Frances Horwich; and a number of soap operas, among other programs.

Chicago programs were marked by originality, and suitability to the medium, as if in compensation for a lack of star glamour. Principally active was NBC, which maintained network production facilities that were known as the Central Division until 1958. In charge was Jules Herbuveaux, one of the showman-broadcasters of the period, who had had an earlier career as a band leader.

Even before film and video tape made live television obsolete, the networks began to concentrate their production bases in New York and Los Angeles, and by the late 1950s Chicago was reduced to a television market, making little more than a profit contribution to the networks. In the 1980s, however, the highly successful *Oprah Winfrey Show* came out of Chicago and, for several years, so did *Donahue.*

***CHICKEN SOUP* ▶** sitcom vehicle for comedian Jackie Mason on ABC that was expected to be an enormous hit when it debuted in the fall of 1989 but that actually fizzled and was canceled after two months. The expectations were based on the huge success of Mason's one-man show on Broadway and the fact that the series was created by the producers of *The Cosby Show* and *Roseanne,* Marcy Carsey and Tom Werner. Also, the show was scheduled by ABC immediately behind *Roseanne,* one of the top-rated shows on the networks. But apparently Mason's ethnic style of comedy wasn't readily accepted around the country. Even though it was the highest-rated new show of the 1989 fall season, it regularly lost one-third of its lead-in audience from *Roseanne,* indicative of audience rejection.

***CHICO AND THE MAN* ▶** popular comedy series on NBC (1974-78) centering on the relationship between the crotchety owner of an automobile garage (Ed Brown) and the high-spirited young Chicano who worked with him (Chico Rodriguez). With Jack Albertson and Freddie Prinze in the leads, it became one of NBC's highest-rated shows. But Prinze died, a suicide, in February 1977. NBC decided to renew the show the following fall incorporating other characters but not recasting Prinze's role. The series could not survive the loss.

James Komack was executive producer for The Wolper Organization in association with The Komack Co.

CHILDREN'S ADVERTISING ▶ commercials directed specifically at children. These became a highly controversial aspect of television, raising questions on the morality of subjecting children to sophisticated advertising techniques. In the 1970s, consumer groups successfully protested the differing commercial standards for children and adults, as well as other allegedly abusive practices, among them promoting nutritionally inadequate foods, using program hosts as salespersons, tempting purchases by offering premiums and advertising expensive toys in a deceptive manner.

Many of these reforms were forgotten as the NAB's code was outlawed and the Reagan-era FCC signalled that the reins were off. Widespread opposition from parents and educators led to passage of the Children's Television Act of 1990, which placed limits on the amount of commercialization and somewhat restricted toy-based programs.

Most of the deplorable practices began in the 1960s when advertisers perceived, through demographic research, that the juvenile viewer could be reached separately and sold specialized products, from Froot Loops to Barbie Dolls. At the same time the networks began to concentrate children's programs on Saturday mornings where a potential audience of 16 million youngsters was found to exist. In 1974 the three networks realized around $80 million in gross advertising revenues from Saturday daytime alone.

Until 1973, the NAB code permitted 16 minutes of nonprogram material per hour in children's weekend television in contrast to a maximum of 9.5 minutes in adult prime time. Network commercial rates for children's time ranged up to $22,000 a minute, depending on the program ratings and the time of year. Saturday morning had become a tremendous profit center.

According to a study by the Council on Children, Media and Merchandising, approximately 50% of the ads in children's programming (from 1965 to 1975) were for food, primarily sugared cereals, cookies, candies and soft drinks; 30% were for toys and 10% for vitamins, often in novelty form.

In 1970, Action for Children's Television (ACT) filed a petition with the FCC asking for the elimination of all commercials on children's programs and for a requirement that all TV stations provide at least 14 hours a week of children's programming geared to the needs of the various age groups. Four years later, the commission responded by issuing a set of guidelines for children's programs.

Pressure from the consumer groups prompted drug companies to withdraw vitamin advertising from children's shows as potentially dangerous to the young. Also in response to the criticism, the NAB Code Authority and the networks agreed to reduce the amount of nonprogram material (chiefly commercials) in children's weekend television from 16 minutes an hour to 12 minutes an hour, effective Jan. 1, 1973, and proposed further to cut back to 9 or 9.5 minutes an hour, the approximate level in adult prime time.

Revisions in the code also did away with "tie-ins," the mention of products in a program context, and with the use of program hosts or cartoon characters from the shows as the commercial spielers.

CHILDREN'S PROGRAMMING ▶ material designed expressly for the juvenile audience, which generally is defined as ages 2 to 11. During the early years of the medium, the appeal of television to children was exploited for the sale of TV sets; later, when most households had but a single TV set, programs were aimed at children on the theory that the young controlled the family viewing until bedtime; and even now, independent stations—particularly those on UHF—schedule blocks of children's programs, because the young help the stations to be discovered.

Although children helped to build circulation for stations and good will for the new television medium, they were not initially perceived as a major marketing group for products. Television was considered too high-priced for child-oriented products in the 1950s and early 1960s when the single or dual sponsorship of programs was the rule. Prime-time programs were particularly expensive, considering that they reached a large proportion of adults who were not targets of the advertisers. But a number of factors converged around 1965 to make children's programs a major profit center of networks: first, the proliferation of multiset households, which broke up family viewing and loosened the child's control over the program his or her parents would watch; second, the drift to participation advertising as opposed to full sponsorships, which encouraged more advertisers to use the medium; and third, the discovery that a relatively "pure" audience of children could be corralled on Saturday mornings (and to a lesser extent on Sundays) where air time was cheaper, advertising quotas were wide open and children could be reached by the devices used years before by the comic books.

By the late 1960s television programming aimed at children was confined, with few exceptions, to Saturday mornings in the form of animated cartoons. Moreover, the animation studios developed a form of limited animation for the undiscriminating youngsters, involving fewer movements per second, which was cheaper than standard animation. Recognizing that children enjoy the familiar, the networks played each episode of a series six times over two years, substantially reducing costs. And while prime-time programs, under the Television Code, permitted 9.5 commercial minutes per hour, Saturday morning children's shows carried as many as 16 commercial minutes per hour. Citizens groups did not become aroused, however, until the networks began to deal excessively—in their competitive zeal—with monsters, grotesque superheroes and gratuitous violence to win the attention of youngsters. Advertisers, by then, were making the most of the gullibility of children by pitching sugar-coated cereals, candy-coated vitamins and expensive toys (some retailing for as much as $50) in shrewdly made commercials that often verged on outright deception.

Such patent abuses of the child market—while Saturday morning grew into one of television's largest profit centers—prompted the formation of watchdog groups such as Action for Children's Television (ACT), whose pleas for reforms could hardly go unheeded by Congress or the FCC. In response to such pressure groups, the industry reduced advertising quotas in children's shows to 9.5 minutes per hour, toughened its code for advertising and reduced the violence content.

When public television introduced *Sesame Street* in 1969 and proved that it, and others such as *Mister Rogers' Neighborhood* and *The Electric Company,* could teach while they entertained, the commercial networks then strived to develop shows and inserts that promoted prosocial values (*Fat Albert and the Cosby Kids*), learning concepts (*Pop Ups, Go, Multiplication Rock*) or even current events, via CBS News. From syndication came such educational series as *The Big Blue Marble* and *Call It Macaroni.* The efforts of ACT and other citizens' groups led the FCC to issue guidelines for children's programming in 1974. This spurred local production of educational shows for the young on weekdays, in recognition of the fact that children are a daily audience.

But the only regularly scheduled weekday program on the networks remained *Captain Kangaroo,* an early morning show for preschoolers which began in 1955 on CBS and which has been exemplary in its treatment of the young viewer.

Among the earliest hit shows for children in the medium were *Kukla, Fran and Ollie, Howdy Doody, Ding Dong School, Mr. I. Magination, Superman* and *Hopalong Cassidy.* Some were uplifting and some simply entertaining, but all were relatively harmless and contributed to television's popularity. In 1949 around half the children's programs on the networks were sustaining—that is, presented without commercials.

In the second wave came *Rootie Kazootie, Time for Beany, Zoo Parade, Super Circus, Pinky Lee, Big Top, Watch Mr. Wizard, Rin Tin Tin, Captain Video, Lucky Pup* and *Juvenile Jury.*

And then, *Lassie, Disneyland, The Shari Lewis Show* and *Captain Kangaroo.*

Meanwhile, at local stations, the stock children's show featured a host designated as Sheriff Sam or Fireman Fred whose chatter inevitably led to the unspooling of old moviehouse cartoons. These were the "wraparound" hosts, who sometimes brought in a live audience of children or worked with puppets. The syndication hits were the movie shorts of *The Three Stooges* and *Our Gang* (repackaged for television as *The Little Rascals*).

More pretentiously produced were the prime-time children's series, such as *Fury, National Velvet, My Friend Flicka, Dennis the Menace, Leave It to Beaver, Flipper, Daktari* and *International Showtime,* among others. Animated situation comedies, such as *The Flintstones* and *The Jetsons,* became popular both with children and adults, and *The Wonderful World of Disney* on NBC, which grew out of ABC's Disneyland, became the "perfect" all-family series, although it has always been aimed primarily at children. *Batman,* too, spanned the generations in its initial network run as a campy entry, but the syndicated reruns have fallen distinctly into the children's program blocks.

In 1990 the major Hollywood studios began competing for afternoon time periods on the independent stations. The Fox network sent out *Peter Pan and the Pirates* as a daily strip to the independents carrying its evening shows, Disney began syndicating a two-hour block that included *Duck Tales* and *Gummy Bears,* and Warner Bros. offered Steven Spielberg's *Tiny Toon Adventures.* Turner Broadcasting's syndication arm weighed in with the animated environmental series, *Captain Planet and the Planeteers.*

But where the major networks were concerned, prime time for children was Saturday morning, where the young could dependably be corralled as a relatively pure market. Combined annual revenues for the three networks averaged around $250 million from the children's ghetto in the late 1980s. This represented about 3% of their total advertising revenues. Fox joined the sweepstakes in 1990, going up against the other networks with a three-hour block of animated shows under the rubric of the Fox Children's Network.

The Saturday morning shows fostered something of a national children's culture; indeed, across the country the most popular shows developed a cult following. Animated shows remained the most appealing to the very young, but occasionally a live-action series was able to break through, as *Pee Wee's Playhouse* did in the late 1980s.

During the 1980s, with the explosion of independent UHF stations, large blocks of afternoon children's programs became standard strategy at local stations. Most of these animated programs were offered on a barter basis—payable in advertising air time rather than in cash—that suited the new stations perfectly. And a great many of the series were built around toys—the doll Strawberry Shortcake, for example—so that in addition to the advertising spots they carried, the programs themselves amounted to advertisements. The practice raised protests from parents groups and eventually led to the Children's Television Act of 1990, which not only put limits on the amount of commercial time used in children's shows but also laid down a requirement that stations program some amount of intellectually or culturally nourishing programs for the young.

The toy-to-program issue effectively vanished when it became apparent that television was a promotional agent whether the toy existed before the telecast or was created afterwards. The big money in children's television came from the licensing of products, beyond toys, such as T-shirts, underwear, towels, sheets, curtains, lamps, posters, games, school supplies, tableware, vitamins, food products and soap. Programs like *The Smurfs* and *Teenage Mutant Ninja Turtles,* which were popular on television systems around the world, hit the licensing jackpot for merchandise. Indeed, the revenues from product licensing are what have helped sustain public television's exemplary children's series, *Sesame Street.* More than two-thirds of the cost of producing and delivering the shows are covered by income from product licensing. In 1990 sales in the U.S. alone of character-licensed products totaled $65 billion.

The commercial exploitation of the child market by broadcast television proved of considerable benefit to cable, as concerned parents subscribed in order to receive the wholesome fare promised by The Disney Channel, Nickelodeon and The Family Channel. Children's programs also became one of the best-selling lines in the home video field because the cassettes gave parents some control over the television their children would be exposed to.

See also Appendix.

CHILDREN'S TELEVISION ACT OF 1990 ▶ a law that imposes limits on the amount of commercialization in children's television programming (including cable) and requires operators to carry at least some programming designed to meet children's "educational and informational needs." Based upon a negotiated compromise between industry and broadcast reformers, the law came into effect without the signature of President Bush. Bush's predecessor, Ronald Reagan, pocket vetoed an earlier version passed by Congress in 1988.

The law set hourly commercial limits above those employed by most stations at the time of enactment: 10.5 minutes on weekends and 12 minutes on weekdays. It also directed the FCC to study and reform toy-based programs that were considered to be no more than half-hour commercials.

CHILDREN'S TELEVISION POLICY STATEMENT ▶ an FCC report issued in 1974 that offered guidelines for children's programming, emphasizing the obligation of broadcasters to serve children because of their immaturity and special needs. The guidelines came in response to a petition by Action for Children's Television (ACT), a consumer group, for rules banning advertisements on children's programs and requiring certain amounts of children's programming at specific times.

The guidelines state that all television stations must provide a reasonable amount of programming for children and that a significant part of it should be educational. The report pointed out that the lack of weekday children's programs is recent. In the early 1950s the three networks broadcast 20-30 hours of children's programs during the week, but during the late 1950s and early 1960s many popular shows such as *Howdy Doody, Mickey Mouse Club* and *Kukla, Fran and Ollie* disappeared, leaving *Captain Kangaroo* the only weekday show regularly presented by a network. The report said that children's programming should not be shown only on weekends and that hosts should not serve as salespersons.

Although critics of the FCC were disappointed that rules were denied, the commission defended its decision, saying that issuing rules would not be consistent with its court-sanctioned role of imposing only general affirmative duties on broadcasters in return for their right to use the public airwaves.

In offering the policy statement, the commission also accepted the code worked out by the National Association of Broadcasters that reduced advertising minutes on children's weekend programming from 12 to 9.5 minutes per hour beginning Jan. 1, 1976.

CHILDREN'S TELEVISION WORKSHOP (CTW) ▶ a nonprofit organization created in 1967 for the purpose of producing the experimental program, *Sesame Street,* which revolutionized children's programming when it debuted in 1969. The "workshop," headed by Joan Ganz Cooney, attracted $8 million in original funding from the Federal Government through HEW and from private foundations, mainly Carnegie and Ford, and the Corporation for Public Broadcasting.

CTW went on to produce *The Electric Company* for public television and foreign-language adaptations of both shows. To free itself of financial dependency, CTW went into production of related materials in other media, such as books, magazines, teaching guides, posters, puzzles and games based on the content of *Sesame* and *Electric.* This generated some funds but still left CTW highly dependent on grants. In 1974 the workshop began a third series, *Feelin' Good,* to convey health information to adults, and produced an NBC special with the Muppets, its first for the commercial medium. In 1977 CTW produced for PBS an adult history series, *The Best of Families.* Three years later it produced a new series, *3-2-1 Contact,* which ran for one season on PBS. *Square One TV* premiered in 1987 and *Ghostwriter,* CTW's new reading and writing series, was scheduled to be aired in 1992, both on PBS. *Encyclopedia,* an information series for families, was broadcast on HBO during the fall of 1988.

The CTW idea began in 1966 with Cooney, a TV producer and foundation consultant, who recognized television's untapped ability to teach. With Lloyd Morrisett, head of the Markle foundation, she developed the proposal that led to CTW and *Sesame Street.*

CHINA ▶ by far the largest television market in the world, with 178 million TV sets watched by some 800 million viewers. According to official estimates, TV receivers are being produced for sale at the rate of 15 million a year. If China, with its population of 1 billion people, were a fully developed commercial market it would have a commanding position in the world.

Television services are provided by China Central Television (CCTV), a network operated by the national government with regional subsidiaries. Of the three channels run by CCTV, one concentrates mainly on educational programs while the other two offer general entertainment, with quite a lot of programming imported from the West, including U.S. series dubbed into Mandarin. Distributors generally sell programs to China on a barter basis, giving CCTV the programs free in exchange for advertising positions that are then sold to American or European companies that distribute products in China. The country has two transponders on the AsiaSat satellite to distribute CCTV's signals to the most distant provinces.

CHINA BEACH ▶ hour-long ABC Vietnam War drama series (1988-1991) that was the first to center on the life of women in a MASH unit near combat. Dana Delaney starred as hardboiled nurse Colleen McMurphy, who regularly tended to the wounded and dying as they passed through her MASH unit. Featured were Marg Helgenberger, Robert Picardo, Concetta Tomei, Brian Wimmer, Tim Ryan and Jeff Kober.

The show received numerous awards from various women's organizations, including the Alliance of Women Veterans and the National Commission on Working Women. John Sacret Young, who wrote the screenplay for *A Rumour of War,* was executive producer with William Broyles, Jr., for Warner Bros. Television.

CHiPs ▶ hour-long NBC police drama (1977-83), which was one of the few hits to emerge from dozens of new series to be introduced by the network from 1976 to 1979. The title is an acronym for California Highway Patrol, of which the two leading characters, bachelor motorcyclists Jonathan Baker and Francis "Ponch" Poncherello, were members. Larry Wilcox and Erik Estrada were the principals.

CHOMSKY, MARVIN J. ▶ much sought-after director of motion pictures and TV movies and mini-series. His TV movies include *Attack on Terror: The FBI vs. the Ku Klux Klan* and *The FBI vs. Alvin Karpis, Public Enemy Number One,* while his mini-series include *The Billionaire Boys Club, Evita Peron, Mussolini: The Untold Story,*

Brotherhood of the Rose, and *Peter the Great.* Among his notable series credits are episodes of *Star Trek, Gunsmoke,* and *Roots.* He was a frequent choice to direct the quality dramas produced by Herbert Brodkin and won an Emmy in 1979 for *Holocaust.*

CHRISTENSEN, BRUCE L. ▶ executive who succeeded Lawrence Grossman as president of PBS in 1984, after having served two years as public broadcasting's chief lobbyist in the post of NAPTS president. The native of Utah began his career as a reporter at Salt Lake City's KSL. He then headed Brigham Young University's radio-television operations (KBYU) and later moved to a similar post at the University of Utah (KUED).

CHRISTIANSEN, ROBERT W., and ROSENBERG, RICK ▶ producing team for Tomorrow Entertainment, until the company folded in 1974. They were executive producers of *The Autobiography of Miss Jane Pittman, Queen of the Stardust Ballroom, The Man Who Could Talk to Kids* and *Born Innocent,* among other filmed dramas.

CHRISTMAS IN KOREA ▶ CBS News documentary (Dec. 29, 1953) in the *See It Now* series, unusual for the fact that it did not present events or probe issues but simply recorded the faces, voices and sights of Korea to reveal the impact of the war upon that country and its people. Edward R. Murrow, Ed Scott and Joe Wershba were the reporters, and Murrow produced with Fred W. Friendly.

CHROMA-KEY ▶ a special effect which permits the electronic superimposition of an object or person in front of a background by using a saturated color (usually blue) to form a "hole" in the picture, so that a second video source (camera, VTR or film) is keyed into the hole. More sophisticated technologies such as Ultimatte are able to create a hole and insert an image of a different size, yielding a more natural-looking superimposition.

CHUBBUCK, CHRIS (d. 1974) ▶ anchorwoman of a local program on WXLT-TV Sarasota, Fla., who, on July 15, 1974, put a gun to her head and committed suicide on camera. The incident took place a few minutes after the start of the morning program, *Seacoast Digest.* Chubbuck reportedly said, before producing the gun: "In keeping with Channel 40's policy of bringing you the latest in blood and guts in living color, you're going to see another first—an attempt at suicide."

Connie Chung

CHUNG, CONNIE ▶ correspondent and anchor of the CBS *Evening News* Sunday edition. In 1990 she anchored the CBS News prime-time magazine *Face to Face with Connie Chung,* designed as a weekly investigative magazine, airing such segments as the Bush administration's signals to Iraq prior to Saddam Hussein's invasion of Kuwait, issues surrounding breast implants, and the controversy over testing rapists for HIV. The series was cut back to six specials a year when Chung made an agreement with the network to alter her schedule so that she "could take a very aggressive approach to having a baby."

The previous season, Chung anchored *Saturday Night with Connie Chung,* which featured cover stories and interviews with such subjects as the actor Marlon Brando and the Exxon Valdez captain Joseph Hazelwood. While both *Face to Face* and *Saturday Night* were heavily promoted, the overriding Connie Chung story was about the anchor herself, particularly as two networks engaged in a tug-of-war in the late 1980s for her services, anxious to have an important woman anchor's presence.

Chung joined CBS News in 1971 as a correspondent, then left for KNXT (now KCBS-TV), the CBS Los Angeles station, as anchor. In August 1983 she left for a larger network landscape, joining NBC News as correspondent and anchor of the Saturday edition of *Nightly News,* NBC *News at Sunrise* and one of the many transitory NBC News magazines, *1986.* In 1988 she covered the presidential campaign and elections. In 1989, when Diane Sawyer moved from CBS's *60 Minutes* to ABC's *PrimeTime Live,* CBS was desperate for a luminous woman as star correspondent. For an enhanced salary (estimated at close to $1 million a year) and the option to choose an anchor role from various network storyboards, Chung rejoined CBS.

Chung began her career in 1969 at WTTG in Washington, D.C., where she became a newswriter and on-air reporter. She is married to Maury Povich, host of the syndicated talk show *The Maury Povich Show.*

CHURN ▶ a term used in the cable industry for subscriber cancellation of the premium services such as HBO and Showtime. All pay cable networks program their schedules with a view to keeping churn at a minimum.

CINADER, ROBERT A. (d. 1982) ▶ an executive producer for Jack Webb's Mark VII Ltd. production company, whose credits in that capacity included *Emergency, Chase* and *Sierra.*

***CINDERELLA* ▶** a Rodgers & Hammerstein musical created expressly for television in 1957. The 90-minute show starred Julie Andrews as Cinderella and featured Jon Cypher, Howard Lindsay, Dorothy Stickney, Ilka Chase, Kaye Ballard and Alice Ghostley. It was directed by Ralph Nelson.

CINEMAX ▶ see HBO/Cinemax.

CIRCULAR POLARIZATION ▶ a transmission technique designed to improve reception, particularly in areas subjected to "ghosting." Broadcast antennas in the U.S. normally emit signals on a horizontal plane, but circular polarization transmits both vertically and horizontally. CP tests have been conducted by WLS-TV Chicago and KLOC-TV Modesto, Calif.

If CP is authorized by the FCC, stations electing to transmit in this mode will require new antennas and, in most cases, larger transmitters. Viewers will require newly designed antennas to realize the full benefits of CP, but reception is immediately improved for many viewers using indoor antennas. CP has been in widespread use by FM stations since 1964.

***CISCO KID, THE* ▶** popular syndicated western (1951-56) based on a character created by O. Henry. Duncan Renaldo played the title role and Leo Carillo his sidekick, Pancho. The series was one of the leaders in the Ziv TV stable, and the reruns continue to play in syndication, the films having been reconditioned and reprocessed in 1965.

CITIZENS' AGREEMENTS ▶ formal agreements between stations and local citizens' groups, entered into mostly at renewal time, in which the stations promise to be responsive to the needs of the concerned groups to head off a petition to deny. Frequently this takes the form of an agreement not to play certain programs, such as movies offensive to a minority group or syndicated programs deemed by the complainants too violent or otherwise unsuitable for children. About such agreements, the FCC has been emphatic that the licensee not assign away to outside parties his responsibilities to make broadcast judgments.

Such agreements became less common as deregulation denied citizens the necessary clout to insist on them. With the support of both industry and most broadcast reformers, the FCC in 1988 adopted several reforms designed to address complaints that the process was sometimes abused. Agreements must now be documented in writing and submitted to the FCC for formal approval. Citing First Amendment concerns, the commission also announced that it would no longer enforce agreements involving programming, leaving the matter to local contract law.

Runaway slave-turned-Union drummer, from *The Civil War*

***CIVIL WAR, THE* ▶** Ken and Rick Burns's 11-hour documentary on America's tragic and perilous war. Aired on public TV in five episodes on successive nights, the documentary attracted record audiences, the largest ever for the debut of a PBS series, giving the public medium an unprecedented level of attention. In some markets the show's ratings were higher than its commercial competition.

The makers deftly combined more than 3000 still images with eye-witness accounts voiced by professional actors, plus the music of the period and the narration of historian

Shelby Foote, to tell a Homeric tale of the war from the perspective of the generals, the politicians and ordinary people. The television series also produced a companion best-selling book and a popular album of the show's music, *Ashokan Farewell,* composed by Jay Ungar.

The Civil War was six years and $3.5 million in the making and was produced by Ken Burns's own company, Florentine Productions, in collaboration with WETA-TV Washington. Funding came from a variety of sources, including a $1 million underwriting grant from General Motors.

CIVILISATION ▶ 13-part BBC cultural series (1970) that created a sensation on PBS for its scope, informational content and viewing appeal. With it, Lord Kenneth Clark, who created, wrote and hosted the series, broke ground for a raft of other series examining aspects of life from a historical perspective, notably Jacob Bronowski's *The Ascent of Man* and Alistair Cooke's *America.*

Civilisation, which had several repeats on PBS, traced the development of Western culture from the seventh to the 19th centuries through paintings, sculpture, architecture and music. Apart from his scholarly achievement, Lord Clark was appreciated for his effective TV projection, which was neither priggish nor condescending. Testifying to the success of the series was the fact that a Harper & Row book based on the scripts was on the best-seller list for eight months and sold 230,000 copies at $15 each.

CLAMPETT, BOB (d. 1984) ▶ creator of classic cartoon characters, including Bugs Bunny, Tweety Bird and Porky Pig for Warner Bros. and Beany & Cecil for his own company. He not only produced, directed and wrote episodes featuring these characters but also performed some of the voices and composed the music.

CLARK, DICK ▶ TV show host and head of Dick Clark Productions, a company specializing in youth-oriented programs and rock artist tours. Best known for his teenage pop music series *American Bandstand,* which has run continuously on ABC since 1957, Clark branched out in the 1970s to hosting daytime game shows such as *The $10,000 Pyramid* on ABC. He began his career as a radio disc jockey and in the 1950s hosted a local TV record hop show, *American Bandstand,* for WFIL-TV Philadelphia, enjoying uncommon success with a common local program form. In 1957 the show began to be carried by ABC, and Clark became a national TV personality.

With considerable fanfare, NBC in 1978 signed Clark to a contract for a series and specials, but his series for the network that fall, *Dick Clark's Live Wednesday,* failed and was canceled before mid-season. During the 1980s Clark hosted the CBS game show *The New $25,000 Pyramid* and NBC's *TV's Bloopers and Practical Jokes.* In 1984 he celebrated his 30th anniversary as host of *American Bandstand.*

Clark's company also occasionally produces TV movies, such as *A Cry For Help: The Tracey Thurman Story* and *Death In Texas,* a mini-series, both on NBC.

Dick Clark

CLARK, MICHELE (d. 1972) ▶ young CBS News correspondent whose highly promising career ended with her death in a plane crash. In a time when the networks were under pressure to provide opportunities for minorities and women, Clark, who was black, attractive and an able TV journalist, moved to the CBS News forefront almost immediately after her graduation from Columbia's Graduate School of Journalism in 1970. Columbia's broadcast fellowship program for minorities, funded by CBS, NBC and the Ford Foundation, was renamed the Michele Clark Fellowship Program in her honor.

CLEARANCE ▶ the acceptance of a network show by a station. Since stations have the right to reject a program or series from the network, they govern the program's potential distribution. A series that receives inadequate clearance, such as *Calucci's Department* on CBS in 1973, is usually doomed before it goes on the air for lack of access to the full national audience. In some instances, however, new programs with low clearances were so popular in the cities where they were carried that the other stations hastily cleared the time for them.

Network o&os rarely deny clearance to a network show.

CLIO AWARDS (AMERICAN TV FESTIVAL AWARDS) ▶ annual competition by the advertising and commercials-production industries for the best American-made radio and TV advertisements. Awards in television are presented for 34 categories of product campaigns and for 15 craft categories (cinematography, editing, writing, etc.). Radio has 15 product awards and 7 craft categories.

Under the direction of Bill Evans for two decades, the Clios carried considerable prestige. Then came the 1991 fiasco when, with Evans absent, the badly mismanaged ceremonies seemed to doom the awards. The proceedings got so out of hand at the 1991 event that people from the audience swarmed onto the stage and ran off with the statuettes. Several months later, however, an investor group headed by Ruth Ratny, a Chicago publisher, bought a significant interest in Clio Enterprises with a view to resurrecting the awards and restoring their good name.

CLIPP, ROGER W. (d. 1979) ▶ pioneer broadcaster who built and headed the TV and radio stations group for Walter Annenberg's Triangle Publications, expanding from the initial property, WFIL Philadelphia. After working as an engineer for NBC in New York, Clipp moved to Philadelphia in 1935 as business manager of WFIL. Later he became general manager and, in 1943, president. When Annenberg's *Philadelphia Inquirer* purchased the station in 1946, Clipp embarked on acquiring additional stations as head of Triangle's broadcast division. Clipp retired in 1968, and two years later the group was dismantled—some stations sold to Capital Cities and some to Gateway—when Annenberg became President Nixon's Envoy to the Court of St. James's.

CLOSED CAPTIONING ▶ a television signal supplemented with information hidden in the vertical blanking interval that allows sets equipped with decoders to display on-screen subtitles of a program's dialogue. Its purpose is to make television accessible to the hearing impaired. The subtitles remain hidden from the screen unless they are called up with the decoder. After 1992 all sets sold in the U.S. will be required to have closed captioning decoders.

CLOSED-CIRCUIT (CCTV) ▶ a television installation in which the signal is not broadcast but transmitted to a limited number of receivers or monitors by cable or microwave. Closed-circuit systems are widely used in industry, commerce and education. North American Philips Corp., a leading source of closed-circuit television equipment, estimates the CCTV market at $175 million for 1975, rising to a $300-million annual rate by 1980.

CLT (COMPANIE LUXEMBOURGEOISE DE TELEDIFFUSION) ▶ oldest commercial broadcaster in Europe and one of Europe's largest and most international broadcasters today, although it is based in one of the smaller countries of the continent. CLT is involved with television operations in Germany, France, Belgium and the Netherlands, in addition to its native Luxembourg, and seemingly has lines out everywhere.

Founded in 1930, it began commercial radio broadcasting in 1931 and commercial television transmissions in 1954, under an exclusive franchise from the Luxembourg government. Still, only after 20 years when it entered Belgian cable did CLT start earning money from television. Today CLT has major shareholdings in Germany's RTL Plus, French-speaking Belgium's RTL-TVI, and France's M6. It also has interests in a number of European independent production companies, notably France's Hamster, and is always near the top of the list whenever prospective buyers or investors are involved in new European enterprises. CLT also maintains close links to fellow Luxembourg company Societe Europeene de Satellites, which operates the Astra satellite and transmits some of CLT's channels. CLT today is partly owned by the French advertising agency, Havas.

CLUTTER ▶ the congestion of nonprogram matter between shows, including commercials, program credits, previews of next week's episode, promotion for other programs, public service announcements, station identification, network identification, billboards and program titles. All constitute messages and are recognized by the television industry as a source of viewer irritation and by the advertising industry as vitiating the impact of the commercial. Yet, while the clutter menace has been discussed for years, little apparently can be done about it. Station and network identification are necessary, and the craft unions require that credits be given. Moreover, it has been established that on-the-air promotion helps to build audience for other television shows, and public service spots have to be accommodated.

CNBC (CONSUMER NEWS AND BUSINESS CHANNEL) ▶ 24-hour basic-cable network offering business and financial information, with a current audience reach of 17 million homes. It was launched by NBC in April 1989 and soon after was folded into Rainbow Programming Enterprises, when NBC bought a 50% stake in that subsidiary of Cablevision Systems Corp. That was done, at least in part, to increase CNBC's national penetration on cable, since it was paltry at the start. The channel came on as a competitor to FNN (Financial News Network) at the height of a national interest in business news. CNBC took over financially troubled FNN in 1991, following a bout in court with the rival bidder, a partnership of Group W and Dow Jones, which challenged the acquisition on anti-trust grounds. Along with a number of business-oriented programs and news wheels, CNBC created programs revolving around such personalities as Dick Cavett and Morton Downey, Jr. Al Barber is CNBC's president.

CNN (CABLE NEWS NETWORK) ▶ Ted Turner's renowned round-the-clock all-news network founded in 1980 and operated from Atlanta; in a scant few years it established itself as one of the world's premiere news organizations. Delivered worldwide by satellite, it is subscribed to by broadcast stations and hotels on every continent and serves as a visual wire service in newsrooms around the globe. In the U.S., CNN frequently outclasses the three networks at covering major breaking stories, although it operates on a more modest budget. As one of the most desired of the basic-cable services, CNN reaches close to 60 million households in the U.S. and is carried in 90 other countries. It has achieved a profound global influence in a relatively short time and enjoys a prestige abroad surpassing that of the major networks.

CNN Headline News, a companion channel that provides a 24-hour continuing wheel of 30-minute news summaries, is not as widely carried as CNN. It was created to fend off a challenge by a pair of news networks that Group W and ABC were preparing to launch in 1982. With Headline News, then known as CNN-2, Turner beat his rivals to the punch.

The success of CNN has been nothing short of remarkable. Its prospects seemed poor when it was launched: cable's national penetration in 1980 was barely 30%, and Turner himself had no background in news. A number of leading American news organizations, including CBS and Post-Newsweek, had considered starting a cable news channel in 1979 but decided the potential audience was too small to justify it. Turner hired veteran broadcast news executive Reese Schonfeld to create the network, and he featured a single on-air star in Daniel Schorr, who had recently left CBS.

CNN lost millions of dollars the first two years but then turned the corner, and by the end of the decade the two ad-supported channels were making substantial profits. On typical days CNN's ratings are in the low single digits, but when major international news events occur the numbers have been known to soar into the teens, excellent for a cable network.

CNN's greatest journalistic and ratings performance came with the outbreak of the Persian Gulf War in January 1991. For many Americans, watching the channel became an addiction, and it was the primary news source for many world leaders. The coverage catapulted CNN anchor Bernard Shaw and such correspondents as John Holliman and Peter Arnett into the front ranks of broadcast journalism.

Thomas Johnston currently heads the CNN organization. Paul Amos is executive vice president of news programming and Jon Petrovich executive vice president of Headline News.

COACH ▶ ABC sitcom (1989—) that revealed the comedic ability of character actor Craig T. Nelson, whose only other regular TV role was the lead in the short-lived *Call to Glory.* In *Coach* Nelson portrays the inept and obsessive football coach of a Minnesota university whose relationship with a beautiful, level-headed TV reporter, played by Shelley Fabares, reveals both his bull-headed and sensitive sides. Co-starring as Nelson's bumbling assistant coaches are Jerry Van Dyke and Bill Fagerbakke.

Produced by Bungalow 78 Productions for Universal Television, *Coach*'s executive producer is Barry Kemp, the show's creator.

COALITION FOR BETTER TELEVISION, THE ▶ organization formed in February 1981 for the purpose of driving out the kinds of television programs its members considered morally offensive. Led by the Rev. Donald E. Wildmon, a United Methodist minister from Tupelo, Miss., the Coalition—claiming a membership of 300 fundamentalist and conservative groups—announced that it would begin monitoring prime-time programs for three months to determine by consensus which were the most abusive of traditionally wholesome values. Once the list was produced, the organization would identify the advertisers in those programs and urge its members to boycott their products.

The boycott might not have been taken seriously were it not for the fact that a key member of the coalition, and its largest financial contributor, was the Moral Majority, led by the charismatic and politically influential Reverend Jerry Falwell. The Moral Majority, formed in 1979, achieved its visibility initially by attacking television's excesses; it then branched into politics. The principal representative of the Religious New Right, it proved a powerful force in the 1980 elections. Falwell's personal popularity and power was boosted by the election of President Reagan, and the stature of the organization itself rose when Reagan selected as his religious-affairs adviser the Reverend Robert Billings, executive director of the Moral Majority.

In saturating the media to discuss the boycott—arguing that the Coalition was not practicing censorship but free speech—Falwell conveyed a sense of a snowballing movement in the country; and the organization's initiative began to be taken quite seriously. The president of Procter & Gamble supported the Coalition's views in a widely publicized speech, and a number of network advertisers began sending representatives to Tupelo for meetings with Wildmon. These visits convinced the minister that reforms were at hand, and he called off the 1981 boycott.

A year later, however, he revived the threat and in March declared a boycott against NBC, its parent, RCA, and all the RCA subsidiaries, including Hertz auto rentals. Saying that NBC had done the least to clean up its programming, Wildmon cited *Saturday Night Live* and *Hill Street Blues* as shows that were notably objectionable.

But this time, Falwell and the Moral Majority were not supporting the effort, and the boycott was perceived as arbitrary and opportunistic. NBC was considered to have been selected as victim because, as the weakest and most financially troubled of the networks, it would feel the effects of a boycott more than the others and would be most likely to respond to the censorial demands of the Coalition. In some critical circles, Wildmon lost sympathy and credibility.

COAXIAL CABLE (COAX) ▶ a transmission line consisting of a tube of conducting material surrounding a central conductor held in place by insulation, widely used to carry television signals. The first inter-city television networking was via coaxial cable of the American Telephone & Telegraph Co., but these interconnections now have been largely replaced by microwave relays, and in some cases by satellite, both of which have higher signal-carrying capacity and are more economical.

Coaxial cable is still widely used in cable-TV systems, master antenna (MATV) distribution systems in apartment houses and, increasingly, in home color television installations because it is less susceptible to interference than other types of antenna-to-set connections. Fiber optics, which can carry an even wider band of frequencies and cleaner signals, will probably replace coaxial cable as systems are rebuilt or upgraded.

COBB, GROVER C. (d. 1975) ▶ a leading industry figure who served as executive v.p. of NAB from 1973 until his death. He was also v.p. of broadcasting for the Gannett Co. since 1969 and before that part owner and general manager of KVGB Radio in Great Bend, Kan.

COCA, IMOGENE ▶ comedienne whose career held great promise, but actually reached its height when she was teamed with Sid Caesar on NBC's memorable *Your Show of Shows* in the early 1950s. Neither she nor Caesar enjoyed much success in TV after their split in 1954. They reunited for a series in 1958 but it failed, as did Coca's situation comedy *Grindl* (1963), in which she played a housemaid.

COE, FRED (d. 1979) ▶ noted producer of TV plays when drama was in flower in the medium and, in the early years, manager of new program development for NBC. He was executive producer of *Mr. Peepers* (1952-53), producer-director of *Television Playhouse* (1948-53) and producer of *Producers' Showcase* (1954-55) and *Playwrights '56,* among others.

COHEN, ALEXANDER ▶ Broadway producer who occasionally works in television as a producer of specials. He produced the Tony Awards telecasts from 1967 to 1986. Other credits include such specials as *A World of Love* on CBS for UNICEF (1970), *Marlene Dietrich's I Wish You Love* (1972), birthday celebrations for both CBS and NBC, the Emmy Awards shows, *Night of 100 Stars* and *Night of 100 Stars II* (1982 and 1985, respectively), *The Placido Domingo Special* (1985) and the *ACE Awards* show (1987). Cohen has also produced numerous plays on Broadway and in London's West End.

COHEN, FRED M. ▶ president of King World International and responsible for the foreign distribution of King World program properties, including its game shows. He also is charged with exploring international venture opportunities. Cohen has spent most of his career in the international field, having worked previously for Sunbow Productions, HBO Enterprises and Time-Life Films.

COINCIDENTALS ▶ audience research conducted at the time of broadcast, principally by telephone, to give stations a sense of how certain special local programs are performing. Coincidentals were more prevalent in earlier times, before Nielsen began metering key markets for overnight ratings. They are still employed, though rarely, in the markets that are not metered for overnights.

COLE, NAT (KING) (d. 1965) ▶ a top recording artist who became the first black person to have his own network variety series (1957), but it was to be the shame of network television. In a period before the civil rights movement, and in a time when TV shows needed sponsorship to survive, no national advertiser would buy the Cole series for fear of a boycott in the South. Many performers rallied to its support and offered to appear free, but it was to no avail. The NBC show was canceled early in 1958.

COLEMAN, DABNEY ▶ character actor who since 1966 has appeared in off- beat roles in six comedy series, starting with *That Girl,* in which he played Marlo Thomas's neighbor. In the mid-1970s he played the mayor in the bizarre soap parody, *Mary Hartman, Mary Hartman,* and in the 1980s he starred as the self-centered talk show host in *Buffalo Bill,* one of the most repugnant but funny characters on TV. Other roles have included a part in the very short-lived series *Apple Pie* and starring roles in both *The Slap Maxwell Story* (1988) and *Drexell's Class* (1991).

Coleman has also played major roles in motion pictures and made-for-TV movies, notably *Baby M* (1988).

COLGATE COMEDY HOUR, THE ▶ comedy-variety series that ran on NBC from 1950-55. It presented some of the biggest names in comedy of that time as rotating hosts. The show broke ground in other areas as well: it was the first commercial series to originate in Hollywood and the first to be telecast in color.

Principal hosts were Eddie Cantor, Martin & Lewis, Abbott & Costello, Bob Hope, and Jimmy Durante. In the summer of 1955 the sponsor attempted to widen the scope and renamed the show *The Colgate Variety Hour,* allowing for the inclusion of movie clips and film stars, but found it could not sustain the greater cost of production.

COLIN, RALPH ▶ outside counsel to CBS for more than 40 years, a member of its board of directors and personal lawyer to chairman William S. Paley. After a dispute with Paley in 1969, reportedly on matters concerning the Museum of Modern Art, of which both men were trustees, Colin was abruptly dismissed as attorney, and he resigned from the CBS board in anticipation of Paley's next action. Colin had been with CBS even before Paley, having worked for Jerome H. Louchheim, whose interests in the young network Paley purchased.

COLLEGE BASKETBALL ▶ one of the most televised sports with more than 1,000 games delivered each year, though fewer than 90 are provided by the three big networks during the regular season. College basketball is a staple of local TV stations and the national and regional cable TV networks. Rights are negotiated separately by college basketball conferences, but the annual 64-team tournament to determine the nation's number one college team is controlled by the National Collegiate Athletic Association (NCAA).

In 1989 CBS made a move to secure the tournament, considered by many the most exciting of sports spectacles, by paying the NCAA $1 billion for a seven-year contract. Under the previous contract CBS paid an average of $57.7 million a year; the new one averages out to $142.8 million a year. But the tournament with "March Madness" and the "Final Four" was considered vital to the CBS strategy of establishing itself as the network of major events. The $1 billion contract also includes championships for women's basketball, for the men's teams of smaller schools, and other events such as wrestling, soccer and volleyball. Under CBS's former contract, only six such championships aired while under the new 17 were telecast. One of the key changes effected by the contract was that ESPN would no longer do the first round of the NCAA basketball playoffs.

COLLEGE BOWL ▶ see Game Shows.

COLLEGE FOOTBALL ▶ popular sporting events whose television rights were governed by the National Collegiate Athletic Association (NCAA) from Jan. 11, 1952, to June 27, 1984, when the U.S. Supreme Court ended the NCAA's control. The high court agreed with two lower federal courts that the collegiate governing body's exclusive power to regulate the number of television appearances by a football team and to negotiate the price of those appearances was an "unreasonable restraint of trade" that violated the Sherman Antitrust Act.

The verdict was the outcome of a suit brought by the University of Oklahoma and the University of Georgia Athletic Association against the NCAA, charging that the national association's television controls constituted price fixing and other illegalities under the Sherman Act. Both schools belonged to the College Football Association, a group of approximately 60 of the nation's top football schools, which contended that football telecasts are the property rights of the individual colleges.

The Supreme Court action wiped out the final two years of the existing NCAA four-year contract with ABC and CBS, under which each network paid close to $132 million a year for the right to broadcast 35 college games, either nationally or regionally.

The arrangement at issue took root on Jan. 11, 1952, when the NCAA membership voted 163-8 to establish an association-wide television plan. The concern of most members was that if individual colleges were allowed to sell TV rights to the highest bidder, then only the most popular of the football schools—like Notre Dame—would be seen on television each week and earn all the television money. Under the NCAA plan adopted, no college team could appear more than six times in two years, and the network that owned the rights had to schedule appearances for at least 82 schools in each two-year period. No school was permitted to negotiate television rights on its own.

In 1984, after the court's decision, two major college football packages emerged: Big Ten/Pac Ten and the CFA. In addition, other conferences and teams made separate deals with national and regional cable networks and TV stations. The number of college games available to a viewer went from two network games on a weekend in 1983 to twelve or more games in the 1990s for homes with cable.

The CFA won its battle for independence. But after the CFA had signed a $210 million contract with ABC, Notre Dame split from the group and signed a separate contract with NBC starting in 1991.

With the Supreme Court decision, college football on TV went from being a controlled event to a programming commodity. While the sport's explosion on TV was undoubtedly welcomed by the fans, the fragmenting of the audience caused by the tremendous increase in games made it difficult to find the advertising to support all the activity.

COLLINGWOOD, CHARLES (d. 1985) ▶ correspondent for CBS News beginning in 1941 who worked under Edward R. Murrow during World War II. Later he became United Nations correspondent and in 1964 chief European correspondent based in London. His annual *Vietnam Perspective* telecasts (1965-69) won several journalism awards in the field of foreign affairs. In 1968 he became the first network newsman admitted into North Vietnam, which resulted in two specials: *Charles Collingwood's Report from Hanoi* and *Hanoi: A Report by Charles Collingwood.* He also anchored special telecasts on the Middle East conflict, and in 1970 and 1971 was moderator of the CBS year-end reviews featuring its correspondents.

During the 1950s, while based in the U.S., he covered the political conventions, served as White House correspondent, and took a two-year leave of absence to become special assistant to Averell Harriman, then Director for Mutual Security in Washington. He returned to CBS News in 1957 as London bureau chief but was called back in 1959 to succeed Murrow as host of the *Person To Person* series. He was also host of such public affairs series as *Conquest, Adventure* and *WCBS-TV Views the Press* and moderated the first *CBS Town Meeting of the Air* to be transmitted by satellite, which involved a discussion among government officials in New York, Washington, London and Paris. He was also the host for *A Tour of the White House with Mrs. John F. Kennedy* (Feb. 14, 1962).

COLLINS, HAL ▶ comedy writer of the 1950s, who wrote for Milton Berle's *Texaco Star Theatre* (1948-52) and the Red Buttons shows (1952-55). Later he was associate producer of the Berle specials and attempted a comeback on ABC with *Jackpot Bowling* (1960-61).

COLLINS, JOAN ▶ sultry actress who, after more than 50 movies and some 30 TV series, became a big star when she landed the role of super-bitch Alexis Carrington in *Dynasty* in 1981. The mini-series *Sins* (1985), in which she starred, was produced by her own company.

COLLINS, LeROY (d. 1991) ▶ former Florida governor who became president of the National Association of Broadcasters (NAB) in 1961, serving almost four years. He became unpopular within the industry when he mistook what was essentially a lobbying job for an inspirational one and continually exhorted the industry to aspire to higher goals than the pursuit of profit. His calls for more public service in the public interest did not sit well with broadcasters who felt the industry needed a defender and not another critic. Nor did he endear himself to the NAB membership when he advocated the adoption of industry restrictions on cigarette advertising aimed at youth. Collins resigned from the NAB in 1964, after the board voted 22-19 to retain him, to head a new civil rights division in the Justice Department.

COLLINS, REID ▶ co-anchor for CNN's *World Day* and *NewsHour,* in addition to reporting and anchoring major national and international stories. He was at the anchor desk during the Gulf War and covered the Iran/Contra hearings—two of the network's highest-rated events ever.

Prior to joining CNN in 1985, he spent 20 years as a correspondent for CBS Radio, anchoring the *World News Roundup* and news-on-the-hour broadcasts. He was a correspondent for WNEW-AM in New York, where his coverage of President Kennedy's funeral was turned into a record album that became a part of the audio collection of the Kennedy Library. Collins began his career as a radio reporter in Montana.

COLLYER, BUD (d. 1979) ▶ indomitable game-show host whose chief credits, among many, include *Beat the Clock,* which premiered in 1950, and *To Tell the Truth,* the big CBS hit that began in 1956.

COLOMBIA ▶ South American country with a fairly unique television system, one whose three national channels are governed by a single state organization, Inravision, which awards contracts to programmers and assigns them airtime on one or another of the channels. Two of the channels are general interest and the third educational. All broadcast 16 hours a day, and all are based in Bogota. Inravision is responsible for serving the entire country, even the remote areas like the Amazon region, which it does either by satellite or by shipping cassettes. The country has a population of 32 million and approximately 4.5 million television households. Cable penetration is at around 5% and is concentrated in Bogota, Cali and two or three other large cities. The attraction of cable is that it brings in Mexican and U.S. channels.

COLONEL FLACK **▶** early comedy-dramatic series on CBS (1953) about a likeable con-man and his aide, played by Alan Mowbray (Colonel Humphrey Flack) and Frank Jenks (Uthas P. "Patsy" Garvey). Produced by Jody Pam Productions with Stark-Layton.

COLOR TELEVISION ▶ a technology that was in progress but not yet perfected when the television boom occurred in the late 1940s, and which, in the United States, led to a bitter fight between RCA and CBS for the color system that would prevail. The arrival of colorcasting in the U.S. is marked as Dec. 17, 1953, when a modified version of RCA's "compatible," all-electronic (dot sequential) system was approved by the FCC—in a reversal of its decision three years earlier to authorize the CBS "spinning disk" (field sequential) system.

CBS had been the first to perfect color transmission, but although its system offered a superior picture the programs broadcast in color could not be received on existing unmodified black & white receivers. There were, at the time, almost 20 million black & white TV sets in homes and millions more in manufacture. RCA challenged the FCC's approval of the CBS system, arguing that its own engineers were rapidly developing a color system that would be compatible with the black & white sets; and although the courts denied the RCA appeals to set aside the FCC decision in CBS's favor, the time was gained for RCA and others working within the industry-wide National Television System Committee (NTSC) to develop a compatible system which ultimately was approved by the FCC in place of the CBS system. DuMont and Chromatic TV Inc. (CTI) also vied for the commission's approval with their systems.

RCA's successful petition for the American color system stated that the corporation had spent $21 million in research and promised that it would expedite equipment production in its manufacturing division and would promptly begin colorcasting over its network, NBC.

During 1954 only 1% of U.S. homes had color sets, but both NBC and CBS began televising some of their programs in color. The fact that colorcasting raised costs that could not be passed on to the advertiser, since he derived no significant benefits from it, deterred CBS. But NBC steadily increased its color output to help its parent company sell color TV sets. In 1956 NBC's Chicago station WNBQ (now WMAQ-TV) became the first in the world to originate locally all-color signals, as a prototype for the company. Approximately 2% of the homes in Chicago could receive color at the time. Gen. David Sarnoff, chairman of RCA, predicted then that "by 1963, all of America would be blanketed by color, and each and every home will be receiving its entertainment in full color."

The prophesy was not realized on schedule. The high cost of conversion to color production and transmission, coupled with a slowness in the manufacture of color TV sets, found NBC alone offering a regular schedule of color programs through 1964. But by 1965 the penetration of color sets in the U.S. was sufficient to be a significant factor in program ratings, and in the spring of that year CBS made a sudden announcement that it would present virtually all its fall schedule in color, which meant that it would have to reshoot several of its pilots that had been made in black & white. Prompting the CBS action, in part, was the fact that it had just replaced James T. Aubrey with John A. Schneider as president of CBS-TV, and the dramatic move to color underscored the start of a new era. Not to be left behind, ABC immediately tooled up and became a full-color network the following year.

By 1977 more than 75% of TV-equipped homes were able to receive color on one or more sets. By 1990 the market was virtually saturated.

COLORIZATION ▶ the conversion of black-and-white films to color by use of computer technology. Although expensive, the process has been used extensively by such organizations as Turner Broadcasting because TV viewers are thought to be more receptive to color programming. Because the colorizing of old movies and TV shows improves their ability to be programmed in desirable time periods, it enhances their market value. The practice is controversial, however, drawing fire from arts organizations and film directors who protest that it perverts the original intent and artistic vision of a film's creator.

***COLT '45* ▶** western series on ABC (1957-59) produced by Warner Bros. and featuring Wayde Preston as Christopher Colt and, during Preston's temporary absence from the show, Donald May as Christopher's cousin Sam.

COLUMBIA PICTURES TV (CPT) ▶ See Screen Gems.

***COLUMBO* ▶** popular detective series airing approximately once a month in a rotation with three other detective series in the NBC showcase *Sunday Mystery Movie.* A vehicle for Peter Falk, who portrayed a shambling and seemingly ineffectual super sleuth, it premiered in the fall of 1971 and was by far the most successful of the rotating elements. *Columbo* was created by Richard Levinson and William Link, who modeled the character after Petrovitch, the detective in Dostoevski's *Crime and Punishment.* Before it became a series the concept was introduced in two "World Premiere" movies, *Prescription: Murder* (1968) and *Ransom for a Dead Man* (1971). Depending on the network's scheduling needs, the series episodes ran either 90 minutes or two hours. Roland Kibbee and Dean Hargrove were executive producers for Universal TV. The series ended in 1977 because Falk tired of it.

NBC attempted to revive the premise, if not the show, in the spring of 1979 by trying out a limited series entitled *Mrs. Columbo,* in which Kate Mulgrew starred as the wife of Columbo who busies herself solving crimes. The program did well enough to make the fall schedule under the new title, *Kate Columbo,* retitled *Kate Loves a Mystery* before its cancellation at the season's end. In the late 1980s, *Columbo* returned to television on ABC's *Mystery Wheel* and then came back periodically, like *Perry Mason,* in the form of TV movies.

***COMBAT!* ▶** hour-long adventure series on the exploits of an Army unit during World War II that featured Rick Jason as Lieutenant Gil Hanley, Vic Morrow as Sergeant Chip Saunders and guest stars. It premiered on ABC in October 1962 and ran until the spring of 1967 via Selmur Productions.

COMEDY CENTRAL ▶ basic-cable network that started in April 1991 after the merger of two fledgling comedy channels, HA! and The Comedy Channel, that were competing for the same niche in 1990 and for channel space on local systems. The combined channel reached 18 million households the first year. Its programming consists chiefly of sitcom reruns and original stand-up comedy performances.

The merger helped heal some longstanding animosities between Viacom International, HA!'s owner, and Time Warner, which owned The Comedy Channel.

COMMERCIAL TV IN EUROPE ▶ the trend of the 1980s across the continent. After decades of adhering to state-run public television systems, usually with two channels of service, the countries one by one began privatizing in the latter half of the 1980s or authorizing new channels to private interests. The technologies of cable and satellites made it apparent to most European governments that television would eventually have to be opened to commerce. Speeding the process were the large publishing concerns, which through all the previous years had used their power with government to hold back commercial television. Once it became clear that private television was inevitable, the leading publishers pushed for the licenses.

The first of the countries to break ranks was France, which in mid-decade privatized its premier public television network, TF1, and opened its airwaves to seven national channels (two of which were carry-over public stations). By its action, France is considered by Europeans to have started a revolution. Within five years, the entire television landscape of Europe had changed, as the American style of television—programmed for profit—spread terrestrially and by satellite.

Actually it was Italy and not France that was in the vanguard, but Italy's move into commercial television in 1975 did not set forces in motion beyond its frontiers. Italy opened the airwaves to commerce—and to all comers—without regulation for strictly political reasons. It happened after the Communists won the elections in Bologna and demanded a national channel. Interestingly, Italy had had a sluggish economy before it opened itself to commercial television, and 10 years later had prospered to where its standard of living surpassed that of Britain. The U.K. had private television even before Italy, beginning in 1956, but it was limited and was required to conform to public service broadcasting standards.

Germany followed France into the adoption of private TV, and then came Spain, and later Denmark, Greece, and Portugal. By the 1990s, Norway and Sweden had begun to cave in, but tentatively. With the disintegration of the Soviet bloc, much of Eastern Europe seemed disposed to accepting commercial broadcasting in some form.

Commercial television began to spread in Western Europe just as the 12 nations of the European Community began planning for a common market in 1992. In anticipation of the unification of the European market, advertising agencies began to consolidate in the belief, early on, that marketing could address all 12 members at once. But such agencies found that although economic structures and practices might be harmonized in the unified market, the cultural and language differences remained—and probably always will. The ideal of creating one television commercial for all, as can be done in the 50 states of the U.S., proved unrealistic with countries as diverse as those of Europe.

COMMON CARRIER ▶ designating a medium that delivers messages prepared by others for a fee and that is required by law to sell or give access to all who desire it, at posted rates, on a nondiscriminatory basis. Notable examples are telephone, telegraph and certain communications satellites.

The Communications Act of 1934 established that broadcasting would not be a common carrier, but there are many pursuing such a designation for cable TV, believing it would be in the public interest. To a certain degree, cable TV already performs as a common carrier—wherever it provides leased-access channels. But most cable operators are opposed to being given full common carrier status (prohibiting them from operating company channels for program origination) because that would give the FCC the right to regulate profits. They reason that, under those circumstances, investment capital for the expansion of cable would probably dry up.

COMMUNICATIONS ACT OF 1934 ▶ the embodiment of national policy for communications in the U.S.; its basic concept is one of private ownership of broadcasting, telephone and telegraph systems, with an administrative agency overseeing these private interests and regulating them in the public interest.

The goal of the Act was to make available to all people a rapid, efficient, national and worldwide wire and radio communications service with adequate facilities at reasonable charge. To accomplish this goal Congress created the FCC (Federal Communications Commission).

While the agency's predecessor, the Federal Radio Commission, had done much to alleviate the chaotic conditions that had existed in radio, the FRC had no authority to regulate telephone and telegraph companies. The growing awareness that these industries were highly interrelated and that the country was in need of a coherent national policy for communications led to the establishment of the Federal Communications Act in 1934.

The FCC's authority under the Act is clearly limited to interstate communications; those activities that remain local in nature are the responsibility of the states. While states have the right to regulate the rates and services for such communications as local telephone calls, the courts have given an expansive interpretation to this provision. For instance, they have determined that radio and television signals—while they remain strictly within one state's territory—may be regulated by the FCC because those signals may affect or cause interference with other radio and signals. By this reasoning, the FCC is also enabled to regulate significant aspects of the cable-TV industry.

The Act structured the telephone, telegraph and broadcast industries in entirely different ways. Recognizing that telephone and telegraph were national monopolies, the Act designated them common carriers—that is, carriers for hire which must furnish service on request, at reasonable prices as defined by the commission. Broadcasting, however, was conceived as a private ownership system based on a concept of competition and operation in the public interest.

The theory behind the Act is that since broadcasters are allowed to use the public airwaves they must agree to operate as public trustees, serving the public interest, convenience and necessity. The law set up a concept of short-term licenses with no vesting of any rights in the private owner of the frequencies allocated. In fact, the Act specifically notes that the granting of any license is not to be construed as creating any right beyond the terms, conditions and periods of the licenses.

With respect to broadcasting, the FCC's authority is to classify stations, prescribe the nature of the service to be rendered, determine what power and type of facilities shall be used and establish times of operation and the areas to be served.

The most important function of the commission is that of allocating portions of the electromagnetic spectrum to various classes of broadcasting service and of assigning frequencies for station operations. In doing so, the FCC is directed by the Act to make a fair, efficient and equitable distribution of broadcast service among the various states and communities.

The commission thus is empowered with broad licensing authority. In considering whether an applicant will operate a broadcast facility in the public interest, the commission may take into account the character of the applicant and his financial and technical qualifications. The commission has the power to deny an application but is required to give the applicant a public hearing before the decision can be final.

If the commission determines that a licensee fails to operate substantially as required by his license or fails to observe or violates any provisions of the Act or regulations, the FCC may issue Cease and Desist orders and, in cases of willful or repeated failures, may revoke a license. While this provision of the Act is quite explicit, the FCC has been reluctant to revoke licenses and has done so only in rare and exceptional circumstances.

A chief reason for that is an ambiguity of the Act which makes it difficult for the FCC to take program service into account in determining whether a station is serving the public interest. While the Act requires the commission to hold the licensee accountable, it also specifically forbids the commission from censoring broadcast programs or from interfering with the right of free speech.

Since networks are not licensed, the FCC does not have any direct authority over them. But the Act does empower the commission to make special regulations applicable to broadcast stations engaged in network operations. The authority granted to the FCC under this provision gives it a form of indirect control over the networks.

The Act has come under increasing criticism over the last generation as impeding the growth of new technologies, but it remains largely intact. After House Communications Subcommittee chairman Lionel Van Deerlin (D-Calif.) failed in 1978-79 to achieve a deregulatory "basement to attic" rewrite of the law, Congress proceeded on a course of updating only as necessary. Other than the Cable Communications Policy Act of 1984, these amendments have been relatively minor. The Children's Television Act of 1990, while actually quite modest, did generate substantial controversy.

COMMUNITY SERVICE GRANT ▶ mode by which the Corporation for Public Broadcasting passes federal funds directly to PTV stations. Under the "partnership agreement" between CPB and PBS in 1973, a sizable percentage of all monies received by CPB from the Federal Government must be distributed to the stations in the system for their unrestricted use (except for construction or the purchase of equipment). Qualified public TV and radio stations apply for the grant, and the amount of the awards is determined by a complex formula, the key to which is the size of the station and its market.

COMO, PERRY ▶ long-popular TV performer of the past, whose easy manner and casual singing style were ideally suited to the intimate medium. Switching back and forth between NBC and CBS, he was one of the few early stars to remain active and popular in TV through the medium's first quarter century. He made his TV debut Dec. 24, 1948 in *The Chesterfield Supper Club,* a 15-minute, thrice-weekly entry on NBC that was a continuation of his four-year-old radio series. In October 1950 he moved to CBS in a weekly variety series, *The Perry Como Show,* which ran five seasons. For the next eight years he was back on NBC, first in a Saturday night variety show whose ratings overwhelmed those of Jackie Gleason, his competitor on CBS, and then (starting in 1959) in a Tuesday night series, *The Kraft Music Hall.*

Como gave up the grind of a weekly series in 1963 to do three to six specials a year, and again he switched between CBS and NBC. The supporting company for most of his variety shows consisted of Frank Gallop as announcer, Goodman Ace as supervisor of scripts and the Mitch Ayres orchestra. In the late 1970s he confined his TV work to two holiday specials a year and eventually retired.

COMPARATIVE HEARINGS ▶ hearings before the FCC in instances when two or more parties apply for the same license, their purpose being to determine which of the applicants is most qualified for the award. An FCC administrative law judge presides over the hearings and issues an initial decision, which may or may not be accepted by the commission in its review of the proceedings.

Over the years the commission has developed a number of comparative criteria to use as a standard in evaluating the applicants and in 1965 issued its definitive criteria for comparison. The commission said it primarily considers programming proposals and the applicant's ability to effectuate the proposals. Other points of comparison are ownership (whether local or remote), ascertainment efforts, staffing and equipment plans, integration of ownership and management, and management's past broadcast record and broadcast experience if it should be outstanding or very poor. A critical factor in awarding licenses is diversity of ownership.

COMPARATIVE RENEWAL ▶ process by which the FCC decides to renew a broadcaster's license upon its expiration or award it to a rival applicant for the station. In theory the commission weighs both proposals for service to the community, but in practice the incumbent's license is almost invariably renewed.

COMPLAINTS AND COMPLIANCES ▶ a division of the FCC established around 1960 as the commission's own investigative arm and as a watchdog over the stations. It was created when the House Legislative Oversight Committee, in its 3.5-year investigation of regulatory agencies during the late 1950s, uncovered abuses and shady practices in broadcasting that had eluded notice by the FCC.

COMPONENT VIDEO ▶ separate handling within a television system of color signals (chrominance) and light signals (luminance). Component systems enable considerable imaging-processing capability and yield high picture quality. Video formats that use component technology include Betacam, MII and D-1.

COMPOSITE VIDEO ▶ television system in which color signals (chrominance) and light signals (luminance) are not separated but rather combined in a one signal. NTSC, used in North America and Japan, is such a system. While composite video cannot yield the high picture quality of component video, it is less expensive.

COMPRESSION ▶ see Video Compression.

COMPULSORY LICENSE ▶ a blanket fee paid by cable operators, as determined by the federal Copyright Royalty Tribunal, for the operators' use of copyrighted material such as programs carried by superstations. The fees are then divided up among affected copyright holders in amounts determined by the government agency. This is the convenient alternative to negotiated, itemized payments for each specific copyright obligation. The practice was controversial from the start.

COMPUSERVE ▶ on-line information service for modem-equipped PC users. A subsidiary of H & R Block Inc., CompuServe began as a company providing business data, then hitched itself to the growing personal computer market by offering video games, news and information services, and "electronic bulletin boards." To access the service, users need communications software that is offered by CompuServe as well as other vendors. As of 1991 CompuServe had 875,000 subscribers and charged $50 per sign-up. A typical hourly fee to use the service was $12.50.

COMSAT ▶ shareholder-owned U.S. communications company providing services to communications carriers, industry, and government. Created in 1963 under provisions of the Communications Satellite Act of 1962, Comsat is the U.S. representative to the International Telecommunications Satellite Organization (Intelsat) and the International Inmarsat Organization. The company's operations are divided into the following areas: international communications over the multiple satellites of the Intelsat and Inmarsat systems; entertainment distribution of video programming to the hotel industry; communications and information systems integration for government and private clients in the U.S. and overseas; and research and development services. As of 1991 the company had 1,500 employees and annual revenues of $456.8 million.

***CONCENTRATION* ▶** see Game Shows.

CONRAD, WILLIAM ▶ actor who became a producer-director and then returned to acting full-time, as star of *Cannon,* in the early 1970s. Conrad had been the star of the radio version of *Gunsmoke* but lacked physical attributes for the role when the series moved to TV. He found work in television as a director and became producer of the *Klondike* series in 1960, before giving up the medium for motion picture production. His portly build and unheroic appearance were right for *Cannon,* which enabled him to resume his acting career 20 years after the visual medium had brought it to a halt. In the 1980-81 season, he starred in *Nero Wolfe* on NBC and later in *Jake and the Fatman,* a CBS hit in the late 1980s and early 1990s.

CONTAM (COMMITTEE ON NATIONWIDE TELEVISION AUDIENCE MEASUREMENT) ▶ industry group of audience research experts established in 1963 to keep check on how Nielsen arrives at its network viewing estimates.

***CONTINENTAL CLASSROOM* ▶** onetime early morning strip on NBC (6:30 a.m.) that began as an experiment in 1958 in the use of commercial channels to teach university-level academic subjects. The project was funded for a three-year period by $1.7 million in grants from the Ford Foundation, the Fund for the Advancement of Education and several business corporations. The first year's program, a refresher course in physics primarily designed for high school teachers, was estimated to have had an audience of around 500,000 regular viewers, including 5,000 teachers who received credit for the course at 270 cooperating institutions. Subsequent courses were in chemistry and contemporary mathematics.

CONTROVERSIAL ISSUES ▶ a critical factor in Fairness Doctrine complaints, since the FCC was explicit in stating that fairness obligations obtain only in matters involving "controversial issues of public importance." Numerous appeals, under the Fairness Doctrine, for time to answer commercials were denied by the FCC on the ground that the issues in dispute were not those of public controversy, among them: *Green v. FCC* [447 F2d 323 (D.C. Cir. 1971)], a case in which public interest petitioners sought time to present opposing views to military recruitment announcements sponsored by the U.S. Armed Forces. The FCC held that recruitment announcements raised no controversial issue, and its decision was affirmed by the D.C. Court of Appeals and the Ninth Circuit Court of Appeals.

Neckritz v. FCC [502 F2d 411 (D.C. Cir. 1974)], was a case in which a public interest advocate sought time to present opposing views to commercials by Chevron, which urged the use of a gasoline (F-310) that Chevron claimed combatted air pollution. The D.C. Court of Appeals affirmed the FCC's judgment that the use of F-310 was not a controversial issue of public importance.

There have been, however, notable instances when the FCC held a fairness complaint to be valid for advertisements, among them: *Wilderness Society and Friends of the Earth Concerning Fairness Doctrine re National Broadcasting Company* [30 FCC 2d 643 (1971)], which grew out of a commercial message by Esso asserting the need for developing Alaska oil reserves quickly. The commercial stressed the capability of the oil companies to retrieve and distribute Alaskan oil without environmental damage. On a petition by public interest groups, the FCC held that the commercial was subject to fairness obligations, and it directed the station (WNBC New York) to inform the commission of the additional material it intended to broadcast to satisfy its Fairness Doctrine obligations.

CONVERSATION WITH DR. J. ROBERT OPPENHEIMER, A ▶ 30-minute CBS News documentary that aired Jan. 4, 1955, probing the mind and heart of the controversial physicist, who had lost his security clearance as a consultant to the Atomic Energy Commission because he had opposed the building of the hydrogen bomb.

The program, which had started out as a feature story on the intellectual resources at Princeton's Institute for Advance Study, settled on the man who headed it because of Edward R. Murrow's fascination with Oppenheimer's genius and humanity. The program was notable as a profile of a brilliant thinker but created problems for CBS News in the McCarthy era because Red-baiters had doubted Oppenheimer's patriotism. Murrow was the reporter and co-producer with Fred W. Friendly.

CONWAY, TIM ▶ a leading TV sketch comedian in the late 1960s and 1970s who appeared destined to play the second banana. He came to notice first as a regular in the situation comedy *McHale's Navy* (1962-66) and then did numerous skits as a guest on variety shows. In 1970 he was given a variety series of his own on CBS but it ran only 13 weeks. He became a regular featured player on *The Carol Burnett Show* in 1975. When that show folded at the end of the 1977-78 season, CBS built another variety series around him, *The Tim Conway Show,* but it fared poorly. Another hour-long series was essayed in the spring of 1980, then was cut back to a half-hour series without musical acts, and in that form ran the entire 1980-81 season. Conway also starred in the comedy *Ace Crawford—Private Eye* in 1983.

COOK, FIELDER ▶ noted director of quality drama during the "golden age," who later became executive producer of *DuPont Show of the Week* in the early 1960s. His more recent directing credits included *The Homecoming* (from which *The Waltons* was derived) and the pilot for *Beacon Hill.*

COOKE, ALISTAIR ▶ British journalist and U.S. television host whose charm and intelligence contributed to the success of *Omnibus* (1952-60), and more recently *Masterpiece Theatre* (1971—). In the early 1970s he created for NBC a series entitled *America: A Personal History of the United States,* which he also wrote and narrated. A naturalized U.S. citizen, he served until 1972 as chief American correspondent for the British paper *The Guardian.* In 1946 he began broadcasting a weekly radio series for the BBC, *Letter From America,* which continues to be heard in 52 countries. But he is best known today as the host of *Masterpiece Theatre* on PBS, which mainly features British mini-series.

Alistair Cooke

COONEY, JOAN GANZ ▶ president of Children's Television Workshop until 1990 and originator of the proposals leading to the production by CTW of *Sesame Street* and *The Electric Company* for public TV.

Trained as a teacher, she worked for a time as a reporter at the *Arizona Republic,* then as a publicist for NBC and the *U.S. Steel Hour,* and later as a producer of documentaries for public television. All this served as basic training for what was to become a significant career in television, one that was responsible for a major development in entertainment.

In 1966 she and Lloyd Morrisett designed the experimental research project for *Sesame Street* and raised $8 million in foundation grants for it. Formed by *Sesame,* CTW later produced *The Electric Company, Feelin' Good, 3-2-1 Contact, Square One TV, Ghostwriter* and several commercial television specials. Cooney won wide recognition as both an innovator and outstanding executive.

COOPER, JACKIE ▶ actor, director, producer and studio executive. A former child movie star, he came into prominence in TV as a star and co-producer of a successful situation comedy in the late 1950s, *Hennessy,* which led to his appointment as head of production for Screen Gems in that studio's most prolific years. In the 1970s he teamed with Bob Finkel in Cooper-Finkel Co., which created a number of situation comedy pilots that did not sell (Finkel producing, Cooper directing). Returning to acting, he had the starring role in *Mobile One,* a short-lived series in 1975. Since then he has concentrated on directing, and he won an Emmy for developing the *White Shadow* pilot.

COOPERMAN, ALVIN ▶ onetime program executive who served three hitches with NBC-TV and, in the intervals, was variously executive director of the Shubert Theaters, president of Madison Square Garden Productions, chairman of Athena Communications Corp. (a cable-TV company), managing director for the Harkness Theater and a producer of TV specials (*The Bolshoi Ballet: Romeo and Juliet*). He also conceived and produced the format for the 1972 Republican National Convention in Miami Beach.

Cooperman's second return to NBC, in 1976, was as program officer for the *Big Event* series of weekly special attractions, with the title of consultant, but he remained for less than a season. In 1967-68, he had returned to become v.p. of special programs for the network. In the mid-1950s, after working as unit manager for the Milton Berle show and later as an associate producer of *Wide Wide World,* he became manager of program sales for NBC and later executive producer of *Producers' Showcase.*

COORS, JOSEPH ▶ ultra-conservative Colorado businessman (executive v.p. of Adolph Coors Brewing Co.) whose flirtation with TV was frustrated on two fronts in 1975 when the Senate Commerce Committee effectively rejected his nomination by President Ford to the CPB board and when the syndicated news company he financed, TVN, folded after losing $5 million in two years.

Coors created TVN (with Robert Pauley, formerly of ABC Radio and Mutual, as chairman) because he believed network news had a liberal bias. The company in 1974 absorbed a competing news service, UPITN, but there were not enough subscribing stations between them to justify the high cost of news gathering and daily transmission over AT&T long lines. Coors withdrew his financial support in October 1975 and TVN was dissolved.

Ironically, only a few weeks earlier Coors had been asked by the Senate Committee to resign his seat on the TVN board to make him a more acceptable nominee to the Corporation for Public Broadcasting (CPB), but Coors refused to do so. The committee's majority disqualified Coors on the conflict of interest issue, but there were other contributing factors.

While his nomination was pending, Coors had written several ill-advised letters to Henry Loomis, president of CPB. One seemed an attempt to influence CPB on selecting a company to construct its proposed satellite earth stations; another expressed displeasure, on behalf of a mortician friend, with a PBS documentary on the high cost of dying. Coors told Loomis he hoped to steer public TV away from programs critical of business, indicating a misapprehension on his part of the board's function.

COP ROCK **▶** innovative—some would say outlandish—police series on ABC in 1990 that interwove rock, rap and gospel songs into standard police melodrama. The show was a creation of Steven Bochco under his $50 million contract with ABC. The interruption of the action by actors breaking into musical performances left viewers baffled and, in fact, uninterested, and the series was canceled in short order.

The cast included Ronny Cox, Barbara Bosson (Bochco's wife), Peter Onorati, Larry Joshua, James McDaniel and Ron McLarty. William Finkelstein, who was co-creator and co-executive producer, had been with Bochco on *Hill Street Blues.* The show was via Twentieth Television.

COPRODUCTIONS ▶ television programs made in a multi-national collaboration with a view to reducing costs for ambitious projects. While European and Canadian producers, out of economic necessity, have engaged in such creative partnerships for years, international coproductions are a fairly new experience for Americans. Cable networks like HBO, USA and TNT took the lead in the U.S., teaming up with certain foreign companies for the joint production of movies and mini-series, sharing the expense with them while dividing up territories for international sales. The foreign influence is often difficult to detect, since the programs tend to employ American stars in at least one of the lead roles, but the end credits increasingly show the involvement of companies well east or well north of Hollywood.

COPYRIGHT LAW REVISION ▶ [Public Law 94-553 (90 Stat. 2541)] bill enacted in 1976 that substantially revised and superseded the 1909 United States Copyright Law; the earlier law had become obsolete, particularly in its inability to remain relevant to the emerging technologies.

The underlying concept of the new law is a single nationwide system of statutory protection for all copyrightable works, whether published or unpublished. For works already under copyright protection, the new law retains the present term of copyright of 28 years from first publication, but it increases the length of the second term to 47 years. For works created after Jan. 1, 1978, the law provides a term lasting for the author's life, plus an additional 50 years after the author's death.

The new law adds a provision to the statute specifically recognizing the principal of "fair use" as a limitation on the exclusive rights of copyright owners, and it indicates factors to be considered in determining whether particular uses fall within this category. In addition to the provision for "fair use," the act lists certain circumstances under which the making or distribution of single copies of works by libraries and archives for noncommercial purposes do not constitute a copyright infringement.

The new law creates a Copyright Royalty Tribunal whose purpose is to determine whether copyright royalty rates, in certain categories where such rates are established in the law, are reasonable and, if not, to adjust them.

In addition, the Copyright Law retains provisions added in 1972 to the old copyright law, which accords protection against the unauthorized duplication of sound recordings but does not create a performance right for sound recordings as such.

Passage of the new copyright act was delayed by the difficulties in resolving a number of complex policy issues, some of which related to the broadcasting industry. One snag concerned public TV. Under the old law, there was a general exemption for public performance of nondramatic literary and musical works when the performance was not "for profit." This was generally interpreted to include a public television broadcast.

The new law removes the general exemption. Instead, it provides several specific exemptions for certain types of nonprofit uses, including performances in classrooms and in instructional broadcasting. Noncommercial transmissions by public broadcasters of published musical and graphic works would be subject to a compulsory license. Copyright owners and public broadcasting entities who do not reach voluntary agreement will be subject to the terms and rates prescribed by the Copyright Royalty Tribunal.

Broadcasting organizations in general are given a limited privilege of making "ephemeral recordings" of their broadcasts under the new law.

Where cable television is concerned, the new law provides for the payment—under a system of compulsory licensing—of certain royalties for the secondary transmission of copyrighted works on cable systems. The amounts are to be paid to the Register of Copyrights for later distribution to the copyright owners by the Copyright Royalty Tribunal. Although these provisions took effect only in 1978, they have already come under attack from program producers and sports interests, who maintain that the compulsory license deprives them of control over their product and that the levels of compensation set in the Act are far too low. They have proposed that Congress repeal the cable-TV provisions and substitute a direct negotiation system in a new Federal communications act.

Also to be paid in this manner are annual royalty fees by jukebox owners. The new law removes the exemption for performances of copyrighted music on jukeboxes and substitutes a system of compulsory licenses.

As a mandatory condition of copyright protection, the old law required that the published copies of a work bear a copyright notice. Under the new act, notice is required on published copies, but omission or errors will not immediately result in forfeiture of the copyright and can be corrected within certain time limits. Innocent infringers misled by the omission or error will be shielded from liability.

As under the old law, registration is not a condition of copyright protection but is a prerequisite to an infringement suit. Subject to certain exceptions, the remedies of the statutory damages and attorney fees will not be available for infringements occurring before registration.

Copies of phonograph records or works published with the notice of copyright that are not registered are required to be deposited for the collection of the Library of Congress, not as a condition of copyright protection but under the provisions of the law making the copyright owners subject to certain penalties for the failure to deposit after a demand by the Register of Copyright.

CORONATION STREET ▶ early-evening British serial on the commercial network that has been one of the most popular shows in the U.K. for more than three decades but literally could not be given away free in the U.S. Frustrated at the indifference to the series in the States, Lord Sidney Bernstein, head of Granada Television, which produces the show, offered it free in the early 1970s to any American station that would guarantee the serial a substantial run. There were no takers. The program's handicap was not just that the accents were British but that they were in a northern working-class dialect difficult even for some Londoners to understand.

Jill Summers and Jean Alexander in a scene from *Coronation Street*

During its 12th year on the air (it had begun in Britain in 1960), *Coronation Street* finally received U.S. exposure on public TV, but the serial did not develop a strong following among American viewers, and it ran only a year. Its popularity in Britain remains phenomenal, however, even with the competition in the 1980s from two rival serials, the BBC's *EastEnders* and the Australian soap, *Neighbours.* Among those featured in the large cast over the years were Violet Carson, Margot Bryant, Jack Howarth, William Roache, Patricia Phoenix, Jill Summers, Jean Alexander and William Lucas.

CORONET BLUE ▶ series about an amnesiac, Michael Alden, that was purchased by CBS and then rejected after 13 episodes had been shot. When CBS decided not to air the series, although the episodes were already paid for, producer Herbert Brodkin demanded they be aired; the show was slotted as a summer replacement in 1967. Frank Converse starred, along with Joe Silver as Max and Brian Bedford as Brother Anthony. The show was by Plautus Productions.

CORPORATION FOR PUBLIC BROADCASTING (CPB) ▶ the nongovernmental, nonprofit corporation established by the Public Broadcasting Act of 1967, responsible chiefly for administering the federal funds for the system, promoting its growth and keeping it free from political influence. CPB receives and disburses federal funds for the development and production of national programming, arranges for the interconnection of the stations (both TV and radio) and conducts training programs and research for the system.

Although charged with providing insulation between government and broadcasters, CPB has a built-in political coloration that, from the beginning, has made it suspect even to the industry it serves. Appointments to its board—originally 15 members but reduced in 1986 to 10 to conform to a 1981 congressional mandate—are made by the president with the advice and consent of the Senate. The law specifies that no more than six may belong to the same political party. The suggestion of partisan ties has raised doubts that a CPB so constituted would work to safeguard public television from becoming an instrument of government policy.

Appointments to the board are for five-year terms, made on a staggered basis to assure a turnover of two directors every year. The board annually elects its own chairman and vice-chairman and employs the CPB president and other officers. Board members receive no salary but are paid $150 a day while attending meetings and conducting CPB business. They are also allowed travel expenses and per diem.

Born of a recommendation by the Carnegie Commission on Educational Television, CPB was organized early in 1968 with a small federal appropriation of $9 million and a gift from CBS of $2 million. President Johnson, who under the law could appoint the first chairman, named Frank Pace, Jr., onetime Secretary of the Army and Director of the Budget. John Macy, Jr., former chairman of the U.S. Civil Service Commission, was CPB's first president.

The CPB role of insulating the system from political influence, never fully effective, has never been less so than during the presidency of Richard Nixon. Memoranda from the Nixon Administration files, made public in 1979, reveal that appointments to the board were made with a view to having the White House control it, and through it the system. After forcing the resignation of Macy, the board brought in its own man to head CPB, Henry R. Loomis, former director of the Voice of America. The move to take over the system nearly succeeded, stymied only by the intercession of Ralph B. Rogers, a prominent Republican industrialist from Texas and chairman of the rival PBS board. Rogers and CPB board chairman Thomas B. Curtis hammered out a working arrangement between their organizations but, in a surprise move, the CPB board summarily rejected it amid charges that the vote had been directly influenced by the White House. Curtis resigned. The board, in disarray, turned to a political "neutral," James R. Killian, to fill the chairmanship. Killian quickly signed with PBS what was termed "the partnership agreement", the essence of which was a guarantee from CPB that 40% of the federal funds would flow directly to the TV stations, increasing to 50% and 60% as appropriations grew.

In 1979 Loomis was succeeded by Robben W. Fleming. In the wake of the Nixon disclosures, Fleming acted to reduce political influence on public television by reorganizing CPB. He placed its programming function with a separate department, the Program Fund, whose director—initially, Lewis Freedman—would report directly to the CPB board. Poor health forced Fleming to resign in 1981. He was succeeded by Edward Pfister, former president of KERA in Dallas. Pfister resigned four years later when the politically conservative board, chaired by Sonia Landau, former head of the Women for Reagan-Bush Committee, ordered him to drop plans to go to Moscow with a public television delegation to discuss program exchange. His successor, Martin Rubinstein, CEO of the Mutual Broadcasting System, was fired after less than a year and was replaced by the CPB's vice president and treasurer, Donald E. Ledwig, a retired Navy career officer.

An attempt to restructure the corporation was made in 1979 after the Carnegie Commission on the Future of Public Broadcasting (Carnegie II) recommended that CPB be abolished. The House bill to revise the Communications Act similarly proposed its elimination. Both efforts, vigorously opposed by CPB, failed to materialize. In 1988, however, Congress, acting on the recommendations of the Senate Commerce Committee, reduced CPB's authority by ordering it to transfer $6 million of its funds to a consortium of independent producers (ITVS) and another $3 million to a consortium of producers of minority programming. More damaging to its hopes for holding its own was the 1988 congressional directive ordering the president of CPB to consult with the presidents of PBS and NAPTS—the latter representing the local stations—and to return to Congress by January 31, 1990, with a plan for determine how best to distribute CPB's national funds. The plan, *Meeting the Mission in a Changing Environment,* proposed the transfer of half of CPB's program funds to PBS in order to further centralize the program decision process with a single agency.

CPB has never attained the parental leadership that had been ordained for it. Its powers have been hampered not only by the meager funds appropriated by the government, but also by the blatant politicization of its board. Instead of appointing "persons eminent in such fields as education, cultural affairs and civic affairs, or the arts"—as called for in the legislation—presidents of both parties too often have used the appointments to pay off small political favors. Thus, what was intended as a shield against political influence has become the sword with which each administration has attempted to advance its own ideology. But even that power has been attenuated by public television's internal rivalries, in which PBS has control of programming, the stations have control of PBS, and CPB has control of a shrinking proportion (16.5%) of public television's purse.

CORWIN, NORMAN ▶ noted radio playwright whose occasional work for TV included an adaptation of his best known work for radio, *On a Note of Triumph.* He also wrote, directed and produced an anthology series for CBS, *26 by Corwin,* in the early years and, in 1971, hosted and directed a prime-access syndicated series, *Norman Corwin Presents,* produced by Group W.

COSBY, BILL ▶ actor-comedian, who after numerous television successes since the 1960s, weighed in with a monster hit in 1984, *The Cosby Show,* which dominated the Nielsens for most of the decade, anchored Thursday nights for NBC and set up all the shows that followed—a sequence that made for the strongest night in television. Syndicated reruns for *The Cosby Show* fetched all-time record prices, averaging out to $1 million per episode. Three years after the show began, a spin-off, *A Different World* (1987), was started. Airing immediately after *The Cosby Show* on Thursday nights, it too has been a big success.

Bill Cosby and the rest of the cast of *The Cosby Show*

In the show Cosby portrays Dr. Heathcliff Huxtable, while Phylicia Rashad plays his wife, Clair. Other cast members include Lisa Bonet as daughter Denise, Malcolm-Jamal Warner as son Theodore, Tempestt Bledsoe as daughter Vanessa, Keshia Knight Pulliam as daughter Rudy, and Sabrina LeBeauf as daughter Sondra.

Early in the 1990s, when *The Cosby Show* was still popular but had started to feel competition from *The Simpsons,* Cosby signed a contract with Carsey-Werner to revive the old quiz show that was the comedy vehicle for Groucho Marx, *You Bet Your Life.*

Other prime-time shows Cosby starred in include the action-adventure series, *I Spy* (1965-68) and the comedy-variety shows *The Bill Cosby Show* (1969-71), *The New Bill Cosby Show* (1972-73), and *Cos* (1976). He also hosted and was executive producer of the animated *Fat Albert and the Cosby Kids*—a children's show that espoused pro-social values. That program, along with the fact that for years he played the role of an amusing and endearing father figure in Jello pudding commercials, helped to inspire the creation of *The Cosby Show.*

COSELL, HOWARD ▶ TV personality who enjoyed a vogue in the 1970s as the most controversial of sportscasters, favored by some viewers for his outspokenness and annoying to others for his abrasive personality and stentorian speech. A former lawyer, he became a sportscaster on ABC Radio in 1953 and has remained with ABC ever since. He came into prominence during the controversy over the boxer Muhammed Ali (then known as Cassius Clay), who had been denied the title of heavyweight champion in the late 1960s because he had sought an exemption from the draft on religious grounds. Hostile to most other broadcasters, Ali was friendly to Cosell and granted him exclusive interviews.

Cosell later became a commentator for ABC's popular *Monday Night Football,* a contributor to *Wide World of Sports* and host of *Howard Cosell's Sports Magazine.* In 1975 ABC made Cosell host of a weekly prime-time variety show, *Saturday Night Live with Howard Cosell,* but it was not well received and was canceled at mid-season. In 1981 he began a weekly half-hour series, *Sportsbeat,* on Sunday afternoons on ABC. He retired from TV sportscasting in the late 1980s and went on to do a radio interview show at WABC New York and other broadcasts for the ABC Radio Network.

***COSMOS* ▶** 13-part PBS series on astronomy, space exploration and humanity's place in the universe, conceived and hosted by Carl Sagan, which began its run in the fall of 1980. For a time it ranked as the highest-rated regular series in public television history; it also spun off a best-selling book, *Cosmos,* published by Random House, which sold more than three-quarters of a million copies in the U.S. alone. *Cosmos* was perhaps the most successful effort by American public television in the educational documentary genre developed by the British Broadcasting Corp. with *Civilisation* and *The Ascent of Man.*

Sagan, an astronomer at Cornell University, was principal writer of the series and head of the independent company which co-produced with KCET Los Angeles. The funding came from the Corporation for Public Broadcasting, the Arthur Vining Davis Foundation, and the Atlantic Richfield Co. Adrian Malone, who produced *The Ascent of Man* for the BBC and now works in the U.S. as an independent, was executive producer and director of *Cosmos.* The writers, along with Sagan, were Ann Druyan and Steven Soter. Senior producers were Geoffrey Haines-Stiles and David Kennard, and KCET program executive Gregory Andorfer was producer.

Cosmos aimed to reveal the interconnectedness of all things, from the origin of matter to the collision of continents, and dealt with such mysteries as black holes, alternative universes, life on other worlds, time travel and the ultimate fate of the universe.

COST PER THOUSAND (CPM) ▶ the ratio of the cost of a commercial spot to the size of the audience reached reported in thousands. CPM is the advertiser's index of how efficiently he has spent his money. Although a 30-second network announcement may cost as much as $250,000, it may reach such a vast audience that in terms of the cost of reaching 1,000 households it is likely to be cheaper than other forms of advertising. Further, there are CPMs for general audiences and for specific audiences. An advertiser would pay, for example, $4.50 per thousand to reach viewers of either sex and all age groups but perhaps $10 or $12 per thousand to reach either women or men in the age group of 18 to 35. Although the target audiences (teenagers, college graduates, etc.) may matter to some advertisers, the most frequent usage is in cost-per-thousand households per commercial minute.

Bob Costas

COSTAS, BOB ▶ charismatic young NBC personality whose one-on-one interview show *Later with Bob Costas* has gained a sizable following since it began airing after *Late Night with David Letterman* in 1989. Costas's comfortable manner and well-rounded knowledge of sports, entertainment and politics have put him on the fast track at NBC. After anchoring the late-night portion of the 1988 Seoul Olympics, he was assigned to host *NFL Live!* and was designated to anchor parts of the 1992 Barcelona Olympics.

Costas started in radio, first in Syracuse, N.Y., where he had attended university, then at KMOX in St. Louis. He got into professional sports coverage in 1976, doing regional NFL and NBA coverage for CBS Sports. He joined NBC in 1980, doing play-by-play of Major League Baseball and college basketball games. Since 1986 Costas has also hosted a syndicated two-hour weekly radio sports talk show, *Costas Coast-to-Coast.*

COSTIGAN, JAMES ▶ writer of quality dramas such as *Little Moon of Alban, War of Children* and *Love Among the Ruins.*

COTT, TED (d. 1973) ▶ broadcast executive who in a 40-year career headed several New York stations: WNEW-AM (1943-50); WRCA-AM-TV (now WNBC-AM-TV) (1950-55); the DuMont-owned stations (1955-57); and WNTA (now public station WNET; 1957-60). Earlier, he had been a producer-director at CBS Radio and at WNYC-AM, the New York municipal station. In later years, he became an independent producer and consultant.

COUCH POTATO ▶ popular appellation for the heavy user of television, depicted in the metaphor as plopped before the set like a vegetable with eyes. The term was coined in the early 1980s by a group of Baby Boomers in the San Francisco area who playfully glorified their addiction to the tube. Calling themselves The Couch Potatoes, they formed a national club and published a hilarious newsletter on the couch-potato lifestyle—lazy and sloppy, to be sure—containing bizarre recipes for that vital companion to the TV set, the toaster oven. After a burst of enlistments on campuses, the club quietly disappeared. All that remains today is the metaphor, and its current use tends to be more pejorative than self-mocking or affectionate.

COUNCIL FOR UHF BROADCASTING ▶ organization of commercial and public broadcasters formed in 1974 to spur the growth of the UHF band, whose priority status with the FCC and Congress had slipped away with the growing interest in cable and other new technologies. The coalition of public and commercial forces was arranged by Hartford N. Gunn, then president of PBS, and Richard C. Block, then president of Kaiser Broadcasting. Gunn's interest was that almost 65% of PBS stations were on UHF, Block's was that his seven independent TV stations were all on UHF.

In 1975, CUB made recommendations to the FCC that were formalized in "The Action Plan for Further UHF Development," which was sponsored also by CPB, PBS, NAB, NAEB, INTV and AMST. The plan asked the FCC to require improvements in the manufacture of UHF tuners, indoor and outdoor antennas and lead-in wire, and to adopt measures to reduce UHF receiver noise and increase the efficiency of transmitters.

COUNTER COMMERCIALS ▶ TV spots that disputed or rebuted the claims of paid commercials. They were granted under the Fairness Doctrine when the issue involved was deemed a controversial one of public importance. In 1967, responding to a petition by public-interest attorney John F. Banzhaf III, the FCC ruled that cigarette commercials constituted such an issue, and stations broadcasting such advertisements were required to provide time for announcements to discourage smoking. But the FCC said this was a unique case, and it would not apply the Fairness Doctrine to other product commercials that raised a controversy, because the result would "undermine" the commercial system of broadcasting. The FCC also rejected a proposal by the FTC that broadcasters allow citizens to respond to commercials that explicitly or implicitly raise controversial issues of public importance, that make claims based on scientific evidence which is in dispute, or that do not point up the negative aspects of a product. However, it maintained that editorial advertising—time purchased for a commentary on an important public issue—would be subject to counter commercials under the Fairness Doctrine. In the wake of repeal of most applications of the Fairness Doctrine, the only important use of counter commercials since 1987 has been in local and state ballot issues.

COUNTER-PROGRAMMING ▶ the tactic of scheduling programs opposite those of rival stations or networks in a manner that would win the audience away. If two networks are competing with dramatic series in a time period, the third might counter with a comedy or variety show. Sometimes, counter-programming is achieved through bridging, that is, by starting a 60- or 90-minute program a half-hour earlier than the competing hit. If the program proves popular, most viewers will not likely switch away while it is in progress.

COURTROOM SHOWS ▶ a hot syndication trend in the 1980s that peppered daytime television with programs on actual or re-created legal contests that had a certain tabloid-newspaper appeal. The trend started with *People's Court* in 1981, a half-hour syndicated program that was such a roaring success that rival TV stations in every U.S. market competed vigorously for it. Its success inspired the revival in 1984 of *Divorce Court,* a syndicated show that had begun in the late 1950s and ran its course in the 1960s. Next came *The Judge* and then *Superior Court.* All but *Superior Court* survived into the 1990s, and many independent stations programmed the three as a morning block to compete with the network soaps.

The programs were natural for television because the courtroom is clearly a place where human-interest stories unfold, full of conflict and melodrama and involving topical issues and ordinary people with whom TV viewers can readily identify. Moreover, the shows revealed something of how the American judicial system works.

Fictional courtroom programs have long been popular on television, as the many revivals of *Perry Mason* attest. But *People's Court* was an original. The 30-minute daily show presented itself as an actual courtroom that brought an endless array of real small-claims cases before its resident jurist, retired California Superior Court Judge Joseph A. Wapner. Judge Wapner in short order became a household name and a beloved avuncular figure for the way he adjudicated petty cases on camera.

The producers of *People's Court,* Ralph Edwards and Stu Billett, corralled cases that were headed for official small-claims courts to their television court with the promise that the show would pay the financial settlement. If no financial settlement was awarded, the participants in the cases would be given $500 to divide between them. There was no lack of cases, and most were truly of the sort that viewers might find themselves involved in.

Divorce Court used actors to portray the litigants but actual lawyers to argue the cases and another retired California judge, William B. Keene, to decide them. The cases, by and large, were the stuff of soap opera, with sex—illicit or odd—often the key issue.

The Judge, which started in 1986, was concerned with Family Court cases that were entirely fictionalized. The judge was portrayed by Bob Shield.

Superior Court was a scripted half-hour program that reenacted real-life cases with actors for litigants and lawyers, and with the judge's decision also pre-written in accordance with the actual outcome of the cases. For part of the run, Raymond St. Jacques played the judge.

The popularity of the daytime court shows began to fade in the early 1990s, but the factors of their appeal gave rise to a more sophisticated form of courtroom television—current court cases of greater import, recorded by news cameras allowed in the courtrooms and discussed and analyzed by experts. CBS News in 1991 derived a prime-time series, *Verdict,* from the increasing access of news cameras to the courtrooms. Andrew Heyward is executive producer. A year earlier, two cable companies, Cablevision and Warner, came up with the same idea for a basic cable channel that would concentrate entirely on covering actual court cases, usually the hottest ones in the news. Recognizing that their best chance of succeeding was to merge, they did, launching the Courtroom Television Network (Court TV) in 1991.

COURTROOM TELEVISION NETWORK (COURT TV) ▶ basic-cable network devoted to covering high-profile court cases through cameras in the courtroom. Launched in 1991 with an initial reach of about 4 million households, the channel sprang from the merger in 1990 of two proposed channels with similar programming aims—In Court, developed by Cablevision Systems, and American Courtroom Network, developed by Time Warner and American Lawyer Media.

The two channels were conceived at a time when syndicated courtroom-centered shows were enjoying success in commercial television. But rather than offering dramatic re-creations of trials, Court TV sought to present the real thing—live coverage of some trials and excerpted replays of others, with commentary and analysis by legal journalists. Fred Graham, former law correspondent for CBS News and the *New York Times,* is chief anchor and managing editor.

After the merger, the joint venture partners became Cablevision, NBC and Time Warner, with American Lawyer managing the venture and serving as producer.

See also Courtroom Shows.

COURTSHIP OF EDDIE'S FATHER, THE ▶ a "heart" situation comedy about a widower, well-to-do and not lacking for women, and his attempts to raise a young son. It had a fair run on ABC (1969-72). In the leads were Bill Bixby as Tom Corbett and Brandon Cruz as his son Eddie, and the series featured Myoshi Umeki as housekeeper Mrs. Livingston, James Komack as Norman Tinker (and also executive producer), Kristina Holland as Tina Rickles and Jodie Foster as Joey Kelly. It was via MGM-TV.

Jacques-Yves Cousteau

COUSTEAU SOCIETY, THE ▶ company under which Jacques-Yves Cousteau, the famed oceanographer, produces a multitude of documentary series. The first, *The Undersea World of Jacques Cousteau,* began on ABC in 1968 and continued for nearly eight years. The documentary specials centered on the contemporary scientific expeditions of Capt. Cousteau and the crew of his specially equipped vessel, *Calypso.* Episodes examined such phenomena as the Great Barrier Reef and the lobster migration along the Bahama Band. The series was by Marshall Flaum Productions in association with Metromedia Producers Corp., ABC News and the Cousteau Society. ABC dropped the series in 1976, but it continued on PBS on underwriting by Atlantic Richfield Corp.

Since 1981 Cousteau's environmental series and specials have been produced for TBS in a number of short series. *Cousteau/Amazon* consisted of six hours and documented the 18-month exploration of the Amazon River basin. Others were *North American Adventures* and *Cousteau Odyssey.* Specials have included *Lilliput Conquers America,* a program about children and the environment that aired on Earth Day 1990, and *Outrage at Valdez.* The Cousteau Society and TBS have entered into a long-term agreement for the production of environmental programming.

COVERAGE CONTOURS ▶ the official and uniform rough guide to a television station's physical coverage. Upon grant of a station construction permit, the FCC requires each grantee to submit a map showing its predicted coverage based on the Commission's engineering formulas. The three grades of predicted contours required by the FCC are:

Grade B service: the quality of picture expected to be satisfactory to the median observer at least 90% of the time for at least 50% of the receiving locations within the contour in the absence of interfering co-channel and adjacent-channel signals.

Grade A service: satisfactory service expected at least 90% of the time for at least 70% of the receiving locations.

Principal city service: satisfactory service expected at least 90% of the time for at least 90% of the receiving locations.

COWAN, LOUIS G. (d. 1976) ▶ president of CBS-TV from March 1958 to December 1959, and before that a noted producer of programs, among them *Stop the Music, The Quiz Kids, Kay Kyser's Kollege of Musical Knowledge* and *Conversation.* Cowan had created *The $64,000 Question* and was president of the network when the quiz-show scandals erupted. Although he no longer had an interest in any show, he was dismissed by CBS at the height of the scandals in an act many believe was sacrificial. It had become *pro forma* to serve up an executive in a bad moment.

Cowan went on to found book and music publishing companies, and he directed seminars in broadcast communications at the Columbia University Graduate School of Journalism while serving as publisher of the Columbia Journalism Review.

After a career as an independent producer of radio and TV shows, he joined CBS in 1955 as a producer and became v.p. of creative service in 1956. He was succeeded as network president by James T. Aubrey, whose expertise was in Hollywood films while Cowan's was in live game shows and variety.

He and his wife died in a fire in their Manhattan penthouse said to have been caused by faulty wiring in their TV set.

COWDEN, JOHN P. ▶ long-time CBS executive, principally in charge of information services (advertising, promotion, research and press information) but also a key aide and adviser to each of the presidents of the network from the mid-1960s until he retired in 1978. A former child actor in radio, he joined the CBS promotion department in 1938, became an executive in 1951 and a vice-president in 1958. In 1972, he was named v.p. and assistant to the president of CBS-TV.

***COX BROADCASTING CORP. v. COHN* ▶** [420 U.S. 469 (1975)] invasion of privacy case in which the Supreme Court maintained that a broadcaster could not be held liable for accurately reporting the name of a rape victim when that information was part of a public court record.

A Georgia statute prohibited anyone from giving the name of any rape victim. A Ms. Cohn had been raped, and when her assailant was tried for the attack, information surrounding the incident became part of the court record. Cox Broadcasting Corp., in covering the trial, reported the facts of the case, including the name of the victim. The girl's father brought suit against the broadcaster for violating his daughter's right of privacy, and he won a substantial verdict in the state court.

Cox Broadcasting appealed the case to the U.S. Supreme Court, which reversed. The court held that the "public interest in a vigorous press" precluded recovery in this case, although the court refused to decide whether truthful publications could ever be subjected to civil or criminal liability, or whether the state could ever define and protect an area of privacy free from unwanted publicity in the press.

COX, KENNETH A. ▶ scholarly FCC commissioner (1963-70) widely respected by the industry for his independence and intelligence, although he frequently voted for reform measures that were unpopular with broadcasters. Cox, who had been chief of the FCC's Broadcast Bureau before he was appointed to the commission by President Kennedy, was instrumental in forging the Prime Time Access-Rule and the rules and primer for community ascertainment. He and fellow commissioner Nicholas Johnson collaborated on studies of the records of promise and performance by broadcasters in Oklahoma, New York and Washington, D.C., and they were joined on the issue of diversifying media ownership.

A Seattle lawyer, Cox went to Washington in 1956 as special counsel to the Senate Commerce Committee, whose chairman, Sen. Warren G. Magnuson, was from his home state. He directed hearings for the committee that touched on network practices, TV allocations, pay TV, cable and ratings. When Newton Minow became chairman of the FCC, Cox joined the commission as broadcast bureau chief.

When his term on the FCC expired, and he was not reappointed by President Nixon, Cox joined the Washington law firm of Haley, Bader and Potts and simultaneously served as v.p. of MCI Communications Inc., a common-carrier microwave firm offering intercity communications services for business.

COX, WALLY (d. 1973) ▶ bespectacled, schoolboyish comedian who found his niche in TV with the classic series *Mr. Peepers* (1952-55). But his popularity was never to grow, although he starred in another series, *The Adventures of Hiram Holliday* (1956), and was featured in such specials as *Heidi* and *Babes in Toyland* in 1955.

COY, A. WAYNE (d. 1957) ▶ chairman of the FCC (1947-52), appointed by President Truman while he was director of the *Washington Post* stations. He was chairman during four critical years on the commission, when decisions were made regarding allocations, color TV, editorializing (containing the seed of the Fairness Doctrine), the reorganization of the commission and the lifting of the freeze on stations. Upon his resignation, he became consultant to Time Inc. and led that company into buying broadcast stations, the first acquisition being KOB-AM-TV, Albuquerque, N.M., for $600,000. He was succeeded as FCC chairman by Paul A. Walker.

CRAMER, DOUGLAS S. ▶ producer for Aaron Spelling Productions. He shared all executive producer credit with Spelling on all ASP shows since joining Spelling, including the *Dynasty* and *The Love Boat* series. He co-produced NBC's adaptations of Danielle Steel's books for TV, including *Kaleidoscope* and *Changes.* He and Spelling also served as co-executive producers for *Dynasty*'s 1991 mini-series revival, *Dynasty: The Reunion.*

A former ABC program executive and later head of production for Paramount TV, he became an independent producer in the 1970s and was executive producer of such situation comedies as *Bridget Loves Bernie* and *Joe & Sons.* Among his made-for-TV movies are *QB VII, The Sex Symbol, Cage Without a Key* and *Search for the Gods.*

CRANE, LES ▶ brash young host of ABC's first attempt to compete with NBC's *Tonight* show. He had a short-lived TV career. A former disc jockey, he began *The Les Crane Show* in 1965, pinning his hopes on controversy and an abrasive style, but despite ample publicity he failed to build a strong following and was canceled a few months after his premiere.

CRAVEN, T. A. M. ▶ twice an FCC commissioner, serving a term from 1937-44, leaving to establish his own engineering consulting firm in Washington and returning for a second term, 1956-63. He opposed any proposals by the commission that smacked of government control over programming or over business practices, and he held fast to the view that decisions on programming in the public interest were best left to the judgment of broadcasters.

CREAN, ROBERT (d. 1974) ▶ TV playwright whose credits include *A Time to Laugh* (1962), *The Defenders* (1964) and *My Father and My Mother,* among a number of other dramas for *CBS Playhouse* and TV religious series.

CRIME STORY ▶ colorful NBC police drama series (1986-88) from the creator of *Miami Vice* set in the 1960s and centering on an elite squad of detectives fighting the Mob. Considered one of the most expensive series ever produced for network television—with the one-hour episodes budgeted at an estimated $1.5 million—it developed a following among crime-show aficionados but never caught on with a mass audience.

Michael Mann, who brought the pace and style of his successful *Miami Vice* to the series, along with the punctuation of a strong musical track, was the show's executive producer for New World Television. Dennis Farina starred, accompanied by Anthony Denison, Bill Smitrovich, Paul Butler and Stephen Lang.

CRIQUI, DON ▶ sports announcer who has been calling NFL play-by-play for NBC Sports since he joined the network in 1979. He has also hosted NBC's pay-per-view cable coverage of the Summer Olympic Games from Barcelona. In addition to covering the NFL, Criqui handled play-by-play duties on NBC's coverage of the Orange Bowl from 1980 to 1989. He has called play-by-play for NBC's college basketball coverage and for NBC Radio coverage of Super Bowls XX and XXI. Criqui also calls play-by-play for New York Mets games on WWOR-TV on a fill-in basis and handles pre-season Chicago Bears telecasts from NBC-owned WMAQ-TV in Chicago.

CRISIS AT CENTRAL HIGH ▶ 1981 documentary on CBS recounting the heightening of racial tensions in Little Rock, Arkansas, as a high school prepared to become desegregated under a 1957 Supreme Court ruling. The text was drawn from the journals of Elizabeth Huckaby, vice principal of the school. Huckaby was portrayed in the two-hour film by Joanne

Woodward. Featured were Charles Durning, Henderson Forsythe, William Russ and Calvin Levels. Writers were Richard Levinson and William Link, who were also the co-producers along with David Susskind. Lamont Johnson directed.

Walter Cronkite

CRONKITE, WALTER ▶ TV's premier newscaster for two decades, quitting his post at CBS while still the leader at his craft. He relinquished the anchor post to Dan Rather in 1981 but stayed on with CBS as special correspondent. The following year he was host of the short-lived CBS series *Universe.* He also conceived and coproduced for public television a news-education series, *Why in the World.* It began on PBS in October 1981 as a weekly program and the following January went to a twice-weekly schedule.

His avuncular manner and journalistic integrity won him the distinction, in the 1970s, of the most trusted man in America. He became the CBS anchorman on the evening news in 1962 and weathered the popularity of NBC's Huntley and Brinkley to emerge as the medium's No. 1 news star and the CBS "iron man" who anchored, from start to finish, the political conventions (except one in 1964, when he was relieved briefly by the team of Robert Trout and Roger Mudd), every space mission, numerous special reports and the day-long CBS observance of the Bicentennial on July 4, 1976.

Cronkite was named to the CBS board of directors when he gave up his anchor post and served until 1990. He remained under contract with CBS News for special news programs, such as *Solzhenitsyn Revisited* (1984), which he narrated. In 1991 he hosted an international coproduction, the four-part series *Dinosaur!,* which played in the U.S. on A&E, and he began work on a multipart history of the 20th Century.

A former UPI foreign correspondent who later had his own syndicated radio news program, he joined CBS as a correspondent in 1950 and became managing editor as well as newscaster on the first half-hour evening newscast a dozen years later, *The CBS Evening News with Walter Cronkite.* A warm TV personality, "as comfortable as old slippers" according to one description, he occasionally allowed human emotions to interfere with journalistic objectivity, as when he wept on camera during the coverage of President Kennedy's assassination.

Cronkite conducted scores of historic interviews, such as those with Archibald Cox and Leon Jaworski during Watergate, and others with such newsmakers as President Johnson, President Ford, Anwar El-Sadat and Alexandr Solzhenitsyn. He accompanied President Nixon on his summit visits to Peking and Moscow and anchored numerous documentaries and special reports. Winner of a vast number of TV and journalism awards, Cronkite was peculiarly the consummate newsman and popular TV personality.

His familiar sign-off on the newscast, "And that's the way it is," became a trademark. He was noted for his expertise, fairness and restraint rather than for a spry wit or theatrical style.

CROSBY, BING (d. 1978) ▶ radio, recording and motion picture star who was host of numerous TV specials but who—except for a short-lived entry in 1964—eschewed a series of his own. He made his TV debut Feb. 27, 1951, singing on *The Red Cross Program* on CBS. Later he was host of such specials as *Bing Crosby and His Friends* and *The Bing Crosby Golf Tournament* and made guest appearances on scores of other shows. His only series, a domestic situation comedy for ABC entitled *The Bing Crosby Show,* was unsuccessful and ran only one season in 1964.

He founded Bing Crosby Productions in the 1950s, a company that had a fair degree of success producing network and syndicated programs; Crosby sold it in the 1960s to Cox Broadcasting Corp., which retained the Crosby name.

Crosby had been one of the great performing names in radio for nearly two decades. He had been an obscure singer with the Paul Whiteman orchestra when William S. Paley, chairman of CBS, heard him on a recording and, impressed with his crooning style, signed him for the network. As was the fashion among radio stars, he developed a mock feud with Bob

Hope, and their friendly rivalry inspired several motion pictures in which they co-starred, notably the *Road* series.

CROSS, JOHN S. (d. 1976) ▶ FCC commissioner (1958-62) named to succeed Richard Mack when he was forced to resign in a scandal. Cross had previously been chief of telecommunications in the State Department. Cross's statement at his confirmation hearing during the height of the *ex parte* scandals, that he was "as clean as a hound's tooth," became an industry byword. He became an engineering consultant on leaving the FCC.

CROSS-OWNERSHIP ▶ any ownership interest in two or more kinds of local communications outlets by an individual or business concern, such as a newspaper's ownership of a television station or of a cable-TV system. Concern in latter years over media monopolies prompted the FCC to prohibit TV stations and telephone companies from owning cable systems in their service areas, TV networks from owning cable systems at all and existing newspapers from acquiring existing stations in the same cities. While the present rules "grandfather" the existing cross-ownership arrangement, they do not permit the sale of a newspaper and a television station to the same party, and co-owned radio and TV stations must find separate purchasers when sold if the license transfers are to be approved.

Upheld by the Supreme Court in the 1978 *FCC v. NCCB* decision, the FCC's rules remained technically intact through the deregulatory period of the 1980s and early 1990s. In practice, however, "waivers" became readily available upon request, at least until 1989, when Senators Edward Kennedy (D.-Mass.) and Commerce Committee chairman Ernest Hollings (D.-S. Car.) furtively inserted an amendment to the FCC's appropriations bill that prohibited adoption of more liberal waiver policies. The measure was declared unconstitutional in part because the U.S. Court of Appeals held that it was improperly aimed at a particular target—stopping the FCC from giving media mogul Rupert Murdoch permission to keep newspaper-TV cross-ownerships in Boston and New York (*News America Publishing Inc. v. FCC*). Even so, the new law created enough obstacles to force the former Australian (who had become a naturalized citizen so he could obtain FCC licenses) to sell off the *New York Post* and his Boston TV station.

In 1989 the FCC abandoned a proposal for complete elimination of its TV-radio cross-ownership ban. Under congressional pressure, it opted for a "liberalized" waiver policy for the top 25 markets that was so liberally enforced that it amounted to repeal. In 1991 FCC chairman Alfred C. Sikes began twin "inquiries" into radio and TV ownership that he hoped would lead to repeal of all cross-ownership rules.

CRYSTAL, LESTER ▶ executive producer of the *MacNeil-Lehrer NewsHour* since 1983 and former president of NBC News. He had been v.p. of documentaries (1976-77) and for the three previous years executive producer of the *Nightly News.* He was named to head the division by Herbert Schlosser, after the ouster of Richard C. Wald; in turn, he was ousted in the Fred Silverman administration. He stayed on as senior executive producer of political and special news broadcasts.

Crystal joined NBC News in Chicago in 1963 as producer of the local newscast on WMAQ-TV, after having worked in the newsrooms of other stations in Chicago, Philadelphia, and Altoona, Pa. He later was associated with the *Huntley-Brinkley Report,* predecessor to the *Nightly News,* as a regional manager, field producer, London producer, news editor and producer.

C-SPAN (CABLE-SATELLITE PUBLIC AFFAIRS NETWORK) ▶ non-profit basic-cable network created in 1979 by some of the larger cable MSOs to give their new medium a unique public service component, namely live, gavel-to-gavel coverage of U.S. House of Representatives proceedings (C-SPAN II, launched in 1986, covers Senate proceedings). The network was developed by Brian Lamb, whose approach to news is to show rather than tell. When Congress is not in session, C-SPAN airs varied Washington forums and conferences. Lamb himself, who is president of C-SPAN, hosts interview programs such as *Booknotes* and *America & the Courts* as well as several viewer call-in programs. The two public affairs channels are supported wholly by the cable industry and are widely respected.

CTAM (CABLE TELEVISION ADMINISTRATION AND MARKETING SOCIETY) ▶ professional organization devoted to the education and professional development of executives in the cable industry. Founded in 1975, it has a membership of about 2,500 cable system and cable programming executives. CTAM holds an annual conference with seminars and exhibits, plus a series of management seminars, sales courses and pay-per-view conferences throughout the year. Since January 1988 Margaret Combs has been president and chief operating officer.

CTV ▶ Canada's national commercial network, the only one in the world owned by its affiliated stations, which today number 24. CTV began in 1961 as a privately owned program source for eight affiliates, but five years later when 11 stations were in the fold it embarked on an imaginative experiment in cooperative ownership. All the affiliates are involved in the management and financial affairs of the Toronto-based network. The original eight own the principal stake.

CTV is one of the leading foreign buyers of U.S. programs, but its license requires that 60% of its overall programming be Canadian, with a requirement of 50% in prime time. Working with independent producers and its affiliated stations, and engaging early in international coproduction, CTV has been responsible for such internationally distributed shows as *E.N.G, Bordertown, Neon Rider, The Campbells, Night Heat, Young Catherine, The Canadians, Peter Ustinov's Russia,* and *My Secret Identity,* a children's show that won the 1990 International Emmy.

Among the keystones of CTV's news and public affairs programming is *Canada AM,* a long-running early morning show, and *W-5 With Eric Malling,* a venerable news-magazine series. Lloyd Robertson, the network's chief news anchor, regularly is named the nation's most trusted journalist in the Canadian *TV Guide*'s annual readership poll.

John M. Cassaday is president and CEO of CTV, having succeeded the original president, Murray Chercover, in 1990.

CUBA ▶ Communist-ruled island country with two state-run networks, both operating in the service of the Fidel Castro government. The entertainment-based network is InterTV, some of whose highest-rated programs are shows pirated from U.S. networks. The other, Canal Tele Rebele, is essentially oriented to news, political information, and culture. It also provides regional programming through its seven affiliates.

A third network is an uninvited one, being beamed into Cuba from the U.S. both by satellite and from a balloon 10,000 feet above the Florida Keys. Known as TV Marti and funded by the U.S. Congress, the television propaganda service complements Radio Marti, a station that has been broadcasting in Spanish to Cuba since 1985 and that continues to aggravate U.S. relations with Castro.

***CUBA: BAY OF PIGS* ▶** NBC News documentary (Feb. 4, 1964) analyzing the events leading to the disastrous attempt at an invasion of Cuba by an American-assisted military force of exiles in 1961. Irving Gitlin was executive producer of the hour, Fred Freed the producer-writer, Len Giovannitti associate producer and Chet Huntley reporter.

***CUBA, THE PEOPLE* ▶** first news documentary produced on portapak equipment to be presented nationally on television. In 1974 an independent video group in Manhattan, the Downtown Community Television Center headed by Jon Alpert, was admitted into Cuba and permitted to tour the country to record on ½-inch tape the living and working conditions of the people; thus the group became the first TV journalists from the U.S. to work in Cuba after the Revolution of 1959. Brought up to broadcast standards by a time-base corrector, the tape documentary was broadcast on PBS in 1974. A second documentary, *Cuba, The People, Part II,* was produced by the group during a second visit in December of 1975 but was shown in exhibitions and not on TV.

CUKOR, GEORGE (d. 1983) ▶ famed movie director whose rare TV assignments included the film drama, *Love Among the Ruins* (1975), which won him an Emmy.

CULLEN, BILL (d. 1990) ▶ one of the durable emcees of the game-show field, hosting such shows as *Where Was I?, Place the Face, Quick As a Flash, Hit the Jackpot, Give and Take, Down You Go, The Price Is Right* and *Eye Guess.* His most successful association, however, was with *I've Got a Secret,* the long-running CBS prime-time show on which he was a panelist. Cullen began as a radio announcer in Pittsburgh and then became a staff announcer for CBS in 1944. His career took a fateful turn when CBS made him emcee of the radio series, *Winner Take All,* in 1946.

CULLMAN PRINCIPLE ▶ [*Cullman Broadcasting Co.*/40 FCC 516 (1963)] FCC policy requiring access where there is no money to pay for time. The Cullman Principle was developed by the FCC to deal with the Fairness Doctrine in situations in which the broadcaster has sold time to one side to present its views but has not presented, or made plans to present, nonpaid contrasting viewpoints. The FCC determined that the licensee could not properly insist upon payment because of the right of the public to be informed.

CUME ▶ shorthand for cumulative audience, the number of different or unduplicated households that viewed a specific program, time period or station at least once over a specified period of time. Cume ratings are a valuable index for programs that are scheduled daily, since they tell not how many people watch any single installment but how many different people are reached by some part of the program over the course of a week or month. Cumes are also widely used by independents and public TV stations as an indication of their ability to reach different households in the market.

CUMMINGS, BOB (d. 1990) ▶ actor with a flair for comedy who, after a successful movie career in the 1940s, moved into television and had another successful career. His star vehicle, a sitcom called *Love That Bob* in which he played a footloose bachelor, was mounted twice. The first aired on NBC and later switched to CBS between 1955-59; the reruns were carried on ABC in daytime under the title *The Bob Cummings Show.* The series was revived by CBS as *The New Bob Cummings Show* (1961-62). Next he co-starred with Julie Newmar in another sitcom on CBS, *My Living Doll* (1964-65). He made his television debut in 1952 in a short-lived half-hour comedy series, *My Hero.*

Although remembered mainly for playing in romantic comedies, Cummings was in fact a first-rate dramatic actor. He won an Emmy in 1954 for his performance in Reginald Rose's *Twelve Angry Men* on CBS's *Studio One.* He also appeared in dramas on *General Electric Theatre* and *The Great Adventure.* But he was most comfortable in comedy roles and for a time was a guest host on NBC's *Tonight* in 1962, between the tenures of Jack Paar and Johnny Carson.

CUNLIFFE, DAVID ▶ British producer-director noted for his work in drama. In a TV career dating to 1960, which followed several years in the theatre as an actor and director, he has worked for Granada Television, the BBC, London Weekend Television and Yorkshire Television, at the latter as controller of drama. He left Yorkshire in 1988 to join ITC, the international production and distribution company, and when ITC abandoned production after a management buyout, Cunliffe spent a year with an internationally involved American company, DLT Entertainment.

With Yorkshire and ITC he was active in a number of U.S. coproductions, among them *The Attic—The Hiding of Anne Frank* for CBS (1988), *The Glory Boys* and *Romance On the Orient Express* for NBC, *Timeslip* for HBO, and *The Harlequin Romances* and *Frankenstein* for Showtime.

At the BBC in the early 1970s, he developed three TV series, one of them the successful and highly regarded *The Onedin Line,* which he also directed. At Yorkshire he directed such plays as *Hedda Gabler* and *The Potting Shed* and was executive producer of *Harry's Game,* which won a number of international prizes.

CURRAN, CHARLES (d. 1980) ▶ former president of the European Broadcasting Union and, since September 1977, chief executive of Visnews, a London-based international newsfilm agency. From 1969 until 1977, Curran had been director-general of the British Broadcasting Corp.

Born in Dublin and educated in England, he joined the BBC in 1947 as a radio producer, then left for newspaper reporting before returning to the BBC in 1951. He held a series of administrative positions and for a time headed BBC's shortwave services before succeeding Hugh Greene as director-general.

***CURRENT AFFAIR, A* ▶** syndicated, reality-based "current events" show that set the benchmark for "tabloid TV," launching an entire genre of syndicated shows that thrive on titillating or gruesome stories, often including dramatized recreations of the events.

The series' host, Maury Povich, launched his own career when *A Current Affair* became nationally syndicated in 1988, after airing on the Fox Network-owned stations since 1986. Povich, who now has his own syndicated *Donahue*-style talk show, left in 1990.

The half-hour show grew out of a local production at Fox's flagship station, New York's WNYW. As the show picked up steam, expanding to the Fox o&os, it helped create STF Productions, Fox's in-house production unit.

Probably the show's most infamous episode was the airing of exclusive video footage of "Preppy murderer" Robert Chambers frolicking with a group of scantily clad women at a slumber party while free on bail. Interspersed with the video was a recreation of the murder he had allegedly committed.

Gerald Stone and Ian Rae were the series' original executive producers, but Anthea Disney took over at the end of 1990 before becoming editor of *TV Guide.*

CURRLIN, LEE ▶ NBC program executive after having been CBS program chief (1975-76); he had been a sales administration executive when network president Robert D. Wood tapped him to succeed Fred Silverman, who had shifted his alliance to ABC. Currlin presided over the fall schedule devised by Silverman and could not be held accountable for its disappointing results; but when ABC took the ratings lead in the spring of 1976 and NBC answered by bringing in two veteran program executives (Irwin Segelstein and Paul Klein) to mount a new challenge, CBS replaced the inexperienced Currlin with a more seasoned programmer, Bud Grant. Currlin received a new position in the sales department and then became head of programs for the CBS o&os. When Silverman became president of NBC, he promptly hired Currlin away as a program executive.

CURTIS, DAN ▶ producer specializing in action-adventure TV movies and series pilots such as *The Night Stalker, Melvin Purvis, G-Man, The Night Strangler, Trilogy in Terror, The Great Ice Rip-Off, Dracula* and *The Norliss Tapes.* He began his independent production career with the successful ABC gothic daytime serial, *Dark Shadows,* after having been a network program executive. Curtis was also producer of the highly expensive series *Supertrain,* the 1979 fiasco rushed into production by the new president Fred Silverman in hopes that it would be the breakthrough show the network needed. When the program opened to poor ratings and reviews, Silverman fired Curtis, but the change in creative personnel was to no avail. Since then, Curtis has produced several successful mini-series, including *The Winds of War* (1983) and *War and Remembrance* (1987). He revived *Dark Shadows* as a prime-time series in the 1990-91 season, but it failed.

CURTIS, THOMAS B. ▶ chairman of the Corporation for Public Broadcasting from September 1972 to April 1973. A former Republican congressman from Missouri, he was appointed chairman at a time when many suspected the Nixon Administration of attempting a takeover of public television. After repeatedly issuing assurances that the Administration was not involved in CPB affairs, Curtis suddenly resigned during a dispute with PBS, amid charges that members of the Administration had made contact with members of the CPB board and were "tampering." He was succeeded by the vice-chairman, Dr. James R. Killian.

CYCLE SAT ▶ distributor of television commercials via satellite to 600 U.S. TV stations using automated receiver/decoder systems. The stations record the commercials for later playback, eliminating the need for tape shipments. Cycle Sat is owned by Winnebago Industries.

D

DAKTARI ▶ an hour-long color adventure series based on the popular motion picture *Clarence, the Cross-Eyed Lion;* it premiered on CBS Jan. 11, 1966, and remained for 89 episodes before being placed into syndication. Starring were Marshall Thompson as veterinarian Marsh Tracy, Cheryl Miller as his daughter Paula, Hari Rhodes as Mike, Hedly Mattingly as Officer Hedley, Ross Hagen as Bart Jason, Erin Moran as orphan Jenny Jones, Clarence (the lion) and Judy (a chimpanzee). The series was produced by Ivan Tors in association with MGM-TV.

DALLAS ▶ nighttime serial that was a smash hit not only on CBS but also in many countries abroad. It was considered the quintessential series of the self-indulgent Reagan era and entered the mythology of the times. Its anti-hero, J. R. (John Ross) Ewing, came to symbolize greed and decadence and his initials became part of the American vernacular. The series began in 1978 and went on to become a national sensation, regularly the highest-rated show in television. The producers, Lorimar Productions, also pulled off one of the greatest television stunts of all time by ending the 1979-80 season with the shooting of *Dallas*'s principal character, J. R., and building up to the fall premiere by promoting the mystery of who shot J. R. and whether he would survive. The shooting was written into the script because Larry Hagman, who played J. R., was in the midst of a contract dispute and might not have returned in the fall.

The cast of *Dallas,* CBS's popular prime-time serial

The episode that opened the 1980-81 season, a masterpiece of hype, was the highest-rated individual show in history at that time, scoring a 53.3 rating and 76 share audience. Toward the end of the 1980s the ratings began to fall, and the show was canceled after the 1990-91 season.

The series centered on a fabulously wealthy family, in contemporary times, that built an empire on cattle and oil. Prominent in the large cast, in addition to Hagman, were Barbara Bel Geddes (as J. R.'s mother, Eleanor Southworth Ewing, known as Miss Ellie), Linda Gray (J. R.'s wife, Sue Ellen Shepard Ewing), Patrick Duffy (Miss Ellie's youngest son, Bobby), Victoria Principal (Bobby's wife, Pamela Barnes Ewing), Ken Kercheval and Charlene Tilton.

The *Dallas* success provided a windfall of spin-offs and knock-offs for Lorimar Productions: *Knots Landing, Flamingo Road, Falcon Crest* and *King's Crossing.*

DALY, JOHN CHARLES (d. 1991) ▶ newsman and panel-show personality during the 1950s and 1960s who doubled as the suave moderator of the *What's My Line?* series on CBS while serving as v.p. in charge of news, special events and public affairs for ABC. He held the ABC post from 1953 to 1960, resigning in a clash with corporate management over policy matters. His tenure with the panel show spanned 17 years.

Born in South Africa, Daly worked first for NBC as a news correspondent, then for CBS (1937-49), variously as White House correspondent and on foreign assignments. In addition to *What's My Line?,* he hosted such programs as *We Take Your Word* and *News of the Week.* He served briefly as director of Voice of America (1967-68), leaving in a publicized dispute over personnel changes made without his advice. And he made news again in 1969 when he resigned as host of a public TV panel show, *Critique,* because a remark made by one of the panelists, which he considered obscene, was not removed from the video tape. Daly joined the American Institute in 1971, where he remained until 1986.

DALY, ROBERT A. ▶ chairman of the board and CEO of Warner Bros. Inc. since January 1982. He was previously president of CBS Entertainment beginning in October 1977 when, in a major reorganization of the company, the TV network's program department was designated a division. Daly thus became head of programming with scant experience in that field. He joined the network in 1955 in the accounting department, later shifting to business affairs, where he rose to become v.p. in charge. In that post, he demonstrated skill in negotiating program contracts. When Robert Wussler became network president in April 1976, he elevated Daly to executive v.p. of CBS-TV. Then came the move to CBS Entertainment, which involved his transfer to the West Coast.

DAMM, WALTER J. (d. 1962) ▶ head of the *Milwaukee Journal's* radio and TV stations, the WTMJs, and a leading figure in the industry as president of the Television Broadcasters Association until it merged with the NAB in 1951. Later he became president of NAB and also helped to organize the NBC television affiliates board in 1953.

***DAMON RUNYON THEATRE* ▶** anthology based on the works of the noted writer, with different stars weekly. Produced by Screen Gems, the half-hour series premiered in 1955 on CBS with Donald Woods as host and ran one year.

***DAN AUGUST* ▶** hour-long police-action series that was a failure in its first presentation on ABC (1970) but was a success in 1973 when CBS carried the reruns as a summer replacement. In that three-year interval the series' star, Burt Reynolds, had climbed from relative obscurity to fame, largely through his appearances on TV talk shows and through the notoriety he acquired from posing nude for a national women's magazine. The series, by Quinn Martin Productions, featured Norman Fell as Sergeant Charles Wilentz, Richard Anderson as Chief George Untermeyer, Ned Romero as Detective Joe Rivera and Ena Hartman as secretary Katy Grant.

DANCY, JOHN ▶ senior White House correspondent for NBC News since July 1978. For the five previous years, he had foreign assignments and covered three wars—the Middle East (1973), Cyprus (1974) and Lebanon (1975). Later he became the network's Moscow correspondent. From 1968-73, he was a national correspondent.

D'ANGELO, WILLIAM P. ▶ executive producer of *Webster, Alice, Room 222, Sheriff Lobo* and *Sledgehammer!* He was also a producer for *Love, American Style, Barefoot in the Park* and *The Young Lawyers.* Through his own company, D'Angelo Productions, he produced a number of Saturday morning network shows and prime-time specials. Later he joined Grosso-Jacobson Productions.

DANIEL BOONE ▶ frontier adventure series that starred Fess Parker and featured Patricia Blair as Boone's wife Rebecca, Darby Hinton as their son Israel and Dallas McKennan as Cincinnatus. Ed Ames co-starred as Mingo, Boone's Cherokee friend, during the first four seasons. The series debuted on NBC Sept. 24, 1964, and remained six seasons. It was produced by Arcola-Fesspar in association with 20th Century-Fox.

DANIELS, BILL ▶ a cable pioneer who built his first cable system in rural Wyoming in 1952, created and divested a major cable operations company and now runs Daniels Communications, a diversified company based in Denver with interests in the cable and mobile communications brokerage business and in sports programming networks. Daniels's personal fortune was estimated at over $300 million by *Forbes* magazine in 1991, with most of it amassed from his cable interests.

In addition to his early cable operations, which eventually grew into one of the country's top 25 MSOs, Daniels founded a brokerage and investment banking company in 1958, Daniels & Associates, to match buyers and sellers of cable television properties. This company, located in Denver, became the industry's leader. In 1989 the brokerage had its best year ever, completing 55 transactions with an aggregate value of $5.4 billion.

Daniels's sports interests range from the Denver Grand Prix Auto Race, which Daniels owns, to the Los Angeles Lakers basketball team, in which Daniels is a minority owner. In conjunction with cable operator Tele-Communications Inc. and investor John McMullen, Daniels owns Prime Network, a group of regional cable sports networks.

DANN, MICHAEL H. ▶ colorful head of programs for CBS from 1963 to 1970 and one of the thoroughgoing professionals who could provide quality or pap, as higher management required. An embattled executive who survived five changes of presidents during his tenure as v.p. of programs, Dann lost out finally to Robert D. Wood when he took a stand against the wholesale cancellation of such hit shows as those of Red Skelton and Jackie Gleason and *The Beverly Hillbillies, Green Acres, Petticoat Junction* and *Hee-Haw.* Dann believed in preserving the hits; Wood was intent on creating a new youth- and urban-oriented image for CBS.

On leaving, Dann joined the Children's Television Workshop to work on the foreign sales of *Sesame Street* and became a program consultant to a number of large companies, principally IBM and Warner Communications. He left CTW in 1976 and concentrated on helping to develop Warner's two-way commercial cable system in Columbus, Ohio. In 1981, he joined ABC Video as a programming executive.

He started in broadcasting in the late 1940s as a comedy writer, then joined NBC's publicity department as head of trade and business news. Later he joined NBC's program department, where he worked in a number of capacities, and in 1958 he switched to CBS as v.p. of New York programs. In 1963 he became head of programming and in 1966 was named senior v.p. of programs. He built a strong department and was succeeded on his resignation by a protege, Fred Silverman.

DARK SHADOWS ▶ see Soap Operas.

DATING GAME, THE ▶ see Game Shows.

DAVEY AND GOLIATH ▶ long-running 15-minute children's series usually dealing with moral questions. It was produced by the Lutheran Church in America and was offered to stations free for public service use. Beginning in 1961, the puppet animation series aired on more than 350 TV stations in the U.S. and Canada, usually early in the morning before the commercial schedules began, and was also carried widely abroad.

DAVID FROST SHOW, THE ▶ syndicated talk-variety series via Group W Productions (1969-72) which was that company's successor to *The Merv Griffin Show* when that established entry shifted to CBS for the late-night derby. Frost, the noted English interviewer and humorist, was equal to managing a daily talkfest (which ran 60 minutes in some markets and 90 minutes in others) but lacked acceptance in many parts of the country and never amassed the number of markets necessary to make the show a success.

DAVIS, BILL ▶ director specializing in variety shows whose extensive credits include *The Julie Andrews Hour* and *The Lennon Sisters Show* on ABC; *The Smothers Brothers Comedy Hour, The Jonathan Winters Show* and *Hee-Haw* on CBS; *The Lily Tomlin Special,* Marlo Thomas's *Free to Be You and Me* and other specials with Herb Alpert and John Denver.

DAVIS, DAVID M. ▶ one of the leading forces in shaping public TV, first as a pioneer producer-programmer at WGBH Boston, then as head of the Ford Foundation office that supported much of public TV, and more recently as the creator and executive director of PBS's *American Playhouse.*

Davis began his TV career in 1947, in the years of the commercial medium's infancy, first as a producer and director with WFIL-TV Philadelphia, later as head of production with WMAL-TV Washington. He left commercial TV after seven years to create and then direct the Greensboro unit of the University of North Carolina's public TV network, before moving to Boston where he headed WGBH's television division. During his 11 years in that post he also produced and directed some of WGBH's shows, including an Emmy- and Oscar-winning feature film about Robert Frost, *A Lover's Quarrel With The World.*

He took a leave of absence from WGBH in 1967 to help with the development of Israeli TV, but, before the year was out, was called to the Ford Foundation by its newly appointed TV advisor, Fred Friendly, to head the foundation's Office of Communications. In the nine years he administered the Foundation's grants to public TV and related projects—$150 million in all—Davis exercised considerable influence over the organization and output of the public medium.

In 1980, after the foundation was largely phased-out of public TV, Davis created *American Playhouse* and became executive director of its parent company, building much of its success on his creative skill in leveraging limited production funds through coproduction arrangements with film and cable. He is also the executive director of another PBS series, *P.O.V.*

DAVIS, ELMER (d. 1958) ▶ highly respected broadcast journalist known for his dry, unemotional delivery and penetrating analyses of news events. A former *New York Times* reporter, he joined CBS in 1939 and quickly became one of radio's most popular commentators. He left CBS in 1942 to become director of the Office of War Information, and when World War II ended he joined ABC. Davis conducted a nightly newscast on TV until illness forced him to leave it in 1953. He returned a year later with a weekly commentary.

DAVIS, JERRY ▶ producer of *The Odd Couple* its first two seasons; executive producer of *Funny Face;* creator and executive producer of *The Cop and the Kid.*

DAVIS, PETER ▶ documentary producer and writer for CBS News (1965-72), whose credits have included *The Selling of the Pentagon, The Battle of East St. Louis, Hunger in America* and *The Heritage of Slavery.* On leaving CBS he produced the controversial motion picture documentary on the Vietnam war, *Hearts and Minds* (1974), and in 1976 signed with WNET New York to produce a public TV series, *Middletown,* on life in Muncie, Ind. It aired in the spring of 1982 as a six-part documentary. Davis was also the co-writer for the TV film *Haywire* (1980). Since 1983, he has been writing articles for national magazines and became a contributing editor for *Esquire* in 1985. Before joining CBS, he was an associate producer of NBC News and a writer for ABC.

DAVIS, SID ▶ Washington news director for NBC News (1977-82); for nine years previously he was Washington bureau chief for Westinghouse Broadcasting, after having been White House correspondent. He was one of the three reporters to witness the swearing-in of President Johnson aboard Air Force One in Dallas after the assassination of President Kennedy in November 1963. In 1979, he became NBC news bureau chief in the capital.

DAWSON, THOMAS H. ▶ president of CBS-TV from Dec. 15, 1966, to Feb. 17, 1969, having risen through the sales ranks of both CBS radio and television. Dawson entered broadcasting in 1938 as a salesperson for WCCO Radio, the CBS affiliate in Minneapolis. He moved to New York with CBS Radio Spot Sales in 1948 and switched to TV spot sales several years later. In 1957 he became sales v.p. for the TV network and was made senior v.p. of the network in July 1966, a few months before his promotion to president.

After leaving CBS, he became for a time director of radio and TV in the Office of the Commissioner of baseball.

DAY AFTER, THE ▶ chilling TV movie televised by ABC on Nov. 11, 1983, about a fictive nuclear war and its effects on Lawrence, Kansas. Relentlessly grim, the film depicts a rural town before, during and after a nuclear blast. The film was directed by Nicholas Meyer, produced by Robert A. Papazian, and written by Edward Hume, and its large cast was headed by Jason Robards. It provoked a great deal of political debate and media attention. ABC was accused by some shareholders of airing Soviet propaganda. The show also provided grist for the mills of anti-nuclear groups and peace activists in the U.S. and Europe.

John Lithgow and JoBeth Williams co-starred. Others in the cast were John Cullum, Steve Guttenberg, Bibi Besch, Lori Lethin, Amy Madigan, Jeff East and Lin McCarthy.

A scene from the ABC movie *The Day After*

DAY, JAMES ▶ a leading force in public television, as president of NET and previously general manager of KQED San Francisco until he left the executive ranks in 1973. He then created the interview series *Day at Night,* which ran for two years on a number of PBS stations, and in 1975 became a professor of communications at Brooklyn College. He is now professor emeritus.

Day was named president of National Educational Television in August 1969 after managing KQED for 16 years. When NET merged with WNDT New York to form WNET in 1970, Day became president of the new entity. Under Day's leadership, the station took on a vitality it had lacked, while the production center turned out such national series as *The Great American Dream Machine, Black Journal, Soul!, Playhouse New York* and the Frederick Wiseman documentaries. Day was also instrumental in acquiring the British series *The Forsyte Saga* and Kenneth Clark's *Civilisation* for the public TV system.

At KQED particularly, Day combined performing with his executive duties. For 14 years he hosted the local interview program *Kaleidoscope* and conducted nationally televised interviews with Eric Hoffer and Arnold Toynbee on *Conversation.*

DAY PARTS ▶ segments of the broadcast day defined by audience levels and audience composition and affecting advertising rates and types of programming. The day parts are early morning, daytime, early fringe, prime access, prime time, late fringe, latenight and, where applicable, overnight.

***DAYS AND NIGHTS OF MOLLY DODD, THE* ▶** comedy-drama series created by Jay Tarses that was critically acclaimed but unsuccessful commercially. It began on NBC (1987-88), then moved to cable's Lifetime network in 1989. Considered one of the best of the sub-genre of the late 1980s known as "dramedies"—a combination of dramatic and sitcom elements with no laugh-track—the story centered on a divorced woman in her mid-thirties coping with life in New York City. Blair Brown headed the cast that featured Allyn Ann McLerie, William Converse-Roberts, James Greene, Victor Garber, David Strathairn and Richard Lawson. Tarses and Bernie Brillstein were the executive producers.

***DAYS OF OUR LIVES* ▶** see Soap Operas.

***DEAN MARTIN COMEDY HOUR* ▶** high-rated NBC variety series (1965-74) in which Martin starred with at least four guests each week and a resident chorus line, The Goldiggers. It was by Claude Productions in association with Greg Garrison Productions.

***DEAR JOHN* ▶** NBC sitcom based on a BBC series of that title that began in 1988. It stars Judd Hirsch as John Lacey, a divorced man coping with the singles life who seeks guidance through the One-to-One Club, a group therapy support group. The group provides the setting for the show's supporting cast, which includes Isabella Hoffman as Kate, Jane Carr as Louise, Jere Burns as Kirk, and Billie Bird as Mrs. Philbert. The series reunites Hirsch and executive producer Ed. Weinberger, who worked together in *Taxi.* The series comes from Paramount Television.

***DEATH OF A PRINCESS* ▶** two-hour docudrama that created a diplomatic flap, and a domestic one as well, prior to its airing May 21, 1980, in the PBS series *World.* The film attempted to illuminate the Middle East for Westerners through piecing together the story of a 19-year-old Saudi Arabian princess who in 1977 was executed, along with her lover, for committing adultery. Under Islamic law, adultery is a capital crime.

The furor began when the film aired in Britain and the Netherlands a few weeks before the U.S. showing. The Saudis voiced objections to the British government, saying the film misrepresented the social, religious and judicial systems of the country and, additionally, was insulting to the heritage of Islam. The Saudi ambassador then called upon the U.S. State Department to block the showing in this country. Implicit were threats of breaking off diplomatic relations and suspending oil exports at the height of the energy crisis.

Pressures on PBS began to mount from Congressmen, Mobil Oil (a chief benefactor of public television) and at least one unidentified philanthropic foundation, all arguing that in showing the film PBS would be going against the best interests of the United States. But PBS stood its ground, refusing to be censored, especially by a foreign government. Nevertheless, several public stations refused to carry the program, including KUHT Houston, a city where oil interests are concentrated, and eight stations in South Carolina, home state of the Ambassador to Saudi Arabia, John C. West.

The episode received wide attention and debate in the press, a fact that contributed greatly to the large audience for the broadcast. After the airing, the issues quickly evaporated. Mobil did not withdraw its underwriting of public television shows, the Saudis did not suspend oil shipments, and there was no move in Congress to end Federal support of the public broadcasting system.

The film was a coproduction of WGBH Boston, ATV in England and Telepictures Corp. It was written by British journalist and filmmaker Anthony Thomas, in collaboration with David Fanning, the executive producer of *World* for WGBH. The script was taken from interviews conducted by Thomas during 1978. Featured in the program were Paul Freeman, portraying a British journalist (apparently modeled on Thomas) trying to dig out the story of the young princess and why she died, and Suzanne Abou Taleb, an Egyptian actress playing the princess. *World* was funded by the Ford Foundation and the German Marshall Fund.

After the U.S. showing, the film was aired on Israeli TV, whose signal reaches across borders to some eight million Arabs.

DEATH OF A SALESMAN ▶ Pulitzer Prize-winning Arthur Miller play staged twice for television by CBS. The first in 1966 starred Lee J. Cobb and Mildred Dunnock reprising their roles as Willy and Linda Loman from the original 1949 Broadway production. James Farentino and George Segal played their sons Happy and Biff in this Emmy Award-winning production.

The show was revived on Broadway in 1984, with Dustin Hoffman and Kate Reid playing Willy and Linda, and John Malkovich and Stephen Lang playing the sons. CBS filmed the second television version the following year. Volker Schlondorff, director of the German film *The Tin Drum,* directed, and the show was shot at the Kaufman Astoria Studios in Queens, N.Y.

DEATH VALLEY DAYS ▶ long-running western anthology series owned and syndicated by U.S. Borax for its 20 Mule Team products. The sponsor started the series on radio in 1930 and carried it into TV in 1952, usually placing it in around 120 markets. Host for the first 12 years was Stanley Andrews, who was represented as the Old Ranger. Subsequent host-narrators included Ronald Reagan, Robert Taylor and Merle Haggard. Production continued until 1972.

DEBBIE REYNOLDS SHOW, THE ▶ an attempt by NBC (1969) to establish a successor to Lucille Ball in a situation comedy that followed the wacky lines of the various *Lucy* shows on CBS. Although Reynolds had been given a two-year contract, the series ended a failure after 17 episodes. Via Harmon Productions and Filmways, it featured Reynolds as Debbie Thompson, Don Chastain as husband Jim, Patricia Smith and Tom Bosley as Charlotte (Debbie's sister) and Bob Landers and Bobby Riha as young Bruce Landers.

DECEMBER BRIDE ▶ popular CBS situation comedy (1954-59) which served as a vehicle for Spring Byington, who portrayed an attractive widow (Lily Ruskin) living with her daughter and son-in-law. Featured were Frances Rafferty and Dean Miller as Ruth and Matt Henshaw, Harry Morgan as Pete Porter and Verna Felton as Hilda Crocker. It produced a successful spin-off, *Pete and Gladys.* It was via Desilu.

DEC. 6, 1971: A DAY IN THE LIFE OF THE PRESIDENCY ▶ An NBC News special covering President Nixon in a 15-hour working day, reported by John Chancellor. It was broadcast in December 1971 shortly after the filming. Although NBC considered it a news coup, others found the timing of the flattering piece uncomfortably close to the election season of 1972.

deCORDOVA, FRED ▶ TV and motion picture producer and director who after 1970 was producer of Johnny Carson's *Tonight* show on NBC. In the 1940s, deCordova was a film director at Warner Bros. and Universal; in the 1950s he moved into television, winning one Emmy as producer of *The Jack Benny Show* and another as director of *The Burns and Allen Show.* He also directed *My Three Sons* for four years and such other series as *The George Gobel Show, Mr. Adams and Eve* and *December Bride.* In all, before joining *Tonight* as successor to Rudy Tellez, he directed some 500 TV programs.

DEF (DELAYED ELECTRONIC FEED) ▶ also known as ABC/DEF, the newsfilm service syndicated by ABC News to subscribing affiliates for use in their local newscasts, at their discretion. All the networks provide such a service to their affiliates for a nominal charge. The DEF material is sent out over the lines in the manner of a closed-circuit broadcast and is taped by the stations, allowing them to select the items suitable for their newscasts. The DEF feed consists of top national and foreign stories, as well as some that might be classified as overset from the network newscasts, and sports and news items with special regional appeals.

DEFENDERS, THE ▶ highly respected dramatic series that starred E. G. Marshall and Robert Reed as father-son lawyers, Lawrence and Kenneth Preston, and featured noted Broadway and Hollywood guest performers. Produced by Herbert Brodkin's Plautus Productions and Defender Productions, it premiered on CBS in September 1961 and continued until 1965. The series outshone most others on the networks for the quality of writing and acting and for its straightforward treatment of serious themes.

DEFICIT FINANCING ▶ term frequently used by production studios to describe the networks' financial arrangements for shows, referring specifically to the fact that the networks usually license programs for substantially less than they cost to produce. A network may put a ceiling of $2.3 million on made-for-TV movies, although the producer's cost is likely to exceed $2.5 million. The network may also hold the line at $900,000 an episode for an hour series that costs $1 million or more to produce. Studios are expected to make up the difference in foreign and domestic syndication, but shows that fare poorly on the networks rarely are in sufficient demand in secondary markets to recover their costs.

The fact that selling one or more shows to the networks can result in ruinous losses, when seemingly the achievement should guarantee profits, has deterred a number of companies from producing for television.

DeFOREST, LEE (d. 1961) ▶ Inventor of the three-element audion tube in 1906, vital to the development of radio and television and for which he became known as "the father of radio." He was credited with more than 300 inventions, including—in 1948—a device for transmitting color television. But he was disappointed with the uses to which his inventions were put and in later years bitterly criticized the broadcasting industry for what he felt was its excessive commercial orientation.

DEGRASSI JUNIOR HIGH ▶ widely praised Canadian dramatic series about a multicultural group of seventh- and eighth-graders at an urban junior high school. The show, told from the kids' points of view, focused realistically on problems and concerns of that age group and dealt unshirkingly with such issues as child abuse, teenage pregnancy, drug abuse, abortion, homosexuality and AIDS. Televised in the U.S. on PBS, the series, which began in January 1987, was a sequel to *The Kids of Degrassi Street* (1984), about eight- and nine-year-olds. The series followed many of the same characters as they grew older, went to junior-high and on to high-school in the next sequel, *Degrassi High* (1989). Coproduced by Linda Schuyler and Kate Taylor, directed by Kit Hood, and written by Yan Moore (with much input from the young cast members), the show won numerous national and international awards and was sold to over 40 countries.

DEINTERMIXED MARKET ▶ an all-UHF market. In its 1952 table of assignments, the FCC put all stations on UHF in certain markets that previously had been "inter-mixed" with some VHF and some UHF stations. Fresno, Calif., for example, originally had a Channel 12. That station was reassigned to Channel 30 when the market was deintermixed.

DELLA-CIOPPA, GUY ▶ onetime producer and CBS executive whose career with the network ran from the late 1930s through the late 1960s, principally as a vice-president in Hollywood. He served as executive producer of the *Red Skelton Hour* during its last several years on the network.

DEMOGRAPHICS ▶ rating data descriptive of *who* is watching, breaking down the audience by age group, sex, income levels, education and race. For most buyers of TV time desirous of reaching a target audience, demographic information is vital. For example, money may be considered misspent when advertising intended for women is shown in a program that has a large proportion of male viewers.

In rating reports at both the national and local levels, at least 30 demographic breakouts are given. The age breakouts generally occur in these groupings: 2-11, 12-17, 18-49 and 50-plus. On the premise that young married couples with young children are the prime prospects for most of the products and services advertised on television, the advertising industry consensus gives the highest priority to reaching viewers 18-34 and 18-49. Programs reaching those groups predominantly command higher rates per thousand than programs more successful with younger or older viewers.

The purchasing of time according to demographics, which became widespread practice in the mid-1960s, led networks and stations to design virtually all their programming for the most desirable age groups, in the knowledge that older and younger viewers would watch television in any case. A corollary effect is that programs with favorable demographics are often retained in the schedule even if their total audience falls below the required one-third share, while those with unfavorable demographics may be canceled despite substantial ratings.

Demographic data are often referred to as "persons" or "people" ratings.

***DENNIS THE MENACE* ▶** successful CBS situation comedy (1959-63) about a likeable but mischievous child. Inspired by the Hank Ketcham comic strip, it was produced by Darriel Productions and Screen Gems. It featured Jay North in the title role, Herbert Anderson and Gloria Henry as parents Henry and Alice Mitchell, Joseph Kearns and Sylvia Field as neighbors George and Martha Wilson and, after Kearns' death in 1961, Gale Gordon and Sara Seegar as new neighbors John and Eloise Wilson. NBC began carrying the reruns in daytime in 1961.

DENNY, CHARLES R., JR. ▶ FCC chairman (1946-47) who resigned to join NBC as v.p. and general counsel. He became executive v.p. of operations for NBC in 1956 and two years later was made a v.p. of RCA. A lawyer, he had joined the FCC in 1942 as assistant general counsel and was appointed a commissioner in 1945, before being named chairman.

DePASSE, SUZANNE ▶ head of Motown Productions, responsible for a number of TV specials featuring contractees or alumni of Motown Records. Her stature in the business rose substantially when she became the catalyst for the *Lonesome Dove* mini-series, joining with two other production companies, one of them Australian, to make it happen. The mini-series was the surprise hit of the season in 1989, and DePasse established that she was capable of producing more than rock music specials.

DEREGULATION ▶ the reduction or elimination of existing regulation, discussed principally in connection with broadcasting and cable TV. It was born of the real or imagined mood of the FCC under the chairmanship of Richard E. Wiley during the 1970s.

Deregulation fever became a Washington epidemic during the Carter Administration, born of desires from liberals and conservatives alike to diminish the government's involvement with business and to reduce the cost of government by eliminating unnecessary paperwork and scaling down the size of Federal agencies. Under Charles Ferris, the FCC undertook a number of initiatives to cut back the regulation of cable TV and remove outmoded rules for television. But its major effort in this sphere was to propose an experimental, partial deregulation of radio. The spirit of deregulation was also evident in the various bills to rewrite the Communcations Act, the House bill going so far as to propose replacing the FCC with a new and smaller agency.

Under Mark Fowler, in the Reagan Administration, deregulation went into high gear with the elimination of ascertainment procedures and initiatives to eliminate the Fairness Doctrine and Equal Time Law. Fowler declared himself not for deregulation but rather what he termed "unregulation."

As was the case with airline and banking deregulation, some of the shortcomings of reliance on the marketplace became evident toward the end of the 1980s boom period. Despite the carping of broadcast reformers and grumbling by Congress, reduced levels of locally produced public affairs programming were tolerated by a public that increasingly turned to cable and other media. But ownership rules that permitted highly leveraged takeover artists to enter into station ownership came under greater scrutiny. And the FCC actually reversed itself on a number of technical changes that had permitted inadequately capitalized applicants to acquire—and then abandon—new stations.

Original cast members of the CBS series *Designing Women*

DESIGNING WOMEN ▶ successful CBS sitcom (1986—) that is notable for presenting women in a positive light in business and for puncturing a stereotypical view of the South as overrun with ignorant racists.

The storyline revolves around four very different women who run a decorating business in Atlanta. The series started with Dixie Carter, Annie Potts, Jean Smart and Delta Burke in the lead roles, but the latter two were replaced by Julia Duffy and Jan Hooks in the 1991 season. Through the four characters and eventual fifth partner, a black ex-convict played by Meshach Taylor, the show's creator and executive producer, Linda Bloodworth-Thomason, vents opinions on a host of issues, from prejudice and sexism to freedom of speech.

CBS has fared well in pairing the show with *Murphy Brown* on Monday nights, establishing a block with strong female appeal to counter ABC's *Monday Night Football.* Bloodworth-Thomason shares executive-producer duties with husband Harry Thomason, for Columbia Pictures Television.

DESILU ▶ independent Hollywood production company created to produce *I Love Lucy* in 1950 and that went on to provide numerous other series to the networks, such as *December Bride, The Untouchables* and *Mannix,* until it was purchased by Gulf and Western (Paramount TV) in 1967 for about $20 million. The company's name melded the first names of the stars of *I Love Lucy,* Desi Arnaz and Lucille Ball, who were real-life husband and wife until their divorce in 1960. Ball then became president of Desilu Productions and Desilu Studios, the old RKO lot the company had purchased. Over the years Desilu also produced such series as *Our Miss Brooks, The Greatest Show on Earth, Glynis, Fair Exchange* and *Whirlybirds.*

DESILU PLAYHOUSE ▶ dramatic anthology hosted by Desi Arnaz that ran on CBS from 1958 to 1961. It produced 54 films that later were put into syndication by Desilu Productions.

DETECTIVES, THE ▶ police series starring Robert Taylor as Captain Matt Holbrook, which premiered on ABC in 1959 as a half-hour show and in 1961 was expanded to a full hour, terminating in the spring of 1962. Produced by Four Star and Hastings Productions, it featured Tige Andrews as Lieutenant Johnny Russo, Adam West as Sergeant Steve Nelson and Mark Goddard as Sergeant Chris Ballard; it added Ursula Thiess when it went to an hour.

DEWHURST, COLLEEN (d. 1991) ▶ one of America's foremost actresses (originally Canadian) whose career on stage, screen and television spanned 40 years and who was closely identified with the works of Eugene O'Neill. On television she was seen with Candice Bergen on *Murphy Brown* playing Murphy's mother. Other television credits include productions of *A Moon for the Misbegotten, The Price, The Crucible, No Exit, The Women's Room, As Is, Anne of Green Gables, Anne of Avonlea, Between Two Women, And Those She Left Behind,* and *Lantern Hill.*

DIANA ▶ situation comedy on NBC designed for British actress Diana Rigg (*The Avengers*). It ran 13 weeks in 1973, was produced by Talent Associates/Norton Simon Inc. and featured Rigg as Diana Smythe, David Sheiner and Barbara Barrie as Norman and Norma Brodnik and Richard B. Shull as Howard Tolbrook.

DICK VAN DYKE SHOW, THE ▶ a classic situation comedy that overcame initial viewer indifference to run five seasons on CBS, starting in 1961. It was a domestic comedy with show biz wrinkles, since Van Dyke's fictive office life (as Rob Petrie) was as a writer of a television show. Mary Tyler Moore, who played his wife Laura, was propelled to TV stardom by the series. Rose Marie as Sally Rogers, Morey Amsterdam as Buddy Sorrell and Richard Deacon as Mel Cooley portrayed Van Dyke's colleagues, and Carl Reiner, who created and produced the show (also writing and directing some episodes), made occasional appearances as Alan Brady, the star of the TV show within the show. Sheldon Leonard was executive producer. It was via Calvada Productions and T&L Productions.

DICKERSON, NANCY ▶ first female correspondent for CBS News (1962-63) and the first woman on television to report from the floor of a national convention. She moved to NBC in 1963, where she was given a daytime news program of her own, from Washington. She became a favorite of presidents and a television celebrity, matters which became difficult to reconcile with her work as a news correspondent. She left NBC at the end of the decade after a contract dispute.

Later she represented PBS as one of four network correspondents in a live one-hour interview with President Nixon. Since then she has participated in special news programs and an independent production company, Television Corporation of America.

DIEKHAUS, GRACE M. ▶ a producer at *60 Minutes* since January 1982. Previously she was senior producer of *CBS Reports* in addition to being executive producer of *Magazine*, CBS News's monthly daytime informational series, and also of *Your Turn: Letters to CBS News*, a bimonthly letters-to-the-editor broadcast. Earlier she was senior producer of *Who's Who* (1976-77) and a line producer of *60 Minutes*.

DIFFERENT WORLD, A ▶ spin-off of the immensely popular *Cosby Show* that, in tandem with its parent series, helped NBC dominate Thursday nights through the late-1980s.

The series, which started in 1987, initially was built around Cliff Huxtable's second oldest daughter, Denise, entering Hillman College. The role was played by Lisa Bonet, but after the first season she left to return to *The Cosby Show*. Others in the resident cast, led by Kadeem Hardison as Dwayne, Dawnn Lewis as Jaleesa, Jasmine Guy as Whitley, and Sinbad as Walter, assumed the central roles.

Produced by Marcy Carsey and Tom Werner (Carsey-Werner Co.) for Viacom Television, the show consistently ranked in the Nielsen top ten, but many attributed that largely to its audience-inheritance from *Cosby*.

Gary Coleman, Mary Ann Mobley and Conrad Bain in a scene from *Diff'rent Strokes*

DIFF'RENT STROKES ▶ NBC situation comedy (1978-86) that became one of that network's few hits in the 1978-79 season. Produced by Norman Lear's T.A.T. Productions, the show developed as a vehicle for a precocious 12-year-old comedian, Gary Coleman. The premise is that two black youngsters from Harlem, Arnold and Willis Jackson, become residents of Park Avenue and are introduced to upper-middle-class life when they are adopted by a wealthy white gentleman, Philip Drummond, played by Conrad Bain. Coleman and Todd Bridges played Arnold and Willis, and Dana Plato played Drummond's daughter, Kimberly.

DIGITAL RECORDING ▶ process of recording and reproducing video and audio signals digitally, relying on streams of ones and zeros to indicate levels of luminance (light), chrominance (color) and other values instead of on the analog reproduction of these values. The major advantage of digital recording is that copies of a tape—with each copy representing one "generation" of removal from the original—are virtually identical to the master, with no loss in quality. This is especially advantageous in applications such as postproduction and special-effects work that require a lot of copying from tape to tape.

The earliest digital format, D-1, was brought to market by Sony in the late 1980s after years of demonstrations. It uses component video technology, meaning that it processes the chrominance and luminance signals separately, enabling considerable imaging-processing capability and yielding high picture quality. It was followed by the somewhat less expensive D-2 digital format, devised by Ampex and marketed by both Ampex and Sony, which uses composite video technology that does not separate luminance from chrominance. Both the D-1 and the D-2 formats use 19mm-wide (approximately three-quarter-inch) tape housed in cassettes. In 1990 Panasonic began marketing a D-3 digital format. Like D-2 it uses composite technology, but its half-inch tape allows for compact recorders and easier cassette storage. Additional digital formats, including half-inch component systems, are under development.

DIGITAL SIGNALS ▶ information transmitted in discrete pulses rather than as continuous signals. See also Analog.

DIGITAL VIDEO EFFECTS (DVE) ▶ manipulation of a TV image or any portion of it in a manner that affects its shape, size, orientation or position on the screen. In the 1980s DVE devices from such companies as NEC, Quantel and Ampex replaced the older analog special-effects generators (SEG) that merely switched between two images to create, say, a wipe effect. DVEs work by rendering the TV signals digital and manipulating them with a computer.

DILDAY, WILLIAM H., JR. ▶ first black general manager of a TV station, WLBT-TV in Jackson, Miss. He was named to head the station by a nonprofit caretaker group that had been given temporary custody of WLBT when the original owners, Lamar Life Insurance, lost the license in 1969 on race-discrimination grounds. The station, an NBC affiliate, prospered under Dilday's stewardship, increasing its share of the market. Since then he has become general manager of the competing CBS affiliate in the Jackson market, WJTW.

DILL, CLARENCE C. (d. 1977) ▶ former Democratic U.S. Senator from the State of Washington, known as the "Father of the Communications Act." Dill served two terms in the U.S. House of Representatives and in 1922 was elected to the U.S. Senate, where he also served two terms. He was co-author of the Radio Act of 1927 that established the Federal Radio Commission, the predecessor of the FCC. In 1933, Dill was named chairman of the Senate Interstate Commerce Committee and helped draft the Communications Act of 1934, which created the FCC and gave the seven-member Commission authority to regulate all interstate and foreign communication by wire and radio.

DILLER, BARRY ▶ chairman and chief executive of Fox Inc., the huge component of Rupert Murdoch's News Corp. that embraces the 20th Century-Fox film studio; Twentieth Television, the production and distribution arm; Fox Broadcasting Co., the network; and the Fox TV stations.

Diller joined Fox in October 1985. Since then the company has added seven TV stations to its group and successfully launched the Fox Network, which brought forth such popular shows as *Married...With Children, A Current Affair,* and *The Simpsons.* Under Diller the film studio has produced such hits as *Home Alone, Big, Broadcast News,* and *Die Hard.*

After starting his career in the mail room of the legendary William Morris Agency, Diller joined ABC's programming department as an assistant in 1966. He soon became its feature films specialist and developed the 90-minute "Movie of the Week" concept, introduced to great success in 1968. Diller became v.p. of programming and in 1972 oversaw another programming innovation—the commercial mini-series, which ABC introduced with *QB VII* and followed with such shows as *Rich Man, Poor Man* and *Roots.*

In 1975 Paramount hired Diller away from ABC as chairman and chief executive of Paramount Pictures. The move startled Hollywood, which had viewed Diller as simply a middle-echelon TV executive, despite his "Movie of the Week" experience. The choice was vindicated when the studio, under Diller, started turning out such hits as *Saturday Night Fever, Raiders of the Lost Ark, Ordinary People, An Officer and a Gentleman* and *Terms of Endearment.* Diller left Paramount primarily because of operational clashes with the parent company's new chairman, Martin Davis.

DIMBLEBY, RICHARD (d. 1965) ▶ journalist whose unique career over nearly three decades established him as the best-known broadcast personality in Great Britain. His fame crested as the semiofficial voice of the BBC on state occasions ranging from coronations to royal weddings and funerals. He died of cancer in December 1965 at the age of 52.

Born of a newspaper family in the London suburb of Richmond, in Surrey, he began his career in print journalism. He joined the BBC news department in 1936, became its first foreign correspondent and, in 1939, its first war correspondent. During the war he reported from 14 countries, culminating with his entry into Berlin with British troops in 1945. A year later he went from BBC staff status to freelance, launching a career as an "actuality" anchorman commentator that saw him cover everything from the coronation of Queen Elizabeth II to state visits by foreign dignitaries, royal weddings, and the funerals of presidents, prime ministers and popes.

His career benchmarks included participation in the first live Eurovision broadcast, the first pickup by Eurovision from the Soviet Union and the first trans-Atlantic telecast by satellite.

Over the years he also appeared on British television in a variety of specials, as a quiz show panelist and as a public affairs anchorman, notably on BBC-TV's long-run prime weekly documentary hour, *Panorama.*

His famous name is perpetuated in British television by his two sons, David and Jonathan, both prominent as on-camera newscasters.

DINAH! ▶ syndicated talk-variety series featuring Dinah Shore and guests. Sold in both 60- and 90-minute versions, the daily programs began in September 1974 with the CBS o&os as their base. The series was produced by Henry Jaffe Enterprises and syndicated by 20th Century-Fox TV.

DING DONG SCHOOL ▶ an early NBC program for preschoolers (1952-56) conducted by Dr. Frances Horwich, who became widely known to viewers as "Miss Frances." The network series originated in Chicago and was continued (1957-59) on the independent station there, WGN-TV. Later it was syndicated on tape.

The program was celebrated at first for its educational value but later drew some criticism for "talking down" to children. Horwich, who had been a professor of education at Roosevelt University, had a slow, deliberate way of speaking and was very much in the schoolmarm mold. Billed as "the nursery school of the air," the program was essentially instructional. As TV developed more exciting techniques of presentation, *Ding Dong School* seemed ever more talky and heavy, and when cartoon shows for children were placed in competition *Ding Dong* was done.

DIRECT-BROADCAST SATELLITES (DBS) ▶ technology of transmitting broadcast-quality signals from a satellite directly to home antennas, eliminating the TV station or the cable company as intermediary. Japan and Canada began practical experiments with DBS in the late 1970s, using low-powered satellites, as a means of reaching remote rural areas that cannot otherwise receive TV service. In Europe, France, West Germany and the Nordic countries have been considering DBS as an alternative to national television by terrestrial lines, chiefly because it would be the most cost-effective way to reach the last 1% of the population.

DBS is a source of concern to the American broadcast lobby for the obvious reason that it could obviate the need for TV stations. It also poses competition to cable systems. By the early 1980s, DBS technology had evolved to the point of allowing home dish antennas only two feet square to receive a plethora of channels from a single satellite, and private corporations and government bodies around the world proposed a dizzying variety of DBS plans. While many of the early experiments did not work out, by 1991 DBS was delivering news and entertainment to thousands of viewers in Britain, and HDTV programming in Japan.

DIRECTORS GUILD OF AMERICA ▶ union representing directors, assistant directors and unit managers in TV, radio and films, organized in 1960 from a merger of the Screen Directors and the Radio-TV Directors guilds. Later it absorbed unions for a.d.'s and stage managers and in 1965 also was joined by the Screen Directors International Guild. The power of numbers—more than 3,000 members—gave DGA the leverage to bargain effectively with networks and individual production companies.

In addition to providing for minimum wage scales, working conditions, residual payments and screen credits in its contracts, DGA in its 1964 negotiations with the Assn. of Motion Picture and Television Producers established a "Director's Bill of Rights," which in spelling out the director's creative responsibility also guaranteed certain artistic rights. Those included his right to screen the *dailies,* to receive a *director's cut* of the completed film and to participate in the dubbing and scoring process.

DISCOVERY CHANNEL, THE ▶ basic-cable network devoted entirely to non-fiction entertainment, chiefly documentaries on nature, science, technology, travel and history. It was founded in 1985 by John S. Hendricks, with initial financial backing from Group W Satellite Communications, New York Life Insurance and Allen and Company. As it was well received wherever it was available, the network gained crucial support from several major cable operators—TCI, United Cable, Cox Cable and Newhouse—both in the form of a financial transfusion and in expanding its cable carriage. In 1989 three of the four cable operators bought out Group W and the other non-cable investors.

Discovery has become an alternative outlet for kinds of programs that previously had to depend on public television for exposure. The channel's biggest programming success has been its annual *Shark Week* series, which often has raised ratings levels into the 3s and 4s.

The network's penetration passed the 50 million mark in 1990, making it one of the fastest growing cable networks of all time. John Hendricks remains chairman and CEO, and Ruth Otte is president and chief operating officer.

In 1991 Discovery purchased The Learning Channel and relaunched it as a companion service.

DISEASE OF THE MONTH ▶ self-mocking industry term, though probably coined by a critic, for a made-for-television movie whose dramatic premise centers on a medical, psychiatric or sociopathic disorder—especially one recently in the news. In the 1980s, when the networks went full tilt in commissioning television movies, films on such topics as wife-beating, nymphomania, drug abuse, depression and the like—many of them based on actual cases that made news—tended to do well in the ratings. And so began a trend that now may even be considered a genre.

DISNEY CHANNEL, THE ▶ popular pay cable network that was an almost immediate success when it launched in April 1983, reflecting the trust in the Disney name and the desire in many households for quality wholesome entertainment. The channel draws on the Walt Disney organization's huge television and movie library but also provides original programming from independent sources that meets its standards for children's and family fare. The channel had more than 5.5 million paying subscribers in 1991.

Concentrating on children's programming by day, the 24-hour channel graduates in age appeal by early evening. It plays to adults after 9 p.m. by offering movies, specials, mini-series and concerts, none with pronounced sexual or violence content.

John F. Cooke is president and Stephen Fields senior vice president of original programming.

DISNEY, WALT (d. 1966) ▶ founder of the multimillion dollar Walt Disney empire—movies, television, amusement parks, recordings and merchandise—that grew out of the garage studio where he created his famous cartoon characters Mickey Mouse and Donald Duck. His animation studios expanded from shorts to full-length features (*Snow White and the Seven Dwarfs*), television series, and amusement parks (Disneyland in California, Disney World in Florida and Euro Disneyland near Paris).

As one of the first movie producers to move into TV production, Disney produced such programs as *The Mickey Mouse Club, Zorro* and the weekly series running under such titles as *Walt Disney's Wonderful World of Color* and *The Wonderful World of Disney,* which became the anchor of NBC's Sunday night schedule. Disney refused to release most of his movies to television, contending that every seven years there would be a new theatrical audience for them. However, in 1982, with pay cable blossoming into a new market, the entire Disney library was readied for the new premium service, The Disney Channel, which began in 1983.

***DISNEYLAND* ▶** Walt Disney's first show for television, which was probably also ABC's first prime-time smash hit, causing CBS and NBC affiliates in two-station markets to scramble for a secondary affiliation with ABC. The show, which premiered Oct. 27, 1954, was presented in the early evening and included action-adventure segments, animation with the familiar Disney characters and nature sequences. The success of *Disneyland* altered industry thinking about programs designed for children and contributed to raising the overall quality of productions for children.

The following fall Disney added *The Mickey Mouse Club* on ABC, another huge success. *Disneyland,* meanwhile, not only helped the financially ailing network but served to promote the Disneyland amusement park in Southern California, which opened almost concurrently with the TV series. *Disneyland* ran on ABC until the fall of 1958, when it moved to NBC as *Walt Disney's Wonderful World of Color,* with essentially the same format. Becoming a Sunday night fixture, it was later retitled *The Wonderful World of Disney.* NBC gave up the series in 1981 because it had gone into a ratings decline. CBS then entered into a pact with Disney for an occasional series.

DISTANT SIGNAL ▶ a station from another market imported by a cable system and carried locally by it. The right to bring in distant signals on a limited basis has been a selling point for cable TV, especially in areas served by fewer than three networks or in those having no independent stations. Because of their coverage of sporting events and their heavy reliance on vintage movies, the independents have tended to be a desired distant signal for cable systems in the smaller towns and have thereby extended their reach.

***DIVORCE COURT* ▶** a successful low-budget syndicated series, produced on tape, that recreated actual divorce trials in the setting of Los Angeles Domestic Relations Court. The cases were argued by professional lawyers, with actors portraying the plaintiffs, defendants and witnesses. Produced from 1958 through 1961, the series, owned by Storer Programs Inc., amassed a library of 130 programs. Syndication sales were handled by NTA.

On the heels of the rage for *People's Court* in the early 1980s, *Divorce Court* was revived in 1984 for another highly successful syndication run, which continued into the early 1990s. Again the program used actors for the reenactments, actual lawyers to argue the cases, and a retired judge, William B. Keene, to consider the evidence and hand down the verdict. The program's producers include Storer, Blair Entertainment, SCI Programs Inc., Kushner-Locke Productions, and BTM Enterprises. Blair has been handling the distribution.

See also Courtroom Shows.

DIXON, PAUL (d. 1975) ▶ popular local TV personality in Cincinnati whose *Paul Dixon Show,* a live morning variety strip, ran 20 years on WLWT and in its later years on three other Avco TV stations in Ohio.

DLT ENTERTAINMENT ▶ production and distribution company that has thrived on adapting British shows for the American market. The company is headed by Donald L. Taffner, a longtime syndicator who in the 1980s also became U.S. distributor for Britain's Thames Television. Taffner reedited Thames's *Benny Hill* variety series into a fast-paced program of sketches and blackouts and had great success marketing it in the States. He also bought the format of *Three's Company* and reworked it as a winning series for ABC and a best-seller in syndication. These were in addition to many other domestic productions. Taffner in latter years has been venturing in legitimate theatre, both in New York and London.

DMA (DESIGNATED MARKET AREA) ▶ term used by Nielsen to define a geographic area of counties in which the home-market TV stations are dominant in total hours viewed.

DOBBS, LOU ▶ anchor of CNN's *Moneyline* and v.p. and business news managing editor of CNN, responsible for all business news reporting and programming.

Dobbs joined CNN in 1980, its first year, as chief economics correspondent and anchor of *Moneyline.* In 1981 he did an expose of price-fixing in the oil industry and produced and anchored CNN's first special report, a 90-minute program that sought to articulate the federal budget for viewers.

Prior to joining CNN, Dobbs was a news anchor and economic news editor at KING-TV Seattle. He holds a decree in economics from Harvard.

***DOCTOR KILDARE* ▶** a 1961 re-creation of the MGM movie series of two decades earlier. Produced for NBC in response to ABC's hit doctor series *Ben Casey, Kildare* starred Richard Chamberlain as Dr. James Kildare and Raymond Massey as Dr. Leonard Gillespie. It received good ratings and ran through 1966, totaling 142 episodes. Produced by Arena Productions in association with MGM-TV, the series made a TV star of Chamberlain.

DOCTOR WHO ▶ long-running British science fiction series that began on the BBC in 1962 and was first syndicated in the U.S. in 1973. The series started when two BBC-TV department heads, Sydney Newton and Donald Wilson, collaborated on the creation of an educational program to help teach children about history and science. Initially, the series centered on an aging scientist who could travel through time and space with a time machine. Over the years, the format underwent changes, as did the lead actor. Dr. Who has been played at various times by William Hartnell, Patrick Troughton, Jon Pertwee, Tom Baker, Peter Davison, Colin Baker and Peter Cushing. Producers are Graham Williams and Barry Letts. In 1983 five of the actors re-united in a 90-minute special that aired on BBC and PBS.

DOCTORS, THE ▶ see Soap Operas.

DOCU-DRAMA ▶ TV dramas based on actual historical occurrences and real people, blending, as it were, the elements of documentary and theater. With the rise of the mini-series and made-for-TV movies, the form grew increasingly popular during the 1970s, but it created an uneasiness among journalists and historians for the distortions of history and truth that could result from invented dialogue, minor plot fabrications, the rearranging of facts and other uses of literary license. Shakespeare's histories, of course, were a form of docu-drama, and critics of the trend in television cited them as examples of how those imaginative and often careless renderings of history have been widely accepted as true and definitive accounts.

Most of the fact-based dramas on TV were drawn from contemporary history. Among the dozens presented on the networks in the 1970s were *The Missiles of October, Pueblo, King, Ike, Eleanor and Franklin, Blind Ambition, Friendly Fire, Tail Gunner Joe, The Ordeal of Patty Hearst, Fear on Trial, Clarence Darrow, A Man Called Intrepid, Backstairs at the White House, The Trial of Lee Harvey Oswald, The Amazing Howard Hughes, Holocaust* and *Roots* and *Roots II.*

DODD, THOMAS J. (d. 1971) ▶ leader of an intense and widely publicized 1961 crusade against TV violence as chairman of the Senate Subcommittee on Juvenile Delinquency. Formal hearings on the subject, presided over by the Connecticut senator in June and July of that year, produced evidence that network officials continually ordered programmers and film studios to increase the violence content in programs for the sake of ratings. Dr. Albert Bandura, professor of psychology at Stanford, who appeared as a witness, cited studies showing that after watching violent films children played more aggressively than before and tended to imitate the behavior they saw.

But Sen. Dodd suddenly lost his fervor, drew back from the investigation and let the crusade peter out. Disillusioned members of his staff attributed his change of attitude to friendships he had made in the broadcast industry.

DOERFER, JOHN C. ▶ chairman of the FCC from 1957 to 1960 whose resignation came as a result of charges of official misconduct during an investigation of the commission by the House Subcommittee on Legislative Oversight.

Doerfer was accused by Dr. Bernard Schwartz, chief counsel for the subcommittee, of undue fraternization with the broadcasting industry, of taking trips paid for by organizations regulated by the FCC and of receiving honoraria while being reimbursed by the Government for his expenses.

Answering the charges in public hearings on Feb. 3, 1959, Doerfer argued that a commissioner is not to be likened precisely to a judge, since he is also engaged in legislation and rule-making, and therefore must move outside the FCC for information on the problems and conditions of the industry. He noted also in his defense that, under the Communications Act, commissioners were permitted to receive honoraria for the publication or delivery of papers.

Since there was no evidence that any of Doerfer's decisions in official matters had been affected by *ex parte* influences, the subcommittee took no punitive action against him. But the tempest raised by the charges made it difficult for Doerfer to continue to serve on the commission and he resigned on March 10, 1960. He was promptly hired as a vice-president and counsel by Storer Broadcasting Co., the company prominently cited in the investigation as having entertained him lavishly.

DOERFER PLAN ▶ a tacit bargain struck with the networks by FCC chairman John C. Doerfer in 1960 that each would present a weekly one-hour public affairs series in prime time in atonement for the quiz show scandals. Moreover, Doerfer asked the networks to agree not to place those programs in competition with each other. When it was argued that such an agreement would be in violation of the anti-trust laws, Doerfer produced a written opinion from the Justice Department permitting collusion by the networks for such a worthy purpose. The Doerfer plan resulted in a boon for the news documentary that lasted about three years.

The precedent made it possible for future FCC chairmen to suggest that the networks rotate a quality program at the same time each day or that they rotate a noncommercial children's show. Neither of those suggestions was acted upon, but the Doerfer plan did break the ground for network agreements to rotate news coverage of such protracted events as the Senate Watergate hearings, with the provision that any network at any time could duplicate part of the coverage on its own news judgment.

DOLAN, CHARLES F. ▶ chairman and chief executive of Cablevision Systems Corp. and one of the cable industry's most visionary executives, credited with creation of Home Box Office, the pay-movie service, in 1970. He also built the first urban cable system, in Manhattan in 1961, and earlier pioneered the development of hotel pay TV.

Dolan sold the Manhattan franchise to Time Inc. in 1973, along with HBO, which was then a regional service distributed in parts of the northeast by microwave. He proceeded to build Cablevision Systems, starting with a small part of Nassau County, an affluent New York suburb on Long Island, and quickly began to expand the system into one of the country's largest cable installations, serving some 560,000 subscribers on Long Island. There he developed cable's first local all-news channel. Meanwhile, he continued to build Cablevision Systems into a major MSO, winning franchises in such population centers as Boston, Chicago and other parts of metropolitan New York. Cablevision has grown into the ninth largest cable operator in the U.S., with systems in 11 states reaching 1.6 million subscribers. Simultaneously, Dolan established Rainbow Program Enterprises, which operates national and regional cable networks. These include American Movie Classics, Bravo and the SportsChannel services. Cablevision also became partnered with NBC and Hughes Communications in a proposed DBS system, Sky Cable.

Dolan began as a writer of radio scripts and commercials and for a time operated a small sports newsreel business before venturing into cable.

DOLLY ▶ costly variety show starring country singer Dolly Parton that flopped for ABC in 1987. The network made a two-year, $44 million commitment to the star, betting she could bridge the generational gap as one who appealed to all age groups and all geographical areas. The show finished 47th in the Nielsen ratings.

Phil Donahue

DONAHUE, PHIL ▶ host of a long-running syndicated talk show initially emanating from the Midwest. It began on WLWD-TV Dayton in 1967 as *The Phil Donahue Show* and at first was fed to sister Avco stations but soon extended its syndication nationally. After six years the program was retitled *Donahue* and moved its originating base to WGN-TV Chicago. In March 1976 Avco, which had been disbanding its broadcast group, sold the program to Multimedia. The show moved to New York in the mid-1980s.

An hour-long daytime program, it features interviews and discussions with celebrities and notable figures in a broad range of fields but emphasizes political, social and sexual topics.

The program grew to become one of the most successful in syndication, carried on 160 stations, and in 1979 it added a half-hour evening edition—an edited-down version of one of the morning shows—for prime-access slotting. For a time in 1979 Donahue doubled on NBC's *Today* with thrice-weekly interviews. In 1991 he added a weekly talk show with Soviet journalist Vladimir Pozner, called *Pozner and Donahue.*

Donahue is married to actress Marlo Thomas.

DONALDSON, JOAN ▶ head of CBC Newsworld, Canada's 24-hour news and information cable network, which began in 1989. She has held the title since the start-up phase in 1987. Steeped in broadcast journalism, she began at CBC as a reporter and moved up the line to senior positions with various current affairs programs. Then she joined CTV's esteemed

W-5 current affairs series as a field producer and went on to teach at universities before returning to CBC in 1983. In 1990 she met with a freak accident, knocked over by a bicycle as she was leaving the CBC offices in Montreal. She remained in a coma as of the fall of 1991.

Sam Donaldson

DONALDSON, SAM ▶ aggressive ABC correspondent known for his bold and often abrasive style; he became controversial during the Reagan years for seeming to show disrespect for the President in his adversarial questioning at news conferences. In the fall of 1990 he became co-anchor with Diane Sawyer of *Prime Time Live,* a weekly series. He continues as an interviewer and roundtable participant on *This Week with David Brinkley,* which airs Sunday mornings on ABC.

He joined the ABC News Washington bureau in 1967 after six years as a news producer, moderator and sometime anchorman for WTOP-TV Washington. He began his television career in 1959 with KRLD-TV Dallas.

DONNA REED SHOW, THE **▶** wholesome, domestic situation comedy that had a long run on ABC (1958-66) and whose reruns began to be stripped in daytime in 1964. Produced by Todon-Briskin in association with Screen Gems, it starred movie actress Donna Reed as Donna Stone and featured Carl Betz as husband Alex, Paul Petersen as son Jeff and Shelley Fabares as daughter Mary.

DONNY AND MARIE **▶** popular weekly variety hour (1975-78) built around the youthful brother-sister team of Donny and Marie Osmond. It featured the Osmond Brothers vocal group and Shipstad and Johnson's Ice Follies. By Osmond Productions and Sid & Marty Krofft Productions, it was guided by Raymond Katz as executive producer, the Kroffts as co-producers and Art Fisher as director.

DOOGIE HOWSER, M.D. **▶** ABC situation comedy from Steven Bochco Productions about a boy-genius (Neil Patrick Harris) who graduated from college at age 10, finished medical school at 14 and became a doctor at 16. James B. Sikking and Belinda Montgomery play Harris's parents and Max Casella Doogie's scheming friend Vinnie.

The show debuted in 1989 to lukewarm ratings, but ABC kept it on the schedule in the belief it had the potential to build an audience, and the following year the network was vindicated. The series was one of the first from Bochco in his exclusive deal to produce for ABC through Twentieth Television. Bochco co-created the show with David Kelley, with whom he worked on *L.A. Law*.

DORFSMAN, LOUIS ▶ top art director and designer for CBS, serving as v.p. of advertising and design for the Broadcast Group (1968-87) and previously as director of design for CBS Inc. He was responsible for much of the interior decor at the CBS headquarters and for the graphics and design of all printed or packaged matter representing the company. He joined CBS in 1946 as a staff designer and over the years became recognized as one of the country's top graphic designers. When he left CBS after 40 years, he started his own design studio.

DORIS DAY SHOW, THE **▶** a "heart" comedy designed for movie actress Doris Day, in which she portrayed a widow, Doris Martin, first living on her uncle's farm, then working as a secretary, then living in the city, then working as a magazine writer, and raising two sons. Produced by Arwin Productions-Terry Melcher for CBS (1968-72), it featured Denver Pyle as Donna's uncle Buck Webb, Rose Marie as Myrna Gibbons, John Dehner as editor Sy Bennett, Jackie Joseph as secretary Jackie Parker and, in the later seasons, Peter Lawford as romantic interest Peter Lawrence.

DORSEY, JOHN ▶ director associated with Chuck Barris Productions whose work included *The Newlywed Game, The Dating Game, The Game Game, The New Treasure Hunt* and *Dream Girl of '67.* Earlier, as a producer-director for NBC, he directed sports and variety programs.

DORSO, DICK ▶ executive of United Artists TV during the early 1960s who was close to CBS-TV president Jim Aubrey. He was a generally successful supplier of programs to the network, but in 1965, after five of his pilots were rejected by CBS at a cost of more than $1 million, UA began its withdrawal from network production and Dorso left the company and the industry.

DORTORT, DAVID ▶ producer specializing in western series who was executive producer of *Bonanza* and *High Chaparral.*

***DOUBLE DARE* ▶** see Game Shows.

***DOUBLE HELIX, THE* ▶** British-American coproduction about scientists James Watson and Francis Crick, who were responsible for identifying DNA, the code by which all living things reproduce themselves. Set in Britain during the 1950s, the two-hour made-for-TV movie was produced and directed by Mick Jackson and written by William Nicholson. The movie was televised on the Arts and Entertainment network in September 1987 and starred Jeff Goldblum, Tim Pigott-Smith, Alan Howard and Juliet Stevenson.

DOUGLAS, MIKE ▶ uniquely successful syndication performer whose daily talk-variety program, *The Mike Douglas Show,* via Group W Productions, ran more than a decade and was valued by stations for late afternoon or early evening time periods. Though Douglas did not have a single major credit on the networks, he was one of the highest-paid performers in TV. In 1972, when other syndicators tried to woo him away from Group W, he negotiated a new contract paying him $2 million a year. In 1980 Group W dropped Douglas for a younger host, John Davidson. Douglas decided to keep his show going by producing it himself with a different distributor, but he threw in the towel in late 1981. The following year he became host of a daily hour interview show on CNN.

Originally a singer, Douglas acquired experience as host of a celebrity talk-show on radio in Chicago. His 90-minute daily TV show began at the Westinghouse (Group W) station in Cleveland in the early 1960s, and when the FCC ordered Westinghouse and NBC to swap their Cleveland and Philadelphia stations, Douglas's base was moved to KYW-TV in Philadelphia. His show emanated from there until 1978, except for occasional tours about the country, and was such an effective showcase for talent that performers gratefully traveled from New York and other cities to appear on it. Later the show was produced in Hollywood and Las Vegas.

DOWDLE, JAMES C. ▶ president and chief executive officer of Tribune Broadcasting, responsible for the company's powerful group of TV and radio stations (including WPIX-TV New York, KTLA-TV Los Angeles, WGN-TV Chicago and KWGN-TV Denver), and Tribune Entertainment, a production and distribution company. Dowdle's TV career began in ad sales with the Petry and Katz rep firms. From 1964-81 he was with Hubbard Broadcasting, where eventually he became general manager of independent station WTOG in Tampa-St. Petersburg, Fla. He was hired by the Tribune Co. as president of its newly formed corporate broadcast group in January 1981.

Tribune's television efforts have grown increasingly important to the company as its core newspaper business has weakened. The company also owns the Chicago Cubs baseball team, which gets important exposure through WGN-TV, one of the superstations relayed to cable systems across the country. In that they cover the three largest TV markets, Tribune's group of independent stations has also become a crucial link in the distribution chain for syndicated program producers hoping to launch a show nationwide. As often as possible, however, Tribune fills its programming slots with shows produced by its own entertainment division.

DOWNLINK ▶ dish used to receive signals from a satellite.

DOWNS, HUGH ▶ TV personality whose career has had a unique evolution; he started as a network announcer in Chicago and developed into a leading TV journalist as longtime co-host of *20/20.* He became known to the mass audience as Jack Paar's sidekick and foil during Paar's reign on NBC's *Tonight Show* and then as host of *Today* (1962-71). For many of his years with *Today,* he doubled as host of *Concentration.* In semi-retirement, he continued to do commercials, specials and the syndicated series *Not For Women Only* as alternate with Barbara Walters. He has been the host of ABC's newsmagazine *20/20* since 1978 and is considered to have been the key to the program's rise in the ratings. In his Chicago years he was associated with such series as *Kukla, Fran & Ollie* and *Hawkins Falls.* Later he worked on NBC's *Home, The Sid Caesar Show, The Arlene Francis Show* and the radio series, *Monitor.* Since the fall of 1988 he has also hosted numerous telecasts of *Live From Lincoln Center* on PBS. Downs has entered *The*

Guinness Book of World Records for having logged 10,000 hours on commercial TV.

Hugh Downs, host of the ABC newsmagazine *20/20*

DOZIER, WILLIAM (d. 1991) ▶ CBS program executive (1951-64) assigned to the West Coast for most of that period. He then formed an independent company, Greenway productions, which produced *Batman* and *The Green Hornet,* among other series.

***DRAGNET* ▶** hit NBC police series based on actual case histories, carried over from radio in 1952 for a seven-year run and then revived in 1967 for three more seasons. Starring and directed by Jack Webb as Sergeant Joe Friday, the half-hour series was noted for its style, which anticipated cinema verite even on radio and added to American lexicon Friday's workaday line of dialogue: "Just the facts, ma'am." The first version featured Barney Phillips as Webb's sidekick, Sergeant Ed Jacobs, soon replaced by Ben Alexander as Officer Frank Smith. The second version cast Harry Morgan as Officer Bill Gannon. Both shows were produced by Webb's own firm, Mark VII Ltd., but the revival was in association with Universal TV. Reruns went into syndication with the title of *Badge 714.*

***DREAM ON* ▶** HBO sitcom incorporating clips from TV anthology dramas of the 1950s and 1960s, including *General Electric Theatre, Alcoa Premiere* and *Studio 57.* The series, which began in 1989, evolved from a deal between MCA Television and HBO, which agreed to create a comedy series that would use the old black-and-white footage, owned by MCA, of more than 800 episodes from vintage shows. Movie director John Landis agreed to produce. After numerous interviews with writers, he settled on David Crane and Marta Kauffman, whose story idea centered around a neurotic, divorced father in his thirties living in New York. He fantasizes, Walter Mitty-like, envisioning his life as scenes from old TV series and movies. The show stars Brian Benben, who is supported by Wendie Malick, Denny Dillon, Chris Demetral, Dorien Wilson, Jeffrey Joseph and Sydney Walsh. Kevin Bright is executive producer with Landis.

DRINKWATER, TERRY (d. 1989) ▶ veteran of CBS News who joined the organization in 1963 and held the title of senior correspondent at the time of his death. Working mainly from a West Coast base, he served variously as Los Angeles bureau chief, field producer, correspondent and anchor of the West Coast edition of *The CBS Evening News.* He received a duPont-Columbia award for his 1983 series for the evening newscast on cancer treatment, which included his own struggle with the disease. He died of it six years later.

DROP-INS ▶ additional VHF channels that could be "dropped in" to the existing FCC table of allocations without causing interference, according to an engineering study by the White House Office of Telecommunications Policy in October 1973. The OTP study said that 62 VHF channels could be added in the top 41 markets; a subsequent FCC study put the figure at 30 stations in 27 cities. The study argued that the FCC's standards for its table of allocations in 1952 was too conservative for the present state of the art, in requiring a spacing of 170 miles for stations assigned to the same channel in the northeast, 190 miles for those in the west and 220 miles for those in the south. The FCC requirement was also that stations on adjacent channels be a minimum of 60 miles apart. The OTP said that if the distance criteria were reduced 10% to 15%, a substantial number of VHF channels could be added in most major cities.

Because the proposed drop-ins would afford an opportunity for minority ownership of stations, the Office of Communication of the United Church of Christ, petitioned the FCC for a rulemaking on the feasibility of the new channels in 1975. The organization noted that of the 608 licensed VHF stations, only two were owned by blacks, and both stations were outside the continental U.S. (in the Virgin Islands).

In the FCC inquiry on the proposal in 1976, established broadcast interests argued that the proposed drop-ins would cause signal interference with existing stations and that if the FCC adopted the plan it would be a severe setback for UHF and would constitute a "breach of trust" by the commission, which had pledged to help develop the UHF band. The proponents contended that the drop-ins would improve competition and make possible a fourth commercial network.

Drop-ins were recommended for such cities as Miami, Atlanta, Kansas City, Milwaukee, Little Rock, Dayton, Spokane, Dallas-Ft. Worth, Houston, Seattle, San Francisco, Memphis, Nashville, Des Moines and Birmingham, among others. Four cities that received dropped-in channels were Knoxville, Tenn. (Channel 8), Salt Lake City, Utah (Channel 13), Johnstown, N.Y. (Channel 8), and Charleston, West Va. (Channel 11).

DSRC (DAVID SARNOFF RESEARCH CENTER) ▶ a contract research facility specializing in client-sponsored electronics, communications, and imaging research. Formerly RCA Labs and since 1987 a subsidiary of SRI International, DSRC developed the ACTV (advanced compatible television) ATV system for a consortium formed of itself plus NBC and GE (later Thompson) consumer electronics, as well as the ADTV (advanced digital system) ATV system for a consortium formed of the three above clients plus Philips Consumer Electronics and Compression Labs Inc. The latter is a fully digital system using video compression that delivers high-definition television (HDTV) on a 6-MGZ channel.

DUBIN, CHARLES S. ▶ producer-director whose work ranged from productions of Rodgers & Hammerstein's *Cinderella,* the Bolshoi Ballet and segments for *Omnibus* to episodes of *Kojak, M*A*S*H, Toma, Kung-Fu* and *Room 222.* He also directed the *Sanford and Son* pilot.

DUFFY, JAMES E. ▶ former president of the ABC television network, who succeeded Elton H. Rule in 1970 when Rule became president of the parent corporation. Duffy rose from the ranks, having joined ABC in 1949 as a publicity writer for its Chicago stations upon his graduation from Beloit College. He moved into sales for the radio network in 1953 and ten years later became vice-president in charge of sales for ABC-TV.

As network president Duffy gained industry recognition for the upgrading of program and advertising policies in television directed to children.

Under reorganization of the ABC television division in 1972, Duffy's authority as network president was substantially diminished, although his title remained in force. The new organizational structure established a higher new post, president of ABC Television, and at the same time removed the program department from network supervision. The areas left reporting to Duffy were sales and affiliate relations.

In the early 1980s Duffy became a sort of roving ambassador and public spokesman for the network—a role that was eliminated when Capital Cities acquired ABC.

DUKE, PATTY ▶ one of the few child stars who has managed to maintain a successful career as an adult. She starred in three TV series and numerous made-for-TV movies and mini-series, including *Captains and Kings* (1976), *The Miracle Worker* (1979), *The Women's Room* (1980), and *George Washington* (1984). In the early-1960s' situation comedy, *The Patty Duke Show,* she played a dual role as teenaged twins. The series ran three years. Two sitcoms in the mid-1980s, *It Takes Two* and *Hail to the Chief,* were short-lived.

She became a star at the age of 12 when she played Helen Keller in *The Miracle Worker* on Broadway. By 1957 she was appearing regularly on *Kraft Television Theatre, Armstrong Circle Theatre* and *The U.S. Steel Hour.*

Duke was for two terms president of the Screen Actors Guild.

DUKES OF HAZZARD, THE ▶ a "Southern," relative to a Western, specializing in automobile chases at high speeds. A one-hour CBS series (1979-85) set in the South about a pair of car-jockeying cousins who delight in outwitting criminals and harassing the local police, it entered the schedule as a mid-season replacement in 1979 and immediately caught on. Tom Wopat and John Schneider played the Duke cousins, Luke and Bo, Catherine Bach was cousin Daisy Duke, Denver Pyle portrayed Uncle Jesse and Sorrell Booke played the corrupt Boss Hogg. The series was renewed and became the ideal lead-in to *Dallas* during the 1979-80 season, and the popularity of the combination was one of the main reasons CBS returned to prime-time dominance that season.

DuMONT, ALLEN B. (d. 1965) ▶ pioneer television broadcaster and manufacturer of picture tubes and TV sets. An outspoken, brilliant inventor, DuMont transformed the cathode-ray tube (CRT) from a fragile, short-lived device to a reliable piece of equipment around which practical TV receivers could be built. Before World War II his Allen B. DuMont Laboratories was manufacturing picture tubes and television sets, and after the war it took the leadership in developing increasingly larger direct-view tubes. The DuMont Television Network, although it did not survive television's early days, bred much of the industry's programming and business talent. DuMont appeared frequently before the FCC, particularly to oppose the CBS field-sequential color system and the intermixture of VHF and UHF channels in the same areas.

DuMONT TELEVISION NETWORK ▶ a venture into nationwide broadcasting by the Allen B. DuMont Laboratories in 1946. It failed in competition with ABC for third-network position and went out of business as the fourth network in 1955. Its owned stations were later to form the nucleus of a major independent group, Metromedia Television.

While it was in operation, the DuMont Network primarily offered low-budget quiz, variety and sports shows, and on occasion it shared special programs with the other networks. It was DuMont that covered the historic Army-McCarthy hearings, but its leading programs otherwise were those of Bishop Fulton J. Sheen, Jackie Gleason and the Monday night boxing matches.

The network grew out of DuMont's ownership of commercial stations WABD in New York (originally W3XWT) and WDTV in Pittsburgh. Paramount Pictures, which had purchased a half-interest in the parent company in 1938, separately owned two West Coast stations.

But the network was unable to put together fully a competitive lineup of affiliated stations, chiefly because it lacked the radio station relationships that the other networks were able to transfer to television. Nor was its unglamorous array of programs an incentive for uncommitted stations, and even Paramount's own KTLA in Los Angeles declined to clear for the DuMont shows.

The merger of ABC with United Paramount Theaters in 1951 strengthened its position as the third network, leaving DuMont a weak fourth, making it difficult to justify the cost of transcontinental lines. Although its affiliations were variously reported as between 80 and 178 stations, the DuMont Network was a losing operation, and less than two years after building a $5 million studio in New York—the largest production center in the industry at the time—DuMont Labs terminated the network and separated itself from the broadcasting division. The owned stations were operated as the Metropolitan Broadcasting Corp. in 1955, and Paramount's holdings were purchased in 1959 by John Kluge, who later changed the company's name to Metromedia.

DuMont's collapse was a chief reason for a 68% rise in billings for ABC during 1955.

DUNCAN, SANDY ▶ pert singer and dancer on the Broadway stage who crossed into TV as star of a sitcom, *Funny Face,* in 1971. When it failed, CBS tried and failed again the following year with *The Sandy Duncan Show* (1972). Not until *The Hogan Family* in 1987 did she finally have a hit series—and then as the replacement for Valerie Harper in the series that began as *Valerie.* The show had to change its title when Harper left in a dispute with the production company, Lorimar. In the long period between series Duncan appeared frequently on TV in variety specials and TV movies.

DUNN, RICHARD ▶ one of the leading figures in Britain's commercial ITV network, as chief executive of Thames Television, until Thames suddenly lost its franchise in the U.K.'s controversial auction of the television frequencies in 1991. Thames, which had the weekday broadcasting license for the London region, continues as a company with a concentration on production.

After a varied career as a writer and film producer, Dunn joined Thames in 1978 as personal assistant to managing director Jeremy Isaacs. In 1981 he became director or production at Thames and in 1985 managing director and chief executive. He is also chairman of the U.K. independent production company, Cosgrove Hall Productions.

DUOPOLY ▶ the FCC rule limiting ownership to one of each type of broadcast service—TV, AM and FM—in a community. The rule exempts public television, whose licensees are permitted to operate two TV stations in the same market, one on VHF and one on UHF.

The duopoly question is raised whenever the coverage of stations under the same ownership overlap. Waivers are granted if overlap is minimal. If the overlap existed before the present rules, "grandfathering" is applied.

Public TV duopolies exist in Chicago, Philadelphia, Boston, San Francisco, Pittsburgh, Minneapolis, Miami, Milwaukee and Richmond.

The 1987 repeal of the FCC's "Regional Concentration" rule did not directly change the duopoly rule, but it allowed broadcasters to own several properties in adjacent cities. A 1991 "inquiry" started by the FCC chairman Alfred C. Sikes was aimed, in part, at changing or eliminating the bar on duopolies. See also Cross-Ownership.

duPONT-COLUMBIA AWARDS ▸ citations for outstanding broadcast journalism conferred by the Alfred I. duPont Awards Foundation and the Columbia University Graduate School of Journalism. The awards are made by a blue-ribbon jury and carry great prestige largely because they are the by-product of a comprehensive nationwide survey of local, national and syndicated broadcast journalism conducted throughout the year. When the commercial networks gave up the special telecasts for the news and documentary Emmy Awards, PBS moved to fill the vacuum by televising the duPont-Columbia Awards. The first of those telecasts was in 1977.

DURANTE, JIMMY (d. 1980) ▸ comedian with background in nightclubs, radio and films, who became one of TV's preeminent personalities in the 1950s. His trademarks were a substantial nose, earning him the affectionate nickname of "Schnozzola"; a gravelly and tuneless voice that he was able to use effectively singing novelty tunes, such as his theme song, "Inka Dinka Doo"; a weather-beaten fedora and the closing line, "Good Night, Mrs. Calabash, wherever you are." His exit on TV was always made on a darkened stage through three circular spots of light issued from above.

Occasionally his TV shows featured the strutting Eddie Jackson, surviving partner in the famous nightclub act of Clayton, Jackson and Durante, formed in 1920, which started his career as a comic. Durante made his TV debut in *Four Star Revue* on NBC, in which he appeared on a rotating basis from November 1950 to May 1951. That gave way in the fall of that year to *All Star Revue,* on which he appeared until the spring of 1953.

In October 1953 he starred in *The Colgate Comedy Hour,* and the following fall he headlined his own show, *Texaco Star Theater,* which ran a year. A loveable lowbrow, he reached some of his highest TV moments clowning and singing duets with Ethel Barrymore, Helen Traubel and Margaret Truman. When his series ended Durante became a frequent variety show guest and always scored with his old nightclub finale, which involved the passionate destruction of a piano.

DURGIN, DON ▸ former president of NBC-TV (1966-73) and champion of the TV special, the 90-minute series, the rotating series and made-for-TV movies. He came into the presidency after holding a number of executive positions with ABC and NBC in the fields of promotion, research, sales and radio. For seven years before his appointment, he had been v.p. in charge of sales for NBC-TV.

When his administration ended he became corporate executive v.p. of NBC and a year later left to become president of Caffery-McCall Advertising. He resigned from the agency in 1976 and then became senior v.p. for Dun & Bradstreet, overseeing the broadcast subsidiary, Corinthian Broadcasting.

DURR, CLIFFORD J. (d. 1975) ▸ FCC commissioner (1941-48) noted for his vigorous support of the commission's controversial Blue Book in 1946, the document that attempted to define the public interest for purposes of license renewals. Durr also was concerned with reserving TV channels for education. A political liberal from Alabama, he turned down reappointment to the FCC saying he was unable to administer the government's loyalty program in good conscience. He returned to the practice of law in Washington and then moved to Montgomery, Ala., to handle civil rights cases. One of his clients was the late Martin Luther King, Jr.

DUVALL, SHELLEY ▸ sometime screen actress who in the 1980s became a prolific producer of cable programming, particularly the acclaimed Showtime series *Faerie Tale Theatre.* She followed with another anthology series for Showtime, *Tall Tales* (1985-88). In 1988 Duvall created Think Entertainment with backing from four cable operators. Though it has taken on some projects for commercial TV, the company remains predominantly a cable supplier—particularly of children's fare.

DYNASTY ▶ the most popular of the prime-time serials to cash in on the success of *Dallas.* Like *Dallas* it centered on a powerful and wealthy family in the West (in this case, Denver) whose fortune was made in the oil business. The sets and costumes were lavish—its weekly wardrobe budget of $10,000 was the highest in television out of a total weekly budget of $1.2 million per hour. *Dynasty* premiered in January 1981 on ABC and was produced by Richard and Esther Shapiro (who also created and wrote the show), Aaron Spelling, and Douglas Cramer. It became a huge hit worldwide, especially in the U.K.

The show starred John Forsythe as Blake Carrington, Linda Evans as his wife Krystle, and Joan Collins. Collins became a big celebrity for her portrayal of the antiheroine, the ruthless and greedy Alexis. Among the many actors who appeared in the series during its nine-year run (1981-89) were Pamela Sue Martin, Emma Samms, Rock Hudson, Jack Coleman, James Farentino, Heather Locklear, Gordon Thomson, Diahann Carroll, Billy Dee Williams, Catherine Oxenberg, Helmut Berger, John Saxon, Ali McGraw and George Hamilton, Jr.

Dynasty stars John Forsythe and Linda Evans, portraying Blake and Krystle Carrington

E

E! ENTERTAINMENT TELEVISION ▶ basic-cable network devoted to covering entertainment news, information and gossip. Formerly called Movietime, the channel underwent a change of leadership and format in 1990 to become a sort of 24-hour version of *Entertainment Tonight,* the successful syndicated program dedicated to show biz infotainment.

Movietime was launched in 1987 under the management of HBO but with a flock of other majority owners, including Warner Communications and seven of the largest cable MSOs. In its first two years, the channel fared poorly with programming that consisted largely of extended movie promos and interviews. Reorganized and reconceived as E! and reaching some 18.5 million households, it enjoys better success.

Though HBO is responsible for its day-to-day management, the channel is not a subsidiary of either HBO or Time Warner but operates as an independent company. Lee Masters is E!'s president, and Fran Shea senior vice president of programming.

EARLY BIRD ▶ Intelsat I, launched April 6, 1965, the world's first commercial communications satellite and the first synchronous communications satellite. Stationed over the Atlantic, it provided 240 telephone circuits or one television channel, increased trans-Atlantic communications capability by 50% and made live commercial television across an ocean possible for the first time.

EARLY FRINGE ▶ the time period preceding prime time, usually 4:30 to 7:30 p.m., Eastern Standard Time, and 3:30 to 6:30 p.m., Central Time.

EARLY FROST, AN **▶** poignant made-for-TV-movie that was the first major film to deal dramatically with the subject of AIDS. It aired on NBC in November 1985. The story centered on a conventional middle-aged couple in rural Pennsylvania forced to cope with the double shock that their son is dying and is homosexual. It was produced by Perry Lafferty and won director John Erman the Directors Guild Award. Ron Cowen and Daniel Lipman wrote the screenplay from a story by Sherman Yellen.

Aidan Quinn played the young lawyer who returns home gravely ill, Gena Rowlands played the mother, Ben Gazzara the father, and Sylvia Sidney the grandmother. Others in the cast were D. W. Moffett, John Glover, Sydney Walsh and Terry O'Quinn. It was by NBC Productions.

EARTH STATION ▶ installation for transmitting and/or receiving electronic communications (such as television) between the earth and a space satellite. The prominent feature of the earth station, also called a "dish," is a parabolic antenna aimed at the satellite. The station also contains specially designed transmitters and/or receivers and amplification equipment. Earth stations began to proliferate at cable systems around the country in 1977 after the FCC approved the use of five-meter dishes, smaller and considerably less costly than the previously authorized models. In the 1980s the U.S. was swept by a boom of consumer receive-only earth stations, installed by thousands of viewers in backyards. Some of these households were in remote areas with no access to other forms of television. Others, however, with access to cable or terrestrial broadcasting, made program reception a hobby.

EAST SIDE, WEST SIDE ▶ hour-long dramatic series centering on a social welfare agency in New York that starred George C. Scott (as Neil Brock) and featured Cicely Tyson (Jane Porter), both relatively unknown at the time. Premiering on CBS in the fall of 1963, it was respected by discriminating viewers but was only moderately successful in the ratings—a fact attributed by many in the trade to its serious content and depressing themes. The series was produced by Talent Associates-Paramount in association with United Artists Television.

Wendy Richard and Bill Treacher, stars of the British series *EastEnders*

EASTENDERS ▶ phenomenally successful early-evening soap opera in Britain that dared to challenge the longtime dominance of Granada TV's *Coronation Street* in the same working-class genre. It was created by BBC-TV in 1985 when *Coronation Street* was 25 years old and still the country's top-rated show. The show was a hit from the start and for a time overtook *Coronation Street* as Britain's most popular show; since then the lead has gone back and forth between the two.

The success of *EastEnders* lies in how well it has grasped the realities of working-class life in London's East End and the human problems peculiar to that class and culture. The struggles of the young and the heartbreak of the old are played out by a cast of 23 regulars whose breakfast-to-bedtime lives in Albert Square are filled with the troubles of overcrowded housing, unemployment, racism, teenage pregnancy, rape, suicide and the lot. Producer Julia Smith and script editor Tony Holland, creators of *EastEnders,* have given the show a gritty, realistic texture in treating contemporary problems with unflinching candor.

The serial airs in the U.S. on a several major market public TV stations that offer viewers a printed guide to the show's East End accents.

EASTMAN KODAK ▶ largest supplier of film to the television industry. The company's involvement goes back to the medium's early days when it provided black-and-white film for kinescopes. Kodak also provided film to stations and networks for news gathering before the advent of ENG. The company is also a main supplier to the Hollywood studios and the commercial production companies, which shoot most shows and spots on film. Kodak is a strong advocate of film as an origination medium for high-definition television (HDTV).

EBERSOL, DICK ▶ president of NBC Sports since 1989. Ebersol was declared a boy wonder at the network in 1975, when, as director of weekend late night programming, he paired with the youthful independent producer Lorne Michaels to create the landmark comedy showcase, *Saturday Night Live.* He was rewarded with vice presidency, NBC's first vice president under the age of 30, and given charge of late night programming. He went on to become v.p. of comedy, variety and event programming, and then took over as executive producer in 1981, when Michaels and much of the show's creative staff left.

In 1985 Ebersol formed No Sleep Productions, an independent production company that made *Friday Night Videos* and *Later with Bob Costas.* Since 1989 he has served additionally as senior v.p. for NBC News. Before joining NBC in 1974, he worked under Roone Arledge at ABC Sports.

EBSEN, BUDDY ▶ a former novelty dancer who became star of *The Beverly Hillbillies* (1962-71), a bucolic situation comedy, and then star of *Barnaby Jones* (1973-80), an urban private-eye series. In films and variety revues, before TV, he was known for his pretzel-like soft-shoe turns. Before *Hillbillies* he was featured in an adventure series, *Northwest Passage* (1958).

EDELMAN, LOUIS F. (d. 1976) ▶ Hollywood motion picture producer who began producing for TV in 1954. His hits on the networks included such series as *Make Room for Daddy, The Big Valley, The Life and Legend of Wyatt Earp* and various shows with Danny Thomas, including the 1952 remake of the movie, *The Jazz Singer.* Among his films were *White Heat, A Song to Remember* and *Hotel Berlin.* He was president of the Screen Producers Guild (1965-67).

***EDGE OF NIGHT, THE* ▶** see Soap Operas.

EDITORIAL ADVERTISING ▶ commercials intended to promote a point of view or an editorial position on an issue, rather than to stimulate the sale of a product or service. Standards & Practices policies of the networks reject such advertising (although the print media and some TV stations accept it) essentially because it may subject them to claims for response time under the Fairness Doctrine. The Supreme Court has ruled that broadcasters may not be forced to sell time for discussion of controversial public issues.

The networks contend, in defending their policies, that to sell time for editorial commercials ultimately would give those with the most money the loudest voices on the issues. They argue also that the public is better served when the points of view are expressed in news programs or information forums than when the message is wrapped in the manipulative techniques of advertising. ABC, however, experimentally began accepting issue advertising in late night slots in 1981.

EDITORIALIZING ON PUBLIC TELEVISION ▶ (*FCC v. League of Women Voters*) a 1984 Supreme Court decision that held that a congressional ban on editorializing by public broadcasters was unconstitutional. The case was brought by the League of Women Voters and the Pacifica Foundation.

Led by Justice William Brennan, the Court's liberal wing eked out a narrow 5-4 majority to rule that noncommercial broadcasters were improperly singled out and denied the right to speak. The decision was important in that it appeared to preclude the use of congressional purse-strings as a tool to rein in non-commercial stations.

After a more conservative Court began to signal a different approach in cases linking health providers' "gag" rules to federal funding, the decision on editorializing was among those newly targeted for challenge by conservatives who believed that public money should not subsidize controversial speech.

EDUCATIONAL TELEVISION AND RADIO CENTER (ETRC) ▶ early "networking" center for ETV established in Ann Arbor, Mich., in 1952 on a grant of $1.5 million from the Ford Foundation's Fund for Adult Education. Headed by Harry K. Newburn, former president of the University of Oregon, the center stored old educational programs and contracted for new material to serve neophyte educational TV stations. The filmed transcriptions were also rented to schools and private groups.

In 1958 Newburn resigned and was replaced by John F. White, who had operated the Pittsburgh ETV station, WQED. White moved the production arm to New York and renamed it the National Educational Television and Radio Center (NETRC), which in 1962 became National Educational Television (NET), the acknowledged national production center for ETV, supported by annual Ford Foundation grants of $6 million. NET broke with the classroom approach to ETV and provided the system with a broad range of cultural, public affairs, documentary and children's programming, breaking the ground for a network service and for the industry's eventual redesignation as Public TV.

***EDWARD THE KING* ▶** British historical series of 13 half-hours, airing in the U.K. as *The Royal Victorians* but retitled by Mobil Corp. for presentation on 49 commercial U.S. TV stations in January 1979. The series, which spans the reigns of the austere Victoria and her sybaritic son, Edward VII, was originally purchased by CBS in 1974 for $2.5 million, but it sat in storage for nearly five years while the network struggled to keep its ratings up.

Eventually Mobil, which had tried to sponsor the series on CBS, bought the rights for $1.8 million and put together an ad hoc network that was to create discomfort for CBS. As it turned out, 19 of the 49 stations assembled by Mobil were major-market CBS affiliates, which virtually wrecked the network's Wednesday night prospects for three months. Mobil required all stations to carry the program at 8 p.m. on Wednesdays. Of the remaining 30 stations in the Mobil lineup, 22 were independents, seven NBC affiliates and one an ABC outlet.

The program was both a critical and ratings success, beating on some occasions its network competition. The opening program ranked third in New York, second in Los Angeles and first in Washington.

Timothy West played Edward; Annette Crosbie, Queen Victoria; John Gielgud, Disraeli; Michael Hordern, Gladstone; and Helen Ryan, Alexandra.

EDWARDS, BLAKE ▶ producer and writer who left television for movies after making his mark in the 1950s as creator of such series as *Peter Gunn, Mr. Lucky* and *Dante's Inferno.* He became a topflight film producer with the success of *A Shot in the Dark* and the Pink Panther movies. He returned to TV in 1991-92 as executive producer of the ABC sitcom, *Julie,* starring Edwards's wife, Julie Andrews.

EDWARDS, DOUGLAS (d. 1990) ▶ CBS newscaster who delivered the network's 15-minute early evening report *Douglas Edwards with the News* from 1948 until Walter Cronkite replaced him in 1962. Edwards, who had begun his career in radio, remained with CBS News and continued to do daytime newscasts on television into the 1970s.

EDWARDS, RALPH ▶ game-show producer and host of *This Is Your Life,* a popular series in the late 1950s. That show and Edwards's *Truth or Consequences* were both revived for first-run syndication in the 1970s.

EEN (EASTERN EDUCATIONAL NETWORK) ▶ a regional network of public television stations in the Northeastern states serving its members with programs of local or regional interest. From time to time, it serves also as a consortium for the joint purchase of programs not otherwise available through PBS.

EFFECTIVE RADIATED POWER (ERP) ▶ the power of the signal radiated from the transmitting antenna, a function of transmitter power and antenna gain (or loss). The FCC generally permits maximum ERP of 100 kilowatts (100,000 watts) for stations on Channels 2 through 6; 360 kilowatts for 7 through 13; and 5 megawatts (5,000,000 watts) for UHF stations. If the antennas are above specified heights, reduced ERP is required.

EGER, JOHN M. ▶ communications lawyer with a strong international orientation who was a policy advisor to presidents Nixon and Ford and then an executive in the CBS Broadcast Group, doubling as its resident expert on international affairs. Later he entered academia and today holds the Lionel Van Deerlin endowed chair in communications and public policy at San Diego State University.

As a young lawyer, Eger became legal assistant to then chairman of the FCC, Dean Burch. Then he moved on to the White House Office of Telecommunications Policy as deputy director, later becoming acting director, in which capacity he advised two presidents. In 1983 CBS Broadcast Group president Gene Jankowski hired Eger as senior vice president responsible for CBS Broadcast International and the company's cable and teletext operations. Eger left CBS in 1986 and started his own company, Worldwide Media Group. He began teaching at San Diego State in 1990, commuting from Connecticut.

***EIGHT IS ENOUGH* ▶** hit ABC comedy-drama, in one-hour format, which premiered in March 1977 and was a Wednesday night mainstay until 1981. The series centered on a family with eight children ranging in age from eight to 23. Dick Van Patten played the father, Tom Bradford, a successful syndicated columnist, and until her death Diana Hyland was the mother, Joan. Van Patten ran the family as a single parent until Betty Buckley joined the cast as his new wife, Abby Abbott.

The children in the series were portrayed by Grant Goodeve (as David), Lani O'Grady (Mary), Lauri Walters (Joannie), Susan Richardson (Susan), Dianne Kay (Nancy), Connie Newton-Needham (Elizabeth), Willie Aames (Tommy) and Adam Rich (Nicholas). The series was drawn from a book by Tom Braden. Lee Rich and Phil Capice were executive producers, Robert Jacks producer and William Blinn, who created the show, executive consultant. The series was by Lorimar Productions.

***EISENHOWER PRESS CONFERENCE* ▶** (Jan. 19, 1955) the first presidential news conference simultaneously covered by the print press, newsreels and television, and at which candid photographs and direct quotations were authorized for broadcast, as recorded, by the White House.

EISNER, MICHAEL D. ▶ chairman and chief executive officer of the Walt Disney Company since 1984, after eight years as president and chief operating officer of Paramount and 10 years as a program executive for ABC. For several years the highest paid executive in the country, the charismatic Eisner quickly turned a moribund Disney into one of Hollywood's major studios. Under his leadership, the studio stepped up movie production—including the full-length animated features that made Disney a household name—returned to prime-time television, entered the lucrative syndication business and bolstered its theme parks. Company earnings increased 500% in his first four years on the job.

Eisner also oversaw the construction of Euro Disneyland, near Paris, and moved Disney into commercial broadcasting by purchasing the Los Angeles TV station KHJ. During Eisner's tenure at Paramount, that company ventured into the cable television field with a one-third interest in the USA Network and quadrupled its television production, which included the hits *Cheers* and *Family Ties.* He came to ABC in the mid-sixties after a brief stint with the CBS program department, and he served variously as senior v.p. in charge of prime-time production and development, v.p. of daytime programming, v.p. of children's programming, v.p. of program development and manager of specials and talent. He was instrumental in developing a number of series that figured in ABC's banner 1975-76 season, among them *Rich Man, Poor Man, Welcome Back, Cotter, Laverne & Shirley* and *Bionic Woman.*

***ELEANOR AND FRANKLIN* ▶** five-part cycle by ABC on the relationship of Eleanor and Franklin D. Roosevelt through the various stages of their careers. It began as a four-hour adaptation of the Joseph P. Lash book *Eleanor and Franklin,* presented in two parts on a Sunday and Monday night, Jan. 11 and 12, 1976. The ratings and generally favorable response prompted ABC to order two sequels, one covering the Roosevelts during their years in the White House, to be presented in 1977, and a final sequel based on another book by Lash, *Eleanor: The Years Alone,* for 1978. Jane Alexander and Ed Herrmann portrayed the Roosevelts. Executive producer was David Susskind, producer Harry Sherman, director Daniel Petty and writer James Costigan.

***ELECTRIC COMPANY, THE* ▶** a public TV series intended to help teach basic reading skills to slow readers, as a derivation of *Sesame Street.* Produced by the same company, Children's Television Workshop (CTW), it premiered as a daily hour in October 1971, two years after the resounding success of *Sesame Street,* and was itself an educational/entertainment success. According to PBS estimates it reached 6.5 million youngsters regularly, both in school and in the home.

The program was planned to reinforce school reading curricula, using the winning entertainment techniques of television—comic vignettes, animation, electronic effects and music. CTW also produced a variety of support materials, such as teaching guides, books and puzzles, for use in schools and day-care centers.

Produced at a cost of approximately $33,000 per show, it was funded initially by foundations and later was sustained by payments from the Station Program Cooperative and outside grants.

ELECTRONIC MEDIA RATINGS COUNCIL (EMRC) ▶ organization established in the early 1960s to provide users of local or national audience measurement services with an independent auditing function that essentially makes sure that the ratings services do what they say they do. Members of the EMRC include ABC, CBS, NBC and most of the larger group-owned stations. The EMRC grants certificates of accreditation to Arbitron and Nielsen for their local and national ratings services.

Shortly after the EMRC's formation, the U.S. Dept. of Justice granted it an antitrust waiver but said it would monitor the organization for anticompetitive behavior. The EMRC has since established "minimum standards" for accreditation, and from time to time it has tussled with the ratings services about whether such standards cross the line between auditor and regulator.

***ELIZABETH R* ▶** BBC six-part mini-series that played on PBS (1973) tracing the life of Elizabeth I from the ages of 15 to 69. It starred Glenda Jackson and aired in Britain in 1971.

ELLERBEE, LINDA ▶ television journalist of an independent spirit who after 11 years with NBC News and shorter stints with ABC and CNN formed her own company, Lucky Duck Productions. In the 1980s, she wrote a best-selling book, *And So It Goes,* and in 1988 began writing a newspaper column for Hearst's King

Features Syndicate. With Lucky Duck and in association with the magazine *American Heritage,* she is preparing a new quarterly PBS series, *The American Heritage Television Specials,* scheduled to begin in 1992.

After many diverse assignments, her career at NBC News climaxed with her appointment as co-host of an overnight news broadcast, *NBC News Overnight.* Though the program failed, Ellerbee was an acknowledged hit. The du-Pont-Columbia awards cited *Overnight* as "possibly the best written and most intelligent news program ever."

Linda Ellerbee

ELLERY QUEEN ▶ twice-produced series, first during the 1950s and again by NBC in 1975. The original (1950-59) was successful, with the title role passing from Lee Bowman to Hugh Marlowe and then to George Nader and Lee Phillips (it was syndicated under the title *Mystery Is My Business*). The 1975 edition, with the late Jim Hutton and David Wayne, was canceled after one season. It was by Universal TV, with Richard Levinson and William Link as executive producers.

ELLIPSE ▶ Paris-based production and distribution company that is a subsidiary of France's highly successful pay-television channel, Canal Plus, and in which Hearst Corp. has a 20% interest. Ellipse Programme, the production unit, deals in international coproductions such as *The New Zorro* series and the animated *Babar* series. The company also has studio operations, a licensing unit and a distribution arm, Ellipse International. Ellipse operates independently of Canal Plus, and only a small percentage of its programs are broadcast by the pay channel.

EMERGENCY! ▶ NBC adventure series (1972-77) about the heroics of the paramedic unit of the Los Angeles County Fire Department. The program's chief distinction was that it drew a sizable audience in its first two seasons against TV's number-one show at the time, *All in the Family.* An animated version, *Emergency Plus 4,* was spun off by NBC for Saturday mornings. Featured in the original version were Robert Fuller as Dr. Kelly Brackett of Ramparts General Hospital, Julie London as Nurse Dixie McCall, Bobby Troup as Dr. Joe Early, Randolph Mantooth as paramedic John Gage and Kevin Tighe as paramedic Roy DeSoto. It was produced by Jack Webb's Mark VII Productions with Universal TV, in association with NBC-TV, with Robert A. Cinader as executive producer and Ed Self as producer.

EMERSON, FAYE (d. 1983) ▶ a former Broadway actress who became one of early TV's most popular hosts. Somewhat controversial for her decolletage, she worked steadily at both CBS and NBC, with *The Faye Emerson Show* running three seasons at the former (1949-52) while she was a panelist on *Leave It to the Girls* and frequent guest on *Who Said That?* on the latter.

Her other shows were *Fifteen with Faye* and *Faye and Skitch* (with Skitch Henderson, her husband for a time). She also had dramatic roles in *Studio One, Ford Theatre* and *Goodyear Playhouse,* among others, and was a panelist on *I've Got a Secret.* At her popularity peak, she substituted for such personalities as Edward R. Murrow, Garry Moore, Dave Garroway and Arlene Francis on their shows.

EMMY AWARDS ▶ annual awards conferred in recognition of outstanding achievement by the National Academy of Television Arts and Sciences (NATAS), an organization of professionals in the industry. A rift between the Hollywood chapter and the rest of the National Academy caused the 1977 Emmy Awards telecast to be postponed, and a dispute ensued over the secessionist group's claim to ownership of the rights to the statuette and its name. The 1977 awards were conferred in the fall rather than the spring and were made by the Hollywood group rather than the national organization. Since then the prime-time awards have been made by the Hollywood chapter (ATAS) and all others by NATAS and its chapters.

The first Emmy awards were conferred on Jan. 25, 1949, at the Hollywood Athletic Club, with the name "Emmy" adopted for the trophy as a variation on "Immy," a nickname for the image orthicon tube. The name was suggested by Harry Lubcke, a pioneer television engineer who served as president of the Academy from 1949-50. The statuette was designed by Louis McManus.

The awards ceremonies had their first national telecast on March 7, 1955, and thereafter became annual, star-studded TV events rotated among the three networks. Local chapters of the Academy also make awards for TV achievement in their cities, and those ceremonies are sometimes televised.

An Emmy Award

EMPTY NEST ▶ half-hour spin-off from *The Golden Girls,* starring Richard Mulligan as Harry Weston, a widowed pediatrician living with his two adult daughters, one a neurotic divorcee (Carol, played by Dinah Manoff) and the other a sensible police officer (Barbara, played by Kristy McNichol). David Leisure, who made his television mark as Joe Isuzu in a series of car commercials, plays Mulligan's lascivious next-door neighbor, Charley. The show began as an NBC series in 1988, slotted immediately after *Golden Girls* in the network's Saturday night lineup. In 1991 it was moved to a different time period. It is produced by Witt/Thomas/Harris Productions for Disney's Touchstone Television.

ENBERG, DICK ▶ three-time Emmy Award winner as Outstanding Sports Personality/Play-by-Play and 14-year veteran as NBC's primary NFL play-by-play voice. His responsibilities have included Super Bowls XV, XVII, and XXIII, the Rose Bowl (1980 to 1988), the Fiesta Bowl (1989), the Federal Express Orange Bowl (1990 and 1991), the World Series (1982) and the NCAA basketball Championships (1976 to 1981). He shares play-by-play duties on NBC's NBA telecasts with Marv Albert, and since 1991 has served as play-by-play announcer (with analyst Bill Walsh) for NBC's exclusive coverage of all Notre Dame home football games. He has hosted the Breeders' Cup Day since 1984, the World Championships of Track and Field in 1983 and 1987, the French Open since 1983, and Wimbledon since 1979, and co-hosted NBC's weekday-morning and Sunday telecasts of the Barcelona Olympics.

ENCRYPTION ▶ scrambling of a TV signal so that the receiver needs a special device in order to see a coherent picture. Encryption is used by cable TV, pay TV, and pay-per-view services—and will be a major component of any DBS service—to ensure that customers pay for the programming.

ENG (ELECTRONIC NEWS GATHERING) ▶ the use of all-electronic means for television news coverage. Virtually from the start of television, electronic news-gathering techniques have been used on special occasions, when there was opportunity to install portable microwave links from the scene of the news event to the studio, transmitter or networking point. In the mid-1970s, ENG spread throughout network and local station news operations, essentially eliminating the use of film as an intermediate step.

Electronic news-gathering received its biggest impetus after 1973 with the development of the time-base corrector (TBC), which made possible the use of lightweight portable (and usually inexpensive) helical-scan videotape recorders (VTR's) as a substitute for film cameras. The TBC converts the output of the helical-scan recorder into a picture with sufficient stability to be broadcast.

The early ENG components were a miniature color camera (minicam), small VTR and a power supply. The power supply, usually battery-operated, could be carried on the cameraman's back or worn on a special belt. In the late 1980s the use of camcorders (cameras and recorders combined in a single unit) further enhanced the portability of ENG equipment and the mobility of news crews. An additional ENG accessory is a portable microwave transmission station for use in cases where it is desirable—and possible—to send the live picture directly to the television studio, thus eliminating the necessity for the videotape recorder.

In most cases, however, the VTR is an integral part of the ENG outfit. When the news event has been recorded, the footage is often microwaved directly to the station. Alternatively, the tape is taken back to the station, rerecorded, then edited for airing. In some cases the editing is done on a truck in the field.

ENG is sometimes called SNG (satellite news gathering) when the signal from a news source is bounced off a satellite on its way back to the station or network. EFP (electronic field production) refers to the use of electronic, nonfilm equipment for location work other than news gathering.

ENGELBERT HUMPERDINCK SHOW, THE ▶ one of several attempts by the British concern ATV to market a variety show in the U.S.; like most of the others it was unsuccessful. Humperdinck, a popular singer on both sides of the Atlantic, was the focus, with international performers as guests. ABC carried the series in 1970 for 18 weeks.

ENGLANDER, ROGER ▶ director associated with artistic and cultural programs. He directed the CBS *Young People's Concerts, Vladimir Horowitz at Carnegie Hall, S. Hurok Presents, The Bell Telephone Hour* and episodes for *Omnibus, The Great American Dream Machine* and *The Performing Arts.*

The hosts of *Entertainment Tonight*

ENTERTAINMENT TONIGHT ▶ syndicated, half-hour magazine series of entertainment news, celebrity interviews, and on-location coverage of TV programs and feature films. The weekend version, *Entertainment This Week,* runs 60 minutes and recaps weekday highlights. Cohosts are Mary Hart (1982—) and John Tesh (1989—), who is accompanied by Leeza Gibbons (1984—) on the weekend show. *ET* began in 1981 and has been a bonanza for Paramount television ever since. The half-hour roundup of gossip and hype is fed to local stations from Los Angeles each weekday in network fashion by satellite. The stations tape the feed and broadcast it when they want. Executive producers are John Goldhamer, George Merlis, and Jack Reilly.

EQUAL TIME LAW ▶ the provision under Section 315 of the Communications Act that requires broadcast licensees who permit their facilities to be utilized by a legally qualified candidate to provide equal opportunities to opposing candidates if such time is requested. The statute was intended to guarantee that broadcasting will be responsive to the fact that politicians are extraordinarily dependent upon the mass media's portrayal of their candidacy.

Section (a) of 315 states that if any licensee shall permit a legally qualified candidate to use a broadcasting station, he shall afford "equal opportunities" to all other candidates for that office. Thus, if one candidate buys time on a station, his opponents may buy equivalent time, but the station is not required to give free time in response to purchased time. The Equal Time Law differs in this respect from the Fairness Doctrine, with which it is often confused.

A legally qualified candidate is defined as one who has publicly announced his candidacy and who meets the qualifications prescribed by law for the indicated office (*McCarthy v. FCC*). The broadcast licensee has no power of censorship over the material broadcast by a candidate (*Farmers Educational and Cooperative Union v. WDAY*).

As a general rule, any use of broadcast facilities by a legally qualified candidate imposes an equal time obligation on the broadcaster for all other candidates for the office. In 1959, however, Section 315 was amended to exclude certain kinds of programs, namely: bona fide newscasts, bona fide news interviews (e.g., *Meet the Press*), bona fide news documentaries in which the appearance of the candidate is incidental to the presentation of the subject, and on-the-spot coverage of bona fide news events.

To establish whether a program is "bona fide," the FCC looks to a number of elements, such as the nature of the format and content, whether the program is regularly scheduled, when the program was initiated and who initiated, produced and controlled it. The commission has held that a news program scheduled to begin 11 weeks before the start of an election was not exempt.

Beginning in 1975 the FCC began a long series of "reinterpretations" of the law to create ever-broader exemptions from its scope. Prodded from the outside by its former general counsel Henry Geller, the commission held that debates involving only major candidates could be "covered" as "on the spot news events." By 1980 the fig leaf of sponsorship by an outside group (such as the League of Women Voters, which held the 1976 presidential debates) was eliminated, so that debates were considered newsworthy even when held in the station's own studios. Insulation from equal time claims for interview programs was also provided, and by 1989 the FCC was even exempting portions of *The McLaughlin Group* political discussion show on the theory that such shows are "newscasts."

Section (b) of 315 requires that charges made for the use of a broadcasting station cannot—during the 45-day period preceding a primary election or during the 60 days preceding a general or special election—exceed the lowest unit charge of the station for the same class of time. At any other time, the charges made to candidates would be comparable to those for other users. Broadcasters became increasingly adept at designing rate structures that denied candidates cheap air time to which they believed they were entitled. Under congressional pressure, a series of unannounced "spot checks" by FCC enforcement staff were executed in 1990, leading to massive litigation and calls on legislation to eliminate "preemptible" rates.

In 1971 Congress passed the Campaign Communications Reform Act, which added a new sub-section to Section 312 of the Communications Act. The new sub-section specifies that a station license may be revoked for willful and repeated failure to allow reasonable access to candidates for federal elective office or to permit them to purchase reasonable amounts of time on the station. The FCC ruled that these provisions applied as well to noncommercial stations, and public TV stations were challenged to comply by Senator James Buckley of New York during his reelection campaign in 1976. The 1971 law was upheld against First Amendment challenge in *CBS Inc. v. FCC.* That 1981 case arose from President Carter's attempt to buy time to announce his reelection bid in November 1979. Ironically, although Carter won a favorable ruling from the FCC in that case, he canceled the speech because of that year's Iranian hostage crisis.

ERLICHT, LEWIS ▶ former ABC executive who shifted from station management to network programming and in the spring of 1979 became v.p. and assistant to the president of ABC Entertainment, Anthony D. Thomopoulos. In a career with ABC that began in 1969 in the sales department of WABC-TV New York, he held a succession of posts that included manager of research for ABC Television Spot Sales; v.p. and general manager of WLS-TV Chicago (1974-77); v.p. of programs, east coast, for ABC Entertainment; and in July 1978, v.p. and general manager of ABC Entertainment, based in Hollywood. He later became senior v.p. and then president of ABC Entertainment between 1981 and 1985, and president of ABC Circle Films until 1986. Since then he has been CEO of New World Broadcasting.

ESPN (ENTERTAINMENT AND SPORTS PROGRAMMING NETWORK) ▶ basic-cable network specializing in sports programming. Launched in 1979, ESPN is one of the largest and most successful basic channels, and it has been at the forefront in positioning cable as a legitimate competitor to the three broadcast networks in bidding for high-profile sports events. It is carried by virtually every cable system and reaches 57 million households.

ESPN was originally the brainchild of William F. Rasmussen and his son Scott. Getty Oil bought the network before launch, and it was then purchased in several stages by ABC (now Capital Cities/ABC), which sold 20% to Nabisco Brands (now RJR/Nabisco) in 1984. In 1990 RJR/Nabisco sold its 20% share to the Hearst Corp.

Milestones for ESPN include signing the largest early cable advertising contract when Anheuser-Busch made a $1.4 million buy in 1979, and purchasing a National Football League Sunday night schedule of games that debuted in 1987. In 1990 ESPN paid $400 million to Major League Baseball in an ambitious plan to televise nationally 175 baseball games a year for four years. Baseball's first two years on the network were a disappointment from a financial standpoint because ratings were lower than expected, but ESPN drew praise for being the first network to offer viewers a national, rather than a regional, perspective on the American pastime. Steven M. Bornstein is ESPN's president and CEO.

ESTES v. TEXAS ▶ (381 U.S. 532 [1965]) case in which the Supreme Court held that television broadcasting of a criminal trial, either live or on tape or film, denies a defendant his right to due process of law as guaranteed by the Fourteenth Amendment.

The case was brought by Billy Sol Estes after his conviction in a state court in Texas on charges of swindling. Estes had asked that TV cameras and broadcast microphones be barred from covering the trial, but the court denied his motion. However, the court ordered all photographers and cameramen to remain in a constricted press booth that was totally enclosed except for a door and a narrow slit barely wide enough for lenses to fit through. The judge also restricted coverage to certain parts of the trial.

After his conviction, Estes appealed to the Texas Court of Criminal Appeals, arguing that the presence of cameramen and photographers deprived him of his right to a fair trial. His conviction was affirmed, and he then appealed to the U.S. Supreme Court for review.

The Supreme Court reversed his conviction because of the prejudice introduced by the cameras. At the outset the Court noted that, while Canon 35 of the Judicial Canons of the American Bar Association prohibits cameras in courtrooms, the Judicial Canons were not the law. But the Court held that due process of law was violated because of the substantial possibility that the cameras interfered with the court's attempt to determine if the defendant committed a particular crime.

The cameras, the Court suggested, might well have an impact upon the jurors, the witnesses, the judge and the defendant. Since the cameras might well have an adverse effect upon the participants of the trial, and since they in no way aided the trials court in its role as fact-finder, the Supreme Court held that Estes had been denied due process.

ETERNAL LIGHT, THE ▶ religion series on NBC that has presented a variety of interview and discussion programs by Protestant, Catholic and Jewish clergymen on ethics in our time. After more than a quarter century on television it was canceled in 1978.

ETV (EDUCATIONAL TELEVISION) ▶ the name for noncommercial television broadcasting until the Public Broadcasting Act of 1967, which, on the recommendation of the Carnegie Commission, changed "educational" to "public" to broaden the scope and promise of the system. The original noncommercial stations were built in the 1950s with an instructional purpose, but their inability to attract a broad audience was attributed partly to the designation "educational," which connoted dry and didactic television. The term is still occasionally used, and well into the 1970s there were organizations such as the National Association of Educational Broadcasters, but officially ETV has been superseded by PTV.

EUROPEAN BROADCASTING UNION (EBU) ▶ launched in 1950 by 23 nations at a founding conference in Torquay, England, it is essentially a system of international broadcasting cooperation—radio and television—with 34 active and 64 associate members. Among the latter are the major U.S. networks.

With administrative and legal headquarters at Geneva, and a technical center at Brussels, the EBU has been instrumental in the drafting of treaties and conventions covering international broadcasting standards and copyrights. Through its Eurovision interconnect, which now links up 23 countries, the organization coordinates coverage of major actuality specials—coronations, space shots, sports championships, etc. Out of its Brussels technical center come, among other things, twice-daily newsfilm feeds by and for constituent TV systems. EBU also sponsors symposia and workshops as well as regular program-trade markets.

EUROPE'S TELEVISION FESTIVALS AND MARKETS ▶ competitive annual events treating television as an art form and conferring international awards for excellence. Festivals abound in Europe, some of them prestigious and consequential, others little more than chamber of commerce types of promotions. The principal ones annually are the Prix Italia, the Golden Rose of Montreux, the International Television Festival of Monte Carlo and the Prix Jeunesse International in Munich.

What had once been a major event, the annual Cannes festival for news and documentary programs, has been merged into the Monte Carlo Festival, where the categories otherwise spotlight drama and children's programs. The categories at Montreux, in Switzerland, are limited to light entertainment entries, while the Prix Italia is for dramas and documentaries. As the name suggests, the Munich event is for children's shows.

Other European festivals are at Kielce in Poland, for films and TV shows with musical themes; Knokke in Belgium for variety shows;

Leipzig in East Germany for short films and documentaries; Prague in Czechoslovakia for dramas and documentaries; and Nordring in Norway for music shows.

The Prix Danube at Bratislava in Czechoslovakia is for children's shows; the Prix Futura in Berlin for programs themed to the world of tomorrow; the festival at Annecy in France for animation; and the Common Market-sponsored festival in Brussels for programs on European affairs.

Still others are sponsored by religious organizations for programs on themes such as peace and justice. Among these are Monte Carlo's UNDA festival for the International Catholic Federation of TV and Radio Awards; the International Christian TV Festival, a skip-year event promoted by the World Association for Christian Communication and the International Catholic Federation of TV and Radio; the Christian Unity TV Awards in Geneva; and the International Religious Broadcasting Festival at Seville, Spain.

Four other major events for the international television trade are not festivals but program markets at which networks, syndicators and independent producers meet to buy and/or sell programs. They are the MIP-TV in April, and MIPCOM in October, both at Cannes, and the twice-yearly (spring and fall) MIFED events in Milan.

The European Broadcasting Union (of which the three major American networks are associate members) also holds twice-yearly screenings of new products by its constituent broadcasting organizations.

EUROVISION ▶ a permanent network of terrestrial circuits and satellite links to facilitate daily program exchanges among members of the European Broadcasting Union (EBU). Ever since the first Eurovision transmissions in 1954, most of the international news and sports coverage that appears on European screens has been transmitted by Eurovision.

EUROVISION SONG CONTEST ▶ a once-a-year live TV special via the Eurovision interconnect in which European Broadcasting Union member countries compete with nominated songs and singers. Started in 1955, the event annually plays to vast television audiences from Ireland to Israel and from Finland to Portugal.

EVANS, BERGEN ▶ erudite TV host and panelist who was also a professor of English. During the 1950s he moderated, from Chicago, the word game *Down You Go,* and later *The Last Word.* He also appeared on *Superghost, Of Many Things* and *It's About Time,* and he supervised the questions for the big quizzes, *The $64,000 Question* and *The $64,000 Challenge.*

EVANS, LINDA ▶ television actress with varied series credits who snagged a principal role in the glitzy prime-time serial, *Dynasty,* in 1981 and rode to stardom with the show's lasting popularity. She had prominent roles in *Big Valley* (1965-69) and *Hunter* (1977) and played supporting parts in such series as *The Adventures of Ozzie and Harriet* and *My Favorite Martian* in the 1960s. But she became known internationally in the 1980s as the blonde and beautiful Krystle, foil to Joan Collins's evil Alexis, in *Dynasty.*

EVANS, MAURICE (d. 1989) ▶ noted Shakespearean actor from Britain who provided U.S. television with numerous distinguished performances of the classics during the 1950s and 1960s, most of them for NBC's *Hallmark Hall of Fame.* He also directed some of the early *Hallmark* productions and helped set the lasting standard for the series.

Evans made his U.S. TV debut in *Hamlet* in 1953 on the *Hallmark* series, a production that NBC claimed had a larger audience than all the theatrical productions of the play since its Elizabethan premiere. There was, of course, no way to substantiate the claim but it remains part of TV lore.

Evans performed *Macbeth* live on *Hallmark* in 1954 and again on film in 1960; *Richard II* in 1954; *The Taming of the Shrew* in 1956; and *Twelfth Night* in 1957. He also performed Shaw's *Man and Superman, The Devil's Disciple* and *Caesar and Cleopatra,* the latter for *G.E. Theatre.* In the latter part of his career he was a regular on the sitcom, *Bewitched.*

***EVENING AT POPS* ▶** hour-long PBS series produced by WGBH Boston that features the Boston Pops orchestra. It began in 1974 with Arthur Fiedler as host and conductor; when Fiedler died in 1979, John Williams succeeded him. The series originally had a companion in *Evening at Symphony,* which featured the Boston Symphony with Seiji Ozawa and a variety of guest conductors. Each ran approximately three months a year—*Pops* during the warmer months and *Symphony* in the fall-winter. *Symphony* was discontinued in 1980, and *Pops* has held the slot alone since.

EVENING/PM MAGAZINE ▶ innovative prime-time access program syndicated five nights a week by Group W Productions, after it was successfully launched as a local nightly magazine on Group W's five stations. On the originating stations the half-hour series was entitled *Evening Magazine,* in syndication it went by the name of *PM Magazine.*

Evening was developed in 1976 at KPIX San Francisco and a year later spawned local counterparts at the four other stations. Since some of the six- or seven-minute segments in the telecasts were not distinctly local in nature, they were bicycled among the Group W stations to reduce the burden and the cost of producing a nightly half-hour. These "national" segments then were offered in a syndicated package to other stations, which created their own magazines by producing around 50% of the material locally. The concept was successful, and by the fall of 1979 there were 47 stations in the fold.

The original program was created by producer B. Ziggy Stone and KPIX program manager William Hillier, who became executive producer for all *Evening/PM* shows. Hillier left to start his own company in 1979 and was succeeded by Richard Crew. *Evening* was the first local magazine program shot entirely on location. It also had the longest run of any show in prime-time access (1979-90).

EVENT TELEVISION ▶ the medium engaged in the live coverage of something happening in real time, whether a news or sports event, an awards presentation or a beauty pageant. Considered by critics to be television at its purest, the idea was broadened by some networks in the late 1960s to include specials and movies as "events" created by television.

EVR (ELECTRONIC VIDEO RECORDING) ▶ now obsolete, but first demonstrated by CBS Inc. in 1967; a system whereby recorded video material may be played back through a television receiver. The recording medium was cartridged black-and-white photographic film, on which picture information, color and sound were electronically coded. With tape dominating the videocassette field, CBS abandoned EVR in 1971. The system anticipated by a decade the home video phenomenon that overtook home entertainment in the 1980s.

EXECUTIVE STORY CONSULTANT ▶ common designation in the credits for a script "doctor," an independent writer engaged to improve a faulty TV play.

EXECUTIVE SUITE ▶ hour-long CBS prime-time dramatic serial (1976-77) about the internal struggles within a large corporation and the intertwining private lives of its employees. Loosely based on Cameron Hawley's novel of that title, it was one of a number of expensive nighttime soap operas introduced by the networks in 1976 following the success that spring of *Rich Man, Poor Man* and *Family.* Featured were Mitchell Ryan as corporate president Dan Walling, Stephen Elliott as vice president Howell Rutledge, Sharon Acker as Walling's wife Helen, Leigh McCloskey as the Walling's son Brian and Wendy Phillips as daughter Stacey. Norman Felton and Stanley Rubin were executive producers, Den Brinkley producer and Charles S. Dubin and Joseph Pevney directors.

EXPOSE ▶ prime-time NBC News series, begun in January 1991, featuring the company's noted investigative news team of Brian Ross and Ira Silverman, and hosted by *Nightly News* anchor Tom Brokaw. The series entered the schedule in January 1991, a time when the networks were looking to reduce costs by doing more in-house programming and when tabloid news and so-called reality-based programs were the trend of the day. Ideally, however, the program hoped to become for NBC what *60 Minutes* has been for CBS and *20/20* for ABC. NBC had tried for an equivalent for more than a decade, and *Expose* was the 1991 attempt. Paul W. Greenberg was executive producer.

A scene from the PBS series on the civil rights movement, *Eyes on the Prize*

EYES ON THE PRIZE ▶ public television's definitive narrative of America's civil rights struggles during the 1950s and 1960s. The series of independently produced films aired on PBS in two sequences of six hour-long programs: *Eyes on the Prize I* (1987) and *Eyes on the Prize II* (1990).

The series was conceived and produced by Henry Hampton through his own production company, Blackside, and Boston's WGBH-TV. Hampton spent six years putting together 44 separate underwriters to get the $2.5 million needed to produce the first six shows. Using news footage and interviews with participants, the first sequence chronicled the civil rights story up to the 1965 march from Selma to Montgomery. It was followed three years later by a sequel costing $5.8 million to produce and carrying the story through the assassination of Dr. Martin Luther King, Jr., and into the mid-1980s.

EYEWITNESS NEWS ▶ title widely used by local stations for newscasts whose format permits reporters to deliver their own stories on the air. The concept was revolutionary in 1968; before then virtually every newscast had a star newscaster who read the copy written by reporters or rewritten from the wires by staff members.

The concept probably had its origins at the public TV station in San Francisco, KQED, during a newspaper strike in 1968. KQED created a program on which newspaper reporters presented the stories that would have been in the papers and conversed with each other on details. But for practical purposes it began at KYW-TV Philadelphia later that year. When the station's news director, Al Primo, learned that the KYW reporters were members of AFTRA, the performing union, and that no extra fees were involved in putting them on the air, he broke with commercial broadcast tradition and let the news-gatherers report the news under their own bylines. This contributed to a looser, more conversational presentation, which a significant number of viewers found more appealing than the standard formal newscast.

Modifications of the basic idea led to the station's newspersons assuming roles as members of a happy-go-lucky team, who exchanged quips between news items. In its most base form—where the joshing stopped just short of spitball throwing—*eyewitness* became known to journalism critics as "happytalk news."

Contributing to its spread across the country was its demonstrable ability to break the established news-viewing habits. In the years when all newscasts took the formal, single-anchor approach, it was extremely difficult for any challenger to overtake the news leader in the market. The axiom of the time was that the news habit was the hardest of all to change. But *Eyewitness News*—with its comedy, chitchat and conviviality—won new viewers almost overnight and devastated the traditional newscasts that had ruled their markets for years.

The *Eyewitness* concept, which in some markets took other names such as *Action News* or *The Scene News,* was promulgated in many instances by news consultants like Frank Magid Associates and McHugh-Hoffman, who helped their clients break the grip on the news market held by more orthodox competitors.

Primo went on to develop successfully the *Eyewitness News* techniques at the ABC-owned television stations in early 1970s, and in 1976 he left to become a consultant to local stations on implementing the format he invented.

F

F TROOP ▶ ABC military situation comedy (1965-67) set in the post-Civil War West, with Forrest Tucker (Sergeant Morgan O'Rourke), Larry Storch (Corporal Randolph Agarn) and Ken Berry (Captain Wilton Parmenter) as inept cavalrymen, and Edward Everett Horton playing Roaring Chicken. Melody Patterson was also featured as Wrangler Jane. The series was by Warner Bros. TV.

FACE THE NATION ▶ CBS's Sunday morning newsmaking series that probes government officials, world leaders and others in the news for 30 minutes. The series began in 1954 as a knock-off of NBC's *Meet the Press* but evolved differently over the years. Instead of a small panel of journalists interviewing a guest, which had been the format for years, *Face the Nation* today has multiple guests with divergent points of view and a single interviewer. Lesley Stahl, the longtime White House correspondent, performed that role from 1983 until 1991, when Bob Schieffer took over. Stahl had succeeded George Herman, who conducted the program the 13 previous years. Others who moderated in the 1950s and 1960s included Theodore Koop, Stuart Novins, Paul Niven, Howard K. Smith and Martin Agronsky.

FACSIMILE ▶ the electronic transmission of written or still pictorial or graphic material. The first recorded facsimile transmission system was patented in 1843—it used telegraph wires. Facsimile has often been proposed as a consumer service to deliver newspapers and other reading material via television channels during the time when no programs are being transmitted or by using the vertical interval between pictures. Although many broadcast facsimile tests have been conducted successfully—most notably RCA's "Homefax" system—the technique has failed to capture the public imagination. In the 1980s inexpensive "fax" machines using phone lines penetrated the entire business marketplace and even made inroads into home use.

FAIRNESS DOCTRINE ▶ a content-regulation concept that underlies the entire structure of broadcasting in the U.S. and distinguishes the broadcast media from all other journalistic endeavors relative to the guarantees of the First Amendment. The Fairness Doctrine requires a two-fold duty from the broadcaster, namely (1) that the broadcaster devote a reasonable amount of time to the discussion of controversial issues of public importance, and (2) that the broadcaster do so fairly, by affording reasonable opportunity for the opposing viewpoints to be heard.

The concept may be simple, but the judicial and legislative battles that have surrounded the doctrine have given it a symbolic importance for both its adherents and detractors that has far exceeded any actual impact on the day-today operations of broadcasters. This symbolic importance has, if anything, increased since the partial repeal of the doctrine in 1987.

The Fairness Doctrine stems directly from the basic scheme Congress set forth for broadcasting in the Radio Act of 1927 and the Communications Act of 1934. The 1927 act originated because of the need for government to allocate radio frequencies among applicants to prevent problems of interference among transmissions. The statutory scheme that was chosen by Congress was one of short-term licensing with the licensee obligated to operate in the public interest.

Very shortly thereafter, the Federal Radio Commission expressed the view that the public interest required ample play for the free and fair competition of opposing views; it also determined that the principle should apply to all decisions or issues of importance to the public. This tradition was carried on through the development of the FCC (Federal Communications Commission) in 1934, and the doctrine was applied through the denial of license renewals and construction permits.

For a period licensees were obliged not only to cover, and to cover fairly, the views of others but also to refrain from expressing their own personal views. After much confusion about the noneditorial rule, the FCC published its Editorializing Report in 1949, which was the first formal articulation of the Fairness Doctrine.

Ten years after the Editorializing Report, Congress amended Section 315 of the Communications Act and passed language that seemed to codify the Fairness Doctrine. After the 1959 amendment, the FCC continued to enforce the principle in individual cases. Originally it considered fairness complaints only at renewal time. Its procedure was to refer appropriate complaints to the station at the time received, obtain the station's response and then consider the matter definitively at renewal time. But starting in 1962, the FCC began considering complaints as they arose. If it determined that the station had violated the doctrine, the station was directed to advise the commission within 20 days of the steps it had taken to remedy the situation.

In addition, the FCC began to remind broadcasters of their special obligation with regard to personal attacks, first brought to broadcasters' attention in the Report on Editorializing in 1949. In 1967 the FCC promulgated rules on personal attack. These rules and their application—and by implication the entire Fairness Doctrine—were eventually challenged in the Supreme Court in the Red Lion decision, and their constitutionality was upheld. Later attempts to turn the Fairness Doctrine into a concept for enforced access (the BEM case) were defeated in the Supreme Court.

Despite anguished claims that the doctrine impedes journalistic freedom and that it treats broadcasters as second-class citizens of the press, the FCC continued to enforce the Fairness Doctrine well into the 1980s. As the number of broadcast stations multiplied and cable and other media proliferated, the scarcity-based principles underlying the doctrine came under increasing challenge. But, as technological advancements greatly increased the need for spectrum space, more and more broadcasters began to temper their vehement demands for repeal. Their action was rooted in the political value of the trusteeship concept inherent in the Fairness Doctrine, which enabled them to argue that broadcasting serves special needs and, unlike land mobile radio and other users, they should not be forced to bid for spectrum they had always received for free.

In 1984 Reaganite Chairman Mark Fowler took aim at the doctrine as one of the major planks of his deregulatory platform. This delighted most broadcasters and infuriated the bipartisan congressional supporters. After a surprise ruling issued by then-Circuit Appeals Court Judges Robert Bork and Antonin Scalia reinterpreting the 1959 amendment, the commission for the first time found itself with a basis to claim discretion to repeal the doctrine on its own. In early 1987 Congress passed a law to overrule the Bork decision, but it was vetoed by President Reagan. This paved the way for repeal, which was implemented under the aegis of newly appointed chairman Dennis Patrick. An appeals court held that Patrick's sweeping First Amendment analysis was beyond his power but upheld the decision on far narrower grounds, leaving room for Congress to reimpose the doctrine.

A new political war of nerves then began. Patrick attempted to defuse the congressional opposition by announcing his intention to continue enforcing election-related aspects of the doctrine, including its coverage of station editorials, ballot issues and personal attacks. Holding a substantial majority in Congress but not enough Senate votes to override another veto, leaders repeatedly attempted over the next several years to tie the doctrine to budget and spending bills; in 1990 it was among a handful of unresolved issues that led to a shutdown of the entire federal government. In each instance, the White House held firm.

Jane Wyman as Angela Channing in the CBS series *Falcon Crest*

FALCON CREST ▶ one of the prime-time serials that followed on the heels of *Dallas.* It was created by Earl Hamner, who also served as the show's executive producer (he also created *The Waltons*). Like *Dallas,* it was produced by Lorimar and televised on CBS, which scheduled it Fridays at 10 p.m. The series profited from *Dallas*'s strong lead-in and had a long run (December 1981 to May 1990). Set in the wine country of Northern California, *Falcon Crest* centered on the efforts of the strong-willed matriarch to gain control of the Falcon Crest vineyard and winery. The huge cast, headed by Jane Wyman as Angela Channing, also featured Robert Foxworth as her nephew Chase Gioberti, Abby Dalton as Julia Cumson, Lorenzo Lamas as Julia's son Lance, Margaret Ladd as Emma Channing, and Susan Sullivan as Maggie Gioberti. Others in the cast were Jamie Rose, William Moses, David Selby, Stephen Elliot, Morgan Fairchild, Shannon Tweed and Ken Olin, along with movie stars John Saxon, Kim Novak, Mel Ferrer and Lana Turner. The executive producers were Michael Filerman and Hamner, who, along with Sandra Siegal, also headed the large team of writers. Bill Conti wrote the show's theme music.

FALK, PETER ▶ actor who is most famous for his role as the amusing, rumpled private investigator in the series *Columbo* (1971-78). He reprised the character in a new *Columbo* series in 1989, and he appeared often in that role in made-for-TV movies, serving also in latter years as executive producer.

Falk began as a stage actor and started in television in such programs as *Studio One* (1957) and *The Dick Powell Show* (1962). In regular series, he often appeared in gangster roles in such shows as *The Untouchables* and *Naked City.*

FALSE OR LIBELOUS STATEMENTS BY CANDIDATES ▶ [*Farmers Educational and Cooperative Union of America v. WDAY, Inc.*/360 U.S. 525 (1959)] case resolved by the Supreme Court that established that broadcasters cannot be held liable for material that they are statutorily unable to control.

In October 1956, a candidate for the U.S. Senate in North Dakota demanded and received equal time on WDAY-TV Fargo. He then charged that communists controlled the North Dakota Farmers Union. The Farmers Union brought a damage suit against the candidate and the station. The North Dakota Supreme Court ruled that stations were not accountable for false or libelous statements made over their facilities by political candidates because Section 315(a) of the Communications Act prohibits stations from censoring the remarks of candidates.

The case was ultimately appealed to the U.S. Supreme Court, which in a 4-3 decision affirmed the North Dakota Supreme Court and found no liability for the station.

FALSEY, JOHN ▶ see Brand, Joshua and Falsey, John.

FALWELL, JERRY ▶ fundamentalist religious broadcaster from Lynchburg, Va., who gained nation-wide attention during the 1980 national elections as head of The Moral Majority, a quasi-religious organization that campaigned for Ronald Reagan and other ultra-conservative candidates. A television preacher with a nationally syndicated program, *The Old-Time Gospel Hour,* he came into prominence with his off-camera attacks on immorality in television. In 1981, he was a moving force in the Coalition for Better Television, which sought to purge the medium of sex and violence by boycotting advertisers in programs the organization deemed unwholesome. Falwell and the Moral

Majority dropped out of the Coalition the following year.

Falwell founded the Thomas Road Baptist Church in Lynchburg in 1956 and a week later started a radio program. Within six months he was on television with a local program. This grew into his syndicated series. The broadcast exposure led to the growth of the church from 35 original members to a congregation of 17,000, one of the largest in the country.

FAMILY ▶ ABC weekly prime-time serial introduced during the spring of 1976 as a mini-series and brought back in the fall as a continuing weekly entry. Centering on the lives of a contemporary middle-class family, it was created by Jay Presson Allen and was the first TV production by noted stage and film director Mike Nichols, in association with Spelling-Goldberg Productions. Sada Thompson portrayed the mother, Kate Lawrence, and James Broderick her husband, Douglas Lawrence. The children were portrayed by Elaine Heilveil, later replaced by Meredith Baxter-Birney, as Nancy Maitland; Gary Frank as Willie and Kristy McNichol as Buddy. Quinn Cummings was added in 1978 as an adopted daughter, Annie Cooper. The program went on hiatus in 1979 and was not in the fall starting schedule but returned at mid-season before finally giving up for good. Aaron Spelling and Leonard Goldberg were executive producers; Nigel and Carol Evan McKeand were the producers.

FAMILY AFFAIR ▶ hit situation comedy on CBS (1966-71) about a wealthy and worldly bachelor who becomes the foster parent of his orphaned nieces and nephew—the quintessential "heart" comedy. Much of the humor derived from the maternal role that was incumbent upon the British manservant, Giles French, as portrayed by Sebastian Cabot. Produced by Don Fedderson Productions, it starred Brian Keith as Bill Davis and featured child actors Anissa Jones and Johnnie Whitaker as young Buffy and Jody, and Kathy Garver as teenage Cissy.

FAMILY AT WAR ▶ British serial drama, popular on the independent channel there via Granada TV. It played on U.S. public television's Eastern Educational Network in the fall of 1974. The series focused on the lives of a Liverpool family and their friends during World War II.

FAMILY CHANNEL, THE ▶ basic-cable network launched in 1977 as CBN Satellite Service, a religious-only network operated by the non-profit Christian Broadcasting Network. In 1981 the channel was changed to CBN Cable Network, a for-profit service running entertainment programming with an emphasis on what it considered wholesome shows, including many off-network westerns. The service distanced itself from its Christian roots with another name change in 1989 to the Family Channel. The 24-hour service has 53 million subscribers and produces six original prime-time series, including *The Legend of Prince Valiant* and *Maniac Mansion.* Other programming consists of original movies, children's shows, daytime health shows and *The Waltons.* Tim Robertson, son of evangelist Pat Robertson, is president of The Family Channel, which is a division of International Family Entertainment, Inc.

FAMILY FEUD ▶ see Game Shows.

FAMILY MATTERS ▶ ABC sitcom spun off of *Perfect Strangers* and produced by the successful sitcom team of Tom Miller and Robert Boyett. The series concerns a black policeman living with his family in Chicago—his wife, the spin-off character, having been the elevator operator in *Perfect Strangers.* Starring are Jo-Marie Payton-France as Harriette Winslow and Reginald VelJohnson as her husband, Carl. The show might not have survived long had it not been for the addition late in its first season of teenaged actor Jaleel White as neighbor Steve Urkel. With a nasal voice and oversized glasses befitting the consummate "geek," Urkel caught on with viewers and helped lift the show into the Nielsen top-ten during its second season.

Miller and Boyett produce *Family Matters* for Lorimar Television. It debuted in 1989.

FAMILY TIES ▶ highly successful NBC sitcom (1982-89) from Gary David Goldberg about a married couple, who are liberals and former flower children, raising three somewhat more conservative children (eventually four). The series launched the career of Michael J. Fox, who played the arch-conservative, Reagan-loving eldest child, Alex. Often at ideological odds with his parents, Steven and Elyse Keaton (played by Michael Gross and Meredith Baxter), Alex quickly became the most popular character of the series. Alex's two sisters, Mallory and Jennifer, were played by Justine Bateman and Tina Yothers, respectively. Brian Bonsall played the fourth child, Andrew, who joined the show in 1986.

The series at the start was scheduled behind *The Cosby Show,* a tactic that gave NBC a firm hold on Thursday nights through most of the 1980s. It was produced by Goldberg for Paramount Television.

The cast of the NBC series *Family Ties*

FAMILY VIEWING TIME ▶ an industry-wide policy adopted in 1975 designating the first two hours of prime time (7-9 p.m.) for programs that would be suitable to all age groups. The policy, which became part of the television code, was later declared illegal by U.S. District Court Judge Warren J. Ferguson, who ruled that FCC chairman Richard C. Wiley had coerced the industry to adopt such a plan in violation of the First Amendment. The networks said, nevertheless, that of their own choice they would continue the practice of keeping the early evening programming free of excessive sex and violence. They also said they would appeal the court's decision.

The Family Viewing concept had evolved from discussions between network officials and the FCC during a time, late in 1974, when Wiley was under pressure from three congressional committees to take some regulatory steps to protect children from the moral liberties assumed by television. Wiley, a staunch believer in industry self-regulation, chose not to issue rules but instead called for meetings with the network chiefs and sternly made suggestions for procedures they might voluntarily adopt. Some at the networks accused him of arm-twisting and "jawboning."

But during Christmas week, Arthur R. Taylor, then president of CBS, issued a statement that his network would, in the fall of 1975, consider the first hour of network prime time (8-9 p.m. EST) a family hour and, in addition, would post warnings on the screen for shows that were either intended for adults or that required parental guidance. NBC, and then ABC, soon afterwards made similar pledges.

Wiley then persuaded the NAB to add the Family Viewing concept to the television code, making it effective for the hour preceding network time, as well. Then he met with managers of independent stations that did not subscribe to the code and persuaded them to honor the plan. When it was unanimous, Wiley then praised the industry publicly for its achievement in self-regulation. "Family Viewing" had no precise definition, and what it meant besides the elimination of gratuitous violence was left to the broadcasters' judgment.

The policy affected numerous programs that were in development at the time for the new fall schedule and caused some, such as *Fay,* intended as a sophisticated comedy about a middle-aged divorcee, to undergo severe script editing. Series such as *All in the Family* and *The Rookies* were ousted from their accustomed 8 o'clock time periods. All this proved upsetting to Hollywood producers and writers, several of whom challenged the Family Viewing policy in a suit filed in the Federal Court for the Central District of California.

On Nov. 4, 1976, Judge Ferguson, in a lengthy opinion, accused Wiley of overstepping his authority by unconstitutionally pressing upon the networks and stations "a programming policy they did not wish to adopt." He said Wiley's actions, implying a threat if the networks did not respond to his urgings, had primarily intended "to alter the content of entertainment programming in the early evening hours," thereby violating the broadcasters' constitutional guarantee of free speech.

The issue evaporated in the deregulatory climate of the 1980s, although there is still a residual sense in the industry that the hours before 9 p.m. should be off limits to programs that are excessively violent or concerned with sex on adult levels. Nevertheless, NBC scheduled *The A-Team* at 8 p.m. in 1983; CBS likewise offered such action-adventure shows as *Magnum, P.I.* in 1982 and later *Airwolf* and *Tour of Duty,* and ABC programmed *Spenser for Hire.* Except for *The A-Team,* the early-hour scheduling of these shows raised little controversy. But in 1987 Fox was considered to have violated the sanctity of the early evening in scheduling *Married ... With Children* at 8:30. A particular episode in which frontal nudity was suggested so outraged a woman in the midwest, who was watching with her children, that she organized a consumer boycott against the advertisers in the show. Fox moved the program to 9 p.m., but the incident made advertisers, and thus the networks, sensitive to family viewing hours again.

FAMOUS JURY TRIALS ▶ series that appeared in two versions: first in a 1949 production by DuMont and then as a syndicated entry designed for strip presentation dramatizing actual trials and serializing them over a period of weeks. The latter version featured Donnelly Rhodes, Tim Henry, Allen Doreumus and Joanna Noyes and was produced in 1970 and 1971 by 20th Century-Fox in association with Talent Associates.

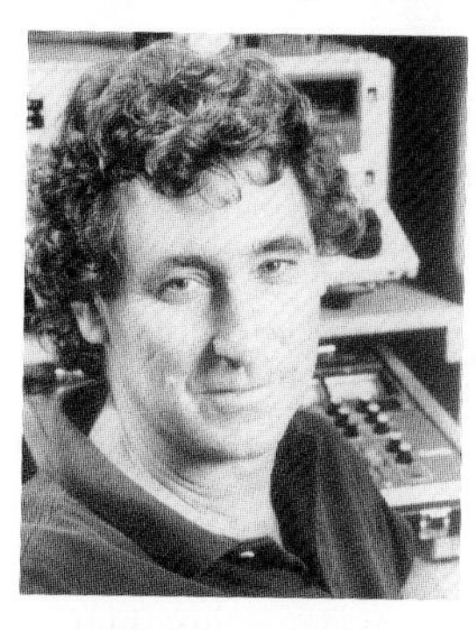

David Fanning

FANNING, DAVID ▶ creator and executive producer of PBS's long-running series *Frontline,* which produces or commissions hour-long, single-topic documentaries on a weekly basis.

Fanning started *Frontline* in 1982 after five years with Boston's WGBH, where he served as executive producer on more than 50 documentaries for an earlier PBS series, *World.* One of the programs in that series, *Death of a Princess,* co-written and produced by Fanning and Anthony Thomas, triggered an international incident that involved the governments of three nations and the Mobil Oil Co.

Before coming to the United States in 1973 from his native South Africa, Fanning produced two films, *Amabandia AmaAfrika* and *May They Be One,* dealing with race and religion in his troubled homeland.

FANTASY ISLAND ▶ moderately successful ABC dramatic series that entered the schedule early in 1978 as a Saturday night parlay with *Love Boat.* It ran until 1984. Ricardo Montalban starred as Mr. Roarke, the mysterious ruler of an island who has the power to make the dreams of his guests come true. His assistant, a dwarf named Tattoo, was played by Herve Villechaize. Wendy Schaal, as Montalban's goddaughter Julie, was added at the start of the 1981-82 season, and Christopher Hewett replaced Villechaize the following season as Lawrence, a new assistant. The series was a Spelling-Goldberg production.

FARMER'S DAUGHTER, THE ▶ ABC situation comedy (1963-66) based on a movie concerning a farm girl who marries a widowed congressman for whom she worked as governess to his two sons. It starred Inger Stevens as Katy Holstrum and featured William Windom as Congressman Glen Morley and Cathleen Nesbitt as Agatha Morley, Glen's mother. Screen Gems produced in association with ABC.

FARNSWORTH, PHILO T. (d. 1971) ▶ one of the two inventors of modern all-electronic television. A contemporary of Vladimir K. Zworykin, he independently demonstrated in 1927 a device similar to Zworykin's iconoscope—the "dissector tube" or orthicon, capable of dividing an image into parts whose light values could be restored to form a reproduction of the original picture. He was founder and research director of the Farnsworth Television and Radio Corp. in 1938. It later became part of International Telephone and Telegraph Co.

FAROUDJA LABORATORIES ▶ equipment company devoted to advanced television (ATV) research and development, and marketer of improved NTSC systems as well as ghost-canceling technology.

FAT ALBERT AND THE COSBY KIDS ▶ animated CBS children's series (1972-77) acclaimed for attempting to promote prosocial values through juvenile situation comedies. It was also a landmark show in minority programming, since its principal characters were black. Hosted by comedian Bill Cosby, the series was based on his monologue routines about the kids he grew up with, including Fat Albert, Weird Harold, Mush Mouth and Rudy. Created in response to mounting criticism over exploitative programs for children, *Fat Albert* was designed for affective rather than cognitive learning and dealt with themes on human feelings, personal relationships, ethics and values. It proved to be very popular with children of all races, and CBS social research found that the prosocial messages usually got through. *Fat Albert* was produced by Lou Scheimer and Norm Prescott of Filmation Associates.

FATAL VISION ▶ acclaimed dramatization of the Joe McGinniss best-seller about on a real-life incident involving Dr. Jeffrey MacDonald, a former Green Beret captain who was accused, cleared, then convicted of the brutal murders of his wife and infant daughters in February 1970. Produced by Daniel Wigutow and Mike Rosenfeld and directed by David Greene, the four-hour mini-series aired in two parts in November 1984. It was critically praised on all levels, notably for the performances of Karl Malden as MacDonald's father-in-law bent on avenging his daughter's murder, and Gary Cole as the manipulative killer. Eva Marie Saint played MacDonald's mother-in-law and Andy Griffith, the government prosecutor. The teleplay was written by John Gay.

The book and mini-series raised some controversy when MacDonald publicly accused McGinniss of, among other things, gaining his confidence as a friend and then manipulating the facts to make a more dramatic story.

FATES, GIL ▶ executive producer for Goodson-Todman of *What's My Line?, To Tell the Truth* and *I've Got a Secret* during the 1950s. Earlier he produced *Stop the Music* and *The Faye Emerson Show.*

FATHER KNOWS BEST ▶ a classic family situation comedy of the 1950s starring Robert Young, a noted film actor, as Jim Anderson, the sensible head of a purportedly normal middle-class American family. It played on all three networks, premiering on CBS Oct. 3, 1954, then switching the following year to NBC, returning to CBS from 1958 to 1962, and continuing in reruns on ABC (1962-67). The films subsequently went into syndication.

NBC attempted to capitalize on the years of popularity of the series in December of 1977 by presenting a 90-minute movie, *The Father Knows Best Reunion.* In the intervening years the family had gone the way of the purportedly normal "middle-class" American family of the 1970s. While the parents were suffering from "empty nest" syndrome, Betty (Princess) was a widow with two children, a career, and marriage on her mind; Bud was in a troubled marriage; and Kathy (Kitten) was in a semi-rebellious relationship with a much older divorced man.

Jane Wyatt portrayed Young's wife Margaret, and the children were played by Elinor Donahue (Betty), Bill Gray (Bud) and Lauren Chapin (Kitten). It was produced by Young's own company, Rodney-Young Productions.

FAULK, JOHN HENRY ▶ folk raconteur and television personality victimized by the anti-communist crusaders of the 1950s. His successful suit for libel contributed to ending the blacklist practices and purges for subversives in the entertainment industries.

In 1956 Faulk was elected a vice-president of the New York chapter of AFTRA, the performers' union, on a platform that deplored the activities of Aware Inc., one of the organizations leading the purge in broadcasting. Aware then issued one of its bulletins, citing Faulk for "communist activities." Although he had been enjoying popularity on both radio and TV, Faulk immediately began losing sponsor support and soon was released by CBS-TV from his panel show. He sued Aware and its principals, Vincent W. Hartnett and Lawrence Johnson, in June 1956. With a contribution of $7,500 from Edward R. Murrow (who called it "an investment in America"), he hired the famed Louis Nizer as his lawyer.

For six years, until the case was decided, Faulk found he was unemployable. Proving in court that the charges made against him by Aware had been either false or based distortedly on half-truths—and with witnesses from the industry testifying to the threats and fear tactics used by the organization to achieve the boycott of an entertainer—Faulk, in June 1962, was awarded damages of $3.5 million. It was the largest judgment ever returned in a libel suit, although it was subsequently reduced by the courts.

In 1976 CBS presented a 90-minute dramatization of Faulk's book, *Fear on Trial,* with George C. Scott as Nizer.

FAWCETT, FARRAH ▶ actress who became a sex symbol overnight in 1976 when she starred for a year in the enormously popular *Charlie's Angels* (1976-81). She quit the series and made a string of mediocre movies, then found a niche in made-for-TV movies, shedding her glamorous image to play a battered wife who kills her husband in *The Burning Bed,* one of television's highest-rated movies ever. She also received acclaim for the off-Broadway production—later a feature film—*Extremities.* Fawcett returned to series television in 1991 playing opposite her live-in partner Ryan O'Neal for the short-lived series on CBS, *Good Sports.*

FAWLTY TOWERS ▶ hilarious British sitcom that aired on public television and starred John Cleese as Basil Fawlty, the pretentious and hopelessly inept proprietor of a British country inn. The series also featured Prunella Scales as Basil's wife Sybil, who always seemed to get the better of him. Connie Booth, Brian Hall and Andrew Sachs played the hotel employees, and Ballard Berkeley, Gilly Flower and Renee Roberts the regular guests, all of whom were constantly trying Basil's patience and driving him to manic excess.

The series, which was created and written by Cleese and Booth, premiered in England in 1975; new episodes appeared in 1979.

FAY ▶ short-lived NBC situation comedy (1975) created as a vehicle for Lee Grant; it stirred a controversy when the network issued a cancellation notice after the fourth episode because its ratings were inadequate. On the *Tonight* show, Grant protested both the hasty decision and the fact that NBC scheduled the program in family hour, forcing the sophisticated dialogue to be tempered. *Fay* concerned a fortyish divorcee, Fay Stewart, determined to make a new life for herself, while her ex-husband, Jack Stewart, continued to bob into the picture. The following summer NBC slotted the previously unexposed episodes outside of family time with a favorable lead-in, but *Fay* failed again to find an audience.

Featured were Audra Lindley as neighbor Lillian; Joe Silver as Jack; Margaret Willock and Stewart Moss as Fay's daughter and son-in-law, Linda and Elliott Baines; Bill Gerber as Fay's boss, Danny Messina; and Norman Alden as lawyer Al Cassidy. The series was by Danny Thomas Productions and Universal TV.

FBI, THE ▶ series dramatizing FBI investigations of crime and subversion, based to some extent on cases from the agency's files. It became a Sunday night mainstay on ABC for eight seasons after its premiere in 1965. Initially, the program was sponsored by Ford, to offset the successful Chevrolet-sponsored Sunday night show *Bonanza.* Automobiles were used abundantly in the series, and most of them were Ford models. Additionally, since the series concerned the workings of a sacred federal agency, the violence employed in the stories was held by some in Congress to be above reproach. A total of 234 episodes were produced by QM Productions and Warner Bros., with a cast headed by Efrem Zimbalist, Jr. as Inspector Lewis Erskine, William Reynolds as Agent Tom Colby and Philip Abbott as Agent Arthur Ward.

A new series, *Today's FBI,* starring Mike Connors as Agent Ben Slater, was introduced by ABC in 1981 in the same Sunday night time period, but it was not really a revival of the old series and was via David Gerber instead of QM.

FCBA (FEDERAL COMMUNICATIONS BAR ASSOCIATION) ▶ organization of lawyers specializing in communications law, many of them alumni of the FCC (Federal Communications Commission). It functions both as a trade association and as the auspices for forums on major communications issues. Founded in 1936, two years after the FRC became the FCC, it has today around 800 members, all of whom practice before the commission. On occasion the association has assisted the FCC, such as in providing ideas for the streamlining of the commission's adjudicatory proceedings. This activity was sometimes criticized as self-serving, as when the Association sought in 1989-90 to reform hearing processes in a way that preserved lucrative settlements.

During the 1980s the Association became increasingly active, pressing its membership to expand employment opportunities for minorities, and in 1991 it formed the Federal Communications Bar Foundation to promote charitable endeavors.

FCC (FEDERAL COMMUNICATIONS COMMISSION) ▶ an independent government agency administered by five commissioners and reporting to Congress, and responsible for regulating interstate and foreign communications by radio, television, wire, cable and newer technologies. Operating as a unit, the five commissioners are charged with interpreting the public interest in broadcasting under a national policy that makes the public interest paramount while providing for private operation of stations without government intrusion.

The FCC has the authority to award broadcast licenses and the power to revoke them when broadcasters have demonstrably failed to serve the public interest, convenience or necessity, or when they are found guilty of serious infractions of commission regulations or of the U.S. Criminal Code.

As the link between the public and the industry—by nature of having selected the trustees for the airwaves, which are in the public domain—the FCC may create rules, conduct hearings and issue guidelines and policy statements to affect broadcast performance in the public interest, but it is forbidden by the Communications Act of 1934 to engage in any form of censorship. This prohibition has kept the commission wary of interference in matters of programming, and the agency has adhered to a policy of trusting the licensee to determine what is best for his community.

While the FCC has no direct regulatory authority over the networks, since they are independent program services and not licensed entities (anyone, in theory, may start a network), historically it has dealt with the networks through the licenses of their owned and affiliated stations and through the regulations for chain broadcasting.

Created by the Communications Act of 1934, the FCC began operating on July 11, 1934, superseding the five-member Federal Radio Commission. The FRC had been formed by the Radio Act of 1927 to undo the chaos that prevailed on the radio band, where signals collided with each other as stations increased power, switched frequencies and extended their broadcast hours as they chose.

The FCC was established when a study of electrical communications, made at the request of President Roosevelt in 1933, recommended that a single agency be created to unify the regulations of all wire and radio communication—telephone and telegraph, as well as broadcast, all of which were engaged in interstate commerce and were to some degree interdependent. Eugene Octave Sykes, a Democrat who had been an original member of the FRC, became the first chairman of the FCC.

Amendments to the Act over the years gave the FCC regulatory responsibility for cable TV, pay-television and communications satellites, and its duties were augmented by a presidential Executive Order in 1963 to ready the communications services under its jurisdiction for possible national emergency situations.

Under its mandate, the FCC allocates TV channels and assigns frequencies with a view to "fair and equitable distribution" of service from market to market, at the same time avoiding the collision of signals. It may also determine the power and types of technical facilities licensees may use and the hours during which they may operate. Licenses or construction permits cannot be transferred or sold without FCC permission, and when licenses are challenged the agency, after holding comparative hearings, must judge which is the most deserving applicant.

Members of the commission are appointed by the president for five-year terms, with approval of the Senate. Anyone who is nominated to fill a vacancy is appointed only for the unexpired term of the predecessor. The president also designates the chairman. No more than three commissioners may be of the same political party and none may own securities of any corporation over which the FCC has jurisdiction.

The chairman presides over meetings, coordinates the work of the commission, represents the agency in all legislative matters and usually is the moving force who imparts a style and working spirit to the commission. Three commissioners constitute a quorum.

Each commissioner has two professional assistants plus three secretaries, while the chairman may have as many as six assistants. Much of the daily work of the agency is delegated to five bureaus and several staff offices. The FCC employs more than 2,000 persons, including its field staff in major cities.

The organization consists of the Mass Media Bureau, Common Carrier Bureau, Private Radio Bureau and Field Operations Bureau. Also, there are the offices of the director, general counsel, engineering and technology, inspector general, administrative law judges, review board, and information. Growing in importance is the office of Plans and Policy.

The Mass Media Bureau, whose responsibilities include processing applications for stations and setting requirements for broadcast equipment, is made up of seven divisions: rules and standards, renewal and transfer, complaints and compliances, research and education, broadcast facilities, license, and hearing. It also embraces the office of network study and administers and enforces cable-TV rules, advises the commission on cable matters, and licenses private microwave facilities used to relay TV signals to cable systems.

Each of the bureaus is responsible for considering complaints, conducting investigations and taking part in commission hearing proceedings, among its other duties.

Administrative law judges, whose appointments are subject to Civil Service laws, conduct adjudicatory proceedings assigned to them by offices of the agency and issue initial decisions. As judges they operate independently and may not be supervised or directed by FCC officials in their investigative work or in the preparation of their opinions.

Most initial decisions are subject to review by the four-member Review Board, a permanent body made up of senior commission employees. Initial decisions may also be reviewed by one or more commissioners designated by the commission. In such cases the board or commissioner issues a final decision, subject to review by the full commission. On occasion the initial decision is reviewed directly by the commission.

The FCC's contradictory mandates—that of looking after the public interest and that of refraining from any involvement with programming that might constitute censorship—have kept the agency under constant criticism from Congress and citizens for failing to exert stricter program controls and for in effect "rubber stamping" license renewals. It has been called weak, bureaucratic and overly protective of the industry it regulates. On several occasions, it has been under formal investigation by Congress. The FCC proceedings follow in these steps:

A Notice of inquiry is issued by the commission when it is asking for information on a broad subject or trying to generate ideas or ascertain points of view.

A Notice of Proposed Rule Making is issued when the commission is ready to introduce a new rule or take steps to change one.

A Memorandum Opinion and Order is issued to deny a petition for rulemaking, conclude an inquiry, modify a decision, or deny a petition asking for reconsideration of a decision.

A Report and Order is issued to state a new or amended rule or to state that the FCC rule in question will not be changed.

See also Appendix.

FCC FEES ▶ a schedule of charges set by the commission in 1970 so that the industries it regulates would cover the costs of operating the agency. But in 1976, the U.S. Court of Appeals for the District of Columbia ruled that the fees were improperly levied and that the basis on which they were collected amounted to taxation. Acting on suits by the NAB, Capital Cities Broadcasting, NCTA and a group of common carriers, the court cited the Supreme Court's ruling in March 1974 that the FCC had been collecting fees in an illegal manner when it based their apportionment on recovering all its budget. Both courts held that the fees charged had to reflect only the direct benefits realized by those receiving them.

After the Supreme Court's ruling, the FCC issued a new schedule in 1975 with expectations of bringing in slightly more than one-third of the commission's annual budget of approximately $45 million. Television stations were charged annually 4.25 times their highest 30-second spot rate, or a minimum of $100, for regulatory services.

The Court of Appeals struck that down, saying that the FCC should base its charges on itemized services and that it should demonstrate the actual costs of those services. The commission was left in a quandary on how to process refunds for the fees collected since 1970. After the court's ruling, it suspended all license fees, including those for the use of citizen's band radio.

FCC PROGRAM POLICY STATEMENT, 1960 ▶ guidelines for programming in the public interest issued by the FCC in July 1960, four years after the controversy over the Blue Book report, which had attempted in broad strokes to define program standards that would bear on license renewals. The 1960 policy statement raised no controversy because the commission made it plain that it would not use the program areas outlined as a definition of service in the public interest for license-renewal purposes. While it was abandoned in 1984, the principles of the statement have served as a continuing benchmark in debates over the adequacy of TV service.

In fact, the Policy Statement was welcomed by broadcasters, not only because it waffled on the question of a licensee's responsibility but because it challenged the Blue Book by declaring that sustaining programs did not constitute, per se, a better service in the public interest than sponsored programs. Without specifying percentages or suggesting that these should be elements of a complete programming plan, the commission listed the following as usually necessary to meet the public interest: programs that provide opportunity for self-expression, programs for children, religious programs, educational programs, public affairs programs, editorials, political broadcasts, news programs, agricultural programs, weather and market reports, sports programs, entertainment programs, service to minority groups and, overall, the development and employment of local talent.

FCC REVIEW BOARD ▶ an intermediate appeals body within the FCC that reviews decisions from the Agency's Administrative Law Judges, typically sitting with panels of three members. Review Board membership is one of the few prizes generally reserved for the agency's career bureaucrats. As the FCC's attention increasingly turned to long-term policy issues through the 1980s, the body has become increasingly powerful.

FECAN, IVAN ▶ head of programming for Canada's CBC with the title of vice president of arts and entertainment. He has been in charge of programming since 1987 and received his new title in 1991. Fecan had schooled in U.S. television as an NBC vice president (1985-87) based in Los Angeles and working for Brandon Tartikoff. Along with movies and series, he had a hand in such NBC Productions offerings as *Saturday Night Live* and *Latenight With David Letterman.*

He has enjoyed considerable success at the CBC and is credited with helping develop such shows as *Where the Spirit Lives, Justice Denied, DeGrassi Junior High, Northwood,* and *Road to Avonlea.* In addition, he set up a feature film unit and fostered the development of three made-for-TV movies that were sold to U.S. networks—*Love and Hate, Conspiracy of Silence,* and *Journey Into Darkness: The Bruce Curtis Story,* all thoroughgoing Canadian productions. This was considered a coup for the CBC, whose dramatic works were usually ignored in the States. He also made possible a weekly arts magazine in prime time, *Adrienne Clarkson Presents.*

FEDDERSON, DON ▶ one of the most successful packagers of family situation comedies through the 1950s and 1960s. He was producer of *Do You Trust Your Wife* and *The Millionaire,* then had a string of sitcoms for which he was executive producer, including *My Three Sons, To Rome With Love, Family Affair* and *The Smith Family.* He was also consultant to the *Lawrence Welk Show* and distributed that series when it went into syndication.

FEDERAL TRADE COMMISSION (FTC) ▶ an independent administrative agency of the government, consisting of a chairman and four commissioners, that is intended to promote free competition by preventing unfair methods of, or deceptive practices in, commerce. Its basic connection with the broadcasting industry is its concern with false and misleading advertising.

Section 5 of the Federal Trade Commission Act, which was passed in 1914, makes it unlawful to broadcast any false advertising relative to commodities that move in interstate commerce. Section 12 of the Act declares that false advertising with regard to foods, drugs, devices or cosmetics are unlawful whether or not they move in interstate commerce. Section 15 of the Act states that any advertisement is false which is misleading in a material respect.

In looking at what is false, the commission can take into account not only what is represented by the ad but also the extent to which the ad fails to reveal material facts with respect to the consequences that may result from the use of the product.

While the FTC has limited authority to punish, it may hold hearings on complaints charging violation of the statutes administered by the commission. If the charges are found to be fact, the FTC issues a cease and desist order requiring discontinuance of the practice. Formal litigation would follow if the order were ignored. Typically, however, voluntary compliance is brought about through advisory opinions by the commission, trade regulation rules, and the issuance of guidelines delineating legal requirements as to particular business practices.

In addition to its concern with unfair advertisements, the FTC aims to restrict discrimination in pricing and exclusive dealing, as well as corporate mergers and joint ventures when they may lessen competition or tend toward monopoly. The agency regulates packaging and labeling within the purview of the Fair Packaging and Labeling Act, supervises the operations of associations of American exporters and protects consumers against circulation of credit reports.

The FTC has issued cease and desist orders on product demonstrations staged to deceive the TV viewer, or that employ devices to enhance the appearance of the product. Such demonstrations have included the substitution of oil for coffee, to make the "coffee" in the commercial look richer and darker than it actually could be, and the placing of marbles in a bowl of vegetable soup forcing the vegetables to the top and making the soup appear more substantial than it was.

The commission also ordered a halt to a TV commercial that represented a brand of shaving cream as capable of shaving sandpaper, after having found that a compound had been added to the sandpaper that allowed a razor to shave it in a stroke. In another case, the FTC held misleading a commercial for a product advertised as affording relief of vitamin and iron deficiency anemia, because the commercial did not disclose the fact that a majority of the people who experience the symptoms noted in the advertisement do not have vitamin or iron deficiency.

Members of the commission are appointed by the President, subject to approval by the Senate. The five commissioners are appointed for staggered seven-year terms. Not more than three commissioners may be members of the same political party, and no commissioner may engage in any other business or employment. The chairman is vested with the administrative responsibility for the agency, headquartered in Washington, and its eleven field offices.

FEELIN' GOOD ▶ the first adult series created by the Children's Television Workshop (CTW) after its success with *Sesame Street* and *The Electric Company*. It sought to convey health care information on public television in the format of a weekly comedy-variety series. A noble idea, researched and tested over a three-year period, it premiered on PBS Nov. 20, 1974, and was withdrawn after 11 episodes for a substantial revision by the Workshop, which admitted that the program was misconceived.

Initially a one-hour program employing songs, comedy sketches, parodies and production numbers, held together by a situation comedy ensemble, it was poorly received by the key critics and was low-rated, even for public television. The program returned on PBS April 2, 1975, by previous arrangement, in a 30-minute format with a more direct approach to health-care information and less concern with entertainment. The situation comedy cast was dismissed in favor of a host, Dick Cavett. It ran 13 weeks in the new form.

Budgeted at $6.1 million, the series was created on grants from Exxon, Aetna Life & Casualty, the Corporation for Public Broadcasting, and a number of other sources.

Its executive producer was William Kobin, and regular members of the original cast were Rex Everhart, Priscilla Lopez, Ethel Shutta, Ben Slack, Marjorie Barnes and Joe Morton.

FELONY SQUAD, THE ▶ half-hour police series on ABC (1966-69) featuring Howard Duff as Detective Sam Stone, Ben Alexander as Sergeant Dan Briggs and Dennis Cole as Detective Jim Briggs. It was via 20th Century-Fox TV.

FELTON, NORMAN ▶ producer whose credits include *Robert Montgomery Presents* in the mid-1950s, *Studio One, CBS Workshop* in the early 1960s and later such series as *Dr. Kildare, Mr. Novak* and *Hawkins.*

FENNELLY, VINCENT M. ▶ producer of *Trackdown, Wanted Dead or Alive, The David Niven Show, Richard Diamond, Dick Powell Theatre, Target: The Corruptors* and *Rawhide.*

FERBER, MEL ▶ producer-director whose credits range from *Studio One, Seven Lively Arts* and *That Was the Week That Was* to episodes of *The Mary Tyler Moore Show, The Odd Couple* and *Alias Smith and Jones.* He directed the pilot for *Happy Days,* was executive producer of the 1972 Democratic national convention and in 1975 became executive producer of ABC's *Good Morning, America.*

FERNS, W. PATERSON (PAT) ▶ one of Canada's most successful independent producers and a pioneer of the coproduction. As president of Primedia Entertainment, based in Toronto, he has developed project partnerships in England and other European countries that allowed for productions on a scale Canadians could not otherwise normally afford. Among them are *Glory Enough for All* and *Heaven on Earth,* the first two dramas ever to play on PBS's *Masterpiece Theatre* that were not produced by the British.

While Ferns has generally concentrated on cultural and dramatic programs of quality, he broadened his scope in 1987 by entering into a joint venture with DLT Entertainment from the U.S. Out of that agreement came Comedia Entertainment, a producer of game shows and other light forms of television.

Though Canadian by birth, Ferns spent much of his youth in England and was educated at Cambridge and Birmingham universities. He returned to Canada in 1968 to join the CBC, where he became a senior producer of two public affairs programs. Four years later he left and with a partner formed an independent production company, Nielsen-Ferns Ltd., which among other series coproduced *Portraits of Power* with the *New York Times.*

Active in industry affairs throughout his career, he was first co-president of the Assn. of Canadian Film and Television Producers and in the 1980s president of the Banff Television Foundation, parent of the international television festival.

FERRIS, CHARLES D. ▶ former chairman of the FCC (1977-81), as President Carter's nominee. A research physicist who decided to become a lawyer, he graduated from Boston University Law School in 1961. He allied himself with the Democratic party and gained prominence on

Capitol Hill first as aide to Senate Majority Leader Mike Mansfield (1964-77) and then as general counsel to Speaker of the House Thomas P. (Tip) O'Neill. Ferris's political backing made his lack of experience with communications matters insignificant.

In recruiting his key assistants from prominent public-interest organizations, Ferris signaled that his would be an activist administration. It proved not to be, however, at least during the first two years of his chairmanship.

As the first Democrat to head the FCC since 1966, and as the liberal successor to the conservative Richard E. Wiley, Ferris endured a difficult two-year period with an agency predominating in Republican appointees. But even when the political balance finally shifted in 1979, he remained unadored by the citizen action groups as well as by the regulated industries. Largely this was an effect of the paradox of a liberal intention to achieve some degree of deregulation. Efforts to deregulate had begun in the Wiley administration, but they were spurred in Ferris's time by mandates from the White House and the Congressional oversight committees.

Ferris adopted a policy of what he called zero-based regulation, which meant examining the existing rules and moving for the elimination of those that were outmoded, unjustly restrictive or otherwise superfluous. Among the more significant regulations to be discarded was the certification procedure for cable television, which permitted cable to spread more rapidly than before. At the same time, Ferris attempted to steer a course that favored neither the broadcaster nor the cable operator, and his addresses to both industries typically were laced with sharp criticism of their unwillingness to aspire to fulfilling their potential. Overall, he positioned himself as an advocate of open competition among the emerging technologies and conventional broadcasting but as an upholder of the public-interest standard for the licensed media.

In the perception of public interest groups, Ferris tilted more toward the doctrine of diversity in the industry than to citizens' causes. His principal innovation at the FCC was to base decisions for deregulation on economic criteria, and to that effect he created staff positions for economists. A study conducted by economist Nina Cornell indicated that most radio stations were broadcasting more news and public affairs than the FCC required of them and that most were operating well within the commission's commercial limits. This led to a commission proposal in 1979 for a general deregulation of radio, at least to the extent of eliminating news percentages, commercial ceilings and the community ascertainment requirement. The initiative did not endear Ferris to the aroused citizen groups, which saw it as an erosion of the people's rights in broadcasting.

FETZER, JOHN E. (d. 1991) ▶ Michigan-based pioneer broadcaster who built one of the larger privately held station groups, Fetzer Broadcasting. In 1965 he entered the cable business with Fetzer CableVision. When the NAB created its Television Code Review Board, he became its first chairman. Fetzer began selling off his holdings in the early 1980s to concentrate on philanthropies, but the station group, under new ownership, retains the original name.

FIBBER McGEE AND MOLLY ▶ unsuccessful attempt by NBC (1959-60) to adapt the hit radio series to TV with Bob Sweeney and Cathy Lewis in the title roles. Featured were Hal Peary as Mayor Charles LaTrivia and Addison Richards as Dr. Gamble. The show was produced by NBC.

A fiber optic cable, right, compared to a copper coaxial cable

FIBER OPTICS ▶ the technique of using very thin flexible fibers of glass or plastic or other transparent materials to carry light. Because the interior of the fiber is reflective, it can convey light around corners. Used with a laser beam or light-emitting diode as the light source, fiber optics can carry wide bands of frequencies—many television channels—and therefore has been proposed as a substitute for coaxial cable.

The use of fiber optics in both telephone and cable-TV installations is on the rise. Because the signal carrier is in the light spectrum rather than in the radio frequencies, a tiny strand of optical fiber can carry as much information as a thick bundle of coaxial cable.

FIELD ▶ one half of a complete television picture constituting every other line. In the NTSC 60-cycle system, a field is transmitted in 1/60 of a second.

FIELD INSPECTION ▶ an examination of a station's broadcast facilities by a representative of the FCC who has the right to make such an inspection "at any reasonable hour." During inspections, stations must make available their technical and program logs, on request. The FCC requires access to station logs for a period of two years after the date of broadcast.

FIELD, SALLY ▶ actress who had two lightweight hit series in her youth, *Gidget* (1965-66) and *The Flying Nun* (1967-70). As she matured, she found the ingenue image difficult to shake because it lingered in reruns of those series. But through award-winning performances in the TV movie *Sybil* and in feature films such as *Norma Rae* and *Places in the Heart,* she established herself finallly as a serious actress. Her other TV series were *Alias Smith and Jones* (1971-73) and *Girl With Something Extra* (1973-74).

FIELD-SEQUENTIAL COLOR ▶ color television system developed by CBS Laboratories under Dr. Peter C. Goldmark and approved for broadcast use in a controversial 1950 FCC decision. In field-sequential broadcasting, the red elements of an entire picture were transmitted, followed by blue elements and then by green. At the receiver, a revolving disc containing red, blue and green filters was mounted over a black and white picture tube and synchronized with similar filters in front of the camera tube.

Although the system had the advantage of simplicity, it suffered from the drawback of incompatibility—that is, the 20 million black and white television sets in use at the time the system was approved would not have been able to receive a field-sequential color broadcast in black and white without a special adapter. After the development of the compatible NTSC system, the FCC reversed its color decision and approved NTSC for color broadcasting.

The field-sequential system is still in use, however, in certain closed-circuit applications, and was used in transmitting color pictures from the moon and from the Apollo space vehicles. The field-sequential signal was converted into standard NTSC color before being broadcast to the public.

FILERMAN, MICHAEL ▶ producer who shared co-executive production credit with Lee Rich and David Jacobs on *Knots Landing* (1979—), the long-running prime-time dramatic serial that spun off from *Dallas* (1978-91).

Filerman started his career in broadcast media at WGN-TV in Chicago in the 1960s. Since then he has been extremely active in producing prime-time dramatic serials, including *Flamingo Road* (1981-82) and *Emerald Point N.A.S.* (1983-84), and such TV movies as *Peyton Place: The Next Generation, Take My Daughters, Please, Coins in the Fountain, The Story Lady, Turn Back the Clock, Assault and Matrimony, The Return of Eliot Ness* and *The Child Saver.*

FILM ▶ always extensively used in television despite the medium's electronic nature. In the 1940s and early 1950s the only way to record live programs was via kinescopes—devices that transferred the output of video cameras onto black-and-white film, which could then be shipped from station to station. Kinescopes were rendered obsolete by the advent of videotape recording in 1956, but 16mm film found a new role in news gathering operations. The telecine, which transfers film to videotape, enabled the extensive use of 35mm color film as an origination medium for dramatic programming. The Hollywood studios that supplied such film became the networks' main source of prime-time programs. Film was phased out of news gathering by the advent of ENG in the mid-1970s.

FILM PACKAGE ▶ a group of feature films assembled by a distributor and marketed at a single price. Packaging is more efficient than selling movies one at a time, and it permits the distributor to dispose of inferior films in a mix with a number of highly desirable titles. When movies first were sold to TV, packages consisted of vast libraries of pre-1948 titles from the major studios; more recently, they have been marketed in groups of from 5 to 30 features, with made-for-TV movies often included among theatrical releases.

Federal law requires that all pictures in a package be priced separately, but as a practical matter stations generally purchase the pictures at the package price and average the costs over the entire group of films.

FILMWAYS ▶ once one of Hollywood's leading independent TV suppliers; it came into prominence during the 1960s when it placed with CBS, in rapid succession, such hits as *The Beverly Hillbillies, Green Acres* and *Petticoat Junction.* Headed by Martin Ransohoff, the company began as a producer of TV commercials and, after a huge success, expanded into series production. Filmways also produced such series as *Mister Ed, The Addams Family, My Sister Eileen, The Phyllis Diller Show* and *Trials of O'Brien.* The company was sold to Orion Pictures in 1983 and became Orion Television.

FINANCIAL INTEREST AND SYNDICATION ("FIN-SYN") RULES ▶ rules adopted in 1970 that prohibited the three major networks from owning or controlling the rebroadcast of prime-time network shows. Originally an afterthought to the hotly debated prime time-access rule, the "fin-syn" rules became the subject of one of the longest running and most heated political battles in Washington regulatory history. The rules ended controversial policies of withholding or delaying ("warehousing") network hits from independent stations that could then program them against network news and prime-time fare, policies that were a major factor in the growth of those stations during the late 1970s and 1980s. Supporters argued that the rules gave important creative freedom and, perhaps more importantly, financial independence to smaller independent producers who had once chafed under heavy-handed network dominance. Charging that the rules were a multi-billion dollar boondoggle for the motion picture studios, the three networks began an all-out attack on the rules in 1981, nearing success within a few years as FCC Chairman Mark Fowler championed their cause. Sudden last-minute intervention by retired film actor-turned-President Reagan was credited with saving the rules in 1983.

The networks' flagging fortunes and the explosive growth of cable gave them new ammunition, and another repeal drive was begun in 1990. The effort seemed destined for success, perhaps because of the impetus given by the new Fox network, which claimed that strict application of the rules would keep it from ever catching up with the three bigger rivals. It was a war of historic excess on all sides. Motion picture starlets were flown in to explain the importance of creative freedom to interested lawmakers. Congressmen and FCC members were flown to New York to meet with network anchors. After the networks hired FCC Commissioner Andrew Barrett's political mentor, former Illinois governor James Thompson, the studios brought musician (and TV producer) Quincy Jones to meet with Barrett.

By the spring of 1991, the Hollywood forces regained the momentum. Barrett, who turned out to be a jazz fan and was offended by the recruitment of his friend Thompson, joined with Commissioners Ervin Duggan and, surprisingly, free-marketer Commissioner Sherrie Marshall (accused at one point of being pro-Hollywood because she had once penned a motion picture script) to adopt a decision largely reaffirming the rules. Among the minor changes was one permitting the networks to compete in syndicating programs overseas, a gesture supposedly adopted to assuage powerful House Energy and Commerce Committee Chairman Dingell, who turned against the Hollywood studios after two were purchased by Japanese electronics giants.

The fight was far from over, as the networks vowed to bring the battle to the courts.

FININVEST ▶ one of Italy's largest conglomerates as the umbrella for Silvio Berlusconi's vast media holdings. Its annual revenues typically are at the $9 billion level. What began as a single local television station on the outskirts of Milan, built by Berlusconi while he was still in the real estate business, has burgeoned into an empire. Today Fininvest owns three national networks—Retequattro, Italia 1 and Canale 5—as well as a 10% interest in the new three-channel pay television service, Telepiu. It is also heavily involved in program production and international distribution through its Milan-based company, Reteitalia.

The key to Fininvest's success in television has been the effectiveness of its advertising sales arm, Publitalia, capitalizing on the expansion of advertising generally in Italy during the 1980s. Outside the country, Fininvest has significant shareholdings in France's La Cinq and Spain's Tele 5. It also owns the largest production facility in Spain, located on the outskirts of Madrid.

FINKEL, BOB ▶ producer-director specializing in variety programs; his credits include *The Colgate Comedy Hour, The Perry Como Show, The*

Tennessee Ernie Ford Show, The Eddie Fisher Show, The Dinah Shore Show and the Emmy Awards telecasts of 1960 and 1963. He was under exclusive contract to NBC in the late 1960s.

FINNEGAN-PINCHUK CO. ▶ production company that has built a reputation for efficiency on location, whether with TV movies or series like *Northern Exposure,* on which it shares a production credit with Falahey-Austin Street Productions. The company's made-for-TV movies include *Call Me Anna* with Patty Duke, *The Two Mrs. Grenvilles, Babes in Toyland,* and *Keeping Secrets* with Suzanne Somers. Principals are Bill Finnegan and Sheldon Pinchuk, with occasional help from Finnegan's wife, Pat.

FIORENTINO, IMERO ▶ TV lighting expert whose independent company has designed the lighting for numerous specials and special events, including the first transmission by the Telstar satellite and the 1976 presidential debates. After the first of the Great Debates in 1960, when Nixon's advisors felt he had been victimized by the electronic medium's cosmetics, Fiorentino personally was retained to supervise the lighting of Nixon in subsequent debates and in his other TV appearances. Fiorentino was a lighting designer for ABC during the network's early years, then left in 1960 to start his own consultancy, Imero Fiorentino Associates. The company employs experts in a number of staging and production services besides lighting.

***FIRING LINE* ▶** interview and discussion series on current issues hosted by William F. Buckley, Jr., the politically conservative publisher and columnist. The program began in 1966 on WOR-TV New York, which offered it in commercial syndication; in 1971 it shifted to PBS while public TV was under fire from the Nixon Administration for favoring the liberal view. Although Buckley resided in New York, the series was produced by SECA, the Southern Educational Communications Assn. in South Carolina. Warren Steibel was producer. Annoyed with the poor time periods the program received from many PBS stations, Buckley in 1975 switched the syndication of the program to a combination of commercial and PTV stations, with the RKO General stations as its base. In the fall of 1977 it became exclusively a PBS series again; eventually it petered out.

FIRST AMENDMENT AND DEFAMATION ▶ the First Amendment to the United States Constitution provides that "Congress shall make no law abridging the freedom of speech, or of the press...." Although this prohibition was written in seemingly unambiguous terms, it was never considered a bar to civil liability for a defamatory falsehood by a newspaper or broadcaster [*Chaplinsky v. New Hampshire,* 315 U.S. 568 (1942) and *Beauharnais v. Illinois,* 343 U.S. 250 (1952)]. This assumption was dispelled in *New York Times v. Sullivan* [376 U.S. 254 (1964)], when the Court determined that one may not be held liable for the "publication" (or broadcasting) of defamatory falsehoods about "public officials" as long as the publisher did not publish with malice. Malice was defined as either having actual knowledge of the falsehood or acting in "reckless disregard" of whether the defamatory statement was true or false.

The case arose in the context of an advertisement published in the *Times* that allegedly defamed the police commissioner of Montgomery, Alabama. He sued the *Times* and collected a judgment of $500,000 in the Alabama courts. The *Times* appealed to the Supreme Court of the United States, which reversed the judgment because, it wrote, the First Amendment required protection for those criticizing "public officials" acting in the course of their public duties.

The *Times* rule was subsequently broadened to include "public figures" [*Curtis Publishing Co. v. Butts,* athletic director at the University of Georgia; and *Associated Press v. Walker,* retired Army General, 388 U.S. 130 (1967)], and there were indications that it would be used to protect publishers of defamatory falsehoods whenever the subject matters under discussion were "issues of public importance" [*Rosenbloom v. Metromedia,* 403 U.S. 29 (1971), plurality opinion of Justice Brennan]. However, this expansion of protection, which at the same time prevented those who were defamed from compensation for their injuries, came to a halt in *Gertz v. Robert Welch Inc.* [418 U.S. 323 (1974)]. In Gertz, the plaintiff was a prominent lawyer who had been defamed in Welch's publication *American Opinion* because of his participation in an unconnected civil damage suit against a policeman. As a threshold matter, the Court reasserted its prior position that only "public officials" and "public figures" triggered the rule announced in *Times v. Sullivan* protecting the publisher of a defamatory falsehood. Gertz, though, was not a public figure despite his prominence among those in the legal profession.

The Court noted that the limited protection for defamations of public figures was in part due to their "significantly greater access" to the media, affording them an opportunity to reply. More importantly, "public figures" generally have "thrust" themselves to the forefront of particular controversies in order to influence the resolution of "issues involved." As a result, the Court indicated that the communications media are entitled to assume that public figures "have voluntarily exposed themselves to increased risk of injury from defamatory falsehoods." Gertz did not have any meaningful access to the media, nor had he "thrust himself" in the arena of public controversy. Therefore, the *Times* privilege did not apply to the defamation, and the *American Opinion* would be liable if Gertz were able to show that the publisher did not act reasonably.

As an increasingly conservative Supreme Court abandoned more and more of the liberal Warren Court doctrines, the mass media became fearful that the protections of the *Times* case would be removed. Indeed, over time the Court did chip away at some of these principles. Of particular concern was the 1990 decision issued in *Malkovich v. Lorain Journal,* in which a newspaper columnist's statement, clearly labeled as opinion (in this case, that a high school wrestling coach had lied under oath), was considered actionable.

There were sighs of relief in the Supreme Court's next term, when the justices declined the opportunity to narrow journalist's First Amendment protection. A generation after the *Times* case, juries continued to be confused by instructions that "actual malice" in the law did not necessarily mean hostility. However, in *Masson v. New Yorker Magazine,* decided in 1991, the Supreme Court left the basic rules in place and instead permitted trial courts to substitute the less confusing standard of "reckless disregard for truth or falsity."

***1ST & TEN* ▶** ensemble sitcom set in the world of professional football, which is scheduled annually by HBO to run throughout the NFL season. The series, which premiered in 1984, follows the fortunes of a bumbling team that is owned by a socialite who received it as part of her divorce settlement. Three actresses have played the role of the owner since the series began: Delta Burke, Ruta Lee and Shannon Tweed. O. J. Simpson and Reid Shelton head the cast as general manager and head coach, respectively. The team has a number of oddball characters, making for several plot strands. Among those featured in the large and ever-changing cast have been John Matusak, John Kassir, Tony Longo and Prince Hughes. Rod Pederson is the executive producer.

FIRST COMMERCIAL TELECASTS ▶ inaugurated by WNBT New York (now WNBC-TV) on July 1, 1941, the day its experimental call letters were changed from W2XBS. The station had been operating experimentally under RCA ownership since 1928 and actually began a schedule of regular service under NBC in 1939, two years before it embarked on commercial service. There were about 4,000 TV sets in the New York area for the first commercial telecast.

The first advertiser was Bulova Watch, which paid $9 for a 10-second Bulova Watch Time announcement superimposed on the test pattern at 2:29:50. The charge was broken down to $4 for the time and $5 for facilities. At 2:30, the telecast began from Ebbetts Field in Brooklyn, with Ray Forrest doing the play-by-play of a baseball game between the Dodgers and the Phillies. The station went off the air at 6:30 and returned 15 minutes later for a simulcast of the Sunoco newscast with Lowell Thomas. Dark again for two hours, it resumed again with a USO program, then *Uncle Jim's Question Bee* sponsored by Lever Brothers, then a Fort Monmouth Signal Corps show followed by Ralph Edwards's *Truth or Consequences* sponsored by Procter & Gamble. Ed Herlihy delivered the Ivory Soap "dishpan hands" commercial. The station signed off at 10:57:19 p.m. with the national anthem.

During the first week of commercial broadcasts, WNBT presented 19 hours of programming, 15 of which were devoted to sports—boxing, baseball and tennis. There were also films: *Death from a Distance, Where the Golden Grapefruit Grows* and *Julien Bryan: Photographer-Lecturer.*

With its commercial development hobbled by World War II, WNBT spent the war years broadcasting about four hours a week, mostly offering instructional programs for air raid and fire wardens on sets installed in New York's police precinct stations. It also presented occasional feature films and live coverage of sports events watched mainly by hospitalized veterans on sets provided by the broadcast industry. But on V-E Day, May 8, 1945, WNBT presented 15 hours of programming on the end of the war in Europe, all of it relayed to WRGB

Schenectady, and WPTZ Philadelphia, on the first TV "network." Similar coverage was provided on V-J Day.

In December 1945 WNBT went to a six-day-a-week operation, with no service on Tuesdays. Early in 1946 Washington joined the network. The first network sponsor on the four-city hookup was Gillette, which underwrote coverage of the Joe Louis-Billy Conn fight on June 19, 1946. This was a five-camera pickup, with Ben Grauer announcing. That same year Standard Brands sponsored the first hour-long variety show, *Hour Glass,* featuring Edgar Bergen, Edward Everett Horton, Joe Besser and a chorus line.

WNBT went off the air from March 1 to May 9, 1946, to switch from Channel 1 to Channel 4. When it returned, it added three days of daytime programming. On June 8, 1946, the historic Milton Berle weekly series began. In 1947 the station carried the World Series between the Yankees and Dodgers. *Howdy Doody* started on Dec. 27, 1947. In 1948 Tuesday joined the schedule, and the programming expanded, with WNBT originating for the network.

FIRSTRUN PROGRAMS ▶ programs or series episodes being presented for the first time on television, without having had previous network or local broadcast exposure. Motion pictures that have played in theaters are considered firstrun in their initial television presentations. Existing network or resurrected series are considered firstrun syndication fare if the episodes offered to local stations have never before been aired.

Through most of the 1950s and part of the 1960s, the accepted practice at the networks was to schedule 39 firstrun episodes of a series and 13 repeats over the lower-viewing summer months. Later, for economic reasons and because rerun programming was found to be acceptable even in high-viewing seasons, the networks changed the formula to 26 firstruns and 26 repeats. By the early 1970s, partly to accommodate specials, the pattern had been reduced to 22 firstruns for most series.

FIRSTRUN SYNDICATION ▶ original programs produced expressly for distribution in syndication, as opposed to network series whose reruns pass into the syndication market. As a notable example, Paramount gambled on producing *Star Trek: The Next Generation* for firstrun syndication, rather than for a network, and won.

FIRSTS **▶** TV broadcasts that were the first of their kind. When TV was new, each "first" carried the sense of history in the making. A list of claimed "firsts" would be endless and many of the claims open to dispute. The following are among the more significant landmarks:

Inaugural of regular television service: by NBC on April 30, 1939, with President Roosevelt appearing in a telecast of the opening of the New York World's Fair.

First professional boxing telecast: Max Baer vs. Lou Nova, June 1, 1939.

First one-hour TV production: Gilbert & Sullivan's *The Pirates of Penzance,* June 20, 1939.

First major league baseball telecast: Brooklyn Dodgers vs. Cincinnati Reds, Aug. 26, 1939, a doubleheader.

First coverage of political conventions and first telecast of presidential election returns: 1940.

First network broadcast: the hookup of WNBT-TV New York, and WRGB-TV Schenectady, N.Y., Jan. 12, 1940.

First TV network sponsor: Gillette, with the telecast of the Joe Louis vs. Billy Conn boxing match, June 19,1946.

First opera telecast from the stage: Verdi's *Otello* from the Metropolitan Opera House by ABC, December 1948, with Texaco as sponsor.

First telecast of a presidential inauguration: President Truman in January 1949.

First telecast from the White House: President Truman's address to the nation on food conservation, October 1949. (This was before there was national interconnection.)

First presidential speech carried coast to coast: President Truman's address at the Japanese peace treaty conference in San Francisco, Sept. 4, 1951. It was pooled by the networks to inaugurate AT&T's coast-to-coast network facilities.

First presidential news conference to be televised: President Eisenhower, January 1955.

First network editorial: delivered by Dr. Frank Stanton, president of CBS Inc., in August 1954. It asked that TV and radio be given the right to cover congressional hearings.

First use of videotape on television: the West Coast feed of *Douglas Edwards With the News* by CBS, Nov. 30, 1956.

FISHER, ART ▶ director associated with comedy-variety shows, pageants and occasionally sports. His credits include *The Sonny and Cher Comedy Hour, The Andy Williams Show, America's Junior Miss Pageant, Miss Teenage America* and specials with Ann-Margret, Bing Crosby, Dionne Warwick and the Jackson Five. He was also producer/director of the coverage of the Ali-Frazier championship fight.

FISHER, EDDIE ▶ a popular singer of the 1950s who starred in *Coke Time with Eddie Fisher,* a 15-minute variety show that aired twice a week on NBC from April 1953 to April 1957. The following September he began an hour-long prime-time series, *The Eddie Fisher Show,* which ran alternate weeks with *The George Gobel Show* for two seasons.

FLAHERTY, JOSEPH ▶ for three decades a major influence in the development of television technology, not only at CBS, where he worked, but throughout the industry. Prior to taking on the position of senior vice president of technology in 1990, Flaherty was CBS's vice president and general manager of engineering and development, a post he held for 23 years. He advocated and presided over the network's and its owned stations' adoption of such technologies as off-line videotape editing, one-inch videotape, electronic production, ENG and minicams.

Flaherty is the recipient of numerous engineering awards in the U.S. and overseas and has published many technical articles on various aspects of television broadcasting. His espousal of advanced television (ATV) technology led him to serve as chairman of the Planning Subcommittee of the FCC's Advisory Committee on Advanced Television Service, as member of the Executive Committee of the Advanced Television Systems Committee (ATSC), and as member of the board of the Advanced Television Test Center (ATTC).

Flaherty joined CBS in 1957 as a design engineer and two years later became the network's director of technical facilities planning. He began his television career at WDAF-TV in his native Kansas City.

FLASHCASTER ▶ device for superimposing written news bulletins over the television picture, usually in a horizontal strip moving across the bottom of the screen.

FLATT, ERNEST ▶ director and choreographer. His credits include *Julie Andrews and Carol Burnett at Carnegie Hall, The Carol Burnett Show, The Lucky Strike Hit Parade, Annie Get Your Gun* and *Kiss Me, Kate.*

FLEISCHMAN, STEPHEN ▶ director, writer and producer of news documentaries, initially with CBS (1957-63) and thereafter with ABC. His credits with the latter include *Close Up: Life, Liberty and the Pursuit of Coal, Assault on Privacy, The Long Childhood of Timmy, Anatomy of Pop—The Music Explosion* and *Close Up: Oil.*

FLEMING, ROBBEN W. ▶ president of the Corporation for Public Broadcasting (CPB) from 1979-81 and for the previous 12 years president of the University of Michigan. His selection to succeed Henry Loomis at CPB came after a long search, but he arrived while public television was in turmoil and at just the time the Carnegie Commission on the Future of Public Broadcasting recommended that CPB be disbanded and replaced by a new organization. Fleming's first acts were to mend fences with PBS and to design a reorganization of CPB that might obviate the need for the legislative changes proposed by Carnegie. He was succeeded at CPB by Edward Pfister.

FLICKER, THEODORE J. ▶ director and writer. His credits include *Dick Van Dyke Show, Andy Griffith Show, The Rogues, I Dream of Jeannie, Night Gallery* and *Man From U.N.C.L.E.*

***FLINTSTONES, THE* ▶** a Hanna-Barbera animated cartoon series of the 1960s that utilized the situation comedy form in a fanciful portrayal of Stone Age domesticity. The first animated sitcom to be presented in prime time, its humor derived chiefly from the anachronism of a prehistoric setting for activities and concerns that were distinctly of modern suburbia.

In the relationships between the two married couples involved—Fred and Wilma Flintstone (voiced by Alan Reed and Jean vander Pyl) and Barney and Betty Rubble (voiced by Mel Blanc, Bea Benaderet and Gerry Johnson)—and in their blue-collar attitudes and styles of speech, *The Flintstones* owed a large debt to Jackie Gleason's *The Honeymooners.* Also modeled on that series was Hanna-Barbera's *The Jetsons,* the reverse image of *The Flintstones* in that it presented modern situations in futuristic times. *The Flintstones* premiered on ABC-TV in the fall of 1960 in an early evening slot; *The Jetsons* followed two years later. The reruns of both have been in continuous syndication.

Hanna-Barbera skirted the high cost of producing animation with both series by developing an assembly-line process, which reduced the number of lip movements with the exclusion of consonants. It sufficed. *The Flintstones* contributed to the English language Fred Flintstone's all-purpose cry: "Yabba dabba doo."

FLIP WILSON SHOW, THE ▶ first comedy-variety hit starring a black performer, which ran on NBC from 1970 to 1974 and during the first three seasons was among the leaders in the Nielsen ratings. Flip Wilson, the star, based much of his comedy on satirical characterizations of Harlem types, such as the chatterbox Geraldine Jones and the Reverend Leroy of the Church of What's Happening Now. The Thursday night hour from Clerow Productions in association with Bob Henry Productions and NBC was bested in the ratings finally by *The Waltons* on CBS. Wilson continued to appear in specials.

FLIPPER ▶ hour-long juvenile interest adventure series on NBC (1964-67) built around a dolphin befriended by two young sons of a marine preserve ranger. Featured were Brian Kelly as ranger Porter Ricks, Luke Halpin and Tommy Norden as his sons, Sandy and Bud, and Susie as Flipper. Filmed in Florida and the Bahamas, the series made a specialty of underwater scenes in which Flipper assisted in the capture of malefactors. It was by MGM-TV and Ivan Tors Films and based on a movie produced by Tors.

FLY, JAMES LAWRENCE (d. 1966) ▶ outspoken chairman of the FCC (1939-44) who made enemies in the broadcast industry when he charged the networks with seeking a monopoly and called the NAB a "stooge organization." Before he became chairman, he was largely responsible for the commission order in 1941 forcing NBC to divest itself of one of its two radio networks, the Red and the Blue. It was the Blue that was sold off, and it became the foundation of the third major network, ABC.

A famous clash with the industry occurred at the NAB convention in 1941, where Mark Ethridge, former NAB president who was then general manager of the *Louisville Courier and Journal*, accused Fly of meddling and of trying to take over the FCC. Fly told newsmen the next day that the management of radio reminded him "of a dead mackerel in the moonlight, which both shines and stinks."

Appointed by President Roosevelt in 1939, Fly, when he became chairman, improved the efficiency of the agency. He was critical of radio soap operas and lotteries and contended that some programs were contributing to juvenile crime. He resigned from the FCC in 1944 to head the Muzak Corporation, from which he retired 10 years later.

FLYING NUN, THE ▶ ABC fantasy-comedy (1967-69) about an American novitiate in a Puerto Rican convent who has the gift of being able to fly. Via Screen Gems, it featured Sally Field in the title role as Elsie Ethrington, ordained as Sister Bertrille, and Alejandro Rey as Carlos Ramirez, Marge Redmond as Sister Jacqueline and Madeleine Sherwood as the Reverend Mother Plaseato.

FLYOVERS ▶ the viewing public, a term coined in the 1960s and still used by producers and network programming executives, usually in a self-deprecating spirit. The term was struck from a widely quoted observation attributed to James Aubrey, then president of the CBS network, in reference to the traffic between New York and Hollywood by those who bought and produced television programs. "The public," he said, "is what we fly over."

FNN (FINANCIAL NEWS NETWORK) ▶ basic-cable service devoted to providing continuous business news that became subsumed in 1991 by its chief competitor, CNBC (Consumer News and Business Channel). FNN had been a publicly traded company owned by Infotechnology. The channel, which was received in 32 million cable homes, prompted a bidding war when it went up for sale. NBC wanted it to increase the penetration of its business-and-consumer channel, CNBC, and also to be rid of its main competitor. Group W Satellite Communications and Dow Jones, in a partnership, were eager to develop the channel as an electronic extension of *The Wall Street Journal*. In a bitter contest, NBC prevailed and promptly merged the channel with CNBC, and FNN was no more. The price was in excess of $150 million. FNN's president was Michael Wheeler.

FOGARTY, JOSEPH R. ▶ former FCC commissioner (1976-83), appointed by President Ford for a seven-year term to fill the non-Republican vacancy of Glen O. Robinson. Fogarty previously was counsel to the Senate Communications Subcommittee while it was headed by Sen. John O. Pastore and for 13 years a staff member of the Senate Commerce Committee. His work on the Commerce Committee had involved transportation, coastal fishing rights and East-West trade but never broadcasting, until Sen. Pastore appointed him in 1975 to succeed Nicholas Zapple as chief counsel of the Communications Subcommittee.

FOLSOM, FRANK M. (d. 1970) ▶ RCA executive who succeeded Gen. David Sarnoff as president in 1949, while Sarnoff retained the title of chairman. Folsom later became chairman of the executive committee board (1957-66).

FOOTBALL ▶ see College Football; Professional Football (the NFL).

FOOTPRINT ▶ the beam of a communications satellite and where it falls geographically. In North America, the footprints of Canada's Anik satellites cover much of the U.S.; conversely, U.S. satellites covering the contiguous 48 states have footprints that fall into Canada. In Europe, a satellite's footprint may cover half the continent, showing no respect for the sovereignty of national borders. When the footprint of an experimental Japanese satellite came down in parts of North Korea, charges were raised of a cultural invasion. Low- and medium-powered satellites have larger footprints than high-powered satellites but require larger receiving dishes.

FORD FOUNDATION AND PUBLIC TV ▶ a relationship that began in 1951 and ended in 1977, except for individual program projects. In that 26-year period, Ford pumped $289 million into the ETV and PTV systems for the development of stations, the building of production centers, the financing of program production, the interconnection of the stations, the perfecting of fund-raising techniques and numerous internal projects.

If Ford is not actually the parent of public TV in the U.S., it is at the very least the godfather. For most of the years educational (later called "public") television has existed, Ford was the single largest source of support for the system. It announced its final four-year phase-out of institutional support in 1973 when it determined that long-range federal funding was in view, that mechanisms had been developed to insulate the system from government interference and that the system had a nucleus of contributing subscribers sufficient for it to stand on its own.

Ford's first activity in broadcasting was the creation in 1951 of the Radio-Television Workshop, conceived as an agency to improve the cultural use of TV and radio in the commercial systems. The Workshop brought forth *Omnibus,* a celebrated weekly series that ran four years on CBS and one on ABC, with its losses covered by the foundation. But as early as 1951, Ford had also contributed to the efforts to secure allocations from the FCC for noncommercial stations that would be dedicated to education.

Ford created the Fund for Adult Education, which in turn financed the National Citizens Committee for Educational Television and made grants to the various organizations working for ETV. Between 1952 and 1961, the Fund made grants of more than $3.5 million to assist 37 new educational stations that were going on the air, and it financed NAEB seminars, workshops and technical consultation services for the new stations. It also provided the backing to establish the Educational Television and Radio Center (forerunner of NET) in Ann Arbor, Mich., as a program supplier and distribution service. From 1953 to 1963, Ford's grants to the center amounted to around $30 million.

A similar amount was distributed during that period for individual experiments with TV as part of formal education, both at the university and public school levels. Meanwhile, the foundation underwrote the *Continental Classroom* early morning series on NBC and made substantial grants to support experiments with the distribution of courses to several states at once from a transmitter in an airplane. By 1963, the total Ford investment in ETV was $80.7 million.

That year, Ford increased its support of NET (which by then had moved to New York) to $6 million a year so that it might provide national programming of a higher quality than before. Next it began to work at interconnecting the stations and allocated $10 million to demonstrate what public TV might achieve with adequate programming funds and a national hookup. This resulted in the creation of the Public Broadcasting Laboratory and its two-hour Sunday evening series, *PBL* (1967-69). Later, when a 24-hour rate was successfully negotiated with AT&T for interconnection by long lines, Ford made a grant to cover some of the expenses and then contributed to the start-up costs of PBS as caretaker of the interconnection system.

Ford contributed to such programs as *San Francisco Mix, The Advocates, Hollywood Television Theatre, Sounds of Summer, Soul!, NET Opera, Black Journal, The Great American Dream Machine, An American Family, V.D. Blues,* Elizabeth Drew's interview series *Thirty Minutes With..., Evening at the Pops, Zoom, Sesame Street, The Electric Company, Visions, The MacNeil-Lehrer Report* and scores of other national and local programs.

Ford also helped to finance national affairs programming through NPACT, created in 1972; the foundation's grants were reflected in such programs as *Washington Week in Review, Washington Connection* and the live coverage of the Senate Watergate hearings and the House Judiciary Committee hearings on impeachment.

Much of Ford's final $40 million grant went toward the support of the Station Program Cooperative, the Station Independence Program, the principal production centers and the plan to interconnect the stations by domestic satellite.

FORD, FREDERICK W. ▶ FCC chairman for one year (1960) of the seven he served on the commission (1957-1964). Although a Republican appointed by President Eisenhower, he held the liberal view that the commission should set up program guidelines for broadcasters in the public interest. After 30 months as a commissioner, following service as an attorney for the FCC, Ford was named chairman by Eisenhower to succeed John C. Doerfer, who resigned by request after the scandals raised by the House Legislative Oversight Committee. When President Kennedy won the election in 1960 and was privileged to appoint his own FCC chairman, Newton N. Minow, Ford returned to his old status as a commissioner. He resigned in 1964 to become president of NCTA at $50,000 a year.

FORD, TENNESSEE ERNIE (ERNEST J.) (d. 1991) ▶ one of few country-music artists to become a major TV personality. His popularity spanned the years from 1955 to 1965 and was enhanced by his recording of "Sixteen Tons," one of the top song hits of the 1960s. Calling himself the "ol' pea-picker," Ford camouflaged his theatrical polish with down-home tales, epigrams and jokes delivered in a becoming country accent.

He came to notice on TV as host of *The Kollege of Musical Knowledge* on NBC upon the retirement of Kay Kyser in the summer of 1954. The following year he began a daytime variety program, *The Tennessee Ernie Ford Show,* featuring country music and comedy. In the fall of 1956 he added a weekly evening series, *The Ford Show,* which was more sophisticated and which ran to the early 1960s. Ford concluded each of his programs with a hymn.

FORREST, ARTHUR ▶ director whose credits include *The Dick Cavett Show,* Jerry Lewis Telethons, David Frost specials and daytime game shows.

FORSYTE SAGA, THE ▶ BBC adaptation of the John Galsworthy novels of 19th-century England, completed in 26 episodes. Its popularity on public television here inspired the commercial networks to experiment with the mini-series form, especially in the adaptation of modern popular novels (*QB VII, The Blue Knight*). The series was produced by the BBC in 1967 and played on National Educational Television (before it became PBS) in the 1969-70 season. MGM-TV, which had been associated with the production, then made it available for commercial syndication.

Featured were Kenneth More, Eric Porter, Nyree Dawn Porter, Ursula Howells, Jenny Laird, Joseph O'Connor, June Barry and John Bennett.

FORTE, CHET ▶ former producer-director specializing in sports coverage; his credits include the Olympic Games on ABC beginning in 1964, events for *Wide World of Sports,* NBC basketball and special events.

FORTNIGHTLY DECISION ▶ [*Fortnightly Corp. v. United Artists Television Inc.*/392 U.S. 390(1968)] landmark ruling of the Supreme Court in a cable copyright case that established that cable systems do not violate a picture company's copyrights when they carry movies broadcast on distant TV stations.

Fortnightly Corp. owned and operated CATV systems in two small West Virginia towns, Clarksburg and Fairmont. When the systems were introduced there were no local TV stations, although two subsequently began to broadcast before the suit by United Artists TV was filed. In the classic use of cable TV, Fortnightly brought in signals from stations in Pittsburgh, Steubenville, Ohio, and Wheeling, W. Va.

United Artists TV, having licensed some of its movies to the stations that Fortnightly imported to the communities it served, brought suit in the mid-1960s to prohibit Fortnightly from showing its copyrighted movies without a license and asked for damages as well. The film company was successful in the District Court and Court of Appeals, but Fortnightly carried the case to the Supreme Court.

The Supreme Court stated that the copyright laws give the holder exclusive right only to "perform in public for profit." It then proceeded to analyze the position of a CATV system to determine if it "performed" the movies for profit. It noted that the broadcaster "selects and procures the program to be viewed" and sends out the broadcast signal. The viewer does not perform; he merely provides the receiving equipment.

The Court felt that a CATV was more like a viewer than like a station, since it did not select programs but merely enhanced "the viewer's capacity to receive the broadcast signals."

Therefore, the CATV presentations were not a performance, the Court said, and Fortnightly did not violate United Artists' copyrights in movies by importing signals from distant stations for its subscribers in Clarksburg and Fairmont.

FOSTER, DAVID H. ▶ president of National Cable Television Association from 1972-75, resigning after policy disputes with the association's board during a period of general frustration for the cable industry. He later joined the Natural Gas Supply Committee as executive director.

FOSTER, NORMAN ▶ director whose credits include *It Takes a Thief, Batman, The Loner, Loretta Young Show, Davy Crockett, Zorro* and *Hans Brinker.*

FOUHY, ED ▶ former v.p. of CBS News in Washington, beginning in 1978, and previously Washington-based producer for the *CBS Evening News with Walter Cronkite.* For five years (1969-74) he produced hard news coverage from the capital for the evening newscast, then went to NBC News where he was first producer of the *Nightly News* and then director of news. He returned to CBS News in 1977. After leaving the network, he served as executive producer for the Commission on Presidential Debates in 1988 and again in 1992.

FOUR STAR PLAYHOUSE ▶ half-hour anthology drama series on CBS (1952-56), from which Four Star Studios was formed. The initial foursome who were to rotate as stars in the series were Charles Boyer, Dick Powell, Rosalind Russell and Joel McCrea. But the latter two dropped out before production and were replaced by David Niven and Ida Lupino. Later Lupino left the group, and though there were only three partners the name Four Star was retained for both the show and production company.

In the anthology series the regulars were usually joined by other well-known actors. Though most of the characters were not reoccurring ones, Powell created a character, Willie Dante, who appeared in most of the playlets as a continuing element. In 1960 NBC premiered a series, *Dante,* that was based on the character but that featured Howard Duff in the role.

FOUR-IN-ONE ▶ an attempt by NBC in 1970 to rotate four diverse hour-long dramatic series, all produced by Universal, in a single time slot. The project was unsuccessful but led to the *Sunday Mystery Movie,* which did well. The rotating series, each of which contributed 6 episodes to *Four-In-One,* were *McCloud* with Dennis Weaver, *The Psychiatrist* with Roy Thinnes, *Night Gallery* with Rod Serling and *San Francisco International* with Lloyd Bridges. *McCloud* went on to become a *Mystery Movie,* and *Night Gallery* became a weekly series on its own.

FOWLER, MARK S. ▶ chairman of the FCC (1981-87), as President Reagan's nominee. Initially underestimated as something of a lightweight because of his rather undistinguished career as a small-time communications lawyer who generally represented small radio stations (such as the Florida outlets at which he spun records under the sobriquet "Mad Mark"), Fowler proved to be an effective and unrelenting ideologue who achieved an almost perfect string of victories in his drive to eliminate all content-oriented regulation and other restraints on operation of free-market forces in broadcasting.

Aided by a conservative Congress and a head start from his Carterite predecessor Charles Ferris, Fowler brought a libertarian zeal to his across-the-board attack, which extended even to eliminating approval of station call letters. Although Fowler left office shortly before his successor Dennis Patrick delivered the *coup de grace* to the Fairness Doctrine, his drive upon this vestige of intrusiveness he so despised was perhaps his most symbolically important endeavor. Among his other major achievements were the relaxation of ownership regulations and repeal of trafficking rules. Two notable failures amidst this record of success were his attack on rules giving preference to minority and female applicants for new stations, and his drive to repeal the "fin-syn" rules restricting network ownership of syndication rights for reruns, which was ended allegedly after direct intervention from President Reagan.

Calling himself an advocate of "unregulation," he acted not only to discard long-standing rules for broadcasting but also to revoke the concept of public trusteeship, which had been the basis for regulation. Fowler argued repeatedly that the public interest would be better served by market forces than by bureaucrats in a federal agency. He minimized television's social influence, describing the TV set in one of his speeches as a mere household appliance, equivalent to "a toaster with a picture."

His commission, dominated by conservatives, did away with many of the procedures that were adopted to hold broadcasters accountable to the public and reduced much of the paperwork. From his first year in office, Fowler pushed against congressional resistance for the abolition of the Fairness Doctrine, the cornerstone of regulation. He finally succeeded in eliminating the doctrine as regulation, leaving it up to Congress to codify it as law.

After leaving the commission, Fowler joined a large Washington law firm. Before his FCC appointment he had been senior partner of a small firm, Fowler & Myers, formed in 1975. Fowler had worked for Reagan's election, serving as legal counsel for communications to the various committees working on the political campaign. He also served on the Reagan transition team.

Before entering the field of law, he worked in broadcasting for about 10 years, chiefly as an announcer and salesman for small radio stations in Florida. Most of these were part-time jobs held during his college years.

FOX BROADCASTING CO. ▶ the budding fourth television network that has succeeded where others had failed largely because of the financial clout and derring-do of media baron Rupert Murdoch and the creative savvy of Hollywood studio executive Barry Diller. The explosion of UHF independents in the 1980s and Murdoch's purchase of the Metromedia independents, all located in major markets, provided the infrastructure on which to build a new network. Murdoch had also purchased 20th Century-Fox Studios, from which the new network and station group took its name.

The Fox television network introduced itself in November 1986 with a single late-night entry, *The Joan Rivers Show,* intended to compete with Johnny Carson's *Tonight,* on which Rivers had been a frequent and popular substitute host. That program failed, but Fox proceeded with a limited prime-time schedule, first staking out Sunday nights. Its programs tended to be innovative and more appealing to young adults than many on the established networks, and in 1989 Fox added additional nights and reported its first profit to enthusiastic affiliates. By the 1991-92 season, Fox was programming four nights a week and placing programs in the Nielsen Top 10. While not a full-blown competitor to the big networks, it has proven itself something more than a minor nuisance.

Diller, along with Fox president Jamie Kellner, took programming risks, especially with shows like *The Simpsons, Married ... with Children* and *America's Most Wanted.* Subjects considered taboo by the big three networks were perfect for Fox. Moreover, Fox used a brilliant strategy for introducing its new shows, scheduling their premieres during August when the three big networks were coasting quietly with reruns.

The idea for a Fox network actually preceded Murdoch's arrival on the scene. After oil magnate Marvin Davis purchased 20th Century-Fox in June 1981 and hired away Barry Diller from Paramount to head the studio in 1984, plans began for a new broadcast network. But the company was having financial problems and had to abandon the idea. Murdoch arrived in 1985, just in time to revive the plan. He paid $250 million to Davis for 50% of the company in 1985, and later bought him out with another $325 million. The plan for a network went into high gear when Murdoch bought the Metromedia group of stations from John W. Kluge for $2 billion, giving him the nucleus of outlets essential for a network. In 1986 Diller hired Jamie Kellner, who previously had been with CBS, Viacom and Orion, to become president of Fox's big new venture.

FOX, IRWIN (SONNY) ▶ one of the few to pass from TV performer to TV executive. He became v.p. of children's programs for NBC in 1976 after having come to prominence as a host of children's programs. He was the star of *Let's Take a Trip* on CBS (1955-58) and during the same period host of the prime-time quiz show, *The $64,000 Challenge.* During the 1960s, he did such shows as *On Your Mark* and *Wonderama.*

He was fired by NBC in 1977 when his attempt at mounting a quality children's schedule was undone by the poor ratings for his shows. Moving to the coast, he became associated with Alan Landsburg Productions and then formed a production company of his own.

FOX, MATTHEW (MATTY) (d. 1964) ▶ motion picture executive and promoter who became a pay-TV pioneer as president of Skiatron, which he acquired in 1954. Fox's promotional skills caused the industry and the investment community to take Skiatron seriously at first, but the company foundered in the FCC's long delay in giving pay TV permission to proceed. Earlier, Fox had been an executive with United Artists, Universal-International Pictures and United World Films.

FOXX, REDD (d. 1991) ▶ veteran comedian who after years of playing nightclubs and making racy party recordings became a television star in 1972 when he was cast as Sanford, the crotchety black junk dealer, in *Sanford and Son* (1972-77). He starred in three failed series after that, two sitcoms and a variety show, until his final series, *The Royal Family,* in which Della Reese co-starred. Barely a month after the program premiered on CBS at the start of the 1991-92 season, Foxx died of a heart attack on the show's set during a rehearsal. He was 68.

***FRACTURED FLICKERS* ▶** syndicated comedy series (1961) built around scenes from silent movie classics with humorous narration delivered by Hans Conreid. It was produced by Jay Ward and Bill Scott.

Characters from Jim Henson's HBO series *Fraggle Rock*

***FRAGGLE ROCK* ▶** spirited and whimsical live-action "muppet" show created by Jim Henson. As HBO's first original children's series (1983-88), it developed a strong following with family audiences. The stories were set among caves beneath the home of a scientist and his dog, inhabited by three kinds of imaginative creatures: the Fraggles, the Doozers, and the Gorgs. A cartoon version ran on NBC from 1987 to 1988.

Lawrence P. Fraiberg

FRAIBERG, LAWRENCE P. ▶ broadcaster and independent producer who served two substantial hitches with Metromedia Television, rising the second time to president of the company (1977-79). He left after a philosophical dispute with higher management and pursued a private venture.

In 1980 he became president of the Group W television stations. He left in 1986 to become president of the newly formed MCA Broadcasting Co., with that company's acquisition of New Jersey-New York station, WWOR-TV. When MCA was sold to Matsushita in 1991, the station was spun off, since it could not be owned by a foreign company. The new broadcasting company took the name of Pinelands, Inc., with Fraiberg as chairman and CEO.

As a broadcaster he was noted as an innovator. For example, while he was v.p. and general manager of WNEW-TV New York, the Metromedia flagship (1965-69 and again from 1971-77), he elevated the station's public image by instituting a successful one-hour newscast in prime time as an alternative to network fare and created campaigns of "total station involvement" for concentrated periods of time with particular issues of public affairs. Later, as president of Metromedia Television, he arranged for annual satellite telecasts of the Royal Ballet.

Fraiberg joined Metromedia in 1959 to assist in the acquisition of additional stations, after having spent the previous decade with KPIX-TV San Francisco in sales and program production. He became v.p. and general manager of Metromedia's Washington station WTTG in 1963 and two years later took over management of WNEW-TV. He left in 1969 to start his own company, Parallel Productions, Inc., then returned in 1971 for another eight-year stretch.

FRAME ▶ a complete television picture, consisting of two interlaced fields, 525 lines in the NTSC system, 625 lines in the CCIR system. Thirty frames are transmitted every second in the NTSC system, 25 in the CCIR system.

FRAME-GRABBER ▶ an adjunct of cable-TV technology that permits the subscriber, using a modified receiver, to call up still pictures or frames of print at will from a local information bank. The subscriber, by means of a selector dial and using a reference guide, may select the set of frames he wishes to view in a wide range of subject areas. The system has a number of applications beyond information retrieval, including programmed instruction and student examinations or quizzes.

FRAMER, WALT ▶ creator and producer of such shows as *Strike It Rich, The Big Payoff, Million Dollar Family, Lady Luck, It's in the Cards* and *Meet the People* during the 1950s. He started in broadcasting as a performer on KDKA Pittsburgh.

FRANCE ▶ one of Europe's grandest television markets for size and productivity, and also one of its most troubled. The country of 20 million television households has seven broadcast TV networks—three general commercial channels, two public TV channels, one pay-TV service, and the last, La Sept, a cultural channel that has been experimenting as a shared venture with Germany, costing each government around $60 million a year. There is as well a burgeoning roster of specialized channels, including one for documentaries, although cable penetration is a scant 2%.

The difficulties come not only from a competitive environment in which advertising growth has lagged but also from France's tangled regulatory structure, which often imposes rules on the television industry in the name of protecting it from foreign influence and maintaining the country's cultural identity. Repeated changes in government policy have kept the industry from achieving any kind of equilibrium and have been a deterrent to investors.

The leading broadcast network is TF1, originally the primary state channel until it was privatized in the mid-1980s. For all the competition, its average share of audience is an enormous 40%, which means it also gets the lion's share of ad revenues. Only TF1 and the pay channel, Canal Plus, are in profit. The commercial rivals, La Cinq and M6, have struggled for years to reach break-even, and La Cinq has been plagued additionally by squabbles among its owners. The two public TV networks, Antenne 2 (which comes in second in the ratings) and FR3, have moved closer together under a joint director general in a bid to streamline their activities and reduce their huge deficits.

FRANCIS, ARLENE ▶ one of the leading female TV personalities of the 1950s, tapped by NBC as hostess of the *Home* show (it was no reflection on her that it was the only one of the *Today, Home, Tonight* trio that did not succeed in the ratings). She was best known as a regular panelist on *What's My Line* but also, for a time, conducted the *Arlene Francis Show* on NBC; a brief entry, *Talent Patrol;* and on radio, *Arlene Francis at Sardi's.* An actress, she also had film and stage credits, including *Once More with Feeling.* Beginning in 1981 she co-hosted *The Prime of Your Life* on WNBC-TV, New York.

FRANCISCUS, JAMES (d. 1991) ▶ TV actor and sometime producer, best known for the title role in the series *Mr. Novak* (1963-65), in which he played a high-school English teacher. This was preceded by a featured role as a detective in *Naked City.* As a producer in the 1970s, he worked on TV adaptations of such classics as *Jane Eyre, Heidi* and *David Copperfield.* Later he portrayed John F. Kennedy in the TV movie *Jacqueline Bouvier Kennedy* (1981).

FRANK, BARRY ▶ senior corporate v.p. of the International Management Group (IMG) and one of the most experienced and accomplished executives in the sports television industry. His wide range of experience began at CBS in 1957 when he was assistant to the v.p. of operations, before becoming an ad agency executive engaged in finding sports events for Ford sponsorship at J. Walter Thompson. Later he was vice president of planning for ABC-TV Sports, and then he did his first stint with IMG as senior vice president of its television arm, Trans World International. In 1976, when Robert Wussler was promoted to president of the CBS television network, he tapped Frank to succeed him in his previous post, as v.p. in charge of CBS Sports. Frank served two years in the post, leaving in 1978 in the wake of the "winner take all" tennis scandal that brought down Wussler, to rejoin IMG. He has been instrumental in the packaging and success of such TV sports staples as *The Superstars, Battle of the Network Stars,* and the World Professional Figure Skating Championships. In 1991-92, he was executive producer of Fox Broadcasting's short-lived prime-time series, *The Ultimate Challenge.*

FRANK, REUVEN ▶ twice president of NBC News, named the second time in March 1982 after the resignation of Bill Small. His first tour (1968-73) ended when Frank asked to return to producing. He subsequently became executive producer of the magazine-style program *Weekend.* Before becoming a news executive in the mid-1960s, Frank had produced more than a dozen documentaries, including *The Tunnel, The Road to Spandau, A Country Called Europe* and *The Daughters of Orange.* He had also been producer of *The Huntley-Brinkley Report* when it began in 1962 and then became its executive producer (1963-65).

Frank joined NBC News as a writer in 1950 after working as a reporter for the *Newark Evening News.* In 1954 he developed such weekly half-hour news programs as *Background, Outlook* and *Chet Huntley Reporting.* His career accelerated when Huntley and David Brinkley were teamed for the first time at the 1956 political conventions, a triumphal event with which Frank was closely associated.

Frank went on to write a book in 1991 titled *Out of Thin Air: The Brief Wonderful Life of Network News.*

Rich Frank

FRANK, RICH ▶ president of Walt Disney Studios who was part of the Disney management team that chairman Michael Eisner brought over from Paramount in the mid-1980s. Joining the studio in 1985, he and division chairman Jeffrey Katzenberg were given the tasks of re-establishing Disney's feature film and television production and distributing and overseeing the company's successful pay-cable Disney Channel. TV production successes included network series *The Golden Girls* and the syndicated *Duck Tales* cartoon series.

Before coming to Disney, Frank was the president of Paramount's Television Group, which developed the hit series *Family Ties* and *Cheers,* the syndication hit *Entertainment Tonight* and the mini-series *The Winds of War.* He came to Paramount from Chris-Craft, where he was the president and general manager of KCOP in Los Angeles. He also co-founded TeleRep, a sales representative firm.

FRANK, SANDY ▶ syndication executive heading his own firm, one of the companies that became prominent distributing shows for prime-time access periods. In 1975 Frank petitioned the FCC to bar strip-programming from the access slots, a move against the low-budget game shows that were able to play nightly; after hearings the FCC denied the petition in 1976. A court appeal did not avail.

FRANKENHEIMER, JOHN ▶ one of the outstanding TV directors of the 1950s who, like many another who developed in the medium, abandoned it for movies. With CBS he was director of *Mama* and *You Are There* and of TV dramas for *Danger, Climax, Studio One, Playhouse 90, DuPont Show of the Month* and other anthologies.

FRANKLIN, JOE ▶ local New York television personality who has conducted a daily program of interviews, chiefly with book- and show-pluggers, almost continuously since 1953. His program *Down Memory Lane* switched stations over the years but settled in at WOR-TV (now WWOR).

FRANK'S PLACE **▶** critically lauded but commercially unsuccessful CBS sitcom (1987-88) from producer Hugh Wilson. The show, one of few comedies made without a laugh track, also had a decidedly serious side, tackling social subjects like racism in off-beat ways. Tim Reid (earlier in *WKRP in Cincinnati*) both starred in the show and served as an executive producer; he played a Massachusetts college professor comically out of his element when he inherits a New Orleans restaurant. Reid's real wife, Daphne Maxwell Reid, played Reid's love interest, Hanna Griffin.

The show won the Television Critics Association's award for outstanding comedy series in

1987, but CBS canceled the show because of poor ratings, even when the show's cast and crew agreed to take a 25% pay cut to keep it in production.

FREDERICK, PAULINE ▶ for 22 years an NBC News correspondent and probably best known of the female journalists during the decades in which there were few in broadcasting. She became prominent as United Nations correspondent for NBC, an assignment she held until her retirement in 1975, but had served earlier as a foreign correspondent, both for NBC and ABC. She joined ABC in a period of freelancing for newspapers and moved to NBC in 1953.

FREED, FRED (d. 1974) ▶ noted producer of documentaries for NBC News, principally those under the rubric of *American White Paper.* He received three George Foster Peabody Awards, two duPont-Columbia Awards and seven Emmys for his programs.

Three of the Freed *White Paper* productions spanned an entire evening of prime-time programming: *NBC Reports: The Energy Crisis* (1973); *Organized Crime In the United States* (1966); and *United States Foreign Policy* (1965). Two others were presented in two parts: *And Now the War Is Over—The American Military in the 70s* (1973) and *Vietnam Hindsight* (1971).

Specializing in major current issues, Freed produced a series of *White Paper* reports examining the urban and environmental crises; these resulted in three programs entitled *The Ordeal of the American City* (1968-69), and two others, *Who Killed Lake Erie?* (1969) and *Pollution Is a Matter of Choice* (1970).

Freed began as a magazine editor and writer, entered broadcasting in 1949 and joining NBC in 1955 as managing editor of the daytime *Home* show. He left to become a documentary producer for CBS, then rejoined NBC in 1961 as producer of *Today* before being assigned exclusively to documentary production.

FREEDMAN, LEWIS ▶ TV drama producer working between PBS and CBS between 1956 and 1974. In the early 1980s he was head of the Program Fund, a newly established division of the Corporation for Public Broadcasting.

He began as a producer on *Camera Three* for CBS (1956-58), then became vice president of programming for WNDT (now WNET), where he produced *New York Television Theatre.* Later he joined the Public Broadcasting Laboratory as director of cultural programming for its Sunday night "network" series *PBL.* In 1970 he became producer of *Hollywood Television Theatre,* a PBS series that originated at KCET Los Angeles. There he produced such plays as *The Andersonville Trial, Awake and Sing, Monserrat, Big Fish, Little Fish* and *Poet Game.* CBS hired him away in 1972 to spearhead its new thrust in drama and mini-series. After producing several full-length plays, he resigned to live in Europe for a few years.

FREEDOMS FOUNDATION AWARDS ▶ citations presented each Washington's birthday for TV and radio programs contributing to an understanding of America in the judgment of Freedoms Foundation at Valley Forge, Pa., source of the awards. Along with programs on patriotic themes, broadcasts on education, ecology, drug abuse and other contemporary topics have qualified for the citation. The Foundation is actively supported by 37 chapters of local volunteers.

FREEMAN, EVERETT (d. 1991) ▶ writer who went from print to radio, then to films and television, and who became co-founder of the Television Producers Guild (later absorbed by the Producers Guild). In the 1950s he created *Bachelor Father,* produced *The Pruitts of Southampton* and wrote for many of the dramatic anthology series.

FREEMAN, LEONARD (d. 1973) ▶ executive producer of *Hawaii Five-O, Storefront Lawyers* and such TV movies as *Cry Rape* as head of Leonard Freeman Productions.

"FREEZE" OF 1948 ▶ a halting of licensing and transmitter construction by the FCC when field studies showed that haphazard channel assignments were creating chaos on the airwaves. Instituted in October 1948, the freeze held until July 1952 while the FCC developed a blueprint for "a fair, efficient and equitable" distribution of service among the states and communities, under its mandate from Congress. Affecting the freeze, along with the need to sort out frequencies and establish engineering standards, was the uncertainty over which of three color TV systems proposed would be authorized for the U.S.

The freeze was lifted with the FCC Sixth Report and Order, issued in April 1952 but effective in July, which presented the commission's frequency allocation plan. That table of assignments, which has guided the regulatory process ever since, envisioned 2,053 stations in

1,291 cities, including 242 noncommercial outlets for ETV. There were to be 617 stations on VHF and 1,436 on UHF, with Channel 1 designated for land-mobile and two-way radio service. The plan also established three geographic zones with different mileage-separation and antenna-height regulations for each.

FRENCH CHEF, THE ▶ long-running public TV series (1963-73) featuring the kitchen artistry and humor of Julia Child, a middle-aged holder of the cordon bleu who succeeded in taking the pomposity out of French cookery. A genial, plain-mannered woman who did not mind taking a swig of the cooking wine after adding the soupcon, she became public television's most popular personality in the 1960s, enjoyed for herself as much as for her ability to instruct. The series emanated from WGBH-TV Boston and went off the air when corporate funding evaporated.

In 1978 Child returned to public television with a new series and simultaneous book, both titled *Julia and Company.* Featuring menu themes rather than individual dishes, the program enjoyed the popularity of her first series.

FRENCH, VICTOR ▶ actor and director who both appeared in and directed episodes of *Gunsmoke, Little House on the Prairie, Carter Country,* and *Stairway to Heaven.*

FRESH PRINCE OF BEL AIR, THE ▶ NBC sitcom about an inner city black teen from Philadelphia shipped out to rich relatives in posh Bel Air, Calif. to keep him out of trouble. Starring Will "Fresh Prince" Smith, a successful rap singer (who performed the show's title song), the show pokes fun at black stereotypes, pitting the streetwise Smith against his more conservative and upright aunt and uncle (Janet Hubert and James Avery) and their two children (Alfonso Ribeiro and Karyn Parsons).

A coproduction between NBC Productions and veteran music producer Quincy Jones's fledgling Quincy Jones Productions, the show's executive producers have been Jones, Kevin Wendle, Susan and Andy Borowitz and Winifred Hervey-Stallworth.

FRESTON, TOM ▶ chairman and CEO of cable's MTV Networks, which consist of MTV, VH-1, Nickelodeon and Nick-at-Nite. A marketing specialist who has been with MTV from its inception in 1980, he made his mark with the young network's immensely effective "I Want My MTV" consumer campaign. From there, he began to rise steadily in the ranks and became president of the MTV Networks in 1987. His affinity with the youth culture, coupled with his M.B.A. from New York University, provided him with the appropriate credentials. After beginning with the Benton & Bowles ad agency, he directed an import business with a partner until 1979. In a career switch, he joined Warner Amex Satellite Entertainment as a marketing manager, in time for the historic launch of MTV.

Tom Freston

FRIEDMAN, PAUL ▶ executive producer of *World News Tonight with Peter Jennings.* After he was named to that post in January 1988, *World News Tonight* rose to become the top-rated network evening news broadcast. In November 1988 he introduced the "American Agenda," a regularly scheduled segment within the newscast covering critical domestic issues of the day, including education, the environment, family, drugs and health.

In his quarter-century career in broadcast journalism, Friedman has been director of ABC News coverage in Europe, Africa and the Middle East, and for the operation of its bureaus in those areas. He joined ABC News in 1982 as a senior producer in London, helping coordinate coverage of such stories as the Falkland Islands War and the Israeli invasion of Lebanon. Prior to joining ABC News, Friedman spent 14 years at NBC News, including three years (1976-79) as executive producer of the *Today* show.

FRIEDMAN, STEVE ▶ executive producer of NBC's *Nightly News* since 1990, after a brief stint as executive producer of the expensive syndicated flop, *USA Today: The Television Show.* Following a six-year tenure with NBC's *Today* in the early 1980s—during which the morning program maintained a firm grasp on the number-one spot—Friedman was thought to have the golden touch in making news programs more entertaining. But the addition of Friedman to the already languishing *USA Today* could not save the GTG Entertainment news program, which folded after losing $40 million.

Steve Friedman

FRIENDLY, ED ▶ independent TV producer since 1967, after having been v.p. of specials in the NBC program department. Initially he teamed with George Schlatter to produce a number of specials, which led to their becoming executive producers of *Rowan and Martin's Laugh-In.* In 1974, after acquiring the rights to the Laura Ingalls Wilder series of "Little House" children's books, he produced the two-hour made-for-TV movie, *Little House on the Prairie,* which became a successful series. He also produced the mini-series *Backstairs At The White House.*

FRIENDLY FIRE **▶** three-hour TV movie on ABC, airing April 22, 1979, which was based on C. D. B. Bryan's journalistic book of that title about a conservative and patriotic Iowa farm couple who become radical antiwar activists after learning that their son was killed in Vietnam by the "friendly fire" of American forces. Despite the bitterness expressed toward the American government by the principal characters, the program attracted a huge audience.

The film received considerable advance press attention because it starred Carol Burnett, the famed comedienne, in a heavy dramatic role, which she carried off brilliantly. Ned Beatty also gave a strong performance as her husband. The supporting cast included Sam Waterston, Dennis Erdman, Timothy Hutton, Fanny Spies and Sherry Hursey.

Martin Starger was executive producer for Marble Arch Productions and Philip Barry coproducer with Fay Kanin, who wrote the screenplay. David Greene directed.

Fred W. Friendly

FRIENDLY, FRED W. ▶ one of the larger-than-life figures in broadcasting who proceeded from a distinguished career as a news producer and partner of the famed Edward R. Murrow, to the executive echelons of CBS as president of CBS News and then on to become a pervasive influence in U.S. public television as consultant to its chief benefactor, the Ford Foundation. Beyond that, as Professor of Broadcast Communication at the Columbia University Graduate School of Journalism, and as author of several books (notably, *Due to Circumstances Beyond Our Control*), Friendly impressed his values on broadcast journalists.

Friendly was president of CBS News for only two years (1964-66), but his tenure was marked with an activism that included publicly discussed clashes with the network for greater news access to the air. Indeed, his departure from CBS ostensibly was over one such battle—the denial of air time for live daytime coverage of the Senate hearings on Vietnam that would have meant the preemption of an old rerun of *I Love Lucy.* But some at CBS maintain that the denial was not really the issue. A layer of management, represented by John A. Schneider, president of the newly formed CBS Broadcast Group, had been placed between the news division and top corporate officials. Friendly, it was said, attempted to regain direct access to Frank Stanton by threatening to resign, and his resignation was accepted.

Soon afterwards, he became TV consultant to the Ford Foundation and professor at Columbia. At Ford, he immediately set into motion a plan to develop a public TV news organization that would be superior to those of the networks in that it would be free of the commercial constraints. This involved first the interconnection of the stations to form a national network (they had not been hooked up at the time) and the creation of the Public Broadcasting Laboratory to develop a prototype program series on current affairs. On Oct. 31, 1967, the two-hour series, entitled *PBL,* made its debut as a Sunday night magazine of the air.

Friendly also developed a proposal to the FCC for a domestic satellite system operated by a nonprofit corporation that would not only provide interconnection for public TV free of charge but also would dedicate a portion of its revenues to the funding of public TV. Friendly's proposal, which became known as his "people's dividend" plan, was not adopted by the FCC, but it did spur the full-time interconnection of stations by land lines.

Friendly's efforts in public TV were resented by many public broadcasters, who considered him a presumptuous outsider determined to reduce the stations to mere carriers of a network. Nor were they as obsessed as he with the idea of creating a great news organization. Their objections forced Friendly to recede into the background, and Ford adopted a policy of noninterference in the affairs of public TV.

Friendly's remarkable career in national broadcasting began with an idea he had conceived for a spoken-history record album in 1948. He was, at the time, an obscure producer at a radio station in Providence, R.I. The project appealed to Edward R. Murrow of CBS, and the album they produced together, *I Can Hear It Now,* was a huge success. It began the legendary 12-year partnership of Murrow and Friendly, through the radio series, *Hear It Now,* and the historic TV version, *See It Now.* Friendly retired from the Ford Foundation in 1980.

Since 1981 Friendly has been Edward R. Murrow Professor at the Columbia University Graduate School of Journalism, now emeritus. Earlier at Columbia he originated a series known as the Seminars on Media and Society, which involve a novel confrontational technique for the exploration of media issues. The format was adapted for a TV series on PBS and for occasional CBS specials on the Constitution.

FRIENDS OF THE EARTH CASE ▶ [*Friends of the Earth and Garie A. Soucie v. FCC and United States of America*/449 F2d 1164 (1971)] Court of Appeals case that expanded the application of the Fairness Doctrine to commercial advertisements after the cigarette commercial decision.

In 1971 Friends of the Earth, an organization dedicated to the protection and preservation of the environment, wrote a letter to WNBC-TV New York asserting that the station had broadcast a number of ads for automobiles and gasolines, which it maintained were heavy contributors to air pollution in New York City. FOE asked WNBC to make time available to the organization to inform the public of its side of the controversy. WNBC turned down FOE's request, claiming that the Banzhaf decision did not impose any Fairness Doctrine obligation on broadcasters with respect to product advertising other than cigarette commercials.

FOE complained formally to the FCC. The commission ruled that the air pollution problem was a complex issue and that Congress had not urged people to stop using automobiles, as it had with cigarettes. The commission refused to extend the Banzhaf Case to other products.

FOE appealed to the D.C. Court of Appeals, which reversed the commission, holding that there was no difference between gasoline and cigarette advertising, since both had built-in health hazards. The court said that although it had indicated the Banzhaf ruling was not to be applied to product advertising generally, the FCC was being too restrained.

Holding that the FOE complaint was not distinguishable from the Banzhaf cigarette complaint, the court remanded the case to the FCC to determine whether WNBC had adequately discharged its public service obligations. After some negotiations, WNBC agreed to broadcast a series of one-minute antipollution announcements.

In a subsequent Fairness Doctrine ruling in July 1974, the commission closed the door on fairness claims with regard to advertising by in effect stating that the cigarette commercial decision was in error. The FCC stated that the interpretation by the Court of Appeals in the FOE Case would essentially destroy the concept of the American commercial system of broadcasting. The commission went on to say that in the future it would apply the Fairness Doctrine only to those commercials that were devoted in an obvious and meaningful way to the discussion of public affairs.

FRIES, CHARLES W. ▶ chairman of Fries Entertainment, which is engaged in TV and feature film production and in domestic and international distribution. Fries founded the company in 1974 on leaving Metromedia Producers Corp. when that company, which he had headed as chairman, curtailed its film producing activities. As an independent, he has been one of the most prolific producers of long-form television in Hollywood. He began his career with Ziv TV, the leading syndication company in the 1950s, and later went to Screen

Gems, Columbia Pictures and Metromedia's MPC. Fries Entertainment filed for bankruptcy protection under Chapter 11 in 1991.

FRINGE TIME ▶ parts of the broadcast day that immediately precede or follow the peak viewing hours of prime time. These tend to be local time periods and are valuable to stations because of the size and composition of the audience. Early fringe is generally considered to be 4:30 to 7:30 p.m. in most time zones, and late fringe 11 p.m. to 1 a.m. In the central time zone, where network prime time begins at 7 and ends at 10, early fringe is truncated but late fringe becomes extremely lucrative because the first hour actually falls during peak viewing time.

FRITO BANDITO ▶ commercial campaign for Fritos corn chips that was pulled off the air in 1970 because of complaints from Mexican-American groups. The commercials featured an animated character representing the stock Mexican bandit speaking in heavily accented English. The groups charged that the commercials were promoting a comic stereotype that was damaging to Mexican-Americans. Their efforts also succeeded in keeping off the air in many markets the film classic, *Treasure of Sierra Madre,* because it depicted a similar stereotypical villain.

Tammy and Jim Bakker in an installment of *Frontline*

***FRONTLINE* ▶** public television's distinguished series of hour-long documentaries, begun in 1982 and continued into a present time when the long-form documentary, once a staple of all three commercial networks, has all but disappeared. Despite the first season's rocky start with an effort to link professional sports and organized crime (*An Unauthorized History of the NFL*), *Frontline* went on to win every available award for journalistic excellence and courage with programs such as *80 Seconds in Greensboro, Abortion Clinic, Crisis in Central America, To the Brink of War, Seven Days in Bensonhurst, High Crimes and Misdemeanors,* and *Innocence Lost.* Its 1991 documentary, *The Election Held Hostage,* revealing new evidence of secret deals to use the Iran hostages in the presidential election of 1980, triggered a congressional investigation into the charges.

Frontline uses what executive producer David Fanning calls a "repertory company" of independent producers, some linked to coproductions with British TV, all of whom are charged by Fanning with turning the day's hot issues into a "rattling good story." Unlike most PBS prime-time series, *Frontline* has no corporate underwriter and is funded entirely from public television's own dollars. Boston's WGBH is the producing station.

David Frost

FROST, DAVID ▶ British TV personality and humorist who became known to U.S. audiences in 1964 when the popular British series he helped to create, *That Was the Week That Was,* spawned an American version on NBC. The program of satire and topical humor was well received by many but fell short in mass appeal; nevertheless, it launched a career for Frost on this side of the Atlantic.

In 1969, when Group W lost the Merv Griffin syndicated talk show to CBS, Frost became host of a talk and interview show for that company with moderate success; his British accent and Cambridge manner were said to have been resisted in mid-America, although the program did well enough in major cities. During the run, Frost developed the reputation of ocean-hopper, doing shows here, in England and in Australia. He became part of the ownership group of London Weekend Television when it was franchised, and he operated his own production company, Paradine Productions, based in London.

Frost made headlines in 1975 when, after the U.S. networks rejected an offer of an exclusive series of talks with former President Nixon for a reported fee of $1 million, he secured the rights for $600,000. The financing, in the main, came from conservative West Coast businessmen who believed that Nixon had been wronged in the Watergate scandal and who wanted him to have a forum to tell his side of the story.

Through Syndicast Services, The Frost-Nixon interviews—four 90-minute programs taped with the former President in his home in San Clemente, Calif.—were syndicated in more than 150 markets on a barter basis. Initially there were to have been six minutes of national commercials in each program, but the resistance of advertisers to an association with a controversial figure resulted in the stations getting an extra minute (a seventh minute) to sell locally. The interviews aired over four weeks in May 1977. Public TV stations carried the broadcasts in certain key markets—such as Buffalo, N.Y., and South Bend, Ind.—where commercial clearances weren't achieved. The first of the telecasts, airing on May 4, attracted the largest audience ever for a news interview program.

FROSTY THE SNOWMAN ▶ Christmas season perennial on CBS since 1969, produced by Rankin-Bass as an hour animated special. The children's story of a snowman who came to life for one day was narrated by Jimmy Durante with character voices by Billy DeWolfe, Jackie Vernon, June Foray and Paul Frees.

FRUCHTMAN, MILTON A. ▶ widely traveled director based in New York who has done work on every continent and who set up a worldwide TV network for the Eichmann trial in Jerusalem. His credits include *Verdict for Tomorrow,* episodes for *High Adventure* series on CBS, *Assignment Southeast Asia* and *Lost Men of Malaya.*

FUCHS, MICHAEL ▶ a leading figure in the cable industry as chairman and chief executive officer of Home Box Office Inc. He joined HBO in 1976, initially in charge of original and sports programming, and had a rapid rise through the ranks. In March 1984 he was promoted to president and chief operating officer of the company and later was elevated to chairman and CEO. He went to HBO following a brief stint at the William Morris Agency, after having practiced entertainment law; Fuchs holds a J.D. degree from New York University Law School.

David Janssen as Dr. Richard Kimble in *The Fugitive*

FUGITIVE, THE ▶ hour-long ABC adventure series that enjoyed great popularity throughout the world and inspired a cycle of man-on-the-run shows (*Run for Your Life, Run, Buddy, Run,* etc.). Running from 1963 to 1967, it starred David Janssen as a doctor, Richard Kimble, who is wrongly accused of murder and relentlessly pursued by police inspector Philip Gerard (played by Barry Morse) as he himself pursues the actual murderer, a mysterious one-armed man. The final episode of the 120 that were produced resolved the story, and it scored enormous ratings here and in every country where the series was carried. After its prime-time run, it was repeated on ABC as a daytime strip and went into syndication in 1970. QM Productions (Quinn Martin) produced it.

FUJISANKEI COMMUNICATIONS GROUP ▶ private Japanese corporation made up of 120 companies, including the Fuji Television Network, the leading commercial network in Japan. Fujisankei also has the largest radio network and controls one of the country's principal newspaper chains. With annual aggregate revenues of $5 billion, it claims to be the fourth largest media organization in the world. Its overseas arm, Fujisankei Communications International, has offices in the U.S. and Europe and is headquartered in New York.

FULL HOUSE ▶ successful ABC sitcom launched in 1987 about a young TV personality, played by Bob Saget, raising his three young daughters after the death of his wife. He has the dubious help of his wild brother-in-law and a friend who wants to be a stand-up comedian, played by John Stamos and David Coulier, respectively. The series is a new switch on the old single parent comedy gambit.

It is produced for Lorimar Television by the producing team of Thomas Miller and Robert Boyett, who along with creator Jeff Franklin are the executive producers.

FUNNY SIDE, THE ▶ a short-lived NBC series (1971) that, with a repertory company of five couples of different ages, attempted to bridge the variety show and the situation comedy. In songs and sketches, each episode attempted to highlight the universal stresses between the sexes. Produced by Bill Persky and Sam Denoff, it yielded 13 episodes. Gene Kelly was host, and Teresa Graves, John Amos, Warren Berlinger and Pat Finley were among the regulars.

FURNESS, BETTY ▶ consumer advocate who began as one of the best-known commercial spielers in the 1950s. A former stage and screen actress (*My Sister Eileen, Doughgirls*), she earned a degree of fame in 1949 as TV spokeswoman for Westinghouse appliances. She became the talk of the nation one evening when, in a live commercial for refrigerators, she struggled in vain with a stuck door.

Later she hosted a number of local shows in New York, among them *At Your Beck and Call* on WNTA-TV and *Answering Service* on WABC-TV as well as such radio programs as *Ask Betty Furness* and *Dimension of a Woman's World.* Active in Democratic party politics, she was appointed by President Johnson in 1967 to be his special assistant for consumer affairs. In 1970 she became head of New York State's Consumer Protection Board but resigned a year later. Soon after she joined WNBC-TV New York as consumer reporter and occasional contributor to network news specials and the *Today* program. When Barbara Walters left *Today* early in 1976, Furness became her temporary replacement through most of the year. Later she became regular consumer reporter for the local newscasts on WNBC-TV New York. She is married to Lesley Midgley, a news executive at NBC.

G

GALAVISION ▶ see Cable Networks.

GALE STORM SHOW, THE **▶** also known as *Oh! Susanna,* a series about the wacky antics of a social director for a luxury liner, carried by CBS (1956-59), and starring Gale Storm as Susanna Pomeroy, with ZaSu Pitts as beautician Elvira Nugent (Nugey), Roy Roberts as Captain Huxley and James Fairfax as first mate Cedric. A hot property in its day, it was involved in several multi-million-dollar transactions. After 99 episodes, ITC bought the films from Hal Roach Studios for a reported $2 million and then produced 26 more, this time for ABC. That network purchased the reruns for its daytime schedule for three years, plus one season's worth of new nighttime episodes, for $5 million.

GALLO, LILLIAN ▶ independent producer whose TV movie credits include *Hustling, What Are Best Friends For* and *Stranger Who Looks Like Me.* She had been executive in charge of ABC's *Movie of the Week* before venturing out on her own.

GALLOPING GOURMET, THE **▶** half-hour syndicated daily cookery series (1969-73) featuring an amusing and good-looking Australian chef, Graham Kerr. The series proved ideal for the barter form of syndication and was placed in more than 130 U.S. markets by Young & Rubicam for its clients, Hunt-Wesson Foods, American Cyanamid and American Can Co. An inexpensive program to begin with, it was produced in Canada, to shave the costs even more. It was also sold in Canada, the U.K., Australia and other English-speaking countries. Fremantle produced and handled foreign distribution.

The set of the popular game show *Jeopardy!*

GAME SHOWS ▶ popular program form from the earliest days of television and one that remains a staple of daytime schedules and early-evening syndication. Over the last 50 years, some 400 different game shows have been essayed, but all have essentially the same mechanics: an exuberant host, a studio audience, contestants from the world outside of television, a certain parlor game device that makes for competition, and prizes of cash or merchandise. The main element that differentiates one from the other is the parlor game device.

Like many another program form, the genre evolved from radio. The popular old *Take It Or Leave It,* which made famous the $64 Question (prize enough in radio days), was grandly translated to television as *The $64,000 Question.* Others that made the passage were *Strike It Rich, You Bet Your Life, Stop the Music, Truth or Consequences, Twenty Questions* and *Winner Take All.* Television's leading creators of game shows, Mark Goodson and Bill Todman, honed their skills in radio.

The appeal of the genre is not only enduring but universal. Game shows are popular in virtually every country, and American formats are big sellers around the world. In countries as developed and sophisticated as England, France and Italy, game shows are still scheduled in prime time. They disappeared from the nighttime schedules of the U.S. networks in the mid-1960s because their appeal is considered too limited to compete with the expensive melodramas and comedies from Hollywood.

Programmers have speculated for years on the reasons for the genre's popularity. Perhaps it is that game shows make for active viewing, since the people at home involve themselves in the guessing. Perhaps, unlike most other program forms, they put real, everyday people on the screen in an entertaining way. Perhaps it is that viewers identify with the contestants and vicariously enjoy winning. Possibly the key is the greed factor, the wish for easy riches. Whatever, game shows have immediacy, some humor, some element of surprise in unexpected behavior, some suspense, some glamour, some interesting characters, and some celebration of the American Dream.

Their appeal, from a producer's standpoint, is that they are relatively inexpensive to make, involving a single set and low talent costs. Moreover, the prizes are often donated for plugs. Given that they hardly require rehearsal, a week's worth of episodes can be shot in a single day. Thus a failure with a new game show venture need not be ruinous, while a success can be fantastically profitable. King World hit television's largest jackpot in the 1980s with the syndicated *Wheel of Fortune.* Few fictional network series have made as much money.

Because the risks are not as great as with other forms of television, old game show successes get retooled every few years, sometimes with new flourishes. Often it is the host who makes the difference (rarely is there a hostess; no woman has yet succeeded in the role, though very few have been offered the opportunity). Game show hosting is a profession in itself, and those who are good at it work constantly—Bob Eubanks, Bill Cullen, Wink Martindale, Chuck Woolery, Alex Trebek, to list a few. Most do nothing else but host game shows their entire careers, but some have found the game show a springboard to a larger career. Johnny Carson began as a game show host, as did Mike Wallace, who became transformed from genial emcee to one of journalism's most dangerous interviewers. Chuck Woolery has been given his own syndicated talk show.

The wheel spins in reverse as well. Groucho Marx, the famed movie comedian, found his niche in television with a game show, *You Bet Your Life.* That show is being revived as a syndicated offering in 1992 with a new host who is one of television's biggest current stars, Bill Cosby. Inventions are endless, and the genre shows no sign of wearing out. Following are some of the notable game shows in the medium's history:

BEAT THE CLOCK—(Mark Goodson-Bill Todman Productions) CBS, 1950-58 and 1979-80; ABC, 1958-61; syndicated, 1969-74. Hosts included Bud Collyer (1950-61), Jack Narz (1969-74) and Monty Hall (1979-80).

BREAK THE BANK—(Wolf Productions) jumped around the three networks in daytime and prime time between 1948-57. Hosts were Bert Parks and Bud Collyer. It originated as a radio show in 1945.

COLLEGE BOWL—(Moses-Reid-Cleary Productions) CBS Sunday afternoon, 1959-63; NBC Sunday afternoon, 1963-70; Disney Channel, 1987. Hosts included Allen Ludden (1959-62), Robert Earle (1962-70) and Dick Cavett (1987). The afternoon versions were sponsored by General Electric.

CONCENTRATION—(NBC, 1958-73; Goodson-Todman Productions, 1973-78) daytime through its NBC-produced run, moving into NBC prime time in 1958 and 1961; syndicated, 1973-78. NBC-version hosts were Hugh Downs, Jack Barry, Bob Clayton and Ed McMahon, and the syndicated version's host was Jack Narz. NBC revived the show for daytime in 1987 as *Classic Concentration* (Mark Goodson Productions) with host Alex Trebek.

THE DATING GAME—(Chuck Barris Productions) ABC daytime, 1965-73, prime time, 1966-70; syndicated, 1973-74, 1978-80 and 1986. Jim Lange hosted from 1965-80, followed by Elaine Joyce and Jeff MacGregor. The show featured a number of celebrities during its run, some before they became famous.

DOUBLE DARE—(MTV Networks) Nickelodeon, 1986—; syndicated, 1987—. Hosted by Marc Summers. It was the first show conceived originally for cable and then jumping to syndication. A short-lived CBS daytime show of the same name but different format aired in 1976.

FAMILY FEUD—(Goodson-Todman Productions) ABC daytime, 1976-85; syndicated, 1989—. The initial run was hosted by Richard Dawson, and the syndicated version hosted by Ray Combs.

THE GONG SHOW—(Chuck Barris-Chris Bearde Productions) NBC daytime, 1976-78; syndicated, 1976-80; repeats aired on USA Network. Chuck Barris and Gary Owens hosted this spoof of talent and game shows rolled into one.

HIGH ROLLERS—(Heatter-Quigley Productions, 1974-78; Merrill Heatter Productions/Century Towers Productions/Orion Television, 1987—) NBC daytime, 1974-76 and 1978-80; syndicated, 1975-76 and 1987—. Hosts were Alex Trebek (1974-80) and Wink Martindale.

HOLLYWOOD SQUARES—(Heatter-Quigley Productions, 1966-81; Century Towers Productions/Orion Television, 1986—) NBC daytime, 1966-80, prime time, 1968; syndicated, 1971-81 and 1986—. Peter Marshall hosted the first production until 1981, and John Davidson took over in 1986.

I'VE GOT A SECRET—(Goodson-Todman Productions) CBS prime time, 1952-67 and 1976; syndicated, 1972-73. Hosts included Garry Moore (1952-64), Steve Allen (1964-67) and Bill Cullen for the syndicated year.

JEOPARDY!—(Merv Griffin Productions) NBC daytime, 1964-75 and 1978-79; syndicated, 1974-75 and 1984—. Art Fleming emceed the show from 1964-79, followed by Alex Trebek from 1984—.

THE JOKER'S WILD—(Barry-Enright Productions) CBS daytime, 1972-75; syndicated, 1977-86, children's version, 1980-81; repeats aired on USA Network. Hosts were Jack Barry and Bill Cullen.

LET'S MAKE A DEAL—(Stefan Hatos-Monty Hall Productions) NBC daytime, 1963-68, prime time, 1967; ABC daytime, 1968-76, prime time, 1969-71; syndicated, 1971-77, 1980-81 and 1984-86; repeats aired on USA Network. Monty Hall hosted all versions.

THE MATCH GAME—(Goodson-Todman Productions) NBC daytime, 1962-69; CBS daytime, 1973-79; syndicated, 1975-82. Gene Rayburn hosted both versions.

NAME THAT TUNE—(Harry Salter Productions, 1953-59; Ralph Edwards Productions, 1974-81; Sandy Frank Productions, 1984-85) NBC prime time, 1953-54, daytime, 1974-75 and 1977; CBS prime time, 1954-59; syndicated, 1974-81, 1984-85. Hosts from 1953-59 were Red Benson, Bill Cullen and George DeWitt; from 1974-81, they were Tom Kennedy and Dennis James, and the most recent was Jim Lange.

THE NEWLYWED GAME—(Chuck Barris Productions) ABC daytime, 1966-74 and 1984, prime time, 1967-71; syndicated, 1977-80 and 1985—. Bob Eubanks emceed the show from 1966-80 and again from 1985 onwards, with Jim Lange in 1984. It's now known as *The New Newlywed Game.*

PASSWORD—(Goodson-Todman Productions) CBS daytime, 1961-67, prime time, 1962-67; ABC daytime, 1971-75. Allen Ludden hosted all versions. A revamped *Super Password* was syndicated in 1984.

THE PRICE IS RIGHT—(Goodson-Todman Productions) on all three networks in various dayparts, 1953—, and syndicated from 1972-80 and 1985-86. Bill Cullen hosted from 1956-65, followed by Bob Barker, who's hosted ever since.

REMOTE CONTROL—(MTV Productions) MTV, 1987-90; syndicated, 1989—. Wacky game show/game-show spoof popular among young adults. Ken Ober has hosted since the show's inception.

THE $64,000 QUESTION—(Entertainment Productions) CBS prime time, 1955-58. Hal March hosted this popular but short-lived game show, which was brought down by scandal.

TIC TAC DOUGH—(Barry-Enright Productions) NBC daytime, 1956-59, prime time, 1957-58; CBS daytime, 1978; syndicated, 1978-86. Hosts included Jack Barry (1956-58), Bill Wendell (1958-59), Wink Martindale (1978-85) and Jim Caldwell.

TO TELL THE TRUTH—(Goodson-Todman Productions) CBS prime time, 1956-67, daytime, 1962-68; syndicated, 1969-78 and

1980-81. Bud Collyer hosted from 1956-68, followed by Garry Moore (1969-77), Joe Garagiola (1977-78) and Robin Ward.

TRUTH OR CONSEQUENCES—(Ralph Edwards Productions) CBS prime time, 1950-51; NBC prime time, 1954-56 and 1957-58, daytime, 1956-65; syndicated, 1966-75, 1977-78 and 1985—. A number of people hosted the show through its various lives, including Ralph Edwards, Jack Bailey, Steve Dunne, Bob Barker, Bob Hilton and Larry Anderson.

WHAT'S MY LINE?—(Goodson-Todman Productions) CBS prime time, 1950-67; syndicated, 1968-75. John Daly hosted from 1950-67, followed by Wally Brunner (1968-72) and Larry Blyden.

WHEEL OF FORTUNE—(Merv Griffin Productions) NBC daytime, 1975—; syndicated, 1983—. Chuck Woolery hosted from 1975-81, succeeded by Pat Sajak. See also separate entry.

YOU BET YOUR LIFE—(Filmcraft Productions for John Guedel Productions) NBC prime time, 1950-61; repeats were syndicated in 1961. Groucho Marx hosted and was the reason the show lasted so long, since it was essentially a catalyst for his wit.

GANNETT CO. ▶ a major media conglomerate with 87 daily newspapers—including the nationally distributed *USA Today*—10 TV and 15 radio stations, and the nation's largest outdoor advertising business. In 1973, the year Allen H. Neuharth, Gannett's colorful chief executive officer, took over, it owned only one TV station. The picture changed in 1979 when Gannett acquired Combined Communications and its seven TV and 12 radio stations.

By 1985 Gannett had added TV stations in Washington, Oklahoma City, Tucson, Mobile and Austin by outbidding Norman Lear and his partner, Jerrold Perenchio, with a $117 offer for the Evening News Association with its TV stations and newspapers, including *The Detroit News.* Later, Gannett spun off the Oklahoma City, Tucson and Mobile stations to Knight-Ridder Newspapers (which later sold off its entire TV group). In 1987 Gannett brought its total ownership to 10 stations when it bought the Harte-Hanks stations in Greensboro, N.C., and Jacksonville, Florida.

In 1986 Gannett set up an ambitious partnership with Grant Tinker, NBC's former chairman, who left the network after it was acquired by General Electric. GTG Entertainment was modelled after Tinker's highly successful MTM Enterprises and was to serve Gannett as a potential source of quality prime-time network series. By 1989 GTG was well underway: Gannett had invested $24 million in a Culver City studio—plus another $15 million for remodelling—and had a five-year deal with CBS. But before the year was out, the focus shifted. Neuharth announced a syndicated TV version of *USA Today,* a dream of his, and hired *Today*'s executive producer, Steve Friedman, to produce it. *USA Today: The Television Program* (later called *USA Today On TV*) was launched on Sept.12, 1988—without a pilot, a tribute to Tinker's reputation—and was carried on 160 stations covering 95% of the U.S. The show proved a disaster from the beginning. Despite three replacements for Friedman, the program failed in the ratings and was canceled effective January 7, 1990. GTG Entertainment, which had cleared another syndicated entry, *Love Thy Neighbor,* in 40% of the country, held two pilot commitments from CBS, and was producing *Baywatch* for NBC, folded a few months later.

When the slowdown in advertising hit in 1990, Gannett joined the parade of those making multi-media pitches to advertisers and their agencies, a technique it had pioneered in 1984 but one that proved to be a solution looking for a problem. By 1990, with the decade's epidemic of acquisitions over, Gannett was buying back its own stock, considering, as did others, their own properties as their best investment.

Gannett's TV properties consist of KARE-TV Minneapolis-St. Paul; KOCO-TV Oklahoma City; KPNX-TV Mesa-Phoenix; KUSA-TV Denver; KVUE-TV Austin, Texas; WFMY-TV Greensboro, N.C.; WLVI-TV Cambridge-Boston; WTLV-TV Jacksonville, Florida; WUSA-TV Washington; and WXIA-TV Atlanta. Allen Neuharth, who stepped down as CEO in 1986, remained as chairman until he reached retirement age in 1989. Cecil L. Walker is president and CEO of Gannett Broadcasting and Ron Townsend is president of the TV Group.

GARAGIOLA, JOE ▶ TV personality whose quick wit and amiable manner propelled him from local sportscasting to a regular spot on NBC's *Today* show and baseball *Game of the Week.* For a time he was also host of the game show *He Said, She Said* and did commercials for national advertisers. A former major league catcher, he started his broadcasting career in 1955 as a sportscaster for the St. Louis Cardinals and then was play-by-play announcer for the New York Yankees before joining NBC. In 1991 he was elected to the Baseball Hall of

Fame and returned to the cast of *Today* after a hiatus of several years.

GARLAND, JUDY (d. 1969) ▶ one of the great motion picture stars for whom television was a bitter experience, partly a function of her temperament. A weekly series that was to have begun in 1957 was scuttled after a round of quarrels with CBS programmers. In 1963 a series finally was produced, *The Judy Garland Show,* but it was plagued with format problems and with a turnover of producers. Worse, it was scheduled opposite the number-one show on TV, *Bonanza,* which demolished the Garland songfest in the ratings. The series lasted one season.

The famed singer had fared considerably better in specials, giving a memorable performance in a 90-minute spectacular in 1955 that drew a large TV audience. Before she undertook her own series, Garland had another successful outing in a special with Frank Sinatra and Dean Martin. Her TV appearances were scant after the flop of the series, but—ironically—she will remain one of the medium's perennial favorites for generations to come through her timeless and inexhaustibly popular movie, *The Wizard of Oz.*

GARNER, JAMES ▶ popular star whose affable, self-deprecating style, ironic humor and rugged good looks have helped make him one of television's most enduring personalities. He has starred in four series, two of which were hits: the off-beat western, *Maverick* (1957-60) and a private detective series, *The Rockford Files* (1974-80). An attempt at a *Maverick* sequel, *Bret Maverick* (1981-82), failed. In 1991 he began a new series, *Man of the People.*

Garner has also appeared in several motion pictures, including such hits as *Victor, Victoria* and *Murphy's Romance.* He starred in two made-for-TV movies, *Promise* (1986) and *My Name is Bill W.* (1989) both of which were produced by the company Garner heads with Peter Duchow, Garner-Duchow Productions. Previously, Garner ran Cherokee Productions with his manager Meta Rosenberg. In 1990 he won the best-actor Emmy for *Decoration Day.*

GARNETT, TAY ▶ director working in movies and TV during the 1950s and 1960s. His TV credits include *The Loretta Young Show, Four Star Theatre, Wagon Train, The Untouchables, Naked City, Gunsmoke, Rawhide, Death Valley Days* and *Bonanza.*

GARRISON, GREG ▶ producer-director and long-time associate of Dean Martin in his series and specials. Other productions include *Golddiggers* and *Country Music,* a summer series.

GARRISON'S GORILLAS ▶ World War II action series that premiered on ABC in September 1967 and ran 26 weeks. Produced by Selmur Productions, it featured Ron Harper as Lieutenant Craig Garrison, and Cesare Danova (as Actor), Brendon Boone (Chief), Rudy Salari (Casino) and Christopher Cary (Goniff) as an Army guerilla band, each fictive member on leave from a U.S. prison.

GARROWAY, DAVE (d. 1982) ▶ one of the early television "personalities," and probably the prime representative of the "Chicago School," whose intelligence and low-pressure style were in marked contrast to the aggressive pitchmen and manic show hosts of the 1950s. A former radio disk jockey for WMAQ, the NBC station in Chicago, he established himself as a refreshingly unconventional TV personality with his first effort for NBC-TV, *Garroway-at-Large* (1949-51). The variety show was startling in forsaking the frills of production; instead of painted backdrops it used the bare studio stage, with a stagehand's ladder as the main prop.

Garroway's success prompted NBC to move him to New York as first host of *Today,* the two-hour morning show, which premiered Jan. 14, 1952. During the 1953-54 season, he doubled as emcee of a nighttime NBC variety series, *The Dave Garroway Show.* Later he hosted *Wide, Wide World* (1955-58) on that network. He also made numerous guest appearances. The strain of his heavy work schedule, combined with a personal tragedy, the death of his wife, led to his retirement from *Today* and NBC in 1961. Later he hosted a series for NET, *Exploring the Universe,* and an entertainment show for CBS. In 1969 he began a syndicated talk show from Boston, *Tempo,* but it was short-lived.

GARTNER, MICHAEL G. ▶ president of NBC News. His appointment to succeed Lawrence K. Grossman in that post in August 1988 was something of a surprise. As a longtime newspaper editor, he, by his own claim, knew everything about news and nothing about television. In choosing him, NBC's new corporate owners put him under pressure to find answers to the networks thus-far-futile quest for a news magazine to match the popularity and profitability of CBS's *60 Minutes* and ABC's *20/20,* and the means to boost the sagging ratings of NBC's nightly news program.

Gartner came to NBC News with a newspaper career that began at the age of 15, answering phones in the sports department of the *Des Moines Register,* and led on after graduation from college to 14 years on *The Wall Street Journal.* He returned to Iowa in 1974 as executive editor of *The Des Moines Register and Tribune,* later becoming president and CEO of the newspaper's parent company. In 1986, after *The Des Moines Register* was sold to Gannett, Gartner joined the new owners as their general news executive in Washington, leaving briefly to edit and then merge Gannett's newly acquired Kentucky newspapers, *The Louisville Courier-Journal* and *The Louisville Times.*

Gartner, a law graduate as well as a self-styled country editor, writes frequently on First Amendment and press issues, including a regular commentary column, formerly in *The Wall Street Journal* and now in *USA Today.*

Michael G. Gartner

GATWARD, JAMES ▶ chairman of Britain's prosperous TVS franchise during the 1980s whose empire came tumbling down after his apparently ill-advised purchase of MTM Entertainment in Hollywood for $320 million in 1988.

TVS (Television South) covered the wealthiest region of England, that south of London, and was enormously profitable. Gatward also created for the company an aggressive and growth-minded subsidiary, Telso, headed by Peter Clark and Peter Thomas. Telso had a potent production arm that produced a number of major films for HBO (among them *Sakharov* and *Mandela*), a leading international distribution company, and a trade publishing operation whose properties included *Cable & Satellite Europe,* two European program guides, and a half interest (with Act III Publishing in the U.S.) in *TBI: Television Business International.* It also acquired the Midem Organization in France, which produced two of the largest international television trade shows, MIP-TV and MIPCOM, in Cannes. The trade shows nicely served the interests of the Telso family of companies and were themselves substantial profit centers.

But Gatward over-reached in buying MTM. He also misjudged the value of its library and the company's ability, without Grant Tinker at the helm, to create hit series for the networks. TVS was so saddled with debt that it had to shed virtually all its Telso properties. The problems increased when the U.S. syndication market went flat in 1989 and the MTM series that had gotten on the networks failed. Gatward was ousted by his board in 1990, and the company lost its broadcasting license in the U.K. franchising auctions of 1991. TVS was left with ownership of MTM.

GAYLORD ENTERTAINMENT CO. ▶ company that operates a broadcast group of key independent stations and cable systems, in addition to a number of potent country music enterprises. It was spun off in 1991 from The Oklahoma Publishing Co. and became publicly traded.

Gaylord Entertainment Co. is the parent of Opryland USA, which owns The Grand Old Opry, the Opryland theme park and hotel in Nashville, and a partnership with Group W Satellite Communications in The Nashville Network (TNN), available to about 54 million cable subscribers. In 1991 the company purchased Country Music Television, which reaches some 15 million cable households, for $24.1 million. The company's distribution arm, Gaylord Syndicom, syndicates *Hee Haw,* among other programs.

The Gaylord family placed 22% of GEC's equity on the market to pay down debt which on June 30, 1991, came to $565.5 million. The biggest part of this debt was incurred in 1989 when the company bought 97.1% of Cencom Cable TV for $417.5 million. Gaylord's cable holdings in 1991 covered 26 franchises servicing 170,000 subscribers, of which more than 153,000 were in Southern California.

The television group consists of four independents: KVTV Dallas-Ft. Worth, KHTV Houston, KSTW Tacoma-Seattle, and WTTV Milwaukee. Oklahoma Publishing Co. of Oklahoma City publishes the *Daily Oklahoman* and the *Sunday Oklahoman.*

GEISEL, THEODOR (d. 1991) ▶ writer of "Dr. Seuss" children's books who also wrote the scripts for all the TV adaptations of his stories, along with original teleplays. His TV credits included *How the Grinch Stole Christmas, Cat in the Hat, Horton Hears a Who* and *The Lorax.*

GELBART, LARRY ▶ veteran comedy writer and playwright who, in TV, worked variously for Jack Paar, Bob Hope, Sid Caesar, Red Buttons, Art Carney and Jack Carson, and in radio for *Duffy's Tavern.* In the 1970s he created the *M*A*S*H* and *Roll Out* series, serving also as co-producer of the former. His plays for the stage included *A Funny Thing Happened on the Way to the Forum, Sly Fox,* and *City of Angels.*

To lure the "dean" of comedy writers back to television, NBC's Fred Silverman gave Gelbart full control of a situation comedy project, letting him write and produce it without network supervision. The program, *United States,* was given a lavish build-up as an adult series combining comedy and drama that would set a new direction for programming. But when *United States* finally went on the air in 1980, it fell far short of its billing and lasted less than two months.

GELLER, BRUCE ▶ late producer of action-adventure series, among them *Rawhide, Mannix, Mission: Impossible* and *Bronk* (as executive producer of the last three).

GELLER, HENRY ▶ one of the leading thinkers on U.S. policy for the electronic media. He was chief adviser to President Carter on telecommunications policy in his capacity as director of the National Telecommunications and Information Administration (NTIA) in the Commerce Department. With the election of President Reagan, Geller founded and became director of the Washington Center for Public Research.

A lawyer and communications savant who had worked 16 years at the FCC, mainly as general counsel, he joined NTIA as acting director when it was created in 1977 from the ashes of the White House Office of Telecommunications Policy. He received his appointment as director, and coincidentally as Assistant Secretary of Commerce, in 1978.

On leaving the FCC in 1974, Geller became a consultant and one-man think tank on a host of issues. In various capacities, as attorney, *amicus curiae* or intervenor, he participated in court proceedings on numerous matters concerning the FCC. During this period, he also worked on a range of telecommunications projects supported by foundation grants. Meanwhile, his personal philosophy underwent change. He became increasingly enthusiastic for First Amendment principles, and this led him away from his previous staunch belief in the Fairness Doctrine and the public trustee concept for broadcasting. In his NTIA post, he became an outspoken advocate of broadcast deregulation in the age of cable and home video, maintaining that there would be larger public benefits if all forms of television were allowed to be governed by market forces. Many of his ideas, with some modifications, found their way into Rep. Lionel Van Deerlin's 1978 and 1979 bills to rewrite the Communications Act.

Geller was consultant to the House Communications Subcommittee for its controversial 1976 policy report on cable TV; one of the authors of the American Bar Association's 1976 report on TV journalism, the First Amendment and the Fairness Doctrine; and a principal figure in the Aspen Institute's program on communications and society, funded by the Ford and Markle Foundations. For two years after leaving the commission he worked on projects for the Rand Corp.

Continuing to work a full schedule long after many colleagues slowed down or retired, Geller became increasingly devoted to helping define the path of telecommunications into the 21st century. He churned out papers on topics such as telephone entry into cable ownership and "information services," and delivery of residential fiber optic service. He successfully pressed for a series of adjustments to the FCC's enforcement of the equal time law so that debates and other candidate appearances would not be hindered.

He served three hitches with the commission, 1949-50, 1952-55 and 1961-73. He began the latter term as associate general counsel, then became general counsel in 1964 and became special assistant to chairman Burch in 1970.

Among his other contributions on the commission, Geller helped write the 1972 cable rules and the definitive explication of the Fairness Doctrine.

GENE AUTRY SHOW, THE **▶** early Western series on CBS (1950-53) starring Autry and featuring his horse Champion and comedian Pat Buttram. It was via Flying A Productions.

GENERAL ELECTRIC THEATER **▶** long-running weekly anthology series on CBS (1953-61) in which top Hollywood film stars appeared, including many who otherwise were holdouts to TV. It began as a one-hour series but in 1955 settled into the 30-minute form, with Ronald Reagan as host. Reagan also starred in some of the playlets. Charles Laughton, Myrna Loy and James Stewart were among those who took part. The series was by Revue Productions.

In 1973 General Electric began a series of occasional dramatic specials, ranging from an hour to 90 minutes in length, under the umbrella title *GE Theater.* Produced by Tomorrow Entertainment and airing on CBS, the series included such fine filmed teleplays as *In This House of Brede, Things in Their Season, Larry, I Heard the Owl Call My Name* and *Tell Me Where It Hurts.*

GENERAL HOSPITAL ▶ see Soap Operas.

GENESIS ENTERTAINMENT ▶ a small syndication company that first made its mark by taking a stock of rarely seen National Geographic specials, repackaging them and selling them to stations nationwide. The shows attracted a small but upscale audience, and the tremendous promotional support president Gary Gannaway provided to stations won them over. Genesis followed up with a first-run court show, *The Judge,* and then won the rights to syndicate the off-network Michael Landon vehicle, *Highway to Heaven,* beating out bigger and better established syndicators.

GENTLE BEN ▶ CBS prime-time adventure series for children (1967-69) featuring a 650-pound bear. It was produced by Ivan Tors Films. In the regular cast were Clint Howard as Mark Wedlow, whose pet bear was Ben. Dennis Weaver and Beth Brickell played his parents, Tom and Ellen Wedlow.

GENUS, KARL ▶ director associated with cultural programs; his credits include *Studio One, DuPont Show of the Month, Robert Herridge Theater, The World of Mark Twain, Sibelius: Symphony for Finland, Duet for Two Hands, I, Don Quixote* and *New Orleans Jazz.*

GEORGE BURNS AND GRACIE ALLEN SHOW, THE ▶ half-hour CBS domestic comedy series (1950-58) built upon the established, daffy vaudeville routines of Burns and Allen, who moved gracefully into TV from radio. The 239 syndicated reruns of the series later became a staple of local programming.

Burns was the consummate straight-man to the dizzy observations and antics of Gracie, his fictive (and real-life) wife. The episodes opened with a monologue by Burns, a champion of the one-liner, which led into the stories. Regularly featured were Bea Benaderet as neighbor Blanche Morton, Fred Clark as her husband Harry Morton and Harry Von Zell as the show's announcer. The series ended Sept. 22, 1958, with the retirement of Gracie from show business.

Burns then began a situation comedy of his own, *The George Burns Show,* on NBC, which ran a single season, Oct. 1958-April 1959. Gracie Allen died in 1964. Admired by most professional comedians for his superb timing and dry style, Burns has remained active with TV guest shots and specials.

GEORGE, PHYLLIS ▶ CBS sportscaster (1972-78), the first female sportscaster on the network's regular staff. She joined CBS after having been Miss America of 1971. In addition to covering football and other sports, she served as co-host of several Miss America telecasts. She became a prime-time performer as host of the *People* series (based on *People* magazine) in September of 1978, but only briefly. The series was canceled after two months. She married John Y. Brown, chairman of the Kentucky Fried Chicken chain, who later became governor of Kentucky.

GEORGE POLK MEMORIAL AWARD ▶ bronze plaques given for special achievement in reporting, writing, editing, photography and production in either the print or electronic media. They are given in memory of the 34-year-old CBS correspondent who was murdered in 1948 in northern Greece covering the civil war. The circumstances surrounding his death are a matter of controversy with a charge by two freelance journalists that the Greek government and the C.I.A. were involved in a cover-up of his murder.

GEOSYNCHRONOUS ORBIT ▶ an orbital path, located precisely 22,300 miles above the equator, in which communications satellites travel at the earth's speed of rotation so that they have the effect of being stationary.

GERALD FORD'S AMERICA ▶ four-part alternate media view of Washington politics presented on public TV (1974-75), notable for having been produced on half-inch video tape. It was by TVTV and the Television Workshop of WNET New York, on grants from the Ford Foundation and Rockefeller Foundation.

GERBER, DAVID ▶ highly successful studio executive who rode out a change of ownership at MGM-UA in 1991 to stay on as head of the television division at MGM-Pathe Communications Co. Before Giancarlo Parretti of Italy made his move to acquire the fabled but declining movie company, Gerber had held the title of chairman and CEO of the MGM Worldwide Television Group. After the takeover, Gerber was retained in a similar capacity but with responsibility for domestic and foreign production for networks and cable.

He joined the company in 1986, after establishing himself as a leading independent producer of network series, to knit together the newly merged television divisions of MGM and United Artists. The company was then represented by a single hour on the networks. Under Gerber's leadership, MGM-UA added such hits as *thirtysomething, In the Heat of the Night, The Young Riders* and *Nightmare Cafe,* among other series. He indicated that the company would continue to make drama, rather than sitcoms, its forte.

Gerber had been one of the top independent producers of the 1970s, after having been a studio executive with 20th Century-Fox TV and Columbia Pictures Television. He was executive producer of *Nanny and the Professor, The Ghost and Mrs. Muir, Cade's County, Police Story, Police Woman, Needles and Pins, Born Free, Joe Forrester, The Quest, Gibbsville* and *Today's FBI.*

Before joining 20th Century-Fox as v.p. of TV sales in 1965, he had been a packaging agent with General Artists Corp. and Famous Artists Corp. He became an independent producer in 1972, working mostly in association with Columbia Pictures TV, where he held the title of executive v.p. for worldwide production.

GERBNER'S VIOLENCE PROFILE ▶ annual study of the extent and nature of violence in network programs conducted for many years, starting in 1967, by Dr. George Gerbner, dean of the Annenberg School of Communications, University of Pennsylvania, and Dr. Larry Gross. The continuing research, funded by the National Institute of Mental Health, was based on observations of a team of trained analysts coding videotaped samples of the "violence content" of each season's programming. A second part of the study, examining the effects of TV violence on viewers, began in 1973 and was based on surveys of child and adult viewers.

A tabulation of violent acts in the programming resulted in a Violence Index, which revealed the extent to which each network dealt in violence and had comparative value with indices of previous years. Among the study's various findings over the years were that heavy television viewers are more apprehensive of becoming victims of violence themselves and more distrustful of other people than are light viewers.

Using the Gerbner Index, The National Citizens Committee for Broadcasting, in its war on TV violence, identified the advertisers whose commercials most often appeared in violence-oriented programs. Partly in response to the NCCB campaign, many TV advertisers eschewed participation in violent programs.

GERMANY ▶ one of Europe's largest and most prosperous television markets, and growing larger with the reunification of the country. Where TV broadcasters are concerned, West Germany has easily had the better of reunification, gaining new markets while East Germany's channels have been faced with job losses and possible shut-downs. West Germany has 26 million TV households, East Germany less than one-third that number.

Upon reunification, the West's public broadcasters, ARD and ZDF, were quick to acquire frequencies in the East and were soon joined by the two largest private broadcasters, RTL Plus and Sat1. ARD began broadcasting on one of the East's two state-run channels (formerly DRF) and in 1992 began broadcasting three regional stations on the second of the East German channels. In the West, ARD has nine regional stations.

ARD leads the ratings overall with a typical audience share of 22.5%, including the viewers for its satellite channel, Eins Plus. It is funded by receiver license fees and advertising, although only 20 minutes a day may be given to commercial spots. ZDF, the other public broadcaster, is a close second with 21.5% of the market, including the viewers of its satellite channel, 3Sat. ZDF's operations are more centralized than those of ARD, which is more regionally configured.

Germany's two leading private broadcasters, Sat1 and RTL Plus, which are distributed both terrestrially and by satellite, went into profit for the first time in 1991, some five or six years after they began. The country's two other private broadcasters, Tele 5 and Pro 7, are still in the process of establishing themselves. In 1991 the pay movie channel, Premiere, was launched in a partnership of three blue-chip media companies: Bertelsmann, the Kirch-Group, and France's Canal Plus.

GET SMART ▶ successful NBC comedy series (1965-69) spoofing the movies and TV shows concerned with international espionage. Comedian Don Adams played bumbling secret agent Maxwell Smart, Barbara Feldon portrayed his partner (and, eventually, wife), Agent 99, and Ed Platt was just called Chief. When NBC canceled, CBS picked up the series for an additional season (1969-70). It was by Talent Associates and Heyday Productions. The series was created by Mel Brooks and Buck Henry.

GHETTO ▶ a period of the week where programs of a single general type tend to be segregated. Mornings and afternoons on Sundays, which historically have had low viewing levels, have come to be the religious, public affairs and cultural ghettos. The period before 7 a.m. on weekdays, where *Sunrise Semester* and *Continental Classroom* became moored, developed into an education ghetto in commercial TV.

Saturday mornings formed a children's ghetto in the mid-1960s when advertisers found it possible to isolate that target group—and economically desirable, since the advertising rates were low for time periods where adult viewing was practically negligible.

GHOST AND MRS. MUIR, THE ▶ fantasy-comedy about a beautiful widow, Carolyn Muir, in love with the handsome ghost who haunts her house, based on the novel and motion picture of that title. It featured Hope Lange as Carolyn and Edward Mulhare as the ghost, Captain Daniel Gregg, with Reta Shaw as housekeeper Martha Grant, Charles Nelson Reilly as the ghost's living nephew Claymore, Harlan Carraher as Carolyn's son Jonathan and Kellie Flanagan as Carolyn's daughter Candy. Produced by 20th Century-Fox TV, it played one season on NBC (1968-1969) and was picked up the next by ABC (1969-70). Although well done, it failed both times.

GHOST CANCELING ▶ technical process for clearing television images of "ghosts," the shadowy figures that appear in the picture when the signal from the transmitter bounces off large objects like buildings or bridges on its way to the home set. Ghost-canceling systems work by identifying the ghost elements that have been added to the picture and then eliminating them.

GIDGET ▶ situation comedy based on the spirited teenager established in a series of motion pictures; it ran for one season on ABC (1965-66). Produced by Screen Gems, it featured Sally Field as Frances (Gidget) Lawrence and Don Porter as her father, Russell Lawrence.

GIFFORD, FRANK ▶ ABC sportscaster most prominent as play-by-play announcer on the *NFL Monday Night Football* telecasts and as a contributor to *Wide World of Sports.* A star football player with the New York Giants for 12 years, he began his broadcasting career part-time with CBS stations in New York well before his retirement from the sport in 1965. After several years as a full-time CBS sportscaster, he was hired away by ABC.

GILL, MICHAEL ▶ producer-director for BBC, best known in the U.S. as producer of *Civilisation* and producer-director of Alistair Cooke's *America* series. He left the BBC in 1978 to produce independently in the States and set up partnership with a fellow alumnus, Adrian Malone.

GILLASPY, RICHARD ▶ director first associated with NBC (*Tonight, Home, America After Dark, Mr. Wizard*) and later v.p. of Ivan Tors Studios. Other credits include *The Chevy Show, Arthur Murray Dance Party, Ernie Kovacs Show* and *Open Mind.*

GILLESPIE, HENRY (d. 1991) ▶ veteran syndication executive who became associated with Turner Broadcasting System in 1982 when he set up Turner Program Services, the company's syndication arm. He served initially as chairman of TBS but was forced by illness into a less demanding role. With the title of vice president of syndication sales for the parent company, he was instrumental in selling CNN services abroad and in acquiring and developing original programming for the company's new cable channel, TNT, from the time it began in 1988.

Gillespie previously held key posts with Viacom Enterprises, Columbia Pictures Television Distribution, and CBS Films.

GILLIGAN'S ISLAND ▶ CBS situation comedy (1964-67) about a group of diverse buffoon types shipwrecked on an island and forced to develop their own society. Created and produced by Sherwood Schwartz for Gladasya Productions, in association with United Artists TV, the series featured Bob Denver as Gilligan and Alan Hale Jr. as Skipper Jonas Grumby, along with Jim Backus and Natalie Schafer as millionaire Thurston Howell III and his wife, Lovey, Tina Louise as movie star Ginger Grant, Russell Johnson as Professor Roy Hinkley and Dawn Wells as Mary Ann Summers. Strongly appealing to children for its low comedy, the series enjoyed a sustained sale in rerun syndication.

GIRL FROM U.N.C.L.E., THE ▶ 1966 spin-off of the popular *Man From U.N.C.L.E.* on NBC; it featured Stefanie Powers as the girl, agent April Dancer, and Noel Harrison and Leo G. Carroll as secret agents Mark Slate and Alexander Waverly. The hour series from Norman Felton's Arena Productions and MGM-TV lasted one season.

GITLIN, IRVING (d. 1967) ▶ news executive for CBS in the 1950s and NBC in the 1960s who developed and headed outstanding documentary production units for both networks. Gitlin's organization was overshadowed at CBS by Edward R. Murrow's *See It Now* unit, and in 1960 NBC president Robert Kintner hired Gitlin away to establish a creative projects unit for NBC News. Moving to NBC with Gitlin was Albert Wasserman, who had produced the stunning *Out of Darkness* on a psychiatrist's progress with a catatonic patient; his first effort for NBC was *The U-2 Affair* (Nov. 29, 1960). Gitlin swiftly put together a team of documentarians and launched the *NBC White Paper* series of specials. He was responsible for such efforts as *Sit-In* and *Angola: Journey to War.*

Gitlin had been a producer and writer in radio and entered TV as a producer of public affairs programs, among them *The Search, Conquest* and *The 20th-Century Woman.*

GLASER, ROBERT L. ▶ longtime broadcasting executive who in 1987 became president of American Film Technologies (AFT), the main business of which is colorizing black & white films. Glaser is the former president of Viacom Enterprises and former president of RKO General, a leading independent station group until it disbanded in the 1980s.

He began in television in Chicago, and in 1955 was midwest manager for ABC Films. Later he joined CBS Films in sales, and then Metromedia. In 1965 he joined the ABC network as midwest sales manager. Two years later he moved to New York as vice president and general manager of RKO's WOR-TV. During his 15-year association with that company, he rose to become president of RKO General and chairman of RKO Television Representatives. Later he joined Viacom as head of its production and syndication operations.

Among AFT's main clients for colorizing film is Turner Broadcasting Co. The company has also developed what it calls "paperless animation," a form of computer animation without cells.

GLASS MENAGERIE, THE ▶ TV production of the Tennessee Williams play on ABC (Dec. 16, 1973), which starred Katharine Hepburn, one of her rare appearances in the medium. It was produced by David Susskind and Talent Associates, was directed by Anthony Harvey and featured Joanna Miles.

GLAUBER, STEPHEN ▶ senior producer of CBS News's *48 Hours* since its 1988 debut, responsible for such broadcasts as *Stolen Memoirs* on Alzheimer's disease, *Gay Bashing* on hate crimes, and *Predators* on law enforcement efforts against repeat sex offenders. Glauber came to *48 Hours* from *The CBS Evening News with Dan Rather,* where he served as senior producer from 1985-87 after eight years producing segments for *60 Minutes.*

He joined CBS News in 1976 as a producer for *Who's Who* and *CBS Reports'* 1977 *Battle Over Panama,* having moved into production from the practice of law two years earlier with New York's public WNET, where he worked on *Behind The Lines, 51st State, Assignment America,* and *Politics: USA.* For the preceding five years he served National Educational Television as general counsel.

GLEASON, JACKIE (d. 1987) ▶ one of TV's great comedy stars of the 1950s and 1960s whose series, *The Honeymooners,* with Art Carney featured, ranks as one of the medium's classics. Portly, brash and enamored of the ambiance of nightclubs and the glitter of chorus lines, Gleason billed himself as "The Great One" and made popular phrases of his patented expressions, "How sweet it is" and "Away we go."

He came into television in 1949, from nightclubs, radio and Broadway, as the original Chester Riley in the NBC situation comedy *The Life of Riley* (which later became the vehicle for William Bendix). After a season, he gave it up for *Cavalcade of Stars* on the DuMont Network. Then came *The Jackie Gleason Show,* a weekly comedy-variety hour in which he developed his repertoire of comic characters, Reggie Van

Gleason, The Poor Soul, Joe the Bartender, Charlie the Loudmouth and Ralph Kramden, the boastful but ineffectual bus driver of a recurring skit, "The Honeymooners." Played against the slow-witted sewer worker portrayed by Carney, Kramden was by far Gleason's most successful creation, and when the variety series closed after three seasons in 1955, the logical next step was for *The Honeymooners* to be transformed from skit to series. The filmed series began Oct. 1, 1955, with Audrey Meadows playing Gleason's wife (as she did in the skits) and ran until Sept. 22. 1956. Gleason went back to the hour live program that fall, but it folded after one season. In 1958 he essayed a new live half-hour series with Buddy Hackett, which ran but a few months.

In the late 1960s, CBS attempted a revival of *The Honeymooners* as a one-hour program, with Sheila MacRae and Jane Kean as the new "wives." It was canceled in 1970, but Gleason received a large annual sum from CBS for several years afterwards, under his contract, which prevented him from signing with another network. In the mid-1970s, he was proposed for other series, but none came to fruition.

Jackie Gleason as Ralph Kramden in *The Honeymooners*

Although Gleason's production tastes ran to the grand and garish, it was noteworthy that *The Honeymooners* achieved its popularity on what was possibly the most drab and depressing of the standing sets in the history of television—a kitchen-living room with an ancient refrigerator, a table in the center and a window looking out on the bricks of the next building.

Gleason played his stardom to the limit. One of his contractual demands was that CBS build for him a one-bedroom circular building in Peekskill, N.Y., at a reported cost of $350,000. Late in the 1960s he determined that he would live in Miami and do his shows from there, although there were no network production facilities in Miami. CBS, which was given to coddling its stars, agreed to build television studios adjacent to Gleason's favorite golf course and to conduct an annual press junket to the site, by train, so that a party could be held going and coming.

GLEN CAMPBELL GOODTIME HOUR, THE ▶ variety show on CBS (1969-72) starring country and popular music singer Glen Campbell, with weekly guests. It was produced on tape by Glenco Productions.

GLITTERING PRIZES, THE ▶ much lauded BBC novel for television, written by Frederick Raphael, which aired on U.S. public TV via the Eastern Educational Network in January 1978 and was repeated the following year. The six 80-minute episodes trace what happens to a group of promising graduates of Cambridge who go after the glittering prizes of the professional world in the 1950s. With Tom Conti as star, it featured John Gregg, Dinsdale Landen, Barbara Kellerman, Natasha Morgan, David Robb and others. Mark Shivas was producer and Warren Hussein and Robert Knights directors.

GLOBAL TELEVISION NETWORK ▶ a TV program service that covers 63% of English-speaking Canada through four owned TV stations (CKND-Winnipeg, CKVU-Vancouver, CFRE-Regina and CFSK-Saskatoon) and a number of affiliates. The system is owned by CanWest Global Communications Corporation, Canada's largest private broadcaster, which was incorporated in 1979.

Global's chairman, Israel (Izzie) Asper, and a consortium of investors bailed out an ailing Global Television in 1974, purchasing a 45% interest. By 1985 it grew to 61%. Following a bitter dispute with partner Paul Morton, CanWest Global obtained 100% ownership in 1989 through a court-ordered auction.

G.L.O.W. ▶ syndicated sports variety show that has proved reasonably popular since its premiere in 1986. Its title is the acronym for Gorgeous Ladies of Wrestling; the show follows along lines of male wrestling with typical over-hyped performers and good versus evil matches. The difference is that these are interspersed with songs and sketches. The show was created by David Lane, who is also host and executive producer.

GLUCKSMAN, ERNEST D. ▶ producer, director and writer associated with comedy-variety programs, principally those starring Jerry Lewis. His credits also include *The Chevy Show, The Saturday Night Revue* and specials with Donald O'Connor, Betty Hutton and Ethel Merman.

GO ▶ NBC Saturday nonfiction series for children which made early practical use of portable video cameras (mini-cams) in programs designed to "go anywhere" for interesting subject matter, whether into the cockpit of a plane or a recording studio. The brainchild of George Heinemann, NBC v.p. of children's programs, *Go* premiered Sept. 8, 1973, in a time when the networks were becoming responsive to public complaints about the low state of children's television. In 1976, for the Bicentennial, the series took a new title of *Go-USA.* Heinemann served as executive producer.

GOBEL, GEORGE (d. 1991) ▶ a comedy sensation in the mid-1950s who became part of NBC's star roster, first in a half-hour series that premiered in 1954, which featured Jeff Donnell as his stage wife and Peggy King as singer, then in *The George Gobel Show* (1957-59), an hour variety program that alternated with *The Eddie Fisher Show.*

Gobel had been an obscure Chicago comic playing in small nightclubs until he did a guest shot on a major TV spectacular. His comedy persona—that of a bewildered innocent, a born loser, gamely coping with the world—and his boyish low-key style won the immediate enthusiasm of the television audience. His trademark exclamation, "Well, I'll be a dirty bird," quickly entered the popular language.

Gobel's overnight success typified how TV made sudden stars of journeyman entertainers; it was part of television's second wave, occurring after the move-over of established radio stars. Gobel's popularity faded in the 1960s, and his TV work mainly consisted of guest shots and occasional dramatic roles until he became a regular on *Hollywood Squares* in the late 1970s. This led to a starring role in the sitcom *Harper Valley.*

GODFATHER, THE ▶ (full title: *Mario Puzo's "The Godfather": The Complete Novel for Television*) nine-hour serialized version on NBC of Francis Ford Coppola's two smash-hit movies, *The Godfather* and *The Godfather, Part II,* reconstructed and interwoven as a single drama about a gangster clan. The TV version, incorporating approximately one hour of material that had been trimmed out of the theatrical presentations, was assembled by Coppola and film editor Barry Malkin. NBC presented it on four consecutive nights in November 1977, but the ratings were somewhat disappointing considering the cost of the project. This may have been because the original movies had already been aired a few years before.

GODFREY, ARTHUR (d. 1983) ▶ one of TV's most successful personalities, who during most of the 1950s conducted two weekly prime-time series for CBS as well as a daily radio show. A master commercial pitchman, with a deep-voiced style, who managed to blend folksiness with sophistication, he was reported by *Variety* to have been responsible for $150 million in advertising billings for CBS in 1959.

Godfrey's first TV venture, *Arthur Godfrey's Talent Scouts,* began Dec. 8, 1948 and ran nearly 10 years. The show presented young professional talent in the traditional amateur show manner, but each was introduced by a celebrity who professed to be the "discoverer." An applause meter determined who won. A month after the premiere, he began a second weekly series, the hour variety show *Arthur Godfrey and His Friends* (changed in 1956 to *The Arthur Godfrey Show*). This involved a resident cast which at various times included Julius LaRosa, Janet Davis, Marion Marlowe, LuAnn Sims, the Chordettes, Haleloke, Frank Parker, the Mariners, Carmel Quinn, Pat Boone and the McGuire Sisters. Tony Marvin was his announcer. His trademarks were a ukulele and the chucklesome greeting, "Howa'ya, Howa'ya, Howa'ya."

Godfrey's firing of LaRosa on the air, with the charge that he lacked humility, was national news, as was his "buzzing" of a New Jersey airport in his private plane. Later, his successful battle with cancer was widely publicized.

In 1959 Godfrey was forced to give up his TV shows because of ill health, although he continued on radio. By the early 1960s the increasing sophistication of TV entertainment had replaced the loose informality of television in the 1950s, and performers such as Godfrey were no longer in demand.

When he was at his height with two prime-time shows, his weekly audience was estimated at 82 million viewers, and in 1954 his combined broadcasts were reported to have accounted for 12% of CBS's total revenues.

GODFREY, KEITH (d. 1976) ▶ leading syndication figure for 20 years, all of them with MCA-TV. He joined in 1955 as a salesman in Houston and retired as executive v.p. in 1975 while ailing with cancer.

***GOING MY WAY* ▶** sentimental dramatic series based on the movie of that title, produced by Revue and Kerry Productions for ABC in 1962. Gene Kelly and Leo G. Carroll starred as Father Charles O'Malley and Father Fitzgibbon, and the series ran for 39 episodes.

GOLDBERG, GARY DAVID ▶ writer-producer who worked his way through various assignments in the Grant Tinker era at MTM Enterprises until he hit paydirt with *Family Ties* on NBC, via his UBU Productions. After the sitcom ended its seven-year run in 1989, Goldberg sold *American Dreamer* to NBC for the 1990-91 season and *Brooklyn Bridge* to CBS for 1991-92.

***GOLDBERGS, THE* ▶** early situation comedy about a Jewish family in the Bronx. It had run 17 years on radio and had inspired a Broadway play when CBS brought it to TV on Jan. 17, 1949. The show was cut down at the height of its popularity during the McCarthy era because a member of the cast, Philip Loeb, who portrayed the father, Jake, was listed in *Red Channels.* Gertrude Berg, who was the star as well as the creator and writer of the half-hour series, refused to fire Loeb, and when advertising support evaporated CBS canceled. NBC then picked up the series, but not for long. The original TV run ended on June 25, 1951.

Loeb, harassed by the Red-baiters and blacklisted in show business, committed suicide in 1955.

The Goldbergs was revived in a 1956 syndicated version, by Guild Films, with Robert H. Harris in Loeb's role and with the original cast virtually intact, Berg as Molly, Arlene McQuade as Rosalie and Eli Mintz as Uncle David. In the brief revival, Tom Taylor played Sammy, the role that had been originated by Larry Robinson.

GOLDEN AGE (OF TELEVISION DRAMA) ▶ appellation commonly used for TV during the 1950s when live studio drama, in the theater tradition, was part of the medium's main nightly fare. Most of the plays were produced in New York under somewhat primitive conditions, but the opportunity to be produced and "discovered" overnight drew scores of young playwrights to television. In yielding a new body of literature, the drama anthologies gave the new medium respectability and prestige, heightened when stage adaptations (and then movies) were made of such TV plays as Reginald Rose's *Twelve Angry Men* (1954), Gore Vidal's *Visit to a Small Planet* (1955), William Gibson's *The Miracle Worker* (1957) and Mac Hyman's *No Time for Sergeants* (1955). Then films were made of Paddy Chayefsky's *Marty* (1953) and *The Bachelor Party* (1955), Rod Serling's *Patterns* (1955) and JP Miller's *The Days of Wine and Roses* (1958), among others.

The era opened with the premiere of the *Kraft Television Theatre* on May 7, 1947, and closed with the final presentation of *Playhouse 90* as a weekly series ten years later. It reached its height between 1953 and 1955, when as many as a dozen original plays were offered by the networks almost every week. As drama flourished, Kraft expanded to two *Theatres,* one on NBC Wednesday nights, the other on ABC Thursdays. *Playhouse 90,* which began on CBS Oct. 4, 1956, was perhaps the most ambitious venture of all, calling for a major 90-minute production every week.

There were also the *Philco Playhouse* (alternating with the *Goodyear Playhouse*), *Studio One, U.S. Steel Hour, Robert Montgomery Presents, Omnibus, General Electric Theater, Motorola TV Hour, Lux Video Theatre, Ford Theatre, Ford Startime, Elgin Hour, Alcoa Theatre, Kaiser Aluminum Hour, Medallion Theatre, Pulitzer Prize Playhouse, Schlitz Playhouse of Stars, Sunday Showcase, Armstrong Circle Theatre, Four Star Playhouse, Four Star Jubilee, Climax!, Producers' Showcase, Matinee Theatre, Revlon Theatre, Breck Golden Showcase, Front Row Center, Playwrights 56, Camera Three, Actors Studio, Hallmark Hall of Fame, DuPont Show of the Month, Desilu Playhouse, Special Tonight* and others.

Out of these showcases came such writers as those mentioned and Robert Alan Aurthur, Robert Anderson, A.E. Hotchner, Tad Mosel, Horton Foote, Calder Willingham, N. Richard Nash, David Shaw, Sumner Locke Elliott, Paul Monash and S. Lee Pogostin. Chayefsky had been writing sketches for nightclub comics, Aurthur was part owner of a record company, Mosel an airlines clerk, Serling employed by a Cincinnati radio station, Nash a teacher, Foote an actor, Miller a salesman and Rose an advertising copywriter. Although writers were usually paid less than $2,500 a script, the wide-open TV market opened new career vistas for each of them.

Directors who came into prominence included Delbert Mann, Arthur Penn, Sidney Lumet, John Frankenheimer, Fielder Cook, George Roy Hill, Franklin Schaffner, Alex Segal, Dan Petrie, Fletcher Markle and Ralph Nelson.

And the era spawned such producers as Fred Coe, Martin Manulis, Worthington Miner, George Schaefer, Paul Gregory, Robert Saudek, Robert Herridge, Herbert Brodkin, Albert McCleery, John Houseman, Norman Felton, David Susskind and Gordon Duff.

Along with the established names at the time, the acting talent included George C. Scott, James Dean, Kim Stanley, Julie Harris, Eva Marie Saint, Paul Newman, Sidney Poitier, Grace Kelly, Lee Remick, E.G. Marshall, Jack Palance, Jack Lemmon, John Cassavetes, Eli Wallach, Rod Steiger, Charlton Heston, Sal Mineo, Dina Merrill, Lee Marvin, Keenan Wynn, Piper Laurie, Rip Torn, Lee Grant, Jack Warden and Lee J. Cobb.

Although the shows were produced live, some of the more successful ones, such as *Patterns* and *A Night to Remember* (1956), which used 107 actors and 31 sets, were repeated weeks after the original telecasts.

But by the late 1950s, virtually all the drama series were gone, having given way to filmed series and quiz shows, and most of the artists who had emerged in the Golden Age fled to movies and the theatre. A few, however, adapted to the new requirements of television and remained; those included Serling, Susskind, Monash, Brodkin, Felton and many of the actors.

Hallmark Cards continued *Hall of Fame* through the decades as seasonal specials, and CBS revived the *Playhouse 90* concept in the late 1960s for two or three plays a year. Studio drama, on videotape, has had sporadic revivals, but never on the scale of the Golden Age, and not with the conviction that it was a natural form for television.

No one can say for certain what caused the wave of drama to pass, but there are several theories. According to one, drama was practical in the years when the wealthier and better-educated families owned most of the television sets, but impractical when sets proliferated to virtually every home in the country, defining a new mass audience. Another holds that advertisers, dealing as they do in their commercials with instant solutions to problems, found it inconsistent with their purposes to sponsor serious plays on human conflicts, which revealed that in real life there are no easy solutions.

Studio drama is costly to produce and inevitably varies in quality from program to program. Networks and advertisers can never be sure how large an audience an original play will attract; episodic series are more predictable. Although many of the more recent drama specials have been sponsored, network officials have indicated that drama is less profitable than other forms of programming because it permits fewer commercial breaks and is usually limited to advertising that is artistically in keeping.

GOLDEN, BILL (d. 1959) ▶ head of advertising for CBS in the 1950s noted for his creativity, impeccable taste and for designing the "CBS eye," the network's distinctive logo. He also played a large role in projecting a classy image for CBS, which wanted to be thought of as the "Tiffany" of the networks.

The stars of NBC's popular sitcom *The Golden Girls*

***GOLDEN GIRLS, THE* ▶** hit series on NBC, created by Susan Harris, which to the surprise of many became the first successful modern sitcom in which all of the central characters were women and, even more unusual, all well over the age of 50. Centered on the lives of four women who share a house in Miami, the stories often derive their humor from going against stereotype. The show premiered in 1985 and stars Bea Arthur as Dorothy, Betty White as Rose, Rue McClanahan as Blanche, and Estelle Getty as Dorothy's mother, Sophia. Executive producers are Paul Junger Witt, Tony Thomas, Marc Sotkin and Susan Harris.

GOLDEN ROSE OF MONTREUX ▶ international TV awards competition for light entertainment programming, held annually in Switzerland since 1961.

Leonard H. Goldenson

GOLDENSON, LEONARD H. ▶ top officer of the American Broadcasting Companies Inc. beginning with its formation in 1953 from the merger of ABC and United Paramount Theatres; he retired in 1986. He held the title of president until January 1972, when he was elected chairman. Goldenson, who engineered the merger, had been president of UPT since its divorcement in 1950 from Paramount Pictures by government order. He had joined Paramount soon after receiving his degree from Harvard Law School; by 1938, at age 32, he was executive in charge of the company's 1,700 movie theaters.

Under Goldenson, ABC not only expanded rapidly in TV and radio but also diversified its activities by adding a phonograph record and distribution company, a network of scenic and amusement parks and publishing subsidiaries. Goldenson steered ABC through a number of financially shaky periods, fending off takeover bids by Howard Hughes and Norton Simon, and finally saw the company attain a secure footing when, in the early 1970s, the ABC network achieved parity with CBS and NBC.

Throughout most of his career at ABC, Goldenson was content to maintain a low profile, saving, perhaps, his most visible role to the end. By 1985, the network locomotives were running low on steam, the advertising economy was entering a deep recession, and competition from cable TV was intensifying. Wall Street had turned predatory, rumors were rampant about network takeovers, and Goldenson feared that his heir apparent, Frederick S. Pierce, would not be able to deal with the changing business environment. Goldenson turned to one of his friends in the industry, the chairman of Capital Cities Communications, Thomas Murphy. Together they hammered out an agreement under which Cap Cities, though the smaller of the companies, acquired ABC for $3.5 billion.

Shortly after the merger's consummation in 1986, Goldenson, then 80, retired from ABC, moved to Florida and with the help of author Marvin Wolf, wrote his autobiography, *Beating the Odds.* It told, among other things, of his reorganizing a bankrupt Paramount Pictures and then running Paramount's movie chain, all by the age of 32. When CBS chairman William S. Paley died in 1990, Goldenson was the only surviving founding father of network television.

GOLDMARK, PETER C. (d. 1977) ▶ a pioneer in the development of new communications technology and, until his retirement in 1971, CBS's resident inventor as head of engineering research and development and, later, as president of CBS Laboratories. On leaving CBS he formed his own company, Goldmark Communications Corp., concentrating on the social uses of broadband communications. His espoused concept of a "new rural society," in which advanced telecommunications technologies would allow a decentralization of business and residences, anticipated changes wrought decades later by such inventions as mobile telephones, fax machines, personal computers and modems.

Joining CBS in 1936, not long after his arrival in the U.S. from his native Hungary, he became involved with more than 160 inventions and is personally credited with developing the 33 1/3 r.p.m. long-playing record, which revolutionized the recording industry. Goldmark also helped create the first successful color TV system for CBS—the so-called "color wheel"—but because that system was not compatible with black-and-white sets, the FCC authorized instead the system developed by RCA for domestic use.

Goldmark also developed EVR (Electronic Video Recording), a form of videocassette using 8.75 mm film instead of tape. CBS created a new division around the invention, in hopes of dominating what seemed to be an emerging home video recording industry, but closed it down when it was clear that the tape systems would prevail.

GOLF ▶ an individual sport that while lacking the broad appeal of major team sports is thought to involve the practitioner-viewer more than most others televised. This is because, except for the professional drives, every golfer at home has been confronted with shots and conditions similar to those facing professionals as they compete. Television contributed greatly to popularizing the sport as a recreational activity for Americans in the 1950s and 1960s, and as the weekend players grew in number, interest in the telecasts increased and over time sent the TV rights soaring.

In 1989 there were 59 different golf events on the three major networks, involving 115 telecasts; some were women's golf events. The cable networks not only had golf events of their own but were partnered with the networks in some of the major golf attractions. Cable networks would carry the early rounds on Thursdays and Fridays for their much-needed sports programming while the big broadcast networks carried the final two rounds on the weekend.

From 1980 to 1990 the PGA Tour purse for approximately 44 events each year grew from $13 million to $46 million. In 1980 Tom Watson was the big money winner with close to $531,000. Ten years later Greg Norman won the honor with close to $1.2 million. This spectacular growth has been guided by PGA commissioner Deane Beman, who assumed the post in 1974.

Another accomplishment of the Beman era has been the creation of the Senior PGA Tour, which grew from two events in 1980 to 40 events a decade later. Some consider it the most successful sports venture of the 1980s. Essentially it involves tournaments played by the established stars of the sport, those most familiar to the lay audience. A huge boost was given to the Senior Tour in 1990 by the reuniting of professional golf's "Big Four": Jack Nicklaus, Lee Trevino, Arnold Palmer and Gary Player.

The Ladies Professional Golf Association did not fare as well as the men's during the 1980s, either in terms of television time or advertising dollars. In November 1990 Charles Mechem, Jr., former chairman and chief executive officer of Taft Broadcasting, became the new commissioner of the LPGA. His television experience, personal style and marketing savvy were looked to for the greater development of this facet of the sport.

Frank Sutton and Jim Nabors in a scene from *Gomer Pyle, U.S.M.C.*

GOMER PYLE, U.S.M.C. **▶** smash hit situation comedy on CBS (1964-68) about a sweet, naive yokel in the U.S. Marine Corps. The countrified antics and dialect of Jim Nabors, in the title role, were the chief interest, and he was nicely foiled by the late Frank Sutton as his tough sergeant, Vince Carter. It was created by Aaron Ruben and produced by Ashland Productions and T&L Productions.

GONE WITH THE WIND **▶** David O. Selznick's 1939 movie classic which, when finally released to TV in 1976 for a single showing, scored the highest rating in history for any television entertainment program. It had only a brief stay at the top, however, being surpassed by *Roots* in February 1977.

NBC paid MGM a reported $5 million for the rights to a single national airing. It was played in two parts on successive nights, Nov. 7 and Nov. 8, 1976. The telecasts scored ratings of 47.7 and 47.4, respectively, reaching an estimated 33,960,000 average households the first night and 33,750,000 the second. *GWTW* retains the distinction as the highest-rated movie on TV of all time. CBS later bought the TV rights for 20 years. When Ted Turner bought the MGM library to supply his new TNT network, *Gone With the Wind* was one of the prize titles. It was scheduled the night the network was launched and has been repeated once a year since, each time scoring well in the ratings.

CBS was assured the sequel, *Scarlett,* when it joined an international consortium in buying the book rights for $8 million in 1991.

GONG SHOW, THE ▶ see Game Shows.

GOOD GUYS, THE ▶ CBS situation comedy (1968-70) about a hash-slinger and a cabbie that was an attempt by the network to establish a blue-collar comedy like Jackie Gleason's *The Honeymooners.* The effort failed. By Talent Associates, it featured Bob Denver as Rufus Butterworth, Herb Edelman as Bert Gramus and Joyce Van Patten as Claudia Gramus.

GOOD MORNING, AMERICA ▶ two-hour early morning show on ABC (7-9 a.m.) that superseded *A.M. America* with a new cast and a largely new creative team. The changes paid off, and the program promptly began to make inroads into the audience for the long-established *Today* on NBC. Within a year NBC had begun to revamp *Today* to keep from losing more ground to the ABC entry.

A key change was the installation of actor David Hartman (who had starred in *Lucas Tanner* and other prime-time series) in the role of host, in place of Bill Beutel and other newscast personalities. Woody Fraser was brought in as executive producer. In general format the program resembled *Today* but with a stronger accent on features. A roster of outside personalities—Jack Anderson, Rona Barrett, Jonathan Winters, Erma Bombeck and John Lindsay—contributed five-minute pieces several times a week. Regulars in the cast were Nancy Dussault, Steve Bell, Margaret Osmer and Geraldo Rivera. Sandy Hill succeeded Dussault in the spring of 1977.

Joan Lunden became co-host in 1980, and Charles Gibson replaced Hartman in 1987. Later, *Good Morning* overtook *Today* in the ratings when the NBC show replaced Jane Pauley with Deborah Norville in a celebrated casting gaffe.

GOOD TIMES ▶ half-hour comedy series concerning an urban black family, which began on CBS in February 1974 as a spin-off of *Maude* by Yorkin & Lear's Tandem Productions. Its debt to *Maude,* however, was chiefly in the appropriation of Esther Rolle, who had portrayed Florida Evans, the maid, in that series. Rolle headed a cast that included John Amos as Florida's husband James, Ralph Carter as son Michael, Jimmie Walker as son J.J., Bern-Nadette Stanis as daughter Thelma and Ja'net DuBois as neighbor Willona Woods. The series made Walker instantly popular as a young black comedian and led to lucrative personal appearances and TV commercials. Amos left in 1976 to take a role in *Roots.* The series was canceled during the 1978-79 season.

Jimmie Walker and Esther Rolle in a scene from the CBS series *Good Times*

GOODMAN, JULIAN ▶ president of NBC from April 1, 1966, until April 1, 1974, when he became chairman. He was an unusual choice for the corporate post—in a time when broadcast leaders were typically drawn from the sales ranks—because his entire training had been with NBC News, where he worked 20 years, latterly as executive v.p. for administration. But while Goodman's background suggested that NBC would strive for even greater achievement in news, in fact news received a lower priority under Goodman than it had had with his predecessor, Robert E. Kintner.

When Fred Silverman and Jane Cahill Pfeiffer were brought into NBC in 1978 to form a new administration, Goodman became chairman of the executive committee. He chose early retirement in 1979, but continued his involvement with media as a director of the Gannett Co. and as a board member of various industry organizations.

Goodman, a Kentuckian, joined NBC in Washington as a news writer for David Brinkley in 1945. He later became director of news and public affairs, v.p. of NBC News and then executive v.p. He produced such programs as *Comment, Ask Washington* and *Report From Alabama* and supervised the *JFK* series that reported periodically on the Kennedy Administration.

GOODSON-TODMAN PRODUCTIONS ▶ company formed in 1946 by Mark Goodson, a former radio announcer, and Bill Todman, former radio writer. It hit the jackpot in the game-show field with a succession of big hits:

What's My Line, I've Got a Secret, Stop the Music, Beat the Clock, To Tell the Truth, The Price Is Right, Password, The Name's the Same, Two for the Money, The Match Game and others. Not only did the shows enjoy long and prosperous runs in the 1950s and 1960s, many of them in prime time, but virtually all were revived in the 1970s either for prime-access syndication or by the networks for their daytime schedules. Goodson-Todman ventured also into the field of episodic filmed series with *The Rebel, Jefferson Drum, The Richard Boone Show, Philip Marlowe* and *The Don Rickles Show.*

Known today as Goodson Productions since the death of Bill Todman in 1979, the company produces *Family Feud, Classic Concentration* and *The Price Is Right.* Virtually all of its game-show formats are sold widely abroad by Fremantle International.

GOSTELRADIO ▶ the state-run television system of what used to be the Soviet Union; it has been undergoing dramatic change since the collapse of Communism and the dissolution of the USSR. When it was the only broadcaster operating in the vast Communist country, it provided three national channels by satellite, in addition to local services in Moscow and Leningrad, and regional programming in some 48 languages. To make all this work Gostelradio maintained 139 studios.

Since the collapse of Communism, Gostelradio has been challenged by a number of cable networks and SMATV systems (satellite master antenna installations in large apartment complexes), and also by the Russian State Television and Radio Company, launched in 1991 in the Boris Yeltsin regime.

Just before the collapse of the Communist regime, President Mikhail Gorbachev had called for an expansion of Gostelradio to five channels—including separate ones for educational and scientific programs and one for news around the clock, in the spirit of *glasnost* and *perestroika.* Gorbachev had also approved the launch of a DBS system called Gelikon, and the country was preparing to legalize reception of direct-to-home satellite transmissions from foreign sources.

GOULD, JACK ▶ radio and TV critic of the *New York Times* (1944-72), one of the first of the daily journalists to recognize that TV required full-time coverage, just as any other major news beat. As reporter, commentator and critic, who at one time headed a staff of eight, he became known as "the conscience of the industry" because his critical observations frequently influenced those who wielded power in broadcasting. At the top of his field in 1957, he received a special George Foster Peabody Award—normally restricted to TV practitioners—for his "fairness, objectivity and authority." Gould joined the *Times* in 1937 after five years with the *New York Herald-Tribune.* He worked initially in the drama department but shifted to radio in 1942 and became critic in 1944. Early in the 1960s he left the newspaper to join CBS in a corporate post but found it an unhappy experience and shortly returned to the *Times.* He retired in 1972 to live in California.

***GOVERNOR AND J.J., THE* ▶** political situation comedy about J.J., the beautiful daughter of William Drinkwater, an elected official who sometimes jeopardized, but always saved, his career. It featured Julie Sommars as J.J. and Dan Dailey as Drinkwater, along with Neva Patterson as secretary Maggie McLeod, James Callahan as press secretary George Callison and Nora Marlowe as housekeeper Sarah. Carried by CBS (1969-71) and then rebroadcast in the summer of 1972, it was by Talent Associates-Norton Simon Inc.

GOWDY, CURT ▶ veteran sportscaster who, in a career that has spanned five decades, has probably broadcast more major events than any other TV announcer. He ended a 15-year stint with NBC in 1979 to sign on with CBS Sports to cover NFL football, among other assignments. His career spans the sporting spectrum and includes coverage of seven Super Bowls, 16 World Series, 12 Rose Bowls and seven Olympic Games. During his years with NBC, he drew on his passions for hunting and fishing to freelance as host of ABC's *The American Sportsman.* After broadcasting sports in Cheyenne, Wyo., and Oklahoma City during the 1940s, he became co-announcer in 1949 with the legendary Mel Allen for the New York Yankees. Three years later he became announcer for the Boston Red Sox and held that position for 15 years. Since then, he has covered a wide range of sports for all three networks and was host of the PBS (1975-77) series *The Way It Was.* In 1984 Gowdy was honored as one of the few broadcasters to be inducted into the Baseball Hall of Fame.

GRADE A SIGNAL ▶ denoting the areas in the coverage pattern of a station where the transmissions should be received best and most reliably. The Grade B Signal denotes the area of secondary service, farther from the transmitter, where reliable service can usually be received with an outdoor antenna.

Grade A conforms to specific electronic criteria established by the FCC: the Grade A perimeter equates to the point at which the field density is 68 dBu for channels 2-6, 71 dBu for channels 7-13 and 74 dBu for channels 14-83.

A station's Grade A contour, usually defined by a circle, is the geographic sphere of coverage where satisfactory service can be expected at least 90% of the time. In the Grade B contour, the quality of the picture is expected to be satisfactory at least 50% of the time.

GRADE, LEW (LORD) ▶ England's grand old man of television, who in his prime ran one of his country's largest commercial franchises, Associated Television (ATV), along with a leading film production studio, and an international distribution company, ITC. No one before or since has produced as much for the U.S. commercial TV market from England as Grade. During the 1960s and 1970s he placed on the U.S. networks such series as *This Is Tom Jones, The Saint, Secret Agent, The Prisoner, The Persuaders, Shirley's World* (with Shirley MacLaine) and *The Julie Andrews Show.* In syndication, he had *The Muppet Show, Interpol Calling,* and *Whiplash.* He also engineered large-scale international coproductions, such as with companies in Italy and the U.S. for such projects as *Jesus of Nazareth* and *Moses the Lawgiver.* Grade promoted his shows with a flamboyance that was not characteristically British.

By the 1970s ITC was probably the largest entertainment empire outside the U.S. The company owned most of the theatres in London and also ATV Music, which among other assets owned The Beatles' music catalog. In partnership with Martin Starger, former head of programming for ABC, Grade founded Marble Arch as a motion picture production company based in the U.S. The company has produced such notable films as *Sophie's Choice, On Golden Pond* and *The Muppet Movie.* Grade's earlier venture in motion pictures, with a string of action films produced by ITC, was one of his biggest failures.

ATV lost its franchise for the Midlands region to Central Independent Television in 1981, and the following year Grade sold off ITC to Australian entrepreneur, Robert Holmes á Court.

Born in Russia in 1906, Grade started in show business as a Charleston dancer in England and later operated a talent agency with his brother Leslie. He entered the television field in 1956 with the advent of commercial television in the U.K. His background as an agent gave him the familiarity with American show business that served him in tailoring programs for both sides of the Atlantic.

GRADE, MICHAEL ▶ chief executive of Britain's Channel 4 Television since 1988, succeeding the channel's founder, Jeremy Isaacs, who had made the unique channel work. Grade is regarded as one of the most talented executives in British television and one of the few who has held high positions in both the commercial and public broadcasting sectors. He also worked for a time in the American industry as an executive of Embassy Television during the early 1980s. When he returned to England he became head of programs for both BBC-1 and BBC-2 and displayed a scheduling prowess that made him a major figure in the industry. He was a natural choice to succeed Isaacs at Channel 4, which, while commercial, has a strong public service component in that it is chartered to serve minority interests.

Grade is the nephew of Lord Lew Grade, who for many years was the dominant figure in British commercial television as head of the regional station, ATV, and of the U.S.-U.K. production company, ITC. At the time of the ITV franchise renewals in 1991, Michael Grade was given an $850,000 "golden handcuffs" contract to keep him at Channel 4 in Britain's new era.

GRADINGER, ED ▶ president of MGM/UA's television production group since October 1991. Former president and chief executive of New World Entertainment until 1989, when the company changed hands, Gradinger was hired by MGM/UA chairman David Gerber, with whom he had worked at Columbia Pictures Television in the late 1970s. Before joining New World, Gradinger was senior executive vice president of 20th Century-Fox Television.

GRAHAM, FRED ▶ chief anchor and managing editor of the Courtroom Television Network (Court TV) since its 1991 launch. The law has long been Graham's specialty; he became a journalist after receiving a law degree. From 1972-87 he was CBS News's law correspondent. Based in Washington, he covered the activities of the Supreme Court, Justice Department, FBI and the legal profession. He also often served as a moderator on *Face The*

Nation. Graham came to CBS News from *The New York Times,* where he had been Supreme Court correspondent from 1965-72. For a time, after leaving CBS, he anchored a local newscast in Nashville, Tenn.

GRAHAM, KATHARINE M. ▶ board chairman and chief executive officer of the Washington Post Co. since the death of her husband, Philip L. Graham, in 1963. In addition to the *Post, Newsweek* magazine and other print properties, she heads Post-Newsweek Stations, a group that includes WDIV-TV-Detroit; WPLG-TV Miami; WJXT-TV Jacksonville, Fla.; WFSB-TV Hartford, Conn.; and WCKY-AM Cincinnati. Her control over the media empire earned her the reputation as one of the most powerful women in America.

GRALNICK, JEFF ▶ v.p. and executive producer of special broadcasts at ABC News, probably best known for having been overseer of *World News Tonight* with Peter Jennings when it became the top-rated network news broadcast in the late 1980s and early 1990s.

Gralnick has also been responsible for coverage of the 1988 election year and such events as the Iran/Contra hearings, the TWA Flight 847 hostage crisis in 1985, the Challenger space shuttle disaster, the summit meetings between President Reagan and Soviet leader Gorbachev in Geneva and Reykyavik, and seventeen-and-a-half hours of special programming marking centennial celebration of the Statue of Liberty.

Gralnick joined ABC News in 1972 as an associate producer of the evening news. For 12 years previously he served CBS News as a special events producer and as an on-air reporter in Vietnam.

GRAMPIAN TELEVISION ▶ regional commercial station in the U.K. licensed to serve northeast Scotland, with headquarters in Aberdeen.

GRANADA TELEVISION ▶ oldest of Britain's regional commercial stations with a worldwide reputation for producing exceptional programming, earned by such efforts as the weekly documentary series, *World In Action,* and such celebrated mini-series of the 1980s as *Brideshead Revisited, Hard Times* and *Jewel in the Crown.* Licensed to the Lancashire region with studios in Manchester, it was founded in 1956 by Lord Sidney Bernstein, whose principal business at the time was renting TV sets to consumers (the British had tended to rent TVs rather than buy them). That business was, and continues to be, the largest in the field in the U.K. and also goes by the name Granada.

Granada Television is the only one of the original regional franchises whose license has been continually renewed. In Britain's harrowing franchise auction in October 1991, the company emerged with its license intact, even though it was substantially outbid by rival Mersey Television. The government gave Granada the edge based on its record of public service.

Along with its documentaries and quality dramas, Granada produces the prime-time soap opera, *Coronation Street,* which portrays working-class life in the Manchester area. It is the longest-running and all-time most popular series in the U.K. Granada also maintains a motion picture division, which provided the backing for *My Left Foot* and coproduced *Prime Suspect* with HBO. Granada Television is part of the Granada Group, which was one of the original investors in British Satellite Broadcasting.

Herbert A. Granath

GRANATH, HERBERT A. ▶ president of Capital Cities/ABC Video Enterprises since 1982. One of the network's more visionary executives, Granath embraced new media, experimented with new technologies and led ABC into new overseas markets. Through the Video Enterprises division, he directed the company's purchase in 1984 of ESPN; its partnership in two other basic-cable networks, Arts & Entertainment and Lifetime; and its financial involvement in the British Screen Sport and the Japan Sports Channel.

Granath got ABC active in such emerging technologies as electronic information delivery, in-store advertising, electronic billboards, videocassette tracking and video publishing. ABC Video Enterprise's international arm invested in three production companies in Europe:

Tele-Munchen, based in Munich; Madrid's Tesauro, and Hamster Productions in Paris.

Granath has been with ABC since 1960 and has served variously as v.p. of ABC Inc., v.p. of program development and marketing for ABC Sports, and as a ABC radio sales executive. He also did a brief stint as senior v.p. for Trans World International and worked in television sales for NBC.

GRANIK, THEODORE (d. 1970) ▶ lawyer who also produced and moderated numerous TV shows, among them *Youth Wants to Know* and *All America Wants to Know* in the 1950s. He also owned WGSP-TV in Washington.

GRANT, B. DONALD (BUD) ▶ former president of CBS Entertainment, the network's programming arm (1980-87). He went into independent production after leaving CBS and in 1990 aligned his company with Tribune Entertainment.

Grant was recruited by CBS in 1972 from NBC-TV, where he had given a good account of himself as head of daytime programs for five years. He was credited with introducing the serial *Days of Our Lives,* which became the pivotal show in the NBC daytime schedule. Grant began with NBC in its executive training program in 1958.

At CBS, he served four years as v.p. in charge of daytime programs, jockeying the schedule into a strong first place and developing a successful youth-oriented soap opera, *The Young and the Restless.* This earned him the promotion to CBS program chief at the start of the Robert Wussler administration in April 1976. However, when the CBS Entertainment division was created in the October 1977 management realignment, Grant yielded the top spot in programming to Robert A. Daly and stayed on as v.p. When Daly resigned in 1980 to become head of Warner Bros., Grant was named president of the division.

GRANT, MERRILL ▶ chairman and CEO of Reeves Entertainment, a successful independent production company that was purchased in 1989 by Thames Television of England. Grant joined Reeves in 1979 and led it to prominence among middle-sized companies, with network, syndication and cable programs of every sort. Grant was executive producer of the *Kate and Allie* series and co-executive producer of *That's Incredible.* Before moving into the production field, Grant had been an advertising executive specializing in television at such major agencies as Benton & Bowles and Grey.

GRAZING ▶ term coined in the late 1980s for a new kind of viewer behavior fostered by the remote-control tuning device that came into wide use with the proliferation of cable. A study by *Channels* magazine and Frank Magid Associates in 1988 confirmed that many viewers flip through the cable channels in the way people flip through magazines, looking briefly at everything rather than settling in to watch anything. In a related style of viewing with the remote control in hand, people may watch several shows in a sitting, dipping in and out of each.

See also Zapping and Zipping.

GREAT AMERICAN COMMUNICATIONS CO. ▶ broadcast and program production and distribution company that was set up in 1987 as a result of the breakup of Taft Broadcasting. Taft was divided at the time between two major investors fighting for control of the company, Carl Lindner's American Financial Corp. and the Robert M. Bass Group.

Lindner got the TV and radio stations and entertainment group, which consisted of Taft Entertainment—a production company that included two animation houses, Hanna-Barbera and Ruby Speers—and Worldvision Enterprises, a major distributor of syndicated programs. That group became Great American Communications Co. The Bass Group got the cable operations, some of which they had already owned in a joint venture with Taft.

The following year, Lindner and Aaron Spelling, a prolific producer of prime-time network TV shows, merged Worldvision with Aaron Spelling Productions. In 1991 another Lindner corporation, Charter Co., a Florida-based firm that sells petroleum products to utilities and commercial users, became the majority owner of Spelling. This was accomplished by acquiring Spelling's 31.67% interest as well as GACC's stake in Spelling, which Lindner sold in order to reduce GACC's $1.1 billion in debt.

Later in 1991 Lindner sold Hanna-Barbera Productions to further reduce GACC's debt. Acquiring the company was Turner Broadcasting System, in a joint venture with Apollo Investment Fund led by Leon Black, a former managing director of mergers and acquisitions at Drexel Burnham Lambert. Turner and Apollo agreed to pay $320 million for H.-B.'s production business. GACC agreed to lay out

$24 million to buy back the distribution rights from Worldvision and turn them over to Turner.

The H.-B. library consists of 3,000 half hours of animated products and 350 TV shows, both series and movies. It was expected that Turner would initially use the library in the form of children's program blocks on the WTBS superstation and/or the TNT cable network, but eventually the library would be the basis of a stand-alone cable network.

Great American Broadcasting, a subsidiary of GACC, consists of five network-affiliated TV stations and 18 radio stations. The TV stations are WTSP-TV St. Petersburg-Tampa, KTSP-TV Phoenix, WDAF-TV Kansas City, WKRC-TV Cincinnati, and WBRC-TV Birmingham.

GREAT AMERICAN DREAM MACHINE, THE ▶ unusual, wry-spirited and sometimes remarkable magazine series on PBS (1970-71). The one-hour episodes successfully combined such disparate disciplines as satire and serious documentary, and there were also dramatic and musical segments. A regular in the series was comedian Marshall Efron. *Dream Machine* disbanded after two seasons for lack of funding. It was produced at WNET New York with A.H. Perlmutter and Jack Willis as executive producers.

GREAT DEBATES ▶ series of four one-hour face-to-face encounters on national TV and radio by the 1960 presidential candidates, John F. Kennedy and Richard M. Nixon, made possible when Congress suspended the equal time law just for the presidential race that year. The debates served to erase Nixon's advantage as the better-known candidate and probably contributed to Kennedy's razor-thin victory that November.

With the three networks carrying the debates simultaneously in prime time, the four programs drew the largest TV audience ever, up to that time—75 million viewers for the first, 61 million for the second, 70 million for the third and 63 million for the final one, according to ARB estimates. The number of different viewers reached by the debates was 101 million. Most analysts attributed the record voter turnout in the national elections of 1960 to the *Great Debates.*

The debates were the fruit of a broadcast industry campaign, led by CBS president Frank Stanton, for the repeal of Sec. 315 of the Communications Act (the equal time rule) because of its stifling effect on political coverage by TV and radio. After the 1960 political conventions, Stanton secured acceptances from Kennedy and Nixon for a televised debate if Congress agreed to remove the obstacle of equal time for the 14 other legally qualified candidates. With the two candidates agreeing to meet on TV, there seemed a chance for the repeal of Sec. 315. But Congress voted only to suspend the rule, on a test basis, and President Eisenhower signed the bill on Aug. 24.

A drawing of lots gave CBS the responsibility for producing the first debate telecast, which was to be limited to the discussion of domestic issues. The event originated at the WBBM-TV studios in Chicago, with Howard K. Smith as moderator and Don Hewitt as producer-director. The panel of news correspondents posing questions to the candidates following their delivery of eight-minute opening statements consisted of Bob Fleming, ABC; Stuart Novins, CBS; Sander Vanocur, NBC; and Charles Warren, Mutual.

The first debate proved to be the most controversial of the four and also the most consequential with respect to its impact on the campaigns. Nixon physically showed the effects of strenuous campaigning, and the loss of weight from a recent illness had made his shirt collar too large. In striking contrast, Kennedy was sun-tanned and full of vigor. When Kennedy refused TV makeup before the broadcast, Nixon did also, although he was pale and needed it. Hewitt's occasional reaction shots during the program found Kennedy relaxed and Nixon perspiring. Overall, Kennedy's TV projection was far superior to that of Nixon, for whom the debate was a catastrophe.

For the subsequent debates, Nixon's entourage included a lighting consultant and a makeup artist, but he could not undo the negative impression he made on the first telecast. The second debate was held at WRC-TV in Washington, Oct. 7, and was produced by NBC with Frank McGee as moderator. The panelists were Edward P. Morgan, ABC; Paul Niven, CBS; Alvin Spivak, UPI; and Harold Levy, *Newsday.*

The third confrontation, produced by ABC on Oct. 13, had Nixon in the Los Angeles studios and Kennedy in the New York studios meeting on the air electronically. Bill Shadel of ABC was moderator and the reporters were Frank McGee of NBC; Charles Von Fremd of CBS; Douglass Cater of the *Reporter;* and Roscoe Drummond of the *New York Herald-Tribune.*

ABC also originated the fourth debate, in its New York studios, on Oct. 21. Devoted entirely to foreign policy, it followed the general format of the first confrontation. Quincy Howe of ABC moderated. The news panel consisted of Walter Cronkite, CBS; John Chancellor, NBC; John Edwards, ABC; and Frank Singiser, Mutual.

J. Leonard Reinsch, representing Kennedy, and Fred Scribner, representing Nixon, had with their aides met more than a dozen times in negotiating sessions to set the procedures for the first debate. The vice-presidential candidates, Lyndon Johnson and Henry Cabot Lodge, had been asked to debate but declined.

The Kennedy-Nixon debates were the last of their kind until the campaigns of 1976, when a change in the FCC's interpretation of the equal time rule permitted TV coverage of debates by major candidates if they were legitimate news events. They were considered to be legitimate news if the debates were conducted by independent organizations, with no direct involvement by the networks. The 1976 debates were held in rented halls, under auspices of the League of Women Voters, and the TV networks were invited to cover them—which, of course, they did.

GREAT GILDERSLEEVE, THE ▶ episodic comedy series brought over from radio in 1955-56, with Willard Waterman as Throckmorton P. Gildersleeve and featuring Ronald Keith and Stephanie Grin as his nephew and niece, Leroy and Marjorie Forrester. It was produced by Robert S. Finkel and Matthew Rapf.

GREAT PERFORMANCES ▶ television's longest-running series devoted to the performing arts, produced by WNET New York. Winner of 43 Emmy Awards, the Peabody Award, and the Prix Italia, the series has aired on public TV since 1973. Executive producer Jac Venza created the series out of two earlier series, *Theater in America* (1973) and *Dance in America* (1975). In addition to funding from public TV sources and the Arts Endowment, the series has received corporate underwriting from Exxon, Martin-Marietta and Texaco.

Rudolph Valentino and Vilma Banky in "The Eagle," a *Great Performances* presentation

GREAVES, WILLIAM ▶ independent filmmaker whose work has expressed the often neglected struggles and achievements of the African-American experience. Greaves has produced over 200 documentaries, including *Resurrections: A Moment in the Life of Paul Robeson,* for Black Entertainment Television; *Frederick Douglass: An American Life;* and the acclaimed *From These Roots,* a study of the Harlem Renaissance of the 1920s. Among his other film and television credits are executive producer and co-host of the series *Black Journal,* for National Educational Television.

Greaves began his career in front of the camera as an actor. Disturbed by the racist stereotypes that tarnished many Hollywood and Broadway vehicles, he went north, apprenticing at the National Film Board of Canada while doing manual labor jobs for income. Eventually he helped make dozens of Canadian films before taking a UN position, which returned him to New York as a television producer in the 1960s.

GREECE ▶ a country whose adoption of commercial television in the late 1980s has created a hotly competitive market in what was once the peaceful domain of the state network, ERT, and its three channels. Publishers predominate in the ownership of the new private networks. Megachannel is owned by the powerful Teletypos publishing concern, New Channel by a publishing consortium, and Kanali 29 by the Kouris Brothers Publishing Group. The fourth commercial channel, Antenna TV, is owned by an FM station operator. There are also two pay channels, TV Plus and Seven X TV. The state network, ERT, supported by receiver license fees, operates two national channels and a third one expressly for the city of Saloniki. Greece has about 3 million TV households.

Eddie Albert and Eva Gabor, stars of *Green Acres*

GREEN ACRES ▶ hit CBS situation comedy (1965-71) about a chic city couple with no aptitude for country living who choose the bucolic life, a straight reversal of the *Beverly Hillbillies* premise while that series was red hot. The two series were a parlay for their creator, Paul Henning, and for Filmways TV. The cast was headed by Eddie Albert and Eva Gabor as Oliver and Lisa Douglas, along with Pat Buttram as Mr. Haney, Alvy Moore as Hank Kimball, Frank Cady as Sam Drucker, Hank Patterson as Fred Ziffel and Arnold, Ziffel's pig.

GREEN HORNET ▶ ABC series based on a radio and comic book hero that was introduced in 1966 on the heels of the network's success with *Batman.* The series failed to last the season, however. The leads were Van Williams as the Green Hornet (grandnephew of the Lone Ranger, known in daily life as newspaper editor Britt Reid) and Bruce Lee as sidekick Kato, and it was produced by Greenway Productions in association with 20th Century-Fox TV.

GREENBERG, PAUL W. ▶ executive producer for NBC News since June 1978, having been recruited from CBS News where he worked 14 years. His particular responsibilities at NBC are in political programs and so-called instant specials—those covering breaking stories of national and international importance. At CBS, where he was a writer and producer, he worked on the *CBS Morning News,* the *Weekend News* and *The CBS Evening News with Walter Cronkite.*

GREENBERG, STANLEY R. ▶ screenwriter noted in television for his work in the docu-drama form. He wrote scripts for *The Missiles of October, Pueblo* and *Blind Ambition,* all dramatic re-creations of modern historical events. Movie credits include *Soylent Green* and *Skyjacked.*

GREENBURG, HAROLD ▶ president and CEO of Astral Inc., a Montreal-based Canadian company involved in broadcasting, entertainment and related retail activities. Greenburg began his career with a photography store in Montreal, building it to a national chain of 145 retail outlets. Then he expanded the company under the name of Bellevue Pathe to include motion picture laboratories and sound studios, and later motion picture packaging and distribution. In 1983 Astral expanded again, this time into television, taking over operating control of First Choice, Canada's eastern pay-television movie service. Its holdings also include Canal Famille, the family channel in Quebec; 50% of the Family Channel in Edmonton, Alberta; the majority interest in the Viewer's Choice Canada pay-per-view service; and a 5% interest in Canal 3 in France.

GREENFIELD, JEFF ▶ ABC News political and media analyst, perhaps best known as the correspondent of the introductory focus pieces that top each evening's *Nightline* with Ted Koppel.

Greenfield's work for *Nightline* has taken him to South Africa, where he contributed to the broadcast's highly acclaimed 1985 and 1990 week-long series, and to Bitburg, West Germany, where he covered the controversial visit of then-President Ronald Reagan to a cemetery containing the graves of former S.S. officers.

Generally considered to be one of the ablest political reporters on television, he has filed stories on the Gary Hart controversy, the Iran/Contra hearings, the 1986 congressional campaigns, the media's coverage of presidential campaigns, including its print reporting and TV editing techniques, and the 1984 Republican and Democratic conventions.

Greenfield's other principle areas of focus are the news and entertainment media, with probing looks at the rationale and aberrations of the ratings system as well as the growth of libel suits against the press.

Prior to joining ABC News, Greenfield was a media critic for CBS News coverage of the 1980 Republican and Democratic conventions and the presidential elections of that same year. Previously, he was an analyst on two PBS programs, *Firing Line* with William F. Buckley and *We Interrupt This Week.* From 1968-70 he served as chief speechwriter for New York Mayor John V. Lindsay, and from 1967-68 in a like capacity for Senator Robert F. Kennedy.

He is author or co-author of nine books, including *Television: The First 50 Years, Playing to Win,* and *The Real Campaign.*

GREENSPAN, CAPPY (d. 1983) and BUD ▶ independent producing team whose credits include the series *The Olympiad* for PBS; the drama *Wilma* for NBC; three one-hour sports documentaries for James Michener's PBS series and a raft of special pieces, including *Olympic Moments* for NBC in connection with the 1980 Moscow Olympics. Bud Greenspan has made a specialty of producing sports documentaries and has become a leading chronicler of the Olympic Games.

GREGORY, PAUL ▶ stage and movie producer who became active in TV in the late 1950s, producing such CBS specials as *Three for Tonight* (1955), an adaptation of his Broadway show, with Marge and Gower Champion; *The Day Lincoln Was Shot* (1956); and *Crescendo* (1957), a musical.

GRIES, TOM (d. 1976) ▶ writer who graduated to director and producer of motion pictures. For TV he directed Truman Capote's *The Glass House* and was producer-director of *The Migrants.* He directed *QBVII,* wrote and created *The Rat Patrol* series for ABC and wrote and directed episodes for *East Side, West Side.*

GRIFFIN, MERV ▶ host of one of TV's most successful syndicated talk shows, who went on to create his own production company that realized a bonanza in the 1980s with *Wheel of Fortune* and *Jeopardy.* As an entrepreneur he ventured also into real estate and resorts, station ownership and film production. He sold Merv Griffin Enterprises to Coca-Cola in 1986 for $250 million, which around that time had acquired Columbia Pictures and Embassy Communications.

The Merv Griffin Show began in 1965 as a Group W syndication stablemate to *The Mike Douglas Show.* More suitable for evening stripping than the Douglas show, and somewhat more sophisticated, it played on a lineup of more than 170 stations by 1968, the year CBS became interested in Griffin as a possible competitor to the Johnny Carson *Tonight* show on NBC. Griffin joined CBS but was unable to dent the Carson ratings. A move from New York to the West Coast midway in the run did not avail and CBS canceled the show in 1972.

Group W bid for Griffin's services again, but he signed instead with MPC, the Metromedia syndication arm, and returned to the prime-time spot on the Metromedia independents that he had held before going to CBS. In 1981, Metromedia began to distribute the show by satellite to stations equipped with satellite-receiving equipment.

Griffin had begun his career as a singer and actor and in 1956 was the vocalist on the *CBS Morning Show* and *The Robert Q. Lewis Show.* Later he hosted a raft of game shows, including *Play Your Hunch* and *Keep Talking* on ABC.

Merv Griffin

GRIMES, BILL ▶ television executive who has held high positions in a range of companies but who is best known as the architect of ESPN's rise in the 1980s to preeminence among the basic-cable networks. In a surprising move he left in 1988 to become president and CEO of Univision, the Spanish-language network that had recently been acquired by Hallmark Cards.

Then in 1991 he left Univision to join Multimedia Inc., a diversified media company, as a vice president of the corporate group.

In the 1970s Grimes was an executive on the rise at CBS, where he started in the radio division. After becoming president of CBS Radio he became a vice president of the Broadcast Group. He was hired away by ESPN in 1981 as executive v.p. and was named president the following year. Under his direction, ESPN became the hot cable network, the first to reach more than 50% of all U.S. homes, a figure it achieved in 1987. Grimes also heightened the profile of the network by adding National Football League games to its schedule, and in addition he brought ESPN to profitability.

His move to Univision in 1988 astonished the industry, because it put him on a quite different path from the one he had been following so successfully and that he appeared to be enjoying. Grimes did not even know how to speak Spanish when he took charge of Univision. While the network was by no means a failure under his guidance, the Hispanic market failed to explode as many thought it would. Grimes left to join Multimedia about three years later.

GRINDL ▶ situation comedy vehicle for Imogene Coca, the former partner of Sid Caesar in the classic comedy series *Your Show of Shows.* NBC introduced the show, about a housekeeper named Grindl, in 1963, but it was unsuccessful. It was by Screen Gems, in association with David Swift Productions.

GROSSMAN, LAWRENCE K. ▶ television executive who was prominent in the 1970s and 1980s and one of the few to swing between public and commercial television. After a long stint as president of PBS (1976-84), he became president of NBC News (1984-88). On leaving he became a lecturer at the John F. Kennedy School at Harvard and then a senior fellow of the Gannett Center for Media at Columbia University (now called the Freedom Forum for Media).

Grossman began his broadcasting career in CBS's advertising department, having come from *Look* magazine. NBC hired him away, and in a few years he became head of that network's ad department and, up to that time, the youngest NBC vice president ever. He left in the early 1970s to start his own advertising agency, one of whose accounts was PBS. In 1976, when there was need for new leadership at PBS with Hartford Gunn's departure, the search committee went outside the system and lit upon Grossman. He was a controversial choice but proved a forceful and productive leader.

When Grant Tinker became chairman of NBC in 1981 and began putting together his own team, he recruited Grossman to head the news division. The two had worked together as young vice presidents at NBC in the 1960s, and Tinker knew Grossman's capabilities. Again the appointment was controversial—a former adman heading one of the world's great news organizations. Grossman had no direct experience in news operations, but as at PBS he proved more than equal to the task. When General Electric bought NBC, Tinker recommended that Grossman succeed him as CEO, but GE had someone else in mind. Tinker's departure from NBC left his successor, Bob Wright, to put together his own team, and Grossman wasn't included.

Lawrence K. Grossman

GROSSO-JACOBSON ▶ successful production partnership of a former New York cop who figured in the famous French Connection case and a Connecticut toiler in the New York television vineyards. Together, since joining forces in 1980, they have produced the CBS reality-based series, *Top Cops,* ABC's *Bellevue Emergency,* NBC's *True Blue,* USA's *Diamonds,* and, at another extreme, the CBS children's series, *Pee Wee's Playhouse.*

The partnership of Sonny Grosso and Larry Jacobson has developed strong ties in Canada and produces many of its programs there, often in coproduction with Canadian companies. With the Canadian network CTV, Grosso-Jacobson produced *Night Heat,* a long-running CBS series in its latenight schedule. With Canada's Alliance and France's Atlantique Productions, it has coproduced the *Counterstrike* series for the USA network. The *Top Cops* series is shot in Toronto. The company has also produced such TV movies as *Out of the Darkness, Trackdown: Finding the Goodbar Killer, The Gunfighter, A Question of Honor,* and *A Family for Joe,* which became an NBC series.

Grosso was a New York policeman who, when assigned to the Narcotics Bureau, became partner of Eddie Egan and helped break the famed French Connection case. He helped write the book and collaborated with William Friedkin and Phil D'Antoni in writing the hit movie. *The French Connection* launched Grosso on a new career, and he was later technical advisor and consultant on *The Godfather.* He also wrote and coproduced stories for *The Marcus-Nelson Murders,* the three-hour pilot for the *Kojak* series, and later worked on the production of *Kojak, The Rockford Files, Baretta* and *Movin' On.* Jacobson, meanwhile, produced shows for a number of syndication companies and in 1977 joined American International Pictures as head of East Coast production. Three years later he teamed with Grosso.

In 1988 their company reorganized as Grosso-Jacobson Entertainment Corp., with William P. D'Angelo as president of the production subsidiary based in Hollywood.

GROUP W ▶ corporate sobriquet for Westinghouse Broadcasting Co. adopted in the mid-1960s to emphasize the group, or multiple-station owner, as a force in broadcasting separate from the networks and individual stations. The new name was sought also because the company initials, WBC, had the ring of station call letters. Under the leadership of Donald H. McGannon, its chairman and president (1955-82), Group W became both prosperous and a power in the industry, for many years recognized as the leading broadcast organization after the three networks.

The power derives partly from the fact that Westinghouse TV stations are concentrated in major markets and are affiliated, variously, with all three networks. This not only gives Group W a voice in the policies of each network but makes it privy to the philosophies and secrets of each.

Moreover, McGannon, who earlier had been an executive with the DuMont Network, was a model broadcaster and earned the status of an industry statesman, a tradition continued by his successors, Daniel Ritchie and Burt Staniar. McGannon gained credibility in Washington for having run a profitable business, while at the same time championing news and public affairs programming.

Group W was also a successful producer and distributor of programs for general syndication and was the source of such talk shows as *The Mike Douglas Show, The Merv Griffin Show, The David Frost Show* and, earlier, *The Steve Allen Show.* Since McGannon was a leading figure in persuading the FCC to adopt the prime time-access rule, limiting the networks to three hours of programming in the peak viewing period, his Group W Productions initially produced syndicated programs for the prime-access period.

Variety dubbed Group W "the Harvard Business School of Television" because so many of its executives went on to head other broadcast groups or to assume high positions at the networks.

Group W dropped cigarette advertising on its stations six months before those commercials were ordered off the air. It also led the opposition of affiliated stations to the networks' proposals to expand their evening newscasts to an hour and it filed a petition on Sept. 3, 1976, asking the FCC to institute a comprehensive inquiry and rule-making procedure into the increasing control of the medium by the three networks.

McGannon, retaining the title of chairman, yielded the titles of president and chief executive officer to Daniel Ritchie in 1979. Ritchie's mandate was to harness the emerging communications technologies for the company's expansion. He moved the company into the new age by acquiring Teleprompter Corp., the second largest cable company, and creating a cable satellite network division, which entered into partnership with ABC in establishing two cable news networks to compete with CNN. Later they were purchased by Ted Turner and immediately were shut down.

In the mid-1970s, Group W produced and syndicated a unique programming cooperative, *PM Magazine* (known as *Evening Magazine* on Group W's own TV stations), a long-running series that made extensive use of ENG cameras in its production and started the careers of numerous producers and performers, including Mary Hart and Maria Shriver. Group W also produced the successfully syndicated daytime program, *Hour Magazine,* and such animated children's shows as *He-Man and the Masters of the Universe* and, in the 1990s, the phenomenally successful *Teenage Mutant Ninja Turtles.*

In 1986 the company sold off its cable systems, and Ritchie retired the following year. Burt Staniar, who had been president of Group

W Cable, was named to succeed Ritchie. Staniar moved Group W Productions into the international sphere, expanded the services of the Satellite Communications group to the cable industry, took an equity position in a number of cable program services, including pay-per-view, and increased the company's portfolio of radio stations to 14. With the acquisition of eight in 1990, Group W became the largest non-network radio operator in the country.

Both Ritchie and Staniar continued the company's early commitment to public service programming. The TV stations group developed a series of public service campaigns—packages of well-focused programs and public service spots—that were offered to stations nationally, serving both to educate viewers on a vital topic and build a public-spirited identity for the stations in their markets. The most popular of these was the *For Kids' Sake* campaign that ran three years in more than 100 markets. Other campaigns dealt with Alzheimer's disease, volunteerism in one's community, and AIDS. Developed at KPIX in San Francisco, *AIDS Lifeline* was distributed nationally as probably the first AIDS education and awareness campaign on television.

Group W owns and operates two CBS affiliates, KDKA Pittsburgh and KPIX San Francisco; two NBC affiliates, WBZ Boston and KYW Philadelphia; and one ABC affiliate, WJZ Baltimore.

GROWING PAINS ▶ a popular family sitcom produced by Warner Bros. for ABC. When the show debuted in September 1985, critics were skeptical of its chances for survival. The star, former talk show host Alan Thicke, seemed ill-suited to the role of Jason Seaver, a psychiatrist-father who practices at home and minds the kids while his wife, Maggie (Joanna Kerns), goes back to work. The show, however, has proven durable, in part because of the teenage appeal of the previously unknown actor, Kirk Cameron. As the son, Mike, he has become a teenage heartthrob and the central figure of the show. The show's original writing team, Neal Marlens and Carol Black, went on to create *The Wonder Years.*

GRUNDY, REG ▶ one of Australia's most successful independent producers in the global marketplace; he has done especially well with soap operas and game shows. His five-a-week soap, *Neighbours,* became a big hit in England in the late 1980s, airing in the early evening hours, and has achieved a devoted following there. The show is also successful throughout Europe. Grundy's company, Grundy International, is also active in international coproductions and has set up production bases in 11 countries, including the U.S., France, Germany, Holland and Spain. In 1991 Grundy tried to buy Australia's Seven Network from the receivers, but his effort failed. His company is based now in Bermuda, where it is in tax exile.

GUDE, JOHN ▶ one-time CBS publicist who became an agent in the 1940s representing such leading news figures as Edward R. Murrow, Raymond Gram Swing and Elmer Davis. It was Gude who brought Murrow into collaboration with Fred W. Friendly, then an obscure radio producer in Rhode Island, for the spoken-history record album *I Can Hear It Now.* That grew into the long Murrow-Friendly partnership on radio's *Hear It Now* and TV's *See It Now.*

GUIDING LIGHT, THE ▶ see Soap Operas.

GUMBEL, BRYANT ▶ a former sportscaster whose intelligence and amiable manner earned him one of the plum assignments at NBC in 1982, anchor of the early morning *Today* show. He has held the post ever since and today owns one of the network's fattest contracts. His credentials in news seemed scant when he became anchor of *Today,* joining a distinguished line that includes Hugh Downs, John Chancellor, Tom Brokaw and Barbara Walters. But Gumbel early on proved himself sufficiently adept at interviewing news figures, and he brought a certain smoothness to the two-hour live daily broadcast. He has traveled widely to report on important international stories from the scene.

Gumbel joined the company in 1972 as a sportscaster for its Los Angeles station, KNBC. Three years later he became host of the NFL pre-game show for NBC Sports, and then was assigned coverage of baseball, basketball and football. His association with *Today* began in 1980, when he was brought on three times a week for a sports report. His promotion to anchor followed the success of that featured segment.

GUMBEL, GREG ▶ host, with former Pittsburgh Steeler Terry Bradshaw, of CBS Sports' *The NFL Today.* Gumbel joined CBS full-time in 1989 after eight years of part-time assignments handling play-by-play on NFL games and college and NBA basketball. He was sports anchor at WMAQ-TV Chicago from 1973 to

1981, then joined ESPN, where he served as co-anchor of *SportsCenter* and hosted *The Week in the NBA* and *The NBA Tonight.* In 1976 he hosted New York Knicks basketball and New York Yankees baseball games and three weekly shows for the Madison Square Garden Network (MSG). In addition to hosting *The NFL Today,* he has hosted major league baseball and college studio shows and provided play-by-play for the College World Series championship games. He is also co-host of CBS's weekday morning coverage of the Olympic Winter Games. He is the brother of Bryant Gumbel, host of NBC's *Today.*

Greg Gumbel

GUNN, HARTFORD N., JR. (d. 1986) ▶ vice-chairman of PBS (1976-79) after having been its first president (1970-76). Earlier he had been general manager of WGBH, the Boston public station. As PBS president Gunn devised the basic plan for the Station Program Cooperative, the apparatus by which member stations chose the national programming for nearly two decades. He also spearheaded the plan for the interconnection of PBS stations by domestic satellite. In 1979, he became the architect of PBS's reorganization as a network, devising the plan by which three program services would be fed out simultaneously over the satellite: one for entertainment and cultural programs, another for educational and instructional programs and a third for special-interest and regional programs.

***GUNS OF AUTUMN* ▶** 90-minute CBS News documentary on hunting (Sept. 5, 1975) that drew letters of condemnation and praise even before the telecast. It aired with virtually no advertising because of a campaign by gun enthusiasts upon the scheduled advertisers. Only Block Drugs, among the advertisers, would not be intimidated. The letters of protest, which came from the National Rifle Association and other pro-gun organizations, expressed certainty in advance of the telecast that the program would be unfavorable to their interests. Although CBS professed to cover the issue of hunting dispassionately and in a balanced manner, several scenes of sheer brutality sufficed for a powerful indictment.

The program was produced, directed and written by Irv Drasnin and narrated by Dan Rather. Perry Wolff was executive producer.

***GUNSMOKE* ▶** classic western built around the fictional Matt Dillon, Marshal of Dodge City, which had a 20-year run on CBS (1955-75) after having established itself as a Saturday night staple on radio. Beginning as a Saturday night half hour, it was expanded in 1961 to a full hour. The series survived a planned cancellation in the late 1960s when William S. Paley, board chairman of CBS, overruled the network's program council and ordered the program reinstated on Monday nights at 7:30. There it was reborn as a hit, placing among the top three series in popularity for several seasons. James Arness starred as the marshal, whose deputy (Chester B. Goode) in the early years was played by Dennis Weaver. Amanda Blake was Kitty Russell, the love interest, for 19 seasons, and Milburn Stone portrayed the running character Doc Adams. Other regulars were Kent Curtis as Festus Haggen, Buck Taylor as Newly O'Brian and Glenn Strange as bartender Sam. The series was owned and produced by CBS.

GURNEE, HAL ▶ director whose credits include *Tonight, The Jack Paar Show, That Was the Week That Was, The Garry Moore Show, The Jimmy Dean Show, The Joey Bishop Show* and the Emmy Awards telecast.

GUY LOMBARDO AND NEW YEAR'S EVE ▶ a radio and TV tradition for ushering in the New Year, which was passed among the networks over the years and became a live syndicated entry by Worldvision in the 1970s. The program featured the dance music of Lombardo and his orchestra, the Royal Canadians, from the ballroom of the Waldorf-Astoria in New York, with shots of the New Year's Eve revelers in Times Square and a countdown of the seconds to midnight with the globe atop the Allied Chemical Tower (originally called Times Tower).

The first of Lombardo's New Year's Eve broadcasts ushered in the year 1930 from the Hotel Roosevelt, the site of many of his later radio broadcasts. In later years, the program emanated from Grand Central Station before settling into the Waldorf. Lombardo reputedly started the tradition of associating *Auld Lang Syne* with New Year's Eve. Though Lombardo died in 1977, the tradition continued.

H

HAGERTY, JAMES C. (d. 1981) ▶ ABC executive who joined the network as v.p. in charge of news and public affairs in 1961 following eight years of service as President Eisenhower's press secretary, a job he handled with distinction and in which he was popular with the press corps. In 1963 he was elevated by ABC to v.p. of corporate relations and served as a liaison to the Nixon White House; Hagerty had come to know Richard Nixon well while he was Eisenhower's vice-president. Illness forced Hagerty into retirement in the early 1970s.

HAGMAN, LARRY ▶ actor whose perfect portrayal of J. R. Ewing, the scheming, amoral anti-hero of *Dallas,* was a big reason the CBS nighttime serial was a huge success and a Friday night fixture for over 12 years. Though the character was disreputable and even hateful, Hagman made him fascinating, an extraordinary achievement in a program that was essentially a soap opera. Previously he had played the male lead in the successful sitcom *I Dream of Jeannie* (1965-70). In the years between those hit shows he starred in two fleeting sitcoms, *The Good Life* and *Here We Go Again.*

Hagman, who has appeared in movies and on the stage, is the son of the late Broadway star, Mary Martin.

HAIMOVITZ, JULES ▶ president of Spelling Entertainment known for his business acumen and ability to turn small assets into large revenues. He helped do so in various positions at Viacom from 1976 to 1988.

Haimovitz began his career at ABC, where he worked in the research department. He joined Viacom in 1976 as director of planning for pay television, helping to launch the pay-cable service Showtime. In 1981 he became v.p. of Viacom International, where he oversaw the MTV Networks and Nickelodeon. He worked in tandem with Ron Lightstone, who eventually moved with Haimovitz to Aaron Spelling's organization.

Jules Haimovitz

HAITI INVASION PLOT ▶ 1966 episode for which CBS was censured following a 1970 House Investigations Subcommittee probe. CBS News had been charged with financing a plot by Caribbean exiles to invade Haiti for the sake of exclusive news coverage of the invasion. CBS denied the charge but admitted paying $1,000 for the maintenance of a three-man news crew on the invasion boat. The network was censured for encouraging the illegal invasion scheme and was charged by the subcommittee with staging scenes for use in a documentary.

HALEY, JACK, JR. ▶ one-time president of 20th Century-Fox TV (from Sept. 1975-June 1976), succeeding Bill Self. The son of actor-comedian Jack Haley (*The Wizard of Oz*), he had been a producer, director and writer of movies and TV programs before joining Fox. Haley worked for Wolper Productions (1959-70), Paramount Pictures, Columbia Pictures and MGM. In TV, he directed a notable Nancy Sinatra special, *Movin' with Nancy* (1967), and in the same year a National Geographic special on insects, *The Hidden World.* His biggest movie was *That's Entertainment* (1974), a knitting together of old MGM movie scenes, which was a box-office smash. In 1976 Haley started his own independent company, which produced a raft of made-for-TV movies and specials.

HALL, MONTY ▶ TV personality known particularly for hosting the hit game show *Let's Make a Deal.* A native of Canada, he began his television career there as emcee and producer of the long-running *Who Am I?* After coming to the U.S. he worked on such shows as *Strike It Rich,* NBC Radio's *Monitor, Video Village* and *Your First Impression.* His popularity through *Let's Make a Deal* led to a Las Vegas nightclub engagement and specials for ABC's *Wide World of Entertainment.*

HALL, WILSON (d. 1990) ▶ longtime NBC News correspondent who joined in 1951 and left in 1978 to head the journalism department at the University of Tennessee. In his first NBC assignment he covered the Middle East from the Cairo bureau. Later he was sent to Cuba, Brazil and Lebanon. After some 20 years of foreign assignments, he returned to the U.S. and worked in NBC's Washington bureau from 1973-78.

HALLMARK CARDS INC. ▶ sponsor of quality dramas, usually of the pastel type, continuously since 1952; but also in latter years a broadcaster and cable operator. A privately held company based in Kansas City, Hallmark made a surprise entry into station ownership in 1987, buying the Spanish International Communications Corp. with its nine Spanish-language stations for $286 million. This put the all-American, midwestern greeting card company into the business of programming and marketing to U.S. Hispanics. A year later it bought Univision Inc., a Spanish programming network, from its Mexican owners for $265 million. Then in the fall of 1991, through its Crown Media subsidiary, Hallmark bought Cencom Cable, whose systems have 550,000 subscribers, for around $1 billion. Added to the 150,000 subscribers of the Wisconsin systems in which Hallmark already had a stake, the acquisition of Cencom made Crown Media one of the top fifty cable concerns in the country.

Keith Carradine and Glenn Close in "Stones for Ibarra," a *Hallmark Hall of Fame* presentation

HALLMARK HALL OF FAME ▶ long-running series of drama specials that began on NBC in 1952 and that over its course has presented some of the medium's most distinguished programs. Its productions—mostly in 90-minute form and offered at the rate of three or four a year—have ranged from Shakespeare, Shaw and Gilbert & Sullivan to modern adaptations from the stage and original plays, the casts made up of leading actors of the American and British stages.

The series ended its exclusive relationship with NBC after the 1978-79 season by mutual agreement. NBC was anxious to be rid of the prestigious series because its low ratings were hampering the network's overall prime-time strategies; Hallmark, meanwhile, was unhappy with the time periods it was being assigned by NBC.

In the 1979-80 season, CBS began airing the *Hall of Fame* specials at the rate of two a season, and scored well with them. Nearly all that played on CBS ranked among the top specials that season: *All Quiet on the Western Front* and *Aunt Mary* in 1979-80, *Gideon's Trumpet* and *A Tale of Two Cities* in 1980-81, and *The Hunchback of Notre Dame* in 1981-82.

The presentations generally are timed for holiday seasons, which are peak marketing times for the sponsor, Hallmark Cards Inc. Although ratings for the plays frequently fall below the base line of success in prime time, the *Hall of Fame* series has proved an immensely effective vehicle for the sponsor. Ratings aside, the company is frequently praised in the press reviews of the shows—a large publicity dividend that TV's scatter-plan advertisers do not receive. Moreover, the quality of the shows reflect on the company and suggest a quality product.

Because of such benefits it scarcely mattered that the productions for the 1961-62 season (*Macbeth, Victoria Regina, Arsenic and Old Lace* and *Give Us Barabbas*) averaged only a 14.5 rating and that those from 1975-76 (*Eric, Valley Forge, The Rivalry, Caesar and Cleopatra* and *Truman at Potsdam*) averaged 14.2. Some of the seasons between were considerably better, averaging as high as 19.0, and some considerably worse, at 11.5, but Hallmark continually reaffirmed its commitment to the series.

Hallmark's beginnings in TV were an extension of its sponsorship of *Hallmark Playhouse* on radio. In January 1952 Sara Churchill hosted *Hallmark Television Playhouse,* a weekly series of half-hour shows. Just before that, however, on Christmas Eve of 1951, Hallmark sponsored NBC's initial production of Gian Carlo Menotti's *Amahl and the Night Visitors,* the first opera to be commissioned for TV, and that signaled the direction it would take in the medium. Hallmark had shifted to a schedule of ambitious productions under the *Hall of Fame* banner.

Over the years Hallmark has presented 10 productions of six works by Shakespeare—*Hamlet* (the first in 1953 with Maurice Evans, the last in 1970 with Richard Chamberlain), *Macbeth, Richard II, The Taming of the Shrew,* and *The Tempest.* There were also six by George Bernard Shaw: *The Devil's Disciple, Man and Superman, Captain Brassbound's Conversion, Pygmalion, Saint Joan* and *Caesar and Cleopatra.*

Among Broadway shows it has offered *Kiss Me Kate, Ah! Wilderness, Arsenic and Old Lace, The Fantasticks, Inherit the Wind, Teahouse of the August Moon, Harvey, The Price, All the Way Home* and *The Green Pastures.*

Outstanding original productions included Rod Serling's *A Storm in Summer,* Allan Slone's *Teacher, Teacher,* James Costigan's *Little Moon of Alban,* John Nuefeld's *Lisa Bright and Dark* and Sherman Yellen's *Beauty and the Beast.*

Mildred Freed Alberg was executive producer of the series for many years and Maurice Evans a frequent director; together they set a standard that was maintained by George Schaefer and others who later assumed charge.

Hallmark switched networks in 1979 for the first time in 27 years. Unable to secure desirable time periods and suitable properties at NBC, in a time when the network was concerned with boosting its ratings, the sponsor bought the three-hour remake on CBS of *All Quiet on the Western Front* for a fall air date. Hallmark explained that it was not severing ties with NBC but would henceforth deal with all three networks to fulfill its advertising needs.

The next two specials, however, wound up on PBS in 1981: *Mister Lincoln* and *Casey Stengel.* For the next decade, all but one of its shows appeared on CBS, including *Sarah, Plain and Tall,* which proved to be the network's highest-rated movie of the 1990-91 season. Among the other *Hallmark* shows to air on CBS were *Witness for the Prosecution* (1983), Steinbeck's *Winter of Our Discontent* (1983), *The Secret Garden* (1987), *Foxfire* (1987), *Stones for Ibarra* (1988), and *April Morning* (1988). Two specials, both starring James Garner and James Woods, drew particular critical praise for their treatment of social problems: *Promise* (1986), the story of a man caring for his mentally ill brother , and *My Name Is Bill W.* (1989), the story of the founder of Alcoholics Anonymous and the one *Hallmark* entry to play on ABC.

HALLS OF IVY ▶ syndicated vehicle (1954-55) for Ronald Colman, about the president of an Ivy League college. Produced by T.P.A. Hall Productions, it featured Colman as President William Todhunter Hall and Benita Hume as his wife, Victoria Cromwell Hall.

HALMI, ROBERT ▶ one-time *Life* photographer who became a noted TV producer, mostly in the made-for-TV movie field. A principal network credit was the CBS series *Nurse* (1981-82). He has also produced such programs as *Cook & Peary: The Race To the Pole, China Rose, Mrs. Lambert Remembers Love, Eyes of a Witness, The Incident, Face To Face, Pack of Lies, Trouble In Paradise, Barnum, Mayflower Madam, Izzy & Moe, Alone In the Neon Jungle, Nairobi Affair,* and *The Murders In the Rue Morgue.* Halmi was also one of the producers of *Lonesome Dove* and in 1991 was part of the group (which included CBS, Reteitalia, and Beta Film) that paid $8 million for the rights to *Scarlett,* the book created as a sequel to *Gone With the Wind.* This positioned him as principal producer of the mini-series, which would be an international coproduction.

Halmi has worked under a number of logos. For a time in the 1980s he was affiliated with Hal Roach Studios. Later the Halmi and Roach companies were acquired by the Australian conglomerate Qintex, but Qintex ran into financial difficulties and the American companies were divested. After that Halmi reestablished his private company under the rubric RHI Entertainment.

HAMILTON, JOE (d. 1991) ▶ Carol Burnett's ex-husband, who was executive producer of her series. Among his other producing credits were *The Garry Moore Show* in the 1960s, *The Smothers Brothers Show* in the 1970s and *The Tim Conway Show* in 1980. He also produced *Mama's Family* (1983-85), a spin-off from the Burnett show.

HAMNER, EARL, Jr. ▶ writer of serious dramas, whose *The Homecoming* gave forth *The Waltons* series, for which he served as narrator and executive story consultant. He also created the series *Apple's Way* and *Falcon Crest,* serving as co-executive producer of the latter, and he wrote the script for *A Dream for Christmas.*

HAMPTON, HENRY ▶ founder and president of Boston-based Blackside Inc. and executive producer of the Emmy Award-winning PBS series *Eyes on the Prize* and *Eyes on the Prize II.* Hampton's first-hand encounter with the civil rights struggle in the South happened in 1965 while he was press officer for the Unitarian Church. The experience left him determined to use television to tell the story of the turbulent times and to give voice to the aspirations of African-Americans, and Hampton acted on that determination by forming Blackside productions in 1968. The idea for *Eyes on the Prize* was born in 1979 but the series was ten years in the making, largely because of the difficulties in aggregating the $2.5 million to produce it.

HAMSTER PRODUCTIONS ▶ one of France's leading independent production companies, whose work is estimated to represent around 15% of the country's independent market. Hamster is run by Pierre Grimblat, a veteran of the French television industry who gets primary backing from the Luxembourg media giant, CLT. ABC Video Enterprises, a division of Capital Cities/ABC, bought a 25% stake in the company in 1989, and HTV of Britain owns 14%. Hamster's ownership is emblematic of the company's international outlook and its intention to produce not just for France but for a world market, as typified by the detective series *Navarro.*

HANGEN, WELLES ▶ foreign correspondent for NBC News, and previously for *The New York Times.* Reported missing in Vietnam in 1970 while on assignment for the network, he is believed dead. Unconfirmed reports had said that he, an NBC soundman and a CBS cameraman had been killed in an ambush set by the North Vietnamese. Hangen joined NBC in 1956 and had worked out of Hong Kong since 1966.

HANNA-BARBERA PRODUCTIONS ▶ principal producer of TV animated cartoons headed by Joseph Barbera and William Hanna, who established the California firm in 1957. During its 35-year history it has produced more than 300 half-hours of animated programming and more than 350 different series. Its productions are syndicated in 80 countries, the most widely circulated being *The Flintstones* and *Yogi Bear.* The company was acquired in 1987 by Great American Communications Co.; in 1991 GACC sold Hanna-Barbera to Turner Broadcasting System and Apollo Investment Fund. Former independent producer David Kirschner became the head of operations in 1989, while Hanna and Barbera remained co-chairmen of the studio.

At a time when soaring costs of full animation forced the closing of most cartoon-producing studios in Hollywood, Hanna-Barbera developed a cheaper method which helped it to dominate the animation market. The system reduced lip movements to simple cycles—vowel to vowel, ignoring consonants entirely—and held body movements to a minimum. This animation stressed plot action and ignored the time-consuming and expensive detail that was superfluous on the small TV screen.

For 20 years prior to the incorporation of Hanna-Barbera Productions, the pair had created and produced the noted *Tom and Jerry* theatrical series of cartoons for MGM. H-B's first TV effort on their own, *Ruff and Reddy,* was followed quickly by *Huckleberry Hound,* which became an immediate success. These led to *The Flintstones,* the "stone-age" situation comedy, and then *The Jetsons,* both of which were big hits in prime time. Other H-B series were *The Pebbles and Bam Bam Show, Yogi's Gang, The New Adventures of Huckleberry Finn, The Banana Splits Adventure Hour, Scooby Doo, Jonny Quest, Top Cat, Magilla Gorilla* and *Quick Draw McGraw.*

Barbera was at first a New York banker, but also a doodler and dreamer who started submitting gag drawings to leading magazines and eventually became a regular contributor. At the first sign of success, he quit banking and mastered animation, then moved to Hollywood to work with MGM—where William Hanna happened to be employed.

Hanna was a structural engineer until he found himself unemployed during the Depression and turned to cartooning. He went to work for Leon Schlessinger's cartoon company in Hollywood and in 1937 was hired away by MGM to be a director and story developer in the cartoon department. Barbera was employed at the same studio as an animator and writer.

Hanna and Barbera began their collaboration in 1938, first in the production of a single, six-minute animated short. Then they created a cartoon entitled *Puss Gets the Boot,* involving a cat and mouse conflict. This subsequently became the *Tom and Jerry* series.

HAPPY DAYS ▶ ABC situation comedy (1974-84) that initially traded on youthful nostalgia for teenage life in the 1950s. Two years after its introduction it exploded into TV's number-one hit, with the focus shifting from a middle-class family to a street-wise tough named Arthur "Fonzie" Fonzarelli, played by Henry Winkler. The series at first centered on the Cunningham family in Milwaukee, and particularly on the teenaged son, Ritchie, played by Ron Howard, and his friends (Anson Williams as Potsie Webber and Danny Most as Ralph Malph). Tom Bosley and Marion Ross played the parents, Howard and Marion, and Erin Moran played little sister Joanie. (An older brother, Chuck, was played first by Gavan O'Herlihy and then by Randolph Roberts but was dropped after the first season.)

During the program's second season, Fonzie, at first a supporting character, caught the fancy of youthful viewers, and the series began to build around him.

It was a Miller-Milkis production in association with Paramount TV, with Thomas L. Miller, Edward K. Milkis and Garry Marshall as executive producers and Tony Marshall and Jerry Paris as producers. Early in 1976 the series spun off a companion hit, *Laverne and Shirley,* which on occasion was cross-pollinated with Fonzie. In 1982, *Joanie Loves Chachi* was spun unsuccessfully off the series.

The reruns of the series, offered in syndication on a "futures" basis while the program was still on ABC, drew record prices. WPIX New York agreed to pay $35,000 an episode, KHBK-TV San Francisco $20,000, and WTTG Washington $15,000.

Henry Winkler and Ron Howard in a scene from *Happy Days*

HAPPY TALK NEWS ▶ derisive characterization of the style of local newscasts, popular in the 1970s, in which the reporters exchange banter between news items. Apart from permitting scarce news time to be consumed by small talk and clowning, the style lent itself to extreme bad taste, as when reports on tragedies were followed by light-hearted repartee. The informal, ensemble approach to newscasting—which in extreme instances involved fun-loving teams dressed alike in blazers, jolly comrades-in-news—swept the country because it allowed last-place stations to overtake the long-established news leaders almost overnight. In self-defense, stations that had prided themselves on serious newscasting and on their journalistic credibility gave in to the trend. The practitioners preferred to call it by other names, such as "eyewitness" or "action" news.

HARD DOCUMENTARY/SOFT DOCUMENTARY ▶ "hard" includes the probing and muckraking documentary on major issues of public importance, as well as in-depth examinations of significant news events or trends; "soft" is without urgency and deals with customs, fashions, sports, culture, history or natural phenomena. Hard documentaries usually provoke controversy; soft documentaries frequently are closer to general nonfiction than to journalism.

HARD NEWS ▶ daily reporting, the occurrences and topical matters covered factually by journalists as items for the regular newscasts. This is as opposed to feature material which also may appear in a newscast, such as opinion pieces (editorials, commentary and reviews), essays, trend stories and human interest items not directly related to international, national or local affairs.

HARDY BOYS, THE **▶** ABC adventure series for children (1977-79), never better than a marginal performer in the ratings, which featured Shaun Cassidy as Joe and Parker Stevenson as Frank. The series was based on the numerous *Hardy Boys* adventure books turned out by Franklin W. Dixon five generations earlier. ABC scheduled it in the early Sunday evening hour, the period designated by the FCC's prime time-access rule for children's shows or public affairs, but it proved no match for CBS's *60 Minutes.*

Initially, the series alternated with *The Nancy Drew Mysteries* and was itself entitled *The Hardy Boys Mysteries.* They premiered in January 1977 as mid-season replacements and were renewed for the fall. *Nancy Drew,* which starred Pamela Sue Martin (later replaced by Janet Louise Johnson) and William Schallert, was not renewed for the 1978-79 season, and *Mysteries* was trimmed from the *Hardy Boys* title. To no avail. The show was a mid-season casualty and ended its run in January 1979.

The series were via Glen Larson Productions, in association with Universal, MCA. Larson was executive producer of both. Michael Sloan was producer, with Arlene Sidaris and Joyce Brotman credited as coproducers.

HARGROVE, DEAN ▶ writer turned producer in the Universal TV stable, with initial credits on *The Name of the Game, McCloud* and *Columbo.* He became executive producer, with Roland Kibbee, of *Columbo* in 1974-75 and the following season of *The Family Holvak* and *McCoy.* Alone, he was executive producer of *Madigan.* During the 1980s and early 1990s, Hargrove's credits included *Matlock, Jake and the Fatman* and the *Perry Mason* movies.

HARLEY, WILLIAM G. ▶ first president of the National Association of Educational Broadcasters (NAEB), who established its headquarters in Washington in 1960 and was chief executive of the association until he retired in 1975. He was succeeded by James A. Fellows, former executive director of NAEB.

HARMON, MARK ▶ actor who has starred in five series, including *Sam* (1978), *240 Robert* (1979-80), *Flamingo Road* (1980-82), *St. Elsewhere* (1983-86) and *Reasonable Doubts* (1991—). He has appeared in several made-for-TV movies, notably *Eleanor and Franklin: The White House Years* (1977) and *Dillinger* (1990-91). His mini-series include leading roles in *Centennial* (1978), *After the Promise* (1987-88) and *The Deliberate Stranger* (1986).

HARPER, VALERIE ▶ actress best known for her portrayal of Rhoda Morgenstern on *The Mary Tyler Moore Show* (1970-74), a part that led to the MTM spinoff, *Rhoda* (1974-78). When the show was canceled, she made a string of TV movies and in 1986 launched another sitcom, *Valerie.* But that series had hardly begun when she left in a dispute with the production company, Lorimar, and was replaced by Sandy Duncan.

HARRINGTON, JOHN B., JR. (d. 1973) ▶ of Harrington, Righter & Parsons (HRP), first station representative firm to handle only TV stations. He and his partners, James O. Parsons, Jr., and Volney Righter, had been with Edward Perry & Co. before starting their own sales representative company in 1949. Harrington retired in 1970.

HARRIS, HARRY ▶ director with extensive credits on prime-time series, including *The Waltons, Kung-Fu, Gunsmoke, Perry Mason, Naked City, Apple's Way* and *Marcus Welby, M.D.*

HARRIS, STAN ▶ producer-director; credits include *The Dick Van Dyke Show, The Smothers Brothers Comedy Hour, That's Life, The Melba Moore Show, The Midnight Special, Music Scene* and *Duke Ellington—We Love You, Madly.*

HARRIS, SUSAN ▶ one of television's hottest writers during the late 1980s and early 1990s, so steeped in success she could sell almost anything she wanted to the networks. In the 1991-92 season she had three hits on NBC—*The Golden Girls, Empty Nest* and *Nurses*—and

Good & Evil on ABC. She made her mark in the 1970s as creator of ABC's *Soap*. Her sitcom series are produced by Witt-Thomas-Harris Productions, which is aligned with Touchstone TV.

Harris's husband, Paul Junger Witt, and Tony Thomas have a separate production company for non-Harris projects, Witt-Thomas Productions. They had *Beauty and the Beast* on CBS in the late 1980s and *Blossom* on NBC in 1991.

HARRY O ▶ hour-long police series on ABC (1974-75) set in San Diego and featuring David Janssen as private eye Harry Orwell, Henry Darrow as police detective Manny Quinlan and Anthony Zerbe as police lieutenant K.C. Trench. The pilot played as a TV movie called *Smile, Jenny, You're Dead.* It was by Warner Bros.

HART, JOHN ▶ veteran correspondent for CBS and NBC who in 1988 became anchor for *World Monitor,* a nightly news program on the Discovery Channel produced by *The Christian Science Monitor.* Hart had actually left the networks several years earlier to anchor a syndicated newscast. He resigned from *World Monitor* in 1991.

HARTFORD PAY-TV EXPERIMENT ▶ one of the major tests of pay TV in the U.S. prior to the FCC's authorization of full-time subscription TV operations (December 1968). The experiment was conducted by Zenith Radio Corp., with its Phonevision system, and RKO General on its Hartford, Conn., UHF station, WHCT, between June 1962 and January 1969. RKO paid the expenses for the test.

The fare consisted of movies at a charge of $.50 to $1.50 per film; sports, cultural events and variety performances at $ 1 to $3; and educational courses at $.25 to $1. Approximately 2% of the TV homes in the area subscribed, and the average subscriber spent only around $1.25 a week for pay programs. As a business venture the Hartford test was a failure with so little penetration into the potential audience, but as a test it revealed that movies would be the dominant programming for pay TV with sports next in importance.

Troubles continued to plague WHCT long after the pay-TV test ended. Until 1981, the station was operated by idiosyncratic California televangelist Dr. EuGene Scott. Facing FCC revocation proceedings, he opted to sell to a minority broadcaster under the FCC's "distress sale" policy. A white male challenger, Alan Shurberg, brought the case to the United States Supreme Court, which ruled in 1990 that the agency's minority ownership preferences are permissible (*Metro Broadcasting Inc. v. FCC*).

HARTMAN, DAVID ▶ TV actor who became a talk-show host when ABC tapped him to anchor its two-hour morning strip, *Good Morning, America,* on Nov. 3, 1975. The renovation of the program (previously called *A.M. America*), which included Hartman's services, boosted its lagging ratings. Hartman has been featured in several prime-time series and played the lead in NBC's *Lucas Tanner* during the 1974 season.

He left *Good Morning, America* in 1987 in a revamp of program and has since concentrated on prime-time specials produced by his own company, Rodman-Downs. Those have included *The Constitution: We Live It Every Day, Early Warning, Seasons of Life* (a five-hour series for PBS) and *Winds of Freedom* for ABC.

HARTZ, JIM ▶ NBC newsman who, for two years (1974-76), served as co-host of *Today,* then became a roving reporter for the program. In 1977, he became co-anchor with Sue Simmons of the local newscasts on WRC-TV Washington, an NBC o&o. Before joining *Today,* Hartz had worked chiefly in local news, initially as a reporter (starting in 1964) and later as anchor for the newscasts on WNBC-TV New York. Since 1981 he has been the host of *Innovation* on PBS.

HARVEST OF SHAME ▶ outstanding investigative hour-long documentary on CBS (Nov. 25, 1960) that revealed the suffering of, and inhumanities against, the agricultural migrant workers in the U.S. and their impoverished families. Edward R. Murrow was the reporter, David Lowe the producer and Fred W. Friendly executive producer.

HARVEY, PAUL ▶ conservative news commentator based in Chicago who for many years had syndicated a successful five-minute TV strip, *Paul Harvey Comments,* which began in 1968. In the 1970s the program was carried in around 100 markets and had a devoted audience in certain parts of the country. In the 1980s, Harvey became one of the country's top radio personalities. Harvey continues his association with ABC Radio, which he had joined in 1944, as news analyst and commentator. In addition, he has written a syndicated newspaper column since 1954.

HASHMARK ▶ in local rating reports, a graphic symbol where normally a number would be, signifying that the program had an audience too small to measure by the methods used. Programs that score hashmarks are usually doomed.

HAUSER, GUSTAVE M. ▶ former chairman and chief operating officer of Warner Amex Cable Corp. (1973-83) and since then chairman of Hauser Communications. A Harvard lawyer, he previously held executive positions with Western Union Intl. and GT&E Intl. and earlier was international affairs counsel for the U.S. Defense Department.

Hauser was the moving force behind Qube, the futuristic interactive cable system that began its commercial test in Columbus, Ohio, in December 1977. It was he who authorized the $20 million test and who shepherded the project almost daily to determine which aspects of it could be turned into profitable businesses. The national attention gained for Qube helped Warner Amex with franchises in Cincinnati, Pittsburgh, Dallas, Houston, and New York.

In 1979 Hauser formed his own cable company, gaining the franchises initially for communities in suburban Washington, D.C. From there Hauser Communications grew to a sizable MSO, ranking 40th in total subscribers in 1991.

***HAVE GUN, WILL TRAVEL* ▶** western hit produced by CBS (1957-62) that rose above the rash of sagebrush series on the networks because of its unusual protagonist, Paladin, an erudite loner who hires out his shooting skills and carries business cards. The inscrutable character was played with finesse by Richard Boone. Paladin's servant, Hey Boy, was portrayed by Kam Tong.

The series, however, brought a successful plagiarism suit from an arena performer who not only billed himself as Paladin and distributed "Have Gun, Will Travel" cards but also bore a strong resemblance to Boone. The courts awarded him damages in 1974, but that was overturned on appeal. The case continued to be pursued and finally was settled in 1991, after 34 years, with an award of more than $3 million.

***HAWAII FIVE-O* ▶** hard-action police series filmed in Honolulu that was a steady but unspectacular winner for CBS from 1968 to 1980. Produced by Leonard Freeman Productions in association with CBS, it starred Jack Lord as investigator Steve McGarrett and featured James MacArthur as sidekick Danny (Dano) Williams, Kam Fong as Chin Ho Kelly, Richard Denning as governor Keith Jameson, Al Eben as Doc Bergman, Peggy Ryan as secretary Jenny Sherman and Khigh Dhiegh as McGarrett's archenemy, Wo Fat.

Jack Lord as Steve McGarrett in *Hawaii Five-O*

***HAWAIIAN EYE* ▶** Warner Bros. adventure series about private investigators working from a swank Hawaiian hotel; it had a successful run on ABC (1959-63). The leads were Robert Conrad as Thomas Jefferson Lopaka and Anthony Eisley (later replaced by Grant Williams) as Tracy Steele. It featured Connie Stevens as singer Cricket Blake, Troy Donahue as Phil Barton and Poncie Ponce as cab driver Kazuo Kim.

***HAWKINS* ▶** 90-minute series for CBS (1973) designed to rotate with *Shaft* as a vehicle for James Stewart. It cast him as country lawyer Billy Jim Hawkins, renowned as an expert in criminal cases, along with Strother Martin as his cousin, R.J. Hawkins. Produced by Arena Productions in association with MGM-TV, *Hawkins* yielded eight episodes.

HAYDEN, JEFFREY ▶ director whose credits range from *Philco-Goodyear Playhouse, Omnibus* and the Max Liebman specials in the 1950s to *Mannix, Ironside* and *Alias Smith and Jones* in the 1970s.

HAZAM, LOU (d. 1983) ▶ documentary producer for NBC, known for the high quality of his work, chiefly in the humanities. He produced *Shakespeare: Soul of an Age, Vincent Van Gogh, The Way of the Cross* and *Michelangelo: The Last Giant.* He traveled extensively for another genre of documentary, which pre-dated the National Geographic specials. Those included *The River Nile, The Sahara, Japan: East Is West* and *Ganges: Sacred River.*

He also worked extensively in the field of medical documentaries, producing the first programs on TV to visit inside a mental hospital and show the birth of a baby; he also produced the first live telecast of a surgical operation.

He began his career in 1933 as a writer of commercials for J. Walter Thompson and then spent a dozen years as a freelance writer for radio and the Federal government before joining NBC as a radio writer. He entered TV in 1952 as associate producer of the political conventions. Hazam took a year's leave of absence from NBC in 1966 and retired from the network several years later.

***HAZEL* ▶** popular situation comedy derived from the *Saturday Evening Post* cartoons of Ted Key about a maid who runs the family she works for. A vehicle for Shirley Booth, it featured Don DeFore and Whitney Blake as George and Dorothy Baxter and was via Screen Gems. NBC carried it 1961-64, and it shifted to CBS in 1965.

HBO/CINEMAX ▶ oldest and largest pay-cable service, which was a driving force in the growth of cable and in legitimizing cable programming. Home Box Office, a subsidiary of Time Warner, was launched in 1972, programming uncut recent theatrical releases and some sporting events, such as title boxing matches and Wimbledon tennis. The service, which usually retails for about $12, presented the first original movie on cable in May 1983 with *The Terry Fox Story* and has gradually increased its original productions with TV movies and original sitcoms, including two series introduced in 1991, *Dream On* and *Sessions.* Bridget Potter, HBO's senior vice president for original programming, has emerged as a leader in the field. In an effort to counter pay cable's flat rate of growth (HBO stands at 17.3 million subscribers) and meet the promise of cable's expansion to 150 channels in the next few years, HBO began experimenting with multiplexing, beaming three separate and varied feeds of HBO to its affiliate systems. Cinemax, a companion pay channel to HBO, was launched in 1980 and boasts of offering its subscribers more movies than any other service, averaging 140 different titles per month. Cinemax stands at 6.4 million subscribers. Michael Fuchs is chairman and CEO of HBO.

***HE AND SHE* ▶** sophisticated situation comedy about a modern young couple, which won favorable critical notice on CBS (1967) but not an audience. Produced by Talent Associates, it featured Paula Prentiss as career woman Paula Hollister, Richard Benjamin as cartoonist Dick Hollister and Jack Cassidy as actor Oscar North.

***HEAD OF THE CLASS* ▶** a classroom-based sitcom about a group of intellectually gifted New York City high school students, produced by Warner Bros. and airing on ABC from September 1986 to January 1991. The popular show starred Howard Hesseman in the 1986-90 seasons as Charlie Moore, a teacher responsible for the high school's Individual Honors Program. When Hesseman quit the cast after four seasons, comedian Billy Connolly took over the class. The series included an episode shot in the Soviet Union, the first ever by an American TV series. It aired as a one-hour special Nov. 2, 1988. The cast included Robin Givens as Darlene, Khrystyne Haje as Simone, Jory Husain as Jawarhalal, Tony O'Dell as Alan, Kimberly Russell as Sarah, William G. Schilling as Dr. Samuels, and Jeannetta Arnette as Bernadette Meara. Michael Elias and Rich Eustis were executive producers.

HEAD-END ▶ a signal-processing facility, or the electronic control center of a cable-television system, often located at the antenna tower. The term usually refers to the land, the building and the electronic processing equipment normally associated with the starting point of the cable operation.

This center contains all the equipment able to receive off-the-air and microwave signals, to change frequencies and to maintain interface between signals and the cable distribution system.

A master head-end and sub head-end are included in some cable networks, since more than one head-end is required in large urban cable systems.

HEADLINE NEWS ▶ see CNN (Cable News Network).

HEADMASTER ▶ an attempt by CBS in 1970 to find a "socially relevant" vehicle for Andy Griffith, once one of its top stars, at a time when social relevance in comedy series was considered essential for success. He was cast as Andy Thompson, headmaster of a school, with Claudette Nevins as his wife Margaret, Jerry Van Dyke as coach Jerry Brownell and Parker Fennelly as custodian Mr. Purdy. The series, produced by ADA Productions, lasted only 13 weeks.

HEARST CORP. ▶ diversified media company whose interests reach far beyond its newspaper publishing origins. Hearst's television operations include a station group; part ownership of the Arts & Entertainment Network, Lifetime and ESPN; and Hearst Entertainment, a TV production and syndication division (formerly known as King Features Entertainment). The company also owns magazines, including *Esquire, Town and Country* and *Good Housekeeping,* in addition to daily and weekly newspapers.

"HEART" COMEDY ▶ a genre of sentimental situation comedy that enjoyed a vogue in the late 1960s and usually involved a bachelor parent (widowed, not unmarried or divorced) and children who in one moment tugged at the heart and in the next triggered the laugh-track. Typical were *Family Affair, The Courtship of Eddie's Father, To Rome, With Love* and *The Doris Day Show.*

HEE HAW! ▶ free-form country-western comedy show, a cornball version of *Laugh-In,* which enjoyed popularity on CBS (1969-70) but was canceled with high ratings in the network's 1970 purge of its rural-oriented shows. Buck Owens and Roy Clark hosted the show, which featured David (Stringbean) Akeman, Cathy Baker, Barbi Benton, Archie Campbell, Harry Cole, Mackenzie Colt, Don Harron (as Charlie Farquharson), Gunilla Hutton, Louis M. (Grandpa) Jones, Zella Lehr, George Lindsey, Sherry Miles, Minnie Pearl, Jeannine Riley, Lulu Roman, Misty Rowe, Junior Samples, Gailard Sartain, Diana Scott, Roni Stoneham, Gordie Tapp, Lisa Todd, the Hagers and Nashville Edition.

Produced by Yongestreet Productions originally for summer fare in 1969, it did well enough to be inserted in the regular lineup as a replacement in December. Yongestreet continued to produce the series for first-run syndication when the network dropped it, finding a reasonable market for it when the FCC's prime time-access rule went into effect in 1971. The show has since been in syndication.

"HEIDI" INCIDENT ▶ a clash of television events on NBC on a Sunday night in November 1968 that distressed millions of viewers and held the network up to criticism for yielding to the tyranny of the clock. With only a few seconds remaining in a football game between the New York Jets and Oakland Raiders, and the Jets leading 32-29, NBC cut away to present, on time, the scheduled children's special, *Heidi,* in a new TV adaptation. But the Raiders, meanwhile, scored two touchdowns in the final 9 seconds of the game, a thrilling and incredible rally that was lost to viewers in the eastern time zone. So numerous were the calls to the network that the Circle 7 exchange in New York was knocked out of service. As a result of the incident, NBC adopted a policy of televising all football games to the end.

That policy backfired on Nov. 24, 1975, when the coverage of a game between the Raiders and the Washington Redskins ran 45 minutes overtime, disappointing millions of children who had tuned in at 7 p.m. for the movie *Willie Wonka and the Chocolate Factory.* In the Eastern time zone, the movie was nearly half over when it came on the screen. NBC had considered showing the film from the beginning in the east but abandoned the idea because it would have kept children up almost until 10 p.m., and would have delayed the evening's other programs.

HEINEMANN, GEORGE ▶ specialist in children's programming, whose career had been with NBC. In 1970 he was named v.p. of children's programs for the network, the first person to receive a vice-presidency in that field; in 1974 he became v.p. of special children's programming, concentrating on experimental and educational fare.

His creations include *Go, Go-USA, Take a Giant Step, NBC Children's Theatre* and *An Evening at Tanglewood.* In 1952, while program manager of WNBQ (now WMAQ-TV) Chicago, he developed *Ding Dong School,* which soon after went on the network. Heinemann joined the New York station, WRCA-TV (now WNBC-TV), in 1956 and gradually moved up to the network, initially as director of public affairs.

In recent years, Heinemann has been actively involved with the NATAS Actor's Dramatic Workshop and teaching at NYU's Tisch School of the Arts.

HELTER SKELTER ▶ four-hour TV adaptation of the best-selling book on the Charles Manson murders. It was the highest-rated telecast of the 1975-76 season despite the reluctance of some affiliates to carry it in prime time, and despite a temporary blackout of the film in the number-two market, Los Angeles.

Presented as a two-part made-for-TV movie (April 1 and 2, 1976), the docu-drama on the mass murders committed by the Manson "family" made many broadcasters uneasy because the subject suggested an exploitation of tabloid headlines in a period when TV was under fire for excesses in violence. Many affiliates delayed it to the late evening and some backed off completely and allowed an unaffiliated UHF station to carry the show. The Los Angeles o&o, KNXT, decided to delay the telecast several weeks because Vincent Bugliosi, the author of the book on which the show was based and the protagonist in the story, was a candidate for local public office at the time (he lost).

Most critics praised the script by JP Miller for downplaying the violence and moderating the sensational in examining the strange life of the group and the bizarre motives for the crimes. The program featured George DiCenzo, Steve Railsback, Nancy Wolfe, Marylin Burnes, Christina Hart and Skip Homeier. Lee Rich and Philip Capice were co-producers for Lorimar Productions and Tom Fries was the producer-director.

HEMION, DWIGHT ▶ a leading music-variety director who has won more Emmy Awards than any other director in that classification and whose credits include specials by practically every top-name performer in show business. Hemion works with Gary Smith, and they are co-producers of any show or series he directs. Series credits include *Kraft Music Hall* and *The KopyKats.* In the early 1970s Hemion and Smith were under contract to Britain's ATV-ITC production company, for which they turned out *Tony & Lena,* the Burt Bacharach specials and numerous others.

HEMION, MAC ▶ director for ABC Sports whose work covered the full range of athletic events. He also directed music-variety latenight shows for ABC telecasts, including the Emmy Awards.

HENDRICKS, JOHN ▶ chairman and chief executive officer of Discovery Networks, which consists of The Discovery Channel, founded in 1985, and The Learning Channel, purchased in 1991. Hendricks previously was head of the American Association of University Consultants until 1982. Part of his duties involved finding television distribution for educational programming, and it was through those efforts that he envisioned a cable TV outlet for the considerable amount of educational and nonfiction programming created each year. He formed the Cable Educational Network in 1982 to develop such a service, and three years later Discovery was launched. The channel foundered and almost went under, but in 1986 four of the country's top cable operators—Tele-Communications Inc., United Cable, Cox Cable and Newhouse Broadcasting—signed on as investors in the service, increasing its distribution and stabilizing its financing.

HENNESEY ▶ series in the wave of service situation comedies featuring Jackie Cooper as Navy doctor Charles (Chick) Hennesey. Running on CBS (1959-62) via Hennesey Co. and Jackie Cooper Productions, it featured Abby Dalton as nurse Martha Hale, Roscoe Karnes as Captain Walter Shafer, Henry Kulky as orderly Max Bronsky and James Komack as dentist Harvey Spencer Blair III.

HENNING, PAUL ▶ writer of comedy series, dating to radio, who struck a mother lode with bucolic situation comedies as creator, writer and producer of *The Beverly Hillbillies* (1962) and *Petticoat Junction* (1963) and as executive producer of *Green Acres* (1965). Earlier he had written for the *Burns and Allen Show* (1942-52), passing with them from radio into TV; and the Ray Bolger, Bob Cummings and Dennis Day TV series. In radio he wrote for Rudy Vallee, Fibber McGee & Molly and Joe E. Brown.

HENNOCK, FRIEDA B. (d. 1960) ▶ first woman appointed to the FCC, a New York lawyer who proved to be an activist, reformer and frequent dissenter. She served (1948-55) spiritedly and flamboyantly and worked particularly at reserving TV channels for education. She had been appointed to a Democratic seat by President Truman and was replaced during the Eisenhower Administration by Richard Mack, who left the commission in disgrace, charged with selling his vote in a Miami license contest. Often Hennock was the lone dissenter on the commission, as when it approved the merger of ABC and United Paramount Theatres.

HENRY, BOB ▶ producer, director and writer specializing in variety programs. Credits include *The Flip Wilson Show, The Mac Davis*

Show, Norman Rockwell's America and specials with Perry Como, Lena Horne, The Young Americans, Andy Williams and Jose Feliciano.

HENRY, E. WILLIAM ▶ chairman of the FCC (1963-66) who adopted the reformist posture of his predecessor, Newton N. Minow, but was never as controversial. Appointed a commissioner by President Kennedy in 1962 and named chairman a year later, Henry was critical of the industry's slavish devotion to ratings and its practice of raising the sound levels for commercials, but his administration in general was moderate. He resigned in 1966 to work in a political campaign in his native state of Tennessee and then became a principal in a closed-circuit TV company.

Jim Henson

HENSON, JIM (d. 1990) ▶ creator and director of The Muppets, described as a cross between marionettes and puppets, which were featured on numerous network shows during the 1960s and achieved great popularity as regulars on *Sesame Street.*

Organic to the celebrated PBS children's program, the principals of the Muppet cast were Big Bird, a seven-foot bird; Oscar the Grouch, the misanthrope who dwells in a garbage can; buddies Ernie and Bert; Kermit the Frog, Grover and the Cookie Monster. Many were specially designed for the show by Henson, who also directed their segments, assisted by Don Sahlin and Kermit Love.

Henson, who was also a painter, sculptor and animator, began puppeteering while a student at the University of Maryland. He introduced the Muppets on a late-night music-comedy show in Washington, D.C. It won them a local series, *Sam and Friends,* that ran for six years.

The Muppets later appeared on *The Ed Sullivan Show* and were featured regularly on ABC's *Jimmy Dean Show* and, for a time, on NBC's *Today.* They were also the stars of several specials, among them *Hey, Cinderella* and *The Frog Prince.* Over the years, Henson made scores of TV commercials and a number of industrial and experimental films.

The Muppet Show, a 30-minute weekly variety series, was produced by ITC for prime-access syndication in 1976 and won a staunch following both in England and the U.S.

In the 1980s Henson Associates shifted into high gear, following up on the 1979 theatrical success *The Muppet Movie* with *The Muppets Take Manhattan.* Henson also created *Fraggle Rock* for HBO, a Sesame Street-like ensemble of puppets with moralistic stories. *Muppet Babies,* a cartoon that featured *The Muppet Show's* principal characters as children, scored on Saturday mornings on CBS, and went on to a syndicated run as well. In 1988, Henson produced *The Storyteller* for NBC, a rendering of European fairy tales hosted by John Hurt. And Jim Henson Productions, the renamed company, co-produced *Dinosaurs* for ABC in 1991.

Not every project was a success, however. Two other theatrical efforts, *The Dark Crystal* and *Labyrinth,* both darker fantasy films, withered at the box office.

As Henson's projects grew, it became clear that he was the successor to Walt Disney; indeed, he had become Disney's main competitor. Henson agreed to enter into a long-term production arrangement with Walt Disney in 1989, but he died suddenly in May 1990 of complications from pneumonia. The deal fell through at year's end, with Henson Associates filing suit against Disney for wrongful use of some Henson characters. The suit was settled with Disney receiving license to use the characters for two Disney theme park shows at Walt Disney World and the Disney MGM Studios in Florida.

HERBERT, DON ▶ former radio actor and writer who became known on TV as "Mr. Wizard" for the educational science series he created and performed in on NBC (1951-65). The series emanated from Chicago.

HERBERT LIBEL CASE ▶ extremely controversial $44 million libel case, with far-reaching First Amendment implications, brought by former Army Lieut. Col. Anthony Herbert, who charged that journalists connected with CBS's *60 Minutes* defamed his character in order to discredit his report of American military atrocities in Vietnam.

Ultimately, Herbert's case was thrown out of court when a judge ruled that he had not presented any triable issues of fact. However, this came only after years of legal wrangling which yielded an important and influential Supreme Court decision. On April 18, 1979, the Supreme Court rejected the arguments of CBS News and ruled that the lawyers for Herbert could inquire during the course of the trial into "the thoughts, opinions, and conclusions" of journalists at CBS News for evidence of malice against him.

This case within a case developed at the pretrial "discovery" proceedings when producer Barry Lando and reporter Mike Wallace refused to answer specific questions about the editorial process involved in their *60 Minutes* segment of Feb. 4, 1973, on Herbert. Because in a libel case the burden is placed on the public figure to prove not just that falsehoods were published but that "actual malice" was intended against him, lawyers for Herbert argued that it was necessary to discover the basis and motivations behind their editorial decisions.

Initially a federal district court judge had ordered Lando and Wallace to answer the plaintiff's questions, but that decision was reversed by a 2-1 vote of a panel of judges from the Second Circuit Court of Appeals on Nov. 7, 1977. In a majority opinion written by Justice Byron White, the Supreme Court overturned the Second Circuit Court reversal and agreed that Herbert's lawyers had the right to obtain "direct evidence" concerning the editorial "state of mind" about Herbert at CBS News.

The Supreme Court's decision came on the heels of its decision in the *Stanford Daily* case that journalists could not protect their files from searches by law enforcement officials. Many members of the journalistic community direly predicted that these decisions at the least were intruding on press freedom and would have a "chilling" effect on the exchange of information and opinion among reporters, editors and sources.

HERBUVEAUX, JULES (d. 1990) ▶ v.p. of NBC's central division (Chicago) during the years of the "Chicago school" of television. He was the executive who made possible such shows as *Garroway-at-Large, Ding Dong School, Studs' Place, Zoo Parade* and *Kukla, Fran and Ollie.* He also helped develop such talents as Hugh Downs, Dave Garroway, Bob Banner and Don Meier. He retired in 1962, after NBC had shut down the central division as a production entity, and became a broadcast consultant.

***HERE COME THE BRIDES* ▶** adventure-comedy series based on the film *Seven Brides for Seven Brothers,* about the importation of women to Seattle in the rugged pioneering days. The hour-long series, produced by Screen Gems, premiered on ABC in 1968 and ran two seasons. It featured Joan Blondell as saloon proprietor Lottie Hatfield, Bobby Sherman as Jeremy Bolt, Robert Brown as Jason Bolt, David Soul as Joshua Bolt, Bridget Hanley as bachelorette Candy Pruitt and Mark Lenard as sawmill owner Aaron Stempel.

***HERITAGE: CIVILIZATION AND THE JEWS* ▶** public TV's 1984 series compressing 5000 years of Jewish history into ten hours of painstakingly researched but sometimes pedantic television. Abba Eban narrated, and Arnold Labaton and Marc Siegel were the executive producers of the $11 million, six-year project. The series, produced by WNET New York, drew the fire of several orthodox Jewish groups for the documentary's secular treatment of their history and traditions.

HERNE, MARY ▶ managing director of Public Television International (PTI) since its founding in January 1990; it is now the largest distributor of PBS programming to foreign markets. Herne previously handled overseas sales for the Pittsburgh public television station, WQED, where she helped form the international distribution organization that represented other PBS stations as well. She came to public TV from the commercial sphere, where she had worked in marketing and advertising for such companies as LBS Communications, ESPN and Ogilvy & Mather Advertising.

HERSKOVITZ, MARSHALL and ZWICK, EDWARD ▶ creators and producers of ABC's comedy-drama series *thirtysomething* (1987-91), which became something of a cultural phenomenon for its accurate portrayal of Yuppie life in the 1980s. Besides prompting the renaming of each decade's generation (twentysomething and fortysomething), it also ushered in further discussion in the print and broadcast media of generational differences in values.

Cinematographically, as well, the series started a trend in off-hand filming techniques, attempting to make each scene more realistic and live-looking. This technique was adopted by advertisers looking to sell products to the very folks that *thirtysomething* portrayed.

Herskovitz and Zwick started out as writers for the dramatic series *Family* and went on to write, direct and produce the noted NBC TV movie *Special Bulletin.* They produced another NBC TV movie, *Extreme Close-Up,* in the 1990-91 season.

HERTZ ▶ unit of frequency equal to one cycle per second. In the U.S. electrical current is 60 hertz. One megahertz equals a million cycles per second, and one gigahertz a billion cycles per second. American VHF television stations are allocated on a band from 54 to 216 megahertz (MHz), UHF stations from 470 to 890 MHz. The term is named for Heinrich Hertz, a 19th-century German physicist who discovered radio waves and pioneered the study of electromagnetic radiation. The principles uncovered by Hertz culminated in the advent of wireless communication, including radio and television.

Don Hewitt

HEWITT, DON ▶ one of TV's premier news and documentary producers who helped develop CBS's *60 Minutes* in 1968 and *Who's Who* in 1977 and served as executive producer of both. As the guiding force of *60 Minutes,* one of the most profitable and consistently popular programs in CBS history, Hewitt has established a unique power base at the network, with a degree of autonomy in the news division that few producers have ever enjoyed. He had been producer-director of *Douglas Edwards with the News* (1948-62) and then executive producer of its successor, *CBS Evening News with Walter Cronkite* (1963-64). During the years before *60 Minutes,* Hewitt produced and directed documentaries and special reports.

He was producer-director of the first of the *Great Debates* of 1960, directed for CBS the three-network *Conversations with the President* (Kennedy in 1962, Johnson in 1964), and produced the CBS coverage of the assassination and funeral of the Rev. Dr. Martin Luther King, Jr. His credits include the documentaries *Hunger in America* (for *CBS Reports*) and Lord Snowdon's *Don't Count the Candles.* Hewitt also directed the CBS coverage of the national political conventions, from 1948 through 1980. Before joining CBS News in 1948, Hewitt had worked for newspapers and news services.

Andrew Heyward

HEYWARD, ANDREW ▶ executive producer of CBS News's *48 Hours* since 1987. Prior to the launch of *48 Hours,* Heyward was senior broadcast producer of the *CBS Evening News with Dan Rather;* he joined CBS News in 1981 as an *Evening News* producer.

Hi8 ▶ video format developed by Sony using 8mm-wide tape housed in cassettes the size of standard audio cassettes. Because the format's memory wavelength has been widened from 5.4 MHZ to 7.7 MHZ, Hi8 picture quality offers more than 400 lines of resolution, yielding an image far superior to that of 8mm consumer camcorders. It allows for the production of news segments and documentary sequences by a single person, a reporter asking questions while operating the camera.

***HIGH CHAPPARAL, THE* ▶** hour-long western dramatic series by the producer of *Bonanza,* David Dortort, in association with NBC. Airing from 1967 to 1970, it starred Leif Erickson and Cameron Mitchell as brothers John and Buck Cannon and featured Linda Cristal as John's wife Victoria, Mark Slade as his son Blue Cannon, Frank Silvera as Don Sebastian Montoya and Henry Darrow as Manolito Montoya.

HIGH CONCEPT ▶ in network/Hollywood parlance, a program idea whose essential premise is so powerful it can be stated in a single sentence.

HIGH ENERGY SHOWS ▶ Hollywood lingo for proposed series that lend themselves to lots of action and activity; the term is suspected of being a euphemism for violent.

HIGH ROLLERS ▶ see Game Shows.

HIGH-DEFINITION TELEVISION (HDTV) ▶ a technology that provides a TV picture and sound vastly superior to present broadcast standards, with an image resolution resembling 35mm motion pictures. HDTV is without question the television of the future, but whether that is to be the near or the distant future is not yet clear. Nor is it clear that stations and networks are eager to switch to some form of HDTV when conversion is bound to involve a large investment in equipment that may not be related to a foreseeable increase in profits. The technology, moreover, is being driven by politics rather than by business.

After Japan's NHK introduced the first high-definition system in the 1970s, American and European companies, spurred on by their governments, began developing other versions of HDTV. The Japanese system worked very well and if universally adopted would have given the world a single, uniform technical standard instead of the three different ones that now exist. The U.S. government, and those of the key European countries, however, began to see that in a worldwide conversion to a new form of television Japan would own the patents to all the transmitting and receiving equipment, which would be worth hundreds of billions of dollars. Rather than accept a form of HDTV that would enrich only Japan, the other countries have held out against that version and given high priority to developing their own.

In the U.S., the Federal Communications Commission has ruled that any HDTV standard ultimately transmitted by broadcasters would have to be compatible with existing home receiving equipment, so that the investments people have made in their television sets would not be lost because the technology changed. The FCC took the same position with color television technologies in the 1950s; the one finally accepted allowed for color transmissions that could be received as well in black & white on the older television sets. This action by the agency eliminated at once the original Japanese HDTV system, since it requires new receiving equipment in the home and renders the old TV sets obsolete.

The key to HDTV's improvement of the broadcast image is a pronounced increase in the number of scan lines used to create the picture. (Behind the television screen, an electron gun scans the image surface from top to bottom, and left to right, in a series of lines. The screen is scanned in this fashion 30 times a second, while actually producing 60 image fields through a process called interlacing. The technical system used in North American and Japanese television, known as NTSC, completes a picture in 525 lines. European television systems create a picture with 625 lines, using either the PAL or Secam standards that were developed after NTSC. The picture quality of Europe's television is far better than that of North America because of the additional 100 lines.)

The NHK system, introduced in the late 1970s and widely demonstrated for several years afterwards, more than doubled the number of scan lines in the North American and Japanese NTSC system. Instead of 525 scan lines, it used 1,125 lines, and the picture was remarkably improved. Also different from conventional television was the aspect ratio—the shape of the screen in point of how height is related to width. In conventional television the aspect ratio on the home receiver is 4:3; in the new system it is 5:3, the wider screen resembling that of the wide-screen movies. As was demonstrated, a screen with a 5:3 aspect ratio can encompass the entire football playing field in a single shot.

In response, a consortium of government and industry organizations in Europe created a multinational HDTV development effort called Eureka. One of the alternative systems it developed was one using 1,250 scan lines. In the U.S., such private companies as Zenith, General Instrument and Sarnoff Labs have developed and demonstrated other variations on HDTV. One of the persistent problems has been that a high-definition signal, in using substantially more scan lines, requires more bandwidth than has been provided for normal television stations. The path required for an HDTV signal, depending on the system used, might be equivalent to one and a half channels. That has been another serious hindrance to its development in broadcast television; ordinary channels, as they have been apportioned among broadcasters, are insufficient for HDTV technology, making it impracticable.

But by the early 1990s, the rapid advances made in digital video compression seemed to obviate the problem. Video compression technology can create multiple channels from existing single channels and thus could accommodate HDTV on any over-the-air station. Advances in digital technology were also incorporated in the U.S. HDTV proposals, which may well have changed the direction of high-definition technology. The NHK 1,125-line system, known as MUSE, involves analog transmission, and the chief rivals to that system now are digital.

The FCC is scheduled to rule upon the several HDTV proposals in 1993, but this will be for a transmission standard that will apply only to over-the-air broadcast television. HDTV standards for cable, direct-satellite broadcasting and home video will not be affected by that ruling, and it is possible that any or all of those media will adopt an HDTV standard incompatible with the system the FCC ordains for broadcasting.

HIGHWAY PATROL ▶ action series produced for syndication by Ziv Television (1955-59) that proved to be one of the highest-rated non-network shows and a precursor to the filmed police series that became standard network fare. It starred Broderick Crawford as Captain Dan Matthews and was narrated by Art Gilmore.

HIKEN, NAT (d. 1968) ▶ one of the outstanding comedy producers of the 1950s, whose masterpiece was *You'll Never Get Rich* (more generally known as the Sgt. Bilko show during its run from 1955 to 1959). Hiken also created and was producer-director of *The Phil Silvers Show* and *Car 54, Where Are You?,* among others.

HILL, PAM ▶ Vice-president and executive producer for CNN's investigative news unit since 1989. Previously, she was v.p. and executive producer of documentaries for ABC News (1978-89) and was responsible for a resurgence of the form in bringing forth a succession of mettlesome reports in the *ABC Close-Up* series, in styles that departed from the conventional. The work she supervised, which was often controversial, contributed to the growing credibility of ABC News in the late 1970s.

She joined ABC in 1973 after eight years with NBC, where she was a director on the *White Paper* series and producer of *Comment,* a half-hour series with Edwin Newman. Earlier, she had been a foreign affairs analyst for Henry A. Kissinger when he was consultant to New York Governor Nelson Rockefeller. She is married to Tom Wicker, columnist and associate editor of the *New York Times.*

At ABC she became a documentary producer, and her 1977 film, *Sex for Sale: The Urban Battleground,* proved the highest-rated ABC documentary up to that time. She was named executive producer of documentaries in January 1978, when Marlene Sanders went to CBS, and she was named a v.p. several months later.

Daniel J. Travanti and Michael Conrad in a scene from *Hill Street Blues*

HILL STREET BLUES ▶ new style of police-drama series (1980-87), introduced by NBC in the fall of 1980, which won the praise of critics and a record number of Emmy awards but little encouragement from viewers its first season on the air. NBC renewed the series despite its poor ratings and was vindicated; the show caught on the second year.

Hill Street Blues was a phenomenon of genre splicing, merging elements of soap opera with police-action melodrama. It also owed a certain debt to a retired MTM Enterprises stablemate, *The Mary Tyler Moore Show,* in focusing on the private lives and interaction of people in a workplace—in this case, a police precinct house. Realism was the series' idiom, reflected in its themes and storylines as well as in its format; individual episodes were never neatly resolved, as in conventional action shows.

The cast included Daniel J. Travanti as Captain Frank Furillo, Veronica Hamel as public defender Joyce Davenport, the late Michael Conrad as Sergeant Phil Esterhaus, Michael Warren as officer Bobby Hill, Charles

Haid as officer Andy Renko, Bruce Weitz as detective Mick Belker, James B. Sikking as Lieutenant Howard Hunter, Joe Spano as detective Henry Goldblume, Rene Enriquez as Lieutenant Ray Calletano, Kiel Martin as detective J.D. LaRue, Taurean Blacque as detective Neal Washington, Barbara Bosson as Fay Furillo, Betty Thomas as officer Lucy Bates and Ed Marinaro as officer Joe Coffey. Also featured were Jon Cypher as police chief Fletcher Daniels, George Wyner as prosecutor Irwin Bernstein and Trinidad Silva as gang leader Jesus Martinez, and joining the cast late in the show's run were Ken Olin as Harry Garibaldi, Mimi Kuzyk as Patsy Mayo, Lisa Sutton as Robin Tataglia, Dennis Franz as Norman Buntz, Peter Jurasik as Sid the Snitch, Robert Clohessy as Patrick Flaherty and Robert Prosky as Sergeant Stan Jablonski. Steven Bochco was executive producer, Gregory Hoblit supervising producer, and David Anspaugh and Anthony Yerkovich episode producers.

By odd coincidence, the president of MTM Enterprises, Grant Tinker, resigned after the first season of *Hill Street Blues* to become chairman of NBC; thus he remained a beneficiary of its success the second season.

HIRSCH, JUDD ▶ one of the stars of the brilliantly funny series *Taxi* (1978-83). He followed up with another hit series, *Dear John,* in 1988. He began his career on the stage, playing the lead in numerous Broadway and off-Broadway plays, among them *Chapter Two, Talley's Folly* and *Hot L Baltimore.* He has also appeared in movies.

HIRSCHMAN, HERBERT ▶ producer whose credits include *Perry Mason, The Man from Shiloh* and *The Zoo Gang* and (as executive producer) *The Doctors, Planet of the Apes* and the film drama *Larry.*

"HIT" LISTS ▶ television shows targeted for exclusion by certain major advertisers out of concern for real or threatened consumer boycotts. The practice began in the late 1980s, when a rash of consumer activist groups around the country used the device of threatening advertisers with a boycott of their products if they continued to run commercials in programs these groups found objectionable. The consumer complaints were usually over programs dealing excessively with violence or sex, but at times they included a program's perceived political leanings. Since advertisers spend heavily in television to make friends and not enemies, many of them complied and supplied their advertising agencies with lists of shows that were off-limits to their commercials. The hit lists identify both specific programs and general categories, such as controversial talk shows, network news programs, and sexy sitcoms.

The practice was first uncovered in June 1989 by a trade newsletter, *Market Shares,* published by *Channels* magazine, which identified dozens of companies and published their hit lists. Previously these were confidential matters between advertisers and their agencies. The practice continues, and the existence of hit lists has influenced what the networks will buy for their schedules.

While most major advertisers have hit lists, not all eschew every kind of controversial programming. Block Drugs and General Foods, for example, withstood enormous pressure from anti-abortion groups and remained advertisers in the NBC made-for-TV movie, *Roe vs. Wade,* in 1989.

Alfred Hitchcock

HITCHCOCK, ALFRED (d. 1980) ▶ famed master of motion picture suspense who became a TV personality, producer and director in the late 1950s with his highly successful anthology *Alfred Hitchcock Presents.*

***HITCHHIKER, THE* ▶** cable anthology series of macabre suspense tales told by a peripatetic young hitchhiker. Spiked with violence and female nudity, the show ran on HBO from November 1983 to December 1988. It was filmed in Toronto and Paris. Executive producers were Richard Rothstein, Jacques Methe, Boudjemaa Dahmane, David Perlmutter and Lewis Chesler (who was also one of the many writers). Nicholas Campbell (replaced by Page Fletcher), played the philosophical hitchhiker-narrator.

HOBIN, BILL ▶ veteran producer-director concentrating on variety shows. His credits range from *Garroway-At-Large, Your Show of Shows* and *Your Hit Parade* in the 1950s; to *Sing Along with Mitch, The Andy Williams Show* and *The Judy Garland Show* in the 1960s; and the Tim Conway and David Steinberg series in the 1970s.

HOCKEY ▶ see NHL (National Hockey League).

HODGE, AL (d. 1979) ▶ actor who played the title role in the *Captain Video* series on the DuMont Network in early TV after having portrayed *The Green Hornet* on radio in the 1940s. One of television's first big stars, enjoying six years of celebrity, he became a victim of typecasting and was unable to find other work in the medium when *Captain Video* folded with DuMont's demise as a network in 1955. Driven to working at odd jobs, such as bank guard and store clerk, while striving continually for a comeback both in Hollywood and New York, he became a television tragedy, living his final years alone, impoverished and suffering from severe emphysema. He was found dead in a downtown New York hotel on March 19, 1979.

A scene from the CBS series *Hogan's Heroes*

***HOGAN'S HEROES* ▶** one of the more successful series in the wave of military situation comedies in the 1960s. It concerned a brash group of Allied soldiers in a German POW camp during World War II who make a luxurious life of imprisonment by constantly outwitting the buffoonish officers in charge. (Similarity to the play *Stalag 17* invited a plagiarism suit.) The series, by Bing Crosby Productions, ran on CBS (1965-71) and featured Bob Crane as American colonel Robert Hogan, Larry Hovis as American sergeant Andrew Carter, Robert Clary as French corporal Louis LeBeau, Richard Dawson as British corporal Peter Newkirk, Kenneth Washington as American corporal Richard Baker and Ivan Dixon as American corporal James Kinchloe. The nutty Nazis were Werner Klemperer as Colonel Wilhelm Klink and John Banner as Sergeant Hans Schultz.

HOGA, TAKASHI ▶ president of Fujisankei Communications International (FCI), the overseas arm of Japan's largest media conglomerate, the Fujisankei Communications Group. Based in New York, he oversees 13 offices in the U.S. and Europe, and his company has developed into an independent profit center through its own business ventures.

FCI produces international news and entertainment programs for the parent company's Fuji TV Network in Japan, along with a daily Japanese-language morning news program in the U.S. that carries English subtitles. The program, *Supertime,* created by Hoga, airs in New York, Los Angeles, San Francisco, Chicago and Atlanta, from 7-9 a.m. every weekday. FCI also serves as the go-between for American and European companies selling products on the Japanese home shopping network.

Hoga has been with Fujisankei since 1957, when he graduated from Waseda University with a degree in literature and drama. He worked for a time with the Fuji Network as a producer and in 1970 arranged for the first telecasts in Japan of American Major League Baseball. He ran the network's New York office from 1979-83, then returned to Japan to head the network's sports division. In 1987 he became president of the company's Japan Executive Center, which organizes special events in Japan. He returned to New York in 1991 as president of FCI.

HOLBROOK, HAL ▶ one of television's most reliable actors for roles of substance. In a span of three decades, he has portrayed an extraordinary range of characters, including Abe Lincoln and Mark Twain, the latter in a TV version of Holbrook's 1960 one-man show on Broadway. Most of Holbrook's TV performances have been in single outings rather than series, and notably in fact-based dramas. Among his numerous credits in docu-dramas, mini-series and TV movies are *A Clear and Present Danger* (1970), *The Senator* (1971), *That Certain Summer* (1972), *Pueblo* (1973), *George Washington* (1984), *North and South* (1985) and *Under Siege* (1986). In 1990, however, Holbrook connected with a hit series, playing Burt Reynolds's irascible father-in-law in the CBS sitcom *Evening Shade.*

HOLLENBECK, DON (d. 1954) ▶ a CBS newscaster associated with Edward R. Murrow. He died, by suicide, while under incessant attack by pro-McCarthy columnists for alleged leftist leanings. He delivered the late evening news on WCBS-TV in New York, worked occasionally with Murrow on *See It Now* and conducted a weekly radio series, *CBS Views the Press,* on which he was frequently critical of Hearst journalism. His own chief critic and accuser was Hearst television columnist Jack O'Brian.

Frail and suffering from ulcers, and said by his colleagues to have been deeply distressed and fatigued by the attacks upon him, Hollenbeck took his life on June 22, 1954.

At the time, Murrow's *See It Now* had contracted for newsfilm with an outside organization, News of the Day, which was jointly owned by Hearst and MGM. On Hollenbeck's death, Murrow and his producer, Fred W. Friendly, decided to end the Hearst relationship and received permission from CBS to hire away all the technicians from News of the Day as the network's own newsreel unit.

HOLLYWOOD FILM COUNCIL ▶ an organization concerned with the common interests of member craft guilds and related unions in the TV and motion picture fields. The Council has lent the support of its numbers to a host of rule-makings and legislative proceedings, usually in the interest of increasing employment. It played an active role, for example, in the Balmuth petition to the FCC to limit the number of network reruns and in the Sandy Frank petition to bar strip programming in the prime-time access time periods. The New York equivalent of the Hollywood Council is the National Conference of Motion Picture and TV Unions (NACOMPTU).

HOLLYWOOD PALACE ▶ ABC Saturday night variety hour (1964-70) mounted as a modern version of vaudeville; it was staged at a refurbished Los Angeles movie house, the El Capitan, which was renamed The Hollywood Palace in honor of the New York theater that was vaudeville's top showplace. Each program featured seven or eight acts and a guest host of star stature. Bing Crosby was host for the premiere show Jan. 4, 1964; others included Maurice Chevalier, Judy Garland and George Burns. Nick Vanoff was executive producer and William Harbach producer.

HOLLYWOOD SQUARES ▶ see Game Shows.

HOLLYWOOD TELEVISION THEATRE ▶ PBS series of drama productions from KCET Los Angeles; it used major actors in adaptations of noted stage plays. Norman Lloyd was executive producer for the entire series. Productions have included *Ladies of the Corridor,* with Cloris Leachman and Neva Patterson; *The Lady's Not for Burning,* with Richard Chamberlain; *Six Characters in Search of an Author,* with John Houseman and Andy Griffith; and *The Chicago Conspiracy Trial,* with Morris Carnovsky, Ronny Cox and Al Freeman Jr.

James Woods and Meryl Streep in the NBC mini-series *Holocaust*

HOLOCAUST ▶ powerful 9 1/2-hour mini-series on the horrors of the extermination of Jews, presented by NBC on four consecutive nights (April 16-20) in 1978, and repeated in September 1979. In the U.S., the initial broadcast reached a total audience of 107 million; worldwide, in the 50 other countries in which it aired—including West Germany, where it provoked a continuing controversy—it was seen by an estimated 220 million viewers. The story, written by Gerald Green, author of *The Last Angry Man,* covers a ten-year period of persecution, centering on one Jewish family and one Nazi family in Berlin. The production won eight Emmy awards, a George Foster Peabody award and two score other citations.

Some critics faulted *Holocaust* for trivializing one of history's darkest episodes with a dramatic scaffolding that too often lent itself to soap opera, but in the main it was hailed as a television landmark, a program that not only brought the reality of Nazi terror to young persons in America but also to many in West Germany who had never learned what had happened before their lifetimes.

Among those top-featured were Michael Moriarty, Meryl Streep, Joseph Bottoms and Rosemary Harris. Others in the large cast included Blanche Baker, Tom Bell, Tovah Feldsuh, Marius Goring, Anthony Haygarth, Ian Holm, Lee Montague, Deborah Norton, George Rose, Robert Stephens, Sam Wanamaker, David Warner, Fritz Weaver and James Woods.

Filmed entirely in Germany and Austria, *Holocaust* was produced by Herbert Brodkin's Titus Productions in association with NBC Entertainment. Brodkin was executive producer, Robert (Buzz) Berger producer and Marvin Chomsky director.

HOLOGRAPHY ▶ a type of three-dimensional photography in which laser light is used to make a picture on an ordinary black-and-white photographic plate. What actually appears on the plate is a light-wave interference pattern, which, when illuminated by a laser beam, produces a three-dimensional image that can be viewed without special glasses. Some have predicted that holography will some day make possible three-dimensional television, but there are still a number of practical obstacles in the way of such a development.

HOME VIDEO ▶ generic term for a range of nonbroadcast television technologies: video recorders, video discs, video games, camcorders, home editing and effects systems, and "media rooms." The explosion of home video in the 1980s altered television viewing habits and is one factor responsible for network loss of audience share.

***HOMECOMING, THE* ▶** two-hour CBS dramatic special (Dec. 19, 1971) subtitled "A Christmas Story," which became the basis for *The Waltons* series although it was not intended as a pilot. The teleplay was an adaptation by Earl Hamner, Jr., of his own novel and was by Lorimar Productions, with Lee Rich as executive producer. The program has been repeated several times as a Christmas special. Featured were Patricia Neal as Olivia Walton, Andrew Duggan as John Walton and Edgar Bergen as Zeb Walton, along with Ellen Corby and Richard Thomas, who continued their roles of Esther (Grandma) Walton and John-Boy in *The Waltons*.

HOMES PASSED ▶ cable-TV term for residences within reach of a cable trunk line that could be wired if the household chose to subscribe. Cable penetration is defined by the number of subscribers in relation to the number of dwelling units passed (i.e., homes capable of receiving cable).

***HONEYMOONERS, THE* ▶** see Gleason, Jackie.

HONG KONG ▶ British colony in Asia whose television operations seem unaffected by the prospect of the country reverting back to Chinese rule in 1997. The colony has awarded the franchise for what will be the largest single cable system in the world, connecting virtually all 1.5 million television households. In addition, Hong Kong is expected to have DBS service during the 1990s from the privately funded Asiasat satellites.

Meanwhile, the colony is served by four commercial networks, owned by two companies, each of which broadcasts one in Cantonese and the other in English. TVB (Television Broadcasts), owned by movie magnate Sir Run Run Shaw, operates the Jade channel in Chinese and the Pearl channel in English. Selina Chow's ATV (Asia Television) competes directly with the Home channel in Chinese and the World channel in English. The Chinese channels are far more popular, with Jade the dominant one. The English-language channels, carrying both British and American shows in the main, together attract only around 5% of the audience.

The state broadcaster, RTHK, has access to the various commercial channels for the transmission of public information and educational programs.

HOOKS, BENJAMIN L. ▶ first black FCC commissioner, appointed to the agency by President Nixon in 1972 in a Democratic seat. An ordained Baptist minister who was pastor of a church in Memphis during the mid-1950s, he was at the same time a lawyer in private practice who eventually became a judge in the

Shelby County Criminal Court (1965-68). He was also a v.p. of a savings and loan association and a producer, host and panelist on TV public affairs programs in Memphis.

Just before the start of the Carter Administration, Hooks accepted the position as head of the National Association for the Advancement of Colored People but stayed on with the FCC until July 1977 in order to qualify for a government pension.

HOOPERMAN ▶ half-hour dramatic comedy starring John Ritter as sensitive San Francisco plainclothes detective Harry Hooperman, who finds himself the owner of an apartment house and a dog when his landlady is murdered. The series was created by Steven Bochco and Terry Louise Fisher, the team that created *L.A. Law,* although they had little direct involvement after the first three episodes and were billed as "executive consultants." The show, which also starred Barbara Bosson and Clarence Felder, aired throughout the 1987-88 season, but was never a solid hit for ABC and was scheduled sporadically the following season, ending its run in September 1989.

HOPALONG CASSIDY ▶ early western series, and one of the medium's first financial bonanzas, drawn from the character created by William Boyd in low-budget movies of the 1930s and 1940s. The shows were enormously popular with children, and "Hoppy," as he was known to them, was extensively merchandised.

Hopalong was introduced on TV in 1948 through the old movies that had been purchased by Boyd. They were so successful that in 1951 and 1952 Boyd produced in 52 low-budget half-hour *Hopalong* films for the series; they are still in syndication. Along with Boyd as Hopalong, Edgar Buchanan starred as sidekick Red Connors.

HOPE, BOB ▶ not so much a comedian as an American institution: the master dispenser of topical jokes, the people's emissary to the troops abroad in time of war, emcee par excellence for black-tie occasions, champion of the American Way of Life threading a patriotic spirit through a web of one-liners, chairman of the board of the entertainment fraternity. Hope's enormous popularity in radio and films carried into television and, if anything, increased with the years over a quarter century.

During the 1970s his specials for NBC—four or five a season—continued to rank among the top shows of the year, not far behind the Super Bowl and Academy Awards. During the Vietnam War, the annual *Bob Hope Christmas Show*—which actually aired in January or February—was fairly consistently the highest-rated special of the year; this was the 90-minute film of his Christmas season tour of military bases with a troupe of entertainers, a Hope tradition that began in World War II.

Like Will Rogers, Hope drew on politics and current events for his monologues, but where Roger's style was folksy, Hope's was urbane. Rogers looked the western country boy, Hope the middle-America businessman.

Bob Hope with Lucille Ball

Hope's TV programs held to the simple format of his radio shows, a monologue followed by skits with guest stars, interspersed with musical performances. He began *The Bob Hope Show* for NBC on Oct. 12, 1952, on a monthly basis, and it continued through 1955. Then came *The Chevy Show Starring Bob Hope* with episodes filmed in Iceland, England, Korea and Japan.

Thereafter, he contracted for a number of network specials each season and made a tradition of hosting the Academy Awards telecast.

HORNER, VIVIAN ▶ v.p. of program development for Warner Cable, a title conferred in 1979 after she mounted Nickelodeon, the company's cable network for children, and Pinwheel, a channel of violence-free programming for preschoolers for Warner's interactive system, Qube. Dr. Horner, who earned a Ph.D. in psycholinguistics for the University of Rochester, joined Warner Cable in 1976 from the Children's Television Workshop, where she was director of research for the children's series *The Electric Company.*

HOROWITZ, NORMAN ▶ colorful veteran of television syndication who was president of MGM-UA Telecommunications Co. until the sale of MGM to Qintex in 1989. Since then he has been working in his own revived company, which he operated before joining MGM in 1986. Prior to that he was president of Polygram Television (1980-84).

Horowitz began in syndication sales with Screen Gems International in 1959, went to CBS Films in 1968 as director of international sales, and returned to Screen Gems (now known as Columbia Pictures Television) two years later as senior vice president, later to become president of the syndication company.

HORWITZ, HOWIE (d. 1976) ▶ producer with Warner Bros. in the 1950s when he was active on such series as *77 Sunset Strip, Hawaiian Eye* and *Surfside 6.* Later, with 20th Century-Fox, he was producer of *Batman,* and with Universal, *Banacek* and several made-for-TV movies.

HOSTETTER, AMOS, JR. ▶ founder and CEO of Continental Cablevision Inc., based in Boston. He started the company in 1963 in partnership with H. Irving Grousbeck, not long after earning an MBA from Harvard. The company expanded rapidly both by building systems and by acquiring franchises, such as McClatchy Cable in 1986 and American Cable Systems in 1988, bringing Continental to 2.7 million subscribers. In 1989 Hostetter bought out Dow Jones's 17% stake for $300 million. His partner Grousbeck left in 1981 but still holds a 10% interest in Continental. Hostetter owns 43%.

HOTTELET, RICHARD C. ▶ former United Nations correspondent for CBS News, holding the assignment for two decades, after having been a foreign and war correspondent for the network since 1944. Before joining CBS , he was a foreign correspondent covering World War II for United Press. After leaving CBS in the mid-1980s he became a commentator for National Public Radio.

HOUSE OVERSIGHT AND INVESTIGATIONS SUBCOMMITTEE ▶ most powerful congressional investigative body for issues related to the communications media, although it has no legislative power. Now known formally as the Oversight and Investigations Subcommittee of the House Energy and Commerce Committee, it has by tradition been a vehicle for the personal agendas of a series of powerful Commerce Committee chairmen, including (since 1981) John D. Dingell (D.-Mich.). One of his predecessors, Harley Staggers (D.-W.Va.), held especially acrimonious hearings on staged TV news in 1972.

HOUSE TELECOMMUNICATIONS AND FINANCE SUBCOMMITTEE ▶ key subcommittee of the House of Representatives with jurisdiction over the FCC. Now known formally as the Telecommunications and Finance Subcommittee of the House Energy and Commerce Committee, its broad power over two disparate but powerful industries has made it one of the most coveted of all congressional assignments. A major reason is that the finance portfolio guarantees members a steady stream of contributions from Wall Street sources interested in the future of the SEC and other agencies regulating stocks, bonds, insurance and commodities trading. Legislative power and oversight over the FCC and other communications agencies has involved the body in broadcasting, cable, reinstituting the Fairness Doctrine, and high definition TV, as well as the restructuring of the telephone industry in the wake of the breakup of AT&T.

From 1976 to 1980, its chairman Lionel Van Deerlin (D.-Calif.) unsuccessfully attempted to pass a deregulatory "rewrite" of the Communications Act. Thereafter, the Subcommittee has generally focused its attentions on narrower agendas. The 1981-86 tenure of Rep. Tim Wirth (D.-Colo.) was marked by the sweeping changes of the 1984 cable bill. His successor, Edward J. Markey (D.-Mass.) has found it necessary to devote more attention to the securities and telephone industries throughout the first years of his tenure, although he played a key role in the passage of the 1990 Children's TV Act and pressed for new legislation on cable and reinstitution of the Fairness Doctrine.

***HOUSE WITHOUT A CHRISTMAS TREE, THE* ▶** 90-minute dramatic special on CBS (Dec. 3, 1972) based on a story by Gail Rock about a Nebraska family in the 1940s. It led to such other CBS holiday sequels as *The Thanksgiving Treasure* and *The Easter Promise.* Jason Robards, Mildred Natwick and Lisa Lucas were featured; the script was by Eleanor Perry. Paul

Bogart directed and Alan Shayne was producer.

HOUSEMAN, JOHN (d. 1988) ▶ noted stage director, producer and writer who occasionally has worked in TV. In the 1950s he produced the Emmy-winning CBS series *The Seven Lively Arts* and a number of dramas for *Playhouse 90.* In 1976 he had one of the acting leads in a PBS production of Pirandello's *Six Characters in Search of an Author* in the *Hollywood Television Theatre* series, and in 1977 he was featured in the ABC serial *Washington: Behind Closed Doors.* But he became best known in television as the star of the CBS series *The Paper Chase* (1978-79), which won the praise of critics but could not muster the support of viewers in its single season on the air.

HOUSER, THOMAS J. ▶ director of the White House Office of Telecommunications Policy (July 1976-January 1977) and for nine months in 1971 a member of the FCC. In the years between he was a partner in the Chicago law firm of Sidley and Austin. Earlier he had been special counsel to Sen. Charles Percy (R.-Ill.), after having been his 1966 campaign manager, and then served as deputy director of the Peace Corps (1969-70).

HOWARD, ROBERT T. ▶ former NBC executive who became president of NBC-TV on April 1, 1974, after seven years as v.p. and general manager of KNBC, the company's station in Los Angeles. He was relieved as president in August 1977, replaced by Robert Mulholland, but instead of leaving the company as many deposed presidents do, he stayed on in the lesser job as v.p. and general manager of the New York station, WNBC-TV.

He left the company after a reorganization by Fred Silverman in 1980 and later became head of United Satellite Television, a new pay-television service using the Canadian ANIK-C satellite.

HOWARD, RON ▶ actor who has been familiar on television since the age of six and quite literally grew up on the medium. In 1960 he played tow-headed Opie on the enormous hit *The Andy Griffith Show,* a role that lasted for eight years. In 1974 he began a six-year role as the all-American teenager Richie Cunningham on *Happy Days,* a part that was spun off from a sketch he played on *Love, American Style* in 1972. Before *Andy Griffith* he had already appeared in numerous television shows, among them *Playhouse 90, The Danny Thomas Show, Dennis the Menace* and *The Twilight Zone.*

In his thirties Howard found success directing movies, including *Splash, Cocoon, Night Shift, Clean and Sober* and *Backdraft.*

***HOWDY DOODY* ▶** one of the earliest network children's series—lively, nonsensical and pretending to no educational value—that was wildly appealing to children. It was to become the symbolic show of the first generation nurtured on television.

The show featured Buffalo Bob Smith, a ventriloquist who was its host and creator; Howdy Doody, a four-foot puppet; and Clarabell, a clown whose voice was an auto horn. (For a time Clarabell was played by Bob Keeshan, who later became Captain Kangaroo.)

Howdy Doody premiered live on NBC on Dec. 27, 1947, as a one-hour Saturday program and remained on the air until 1960. A measure of its success was the overwhelming demand for studio tickets. The waiting list was so long that expectant mothers were reported to have requested tickets for their unborn children. The program was unsuccessfully revived in syndication in 1976.

HTV ▶ British commercial independent serving Wales and West of England, its contract area stretching from Anglesey to the borders of Devon and Wiltshire. Previously known as Harlech TV, the program company has its bases in Cardiff and Bristol and reaches a population of around 4 million. Its chief problems are a difficult terrain, which requires the use of 53 UHF and 12 VHF transmitters, and the fact that the programming must be divided for the English-speaking and Welsh-speaking viewers. Its managing director is Patrick Dromgoole.

HUBBARD, STANLEY S. ▶ president and chief executive of Hubbard Broadcasting since 1983. A second-generation broadcaster, Hubbard took over the Minnesota-based company from his father, Stanley E. Hubbard, and projected himself as a force in the industry by energetically endorsing new approaches and technologies. He has been an outspoken proponent of direct-broadcast satellite (DBS) development since 1981, when he applied for one of the first licenses awarded by the FCC; his United States Satellite Broadcasting hopes to be broadcasting by 1994.

Over the last several decades, the Hubbards sparked such new ideas as the daily newscast, color broadcasting, satellite news gathering and weather radar. The younger Hubbard created Conus Communications, the country's first satellite news cooperative, which provides coverage to more than 150 member stations by satellite.

In Minnesota, Hubbard Broadcasting owns KSTP in St.Paul/Minneapolis, KRWF in Redwood Falls, WDIO in Duluth, WIRT in Hibbing and KSAX in Alexandria. The company also owns three stations in New Mexico: KOB (Albuquerque), KOBR (Roswell) and KOBF (Farmington), as well as WTOG in St. Petersburg, Florida.

HUBERT, DICK ▶ independent producer of TV documentaries, after having been executive producer of Group W's Urban America Documentary Unit and a writer-producer for ABC News. When Group W disbanded the Urban American unit in 1973, Hubert formed Gateway Productions with Paul Galan and Morty Schwartz and produced *It's Tough to Make It in This League,* a football documentary on PBS. In 1979, for Capital Cities Broadcasting, he produced *Inflation: The Fire That Won't Go Out,* a special that was syndicated to 190 commercial stations.

For a time during the 1980s he was executive producer of *Louis Rukeyser's Business Journal,* a producer of news specials for Capital Cities, and producer of a Bill Moyers PBS special, *World Hunger: Who Will Survive?* In 1989 Hubert created a second company, Videoware Corp., which produced *The Dreyfus Roundtable* for the Dreyfus Corp., a business series for the Financial News Network. He also was consultant to Cablevision Systems in the development of the In Court cable channel, which later merged with Time Warner's Court TV. A third company, Medical Economics and Video Publishing, founded by Hubert in 1990, produces specialized programming for health care professionals.

HUBLEY, JOHN (d. 1977) and FAITH ▶ film animators known for their humanistic approach to the craft. A husband and wife team, each with a background in aspects of film production, they formed their own company, Storyboard, in 1955. Their most ambitious film for TV was *Everybody Rides the Carousel* (1976), a 90-minute work adapted from the writing of psychoanalyst Erik H. Erikson and developed at Yale University. It aired on CBS, sponsored by Mobil Oil, with Cicely Tyson as host.

HUGGINS, ROY ▶ action-adventure producer and writer who established his reputation as creator of *Maverick, Colt 45* and *77 Sunset Strip* in the mid-1950s and added to his list *The Fugitive, Run for Your Life, The Rockford Files* and *City of Angels.*

Huggins has been executive producer of *Alias Smith and Jones, Cool Million, Toma, Baretta, Hunter,* and numerous other series and made-for-TV movies. His production company, Public Arts, was associated with Universal TV on such series as *Baretta* and *Rockford Files.*

HUGHES COMMUNICATIONS ▶ manufacturer of communications satellites and a leading marketer of transponder (or channel) time to the U.S. cable television industry. In the early 1980s, when the company was headed by Clay (Tom) Whitehead, Hughes originated the so-called real estate model for satellite occupancy, selling the transponders to cable networks in the manner of condominiums. Prior to that, the practice was to lease satellite transponders to users for periods of years. When Whitehead launched the first Hughes Galaxy satellite, all the transponders he intended to sell had been sold, and the company made a large profit the moment the satellite was successfully placed in orbit. As part of a strategic move into direct-to-home satellite broadcasting (DBS) Hughes obtained in 1991 a $100 million commitment from Hubbard Broadcasting for transponder capacity on a DBS satellite to be launched in 1994.

HUGHES TELEVISION NETWORK ▶ one of the first ad hoc networks to put together lineups of stations for special telecasts, usually of sports events. Most of the stations are regularly affiliated with the major networks but clear time for the HTN events.

Paramount Pictures purchased HTN in 1977 and established a division under Rich Frank to create original programs for the network. That plan was abandoned in 1979 and HTN was put under the wing of the Madison Square Garden Communications Network, with John A. Tagliaferro as general manager. In 1989 HTN was acquired by IDB Communications.

The company started as Sports Network in 1956 and was founded by Dick Bailey, a facilities expert for ABC who had an exceptional understanding of the economics of leasing

AT&T long lines. Initially the company served as a facilities coordinator for sporting events, which usually involved arranging for the transmission of "away" games to a team's home city. But soon it began to distribute golf, college basketball, tennis and other sports around the country over a part-time network. In 1968 Sports Network was purchased outright by the reclusive billionaire Howard Hughes, and given the name of Hughes Sports Network, later changed to Hughes Television Network.

In 1974 the network merged with a number of Hughes's other personal properties, principally Las Vegas hotels (The Sands, Harold's Club, etc.) and real estate to form a single company known as Hughes Television Network Inc. But Paramount purchased the network alone. Most of the sports telecasts are on weekend afternoons, but HTN also has distributed some entertainment programming in prime time, such as *Magic, Magic, Magic* (1976) and *Steve Allen's Laugh-Back* (1976). Starting in 1969 and for several years after, it distributed the weekly series *Outdoors* in 70 markets for Liberty Mutual insurance by means of a tape network.

HULLABALOO ▶ one of the first rock and roll variety series, presented by NBC (1964-66) and featuring a chorus line of wriggling dancers and guest performers. It was by Gary Smith Ltd.

HUME, BRIT ▶ chief White House correspondent for ABC News. A national news correspondent since 1976, Hume was a key ABC reporter in Washington. Prior to coming to the network, he worked on the documentary series, *Close-up,* earning television's first Academy Award nomination in the process. Hume began his career as an investigative reporter for Jack Anderson's syndicated newspaper column.

HUNGER IN AMERICA ▶ CBS News documentary (May 21, 1968) produced by Martin Cart that became the subject of a controversy over an instance of misreporting. In the opening sequence, a baby receiving emergency medical treatment was said by the narrator to be dying of starvation. But the San Antonio hospital at which the sequence was filmed maintained that the baby actually died of premature birth. CBS News explained that the misinformation had been given by a hospital official, an account denied by the party in question. The FCC decided not to resolve the issue since it came down to a choice of whom to believe, the producer or the hospital official. The commission, at any rate, found no evidence of deliberate deception.

HUNTER ▶ crime drama series on NBC set in Los Angeles that followed the exploits of tough cop Rick Hunter (played by Fred Dryer) and his beautiful partner Dee Dee McCall, nicknamed "The Brass Cupcake," (played by Stepfanie Kramer). Created by Frank Lupo and produced by Stephen J. Cannell, the show debuted in September 1984 opposite *Dallas* and suffered poor ratings, but it picked up in the second season with a new executive producer, the veteran Roy Huggins, and a more felicitous time slot. Hunter acquired several new partners after Kramer left the show at the end of 1990. Her first replacement was Darlanne Fleugel, who was eliminated in mid-season and replaced by Lauren Lane. Others featured in the series included John Amos, Charles Hallahan, James Whitmore, Jr., and Garrett Morris.

HUNTLEY, CHET (d. 1974) ▶ anchor on NBC's *Huntley-Brinkley Report,* the network's high-rated evening newscast, which began Oct. 15, 1956, and ran until Huntley's retirement from NBC in July 1970. The format cut back and forth between Huntley in New York and David Brinkley in Washington, and the ritual closing—"Good Night, Chet" "Good Night, David"—entered the lore of television. In 1965 a consumer-research company found that Huntley and Brinkley were recognized by more adult Americans than were such stars as Cary Grant, James Stewart or The Beatles.

Huntley was the straight-man to the dry wit of Brinkley, and he projected sobriety and sincerity. He was selected for the newscasting post and was signed to a seven-year contract by NBC after the triumph over CBS by the Huntley-Brinkley tandem in covering the political conventions of that year. Huntley's penchant for speaking out off-camera on controversial issues drew criticism from both the political left and right. A southern newspaper editor charged him with editorializing on-air with his eyebrows. In the 1960s he raised a controversy for delivering a radio commentary favorable to beef interests when it was learned that Huntley himself owned cattle in his native Montana. Other news reporters faulted him for becoming a spokesperson in commercials after his retirement, calling it a betrayal of the news profession to lend his journalistic credence in support of an advertiser. But he was a respected and unflappable newsperson in his time, and at the height of his career his salary with NBC was estimated at nearly $200,000 annually a huge amount for a newsman at the time.

Huntley began his broadcasting career in 1934 at radio station KPCB in Seattle, as announcer, writer, disk jockey and salesperson for $10 a month. Two years later he joined KHQ Spokane, then KGW Portland, Ore. In 1937 he was with KFI Los Angeles, and later joined CBS News in the West, where he remained for 12 years. He moved to ABC in L.A. in 1951 and remained until NBC News hired him away, to New York, in 1955.

Huntley and Brinkley had what was perhaps their only public difference in 1967 when Huntley crossed AFTRA picket lines while Brinkley refused to do so. Huntley contended that newscasters did not belong in a union that represented "actors, singers and dancers."

He retired on Aug. 1, 1970, to pursue business interests in Montana, including the development of the Big Sky resort, which did not open until after his death. When he left NBC the evening newscast was retitled *The NBC Nightly News.*

HUT (HOUSEHOLDS USING TELEVISION) ▶ a rating company's estimate of the unduplicated households tuned to television during a quarter-hour period. HUT levels vary through the day, from a low percentage of usage in the mornings to a high percentage in the peak viewing hours. The ratings for individual programs take on meaning when measured against the HUT; a high rating when the HUT is low is superb, a low rating when the HUT is high is a disaster.

The term supplanted *sets-in-use* with the advent of multiset households.

HYATT, DONALD B. ▶ producer-director of public affairs programs for NBC whose most notable work was the distinguished *Project 20* series, begun in 1958. He became executive producer of special projects programs for the network in that year and added to his list of credits the *Wisdom* and *World of* series. Hyatt became an independent film producer-director and a TV consultant. He was a visiting lecturer at Yale University in 1980-81.

HYDE, ROSEL H. ▶ long-time commissioner (1946-69) and twice chairman of the FCC, whose service to the agency as a staff member dated back to the Federal Radio Commission. In 1953 President Eisenhower elevated him to chairman for the specified period of one year; he then served several subsequent months as acting chairman until the president named George C. McConnaughey the new chairman in October 1954. The most significant action by the FCC during Hyde's term as chairman was to extend the license renewal interval for television from one to three years.

Hyde, who had several reappointments to the commission, was named acting chairman by President Johnson for two months in 1966 when E. William Henry resigned and then received the full title of chairman a second time. He served as chairman for three years, until his retirement in 1969. During his second administration, the hard line began to be drawn between liberal and conservative factions on the FCC, partly because the radical reformer Nicholas Johnson had joined the commission.

HYLAND, WILLIAM H. ▶ CBS sales executive of the 1950s who exerted a powerful influence on TV program decisions in the 1960s as senior v.p. and director of broadcasting for J. Walter Thompson Advertising. Hyland, who had joined CBS in 1937, became v.p. in charge of sales in 1953 and senior v.p. of the network in 1963, after which he left to join the ad agency.

HYPOING ▶ the practice of scheduling stronger than usual programs and "blockbuster" movies by networks and stations during *sweep weeks,* when the rating services survey most of the markets for the three local rating reports they will receive during the year. The attempt to inflate a station's ratings during those weeks is widely recognized as an act of deliberately distorting the competitive picture in a market and it has been condemned by both the FTC and FCC as fraud. But the age-old practice continues, because the sweep ratings are used by ad agencies in determining where to place their spot business and how much to pay for commercial time.

HYTRON (also CBS-HYTRON) ▶ TV set manufacturing company purchased by CBS in 1951 for $17.7 million in stock—a venture that proved one of the corporation's most embarrassing mistakes. Not only had CBS misjudged the value of Hytron Radio and Electronics, but the company produced an inferior set, under the brand name of Air King, that could not compete with those manufactured by the large electronic companies (RCA, Zenith, etc.). Moreover, CBS-Hytron placed its faith in the vacuum tube when other companies were switching to the newly developed transistor.

CBS commissioned the noted designer Paul McCobb to give its sets a smart external appearance, but to no avail. In 1959 CBS dropped the name Hytron and called the division CBS Electronics. In 1961 it dissolved the manufacturing arm after it had run up losses of about $50 million.

I

I, CLAUDIUS ▶ highly acclaimed 13-hour BBC series, which, for its scenes of violence and sex in ancient Rome, challenged the boundaries of what was acceptable on American television when it aired on PBS in 1978. The series, based on two novels by Robert Graves, *I, Claudius* and *Claudius the God,* covered the reign of the four emperors who followed Julius Caesar and preceded Nero. A political tale played against the background of the dissolute sexual affairs in the courts of the emperors, it chronicled the corruption of Roman life during the years 24 B.C. to 54 A.D.

Using Graves's literary device, the series had Claudius—the fourth of the 12 Caesars who presided over the decline and fall of Rome—narrate the story of his reign and those of his three predecessors: Augustus, Tiberius and Caligula. Adapted for television by Jack Pulman, the series skillfully wove the ingredients of domestic drama and comedy into the fabric of the historical tragedy, and it preserved the author's intended parallels to our times.

Derek Jacobi played Claudius, the presumed court idiot whose shrewd intelligence was camouflaged most of his life by a deformed body and severe stammer. Featured were Sian Phillips, John Hurt, Brian Blessed, George Baker and George Hart. Herbert Wise was the director.

The series made many public television stations uneasy for its beheadings, assassinations, gladiator games and episodes of incest, prostitution, adultery, rape, nymphomania, homosexuality, toplessness, sex orgies and sex tournaments. Nevertheless, all PBS member stations broadcast the series, under the *Masterpiece Theater* umbrella, via WGBH Boston and Mobil Corp.

I DREAM OF JEANNIE ▶ fantasy situation comedy about an astronaut blessed with his own genie, who happens to be a luscious female. Running on NBC (1965-69) via Screen Gems, it featured Barbara Eden as Jeannie, Larry Hagman as astronaut Tony Nelson, Bill Daily as Tony's friend Roger Healey and Hayden Rorke as NASA psychiatrist Alfred Bellows. The reruns proved very successful in syndication.

I LOVE LUCY ▶ the supreme situation comedy, tops in the ratings for most of its years on CBS (1951-57) and popular in almost every country in the world; the reruns continued for years to be prized by local stations as daily fare. Apart from its significance in propelling Lucille Ball to stardom, the series was prototypical; its basic structure—the interaction of two neighboring couples—served such other successful situation comedies as *The Honeymooners* and *All in the Family.* Ball and her husband, Desi Arnaz, played Lucy and Ricky Ricardo, a housewife and her bandleader husband; and William

Frawley and Vivian Vance played neighbors Fred and Ethel Mertz.

I MARRIED JOAN ▶ broadly played but popular situation comedy on NBC (1952-57) that featured Joan Davis as Joan Stevens, the zany wife of Judge Bradley Stevens, played by Jim Backus. It was by Volcano Productions.

I SPY ▶ hour-long espionage series, which featured Robert Culp and Bill Cosby as secret agents on international assignments posing as a top tennis player, Kelly Robinson, and his trainer, Alexander (Scotty) Scott. Notable as the first TV series to star a black actor, the series ran on NBC from 1965 to 1968. It was by Sheldon Leonard Enterprises.

IATSE (INTERNATIONAL ALLIANCE OF THEATRICAL STAGE EMPLOYEES) ▶ AFL-CIO union representing film craftspeople (camera operators, sound crew, editors, remote lighting crews) and certain other technicians at all three networks and at numerous TV stations. About 20% of the total international membership of 60,000 is involved in TV operations or production. The union also represents motion picture projectionists, makeup and wardrobe artists, set designers and screen cartoonists. Founded in 1893, it became international in 1902.

IBEW (INTERNATIONAL BROTHERHOOD OF ELECTRICAL WORKERS) ▶ technical union formed in 1891, which in 1931 began to organize radio engineers and today represents around 12,000 technicians at CBS and at more than 170 local stations. Broadcast representation, however, makes up a small part of the diversified International, whose total membership from all industries is about one million. This is in contrast to the National Association of Broadcast Employees and Technicians (NABET), the technical union at NBC and ABC, which is exclusively in broadcast.

The technicians' unions at the networks are protected from raids upon each other by being signatories to the AFL-CIO nonraiding agreement.

ICM (INTERNATIONAL CREATIVE MANAGEMENT) ▶ a leading talent and packaging agency in the 1970s, formed from mergers the previous decade of several agencies, principally International Famous, Creative Management Associates and Marvin Josephson Associates. The agency represents actors, variety performers, writers, directors, producers, composers and other creative talent in their employment by movie and TV studios, networks, syndicators and other facets of show business. It also represents Washington writers and such former government officials as Henry A. Kissinger. ICM is a subsidiary of Marvin Josephson Associates.

IDB COMMUNICATIONS GROUP ▶ one of the leading suppliers of domestic and international transmission services for the distribution of news, sports, and syndicated programs. Controlling 20 transponders on five satellites, the company also claims to be the largest reseller of satellite time. IDB maintains teleports in Los Angeles and New York, has extensive international links and maintains a vast fleet of transportable earth stations. It is also the parent of the Hughes Television Network, which mainly deals in the transmission of sports events. The company was founded in 1981 by entrepreneur Jeffrey Sudikoff.

Robert A. Iger

IGER, ROBERT A. ▶ president of ABC Entertainment since March 1989. With his TV experience heavily tilted toward sports, he was considered a surprise choice to succeed the respected Brandon Stoddard as chief of the network's prime-time schedule. Prior to moving into the top programming spot, he served for seven months in the post of executive vice president of the ABC Television Network Group.

Iger started with ABC Television in 1974 as a studio supervisor, moved up in two years to ABC Sports where he managed and directed the programming for *ABC's Wide World of Sports,* then in 1987 was named vice president of programming for ABC Sports. During those years, he had a large hand in acquiring major sporting events for the network and was heavily involved in the network's coverage of three Olympic Games.

IIC (INTERNATIONAL INSTITUTE OF COMMUNICATIONS) ▶ nonprofit membership organization involved in communications research and policy analysis and committed to promoting the exchange of communications ideas and concepts between broadcasters and policy-makers worldwide. Begun in 1968 as the International Broadcast Institute, the London-based organization has more than 1,000 individual and corporate members in 75 countries. Its name change in 1977 reflected the Institute's broadened scope of interest and the convergence of electronic technologies to include everything from computers to satellites. By sponsoring research and conferences, and publishing the professional journal *Intermedia* as well as books and reports, the IIC seeks to improve the understanding of communications in the broadest sense and to facilitate free discussion of major problems and policies common to the world's communications systems.

Arthur D. Morse, former CBS News producer-writer, served as the Institute's first executive director until his death in an automobile accident in 1971. The present executive director is Carol Joy.

IKE ▶ six-hour ABC mini-series on the life of General Dwight D. Eisenhower during the World War II years when he became a military hero. It was televised over three nights, May 3, 4 and 6, in 1979 to very good ratings. Drawn partly from Kay Summersby Morgan's memoir, *Past Forgetting,* the serial focused on Ike's close relationship with Summersby while she was his personal driver in London and later an aide in his office, but it was careful not to link them romantically.

Robert Duvall portrayed Ike, Lee Remick was Kay and Bonnie Bartlett played Mamie Eisenhower. The cast included Dana Andrews as Gen. George C. Marshall, Wensley Pithey as Winston Churchill and Ian Richardson as Field Marshal Montgomery. Melville Shavelson was executive producer and writer, and he directed with Boris Sagal.

ILOTT, PAMELA ▶ longtime head of religious broadcasts for CBS News, whose tenure effectively ended with the creation of the *Sunday Morning* series and the general disappearance of noncommercial religious programs on television in the late 1970s. Ilott had joined the network in 1957 and was made a vice president in 1976, the first woman to hold that rank at CBS News. She had been executive producer of such acclaimed weekly series as *Lamp Unto My Feet* and *Look Up and Live.* She had also created *For Our Times,* which was hosted by Douglas Edwards.

ILSON, SAUL and CHAMBERS, ERNEST ▶ comedy writing team, developed in Canadian television, who specialize in music-variety formats. Their extensive credits include producing the *Tony Orlando & Dawn* series.

In the late 1970s, they split and went separate ways. Ilson joined NBC as executive in charge of variety and comedy development, and he left in late 1981 to return to independent production. He produced *The Billy Crystal Comedy Hour* for NBC before signing an exclusive deal with Columbia Pictures TV. Chambers, as a free-lance producer, became supervising producer for *Love, Sidney.*

IN LIVING COLOR ▶ irreverent half-hour comedy-variety show on Fox that was the first prime-time television outlet for Afro-American humor and music. Created by Keenen Ivory Wayans, who attracted notice with a motion picture parody of the black exploitation films of the 1970s, *I'm Gonna Git You Sucka,* the series premiered on Fox in 1990 in a month when the three major networks were running repeats. Its debut was helped by its placement in Fox's Sunday night lineup right after *The Simpsons,* one of the network's most popular shows.

The show features comedy skits that poke fun at black stereotypes and deal as well with other social and ethnic subjects. Favorite targets include Arsenio Hall, Nation of Islam leader Louis Farrakhan, the handicapped, and Supreme Court Justice Clarence Thomas. At each skit's end, just before the commercial break, a group of female dancers, the Fly Girls, perform a choreographed sequence to a rap song.

In Living Color earned a reputation for extending the prime-time boundaries for sexual innuendo and graphic language, and the show has been criticized in some quarters as racist and homophobic. Still, it has succeeded in attracting a large and youthful audience. Wayans, who is black, is accompanied on the show by his brothers Damon and Shawn and sister Kim and an ethnically diverse supporting cast. Wayans is executive producer and chief writer.

IN SEARCH OF . . . ▶ syndicated weekly half-hour series that presented strange and unexplained phenomena in a no-frills documentary style. With fuzzy film clips, interviews and some of the earliest re-creations on TV, *In Search Of*... tackled such subjects as the Loch Ness Monster, Bigfoot, UFOs and witchcraft. It ran from 1976-82 with Leonard Nimoy as host.

IN THE HEAT OF THE NIGHT ▶ a police drama series based on the 1967 film of the same title, centering on the relationship between a small-town Mississippi police chief and his new chief of detectives. The one-hour series stars Carroll O'Connor as Bill Gillespie and Howard Rollins as Virgil Tibbs. It debuted on NBC in March 1988 with veteran programmer Fred Silverman and Juanita Bartlett as executive producers. Carroll O'Connor became active in the production and took an executive producer's role as well in 1989.

INCREDIBLE HULK, THE ▶ hour-long CBS adventure drama on one of the Marvel Comics superheroes, represented in live-action. The role of The Incredible Hulk required two actors—one, Bill Bixby, to portray normal human doctor David Banner; the other, weight-lifter Lou Ferrigno, to play the immense green monster into which he is transformed in situations of stress. *Hulk* was the third comic-book-inspired show on CBS when it premiered in March 1978, having been preceded by *The New Adventures of Wonder Woman* (salvaged by the network when ABC canceled it) and *Spiderman*. In preparing for the 1979-80 season, CBS discarded two of the shows, although they were both doing moderately well, because it did not want the identity of a comic book network. *Hulk* was the program retained because it had developed a youthful cult following. Its network run ended in the 1981-82 season.

INCREDIBLE MACHINE, THE ▶ First of the National Geographic specials to play on PBS (Oct. 28, 1975) and the program attaining the highest rating in public TV history, a 24.8 rating and 36 share in New York, and shares above 25 in most major cities, even some with UHF outlets for PTV. The one-hour program, a documentary on the workings of the human body, produced, directed and written by Irwin Rosten, had been turned down by the commercial networks. When all rejected the four annual National Geographic specials, believing them to have exhausted their commercial popularity, WQED, the public TV station in Pittsburgh, secured underwriting from Gulf Oil and acquired the series for PBS. E.G. Marshall was narrator, Dennis B. Kane executive producer, and Wolper Productions and the National Geographic Society the source.

INDEMNITY CLAUSES ▶ standard provisions in program contracts under which the packagers assume responsibility for claims, liabilities and damages. They protect the networks and their affiliates in lawsuits that may occur over programs supplied by outside studios. There is also a moral turpitude clause allowing a network to void a contract if a principal performer should be involved in a scandal that may affect the value of the property.

INDEPENDENT TELEVISION COMMISSION (ITC) ▶ Britain's new regulatory body for commercial television and cable, created with the government's restructuring of the industry in the early 1990s. The agency replaced the Independent Broadcasting Authority (IBA), which had been created in 1954, and although it retained many of the IBA's responsibilities it was directed to supervise with a lighter touch—that is, with less interference into business practices, allowing market forces to come into play. Named to head the ITC as chairman was George Russell, who also headed the IBA in its final year and engineered the transition. A one-time business executive in other industries, he later became a member of the IBA and sometime later chairman of Independent Television News. Russell was the overseer of the unprecedented auction of the commercial franchises in 1991.

The ITC oversees independent commercial television and radio, and also cable, in England, Scotland, Wales, Northern Ireland and the Channel Islands. Often thought of as the British equivalent of the American Federal Communications Commission, the agency's scope and power is in fact much broader. It is more a parent of the system than the FCC is in the U.S. As the old IBA was a strict parent, and one that assumed ultimate responsibility for the programming, the ITC has been instructed by the government to be more permissive and to encourage competition. The ITC owns the transmitting towers used by the stations, which lease them for a substantial annual fee.

INDEPENDENT TELEVISION NEWS ▶ the international news "department" for commercial television in Great Britain since the mid-1950s. Headquartered in London with its own studios, ITN is consortium-owned by Britain's independent stations and supplies them with several networked news wrap-ups each day, as well as news specials. Its prime nightly feed is the half-hour *News at Ten* show.

INDIE ▶ industry shorthand for independent, whether with reference to TV stations not affiliated with a network or to producers operating on their own.

INFOMERCIALS ▶ TV commercials presented as programs—usually 30 minutes in length, though sometimes longer—in the belief that people interested in a new product or service want to know more about it than can be told in a standard advertising spot. The form blossomed on cable in the 1980s, especially in post-midnight time periods, but it has been eschewed by the broadcast networks and most of the large TV stations. However, frail independent UHFs and other stations hurting in a depressed advertising market have accepted these program-length commercials sufficiently to encourage Home Shopping Network Inc. in 1991 to launch a 24-hour infomercial service called Infonet. Stations may broadcast any part of Infonet, as they choose, and are compensated with commissions on the quantity of products sold in their markets.

INPUT (INTERNATIONAL PUBLIC TELEVISION SCREENING CONFERENCE) ▶ a loosely structured coalition of European and North American public service broadcasters who annually organize a week-long conference to view and discuss innovative programming. The site of the conference varies with the host country and alternates each year between North American and Europe.

INQUIRY INTO THE ECONOMIC RELATIONSHIP BETWEEN TELEVISION BROADCASTING AND CABLE TELEVISION ▶ two-year FCC study of its cable-TV programming rules concluded in April 1979. The commission found that increased competition from cable TV would present no serious threat to the financial health or survival of local broadcast stations, and it initiated a rulemaking proceeding to eliminate its limits on distant-city television signals cable systems may carry and its "syndicated exclusivity" program blackout requirements, both established by the FCC's 1972 Report and Order on Cable Television.

Although technological and legislative developments quickly made much of the commission's work obsolete, it had an important influence on a critical stage of the industry's evolution. The Economic Inquiry was the commission's first thorough assessment of the assumptions underlying its 15 years of cable-TV regulation. Broadcast interests had first sought protection from cable television in the mid-1960s, when cable systems began to offer their first independent, competing service in the form of television stations brought from distant cities via microwave. Beginning in 1965, the Commission issued a series of regulations limiting the number of distant-city television signals cable systems could carry and requiring programming on those signals to be blacked out if it was under contract to local broadcast stations—regardless of whether the local station was showing the program or "warehousing" it for use sometime in the future.

The commission had based its regulations on an "intuitive model" of cable's potential impact on local broadcast stations. The commission assumed that the increased viewing options available on cable TV would cause a decline in local station viewing audience bringing on a serious decline in advertising revenue. Ultimately, the loss in revenue would cause a decline in local programming produced by stations, the commission believed. Beginning in 1977, the FCC set out to test each of these assumptions, seeking evidence from broadcast and cable-TV interests and commissioning its own independent studies from five of the nation's top television economists.

The commission concluded that each of the assumptions was groundless. Even in television markets heavily penetrated by cable, the studies showed, local stations had lost at most 1% of their audience; in the long run, that figure might rise to only about 10% even with tremendous cable growth. In fact, UHF stations were experiencing an average of 5.5% audience increase because of improved reception via cable. On advertising revenues, the commission found that the growth in demand for broadcast advertising continues to grow more than enough to offset minimal audience losses to cable TV. Finally, the commission found that there is little relationship between a broadcast station's revenues and the amount of local or public affairs programming it produces.

The commission also found that its blackout rules, designed to protect the value of syndicated programs to local broadcast stations, were unnecessary and that syndicated programming carried on cable TV has not had any impact on program suppliers' revenues from these productions.

INSIDE NORTH VIETNAM ▶ documentary by Felix Greene, a British citizen residing in the U.S., that stirred a controversy when it was telecast on NET in 1968. The film, which depicted the Vietnam War from the enemy side, was denounced as Communist propaganda by a group of congressmen who had not seen it; they also charged NET with acting against the public interest for showing it.

Greene's film had actually been commissioned by CBS News when it learned that he would be going to North Vietnam for the *San Francisco Chronicle*. CBS used only a few scenes of the film for a report in its evening newscast, and the documentary was offered to NET. Greene swore that the footage had not been inspected or censored by the North Vietnamese and that none of the scenes were staged or recreated.

INSTANT ANALYSIS ▶ the analytical reporting that usually follows a presidential address on the networks. Politicians and partisans have complained about it—particularly during the Nixon Administration (the term in fact was coined by Vice President Spiro T. Agnew in his famous speech denouncing network news, delivered in Des Moines November 1969)—because it appears to give broadcast pundits the last word over that of the President. But journalists point out that although newspaper analyses appear the next morning, they too are written immediately after the President's address.

Apparently in response to objections of the Nixon Administration, CBS chairman William S. Paley banned instant analysis on his network in 1972 but retracted the order five months later.

INSTITUTIONAL OWNERSHIP ▶ shares held in broadcast companies by banks, insurance companies and other financial institutions. Greatly liberalized policies during the 1980s have permitted much increased institutional holdings. The FCC considers an investor holding 5% of a company to be an "owner" subject to the commission's multiple ownership rules. The limit used to be 1%; this and other changes in defining "active" and "passive" ownership have also expanded the degree of permissible institutional involvement.

INTELSAT ▶ the International Telecommunications Satellite Organization, established in 1975, which owns and operates the global telecommunications system used by most countries of the world for international communications. The entire system is managed by the U.S. signatory, Comsat (Communications Satellite Corp.), under a contract with Intelsat. Comsat is also the largest owner, with a 38.5% investment share.

In all there are 121 member countries in Intelsat, served by a system of 17 satellites covering virtually all points of the globe. A new satellite to be launched in the early 1990s, Intelsat K, will have a footprint covering all of Europe, the eastern part of the U.S. and most of the major cities in Latin America. There are also spare satellites that are back-ups for the primary satellites over each of the oceans; these are used in instances of heavy traffic, such as during a war or during the World Cup soccer matches.

INTERACTIVE TELEVISION ▶ kinds of television that allow for direct viewer participation rather than mere passive consumption. The definition is broad enough to include home shopping channels, game shows that provide 900 numbers for viewer participation and cable's pay-per-view feature. But the truest forms are videotext and teletext that allow for information retrieval from the screen, optical video discs that permit random access, and Warner's noble experiment in the late 1970s with two-way cable, known as Qube. Interactive systems exist today that allow viewers to direct the course of a drama or to choose the stories they want to know more about in a newscast. Many TV professionals believe interactive television will come into its own by the end of the 1990s, when a generation that grew up on Nintendo video games, sophisticated telephones and home computers comes of age.

INTERCONNECTION ▶ the hooking up, or linking, of TV stations or cable systems through microwave, cable relay or satellites so that they may simultaneously carry the same programs or exchange their services. Interconnection on a national scale is represented by the three TV networks, but in public TV and cable there are also statewide and regional interconnections, and cable systems in different franchise areas of the same city maintain an interconnection in order to share certain programs. Interconnection is not synonymous with network, although as a physical capability it may imply a network.

INTERLACE ▶ the method by which scanning is accomplished in alternate sets of lines on broadcast television. Instead of scanning each line consecutively, the television system scans alternate sets of lines. For example, in the NTSC system, 1, 3, 5, 7, etc., are scanned, down to line 525, in 1/60 of a second; then the alternate lines—2, 4, 6, 8, etc.—are scanned, producing a complete picture in 1/30 of a second. Each set of lines is a field. Two fields, comprising a full picture, comprise a frame. One major purpose of interlace is elimination of the flicker that would occur if all 525 lines, or 625 lines in the CCIR system, were scanned consecutively.

INTERNATIONAL SHOWTIME ▶ family series on NBC in which Don Ameche hosted performances by foreign circuses, aquacades, ice shows and other spectacles. The hour-long series premiered on Sept. 15, 1961, and ran through 1965.

INTERTEL ▶ a step toward international communication taken in 1960 when broadcast organizations in four English-speaking countries agreed to produce a stream of documentaries in concert as the International Television Federation. The conditions were that the documentaries be presented on a bimonthly basis, be given prime-time exposure and be distributed nationally in each country represented. Each group financed its own production. Although some brilliant work resulted, and talented documentarians received exposure outside their own countries, the arrangement was fraught with problems, and Intertel disbanded in late 1968.

The participants were Westinghouse Broadcasting and National Educational Television in the U.S.; Associated Rediffusion Ltd. of the U.K.; the Canadian Broadcasting Corp.; and the Australian Broadcasting Commission. Intertel's demise was brought on in part by the withdrawal of Westinghouse, which found it difficult to carry some of the foreign programs, and by Rediffusion's loss of its license when Britain revamped its broadcast assignments.

Although one of the ideals of Intertel was to promote international understanding, it developed that some countries took exception to the way they were represented by producers of other participating countries. A Canadian documentary on Castro's government, *Cuba, Si!,* was scheduled but never shown. Another CBC film, Douglas Leiterman's *One More River,* on racial problems in the U.S., was rejected by both Westinghouse and NET as sensationalized.

Britain had some problems with Michael Sklar's *Postscript to Empire,* an American view of the changes in English life and of the conservative-liberal polarity there, and neither Canada nor the U.S. was altogether comfortable with the Rediffusion entry, *Living with a Giant,* produced by Rollo Gamble, which pointed up Canada's economic, cultural and political dominance by the U.S.

There were a number of outstanding programs from each country, however, including such NET-Westinghouse offerings as Sklar's *A Question of Color* and Dan Klugherz's *Canada in Crisis* and *American Samoa: Paradise Lost?*

INTV (ASSOCIATION OF INDEPENDENT TELEVISION STATIONS) ▶ organization formed in 1972 to represent the interests of stations that were not network-affiliated, particularly with respect to regulatory matters and the promotion of sales. While at first a small and fairly insignificant industry association, INTV came into prominence during the early 1980s with the boom in new UHF stations, most of which were independent. With cable delivery, UHFs became as easy to receive as VHF channels, and that helped spur the growth. From representing a relative handful of stations, INTV found itself with hundreds of members, and its annual conventions during the boom years attracted the syndication companies that built around it one of their primary trade shows.

But during the latter part of the decade some of the UHFs began to fail, and with dozens filing for bankruptcy the growth period ended. The same cable that gave UHF stations efficient distribution into homes was also delivering more cable networks to those homes that competed for their audience. The glory years of INTV effectively ended with the success of the Fox Network, which claimed around one-third of the country's independent stations as affiliates. While technically these stations were still independents, their circumstances were quite different from the non-affiliated stations, and INTV was not as cohesive as before. Moreover, the syndicators lost about a third of their prime customers for nighttime programming, and to them the INTV trade show became optional rather than mandatory.

INTV was founded by Roger Rice, then v.p. and general manager of KTVU Oakland. He later became president of the Television Bureau of Advertising (TvB). When Rice left, Herman Land, a broadcast consultant, became INTV's first executive director and later its president. On Land's departure for a new career in academia, the association came under the leadership of Preston Padden, who was forceful, energetic and charismatic, and his arrival was timed perfectly for the UHF explosion. Padden headed the organization through most of the 1980s and left in 1990 to join the Fox Network as vice president of affiliate relations. He was succeeded at INTV by James Hedlund.

INVENTORY ▶ commercial spot positions at a station or network that are still available for sale in a given quarter-year sales period.

IRELAND ▶ country with just under 1 million television households served by two channels of a state-run network, Radio Telefis Eirann (RTE), and a new private network, TV3, started in 1990. The two national channels, RTE 1 and Network 2, are complementary services programmed not to clash with similar kinds of shows in any hour. Emanating from Dublin, both carry commercials and a large amount of domestically produced programs. The private network, TV3, is owned by Windmill Lane Pictures and is distributed by cable and MMDS for around eight hours a day. It features a good deal of original programming by independent producers. The country also has 50 licensed cable operators mainly serving the larger population centers. They carry, along with the domestic channels, the four British terrestrial networks and the available satellite services, such as Sky and Superchannel.

IRELAND, CHARLES T., JR. (d. 1972) ▶ president of CBS Inc., successor to Dr. Frank Stanton, for nine months. Three months after being hospitalized with a heart spasm and then returning to work, he died in his sleep. Ireland came to the company, after a long executive search by CBS, as a specialist in finance and acquisitions for ITT. His selection in October 1971 indicated the direction CBS intended to take preparatory to the eventual retirement of William S. Paley, its founder and chairman. Ireland had been senior v.p. of the ITT conglomerate and its moving force in the expansion with new companies. A consummate businessman, he was, however an "outsider" to the show business activities of CBS—television, radio and recordings. Death came while he was still learning the ways of the company, and he was succeeded soon after by Arthur R. Taylor, a young executive previously with International Paper Co. Taylor was fired by Paley in October 1976.

***IRONSIDE* ▶** hit hour-long detective series on NBC (1967-74) whose principal character, a special consultant to the San Francisco Police Department, is confined to a wheelchair. Raymond Burr portrayed former detective chief Robert T. Ironside, who becomes a consultant, with his own crime-solving team, when an attempt on his life leaves him paralyzed from the waist down. Featured were Don Mitchell as personal assistant Mark Sanger, Don Galloway as Lieutenant Ed Brown and Elizabeth Baur as Officer Fran Belding (Barbara Anderson appeared in the first four seasons as police officer Eve Whitfield). It was by Harbour Productions and Universal TV in association with NBC-TV.

IRTS (INTERNATIONAL RADIO AND TELEVISION SOCIETY) ▶ a grandiose name for New York City's version of the broadcast advertising clubs common to many of the larger television markets. The Los Angeles equivalent is called the Hollywood Radio and Television Society and the Chicago counterpart the Chicago Broadcast Advertising Club. Although formed to bring together members of the advertising industry with executives of broadcasting, the IRTS membership also includes representatives of foreign systems and communications faculty from universities. The IRTS monthly luncheons, which traditionally begin in September with an address by the chairman of the FCC, serve as a forum for speakers on diverse broadcast subjects. One of the annual features of both IRTS and HRTS is a panel discussion with the program chiefs of the networks. Through its IRTS Foundation, IRTS also underwrites college-industry and faculty-industry seminars, as well as a number of in-service training programs for younger people in the broadcast and related communications fields.

IRVING, RICHARD (d. 1991) ▶ prolific producer-director long associated with Universal TV, where he was executive vice president until 1979. In the medium's early years, he helped set up Revue, the MCA/Universal TV production arm, from which he produced shows in such anthology series as *Mystery Theater, Chevron Theatre* and *Pepsi-Cola Playhouse.* Later he produced for *Wagon Train, The Name of the Game* and *Columbo* and directed the pilot for *The Six Million Dollar Man.* After leaving Universal, he directed *The Jesse Owens Story* and *Hell Town* and produced a remake of *The Last Days of Pompeii.*

ISELIN, JOHN JAY ▶ former president of WNET New York, largest of the public TV stations and a leading producer of national programming, from 1973-86. He succeeded James Day as president after having served two years as general manager. With a background in publishing and journalism, and with no previous experience in broadcasting, Iselin joined WNET in 1971 with the initial assignment of creating a strong local identity for the New York station after its merger with another PTV entity, National Educational Television. One of the results was the innovative nightly news magazine *51st State.*

As president, Iselin proved an effective fund-raiser, willing to invest funds on high-risk projects. Under his aegis WNET introduced such major national series as *The MacNeil/Lehrer NewsHour, The Brain, Civilization and the Jews,* and *Innovation.* As an effective impresario and promoter, Iselin increased the station's audience and its financial base, though he was also forced to steer it through several financial crises. Before coming to WNET Iselin was a v.p. with Harper & Row and senior editor for national affairs with *Newsweek.* Following his 1986 resignation from WNET he became president of New York's Cooper Union.

ISRAEL ▶ a country with two national terrestrial channels that appears on the brink of a cable explosion. On the first channel, run by state broadcaster Israel TV, three services share time—Arabic, Educational and Hebrew. On the second, which began in 1986, three franchise-holders get two days of airtime each and split up Saturdays. But cable has begun to take off in Israel with several alternative channels on offer, and analysts believe that some 90% of the country's 700,000 TV households will have cable by 1996.

ISRAEL, LARRY H. ▶ broadcast executive who became president and chief operating officer of the *Washington Post* Co. in 1973 and resigned in early 1977, apparently after a dispute with the chairman, Katherine Graham. A businessman with a journalism background and a scholarly aspect, Israel earlier had risen to top positions with Group W and the Post-Newsweek Stations. On leaving the *Washington Post,* he proceeded to work at acquiring stations in forming a new broadcast group.

ISSUES AND ANSWERS **▶** ABC's Sunday morning newsmaker show that ran from 1960 until 1981, when it was supplanted by *This Week With David Brinkley. Issues and Answers* was mounted in a time when ABC was seeking parity with the other networks. As NBC had *Meet the Press* and CBS *Face the Nation,* ABC was determined to have something of the kind that might make Page One news the next day. Like its counterparts, it originated in Washington for 30 minutes and usually featured a guest from government. Bob Clark was the permanent panelist who usually was joined by another ABC News correspondent. Peggy Whedon produced the program from the time it began until it gave way to *This Week.*

When Brinkley left NBC, he was immediately hired by ABC News president Roone Arledge, who designed a new one-hour Sunday morning program to suit Brinkley's talents and experience. *Issues* was dropped to make room for *This Week,* and Dorrance Smith became producer. In addition to Brinkley the regulars on the program are Sam Donaldson, Cokie Roberts and George Will, who are joined from time to time by other journalists.

Arledge's efforts have been vindicated. Although it was the latest to enter, Brinkley's has become the dominant network news panel show on Sunday morning in ratings, critical attention, and perceived importance.

IT TAKES A THIEF **▶** hour-long series taking a tongue-in-cheek approach to counter-espionage, starring Robert Wagner as Alexander Mundy, a master thief paroled to ply his trade solely for a government intelligence agency. Fred Astaire appeared in several episodes as his father, Alistair Mundy, the greatest thief of them all. Produced by Universal TV, it played on ABC (1968-70).

ITALY ▶ a country whose television is dominated by two forces: the state-run RAI (Radiotelevisione Italiana), which operates three national channels, and Silvio Berlusconi's Fininvest, which also operates three in the private, commercial mode. Together they account for 90% of advertising revenue and nearly 90% of viewing audience, although there are also around 1,000 independent television stations spread throughout the Italian peninsula, and additional competition from Tele Monte Carlo, beaming into Italy from the principality of Monaco. None of the competitors have made a dent in the country's essential duopoly. RAI's three networks typically aggregate 50% of the viewing audience; Berlusconi's channels, collectively, typically 40%.

Italy was the first European country to deregulate. In 1975 the Italian government threw open all the available frequencies to all who might claim them for commercial use. In short order hundreds of local commercial stations were built without any government oversight or restrictions and before there was sufficient advertising in the marketplace to support any of them. Some of the stations found they could attract an audience by airing X-rated movies at night; stations in Milan and Turin inaugurated amateur stripteases by housewives, while others created game shows that were variations on strip poker.

Alignments of stations to form a national network were attempted by several companies, but the only one to succeed was Berlusconi. Since government rules did not allow a network interconnection of local stations, Berlusconi built the first of his networks by servicing the member stations with cassettes for the programming and advertising in every hour. Then he bought up other assembled networks of stations that were failing, and had three running simultaneously. RAI-TV, meanwhile, expanded from two channels to three.

In 1990 the Italian government developed legislation that intended to break up the RAI/Fininvest duopoly. But after all the pulling of political strings in a country whose politics, business and media have strong links, the bill that was finally passed scarcely diluted the power of the two principal broadcasters. In fact, it strengthened Berlusconi's position by allowing his networks to interconnect their stations, giving them the ability to carry live sports and national newscasts.

In 1991 a three-channel pay TV network known as Telepiu was launched. The brainchild of Berlusconi, it is owned by a consortium of his closest friends and business associates. Berlusconi's Fininvest could not actively participate in the ownership because the Italian law adopted in 1990 for media ownership sets the limit at three networks.

ITC ENTERTAINMENT GROUP ▶ production and distribution company with an international pedigree and a long history of ownership changes. The company was formed in 1958 as a British-American partnership of Lew Grade's ATV and the Jack Wrather organization. Called the Independent Television Corp., it was established essentially for the international distribution of programs. Later Grade bought the entire company and made it both the distribution arm of his regional TV station in England, ATV, with key offices in the U.S. headed by Abe Mandel, and an independent producer of program series. Among the early ITC shows to play both sides of the Atlantic were *The Adventures of Robin Hood* with Richard Greene, *Ramar of the Jungle*, *The Saint*, *Secret Agent*, and *The Prisoner*. Later the company scored with such hit series in U.S. syndication as *UFO*, *Space 1999*, and *The Muppet Show*.

In 1982 Grade sold ITC to Australian entrepreneur Robert Holmes á Court, who appointed Jerry Leider and Chris Gorog to run it. They concentrated primarily on the production of TV movies and mini-series for the U.S. networks, among them *Billionaire Boys Club*, *Sidney Sheldon's Windmill of the Gods* and *Poor Little Rich Girl*. When Holmes á Court's other financial interests suffered in the "Black Monday" market reversal of 1987, he sold ITC some months later to fellow Australian, Alan Bond. The following year, Bond sold the company to senior management. In leading the buyout, Gorog raised the entire financing, $125 million, from Midland-Montagu Ventures of London.

Just prior to the buyout, the company had again been restructured, with management centralized in Los Angeles and the London and New York operations turned into regional offices. Leider left the company when, after the buyout, ITC retreated somewhat from the risky business of production to concentrate on acquiring movies and programs for domestic and international distribution. Gorog became president and CEO in 1990.

ITFS (INSTRUCTIONAL TELEVISION FIXED SERVICE) ▶ omnidirectional microwave system utilizing channels in the 2.5 to 2.69 gigahertz frequency range, which was established by the FCC in 1963 expressly for use by educational institutions. An ITFS station at a school district headquarters may transmit up to four programs simultaneously to its schools. "Fixed service" denotes reception by special receivers at the intended institutions. The Catholic Television Network, established in several major cities, broadcasts on ITFS to its parishes and schools.

In 1976, more than 150 of these point-to-point stations were in use. Operating on frequencies above the UHF band, with their power generally limited to 10 watts, the ITFS stations in most cases carry less than five miles. The successful utilization of ITFS made it possible for ETV to become public television, since the dependency on it for instructional programming was lessened.

***IT'S GARRY SHANDLING'S SHOW* ▶** offbeat sitcom with youthful comedian Garry Shandling that originated on pay cable network Showtime in 1986 and then moved to the Fox Network. The program's unusual characteristic was that Shandling occasionally stepped out of the story to address the audience directly in the manner of George Burns in the old *Burns and Allen Show* of the 1950s. Created by Shandling and former *Saturday Night Live* writer Alan Zweibel, the series had Shandling playing himself, a standup comic and star of a TV show. Featured were Molly Cheek, Scott Nemes, Michael Tucci, Bernadette Birkett, Barbara Carson, Paul Willson, Ian Buchanan and Jessica Harper. Executive producers were Bernie Brillstein, Brad Grey, and Shandling.

ITVS (INDEPENDENT TELEVISION SERVICE) ▶ a public TV organization created in 1990 to administer the $6 million (plus administrative costs) of the Corporation for Public Broadcasting funds that Congress said must go to independent producers. ITVS, with its own board and executive staff, was the product of intensive lobbying by independent producers who felt they were not getting a fair shake from CPB's grant policies.

I'VE GOT A SECRET **▶** see Game Shows.

Garry Shandling on the set of *It's Garry Shandling's Show*

J

JACKER, CORINNE ▶ playwright whose work in TV has included the American adaptation of Ingmar Bergman's *The Lie* and episodes for *Visions, The Adams Chronicles* and the CTW drama series on PBS. She also served as head writer and editor of *Bicentennial Minutes* on CBS.

JACKSON, KEITH ▶ ABC sports commentator, known especially for announcing the NCAA football series and the Monday night baseball games. His other credits include the *Pro Bowlers Tour, ABC Championship Auto Racing,* major league baseball and events for ABC's *Wide World of Sports.* Before joining ABC Jackson had announced sports events for the University of Washington for eight years, the football games of Washington State for four years and the games for several AFL teams in the west. He had also worked 10 years at KOMO-TV, the ABC affiliate in Seattle.

JACOBI, WILLIAM G. ▶ president and chief operating officer of Nielsen Media Research, the TV ratings company, since January 1991. In 1984, as senior vice president for planning and acquisitions at Dun & Bradstreet Corp., he directed the company's $1.3 billion acquisition of A.C. Nielsen.

JACOBS, DAVID ▶ writer-producer for television who created such prime-time soap operas as *Dallas* (1978-91) and its spin-off *Knots Landing* (1979—), as well as the TV movie *Dallas: The Early Years.* He has produced several other prime-time serials, including *Secrets of Midland Heights* (1980-81), *Berrenger's* (1985), and *Guns of Paradise* (1990-91). Jacobs also serves as executive producer for *Knots Landing* and *Homefront,* which premiered in the 1991-92 season.

JAGODA, BARRY ▶ special assistant and chief television advisor to President Carter for the first two years of his administration. Previously, he had been an independent producer and for several years a producer in the CBS News special events unit.

***JAKE AND THE FATMAN* ▶** serviceable CBS detective series in the tradition of *Barnaby Jones, Quincy* and *Ironside* to the extent that an older detective provides the brainpower while his young sidekick does the legwork and fighting. The series premiered on CBS in 1987 and stars veteran TV actor William Conrad (*Cannon*) as the Fatman and Joe Penny as Jake. The series is produced by the Fred Silverman Company, in association with Dean Hargrove Productions and Viacom.

***JAMES AT 15* ▶** NBC series written by novelist Dan Wakefield, as his first TV effort, about the growing-up process of a sensitive teenager, played by Lance Kerwin. The series entered the schedule in October 1977 to replace an

NBC failure but was itself a marginal performer. After Wakefield resigned in a clash with NBC, the program's days were numbered, and it ran out its skein in the spring of 1978.

The dispute occurred after Paul Klein, then NBC program chief, offered an idea to perk up the ratings: James would turn 16 and lose his virginity on his birthday. Wakefield proceeded to write the script, but he quit the show when NBC Standards & Practices would not accept dialogue between the boy and girl on the matter of contraception, even when the euphemism "responsibility" was used for birth control. When the episode aired in February 1978, after Wakefield had left, the title of the series was changed to *James at 16.* Presumably, if it had continued to run, the title would have changed annually.

Featured in the cast were Linden Chiles and Lynn Carlin as parents Paul and Joan Hunter, and David Hubbard and Susan Myers as friends Ludwig (Sly) Hazeltine and Marlene.

JAMES, DENNIS ▶ veteran emcee of daytime game shows who came into prominence in TV in the early 1950s as commentator of the wrestling matches on the DuMont Network, adding sound effects and generally contributing to the comedy that was part of the grappling exhibitions in those times. He went on to host a flock of game shows over more than two decades, including *What's My Line, Chance of a Lifetime, High Finance, The Name's the Same, People Will Talk, Haggis Baggis* and *Judge for Yourself.* He also emceed a daytime variety show, *Club 60,* and early in his career was announcer for *Ted Mack's Original Amateur Hour.*

***JANE GOODALL AND THE WORLD OF ANIMAL BEHAVIOR* ▶** umbrella title for an ABC series of nature documentaries featuring Goodall, who came to national attention through a *National Geographic* article and TV special as a scientist who lived among the apes. Her first effort in the ABC series, narrated by Hal Holbrook, was *The Wild Dogs of Africa* (January 1973) and her second was *Baboons of Gombe* (February 1974). The two were produced by Marshall Flaum for Metromedia Producers Corp.

***JANE WYMAN THEATER* ▶** half-hour dramatic anthology series on ABC (1955-58) with Jane Wyman as hostess and star. Some of the playlets were rerun on CBS in what was entitled *Jane Wyman's Summer Playhouse.* The series was via Lewman Productions.

JANKOWSKI, GENE F. ▶ former president of the CBS Broadcast Group (1977-88), who not long after Laurence Tisch's acquisition of the company was replaced by Howard Stringer. During his tenure through the tempestuous 1980s, Jankowski acquired the reputation at CBS of an eternal optimist who saw no real danger to the existing system. He seriously misjudged cable's impact on the networks. On leaving CBS, he started a company that sought to buy broadcast properties.

In the top CBS broadcast post, Jankowski succeeded John F. Schneider, under whom he had previously served as executive vice president. Later he was also named a vice president of CBS Inc. and a director of the corporation. His appointment as president was accompanied by the most extensive management reorganization in the company's history, with the creation of new divisions and the appointment of five divisional presidents, all reporting to him.

Jankowski rose in the company through sales, having started in 1961 as an account executive with the radio network, rising there to eastern sales manager. In 1969 he joined the CBS-TV sales staff, then became general sales manager of WCBS-TV, New York. He was named v.p. of sales for the owned stations division in 1973 and the following year became v.p. of finance and planning for the division. That proved the springboard to CBS Inc. two years later he was elevated to v.p. and controller for the corporation and a year after that v.p. of administration.

Jankowski attracted notice in the company in the early 1970s when, in the wake of the ban on cigarette advertising, he conducted a successful effort to bring new advertisers into television. Affable and businesslike, he maintained a low profile as president of the broadcast group and was not an autocratic leader, deeming management a team effort. Thus while the cult of personality flourished at NBC with Fred Silverman and at ABC with Frederick Pierce, Roone Arledge and Tony Thomopoulos, it was muted at CBS.

JAPAN ▶ dynamic TV market of the Pacific Rim whose 37.9 million television households are served by a two-channel state network, NHK (Japanese Broadcasting Corp.), five private national networks, and one pay-television network, along with cable and direct-broadcast satellite (DBS) services. NHK is funded by receiver license fees and operates a general entertainment and an educational network.

Among the commercial channels, the ratings leader for years has been Fuji TV, but it is not so dominant as to eclipse the other networks: Asahi National Broadcasting, Nippon Television Network, Tokyo Broadcasting System, and TV Tokyo Channel 12. All were created to serve regions, or prefectures, but each has sufficient local affiliates to achieve near national penetration. Most are owned or partly owned by newspaper interests. The pay-TV network, whose programming consists entirely of movies, is known as Star Channel.

Cable penetration by the end of 1991 was at around 16%, but it and direct-to-home satellite broadcasting are expected to expand rapidly in the 1990s with the introduction of new program services. NHK has been permitted to operate two DBS channels, one offering entertainment, the other a 24-hour news and sports service, and with those has been pioneering the burgeoning DBS field. Japan Satellite Broadcasting's channel, called Wowow, made a strong entry in DBS with a schedule of around 500 movies a year, most of them foreign.

For one of the world's most populous and prosperous countries, Japan as represented by its networks has scarcely been involved in the buying and selling of programming in the world marketplace. The language and cultural barriers have been the chief reasons. But in recent times, young Japanese have become involved with western pop culture, and the new pay-channels and DBS services are bringing more North American and European programming to Japan.

Japan's giant electronics companies may be hastening the process of westernizing the East by buying up much of Hollywood. At the end of 1991 three of the major studios were owned all or in part by Japanese companies: Columbia going to Sony, MCA to Matsushita, and part of Warner Bros. to Toshiba and C. Itoh. This might be viewed another way, however, as the start of easternizing the West.

JARRIEL, TOM ▶ veteran broadcast journalist for ABC News since 1965, familiar to viewers as a regular contributor to the prime-time weekly magazine *20/20.*

During the 1990-91 television season, Jarriel's reports included a piece purporting to be an actual exorcism that ABC claimed was sanctioned by the Roman Catholic Church; a study of education about death in public schools; and a look at Romania's squalid orphanages and the desperate efforts of American couples to adopt Rumanian children. In 1988 Jarriel anchored two ABC News specials, "The Business of Defense: Flaws in the Shield," critically focusing on the Pentagon, the military contractors who build the weapons, and their middlemen; and "Life After Death Row," on the 102 men and women then awaiting execution in California who, because of a change in the law, became eligible for parole.

Since arriving in Washington in 1968, Jarriel has covered national politics, serving as ABC News White House correspondent from 1969 until the inauguration of Jimmy Carter and covering President Nixon on his historic trip to China, as well as reporting on various summit meetings in Moscow. From 1979-90 Jarriel served as anchor for ABC News *Weekend Report* and ABC *Newsbrief.*

He first received national attention for his coverage of the civil rights movement in the South, and was, according to ABC, the only network news correspondent covering the Rev. Martin Luther King, Jr., on the night of his assassination.

JARVIS, LUCY ▶ documentary producer for NBC News (1960-76), whose notable achievements include filming the Kremlin, China's Forbidden City, Scotland Yard and The Louvre. Her work has spanned the political and cultural spheres, and her videography has an international flavor. She produced, among other TV specials and films, the following: *The Kremlin* (1963), *The Louvre* (1964), *Who Shall Live?* (1965), *Mary Martin: Hello Dolly! Around the World* (1965), *Dr. Barnard's Heart Transplant Operations* (1968), *Khrushchev in Exile: His Opinions and Revelations* (1967), *Bravo Picasso!* (1967) and *Trip to Nowhere* (1970).

In 1976 she left NBC to produce independently, her first assignment being to produce prime time specials with Barbara Walters for ABC. That relationship ended after the first program. In the 1981-82 season she produced *Family Reunion,* a four-hour mini-series starring Bette Davis.

***JEFFERSONS, THE* ▶** situation comedy on CBS (1975-85) centering on a middle-class black family in a luxury apartment building; its characters, in certain respects, parallel those of *All in the Family,* from which the series was spun off. Slotted immediately following *All in the Family* and preceding *Mary Tyler Moore,* the series established itself at once and in 1976 took over the Saturday evening leadoff spot long held by the Bunkers. *The Jeffersons* broke new ground in TV by introducing a biracial couple as neighbors of the principals.

Featured were Sherman Hemsley and Isabel Sanford as George and Louise Jefferson, Mike Evans—succeeded by Damon Evans—as son Lionel, Roxie Roker and Franklin Cover as neighbors Helen and Tom Willis, Berlinda Tolbert as their daughter Jenny Willis (who eventually married Lionel) and Zara Cully as Mama Jefferson. It was by Norman Lear's T.A.T. Communications with NRW Productions.

JENCKS, RICHARD W. ▶ high-ranking executive of CBS during the early 1970s who, for a time, was a leading candidate to succeed Frank Stanton as president of the corporation. But his star fell suddenly, and two years after attaining the post of president of the CBS Broadcast Group he was assigned in 1972 to Washington as corporate v.p. He asked for early retirement in 1976.

JENKINS, CHARLES FRANCIS (d. 1934) ▶ inventor and entrepreneur who in 1928 inaugurated the first regularly scheduled television broadcasts. Already known as the inventor of the basic motion picture theater projector, he regularly broadcast "radiomovies" from Washington, D.C., using a spinning disc that provided one-inch-square pictures with 48 lines of resolution to eager hobbyists who modified their radio sets to receive the silhouette images. As early as 1923 he had received recognition for transmitting a picture of President Harding by wireless from Washington to Philadelphia. The Jenkins broadcasts continued until 1932. Jenkins Television Corp., which manufactured receivers, was taken over by De Forest Radio Co., which later was declared bankrupt. In 1929 Jenkins forecast: "The folks in California and Maine, and all the way in between, will be able to see the inauguration ceremonies of their President in Washington, the Army and Navy games on Franklin Field, and the struggle for supremacy in our national sport, baseball."

JENNIE: LADY RANDOLPH CHURCHILL ▶ seven-part mini-series on the life of Jennie Jerome, the wealthy American who married Lord Randolph Churchill and became mother of Winston Churchill. Produced by Britain's Thames TV, and starring Lee Remick, it drew high ratings in its U.S. run on PBS in 1975. More than a biography, the serial marked the social changes that occurred from the late 19th to the early 20th centuries. The hour episodes were written by Julian Mitchell and directed by James Cellan Jones.

Peter Jennings

JENNINGS, PETER ▶ since 1983, anchor and senior editor of ABC's *World News Tonight.* In a career that has spanned most of the major news events of our times, the Canadian-born journalist brought to the ABC anchor desk years of first-hand experience covering stories as a foreign correspondent. His thoughtful, dispassionate style and sensitivity to the news anchor's special responsibility in mediating the world of sometimes cataclysmic events won him the widest viewership among the networks during the Persian Gulf War. During that war, he also anchored a special broadcast, *War in the Gulf: Answering Children's Questions,* to ease fears created in youngsters by television's war coverage.

A high-school dropout, Jennings began his broadcasting career in one of Canada's local radio stations, rose quickly to become co-anchor of the national newscast on CTV, the country's commercial network, and, with less than six years in broadcasting, was snapped up by ABC News and in 1964 made the anchor of its evening news. He was 26 at the time. Three years and many disappointing ratings later, the youthful Jennings was replaced by Frank Reynolds and sent into the field "to mature" and get more experience. He spent most of the next decade as an ABC correspondent, covering stories in the U.S. and abroad—the Kennedy assassination and funeral, the civil rights movement in the South, and several presidential campaigns. But it was as a foreign correspondent, covering the "hot spots" of the world, that he grew into national stature. In 1969 he established ABC's news bureau in Beirut, the first American television news bureau in the Arab world, and began a seven-year tenure as its chief.

In the late 1970s ABC News made him the London-based co-anchor of its three-man team on *World News Tonight,* and then in 1983, on the death of Frank Reynolds, returned him to New York as the sole anchor on the show he had left 15 years before.

JEOPARDY! ▶ see Game Shows.

JESUS OF NAZARETH ▶ 6-hour and 37-minute film on the life of Jesus, directed by Franco Zeffirelli and coproduced by Britain's ATV and Italy's RAI-TV; it premiered in the U.S. in 1977 as a two-parter on NBC on Palm Sunday (April 3) and Easter (April 10), dominating prime time. The film, reported to have cost $18 million to produce, drew a 50 share both nights in its debut and had an estimated cumulative audience of 90 million viewers.

The U.S. rights had been purchased by General Motors for $3 million two years before the telecast, and G.M. had an additional investment of $1.5 million for air time on NBC when it decided to withdraw its sponsorship. The automotive company was reacting to a national campaign by a number of evangelical religious groups to block the telecast because they objected to the idea that Jesus was being presented as an ordinary human being in the film biography. Led by Bob Jones III, president of Bob Jones University, the protestors—who had not screened the film—had formed their opinion from a statement Zeffirelli had made in a press interview. In literature that was widely circulated around the country to fundamentalist groups, those who opposed the film called for a boycott of General Motors products.

Procter and Gamble then purchased sponsorship of the premiere telecast at bargain rates, although G.M. retained the rights to repeat showings. By the time it went on the air, the film, after special screenings by NBC, had the endorsement and praise of religious leaders of the major faiths.

In the film, Robert Powell portrayed Jesus; Olivia Hussey, the Virgin Mary; Yorgo Voyagis, Joseph; Peter Ustinov, Herod; Isabel Mestres, Salome; Michael York, John the Baptist; and James Farentino, Simon Peter. The international cast also included Claudia Cardinale, Anthony Quinn, James Earl Jones, Donald Pleasence, Laurence Olivier, James Mason, Christopher Plummer, Stacy Keach, Rod Steiger, Ernest Borgnine, Ian Holm, and Fernando Rey.

The program has been repeated several times by NBC at Easter time, with good ratings every time out.

Bernard J. Kinham was executive producer, Vincenzo Labella producer, and Anthony Burgess, Suso Cecchi d'Amico, and Zeffirelli the writers.

JETSONS, THE ▶ animated situation comedy about a family in the 21st century whose concerns and spoken idiom were of the 1960s. Premiering on ABC in 1962 as an offshoot of Hanna-Barbera's *The Flintstones,* it enjoyed a successful run, was purchased by CBS in reruns and in 1971 was scheduled by NBC on Saturday mornings. The voices were by George O'Hanlon (George Jetson), Penny Singleton (Jane, his wife), Janet Waldo (daughter Judy), Daws Butler (son Elroy), Mel Blanc (George's boss, Cosmo Spacely) and Don Messick (Astro, the dog).

JEWISON, NORMAN ▶ producer-director who was active in New York network originations in the late 1950s and early 1960s specializing in music-comedy specials such as *Tonight with Belafonte* (1959) and *An Hour with Danny Kaye* (1960). He gained his initial reputation in the medium in his native Canada as a director for the CBC. Like many another accomplished TV director, he quit the medium for motion pictures. His film credits include *Fiddler on the Roof* and *Rollerball.*

JIGGLIES ▶ programs that trade to some degree on attractive women whose distinctive body parts bounce or wiggle. The term was used derisively by an NBC executive in the 1970s to describe certain ABC shows that were beating his—*Charlie's Angels,* for one—and the critics borrowed it. It has since become part of the television lexicon.

JIM NABORS HOUR ▶ hour-long comedy-variety show starring Jim Nabors and Frank Sutton, with Ronnie Schell and Karen Morrow. It was produced by Naborly Productions for CBS (1969-71).

JIMMY STEWART SHOW, THE ▶ half-hour situation comedy presented on NBC (1971-72) that failed to catch on despite the long movie stardom of James Stewart. In the series he portrayed a college professor faced with the problems of generation gap both on campus and at home. Featured were John McGiver, Jonathan Daly and Julie Adams. It was by

Warner Bros. in association with AJK Ablidon Productions.

JOEY BISHOP SHOW, THE ▶ situation comedy vehicle for Joey Bishop that underwent several changes of format, cast and network—all to no avail. Nevertheless, it ran from 1961 to 1965. Featured were Bishop as comedian Joey Barnes and, beginning with the second season, Abby Dalton as Joey's wife, Ellie, and Corbett Monica as his writer, Larry. Produced by Danny Thomas's Bellmar Productions, the series started on NBC and two seasons later moved to CBS.

JOHNNY CASH SHOW, THE ▶ country-music variety series on ABC, produced in Nashville by Screen Gems. It had a successful run as a summer replacement in 1969 and was brought back as a mid-season entry the following January. Although successful at first, it faltered the next season and was canceled.

JOHNSON, NICHOLAS ▶ Enemy Number-One to the broadcast industry for the more than seven years he served as an FCC commissioner (1966-73). He was a noisy reformer who campaigned for virtually everything the industry feared: counter-commercials, license challenges by citizens at renewal time, the break-up of media monopolies, an informed and activist FCC and access to the airwaves for minorities, political dissenters and representatives of the counter-culture.

He remained on the commission several months beyond his term of appointment because his successor had not yet been named; then he swung into action to oppose (unsuccessfully) the confirmation of the nominee, James Quello, because he was a former broadcaster.

On leaving the commission, Johnson—who had developed a following among youth—entered politics but was defeated in a bid for the Democratic nomination for congressman in his home district in Iowa. He then continued his work in broadcast reform as chair of the National Citizens Committee for Broadcasting in Washington, publisher of the magazine *Access* and media commentator on the NPR program *All Things Considered.* When Ralph Nader took over NCCB as chair in 1978, Johnson became head of a new, related organization, the National Citizens Communications Lobby.

Johnson was the most unorthodox and flamboyant of commissioners, boldly taking his dissents to the press, writing magazine articles critical of the FCC and of the industry and making speeches to citizens groups, stirring their participation in license renewals and advising them of their rights to challenge broadcast licenses. He even wrote a book as a commissioner, *How to Talk Back to Your Television Set,* which detailed the public's rights in broadcasting. Unfazed by the industry's attacks upon him as a censor and a dictator, or by the anger he aroused in FCC chairperson Dean Burch with his brashness and his ridiculing of the commission, Johnson pursued his causes in public, taking advantage of the print media's receptivity to any denunciation of broadcasting by a public official.

Proclaiming himself the public's advocate on the FCC, he accepted the appellation of "radical" and grew a mustache and wore his hair long as a message that he was not of the establishment. He was faulted, even by admirers, for being given to hyperbole, as when he called television "a child molester" in building a case for reforms in children's programming.

Although he was thought of as a dissenter, he voted with the majority on such critical issues as the denial of the WHDH license to the *Boston Herald-Traveler* and the adoption of the prime time-access rule.

Johnson was only 32 when he was appointed to the FCC by President Johnson. But by then he had already served as administrator of the U.S. Maritime Administration (1964-66), practiced law with the Washington firm of Covington and Burling, taught law for three years at the University of California at Berkeley and served as law clerk to the late Supreme Court Justice Hugo L. Black.

JOHNSON, ROBERT ▶ founder and president of Black Entertainment Television (BET), a basic-cable network programmed for the black community. A former press secretary to District of Columbia congressional delegate Walter Fauntroy, and erstwhile vice president of government relations for the National Cable Television Association (1976-79), Johnson launched BET in January 1980, initially as a part-time service (it programmed just one night a week, Fridays, from 11 p.m. to 2 a.m.). Later that year he also established District Cablevision to pursue a cable franchise in Washington and was able to begin construction in September 1986. BET has become a 24-hour, seven-day service, programmed with a mix of talk shows, music videos and series, and reaching more than 30 million subscribers.

JOHNSON, TOM ▶ president of CNN (Cable News Network) since August 1990. Johnson's predecessors were Burt Reinhardt (1982-90) and the founding president, Reese Schonfeld (1979-82), who was present at the creation with Ted Turner.

Johnson came from publishing, where he had been with the *Los Angeles Times* since 1977. In 1980 Johnson became its chief executive officer and the first non-Chandler to head the newspaper. During his nine years as a publisher, the *Times* won six Pulitzer prizes, and with a 1990 daily circulation of 1.2 million, and 1.5 million Sunday, it became the largest metropolitan newspaper in America.

A native of Macon, Georgia, Johnson began his career on the *Macon Telegraph and News,* later going to Washington, where he worked for President Lyndon B. Johnson as deputy press secretary and special assistant to the president.

JOKER'S WILD, THE **▶** see Game Shows.

JONES, ANNE P. ▶ FCC commissioner (1979-83), appointed by President Carter to the female seat previously held by Margita White. She had been general counsel for the Federal Home Loan Bank Board and earlier, for 10 years, on the staff of the Security Exchange Commission. A Democrat from Boston, she had been recommended to the White House as a possible nominee by FCC chairman Ferris, with whom she had been a classmate at Boston College Law School. Despite that connection, she won confirmation easily on the judgment that she was a person of independent spirit who would not automatically cast her vote with the chairman. She became the third Boston Law School alumnus on the commission, along with Ferris and Joseph Fogarty.

JONES, CHARLIE ▶ veteran sports announcer whose broadcasts of professional football on network television for more than thirty years is a record. He worked the very first American Football League game in 1960 and the first AFL Championship Game and Super Bowl I. He was the play-by-play announcer on ABC's coverage of the AFL from 1960 to 1964 and the commentator on the network's *Wide World of Sports.* In 1965 he joined NBC for its coverage of the AFL and continues to do play-by-play for NBC's NFL games. Jones has described 25 different sports for NBC, including Wimbledon tennis, figure skating and various events for NBC's *SportsWorld,* in addition to calling the track-and-field action for NBC's coverage of the Seoul Olympics.

JONES, CHARLOTTE SCHIFF ▶ one-time v.p. of CBS Cable and former producer of the short-lived CBS series *People,* based on *People* magazine. Before joining CBS Cable as one of its original staff when it was organized in 1980, she had been an executive of Time Inc., first with Manhattan Cable, then as assistant publisher of *People* at the time of the network series. Before joining Time, she was director of community programming for Teleprompter Cable in New York.

JONES, CHUCK ▶ animation producer-director who for a time in the late 1960s served as head of children's programs for ABC-TV. Most of his career had been spent with the cartoon division of Warner Bros. (1938-62), where he created the Roadrunner and Pepe LePew cartoon series and helped to develop Porky Pig and Daffy Duck. His association with ABC began while he was co-producer, writer and director of *The Bugs Bunny Show* on that network. He was producer of *Cricket on Times Square* and *A Very Merry Cricket* and was writer, director and producer of the *Jungle Book* animated specials.

JONES, MERLE S. (d. 1976) ▶ long-time CBS executive who for 14 months was president of the network (1957-58) and then became president of the owned-stations division for 10 years until his retirement in 1968. His career with CBS spanned 32 years, beginning in 1936 as assistant to the g.m. of KMOX, the CBS-owned radio station in St. Louis. Except for three years with Cowles Broadcasting in Washington, D.C. (1944-7), his entire subsequent service was with CBS. He was g.m. of WCCO Minneapolis St. Paul (1947), when it was owned by CBS; then headed KNX Los Angeles and the Columbia Pacific Network (1949); and then the TV counterpart, KTSL (now KNXT), before becoming v.p. in charge of the CBS-owned TV stations. In 1956 he was named executive v.p. of the network, and a year later became president. He was a director of CBS from 1957 to 1968.

JONESTOWN MASSACRE ▶ ambush at the airport outside Jonestown, Guyana, on Nov. 18, 1978, which set in motion the events leading to the incredible mass suicides of the cult followers of the Rev. Jim Jones. Killed in the ambush, along with California Congressman Leo Ryan, who was investigating the cult, were two members of NBC News, Don Harris and Bob Brown. Also a victim was Greg Robinson, a photographer for the *San Francisco Examiner.*

Harris, a reporter based on the West Coast, had previously reported on Southeast Asia for NBC. Brown, a newsreel cameraman, had come on staff six months before the fatal episode, having previously worked as a free lance for CBS and other organizations. Brown filmed the ambush even as he was being shot, and that footage received wide exposure on network newscasts and special reports on Guyana. Harris's posthumous scoop was the final interview with the Rev. Jones, preserved on film. Bob Flick, an NBC News field producer who escaped the massacre, provided the eyewitness account of it for reporters.

JOSEPHSON, MARVIN ▶ major figure in the field of talent representation and program packaging; through a series of mergers, he parlayed a small personal management business into the country's second largest talent agency, ICM (International Creative Management), behind only CAA. The firm represents hundreds of performers, writers, producers, directors and production companies for the standard 10% commission and has been responsible for packaging scores of TV series. In 1973 Josephson negotiated the sale of the TV rights for the Montreal Olympics to ABC for a record sum of $25 million. In 1977 he negotiated the literary and TV contracts, said to total more than $5 million, for Henry A. Kissinger. He also represents Jimmy Carter, Barbara Walters, and Gen. Norman Schwarzkopf.

In 1955, after working briefly for CBS as an attorney, Josephson started a personal management office, Broadcast Management Inc., with Bob Keeshan (*Captain Kangaroo*) as his first major client. Six years later the rapidly growing company merged with a West Coast firm, Roenberg, Coryell Inc., and changed its name to Artists Agency Corp. In 1967 Josephson bought out his partners and renamed the agency Marvin Josephson Associates. Two years later he acquired the large Ashley-Famous Agency that earlier had been formed in a merger of the old International Famous Agency and the Ted Ashley organization.

JOURNAL, THE **▶** nightly news-perspective program that follows the 10 p.m. newscast on Canada's CBC and has grown into a national institution since its debut in 1982. The program examines national and international news developments and is remarkable for its production of timely documentaries on short deadlines. *Journal* documentaries have sold widely abroad and on occasion to the *MacNeil-Lehrer Newshour* in the U.S.

The programs also contain news analyses, feature stories and arts coverage. News interviews are conducted by the *Journal*'s host, Barbara Frum. The program's ratings have, from the first, exceeded the CBC's expectations. Mark Starowicz has been the executive producer since the first broadcast.

JUDD FOR THE DEFENSE **▶** dramatic series of a larger-than-life lawyer, represented as the most successful in the world, featuring Carl Betz as Clinton Judd, with Stephen Young as his junior partner, Ben Caldwell. It was produced by 20th Century-Fox TV in association with Vanadas Productions for ABC (1967-69). The series was carried in 13 international markets.

JUDGE, THE **▶** see Courtroom Shows.

JUDGMENT **SERIES ▶** series of docu-drama specials for ABC (1974-75) by Stanley Kramer in association with David L. Wolper. The programs dramatized critical trials of modern history and consisted of *Judgment: The Court-Martial of the Tiger of Malaya—General Yamashita* (June 11, 1974); *Judgment: The Trial of Julius and Ethel Rosenberg* (Jan. 28, 1974); and *Judgment: The Trial of Lt. William Calley* (Jan. 12, 1975). All were 90-minute specials offered under the rubric of *ABC Theatre.*

JUDSON, ARTHUR (d. 1975) ▶ prominent concert manager from the 1920s through the 1960s who was a founder of the small radio network in 1926 that was to become CBS. To create opportunities for the artists he managed, Judson purchased New York radio station WABC for $75,000 at a time when radio was a new and expanding field, and he organized a network of 16 stations by paying each $500 a week to carry his programs. With financing from the Columbia Phonograph Company, the network began operations on Sept. 19, 1926 as the Columbia Phonograph Broadcasting System. When William S. Paley acquired controlling interest in the failing company in 1928, "Phonograph" was dropped from the name. Judson remained the second largest stockholder in CBS.

He later founded and headed Columbia Concerts Corporation and its subsidiary, Columbia Artists Management, and in 1938 became sole owner of Columbia Records, which was eventually to become a division of CBS.

JULIA ▶ NBC situation comedy (1968-71) built around a black star, Diahann Carroll. Its success opened the way to other shows with black principals. Though Carroll was not TV's first black star, she was the first to carry a show on the same terms as a white star with good ratings and ample advertiser support.

Amos 'n' Andy, a syndicated TV series drawn from the radio program, had been an audience favorite during the 1950s with an all-black cast, but it was driven off the air by black citizens groups as patronizing and embarrassing to the race. In 1965 Bill Cosby partially broke the color barrier with billing as co-star of the NBC action-adventure hour *I Spy,* but in fact he was the second lead to Robert Culp, and the billing was really cosmetic. In 1957 Nat King Cole, like every other top recording artist, was given a show of his own on network TV, but that was before the civil rights movement; no sponsor would touch it, and some southern stations declined to carry it. *Julia,* in 1968, was the breakthrough program.

At that, it was widely criticized as unrealistic and unrepresentative of black life in America. Carroll portrayed a beautiful widow, Julia Baker, raising a young son, Corey; she worked as a nurse and lived in an integrated housing project. On TV, however, her living quarters were idealized to the level of floor-wax commercials, and it was felt that the character could have been white but for the fact that a light-skinned black had been assigned to play it.

In the integrated supporting cast were Marc Copage as Corey, Michael Link as Corey's friend Earl J. Waggedorn, Betty Beaird as Marie Waggedorn, Lloyd Nolan as Dr. Morton Chegley and Lurene Tuttle as chief nurse Hannah Yarby. It was produced by 20th Century-Fox TV.

The pilot for Julia had actually been rejected by NBC at first sight. But a half-hour slot was open on the network opposite *The Red Skelton Show,* a long-time hit on CBS, and several other situation comedies had been under consideration. NBC programmers gave themselves no chance of beating Skelton and chose *Julia* to salvage something from the loss—the appearance of having tried to do a program with a black lead. To their, and the industry's, surprise, *Julia*—with all its faults—turned out to be a hit.

JUNE ALLYSON SHOW, THE ▶ half-hour dramatic anthology on CBS (1959-61) with movie actress June Allyson as hostess and occasional star. Originally titled *DuPont Show with June Allyson,* it was by Four Star and Pamric Productions.

JUSTICE DEPARTMENT ANTITRUST SUIT ▶ identical lawsuits filed April 14, 1972, by the Department of Justice against ABC, CBS and NBC charging them with illegally monopolizing prime time and with restraint of trade. The suits sought to bar the networks from securing financial interests in programs and from producing shows of their own.

In 1976 NBC agreed to a settlement, one whose terms appeared to have no serious economic implications for the network. Many of the restrictions, however, were conditional on the other networks reaching a similar settlement. ABC and CBS at first declined to settle in the manner of NBC, but eventually they too reached agreements.

The department's case, which had been prepared in 1970 but was withheld for two years, contended that the networks use their control over prime time to keep off the air programs in which they have no financial interests, that they thereby force producers to grant them part ownership of the shows and that they control the prices paid for programs and movies.

The networks struck back with the contention that the suit was politically motivated, brought against them by the Nixon Administration in retaliation for the news coverage of the government that President Nixon had felt was biased against him.

The networks cited as suspicious the fact that the suit might have been filed earlier but instead had been laid aside by previous Attorneys General and that it was entered even after a similar civil suit by Hollywood studios that was still pending. Moreover, they pointed out, the research that had been the basis for the suit was applicable to the year 1967 but not necessarily to 1972 since, in the interval, the FCC had already taken steps to drive the networks out of syndication and the ownership of programs for post-network sale.

In November 1974 motions to dismiss the Justice Department's lawsuits were entered in U.S. District Court in Los Angeles, after the networks were denied their petition for access to President Nixon's tapes, which they maintained would have substantiated their claim that the suit was politically motivated. U.S. District Court Judge Robert J. Kelleher dismissed the cases against the networks because the Ford Administration would not provide the tapes, since the question of whether they were owned by the government or by Nixon was still under debate. But the judge's dismissal was "without prejudice," which meant the Justice Department could file the suits again, under a new administration—and it did. The networks then appealed to the Supreme Court to bar the department from prosecuting its case. In April 1975 the Court dismissed the appeal, permitting the case to proceed.

Under NBC's settlement agreement, the network would be limited in program ownership to 2 1/2 hours of entertainment programs a week in prime time; to no more than 11 hours in fringe time; and no more than 8 hours in daytime (8 a.m. to 6 p.m.). The network's production of news programming would be exempt.

The agreement also limited to one year any contract between the network and a supplier that a program be produced at NBC's facilities. It limited the number of years over which a network could obtain exclusive rights to a program before it was developed. Further, the network was prohibited from retaining exclusive options on more than 35% of the shows presented to it that had not yet been selected for broadcast. ABC and CBS were bound by similar limitations.

The 1989 expiration of several key provisions of the agreements became a central element in the networks' drive to seek repeal of the FCC's "fin-syn" rules. The prospect of increased network production was important leverage in the fight with Hollywood interests. By the summer of 1991, the drive escalated, with the networks formally seeking Justice Department permission to dissolve other portions of the agreements.

K

KAHN, IRVING B. ▶ a noted cable pioneer who in 1976 entered the fiber optics field and, through his company, Broadband Communications, has been active ever since in advanced communications technologies. In 1977 he founded General Optronics Corp., which manufactured laser diodes for use in fiber optic systems and which he headed as chairman until it was sold in 1988.

Kahn had been a dominant figure in cable TV and its leading visionary as president of Teleprompter Corp. during the 1960s, until he was convicted of bribery and perjury in connection with an attempt to secure a cable franchise in New Jersey. In 1975, after serving a 30-month prison sentence, he formed his own company, Broadband Communications Inc., to secure films and other programs for pay cable. He also began to work at developing fiber optics technology for cable TV, and meanwhile built a large cable system in Camden, N.J., and surrounding communities. In 1980 he sold these franchises to the *New York Times* for $100 million, a record price, based on subscribers served. The system involved 55 franchised areas in Southern New Jersey and pitched the *New York Times* into the cable business.

Under Kahn's leadership, Teleprompter grew to the largest and most powerful of the MSOs. Not long after his conviction and his total separation from the company, Teleprompter experienced a financial crisis when the expected cable boom in the cities did not materialize. Kahn became president and chairman of Teleprompter in 1951, after 16 years in show business advertising and publicity, chiefly with 20th Century-Fox.

KALB, BERNARD ▶ widely traveled CBS News correspondent specializing in foreign affairs who left in 1980 to join NBC News, following his old boss Bill Small there. He left NBC in 1984 to become Assistant Secretary of State for Public Affairs under George Schultz. When he resigned from that post in October 1986, he said it was in protest of a secret "disinformation program" by the Reagan Administration.

Kalb joined CBS in 1962, after 15 years as foreign correspondent for the *New York Times,* as chief of the Southeast Asia and India bureau. Except for a year as Paris correspondent, his base was Hong Kong until 1970, when he was reassigned to the Washington bureau. For nearly two years (1970-72), he was Washington anchor for the *CBS Morning News* with John Hart. With his brother, Marvin Kalb, CBS diplomatic correspondent, he wrote the political biography, *Kissinger.*

KALB, MARVIN ▶ former NBC News diplomatic correspondent (1980-87), hired away from CBS News after a distinguished 23-year career at the network. The Kalb brothers, Bernard and Marvin, defected to join Bill

Small when he became president of NBC News, and they represented Small's prize catch. They were, however, resented at NBC News, which has proud traditions of its own. Small's ouster from NBC in 1982 was attributed in part to the morale problems resulting from what was perceived as his attempt to remake NBC News with old CBS colleagues.

Marvin Kalb's transfer to NBC was controversial also for another reason: reportedly, his new contract contained a guaranteed quota of air time. This raised the issue, in media circles, of star power superseding news judgment in television.

Kalb became diplomatic correspondent for CBS News in 1963, after extensive experience in foreign affairs dating back to the State Department post he had held at the American Embassy in Moscow. He joined CBS as a journalist in 1957. Fluent in Russian, Kalb is a specialist in Soviet-American relations and is the author of five books. Since 1987 Kalb has been the director of the Joan Shorenstein Barone Center for Press, Politics and Public Policy at Harvard University.

KANE, DENNIS ▶ director with varied entertainment credits (Joyce Brothers's *Living Easy, Dark Shadows,* Thanksgiving Day parades). He also directed network political specials for Republican candidates—Eisenhower, Goldwater, Nixon and others.

KANE, JOSH ▶ producer of prime-time series and TV movies in a production partnership with Michael Ogiens since 1986. Previously he was an executive of NBC Entertainment, before switching to CBS as a vice president of programs. The partnership with Ogiens resulted in a successful ABC series, *The Young Riders,* for which they were co-executive producers during the show's first season (1989-90). They also served as executive producers for several TV movies, including *Trenchcoat in Paradise* and *Into the Badlands.*

Kane began at NBC as a page in 1965, then worked in the network's press department for ten years. After shifting to the program department he became v.p. of East Coast programs in 1977 and assistant to the president of NBC Entertainment in 1981.

KANTER, HAL ▶ comedy writer and producer who, after writing radio programs and screenplays for Bob Hope, made his mark in TV as producer-writer-director of *The George Gobel Show* in the 1950s. He later became executive producer of *Julia* (1968-71) and in 1976 was named supervising producer of an established hit series, *Chico and the Man.* Kanter's credits also include *Valentine's Day, The Jimmy Stewart Show* and episodes of *All In the Family.*

KAPLAN, RICHARD (RICK) ▶ executive producer of ABC News' *Prime Time Live.* Since its fitful start in August 1989, replete with self-conscious star dialogue between anchors Diane Sawyer and Sam Donaldson and a studio audience no one knew quite what to do with, Kaplan has helped the show to become ABC's second successful newsmagazine, along with its forerunner, *20/20. Prime Time Live* features a wide range of news, feature stories and investigative reports, with an emphasis wherever possible on immediacy.

From 1984-1989, Kaplan was executive producer of *Nightline* with Ted Koppel, and he was generally praised for guiding the series through a period of innovation and scoring an impressive number of exclusive interviews.

Stuart Karl

KARL, STUART (d. 1991) ▶ noted home video entrepreneur who put his Karl Home Video on the map in the early 1980s with the release of the *Jane Fonda Workout* series, the first giant hit in the field. In 1984 he sold the company he had started only four years earlier, while still in his twenties, to Viacom. He continued to head it until 1987, when he was forced to resign over a conflict of interest. Viacom later sued Karl and several of his colleagues in the company for improper practices that allegedly resulted in huge losses for the video division. In 1988 he was fined and placed on probation for making illegal political campaign contributions. At the time of his death, at age 38, he was president of the NAC home video company.

***KATE & ALLIE* ▶** successful CBS sitcom about two divorced women, friends since high school, who with their children share a New York apartment. The show debuted in 1984, lasting five seasons on CBS. It starred Jane Curtin as and Susan Saint James.

Comedic themes usually revolved around new male relationships and dealing with their children's adolescent crises. Towards the end of the series' run, Curtin's character Allie remarried but still lived with Kate, since her husband was often on the road.

Reeves Entertainment produced, and MCA Television syndicated the half-hour show. Mort Lachman, Merrill Grant, Saul Turtletaub and Bernie Orenstein were executive producers.

KATZENBERG, JEFFREY ▶ chairman of the Walt Disney Studios since October 1984 and credited with leading the studio out of its dormant state into a prominent position in motion picture and television production. Katzenberg left his post as president of production at Paramount Pictures to follow his boss, Michael Eisner, to The Walt Disney Co., where Eisner was installed as chairman and CEO.

Katzenberg, skillfully using several stars of a lesser magnitude at Disney, turned the studio around in short order with a string of box-office hits, including *Down and Out in Beverly Hills, Good Morning, Vietnam, Honey, I Shrunk the Kids* and *Pretty Woman.* On the TV syndication side, under Katzenberg's oversight, Buena Vista Distribution increased its share of the market from 3% to 20%, making it one of the top distributors in the business. The company also became enlivened as a supplier to network television with such shows as *Golden Girls, Empty Nest* and *Carol & Company.*

Katzenberg came to the motion picture business after a stint with New York Mayor John Lindsay's political campaign. He started as assistant to United Artists' president David Picker and moved with Picker to Paramount, where he was assistant to studio chairman Barry Diller. Later he moved into the production division and rose to the presidency of that division in 1982.

KAYE, DANNY (d. 1987) ▶ noted movie comedian who made TV appearances sparingly until 1963, when he began a weekly variety series on CBS that ran four seasons. The series did well enough in the ratings scheduled at 10 p.m. on Wednesdays, but many believed it would have been a smash at an earlier hour since Kaye was enormously appealing to children.

One of his memorable TV appearances was in a 1957 *See It Now* program, entitled *The Secret Life of Danny Kaye,* on which he appeared with children of various countries to demonstrate the work being done by UNICEF.

KEARNEY, MICHELLE ▶ a specialist in foreign television sales to the Latin American markets, first for Lorimar Telepictures, where she was a vice president of international sales for 10 years, and later for London-based Carolco Films International, whose New York office she joined in 1989. Two years later she was promoted to senior vice president of international television for Carolco, with responsibility also for the Asian territories. A native of Colombia, she began her career in the Spanish unit at the United Nations.

KEESHAN, BOB ▶ creator and star of *Captain Kangaroo,* daily children's program on CBS that had a 24-year run. After working as a page for NBC, he became an assistant to Bob Smith on the *Howdy Doody* show and soon created the popular clown character Clarabell, which he played for five years. In the early 1950s, he developed characters for his own TV series, *Time for Fun* and *Tinker's Workshop,* but on Oct. 3, 1955 he launched *Captain Kangaroo* and was on his way to becoming an institution.

In 1959, as an adjunct to the program, he conducted symphony orchestras in major cities for a series of classical concerts for children. In 1965 he added a Saturday morning program, *Mister Mayor,* which two years later gave way to a sixth day of *Kangaroo.* The series was frequently cited for its good taste and promulgation of positive social values. CBS canceled it in 1984.

KEMP, BARRY ▶ executive producer of the *Newhart* series in its early years. Through his Bungalow 78 Productions he has supplied ABC with the series *Coach* and CBS with *Princesses.* Bungalow 78 has worked in association with Universal Television.

KENT, ARTHUR ▶ NBC News correspondent cast into the limelight for his live reporting from Saudi Arabia during the Iraqi missile attacks in the Persian Gulf War. Dubbed "the Scud Stud," "the satellite dish" and "Arthur of Arabia," either by admiring female viewers or a zealous network p.r. department, Kent was assigned to some high-profile network duties after the war, including substituting for Bryant Gumbel on *Today* and sitting in for Tom Brokaw on *Nightly News.*

Kent became a full-time NBC News correspondent in August 1989, based in Rome.

Previously he worked as an independent cameraman and reporter, performing as a stringer for NBC News in reporting on the combat between Afghan guerrillas and Soviet-backed Afghan government forces. Other non-studio, on-site coverage included the 1989 Chinese student uprising in Tiananmen Square in Beijing and the collapse of the Ceaucescu regime in Romania.

Kent's first job in journalism, at age 19, was at the Ottawa affiliate of Canada's CTV network. He became the Canadian Broadcasting Corp.'s youngest correspondent ever at 21.

KENT, MORTON J. ▶ a former insurance executive who, with no previous experience in broadcasting, rapidly assembled a group of eight independent UHF stations in the early 1980s and then went bankrupt later in the decade. The failure of the group, known as Media Central Inc., shocked the station sector of the industry, which long had felt invulnerable to financial disaster. It also created a crisis for certain syndicators who had supplied programs to the group.

Kent entered television at a time when UHF stations were proliferating in the country and winning sizeable audiences through their carriage on cable. Believing he could make money by operating a group of stations from a central management structure, Kent built stations in Kansas City, Honolulu, Canton, Oh., Columbus, Ga. and Cape Girardeau, Mo. He also signed management agreements with stations in Jackson, Miss., Knoxville, Tenn. and Huntsville, Ala. The company itself was headquartered in Chattanooga. MCI initially was perceived as a hot station group, but in July 1987 it filed for bankruptcy protection under Chapter 11. All the stations later were sold, except the one in Canton.

KESTEN, PAUL W. (d. 1956) ▶ a key management figure at CBS as head of promotion and public relations, until ill health forced his retirement in 1946. Apart from having the distinction of hiring Frank Stanton, who later became president of the corporation, and Peter Goldmark, who developed a color-TV system and the LP recording, Kesten was the father of the CBS "image," having determined that CBS could compete with NBC on a basis other than circulation. In the late 1930s, years before commercial TV began, Kesten became the CBS officer in charge of developing color TV, a project for which he had brought in Goldmark.

KEYES, PAUL W. ▶ comedy writer-producer who wrote for Jack Paar in his late-night NBC show and later became producer and head-writer of *Laugh-In.* He was producer of the American Film Institute's *Salute to James Cagney* and the *Salute to John Wayne.*

KIBBEE, ROLAND (d. 1984) ▶ veteran producer-director who began as a radio writer for Fred Allen, Groucho Marx and Fanny Brice. He was executive producer of *Columbo,* co-exec producer of *The Family Holvak* and *McCoy,* and producer of *Barney Miller* for the 1976-77 season. He was also producer-writer for *It Takes a Thief* and *The Bob Newhart Show.* He returned to *Barney Miller* in the 1981-82 season as co-executive producer.

KIHN, ALBERT (d. 1974) ▶ news cameraman who, while in the employ of KRON-TV, San Francisco, filed a petition to deny against that station and KRON-FM, charging undue media concentration by the parent Chronicle Publishing Co. He was joined in the petition by an employee of the *San Francisco Chronicle,* Blanche Streeter. They charged that the company ordered journalists to avoid some stories and to cover others to advance the Chronicle Company's private interests. The FCC resolved the various issues in the stations' favor and renewed the licenses in May 1973. Kihn and Streeter pursued the case through court appeals, but before the case could be heard Kihn was killed in a plane crash in March 1974 with other members of a film crew while on a documentary assignment for Wolper Productions. His widow and Streeter abandoned the appeal the following year, upon receiving a settlement of $150,000 from the *Chronicle* to cover their legal expenses.

KIKER, DOUGLAS (d. 1991) ▶ NBC News correspondent mainly assigned to Washington after having been White House correspondent for the *New York Herald Tribune* and director of information for the Peace Corps. He joined NBC News in 1966, went to Rome for two years in 1969 and, after his return, became prominent on the network in covering the Watergate developments. He was named Washington correspondent for the *Today* show in 1975.

A sometime novelist, he was the author of *The Southerner* and *Strangers on the Shore,* both published in 1959.

KILLER C's, THE ▶ a bloc of cable MSO's—Cox, Comcast and Continental—comprising the third power in the industry after John Malone's TCI and Time Warner's ATC. The cable industry refers to them as the Killer C's because, in acting jointly (sometimes with Newhouse Cable strengthening the bloc), they have been known to kill projects.

KILLIAN, JAMES R., JR. (d. 1988) ▶ frequently called "the father of public television" because of his chairmanship of the important Carnegie Commission on Educational Television, whose study and recommendations led to the Public Broadcasting Act of 1967. A distinguished science administrator—he was president of MIT, the first presidential assistant for science, and the architect of NASA—Killian was appointed to the original board of the Corporation for Public Broadcasting by President Johnson and served as its chairman from May 1973 until he resigned in December 1974. His chairmanship resolved a bitter internal board struggle prompted by charges that the Nixon Administration had sought to influence its decisions. Following his resignation he was made chairman emeritus of the CPB board.

KINESCOPE RECORDING ▶ a record of a television program made by filming it from a television monitor. Before the development of video tape, it was the means of preserving live television programs and news coverage. Although programs were sometimes repeated or syndicated by kinescope recording (or "kinnie"), the poor picture quality discouraged extensive use. The word *kinescope* is actually a synonym for "picture tube," but it became the accepted abbreviation for *kinescope recording.*

***KING* ▶** a six-hour NBC docu-drama serial airing on three consecutive nights in February 1978 to very disappointing ratings. The series, tracing the life of Martin Luther King Jr. from 1953 to his murder in a Memphis hotel in 1968, was actually a portrait of the civil rights movement. Written and directed by Abby Mann, it starred Paul Winfield as King and Cicely Tyson as his wife, Coretta Scott. Others in the cast were Howard Rollins, Kenneth McMillan, Dick Anthony Williams, Ossie Davis and Al Freeman Jr.

***KING FAMILY, THE* ▶** ABC music-variety series (1964-6) that grew out of a guest appearance on *Hollywood Palace* of the six King Sisters and their husbands and children—36 in all. They later produced a series of specials for syndication, each keyed to a holiday theme, including back-to-school—12 in all.

KING, LARRY ▶ TV and radio interviewer with an extraordinary range of knowledge and remarkable stamina. For a number of years he conducted both a nightly half-hour program on CNN and a midnight-to-5 a.m. broadcast on the Mutual radio network. He is equally adept at interviewing government officials, authors, celebrities, jazz musicians and sports figures.

Talk-show host Larry King

He won a strong national following with his nightly Mutual marathon, the *Larry King Show,* which began in 1978, and he joined the CNN lineup in 1985 with *Larry King Live.* That program has consistently been one of the highest-rated half hours on CNN. King also writes a weekly column for *USA Today.* His strong showing on CNN prompted his selection by TBS in 1990 to host the Goodwill Games, Ted Turner's answer to the Olympics.

King started in radio in Miami, hosting a morning talk show at age 25. His quick wit and engaging style landed him the color commentary in the Miami Dolphins football telecasts. At the same time, he was writing entertainment columns for the *Miami Herald* and *Miami News.* He started his Mutual radio show with 28 affiliates, but the number has grown to well over 200.

KING, ROGER M. and MICHAEL ▶ as chairman and president/CEO, respectively, of King World, the two brothers sit atop television's leading distribution company with three of television's most popular and profitable syndicated first-run hits: *Wheel of Fortune, Jeopardy!* and *The Oprah Winfrey Show.*

Their meteoric rise to wealth and power began when the brothers—there were originally four—took over a company begun much earlier by their colorful father, Charles, whose fortunes as a producer and syndicator in radio plummeted with the advent of TV. Its major asset at his death was the rights to a series of film shorts, *The Little Rascals.* With a competitive spirit that was unusual even for the fast-dealing world of syndication, the brothers tied up the rights to two Merv Griffin shows, syndicating the first, *Wheel of Fortune,* in the fall of 1983 and following up a year later with *Jeopardy!* The shows, which had aired on the networks in daytime, proved to be blockbuster hits in the early evening.

Roger M. and Michael King

After introducing *The Oprah Winfrey Show* in 1986, King World was a formidable force in the TV industry worldwide with distribution rights to the three shows that consistently topped the ratings in syndicated fare. The three shows accounted for 83% of the company's revenues in 1991, with their future further into the 1990s seemingly assured by renewals on stations covering more than 95% of U.S. households.

In the late 1980s King World became producers as well as distributors with the tabloid-style newsmagazine strip *Inside Edition* and later with the half-hour comedy strip *Candid Camera.* In 1988 the company bought WIVB Buffalo, set up a subsidiary, Camelot Entertainment, to sell barter spots in its own shows, and created an international division.

Not all of the King World shows have been hits. Among its failures were *Monopoly, Instant Recall, Nightlife, True Confessions, Headline Chasers,* and *Soap World.*

KINOY, ERNEST ▶ prolific New York based writer of plays for TV, radio, films and the Broadway stage who contributed to such acclaimed series as *Studio One, Playhouse 90, Naked City* and *DuPont Show of the Week.* In 1965 he won an Emmy for an episode of *The Defenders,* entitled "Blacklist," about a victim of the anticommunist campaigns of the McCarthy era. In the 1950s he wrote a TV series, *The Marriage,* which starred Hume Cronyn and Jessica Tandy. His credits in the 1970s included scripts for *The Story of Jacob and Joseph* and *Roots.* Kinoy's writing credits during the 1980s included *Murrow, Skokie* and *Stones for Ibarra,* and in 1990 a TNT made-for-TV movie, *Chernobyl: The Final Warning.*

Kinoy served for a time as president of the Writers Guild of America, East (1969-71).

KINTNER, ROBERT E. (d. 1980) ▶ forceful president of the National Broadcasting Co. (1958-65), noted for giving high priority to the network's news operations. During his administration, NBC achieved leadership in news and special events coverage. Earlier (1949-56), he had been president of ABC-TV.

Kintner was given the title of chairman and chief executive officer of NBC in 1966 but, owing to illness, never served in that capacity and went into retirement shortly afterward.

His shibboleth for NBC News was "CBS Plus 30," mandating 30 minutes more coverage of an event than CBS would provide. Kintner's emphasis on network news traced to his early career in the 1930s as Washington correspondent for the *New York Herald Tribune* and later as writer of a nationally syndicated column with Joseph Alsop. With Alsop, he also wrote two best-selling books, *Men Around the President* and *Washington White Paper.*

In 1944, following military service, he joined ABC as v.p. of programming, public relations and advertising. Two years later he was promoted to executive v.p. and in 1949 to president. He resigned in 1956 and the following year joined NBC as executive v.p. responsible primarily for coordinating all color TV activities. In February 1958 he was put in charge of the television network and five months later became corporate president.

KIRCH, LEO ▶ sole owner of the KirchGroup, an independent German production and distribution concern and one of the most powerful media organizations in Europe. Established in Munich in the mid-1950s, it is primarily known by the operations of its flagship companies, BetaFilm, Taurus Film and Unitel.

Kirch, who personally maintains a low profile in the industry although his companies are highly aggressive and prominent, built his business on acquiring rights; today he owns more film and television rights than anyone in Europe. The son of a Bavarian vine-grower, Kirch made his entry into the entertainment business in 1954 when he paid $11,000 for German theatrical and television rights to Federico Fellini's movie classic, *La Strada.* Later he began acquiring performing arts programs as well as feature films and securing rights not only for Germany but for worldwide distribution.

The library he has amassed, which today is valued at an estimated $2 billion, has been the foundation of Kirch's empire, leading to the KirchGroup's expansion into production, coproductions, and station ownership. Kirch controls global distribution rights to some 80,000 hours of feature films and television programs, and in addition produces or coproduces around 400 hours of original programming a year.

The KirchGroup has been a driving force in the expansion of commercial television in Europe. It holds a major stake in Sat 1, one of the two leading private stations in Germany. It also owns, with France's Canal Plus and Germany's Bertelsmann, the pay movie channel, Premiere (formerly Teleclub, when Kirch was sole owner). Later Kirch invested in Italy's new pay channel, Telepiu, for an 8% stake. KirchGroup also has an equity position in Germany's largest newspaper publishing company, Axel Springer Verlag, and runs Germany's largest book club, Deutscher Bucherbund.

KIRSHNER, DON ▶ rock music publisher, record producer and promoter who branched into TV in the early 1970s and was responsible for *In Concert,* the ABC monthly 90-minute rockfest that began in 1973; the syndicated *Don Kirshner's New Rock Concert;* the annual *Rock Awards* telecasts; and the Saturday morning children's series, *The Kids From C.A.P.E.R.* Kirshner's first major work in TV was as music supervisor for the 1967 NBC series *The Monkees,* a situation comedy about rock musicians that was designed to introduce a new number every week. Kirshner was head of Colgems Records at the time and reaped three number-one singles from the series.

***KITCHEN DEBATE* ▶** a spontaneous exchange between Soviet Premier Nikita Khrushchev and Vice-President Richard M. Nixon that took place at an exhibition hall in Moscow in July 1959, while RCA color cameras and Ampex video tapes were being demonstrated. The two men had dared each other to record a discussion that would be televised in their respective countries without editing.

As they walked through the American exhibits, trading taunts and criticism of each other's political ideology, with the cameras following them, they stopped to argue before a display of American kitchen appliances. It was at this point that Nixon gesticulated in a manner in which he appeared to be poking a finger at Khrushchev's chest. The moment, preserved also in still photographs, suggested that he was standing up to the Soviet leader.

The kitchen exhibit gave the Cold War videotape event its name, and it served Nixon's future presidential campaigns.

KITMAN, MARVIN ▶ television critic for *Newsday* since 1969, syndicated nationally by the *Los Angeles Times* Syndicate. Kitman's approach to daily television criticism is through trenchant humor. Perhaps his greatest criticism has been leveled at public television, possibly because he believed it had great promise.

Kitman began covering television in 1967 when he was hired as a TV critic by *The New Leader* magazine. Previously, Kitman was a Madison Avenue copywriter and a free-lance magazine writer. He has written six books, including *George Washington's Expense Account* and *The Marvin Kitman TV Show.* He is one of the few television critics to have actually worked in the business. For six years he was a commentator about television on the *Ten O'Clock News* on WNEW-TV in New York, and the co-creator with Jim Bouton of a sitcom, *Ball Four,* on CBS in 1976. It failed to earn decent ratings or favorable reviews.

***KKK: THE INVISIBLE EMPIRE* ▶** noted CBS documentary broadcast Sept. 21, 1965, probing the history and workings of the Ku Klux Klan, the first TV film report to do so. It was produced by David Lowe under the *CBS Reports* banner, with Charles Kuralt as reporter.

KLAUBER, EDWARD (d. 1954) ▶ executive v.p. of CBS during the 1930s, considered by some to be "the father of broadcast journalism" because of his pioneering initiatives with radio network news. With Paul White as his chief aide, Klauber in 1933 organized the Columbia News Service (the forerunner of CBS News) when General Mills offered to sponsor daily news broadcasts. Klauber spurred the growth of the news organization, and by World War II it was one of the largest and most distinguished news services in the world.

Klauber joined CBS in 1930 as top assistant to the network's young president, William S. Paley, after having been night city editor of the *New York Times*. Intrigued with the possibilities of disseminating news by radio, he convinced Paley of its value to the network and then hired White to help build the staff. Klauber also served as the corporate force to insulate news judgments from advertiser interests.

When he was passed over for the position of wartime manager of CBS (Paley having gone to London to work for General Eisenhower), Klauber resigned from the network and joined the Office of War Information.

KLEIN, HERBERT G. ▶ former director of communications for the Nixon Administration who, on resigning in July 1973, became v.p. of corporate relations for Metromedia Inc. From 1977-80 he was the company's media consultant. He then went on to become editor-in-chief and v.p. of Copley Newspapaers Inc. Klein—a longtime friend of Nixon, having helped him in every campaign since his first race for Congress in 1946—had been editor of the *San Diego Union* when he was named to the newly created post in the executive branch in 1968.

The job involved, among other things, receiving complaints from the news media and in turn forwarding the complaints of the Administration to the media. Klein's resignation after five years was prompted partly by Ron Ziegler's preemption of his role as confidant to the President.

KLEIN, PAUL L. ▶ creator and former president of the Playboy Channel, the Hi-Life Channel and Home Dish Satellite Networks (adult-oriented cable channels and systems), who started out at NBC-TV, first as an audience research expert (1965-70) and then returning in 1976 as v.p. of programming. In the interval he founded and was chairman of Computer Television Inc., a company that pioneered *Hotelvision* (movies for pay over hotels' master antenna systems). He also produced *Pop-Ups,* educational spots for children carried by NBC, and was periodically a consultant to PBS, the Ford Foundation, Lincoln Center and Janus Films.

Klein came up short of hits as NBC programmer, and his gamble that a schedule of specials, movies and mini-series would prevail over stock weekly series was a chief reason for NBC's slide into third place. Fred Silverman kept him on as program chief when he came in as president of NBC, but Klein resigned in 1979 to become an independent producer and, later, creator of the Playboy Channel.

Klein became widely known among media buffs for his "LOP Theory," which holds that most viewers do not turn on the set for a specific program but instead select what Klein termed "the Least Objectionable Program" after making a decision to watch television. The theory was first articulated in an article for *New York Magazine.*

Klein left Playboy in 1984 to start his own satellite-delivered channel, Hi-Life, which went beyond Playboy in so-called adult-orientation with "X"-rated films. By 1990 he was president of a larger system, Home Dish Satellite Networks Inc. Early in that year, the District Attorney of Montgomery, Alabama, brought the law down on Home Dish and its satellite carriers and owners, including the Tuxxedo Channel and American Exxxtasy Channel. Apparently, the adult material violated state law, and the illegal reselling (by people independent of Home Dish) of tapes of the shows to minors violated federal law. This litigation impaired Klein's ability to do business as before, and his company folded.

KLEINERMAN, ISAAC ▶ prolific producer-director of documentaries for CBS News (1957-76) and earlier for NBC (1951-57); he resigned from CBS in the summer of 1976 over differences with management and became an independent producer. Kleinerman joined NBC from RKO-Pathe and became film editor of *Victory at Sea* and a producer in the *Project 20* unit (*The Great Way, The Twisted Cross, The Jazz Age, Nightmare in Red*). He also produced episodes for the *Wisdom* series.

CBS hired him away in 1957 to help organize *The Twentieth Century* unit; he was to produce close to 200 films for that series, as well as others for *CBS Reports* and *The 21st*

Century. Overall, in a 25-year career with the two networks, Kleinerman was responsible for more than 400 documentaries covering a broad spectrum from history and current events to the humanities and sports.

As an independent he produced *The Unknown War,* a syndicated series created from footage of World War II shot by Russians, which was distributed by Air Time in 1978-79.

KLUGE, JOHN ▶ former broadcaster who parlayed his TV and cellular radio licenses into an enormous fortune. *Forbes* magazine named him the richest man in America in 1991, estimating his net worth at $5.9 billion. Kluge is the head of Metromedia, now largely a shell company but formerly the operator of an important group of independent TV stations and, later, a cellular telephone concern.

In 1959 Kluge bought a controlling interest in the Metropolitan Broadcasting Corp., which was what remained of the recently expired DuMont network. Essentially it consisted of the owned-and-operated TV stations. Kluge changed the name of the company to Metromedia and created a production subsidiary, Metromedia Producers Corp. He expanded the company into other media ventures, and then in 1984 took the group of seven stations private in a leveraged buyout worth $1.3 billion. He surprised everyone by turning around the next year and selling the stations (six of them to Rupert Murdoch, who used them to build the Fox Network) for more than $2 billion and divesting of other Metromedia assets for additional billions. That left him with a growing cellular telephone business, but he sold that off as well in the summer of 1986, for some $1.2 billion.

Since then Kluge has made no major deals, though he acquired an interest in Orion Pictures from his friend Arthur Krim. In 1991, as the studio (and therefore his deal) went sour, he was forced to take a more active role in the studio's operation.

KNOTS LANDING **▶** long-running CBS prime-time serial (1979—) that was spun off the hugely successful *Dallas.* From the stable of nighttime soap operas Lorimar Television provided CBS in the 1970s and 1980s, *Knots Landing* has run longer than all save *Dallas.* The story initially centered on the domestic conflicts of Valene and Gary Ewing (played by Joan Van Ark and Ted Shackelford), outcasts from the Ewing clan familiar to *Dallas* followers, who move to Knots Landing in California to begin a new life. The focus of the story lines shifted year by year with the addition of new characters. Others in the cast were Michele Lee as Karen Fairgate, Kevin Dobson as Mac MacKenzie, Pat Petersen as Michael Fairgate, Steve Shaw as Eric Fairgate, Donna Mills as Abby Cunningham and William Devane as Gregory Sumner. Howard Duff and Ava Gardner were guest stars in 1985.

The show is produced by Roundelay/MF Productions for Lorimar Television. Executive producers include Lee Rich, Michael Filerman and David Jacobs.

KOJAK **▶** highly popular detective series, both in the U.S. and abroad, that began on CBS in the fall of 1973 and ended in 1978. Although the series made extensive use of location footage, it was the Savalas persona—the stocky, totally bald, unglamorous rendition of hero—that gave the series its realistic edge. Telly Savalas achieved true stardom with the series and was the source of its great appeal around the world.

Along with Savalas as Lieutenant Theo Kojak, the show featured Dan Frazer as Captain Frank McNeil, Kevin Dobson as detective Bobby Crocker and Demosthenes (the middle name of Savalas's brother, George Savalas) as detective Stavros. Matthew Rapf was executive producer for Universal TV.

KOMACK, JAMES ▶ a leading producer of situation comedies in the 1970s whose independent production company, The Komack Co., turned out *The Courtship of Eddie's Father, Chico and the Man, Welcome Back, Kotter* and *Mister T and Tina.* A former nightclub comedian, he became an actor in situation comedies before turning to producing.

KOMODIKIS, MARIA D. ▶ vice president of international television sales for ABC Distribution Co. in New York and liaison with ABC News for the offshore sale of its programs. Prior to joining ABC in 1989, she served three years in a similar capacity at CBS Broadcast International. Before joining CBS, initially as director of news service marketing, she held managerial positions at Time-Life Films and Metromedia.

KONIGSBERG, FRANK ▶ producer of such mini-series as *Onassis: The Richest Man In the World* and *Ellis Island.* His movies-for-TV include *Surviving, Night of the Hunter* and *Rock Hudson.*

KONNER, JOAN ▶ veteran producer of documentaries and public affairs series who in 1988 became Dean of the Graduate School of Journalism at Columbia University, her alma mater. Prior to her appointment, she was partnered with Bill Moyers in a company called Public Affairs Television Inc., holding the title of president and executive producer. With Moyers she produced *Moyers: In Search of the Constitution, God and Politics, The Secret Government: The Constitution in Crisis,* and *Joseph Campbell and the Power of Myth.*

Initially she worked in commercial television as a writer, director and producer for NBC News, starting in 1965. After 12 years she left to join public television station WNET New York as executive producer for *Bill Moyers' Journal* (1977-81). Later she became vice president of programming for WNET's metropolitan division, a post she held for three years, until she rejoined Moyers and helped to set up their production company.

Her titles at the Graduate School of Journalism include publisher of *The Columbia Journalism Review* and duPont Professor of Broadcast Journalism.

KOOP, THEODORE F. ▶ long-time Washington v.p. for CBS (1961-72) responsible for government relations. While holding the post, he also served through the administrations of Kennedy, Johnson and Nixon as standby censor in the event of a national emergency; in that capacity, he was to have interdicted the dissemination of information that might aid the enemy. While the position was classified, for security reasons, the secret got out in 1962 during the Cuban missile crisis; Koop remained on standby, nevertheless. He was tapped by President Kennedy because he had served as deputy to Byron Price, director of censorship during World War II.

Koop had been a journalist before his corporate assignment. From 1948 to 1961 he was director of news and public affairs in the CBS Washington bureau. Before the war he had been with AP and on the editorial staff of the National Geographic Society. He retired from CBS in 1972.

KOPLOVITZ, KAY ▶ president and chief executive officer of the USA cable network since April 1980, the first female to head a network in the U.S. As one of the pioneers of satellite-delivered program services, she is also a highly visible spokesperson for the industry. She previously was vice president of UA-Columbia Satellite Services, in which capacity she was instrumental in starting the original Madison Square Garden Sports Network, the precursor to USA, in 1977.

The all-sports network was repositioned as a general interest network and renamed USA in 1980, with Koplovitz installed as president. The following year, when USA was purchased by a consortium of MCA, Paramount Pictures, and Time Inc., Koplovitz was retained as the operating head of the channel. She developed the network along the lines of a major market independent station, with popular off-network series, professional sports and movies, and built it into one of the leading basic-cable networks in the country. Later USA began financing original series and TV movies.

Kay Koplovitz

Early in her career she was a producer-director for WTMJ-TV Milwaukee and later worked at Comsat in Washington. In 1973 she started her own communications management and public relations firm, through which she became involved with cable. Her husband, William Koplovitz, Jr., is v.p. of corporate development for Rogers-UA Cablesystems Inc.

Ted Koppel

KOPPEL, TED ▶ one of TV's leading journalists as anchor of ABC News' *Nightline,* a live-interview news show airing each weeknight. As a

Washington-based correspondent, Koppel spent 17 years with ABC before bursting into national prominence in November 1979 as anchor of the late-night series *The Iran Crisis: America Held Hostage.* When the crisis specials became a regularly scheduled nightly news program, *Nightline,* Koppel emerged as the journalist viewers depended upon for news and analysis of the Americans held hostage in Iran and later on other issues facing the nation. He quickly earned a reputation as one of television's best interviewers, based on his intense preparation, his ability to listen, and the courage to tell his guests that they had been unresponsive to his precisely framed questions.

Among his honors, Koppel counts two Peabody awards and seven duPont-Columbia awards, including the first Gold Baton in the history of that prize for his 1985 week-long series from South Africa.

Before his *Nightline* assignment, Koppel worked as an ABC News anchor, foreign and domestic correspondent, and Hong Kong bureau chief, after reporting from Vietnam. He joined ABC News in 1963, at the age of 23, as a full-time general assignment correspondent. Prior to ABC, he worked at WMCA Radio in New York, where he was a desk assistant.

A native of Lancashire, England, Koppel moved to the United States with his parents when he was 13. He holds a B.A. degree in liberal studies from Syracuse University and an M.A. in mass communications research and political science from Stanford.

KOPYKATS, THE ▶ hour-long comedy-variety series on ABC (summer, 1972) on which noted impressionists enacted great stars. Produced by Gary Smith and Dwight Hemion for ITC, the summer series grew out of a special that seemed to have possibilities for an ongoing series, but it was never adopted for the regular season. Taking part were Rich Little, Frank Gorshin, George Kirby, Marilyn Michaels, Charlie Callas, Joe Baker and Fred Travalena. In January 1976 Little began a series of his own on NBC, but it was short-lived.

KOTLOWITZ, ROBERT ▶ vice president of programming for WNET New York beginning in April 1973, having previously been editorial director responsible for all national programming from the PTV station in the cultural and public affairs spheres. Before joining public TV, he had been managing editor of *Harper's* magazine (1967-71) after serving as senior editor for three years. Earlier he was senior editor of *Show* magazine. Kotlowitz is also a novelist (*Somewhere Else* and *The Boardwalk*).

Ernie Kovacs

KOVACS, ERNIE (d. 1962) ▶ innovative comedian whose fanciful and often irreverent sight comedy made creative use of video effects more than a decade before the techniques became voguish with *Laugh-In.* His career was ended before reaching full bloom by his death in an auto crash in Hollywood. He had been married to Edie Adams, a rising comedienne.

His first programs, on NBC, *It's Time for Ernie* (March 1951) and *Ernie in Kovacsland* (summer, 1951), emanated from Philadelphia. Though short-lived, *The Ernie Kovacs Show,* produced in New York for NBC (December 1955 to July 1956), established his reputation for zany originality and won him wide admiration, if not the general popularity required by television. His trademark became a cigar and mustache under a pair of horn-rimmed glasses.

PBS mounted a retrospective of his programs in the spring of 1977.

KRAFT MUSIC HALL ▶ hour-long NBC musical variety show (1967-71) that sprang from a popular radio program so named that ran from 1933-49. Both were the principal ad vehicle for Kraft Foods, which also sponsored *Kraft Television Theatre* (1947-58).

Actually, the television version first appeared in 1958 under the title *Milton Berle Starring in the Kraft Music Hall* and *Kraft Music Hall Presents: The Dave King Show.* Then came a version hosted by Perry Como, which ran from 1959-1963.

When the show reappeared in 1967, hosts and themes changed every week, including George Burns hosting "Tin Pan Alley Today" and Dinah Shore hosting "The Nashville Sound." Music during this run of the show wasn't the only focus, however. Woody Allen and Groucho Marx each hosted an evening of comedy, and Dean Martin's "Celebrity Roasts" evolved from the program, too. The show's last host was British TV personality Des O'Connor.

KROFFT, SID and MARTY ▶ brother team of puppeteers who head a successful TV production company responsible for such children's shows as *H.R. Pufnstuf, The Bugaloos, Lidsville, Lost Saucer, Far Out Space Nuts* and *The Krofft Supershow.* The Kroffts also produced *Donnie and Marie* and *Barbara Mandrell and the Mandrell Sisters* in prime time.

Born into a European family of puppeteers, the Kroffts made their mark at the New York and Seattle World's Fairs with their adult puppet show, "Les Poupees de Paris." In 1969, when the networks were responding to pressure for more wholesome Saturday morning children's shows, the Kroffts created *Pufnstuf,* an NBC fantasy series combining live actors and life-size puppets. Its success led to the other series. The Kroffts later created the first indoor, high-rise amusement park, "The World of Sid and Marty Krofft," in Atlanta's Omni International structure; it opened in 1976.

KTBC ▶ Austin, Tex., station owned by Lady Bird Johnson. Its history came to public light, raising eyebrows, when Lyndon B. Johnson became President. The station, which was the source of the family fortune, appeared to have had unusual advantages, perhaps because of Lyndon B. Johnson's power in the Senate, first as Democratic Whip and then as Majority Leader. KTBC-TV was one of the first 18 licenses to be awarded in 1952 after the FCC's four-year freeze, and it was the only VHF assigned to the market, giving it a virtual monopoly there against only UHF competition. It became a CBS affiliate.

The Johnsons had acquired radio station KTBC in Lady Bird Johnson's name in 1943 for $17,500. The station was a daytime-only operation with no network affiliation, therefore seriously handicapped. Soon, however, the FCC granted Johnson's application for a power increase from 250 watts to 1,000 watts and for unlimited broadcasting hours. The station then acquired a CBS affiliation and became hugely profitable.

Lady Bird Johnson gave up control of the stations in 1963, putting the stocks in trust while she was in the White House. She resumed control in 1969, after the Johnson presidency. The station later was sold to the Times-Mirror group.

KTTV AGREEMENT ▶ controversial pact negotiated in 1972 by Metromedia's KTTV Los Angeles and the National Association for Better Broadcasting (NABB), a citizens group, under which the station agreed to ban from the air a list of violent children's programs drawn up by NABB. The agreement was reached to call off a petition to deny by NABB, which argued that KTTV did not deserve to hold the license because, with its concentration on violence, it did not properly serve the child audience.

Among the 42 series KTTV agreed not to play were *Batman, Superman* and *Spiderman.* The station also said it would comply with NABB demands that it post warnings to parents for a list of 81 other shows—many of which it did not own—if they were played before 8:30 p.m.

In December 1975, the FCC shot down the agreement saying that "deals" could not be made between a citizens group and station, because under law a station could not delegate its program responsibilities. The commission was also troubled that the agreement sought to bind not only the parties involved but also future licensees and that the pact would generally have the effect of program censorship.

Ku-BAND ▶ narrow-beam signal from a high-powered satellite that can be picked up by a dish as small as a foot square. Because they do not require expensive ground installations, Ku-band signals are used for direct-broadcast satellite in home entertainment and in corporate communications.

KUKLA, FRAN AND OLLIE **▶** an artful puppet series, not strictly directed at children, that was highly popular in the early 1950s for its endearing characters, topicality and gentle humor, sometimes verging on satire. A television classic of the "Chicago School," and uniquely suited to the medium, it had sporadic revivals and during the 1970s was used by CBS as the wraparound in its Children's Film Festival.

KFO, as it was known in the trade, featured a live performer, Fran Allison, in the company of puppets created by Burr Tillstrom, and dealt with their foibles and concern for each other. Featured were the gnomish Kukla and the vain dragon, Ollie. Others in the Kuklapolitan Players included Beulah Witch, Delores Dragon, Madame Ogelpuss, Fletcher Rabbit and Cecil Bill. From time to time, they performed musicals, such as *St. George and the Dragon* and *The Mikado.*

Beginning as a local show on Chicago's WBKB on Oct. 13, 1947, it was so well received that it was carried on a midwestern network and then went to NBC, premiering there on Jan. 12, 1949. The show ended its NBC run on June 13, 1954, and the following September resumed on ABC, where it remained until Aug. 30, 1957. It was produced by Beulah Zachary until her death in a plane crash in 1959. An important contributor was the musical director and pianist, Joe Facianato.

Tillstrom had created Kukla in 1936 while he was performing in Chicago with the WPA Parks District Theatre. Allison had been a Chicago radio actress when she teamed with the Kuklapolitans for the TV show. Tillstrom also perfected a hand ballet, which he performed occasionally on TV after the series was canceled. Burr Tillstrom died in 1985, Fran Allison in 1989.

KULIK, BUZZ ▶ director of made-for-TV movie specials, whose credits include *Brian's Song, Cage Without a Key, From Here to Eternity, Rage of Angels, George Washington, Kane and Abel* and *Women of Valor.*

***KUNG FU* ▶** hour-long adventure series on ABC (1973-75) about a Buddhist priest trained in the martial art of Kung Fu traveling the American frontier in the 1870s. David Carradine played the lead, Kwai Chang Caine, and Keye Luke and Philip Ahn were featured as Master Po and Master Kan. Radames Pera appeared as a youthful Caine, affectionately called Grasshopper. It was by Warner Bros. TV.

KURALT, CHARLES ▶ CBS News correspondent since the 1950s, now best known for his anchor role on *Sunday Morning,* to which he brings an amiable quality and unhurried style that is perfectly suited to the time period. Kuralt has anchored the program since its premiere in January 1979, helping it gain viewer loyalty with its comfortable Sunday morning mix of essays on events and issues, the arts and nature.

Kuralt is also known for his patented news feature *On the Road,* in which he reports on American life in towns and hamlets around the country, traveling with a crew in a battered motor home. His journeys on the backroads were periodic features on the *CBS Evening News* and were popular with viewers. About once a year they were presented in a one-hour prime-time special. While Kuralt continues to do *On the Road* pieces, the demands of his Sunday broadcast have made them infrequent.

Before beginning *On the Road* he had been a political reporter, foreign correspondent and reporter on such documentaries as *Mayor Daley: A Study in Power, You and the Commercial, Misunderstanding China* and *Destination: North Pole* (the latter resulting in a 1968 book by Kuralt, *To the Top of the World*). He joined CBS as a news writer in 1956. Formerly he had been with North Carolina's *Charlotte News.* In 1977 he became one of the regular correspondents for the CBS prime-time series *Who's Who.*

Veteran CBS correspondent Charles Kuralt

KUSHNER-LOCKE CO. ▶ since 1983 a prolific producer of shows for the networks, syndication and cable, noted for the variety of its output: movies-for-TV, mini-series, game shows, and animated and live-action children's programs. Founded by Donald Kushner, a former attorney specializing in theatrical law, and Peter Locke, a film school graduate, the partnership's first collaboration was with *Automan,* a prime-time series for ABC, and then with a game show for The Disney Channel, *Contraption.*

Kushner-Locke's prime-time TV movies include *Sweet Bird of Youth* and *Good Cops, Bad Cops* for NBC and *Liberace: The Man Behind the Music* and *Fire in the Dark* for CBS. The company also produced several daytime shows, among them the weekday series *Barbara DeAngelis* (CBS) and *TrialWatch* (NBC), and in syndication, *Divorce Court.* One of its children's shows, *Krypton Factor,* is in syndication, while another, the animated series *Brave Little Toaster,* is produced for The Disney Channel.

L

L.A. LAW ▶ popular hour-long ensemble drama centering on the private and professional activities of attorneys in a prestigious Los Angeles law firm. The series premiered on NBC in 1986 and remained one of the strongest hours on any of the networks until 1991, when two of its main characters left the show and ratings began to slide.

Following on the ensemble success of his previous hit series, *Hill Street Blues,* co-creator Steven Bochco assembled an interesting mix of attractive and ambitious lawyers working on cases that often dealt with contemporary social issues, such as AIDS and sexual discrimination. The cast was headed by Harry Hamlin as Michael Kuzak, Susan Dey as Grace Van Owen, Jimmy Smits as Victor Sifuentes and Corbin Bernsen as Arnie Becker.

Shortly after the first season, both Bochco and co-creator Terry Louise Fisher left the series, apparently in a disagreement with Twentieth Television over the show's direction. David Kelley and Gregory Hoblit took over as executive producers. Twentieth Television sold the syndicated reruns to the Lifetime cable network in 1990.

LACHMAN, MORT ▶ head writer and producer for Bob Hope specials for more than 20 years. He was also executive producer of *One Day at a Time* (1975-76), *All in the Family* (1976-77) and other comedy series, the most recent being *Gimme a Break, No Soap Radio, Kate and Allie* and *Bagdad Cafe,* which was canceled mid-season (1990-91) when Whoopi Goldberg left the series.

LACK, ANDREW ▶ executive producer at CBS News who created such prime-time magazine series as *West 57th Street,* which was broadcast from 1985-89, and *Face To Face with Connie Chung.* Lack previously was the senior executive producer of *Crossroads* (1984), a weekly series co-anchored by Bill Moyers and Charles Kuralt, and executive producer of *Our Times with Bill Moyers* (1983).

Earlier he served on *CBS Reports* in various posts, including producer and correspondent. He was responsible for such broadcasts as *The Politics of Abortion, The Boat People,* and *Teddy,* the 1979 Roger Mudd one-hour interview with Sen. Ted Kennedy, a broadcast that was felt to have seriously damaged Kennedy's White House ambitions. Lack joined CBS News in 1976 as a producer for *Who's Who* and the following May became a producer for *60 Minutes.*

LAFFERTY, PERRY ▶ veteran producer and director who became CBS v.p. of programs in Hollywood (1965-76) and then returned to production until NBC recruited him in the summer of 1979 as its v.p. of programs in Hollywood. Lafferty thus was reunited with

Fred Silverman, new president of NBC, under whom he had worked for part of his tenure at CBS. Silverman chose Lafferty to strengthen the network's ties with the creative community on the Coast and to gain from Lafferty's extensive experience with TV programs.

Before taking the executive position he had been producer of *The Danny Kaye Show* for its first two seasons and earlier of such programs as *The Andy Williams Show, Your Hit Parade* and several Arthur Godfrey specials. He also directed dramas for *Studio One, The U.S. Steel Hour, Twilight Zone* and *Robert Montgomery Presents* and episodes of *Rawhide.* Lafferty wrote and directed radio programs while studying music at Yale and began working in TV after graduation in 1947.

Lafferty left NBC in 1985 as senior v.p. of movies, mini-series and special projects. He went on to produce two TV movies for NBC in the 1990-91 season, *Murder C.O.D.* and *Maybe Baby.*

LAIRD, JACK ▶ producer, writer, and director for TV and film, whose credits include producing *Ben Casey* and *Rod Serling's Night Gallery.* Later he was supervising producer of *Kojak* and produced the series *Doctors Hospital* (1975-76), *Switch* (1976-77) and *The Gangster Chronicles* (1981). He also produced the TV movies *See How They Run, Destiny of a Spy,* and *The Dark Secret of Harvest Home.*

Laird started his career as an actor in radio, TV, film and theater on the west coast, and later he became a producer with Bing Crosby Productions (1961-63) and with Universal Studios. He has written plays, films, TV movies and series episodes.

LaLANNE, JACK ▶ host of a leading syndicated physical fitness series from the late 1950s through the 1970s. Assisted by his wife, Elaine, LaLanne demonstrated systematic exercises, or "trimnastics," for an early morning audience of housewives. The series was produced by Filmline Productions in association with the American Physical Fitness Institute. The program led to the creation of a national chain of Jack LaLanne health clubs.

***LAMP UNTO MY FEET* ▶** long-running and prestigious CBS religion series that was canceled in January 1979 along with two other Sunday morning programs to make way for the news series *Sunday Morning. Lamp* was doused because the vast majority of CBS affiliates had stopped carrying it, most of them choosing instead to play paid religious programs. CBS hoped to regain its clearances with the news program.

During more than a quarter-century on the air, *Lamp* aimed to illumine the common aspects of all religions. Employing theological discussions, programs on the arts and dramatic and documentary forms, the programs featured representatives of the Syrian Orthodox, Quaker, Hindu and Buddhist religions, as well as other major faiths. Pamela Ilott was the producer.

***LAND OF THE GIANTS* ▶** adventure series by Irwin Allen, master of special effects. It concerned the passengers and crew of a commercial rocket ship that had crashed on a planet inhabited by a race of giants. Produced by Allen in association with 20th Century-Fox TV, it was carried on ABC from 1968 to 1970 and featured Gary Conway as Captain Steve Burton and Kurt Kasznar as Alexander Fitzhugh.

LANDAU, ELY ▶ syndication executive in the 1950s who later became a film producer (*The Pawnbroker, The Fool Killer*). In 1953 he organized National Telefilm Associates, which for several years was a leading and innovative syndication concern. Landau, as chairman of NTA, created in 1956 the NTA Film Network, an attempt at bridging syndication and networking. He also was the moving force behind *Play of the Week,* a high-quality videotape series of two-hour stage dramas distributed by NTA and produced at the station the company owned, WNTA-TV New York (now WNET, the public TV station). Landau sold his interest in WNTA in 1961 to produce theatrical movies.

Michael Landon

LANDON, MICHAEL (d. 1991) ▶ actor, director and producer who for more than 25 years was almost continuously on view in three hit series. Twelve of those years were spent playing Little Joe Cartwright in the immensely popular *Bonanza* (1959-1973), many episodes for which he also wrote and directed. He was the creator, writer, director and executive producer of two other series in which he also starred, *Little House on the Prairie* (1974-82) and *Highway to Heaven* (1984-88). He also wrote, directed and was executive producer of the series, *Father Murphy* (1981-82), as well as a number of made-for-TV movies including *The Loneliest Runner, Sam's Son, Love is Forever,* and *Where Pigeons Go to Die.* Landon's last television credit was as producer and actor in the CBS pilot *Us,* just before he died of cancer in 1991 at the age of 54.

LANDSBURG, ALAN ▸ writer-producer who has worked mainly in non-fiction forms of programming. He was producer-director for the National Geographic specials *Undersea World of Jacques Cousteau* and *In Search of Ancient Astronauts,* among others. He was executive producer of *That's Incredible* and *Those Amazing Animals* and produced the series *Gimme a Break.* In 1988 Landsburg was executive producer of the CBS mini-series, *Bluegrass,* and in 1991 produced *Triumph of the Heart: The Ricky Bell Story.*

Landsburg started out as a producer at NBC in New York in the 1950s and then moved to CBS. He was a writer-producer for Wolper Productions in the 1960s and then executive producer at Metromedia Producers Corp. In 1970 he left to start his own company, Alan Landsburg Productions, specializing in documentaries. When the company was bought in 1985 by Reeves Productions, Landsburg began another production house, The Landsburg Company.

LANI BIRD ▸ first Pacific satellite launched by Intelsat (Jan. 11, 1967) establishing satellite communication between the U.S. mainland and Hawaii and making live network TV transmissions possible there for the first time. Its formal name was Intelsat II.

LANTOS, ROBERT ▸ one of Canada's leading producers in international markets as chairman and CEO of Alliance Communications Corp. His company was one of the first from Canada to break through significantly in producing series for the U.S. market, notably *E.N.G., Night Heat* and *Slick* for CBS latenight. Alliance was formed of a number of independent companies over a period of years. In 1975 Lantos co-founded RSL Entertainment, which later merged with ICC Cinema to form Alliance. Lantos's Vivafilm, a Montreal-based distribution company, also was brought into Alliance. In the late 1980s Lantos's partners in the company departed one by one, and in 1989 he became its sole head.

LAR DALY DECISION ▸ a 1959 FCC decision on a political equal time claim that caused Congress to amend the Communication Act exempting legitimate news coverage from the Sec. 315 requirements.

As a minor candidate (America First Party) for Mayor of Chicago that year, Lar Daly claimed equal time on television to the routine newscast coverage of several ceremonial acts performed by the incumbent, Mayor Richard J. Daley. The FCC, by a 4-3 vote, held that Daly was entitled to the time, a decision widely interpreted as meaning that elected officials could not receive legitimate news coverage during a campaign period without creating free time situations for all their rival candidates.

Congress moved then to amend the law, making newscasts, news interviews, news documentaries and spot coverage of news events exempt from equal time considerations.

***LARAMIE* ▸** western on NBC (1959-62) with John Smith as rancher Slim Sherman, Robert Fuller as rancher Jess Harper, Spring Byington as housekeeper Daisy Cooper and Hoagy Carmichael as Jonesy. It was produced by Revue Productions.

LARGE-SCREEN TV ▸ display system used by consumers who want a theater-like viewing experience and in corporate and institutional presentations before large audiences. For consumers the two options in large-screen sets are two-unit projection TVs, in which the picture emanates from a projector onto a reflective screen as it does in film projection, and single-unit direct-view TVs, in which projection takes place within the set's cabinetry.

LaROSA, JULIUS ▸ pop singer of the 1950s who earned a paragraph in TV history when he was fired on the air by Arthur Godfrey as a regular member of the weekly series *Arthur Godfrey and His Friends* in 1953. Bounced for an alleged lack of "humility," LaRosa had reason to be thankful for the firing, since for a brief time it made him a national folk hero and won him an RCA Victor contract. In 1955 he began his own 15-minute summertime TV show three times a week, as well as a half-hour series with Kitty Kallen, *TV's Top Tunes.* His popularity declined in the 1960s and, by the end of the decade, he had become a disc jockey for WNEW-AM New York.

LARSON, GLEN A. ▶ an original member of The Four Preps singing group in the late 1950s who moved into TV writing and then producing, becoming one of Hollywood's biggest hit-makers. He produced *Alias Smith & Jones* and *It Takes a Thief* and was executive producer of *McCloud, Six Million Dollar Man, Get Christie Love, Switch* and *Quincy.* He joined 20th Century-Fox Television in 1981 and produced *The Fall Guy* there. Larson's other credits include *Magnum, P.I.* (1980-88), *Knight Rider* (1982-86), and the CBS comedy-drama *P.S. I Luv U* (1991—).

LASER ▶ acronym for "Light Amplification by Stimulated Emission of Radiation," a device which converts power into an intense, narrow beam of light. It has several potential uses in television: (1) because the laser beam can carry large bandwidths, it can be used in conjunction with fiber optics as a substitute for cable, (2) as a pickup device in optical videodisc player systems and CD players, 3) as a potential key component of three-dimensional television.

LASSIE ▶ long-running weekly adventure series with particular appeal to children. Derived from the movie series about an intelligent and heroic collie, it was a Sunday night fixture on CBS from 1955 to 1970. A casualty of the FCC's prime time-access rule, which forced the networks to cut back their programming, *Lassie* continued in production three more years as a bartered prime-access entry, under Campbell Soup sponsorship. The series was owned and produced by the Wrather Corp.

The original cast featured Tommy Rettig as Jeff Miller, the young owner of the collie, Jan Clayton as his mother, Ellen Miller, and George Cleveland as his grandfather. The cast changed at various times in the show's long run, and over the course of it at least six different dogs, descended from the same line, played the title role. Although Lassie was supposed to be female, male collies were used.

The second Lassie family featured Jon Provost as the young boy, now named Timmy Martin, and Jon Shepodd and Cloris Leachman as his parents, Paul and Ruth Martin. In the third and probably best-known of the families, June Lockhart and Hugh Reilly were the parents (still Ruth and Paul Martin) and Provost continued as Timmy. Later episodes had Lassie traveling with an adult master, a ranger played by Robert Bray.

Reruns of the early black-and-white version were syndicated as *Jeff's Collie,* and those starring Provost as *Timmy and Lassie.* The remainder were syndicated as *Lassie.* The show was revived again in 1988.

LAST KING OF AMERICA, THE ▶ an attempt by CBS News at reaching into history with the news interview; the effort, on June 6, 1973, fell short of a critical success. Eric Sevareid as a contemporary reporter attempted an impromptu interview with King George III of England, who lost the colonies, portrayed by actor Peter Ustinov. It was filmed near Stratford-on-Avon, with Perry Wolff as producer for CBS News.

David Letterman

LATE NIGHT WITH DAVID LETTERMAN ▶ offbeat and often hilarious post-midnight desk-and-sofa show that, in its parlay with *Tonight,* has given NBC a powerful late-night block. NBC had looked for a way to use the young comedian, whose irreverent brand of humor was considered both too special and too dangerous for prime time. Letterman made a strong impression in the 1979-80 season as a frequent guest host (replacement) for Johnny Carson on *Tonight,* and in 1982 when the network canceled Tom Snyder's *Tomorrow,* Letterman got the slot. He has built a staunch following among young viewers. In 1987 the show was expanded from four nights a week to five.

The show is a melange of mischief, interviews, music, satire, foolishness and Letterman's acerbic wit, all performed live and much of it spontaneous. Letterman's resident cast includes bandleader (and sidekick) Paul Shaffer and comedy actor Calvert DeForest. Guests are celebrities, budding comedians and musical performers.

Among Letterman's favorite targets for his humor have been Bryant Gumbel, host of NBC's *Today* show, and General Electric, parent of NBC.

LAUGH-TRACK ▶ laughter mechanically inserted on the soundtrack of a show by mixing "canned" or prerecorded audience responses into the final audio track of a show that had been filmed without audience. The device used is a portable console consisting of multiple cassette players containing a range of laughter from mild titters to uncontrollable guffaws. Working in an audio recording studio while the film or tape of the program is projected, the operator assesses scenes for the type of laughter indicated and activates the appropriate cassette to be mixed into the sound track. Laugh-tracks are mainly used for comedy, game and variety programs.

Cindy Williams and Penny Marshall, stars of the ABC series *Laverne and Shirley*

***LAVERNE AND SHIRLEY* ▶** ABC smash-hit situation comedy (1976-83) that was a spin-off of *Happy Days.* It concerned two young female blue-collar workers, Laverne DeFazio and Shirley Feeney, in Milwaukee during the 1950s, played by Penny Marshall and Cindy Williams. Also featured were David L. Lander and Michael McKean as dopey pals Andrew (Squiggy) Squigman and Lenny Kowznovski, Phil Foster as Laverne's father Frank, Eddie Mekka as Shirley's boyfriend Carmine Ragusa, and Betty Garrett as landlady (and, eventually, Frank's wife) Edna Babish. Thomas L. Miller, Edward K. Milkis and Garry Marshall were co-executive producers and Mark Rothman, Lowell Ganz and Tony Marshall the producers. It was by Paramount TV and Miller-Milkis Productions.

LAWRENCE, BILL (d. 1972) ▶ ABC News correspondent and national affairs editor, noted for his raspy style, wit and accurate prediction in 1966 that President Johnson would not run for reelection. He joined ABC in 1961 as White House correspondent after 20 years with the *New York Times,* variously as a war, foreign and national correspondent. He became the network's national affairs editor in 1965 and in the years before his death broadened his activities to include some sports reporting, such as covering the Triple Crown of racing and the World Series. His only book, *Six Presidents, Too Many Wars,* was published shortly after his death.

***LAWRENCE WELK SHOW, THE* ▶** music-variety series that was a Saturday night fixture on ABC for 15 years (1955-70) and had a large enough following to continue in first run syndication as one of the more popular entries in prime-access time. Welk lost his ABC berth despite healthy ratings because he tended to attract older viewers.

Featuring traditional popular music and the continental but unsophisticated bandleader, Welk, the program made its debut on July 2, 1955, as the *Dodge Dancing Party* and three years later changed the title to *The Plymouth Show Starring Lawrence Welk.* The following year it became *The Lawrence Welk Show.*

Adhering to an old and simple format, the series presented Welk's 27-piece band, soloists and singers doing individual turns and Welk performing on an accordion or doing a fox trot with a cast member. Welk billed his style as "champagne music" and used "I'm Forever Blowing Bubbles" as his theme, but he was best known to TV audiences for his musical cue: "a-one, a-two!"

Among the featured performers over the years were Alice Lon, the Lennon Sisters, Joe Feeney, Larry Hooper, Myron Floren, Tiny Little Jr. and Jerry Burke. Lon, who was the original "Champagne Lady'" on TV, was fired by Welk for exposing her knees too often.

At his height, Welk had a second TV series, *Top Tunes and New Talent,* which began in 1956 and lasted two seasons. He gave up making original programs in 1982, but specially selected reruns continued to be offered in syndication.

LAWSON, JENNIFER ▶ senior executive vice president for programming at PBS, a position created in 1990 with the move within public broadcasting to partially centralize program decision-making. She was thus invested with the power to make major programming decisions for the system. Lawson moved to PBS after nine years as a program officer with the Corporation for Public Broadcasting's Program Fund, serving briefly as its head before her departure. Prior to that she headed the Film Fund in New York City.

Geraldine Laybourne

LAYBOURNE, GERALDINE ▶ president of cable networks Nickelodeon, a children's service, and Nick at Nite, the channel's nighttime designation for a family-viewing schedule of vintage TV reruns like *Mr. Ed* and *My Three Sons.*

Laybourne previously was a teacher who developed an interest in the relationship between media and education. She co-founded the Media Center for Children, a nonprofit resource library for schools and media producers, and eventually became a producer herself. She signed on with Nickelodeon as program manager when the network was only a year old.

Originally noncommercial, Nickelodeon a few years later became a commercial venture owned by Viacom, and it accepts advertising aimed at children. But it generally receives high marks for careful handling of its young audience. The network has occasionally been criticized for favoring entertainment programming in comparison to educational fare, but Laybourne maintains that providing respectful entertainment for children can have value as education. The network has added educational fare as it has matured, including news programming specifically for a young audience.

LBS COMMUNICATIONS ▶ distributor and producer of syndicated programs, known particularly for its role in the growth of barter syndication and for its hard-driving president, Henry Siegel. The company reached a peak of success in the mid-1980s but ran into financial difficulties at the end of the decade, due partly to the debt taken on in a leveraged buyout from Grey Advertising. With the advertising market having turned soft, it was not an opportune time for an LBO.

LBS was established as a subsidiary of Grey Advertising in 1976, when Siegel persuaded management that barter syndication, then in seminal form, offered special opportunities for the agency's clients. It was named Lexington Broadcasting Service to differentiate it from the agency, whose offices were on Lexington Ave. in New York. LBS scored its first coup a year later when it convinced client Procter & Gamble to sponsor a syndicated program built around the rock group, Sha Na Na. The program, *Sha Na Na,* became a big hit in the late 1970s. In 1980, when P&G decided the show no longer met its marketing needs, LBS took the risky step of producing the program on its own and giving it free to stations in exchange for spots that LBS would sell to national advertisers. The barter scheme worked beautifully, and for a while the show was a cash cow for LBS.

The company made another bold and unprecedented move in 1983 by taking on the canceled network series, *Fame,* and backing its continued production by MGM expressly for the syndication market. This too worked well. But one of the ambitious LBS schemes that failed was the creation of an afternoon daytime network, called INDAY, which provided a block of programming, mostly talk shows, to independent stations. It barely lasted half a year.

With the aid of the venture capital firm of Warburg Pincus, Siegel engineered the $38 million LBO in 1988. Siegel's twin brother, Paul, is president of the Hollywood-based LBS Entertainment.

LEACHMAN, CLORIS ▶ actress who has had an enduring career on television since the early 1950s. She is best known for her portrayal of busybody Phyllis Lindstrom in *The Mary Tyler Moore Show,* a role that was spun off to *Phyllis* (1975-77).

In the 1950s and 1960s she appeared in a wide range of programs, including *The Bob and Ray Show, Zane Grey Theater, Alfred Hitchcock*

Presents and *The Donna Reed Show.* From 1986-89 she was a regular on *The Facts of Life.* In 1991-92 she starred in the NBC sitcom *Walter and Emily.* She has also appeared in made-for-TV movies and motion pictures.

LEAD-IN ▶ the preceding program. In rating analysis, a program's performance is assessed with attention to the audience inherited from its lead-in. A show that overcomes a weak lead-in demonstrates that it has extraordinary appeal; one that cannot hold the audience of a strong lead-in is considered lacking in inherent appeal and is usually a candidate for cancellation.

LEAHY, THOMAS F. ▶ longtime CBS senior executive whose early retirement in spring of 1992 ended 30 years of service with the network in a variety of key posts. His most recent appointment, in October 1990, was to the post of senior vice president of the CBS Broadcast Group. Earlier, he had held such positions as president of the CBS Marketing Division (from 1988), president of the CBS Television Network (from 1986), and executive vice president and senior broadcasting vice president of the CBS Broadcast Group (from 1981), with responsibilities for the CBS Entertainment Division and the CBS Television Network Division.

He joined CBS in 1962 as salesman for the television network, rising to director of daytime sales in 1969. In 1971 he switched to the stations division as vice president and general manager of WCBS-TV, the flagship station, which served as his springboard to the presidency of the station division in 1977. From there he was elevated to the Broadcast Group.

LEAR, NORMAN ▶ TV's most successful producer in the 1970s who, in pioneering the mature and frank-spoken situation comedy, led the medium into new directions of sophistication. Flouting the old broadcasting taboos and finding a huge audience highly receptive to his "adult" approach to TV comedy, Lear triggered the massive reappraisal of program standards that led to the "new boldness" that characterized prime time in the early 1970s.

Coming to TV from motion pictures with his partner Bud Yorkin (together they were Tandem Productions), he had an explosive hit in 1971 with *All in the Family,* which broke new ground in dealing with such subjects as bigotry, menopause, homosexuality and impotence, as well as with political issues. A string of successful spin-offs—*Maude, Good Times, The Jeffersons*—and another blockbuster, *Sanford and Son,* quickly made him the hottest independent program supplier to the networks and broadened his license to explore the outer boundaries of acceptability for the use of the language and subject matter. Usually, his ventures beyond the normally accepted limits were justified by well-crafted scripts that attempted to deal realistically and responsibly with contemporary society.

In 1974, with former talent agency Jerry Perenchio, Lear co-founded another company, T.A.T. Productions, separate from his partnership with Yorkin. T.A.T. also began generating hits—notably *One Day At a Time* and *Mary Hartman, Mary Hartman,* whose impact on syndication in 1976 was comparable to that of *All in the Family* on network TV five years earlier. There was also a slew of failures: *Hot l Baltimore, The Dumplings, All's Fair, The Nancy Walker Show, All That Glitters, In the Beginning,* and *Apple Pie.* But in a business in which, on average, four out of five new series fail every season, Lear's hit percentage in the 1970s was extraordinary. He was clearly the dominant producer of the decade.

At least one of his shows placed in the prime-time top ten for 11 consecutive seasons (1971-82), and in the 1974-75 season Lear had five of the top ten shows. His off-network series were also red-hot in syndication; between 1975 and 1985 his off-network sales exceeded $1 billion. But instead of continuing on the television path that began in the medium's early years, when he was a comedy writer for Martha Ray, George Gobel and other comedians, Lear gave vent to his penchant for business.

In 1982 he and Perenchio purchased Avco/Embassay Pictures and formed Embassy Communications as successor to T.A.T. They became successfully involved in motion pictures, home video, pay television, cable ownership, and Spanish-language broadcasting with WNJU-TV New York. In 1984 they sold their cable systems to TCI for a large profit and a year later sold Embassy and Tandem Productions to Coca-Cola for $485 million. In 1986 they made a $50 million profit on the sale of WNJU.

That same year, Lear acquired *Channels* magazine and began to build a new company on his own, Act III Communications. In addition to a trade magazine group headed by Paul David Schaeffer that went on an acquisition spree, Lear acquired a chain of motion picture theaters in Texas and assembled a group of UHF television stations. He also started his own motion picture company. Act III, however, was not one of Lear's great successes. The publishing and motion picture ventures were costly failures and were shut down in the winter of 1990.

Meanwhile, Lear's magic touch in television eluded him in several sporadic projects. Two sitcoms that made it to the networks, *a.k.a. Pablo* and the somewhat autobiographical *Sunday Dinner,* flopped, and the pilot for another sitcom, *Balls,* was rejected in 1991. A late-night series in the eccentric tradition of *Mary Hartman* had been accepted for a trial on CBS but eventually was withdrawn by Lear as unworkable.

He was far more successful in the 1980s as a social activist. In 1981 he began devoting much of his time to counteracting the influence of the Religious New Right in politics. He co-founded a national organization, People for the American Way, that created literature and commercials to offset the media campaigns of the Moral Majority and kindred groups. The organization, and Lear personally, were credited in some quarters with having foiled President Reagan's attempt to appoint Judge Robert Bork to the Supreme Court. In 1989, with James Burke and Warren Buffett, he founded The Business Enterprise Trust, an organization that would make awards, like the Oscars and Emmies, to corporations for courage, integrity and social vision. He was unable, however, to find a network that would pay for the exclusive right to broadcast the awards ceremonies.

LEASED CHANNELS ▶ channels made available on cable systems, usually at the behest of the franchising authority, for leasing to members of the public at posted rates, on a common carrier basis. As a form of paid public access, leased channels permit individuals or companies to present programs of their own with advertising sponsorship and with no interference from the cable operator except for reasons of obscenity.

In principle, the leased channel concept permits every citizen to become a broadcaster, or video publisher, at a relatively low fee—in marked contrast to over-the-air television which is a closed shop for a limited number of licensees. The FCC regulations require that leased cable channels be made available on a nondiscriminatory first-come, first-served basis according to posted rates applicable to all.

***LEAVE IT TO BEAVER* ▶** family situation comedy of the late 1950s whose reruns continue to play on local stations. It premiered on CBS in October 1957 and moved to ABC a year later, where it ran until August 1963. Jerry Mathers played Theodore (Beaver) Cleaver, a young boy, and Tony Dow his older brother, Wally. Hugh Beaumont and Barbara Billingsley were their seemingly perfect parents, Ward and June Cleaver; Ken Osmond played Wally's unwholesome friend, Eddie Haskell; Frank Bank was Wally's friend Clarence (Lumpy) Rutherford; and Richard Deacon portrayed Lumpy's father (and Ward's boss), Fred Rutherford. It was by Gomalco Productions and Universal. The show was revived as *The New Leave It To Beaver* in the mid-1980s.

The cast of *Leave It To Beaver*

LEE, H. REX ▶ FCC commissioner (1968-73) who was appointed by President Johnson to a Democratic seat and resigned 18 months before the end of his term to benefit from an early retirement plan for government officials with long years of service. Lee entered government in 1936 as an economist with the Department of Agriculture. Later he served with the Department of Interior and in 1961 was appointed, by President Kennedy, governor of American Samoa. On the FCC he was public television's leading advocate. He later became head of the Public Service Satellite Consortium.

LEE, PINKY ▶ burlesque comedian who was popular in the early years of TV. He starred with Martha Stewart (later replaced by Vivian

Blaine) in the variety show *Those Two* from 1951 to 1954, which was followed by a successful children's series, *The Pinky Lee Show*.

LEE, ROBERT E. ▶ FCC commissioner (1953-81) appointed to a Republican seat by President Eisenhower. He was reappointed by Presidents Eisenhower, Johnson and Nixon. Through all those years he was the commission's staunchest believer in the development of UHF and approached many issues with a view to their potential impact on UHF. Before joining the FCC, he was a special agent for the FBI, administrative assistant to J. Edgar Hoover at the FBI and director of surveys and investigations for the House Appropriations Committee. Lee served longer on the FCC than any previous commissioner. Before retiring, he served for one month as chairman of the Commission while Mark S. Fowler was preparing to take the office.

LEGALLY QUALIFIED CANDIDATES ▶ [Letter to Mr. Larry Seigle/FCC 72-924 (1972)] vital to claims for equal time, determined by reference to whether the candidate can be voted for in the state or district in which the election is being held, and whether he is eligible to serve in the office in question.

The FCC made a key ruling in 1972 when it denied appeals by Socialist Workers Party candidates for president and vice-president for equal time to respond to broadcasts by the Democratic candidates. The appeals were by candidates who were 31 and 21 years old. The commission found, with one dissent, that since the Constitution states that a person under 35 years of age is ineligible to hold the office of president, neither candidate could serve and therefore neither was a "legally qualified candidate."

LEGEND OF MARILYN MONROE, THE ▶ re-creation of the life of the legendary actress through stills, newsreel and candid footage and clips from her films. The hour was produced in 1965 by Wolper Productions, with John Huston as narrator.

LEHRER, JAMES C. ▶ Washington-based co-anchor of the successful PBS nightly program *The MacNeil-Lehrer Newshour* (formerly *The MacNeil-Lehrer Report*). Previously he was correspondent for NPACT and moderator of many of its programs. He came to the Washington public affairs arm of PBS in 1972 from KERA, the PTV station in Dallas, where he was news director and executive producer of *KERA Newsroom*. With NPACT he held the title of public affairs coordinator. Lehrer and Robert MacNeil formed their own production company in 1982 for commercial as well as public television.

LEISER, ERNEST ▶ former vice president and assistant to the president of CBS News beginning in 1981. Before that he had been a leading producer for CBS News for most of the years since he joined in 1953. From 1964 to 1967 he was executive producer of *The CBS Evening News with Walter Cronkite* and then executive producer of the CBS Special Reports Unit. He left in 1972 to become exec producer of *The ABC Evening News* and *The Reasoner Report* but returned to CBS after three years to work on special news projects, such as the all-day Bicentennial spectacular on July 4, 1976. He won Emmys for two documentaries, *Father and Sons* and *The World of Charlie Company,* and for producing the coverage of the assassination and funeral of Dr. Martin Luther King Jr. In 1979, he was named CBS News v.p. of special events and political coverage. He retired from CBS in the mid-1980s and became a Gannett senior fellow at the Gannett Center for Media Studies (1987-88).

LENO, JAY ▶ comedian tapped for the coveted top spot on NBC's *Tonight Show* with Johnny Carson's retirement (after 30 years) in the spring of 1992. Smart and hip, Leno is one of those unusual talents, like others in the *Tonight* line (Steve Allen and Jack Paar), whose appeal cuts across barriers of age and education levels. His forte is poking fun at American mores and the consumer culture. Leno first appeared on *Tonight* in 1977, when he began making the rounds of talk-variety shows including several guest spots on *Late Night with David Letterman.* He started in show business as the warm-up act for entertainers like Johnny Mathis, John Denver and Tom Jones. Leno got his start in television writing for Jimmie Walker in the 1970s situation comedy *Good Times.*

LEONARD, BILL ▶ longtime CBS News executive who in April 1979, after more than 30 years with the company, became president of the division, succeeding Richard S. Salant, forced to retire on reaching age 65. Leonard himself, when he assumed the post, was two years away from mandatory retirement. He was tapped by a relatively new CBS management that had not yet evaluated the longterm candidates for the presidency of the news division. Prior to his appointment, Leonard had been

CBS Washington v.p. and chief liaison with the government and its agencies. He succeeded Richard W. Jencks in the post in 1975.

Leonard stayed on beyond his 65th birthday, under a waiver by the CBS board, and retired in March 1982, yielding his post to Van Gordon Sauter.

Starting in radio in 1946, with the CBS station in New York, Leonard conducted the *This Is New York* series that later shifted to WCBS-TV as *Eye on New York.* He moved on to the CBS News division in 1959 as producer-correspondent of *CBS Reports* and until 1962 produced, wrote and narrated those programs. He then formed the CBS News Election Unit and in 1964 became an executive with initial responsibility for editorial policies, production planning and special events coverage. In 1968 he was placed in charge of all special and documentary production and three years later became senior v.p. Among the *CBS Reports* documentaries produced and narrated by Leonard before 1962 were *Trujillo: Portrait of a Dictator, Thunder on the Right* and *The Beat Majority.* Leonard, who married the former wife of CBS correspondent Mike Wallace, is the stepfather of Chris Wallace, a rising star at ABC News.

LEONARD, HERBERT B. (BERT) ▶ highly successful producer of adventure series in the 1950s and 1960s, whose credits include *Naked City* and *Route 66* (through his Shelle Productions), *Rescue 8* (through Wilbert Productions), *Tales of the Bengal Lancers* (through Lancer Productions) and, earlier, *Circus Boy* and *Rin Tin Tin* (Herbert B. Leonard Productions).

LEONARD, SHELDON ▶ character actor in movies and comedy actor in radio whose chief success in television has been as a producer and director. His credits in that sphere began in 1953 when he became executive producer and director of the Danny Thomas series during its first year. Later he and Thomas became partners in a production company. Leonard developed *The Andy Griffith Show* for CBS, then spun off *Gomer Pyle, USMC* and put together such other hits as *The Dick Van Dyke Show* and *I Spy,* all of which he supervised as exec producer. He was also exec producer of *My World and Welcome to It.* In 1975, he returned to acting, playing his most familiar character role, that of a Runyonesque gambler in *Big Eddie,* a CBS situation comedy. The show flopped, however. During the 1930s Leonard had been featured in a number of Broadway shows, including *Three Men on a Horse.* He went to Hollywood in 1939 and made more than 140 movies, frequently playing gangsters or gamblers. He then began making radio appearances and was a frequent guest on the comedy programs of Jack Benny, Phil Harris, Bob Hope and Judy Canova. He also dabbled in writing radio plays and in the 1950s switched to television writing and directing.

LESCOULIE, JACK (d. 1987) ▶ TV personality who was a regular on NBC's *Today* from 1958 to the late 196Os and earlier had been a TV sidekick to Jackie Gleason. He also hosted several daytime shows and in 1975 was anchorman for NBC's latenight experiment *America After Dark.* On leaving *Today* he moved to Cincinnati to work on television projects there.

***LESLIE UGGAMS SHOW, THE* ▶** a CBS music-variety series (1969) that represented an early attempt to build a program of that type around a black star. But Uggams, although fresh from a triumph on Broadway, lacked a national following, and her series was canceled after 13 weeks. It was produced by Ilson & Chambers.

LESTER, JERRY ▶ rowdy comedian who made an impact on TV in 1950-51 as emcee of *Broadway Open House,* the pioneer latenight show on NBC. As a nightly show it drew heavily on Lester's broad comedy resources—and those of Dagmar, Wayne Howell and Milton Delugg, as well—but while it marked the height of his career, it also caused him to suffer from overexposure. Lester faded from prominence soon afterwards, while NBC learned that comedy in a lower key would sustain better on a nightly basis.

***LET'S MAKE A DEAL* ▶** see Game Shows.

LETTERMAN, DAVID ▶ see *Late Night with David Letterman.*

LEVANT, OSCAR (d. 1972) ▶ concert pianist, literary wit and raconteur who in the late 1950s became host of a popular syndicated talk show emanating from the West Coast. But the program was considered in poor taste by many because it seemed to exploit Levant's neuroses and his eccentric behavior more than it made use of his conversational or musical talents. He guested frequently on other shows and for a time was panelist on *General Electric Guest House.*

LEVATHES, PETER G. ▶ commercial TV and motion picture executive who became director of program development for the Corporation for Public Broadcasting (1976-77). He had previously been with 20th Century-Fox TV as executive v.p. of all production for the studio, movies as well as TV.

LEVIN, GERALD ▶ chief operating officer and vice chairman of Time Warner Inc. who had a significant hand in structuring the 1989 merger of the two companies and who has continued to focus on the financial aspects of the combined entity.

Levin started in programming at HBO in 1972, was named its president in 1973 and chairman in 1976. It was he who took the daring step of putting the small three-state pay cable operation on satellite in 1975, creating the first national cable network. *Channels* magazine dubbed him "the Lenin of video ... the man who started the revolution." Levin's gamble on satellite distribution enabled him to build HBO into the nation's largest pay-television service. The perceived demand for HBO around the country also prompted the rapid spread of cable in the late 1970s and early 1980s. HBO was described then as the engine that was pulling cable. In stimulating the creation of a wide variety of new satellite networks, Levin's move was a major leap forward for the cable medium, which until then had been primarily local.

Levin was promoted to vice president of the Time Inc. video group in 1979 with Time's cable operations, ATC, and other video interests added to his responsibilities. From the mid-1980s on he was Time's chief strategist.

A graduate of Haverford College and the University of Pennsylvania Law School, Levin worked as an attorney from 1963-67 and later was COO of Development and Resources Corp., an international investment and management company.

LEVINE, IRVING R. ▶ veteran NBC News correspondent (since 1950) who became economic affairs correspondent in Washington in 1971 after covering foreign beats for nearly two decades. He was based in Rome for ten years, in Moscow for four and in Tokyo for two. He also served a year in London.

LEVINSON-LINK ▶ producer-writer team of Richard Levinson and William Link, who created *Mannix, Columbo, Ellery Queen, Tenafly* and *Murder She Wrote* and served as executive producers of the latter four. They were also the writers and executive producers for such made-for-TV movies as *The Execution of Private Slovik* and *The Gun.*

Levinson went on to write and produce several TV movies before dying of lung cancer in 1987. Link served as executive producer for the *ABC Saturday Mystery Movie* from 1989 to 1990. He wrote a TV movie in 1990, *The Boys,* with an anti-smoking theme. It depicted the Levinson-Link partnership, which began while they were in college.

LEVITAN, PAUL (d. 1976) ▶ director of special events for CBS (1961-72), responsible for coverage of such spectacles as the America, Universe and Teenage America pageants and the Rose Bowl and Thanksgiving Day Parades. During the 1950s he had been an executive producer for CBS News, principally on special events coverage, and before that worked with Fred Friendly on producing *See It Now.*

LEVY, DAVID ▶ one-time program v.p. for NBC (1959-61), having joined from the broadcast department of Young & Rubicam. He later went to Goodson-Todman Productions on the West Coast and then to Filmways, serving as executive producer of such series as *The Double Life of Henry Phyfe, The Pruitts of Southhampton* and *The Addams Family.* In a novel, *The Chameleons,* published in 1964, Levy described with some acrimony the executive suite intrigues at a network.

LEVY, ISAAC (d. 1975) and LEON (d. 1978) ▶ pivotal figures in the evolution of CBS and later members of its board of directors; they were instrumental in William S. Paley's acquisition of the struggling radio network in 1928.

In 1922 Isaac bought Philadelphia's WCAU and Leon became chief administrator of the station. A few years later Leon married Blanche Paley, whose family owned Philadelphia's Congress Cigar Co., which soon became a major advertiser on WCAU. In 1927 Leon made the station an affiliate of the newly formed network United Independent Broadcasters, which sought to compete with RCA's network. That same year the operating rights of UIB were purchased by the Columbia Phonograph Co. and the network was renamed the Columbia Phonograph Broadcasting System.

A year later the Levy brothers persuaded Leon's brother-in-law, William Paley, to buy the controlling interest in the network while they bought large shares in it themselves. Through the years they remained major shareholders of CBS. Ike Levy left the board of directors in 1951 but Leon continued to serve as a director, and in 1975 his holdings in the company came to 330,756 shares.

LEVY, RALPH ▶ producer-director of the 1950s who guided the programs of Jack Benny, Ed Wynn and George Burns and Gracie Allen, among others. But his most significant credit was producing the pilot film for *I Love Lucy* in 1951.

LEWINE, ROBERT F. ▶ former ABC, NBC and CBS program executive; later executive v.p. of the talent agency CMA; and for many years an official of the Academy of Television Arts and Sciences, serving twice as national president. He was an ABC program exec from 1953 to 1957, rising to v.p. in charge, and then moved to NBC and became its program chief (1957-58). After a year in independent production he joined CBS and became the network's program v.p. in Hollywood. He joined CMA in 1964 and returned to NBC in 1977.

LEWIS, JERRY ▶ see Martin and Lewis.

LEWIS, ROBERT Q. ▶ ubiquitous TV personality during the 1950s who hosted or was a panelist on numerous game shows and conducted daytime variety shows known as *Robert Q's Matinee* and *The Robert Q. Lewis Show*.

LIBERACE (d. 1987) ▶ pianist and entertainer who achieved an intensely devoted fan-following during the 1950s with a 15-minute nationally syndicated program on which his ornate semiclassical playing style was abetted by his personal effusiveness, extravagant smile and outrageous wardrobe. His vast appeal, which from 1953 to 1955 made his program one of the most popular on television, was demonstrably with older women.

Although he was born and educated in Wisconsin, his persona was continental, an image that was also served by his trademark—a candelabra on his piano—and his use professionally of his surname only. His given names were Wladziu Valentino. Working with him always was his brother, George Liberace, as a violinist and conductor of the orchestra.

Liberace's excesses were frequently ridiculed, but he generally took the insults good-naturedly with a response that is now famous: "I cried all the way to the bank."

He did, however, sue the British columnist Cassandra for libel.

LICENSE CHALLENGE ▶ procedure by which an individual or group may oppose the renewal of a license for a particular existing station and apply to receive it instead. A license challenge—also called a strike application—differs from a petition to deny essentially in the fact that it asks for the license while the petition to deny does not, although both contend that the incumbent is not worthy of the right to broadcast.

Because of the high stakes—a major market TV station can be worth several hundred million dollars—and the cost of mounting a years-long defense, the prospect of a license challenge is nerve-wracking. However, because of the FCC's pro-incumbent bias, the fear is more theoretical than real, except for a broadcaster already in regulatory hot water.

LICENSE RENEWAL ▶ approval by the FCC of a broadcaster's privilege to operate for another five-year term upon the expiration of his license. Technically the licensee must demonstrate in his application for renewal that his continuance would serve the public interest. Licensees are required to give adequate notice to the public of the application for renewal, and if the incumbent's license should be challenged by a competing applicant at license renewal time the FCC must hold a comparative hearing to determine who will get the license.

Historically, a proven—even though unexceptional—record of performance by an incumbent has been preferred, in comparative renewals, to the untried proposals of a challenger. Even so, bills were introduced in Congress during the 1970s to amend the Communications Act in ways that would establish that an incumbent is not to be treated as a new applicant. Legislation in 1981 lengthened the licensing period for television stations from three years to five.

Throughout the 1980s, renewal became virtually automatic. As a consequence of Reagan-era deregulation that defanged citizens' petitions to deny, and the insulation against competing applications provided by the U.S. Court of Appeals' 1982 *WESH-TV* decision, broadcasters' anxiety over the security of their licenses was greatly reduced. While occasional challenges were filed, the challengers often seemed more interested in obtaining a financial settlement than in seriously litigating the case. This residual problem was addressed by the FCC in the latter part of the 1980s in a series of actions that eliminated the opportunity to press for substantial payments, and created a number of new procedural obstacles for challengers to overcome.

In a notable comparative renewal case in the early 1950s [*Hearst Radio Inc. (WBAL),* 15 FCC 1149 (1951)] the FCC favored an existing license over a challenger even though the incumbent's performance had not been outstanding. This decision of the commission so discouraged challengers that during the 1950s and 1960s, with one exception, no TV licensee in the regular renewal process faced a comparative hearing.

But in 1965 the FCC issued its policy statement on comparative hearings that said that past broadcast experience would not be an important factor unless it was unusually good or poor. The FCC also stressed that integration of management and diversity of ownership would be important considerations in assessing an incumbent's qualifications.

In the WHDH case, the standards enunciated in the 1965 policy statement were directly applied in a comparative renewal hearing, and although WHDH was far from a normal renewal situation, the FCC's refusal to consider the incumbent's past performance caused great consternation in the industry. It also opened the floodgates to other license challenges.

Broadcasters immediately began lobbying Congress for some relief and in 1969 Sen. John O. Pastore, chairman of the Senate Communications Subcommittee, proposed a two-stage hearing for comparative renewals. Under this bill, the FCC would examine the incumbent's record to determine if the licensee had met the public interest standard; if it had, then the commission would authorize renewal. Competing applications would thus be considered only if the incumbent had failed to meet the standard.

After opposition to the bill stalled its progress, the FCC in 1970 issued the Policy Statement Concerning Comparative Hearings Including Regular Renewal Applications. Here the commission stated that if an incumbent could show that its program service had been "substantially" attuned to the needs and interests of its area, and that the operation of the station had not otherwise been seriously deficient, its application will be preferred over that of the newcomer.

In June 1971, the D.C. Court of Appeals held the 1970 policy statement invalid because it operated to deprive the competing applicant of its statutory right to a full hearing (*Citizens Communications Center v. FCC* [477 F2d 1201 (D.C. Circuit 1971)]). In addition, the court stated that the commission was attempting to establish by policy statement what Congress had not done by legislation.

The court suggested that "superior" service should be of major significance and that the commission in its rulemaking proceeding should try to clarify what constitutes "superior" service.

The only major station licenses remaining in jeopardy after the WESH-TV decision were the long-endangered franchises held by the RKO group. The only other exception to the general rule involved WSNS-TV, a Chicago UHF station, which was really no more than a skirmish in a long war between two family-owned movie theater operators. The challengers, Monroe Communications, charged that during the 1970s, while the station was operated as a pay-TV outlet, it carried obscene films and did no public service programming. The FCC renewed the license because the station started carrying an early morning service program in the last six months of its license term. The U.S. Court of Appeals reversed, and virtually directed the commission to award the license to Monroe.

LICENSE TRANSFER ▶ the passing of a broadcast license from one owner to another, normally through the sale of the station, which cannot be consummated without FCC approval. Section 310 of the Communications Act specifies that application must be made to the FCC for the transfer of licenses or construction permits and that the FCC should approve only if it finds that "the public interest, convenience and necessity will be served thereby."

For five decades, the process of buying and selling broadcast properties was so closely regulated that purchase of a station was one of the most common techniques employed as a defense against hostile takeovers of publicly traded companies. The FCC gave long and close scrutiny to purchasers' character and financial qualifications, and it forbade "trafficking" by establishing a minimum three-year holding period before a station could be sold.

All this changed abruptly under the Reagan Administration's deregulation policies. Chairman Mark Fowler repealed the trafficking rule and enthusiastically encouraged speculative ventures such as limited partnership investment pools to bring additional capital into the industry, promising them quick profits as prices rose. In 1985, making light of warnings from broadcast reformers and group owners worried about takeover problems of their own, Fowler and his colleagues paved the way for a hostile takeover of Storer Communications, one of the oldest broadcast groups, by allowing the temporary transfer of its stations to a group of independent trustees pending the outcome of the proxy fight and approval of the new management once it was voted in. Ironically, although the Storer precedent led to numerous similar deals, it ultimately went bust, and within a few years the junk bonds that Drexel Burnham's Michael Milken packaged to finance the deal were worth pennies on the dollar.

LICENSING (OF PROGRAMS) ▶ lease basis on which producing companies "sell" their programs to networks or stations. In ordering a program or series from a studio, a network merely secures the rights for two air plays under a standard agreement, but the property remains under the ownership and control of the producing concern. The studio may simultaneously license the rights to foreign systems but must wait until the network has completed its use of the property before releasing it in domestic syndication. There, individual stations may license the rights to the reruns for a specified time in their specific markets.

LIE, THE ▶ drama written for Swedish TV by Ingmar Bergman, which was translated and produced for the U.S. by CBS (April 4, 1973) as a 90-minute *CBS Playhouse 90* special. Lewis Freedman produced, and George Segal and Dean Jagger were the stars.

LIEBERTHAL, GARY ▶ chairman of Columbia Pictures Television, a unit of Sony-owned Columbia Pictures Entertainment. A longtime syndication executive, he remained at the head of his organization despite a rash of ownership changes.

Lieberthal got into TV syndication in an unusual way. In 1968 he went to work for Arbitron, the local ratings service, producing the company's television market surveys. A later Arbitron assignment gave him unique insights into the syndication marketplace, which eventually led to his appointment in 1976 as v.p. of syndication for T.A.T. Communications. That was when T.A.T. was about to launch Norman Lear's latenight syndicated spoof, *Mary Hartman, Mary Hartman.*

Then, when the company acquired Embassy Pictures, T.A.T. became Embassy Telecommunications. In 1983 Lieberthal successfully launched "Embassy Night at the Movies," an ad hoc syndication network that provided stations with the TV premieres of theatrical motion pictures. In 1985 Embassy was purchased by the Coca-Cola Company and later merged with Columbia Pictures Television, also owned by Coca-Cola. Sony USA acquired Columbia in September 1989. Lieberthal survived all the changes intact.

LIEBMAN, MAX (d. 1981) ▶ a Broadway theater and film producer known principally in TV for his work as producer of the famed *Your Show of Shows* comedy series with Sid Caesar and Imogene Coca. In 1955 he produced a number of color "spectaculars" for NBC and in the late 1960s was creative supervisor of *The Jackie Gleason Show.*

LIFE AND LEGEND OF WYATT EARP, THE ▶ hit western series on ABC (1955-60) about the marshal of Tombstone, Arizona, starring Hugh O'Brian. It was by Louis F. Edelman and Wyatt Earp Enterprises.

LIFE GOES ON ▶ hour-long ABC drama series that broke new ground when it was introduced in 1989 because its central character, Corky Thatcher, is an 18-year-old retarded teenager. The role is played by Christopher Burke, who has Down Syndrome. The show was generally well received but it has struggled in the ratings opposite CBS's *60 Minutes* on Sunday nights. It has been lauded by mental health authorities for illustrating the capabilities of the mentally handicapped.

The series is produced by Warner Brothers Television, and its executive producer is Michael Braverman.

LIFE OF RILEY, THE ▶ the prototypical early situation comedy of the Bumbling Father school: it bloomed twice on NBC, first with Jackie Gleason and Rosemary DeCamp as Chester A. and Peg Riley (1949-50), and then with William Bendix and Marjorie Reynolds (1953-58) in the leads. The protagonist was a likeable but stupid working-class head of the family who managed always to muddle through mild trouble. The show was popular and the repeats sold well in syndication.

LIFE ON EARTH ▶ remarkable 13-episode British natural history series tracing the evolution of life on this planet over millions of years; it had its U.S. premiere on PBS in January 1982 and quickly became one of public television's most watched series ever. David Attenborough, former program director of the British Broadcasting Corporation, wrote and narrated the series.

In the tradition established at the BBC by *Civilisation* and *The Ascent of Man,* Attenborough's documentary series was meticulously researched and was filmed on locations in 30 countries, employing the most advanced photographic techniques. It took three years to produce. Christopher Parsons was executive producer and John Sparks and Richard Brock co-producers. It was the biggest production ever undertaken by the BBC's Natural History Unit in Bristol, England.

Life on Earth was produced in association with Warner Bros. Television, which invested in the project, and was presented on PBS by WQLN, Erie, Pa., on funding by Mobil Corp. Attenborough's book based on the series was published in the U.S. by Little, Brown & Co. in 1981.

LIFE WITH FATHER ▶ situation comedy based on the popular book and play by Clarence Day. It aired on CBS (1953-55) with Leon Ames as Clarence Day Sr. and Lurene Tuttle as his wife. The Day sons were played by Ralph Reed (replaced by Steven Terrell) as Clarence Jr., Freddie Leiston (replaced by Malcolm Cassell) as John, Ronald Keith (replaced by B.G. Norman and Freddy Ridgeway) as Whitney and Harvey Grant as Harlan. Dorothy Bernard played the housekeeper, Margaret.

LIFE WITH LUIGI ▶ popular early CBS situation comedy that moved over from radio in 1948. In it, J. Carrol Naish portrayed a newly arrived Italian immigrant, Luigi Basco. Alan Reed was featured as Pasquale.

LIFELINE ▶ weekly prime-time nonfiction series on NBC (1978), in the cinema verite style, focusing on the professional and private lives of actual doctors. The pilot had caught the fancy of Fred Silverman after he joined NBC as its new president in June 1978, and he altered the fall schedule that had already been set to make room for it.

An unusual program for prime time, it seemed to represent what Silverman promised NBC affiliates in his maiden speech to that body: innovative, high-quality fare—programming that would take the high road rather than pander to the youth market. NBC purchased 13 episodes from Tomorrow Entertainment and the Medcom Co., which produced it jointly, but was unable to spark the interest of the viewership.

The series was shifted to various time periods in hopes that it would find an audience somewhere, and one week, in a patented Silverman "stunt," it aired three times. But always, despite generally favorable notices, it landed at or near the bottom of the Nielsens. *Lifeline* was dropped at mid-season. Thomas W. Moore and Dr. Robert E. Fuisz, chairman of Medcom and a practicing physician, were the executive producers.

Robin Leach, host of *Lifestyles of the Rich and Famous*

LIFESTYLES OF THE RICH AND FAMOUS ▶ one-hour syndicated magazine series that visits celebrities at their opulent homes. It was created by former *Entertainment Tonight* reporter Robin Leach, the show's host and executive producer, who shamelessly revels in the ostentatious excesses of the stars, managing to keep a straight face as he outdoes himself each week with superlatives and hyperbole. His loud voice and cockney accent are often parodied on comedy shows. The show began in syndication in 1984, and in 1986 it was run on ABC both in a daytime and nighttime slot.

LIFETIME ▶ basic-cable network dedicated to providing entertainment and information programming of particular interest to women. Lifetime was created by the 1984 merger of Daytime and Cable Health Network. Daytime, launched in 1982 by Hearst/ABC Video Services, featured four hours a day of self-help, relationship and female-oriented programming, and Cable Health Network, started by Viacom in 1982, was a 24-hour health and fitness service. Lifetime, which is headquartered in Kaufman Astoria Studios in Queens, N.Y., serves 52 million subscribers. The network has been aggressive in recent years in buying high-profile shows, such as *L.A. Law* and *Moonlighting,* straight from their broadcast runs and before a syndication window. Lifetime received accolades for producing 13 new episodes of the critically acclaimed *The Days and Nights of Molly Dodd* after broadcast cancellation in 1989. In 1990 the network began airing original movies, and several of these, such as *The Killing Mind* starring Stephanie Zimbalist, boosted the network's ratings into the 5 range (in cable homes). The network's entire Sunday schedule, called Lifetime Medical Television, consists of medical programs targeted to doctors and nurses. Thomas F. Burchill, president and CEO of Lifetime's parent company, Hearst/ABC-Viacom Entertainment Services (HAVES), has expressed interest in moving "Doctor's Sunday" to another cable channel to make room for a seventh day of Lifetime programming.

LIGHT ENTERTAINMENT ▶ a category of programming that, in an international definition, embraces pop music, comedy and what Americans call variety shows. Light entertainment series have been scarce on the mainstream U.S. networks for nearly two decades, largely because of the cultural differences among the generations. Since youthful tastes in comedy and music do not agree with those of older adults, a network seeking a mass audience cannot expect to succeed serving either group. Attempts to build programs around performers who appear to bridge the generations—such as ABC had done with Dolly Parton in 1988—were unavailing. Rock music shows and comedy programs like *Saturday Night Live* and *The David Letterman Show* have been consigned to the late hours, when the youth audience predominates.

Light entertainment has thus become niche programming for the cable networks, which can succeed with ratings that would be disastrous for commercial television. MTV and VH-1 provide what youth requires in music, while A&E, HBO and Showtime have showcased young stand-up comedians who otherwise would have scant opportunities for television exposure.

***LILLIE* ▶** 13-hour British series, produced by London Weekend Television, on the life of Lillie Langtry, the legendary British actress and professional beauty who became mistress of the Prince of Wales, later Edward VII. It began its U.S. run in March 1979 as an entry in the PBS *Masterpiece Theatre* series. Based on James Brough's book, *The Prince and the Lily,* it was developed and largely written by David Butler and directed by John Gorrie. Francesca Annis starred in the title role, with Patrick Holt, Peggy Ann Wood, Anton Rogers and Simon Turner featured.

LINDEMANN, CARL, JR. (d. 1985) ▶ former network sports executive. He was v.p. of CBS Sports for a brief time from 1978 to the early 1980s, after a long association with NBC where he was head of sports from 1963 to 1977. Lindemann's departure from NBC was sudden and never fully explained by the network, but it appeared to have been precipitated by a dispute over who would supervise coverage of the 1980 Moscow Olympics.

One of Lindemann's notable achievements at NBC was to gain the network a share of the professional football market at a time when CBS had an exclusive on the glamour package of sports, the National Football League. Lindemann persuaded NBC to put up $42 million for a five-year contract with the new American Football League in 1964, which was five times what ABC had been paying for the struggling second-class league. The money and TV exposure helped the AFL grow into a full-fledged competitor with NFL, which eventually produced a merger of the two into separate conferences of a single league.

Lindemann also formulated an extensive college basketball schedule for NBC and secured the rights to the World Series, Rose Bowl, Orange Bowl, Senior Bowl, Wimbledon Tennis Tournament and, on alternating years, the baseball All-Star game and the Super Bowl.

He began with NBC as a student engineer, became an associate producer of *The Kate Smith Hour* in 1953, unit manager of the *Home* show in 1954 and then business manager of the program department. In 1957 he was director of daytime programs.

***LINEUP, THE* ▶** half-hour crime series on CBS (1954-59) and one of the first to make use of an authentic setting, in this case San Francisco. It featured Warner Anderson and Tom Tully as police detectives Ben Guthrie and Matt Grebb and was produced by Desilu. Later joining the cast were Marshall Reed as Fred Asher, Rachel Ames as Sandy McAllister, Tod Burton as Charlie Summers, William Leslie as Dan Delaney and Skip Ward as Pete Larkins. The syndicated reruns wisely gave billing to the colorful city, taking the title *San Francisco Beat.*

LINKE, RICHARD O. ▶ producer long associated with Andy Griffith, serving as co-executive producer with Griffith of *Mayberry RFD,* as producer of the *Lawrence Welk Show,* and as executive producer of *The Jim Nabors Show, Headmaster* and the made-for-TV movie, *Winter Kill.*

Art Linkletter

LINKLETTER, ART ▶ daytime TV personality whose *Art Linkletter's House Party,* a program of interviews and features for housewives, ran almost 20 years on CBS after establishing itself on network radio. Linkletter, who entered TV in 1952, mined a rich lode from interviewing children. It not only made for amusing television but served for several books, including *Kids Say the Darnedest Things.* In 1954 he added to his TV exposure with *People Are Funny,* a popular NBC entry in which contestants were asked to perform stunts.

"LITTLE ANNIE" ▶ see Stanton-Lazarsfeld Program Analyzer.

***LITTLE HOUSE ON THE PRAIRIE* ▶** hour-long NBC dramatic series based on the *Little House* books of Laura Ingalls Wilder that recalled her life in the West in the late 19th century. The series began in September 1974 after its two-hour pilot drew an impressive rating in March of that year. Michael Landon, featured in the series as the father, Charles Ingalls, served also as co-executive producer with Ed Friendly and occasional director. Friendly later dropped out after a series of "artistic differences" with Landon. Also in the regular cast were Karen Grassle as the mother, Caroline Ingalls, Melissa Gilbert as middle daughter Laura, Melissa Sue Anderson as elder daughter Mary, twins Lindsay and Sidney Greenbush as baby Carrie, Richard Bull and Katherine MacGregor as shopkeepers Nels and Harriet Oleson, and Alison Arngrim and Jonathan Gilbert as the bratty Oleson kids, Nellie and Willie.

The series became a Monday night fixture for NBC and was the network's highest-rated weekly program during 1978 and 1979, its only show to rank regularly in the Nielsen Top 10. In 1981-82, supporting player Merlin Olsen (who played Jonathan Garvey) was spun off to another series, *Father Murphy,* which was created and produced by Michael Landon. Both series were via NBC Productions.

***LITTLE RASCALS* ▶** TV title for the *Our Gang* movie shorts produced in the 1930s. Repackaged with great success as a syndicated children's series, the old films continue to be purchased by stations for the new generations.

Warren Littlefield

LITTLEFIELD, WARREN ▶ president of NBC Entertainment since July 1990 when he succeeded the legendary Brandon Tartikoff, who moved slightly aside into a somewhat higher post at the time. Littlefield did not fully take over programming for NBC until the summer of 1991, when Tartikoff left to become head of Paramount. Previously, Littlefield had been executive vice president of prime-time programs under Tartikoff, beginning in 1987. For two years earlier, he was senior vice president of series, specials and variety programming.

Littlefield joined NBC in 1979 as manager of comedy development, having come from Warner Bros. Television in a similar capacity. During his tenure, and largely under his supervision, NBC developed such hit series as *Cheers, Family Ties, The Cosby Show* and *The Golden Girls.* These were among the shows that carried NBC from last place to first.

***LIVE FROM LINCOLN CENTER* ▶** occasional series of PBS telecasts of concerts, operas, ballets and chamber music direct from the Lincoln Center for the Performing Arts in New York City. The series premiered in 1976 after Lincoln Center, anxious to extend the audience for the performances of its constituent companies—and to increase its revenues as well—devoted two years to experiments with techniques that permitted telecasts from the stage that would neither alter the atmosphere of the theater nor compromise the integrity of the performances. The techniques involved the use of unobtrusively placed shotgun microphones and newly developed studio cameras able to provide a picture with normal stage lighting.

The premiere live broadcast on Jan. 30, 1976, presented a New York Philharmonic concert conducted by Andre Previn with Van Cliburn as soloist. In the years since, *Live From Lincoln Center* has provided audiences with a front-row seat at performances—now six a year—with many if not most of the concert stage's foremost artists. The range runs the gamut from comedian Danny Kaye conducting a concert of the New York Philharmonic (1981) to the very popular concerts featuring tenor Luciano Pavarotti.

All of the Lincoln Center constituent companies participate in the series except the Metropolitan Opera, which has a separate and long-standing funding arrangement with Texaco. *Live From Lincoln Center* gets its funding from the National Endowment for the Arts, the Robert Wood Johnson, Jr., Charitable Trust, and the corporate underwriting of General Motors. Executive producer John Goberman heads a veteran production team that includes Kirk Browning as telecast director.

LIVE FROM STUDIO 8H ▶ series of cultural specials begun at NBC during the Fred Silverman administration in an effort to revive the network's great traditions. Studio 8H in Rockefeller Center was the largest radio studio in the world when it was built in the 1930s; it was converted permanently for television in 1950.

8H was the studio from which Arturo Toscanini conducted broadcasts of the NBC Symphony Orchestra for 17 years, and so, appropriately, the premiere of *Live from Studio 8H* on Jan. 9, 1980, was a 90-minute tribute to Toscanini featuring Zubin Mehta and the New York Philharmonic, with soloists Leontyne Price and Itzhak Perlman. Martin Bookspan was commentator and Judith DePaul and Alvin Cooperman producers.

The second in the series, airing July 2, 1980, presented five ballets and was entitled *An Evening with Jerome Robbins.* Subsequent programs, all running 90 minutes, included *Caruso Remembered* and *100 Years of America's Popular Music.*

LIVE WITH REGIS AND KATHIE LEE ▶ daily, syndicated magazine show featuring Regis Philbin and Kathie Lee Gifford, which grew out of their local "chat show" that originated on WABC New York. The programs are light in content, involving interviews with entertainment celebrities and discussions with experts on topics such as health and fitness, cooking ideas, home-improvement, and a myriad of other practical issues for a daytime audience. Much of the success of the show owes to the breezy style of the hosts and the good personal chemistry between them. Pleasant folks and apparently comfortable with each other, they represent an alternative to the prevailing sensationalist talk shows of the 1980s and 1990s. The show premiered in 1988 and is produced by Buena Vista.

Regis Philbin and Kathie Lee Gifford

LOEVINGER, LEE ▶ scholarly FCC commissioner (1963-68) who, although a Democratic appointee, held to the conservative view that the commission may not undertake regulation of program content in any form in broadcasting. He subscribed to the belief that broadcasters give the public what it wants and on the whole serve the public well. He left the FCC to practice communications law. Before joining he had been an Associate Justice of the Minnesota Supreme Court and Assistant Attorney General in charge of the antitrust division of the Justice Department.

LOHR, LENOX RILEY (d. 1968) ▶ president of NBC from 1936 until his resignation in July 1940. He had come to the network after serving as general manager of Chicago's successful Century of Progress exposition.

LONDON WEEKEND TELEVISION ▶ commercial company licensed to serve London on weekends, from 7 p.m. Fridays to sign-off on Sundays, while Thames TV has the franchise on weekdays. A major contributor to the ITV network and exporter of such hit series as *Upstairs, Downstairs* and the *Doctor* cycles, it operates from the South Bank Television Centre situated on the south bank of the Thames between Waterloo Bridge and Blackfriars Bridge.

LONE RANGER ▶ half-hour filmed series that carried over into TV the classic radio series created by Fran Striker in 1933. ABC carried the first runs (1952-57). CBS picked up the reruns, and then NBC licensed them, giving the 182 films produced by the Wrather Corp. a network run until 1961. Clayton Moore (and occasionally John Hart) played the lead—ranger John Reid, the lone survivor of an ambush, who dons a mask and pledges to protect the citizens of the West—with Jay Silverheels as his friend Tonto.

A second version, in animated cartoon form, was introduced on CBS as a Saturday morning entry in 1966.

LONESOME DOVE ▶ an ambitious eight-hour mini-series centering on a cattle drive, which CBS televised in four parts on consecutive nights in February 1989 and found itself, unexpectedly, with the season's big hit. The program's success surprised the entire industry because it was a Western, a genre generally considered to have been passe.

The mini-series was an adaptation of Larry McMurtry's Pulitzer Prize-winning novel about two ex-Texas Rangers after the Civil War who drive their cattle from Lonesome Dove, Texas, to Montana to establish a ranch in undeveloped territory. Robert Duvall headed the large cast, which included Anjelica Huston, Danny Glover, Tommy Lee Jones, Robert Urich, Frederic Forrest, Ricky Schroder, William Sanderson, Chris Cooper, and Diane Lane.

The mini-series was a collaboration of Motown Productions, Pangaea Productions and Qintex Entertainment, with Suzanne DePasse, Bill Wittliff and Robert Halmi, Jr. as executive producers. Dyson Lovell was producer and Simon Wincer the director.

LONGFORM ▶ term used for programs that exceed an hour's length. It's generally used today in reference to movies made for television.

LOOK UP AND LIVE ▶ CBS series on religion which incorporated sub-series by the major faiths, with production cooperation from each. Thus, the National Council of Churches assisted in the *Image of Man* series, which presented an overview of man as currently shown in stage, film, TV and musical productions; the National Council of Catholic Men cooperated in a two-program discussion on freedom within the Church and the relationship of Church to society; and the New York Board of Rabbis presented poetry and drawings by some of the doomed children of Terezin Concentration Camp in Czechoslovakia in the 1940s.

It went off the air in January 1979, with *Lamp Unto My Feet* and *Camera Three,* to create a time block for the new CBS newscast *Sunday Morning.* Essentially the series died for lack of station clearances.

LOOMIS, HENRY ▶ president of the Corporation for Public Broadcasting (1972-79) after the departure of John W. Macy. Loomis, a physicist who spent most of his career in public service, had been a Deputy Commissioner of Education, director of the Voice of America, deputy director of the USIA and part of a group of policy advisors to President Nixon in 1968, before joining CPB. He was an advocate of the White House position to decentralize public television and spent virtually all his career on the CPB trying to preserve the legislated powers of the organization against the usurpation of most of them by PBS, the organization of public TV stations. But if Loomis failed to bring inspired leadership to the system, he played a key role in the effort to convert the system to satellite distribution from its dependency on AT&T long lines for interconnection.

LOPER, JAMES L. ▶ former president and general manager of KCET, the Los Angeles public TV station and production center. Loper had been assistant to the president when KCET went on the air in September 1964 and became v.p. and general manager in 1966. He became president in 1971.

Loper had been director of the educational television department at California State University at Los Angeles when he became involved in 1962 with a committee seeking to establish a noncommercial TV station in L.A. He subsequently was hired full-time to help put together the license application and became an officer of the licensee, Community Television of Southern California. Loper served as chairman of PBS from 1969-72 and later became a director on the PBS board of managers.

When he left KCET in the mid-1980s, he became president of NATAS. Bill Kobin succeeded him at KCET.

LORAIN JOURNAL DECISION ▶ case in which the *Lorain Journal* of Lorain, Ohio, was found by the U.S. Appeals Court to be in violation of antitrust laws for refusing to sell space to local advertisers who also bought time on local radio. The suit, charging unfair competition, was brought by WEOL Radio in Elyria, Ohio. The Appeals Court decision was upheld by the Supreme Court in 1951.

LORD, WILLIAM E. ▶ veteran ABC News executive who in the late 1980s became vice president of ABC News InterActive, a unit exploring the new technological frontier. From 1984 to 1988 he was executive producer of *World News Tonight With Peter Jennings,* and previously he was executive producer of *Nightline* from the time it began in 1980. He also served as executive producer of *Viewpoint,* ABC's forum for criticism of television news. Earlier he was head of news for *Good Morning America* and from 1976-78 v.p. in charge of news for ABC, after having been Washington bureau chief. He joined ABC News in 1961 as a writer-reporter.

***LORETTA YOUNG SHOW, THE* ▶** long-running NBC anthology series (1953-60) with Loretta Young as hostess and star. The show became noted for Young's swirling entrances in dazzling gowns. In its first year the series was entitled *A Letter to Loretta.* The reruns went into syndication as *Loretta Young Theatre.* It was produced by NBC.

LORIMAR PRODUCTIONS ▶ independent Hollywood company founded in 1968 by Lee Rich, former advertising executive, and Merv Adelson, financier and movie producer. The company has produced such series as *The Waltons, Doc Elliott, Apple's Way* and *The Blue Knight* and made-for-TV movies, including *Helter-Skelter, Sybil, Eric* and *The Widow.*

One of the leading independent producers in the 1970s, Lorimar went into high gear in the 1980s with the blockbuster *Dallas* and all its spinoffs—*Knots Landing, Flamingo Road, Falcon Crest* and *King's Crossing.* The company merged with Telepictures in 1985 and later was acquired by Warner Communications. It continues to operate as a unit of Time Warner.

In the late 1980s and early 1990s, Lorimar became successful with the sitcom genre, mostly with shows from Miller-Boyett Productions, such as *Full House, Step By Step, Family Matters, Perfect Strangers,* and *The Family Man.*

***LOST IN SPACE* ▶** science-fiction series on CBS (1965-68), with plot characteristics of *Swiss Family Robinson,* produced by Irwin Allen Productions in association with Van Barnard Productions and 20th Century-Fox TV. Its regular cast—featuring a family marooned in outer space—was Guy Williams as astrophysicist John Robinson, June Lockhart as his wife Maureen, Marta Kristen as daughter Judy, Billy Mumy as son Will, Angela Cartwright as daughter Penny, Mark Goddard as pilot Don West, Jonathan Harris as cowardly enemy agent Zachary Smith and Bob May as the robot.

LOTTERY ▶ either as a category of information or as a form of station promotion, barred from broadcasting under Section 1304 of the United States Code. The prohibition against the broadcast of lottery information was eased somewhat, however, when state-sponsored lotteries became prevalent. The courts held that the winning number in a state lottery was "news" and therefore protected by the First Amendment. Under a congressional amendment in 1975, it became possible for stations to televise the final drawings in state lotteries as a form of entertainment programming. Further expansion followed, permitting advertising for state lotteries, for lotteries conducted by state-sanctioned charities and later for "gaming conducted by an Indian tribe...."

Section 1304 states that a licensee may not broadcast "any advertisement or information concerning any lottery." In several instances, promotional activities by stations were held to be violations of the law because they constituted lotteries in that they involved (1) a prize, (2) chance and (3) consideration. Court tests have determined that if one of the three elements is lacking, the activity is not a lottery under federal law.

The prohibition against the broadcast of lottery information was challenged early in the 1970s in a petition by the New Jersey Lottery

Commission, joined by New Hampshire and Pennsylvania. It called for a declaration that broadcasting the winning numbers from the weekly state drawings would not violate the statute [*New Jersey State Lottery Commission v. United States,* 491 F2d 219 (Third Circuit, 1974)].

The Court of Appeals for the Third Circuit held that the winning ticket number was of interest to nearly 3 million ticket holders, and therefore it was "news," protected both by the First Amendment and by Section 326 of the Communications Act, which prohibits censorship. The court felt that Section 1304 should apply only to the "promotion of lotteries for which the station receives compensation."

While the New Jersey Lottery case was pending before the Supreme Court, Congress enacted Section 1307(a), which created certain exemptions to the blanket prohibition in Section 1304. These exemptions applied to lotteries that were conducted by a state and to broadcasts on stations in that state, or in an adjacent state that also conducts a lottery.

The Supreme Court thereupon remanded the case to the Court of Appeals to determine if the new statute would cover the New Jersey situation [420 U.S. 371 1975].

On remand, New Hampshire argued that although it did conduct a state lottery, its western neighbor did not. Therefore, even under Section 1307 Vermont stations would be barred from broadcasting New Hampshire lottery results, thus hurting its sales. The Court of Appeals [34 RR2d 825 (Third Circuit, 1975)] held that the question was not moot, and its original decision was reinstated. The Supreme Court has not yet decided whether to hear an appeal.

LOU GRANT ▶ much respected hour-long dramatic series on CBS (1977-82), created as a vehicle for Ed Asner in the 1977-78 season after the demise of *The Mary Tyler Moore Show,* in which he played newsroom boss Lou Grant. Asner continued the role in the new series, but in a less comic fashion, as city editor of a Los Angeles newspaper. Nancy Marchand was featured as publisher Margaret Pynchon, and newsroom colleagues were played by Mason Adams as managing editor Charlie Hume, Robert Walden as reporter Joe Rossi, Linda Kelsey as reporter Billie Newman and Daryl Anderson as photographer Dennis (Animal) Price. The series survived a shaky start in the ratings and gradually built a loyal audience. Its run ended in 1982.

The series was produced by MTM Productions, with Gene Reynolds, James L. Brooks and Allan Burns as executive producers.

The cast of the CBS series *Lou Grant*

LOVE, AMERICAN STYLE ▶ successful comedy anthology series on ABC (1969-73) that featured playlets, sketches, vignettes and blackouts, all on the general theme of love, with no regular performers. The series began in a one-hour format, was cut back to 30 minutes during 1970 and then was returned to its original length. It was produced by Paramount TV.

LOVE BOAT, THE ▶ ABC hit series (1977-86), an anthology of light romantic stories taking place on a luxurious cruise ship, which became a Saturday night fixture. Several stories were interwoven in each episode, all of them featuring guest stars. The regular cast was the ship's crew: Gavin MacLeod as Captain Merrill Stubing, Lauren Tewes as cruise director Julie McCoy (replaced in 1984 by Pat Klous as Judy McCoy), Bernie Kopell as Dr. Adam (Doc) Bricker, Fred Grandy as Burl (Gopher) Smith and Ted Lange as bartender Isaac Washington, along with Jill Whelan as Stubing's daughter Vicki. The series frequently drew its guest stars from other ABC hits. Aaron Spelling and Douglas S. Cramer were executive producers for Aaron Spelling Productions.

LOVE IS A MANY SPLENDORED THING ▶ see Soap Operas.

LOVE OF LIFE ▶ see Soap Operas.

LOVE THAT BOB ▶ a high-rated situation comedy of the late 1950s in which Bob Cummings (who had been Robert Cummings in movies) played a libidinous bachelor working as a commercial photographer. The series won a moment of fame for Ann B. Davis (who became the *Brady Bunch* housekeeper) as his homely secretary, Schultzy. Also featured were Rosemary DeCamp as Bob's sister, Margaret MacDonald, and Dwayne Hickman as her son Chuck.

Premiering on NBC in January 1954, it moved to CBS for two more seasons, terminating in July 1959. ABC then picked up the reruns for its daytime schedule and carried them for two years. In reruns, the series was retitled *The Bob Cummings Show.* That was also the title of a new CBS series Cummings began in October 1961, which cast him as a troubleshooting adventurer and featured Roberta Shore as Hank Geogerty and Murvyn Vye as Bob's pal Lionel. That show ran only four months.

LOVING ▶ see Soap Operas.

LOWE, DAVID (d. 1965) ▶ producer of bold investigative documentaries for *CBS Reports* who, in 1960, contributed one that is considered a classic, the disturbing *Harvest of Shame,* narrated by Edward R. Murrow. A few days after his death, he won an Emmy for *KKK: The Invisible Empire.* Other of his documentaries were reports on such matters as the racial strife in Birmingham, Ala., the threat of nuclear war, the right to bear arms, abortion and the law, the funeral industry in the U.S. and the racial situation in South Africa. He was married to columnist Harriet Van Horne.

LOWER, ELMER W. ▶ retired TV news official who held posts at all three networks; he became v.p. of corporate affairs for the American Broadcasting Companies Inc. in 1974 after 11 years as president of ABC News. Lower was responsible for building the modern ABC News operation and for raising its stature from a routine service to one of the major news organizations in the world.

While he was with NBC News, Lower developed the modern electronic tabulating methods for election returns that became the foundation of NES (National Election Service), a cooperative of the three networks and the two U.S. wire services.

Lower joined ABC News in 1963 after a four-year stint with NBC News, during which he served first as Washington bureau chief and then as v.p. and general manager of the division in New York. Earlier (1953-59), Lower had been with CBS News as director of special projects in New York. He entered broadcasting after a career in print journalism, as foreign correspondent for *Life* magazine (1945-51) and previously as a reporter and editor for newspapers and wire services. In 1988, Lower joined the PBS Board of Directors.

LOW-POWER TELEVISION (LPTV) ▶ television station licensed to cover a limited geographical area in a radius of 10 to 15 miles and capable of being inserted into the VHF and UHF bands without interfering with an existing full-powered station.

The concept of low-power television was advanced by the FCC under Charles Ferris in the Carter Administration, both to increase over-the-air competition and to provide minorities with new opportunities to become broadcasters. Low-power stations, which are modeled on the translators (or repeater stations) that have existed for years in rural areas, are estimated to cost as little as $100,000 to construct. In short order, there were more than 40,000 applications for the 3,000 to 4,000 frequencies that might become available.

The first low-power station to be licensed was in Bemidji, Minn., and began operations in 1982; but a freeze was put on all other licensing because there were so many competing applications for the choicest frequencies.

The freeze was lifted in the Reagan Administration, in March 1982, when the FCC opened the way to licensing via a lottery system weighted in favor of minorities and nonbroadcast interests. But it also envisioned competition for the major networks through the interconnection of low-power stations by satellite.

The LPTV stations are subject to fewer restrictions and regulations than conventional television stations, but they never came under the FCC's "must carry" rules for cable television, which means that most of them still have to survive strictly on over-the-air transmissions and cannot be received on sets hooked up to cable. As of 1991 there were 1,100 LPTV stations on the air and construction permits had been granted for another 1,800.

LOXTON, DAVID (d. 1988) ▶ director of the Television Laboratory, the experimental unit at WNET New York, beginning when it was established in 1971. In that capacity he served as executive producer of the series *VTR: Video and Television Review* and supervised such alternate video documentaries as *Gerald Ford's America, Lord of the Universe, The Good Times*

Are Killing Me and *Super Bowl.* Earlier (1966-71) he had been an associate producer and producer for National Educational Television. He made his commercial TV debut in 1976 as coproducer, with Frederick Barzyk, of a late-night NBC project, *People.*

***LOYAL OPPOSITION* SERIES ▶** a plan by CBS president Frank Stanton in 1970 to grant 25 minutes of free TV time several times a year to permit the opposition political party to express its views on presidential policies. What was to have been a sporadic series was canceled after the first installment because of the controversy it raised.

Stanton's purpose with the series was to offset, in a two-party system, the natural advantage enjoyed by a President to command air time for the promulgation of his views on issues. At the time, the networks were under pressure from several Democrats in Congress who opposed the war in Vietnam and wanted air time to challenge the Administration's policies; the networks were in the position of accessories to the pro-war policies if they did not balance President Nixon's telecast with the views of the significant opposition.

CBS aired the first and only *Loyal Opposition* telecast on July 7, 1970, having left the use of the time to the discretion of the Democratic National Committee. DNC chairman Lawrence O'Brien chose to go on the air personally, and his presentation was sharply critical of President Nixon on a number of issues, beyond that of the war.

The 25-minute program was followed in many cities by a paid five-minute spot soliciting funds for the Democratic party.

The Republican National Committee immediately demanded time from CBS to reply to the O'Brien broadcast, calling it an attack on the President rather than a discussion of the issues. When CBS refused to grant the time, the RNC complained to the FCC. After agonized deliberations, the commission held that under the Fairness Doctrine the RNC was entitled to the time. CBS then appealed to the courts, and the FCC decision was reversed. But the problems raised by *Loyal Opposition* caused CBS to abandon the plan for a series.

LUCAS, GEORGE ▶ noted motion picture director (*Star Wars*) who occasionally contributes to television. Among his made-for-television movies were *The Ewok Adventure* and *Ewoks: The Battle for Endor.* He also essayed a series, *The Young Indiana Jones.* All were for ABC.

LUDDEN, ALLEN (d. 1981) ▶ game-show host and moderator, whose principal credits include *Password* and *G.E. College Bowl,* although he was ubiquitous in daytime TV after 1961. Earlier he had done multiple duty as program director for the CBS-owned radio stations, executive of CBS News and director of the network's creative services, while moderating the radio and then the TV versions of *College Bowl.* Ludden and his wife, actress Betty White, formed their own production company, Albets, which produced her syndicated series, *The Pet Set.*

LUMET, SIDNEY ▶ noted film director who developed his skills with CBS during the 1950s in such programs as *Mama, Danger, You Are There, Omnibus, The Best of Broadway* and *Alcoa-Goodyear Playhouse.* The plays he directed on TV included *Twelve Angry Men, All the King's Men, The Iceman Cometh, The Sacco and Vanzetti Story* and *The Dybbuk.* Like many others of TV's "Golden Age" who went into film, he never returned to television.

LUND, PETER ▶ executive vice president of the CBS Broadcast Group, which he rejoined in 1990. Long highly regarded in the company, he left CBS in 1987 to become president of Multimedia Entertainment, which produced and distributed such talk shows as *Donahue* and *Sally Jessy Raphael* for syndication. Lund was wooed back to CBS by chairman Larry Tisch and Broadcast Group president Howard Stringer. He holds a key position, responsible for marketing, network sales, the CBS-owned TV stations and CBS Radio. In his earlier years with CBS, Lund was variously president of the owned-TV stations, president of CBS Sports, vice president and general manager of WBBM-TV in Chicago and then of WCBS-TV in New York. He joined CBS in 1977 on the radio side.

LUNDQUIST, VERNE ▶ CBS Sports play-by-play announcer for college football, the NFL, the NBA, the NCAA men's basketball tournament, the Masters and other PGA Tour events, the World Figure Skating Championships, boxing and the U.S. Open Tennis Championships. Lundquist was sports director of WFAA-TV in Dallas for 16 years beginning in 1960 and is best known there as the former radio voice of the Dallas Cowboys, a role he held from 1972 to 1984. During that period he was recognized with seven consecutive Texas Sportscaster of the Year Awards. From WFAA-TV, Lundquist joined ABC Sports and after an 8-year stint he jumped to CBS. He also serves as the lead CBS play-by-play announcer for figure skating for the network's coverage of the 1992 Olympic Winter Games in Albertville, France.

M SQUAD ▶ high-rated NBC police series (1957-60) starring Lee Marvin as Chicago plainclothes lieutenant Frank Ballinger. Paul Newlan was featured in the other key role as Capt. Grey. The half-hour series was from Latimer Productions and Revue Studios.

MACDONALD, TORBERT H. (d. 1976) ▶ chairman of the House Communications Subcommittee in the early 1970s, responsible for a number of significant bills affecting TV and radio. In 1967 he sponsored the legislation in the House that led to establishing the Corporation for Public Broadcasting. Later he was a force behind the Federal Election Campaign Act of 1971, which limited media spending by candidates for federal office. He also introduced the bill in 1973 that banned TV blackouts of professional football home games and other sports events if they were sold out in advance. Before illness forced him to resign in the spring of 1976, his major project was to clear away many of cable TV's regulatory obstructions so that it might grow. A Democrat from Massachusetts, Macdonald served eleven consecutive terms in the House. He had close political and personal ties to President Kennedy, having been his roommate at Harvard from 1936 to 1940.

MacGYVER ▶ hour-long action-adventure series from Paramount about a canny modern-day hero, engaged for secret missions by the government and others, with an improbable knack for resolving intricate crises at just the last moment—disarming a missile with moments to spare, staging a daring mountaintop rescue, and the like. The series stars Richard Dean Anderson as MacGyver and Dana Elcar as Peter Thornton. Henry Winkler and John Rich are the executive producers. It debuted on ABC in September 1985.

MACK, CHARLES J. (d. 1976) ▶ one of the chief cameramen for CBS News dating to the beginnings of the Edward R. Murrow-Fred W. Friendly *See It Now* unit. Mack, in fact, had been part of the Hearst *News of the Day* newsreel team that had been contracted for *See It Now* and later signed on with CBS when Murrow severed relations with Hearst. Mack remained a leading cameraman for the network until he retired in 1971. Among his credits was the documentary *What Really Happened in Tonkin Gulf,* which won an Emmy for CBS News.

MACK, RICHARD A. (d. 1963) ▶ an FCC commissioner who was forced to resign in March 1958 under charges that he had sold his vote to an applicant for Channel 10 in Miami. The House Legislative Oversight Committee, headed by Rep. Oren Harris (D.-Ark.), had produced checks made out to Commissioner Mack by Thurman Whiteside, who was alleged to be acting for National Airlines, the winning applicant for the station. The case was tried in federal court but resulted in a hung jury, and the retrial was never held. Whiteside committed suicide and Mack, who had become an alcoholic, died in a cheap rooming house.

In 1960 the FCC canceled its grant of the Channel 10 license to National Airlines and awarded it instead to L.B. Wilson Inc.

MACK, TED (d. 1976) ▶ host of *The Original Amateur Hour* for 22 years, taking it from radio to TV. When CBS canceled the show in 1970, Mack tried to revive it in syndication, without success. Among the 10,000 amateurs who appeared on the program over the years, around 500 became professionals, among them Maria Callas, Frank Sinatra (as a member of a quartet known as the Hoboken Four), Robert Merrill, Ann-Margret, Pat Boone, Paul Winchell, Vera-Ellen, Regina Resnik, Mimi Benzell, Jerry Vale and Jack Carter.

Amateur Hour started as a radio program in 1934 and soon was taken over by Major Edward Bowes. Mack became its talent scout and Bowes's assistant, eventually taking over the show when Bowes died in 1946. Two years later he moved it into TV where initially it played on four stations of the DuMont Network before becoming a fringe-time staple on CBS.

Mack began in show business as a clarinetist and saxophonist with a number of big bands and for a time headed a band of his own.

MACKIN, CATHERINE (CASSIE) (d. 1982) ▶ political correspondent for NBC News and later for ABC News, having previously worked in print journalism. She first attracted notice in covering the 1972 presidential campaign and was tapped as one of the floor reporters for the Republican national convention. In 1976 she became regular anchor for the Sunday edition of the nightly news. ABC News hired her away in 1977. Five years later she died of cancer at age 42.

MACLEAN HUNTER CABLE TV ▶ Canadian cable operator whose properties include seven systems in the U.S., all noted for community service in accordance with the company's operating philosophy. Unlike the systems of most American-owned MSOs, those of Maclean Hunter encourage community programming and promote local shows. Maclean Hunter's U.S. systems are in New Jersey, Florida and the Detroit area and all are frequent winners of the cable industry's ACE awards for local programming.

A division of Maclean Hunter Ltd., a Toronto-based diversified media company, Maclean Hunter Cable TV serves about 700,000 subscribers in the U.S. and about the same number in Canada. All the systems provide remote camera equipment, remote trucks, editing suites and extensive training to citizens interested in producing their own shows on the local access channels.

J. Barry Gage is president of the cable division, Philip Patterson heads up U.S. operations as senior vice president and Merle Zoerb is vice president of community programming.

MacLEISH, ROD ▶ news commentator for CBS since the fall of 1976, noted for his writing style and his perceptive essays on social change in the U.S. He joined the network after a 21-year association with Group W Broadcasting.

After serving as news director of the Westinghouse station in Boston, WBZ, MacLeish organized and headed the company's Washington bureau (1957-59) and then did the same with its foreign news service (1959-66). He became a commentator in 1966 but continued to go abroad from time to time on reporting assignments as events warranted. He is nephew of the poet Archibald MacLeish.

MacNEIL, ROBERT ▶ TV journalist mainly with public TV in the U.S. but whose career also included stints with NBC, Britain's BBC and Canada's CBC. In August 1975 he left the BBC to become anchor and executive editor of a nightly news and commentary program on WNET New York, *The MacNeil Report.* The program later was sent out over PBS as *The MacNeil-Lehrer Report,* becoming *The MacNeil-Lehrer NewsHour* in 1983.

A native Canadian, he began his career with the CBC and in 1955 went to England for Reuters. He joined NBC News as a London correspondent in 1960 and three years later was transferred to the Washington bureau and then to New York. There he anchored WNBC's local evening newscast and coanchored NBC's weekend *Scherer-MacNeil Report.* He left to join the BBC the first time in 1967, then returned to the U.S. to narrate and write a documentary for the Public Broadcasting Laboratory on the 1968 Democratic National Convention, *The Whole World Is Watching.*

In 1971 MacNeil became senior correspondent for public TV's NPACT, anchoring several of its shows, including *Washington Week in*

Review and the coverage of the Senate Watergate hearings. He rejoined the BBC in 1973 to make a series of documentaries about the U.S. and to participate in several co-productions of the British and American public systems.

His credits include numerous documentaries and a book on TV's influence on American politics, *The People Machine.*

Jim Lehrer and Robert MacNeil of *The MacNeil-Lehrer NewsHour*

MacNEIL-LEHRER NEWSHOUR, THE ▶ nightly hour news program on PBS that premiered in 1976 as a coproduction of WNET New York and WETA Washington, cutting between the studios of both. The program actually had begun the previous year as a local origination for the two cities but gradually gained other outlets and eventually was adopted by the whole system as its nightly news program. Originally a 30-minute program called *The MacNeil-Lehrer Report,* it was expanded to an hour in the fall of 1983, making it the first national evening news program of that length.

Leaving to the commercial networks and stations the task of delivering the laundry list of news items, *MacNeil-Lehrer* concentrates on covering the major stories in depth each night, using guest experts for the discussions, including other journalists. Robert MacNeil anchors from New York and Jim Lehrer from Washington. The program is scheduled at 7 p.m., Eastern time.

The program's regular correspondents are Charlayne Hunter-Gault, formerly of the *New York Times,* and Judy Woodruff, formerly of NBC. Les Crystal, a former president of NBC News, became executive producer with the expansion of the program to an hour. He succeeded Al Vecchione, who became president of MacNeil-Lehrer Productions. In addition to the evening news program, the company produces documentaries and documentary series, such as *The Story of English, The Heart of the Dragon,* and *C. Everett Koop, M.D.* Among its other distinctions, the *MacNeil-Lehrer NewsHour* is the only major news program owned by its anchors, the two having bought out Gannett's half-interest in 1986.

MacPHAIL, WILLIAM C. ▶ one-time head of sports for CBS (1955-1974), receiving the title of v.p. in 1961 when the sports unit shifted from CBS News to become a separate department of CBS-TV. For nearly 10 years before joining CBS he was a baseball executive like his father, Col. Larry MacPhail, and his brother, Lee, both of whom were officials of the New York Yankees. On leaving CBS he became a v.p. of the Robert Wold Co. and, in 1979, joined Ted Turner's Cable News Network as chief sports executive.

MACY, JOHN W., JR. (d. 1986) ▶ first president (1969-72) of the Corporation for Public Broadcasting (CPB) who resigned in frustration after a number of difficulties with the Nixon Administration, which disapproved of the direction public TV was taking, and after failing to win the support of PTV stations in trying to build CPB into a strong national organization. He went on to become president of the Development and Resources Corp.

Macy was appointed to the CPB by President Johnson when the organization was formed, after having been executive v.p. of Wesleyan University, chairman of the Civil Service Commission under Presidents Kennedy and Johnson and a recruiter for Johnson for government positions. He was driven from PTV when the Nixon Administration accused PBS (then an arm of CPB) of a liberal political bias, wanted federal funds to be funneled directly to the stations rather than to PBS and finally vetoed the $155 million authorization bill for CPB. On leaving, Macy said he believed the reelection of Nixon would be the deathblow to public TV.

MADDEN, JOHN ▶ popular sportscaster on CBS's National Football League telecasts since

1979. Partnered with play-by-play announcer Pat Summerall since 1981, Madden is known for his insider analysis of football—gained from 10 years as head coach for the Oakland Raiders—as well as for his shrill, enthusiastic announcing style. In 1991 he won his eighth Emmy Award as television's Outstanding Sports Personality-Analyst. Madden also hosts an annual post-season football special called *The All-Madden Team.*

John Madden

MADISON SQUARE GARDEN NETWORK (MSG) ▶ largest and oldest regional cable sports network and the progenitor of the USA Network. MSG, which reaches 4.5 million subscribers in metropolitan New York, most of whom receive it as a basic service, is known mostly for carrying Knicks basketball and Rangers hockey from the Garden. The service is also one of the most expensive for cable operators to carry, since it charges around $1 per subscriber each month. Cablevision Systems reacted to the high cost by making MSG a pay service.

In 1985 MSG gained the rights to televise the Knicks and Rangers road games in addition to their home schedules. Marv Albert, the longtime radio voice of the Knicks, covers the games for MSG along with analyst John Andariese. In 1990 the channel added New York Yankees baseball to its events. Owned by Paramount (formerly Gulf & Western), parent of the famed sports arena in New York City, MSG launched on Manhattan Cable in 1969 to 18,000 subscribers, all in lower Manhattan. The USA Network was spun out of MSG in 1981 as a separate basic-cable entertainment network co-owned by Paramount and MCA.

***MAGAZINE* ▶** occasional CBS daytime series in newsmagazine format, which began in 1973 on a schedule of four-a-year and later expanded to six. With Sylvia Chase as anchorwoman, and with a predominantly female staff, the series concentrated on issues of specific interest to women, such as unnecessary hysterectomies and profiles of prominent women. The one-hour shows were presented as daytime specials, preempting regular soap operas and game shows. They ran for several years and then evaporated.

MAGAZINE CONCEPT ▶ commercial policy that permits advertisers to buy spots in programs the same way they buy pages in magazines, strictly on a circulation basis with no direct association with the program (or article) or its content. The opposite of program sponsorship, the magazine concept or participating advertising has prevailed in TV since the mid-1960s.

A pioneer of the concept was Sylvester (Pat) Weaver who, while he was president of NBC in the early 1950s, developed the *Today, Home* and *Tonight* shows to be sold in that manner. But the great impetus came from ABC around 1965 when, in desperation for prime-time sales, it began to sell insertions in programs on scatter plans where it was unable to find sponsors.

The magazine concept served to give the networks full control over programs and overall has proved more profitable to them. At the same time it has afforded greater access to television for the smaller advertisers and has benefitted the larger ones by eliminating the risks inherent in program sponsorship.

MAGAZINE FORMAT ▶ a program made up of varied segments, long and short, on a variety of subjects or themes, just as magazines are made up of assorted articles, departments and graphic materials, some serious and some not. The application is usually to news or public affairs programming: *60 Minutes, 20/20, Weekend, PBL* and *The Great American Dream Machine,* for example. But in the late 1970s it was adopted for straight entertainment with *Real People, That's Incredible,* and *Those Amazing Animals.* The longest-running magazine show of all is the ABC anthology *Wide World of Sports.*

Magazine programs with an entertainment accent began to proliferate in local TV during 1976, and several syndicated shows in the format came on the market for the 1977-78 season. At the local level the form was pioneered by such stations as KCRA Sacramento, KGW Portland, Ore., WMAL-TV Washington and KPIX San Francisco. These efforts spawned Group W Productions' *PM Magazine,* one of the most potent syndicated programs of the 1980s.

The magazine became epidemic in the 1990s with such shows as *Prime Time Live, 48 Hours, Inside Edition, A Current Affair, Expose, Unsolved Mysteries, America's Most Wanted, Cops, Hard Copy* and *Rescue 911.*

MAGID ASSOCIATES ▶ market research firm specializing in consulting TV stations on improving the appeal of their newscasts. Based in suburban Cedar Rapids, Ia., and headed by Frank N. Magid, whose graduate school field was social psychology, the company became the industry's leading "news consultant" in the 1970s with clients in more than 100 markets. Contributing to its growth was the discovery by the industry that stations which led their markets in news were usually first in overall ratings, regardless of their network affiliations.

The Magid influence was felt primarily in the explosion of "Action News" formats around the country and in the technique of presenting news items tersely, among banter between members of a newscasting "team." The Magid recommendations extended to news content as well as to the manner of presentation and the selection of personnel.

MAGNETO-OPTICAL DISC ▶ recording medium that combines the advantages of magnetic and optical technologies, using laser beams and magnetism to read, record and erase large quantities of data.

MAHONY, SHEILA ▶ lawyer who became executive in charge of franchising activities for Cablevision Corp., after having been executive director of the Carnegie Commission on the Future of Public Broadcasting (1977-79). For the previous two years she was executive director of the Cable Television Information Center in Washington, a nonprofit organization devoted to assisting state and local governments with cable television franchising, and before that she worked for the City of New York in cable television matters.

MAJOR MARKET ▶ one of the 50 largest television markets, the designation having importance both in national spot sales and in the application of certain FCC regulations. Many spot advertisers specify only the major markets, which means that those below 50 will not be purchased. The FCC occasionally will establish rules that apply only to stations in the top 50 markets: the prime time-access rules, for example. A market is defined by the effective reach of a station's television signal, and it is measured for size by the density of TV households.

***MAKE A WISH* ▶** ABC half-hour informational children's series scheduled Sunday mornings (1971-77). Hosted by Tom Chapin, it was produced, directed and written by Lester Cooper of ABC Public Affairs.

***MAKE ROOM FOR DADDY* ▶** early situation comedy vehicle (1953-64) for Danny Thomas on ABC in which he portrayed Danny Williams, a family man working as a nightclub comedian, with Jean Hagen as his wife, Margaret. When Hagen left the cast in 1956 the series was retitled *The Danny Thomas Show;* in this version, Marjorie Lord played a widow, Kathy O'Hara, who eventually married Williams. The series moved to CBS the following year and ran until 1964. Reruns were purchased by NBC for daytime stripping in 1960, and the repeats then went into syndication. Sherry Jackson (later replaced by Penney Parker) and Rusty Hamer portrayed Thomas's children, Terry and Rusty, and Lelani Sorenson and Angela Cartwright were added as Kathy's children, Patty and Linda.

In 1970 ABC made an attempt to revive the series as *Make Room For Granddaddy,* with the members of the previous cast a generation later, but it did not fare well and was canceled after a season.

MAKE-GOODS ▶ commercial spots from the network inventory given free to advertisers who did not receive full value on their original purchases. Since the networks sell programs well in advance of their airing, they price the spots according to their own projections for size and composition of audience. The advertiser is given a guaranteed cost-per-thousand and runs no risk. If, when the ratings arrive, the program should fail to deliver on its promise of audience, the network pays back in the form of make-goods in other parts of the schedule. This, of course, depletes inventory, sometimes severely, and a highly touted program or sporting event that flops can wreck the network's quarterly business performance because of the obligation to make good on the advertising contracts.

***MAKING OF THE PRESIDENT, THE* ▶** (1960 and 1964) 90-minute CBS documentaries based on Theodore H. White's quadrennial best-selling books on the campaigns for the Presidency. The first, *The Making of the President—1960,* centering on John F. Kennedy, was produced in 1961 by Metromedia Producers Corp. The second (1964), covering the political race between Lyndon B. Johnson and Barry Goldwater, was televised in October 1965 and was produced by Wolper Productions. Both were narrated by Martin Gabel.

The Making of the President—1972, documenting Richard M. Nixon's smashing victory over George McGovern, was produced by Metromedia but rejected by the networks, apparently because it was offered while the Watergate scandal was unfolding.

MALONE, JOHN C. ▶ president and chief executive officer of Denver-based Tele-Communications Inc. (TCI), the country's largest cable operator. Often called the most powerful man in cable because of his company's incredible clout in buying programming and equipment, Malone acknowledges his influence and rarely hesitates to use it, often in controversial ways.

Malone joined TCI in 1973, when the company was a small, nearly bankrupt cable operator, but he came complete with a resume most executives would envy at the end of their careers. After graduating from Yale in 1963 with a degree in electrical engineering and economics, Malone went on to get two masters degrees (in industrial management and electrical engineering) and a PhD. in operations research, which he received in 1967. During those years he also worked at Bell Telephone Laboratories in planning and research, and in 1968 joined management consultants McKinsey & Co. His cable experience began in 1970, when he joined General Instrument, a leading equipment supplier. Later he became president of GI's Jerrold Electronics division.

When Malone took charge of TCI he began building it steadily, largely through acquisitions, swallowing up scores of smaller companies. With around one-fourth of all U.S. cable homes served by TCI or an affiliated company, TCI has become cable's supreme gatekeeper, determining to a large extent which new networks may receive national distribution and which may not.

MAMA ▶ popular sentimental comedy on CBS from July 1949 to March 1957, based on the play *I Remember Mama,* which had been drawn from the book *Mama's Bank Account.* Thousands of letters from viewers brought the program back, after a brief cancellation, in December 1956, but the revival lasted only three months. Presented live, it played on Friday nights under sponsorship by Maxwell House coffee.

It starred Peggy Wood as Marta Hansen, the immigrant matriarch from Norway who, with her husband Lars (played by Judson Laire), learned to adapt to American ways through their three children. Set in the early 1900s, it dealt not so much in humor as in the commonplace problems of youth that could be resolved by parental wisdom, and in the personal wounds that could be healed by family love. *Mama* brought on a wave of domestic comedies on TV.

Featured were Rosemary Rice as Katrin, Dick Van Patten as Nels, Iris Mann (for the first season), Robin Morgan and Toni Campbell (for the final few episodes) as Dagmar and Ruth Gates as Aunt Jenny.

The cast of the CBS comedy series *Mama*

MAN AGAINST CRIME ▶ early police series on CBS (1949-53) starring Ralph Bellamy as investigator Mike Barnett, and produced by MCA-TV. The reruns were syndicated as *Follow That Man.*

MAN ALIVE ▶ inspirational documentary series on Canada's CBC that has been running weekly since 1966. The half-hour series is dedicated to celebrating the human spirit and to examining such traits as courage and moral strength, often through extraordinary people like Mother Teresa and the Dalai Lama. The executive producer is Louis Lore.

MAN FROM U.N.C.L.E., THE ▶ popular NBC action-adventure series on international espionage (1964-68), which featured Robert Vaughn and David McCallum as secret agents Napoleon Solo and Illya Kuryakin, and Leo G. Carroll as their superior officer, Alexander Waverly. In 1966 the series spun off *The Girl from U.N.C.L.E.,* with Stefanie Powers as April Dancer and Noel Harrison as Mark Slate, which lasted only a single season. *Man's* demise was attributed by some to the frequent shifting of its time period by NBC. Norman Felton was executive producer of both *U.N.C.L.E.* series, which were by MGM-TV in association with Felton's Arena Productions.

MANDEL, LORING ▶ New York-based dramatist who wrote original plays for the quality showcases of the 1950s and 1960s and more recently for *CBS Playhouse,* the Benjamin Franklin series, *Sandburg's Lincoln* and the CTW drama series, *The Best of Families.* He received an Emmy for *Do Not Go Gentle Into That Good Night.* He also has written screenplays and stage dramas, including the Broadway version of *Advise and Consent.*

MANN, ABBY ▶ writer and producer, noted for such TV dramas as *Judgment at Nuremberg, The Marcus-Nelson Murders* (which led to the series *Kojak*) and *A Child Is Waiting,* in addition to plays for *Studio One, Playhouse 90, Robert Montgomery Presents* and other showcases of the "golden age" of TV drama. He also created *Medical Story,* an anthology series for NBC (1975) that won praise but fell short in the ratings. Mann then set about working on a four-hour TV dramatic special for NBC, *King,* on the life of the Rev. Dr. Martin Luther King, Jr., for presentation in 1977 on the eighth anniversary of the civil rights leader's death. Mann was writer, director and executive producer of the film.

MANN, DELBERT ▶ one of the group of motion picture directors who received their grounding in the live TV drama anthologies of the 1950s. Mann directed both the TV and movie versions of such plays as *Marty, Bachelor Party* and *The Middle of the Night* and has concentrated on movies since the 1960s. He had been staff director for NBC in the early years (1949-55) and worked on such series as *Lights Out, Philco-Goodyear Playhouse* and *Producer's Showcase;* later he did *Playhouse 90, Playwrights '56* and *Ford Star Jubilee,* among others. His TV directing credits include *The Day Lincoln Was Shot, Our Town, Heidi, The Man Without a Country* and a 1955 production of *The Petrified Forest* with Humphrey Bogart, Lauren Bacall and Henry Fonda. In 1980, he directed *Playing for Time.*

MANNING, GORDON ▶ longtime news executive with NBC and CBS who was credited with scoring numerous journalistic coups in his career, such as setting up a conversation between Tom Brokaw and Mikhail Gorbachev and arranging a live *Today* coverage from Moscow in 1984. Though formally retired from NBC News after 12 years, he remains active as consultant on editorial projects. Before joining NBC he was with CBS News as a vice president.

MANNIX ▶ long-running CBS private-eye series (1967-76) with Mike Connors as Joe Mannix and Gail Fisher as his secretary, Peggy Fair. Other regulars were Joseph Campanella and Robert Reed. The show was produced by Paramount TV.

MANSFIELD, IRVING ▶ producer of *Your Show of Shows* and *Talent Scouts,* two outstanding hit series of the 1950s. Later he became business manager for his novelist-wife, the late Jacqueline Susann.

MANSFIELD JOURNAL CO. v. FCC ▶ [180 F2d 28 (D.C. Cir. 1950)] case that strengthened the policy of the FCC to diversify control of the outlets of mass communications in a community.

The Mansfield Journal Co., which published the only newspaper in Mansfield, Ohio, refused, as a competitive maneuver, to accept advertising from any firm that advertised on the town's only local radio station. When the Journal Company later applied for radio licenses in several areas outside its immediate community, the FCC denied all its applications because the newspaper's advertising policy bespoke an attempt to suppress competition and to secure a monopoly of mass advertising and news dissemination.

The Journal Company appealed to the courts, charging the commission with acting beyond the scope of its power by enforcing the antitrust laws. The D.C. Court of Appeals disagreed with the Journal Company, holding that a formal violation of the antitrust laws was irrelevant to the *Journal*'s case because the commission never made such a determination. The only question had been the *Mansfield Journal*'s ability to serve the public, and the commission had every right to consider whether the *Journal*'s advertising policies, as an attempt to monopolize mass communications, were in the public interest.

MANULIS, MARTIN ▶ prominent producer-director of the 1950s and early 1960s associated with *Studio One, Playhouse 90, Suspense, Climax* and others, chiefly as a staff producer-director for CBS (1951-58). He later became head of production for 20th Century-Fox TV and then formed his own motion picture company.

MANY LOVES OF DOBIE GILLIS, THE **▶** CBS situation comedy (1959-63) created by humorist Max Shulman, which starred Dwayne Hickman and featured Bob Denver as his buddy, Maynard G. Krebs, and Frank Faylen as Dobie's dad, Herbert T. Gillis. It was via 20th Century-Fox TV.

MARCH, ALEX ▶ producer and director of TV dramas, prominent during the 1950s as producer of the *Studio One Summer Theater* on CBS. In 1960 he produced *The Sacco and Vanzetti Story* and directed *The Story of Margaret Bourke-White.* In 1982 he was named supervising producer for *Nurse.*

MARCH OF TIME **▶** documentary series produced for syndication in 1966 by Wolper Productions as an attempt to revive, for TV, the series that had played movie houses in the 1940s. Eight films were produced, all narrated by William Conrad. They included *And Away We Go,* on the proliferation of the auto; *Search for Vengeance,* on the international underground pursuing Nazi war criminals; and *Seven Days in the Life of the President,* on President Lyndon Johnson during a week of crisis.

The original *March of Time* films that were shown theatrically in the 1930s and 1940s were acquired by SFM Entertainment for television distribution.

MARCUS, ANN ▶ writer of comedy serials who made her mark with Norman Lear's T.A.T. Productions in the mid-1970s as co-creator of *Mary Hartman, Mary Hartman* and *All That Glitters,* then joined Columbia Pictures Television to write the NBC daytime serial *Days of Our Lives.* Teamed with her husband Ellis, she created a new late-night syndicated strip in 1979, *Life and Times of Eddie Roberts,* known also by the acronym *L.A.T.E.R.* It was unsuccessful.

MARCUS WELBY, M.D. **▶** highly successful medical melodrama on ABC (1969-76) that served as a second TV vehicle for Robert Young almost a generation after the first, *Father Knows Best.* The hour-long series cast him as a general practitioner of the old school working with a young associate who made house calls on a motorcycle. The series was a big hit from the start, but many attribute that to the fact of weakish competition; CBS had scheduled its newsmagazine *60 Minutes* in that Tuesday night timeslot and NBC its monthly newsmagazine, *First Tuesday.* James Brolin portrayed the younger doctor, Steven Kiley, Elena Verdugo was featured as receptionist and nurse Consuelo Lopez, Sharon Gless appeared as nurse Kathleen Faverty and Pamela Hensley played public relations director Janet Blake. *Welby* was created by David Victor, who served as executive producer for Universal TV.

MARK RUSSELL COMEDY SPECIALS **▶** public TV's every-other-month half-hour comedy specials with the political satire and song spoofs of comic Mark Russell. Produced by WNED before a live audience in Russell's native Buffalo, the show capitalizes on the 20 years Russell spent as a lounge comic in Washington's Shoreham Hotel, commenting on the news and satirizing the capital city's newsmakers. The specials, which debuted in 1979, are virtually public television's only original contribution to the craft of television comedy.

MARK SABER MYSTERY THEATER **▶** half-hour detective series (1951-54) drawn from radio's *Mystery Theater* with Tom Conway as Inspector Mark Saber of the homicide squad, and James Burke featured as Sergeant Tim Maloney. The series was produced by Roland Reed Productions. A new version, *Saber of Scotland Yard,* was produced for syndication by Sterling Drug from 1957 to 1960, and it turned Mark Saber into a one-armed British private eye. The role was played by Donald Gray, and the producers were Edward J. and Harry Lee Danziger.

MARKELL, ROBERT ▶ drama producer who had started as a scenic designer in the early days of TV, notching his first producing credits with *Playhouse 90.* He was producer of *The Defenders* in the 1960s and in 1975 became executive producer of *CBS Playhouse* and the network's nightly *Bicentennial Minutes.* For *CBS Playhouse* he produced *20 Shades of Pink* and *The Tenth Level,* among other original plays. In 1981, he supervised the production of the CBS mini-series, *The Blue and The Gray.*

MARKLE, FLETCHER (d. 1991) ▶ writer, producer and director from Canada who was also prominent in the "golden age" of studio drama and directed such series as *Life with Father* (1953-55) and *Father of the Bride* (1961). He had been director for *Studio One* on CBS in 1947-48 and returned to that series as producer in 1952-53. His initial broadcasting experience had been with CBC and BBC, chiefly in radio. Other U.S. credits include *Ford Theatre, Front Row Center Mystery Theatre, Panic, Colgate Theatre, Lux Playhouse, Thriller* and *Hong Kong.*

MARRIED ... WITH CHILDREN ▶ somewhat controversial sitcom (1987—) created by the team of Ron Leavitt and Michael M. Moye, which became one of the first solid hits on the Fox Network. In a marked departure from the idealized, suburban domestic comedy, the show centers on a quarrelsome working-class family in an unkempt household. Ed O'Neill and Katey Sagal play the ever-bickering Al and Peg Bundy, whose complaints about each other often have to do with sexual dissatisfaction. Christina Applegate and David Faustino play their less-than-wholesome children, Kelly and Bud. David Garrison and Amanda Bearse portray their white-collar neighbors, the Rhoades.

The program received extraordinary publicity in January 1989 when a Michigan housewife, Terry Rakolta, received considerable press attention (including the front page of *The New York Times*) for her attempt to organize a boycott of advertisers in the show. Rakolta was outraged by an episode involving the purchase of a bra, during which she had been watching with her children. In response, Fox moved the show from 8:30 to 9 p.m., where its ratings improved.

MARRINAN, JAMES P. ▶ veteran executive of international TV distribution. Since 1986 he has been senior executive vice president of ITC Entertainment Group's international division, based in Los Angeles. Previously he was with Viacom Worldwide Ltd., a subsidiary of Viacom International, for more than 12 years. He held a number of executive positions at Viacom, including vice president of the company's Latin American operations.

MARSHALL, GARRY ▶ film producer and prolific comedy writer who hit a jackpot in the mid-1970s as creator and co-executive producer of *Happy Days, Laverne and Shirley, Mork and Mindy* and *Angie.* He also created and co-produced *The Odd Couple* series and *The Little People* (later retitled *The Brian Keith Show*).

Unlike other successful producers who started their own companies, Marshall continued to work through Paramount TV. His father, Tony Marshall, was on his staff as a producer and his sister, Penny, played Laverne in *Laverne and Shirley* before becoming a film director. Another sister, Ronny, served as an associate producer.

Marshall began his TV career as a comedy writer for Jack Paar in 1960 and then became a writer for Joey Bishop's late-night show on ABC. For seven years he teamed with Jerry Belson in the writing of movies, specials and comedy series, one of which was the situation comedy adaptation of *The Odd Couple.* Marshall then became executive producer of that series for Paramount and in 1974 created *Happy Days.* Since 1982, Marshall has concentrated on motion pictures.

MARSHALL, PENNY ▶ comedy actress who became a film director after the success of *Laverne and Shirley.* After an early career of supporting roles and minor parts in a number of TV series, she made some guest appearances in the hit series *Happy Days,* produced by brother Garry Marshall, which turned out to be fateful. Her character Laverne was spun off to create the situation comedy *Laverne and Shirley,* which ran from 1976 to 1983. Later she directed such films as *Big* and *Awakenings.*

MARTIN and LEWIS ▶ red-hot comedy act of Dean Martin and Jerry Lewis which in 1950 began successful seasons in NBC's *Colgate Comedy Hour* rotation. The act was an outstanding modern vaudeville pairing of a suave and handsome singer (Martin) with a frantic buffoon (Lewis). The team split up in 1956. Martin went on to make films and had great success with his own NBC variety show (1965-74), which projected him as a likeable roué. Lewis was also successful as a solo but on a different scale. His movies appealed chiefly to youngsters and rural folk, and his TV triumphs were an animated Saturday morning children's show, which starred his likeness, and the annual Muscular Dystrophy Telethons, which he hosted. His venture in a weekly Sunday night variety series on ABC failed.

MARTIN, DEAN ▶ see Martin and Lewis.

MARTIN KANE, PRIVATE EYE ▶ progenitor of the long line of TV detective series, airing from 1949 to 1954 and revived by United

Artists TV in 1957 as *The New Adventures of Martin Kane.* The actors who succeeded one another in the lead role were William Gargan, Lloyd Nolan, Mark Stevens and Lee Tracy.

MARTIN, MARY (d. 1990) ▶ Broadway musical-comedy star whose occasional TV appearances resulted in some of the medium's memorable hours during the early years. One of her stunning contributions was on *Ford's 50th Anniversary Show* on June 15, 1953, carried on both CBS and NBC, when she and Ethel Merman sang a Broadway catalog, seated on stools on a bare stage. But even more potent was her performance in *Peter Pan,* in the title role, offered first on March 7, 1955 on NBC (before the video tape era) and repeated live on Jan. 9, 1956. Once taped, Mary Martin's *Peter Pan* was repeated on NBC for several years.

Later she co-starred with Helen Hayes in *The Skin of Our Teeth* for an NBC *Sunday Spectacular* and starred in a TV version of *Annie Get Your Gun.* Her specials included *Magic with Mary Martin,* a program which traced her career in music, and *Mary Martin at Easter Time.*

MARTIN, QUINN (d. 1987) ▶ highly successful producer of adventure series, usually with police themes, whose QM Productions was one of the most active independent companies on network TV through the 1960s and 1970s. His first major hit, *The Untouchables,* was produced for Desilu Productions in 1959. On his own, he scored in 1963 with *The Fugitive* and in 1965 with *The F.B.I.* Then came *Cannon, Barnaby Jones, Streets of San Francisco* and *Bert D'Angelo/Superstar,* all of them running simultaneously in 1976 with Martin as executive producer. Among his lesser shows were *Banyon, The New Breed* and *Caribe.*

Earlier in his career he wrote for *Four Star Playhouse* and produced *The Jane Wyman Show* and *Desilu Playhouse. The Untouchables* emerged from the latter and started Martin on his way as a specialist in crime-adventure shows.

MARTIN, STEVE ▶ comedian whose slow-advancing career took off when he began making regular appearances on *Saturday Night Live* in the 1970s. His "wild and crazy guy" routine caught fire with the audience and gained him frequent appearances on the *Tonight Show* and starring roles in a number of movies, including *Roxanne* and *L.A. Story,* both of which he directed. Early in his career, after years on the nightclub circuit, Martin became a writer for *The Smothers Brothers Comedy Hour.* He performed his own act on a number of variety shows before hitting it big on *SNL.*

***MARTY* ▶** a Paddy Chayefsky masterpiece and one of the most famous teleplays of all time. The story of a heavyset, middle-aged butcher hanging out with other lonely, rejected men who seem destined never to marry was realistic drama at its best in the early years of television. When Marty meets his female coordinate—a plain-looking, wallflower schoolteacher—the play becomes a love story that turns on inner beauty. Though the title role is often associated with Ernest Borgnine, who starred in the 1955 movie version, the live TV production in 1953 for the *Goodyear Television Playhouse* starred Rod Steiger. The woman who played "the dog" Marty's friends derided was Nancy Marchand. The supporting cast included Betsy Palmer, Nehemiah Persoff and Lee Phillips.

MARX, GROUCHO (d. 1977) ▶ the wisecracking member of the four Marx Brothers of vaudeville and films, whose singular talents were harnessed for television in the half-hour quiz show *You Bet Your Life,* which began Oct. 5, 1950, and ran for 10 seasons. The program, which offered modest prize money and often featured bizarre contestants, succeeded not for the intrigues of the game but for the opportunities it presented for Marx's brash, ad-lib humor in his interviews with the guests. Marx was noted for outrageously candid quips that verged on insult. His comic trappings were a morning coat, an aggressive cigar and a broad, rectangular mustache. His show had a single extra gimmick that became famous: If a contestant chanced to speak a predetermined "magic word," an absurd stuffed duck descended to signify the winning of a bonus prize. *You Bet Your Life* was Marx's only TV series, although he made numerous guest shots. In 1974 video tapes and kinescopes of the old shows were syndicated to stations with a reasonable degree of success.

MARX, MARVIN (d. 1975) ▶ TV comedy writer and producer, noted for writing the Jackie Gleason-Art Carney classic, *The Honeymooners.* His association with that series, which had periodic revivals, spanned 17 years. In 1968 Marx created a novel musical-comedy series for NBC, *That's Life,* which lasted a single season. He died in a nursing home in Miami at the age of 50.

***MARY HARTMAN, MARY HARTMAN* ▶** phenomenal syndicated strip that was part legitimate soap opera and part spoof. It enjoyed a vogue in around 100 markets during 1976 and would have had wider distribution but for its sex-oriented themes, which deterred many stations from buying it. Producer Norman Lear, who was the leading television independent with a string of situation comedy hits on the networks, had put the daily half-hour series into syndication after all three networks had turned it down (CBS financed the pilot). *Mary Hartman, Mary Hartman* became .one of the most talked-about shows in television, but because the 26-week charter contracts were for a low try-out fee, the series, paradoxically, was losing around $50,000 a week while it was scoring well in all the ratings, whether scheduled by stations in the afternoon or the late evening. Desirous of keeping it going, such groups as Metromedia and Kaiser, enjoying the benefits of its success, offered to renegotiate their contracts at higher fees.

The cast was headed by Louise Lasser and featured Phil Bruns and Dody Goodman as George and Martha Shumway, Mary's parents; Debralee Scott as Mary's little sister, Cathy Shumway; Greg Mullavey as Mary's husband, Tom Hartman; Claudia Lamb as Mary's daughter Heather; Mary Kay Place and Graham Jarvis as Mary's best friend and her husband, Loretta and Charlie Haggers; and Victor Kilian as the "Fernwood Flasher," Mary's grandfather, Raymond Larkin. Lear's T.A.T. Productions was its source, and it was distributed initially by Rhodes Productions. The series ended its run, voluntarily, in the summer of 1977 because of the strain of producing five shows a week. It gave way to a new fictional talk show, with characters from *Mary Hartman,* entitled *Fernwood 2-Night.*

MARY TYLER MOORE SHOW, THE ▶ CBS situation comedy (1970-77) considered by many to have come closest of all sitcoms to perfection in the form, partly a function of superb casting. Moore, best known previously as the wife and second lead in the original *Dick Van Dyke Show,* was presented here as a single young woman rebounding from a romantic disappointment and trying to build a career as a functionary in the newsroom of a second-rate Minneapolis TV station. The programs relied on two principal sets, each with its own cast of characters: the newsroom and Moore's apartment. The latter resulted in spin-off series for two neighbors, Rhoda Morgenstern and Phyllis Lindstrom, played respectively by Valerie Harper and Cloris Leachman.

But TV stars were spawned by the newsroom as well. Edward Asner, a previously obscure character actor, won a batch of Emmys for his role as crusty but kindly news director Lou Grant, and he became an actor in high demand. He went on to star in his own series, *Lou Grant.* Likewise, Gavin MacLeod, who played sarcastic news writer Murray Slaughter, got his own series, *The Love Boat.* Ted Knight, a virtual unknown until the series, became a household word as Ted Baxter, the vain and obtuse anchorman; and Georgia Engel (who played Baxter's wife, Georgette) and Betty White (as Sue Ann Nivens, host of the station's *Happy Homemaker* feature) received strong career boosts from the show.

The series became the keystone of the powerful CBS Saturday night lineup and was terminated at its height of popularity at the will of the star. As for Moore, symbol of the wholesome, determined and humane middle-American woman, she not only enjoyed great personal popularity from the series but built from it (with her husband, Grant Tinker) one of the leading independent production companies in Hollywood, MTM Enterprises.

James Brooks and Allan Burns, the creative nucleus, received continuing producer-writer credit.

The cast of the classic CBS series *M*A*S*H*

M*A*S*H ▶ immensely popular CBS series (1972-83) based on Robert Altman's 1970 hit movie of that title concerning war-weary surgeons during the Korean War who labor to keep their sanity with dark jokes, pranks and irreverent wisecracks. After a slow start in 1972 and several uncertain subsequent seasons, the half-hour series caught fire in 1975 when it was given a Monday night timeslot. For the next seven years it ranked regularly in the Nielsen top ten, despite a succession of cast changes. But it has had even greater success in syndication, where it seemed destined to earn more money than any program ever. Its network run ended with a bang in February 1983. The final episode was a 2 1/2 hour special so widely publicized that it became a national event. The telecast drew the largest audience for a single program in TV history.

*M*A*S*H* belonged to a long line of war sitcoms (*You'll Never Get Rich, Hogan's Heroes, F Troop, McHale's Navy*) but differed from the others because it adhered to realism rather than contrived situations, and because it was black comedy, with pain and death always on hand. Moreover, its philosophical roots were in the anti-establishment, anti-war movements of the 1960s, making it an anachronism in the conservative climate of the subsequent decades in which it flourished. To a large extent, the program's appeal flowed from the high quality of its scripts, the excellent production standard that was consistently maintained, and the superb ensemble playing of its cast. Among its other virtues, *M*A*S*H* did not strain for laughs.

What was most remarkable about the program, and helped to explain its phenomenal success in syndication, was that it appealed to all levels and age groups of the audience. Thus its reruns pull high ratings wherever they are scheduled by stations in the early evening, when children and the elderly are watching, or in late night time periods frequented by teenagers and young adults.

Reportedly, 20th Century-Fox Television reaped $25 million from the first round of syndication, and after the program's proven success on local stations asked five times the original price for the second round in 1982. As the star of the series with a sizeable profit participation, Alan Alda is believed to have earned $30 million from syndication alone.

In addition to Alda as Captain Benjamin Franklin (Hawkeye) Pierce, the regular cast at the 4077th M*A*S*H Unit included Loretta Swit as Major Margaret (Hot Lips) Houlihan, Mike Farrell as Captain B.J. Hunnicutt, Harry Morgan as Colonel Sherman Potter, David Ogden Stiers as Major Charles Emerson Winchester III, Jamie Farr as Corporal Max Klinger and William Christopher as Father Francis Mulcahy. Gary Burghoff (Corporal Walter "Radar" O'Reilly), Larry Linville (Major Frank Burns), Wayne Rogers (Captain John F.X. "Trapper John" McIntire) and McLean Stevenson (Lieutenant Colonel Henry Blake), who were in the original cast, dropped out at various points during the run to pursue other performing opportunities. Also appearing in several episodes were Tim Brown, reprising his motion picture role as football great and surgeon Spearchucker Jones, Odessa Cleveland as Lieutenant Ginger Ballis, Karen Philipp as Lieutenant Maggie Dish, G. Wood as General Hammond, Patrick Adiarte as Ho Jon, Alan Arbus as psychiatrist Sidney Freedman, Jeff Maxwell as cook Igor Straminsky, Kellye Nakahara as Lieutenant Kellye Nakahara and G.W. Bailey as Sergeant Luther Rizzo.

Larry Gelbart was creator of the series and writer of its earliest episodes, and Gene Reynolds was original executive producer. Both left after several seasons. Burt Metcalfe, who was the program's first casting director, succeeded Reynolds as executive producer.

A sequel to the sitcom, *AfterMash,* presented several members of the original ensemble adjusting to civilian life. It began on CBS in the fall of 1983 and was canceled in December 1984.

MASINI, AL ▶ president and chief operating officer of TeleRep, a leading TV station rep firm and program syndicator. Masini became known in the industry for his programming prowess. In 1977 he conceived and organized Operation Prime Time, a mechanism by which independent stations invested in a pool that funded highly promotable, network-quality dramatic specials and mini-series. OPT lasted about 10 years. Masini created the weekly music show *Solid Gold* in 1980 and was instrumental in the development of *Entertainment Tonight* in 1981. He was also the creative force behind *Star Search* and *Lifestyles of the Rich and Famous.*

Masini built his career, however, in the rep business, acquiring national spot advertising for client TV stations. He had worked for the Petry company before founding TeleRep in December 1968.

MASTER ▶ an original video tape recording, from which copies are made.

MASTER ANTENNA (MATV) ▶ a single receiving system serving multiple television receivers within the same building or group of buildings. MATV systems are widely employed in apartment houses and projects, hotels and motels, and office buildings. MATV differs from cable TV (CATV) in that the latter connects a number of separate and distinct homes or buildings to a single antenna system.

Dame Peggy Ashcroft and Tim Pigott-Smith in "The Jewel in the Crown," a *Masterpiece Theatre* presentation

MASTERPIECE THEATRE ▶ long-running, year-round public TV series of single dramas and dramatic series imported mainly from British television and traditionally aired on PBS stations Sunday evenings. The series began in 1969 when WGBH Boston, witnessing NET's failure to follow up on its success with *The Forsyte Saga,* seized the initiative and persuaded the Mobil Oil Company to underwrite a series of British imports, with introductions by Alistair Cooke acting as series host.

Though some critics have cavilled with the aptness of "masterpiece" to describe every show in the series, *Masterpiece Theatre* has established a reputation for quality entertainment and is credited with influencing the acceptance of the serial form by the commercial networks. By far its most popular presentations were *Upstairs, Downstairs,* which ran in four successive seasons (1973-77), and *The Jewel in the Crown* (1981). In addition, the series has included a large number of unquestioned literary masterpieces, among them *Vanity Fair, Crime and Punishment, Silas Marner, Goodbye Mr. Chips, A Tale of Two Cities,* and *David Copperfield.*

MATCH GAME, THE ▶ see Game Shows.

MATLOCK ▶ folksy courtroom drama series that brought Andy Griffith back to the screen as Benjamin Matlock, an Atlanta lawyer who mixes country charm and a canny legal mind to solve murders in headline-making trials. The series, on NBC, was inspired by the TV movie *Diary of a Perfect Murder,* which aired March 3, 1986. The series debuted that fall and was a steady but not spectacular performer for NBC. The network scheduled it opposite a show with high youth appeal on another network, since its own audience tended to be weighted with older viewers. Former network programmer Fred Silverman is the executive producer.

MATSUSHITA ▶ large Japan-based conglomerate that fully or partially owns several consumer and professional TV equipment manufacturers—Panasonic, Quasar, and JVC among them. In 1990 the company followed the lead of its archrival Sony and acquired a large Hollywood studio, MCA/Universal, in an effort to gain some control of the programming, or "software," that runs on video hardware systems.

MAUDE ▶ highly successful and frequently controversial spin-off of *All in the Family* on CBS (1972-78) about an aggressive middle-aged woman, Maude Findlay, in step with the times and committed to the liberal viewpoint. The series, which projected veteran actress Bea Arthur to stardom, once involved her confronting the explosive question of abortion and on another occasion being helped by modern psychiatry and medicine for manic-depressive illness. On yet another program, she was permitted to curse her husband as a "son of a bitch."

Bill Macy played her somewhat erratic fourth husband, Walter Findlay, and other regulars were Adrienne Barbeau as daughter Carol Traynor, Brian Morrison (replaced by Kraig Metzinger) as Carol's son Philip, Conrad Bain and Rue McClanahan as the Findlay's neighbors, Arthur and Vivian Harmon, and Hermione Baddeley as their maid, Nell Naugatuck. Esther Rolle had portrayed housekeeper Florida Evans for two seasons, until she was spun off in a new situation comedy, *Good Times.* It was produced by Norman Lear's Tandem Productions.

MAVERICK ▶ highly successful offbeat western whose hero was cowardly, unskilled in the orthodox heroic arts and something of a rogue. The perfect casting of James Garner in the lead shot him to stardom. He was later joined by Jack Kelly as brother Bart Maverick and Roger Moore as cousin Beau Maverick. Produced by Warner Bros., the series ran on ABC (1957-62) when the network had little else going for it.

The series was revived for ABC in the 1981-82 season under the title *Bret Maverick,* with

Garner repeating the role. Featured were Darleen Carr as photographer Mary Lou (M. L.) Springer, Richard Hamilton as Cy Whitaker, Stuart Margolin as Philo Sandine, Ed Bruce as Tom Guthrie and John Shearin as Sheriff Mitchel Dowd.

Warner attempted to revive the series in 1979 with a made-for-television movie, *The New Mavericks,* also starring James Garner. Instead it resulted in a spin-off series without Garner. It featured Susan Blanchard and Charles Frank.

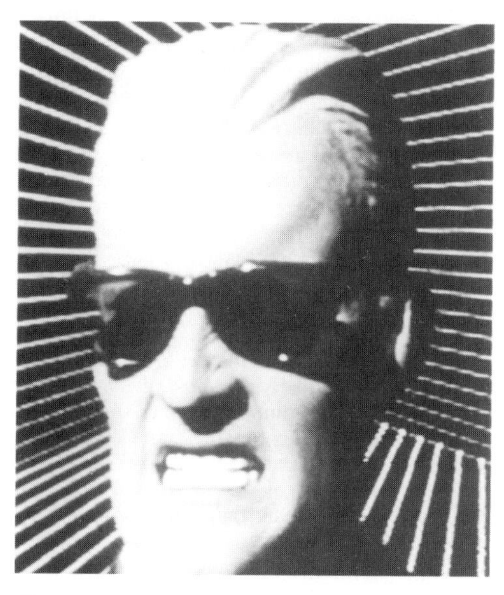

The computer-generated title character of *Max Headroom*

MAX HEADROOM ▶ innovative but short-lived futuristic ABC series about a TV reporter and his computer-generated alter ego, Max Headroom. A creation of British producer Peter Wagg, the ever-wisecracking and stammering character Max Headroom first appeared in the U.S. on Cinemax in a talk show—also called *Max Headroom*—which was unusual for the genre, given that the character only existed within a TV set like an animated character. Headroom was also used in Coca-Cola commercials before the series appeared.

The one-hour series' bleak premise had the world taken over by television networks. Ace TV reporter Edison Carter (Matt Frewer) constantly hunted for hot crime and corruption stories with his portable minicam, getting either advice or ridicule along the way from Max, who zapped in and out of the network feed.

Produced by Lorimar Television, *Max Headroom* had an unusual look and pace, interspersing grainy video footage from Carter's reportage with rapid-fire dialogue. It first aired as a mid-season replacement in early 1987, but it went off the air shortly after the beginning of that year's fall season.

MAY SCREENINGS ▶ an international TV market of sorts, held in Hollywood immediately after ABC, CBS, NBC and Fox announce their fall schedules. Through an organizing group, the studios and other producers of the selected shows host foreign buyers in a week or more of sales screenings. Most of the foreign networks, public or private, are anxious to secure what they hope will be the next big American hit, so the turnout is assured. The studios pool money to pay for the transportation and accommodations of the foreign guests and then each in turn, by prearrangement, may host the group for about a day to pitch the pilots the networks bought. Foreign networks may carry the shows at the same time as the American networks, and in many cases their purchases represent the shows' profits. The network schedules are usually completed in May, but sometimes the deadline is extended with the odd result that the May Screenings are held in June. The British industry does something similar—known as the London Screenings—but the event occurs much later in the year. Following those come the German screenings, at which the main producing organizations present their programs.

***MAYBERRY, R.F.D.* ▶** countrified situation comedy on CBS (1968-70) that was salvaged from the *Andy Griffith Show* when Griffith decided to leave. It was successful but fell to a CBS decision in 1970 to weed out the rural-oriented and demographically undesirable shows. The series starred Ken Berry as town councillor Sam Jones and featured Arlene Golonka as Sam's girlfriend Millie Swanson, George Lindsay as Goober Pyle, Jack Dodson as county clerk Howard Sprague, Paul Hartman as repairman Emmett Clark, Frances Bavier as Aunt Bee Taylor, Sam's housekeeper, and, after Taylor left the show, Alice Ghostley as the new housekeeper, Alice. It was by RFD Productions and Paramount.

MAYFLOWER DECISION ▶ [Mayflower Broadcasting Corp./8 FCC 333 (1940)] an FCC opinion that stood as a rule through most of the 1940s, which prohibited all licensees from taking positions of advocacy on the air. The decision was later reconsidered and reversed in the Report on Editorializing, issued on June 1, 1949.

The episode began when a radio station in Boston, owned by Mayflower Broadcasting Corp., was charged with making political endorsements and supporting partisan politics in public controversies, with no effort toward fairness and balance. After lecturing the licensee about its onesidedness and bias, the FCC renewed the license on securing a promise from the licensee not to editorialize in the future. This stood as a rule for the industry. The FCC's opinion appeared to define public interest as the obligation to present all sides of important public questions fairly, objectively and without bias. That definition was laid aside along with the ban on editorializing in 1949.

MCA ▶ one of the Hollywood "majors" as owner of Universal Pictures. In November 1990 it became the fourth of the big studios to be taken over by a foreign buyer (after 20th Century-Fox, Columbia and MGM/UA). The acquisition by Matsushita Electrical Industrial Co., the world's largest manufacturer of consumer electronics products, was the largest of a U.S. company by a Japanese concern. The price was $6.3 billion.

In the purchase, Matsushita acquired virtually all the company's many parts: the MCA Television Group, Universal Pictures, MCA Records and Geffen Records, a half-interest in the USA Network (Paramount owns the other half of the cable network), Universal Studios Hollywood and Universal Studios Florida, MCA Home Entertainment (video), publishing companies, retail stores and 49% of the Cineplex Odeon movie theater chain. The MCA Television Group consisted of five divisions: Universal Television, producer of network TV programs; MCA TV, domestic distributor of TV programs and movies to stations; MCA TV International, the foreign distribution arm; MCA Television Entertainment, the cable production unit; MCA Family Entertainment, the animation unit. Of greatest value was the MCA library of 2,900 movie titles and 13,000 television shows.

What Matsushita did not get was WWOR-TV New York, because of the government restriction on foreign ownership of broadcast licenses, and MCA's concession stands at Yosemite National Park, because of the negative public response to the idea of foreign-owned businesses in a national park. The television station was spun off as Pinelands Inc., its stock traded separately. It was MCA's only station and represented a valuable tool in testing MCA programs in the nation's No. 1 market.

At the time of the acquisition, Universal Television had seven series on three networks in addition to three series in first-run syndication: *Charles In Charge, New Dragnet* and *New Adam 12.*

MCA's history dates to 1924, when as Music Corp. of America it was founded by optometrist Jules Stein as a booking agency for orchestras playing popular dance music. Over time it expanded into one of the country's largest talent agencies, representing a huge roster of performers, writers, producers and directors.

During the 1950s and 1960s, the company grew to even greater power in the entertainment world, earning itself the nickname of "The Octopus" by acquiring, in order, Revue Productions, which turned out low-budget TV series, Universal Pictures and Decca Records. This put it in the business not only of selling talent but also of buying it. With television, MCA expanded into packaging—putting together the property, the actors and the creative unit. It also set up its principal clients in their own production companies, and then represented both the companies and the stars. Ordered by the government to divest itself of either the buying or selling function, as required under the Sherman and Clayton antitrust laws, MCA elected to give up the talent agency. With the decision, it surrendered its original corporate name.

Lew Wasserman is the longtime chairman of MCA and Sid Sheinberg its president.

McANDREW, WILLIAM R. (d. 1968) ▶ head of NBC News from 1951 until his death, a respected executive under whose guidance the division grew both in stature and size. McAndrew assembled a topnotch roster of correspondents and producers as the division grew during his administration from 70 employees to nearly 1,000. Through much of the 1960s NBC was widely regarded as the leading news network in journalistic initiative and achievement, and it led as well in the ratings. The organization's drive and esprit were largely attributed to McAndrew's almost fatherly leadership.

McAndrew began with the NBC Washington bureau in the late 1930s, then went to work for *Broadcasting* magazine and later ABC News. He returned to NBC News in 1944 as director of the Washington bureau and five years later became station manager of the Washington o&os, WRC and WRC-TV. In 1951 he moved to New York as manager of news and special events for the radio and TV networks and received a succession of new titles in the post until he was named president in 1965.

McAVITY, THOMAS A. (d. 1972) ▶ v.p. in charge of programs for NBC and later general program executive until his retirement in 1971. In three stints with the network, the first dating to radio days, he helped develop numerous shows, among them the Bob Hope specials and *Your Hit Parade.* In the 1940s he left NBC to work in the advertising and talent agency fields, then took a position with CBS in 1950 and a year later rejoined NBC as director of talent and program procurement. He became v.p. of programs in 1954 and two years later head of both programs and sales. He left soon afterward to join McCann-Erickson Advertising, and then J. Walter Thompson, but he returned to NBC again in 1963 as a general program executive.

McCARTER, WILLIAM J. ▶ president and general manager of WTTW Chicago since 1972 and a leader in shaping the programming and policies of public television. Under his leadership WTTW became one of public TV's national production centers, with *Sneak Previews* and *Soundstage,* among other series. It also became one of PTV's most-watched stations. Prior to joining WTTW, McCarter was president of WETA-TV and -FM in Washington, where he created public TV's longest-running show, *Washington Week in Review.*

***McCARTHY v. FEDERAL COMMUNICATIONS COMMISSION* ▶** [390 F2d 471 (D.C. Circuit 1968)] a Court of Appeals case that laid down the general proposition that a President is not a candidate for reelection until he announces his decision to run.

Following a practice that began in 1962 with a year-end interview with President Kennedy, the three TV networks in December 1967 carried a joint hour-long interview with President Johnson. Sen. Eugene McCarthy, who, prior to the broadcast, had announced his own candidacy for the Democratic party nomination, requested equal time. The FCC denied the senator's request, saying that Section 315 only applied to legally qualified persons who had, among other things, publicly announced their candidacies. Since President Johnson had not officially announced his own candidacy, the commission felt there was no equal time requirement.

The Court of Appeals, while warning the commission not to adhere to arbitrary formulas, affirmed the commission because it felt the FCC's ruling was not unreasonable.

McCARVER, TIM ▶ commentator for CBS Sports and WWOR-TV in New York, considered by many to have raised the sophistication level of baseball broadcasting. A longtime catcher in the big leagues, McCarver first gained notice as a broadcaster when he started doing Mets games for WWOR-TV in New York, a superstation transmitted via satellite to over 13 million cable subscribers. He also served as an analyst for ABC's baseball coverage for six years, working the 1984 and 1986 National League Championship Series, the 1985 and 1987 World Series, and the 1986 and 1988 All-Star Games. He joined CBS in 1990 and is teamed with play-by-play announcer Jack Buck. McCarver, a native of Memphis, Tenn., had a distinguished career as a Major League catcher from 1959-80. He played 12 years with the St. Louis Cardinals, eight and a half with the Philadelphia Phillies and had brief stints with the Montreal Expos and Boston Red Sox. McCarver also served as a prime-time co-host of CBS's coverage of the Olympic Winter Games, held in Albertville, France, in February 1992.

***McCLATCHY BROADCASTING CO. v. FCC* ▶** [239 F2d (D.C. Cir. 1956)/ *rehearing denied,* 239 F2d 19,/ *cert. den.,* 353 U.S. 918 (1957)] case which established that, when other factors balanced out, the FCC may award a license to one applicant rather than another because it would lead to greater diversification of media ownership.

McClatchy and Sacramento Telecasters each submitted an application for a single TV license in Sacramento, Calif. The FCC's hearing examiner found that McClatchy was the licensee of several radio stations in central California and that it was a wholly owned subsidiary of McClatchy Newspapers, which published a number of newspapers in the same area. Telecasters, on the other hand, had no other media interests and would have been a newcomer in the field. The hearing examiner found, however, that since McClatchy had not used its concentration of media in a monopolistic way the fact of concentration should not be held against it.

But the commission itself disagreed. In finding only slight differences between the applicants in terms of their programming and staff proposals, the commission therefore considered the diversification question to be crucial. Since granting Telecasters the license would add a new media voice to Californians and since granting the license to McClatchy would not, the FCC awarded the license to the former because all other factors were virtually equal.

McClatchy appealed. The D.C. Court of Appeals held that the FCC had every right to consider diversification as the "decision" factor. The court reasoned that determination of the "public interest" required a series of ad hoc tests and that the commission should not be "imprisoned in a formula of general applications." The commission's obligation, the court said, was to avoid acting in an arbitrary fashion, and as long as it decided in a reasonable manner the court would not overrule its judgment.

Kerry McCluggage

McCLUGGAGE, KERRY ▶ president of Paramount Television Group since August 1991, brought in by Brandon Tartikoff shortly after he became chairman of Paramount Pictures. McCluggage previously had been president of Universal Television, overseeing the production of such successful series as *Coach, Major Dad* and *Northern Exposure.* In a 13-year career with MCA/Universal McCluggage was involved in all levels of production before becoming a studio executive. He was executive producer of *Miami Vice.*

The Paramount Group consists of the network, syndication and international television production and distribution units and the six stations owned by Paramount known as the TVX group. McCluggage also looks after Paramount's 50% stake in the USA Network and its 49% stake in Zenith Productions in England. Also reporting to McCluggage is Wilshire Court Productions, which produces exclusively for cable.

McCONNAUGHEY, GEORGE C. (d. 1966) ▶ chairman of the FCC from 1954 to 1957, having been appointed to the commission in 1953 by President Eisenhower. He became embroiled in a scandal over alleged improper contacts between FCC officials and broadcasters, the so-called "$100 million lunch," which jeopardized the license of WHDH-TV Boston. The scandal resulted in the establishment by the Justice Dept. of a guideline for the commission that any applicant who met with an FCC commissioner outside of normal proceedings would automatically lose his case.

McConnaughey denied under oath charges made in House Subcommittee hearings that he had solicited bribes from some license applicants and that he often had lunched with applicants. Those charges were never substantiated, but McConnaughey did admit having private meetings with applicants. He left the commission when his term expired June 30, 1957, to return to practicing law.

McCONNELL, JOSEPH H. ▶ president of NBC from Oct. 7, 1949, to Dec. 31, 1952, a period of expansion and transition for the company. McConnell reorganized NBC into three major units—the radio network, the TV network and the broadcast stations owned and operated by NBC. He then proceeded to enlarge the television network. McConnell had practiced corporation law in Washington and New York before joining the legal department of RCA, parent of NBC, in 1941. He rose to general counsel and executive v.p. of RCA before receiving the NBC assignment. McConnell resigned in 1952 to become president of Colgate-Palmolive-Peet Co.

McCORMACK, MARK ▶ founder of the International Management Group (IMG) who, as its chairman and owner, is considered the most powerful man in sports and the creator of today's multi-billion dollar sports marketing and management industry. Starting with one client, Arnold Palmer, and a small office in the early 1960s, he now has 42 offices in 29 countries doing over $700 million a year in volume.

IMG is the world's largest independent source of televised sports. It also promotes a wide variety of sports and cultural events and is sports marketing consultant to major corporations and sports leagues. One of IMG's divisions, Trans World International (TWI), founded in 1966, is the largest independent source and distributor of sports programs in the world, providing programming to television networks everywhere on the globe. IMG also represents numerous major sports organizations, including those owning the rights to such events as the U.S. Open, the British Open, Wimbledon, and the PGA Championship.

One of TWI's most publicized associations is with Olympic television rights. The company was retained by the Olympic Organizing Committees of Calgary (1988), Seoul (1988), Albertville, France (1992), and Lillehammer, Norway (1994).

McDERMOTT, THOMAS ▶ production executive who served as program director for RCA's videodisc subsidiary, SelectaVision (1970-76), after having been president of (and partner in) Four Star International, the TV production company. Earlier he had been v.p. for broadcasting of Benton & Bowles Advertising. He returned to TV production on leaving RCA.

McDONALD, EUGENE JR. (d. 1958) ▶ board chairman of Zenith Radio Corp. and an early and ardent advocate of pay TV. Under McDonald, Zenith developed the over-the-air pay system Phonevision (used in the 1962-68 experiment in Hartford, Conn.) and established a pay-TV subsidiary, Teco, to pursue the cause for subscription TV.

McEVEETY, BERNARD ▶ director with numerous prime-time credits, principally in western series: *Death Valley Days, The Virginian, Rawhide, Laredo, Gunsmoke, Wild, Wild West* and *Dirty Sally,* among others.

Donald H. McGannon

McGANNON, DONALD H. (d. 1984) ▶ longtime chairman and president of Group W (1955-1982) and a forceful, independent figure in the industry whose views affected network and FCC policies. While building Group W into the most potent station group outside those owned by the networks, he also established Group W Productions as a major syndicator, producing and distributing such widely used fare as *The Mike Douglas Show, The Merv Griffin Show* (until 1970), *The David Frost Show, The Steve Allen Show, PM East* and *PM West, The Regis Philbin Show, PM Magazine,* numerous documentaries and such notable children's series as *Call It Macaroni.*

Early in 1979 McGannon yielded the titles of president and chief executive officer to Daniel Ritchie and withdrew from the day-to-day operations of the company. He retained the chairmanship, however, until his retirement in 1982. Two years later he died of Alzheimer's disease.

As an industry statesman, McGannon fell in and out of favor with his fellow broadcasters, depending on his latest cause. In 1964 he received the NAB's distinguished service award, then angered his fellow station operators by pushing for a rule that would limit network dominance over prime time. His efforts led to the FCC's adoption of the prime-time access rule in 1970, which at first made McGannon a pariah with fellow broadcasters and then a saint, when the PTAR arrangement proved more profitable to them than network service. For the first year of prime-access, Group W Productions, at McGannon's behest, produced such series as *Norman Corwin Presents, The David Frost Revue, The Tom Smothers' Space Ride* and other series that reportedly ran up a loss of $3 million for the company.

McGannon also fought the networks on increasing sex and violence in prime time and, in 1969, withdrew his stations from the TV Code because its provisions were not strict enough. Earlier, he successfully led the industry opposition to ABC's attempt to ramrod a fourth commercial minute in the half-hour prime-time series, *Batman.* During the early 1960s he canceled all of his radio stations' connections with the networks and made them all independent. To provide them with news, he built his own national and foreign news organization and then adopted the all-news format for several of the Group W stations. He was also in the forefront of the fight in 1976 to block the networks from attempting to increase their newscasts from 30 minutes to an hour a night. Group W had TV stations affiliated with all three networks. A McGannon petition for a new FCC inquiry into network practices led to such a probe in May 1977.

A lawyer, McGannon made his initial mark in broadcasting as an executive of the old DuMont Network (1952-55) before moving on to Westinghouse. Under his stewardship, the company sponsored six annual public service conferences for the entire industry. McGannon also founded the Broadcast Skills Bank, an organization dedicated to discovering and recruiting able black personnel for the broadcast industry, which later became the Employment Clearing House under the NAB. He served also as president and trustee of the National Urban League, chairman of the Advertising Council and chairman of the Connecticut Commission for Higher Education. He is memorialized by the Donald McGannon Communication Center at Fordham University, his alma mater.

McGEE, FRANK (d. 1974) ▶ NBC newsman who drew major domestic assignments during the 1960s and, from 1971 until his death, served as host of *Today.* In a 17-year career with NBC, McGee had variously been a Washington correspondent, anchor for the WNBC newscast in New York, Sunday anchor for the network and (1970-71) coanchor of the *Nightly News.* He also covered Apollo moon-shots, presidential elections, political conventions and the assassinations. McGee was moderator of the second of the Kennedy-Nixon "Great Debates" in 1960. He came to the network's attention with his coverage of racial friction in Montgomery, Ala., while working as news director there for NBC affiliate, WSAF-TV, in 1957.

McGINNIS, MARLENE ▶ president of two small production companies that could hardly be more different from one another. The first, founded in the late 1970s, produces *VideoFashion!*, which claims to be the first monthly magazine produced on video. It is distributed in some 40 countries and narrated in 19 languages. The second, Video Ordnance, formed in 1983, produces documentary magazine series on advanced military weaponry—tanks, fighter planes, missiles and other tools of war, with an accent on high-tech developments. The series *Firepower* has aired in several 13-week flights on the Discovery Channel. Both companies have flourished in the international market and with video cassette sales.

Video Ordnance came into prominence during the 1991 Persian Gulf War, when its footage was in high demand around the world as well as in the U.S. While much of the footage is original, a good deal of it is supplied by the Pentagon and defense contractors. Video Ordnance produced three documentaries for A&E immediately after the Gulf War, in what the cable network billed as "Desert Storm Week." The three were *The Air Assault, The Ground Assault* and *Desert Victory.* In the first week of the Gulf War, two videos on American military technology reportedly realized more than $500,000 in sales around the world.

McGinnis, a native of South Africa who is of Chinese descent, moved to New York in the 1960s and landed a job in the advertising industry as personal assistant to George Lois, following him from Papert, Koenig & Lois to Lois, Holland & Callaway. She eventually became an account executive before leaving to start her production company.

McHALE'S NAVY ▶ one of the more potent items in the service comedy vogue of the 1960s featuring Ernest Borgnine as Lieutenant Commander Quinton McHale, Joe Flynn as Captain Wallace Binghamton and Tim Conway as Ensign Chuck Parker—all broadly inept officers of a PT boat. Produced by Sto-Rev, it ran on ABC from 1962 to 1965 and then in syndication.

McINTIRE, JOHN (d. 1991) ▶ veteran character actor probably best known for his continuing role in *Wagon Train* from 1961 to 1965. He also appeared in such series as *Naked City* and *The Virginian,* as well in some 100 motion pictures and mini-series.

McKAY, JIM ▶ veteran sports commentator for ABC Sports since his 1961 appearance on the premiere program of ABC's *Wide World of Sports,* a role he has continued to play for that network in the years since. Before joining ABC, he spent 10 years covering sporting events for CBS, including the 1960 Olympic Games in Rome.

McKay has hosted a wide variety of televised events in the course of his long career in broadcast sports, among them the Kentucky Derby, the British Open, the Indianapolis 500, and eleven Olympic Games. None was more memorable, however, than his unexpected role as a newsman reporting the tragic events surrounding the 1972 Black September terrorists' attack on the Israeli athletes in the Olympic Village in Munich.

His other claim to immortality: his was the first voice Baltimoreans heard on their television. In 1947 he gave up his job as a reporter for the *Baltimore Sun* newspapers to join that organization's new TV station, WMAR-TV, where he wrote and produced news and sports for two years until he joined the CBS network in New York.

McLAUGHLIN GROUP, THE ▶ one in the 1980s wave of news discussion shows that examine topical issues with panels of liberal and conservative journalists, on the presumption of achieving a balance of views. But often, as also with CNN's *Crossfire,* the programs generate more heat than light, and the issue at hand becomes a matter of secondary interest to the heated interaction of the discussants. This makes for good, if noisy, television, though not necessarily for nourishing news analysis.

The McLaughlin Group is moderated by John McLaughlin, a former assistant to Presidents Nixon and Ford. Among the regulars on the liberal side are Jack Germond and Morton Kondracke; a frequent participant on the right is Pat Buchanan, who is also a regular on *Crossfire.*

What is unusual about *McLaughlin* is that it's a hybrid of commercial and public television and is syndicated to both systems, claiming some 200 stations overall. The series is a coproduction of commercial station WRC-TV Washington and public WTTW Chicago, along with an independent company, Oliver Productions.

McLUHAN, MARSHALL (d. 1980) ▶ professor at the University of Toronto, author and avant-garde interpreter of the media and their cosmic meanings. He contended that societies have always been shaped more by the nature of the media by which people communicate than by the content of the communication. The now familiar phrase that summarizes his position, "the medium is the message," embodies the historic view that the means by which humans communicate have always determined their actions.

In *Understanding Media: Extensions of Man* and his other books, McLuhan's underlying theme is that media—speech, printing, art, radio, telephone, television—function as extensions of the human organism to increase power and speed. He used the words "hot and cool" to describe the mode of impact of a particular medium on people's senses (television in his view is "cool"), and he observed that the mass media of today are turning the world into a "global village," shrinking the globe with respect to shared experience and the passage of news.

McMAHON, ED ▶ sidekick to Johnny Carson on the *Tonight Show* for 30 years and a familiar face on television since the early 1950s, having started his career as a circus clown on *Big Top* (1950-51). He first appeared as Carson's straight man on the daytime quiz show *Who Do You Trust?* (1957-63). He hosted three daytime game shows in the 1960s and 1970s and has played minor parts in a number of TV movies. He and Dick Clark co-hosted *TV's Bloopers & Practical Jokes* (1984-86), and he has been the host of *Star Search* since it started in 1983.

McMULLEN, JAY ▶ former *CBS Reports* documentarian noted for his bold investigative reporting with such works as *Biography of a Bookie Joint* (1961), *The Tenement* (1967), and *The Mexican Connection* (1972).

McNEELY, JERRY C. ▶ writer and producer-director who created the *Lucas Tanner* series and was co-creator of *Owen Marshall.* A former professor of communications at the University of Wisconsin, with a Ph.D. in drama, he served as executive story consultant to Universal Studios before branching into production.

McQUEEN, TRINA ▶ head of all news operations for Canada's CBC, with the title of vice president, the first woman to hold such a senior position in Canadian television. So far as is known, she is also the first woman to head a major TV news organization in the developed world. Prior to her appointment, on which a vice presidency was conferred in 1991 (in an organization that gives out such titles sparingly), McQueen had been director of network television for CBC for five years—responsible for budgets, planning, policy, commercial sales and business affairs. For the four years previous, she was director of TV network programs.

Her background, however, was in journalism. She worked as a reporter both locally and nationally for the CBC, after having been a co-host of *W-5,* the popular current affairs program on the commercial CTV network. Before that she worked in print journalism on daily newspapers.

McRANEY, GERALD ▶ an unusual Hollywood hyphenate: actor-producer. He stars in the CBS hit *Major Dad* (1989—), and serves as well as co-executive producer. He was also executive producer for two CBS TV movies, *Love and Curses and All That Jazz* and *Vestige of Honor.*

MDS (MULTIPOINT DISTRIBUTION SERVICE) ▶ a specialized private service in the superhigh frequency band (2,150-2,160 megahertz). MDS is a common-carrier service authorized to transmit special private television programming, data and facsimile to locations within a metropolitan area, on order from customers. MDS is widely used to transmit special television channels to hotels and has also been used to beam pay-TV programs to cable systems. In the late 1970s, there was a growth spurt in STV (subscription television) and pay-TV services using MDS to transmit, but most of these were choked off by the growth of cable.

MEAD, ROBERT ▶ former TV adviser to President Ford, appointed at the start of the Administration but discharged by press secretary Ron Nessen in July 1976 when a live special on Queen Elizabeth's visit to the White House, carried by PBS, went badly. Mead had been a news producer for CBS at the White House when he was appointed. In addition to handling arrangements for the president's televised speeches and press conferences, and selecting the times of broadcast, Mead also coached the new president in advance of the telecasts to help him perform effectively.

MEADE, E. KIDDER, JR. ▶ former vice-president of corporate affairs for CBS Inc. (1957-1981). He joined the company after serving with its outside public relations counsel, Earl Newsom & Co. A graduate of West Point and a lieutenant colonel during World War II, he became a member of the staff of the Secretary of Defense and later (1950-53) a special assistant to the Under Secretary of State. He then became v.p. of Colonial Williamsburg Inc.

MEADOWS, AUDREY ▶ actress and comedienne best known for her role as Jackie Gleason's wife (Alice Kramden) in *The Honeymooners.* She was also featured on the *Bob & Ray Show* in the early 1950s and with Sid Caesar, Red Skelton and Jack Benny. She was a regular on CBS's short-lived *Uncle Buck* series in 1990-91.

MEDIA ACCESS PROJECT ▶ Washington-based public interest law firm affiliated with the Center for Law and Social Policy and concentrating on communications matters before the FCC, other regulatory agencies and the courts. The organization is headed by Andrew Jay Schwartzman.

MEDIA LAB AT MIT ▶ institution conducting research into new communications technologies, including advanced television (ATV) and interactive and entertainment technology. Headed by Dr. Nicholas Negroponte, the lab produced remarkable experiments with the optical video disc during the 1970s that served to advance the technology's educational use.

***MEDIC* ▶** artful and meticulously researched medical-drama series which had been produced for syndication (1954-56), with Richard Boone as narrator and star, playing Dr. Konrad Styner, of the first episode. In a fictional framework, the programs examined medical practices and problems and were filmed on location at Los Angeles hospitals. The 30-minute programs were written by James Moser and produced by Worthington Miner for Medic TV Productions.

***MEDICAL CENTER* ▶** hour-long series of dramas set in a fictional medical center within a large university. It premiered on CBS in 1969 and performed well enough in the ratings to earn an annual renewal up until 1976. Produced by MGM-TV in association with Alfra Productions, it starred Chad Everett as young Dr. Joe Gannon and James Daly as chief of staff Dr. Paul Lochner.

***MEET MILLIE* ▶** a 1952-56 situation comedy on CBS about the business and romantic life of a Manhattan secretary. Elena Verdugo played the title character, Millie Bronson, Florence Halop her mother and Ross Ford the boss's son, Johnny Boone Jr.

***MEET THE PRESS* ▶** prestigious 30-minute newsmaker series airing Sunday mornings on NBC since 1947, and the oldest series on network television. A kind of made-for-TV news conference, the Washington-based program typically has a single guest—usually from government—who is interviewed by a panel of print journalists. The programs frequently elicit information and statements that make front-page news on Monday mornings. This may have prompted CBS's introduction of a similar program, *Face the Nation,* in 1954. ABC followed in 1960 with a news forum of its own, *Issues and Answers*, which gave way to *This Week with David Brinkley.*

Meet the Press actually began in 1945 as a radio program, created by Lawrence E. Spivak and Martha Roundtree. Spivak's interest initially was in promoting his magazine, *American Mercury,* of which he was editor and publisher. In the early years he was producer and a permanent panelist and Roundtree the moderator. When the program moved to television,

Spivak sold the magazine and in 1953 bought out Roundtree's interest. Two years later he sold the program to NBC but stayed on for the next 20 years as executive producer and moderator.

When Spivak retired in 1975, NBC Washington correspondent Bill Monroe succeeded him as executive producer and moderator. Monroe in turn was replaced by Marvin Kalb, who in 1984 was joined by Roger Mudd as what the network called "principal interviewers." The program is conducted now by Tim Russert.

Meet the Press began as a nighttime show, for a while on Wednesdays after 10 p.m., then on Mondays and then Saturdays. In the mid-1950s, it found its niche on Sundays in the daytime hours, where it remains today.

Bill Monroe with guest Golda Meir on the set of *Meet the Press*

MELCHER, MARTIN ▶ producer and talent agent who, after selling his agency to MCA in 1948, concentrated on representing his wife, actress Doris Day. Their own company, Arwin Productions, produced *The Doris Day Show* on CBS (1968-73), as well as some of her films.

MELENDEZ, BILL ▶ see Mendelson, Lee and Melendez, Bill.

"MEN IN WHITE" COMMERCIALS ▶ advertisements that used actors to simulate doctors, suggesting that their patented medicines were recommended by medical authorities. The practice ended in 1958 when, in response to pressure, it was outlawed by the NAB Code. But it resumed in the 1980s with deregulation.

MENDELSON, LEE and MELENDEZ, BILL ▶ producers of all the *Charlie Brown* specials since the first in 1965; they work in association with Charles M. Schulz, the cartoonist who created the *Peanuts* strip on which the programs are based, and United Features Syndicate. All have been done for CBS, including a motion picture when CBS had a theatrical film division, and the much-lauded mini-series *This Is America, Charlie Brown*. Mendelson serves as executive producer and Melendez supervises the animation and also performs the voice of Snoopy. Schulz writes the programs.

MEREDITH, DON ▶ former star football quarterback who became a star ABC sportscaster on *Monday Night Football* and in 1974 was hired away by NBC on a sports and entertainment contract. Meredith not only provided football expertise as color commentator for ABC but also displayed a lively, countrified wit. This prompted NBC to sign him for occasional acting roles and hosting assignments on *Tonight* as well as for its coverage of football and tennis. He returned to ABC Sports in the summer of 1977.

MERRIMAN, JOHN (d. 1974) ▶ editor, producer and reporter for CBS News since 1942 who served as news editor of the *CBS Evening News* from 1966 until his death eight years later in a plane crash. In 1973 he was president of Writers Guild—East.

MESTRE, GOAR ▶ founder of two television networks in Cuba during the early 1950s, each consisting of seven stations, which made him the first person in the world to create a national television system. When his broadcast properties were taken over by Fidel Castro's government, Mestre emigrated to Buenos Aires with his Argentine wife and there started a successful production company, Proartel, which created programs for the country's Channel 13. His wife, with financial support from CBS, was part owner of the station. *Variety*'s headline for Mestre's reemergence in television was "Mestre Rides Again."

CBS helped to sponsor Mestre's Argentina enterprise out of gratitude, as Mestre, a graduate of Yale, had sold his Cuban properties to the American network and then called off the deal when he realized the stations were about to be confiscated by Castro. His gentlemanly act spared CBS a huge loss.

MEXICO ▶ a country whose television from the beginning has been dominated by Televisa, owned by the Azcarraga family (both the late founder and his son, who now runs the company, are named Emilio Azcarraga). Televisa operates four national TV channels, and fulfills its statutory obligation to devote airtime to cultural and educational programming by dedicating one of its networks, Channel 9, strictly to that purpose.

The other channels thus are free to go about their business. Televisa is one of the world's leading producers of telenovelas, which sell internationally, and it is also a chief supplier of programming to the Spanish-language networks in the U.S., Telemundo and Univision. It also owns Galavision, the Hispanic U.S. cable channel.

The other networks of consequence in Mexico are those of the state-run Imevision, which operates five national channels in all and accepts advertising. Its accent is on education and culture. Mexico also has around 30 independent regional stations.

All told there are 9.5 million television households in a country with a population of 88 million people. Unlike Canada, which is culturally threatened by its proximity to the U.S., Mexico sends its culture past the northern frontier to the American-based Hispanic stations that are coming to represent a significant market of their own.

MIAMI VICE ▶ one of the most popular cop shows of the 1980s, which had the added dimension of trendiness. The series ran on NBC from September 1984 to July 1989, powered more by its form than its content. The show paid particular attention to sound, color, and camera angles. It had a distinctive look that reflected what was indicated in the two-word source of its concept: "MTV cops."

Miami Vice was launched with two relative unknowns in starring roles, Don Johnson as the white Detective Crockett and Philip Michael Thomas as his partner and buddy, the black Detective Tubbs. Playing two undercover vice cops, the stars were hip, hard-boiled and extremely well-dressed. The show itself was instantly recognizable by its lush Miami settings and a predominance of pastel colors. Contemporary music, much of it played by the reigning rock bands, was closely integrated with the storyline. Occasional segments, looking much like music videos, may even have had their influence on that genre.

The series was a hit in its first two seasons, finishing in the top ten, but slipped when NBC placed it opposite *Dallas*. By its fifth and final season it had fallen into 53d place. The decision to take it off the air was largely a financial one. Michael Mann, the show's creator and executive producer, had spent lavishly, an estimated $1.2 million per episode. Universal TV, anxious to recoup its investment in the off-network syndication market, sold the show to USA Network, which started its run on cable in 1989.

Philip Michael Thomas and Don Johnson on *Miami Vice*

MICHAELS, AL ▶ ABC sportscaster and three-time winner of the media's "Sportscaster of the Year" award, best known for his professional baseball and football coverage including six World Series, five All-Star games and six League Championship Series. He started his broadcasting career in 1969, covering the Hawaii Islanders in the Pacific Coast League. He moved to Cincinnati in 1971, where at the age of 26 he was the lead announcer for the Reds and covered them for NBC Radio and TV in the 1972 World Series. Before signing with ABC Sports in 1977, he spent four years broadcasting the San Francisco Giants games on local radio and TV. In 1980 he covered the U.S.A. hockey team's successful quest for the gold medal in the Winter Olympic Games, and four years later he covered figure skating and hockey at the Winter Games in Sarajevo and track and field and road cycling at the Summer Games in Los Angeles. He joined the *Monday Night Football* announcing team in 1986. His coverage of the opening game of 1989's World Series in San Francisco, when that city was rocked by a disastrous earthquake, cast him briefly in the unexpected role of an eye-witness newscaster.

Al Michaels

MICHAELS, LORNE ▶ youthful producer of the original NBC *Saturday Night Live,* credited with being most responsible for its success. When Michaels left the show in 1980 for other pursuits, virtually the entire cast and creative staff followed. He returned as producer in 1985, however, bringing an entirely new cast with him.

A Canadian, Michaels had honed his skills in Toronto (1967-73) writing, producing and performing in a number of CBC comedy specials with a partner, Hart Pomerantz. He broke into American TV, while still in his 20s, as a writer for *Laugh-In* and later for Lily Tomlin specials.

On leaving *Saturday Night Live* in 1980, he formed his own production company with a view to making movies and creating programming for cable TV as well as commercial TV. Later in the decade he served as executive producer of an HBO comedy series, *The Kids in the Hall.*

Lorne Michaels

MICKELSON, SIG ▶ first to hold the title of president of CBS News, serving in that capacity from 1951-1961. He produced *The Great Debates* between John F. Kennedy and Richard M. Nixon in 1960 and was a founder and early president of the Radio-Television News Directors Assn.

Mickelson joined CBS as a reporter in 1941, after having taught journalism. On leaving the company, he became head of international broadcasting operations for Time Inc. and later moved to Chicago as v.p. of international operations and TV for Encyclopaedia Britannica Educational Corp., teaching journalism part-time at Northwestern University. Later he became president of Radio Free Europe and Radio Liberty.

***MICKEY MOUSE CLUB* ▶** a popular early evening series on ABC in the late 1950s that employed a cast of juvenile actors known as Mouseketeers and offered varied entertainment, both live and filmed, including Walt Disney cartoons and episodic series (such as "The Adventures of Spin and Marty," starring Tim Considine and David Stollery, and "The Hardy Boys," starring Considine, Tommy Kirk and Florenz Ames).

Legions of children around the country became members of the club, wore its mouse-eared beanie and sang the club song. The program premiered Oct. 3, 1955, as a daily one-hour entry and ran through 1959. It not only provided ABC with a major show in a time when the youngest network was struggling for audience attention, but it was also a windfall for Mickey Mouse merchandise and served to promote the newly opened Disneyland, Walt Disney's amusement park in Southern California.

Some of the reruns were syndicated for a few years during the early 1960s. On Jan. 20, 1975—almost 20 years after it began—*Mickey Mouse Club* was brought back into syndication by SFM Media Service Corp. on the theory that its original audience would watch it nostalgically along with a new audience of children. Later a new series was mounted, but the revival was only moderately successful, and production ceased in 1977.

A movie career grew out of Annette Funicello's performance as a Mouseketeer. Others of the original cast were Sharon Baird, Bobby Burgess, Lonnie Burr, Tommy Cole, Dennis Day, Darlene Gillespie, Cheryl Holdridge, Cubby O'Brien, Karen Pendelton and Doreen Tracey.

***MICKEY SPILLANE'S MIKE HAMMER* ▶** private-eye series (1957-59) based on the character in Spillane's novels, portrayed by Darren McGavin. By Revue Studios, it played on CBS.

The network revived it in 1984 with Stacy Keach as Mike Hammer. That series ran sporadically until the fall of 1987. The series was interrupted by Keach's imprisonment for six months. He served the term in England for possession of cocaine.

MICO (MEDIA INTERNATIONAL CORP.) ▶ commercial company formed in 1990 by Japan's noncommercial television network, NHK, to invest in motion pictures and TV coproductions in the U.S. and other parts of the world. NHK, Japan's equivalent of the BBC and the country's largest broadcaster, operates three direct-broadcast satellite (DBS) channels in addition to its terrestrial network. MICO was formed with a view to securing attractive programming for the DBS channels, one of which is transmitting high-definition television (HDTV); but as the profit-making arm of NHK it also stands to help finance the public broadcaster's other ambitious projects.

In addition to the public funds it receives from NHK, MICO's bankroll has been fattened by capital from such commercial enterprises as C. Itoh & Co. (one of the Japanese companies that purchased a stake in Time Warner), Sumitomo Bank and Dai-Itchi Kangyo Bank. Some believe MICO is potentially the largest investor in TV programming in the world.

MICROWAVE, or MICROWAVE RELAY SYSTEM ▶ a system of radio repeaters mounted on towers, each consisting of a receiving antenna and transmitter, spaced up to 50 miles apart. This is the principal means of interconnecting television stations as well as cable systems within continental boundaries. The microwave frequencies are 890 megahertz and above and give their name to this relay system. Microwaves are also used to connect studio to transmitter and for remote television origination equipment to the studio or transmitter.

MIDEM ORGANIZATION, THE ▶ Paris-based owner and operator of leading international trade shows: MIP-TV and MIPCOM for television and MIDEM for the music business. MIP is the French acronym for Marche International Programmes and is an April event that typically draws close to 9,000 participants. MIPCOM is the fall edition, held in October, with a slight added emphasis on home video and "new" media. It tends to draw around 7,000. Both program markets are held in Cannes and are aimed at bringing together television leaders from all parts of the world to buy and sell programs, negotiate coproductions and otherwise advance cross-border activity. Midem was acquired by Reed International in June 1989 from Telso, a subsidiary of the former U.K. broadcaster TVS.

MIDGLEY, LESLIE ▶ CBS News executive principally responsible for producing the "instant" news specials until NBC News hired him away in 1979 as v.p. of documentaries and such programs as *Tomorrow* and *Prime Time Sunday.* He retired from NBC in 1982, following Bill Small's departure as president of the news division.

When CBS suspended all commercial programming following the assassination of President Kennedy in 1963, Midgley produced the network's nighttime schedule for four evenings. He also produced the four one-hour specials on the Warren Report in 1967, a number of programs on the energy crisis in 1973-74 and 10 hour-long special broadcasts on the unfolding Watergate story in 1973.

Midgley joined CBS News from *Look Magazine* in 1954 and became producer of the *CBS Sunday News,* then anchored by Eric Sevareid. In 1960 he produced the series, *Eyewitness to History* (later entitled *Eyewitness*), and from 1967 to 1971 he was executive producer of *The CBS Evening News with Walter Cronkite.* Midgley married Betty Furness, NBC consumer affairs reporter.

MIDNIGHT SPECIAL, THE **▶** 90-minute contemporary music series on NBC that was scheduled at 1 a.m. Saturdays (following the Friday *Tonight Show*) as part of the network's exploration of postmidnight television. The series premiered Feb. 3, 1973, with Burt Sugarman as executive producer and Stan Harris as producer and director. Wolfman Jack, nationally known rock disk jockey, was regular announcer, and an array of pop music and comedy stars served as hosts. Each program presented approximately 10 acts from the various fields of pop music.

MIDWEST VIDEO CORP. CASE ▶ [*United States v. Midwest Video Corp.*/406 U.S. 649 (1972)] test in which the Supreme Court affirmed the authority of the FCC to create statutory policies for cable TV, including requiring the systems to originate their own programming.

Rules issued by the FCC in 1969 mandated "significant amounts" of cablecasting from all systems with more than 3,500 subscribers. Midwest Video Corp., which operated a system of that size, challenged the rule in the Court of Appeals for the Eighth Circuit and won a decision that the FCC had not the authority to require cablecasting. Moreover, the court held that such a rule was not in the public interest.

On the FCC's appeal, the decision was reversed by the Supreme Court. No majority was assembled, but a four-justice plurality said its decision rested upon whether or not the rule was "reasonably ancillary to the effective performance" of the commission's regulation of television broadcasting. The plurality held that the commission's concern with cable TV is not merely prohibitory by avoiding adverse effects but extends also "to requiring CATV affirmatively to further statutory policies." It maintained also that since cablecasting would assure more diversified programming, the FCC's rule furthers the goal of the Communications Act generally.

Chief Justice Burger concurred in the result, and four justices dissented, saying that congressional action was required to make cablecasting compulsory.

MIDWEST VIDEO II ▶ [*Federal Communications Commission v. Midwest Video Corporation et al.*/47 U.S.L.W. 4335 (1979)] case in which the Supreme Court struck down the FCC's cable-TV access rules and production facilities and channel capacity requirements. At issue were the FCC's 1972 rules requiring cable-TV systems with over 3,500 subscribers to offer access channels to the public, local governments and educational institutions, over which the cable system had no program control; to maintain production facilities for public use for a minimal fee; and to provide a minimum of 20 channels by 1986.

Midwest Video Corp. challenged the FCC rules as beyond the commission's authority on statutory grounds and was joined by the NCTA, which sought a ruling that would have established First Amendment rights for cable programmers akin to those of broadcasters. The court upheld the ruling of the Eighth Circuit Court of Appeals, striking down the regulations, on statutory grounds alone, but specifically deferring judgment on any constitutional questions of a cable operator's right to control the programming on his system. The court held that the FCC's authority over cable TV derived from the 1934 Communications Act's grant of jurisdiction over broadcast television. However, the Act specifically forbids the commission to impose common carrier-like obligations—i.e. first-come, first-served access at federally regulated rates, like those prescribed for telephone companies—on broadcast entities. The court found the commission's cable-TV access rules to be common carrier-style regulations. Rules requiring maintenance of production facilities and prescribing future channel capacity were struck down because they were so intertwined with the access rules that they could not reasonably be separated, although the justices did not find them to be beyond the FCC's current statutory jurisdiction.

Because the court did not rule on constitutional questions but confined itself to judgment on the basis of the 1934 Communications Act, it left the door open for Congress to reimpose the access requirements through new legislation. In addition, state and local authorities may still require access channels through legislation or in new cable-TV franchises. In communities where current franchises already require access channels and facilities, cable operators must continue to honor the franchise provisions even though the federal requirement has been struck down.

MIGRANT **▶** controversial NBC News documentary (1970) produced by Martin Carr as a followup ten years after *Harvest of Shame*, the famous CBS documentary by Edward R. Murrow and David Lowe on the plight of migrant workers. Carr's one-hour film demonstrated that living and working conditions for the Florida agricultural migrants were still wretched and had scarcely improved at all in the decade—a conclusion challenged acrimoniously by the Florida Fruit and Vegetable Association, which asked NBC for reply time under the Fairness Doctrine.

Meanwhile, executives of Coca-Cola Foods—a company with vast interests in the Florida citrus industry through such orange juice brands as Minute Maid, Hi-C, Tropicana and Snowcrop—on learning in advance that theirs was one of the companies cited in the film as exploiting the migrant workers, applied pressure on NBC to make certain excisions. NBC did not, nor did it grant the association reply time. The program was televised without commercial support. Perhaps it was a coincidence, but the following quarter Coca-Cola shifted its scatter-plan billings from NBC to ABC and CBS.

In later hearings by the Senate Subcommittee on Migratory Labor, the program's revelations were upheld as valid, and Coca-Cola was the first company to announce a plan to transform the migratory work force into a stable year-round group with the same fringe benefits as were received by other Coca-Cola employees.

MII ▶ video format introduced by Panasonic in 1986 to compete with Sony's Betacam format. The two are both component, half-inch-cassette-based systems but are incompatible with one another. MII was adopted by NBC as its internal "universal" format but found few other adherents in the U.S.

MILEAGE SEPARATION ▶ minimum distance formula used by the FCC as a guide for allocating TV channels in its 1952 Table of Assignments. The commission determined that stations on the same channel would have to be at least 170 miles apart, and it set the minimum separation for adjacent channel assignments (e.g., Channel 2 and Channel 3) at 60 miles.

MILLER, JP ▶ one of TV's leading playwrights, perhaps best known for *The Days of Wine and Roses.* Active with *Philco-Goodyear Playhouse* and other drama showcases during the "golden age," he took to writing novels when TV drama went into its decline, although he has returned from time to time. He wrote the script for the two-part TV dramatization of the book *Helter-Skelter* (1976), for which he won critical praise. The show ranked number-one in the Nielsens that season.

MILLER, WILLIAM E. ▶ president of Hearst Entertainment Distribution Inc., which until 1990 was known as King Features Entertainment. Since 1980 Miller has been responsible for all domestic and foreign program sales activities and also is in charge of program acquisition and production. He was schooled in the Time Inc. organization, which he joined in 1968. In 1972 he was assigned to Time-Life Films and three years later became senior vice president. When Time-Life Films dissolved in 1980, he followed his boss, Bruce Paisner, to King Features.

MILLER-BOYETT PRODUCTIONS ▶ production company founded by Thomas L. Miller and Robert L. Boyett. Most recently with the house of Lorimar, the team's prolific output of prime-time comedies has included *Full House, Family Matters, Perfect Strangers, Step By Step, Going Places, The Family Man,* and the long-running *The Hogan Family.*

It was while they were at Paramount Studios in the 1970s, and with an additional partner, Edward Milkis, that the Miller-Boyett team produced their biggest hits with *Happy Days, Laverne and Shirley,* and *Mork and Mindy.* Previously, Miller was a development executive with both Paramount and 20th Century-Fox. Boyett was formerly senior vice president of television at Paramount and prior to that served as a development executive with ABC television. Miller-Boyett Productions includes the writer-producer team of William Bickley and Michael Warren.

***MILLIONAIRE, THE* ▶** big CBS hit (1954-59) whose stories involved the sudden gift of $1 million to ordinary persons by an anonymous donor, an eccentric billionaire named John Beresford Tipton. Marvin Miller played the sole continuing character, Michael Anthony, the dour presenter of the gift as secretary to the billionaire. (Though Tipton was never seen, his voice—provided by Paul Frees—was heard.)

MILNE, ALISDAIR ▶ chairman of the British Broadcasting Corp. and previously managing director for television (1977-81). Earlier he was its director of programs for several years.

Born in India of Scottish ancestry, he joined the BBC in 1954 as a public affairs producer. A high point in his programming career came as executive producer of *That Was the Week That Was,* the topical satire series that later transferred to the U.S.

MINER, WORTHINGTON ▶ a leading creative force in the early years of TV as writer, producer and executive. With a background in theater, he became manager of TV program development for CBS in 1948 and was responsible for the creation of *Studio One, Toast of the Town (The Ed Sullivan Show), The Goldbergs* and *Mr I. Magination.* Miner produced and wrote many of the early plays for *Studio One* and was also producer of the other three series. In 1952 he was hired away by NBC but later became a freelancer. He was executive producer of the syndicated series *Medic,* then of *Frontier* and, in the later 1950s, the syndicated drama series *Play of the Week.* He later worked in motion pictures (*The Pawnbroker, The Fool Killer*).

MINI-SERIES ▶ program series designed for limited runs, over several nights or several weeks, as opposed to those created in hopes of running indefinitely. The mini-series came into vogue in U.S. commercial television during the

1970s after the success on public television of such short-term British series as *The Forsyte Saga, Elizabeth R, The Six Wives of Henry VIII* and *Civilisation.* Lending themselves particularly to short-term serialization were popular novels, and with the success on U.S. networks of the adaptations of Leon Uris's *QBVII* and Joseph Wambaugh's *The Blue Knight,* a raft of other best sellers were produced as TV mini-series.

The mini-series came into full flower with ABC's adaptation of Irwin Shaw's *Rich Man, Poor Man* in 1976. That inspired numerous others, and NBC even created a regular weekly series of mini-series under the title of *Best Sellers.* But the crowning achievement in the form, in terms of its ratings and public impact, was ABC's serialization of Alex Haley's *Roots* over eight consecutive nights in January 1977. It drew the largest audience for an entertainment program in the history of television.

MINOW, NEWTON N. ▶ chairman of the FCC (1961-63), on appointment by President Kennedy, who shook the industry with his "vast wasteland" speech at the NAB convention shortly after he took office. Minow, 34 at the time and a former Chicago law partner of Adlai Stevenson, made it plain at once that the FCC in his administration would consider program performance as a condition for license renewal. While there were a number of fines, short-term renewals and a few radio license revocations administered, no major licenses were lost during Minow's term, but the climate he set nevertheless had broadcasters on edge. Later in his career he became involved in public television and was elected chairman of PBS in 1978. He had been a member of the PBS board since 1973.

In his famous 1961 speech—which instantly won him high visibility with the public—Minow described the TV programming landscape as a "vast wasteland" and went on to say that he would not abide a "squandering of the public airwaves." He said broadcasters would be held to their program promises at license-renewal time, and he put the industry on notice that it was expected to do a better job in the public interest. From the industry view, his most teeth-rattling statement was, "There is nothing permanent or sacred about a broadcast license." FCC chairmen did not normally assume the role of TV critics, and because of the sensitivities toward government censorship they usually avoided making evaluations of the general programming.

Part of Minow's strength derived from his support by the press; unlike most FCC chairmen, he was able to make news at will. But he left the FCC without many lasting achievements to take a high-paying position with Encyclopaedia Britannica in Chicago. In 1965 he returned to law practice, with CBS as one of his clients; became chairman of the organization operating Chicago's public TV station, WTTW; and taught classes at Northwestern University. He has been the director of the Annenberg Communications Program in Washington since 1987.

MISS AMERICA PAGEANT **▶** premier national beauty competition televised live from Atlantic City since 1954 and consistently one of the highest-rated programs of the year. Occurring early in September, it has traditionally marked the opening of every new season. Among the event's own traditions was the singing of the pageant's anthem, "There She Is, Miss America," at the finale by ex-master of ceremonies Bert Parks. The song dates to the second telecast (1955), which was Parks's first as emcee.

A few of the Miss Americas went on to build modest careers as TV performers, among them Marilyn Van Derbur and Lee Ann Merriwether, winner of the first pageant to be televised. Bess Myerson has had the largest success in TV, ranging from panelist on *I've Got a Secret* to syndicated talk shows of her own, but she was crowned in 1945 and was not a TV Miss America.

The telecasts were carried first by ABC for three years, then by CBS (1957-65) and by NBC ever since. Although the event was popular with viewers from the start, it did not become blockbuster fare until 1958, when it scored a 49.2 rating (Total Audience), and 66 share, and reached 21.4 million homes over the course of the telecast. Since then it has typically been received in 25 to 28 million homes each year and in 1973 hit a high of mote than 30 million homes. The ratings are remarkable for the fact that the telecasts occur after prime time and run past midnight.

In an effort to rejuvenate the event, the promoters fired the aging Bert Parks and made Ron Ely the host in 1979. After two seasons, Ely gave way to Gary Collins. In 1991, Regis Philbin and Kathie Lee Gifford were hosts.

MISSILES OF OCTOBER, THE **▶** landmark ABC documentary drama (Dec. 18, 1975) concerning the political maneuverings in the 1962

Cuban Missile crisis, with actors portraying the world figures involved. William Devane played President John F. Kennedy; Martin Sheen, Robert F. Kennedy; Howard da Silva, Khrushchev; and Ralph Bellamy, Adlai Stevenson. The three-hour teleplay was written by Stanley R. Greenberg. Herbert Brodkin and Buzz Berger were coproducers and Anthony Page director. Irv Wilson was executive producer for Viacom.

MISSION: IMPOSSIBLE ▶ hour-long series on CBS (1966-73) of foreign intrigue and intricately executed feats of espionage, produced by Bruce Geller for Paramount TV. The original unit, for the first four seasons, featured Barbara Bain, Martin Landau, Peter Graves, Greg Morris and Peter Lupus. When Bain and Landau dropped out, Leonard Nimoy and Lesley Warren took their places. Lynda Day George appeared for one season, and Steven Hill took part in the first 18 episodes. Dubbed in 15 other languages, the series has been sold in 71 countries.

ABC revived the adventure series in 1988 following the Writer's Guild Strike, producing new episodes—and in some cases using old scripts—in Australia in order to have fresh programming for the 1988 fall season. The rehash starred Peter Graves of the original cast together with Phil Morris, the son of original cast's Greg Morris. Even the show's trademark introduction—a self-destructing audiotape—was updated with a self-destructing laser disc. ABC, however, retired the show in 1990, once the regular Hollywood pipeline was again pumping out shows for the networks.

MR. BELVEDERE ▶ ABC family sitcom (1985-90) whose pivotal character was an imperturbable British butler based on the character Clifton Webb had portrayed in a series of movies during the 1940s. Played by Christopher Hewitt, Mr. Belvedere attended to a middle-class American family with two busy parents and their three precocious children. Former baseball player Bob Uecker and Ilene Graff played the parents, George and Marsha Owens. Also featured were Rob Stone, Tracy Wells, Brice Beckham, Tricia Cast, and Michele Matheson. The show was produced by Lazy B/FOB Productions.

MISTER DUGAN ▶ unborn situation comedy with an unusual story of its own: it was canceled by its producers a few days before its scheduled premiere, although the network was eager to air it. The bizarre incident occurred in the spring of 1979 when Norman Lear and Alan Horn of T.A.T. Productions determined that the show, which was about a black freshman Congressman from Philadelphia, did not depict the lead character with sufficient dignity or as a "positive and accurate role model." A screening for the Congressional Black Caucus confirmed their own reservations, and they withdrew the program from CBS-TV and ordered production stopped after three episodes. CBS, which had no objection whatever to the portrayal of the Congressman by Cleavon Little, and which had promoted the show's May 11 debut in its Sunday lineup, was forced to fill the time with the second part of a two-part episode of the preceding show, *Alice*.

The setback was the third for the project that became *Mister Dugan*. The idea was born as a way to refurbish the faltering *Maude* series—Maude would become a freshman Congresswoman. But Bea Arthur, who portrayed Maude, elected not to continue for another season. The role was then adapted to a black Congressman and was to have been a vehicle for John Amos. But Amos withdrew before the shooting, and he was replaced by Little. Lear indicated, after his action, that the project was not dead but would have to be redesigned. It never was.

MISTER ED ▶ one of the first of the fantasy situation comedies, a successful CBS entry (1961-66) about a talking horse, whose voice was provided by Allan "Rocky" Lane. Alan Young played Wilbur Post, the only one to whom Mr. Ed ever spoke. Also featured were Connie Hines as Wilbur's wife, Carol, and Leon Ames and Florence MacMichael as neighbors Gordon and Winnie Kirkwood (Larry Keating and Edna Skinner were regulars, as neighbors Roger and Kay Addison, for the first two seasons). It was from Filmways.

MR. NOVAK ▶ hour-long dramatic series on NBC (1963-65) about an idealistic young English teacher named John Novak. It broke the ground for numerous other teacher shows. James Franciscus appeared in the title role, with chief support from Dean Jagger as school principal Albert Vane (replaced by Burgess Meredith, as new principal Martin Woodridge, in the final 13 episodes). MGM-TV produced it.

MR. PEEPERS ▶ a TV comedy classic despite its failure to win a vast audience in three seasons on NBC (1952-55). Commended for its casting, intelligent scripts and humor in a low key, it concerned a bookish science teacher, Robinson J. Peepers, and some of his quirky colleagues at a small town junior high school. Wally Cox starred, and featured were Tony Randall as English teacher Harvey Weskitt, Marion Lorne as Peeper's landlady, Mrs. Gurney, and Patricia Benoit as the school nurse, Nancy Remington, who married Peepers.

Mr. Peepers began as a summer replacement in July 1952 and impressed NBC sufficiently to win a premium slot in October. The programs were presented live.

Pat Benoit and Wally Cox as Nancy and Robinson Peepers in *Mr. Peepers*

MR. ROBERTS ▶ short-lived comedy-drama series on NBC (1965-66) based on the characters of the movie and play of that title (from Thomas Heggen's book) and inspired by the success of other military situation comedies in the 1960s. Roger Smith starred as Lieutenant Douglas Roberts, and Steve Harmon played Ensign Frank Pulver, George Ives was Doc and Richard X. Slattery portrayed Captain John Morton. It was by Warner Bros.

MISTER ROGERS' NEIGHBORHOOD ▶ a low-key public television children's series devoted to examining values, feelings and fears through the company of Mister Rogers (Fred Rogers) on a set representing his home. Rogers, a Presbyterian minister, employed an easy manner, gentle conversation, puppet plays and soothing songs in dealing with matters that were likely to concern children emotionally, such as nightfall, rejection, physical handicaps, going to the dentist, disappointment and death.

The program began locally on WQED Pittsburgh and then spread to other public stations until it became part of the regular weekday PBS children's fare, along with *Sesame Street* and *Electric Company*. In addition to performing in it, Rogers also wrote and produced the series.

After eight years, believing he had covered the full range of pertinent themes, Rogers suspended production to package the best of his 460 programs for repeat showing. However, he resumed production again in 1979 and by 1991 had produced an additional 190 shows, among them the first shows shot in selected locations. During the Persian Gulf War, he created special shows to calm the fears of young children, though his continuing theme, expressed as "people will like you just the way you are," is directed at building the child's self-esteem. His trademark sweater now resides in the Smithsonian.

Fred Rogers

MMDS (MULTICHANNEL MULTIPOINT DISTRIBUTION SERVICE) ▶ also known as wireless cable, this MDS service delivers multiple channels of programming, including pay TV and pay-per-view, via microwave directly into apartment buildings and homes. Able to offer a channel mix similar to that of a typical cable-TV system, MMDS was made possible in 1983 when an FCC frequency reallocation enabled MDS services to avail themselves of at least eight and as many as 33 high-frequency six-MHZ channels. Video compression techniques can significantly increase that capacity. Because it transmits over the air and uses no public right-of-way, MMDS is not locally regulated.

MNA RATINGS (MULTI-NETWORK AREA) ▶ a regular audience survey report of the A.C. Nielsen Co. indicating the relative potency of the networks in the top 70 markets where the programs of all three are in direct competition. (Daytime MNA ratings are drawn from 63 of those markets.) Covering a Sunday through Saturday period and issued approximately seven days after the broadcast week, the MNA report contains demographic breakdowns by age and sex, along with household viewing estimates for time periods. The populations of the MNA markets represent 65.7% of the total national audience.

MOD SQUAD ▶ successful hour-long series about a young trio with counterculture proclivities who channel their rebelliousness into useful police work. Produced by Thomas-Spelling Productions and playing on ABC (1968-73), it featured Peggy Lipton as Julie Barnes, Michael Cole as Pete Cochrane, Clarence Williams III as Linc Hayes and Tige Andrews as Captain Adam Greer.

MOLINE RENEWAL ▶ [Moline Television Corp./31 FCC 2d 263 (1971)] instance in which the FCC excused a licensee for failing to fulfill its license promise. In the comparative hearings in 1963 in which the Moline Television Corp. was awarded the license for Channel 8 in the quad-cities of Moline, East Moline and Rock Island, Ill., and Davenport, Ia., the company had proposed 12 locally produced public affairs series. By the conclusion of its initial three-year license period, the station, WQAD, had aired none of the promised programs. When Moline applied for renewal, a competing applicant, Community Telecasting Corp., also filed and the FCC scheduled a comparative hearing.

The commission, in considering Moline's application for renewal, excused the marked difference between promise and performance by noting that Moline's network, ABC, had substantially upgraded its public affairs programming during the three-year period. Additionally, the FCC found persuasive Moline's argument that its decision to spend money on its evening news program precluded financing the promised public affairs series.

In examining Moline's financial situation, the FCC found a substantial operating deficit, supporting the excuse for failure to produce the local series. The FCC held that these factors resulted in only a "slight demerit" against Moline. Since Moline integrated its ownership with its management very well, and because its owners were local residents, the commission awarded Moline a renewal of its license.

Commissioner Nicholas Johnson filed an angry dissent in which he chastised the majority for granting a renewal to an unqualified licensee when a qualified challenger stood ready to run the station. He felt that awarding a renewal to Moline in this instance indicated that the commission would never deny a renewal to an existing licensee, no matter how dismal his performance had been or how promising the challenger.

MOLNIYA (LIGHTNING) ▶ Soviet Union's domestic satellite system, the first domsat system inaugurated by any country. Since 1965, multiple Molniya satellites, in random elliptical orbits, have been relaying television and other telecommunications within the Soviet Union's borders.

MONASH, PAUL ▶ drama producer whose TV credits include *Peyton Place,* an ABC series in the mid-1960s, and *Judd for the Defense,* a legal drama series. In 1976, after producing a string of motion pictures, including *Butch Cassidy and the Sundance Kid* and *Slaughterhouse Five,* he joined CBS as a program v.p. in charge of movies for television and mini-series, but two years later he returned to independent production of TV movies.

MONITOR CHANNEL, THE ▶ news-oriented basic-cable network launched May 1, 1991, by Monitor Television, an offshoot of the *Christian Science Monitor.* The channel, currently with 3.5 million subscribers, debuted when available cable channels were in short supply and in order to gain carriage was forced to offer itself free to cable systems, unlike most other basic channels, which receive fees on a per-subscriber basis. As a result, the service was faced with surviving on the single revenue stream of advertising sales. Even as a give-away to cable systems, however, Monitor was reaching fewer than 4 million households by the end of 1991. Its programming involves news coverage, analysis, discussion and commentary, approaching current events in greater depth than CNN. John Hoagland, Jr., is chairman and CEO and Netty Douglass president.

MONKEES, THE ▶ musical situation comedy on NBC (1966-68) about a wild rock quartet, not unlike the Beatles. A group of singer-musicians was assembled for the series and their first recording promoted into a hit before the program premiered. The group then became, for several years, popular rock artists outside their fictive portrayal on TV. It consisted of

Davy Jones, Peter Tork, Mickey Dolenz and Mike Nesmith. The series was produced by Raybert Productions and Screen Gems. CBS carried the reruns in 1969 and ABC in 1972. *The Monkees* went into syndication in 1975.

MONOCHROME ▶ black-and-white television.

MONROE, BILL ▶ executive producer and moderator of NBC's *Meet the Press* (1975-84), having previously been Washington editor for *Today*. He joined NBC News in 1961 as Washington bureau chief, after having been news director of WDSU-TV New Orleans for six years. Monroe created the letters-to-the-editor segment for the *Today* show in 1984. In 1986, he retired after 25 years with the network.

MONTANUS, EDWARD (d. 1981) ▶ key executive of MGM-TV until his death, he was promoted to executive v.p. in 1976, and president in July 1977. He joined MGM-TV as director of syndication sales, then became head of network sales in 1970. Earlier he had been with ABC-TV sales and NBC Films in Chicago.

MONTE CARLO INTERNATIONAL TELEVISION FESTIVAL ▶ TV awards competition organized in 1961 by the Monaco principality, whose prizes (called *Golden Nymphs*) are awarded to writers in the fields of news and dramas, to directors and to actors and actresses. There are also other categories that vary from year to year.

MONTGOMERY, ROBERT (d. 1981) ▶ motion picture star who became prominent in TV in 1950 as host of a popular NBC drama anthology, *Robert Montgomery Presents,* which he also produced and in which he occasionally starred. He later became staff consultant to President Eisenhower for television—the first person to serve a President in that capacity—and a severe critic of the networks for what he considered their abuses of power.

Robert Montgomery Presents, slotted opposite *Studio One* on CBS, ran for six seasons with an assortment of one-hour adaptations and original TV plays. The series was to provide a springboard for the star's daughter, Elizabeth Montgomery, who was part of a stock company Montgomery had organized for the summer presentations in 1956.

Montgomery joined the White House at the urging of press secretary James Hagerty and functioned primarily as an acting coach to the President, who had felt uneasy before the TV cameras. Through Montgomery's instruction, Eisenhower gained the confidence to hold televised press conferences, and the coaching was also of benefit to the President's 1956 reelection campaign.

Montgomery had little to do with TV thereafter, except to denounce it, and his entry for *Who's Who in America* makes no mention of *Robert Montgomery Presents.* In 1969 he became president of the Lincoln Center Repertory Theater.

The members of the Monty Python comedy troupe

***MONTY PYTHON'S FLYING CIRCUS* ▶** BBC series of madcap and irreverent comedy, which, after enormous success in England, was sold to the Eastern Educational Network in 1974 by Time-Life Films. Its popularity on public stations, especially among the young, prompted a few sales to commercial stations and then a sale to ABC for two late-night specials in 1975. The 30-minute programs were free-form, consisting of sketches and blackouts. In the regular cast were Graham Chapman, John Cleese, Terry Gilliam, Eric Idle, Terry Jones and Michael Palin; they were also the writers. Ian Macnaughton was producer. When the group split up, Cleese and Palin went on to make movies in the U.S. Chapman died in 1989.

***MOONLIGHTING* ▶** stylish romantic comedy produced by ABC (1985-89) that revived Cybill Shepherd's flagging career and projected Bruce Willis to stardom. Shepherd played a former model, Maddie Hayes, who starts a detective agency after losing her fortune to an embezzler, taking in the brash and lascivious Willis as her partner, David Addison. Their antagonistic relationship was the motif of the series, with the sense of a powerful sexual attraction between them always evident. Eventually, by the end of the second season, the characters gave into it. The love-making episode received a great deal of advance publicity and drew a large audience. Other cast members included Allyce Beasley as Agnes Dipesto and Curtis Armstrong as Herbert Viola.

Inspired by the 1940 film *His Girl Friday,* the series was created by Glenn Gordon Caron and produced by Picturemaker Productions. Despite a devoted audience, the show was beset with production problems and personality conflicts that led to a hasty cancellation in 1989. The episodes often were not produced on time, while running over budget, and repeats were frequent during the regular season.

Bruce Willis and Cybill Shepherd, stars of the ABC series *Moonlighting*

MOONVES, LESLIE ▶ president of Lorimar Television since 1991, having had a rapid rise in the company he joined in 1986. Indeed his rise in Hollywood was itself swift.

After having worked briefly in theatre in Los Angeles, first as an actor and then as a producer, Moonves was hired by Columbia Pictures Television to work in comedy series development. Less than two years later he joined 20th Century-Fox to work on TV movies and soon became head of the department. His success in that area led to his being hired away by Lorimar. Before long he was asked to head TV series production as well as the movies-for-TV unit. A year after he took over, Lorimar became the top supplier of series to the networks. Later Moonves was named executive vice president in charge of all program production. When he was named president, Lorimar had 12 series on the networks and several others in the wings. The network series included *Knots Landing, Full House, Family Matters,* and *I'll Fly Away.*

MOORE, GARRY ▶ amiable personality and program host who thrived during a period when the ability to maintain a friendly rapport with the audience mattered more than having musical, acting or comedy talent. For a period during the late 1950s, when he was ubiquitous on CBS, Moore was reputed to have had the highest income of any TV performer.

His mainstay was *I've Got a Secret,* the Goodson-Todman panel show he moderated from 1952 to 1964, but the high point of his career was the prime-time *Garry Moore Show,* a popular variety series on CBS that began in 1958 and that was otherwise notable for launching the comedienne Carol Burnett.

One of the many who moved from network radio to TV, Moore made a number of efforts to establish a daytime variety show for CBS during the early 1950s before finding his niche with *Secret.* In the late 1960s an attempt was made to revive his Sunday night variety series; its failure marked his virtual retirement from the medium.

MOORE, MARY TYLER ▶ star of the CBS situation comedy *The Mary Tyler Moore Show,* which became a fixture in the network's Saturday night lineup through most of the 1970s before voluntarily canceling itself in 1977. In her portrayal in the series of Mary Richards, she came to represent the quintessential clean-cut single woman striving for a career and coping with life in the big city. The success of the series helped MTM Productions (the company in which she was partnered with her then-husband, Grant Tinker) to flourish as one of the leading independent suppliers to the networks.

Her first role in a TV series was as Sam, the secretary in *Richard Diamond, Private Eye,* but it called for only her legs to be shown and she left the series after 13 weeks. She attempted, unsuccessfully, two comedy-variety series in the 1978-79 season, the first called *Mary,* the second *The Mary Tyler Moore Hour.* She had been a professional dancer since the age of 17 and displayed that talent in several TV specials.

Moore achieved her first prominence in TV on *The Dick Van Dyke Show,* which ran five years on CBS in the 1960s. Following that she appeared in several movies and a Broadway show. Returning to television, she won an Emmy for the drama *First You Cry.* She also played opposite Robert Preston in the HBO film *Finnegan Begin Again* (1985), and was Mary Todd Lincoln in the NBC mini-series *Gore Vidal's Lincoln.* She attempted another series, *Annie McGuire,* for CBS in 1988-89, but it only lasted one season. In 1990 she starred in the made-for-TV movie *Thanksgiving Day.*

Mary Tyler Moore

MOORE, RICHARD A. ▶ president of KTTV Los Angeles during the 1950s and part of the 1960s who became part of the White House inner circle during the Nixon Administration and thus a witness in the Watergate proceedings. During his broadcast career, Moore helped organize the Television Advertising Bureau, the sales promotion organization for the industry that later became TVB. After the election of Nixon he became first a consultant to Robert Finch, when he was Secretary of HEW, and then special assistant to Attorney General John N. Mitchell in 1970. Before joining KTTV, Moore had been an attorney for ABC.

MOORE, THOMAS W. ▶ onetime president of ABC-TV (1963-68) and later founder and head of Tomorrow Entertainment, a General Electric subsidiary involved in motion picture and TV production. When GE disbanded the company in 1975 because of dissatisfaction with its profits, despite the production of a number of distinguished shows, Moore retained the name and continued to operate as an independent producer. The company had been responsible for such acclaimed filmed dramas as *The Autobiography of Miss Jane Pittman, In This House of Brede, Larry* and *I Heard the Owl Call My Name.* In association with Medcom, it produced the *Body Human* series of occasional specials.

Moore had been president of ABC during the network's desperate years, when it perennially ran third, and he jockeyed ABC into near contention with the leaders in 1965. The former program chief of ABC (1957-63), he became president when Ollie Treyz was dismissed after congressional criticism of an overly violent episode of *Bus Stop.*

Moore was the loser in an internal power struggle that occurred in 1968 when the expected merger with ITT fell through. Although he had appeared to be receiving a promotion as head of all ABC broadcast operations, he was in fact shunted aside. He resigned in the summer of 1968. Before Tomorrow Entertainment was organized, he served for a brief time as head of Ticketron.

During the election campaigns of 1972, he was TV advisor to Vice-President Agnew and later was appointed by President Nixon to the board of the Corporation for Public Broadcasting. In 1976 he became vice-chairman of the board. His CPB term ended the following year.

MORGAN, EDWARD P. ▶ ABC newsman, prominent in the 1950s and 1960s, who became known as the "voice of labor" through his 15-minute radio program of news and commentary sponsored by AFL-CIO because of his liberal views. As if to prove that his labor sponsors did not influence his editorial opinions, Morgan often was critical of organized labor in his commentary.

Before joining ABC in 1955, Morgan had been a correspondent for CBS News. In 1967 he took a two-year leave of absence from ABC to become senior correspondent of the Public Broadcasting Laboratory and anchorman of its TV news-magazine, *PBL.* A critic of commercial broadcasting even while working in it, Morgan had been a board member of the National Citizens Committee for Broadcasting, an activist group. He retired from ABC in 1975.

MORITZ, REINER ▶ one of the world's most successful producers of arts programs for television who was never tempted to depart into more popular areas. His production company, RM Arts, is based in Munich, and his distribution company, RM Associates, in London.

Moritz began as a music journalist for German newspapers and regional TV station NDR. In the 1960s he became involved in the production of music programs for Leo Kirch's company, Beta Film. He set up an independent company in 1970 with backing from Polygram, and 12 years later went out on his own as RM Arts. Though he could not take with him the catalog of already-produced arts programming, he was prolific enough in producing new programs to start his own distribution company in 1987. That company, RM Associates, is based in London in part because Moritz has been coproducer of *The South Bank Show,* an arts omnibus in which he is partnered with U.K. franchise holder, London Weekend Television.

MORK AND MINDY ▶ the runaway hit of the 1978-79 season, bringing instant stardom to comedian Robin Williams, who played an explorer from the planet Ork learning the ways of earthlings in Boulder, Colo. The character of Mork was introduced in an episode of *Happy Days* in the 1977-78 season, with such pleasing results—thanks to Williams's gift for sight comedy and verbal acrobatics—that a new series was immediately developed as a vehicle for him. Mindy McConnell, a young single woman, was played by Pam Dawber.

The show was so popular in its freshman season that it won ABC dominance of Thursday nights. Confident that Mork's audience was a loyal one, ABC programmers moved it to Sundays for the 1979-80 season, pitting it against *Archie Bunker's Place* (the continuation of *All in the Family*) in a showdown of sitcom giants. Ratings plummeted. In 1981 Jonathan Winters joined the cast as the son (a fully grown hatchling named Mearth) of Mork and Mindy, by now married. Ratings did not improve with the addition, however, and the show ended in 1982.

Garry K. Marshall, creator of *Laverne and Shirley* and *Happy Days,* and Tony Marshall were the executive producers. Bruce Johnson and Dale McRaven were the producers. The series was via Miller-Milkis Productions and Henderson Production Co., in association with Paramount Television.

MORSE, ARTHUR D. (d. 1971) ▶ former CBS News producer-writer who in 1967 became the first director of the International Broadcast Institute, a nonprofit organization, then based in Rome, which undertook studies of communications technologies. While serving in that capacity, Morse was killed in an automobile accident in Yugoslavia.

At CBS, he had worked for the *See It Now* series as a reporter and director during the 1950s, his credits including *The Lost Class of 1959* and *Clinton and the Law,* a report on integration in Clinton, Tenn. In 1960 he was assigned to *CBS Reports* as a producer-writer and worked on such programs as *Who Speaks for the South?, The Other Face of Dixie* and *The Catholics and the Schools.* He resigned from CBS in 1964 because of what he felt was a lack of support from the network for a report he was preparing on the tobacco industry and the health hazards of cigarette smoking.

MORTON, BRUCE ▶ CBS News correspondent, with the network since 1964, generally recognized as one of the ablest, albeit low-key members of the CBS panoply of journalists.

Morton's CBS career has included reporting on Vietnam, the space program from the Gemini through the Apollo missions, and major political stories throughout almost three decades of election campaign years. He covered House Judiciary Committee hearings on the impeachment of President Nixon, congressional hearings on the confirmations of Supreme Court Justices Powell and Rehnquist, and urban uprisings in Watts, Detroit, Philadelphia, Chicago and Washington, D.C.

Prior to CBS News, Morton was based in London for ABC News, covering events in the Congo as well as the conflicts in Cyprus and between Algeria and Morocco. He reported for Radio Press from Washington in 1959 and 1960. While still a student at Harvard College, from which he was graduated in 1952, Morton wrote and read newscasts for WORL, Boston.

MORTON DOWNEY, JR., SHOW, THE ▶ confrontational talk show of the late 1980s that was built around the contentious, abrasive personality of chain-smoking Morton Downey, Jr. Its purpose was to create angry verbal conflict on the screen, sometimes verging on physical conflict, rather than to illuminate issues. Downey presented himself as a liberal-hating arch-conservative who was known on occasion to order a guest off the set because he could not stand the person's views.

After a tryout locally on WWOR-TV New York in 1987, the nightly program went into national syndication the following year, usually scheduled at a late hour. It developed a cult following among young people, who enjoyed Downey's unorthodox, insulting style and perhaps also his jingoist politics. The show's studio audience of mostly young people cheered his antics and arguments. The program was controversial in itself, and never lacked for fireworks.

He gained much publicity from his sometimes scandalous behavior on the show. For example, in 1988 Downey wrapped an American flag around his buttocks and challenged his Iranian guest to "kiss it." On another occasion a fight broke out between the black minister Al Sharpton and black activist Roy Innis.

The show never ran out of energy but it did run out of viewer interest. Its syndication run ended after 14 months.

Morton Downey, Jr., in action on his talk show

MORTON, GARY ▶ former comedian who, on marrying Lucille Ball, became producer of her *Here's Lucy* series and her subsequent TV specials.

MOSEL, TAD ▶ dramatist who in the 1950s wrote for such series as *Omnibus* and *Playhouse 90,* his TV works including *Who Has Seen the Wind?, The Playroom, The Lawn Party* and *My Lost Saints.* In 1971 a TV version of his Pulitzer Prize-winning Broadway play, *All the Way Home,* was presented on *Hallmark Hall of Fame.*

***MOSES, THE LAWGIVER* ▶** six-part dramatization of the Biblical episode carried by CBS in the summer of 1975. The series was produced by Italy's RAI-TV in association with Britain's ATV-ITC and was filmed in Israel with an international cast. Burt Lancaster played Moses; Anthony Quayle, Aaron; Ingrid Thulin, Miriam; Irene Papas, Zipporah and Laurent Terzieff, Pharaoh. Richard Johnson was narrator. The script was by Anthony Burgess and Vittorio Bonicelli. Vincenzo Labella was producer and Gianfranco DeBosio director.

***MOTHERS-IN-LAW* ▶** NBC situation comedy (1967-69) about suburban neighbors who become in-laws. A vehicle for Eve Arden and Kaye Ballard, who played Eve Hubbard and Kaye Buell, it also featured Herb Rudley as Eve's husband Herb, Roger C. Carmel (for the first season) and Richard Deacon (for the second season) as Kaye's husband Roger, and Jerry Fogel as Kaye and Roger's son Jerry, who married Suzie Hubbard, played by Deborah Walley. It was via Desi Arnaz Productions.

***MT. MANSFIELD TELEVISION INC. v. FCC* ▶** [442 F2d 470 (2nd Circuit 1971)] Court of Appeals action upholding the constitutionality of the prime time-access rules. After the rules were introduced in 1970, the networks brought suit claiming that the rules violated the First Amendment. The U.S. Court of Appeals for the Second Circuit upheld the validity of the rules, claiming that the Red Lion case had held that the public's First Amendment rights took precedence over the broadcasters', and that under that implied theory of access the prime time-access rules appeared to be a reasonable attempt to fulfill that concept.

MOVIE CHANNEL, THE ▶ see Showtime/The Movie Channel.

***MOVIE OF THE WEEK* ▶** series of 90-minute features made expressly for ABC under arrangements with independent producers and various studios. Originally scheduled one night a week, the anthology did so well it was expanded to two nights. Each showcase carried approximately 24 originals and repeats. *MOW,* as it was abbreviated in the trade, ran from 1969 to 1975. But well before the ABC series ended, its title became generic, and it continues to be used as a synonym for made-for-TV movies.

MOVIES ON TV ▶ a program staple from the earliest days of commercial TV (to the extent that films were available before 1956) and since the mid-1960s a staple of the network prime-time hours as well. As late-vintage theatrical movies entered TV, with their mature themes and racy dialogue, television's program standards were forced to loosen; movies thus were a chief influence in the revolution in TV mores that took place in the early 1970s.

Television, which in the beginning was viewed as a threat to movies, has instead prolonged the life of motion pictures and indeed has given some of them perpetual life. It has also become a second market for movies (and pay cable a third, with home video a fourth), which for a time represented a virtual guarantee to producers of at least $1 million in advance of production for even average pictures.

William Boyd's old *Hopalong Cassidy* films, and other "B" westerns that had been sold to

TV by Republic Studios, proved as early as 1948 that movies were dynamite in the new medium. The major studios held back their libraries, however, for fear of helping the rival medium seal their doom.

Until 1956 movies trickled into TV from small companies and private owners. In 1955 ABC purchased 100 British films from J. Arthur Rank for an afternoon film festival. But the dam burst the following year when RKO Teleradio Pictures sold 740 movies and 1,000 shorts to C&C Super Corp., which then leased them to stations. Soon after, Columbia Pictures released a batch of pre-1948 titles through its syndication subsidiary, Screen Gems, and the other majors followed in rapid order—some packages going for as high as $50 million. All held the line at the theatrical release year of 1948 and were able to sell the films without payment of residuals.

Local stations fed heavily on the movies during the 1950s and the early 1960s, the feature-length films solving innumerable program problems for 90 minutes and two hours at a time. Independent stations used them to compete with the networks in prime time. WOR-TV New York developed the *Million Dollar Movie,* repeating the same film every night of the week. WGN-TV Chicago tailored a batch of old *Bomba, The Jungle Boy* movies into a successful one-hour prime-time series, and then assembled some odd-lot juvenile titles (*Tom Sawyer,* etc.) into a Friday evening series, *Family Classics,* which outrated some network shows.

The CBS o&os invested heavily in choice titles and created the parlay of *Early Show, Late Show* and *Late, Late Show* (late afternoon, post-prime time and post-midnight), which other stations adopted. Each film was rotated among the three showcases, then was rested and then repeated. The release of a library of Shirley Temple movies in 1957 proved a bonanza for the stations, and especially for the Ideal Toy Co., which sponsored.

When the major studios began selling their post-1948 titles after 1960, the networks began buying. NBC started the tide with *Saturday Night at the Movies,* and by 1966 each network had staked out one or two nights for movies. But the prime-time movies were a Pandora's Box: They wiped out most TV series in competition, leaving each network the problem of scheduling against them; their success brought escalations in price (by 1967 films of no particular distinction were fetching $800,000 for two plays); and, worst of all, there was a looming shortage of supply, made even more critical by the fact that the theatrical movies then in vogue were of a sophistication that made them unplayable under TV's program standards at the time.

NBC prepared to beat the shortage by contracting with Universal TV in 1966 for a steady supply of movies that would be made expressly for television at approximately $800,000 per title. The long-range deal resulted in the two-hour *World Premiere* anthology. ABC also dabbled in made-for-TV pictures by ordering three from MGM before devising the highly successful *Movie of the Week,* which arranged for the production of 90-minute features from a variety of producers at half the price NBC was paying Universal. CBS, ABC and Westinghouse Broadcasting all started their own motion picture production companies, but none was a financial success.

On the local level, the movie shortage was being felt even before the networks began buying features. The dwindling supply gave rise to the 90-minute talk shows—principally those of Mike Douglas and Merv Griffin—to fill the long gaps in the schedules. A number of syndicators speculated with dubbed foreign films but lost money in a market that rejected them.

In the early 1970s the movies that had previously been considered too mature for TV (*The Graduate, Love Story* and scores of others) found their way onto the home screens, some with a bit of editing. The networks rationalized their change of heart by citing the changing morality in the country and asserting their need to be in step with the times. But it was also true that the movie houses had been getting precisely the audience television and its advertisers were most eager to reach—-young adults in the 18-34 age group. To win them back to TV, the networks would have to alter their standards. The new permissiveness then was extended to TV's own series to make it possible for them to compete with movies.

By 1974 an average sort of movie no longer sufficed for prime time and the networks grew selective with titles and trimmed down to fewer showcases. The new mania was for blockbuster movies, preferably fresh out of theatrical release, to be shown as specials. ABC had provided the eye-opener in 1966 with *The Bridge on the River Kwai,* for which it had paid $2 million for two showings. The first outing on Sept. 25, 1966, drew a tremendous audience of more than 60 million, a record at that time for a televised movie. Later it was exceeded by *The*

Birds and a number of big theatrical hits purchased by the networks for astronomical amounts.

NBC paid $7 million for a single airing of *The Godfather,* $5 million for a single play of *Gone with the Wind,* and $3 million for the first TV rights to *Dr. Zhivago.* ABC paid $3.3 million for *The Poseidon Adventure* and charged advertisers $150,000 a commercial minute in that film. NBC charged $250,000 a minute for spots in *Gone with the Wind.*

The climate changed in the 1980s, and the networks' enthusiasm for Hollywood movies waned because the prior release of the films to pay cable and home video severely diminished the audience for even the top titles. The networks concentrated instead on exploitable made-for-television movies and mini-series (which are really movies in longer form), except in some instances when they paid enough to buy the pictures ahead of pay cable. Local stations, except for the independents, also began using fewer movies and turned instead to syndicated talk shows.

The availability of motion pictures to the new media was a prime factor in the steady erosion of the network audience during the 1980s. HBO, Cinemax, Showtime, The Movie Channel, Disney, American Movie Classics, TNT, WTBS, Lifetime, and USA all reached sizable audiences with movies. Moreover, as pay-per-view develops, it too may make a significant claim on television's viewership with movies recently out of theatrical release.

But perhaps the most significant incursion into television viewing was made by home video, especially on Friday and Saturday nights, as young people everywhere began gathering over rented videos in preference to watching television. *Saturday Night at the Movies,* which started it all at the networks, paradoxically took on a pesky new meaning.

See also Appendix.

MOVIETIME ▶ see E! Entertainment Television.

M.O.W. ▶ acronym for Movie of the Week but used in the industry as generic for any made-for-television movie.

MOYERS, BILL D. ▶ public television's master interviewer and essayist whose peripatetic shifts between PBS and CBS during the 1970s and 1980s gave ulcers to executives in both venues. After two stints with CBS, the first as chief correspondent for *CBS Reports,* the second as senior news analyst for the *CBS Evening News,* Moyers returned in 1986 to public TV, where his television career began.

When he returned to PBS, Moyers became a frequent and effective presence in both the documentary and interview programs. Working through his own production company, Public Affairs Television Inc., Moyers focused his critical eye on a wide range of topics in the social, political and international spheres. Some tended toward investigative journalism, namely *The Secret Government, God and Politics,* and *The Public Mind;* others were of cultural interest, such as *A Gathering of Men, Amazing Grace,* and *The Songs are Free with Bernice Johnson Reagon.* Two of his major interview series—*Joseph Campbell and the Power of the Myth* and *A World of Ideas*—resulted in best-selling books.

Moyers began his varied career at the age of 15 as cub reporter in the small East Texas town where he grew up. After college, he was tapped by President Kennedy to be Deputy Director of the Peace Corps and went on to become Special Assistant to President Johnson. He left the White House in 1967, became the publisher of *Newsday,* the Long Island daily, and then in 1971 entered public television as the host-moderator of the weekly public affairs series, *This Week,* produced by WNET New York. Not until the following year, however, with *Bill Moyers' Journal,* did he find the format that made best use of his unique talents, of which his *Essay on Watergate* gave convincing proof.

Bill Moyers

MOZARK PRODUCTIONS ▶ company name for the husband and wife team of Harry Thomason and Linda Bloodworth-Thomason, who wrote and produced the CBS sitcom *Designing Women* (1986—). Linda, the writer of the team, became an instant legend in the business by writing each of the first season's 22 episodes. She was also the creator of the CBS sitcom *Evening Shade* (1990—). Mozark Productions signed a contract with CBS to produce an additional six series.

MPAA (MOTION PICTURE ASSOCIATION OF AMERICA) ▶ organization formed in 1922 to represent the principal distributors and producers of movies in the U.S. and to preserve and enlarge the global market for their films. Television is one such market, and MPAA, under its president Jack J. Valenti, has aggressively sought FCC regulations that would promote the growth of pay cable as a potentially lucrative new market for feature films. It also led the film industry's battle to preserve the Financial Interest and Syndication Rule.

MSO (MULTIPLE SYSTEM OPERATOR) ▶ a cable-TV company that owns and operates more than one cable system. Most of the early cable installations were known as "mom and pop" operations, small systems locally owned. But a wave of acquisitions and consolidation in the 1980s concentrated ownership in a handful of large companies. In fact, the nation's top MSO, Denver-based Tele-Communications Inc., serves nearly 25% of all cable subscribers. The largest MSOs also operate within a tangled web of investments in other cable operations and in the networks that supply programming. The ownership of Turner Broadcasting System, for example, includes a group of 16 cable operators.

See also Appendix.

MSTV (ASSOCIATION FOR MAXIMUM SERVICE TELEVISION) ▶ organization of local broadcasters formed in 1956 to preserve the coverage, range and power of their stations against proposals by the FCC to increase the number of VHF stations by reducing the distances covered by existing stations. Formerly known as AMST, the organization is essentially concerned with protecting the maximum effective radiated power permitted for stations by the FCC rules adopted in July 1956. It was instrumental in securing passage of the All-Channel Receiver legislation in 1962 and has mounted resistance to proposed reallocations of the television broadcast spectrum to non-broadcast frequency use.

In recent years the 250-member association, whose president is Margita White, has involved itself in the testing of several proposed HDTV broadcast systems.

MTV/VH-1 ▶ in concept and execution, one of the medium's most influential television channels, not only in the U.S. but internationally. With satellite-distributed versions in all parts of the globe, it has become the nearest service in existence to a world network, largely because interest in rock music is high among youth everywhere. Rock music is what MTV is about.

MTV established the music video as a popular entertainment form, and the production styles and techniques have been borrowed by TV commercials and to some degree by mainline shows. The videos have also become vital in the promotion of new recordings. The basic-cable channel, which made the term "VJ"—short for video jockey—a household word, was launched in 1980 by Warner Amex Satellite Entertainment and acquired in 1987 by Sumner Redstone's Viacom. While music videos are the staple of MTV's around-the-clock programming, introduced by on-camera VJs, the network also carries certain long-form programs, such as its pop culture game-show *Remote Control,* that are consistent with its rock 'n'roll image.

Reaching 56 million cable homes in the U.S., MTV has had such an impact on American pop music culture that its playlist, rather than those of radio stations, now sets musical trends and launches new artists. Its critics charge that MTV's glorification of music videos has placed a greater importance on the visual appeal of artists, resulting in popular tastes being more influenced by a group's style of dress, rather than the substance of its music.

In 1991 MTV announced its intention of spinning itself off into three separate channels, each focusing on a musical genre. Sister channel VH-1 was launched in 1985 with an effort to appeal to the musical tastes of the somewhat older "baby boomers," but has floundered through several attempts at determining the precise measure of those tastes. The 1991 format change to "The Greatest Hits of Music Video" is the most recent effort to strike a chord with the thirtysomething-and-beyond audience.

Tom Freston is chairman and CEO of MTV Networks and Edward Bennett the president of VH-1.

MUDD and TROUT ▶ news-anchor team mounted by CBS in 1964 in response to the popularity of Huntley and Brinkley on NBC, to no avail. Roger Mudd and Robert Trout had a short run as a team. They replaced Walter Cronkite as anchor for the 1964 Democratic national convention, but Cronkite was back at his post for the Republican conclave that year.

MUDD, ROGER ▶ congressional correspondent and essayist for *The MacNeil-Lehrer NewsHour.* Prior to joining the PBS nightly program in 1987, Mudd spent seven years at NBC News, where he was variously chief Washington correspondent, chief political correspondent, co-host of *Meet the Press,* anchor of *American Almanac* and, briefly, co-anchor with Tom Brokaw of *NBC Nightly News.* Mudd joined NBC from CBS News in 1981 after CBS selected Dan Rather, and not him, to be succeed Walter Cronkite as the national newscast anchor.

When hired by NBC, he was assured of becoming John Chancellor's successor as anchor of *Nightly News.* Mudd later agreed to team up with Brokaw to smooth the way for Brokaw's new contract with NBC. They made their debut together in April 1982. A year later, Brokaw was made sole anchor.

Mudd became a CBS News correspondent in 1961. Handsome, articulate and respected by his peers for his writing abilities, he was considered by many to be heir-apparent to Cronkite as the network's premier anchorman.

Mudd, who joined CBS from its Washington affiliate, WTOP-TV, covered all political conventions and elections since 1962 and served as anchor or reporter for documentaries such as *The Selling of the Pentagon* (1971) and special reports in 1973-74 on the unfolding of the Watergate story, the resignation of Spiro Agnew, the appointment of Gerald Ford as Vice President, the Senate Watergate hearings and the resignation of President Nixon.

With the primary assignment of covering Congress, Mudd was anchor of the Saturday edition of *The CBS Evening News* (1966-73) and also the Sunday edition (1970-71).

MUELLER, MERRILL ▶ broadcast journalist (1945-74), working first for NBC News and then, for six years, ABC News. Between the two networks, he was a floor reporter at all political conventions from 1952 to 1974. At NBC, he was variously news director for London, Asia and the Mediterranean and newscaster for the *Today* program, preceding Frank Blair. From 1957 until he joined ABC in 1968, he was a senior correspondent in New York and worked on numerous major stories, including the assassination of President Kennedy. With ABC, he was a roving correspondent, based in New York and, for a time, in Los Angeles.

On leaving the network, he became a consultant to the federal government in Washington for two years and then Newhouse Professor of broadcast and print journalism at Syracuse University.

MUGGS, J. FRED ▶ chimpanzee who received a five-year contract from NBC for appearances on the *Today* show in the early 1950s and who later had his own local TV show in New York for a brief period. In 1972 he joined Busch Gardens, a family entertainment park in Tampa, Fla., but continued to do occasional TV guest shots. His trainers were Bud Mennell and Roy Waldron, pet shop owners who had purchased him as a baby for $600.

MULHOLLAND, ROBERT E. ▶ former president of the National Broadcasting Company (1981-84), named to the post when Grant Tinker succeeded Fred Silverman as head of the company with the title of chairman. Tinker chose to continue living on the West Coast, and Mulholland was in day-to-day charge of the company's New York headquarters. Previously he was president of the television network (since 1977), after having briefly been executive v.p. in charge of the Moscow Olympics. Most of his career was spent as an NBC News executive.

Mulholland, who began as a news writer for WMAQ-TV, the NBC o&o in Chicago, had risen in 13 years to executive v.p. of NBC News with overall responsibility for all TV news gathering operations, news documentaries and news at the owned stations. From 1963 to 1967, he acquired a background as a field producer in Chicago and then in Europe, and for the next four years served as West Coast news director, in which capacity he launched the first two-hour local news program in a major market. This earned him a chance to become producer of the *NBC Nightly News* and then, in 1972, executive producer.

MULL, MARTIN ▶ comedian who first gained attention as the fictional host of the mock talk show *Fernwood 2-nite* (1977-78) and later as the real occasional guest host of *Tonight.* Mull made his television debut in the offbeat comedy series *Mary Hartman, Mary Hartman* (1976-77). In 1984 he produced and starred in his own situation comedy series, *Domestic Life,* but it was unsuccessful.

MULTIMEDIA ▶ combination of more than two media in any single application, most often used with reference to a combination of video, audio, text and graphics available on a single desktop system.

MULTIPLE OWNERSHIP RULES ▶ limits on station ownership imposed by the FCC to prevent undue concentration of economic power and to promote a diversification of viewpoints. Under present rules, any single licensee may have ownership interests of more than 5% in no more than twelve full-power, full-service AM, FM and TV stations (the "12-12-12" rule). Absent a waiver, commercial broadcasters may not own more than one station in a community (the "one-to-a-market" rule). Public broadcasters are exempt from the one-to-a-market rule to the extent that they may operate one VHF and one UHF in the same community.

The first multiple ownership rule was adopted in 1940. It pertained only to FM stations and forbade ownership by any one person of more than one station serving substantially the same area. The rule also provided that ownership of more than six stations would be a concentration of control inconsistent with the public interest.

In 1953 the commission adopted a revised multiple ownership rule that provided that no person may hold any interest, direct or indirect, in more than five TV, seven AM and seven FM stations. The validity of these rules was sustained by the Supreme Court (*U.S. v. Storer Broadcasting Co.*). In 1954 the FCC amended the rules to permit ownership of seven TV stations but restricted ownership of VHF stations to five. This was designed to promote the development of UHF.

While the FCC has never decided to bar newspapers as a class from ownership, it has consistently favored applicants without newspaper experience in selecting among competing applicants for a license. In addition, the commission has also followed the consistent practice of considering whether an applicant already has other broadcast interests even though such interests were permitted by multiple ownership rules.

In 1970 the commission proposed a controversial rule that would require divestiture within five years to reduce one party's media holdings in any market to one or more daily newspapers, or one TV station or one AM-FM combination. The rule would require that if a broadcast station were to purchase one or more daily newspapers in the same market, it would be required to dispose of any broadcast station. No grant for a broadcast station license would be made to a newspaper owner in the same market.

After much discussion of this rule, the FCC, in 1975, adopted a modified version which would require divestiture by 1980 only in instances where the degree of media concentration could be considered egregious. The FCC defined an egregious situation as one in which a party owns and operates the only newspaper published in a community, as well as the only TV or radio stations in that community. A newspaper could own the only radio station if there is a separately owned TV station.

In 1977 the D.C. Court of Appeals, in *NCCB v. FCC,* determined that the FCC has the authority to forbid future formation of jointly owned newspaper-broadcasting combinations located in the same communities. However, the court ruled that the FCC erred in its reasoning that divestiture should be ordered only when it can be demonstrated that the public interest is harmed by the combinations. The court concluded that exactly the opposite standard should apply—that divestiture should be required except in those cases where evidence clearly shows cross-ownership to be in the public interest.

MULTIPLEXING ▶ in cable, the use of two or more channels to present the same lineup of programs but at different times, to make programs more available to viewers. Thus if HBO were able to acquire two additional channels, it might present the same movie at 8, 9 and 10 p.m. Companies engaged in pay-per-view were the first to recognize the need for more than a single channel, not only to give the consumer a range of tune-in options but also to get around the problem of the three-hour time difference from coast to coast. Multiplexing became a hot idea in the early 1990s with the prospect of digital compression technology, which could turn 30-channel cable systems into 150-channel systems without the need to rebuild. The same technology is applicable to satellite transponders, giving each the capacity for at least five channels instead of only one. The coming multiplication of capacity has virtually every major cable network contemplating some form of multiplexing, and the major terrestrial networks as well. It is expected to be used initially in satellite distribution to the different time zones.

MULTIPOINT DISTRIBUTION SERVICE ▶ see MDS (Multipoint Distribution Service).

MUNRO, J. RICHARD ▶ former co-chairman and CEO of Time-Warner Inc. who retired in the spring of 1991. Prior to the merger of

Time and Warner in 1989, Munro was chairman and CEO of Time Inc. He had been elevated to president in 1980, after having been head of all video enterprises of Time Inc. since October 1975. The Video Group flourished under Munro's direction and rose from the smallest of Time's three main divisions to the largest, in terms of revenues and profits. Its extraordinary success—especially that of HBO—pointed the way to Time Inc.'s future and made it possible for Munro to leap over executives of the publishing division to the presidency when Andrew Heiskell retired.

Munro joined *Time* in 1957 in the magazine's circulation department, then moved to *Sports Illustrated* where he rose to become general manager and, eventually, publisher.

MUNSTERS, THE ▶ fantasy situation comedy about a family of monsters living ordinary domestic lives. The head of the family, Herman Munster (Fred Gwynne), was physically modeled on the Frankenstein monster. Other regulars were Yvonne DeCarlo as Lily Munster, Butch Patrick as Herman and Lily's son Eddie, Beverly Owen (for the first half-season) and Pat Priest as their niece Marilyn and Al Lewis as Grandpa. Produced by Universal, it ran on CBS (1964-65) and had been created by Joe Connolly and Bob Mosher.

MUPPET SHOW, THE ▶ syndicated variety series (1976-81) featuring Jim Henson's large cast of Muppets (moppet-like marionette/puppets, including Kermit the Frog, Miss Piggy and Fozzie Bear) and a live guest star each episode. As a prime-access entry, it opened on around 160 stations domestically, including those owned and operated by CBS, and in scores of foreign markets. It was produced in England by ITC and Henson Associates, with Gary Smith and Dwight Hemion as creative consultants and Jack Burns as producer-writer. It grew to be a tremendous hit in England and Europe, while in the U.S. it ranked consistently among the top-rated prime time-access series. By 1978, with its global spread having reached about 100 countries, it had become one of the most popular television shows in the world. In 1979, the TV series spun off a theatrical feature, *The Muppet Movie.*

MURDER, SHE WROTE ▶ highly successful hour-long mystery series on CBS (1984—) built around a writer, Jessica Fletcher, whose everyday life plays out like one of her best-selling detective novels. Although the episodic storylines are somewhat formulaic, which is often the case in the whodunit genre, the series has been a splendid vehicle for the veteran actress, Angela Lansbury. The show is one of the few in TV history in which the sole lead character is a middle-aged woman.

Created by Richard Levinson (now deceased), William Link, and Peter S. Fisher (who also did *Columbo* and *Ellery Queen*), *Murder She Wrote* was one of the most durably popular series of the decade. Supporting players have included Tom Bosley as Sheriff Amos Tupper, William Windom as Dr. Seth Haslett, Michael Horton as Grady Fletcher, and Ron Mazak as Mort Metzger. The show is produced by Link and Fisher, and Universal Television.

Angela Lansbury as writer-sleuth Jessica Fletcher in *Murder, She Wrote*

MURDOCH, RUPERT ▶ as chief executive of News Corporation Ltd., a one-man worldwide media conglomerate with newspaper and television holdings on three continents, and arguably the world's most powerful media baron. Building on a foundation in his native Australia, Murdoch has assembled a newspaper, magazine and TV empire with, at one time or another, such disparate holdings as New York's untamed *Village Voice* and the sobersided London *Times.* Two of Murdoch's contributions have forever altered the media landscape: his against-the-odds creation of a fourth American television network—a gamble many have tried but none have won—and his equally high-risk success in establishing Sky Channel, Europe's first direct broadcast satellite.

The Fox Television Network began challenging the "big three" in 1986, soon after Murdoch spent $575 million to purchase Twentieth Century Fox—together with its highly innovative chairman, Barry Diller—and another $2 billion to acquire Metromedia's TV stations in six of America's key markets. It is a measure of the man that he gave up his Australian citizenship and swore allegiance to the U.S. to comply with the law prohibiting foreign ownership of broadcast stations.

Rupert Murdoch

In his efforts to launch a cable and DBS service, first for all of Europe (Sky Channel), later for the U.K. only (Sky Television), Murdoch faced the problem of winning over viewers already paying for their TV through a license fee. He succeeded, however, in building an audience for Sky Television with four channels of lively programming. He then beat off the challenge of a competing satellite, British Sky Broadcasting (BSB), by merging with his rival to create British Sky Broadcasting (BSkyB).

MURPHY BROWN ▶ sophisticated hit comedy series set in a Washington, D.C., newsroom, which revolves around an appealing but somewhat neurotic star reporter of a successful news-magazine show. Candice Bergen plays the title character, but the show is otherwise an ensemble piece deriving much of the comedy from the characters in the newsroom. The resident cast includes Grant Shaud as Miles Silverberg, Faith Ford as Corky Sherwood, Joe Regalbuto as Frank Fontana, Charles Kimbrough as Jim Dial, Pat Corley as Phil and Robert Pastorelli as Eldin Bernecky. The show premiered on CBS in 1988 and won a staunch following. It was created by Diane English and Joel Shukovsky, who are also its executive producers.

MURPHY, EDDIE ▶ big box-office comedy star in films who, like many another, was lifted from obscurity by television. He was one of several to hit it big on *Saturday Night Live,* appearing as a regular from 1981-84. Since then his work has largely been confined to movies, although he did a two-hour, one-man comedy concert for HBO where he gave free rein to his own brand of humor, which was far too scatological to have played on conventional TV. His production company sold *The Royal Family* to CBS for the 1991-92 season.

The cast of the popular CBS series *Murphy Brown*

MURPHY, THOMAS S. ▶ chairman and former CEO of Capital Cities/ABC. A onetime Brooklyn Democratic politician, he walked away from a career in politics in 1954 for a job in broadcasting with a new UHF television station in Albany, WROW-TV. Ten years later he was chairman/CEO of the station's parent, Capital Cities Communications, which he continued to build into one of the country's leading media companies. Highly regarded in the business world generally, as well as in the broadcast and publishing industries, Murphy was often singled out as a model chief executive.

In 1985 Murphy engineered the acquisition of ABC by Cap Cities for $3.5 billion. Murphy never forgot his roots in broadcasting, and despite leading ABC through a painful period of cost-cutting and layoffs, he frequently spoke about the need to preserve broadcasting's "public trust" responsibilities. In 1990 Murphy stepped down as CEO and handed the responsibility to his longtime colleague, Daniel Burke, who had been his second-in-command at Cap Cities as well as at ABC.

Thomas S. Murphy

MURRAY, BILL ▶ one of the several alumni of NBC's *Saturday Night Live* who hit it big on the show and then all but abandoned television for movies. Murray's showcase years on *SNL* were 1978 and 1979. From there he made an easy transition to such youth-appeal films as *Meatballs* (1979), *Stripes* (1981) and *Ghostbusters* (1984). The films continue almost annually because Murray is box-office gold. But the trigger for his stardom was two seasons on television.

MURRAY, KEN ▶ early variety-show emcee who had three seasons (1950-53) with *The Ken Murray Show.* Later he did guest shots on other programs showing his home movies of celebrities.

MURROW, EDWARD R. (d. 1965) ▶ broadcasting's supreme journalist, whose verbal gifts and superb delivery were matched by his humane values and high professional standards. He not only was radio's premier reporter in covering World War II for CBS—famous for his broadcasts from the rooftops of London in language one commentator called "metallic poetry"—but also was responsible for assembling the crackerjack team of foreign correspondents that served as a cadre for CBS News for the next quarter century.

Murrow's greatest work, however, was on the domestic front, principally with the series *See It Now,* on which, in 1954, he succeeded in exposing the ruthless tactics of and injustices perpetrated by Sen. Joseph McCarthy. It was undoubtedly the most courageous undertaking in TV history. Several years later, for *CBS Reports,* he contributed the memorable documentary expose of the inhumanities suffered by migrant workers in the U.S., *Harvest of Shame.*

Legendary broadcast journalist Edward R. Murrow

Murrow also was host of a popular prime time series, *Person to Person,* on which he visited electronically the residences of the famous for live interviews. His two nighttime series ran concurrently, *See It Now* for eight seasons and *Person to Person* for five.

Fascinated with TV's ability to broadcast from several places at once, Murrow extended the *Person to Person* concept to other continents for a weekend discussion series, *Small World* (1958-59).

He had two trademarks: the closing line, "Good night ... and good luck," and the cigarette. Often on the screen he was engulfed in a cloud of smoke. He died of lung cancer at just about the time the advertising of cigarettes on TV had grown into a controversial issue.

Murrow had joined CBS in 1935 as director of talks and education, and two years later he became European director. His distinguished work during the war, both in reporting and managing the CBS forces, earned him a promotion in 1945 as v.p. and director of public affairs and member of the board of directors. He gave up the vice-presidency, however, to do *See It Now.*

Murrow left CBS in 1961 to become director of the U.S. Information Agency in the Kennedy Administration. By that time he had become disenchanted with commercial television and openly critical of its devotion to escapism. The cancellation of *See It Now* in 1958, for competitive reasons, had had a damaging effect on his spirit.

Brent Musburger

MUSBURGER, BRENT ▶ sports announcer for ABC Sports since 1990 after being dropped by CBS Sports, where he had been since 1975 and where he was best known as the anchor of CBS's *NFL Today*. He was the lead play-by-play announcer for the NCAA Final Four Basketball Tournament and hosted *CBS Sports Saturday/Sunday*, the U.S. Open Tennis Championships, The NBA Finals, the Masters Tournament and the Pan American Games. He started in broadcasting in Chicago in 1968 as sports director for WBBM Radio. Later he worked for WBBM-TV, before moving to Los Angeles to co-anchor the nightly news for KNXT-TV.

MUSEUM OF TELEVISION AND RADIO ▶ a repository of audio tapes, video tapes, scripts, books and other written materials from broadcasting's seventy-year history. Formerly the Museum of Broadcasting, the institution changed its name in 1991 to embrace the burgeoning world of nonbroadcast video, moving at the same time into larger and more elegant quarters, designed expressly for its needs, at 25 West 52nd in New York's midtown. Established in 1975 under a personal grant from the late CBS chairman William S. Paley, the museum opened its doors the following year with a modest collection of tapes from all three networks and independent sources. It has continued to expand its collection and regularly programs exhibits of its audio and video holdings. The museum is governed by a board broadly representative of the industry. Its president since 1981, Robert Batscha, succeeded the museum's first president, Robert Saudek, one-time producer of *Omnibus*. Its collection, partly supported by individual memberships, is open to the public.

MUSIC, LORENZO ▶ performer and sometime writer and producer. He and his partner, David Davis, created *The Bob Newhart Show*, produced *Rhoda*, and were line producers of *The Mary Tyler Moore Show*. Music wrote episodes of all three series.

In *Rhoda*, Music played the voice of Carlton, the doorman, which he later turned into an award-winning animated series. In 1976 he and his wife starred in a syndicated series, *The Lorenzo and Henrietta Music Show*, but it was unsuccessful and had only a brief run. In the 1980s Music played the voice of Garfield the cat on animated TV specials and occasionally wrote these shows.

***MY FAVORITE MARTIAN* ▶** moderately successful CBS fantasy series (1963-66) in which Ray Walston portrayed a whimsical visitor from Mars who attaches himself to newspaper reporter Tim O'Hara, played by Bill Bixby. The two decide to name Walston's character Martin O'Hara, and they tell people he's Tim's uncle. Featuring Pamela Britton as their landlady, Lorelei Brown, and Alan Hewitt as police officer Bill Brennan, it was by Jack Chertok Productions.

***MY FRIEND FLICKA* ▶** sentimental half-hour series that ran several times on all three networks, and then in syndication, although only one season's worth of episodes had been produced. CBS carried it initially in 1956, NBC played the reruns the following year, then ABC purchased the 39 episodes for the 1959 and 1960 seasons. The reruns went to CBS in 1961, then back to NBC in 1963 and back again to CBS for the next two years.

Flicka, concerning a boy's love for his horse, was based on the book by Mary O'Hara and the subsequent motion picture. It featured Johnny Washbrook as the boy, Ken McLaughlin, Gene Evans and Anita Louise as his parents, Rob and Nell, Frank Ferguson as Gus and an Arabian sorrel called Wahama as Flicka. It was by 20th Century-Fox TV.

***MY FRIEND IRMA* ▶** early situation comedy (1952-54) that featured Marie Wilson as a voluptuous and naive good samaritan, Irma Peterson. Others in the cast were Cathy Lewis as Irma's sensible roommate, Jane Stacey, then (after Lewis's departure) Mary Shipp as her new roommate, Kay Foster; and Sid Tomack as Irma's crafty boyfriend, Al, followed by Hal March as her new boyfriend, Joe.

***MY LITTLE MARGIE* ▶** father-daughter situation comedy (1952-55) produced for syndication by Hal Roach Jr. and Roland Reed. It proved a durable item and was one of the first filmed shows whose reruns were "stripped," i.e., presented daily. It featured Charles Farrell as Vern Albright and Gale Storm as his daughter, Margie Albright.

MY THREE SONS ▶ highly successful situation comedy vehicle for film star Fred MacMurray that ran six seasons on ABC (1959-65) and then seven more on CBS. MacMurray portrayed a widower, Steve Douglas, raising three sons with the help of a housekeeping uncle (Charley O'Casey, played by William Demarest), who was preceded in the early seasons by a housekeeping grandfather (Bub O'Casey, played by William Frawley). The sons were Tim Considine as Mike, Don Grady as Robbie, and Stanley Livingston as Chip; later, Stanley's brother Barry Livingston joined the family as an adopted son, Ernie. As the boys aged, the initial premise of the series changed. In the 10th season, Beverly Garland joined the cast as MacMurray's new wife, Barbara Harper. Meanwhile, marriage involving the sons brought other women into the cast, as well as children. The series was by Don Fedderson Productions.

MYSTERY! ▶ the umbrella title for a weekly public TV series, on PBS since 1979, presenting a variety of multipart dramas imported from British television by WGBH Boston and hosted in its American incarnation by actor Vincent Price, and later, Diana Rigg. *Mystery!* is closely identified with five of its best-known fictional programs, *Rumpole of the Bailey, Poirot, Reilly, Ace of Spies,* Agatha Christie's *Miss Marple,* and Dorothy Sayers's *Lord Peter Wimsey.*

N

NAKED CITY ▶ realistic police series, based on Mark Hellinger's motion picture, that had a season's run in half-hour form on ABC (1958), then was revived successfully with a new cast in hour-long form (1960-63). The shorter version starred John McIntire as Lieutenant Dan Muldoon and James Franciscus as Detective Jim Halloran; the longer, Horace McMahon as Lieutenant Mike Parker, Paul Burke as Detective Adam Flint and Nancy Malone as Libby, Flint's girlfriend. Both were by Herbert B. Leonard's Shelle Productions and Screen Gems.

NAKED HOLLYWOOD ▶ a six-part documentary series produced by the BBC that afforded a candid and somewhat embarrassing view of the Hollywood movie business behind the scenes. The series aired in the U.S. on the Arts & Entertainment network, premiering in July 1991. Each one-hour episode examined a different aspect of the film industry through interviews and movie footage, examining the roles of actors, producers, directors, agents and writers and featuring many of the major players in Hollywood. Executive producers were Michael Jackson, John Whiston, and Abbe Raven.

NAME OF THE GAME ▶ an attempt by NBC to create three 90-minute series (1968-70) in one by rotating three heroes of a single publishing empire. Gene Barry had every third episode as *Crime* magazine publisher Glenn Howard, Robert Stack portrayed senior editor Dan Farrell and Tony Franciosa was investigative reporter Jeff Dillon. Regularly featured were Susan Saint James as research assistant Peggy Maxwell and Ben Murphy as assistant Joe Sample. The series was produced by Universal TV and grew out of a made-for-TV movie, *Fame Is the Name of the Game.*

NAME THAT TUNE ▶ see Game Shows.

NARROWCASTING ▶ in theory, the opposite of broadcasting, directing the programming to an intensely interested specific viewership rather than to the broadest possible mass audience. Cable promulgated the term in a marketing pitch to suggest that its approach was different from broadcast television's—in effect promising channels to serve virtually every interest. But nearly all basic-cable channels need advertising, and most TV advertisers want larger audiences than the narrowcasting ideal can provide. So, as an example, a channel that purported to serve the arts buff merged with another and renamed itself Arts & Entertainment. With concessions made continually to expanding a channel's audience, what may have been intended as genuine narrowcasting has, in the main, become essentially niche programming.

NASHVILLE NETWORK, THE (TNN) ▶ basic-cable network whose programming centers on all things "country": country music, auto racing, cooking, fishing, tractor pulls and the reruns of *Hee Haw*. TNN, which reaches 54 million cable homes, began in 1983 under the ownership of Opryland USA, parent of the Nashville institution, the Grand Ole Opry, and Group W Satellite Communications, which provides the marketing and distribution. In 1988 the two companies launched a radio program service based on the cable channel and joined with Meredith Corp. in publishing a magazine, *Country America*. In January 1991 Opryland and Group W Satellite bought a small cable program service, Country Music Television (CMT), from James William Guercio and Sillerman Magee Communications Management. CMT, reaching 14 million homes, is a country-western version of MTV, playing country music videos around the clock.

Tom Griscom is senior vice president of broadcasting for Opryland, but the day to day operations of the two channels are the responsibility of Group W Satellite, of which Don Mitzner is president and Lloyd Werner, senior vice president for sales and marketing.

NATIONAL ACADEMY OF TELEVISION ARTS AND SCIENCES (NATAS) ▶ national organization formed in 1957 to confer annual awards of excellence (Emmy awards) in TV production and performance in the manner of the older motion picture academy. Until a rift developed in 1976 between East and West Coast factions, NATAS consisted of 13 chapters in major cities and had a total membership of about 11,000, representing both the creative and technical sides of the medium. The chapters not only participated in the national voting for awards but also presented local awards.

The schism occurred when the presidency of NATAS shifted from Robert Lewine of the Hollywood chapter to John Cannon of New York who derived his support chiefly from the hinterland chapters. The Hollywood group rebelled and mounted a boycott of the 1977 awards, arguing that its members were the ones who performed in and produced, wrote and directed virtually all the shows that would be considered for awards. The Hollywood members maintained that those who belonged to the hinterland chapters were not really peers and should not have had the right to oust a president who, in their view, had performed outstandingly.

Also vexing to the dissidents was the fact that Hollywood, as the largest chapter with 4,800 members, had only 10 trustees and therefore could not control an organization in which New York and the regional chapters together had 20 trustees.

When all attempts to resolve the differences failed, the Hollywood unit withdrew from NATAS and created a separate organization called the Academy of Television Arts and Sciences. In addition, it sued to retain the exclusive use of the name "Emmy" for its awards, basing the claim in that the Hollywood unit had been presenting Emmy awards for several years before the national academy was formed.

All suits were dropped and the matter settled with a compromise. ATAS, the Hollywood organization, would have the rights to the Emmy awards for nighttime programs. The National Academy of Television Arts and Sciences, with headquarters in New York, would control the Emmy awards for daytime, sports, news and local programs. It would also continue to publish the *Television Quarterly*.

NATIONAL ASSOCIATION OF BROADCAST EMPLOYEES AND TECHNICIANS (NABET) ▶ union representing engineers and certain non-technical personnel at NBC, ABC and more than 75 local TV stations, with a total membership of around 9,500 employees. NABET grew out of the Association of Technical Employees, organized in 1933, which became the bargaining agent at NBC. When NBC was forced to split off its Blue Network, NABET found itself with built-in jurisdiction at the new company, which became ABC. An attempt in the early 1950s to gain jurisdiction over CBS technical personnel, represented by IBEW (International Brotherhood of Electrical Workers), failed.

The union adopted the name NABET in 1940 when it began to extend its representation beyond technical workers to other job classifications, including news writers, publicity writers and clerical departments. NABET struck NBC for three weeks in 1959 and, in a contract dispute with both networks, struck ABC in the fall of 1967. A protracted strike at ABC in 1977 chiefly concerned the extent to which the network would be allowed to use freelance crews for electronic news-gathering. In 1987, NBC's new General Electric management stood tough against NABET's new contract demands. It was a fairly long and bitter dispute but G.E. was considered ultimately to have won.

NATIONAL ASSOCIATION OF BROADCASTERS (NAB) ▶ the major trade association of the U.S. broadcast industry; headquartered in the capital, it represents the interests of the 4 networks, some 940 TV stations and more than 4,900 radio stations. The NAB speaks for the industry in national and policy matters relating to legislation and governmental regulation, and provides legal, labor relations and research services for its members. Edward O. Fritts has been its president since 1982. Until the practice was declared illegal in 1982, one of the body's primary functions was its issuance of voluntary "codes" defining "acceptable" practices on commercialization, program subject matter and the like.

NAB's annual convention, generally devoted to management and engineering aspects of the industry, is usually held in March or April and is the largest broadcast conclave of the year.

Despite the awesome power the industry has as a result of its control over hometown coverage of members of Congress, the group lobbying effort is frequently cited as disproportionately ineffective. The cumbersome governing structure of the NAB is undoubtedly a contributing factor. In order to represent a membership ranging from the TV networks down to "mom and pop" daytime radio stations, the NAB operates with a radio board, a television board, a joint board and an executive committee.

NATIONAL ASSOCIATION OF TELEVISION PROGRAM EXECUTIVES (NATPE INTERNATIONAL) ▶ an organization for TV program directors, formed in 1962, whose annual conference serves also as a domestic program exposition for syndicators. Although its original purposes merely were to raise the status of the program director in the industry and to foster an exchange of local program ideas, the organization gained prominence through the FCC's prime time-access rule, for which it provided the industry's chief forum and program market. By the mid-1970s NATPE's conferences, drawing general managers as well as program directors, rivaled in importance those of the National Association of Broadcasters for the discussion of industry issues. The organization's presidency passes each year to an active program director.

NATIONAL ASSOCIATION OF THEATER OWNERS v. FCC ▶ [420 F2d 922 D.C. Cir. (1969), cert. den/397 U.S. 922 (1970)] case in which the Court of Appeals held that the FCC had the power to regulate pay TV and that pay TV was a permissible medium.

In late 1968, after many years of consideration, the FCC issued a report that stated its authority to regulate subscription television and then established regulations for pay broadcasting. The National Association of Theater Owners challenged both the regulations and the power of the commission to issue such regulations.

The Court of Appeals for the District of Columbia Circuit affirmed the FCC's regulations, citing statutory requirements that the FCC act to "encourage the larger and more effective use of radio in the public interest" and the Supreme Court's holding that the FCC could regulate cable TV. The regulations, the Court said, did not constitute a general assertion of control over the rate-making decisions of conventional TV stations, nor were the regulations arbitrary because the FCC was not required to employ measures "less drastic" than rate-making.

Finally, the Court rejected a claim that even if the regulations were within the power of the commission, they were unconstitutional. The court held that the regulations were not discriminatory against the poor or in violation of the equal protection clause of the Fourteenth Amendment, as had been claimed, because the FCC had promulgated a number of safeguards to protect free TV. Nor, it said, did the program restrictions placed upon pay TV violate the First Amendment as a prior restraint of free speech. The court indicated that the rules did not ban speech.

The Theater Owners sought review in the Supreme Court but the court denied certiorari.

NATIONAL BROADCASTING CO. ▶ see NBC.

NATIONAL BROADCASTING CO. v. UNITED STATES ▶ [319 U.S. 190 (1943)] case in which the Supreme Court affirmed the power of the FCC to issue rules restricting the scope of agreements between the networks and their affiliates. Suit was brought by all the networks following the FCC's issuance in 1941 of regulations that greatly restricted the future scope of the national radio networks and their respective affiliates.

The FCC's new rules prohibited exclusive affiliation between a local station and a network; barred local stations from restraining other stations in the area from broadcasting a network show that it chose not to air; prohibited the networks from requiring affiliates to air a particular program at a particular time; and established that networks could not regulate the local advertising rates of affiliates. The rules also set a maximum of two years for affiliate contracts.

In their suits the networks challenged the regulations as being beyond the scope of the commission (since the networks are not licensed) and unconstitutional. The Supreme Court, as a threshold matter, decided that the FCC had the power to issue such regulations. This power, it said, came from the general powers inherent in the commission's congressional mandate to act within the "public interest, convenience and necessity" and to promote the "more effective use of radio." Additionally, Congress gave the commission power to make regulations concerning chain broadcasting. The court concluded that the regulations comported with the Communications Act of 1934.

In dealing with the constitutional challenge, the court held that the "public interest" standard was not too vague to constitute an overt delegation of power from Congress to a regulatory commission. Nor did the regulations conflict with the First Amendment prohibition of speech abridgments. The court held that some regulation of radio was necessary to create an orderly system of radio broadcasting, and that the regulation need not be limited to technical considerations alone.

The court stated, bluntly, that the "right of free speech does not include ... the right to use the facilities of radio without a license." Since the court rejected the assertions of the networks on these two major points, it affirmed the power of the FCC to issue guidelines relating to the practices of radio networks.

NATIONAL CABLE TELEVISION ASSOCIATION (NCTA) ▶ trade association founded in 1951 for the cable-TV industry representing its interests before Congress, the FCC and state regulatory agencies. As cable's equivalent of the NAB, NCTA was successful in countering the broadcast industry's propaganda war on pay cable in the mid-1970s and marshaled its forces to fight for recognition of cable TV as an independent medium in Congress' efforts to rewrite the nation's basic communications law.

James P. Mooney, its president and chief executive officer, a lawyer and former congressional staffer, joined in 1984. NCTA was highly effective during most of the 1980s, winning significant regulatory concessions for its industry (in 1984, in particular), but its influence has decreased as new powers, such as the telephone companies, have sought a role in its businesses. In 1991 the association mounted a multimillion dollar public-relations campaign, including TV commercials created by the Bozell Inc. ad agency, in an attempt to improve its members' image and avert a move in Congress toward reregulation of the cable industry. NCTA members operate cable systems serving over 90 percent of the nation's close to 55 million cable TV subscribers.

NATIONAL CITIZENS' COMMITTEE FOR BROADCASTING (NCCB) ▶ a nonprofit public interest action group that served for a decade as a central service organization for the various citizens groups in the broadcast reform movement. Essentially, the aim of the movement was to make radio and TV more responsive to the needs and interests of the public.

NCCB had begun in the late 1960s as a citizens' organization to support legislation for public broadcasting and was originally the National Citizens' Committee for Public Broadcasting. Dropping "public" from its name in 1968, and headed by Thomas P.F. Hoving with Ben Kubasik as executive director, it became a watchdog organization on commercial broadcasting practices. NCCB went into a decline after a few years but was reorganized in 1974 with Nicholas Johnson as its chairperson, giving the former FCC commissioner a base from which to continue his potent criticism of the industry and the regulatory process.

In 1978, the NCCB became part of the Ralph Nader organization, with Nader becoming its chairperson. Johnson left to head the new National Citizens' Communications Lobby, which derived funding from NCCB.

NATIONAL EDUCATIONAL TELEVISION (NET) ▶ once the principal supplier of national programming for the noncommercial system through all the phases of ETV and PTV. Until the Public Broadcasting Service began in 1970, many regarded NET as the public "network" although it had to deliver its programs by post since the stations were not interconnected. For economy reasons, it merged in April 1972 with New York station WNDT, which then changed its call letters to WNET.

NET grew out of NETRC, the National Educational Television and Radio Center created in December of 1952 by the Fund for Adult Education, and an original grant of more than $1 million. Its purpose initially was to facilitate an exchange of films and kinescopes between ETV stations, from a processing center at Ann Arbor, Mich. Later, for purposes of developing new programs, it expanded to New York, with the annual funding assumed largely by the Ford Foundation. In October 1962, it dropped the radio function and became simply NET, headed by John F. White.

Ford regularly contributed $6 million toward NET's annual $8 million operating budget, and the organization supplied approximately half the general programming for the typical ETV station in the years before the Public Broadcasting Act of 1967. Exclusive of reruns, NET normally provided five hours of original evening programming a week—divided between cultural and public affairs—and 2.5 hours a week of children's programs. Most of the production was by staff or independent producers in New York, but some was contracted to local stations in various major cities. NET also imported programs from foreign systems, principally the BBC.

Although the programs were needed by all stations, many regarded NET as having a liberal bias on political issues and were wary of its documentaries. The establishment of PBS served to give individual stations a greater voice in what was being produced for the system nationally, but NET (as WNET) continued to be a major supplier of programs chiefly because it had the support of the Ford Foundation and access to the New York talent pool.

NATIONAL FILM BOARD OF CANADA ▶ an internationally renowned film and television production institution that has produced some 9,000 documentary, feature and animated films in its first 50 years. It was created in 1939 by an act of Canadian Parliament for a seemingly simple purpose—to interpret Canada to Canadians and others throughout the world. But even though it is a government agency, it is far from being a government mouthpiece. From its beginnings under the direction of documentary pioneer John Grierson, the NFB has operated as a unique entity, a publicly funded organization with the creative freedom to produce films that challenge and disturb. As a film studio it has been saluted by Hollywood with nine Oscars.

No institution like it exists in the U.S. The Film Board produces and commissions works with no assurance they will be broadcast. Having no direct access to a broadcast outlet, it must sell or distribute its productions to the Canadian television networks, or enter into coproduction arrangements with North American or international broadcasters.

Although some of its productions are seen by millions throughout the world, few are big commercial successes. But financial return on investment is not the Board's prime objective or its criterion for a project.

Throughout its existence, the NFB has subsidized the work of many of Canada's finest filmmakers. Its animation unit, established by Norman McLaren, whose multiple-imaged *Pas de Deux* endures as a classic, still nurtures the work of such artists as Richard Condie, Co Holdeman and Caroline Leaf. The Board's innovative photo-animation techniques in its *City of Gold* (1957) have influenced much of television's production vocabulary, including NBC's *Project 20* and the more recent PBS series, *The Civil War*.

Before the arrival of television, traveling projectionists equipped with their own generators brought the work of the Film Board into hundreds isolated communities throughout Canada. For years it has been as much a part of Canada's culture as maple syrup, hockey and the Royal Mounted Police. The NFB's chairman is Joan Pennefather.

NATIONAL GEOGRAPHIC SPECIALS ▶ series of specials on natural history, anthropology and explorations, produced in association with the National Geographic Society and carried first on CBS (1965-73), then on ABC (1973-74) and later on PBS (1975—). The nonfiction hours were produced at the rate of four a year and were a surprising success when they began, since programs of their type did not usually draw high ratings in prime time.

CBS dropped the series after eight years when the ratings went into a decline, and after a lukewarm season on ABC the Geographics were no longer of interest to the commercial networks. Meanwhile, four new programs had already been produced. They eventually wound up on PBS on underwriting from Gulf Oil, through the Pittsburgh station, WQED. The first of the four, *The Incredible Machine,* a documentary on the workings of the human body, was an enormous hit, scoring the highest rating in the history of public television and in some markets outdrawing programs on the commercial networks. Thus the series was reborn, as a noncommercial entry.

The initial group of programs on CBS was produced by Wolper Productions. Metromedia Producers Corp. then took over for several years, and Wolper had the project again in

1973. The programs were narrated by Alexander Scourby, Orson Welles, Leslie Nielsen and Joseph Campanella, and they included such titles as *Grizzly!, The Amazon, Dr. Leakey and the Dawn of Man, Holland Against the Sea, Polynesian Adventure* and *Miss Goodall and the Wild Chimpanzees.*

The four that played on ABC, all by Wolper, were *The Big Cats, Bushmen of the Kalahari, Journey to the Outer Limits* and *Wind Raiders of the Sahara.*

The PBS group, produced independently by such talents as Irwin Rosten and Nicolas Noxon, featured E.G. Marshall and Joseph Campanella as hosts and included *Treasure!, Voyage of the Hokule'a, The Volga, The New Indians* and *Search for the Great Apes.* National Geographic also produces a magazine show, originally seen on Nickelodeon and later switched to WTBS in 1986.

NATIONAL NEWS COUNCIL ▶ an independent organization founded in August 1973 to receive, examine and report on specific complaints concerning the accuracy and fairness of news reporting by the press and broadcast media. The 15-member council had no power of enforcement over the media beyond the release of its findings. It was formed on the recommendation of a task force selected by the Twentieth Century Fund and was supported by the Fund and other foundations. It shut down in 1984.

NATIONAL PUBLIC AFFAIRS CENTER FOR TELEVISION (NPACT) ▶ former designation for the Washington-based news and public affairs production arm for public television. The name NPACT was dropped in 1976 as a delayed effect of the merger of the organization with the Washington station, WETA. The NPACT programs—*Washington Week in Review, Washington Straight Talk* and live special events—continued to be produced, but under the WETA banner.

NPACT had been created as an independent production agency for the PTV system in July 1971 from what had been the Washington bureau of NET, on grants totaling $3 million from the Ford Foundation and CPB. It was a step taken toward diversifying the production sources for PBS. But shortly after NET was merged with WNDT New York in 1972 to conserve costs, NPACT was similarly merged with WETA, although it retained its own administration under James Karayn, the former Washington bureau chief for NET.

Karayn resigned in 1975 and WETA absorbed the organization totally. Wallace Westfeldt, former NBC News producer, in effect took Karayn's place but with the title of executive producer. He left in 1977 to join ABC News.

Frequently at the center of controversy during its early years, NPACT was attacked by aides to President Nixon for an alleged liberal bias, and it was a target of OTP director Clay T. Whitehead, who contended that it was improper for a system receiving federal funds to deal in news and public affairs programming.

A source of congressional indignation was the revelation that NPACT's principal anchors, Sander Vanocur and Robert MacNeil, were being paid $85,000 and $65,000 a year, respectively. Although these fell below comparable salary levels in commercial TV, they were considered extravagant for a system that had been pleading with Congress for larger funds. This prompted the CPB board to put a ceiling of $36,000 on public TV salaries, which could be exceeded only with explicit approval of CPB.

When Vanocur and MacNeil left, they were succeeded by Jim Lehrer and Paul Duke, the latter, like his predecessors, an alumnus of NBC News. NPACT's other correspondents included Carolyn Lewis, Peter Kaye and Christopher Gaul, and the agency drew regularly from newspaper and magazine correspondents in the capital for on-air assignments.

NATIONAL TELECOMMUNICATIONS AND INFORMATION ADMINISTRATION (NTIA) ▶ an agency of the Commerce Department established in 1977 by the Carter Administration to assume the functions of the disbanded Office of Telecommunications Policy in the White House. NTIA is responsible for keeping abreast of developments in communications and the common-carrier field and for recommending policy and legislation. The OTP had lost its influence and was discredited when its first director, Clay T. Whitehead, used the office to advance the broadcast strategies of the Nixon White House.

Henry Geller, a former FCC general counsel and public interest lawyer, became acting director of OTP before the changeover and also of NTIA when the agency moved to Commerce. He was officially named Assistant Secretary of Commerce and director of NTIA early in 1978. In that capacity, he was also the President's chief advisor on telecommunications matters. Geller was succeeded in the Reagan administration by Bernard Wunder, and he by Janice Obuchowski in 1989.

NAVY LOG ▶ series of documentary-like dramas produced for syndication (1955-57) by Sam Gallu Productions with the cooperation of the Department of the Navy. The 30-minute stories, each with a different cast, formed an anthology that enjoyed a wide sale overseas as well as domestically.

NBC ▶ RCA's broadcasting subsidiary, created in the 1920s as America's first national network to help sell the radio sets and other broadcast equipment RCA manufactured; in the 1940s it was television sets and studio equipment. In the 1950s NBC (National Broadcasting Co.) was vital to RCA's promotion of color. As television grew, however, NBC became responsible for more and more of RCA's total profits. In 1986 GE bought RCA for a staggering $6.3 billion in cash, at that time the largest non-oil industry transaction in American history.

Throughout most of its early years in television, NBC ran second in ratings and glamour to CBS. Yet NBC was usually more innovative. It was the network that brought TV to the masses with Milton Berle and developed the desk & sofa talk-variety shows, *Today* and *Tonight.* Later it pioneered the after-midnight frontier with *Tomorrow* and *Saturday Night Live.*

NBC also invented the TV special, originally called the "spectacular"; commissioned an opera for television, *Amahl and the Night Visitors;* brought recently produced theatrical movies to prime time (*Saturday Night at the Movies*); and initiated the made-for-TV movie, the Sunday press conference (*Meet the Press*), the free-form comedy show (*Laugh-In*), the 90-minute series (*The Virginian*), the rotating dramatic series (*Name of the Game, Sunday Mystery Movie*), the dual-anchor newscast (*Huntley-Brinkley*), the one-minute newscast (*Update*) and the one-hour soap opera.

Because of RCA's manufacturing interests, and because the RCA color system had beat out CBS's in the early 1950s, NBC was the first network to push color and to present all its programs in color.

CBS built its ratings supremacy on programs and stars spirited away from NBC. But NBC withstood further raids, and in the early years of TV was able to field such stars as Bob Hope, Fred Allen, Eddie Cantor, Kate Smith, Groucho Marx, Sid Caesar, Jimmy Durante and Milton Berle. It pioneered latenight programming, developing such stars as Jerry Lester, Steve Allen, Jack Paar and Johnny Carson.

The character and stature of NBC as a company was molded by Gen. David Sarnoff, who headed RCA for nearly 40 years, and his son Robert, who moved up the executive ladder at NBC and then followed his father into the chairmanship of RCA. (He was ousted in a corporate shakeup in November 1975.) But the network's personality was forged by two other men—Sylvester Weaver and Robert E. Kintner. Both broke new ground: Weaver in entertainment, Kintner in news.

Weaver, the imaginative and venturesome NBC president in the 1950s, created the TV spectacular (later dubbed the special), the intimate talk show (*Today, Home, Tonight*) and the TV magazine (*Wide, Wide World*). Kintner, a former newspaper columnist who had become president of ABC-TV before NBC hired him away, countered the CBS leadership in entertainment by setting out to trounce that network in news.

Kintner gave news a priority it never enjoyed before or since in television, and through it he won a new kind of respect for the medium generally. His standing order to the news forces was "CBS Plus 30"—which meant that in all instances of common coverage NBC was to offer 30 minutes more than CBS. The Huntley-Brinkley team emerged during Kintner's administration, backed by a platoon of TV journalists who became star byliners—Frank McGee, John Chancellor, Edwin Newman, Sander Vanocur, Nancy Dickerson, Irving R. Levine, Pauline Frederick—and a battalion of crackerjack executives, writers and documentary producers. It was on Kintner's approval that Barbara Walters was allowed to develop as the female star of *Today.*

When Kintner left in 1966, NBC retreated from flamboyancy and one-man rule and experimented instead with a tripartite system of management and other forms considered more businesslike. Kintner was succeeded by a former news executive, Julian Goodman, but the company's dominant figure for the next decade was David C. Adams, an erudite attorney who functioned under various titles—chairman, vice-chairman, executive v.p.—but served in all as the grey eminence.

Adams, who always preferred to remain in the background personally, manifested a distaste for high visibility in management generally. But he yielded eventually to the peculiarities of the TV business, which has always thrived best on the cult of the personality. In 1975 Herbert S. Schlosser, a lawyer and former NBC program executive, was elevated to president of NBC with a clear mandate to provide aggressive personal leadership. Two years later, he became also chief executive officer. Goodman, as chairman, assumed the role of statesman. Adams directed the corporate staff.

Later came the chaotic era of Fred Silverman, then that of Grant Tinker, which made NBC the commanding network. The Tinker era was followed by a drastic cultural change when General Electric acquired the network.

HISTORY—Oldest of the networks, NBC was inaugurated on Nov. 15, 1926, with a special four-hour program originating from the ballroom of the Waldorf-Astoria Hotel in New York that included cutaways to other cities. The station lineup consisted of 21 charter affiliates and four other outlets, reaching as far west as Kansas City. CBS was organized the following year.

RCA had entered broadcasting in 1926 when it purchased WEAF (now WNBC) in New York from AT&T for $1 million plus an agreement to use AT&T for network interconnection. NBC was incorporated Sept. 9, 1926, by a consortium consisting of RCA, which owned 30% of the stock, Westinghouse, which owned 20% and General Electric, which owned 50%. At the time, an estimated 5 million homes were equipped with radio.

That same year, NBC acquired a second New York station, WJZ (actually licensed to Newark, N.J.), which had been owned by Westinghouse. Rather than duplicate the network programs on two New York stations, NBC created a second network. Stations hooked into the programs originating at WEAF became the Red Network; those carrying the WJZ feed, the Blue Network. The color designations resulted from the switchboard's use of red and blue to separate the networks. The Blue Network began Jan. 1, 1927, with six affiliates. (On FCC orders, it was divested by RCA in 1943 and became ABC.)

In 1930 RCA bought out the Westinghouse and GE interests and became sole owner of NBC, with Sarnoff doubling as its and RCA's president.

Radio not only developed the stars and program formats that were to be adopted by commercial television but also the entire modus operandi, including the economic system and the affiliate relationships.

NBC began its first TV transmission on Oct. 30, 1931, on experimental station W2XBS New York, and it inaugurated regular TV service on April 30, 1939 with a telecast of President Roosevelt at the opening of the New York World's Fair. The first "network" broadcast on Jan. 12, 1940, linked the New York station, WNBT (now WNBC-TV),with WRGB in Schenectady. World War II all but halted the development of TV, but the post-war spurt began around 1947, when *Kraft Television Theatre* and *Howdy Doody* started in the medium (along with other dramatic series on CBS and DuMont). But the medium's proliferation among working-class households was propelled in 1948 by the start of *The Texaco Star Theater* with Milton Berle. Then began the wholesale transfer of shows and stars from radio to TV—everything from *The Voice of Firestone* to the soap operas.

The network fanned out as AT&T facilities permitted and as new stations signed on the air when the FCC lifted its freeze on licenses in 1952. On Sept. 4, 1951, NBC and the other networks pooled coverage of the signing of the Japanese peace treaty in San Francisco, an event that inaugurated coast-to-coast service.

The great years of network television were the decades of the 1950s, 1960s and 1970s. By the late 1970s, with advertising demand for national air time growing greater every year and only three networks to divide the pie, television had become—or so it appeared—a failure-proof business. One year NBC finished third in the ratings and wound up with record profits.

But the changes brought by the 1980s were a cause for concern. By mid-decade, when RCA chairman Thornton F. Bradshaw had been at the helm of the $10 billion company for five years, he began to worry about its future in the new environment. Notorious predators such as Donald Trump, Irwin L. Jacobs and T. Boone Pickens had been rapidly buying stock.

Bradshaw's proudest accomplishment had been to recruit Grant Tinker from Hollywood and MTM Enterprises to be president of NBC in 1982. Tinker had been a programmer and was a keen judge of talent, and he restored stability to the organization while leading NBC to first place with a strong team of key executives. His choice of Brandon Tartikoff to run the network entertainment division was inspired, and his choice for president of NBC News, Lawrence Grossman, proved a canny one.

Bradshaw came close to merging RCA with MCA in 1984, and a year later held talks with the Disney Co., but neither bore fruit. The discussions with General Electric chairman Jack Welch did, however. GE had 1984 earnings of over $2 billion and lots of cash on hand. Welch also had a reputation for toughness—even ruthlessness—in business that was never compromised by sentimentality or love of tradition. The GE corporate culture was nothing like that of RCA/NBC. A year later the purchase was consummated for $6.3 billion, and RCA ceased to exist. After this point NBC was a new company, run differently than before.

When Tinker departed in 1986, Welch named Robert C. Wright, who had been president of GE financial services, to succeed him, but with the title of president of NBC (Tinker had been chairman). Wright had worked his way up in the organization, had some previous cable experience, and most importantly was an executive whom Welch liked and trusted. In the new culture, which in fact prevailed at all three networks after they changed hands, the idea of the company having a public trust gave way to that of the company's responsibility to its stockholders.

Not long after the acquisition, Welch sold off the NBC radio properties, including the network that had started it all.

NBC MAGAZINE ▶ weekly series begun in the fall of 1980 that represented the third try by NBC News to establish a weekly prime-time newsmagazine comparable to CBS's *60 Minutes* and ABC's *20/20.* These efforts started with *Weekend* in 1978. The following year it became *Prime Time Sunday,* with Tom Snyder as host-anchor and with an emphasis on live explorations of news stories through interviews by satellite. When this failed after eighteen months the series was revised and built around a new anchor, the veteran David Brinkley. It was slotted Fridays at 10 p.m. for the 1980-81 season and retitled *NBC Magazine with David Brinkley.*

The new format was less formal and more chatty than the previous ones. Between feature stories, Brinkley bantered with the principal correspondents—Jack Perkins, Garrick Utley, Douglas Kiker and Betsy Aaron. The critical response to the program improved, but the ratings did not, and the show was shifted to Thursdays at 8 p.m.

When Brinkley suddenly left the network to join ABC News at the start of the 1981-82 season, the program proceeded without a host-anchor and with a shorter title, *NBC Magazine.*

NBC TELEVISION STATIONS ▶ one of the leading broadcast groups,with six major market stations; it operates as a division of the National Broadcasting Company. NBC is the only network with an o&o in the nation's capital, Washington, D.C.

The stations are WNBC-TV New York, KNBC-TV Los Angeles, WMAQ-TV Chicago, WKYC-TV Cleveland, WTVS Miami, and WRC-TV Washington, D.C. John Rohrbeck became president of the group in 1991.

NBC-WESTINGHOUSE SWAP ▶ an exchange of stations between NBC and Westinghouse Broadcasting in 1955 that was held suspect for 10 years and finally led to an order by the FCC to reverse the deal. Thus, NBC became a sojourner in Philadelphia and Westinghouse in Cleveland.

The original exchange involved NBC giving up its Cleveland station WNBK-TV and $3 million in 1955 for Westinghouse's Philadelphia properties, WPTZ-TV and KYW-AM. The FCC approved the transaction but the agreement raised some eyebrows because it allowed NBC to trade up from the 6th largest market to the 4th, which was not a logical move for Westinghouse. Becoming concerned with possible antitrust implications, the Justice Department found a Westinghouse executive who said the trade was "forced" upon his company, and a federal grand jury probe into the alleged coercion was begun in 1956. Three years later the Supreme Court ruled that NBC would have to stand trial for the allegation. In 1964 the FCC said it would renew the licenses of the stations if the two companies would switch back, and the following year they did. NBC's Cleveland station then became WKYC-TV and Westinghouse's Philadelphia outlet, KYW-TV.

NBC *WHITE PAPER* ▶ NBC's answer to *CBS Reports* in the years when the two networks battled for journalistic supremacy and competed for prestige as well as for ratings. *White Paper* was a distinguished occasional series of documentaries and investigative reports that began in 1960 with *The U-2 Affair,* an examination of the crash of an American spy plane in the Soviet Union, and its implications. Well over a hundred other programs were produced under the *White Paper* rubric in the next three decades, although they grew fewer and fewer in the 1980s and have practically vanished with the tightening of the news budgets by the new network owners.

Programs in the *White Paper* series often dealt with large issues, such as U.S. foreign policy, race relations, organized crime, and the energy crisis. When the issue was big enough, the program sometimes spanned the full three hours of prime time.

Irving Gitlin, who had joined NBC from CBS, was executive producer of the *White Papers* until he died in 1968. He was followed by Fred Freed and then Reuven Frank. Among those who produced for the series were Lou Hazam, Albert Wasserman, Don Hyatt, Lucy Jarvis and Shad Northshield.

NEBRASKA GAG RULE ▶ a controversial order by a Nebraska court restricting media coverage of the 1975 trial of a mass murderer, in order to preserve the defendant's right to a fair trial. The networks and RTNDA joined with members of the print press in opposing the prior restraint as a violation of the First Amendment and one that would establish a dangerous precedent. In 1976 the Supreme Court ruled the gag order unconstitutional.

The order by Judge Hugh Stuart, in the case in which Erwin Charles Simants was accused of murdering six members of a family and sexually assaulting two of them, barred the media from reporting certain matters that were discussed in pretrial proceedings (including confessions by the defendant) and aspects of the case discussed in open court. The case was brought to the Supreme Court by newspapers and broadcasters in Nebraska.

NELSON, GENE ▶ veteran writer-director whose credits include made-for-TV movies, pilots (*I Dream of Jeannie*) and episodes for such series as *Mod Squad, The FBI, Dan August* and *The Rookies.*

NELSON, OZZIE (d. 1975) ▶ actor, producer and director who starred in ABC's long-running family situation comedy *The Adventures of Ozzie and Harriet,* and also in the short-lived *Ozzie's Girls.* He also produced and directed both series and earlier had been producer-director of *Our Miss Brooks.* Before entering TV, he had been a popular bandleader on radio, with his wife, Harriet Hilliard, as vocalist.

NELSON, RALPH ▶ one of the outstanding early directors in the medium, who directed the entire *Mama* series, the first production of Rodgers & Hammerstein's *Cinderella* (1957) and dramas for *Playhouse 90, Climax!* and other anthologies of the time. He received an Emmy for *Requiem for a Heavyweight* and also directed the movie version. Like many creative talents of the "golden age," he gave up TV for movies and directed such notable films as *Charly* and *Lilies of the Field.*

NESSEN, RON ▶ NBC News correspondent who in 1970 was appointed press secretary to President Ford, the first TV newsperson to hold that position. A former reporter for UPI, he had joined NBC in 1962 and was White House correspondent during the Johnson Administration.

NETHERLANDS ▶ a country with one of the oddest television systems in the world. Its three national state channels, run by NOS, are programmed by 34 companies that represent special interest groups. Access to the air and the amount of airtime accorded is based on the groups' membership figures. The country has 5.5 million TV households and a cable penetration of 90%.

The system is being shaken up, however, by a commercial channel, RTL 4, which has been broadcasting from Luxembourg since 1989. Within two years the new channel has claimed 21% of the audience and a large share of the advertising revenues. NOS, which is supported by a combination of receiver license fees and advertising, limits commercial time to 10% of its schedule. It may be forced by the erosion, however, to adopt the European Community standard of 15%. The three networks have annual revenues of $500 million, some 60% of which comes from advertising.

NETWORK SYNDICATION ▶ the resale of off-network series and specials by the syndication divisions of CBS, NBC and ABC, until the FCC forced the networks to end those operations in June 1972. The commission's purpose was to reduce network control over programs and to remove a potential for anticompetitive developments in the syndication market. The networks were given until June 1973 to cease distributing programs for non-network exhibition. The ban remained largely unchanged until 1991, when it was liberalized after the epochal network-Hollywood "fin-syn" debate.

CBS Films was spun off, along with the CBS cable-TV division, into a new company, Viacom. ABC Films was purchased for close to $10 million by a group of its executives and became Worldvision. The syndication properties of NBC Films (known during the 1950s as California National Productions, or CalNat) were sold outright to NTA.

Until the FCC action, the networks had made a regular practice of sewing up the subsidiary rights to programs before putting them on the air, or at least of acquiring financial interests in the programs to enable them to share in the syndication revenues. Because the networks provided a steady stream of desirable programming, their syndication operations exerted a unique power in the syndication market; and stations were known to buy programs they did not want, to remain in the good graces of the network syndicators.

The FCC rules forcing divestiture were actually adopted in 1970, at the same time the prime time-access rule was hatched, but the measure was stayed pending an appeal by the networks to the U.S. Court of Appeals in Washington. In 1972 the court upheld the commission.

NETWORKS ▶ chains of stations interconnected today by satellite for the efficient distribution of programs and advertising from a central source. Because the economies of scale permit more ambitious and expensive production than individual stations could normally afford, and because they tend to be highly promotable, network programs traditionally have drawn greater audiences than local or syndicated shows in any TV market.

The three major national networks, ABC, CBS and NBC, are each affiliated with approximately 200 stations and through them cover virtually the entire country. From early times, the stations have been compensated by the networks for the use of their air time at a rate that usually makes it more profitable for them to be affiliated than to buy or produce, and then sell, their own programs. Affiliates also receive spot positions around the network programs to sell locally, and since audience levels are usually high in the network time periods, the spots allotted to stations command high rates. Moreover, the resale value of a network-affiliated station is usually more than double that of a nonaffiliated station.

Under this economic system, the networks for many years have supplied some 60% of the programs that affiliated stations broadcast, and the networks became the dominant force in American television although broadcasting in the U.S. was founded on the doctrine of localism. The affiliates provide an infrastructure for national broadcasting.

The system of three networks and 600-plus affiliates worked nicely until competition from cable, new UHF stations, the new Fox network and home video made itself powerfully felt in the 1980s. The networks' new business-minded owners, struggling against the erosion of audience and sinking profits, began tampering with the system by instituting cutbacks in affiliate compensation and eliminating much of the hospitality that was lavished on affiliates at their annual meetings and on their visits to New York. On a number of issues, including the increasing involvement of ABC and NBC in cable channels that compete for the audience, the old, harmonious network-affiliate relationships have grown somewhat strained in the 1990s.

An official definition of a true network was articulated by the Federal Communications Commission in 1990 when it attempted to clarify which broadcasters were actually affected by the 20-year-old Financial Interest and Syndication Rule, commonly known in the trade as fin-syn. The rule prohibits the networks from engaging in domestic syndication and taking equity positions in programs they put on the air. Rupert Murdoch's new Fox Network seemed to violate the rule since it was a sister company to the 20th Century-Fox studios, which both owned programs and syndicated them. The FCC placed Fox outside the rule by defining a network as one that programmed more than 15 hours a week during the peak viewing hours. Fox at the time was distributing programs to affiliates only four nights a week for a total of 12 hours.

The FCC definition was significant in giving the major networks the option of getting under the rule themselves by cutting back their prime-time broadcasts to five nights, or by selling off a weekend service to another operator. By programming fewer than 15 hours in prime time, any network, while fin-syn exists, could be acquired by an American-owned Hollywood studio such as Disney or Paramount, or by a prosperous syndicator like King World.

Some network officials have publicly expressed doubt that more than two major networks will survive into the 21st century, though no one can safely predict which one might fail.

NEUFELD, VICTOR ▶ executive producer of ABC News's *20/20* since September 1987, overseeing the daily operation of the prime-time magazine show. Previously he was senior producer of *20/20,* beginning in 1979. He joined ABC News as a producer in 1973, holding a variety of positions including senior producer of *ABC Evening News*. He began his career at WNEW-TV in 1969.

NEUMAN, ALAN ▶ veteran director who worked on such series of the 1950s and 1960s as *Person to Person, Wide, Wide World, This Is Your Life, Colgate Comedy Hour, NBC Opera, Wisdom* and *Producer's Showcase.*

NEUMAN, E. JACK ▶ lawyer turned writer-producer who created such series as *Police Story, Petrocelli* and *Kate McShane.* He also served as executive producer of *Kate McShane* and of the *Law and Order* pilot, which he wrote. He works through his independent company, P.A. Productions.

***NEW ADVENTURES OF PERRY MASON, THE* ▶** futile attempt by CBS to re-create, in 1973, its old and amazingly durable hit of the 1950s. The second version featured Monte Markham as Erle Stanley Gardner's famous fictional attorney and was short-lived, running less than a season. The regular cast included Harry Guardino as prosecutor Hamilton Burger, Sharon Acker as secretary Della Street, Brett Somers as receptionist Gertie, Albert Stratton as investigator Paul Drake and Dane Clark as Lieutenant Arthur Tragg. It was produced by 20th Century-Fox TV and Cornwall Jackson.

***NEW DICK VAN DYKE SHOW, THE* ▶** unsuccessful attempt by CBS (1971-73) to equal the star's initial success in the situation comedy form. Produced in Arizona, the series starred Van Dyke and Hope Lange as Dick and Jenny Preston and was created by Carl Reiner. It was produced by Cave Creek Enterprises.

NEW JERSEY COALITION FOR FAIR BROADCASTING ▶ citizens' organization formed in 1971 to campaign for adequate VHF television service for New Jersey, one of two states without a commercial VHF assignment (Delaware is the other). Ultimately the group accomplished its primary objective not through public pressure, but through a back-room deal under which its senator, Bill Bradley (D.-N.J.), saved RKO from the imminent loss of its license for WOR, its flagship New York City TV station, on the condition that it be immediately moved to (Seacaucus) New Jersey.

Situated between two of the largest urban centers, New Jersey has been blanketed by the New York City stations in the north and the Philadelphia stations to the south. Because the state's residents constituted approximately 30% of the viewership in each market, the Coalition was formed by 18 organizations of the larger cities to demand from the stations commensurate coverage of New Jersey news events and state issues. Public officials argued that the lack of a television station not only created a news vacuum in the state but mitigated against a sense of state identity among Jerseyites.

Although it is a more populous state than Florida, Wisconsin, Minnesota and most others, New Jersey wound up without a major TV station by accident of geography and the FCC's allocation policies in 1952, when it lifted the four-year "freeze" on station licenses. Attending first to the major urban centers, the agency set up a schedule of allocations based on market size and suitable mileage separation for the signals.

New York was assigned channels 2, 4, 5, 9 and 11 and Philadelphia channels 3, 6 and 10—the frequencies fitted, as interlocking fingers. Channel 8 was allocated to New Haven, Conn., Channel 12 to Wilmington, Del., and Channel 13 to Newark, N.J., as a commercial operation.

But in 1961, as educational television was spreading, Channel 13 was sold to the newly formed noncommercial Educational Broadcasting Corporation and has since served as the New York area's public TV station (first as WNDT, later as WNET). Similarly, Wilmington's Channel 12 went educational and, as WHYY-TV, is generally identified as Philadelphia's public station.

On pressure from the Coalition, several of the New York stations assigned full-time news reporters to New Jersey, and others created weekly public affairs programs devoted to issues of the state. But the organization, regarding the efforts as token, petitioned the FCC in 1974 to reassign one of the existing New York stations to New Jersey or to determine whether a completely new station could be "dropped in" on the VHF band. Otherwise, it recommended that the agency "hyphenate" the New York and Philadelphia markets, designating them officially as the New York-northern New Jersey and Philadelphia-southern New Jersey, which would require that all stations establish studios in the state.

In 1976 the FCC denied all those requests but ruled the New York and Philadelphia stations would, in some manner, have to establish a "presence" in New Jersey.

NEW WORLD TELEVISION ▶ one of the most watched independent studios of the 1980s, producing such critically popular shows as *The Wonder Years, Crime Story* and *Tour of Duty.*

When the parent company New World Pictures (now called New World Entertainment) was formed in the mid-1980s, its goal was the production of cheap, low-budget fare to fill the void in B-grade motion pictures. The philosophy worked well until the highly leveraged company was called upon to begin repaying the debt it had acquired, a huge problem despite its efforts to keep costs low by skimping on production quality.

New World's entry into television also cost the company heavily in production expense, with *Tour of Duty* and *Crime Story* each costing over $1 million an episode to produce. To make matters worse, all of New World Television's network entries except ABC's *The Wonder Years,* New World Television's first prime-time ratings success, were canceled before they had accumulated enough episodes for syndication.

In late 1991 the bulk of New World Television was folded into Sony Pictures Entertainment's TriStar Television, while parent company New World Entertainment concentrated its efforts in the international distribution market.

NEW ZEALAND ▶ a small country with a mere one million television households, yet focal in the international industry as the first to have deregulated completely. The country's first commercial network, TV3, which began in 1989 to great hoopla, proved a fiasco and went into receivership just three months after launch.

New Zealand television remains dominated by an energetic public broadcaster, TVNZ, which operates two channels and accepts advertising on both. The commercial network, TV3, had by 1991 strengthened its position with audiences and advertisers and has begun posing a threat to the old system. A three-channel pay-TV service and a regional broadcasting service from Canterbury Television, founded in 1991 and broadcasting to the south island, have pitched the country into the second age of television. The country is also served today by a satellite system called Sky Networks, whose investors include America's ESPN and Time Warner, as well as public broadcaster TVNZ.

NEWHART, BOB ▶ low-key comedian whose TV sitcoms have been quiet successes, usually ranking in the top 20 and running for years but without notoriety. Newhart began as a stand-up comic whose routines were usually one side of a dialogue. They were used to hilarious effect on the 1960 LP, *The Button-Down Mind of Bob Newhart.* This success, combined with an appearance that same year on the Emmy Awards telecast, gave him a shot at a TV series in the 1961-62 season; the series suffered modest ratings. After ten years during which he made guest appearances on variety shows, he launched *The Bob Newhart Show* (1972) on CBS, in which he portrayed a psychologist playing off a cast of off-beat characters. The show lasted six seasons. In 1982 he returned in another CBS sitcom, *Newhart,* this time playing the owner of a small inn in Vermont. The series ran until 1990.

NEWLYWED GAME, THE **▶** see Game Shows.

Edwin Newman

NEWMAN, EDWIN ▶ former NBC newscaster with a raspy voice and dry wit, considered one of the most literate members of the electronic journalism fraternity. He joined NBC News in London in 1952 and later became bureau chief there (1956-57), then in Rome (1957-58) and then in Paris (1958-61). Based in New York since 1961, he was one of the regular reporting stars of the national political conventions, reported on other special events, and was narrator of documentaries. Newman was a frequent substitute on *Today* and also hosted a weekly interview show, *Speaking Freely.* For a time he was drama critic for WNBC-TV. His first book on the use of language in news media, *Strictly Speaking,* was a best seller in 1974.

NEWMAN, SYDNEY ▶ Canadian broadcast executive who made his mark in British television as a drama producer and later as a program executive. For independent television there, he created and produced *Armchair Theatre,* a highly successful weekly showcase with a strong bias for gritty, realistic drama. As such it was a benchmark for the British medium and helped put many a young writer and director on the map. Newman subsequently shifted to BBC-TV as a program executive in charge of anthology and series drama. His major achievement in that capacity was to establish the *Wednesday Play* as a slot for contemporary drama. On his return to Canada in the late 1960s he took over the leadership of the National Film Board of Canada, and more recently he has been serving as an independent film and television consultant.

NEWS ▶ television's noblest service, the leading source of the medium's prestige and, as it proved during the turbulent 1980s, the program form most vulnerable to surgical procedures during severe downturns in the television economy. At the network level, news suffered also from the new corporate cultures that established themselves in mid-decade. The new owners at CBS and NBC particularly, being wholly oriented to the imperatives of business, displayed little tolerance for the high-cost journalistic functions of the networks that made them loss leaders instead of profit centers.

Network news was diminished in the 1980s both by severe budget cuts and a general denial of air time. At each network, soon after the new managements were installed, the news divisions were forced to execute deep cutbacks in staff, eliminate a number of domestic and foreign bureaus, and practice other budgetary austerities that restricted travel and often limited the quality of coverage. Social and topical news documentaries all but vanished, and only rarely was prime evening time given to news specials or to the examination of current events. What many believe to be the single biggest news story of the century—the failure of Communism—was duly noted in the regular news programs but not given the all-stops-out prime-time treatment it would have received in a previous time.

Moreover, many affiliates and even some of the networks' owned stations took to rescheduling the evening newscast in an earlier time period so that the 7-8 p.m. hour might be opened fully to more lucrative syndicated programming. The news divisions were mandated to help pay their own way by developing popular prime-time magazine programs to take the place of Hollywood-supplied entertainment shows and to keep stride, though of course on a higher plane, with the hot syndication trend of the early 1990s, Tabloid Television. The comedown was precipitous for news organizations that had painstakingly developed their credentials and credibility over more than three decades and that had grown to be respected worldwide.

That ABC should have taken the lead in news from its better-established rivals may be attributed only partly to the on-screen appeal of its anchor, Peter Jennings, and to the edge ABC News has gained from its late-night *Nightline* with Ted Koppel. The organization itself has remained stable under the Roone Arledge administration, which began in 1977, in contrast to the other networks. In that time span, NBC News had five presidents and CBS News seven. It is also relevant that when ABC Inc. changed hands, it went to a company, Capital Cities, that was steeped in broadcasting and understood journalism as a profession. The other networks went to owners who regarded news as a business.

While network news experienced a humbling decline in the 1980s, local newscasts continued as potent and profitable forms of programming in virtually every television market. Stations by and large derive their local identities from news, and in many markets the station with the top-rated newscast is the top-rated station overall, regardless of its network affiliation, a curiosity that was discovered in the late 1960s. New sources of news material became available to stations in the 1980s, in addition to the special feeds from the networks for their local newscasts. CNN began syndicating its news coverage to broadcast stations, and the Conus cooperative facilitated a kind of news exchange among stations that were most seriously engaged in the news function of broadcasting.

CNN emerged as a leading news organization in the 1980s

The success of CNN was clearly the most positive development in television journalism during the 1980s. The availability of television news around the clock proved a strong selling point for cable, and Ted Turner's Cable News Network established itself as a leading American news organization in a remarkably short period of time. Without a star system and other such vices of the network news organizations, CNN was able to operate two full-time channels on half the budgets of network news and turn a profit, besides. In head-on competition with the three networks during the Persian Gulf War, CNN outshone them all and was the focal network not only with the viewership but also with government and military officials.

CNN's influence, moreover, is worldwide through the global satellite distribution of its programming. Some broadcast systems abroad subscribe to CNN as a kind of news agency, like Reuters or Associated Press, and use some of its reports on the air. But even the foreign networks that do not subscribe carry CNN in their newsrooms, and many of the newer stations use it as a teaching laboratory for their own young journalists, on matters of content, presentation and pacing. The full CNN channel is carried on hotel systems in most major countries, allowing American travelers to remain in daily touch with developments back home.

The 24-hour news concept has been adopted by cable and DBS channels in Canada, the United Kingdom and other countries, but none has anything like CNN's worldwide penetration. That news presented by an American network should be so internationally pervasive is alarming to other countries, and CNN's dominance in the field will be challenged in the 1990s with global news networks from Britain's BBC, if not by others as well.

HISTORY—TV network news began on CBS in 1948 with *Douglas Edwards and the News.* NBC followed soon after with *The Camel News Caravan* with John Cameron Swayze. Both were 15 minutes in length and essentially involved a recitation of the stories by a news reader. Edward R. Murrow was the CBS news star at the time but did not appear on the evening newscast, confining his work to the weekly *See It Now* series and CBS Radio. ABC entered later with John Daly but was hobbled by a short affiliate lineup and a comparatively small news organization.

Network newscasts doubled in length in the fall of 1963, fronted by Walter Cronkite on CBS and Chet Huntley and David Brinkley on NBC. ABC had a large turnover in anchors—including Bob Young, Peter Jennings, Howard K. Smith and Frank Reynolds—until it hired away Harry Reasoner from CBS in 1970. In 1976 Reasoner was teamed with Barbara Walters, first female news anchor on the networks, who was hired away from NBC's *Today* show. By then, John Chancellor had become NBC's anchor, teamed with Brinkley. Cronkite remained CBS's ace.

Over the years, the ratings lead switched between NBC and CBS, while ABC made slow progress toward parity. NBC held the lead from 1953 to 1956, then lost it to CBS, which held it until 1960. That year, Huntley and Brinkley forged ahead and gave NBC the most popular newscast for five years. From 1965 to 1967, NBC and CBS ran neck and neck, until Cronkite moved in front, holding the lead for about nine years. In 1976, CBS and NBC were close again, each reaching around 20 million viewers a night to ABC's 15 million. ABC News, with Roone Arledge as its new president, began a build-up of staff in the summer of 1977 for a new assault on the news ratings of CBS and NBC. In 1979, ABC's *World News Tonight,* chiefly anchored by Frank Reynolds, closed in on NBC's *Nightly News* for second place and on several occasions passed it in the ratings. ABC's rise, and its attempts to raid the other networks for news stars, led to changes at CBS and NBC.

In 1981, Cronkite yielded the anchor post on the evening newscast to Dan Rather, who was joined within the year by Bill Moyers, serving as commentator. Meanwhile, Roger Mudd moved to NBC News and in 1982 became co-anchor with Tom Brokaw of *Nightly News.* In the wave of personnel changes, David Brinkley ended a long career at NBC News and switched to ABC.

When Frank Reynolds died in 1983, Peter Jennings became permanent anchor of *ABC World News Tonight,* and the newscast continued its steady advance in the ratings. Tom Brokaw was made sole anchor of *Nightly News,* and Roger Mudd, who had been passed over at CBS and now again at NBC, worked for a time at other assignments and eventually left to join the *MacNeil-Lehrer NewsHour* on PBS. Rather remained the CBS anchor.

In 1989 the ABC newscast moved into first place, and by 1991 it was decisively ahead.

NEWS AT TEN ▶ across-the-board 10 p.m. half-hour news program in Britain originated by Independent Television News and cleared by all independent stations in that country. Introduced in the late 1960s, it has consistently won high audience shares and enjoyed a reputation for journalistic hustle, ingenuity and showmanly presentation. Not long after its inception, the show went to a two-person anchor format, the first in Britain, admittedly modeled after NBC's prime nightly newscast. The program's graphics include an opening shot of "Big Ben" and the houses of Parliament.

NEWS OF THE DAY ▶ newsreel company jointly owned by Hearst and MGM which had been contracted by the CBS *See It Now* unit in the 1950s for all the film and post-production work. Edward R. Murrow canceled the arrangement, however, after the suicide of his protege, Don Hollenbeck, who had been under constant attack by Hearst columnists accusing him of slanting the news to the left. The same columnists had been critical of Murrow's devastating programs on Sen. Joseph McCarthy. When Murrow dropped the services of the Hearst newsreel, the News of the Day technicians resigned to join *See It Now.*

NEWSROOM **▶** public TV program created by KQED San Francisco during a newspaper strike in the 1960s. It was the precursor to the *Eyewitness News* format that spread throughout the commercial TV system. Central to the *Newsroom* concept is the gathering of reporters around a desk to discuss the day's news and its significance. Several public stations borrowed the format, but none was able to equal the bold, straightforward tone of the original.

NEWSROOM COMPUTERS ▶ systems set up inside network and station news operations that help organize and process the flow of information and the management of the news gathering and reporting process. These systems perform such functions as controlling the flow of news copy from writers through editors and into the teleprompter read by the anchor, organizing material that comes in on microwave signals or cassette from ENG crews, and coordinating the selection of news graphics.

NEWSWORLD ▶ Canada's 24-hour all-news national cable channel. Operated by the public network, CBC, it began on July 31, 1989. But unlike the CBC, which delays its broadcasts for Canada's six time zones, Newsworld broadcasts entirely in real time. Moreover, it has origination points in major centers all across the country so that it is genuinely national. Although it covers international developments as well as national, more than 90% of its programming has Canadian authorship. It also offers 30 hours a week of closed-captioned programming for the hearing impaired.

Newsworld receives its operating revenues both from cable subscription fees and the sale of advertising. It is licensed to carry eight minutes of advertising an hour, about one-third less than conventional broadcasting. Joan Donaldson has headed Newsworld from its inception.

NFL INSTANT REPLAY ▶ the use of familiar television technology as a tool in officiating professional football games. After many years of discussion and several of experimentation, the system of using television's instant replay techniques in overturning calls by field officials was adopted in 1986. The objective of the system is to allow the officials to review plays in the manner that television viewers are able to. The system is employed to reverse an on-field decision only when the visual evidence in a video replay is indisputable.

Thus a new member is added to the game's officials—the replay official, who is positioned in a sideline booth equipped with two television monitors and two high-speed VCRs, plus radio communications with the field officials. The network carrying the game is not part of the review process. The replay official watches the live network feed but does not hear the commentators. Whenever a replay official believes an error has been made in a call, he contacts the head field referee via a headset. During a three-year period in which approximately 510 plays were reviewed, a total of 63 field calls were reversed.

NHK (NIPPON HOSO KYOKAI) ▶ the Japan Broadcasting Corporation, that country's behemoth public broadcaster and a world leader in television technology with its development and use of high-definition television (HDTV). Together with the BBC one of the last remaining public systems without advertising, NHK is sometimes compared with the British public broadcaster because of the sweep and range of its programming. The two are alike also in deriving their support entirely from license fees, though in NHK's case the fee is paid directly to the broadcaster. In Japan, this amounts to almost 40 million TV households.

For many years a monopoly broadcaster, NHK has since the end of World War II faced competition, first in radio and then in TV.

Operating Japan's only two national TV networks—one educational, one general—each with 100% coverage of Japan's four islands, plus an experimental DBS service, the public broadcaster has managed to hold its own against the commercial competition, particularly in news broadcasting. NHK's DBS service, begun in mid-1988, offers two pay channels, one a 24-hour news and sports service, the other an entertainment channel. The NHK Symphony, which performs worldwide, is Japan's oldest concert orchestra.

After years of experimentation, NHK's technical laboratory developed the world's first HDTV system, heavily promoted by the public broadcaster as a major contender in the fight for a universal standard of HDTV. NHK is itself a pioneer in its use, broadcasting HDTV programs from its DBS satellite for brief periods each day.

NHL (NATIONAL HOCKEY LEAGUE) ▶ one of the few professional sports competitions that does not live or die by television. The NHL has been able to maintain its traditions and economic stability, and in fact to continue its program of expansion, even though U.S. television is largely indifferent to the sport. In at least one year during the 1980s, the finals of the championship Stanley Cup Playoffs could not find a commercial TV outlet in the U.S. and were carried, if at all, on non-paying public television stations.

Though the teams are divided between Canada and the U.S., the level of interest in the sport between the two countries is wildly out of balance. In Canada, during hockey season, few television programs can compete for interest; the NHL games dominate the Nielsens and are a coup for the beer company that has nailed down the sponsorship. In the U.S., on the other hand, the viewing is traditionally so scant that there is almost no competition for the rights. The Los Angeles Kings' acquisition of superstar Wayne Gretzky from Edmonton did not succeed in boosting the viewing.

During the late 1980s the NHL found its outlets finally in cable's regional pay channels, the affiliates of SportsChannel America. In the final year of the initial contract, the SportsChannel regional channels collectively paid $17 million for the rights. The 1991-92 renewal, however, was a one-year contract for $5.5 million—in the sports world, a rare severe cut in rights fees. The NHL was able to withstand the slight from television since it still survives nicely on arena admissions and the sale of merchandise and, in fact, is looking towards expansion from 22 teams to 28 by the end of the 1990s.

NICHOLAS, N. J. (NICK) ▶ president and co-chief executive officer of Time Warner Inc. He joined Time Inc. in 1964 straight from Harvard Business School, and by 1971 he was an assistant treasurer of the company, overseeing its cable and pay-television businesses. He later was president of Time's Manhattan Cable Television, a cable system operator, and in 1981 he was named chairman of HBO. After becoming an executive vice president of Time Inc. in 1984, overseeing all the company's video operations, Nicholas was named president in 1986. Following Time's merger with Warner Communications in January 1990, Nicholas became co-chief executive in May 1990, sharing the title with Warner's Steve Ross, who is chairman of the company.

NICHOLL, DON (d. 1980) ▶ writer associated with Norman Lear who was co-creator and co-producer, with Michael Ross and Bernie West, of *The Jeffersons* and *The Dumplings.* He was also executive producer of *All in the Family* for the 1974-75 season.

NICHOLS, MIKE ▶ noted stage and motion picture director who made his entry into TV production as co-executive producer of *Family* in 1976. Earlier in his career he frequently appeared on TV as a comedian teamed with Elaine May.

NICKELODEON/NICK AT NITE ▶ basic-cable network for children launched in 1979 by Warner Amex and later acquired by Viacom. Nickelodeon has succeeded in dominating the children's niche and providing a service that has attracted subscribers for cable. The network offers along with varied animation shows a number of live-action programs that create a kind of club atmosphere for Nickelodeon devotees. Among them are game, panel and discussion shows that feature young people. Nickelodeon won praise and good ratings for the original Sunday morning cartoon block it introduced in 1991. The network began as a commercial-free service, but in the early 1980s it reversed the policy and began soliciting advertising. It has been careful with its advertising practices, however, recognizing that advertising abuses by commercial television have made Nickelodeon the acceptable alternative for many concerned parents.

In 1985 MTV Networks expanded Nickelodeon from a 13-hour, essentially daytime service to a 24-hour schedule with the introduction of Nick at Nite. The nighttime service, featuring vintage off-network shows that stations thought were passe, such as *Mr. Ed* and *Get Smart*, created new interest in the oldies by packaging them in a campy homage to the Golden Age of Television. The service broke new ground in 1991 by coproducing a series with ABC called *Hi Honey, I'm Home*, episodes of which debuted on ABC and appeared as "instant reruns" the following week on Nick at Nite. Nickelodeon reaches 55.4 million cable subscribers while Nick at Nite reaches 50.2 million. Geraldine Laybourne is the president of both services.

NIELSEN CO., A.C. ▶ a company whose best-known service is the measurement of TV audiences and whose reports are recognized as the index to success or failure in TV programming. In the television ratings business, Nielsen Media Research has four main services: NTI (Nielsen Television Index), which produces ratings for network shows; NSI (Nielsen Station Index), which concentrates on local market reports; NSS (Nielsen Syndication Service), which reports on syndicated shows; and NHI (Nielsen Homevideo Index), which reports on cable, pay cable and VCR programs.

Since its founding in 1923 by Arthur C. Nielsen, Sr., however, Nielsen's main business has been the tabulating and reporting, via electronic scanning, of consumer consumption of groceries, health and beauty aids, drugs and other packaged goods. This business is handled by Nielsen Marketing Research, which is headquartered in Northbrook, Ill., with offices in more than 20 other countries.

It was Nielsen's success in pinpointing the flow of retail merchandise that prompted manufacturers, in the 1930s, to ask Nielsen to evaluate radio advertising, in which manufacturers were beginning to invest heavily. Nielsen purchased the rights to an audience-counting device, a black box attachment to radio sets known as the Audimeter, and then bought out the methodology of an existing ratings company. In 1942 Nielsen introduced an audience measurement service that could document which stations were being listened to by the slow-crawl film contained within the Audimeters. In the late 1940s, with television's emergence, Nielsen adapted its methodology to the new medium.

The increase in the number of independent radio stations, coinciding with the expansion of TV, forced Nielsen out of radio measurement by 1964. Thereafter, Nielsen ceased producing radio ratings and concentrated on network and local market audience data for television.

A.C. Nielsen was acquired by Dun & Bradstreet Corp. for $1.3 billion in 1984. John C. Holt, a senior executive of D&B, became chairman and CEO of A.C. Nielsen in 1987; and William G. Jacobi, also a D&B executive, became president and COO of Nielsen Media Research in 1991.

While in local television Nielsen has stiff competition from Arbitron, in network television Nielsen has the field virtually to itself. Thus, Nielsen is not only the scorekeeper in the TV game; its numbers are, in fact, the score.

Founder A.C. Nielsen, Sr., died in 1980 and was succeeded by his son, A.C. Nielsen, Jr.

NIELSEN TELEVISION INDEX (NTI) ▶ the basic national audience measurement service of the A.C. Nielsen Co. that publishes estimates of network programming, as opposed to the local market audience estimates. The 1,200 households used for the NTI metered sample are drawn from census tracts.

The cast of NBC's hit comedy series *Night Court*

NIGHT COURT ▶ comedy series on NBC (1984—) built around a youthful, unconventional judge, Harry T. Stone (played by Harry

Anderson), who presides over a Manhattan courtroom that has an endless parade of oddball lawyers and defendants with complaints peculiar to nocturnal life. The resident cast includes a raft of previously unknown talent, such as John Larroquette as the lascivious prosecutor Dan Fielding, Markie Post as the idealistic public defender Christine Sullivan, Marsha Warfield as the tough court officer Roz Russell, and Richard Moll as the thick-skulled court officer Bull Shannon. Other members of the cast have included Selma Diamond, Florence Halop, Ellen Foley, Mike Finneran, Denice Kumagai, Jolene Lutz, John Astin and Mary Cadorette.

NIGHT GALLERY ▶ anthology series of bizarre tales of the occult, with Rod Serling as host-narrator. It began on NBC in 1970 as one of four rotating one-hour series under the umbrella title of *Four in One.* The following season it became a full-time series under its own title. In 1972 it was reduced to half-hour form and canceled in 1973. Universal TV produced it.

NIGHTLINE ▶ ABC's latenight news program, anchored by Ted Koppel, which grew out of the network's special nightly coverage of the Iranian crisis in the winter of 1979. The program represented a major expansion of network news and proved surprisingly successful as a competitor to NBC's *Tonight* with Johnny Carson and CBS's reruns of action-adventure shows in the 11:30 to midnight time period.

As a series *Nightline* was a fluke. ABC had been carrying rerun programming in latenight and ABC News, under the relatively new leadership of Roone Arledge, was struggling to be regarded seriously when the American hostages were taken at the embassy in Iran on Nov. 4, 1979. The story was of enormous interest to the American people, and Arledge persuaded the network to give up some of the latenight time to a daily series of updates, *The Iran Crisis: America Held Hostage.* It is doubtful that the commitment would have been made if anyone had imagined the hostages would be held for more than a few months: ABC found itself stuck covering a news story that had few developments day by day and that seemed to threaten its profits. But *America Held Hostage* proved surprisingly successful, and in short order Koppel, who had been with ABC News since 1963, became popular. By February 1980, ABC discovered it had a new regular latenight program and a month later dubbed it *Nightline.* William E. Lord, a longtime executive of ABC News, became its executive producer. The program reaped a number of awards in its first year, including an Emmy, a duPont-Columbia, and a Christopher.

ABC had so little faith in the news program that it deliberately scheduled the broadcasts in 20-minute lengths, instead of the customary half-hour, to frustrate local stations that might have chosen to preempt the news show for a syndicated program. Since there are no 20-minute syndicated programs, the ABC affiliates stayed with *Nightline* so as not to lose out on the entertainment programs that followed. When it was clear to all that *Nightline* had won the viewers' acceptance and that it could compete with *Tonight,* ABC was able to expand it to a full half-hour without fear of losing affiliate clearances.

Nightline differs from the typical newscast in that it generally develops a single story in the news through interviews with guests and reports from correspondents. The program is structured to respond to late-breaking stories.

The show has evolved into a forum for many of the world's most prominent people in national and international affairs. Its notable guests have included South African President F. W. de Klerk, Nelson Mandela, King Hussein of Jordan, Austrian President Kurt Waldheim, Libyan colonel Muammar Qaddafi, Nobel Peace Prize winner Desmond Tutu, India's Prime Minister Rajiv Gandhi, PLO leader Yasir Arafat, and Presidents Bush, Reagan, Carter, Ford, and Nixon.

Nightline has introduced a new programming idea with the concept of the "town meeting," wherein the network combines panelists, call-ins, radio simulcasting, and assistance from its numerous affiliates to create a unique participatory style broadcast. "Town Meeting" topics have included AIDS, Wall Street and the economy, the question of legalizing drugs, and South Africa.

NIMOY, LEONARD ▶ actor best known for his role as the Vulcan extraterrestrial Mr. Spock in the popular series of the late 1960s, *Star Trek,* after which he did a two-year stint on *Mission: Impossible,* replacing Martin Landau as the team's master of disguises. In later years he narrated a cartoon version of *Star Trek* and hosted the syndicated show *In Search Of....* More recently Nimoy has turned his talents to directing movies, including *Three Men and A Baby* (1987) and *The Good Mother* (1988). He also directed two and appeared in all five movie versions of *Star Trek.*

Nimoy's early television work consisted of small parts in a variety of series. It was a guest appearance in 1964 in *The Lieutenant* that led its producer Gene Roddenberry to cast Nimoy in a new science fiction series, which turned out to be *Star Trek.* The part of Spock was one from which Nimoy could never quite break free; in 1975 he published his autobiography, *I Am Not Spock.*

90 BRISTOL COURT ▶ a trio of related situation comedies mounted by NBC in 1964 in an attempt to penetrate the CBS dominance of Monday night. The comedies, scheduled in successive half hours, were linked by the fact that their characters all lived at the same address. The three series—entitled *Karen; Tom, Dick & Mary* and *Harris Against the World*—all failed in their first season.

NIXON, AGNES ▶ packager and head writer of two long-running ABC soap operas, *One Life to Live* and *All My Children.* She became heiress to the title of "Queen of the Soaps" with the death of her former employer, Irna Phillips. In the 1950s she became a dialogue writer for Phillips and for several years wrote the daily episodes of *As the World Turns.* Later she became head writer for serials owned by Procter & Gamble. In 1968 she struck out on her own, creating and packaging *One Life to Live,* which premiered July 15, 1968. *All My Children* followed on Jan. 4, 1970. She wrote the story for *The Mansions of America* mini-series, which aired on ABC in 1981. In 1983 Nixon created another successful daytime drama on ABC, *Loving.*

NIXON INTERVIEWS WITH DAVID FROST, THE ▶ series of four 90-minute telecasts in May 1977 in which the British talk-show personality David Frost interviewed former President Nixon over a special U.S. network of 155 TV stations. Representing Nixon's emergence from nearly three years of seclusion after resigning from office in disgrace, the broadcasts stirred up the press and national magazines, helping to build the programs a tremendous audience.

The first of the telecasts, airing on May 4 and devoted to issues surrounding the Watergate episode, scored shares of 47 in New York and 50 in Los Angeles—and an estimated national audience of 45 million people—making it the highest-rated news interview program in TV history and one of the most watched news programs ever (excepting events covered simultaneously by all three networks).

Under an intense prosecutorial barrage from Frost, Nixon admitted to having done some lying as Watergate was unfolding but continued to deny an involvement in the Watergate conspiracy and cover-up. Nixon confessed only to letting the American people down and said he impeached himself.

Frost secured the rights to the interviews in 1976 by offering Nixon a guarantee of $600,000 and 10% of the profits, after CBS News and ABC News turned away the ex-President's agent, Irving (Swifty) Lazar, who had asked $1 million for TV access to Nixon. NBC News made an offer of $400,000 for two telecasts with the ex-President and then learned, before it could raise its bid, that Frost had won the rights. For Frost the project was a chance for a comeback in the U.S., where his star had fallen after his syndicated shows for Westinghouse had been canceled three years before.

CBS and ABC both rejected the program on the principle of "checkbook journalism," and ABC was particularly averse to the idea of paying a former president for his accounting to the public.

Frost secured financial backing from a group of affluent Nixon followers in Southern California and engaged the syndication firm Syndicast Services to put together an ad hoc network. Meanwhile, his own company, Paradine Productions, sold the radio rights to the Mutual Broadcasting System, the 16-millimeter educational film rights to Universal Pictures and the foreign rights to 10 countries. The broadcasts were carried in Britain on the BBC on a one-day delay.

Using the barter incentive and scheduling the programs for a month when the networks were expected to be given over largely to reruns, Syndicast lined up stations sufficient to cover 90% of the country. It also arranged for the Robert Wold Co., specialists in arranging the simultaneous distribution of programs for special networks, to handle the interconnection.

Initially, the commercial time was to have been divided evenly between national and local spots—six minutes for each—but when advertisers resisted the network buy at $125,000 a minute, Syndicast sold one of the minutes of national time to the stations.

After a masterfully engineered publicity campaign at the 11th hour, which through selective leaks of the program's content gained Frost/Nixon the covers of *Time, Newsweek* and

TV Guide, the first program was sold out by broadcast time.

With $2 million from "network" advertising sales, $1 million from foreign sales, and substantial other amounts from the sale of radio and educational rights, the entire project was in the black.

Moreover, Frost exercised his contractual right to create a fifth program from the outtakes. He had taped 28 hours with Nixon at the ex-President's home in San Clemente, Calif., and was privileged to use a total of seven hours on the air. The four original broadcasts covered only six hours. The fifth program was put on the syndication market as a straight sale to stations for airing during the week of September 5, 1977.

To protect what he believed to be the rerun value of the program, Frost denied the networks excerpt rights for their newscasts. Estimates were that Nixon would realize at least $1 million overall from the telecasts.

Marvin Minoff of Paradine Productions was executive in charge of the production and Jorn Winther the director.

NO TIME FOR SERGEANTS ▶ television play airing live on CBS in 1955 that started the career of Andy Griffith. A comedy about draftees in the Air Force, in which Griffith played an endearing country bumpkin, it scored so well on the small screen that it was soon remounted for the Broadway stage and was a hit there as well. The play was written by Ira Levin and produced and directed for television by Alex Segal. Others in the TV cast were Harry Clark, Robert Emhardt and Eddie LeRoy.

NOBLE, EDWARD J. (d. 1958) ▶ founder of the American Broadcasting Company and its first board chairman. A multi-millionaire who made his fortune manufacturing Life Savers candies, Noble purchased the NBC Blue Network from RCA for $8 million in 1943, when the FCC ordered the company to give up one of its two radio networks. At the time the Blue Network had 155 affiliated stations. Noble's prior experience with broadcasting had been as owner, for two years, of WMCA in New York, a station he sold in 1943. Noble served as chairman of ABC until 1953 when it merged with United Paramount Pictures. He remained a director of the company until his death.

NORTHERN EXPOSURE ▶ light-hearted drama series on CBS that is representative of the creative cultural wave emanating from the Pacific Northwest. Reminiscent in its oddness of another example of Northwestern bizarre, *Twin Peaks,* the show looks at life in a sleepy Alaska town in the middle of nowhere. The show has an assortment of offbeat characters, including a displaced obsessive New York doctor, Joel Fleischman (played by Rob Morrow), a beautiful but icy pilot, Maggie O'Connell (Janine Turner), an ex-astronaut, Maurice Minnifield (Barry Corbin), a handsome poetic disk jockey, Chris Stevens (John Corbett) and a couple—about forty years apart in age—who own the town bar.

Shot entirely in Washington state, the series was co-created and produced by Joshua Brand and John Falsey, both veterans of *St. Elsewhere.* It debuted originally in the summer of 1990, and returned to the schedule in early 1991. The Finnegan-Pinchuk Company, Falahey/Austin Street Productions and Cine-Nevada Productions produced for Universal Television.

Robert (Shad) Northshield

NORTHSHIELD, ROBERT (SHAD) ▶ noted producer of news programs whose career has swung between CBS and NBC, with a brief stint at ABC. After developing and producing the successful 90-minute *Sunday Morning* news broadcast on CBS in 1978, Northshield was rewarded with responsibility for revamping the weekday morning news program, retitled *Morning,* in January 1979. Three years later, when the weekday edition failed to rise to ratings parity with *Today* and *Good Morning, America,* Northshield's responsibilities were reduced to *Sunday Morning* and a new executive producer, George Merlis, was brought in for the daily shows. In 1987 Northshield left *Sunday Morning* to work as the executive producer on pilot programs with Charles Kuralt. He also produces CBS special news programs.

Northshield had rejoined CBS in 1977 after a 17-year absence. He worked initially as an executive producer in sports and then as a documentary producer for CBS News, before receiving the *Sunday Morning* assignment. He had spent the previous years, since 1960, with NBC News. In the early 1960s, he was producer of *Today* with occasional documentary assignments. He was made general manager of NBC News in 1964, supervising political coverage, and a year later became executive producer of the *Huntley-Brinkley Report.* He produced such documentaries as *Suffer the Little Children* (1972), *And Who Shall Feed This World?* (1974) and *The Navaho Way* (1974).

He began his TV career with CBS in 1953 and was producer of the *Adventure* series and of *Seven Lively Arts.* Later he became a columnist for the *Chicago Sun-Times* and then produced public affairs programs for ABC (1958-60) before joining NBC.

NORVILLE, DEBORAH ▶ former co-anchor of NBC's *Today* show (1989-91). Critics and viewers called her The Other Woman when she replaced fixture Jane Pauley as Bryant Gumbel's co-anchor. Viewers responded by dropping *Today* to number two in the ratings.

In April 1991 Norville, who had been on maternity leave since February of that year, was herself replaced by Katie Couric. NBC claimed the leave-taking was Norville's own idea, "to give my son the best possible start on life."

Norville started her broadcast career in 1978 while still a student at the University of Georgia, reporting for WAGA-TV in Atlanta. In 1987 after six years at the NBC-owned Chicago station, WMAQ-TV, she anchored NBC's *News at Sunrise* and substituted for both Gumbel and Pauley on *Today.* Norville went on to host a three-hour ABC Radio talk show.

NOTICE OF INQUIRY ▶ an FCC procedural device preliminary to rule-making, which is its means of alerting the public to the prospective adoption of new rules or to possible changes in existing rules. The Notice of Inquiry is issued for information on a broad subject or when the commission is seeking ideas on a given topic.

NOTRE DAME FOOTBALL ▶ one of the sought-after collegiate gridiron attractions because of the school's cachet in the sport, based on its history of fielding exceptional teams. In 1991, just after the College Football Association signed a five-year contract with ABC for $210 million (to be divided among 63 college organizations), Notre Dame announced it was withdrawing to go it alone. The university then signed a $38 million five-year contract with NBC, which figures out to $17.5 million more than it would have gotten from its cut of the CFA package. Notre Dame splits $1.2 million with each visiting team.

According to Notre Dame officials, the reason for the university's surprise pull-out from the CFA deal was not a matter of money but rather that ABC had a regional system of telecasts in mind, and Notre Dame wanted its games to be televised nationally. ABC's position is that the regional concept ensures exposure for all the member colleges in CFA, and since viewer interest in the teams tends to be regional, the plan will maximize ratings.

***NOVA* ▶** major PBS series with the distinction of being the longest-running nationally broadcast science program on television. Begun in March 1974 by WGBH-TV producer Michael Ambrosino and modelled on a similar BBC series, *Nova* is noted for examining complex questions of science, nature and technology in a manner comprehensible to ordinary citizens and in a relatively entertaining fashion. The treatment of new developments in science runs the gamut from attempted cures for baldness in "Sex, Lies and Toupee Tape" to the controversy surrounding the "Secrets of the Dead Sea Scrolls." The series, underwritten by the Johnson & Johnson Family of Companies and Lockheed, is produced by WGBH-TV Boston with Paula S. Apsell as executive producer and Bill Grant as executive editor.

NOXON, NICOLAS ▶ producer-director-writer specializing in nonfiction programs who, with Irwin Rosten, headed the MGM documentary department in the early 1970s, chiefly responsible for the *GE Monogram Series.* That unit yielded three programs a year for NBC. Earlier, at Wolper Productions, where he had met his partner, Noxon produced and wrote such shows as *Doctor Leakey and the Dawn of Man, Voyage of the Brigantine* (both programs winners of Peabody Awards), *Epic of Flight,* seven half-hours of *Hollywood and the Stars* and 17 half-hours of the *Biography* series.

NTSC ▶ initials commonly used to designate the American-developed systems of both monochrome and color television. The letters stand for National Television System Committee, first established in 1936 to develop monochrome television standards and reconstituted in 1950 to recommend a compatible color television system. Both groups consisted of engineers from a variety of receiving and transmitting equipment manufacturers and were formed under the aegis of the Radio Manufacturers' Association (now the Electronic Industries Association).

The first NTSC recommended the 525-line, 60-field-per-second black-and-white system currently in use. The second group developed a color television system compatible with these monochrome standards. Both recommendations, based largely on systems developed by RCA, were adopted by the FCC for American television. The NTSC monochrome system has a 6-megahertz channel bandwidth, amplitude-modulated picture and frequency-modulated (FM) sound.

The major countries using NTSC monochrome and color standards, in addition to the United States, include Canada, most Western Hemisphere nations, Japan and other Far Eastern countries in the American sphere of influence. NTSC color broadcasting started in the United States on January 1, 1954. The other major television system is the European CCIR, which is used with two different color standards—PAL and SECAM.

NURSES, THE ▶ drama series on CBS (1962-65) set in a large hospital. Produced by Plautus Productions, it featured Shirl Conway as supervising nurse Liz Thorpe, Zina Bethune as new nurse Gail Lucas, Edward Binns as Dr. Kiley, Stephen Brooks as Dr. Lowry, Michael Tolan as Dr. Alexander Tazinski and Joseph Campanella as Dr. Ted Steffen. In 1964, when Tolan and Campanella joined the cast, the show changed its title to *The Doctors and the Nurses.*

N.Y.P.D. ▶ half-hour ABC series (1967-68) produced on 16mm film, drawing its stories from cases of the New York City Police Department. It starred Jack Warden as Detective Lieutenant Mike Haines, Robert Hooks as Detective Jeff Ward and Frank Converse as Detective Johnny Corso and was produced by Talent Associates.

O

O&O ▶ trade shorthand for an owned-and-operated station, usually in reference to those owned by the parent corporations of the networks but applying also to group-owned stations. WBBM-TV Chicago is a CBS o&o; WBZ-TV Boston is a Group W o&o.

OATER ▶ nickname for a TV western and in popular use in the early 1960s when westerns were the dominant form of prime-time entertainment on the networks. Other pet names for the form were oatburner, horse opera and thatawayer (from the western movie cliche, "They went thataway.") These terms applied mainly to shows that were riding the western trend and were otherwise undistinguished.

Eric Ober

OBER, ERIC ▶ president of CBS News since August 1990, succeeding David W. Burke, whom CBS had hired away from ABC four years earlier. Ober's career at CBS, which began in 1966, has shifted between news and managerial posts. After working in various areas of local station news, he was named general manager of WBBM-TV, CBS's Chicago station, in 1983. A year later he was assigned to CBS News as vice president of public affairs. Then he became v.p. of news for the owned-TV stations. In 1987 he became president of the owned-stations division, his last stop before becoming the CBS News chief.

"OBJECTIONABLE" MATERIAL ▶ [Pacifica Foundation/ 1 R.R. 2d 747 (1964)] programs found offensive by some people but otherwise well within the public interest standard for broadcast. The FCC decided in the Pacifica case that broadcasters have a right to air "provocative" programs but suggested that they be confined to the later evening hours when children presumably are asleep. The opinion in this case established the legal framework which the Supreme Court later adopted in another case involving the same license.

The Pacifica Foundation, licensee of several noncommercial FM stations, frequently broadcasts avant-garde programs. When the foundation sought to renew its licenses, the FCC questioned it about five programs that had drawn complaints. They included two programs in which poets read from their works; a reading of Edward Albee's play *Zoo Story;* a discussion group in which homosexuals spoke of their problems and expressed their attitudes; and readings of an unfinished novel by its author.

Pacifica defended most of the broadcasts by stating that they fell well within the public interest standard. The commission recognized that while such programs may tend to offend some listeners, "this does not mean those offended have the right, through the commission's licensing power, to rule such programming off the air waves." The commission also noted that the programs had been broadcast at hours when most children had gone to sleep.

Pacifica did not defend the two programs of poetry, which it admitted contained some passages that did not conform to its own standards of acceptability. It said the programs were aired through errors in the screening process. The FCC found the explanation to be "credible" and decided that two isolated errors over a period of four years were hardly sufficient to question seriously a licensee's fitness to continue broadcasting. There was no appeal, and Pacifica's licenses were renewed.

See also Carlin "Seven Dirty Words" Decision.

OBSCENITY AND INDECENCY ▶ Section 1464 of the U.S. Criminal Code makes it a federal crime to broadcast "any obscene, indecent, or profane language...." The FCC has the power to revoke the license of a broadcaster it finds to have violated this law.

The prohibition on "profanity" is indisputably unconstitutional, and it is universally ignored. "Indecency," which includes vulgar and offensive language, often of a political nature, is entitled to some degree of constitutional protection. "Obscenity," which typically involves "hard core" or explicit sexual content, is not considered to be "speech" subject to the protection of the First Amendment, and can be lawfully prohibited in all forms.

Obscenity has rarely appeared on over-the-air TV or on cable networks, although the latter have often carried "hard-R" feature films that many regard as close to the line. A highly publicized exception occurred when a station in Milwaukee paid a fine in 1988 for the purportedly mistaken broadcast of an explicit film called *Private Lessons.*

Until 1987, the FCC followed a relatively lenient approach to enforcing the prohibition on broadcast indecency. Although the Supreme Court's 1978 *Pacifica* decision upheld a bar on "material that depicts ... in terms patently offensive as measured by contemporary community standards ..., sexual or excretory activities or organs ...," the commission took a literalist stance by acting only upon the repeated daytime or prime time broadcast of seven specific "dirty words." This changed suddenly in April 1987 when outgoing FCC chairman Mark Fowler announced a new policy under which the commission's *de facto* recognition of a "safe harbor" for broadcast of indecent material after 8 p.m. was changed to midnight, and the commission began issuing fines to broadcasters carrying objectionable material other than the seven "dirty words."

A coalition of broadcast reform and civil liberties groups, along with the networks and major public and commercial broadcast owners, successfully challenged the new policy in the U.S. Court of Appeals. Although the unanimous *Action for Children's Television v. FCC* decision upheld the FCC's broader definition of indecency, it held that the ban on all indecent broadcasts until midnight violated the First Amendment, since it unnecessarily denied adult access to stronger material. The Court directed the FCC to come up with a new and defensible "safe harbor."

Congress intervened. Just prior to election day in 1988, it adopted the "Helms Amendment," named for its sponsor, North Carolina Senator Jesse Helms, whose political career was built upon his years as an editorialist on Raleigh's WRAL-TV. The law directed the FCC to ignore the Court decision and instead adopt a blanket ban on any broadcast of indecency. The Helms amendment was declared unconstitutional by the Court of Appeals in 1991, in a second *Action for Children's Television v. FCC* decision.

OBSCENITY CASES AND THE SUPREME COURT ▶ the Supreme Court has attempted to define First Amendment protection of allegedly obscene speech for many years without success, owing primarily to the difficulty of defining "obscene" in the first instance. Originally it was assumed that obscenity, like defamation and "fighting words," was not "speech" within the meaning of the First Amendment protections [*Chaplinsky v. New Hampshire,* 315 U.S. 568 (1942)]. This was subsequently affirmed in *Roth v. United States* [354 U.S. 476 (1957)], a landmark decision because it was the first case in which the Supreme Court was required to decide if obscenity was protected speech.

Roth, a New York publisher, was convicted of mailing obscene advertising material and an obscene book in violation of Federal law. His conviction was appealed to the Supreme Court, which affirmed. The court reasoned that the First Amendment "was not intended to protect every utterance," and that obscenity was "utterly without redeeming social importance," and was not protected by the Constitution.

Subsequent cases focused sharply on the word "utterly," and the court found itself reviewing dozens of cases to decide whether allegedly obscene matter was "utterly without redeeming social value" [*Memoirs v. Massachusetts,* 383 U.S. 413 (1966)]. Since a majority of the Justices were unable to agree upon criteria which made material obscene under this "definition," the court disposed of case after case by refusing to grant certiorari, or reversing in per curiam opinion.

This ad hoc approach, which continued to leave undefined the parameters of protected communication, was generally unsatisfactory to the bench and bar alike because it required the Supreme Court to sit in review of *factual* determinations of state and Federal trial and appellate courts. The Supreme Court attempted to rectify this situation in *Miller v. California* [413 U.S. 15 (1973)] and *Paris Adult Theater I v. Slaton* [413 U.S. 49 (1973)].

In the Miller case, the defendant was convicted of violating a California obscenity law by conducting a mass mailing campaign to advertise "adult material." These advertisements explicitly depicted sexual activities and included prominent display of genitals. The Supreme Court, speaking through Chief Justice Burger, not only affirmed Miller's conviction but established general guidelines for lower courts to follow in future obscenity cases. The guidelines required the application of "contemporary community standards" to determine whether the material appealed to prurient interest by a "patently offensive" display of sexual conduct where the work, "taken as a whole, lacks serious literary, artistic, political or scientific value."

In the Paris Theater case, the court held that a movie theater owner could be held liable for showing obscene movies despite warnings at the theater entrance that admission was limited to people over 21 because the films displayed explicit sexual acts. The individual, said the court, had no fundamental privacy right to view obscene movies in places of public accommodation.

If the court hoped by these two decisions to rid itself of the chore of examining material to review lower court findings of obscenity, it was mistaken. In *Jenkins v. Georgia* [418 U.S. 153 (1974)], the Supreme Court was required to apply its Miller test to the film *Carnal Knowledge,* which had been found obscene in the Georgia courts. Jenkins, a theater owner, was convicted by a jury of displaying an obscene film. The Georgia Supreme Court affirmed the conviction because, it said, a jury's determination of obscenity precluded all further review. The U.S. Supreme Court disagreed and held that juries simply do not have "unbridled discretion in determining what is patently offensive." Since the Justices did not find that the film was "obscene," the court reversed the conviction, reaffirming an earlier pronouncement of a distinction between sex and obscenity.

Although majorities of Justices have consistently agreed that obscene speech is not entitled to the protection given to other kinds of speech by the First Amendment, the Supreme Court has not as yet successfully delineated the bounds of this limitation, and until it does the court will continue to review lower court decisions by substituting its own moral judgment.

With the gradual replacement of more liberal members, the Supreme Court has become increasingly stern in its view of obscenity. Ruling in cases involving "dial-a-porn," the Court has made plain its disapproval of explicit sexual material. A new threat emerged in 1991, when the Court outlawed nude dancing under a theory that its action was directed not at speech or artistic expression, but at a public nuisance. Conservatives immediately began to press for extension of this principle to broadcasting.

OBUCHOWSKI, JANICE ▶ administrator since 1989 of the National Telecommunications and Information Administration (NTIA), with the formal title of assistant secretary for Communication and Information for the Department of Commerce. Moving between the regulators and the regulated, Obuchowski spent four years with a Washington antitrust litigation firm before joining the FCC as chief of its Common Carrier Bureau. Later she became senior advisor to FCC chairman Mark Fowler. She left government in 1987 to serve NYNEX, the East Coast telephone complex, as its executive director for international affairs, immediately prior to her confirmation as NTIA administrator in September 1989.

O'CONNOR, CARROLL ▶ actor who apparently has succeeded in escaping imprisonment in a single, hugely successful role. His ten-year identification with the character Archie Bunker in *All in the Family* and its sequel, *Archie Bunker's Place,* was so strong that many believed he could not be credible playing any other character. O'Connor, being an accomplished actor, seems to have surmounted the type-casting. He wrote and starred in the TV version of *The Last Hurrah* (1977) and co-starred in the TV movie, *The Father Clements Story* (1990). Since 1988 he has played one of the leads in the NBC series, *In the Heat of the Night.*

Before *All in the Family,* he had appeared in some 30 feature films and around 100 TV programs, mostly in supporting roles. He attended college in Ireland and began his career on the stage, playing in Dublin, London and Paris before making his Broadway debut in 1958.

O'CONNOR, JOHN J. ▶ veteran television critic for *The New York Times* who succeeded Jack Gould in 1971. His concentration through the years has been on the more intellectually nourishing works for the medium rather than on the mass-appeal entertainments. Though he of course reviews the run-of-the-mine sitcoms and police shows on the networks, O'Connor is clearly more comfortable with the general offerings on PBS and some of the cable channels, and he is the country's leading television reviewer of serious drama and arts programming. For many years he was responsible for all areas of television, but in the early 1980s the *Times* relieved O'Connor of reviewing news, documentaries and other non-fiction and assigned those duties to John Corry. Later Corry was replaced by Walter Goodman.

O'Connor came to the *Times* from *The Wall Street Journal,* where he had started as a cultural critic in 1960 and became arts editor in 1966.

***ODD COUPLE, THE* ▶** ABC situation comedy (1970-75) drawn from Neil Simon's Broadway comedy hit of that title, concerning a compulsively neat photographer, Felix Unger, sharing an apartment in New York with a slovenly sportswriter, Oscar Madison. The roles were played by Tony Randall and Jack Klugman, respectively, with Al Molinaro featured as policeman-friend Murray Greshler. The series was always only marginally successful, but the syndicated reruns did well. It was by Paramount TV, with Garry Marshall as executive producer and Tony Marshall as producer.

Jack Klugman and Tony Randall, stars of the ABC series *The Odd Couple*

OFFICE OF TELECOMMUNICATIONS POLICY ▶ a White House agency established in 1971 as principal advisor to the President on national telecommunications matters, with the additional responsibility of formulating policies and coordinating cost-effective operations for government communications systems. OTP was dissolved in 1977 and its functions assumed by the new National Telecommunications and Information Administration (NTIA) in the Department of Commerce. OTP assigned the frequencies used by federal agencies and provided policy direction for the national communication system and emergency communications.

The office was politicized by its first director, Clay T. Whitehead, who used it to carry out the media strategies of the Nixon Administration. In his well-publicized speeches, he intimidated the networks and their affiliates with charges that network news dealt in "ideological plugola" and "elitist gossip," and he admonished public broadcasters against centralizing under a fourth network. He made it plain that the Administration would not support a long-range funding bill for public television if that industry did not adopt a system based on "grassroots localism." Whitehead resigned in 1975, after producing several important studies that redeemed the office, but the damage to the image of the agency during his tenure nearly caused it to be abolished during the Ford Administration.

With John Eger as acting director, OTP later made policy recommendations to the FCC regarding cable TV, domestic satellites, land-mobile radio service, VHF spectrum allocation and the economic impact of competition in certain telecommunications markets. Thomas J. Houser, a Chicago lawyer who once had served briefly on the FCC, was named director by President Ford in 1976. He resigned in January 1977 at the start of the Carter Administration. William Thaler then became acting director.

OTP maintained a staff of around 48 people and operated on an annual budget of about $8.5 million, although nearly three-fourths of that amount went to the Office of Telecommunications of the Commerce Department, from which OTP received support services. More than 100 employees of the Commerce OT were assigned to OTP on a full- or part-time basis in connection with spectrum management and general policy-making.

OFF-NETWORK ▶ syndicated series that had their original runs on the networks in prime time, and after four or five years on the air amassed a library worthy of repeating in fringe time periods. When sold to stations, the reruns are presented in different form as strips, airing in the same time period every weeknight. Off-network shows usually are the most attractive in the syndication market because their popularity is proven.

O'HANLON, JAMES ▶ writer who created *Maverick.* He also wrote for *My Favorite Husband, 77 Sunset Strip, Cheyenne* and *Going My Way.*

OHLMEYER, DON ▶ former high-ranking sports executive with NBC and ABC and now chairman and CEO of Ohlmeyer Communications Co. He formed his production company in 1982 and has since served as executive producer of numerous sports events and TV movies, including *Right to Die, Under Siege* and *Special Bulletin* (written and directed by Marshall Herskovitz and Edward Zwick). He has also produced the Emmy and MTV awards shows and has directed the TV movie *The Heroes of Desert Storm.*

At the networks Ohlmeyer was a production executive with extensive experience in covering the Olympic Games, and thus a prize catch for NBC Sports after it had acquired the rights to the 1980 Moscow Olympics for $100 million. He joined NBC as executive producer of sports in 1977, at the age of 32, after spending ten years with ABC Sports in a variety of production capacities.

He was producer-director of the summer Olympics in Munich (1972) and Montreal (1976), as well as the 1976 Winter Olympics telecasts from Innsbruck. In 1968, only a year out of Notre Dame, he was associate director of the Summer Olympics from Mexico City. At ABC he also produced the NFL Monday night football coverage, NCAA football, NBA basketball, coverage of several world heavyweight championship fights and segments for *Wide World of Sports.* Other credits include such prime-time specials as *Battle of the Network Stars, Superstars* and the harlem Globetrotters specials.

With such a background, he was given overall creative control of NBC's coverage of the 1980 Moscow event. In addition to his position as executive producer of all NBC Sports programming, he served as a program packager for the TV network. Ohlmeyer is known for having widened the scope of sports coverage on television by introducing live coverage of the Wimbledon Men's Tennis Finals, as well as televising AIAW (Association for Intercollegiate Athletics for Women) events, Championship Auto Racing Team events and downhill skiing. He was also the first to introduce the announcer-free televised football game. His work has netted him a passel of Emmy awards.

OLYMPICS, THE ▶ a quadrennial international sporting event and television extravaganza whose rights are so sought-after by the U.S. networks that they have become the most expensive rights in all of television. Moreover, they have risen steeply every four years for both the summer and the winter broadcasts. In 1972 ABC secured the rights to the summer games from Munich for $13.5 million. Twenty years later, for the 1992 summer games in Barcelona, NBC's winning bid was $401 million.

In order to justify the increases, the networks each time schedule more and more hours of coverage. This puts a strain on advertising budgets for the companies that want to participate in the Olympics, since the schedule of broadcast hours for both the summer and winter games are expanded in the same year. In an effort to lessen the strain, the International Olympic Committee—which derives its greatest financial support from U.S. television—changed the pattern of the games so that the summer and winter events occur two years apart. This staggered schedule goes into effect with the winter games in 1994, to be followed by the summer games from Atlanta in 1996. Each will continue at four-year intervals.

The Olympics became a hot television event in the summer of 1968 when ABC was providing the coverage and, for the first time, captured the interest of a broad public with its telecasts of games and amateur track events that were minor sports at best, and some even obscure. ABC Sports, under Roone Arledge, proved just the right network to popularize the Olympic games. For many years, one of ABC's most consistently successful shows was Arledge's *Wide World of Sports*, a magazine series that had covered every kind of athletic event on the globe. ABC had become so proficient at shooting these events and packaging them for an American audience that the Olympics were almost an extension of *Wide World of Sports*, although, of course, much more complex.

ABC's success with the Olympics that year had an unexpected dividend. It gave the network a clear running start on the fall season. Not only had viewers formed a habit of tuning into ABC for the coverage but they were also substantially exposed to the network's promotional spots for its new shows. As the perennially third-ranked network, ABC had one of its most successful seasons that fall. Eight years later, the 1976 summer Olympics were credited with giving ABC the boost that made it the top-rated network during the fall season.

In 1980 NBC executives committed what was then an astronomical $100 million to Olympics coverage from Moscow, in hopes it would do for their network what the summer games had done previously for ABC. But to NBC's misfortune, the U.S. boycotted the 1980 Olympics after the Soviet invasion of Afghanistan. The network recovered much of its prepaid investment from insurance but the loss of the event upset the NBC strategy of presenting 150 hours of coverage, which would have meant more than 10 hours a day for two weeks.

Whichever network telecasts the Olympics typically captures some 50% of the audience each night for the two week duration and also receives a large tune-in for the day-long coverage on weekends. During the course of their immersion in the coverage, viewers develop a relationship with the network that tends to carry over to the new season, which is why the networks bid so vigorously for the rights.

In part because the American networks are so avid for the event, the U.S. contributes an inordinate share towards the Olympics' financial support, many times more than the rest of the world. In 1988, for example, the countries of Western Europe (through Eurovision) together paid $5.7 million for broadcast rights to the Winter Olympics from Calgary, while ABC paid $309 million, or 50 times more. Globally, the audience for the two-week period is estimated at around a billion.

From the inception of the modern Olympics in 1896, politics and nationalism have been interwoven in the games. The worldwide attention provided by television has heightened the temptation of countries to use the Olympics for some manner of political statement. Thus the world watched in horror as members of the Israeli delegation to Munich in 1972 were killed by Palestinian terrorists. In 1976 25 nations shattered the dreams of their 697 athletes by pulling out of the games at the last minute because New Zealand had been allowed to participate after sending a rugby team to South Africa. Then, in 1980, came the U.S. pullout from the Moscow games, and for hundreds of athletes the many years of rigorous training came to naught.

Negotiations for the 1980 games covered six months, with the Soviets first appearing to have awarded the rights to Satra, an American company that had specialized in trade with the U.S.S.R. But the IOC rejected Satra because its rules require the rights to go to actual broadcast companies and not to middle-men. Lothar Bock, a West German entrepreneur who had been representing CBS in the negotiations before the network decided to drop out, offered his services to NBC and quietly wrapped up the $100 million deal in January 1977 before ABC could make a move. Bock received a commission of $1 million.

Rights fees have so escalated that NBC's winning bid for the Barcelona games in 1992 is quadruple the $100 million bid for the Moscow games 12 years earlier, an amount that was astounding at the time. It is no longer possible to amortize the larger investment by adding yet more hours of airtime for coverage because the saturation point has virtually been reached on the networks. CBS, which bid $243 million for the 1992 winter Olympics from Albertville, France, and another $300 million for the 1994 winter Olympics from Lillehammer, Norway, is expanding coverage hours through the enlistment of cable. CBS has recruited Turner Broadcasting to carry a package of events from the two winter competitions. NBC has taken an even bolder step in allotting some of the

Barcelona coverage to a huge three-channel pay-per-view operation on cable. If the ploy works, pay-per-view is bound to figure in all future calculations for Olympics rights.

OMMERLE, HARRY G. (d. 1976) ▶ a key CBS executive in the 1950s who became v.p. of programs in 1958. He left a year later to head the radio-TV department of the ad agency SSC&B, and in 1966 was named executive v.p. He retired in 1970. Before joining CBS he operated his own talent and program packaging firm.

OMNIBUS ▶ one of commercial TV's most honored series (1951-56), created by the Ford Foundation's Radio-Television Workshop and underwritten by the foundation to demonstrate that a program of cultural and intellectual value could attract a grateful audience and sponsorship. Hosted by Alistair Cooke and produced by Robert Saudek, former head of public affairs for ABC, the program took in $5.5 million in advertising revenues during its five years on the air, against $8.5 million in costs, Ford making up the difference.

The series—featuring documentaries, dramas, musicals, concerts and other programs—began on CBS, which scheduled it Sunday afternoons, and went to ABC its final year in a Sunday evening berth. As Sundays became more lucrative to the networks, none felt it could afford any longer to carry a program like *Omnibus,* which had virtually no potential for profits. Ford withdrew from the series, giving the rights to any future production to Saudek, and turned its attention to building up educational (now public) TV.

The title and concept were reviewed for a limited series of specials in 1980 and 1981 on ABC. Produced by Martin Starger for Marble Arch Productions, with Hal Holbrook as host, the specials were neither critical nor ratings hits, and production was abandoned.

ONE DAY AT A TIME ▶ Norman Lear situation comedy (1975-84) on the trials of an independent, middle-aged divorcee raising two teenaged daughters; it was introduced by CBS as a mid-season replacement in 1975 and ran until 1984. Featured were Bonnie Franklin as Ann Romano, Mackenzie Phillips and Valerie Bertinelli as daughters Julie and Barbara Cooper, Richard Masur as neighbor David Kane and Pat Harrington as apartment building superintendent Dwayne Schneider. The series was by Lear's T.A.T. Communications and Allwhit Productions, with Jack Elinson and Norman Paul as executive producers; Dick Bensfield and Perry Grant, producers; and Herbert Kenwith, director. Subsequently Bensfield and Grant became executive producers, along with director Alan Rafkin.

ONE LIFE TO LIVE ▶ see Soap Operas.

ONE STEP BEYOND ▶ dramatic anthology series based on investigated cases of ESP, hosted and produced by John Newland. It was on ABC (1959-61).

O'NEIL, TERRY ▶ executive producer of NBC Sports since 1989, credited with emphasizing the "news and information" aspects of NBC Sports telecasts and instituting the *NBC Sports Prudential Update.* He brought to the NBC network NFL commentators Bill Walsh, Will McDonough, Bill Parcells and Todd Christensen, as well as golf analyst Johnny Miller and tennis analysts Jimmy Connors and Chris Evert. O'Neil began his career in sports TV as a researcher for ABC's coverage of the 1972 Olympic Games, later becoming a producer for ABC Sports, earning Emmy Awards for coverage of NCAA football and the 1980 Winter Olympics. In 1981 he became executive producer at CBS, where he introduced an on-screen diagramming device, the Telestrator, and brought together the broadcast team of Pat Summerall and John Madden. Before rejoining NBC in 1989, O'Neil headed his own independent production company, which created the show *The Sports Reporters.* He is the author of "The Game Behind the Game," an account of his 15 years in network sports TV, and the co-author (with Rocky Bleier) of "Fighting Back."

ONE-INCH TAPE ▶ video recording format launched in the mid-1970s that replaced two-inch quadruplex tape. In the U.S. a version known as one-inch Type C became the de facto standard at most broadcast operations during the decade of the 1980s. One-inch systems were more economical and easier to operate than two-inch at no sacrifice in quality.

ONE-OFF ▶ British term for a single standalone drama or documentary that is not part of an anthology series. The nearest American equivalent is called a special.

ONE-TO-A-MARKET RULE ▶ FCC policy barring owners of a TV or radio station in a particular city from acquiring a second station in that metropolitan area. In the early days of television, successful radio station owners were encouraged to start TV stations wherever they had radio stations, running the two as companions. By the mid-1960s the FCC sought to increase diversity by separating this ownership. The rule, as adopted in 1970, "grandfathered" existing combinations, but required that any sales of those properties would have to be made to separate purchasers. During the 1980s the FCC's deregulators made waivers of the rule freely available. Outright repeal was proposed in 1987, but the commission yielded to Congressional pressure and, in 1989, adopted instead an even more liberalized waiver policy for stations in the 25 largest markets.

In 1991, FCC chairman Alfred C. Sikes began a new "inquiry," which he hoped would create the political and regulatory framework for abolishing the 12-12-12 rule.

OPEN END ▶ free-wheeling syndicated conversation show, hosted by television producer David Susskind, which broke new ground in the medium in 1958 by allowing its discussions with varied guests to be oblivious of the clock and to run indefinite lengths, usually for several hours. By the mid-1960s, however, it was given a fixed one-hour format and eventually took the title of *The David Susskind Show.*

OPERATION PRIME TIME ▶ a nebulous cooperative of independent stations formed in 1976 to finance the production of significant prime-time programs to compete with those of the networks. The effort was joined by MCA-TV, the syndication arm of Universal TV, and was spearheaded by Al Masini, president of Telerep, the station representative firm. Masini had suggested the idea at an INTV convention.

The project bore fruit in May 1977 with the presentation by 95 stations of a six-hour adaptation of the Taylor Caldwell novel, *Testimony of Two Men.* Twenty-two of the stations were independents and the rest network affiliates; all had put up money to finance the Universal production in exchange for the right to play the serial six times. Most were able to recoup their investment with the first showing.

Among the independents active in starting the cooperative were WPIX New York, WGN Chicago, KCOP Los Angeles and KTVU San Francisco. The linking of independents in this manner caused word to spread in the industry that a "fourth network" was being born, but that characterization of the effort was largely promotional hyperbole.

OPT was significant because it represented a new way to generate national programming, but as an ongoing venture it was limited by the scarcity of independents and the high risk of mounting programs on network-scale budgets.

Testimony had a production budget of $550,000 an hour. Its cast included David Birney, Steve Forrest, Inga Swenson, Barbara Parkins, William Shatner, Margaret O'Brien, Cameron Mitchell, Dan Dailey, Ralph Bellamy and Ray Milland. It was produced by Jack Laird and directed by Larry Yust and Leo Penn.

Subsequent presentations included serial adaptations of John Jakes's *The Bastard, The Rebels* and *The Seekers,* Irwin Shaw's *Evening in Byzantium* and Howard Fast's *The Immigrants.* The project began to run out of steam in the 1980s and shut down in mid-decade.

OPTION TIME ▶ periods of a station's schedule that for many years were effectively controlled by a network, because affiliation contracts specified blocks of time that a network might claim for its use. Local programs would evacuate those time periods whenever the networks exercised their options.

In 1963 the FCC banned "network option" clauses from affiliation contracts as a practice with "anti-competitive effects" which involved an abdication of the licensees' responsibility to program the station in what they consider to be the public interest.

ORACLE ▶ system developed by Britain's ITA, almost concurrently with the BBC's Ceefax, which permits the viewer to call up printed news bulletins and other reading material on the screen by means of a decoder attachment.

ORIGINAL AMATEUR HOUR, THE ▶ a fringe-time variety show featuring amateur talent sought out from all parts of the country. It had a 21-year run on TV (1949-70) as a carry-over from radio. Its host was Ted Mack. The program switched back and forth among the networks. It had its TV premiere on NBC Oct. 4, 1949, switched to ABC (1954-57), went back to NBC for a season and then went to CBS for a long run (1958-70). In its final years its title became *Ted Mack's Original Amateur Hour.* An attempt was made to keep the show going in syndication, but it was unsuccessful.

ORION TELEVISION ▶ independent Hollywood production and distribution company that was hot in the early 1980s with the CBS hit *Cagney and Lacey* and a revival of the syndicated *Hollywood Squares.* Orion TV's fortunes later declined, however, when the syndication business softened and some of its new network contenders failed.

Orion Television was created in 1983 when its year-old parent company, Orion Pictures Corp., purchased Filmways, a small independent production company that had flourished in the late 1960s. By 1985, Orion had a big hit in its first attempt at a network series. *Cagney and Lacey* won awards and lasted six seasons. But the reruns went into syndication at a time when stations were rejecting hour-length off-network shows, favoring half-hour sitcoms. In that same weakened syndication market, Orion's *Hollywood Squares* struggled and then quit. Meanwhile, two prime-time series, *Equal Justice* and *WIOU,* were canceled by the networks.

In 1991 Orion TV was sold off in parcels, with Group W acquiring *The Chuck Woolery Show* and Lorimar Television the rest of the production group, including Gary Nardino, who had headed Orion Television. The distribution arm was retained to concentrate mainly on foreign sales. Orion Pictures, the parent company, also ran into difficulty despite having produced the 1990 Oscar winner *Dances With Wolves.* Laboring under a heavy debt load, it released a number of disappointing films and was in sore need of more box-office winners.

ORKIN, HARVEY (d. 1975) ▶ writer of *You'll Never Get Rich,* the Phil Silvers hit situation comedy (1955-59); later he became head of the creative services department for Creative Management Associates, the talent agency.

ORR, WILLIAM T. ▶ head of TV production for Warner Bros. whose deals with ABC for *Cheyenne* and other series in 1955 opened the way for the major Hollywood studios to produce films for television. A sometime actor who was also son-in-law to Jack L. Warner, Orr rose to executive assistant to Warner after his coup in opening an important new market for the company.

***OSCAR LEVANT SHOW* ▶** West Coast talk show that began in the late 1950s contemporaneously with David Susskind's *Open End* in New York and Irv Kupcinet's *At Random* in Chicago. Levant—concert pianist, author, actor, wit and raconteur—invariably was more interesting than his interview guests and after a few years the program degenerated into a kind of psychiatry session in which the host discussed his own neuroses.

Charles Osgood

OSGOOD, CHARLES ▶ co-anchor of *CBS Morning News,* Osgood earned a reputation as a wordsmith for his contributions to *CBS Evening News* and Charles Kuralt's *Sunday Morning* and for his own radio commentaries on *The Osgood File,* which became a weekly feature on *CBS This Morning.* Osgood has been with CBS News since 1971; his reports occasionally have been delivered in verse. Osgood began his career at WGMS Radio, a classical music station in Washington, D.C. Later he was a general assignment reporter for ABC News for four years.

Soon after Army service, he and some friends opened their own commercial recording studio with artists such as Charlie Byrd. Osgood is a composer, as well, writing "Black Is Beautiful," sung by Nancy Wilson, and "Gallant Men," narrated by the late Sen. Everett Dirksen.

OSMONDS, THE ▶ family of singers from Utah who received their first regular television exposure on *The Andy Williams Show* in the 1960s and later had several regular series and specials of their own. Their biggest show, *Donny and Marie* (1975-78) on ABC, produced by Sid and Marty Krofft, gave way to *The Osmond Family Show,* produced by The Osmond Brothers and Dick Callister. ABC slotted it early Sunday evening, opposite *60 Minutes,* as a mid-season replacement for *The Hardy Boys,* but without success. When the series was canceled, the Osmonds, through their own production company, kept it going in syndication.

OTTE, RUTH ▶ president and chief operating officer of Discovery Networks, parent of two basic-cable services, The Discovery Channel and The Learning Channel. Joining Discovery in 1986, she helped shape the network's identity and established a collegial management style. Otte began her career in financial and internal auditing with ITT in Madrid. After earning an MBA at Georgia State University, she worked for Coca-Cola and then in marketing for Warner Amex, where she rose to vice president of marketing for MTV and VH-1. She joined Discovery as president in 1986.

OUR MISS BROOKS ▶ a CBS situation comedy (1952-57) about a high school teacher, Connie Brooks, that served as a vehicle for Eve Arden, a movie comedienne noted for her wisecrack delivery. Produced by Desilu on film, the series enjoyed great popularity for several years and had a successful syndication run when it was retired by CBS. Gale Gordon was regularly featured as the school's principal, Osgood Conklin, and Bob Rockwell played a fellow teacher, Philip Boynton. A young Richard Crenna was a regular for the first four years.

OUT OF DARKNESS ▶ noted CBS documentary (1956) produced by Albert Wasserman that traced the progress of a psychiatrist with a catatonic patient in a mental hospital, leading to a powerful climactic scene in which the woman begins to speak again. The commentary was by Orson Welles.

OUTER LIMITS, THE ▶ science fiction anthology series created by Leslie Stevens. Vic Perrin introduced and concluded the program. Produced by Daystar-United Artists TV, the series ran on ABC (1963-65).

OVERBUILD ▶ a cable system constructed in a community in which another cable system already exists. This happens rarely because of the high cost of cable construction, but it has occurred in a few situations in the U.S. So far as is known, none has knocked out the original system.

OVERMYER NETWORK (UNITED NETWORK) ▶ a short-lived commercial TV network formed by UHF station owner Daniel H. Overmyer and one-time ABC-TV president Oliver Treyz, which broadcast for 11 nights in May 1967 before collapsing under the high cost of line charges. Overmyer and Treyz laid plans for the network in 1966, projecting a nighttime service that would be carried chiefly by independent stations and that would feature mainly a two-hour variety show from Las Vegas. While preparations were underway, a West Coast group of investors gained control of the project and renamed it the United Network. The two-hour *Las Vegas Show* premiered on 127 stations with support from 13 advertisers, but the audience response was slight, and the venture collapsed during its second week on the air.

OWEN MARSHALL: COUNSELOR AT LAW ▶ hour-long series on ABC (1971-74) about a brilliant lawyer portrayed by Arthur Hill. Lee Majors, who played Jess Brandon, his young law partner, for two seasons, left the cast for his own series, *The Six Million Dollar Man,* and was replaced first by Reni Santoni as Danny Paterno, then by David Soul as Ted Warrick. Featured were Christine Matchett as Marshall's young daughter, Melissa, and Joan Darling as his secretary, Frieda Krause. David Victor, who produced *Marcus Welby, M.D.,* fashioned *Owen Marshall* as a legal counterpart, both for Universal TV.

P

PAAR, JACK ▶ volatile TV personality who became a nightly institution as host of NBC's *Tonight* show, which he took over in 1957. He frequently made news with his capricious behavior on camera and his feuds with the press and other show business personalities. Paar was known to weep on camera, and on one occasion he walked off the show when the network censored one of his jokes which made reference to a water closet. Paar's hallmarks were his emotionality, his adeptness at conversation and his penchant for irritating both his guests and his audience. He grew so popular that after his first year on *Tonight* the network changed the title to *The Jack Paar Show.* He had done four network daytime shows previously, including a quiz program, *Bank on the Stars,* but had not caught the public fancy until he became the late-night host. He was selected by NBC after making four impressive appearances as guest host. On the nightly program he developed a roster of regular guests—among them Zsa Zsa Gabor, Cliff Arquette, Genevieve, Dody Goodman, Hans Conried, Alexander King and Hermione Gingold—some of whom were faded celebrities reborn.

Tired of the grind, Paar gave up the show in 1962 and switched to a weekly variety series on NBC that failed. He purchased a TV station in Poland Springs, Me., and sold it several years later. Meanwhile, Johnny Carson took over *Tonight* and was even a bigger hit than Paar. In 1973 Paar signed with ABC to compete with Carson on a limited schedule of one week a month and failed to recapture his earlier glory.

PACKER, BILLY ▶ CBS Sports broadcaster best known for his coverage of college basketball. Packer covered the NCAA Division I Men's Basketball Tournaments after joining NBC in 1973 and continued to do so after moving over to CBS in 1980. With NBC, he was a regular-season and tournament analyst with Dick Enberg and Al McGuire. Packer learned basketball through experience. At Wake Forest University he was an All-Atlantic Coast Conference guard (1960-62) and led his team to the Final Four in 1962. He graduated with an economics degree but returned to the gym as a Wake Forest assistant coach from 1965-1969.

PAIK, NAM JUNE ▶ Korean-born avant-garde video artist who fathered the video arts movement in the U.S., conducting experiments with abstract images on the screen as early as 1963 and producing the first non-professional works on half-inch portapak equipment in 1970. Working with old TV sets whose circuitry he modified, Paik developed the technique of creating fantastic abstractions by moving a magnet across the screen. Later he achieved complex kaleidoscopic effects through electronic "feedback," a circular electronic process that occurs when a TV camera is focused upon a TV monitor. Collaborating with Shuya Abe at the studios of WGBH Boston, he built the first video synthesizer, a device to add color to black-and-white images, which was yet another boon to video artists. Paik's own works are largely electronic collages flavored with humor and a sense of the absurd.

PAISNER, BRUCE ▶ chairman and CEO of Hearst Entertainment, formerly known as King Features Entertainment, which is involved in the domestic and international production and distribution of programs ranging from mini-series to animated shows. He is also a vice president of the parent Hearst Corp.

A graduate of Harvard Law School, Paisner went directly to work for Time Inc. in 1968 as an assistant to the chairman of the corporation, Andrew Heiskell. Prior to law school, he worked for the company as reporter for *Life* magazine. In 1973 Paisner was named president of Time-Life Films, engaged in marketing BBC programs in the U.S., co-financing new programs with the BBC, and developing domestic shows, including those based on the magazine properties of Time Inc. Seven years later, when Time-Life Films folded, Paisner formed an independent production and distribution company, Novacom, in partnership with Boston public-TV station WGBH. In 1981 Novacom was acquired by Hearst Corp., which brought in Paisner as president of its King Features Entertainment.

PAL ▶ Phase Alternate Line color television system, developed by Germany's Telefunken and widely in use in Western Europe. An offshoot of the American NTSC system, it is nonetheless incompatible with NTSC and with the other major color system, SECAM. The PAL system has been adopted by all Western European countries except France, and by Brazil and China. It was first broadcast in the United Kingdom in 1967.

PALEY, WILLIAM S. (d. 1990) ▶ legendary patriarch of CBS for six decades, and for most of that time the company's largest stockholder. He continued to exert tremendous influence over the company until his death at age 90 in 1990. Paley purchased a floundering radio network with 16 affiliates in 1928 and built it into an enormously powerful and profitable broadcast organization. Paley's ability to deal with stars and keep them content, his instinct for what would succeed in mass entertainment and his keen eye for the extraordinary executive were among the factors in CBS's rise to preeminence in a field that had been dominated by NBC and its former parent, RCA.

More than chairman, Paley was monarch of CBS, and under his demanding leadership the television network was first in ratings for 20 consecutive years, during which it billed itself as "the largest advertising medium in the world." Scheduled to retire in 1966 on reaching age 65, Paley waived the company's mandatory retirement rule for himself and, with the board's approval, stayed on to chart a line of succession and to put CBS on a new economic footing through business acquisitions that would reduce the corporation's dependency on profits from broadcasting.

William S. Paley

Ten years later, just after his 75th birthday, Paley fired the executive who had been in line to succeed him—Arthur R. Taylor, recruited in 1972 from International Paper Co.—and named John D. Backe, head of the CBS Publishing Group, the new president of CBS Inc. Paley fired Backe in 1980 and brought in Thomas H. Wyman from the Pillsbury Co. By this time, however, Paley's habit of spitting out presidents was irritating other members of the CBS board. In 1983 Wyman, with the board's backing, eased Paley out with the new title of "founder chairman" and effectively isolated the aging leader from the company. Embittered and in failing health, Paley summoned all his strength for one last fight. In an unexpected move, Paley threw his support behind Larry Tisch's takeover of CBS in 1986 and Wyman was ousted. By that time, Tisch was CBS's largest single stockholder, controlling 24.9% of the shares, and Paley was second with 9%. The Tisch-Paley alliance briefly restored Paley to power, but Tisch quickly solidified his power and took over day-to-day control of the company. Whatever Paley's true motives, his decision to form an alliance with Tisch to oust Wyman resulted in the transfer of control of CBS to the Tisch family.

Paley began in commercial broadcasting as a sponsor, purchasing air time in Philadelphia for La Palina and other brands of the Congress Cigar Co., his family's concern. Intrigued with radio's possibilities, he purchased for $300,000 the failing Columbia Phonograph Broadcasting Co., a small network formed earlier from what had been United Independent Broadcasters. On Jan. 8, 1929, he renamed the company the Columbia Broadcasting System and, from five floors of office space in Manhattan, began building his communications empire by purchasing stations, establishing affiliations with scores of other stations around the country and selling sponsors on the concept of network radio.

When CBS purchased the Columbia Phonograph and Records Co. for $700,000 in the 1930s, Paley hired away the president of RCA Victor, Edward Wallerstein, to run it. Thus he acquired the most experienced executive in the recording business and with the same stroke eliminated his most formidable competitor. Under CBS ownership, Columbia Records grew to become the most successful recording company in the world. (In 1987 CBS sold its record division to Sony for $2 billion.)

With a $5 million bank loan, Paley executed the coup in 1948 for which he became famous and which was to propel CBS to the forefront of broadcasting. In startling succession, he raided NBC for some of its biggest stars, among them Jack Benny, Amos 'n' Andy, Red Skelton, Edgar Bergen and Charlie McCarthy, and Frank Sinatra. As the audience followed the stars, the CBS penetration grew. *Variety* dubbed the phenomenon, "Paley's Comet."

World War II crystallized Paley's idea for the *CBS World News Roundup,* a daily program around which formed an army of stellar foreign correspondents organized by news director Paul White and headed by Edward R. Murrow. Among them were William L. Shirer, H. V. Kaltenborn, Raymond Gram Swing, Eric Sevareid, Robert Trout and Charles Collingwood, a group that formed the nucleus of what later became CBS News.

Paley's influence on the company extended to styles of dress and office decor, which he chose to describe as "modern but conservative." Although he lived in a patrician manner, moved in high social circles and was president of the Museum of Modern Art and the guiding force behind the creation of the Museum of Television and Radio, he maintained throughout his career a mastery of the popular entertainment objectives of broadcasting and was the industry's foremost impresario.

PALMER, BETSY ▶ ubiquitous TV performer during the 1950s and 1960s who appeared in dramas as an actress, on game shows as a panelist and on *Today* as one of Dave Garroway's regular sidekicks. She was a regular panelist on *I've Got a Secret* and had dramatic roles in productions for *Studio One, Danger* and the *U.S. Steel Hour* and in the series *Martin Kane.*

PANAMSAT ▶ world's only privately owned, trans-oceanic satellite, established in 1984 by Rene Anselmo, a successful American broadcasting entrepreneur. PanAmSat's PAS 1 satellite, known as Alpha Lyracom, was launched in 1988 and covers Europe, North America, the Caribbean and Latin America. Among the satellite's customers, beamed into Europe, is Galavision, the Hispanic U.S. cable channel Anselmo created when he was head of the now defunct Spanish International Network (SIN).

In founding PanAmSat, Anselmo has had to go up against Intelsat, the powerful international cartel that has had monopoly control over rates for international satellite traffic. Because Intelsat and the local PTTs of the signatory countries represented an almost insurmountable wall of resistance to any private company that might presume to compete, Anselmo was unable to raise outside capital for the venture. So he invested the major portion of the $75 million he received when SIN was sold to Hallmark Cards. On the whole, the battle has gone well for PanAmSat, especially in Latin America. A second Alpha Lyracom satellite is scheduled to be launched into a transatlantic orbital slot in 1994.

***PAPER CHASE, THE* ▶** widely praised CBS dramatic series (1978-79) that ran the full season despite anemic ratings but was not renewed beyond that. The series was drawn from the 20th Century-Fox movie of that title, which in turn was inspired by John Jay Osborn Jr.'s novel about the trials of first-year law students with an intimidating, autocratic professor, Charles W. Kingsfield Jr. John Houseman, who had played Kingsfield in the movie and won an Oscar for the performance, recreated the role for the TV series. Robert C. Thompson, producer of the film, was executive producer of the series for Fox.

The intelligent scripts and high level of acting endeared the series to many TV critics, but the subject matter was not the stuff of which television hits are usually made, and the series was handicapped further by its placement in the schedule. CBS assigned it the Tuesday night slot opposite two of ABC's top-rated shows, *Happy Days* and *Laverne and Shirley.* Later in the season the series was shifted experimentally to other time periods to no avail. The regular cast included James Stephens as James T. Hart, Francine Tacker as Elizabeth Logan, Tom Fitzsimmons as Franklin Ford, Robert Ginty as Thomas Anderson, James Keane as Willis Bell, Jonathan Segal as Jonathan Brooks and Deka Beaudine as Asheley Brooks.

Reruns of the series aired on PBS in 1981.

PAPP, JOSEPH (d. 1991) ▶ famed theater producer and head of the New York Shakespeare Festival who produced an embarrassing episode for CBS in 1973. In pursuing leadership among the networks in the sphere of serious contemporary drama, CBS had signed Papp in 1972 to produce 13 plays for the network over a period of four years. He delivered only two, canceling the contract after a widely publicized row with CBS when it postponed the showing of his production of David Rabe's antiwar drama, *Sticks and Bones.*

The two-hour TV adaptation of the prize-winning Off Broadway drama had been scheduled for broadcast March 9, 1973. But after a closed-circuit preview, dozens of affiliates indicated that they found it too rough to carry, or too difficult for viewers to comprehend. CBS itself became concerned over the timing: The program was airing the week that Vietnam POWs were being released and returning home, a week when patriotic sentiment was running high. Moreover, there was the worry that President Nixon, who was personally greeting the returning prisoners, might construe the showing of *Sticks and Bones* as an impertinent attempt by CBS to undermine his effort to create a national celebration around the event.

When the network decided to put off the broadcast indefinitely, while as many as 69 affiliates were on record as refusing to carry it, Papp called CBS "cowardly" and charged the network with censorship. CBS finally did present the play, without commercials and in the light viewing month of August; more than 90 affiliates preempted it, some delaying it to a time period around midnight. But by then, the relationship with Papp had ended.

In November 1973 ABC announced that it had signed Papp to produce two dramas for prime time and to develop other shows for children and for late evening viewing. None ever appeared, however.

Papp's first program for CBS was a three-hour TV adaptation of his stage hit, Shakespeare's *Much Ado About Nothing,* in turn-of-the-century dress. The program was charming and was generally well-received by the critics, but it drew anemic ratings. Papp later complained that in giving the show away free on TV he hurt the box office for the stage version, forcing it to close nine days after the telecast. The program aired on Feb. 2, 1973.

PARIS, JERRY (d. 1986) ▶ actor-turned-director who first made his mark directing and acting in episodes of *The Dick Van Dyke Show* in the 1960s, becoming thereafter a busy director of situation comedy episodes and of pilots. He was director of *Happy Days* from 1975 to 1986, adding the co-producer credit in 1976.

PARKER, EVERETT C. ▶ a leading crusader for the public's rights in broadcasting, as director (1954-83) of the Office of Communication of the United Church of Christ. With some notable success, his continuing effort had been to make broadcasters accountable to the public; to gain employment and access on the air for blacks and other minorities, and for women; and to oppose the broadcasting of extremist views when voice is not given to opposing opinions.

His office filed the petition to deny the license renewal of WLBT-TV Jackson, Miss., for discriminating against blacks, who constituted more than 40% of the local population. This led to two landmark decisions by the Court of Appeals for the District of Columbia Circuit: the first, granting members of the public the right to intervene in license-renewal proceedings; the second, revoking the WLBT license for disobeying the Communications Act requirement that it serve "the public interest, convenience or necessity."

Working with citizens groups in local communities, Parker's office brought pressure upon a number of stations to correct alleged abuses and in several instances obtained agreements from the stations to perform certain specified services for minorities. Parker was also instrumental in causing the FCC to adopt rules requiring stations to maintain a "continuous dialogue" with members of the public so that dissatisfaction with the station's perception of community needs might be resolved locally.

PARKS, BERT ▶ TV personality who, despite numerous daily programs, came to be best known for a single annual appearance as master of ceremonies for the Miss America Pageant. His singing of the ritual song, "There She Is, Miss America," had been one of the medium's constants through two decades. His ouster from the pageant for a younger host in 1979 became a national scandal. Outgoing and exuberant, Parks was an ideal game-show host. He had a program of his own on NBC, *The Bert Parks Show* (1950-52), after which he hosted *Stop the Music* on ABC (1954-56) and later *County Fair, Masquerade Party* (in the original version) and *Break the Bank.*

PARRETTI, GIANCARLO ▶ the Italian entrepreneur who burst on the international motion picture and television scene in late 1990 when he bought MGM and its famous roaring lion trademark from Kirk Kerkorian. He was a Hollywood mogul for less than a year. When he continually strained to meet the loan repayments over the next few months, the banks stepped in and removed him from control. During Parretti's brief tenure, the name of the international television distribution company became MGM Pathe.

Although Parretti's financial dealings over the years have frequently had him under legal investigation both in Italy and France, at least once with charges of bank fraud, he has successfully bought and sold European media properties with his partner Florio Fiorini. Most of Parretti's dealings have been financed by selling off parts of his two major assets—theatrical distributor Cannon in France and Pathe Cinema in Italy—or by using them as collateral. Parretti long had close links with French bank Credit Lyonnais, though these connections were strained to the breaking point with the MGM-UA acquisition.

PARTNERSHIP AGREEMENT ▶ a joint resolution adopted on May 13, 1973, by the Corporation for Public Broadcasting (CPB) and the Public Broadcasting Service (PBS), the two governing bodies of public television, establishing ground rules for working together. Although CPB had been deeded leadership over the system in the Public Broadcasting Act of 1976, PBS asserted its primacy as the representative body of the licensed television stations. The PBS claim to equal power drew from the "bedrock of localism" principle affirmed in the agreement as "mutually desired."

A key provision of the agreement was that CPB distribute a substantial portion of the federal funds it received directly to the PTV stations, as Community Service Grants, under the following formula: 30% at a $45 million funding level, 40% at a $60 million level, 45% at a $70 million level and 50% of funds exceeding $80 million.

The partnership was strained in the fall of 1976 when CPB acted on a number of projects that had not received PBS approval, among them the allocation of $1 million to the BBC to help finance the production of the complete dramatic works of Shakespeare. The conflict led to another round of negotiations between committees of both organizations. They resolved to reaffirm the agreement, with modifications that would give CPB discretion only in the financing of pilots but otherwise requiring joint approval for grants to programs that would actually be aired.

***PARTRIDGE FAMILY, THE* ▶** ABC musical situation comedy (1970-74) about a family that becomes a professional rock group. Via Screen Gems, it starred Shirley Jones as Shirley Partridge and featured David Cassidy as Keith, Susan Dey as Laurie, Danny Bonaduce as Danny, Jeremy Gelbwaks—replaced by Brian Forster—as Chris, Suzanne Crough as Tracy and Dave Madden as Reuben Kincaid, their manager.

PASETTA, MARTY ▶ director specializing in musical variety. He has directed, and sometimes produced, the Emmy, Oscar and Grammy Awards shows since the 1970s and scores of star-centered specials, among them *Sandy in Disneyland, Bing Crosby and His Friends, Barry Manilow in Concert,* and *Ole' Blue Eyes Is Back.* He was director of the weekly series with the Smothers Brothers, Andy Williams and Glen Campbell.

Pasetta began his career in local television at KGO-TV, San Francisco, where he directed and created a wide range of shows. After 16 years with KGO-TV, he moved to Hollywood in 1968 and soon began receiving choice assignments.

***PASSWORD* ▶** see Game Shows.

PASTORE, JOHN O. ▶ feisty Rhode Island senator who held great power over the broadcast industry during his 21 years as chairman of the Senate Communications Subcommittee as its principal legislative force. Pastore, who retired from the Senate in 1976, was perhaps best known for his unrelenting war on excesses of sex and violence in TV, and the pressures he exerted played a part in the industry's adoption of *family viewing time* in 1975. But he figured importantly in much communications legislation over the two decades, concerning such matters as public broadcasting, communications satellites and the Fairness Doctrine. His power also derived from his committee's oversight of the FCC and its confirmation of appointees to communications-related posts in the Government. Not the least of his strength was his profound knowledge of the issues and his readiness to trade something the industry desired, such as longer license periods, for the reforms he sought.

Pastore was a vigorous defender of the Fairness Doctrine, and he successfully fought bills offered in 1975 by Sen. William Proxmire (D.-Wis.) and Sen. Roman Hruska (R.-Neb.) to abolish the doctrine. On the other hand, he opposed the equal-time law and was unsuccessful in his efforts to have it repealed.

It was Pastore's inquiry in the late 1960s into the possible influence of TV violence on violent behavior—and his questioning of William H. Stewart, Surgeon General of the Public Health Service—that led to the $8 million, three-year government study of the subject, culminating in the publication in 1972 of the five-volume *Surgeon General's Scientific Advisory Report on Television and Social Behavior.*

In the midst of confusion about the conclusions of the report, caused partly by accounts in the press, Pastore managed to preserve the credibility of the work through hearings with members of the advisory committee that established a reasonable consensus on the social effects of TV violence.

PATTERNS ▶ 1955 TV drama that aired live on NBC in the *Kraft Television Theatre* series and effectively launched the career of writer Rod Serling. The critical response was so great that the network restaged the show with the same cast for an encore performance a month later, unprecedented in the pre-videotape era of television. A story of executive suite power plays and the tension between ambition and morality in the corporate world, the play starred Everett Sloane, Ed Begley, Richard Kiley and Elizabeth Montgomery. Fielder Cook was producer and director.

PATTY DUKE SHOW, THE ▶ ABC situation comedy (1963-66) in which Patty Duke played two roles, that of an American teenager, Patty Lane, and her look-alike British cousin, Cathy Lane. Featuring William Schallert and Jean Byron as Patty's parents, Martin and Natalie Lane, Paul O'Keefe as Patty's brother, Ross, and Eddie Applegate as her boyfriend, Richard Harrison, it was by Chrislaw and United Artists TV.

PAULEY, JANE ▶ NBC News correspondent whose career blossomed in 1990 after it had appeared to have been dealt a blow. For 13 years, beginning in 1976, she had been the regular female host on NBC's *Today,* given the title of co-anchor in 1982 when Tom Brokaw left to become co-anchor of the *Nightly News.* When the *Today* ratings began to slip in 1989, the producers brought in an attractive and much younger journalist, Deborah Norville, who apparently was being groomed as Pauley's successor. The move backfired on NBC News. Faced with decreasing visibility, Pauley resigned. Her replacement by the largely inexperienced Norville was widely resented, and the press made much of the episode. Norville was portrayed as "the other woman," and the public sympathy for Pauley gave her the star stature she never really enjoyed on the morning program.

Rather than washed-up, Pauley became a bankable name at NBC, and in the summer of 1990 a series of five prime-time specials called *Real Life With Jane Pauley* was given a tryout. It proved successful and was installed as a weekly series in the NBC prime-time lineup in January 1991. A magazine show on American life in the 1990s, with contributions by other NBC correspondents, it presents Pauley as host, reporter and interviewer of celebrities.

Overlooked in the vilification of Norville by the press was the fact that Pauley was picked for *Today* for much the same reasons—her youth and good looks—in 1976. She too had had scant experience as a journalist, having been a co-anchor at the NBC Chicago station, WMAQ-TV, for only a year before winning the *Today* job in an extensive search for a successor to Barbara Walters. Before that she had worked briefly as a reporter and co-anchor at WISH-TV in her native Indianapolis.

Pauley is married to *Doonesbury* cartoonist and sometime playwright, Gary Trudeau.

PAY CABLE ▶ pay television by means of cable TV, which results in the consumer paying first for basic-cable service and then additional monthly amounts for the desired pay channels. The scrambled pay signals are decoded by the cable operator for the channels the consumer desires, with the charges added to the monthly cable bill. Cable fees vary from system to system, but most systems package the premium channels in some fashion. On Manhattan Cable in New York, for example, where the fee for the basic service is $20.95, the added charge for any single pay channel is $12.95, for the second one $10.05, and for the third $9. Subscribers can receive the entire package of basic cable and seven pay services for $69.80 a month.

The leading pay-cable network from the start has been HBO, which in 1975 revolutionized the entire television business when it became the first satellite-delivered national channel. The field also includes Showtime, The Movie Channel, The Disney Channel, Encore, and HBO's sister channel, Cinemax, along with a number of regional sports channels. Bravo remains a pay channel on some systems, but has converted to basic on others.

With its ever-expanding channel capacity, the cable medium can accommodate a good many more pay services, and probably will over time to serve more specialized tastes and needs. But in the 1990s the cable industry has become eager to develop the more interactive form of pay television, pay-per-view, which permits the impulse-buying of programs by the consumer and allows the systems to charge subscribers on a per-program basis. The future stage, beyond pay-per-view, is programming-on-demand, by which subscribers may call up from a vast catalog of new and old movies, and other kinds of programs, whatever they wish to see, at the posted price. Programming-on-demand would turn cable systems into electronic video rental shops.

Pay cable has come a long way from its difficult beginnings. To retard its development, and that of cable, television broadcasters in 1975 assembled a war chest of $1 million for a campaign led by the National Assn. of Broadcasters to keep the FCC from liberalizing the stringent rules it had imposed on pay TV and pay cable. Seeking the support of the public, the TV industry in its newspaper and magazine ads portrayed pay cable as a menace to the elderly and the poor, and a malignancy that would ultimately force all viewers to pay for what they were receiving free. The FCC's rationale for its strict cable rules was that pay TV should supplement conventional television and not replace it.

The fact that theater TV, a form of pay TV, had sufficient resources to outbid commercial television for heavyweight boxing matches seemed to the commission to bear out the NAB's contention that when cable TV achieved adequate penetration it would begin to outbid commercial TV for many of its regular attractions—new movies, the Super Bowl and even its most popular series. Thus, the FCC rules for cable were designed to keep such a "siphoning" of programs from happening.

Aligning with the cable industry for a relaxation of the rules was the motion picture industry, which saw in pay cable a whole new market to take the place of the neighborhood movie house that was eliminated by commercial television. To be able to deliver motion pictures into the house with virtually no distribution or advertising costs and no extra production costs—and to reach the movie consumer who no longer went to theaters—was highly appealing to the film studios, which saw also the possibility of producing films especially for pay TV.

In 1975 the FCC did somewhat ease its pay-cable rules—not enough to suit the cable industry but too generously in the view of the NAB. Both went to court to appeal the rules. On March 25, 1977, the U.S. Court of Appeals for the District of Columbia held that the rules were unconstitutional and improper and ordered them vacated. The court said the FCC acted without knowing whether the siphoning threat was real or fanciful. The TV industry then mounted a legal challenge of the opinion.

Under the original rules, pay cable was able to play movies only within two years of their theatrical release and otherwise not until ten years after their release. the new rules changed the formula to three and ten, on the premise that most movies purchased by commercial television are between three and ten years old.

In January 1976 the House Communications Subcommittee issued a staff report on cable TV—the first Congressional assessment of the industry in 15 years—which favored cable's growth and which concluded that "constraints should not be imposed upon cable to protect broadcasting from competition."

See also Appendix.

PAY TELEVISION ▶ known also as Subscription Television or STV, an alternative form of commercial television that, when it was operating, sold its programming directly to the consumer over specially designated broadcast stations. The STV stations sent out a scrambled signal locally that could be decoded by a black-box device attached to the TV set.

For a time in the early 1980s, it seemed possible that STV would beat out cable as the pay TV of choice with the consumer, especially in urban areas. Cable had not yet been franchised in most of the larger cities, and STV could be tooled up swiftly, without franchising procedures or the stringing of wires. STV stations began springing up on the UHF band around the country. Dallas, at one point, had three such stations and Philadelphia and several other cities two. But cable, with HBO and Showtime, proved the preferred mode of pay TV when it finally arrived in the cities, and by the latter part of the decade the STV stations fell away—some of them converting to home shopping channels and others to conventional TV independents—and STV effectively vanished as a form of broadcasting.

Its fortunes might have gone differently had the Federal Communications Commission not stifled its development for more than two decades. Pay-TV promoters had sought the right to broadcast as early as 1950, but the FCC did not authorize the service, except in isolated experiments, until Dec. 12, 1968. A further delay occurred when the National Assn. of Theater Owners and the Joint Committee Against Toll TV appealed to the courts to block the authorization. That ended on Sept. 30, 1969, when the Supreme Court denied a petition for review of a lower court's decision upholding the FCC action.

Pay cable began in 1972, but the over-the-air form was slower to get started. The FCC authorized three over-the-air systems—Zenith's Phonevision, Teleglobe's Pay TV Systems and Blonder-Tongue Laboratories' BTVision—as technically suitable for stations applying to broadcast pay TV. Subsequently, UHF stations in Los Angeles, Chicago, Newark, Boston, Milwaukee, San Francisco and Washington, D.C., were granted approval to operate pay television, but it was not until 1978 that STV caught fire. National Subscription Television's KSBC-TV, Corona-Los Angeles, started in April 1977 with 800 subscribers and a year later had more than 100,000 and was in the black. By mid-1979 the total swelled to 177,000 subscribers. Meanwhile, in the East, Wometco Broadcasting purchased Blonder-Tongue's ailing Newark STV station, WBTB, and similarly found the market highly receptive to its pay service, Wometco Home Theater. The station found its audience in the areas of metropolitan New York that were not yet wired for cable TV. Its subscribers were charged $45 for installation, a $25 deposit for the decoding unit and $15 a month for the programming.

These twin successes, and those of a second Los Angeles station, sparked such interest in STV that Time Inc., already heavily involved in pay cable as owner of HBO, purchased 50% of Chicago UHF Station WSNS in 1979 with intentions of converting it to pay TV. In July of 1979, NST's second STV station, WXON-TV Detroit, began its operations. Major commercial broadcasters, who once had fought pay TV, began eyeing it for their own expansion—until the bubble burst.

The vigorous opposition to pay broadcasting by theater owners and advertising-supported TV, which through their "Save Free TV" campaigns often won allies among the general public, posed a dilemma to policy-makers from the earliest years. Sporadically, the FCC authorized pay-TV tests but did not permit pay broadcasting to enter the marketplace until advertiser-supported television was firmly and securely entrenched.

The commission was obliged to permit over-the-air experiments because Section 303 of the Communications Act requires the agency to "study new uses of radio, provide for experimental uses of frequencies, and generally encourage the larger and more effective use of radio in the public interest."

In 1950 Skiatron tested its system briefly on WOR-TV New York; a year later, Telemeter experimented over KTLA Los Angeles and Zenith on its own experimental station in Chicago. Other tests were conducted on a Bartlesville, Okla., cable system (1957); on a broadcast station in Etobicoke, Canada, a suburb of Toronto; and in Hartford, Conn., on the RKO station WHCT (Channel 18). The latter experiment, which involved the participation of Zenith with its Phonevision system, ran from 1962 to 1969.

The movie and TV industries marshaled their forces to frustrate an attempt in 1962 by an independent company, Subscription Television Inc., to wire up sections of Los Angeles and San Francisco for a pay-TV service. The well-organized campaign by the powerful forces resulted in a California referendum to prohibit pay TV, which was passed by the state's voters in November 1964. By the time the state supreme court ruled the proposition unconstitutional, Subscription Television had lost $10 million and was in bankruptcy.

The rules for pay TV finally adopted by the FCC late in 1968 were restrictive and designed to minimize the threat to the existing TV system. The commission's rationale was that it would not betray the millions of people who had purchased sets to receive free TV. Essentially, the rules specified that there be only one over-the-air pay-TV station licensed to any market; that only markets already receiving four commercial TV stations or more be authorized a pay-TV outlet; that the stations may not sell decoders but only lease them to subscribers; and that along with their pay services the stations must carry a schedule of free, unscrambled programs (which could carry advertising) a minimum of 28 hours per seven-day week.

Added to these were the "anti-siphoning" rules pertaining to programs. The initial rules barred the use of movies that were between two and 10 years out of theatrical release (later that was eased to three and 10) and required that at least 10% of the pay fare offered be something other than movies and sports. Also barred initially were continuing series, although that restriction was later lifted. Over-the-air pay TV was prohibited from carrying sports events that had appeared locally on conventional TV the previous five years. Most of these rules were later abolished.

PAY-PER-VIEW TELEVISION ▶ cable-related technology that makes for a true home box office, allowing telecasts of individual movies, concerts or sports events to be sold as if to purchasers of tickets. Cable households equipped with addressable converters make a phone call to order the event and, on a designated channel at the appointed time, the scrambled signal is decoded expressly for those who have called for it. The charge, which varies with the event, is added to the subscribers' cable bill.

The cable industry regards pay-per-view as its great new frontier, and the motion picture and sports industries see it as an electronic extension of the theatre and arena box office, potentially a huge new revenue source. By the early 1990s, with close to 20 million addressable homes available, pay-per-view's record was spotty. The Evander Holyfield-Buster Douglas heavyweight championship fight in October 1990 grossed $35 million from pay-per-view, attracting 7% of the addressable households. This was topped in 1991 by the Holyfield-George Foreman match, which exceeded $50 million, a record PPV box office. However, many movies offered shortly after their theatrical release have met with disappointing results, as had a 1991 all-star Metropolitan Opera concert. Periodic extravaganzas staged by the World Wrestling Federation, billed as *Wrestlemania,* have done extraordinarily well, grossing in some instances over $13 million. On the other hand, even the most successful movies on offer barely realize $1 million.

Some of the movie studios attribute this to the limitations of channel capacity; the rigid scheduling of a movie at 8 p.m., they believe, loses all the customers who cannot be there precisely at that hour. The studios consider a multi-channel pay-per-view system ideal, since it would allow for the film to be offered at a variety of times. That may come with the adoption by the cable industry of video compression, which could increase their present channel capacity five-fold. Top executives of Warner Communications expect that, when cable is able to offer 150 channels, each of the Hollywood studios will lease as many as five to sell their films in the homes.

NBC made a large gamble on pay-per-view when it paid dearly for the rights to the 1991 Olympics from Barcelona. Unable to realize a profit from carrying the games solely on its own network, NBC has designated part of the package for pay-per-view. The network's revenue projections from PPV were predicated on an addressable universe of 25 million homes, but the actual number appeared to fall a few million below that.

There are two national pay-per-view networks, each with two channels: Viewer's Choice, owned by a consortium of leading cable companies, along with Walt Disney and Warner Bros.; and Request TV, owned by Group W and Reiss Media Enterprises. Graff Pay-Per-View operates three channels in various parts of the country, and Playboy and Avalon Pictures one each.

Pay-per-view is expected by the cable industry to evolve ultimately into programming-on-demand, envisioned as the ideal pay system, allowing viewers to decide what they want to see from thousands of options and ordering it up. This is expected, when it develops, to render video rental shops obsolete, since any tape they may have in stock could be called up electronically.

PBS (PUBLIC BROADCASTING SERVICE) ▶ public television's central source of national programming, created in 1969 by the Corporation for Public Broadcasting (CPB) primarily to manage the newly established interconnection system. Although PBS replaced NET as the distributor of national programming, it was restricted from assuming NET's role in producing and acquiring programming. To avoid centralized control of programming, the CPB assigned responsibility for program production and acquisition to the stations, initially to the seven largest—including NET, which by then had been merged into New York's Channel 13—but after protests from the excluded stations, to all PBS stations.

PBS was created as a membership organization and remains so today. Its 340 member stations support it through dues and assessments and elect its governing board, originally limited to station chief executives. PBS was restructured in 1973 after the CPB, dominated by the Nixon White House and bent on seizing control of programming, threatened to take over the PBS functions. Ralph B. Rogers, a millionaire industrialist and chairman of the Dallas public station, assumed the leadership of PBS, reorganized it with an expanded board that included 25 local lay leaders in addition to the 21 station professionals, and persuaded the stations to merge their trade association—the ETS division of the National Association of Educational Broadcasters—into the reorganized body. As the elected chairman of the greatly strengthened PBS, Rogers confronted CPB's leaders and forced a compromise solution to the differences between the two rivals in which PBS was given a consultative role in choosing which programs were to be funded from CPB's federal dollars and the freedom to use the interconnection for programs not funded with federal dollars.

The Nixon years were characterized by the administration's determined attacks upon PBS as a "network" and repeated calls for its "decentralization." Documents, later released under the Freedom of Information Act, revealed that the White House's aim was to shift control of programming to the individual stations, believing the stations would act more conservatively in political terms. The stations, on the other hand, were less interested in control than in getting their hands on a larger share of the congressional appropriation. They lobbied Congress to mandate a proportion that was to rise annually, reaching from 40% to 60% as the size of the appropriations grew. PBS president Hartford Gunn used the situation to satisfy the need for decentralization, at the same time reducing CPB's influence over programming. In 1974 he created the Station Program Cooperative (SPC), an ingenious mechanism by which stations voted to choose which national programs would be produced and then shared proportionately in their production costs. For more than 15 years, the SPC remained a principal source of PBS national programming.

In 1976 Gunn was succeeded by Lawrence K. Grossman, an advertising executive, whose seven-year tenure was marked by efforts to strengthen programming and to build audiences for PBS. His proposal to finance additional programming by allying PBS with performing arts organizations in a pay-TV scheme failed to materialize. When he resigned in 1984 to become president of NBC News, he was succeeded by Bruce Christensen, chief lobbyist for the public stations and the former director of both the Brigham Young and University of Utah television and radio stations.

PBS's role in programming underwent another major change in 1990 when its member stations, concerned that the SPC's balloting process did more to sustain established series than to produce new or innovative programming, voted to give PBS a stronger voice in program production. The stations turned over $78 million from the SPC fund for PBS's discretionary use in building a stronger national schedule. Another $26 million was added when the CPB, responding to congressional pressures to rethink the process of national program production, transferred half its programming funds ($23 million) to its old rival. In this modest move toward greater centralization, PBS named a former CPB program executive, Jennifer Lawson, to the post of senior executive vice president of national programming and promotion, with advice and oversight from a 17-member station-dominated Program Policy Committee. The PBS lineup for the 1991-92 season was the first to reflect Lawson's new role as the system's "programming czar."

PEABODY AWARDS ▶ annual awards recognizing distinguished and meritorious public service that are regarded as among the most prestigious in broadcasting. Administered by the Henry W. Grady School of Journalism at the University of Georgia, with the aid of a national advisory board, the awards were established in 1940 to perpetuate the memory of George Foster Peabody, a native of Columbus, Ga., who became a successful New York banker and philanthropist. The awards are made to programs, stations, networks and individuals.

PEACOCK, IAN MICHAEL (MIKE) ▶ British programmer who, after a spectacular career with the BBC, switched briefly to the U.K.'s commercial system and then came to the U.S. in 1974 as executive v.p. of network programs for Warner Bros. TV. He held that post for less than two years.

He rose at the BBC from a trainee in 1952 to program chief and head of the creative staff in the mid-1960s. On his way up, he was a producer, then editor of BBC News and head of programs for BBC-2 when it was established. During his BBC career he was instrumental in developing such programs as *Panorama,* the prestigious weekly public affairs series, and the comedies *Till Death Us Do Part* and *Steptoe and Son,* from which *All in the Family* and *Sanford and Son* were drawn in the U.S.

Peacock left the BBC to become managing director of London Weekend Television in 1967 but resigned within a year after a dispute with the board of directors. He became a consultant and independent producer for five years and then joined Warner Bros. Ltd., London, in 1972, transferring to the U.S. two years later.

PEE-WEE'S PLAYHOUSE ▶ fanciful live-action children's show that entered the CBS Saturday morning lineup in 1986 and quickly became a cult favorite with teenagers and young adults because of the unique appeal of Pee-wee Herman, as a man portraying (or behaving as) a child. A nutty, nasal-voiced, bow-tied character in a shrunken suit, Pee-wee Herman was created by actor Paul Reubens. Staged on a cleverly designed set, the programs consisted of live sketches and animated shorts using claymation and computer graphics. Augmented at times by celebrity guests, the regular cast included Phil Hartman, Gregory Harrison, Ric Heitzman, Alison Mork, Roland Rodriguez, Jon Paragon, Lynne Stewart, Johann Carlo, Gilbert Lewis, and Shirley Stoler.

In April 1991, CBS canceled the show after the network and star mutually agreed not to continue with a sixth season. In July of the same year, Reubens was arrested for exposing himself in a Florida adult movie theater, an episode that was widely covered in the tabloid press. CBS immediately canceled the five reruns that were to have aired through August.

PENNIES FROM HEAVEN ▶ a dark and most unusual mini-series, created by noted British writer Dennis Potter, on the tacky life and strange encounters of a traveling sheet-music salesman during the Great Depression. The drama, which involves murder and adultery, among other evils, was startling in its use of music. Often the song-plugger's fantasies are expressed in songs of the period, the songs he sells, which are in ironic contrast to his drab life in the English midlands. The six episodes, each 75 minutes in length, aired in the U.S. on PBS in 1979.

Produced by Kenith Trodd of the BBC, directed by Piers Haggard and choreographed by Tudor Davies, the series starred Bob Hoskins, supported by Gemma Craven, Cheryl Campbell, Kenneth Colley, Hywel Bennett, Ronald Fraser, Freddie Jones, Rosema Martin and Dave King. A feature film, starring Steve Martin, was adapted from the series a couple of years later.

PENSIONS: THE BROKEN PROMISE ▶ NBC News investigative documentary on abuses in some private pension plans, narrated by Edwin Newman and broadcast Sept. 12, 1972. The program gave rise to a major Fairness Doctrine case, which was not resolved until February 1976, when the Supreme Court refused to hear the case, letting stand a lower court's decision in favor of NBC's position that the program was reasonably balanced for a journalistic expose.

The case began shortly after the broadcast when Accuracy in Media, a news-media watchdog group with a conservative orientation, filed a fairness complaint with the FCC arguing that the program maligned the private pension industry and was not properly balanced with material on the pension plans that had kept their promises to retired persons. Although Newman had mentioned several times in the program that most pension plans were honest, the FCC upheld the AIM petition and ruled that NBC was obliged to tell the positive side of the pensions story, under the Fairness Doctrine. Ironically, the day after the FCC staff deemed the program one-sided, *Pensions* won a Peabody award as "a shining example of constructive and superlative investigative reporting."

NBC appealed the FCC's ruling in the U.S. Court of Appeals in Washington and in September 1974 the court in a 2-1 opinion overturned the FCC's decision. Judge Harold Leventhal, who wrote the court's opinion, held that judgment in an investigative report intending to uncover abuses should not be disturbed if reasonable and in good faith.

AIM appealed to the court for a rehearing, arguing that the three-man panel had made factual and legal errors; and in December 1974 the court agreed to hear the case *en banc,* by the full bench of nine judges. Later, however, the court sent the case back to the original panel to decide whether the case had become moot because legislation had been enacted to regulate private pension systems. In July 1976 the panel directed the FCC to dismiss the complaint. AIM then carried the matter to the Supreme Court, appealing for a decision that would clarify the application of the Fairness Doctrine to documentaries. The court's denial closed the case, and the FCC vacated the complaint.

PEOPLE METER ▶ see Audimeter.

PEOPLE'S CHOICE, THE **▶** an early Jackie Cooper situation comedy vehicle in which he portrayed a small-town mayor, Socrates (Sock) Miller, with a talking basset hound named Cleo. On NBC (1955-58), it was via Norden Productions and featured Patricia Breslin as Sock's girlfriend, Amanda (Mandy) Peoples.

PEOPLE'S COURT **▶** see Courtroom Shows.

PEPPIATT-AYLESWORTH ▶ writing and producing team of Frank Peppiatt and John Aylesworth, who have worked chiefly on variety shows and were creators and executive producers of *Hee-Haw.*

PERFECT STRANGERS **▶** successful if standard ABC sitcom from the team of Thomas Miller and Robert Boyett, producers of *Full House* and *Family Matters.* The series premiered in 1986 with Bronson Pinchot as Balki Bartokomous, a Greek immigrant who moves to the United States and settles in with a distant American cousin, Larry Appleton (played by Mark Linn-Baker). The show derives its humor from the clash of cultures, styles and habits of the two roommates in the manner of *The Odd Couple.* The show's executive producers are Miller and Boyett, as well as Dale McRaven, William Bickley and Michael Warren, in behalf of Lorimar Television.

PERLMUTTER, ALVIN H. ▶ documentary producer whose career swung between commercial and public television before he formed his own production company in 1977. As an independent, he produced the PBS series *Global Papers.* From 1975 to 1977, he was v.p. of NBC News in charge of documentaries. Before that, working in public TV for WNET, New York, he was associated with scores of documentaries and was executive producer of *The Great American Dream Machine, Black Journal, NET Journal* and *At Issue.* Earlier, he was director of public affairs and then program manager of WNBC-TV New York.

His own company, AHP, produces the weekly series *Adam Smith's Money World* along with news-oriented documentaries. Among AHP's more notable works have been two series with Bill Moyers, *Joseph Campbell and the Power of Myth* and *The Public Mind.*

When the Markle Foundation in 1990 proposed a large public television project for the 1992 election year, to which it planned to contribute $5 million as a spur to other contributions, it chose Perlmutter to do the feasibility study and then named him to oversee the development. The project, which had the working title of *The Voter's Channel* and the aim of improving the information content of the election campaigns, became derailed when PBS and Markle could not agree on the dimensions of the plan or on the commitment of airtime.

PERRY MASON **▶** vastly successful hour-long series based on Erle Stanley Gardner's stories of a crime-solving criminal lawyer; it had a nine-year run on CBS (1957-66) and made a star of Raymond Burr. One of TV's most enduring series, it has never ceased running in syndication and is a staple in virtually every television market, although the 245 episodes have played numerous times and only a few are in color.

Featured were Barbara Hale as Mason's secretary, Della Street, and William Hopper as detective Paul Drake, with William Talman portraying Hamilton Burger, the district attorney who was Mason's weekly opponent in the courtroom. The series was produced by Paisano Productions.

CBS attempted to revive the series in 1973 as *The New Adventures of Perry Mason,* with Monte Markham in the title role, but it failed and was canceled at mid-season. In 1985, NBC aired a reunion movie, *Perry Mason Returns* which led to a series of feature-length Perry Mason movies, again starring Burr and made this time by the Fred Silverman Co., Dean Hargrove Productions and Viacom.

PERSIAN GULF WAR ▶ pictorially, on the television screen, a technology war, eerily close to a child's Nintendo game, with monochromatic images of "smart bombs" homing in on precise targets, "surgically" avoiding "collateral" damage to civilians and non-military structures, all dramatically portrayed in film supplied by the Department of Defense. The images created a sense of awe and pride in America's military technology, never more so than the moment the TV screen was filled with images of Israel's dramatic rescue from the threat of Iraqi Scud missiles by the U.S. military's wonder weapon, the seek-and-destroy Patriot missile. The Nintendo effect was further heightened by the networks' dazzling on-screen graphics, a heritage of TV's coverage of sporting events.

Virtually nothing was visible on the TV screen of the war's human tragedy, not even the return to U.S. soil of its fallen men and women, since those pictures were banned by the military. What was seen mainly were sober, monochromatic, and later increasingly jaunty press conferences. In TV studios there was an endless parade of experts engaging in "the talking heads war," in which former military brass were trotted out. In the war zone itself, reporters were required by the military to remain with small pools, selected by the military, and accompanied at all times by military censors. In this atmosphere, enterprise journalism was almost impossible. But there was some.

On CBS, after a slow start getting off the mark, Bob McKeown's early reports from Kuwait City were uncensored, a feat he achieved by breaking away from "pack journalism." Another CBS correspondent, Bob Simon, also went off on his own, but he and his crew were captured by an Iraqi patrol and held for 40 days during which they were interrogated and tortured. On ABC, viewers saw early live reports and hostage interviews from Forrest Sawyer and the extraordinary scene of Iraqi soldiers surrendering to his camera crew. On NBC, correspondent Arthur Kent, movie-star-handsome and reporting live as Scud missiles were fired into Saudi Arabia, earned the nickname of the "Scud Stud."

But the television war belonged, clearly and decisively, to CNN. With the Persian Gulf War, the cable network moved out of the periphery and into the center of the nation's principal news and information sources. Its ratings were big league, and they held up for the duration of the war. People began describing themselves as CNN addicts.

From the first moments of the bombing of Baghdad on Jan. 16, 1991–reported with audio only by Bernard Shaw, Peter Arnett and John Holliman—until the truce two months later, CNN was the only network permitted by Iraq to remain and report from that country. Arnett's reports always bore the lower-third legend "Cleared by Iraqi Censors." Some critics charged him and CNN with serving as a conduit for Saddam Hussein's propaganda, but other journalists felt it was essential to see and hear what effect the war was having upon Iraq. CNN responded with "we will look through any window made available to us to see, even if darkly, something of what is going on." And it did, throughout the 100 days of Operation Desert Storm.

However, the efforts of a beleaguered press to provide a truthful picture of the Persian Gulf War were minor victories in what might be termed The War Between the Networks & The Defense Department. It was a war the Defense Department won. As it had earlier in Grenada and Panama, the Pentagon succeeded—albeit on a much larger scale—in getting a favorable press by not allowing the press free access to the war. Instead, through pictures supplied by the Pentagon and frequent but carefully managed press conferences, the military presented an image of a sanitized war devoid of the human horrors and carnage. The strategy of waging war but not allowing it to be shown was a way, as some critics believed, of avoiding a repetition of what had happened with Vietnam. In that war, with its heavy television coverage of death, destruction and political disarray, the American public eventually turned against the war's continued prosecution.

PERSKY-DENOFF ▶ producing team of Bill Persky and Sam Denoff active mostly in situation comedy. After coming into prominence as writers on the first *Dick Van Dyke Show,* they became producers of *The Funny Side* and then executive producers of *That Girl, The Montefuscos, Big Eddie* and others.

PERSON TO PERSON **▶** a live weekly interview series on CBS (1953-59) that was conducted informally at the homes of the famous and always involved a brief tour of those residences for what they might reveal of the subjects. Edward R. Murrow, the network's premier journalist, urbanely hosted from the studio, so that his vantage was the same as the viewer's.

Uniquely suited to TV, and highly popular, the show visited over the years such notable persons as former President Truman, Maria Callas, Marilyn Monroe, Jackie Robinson, Marlon Brando, Robert Kennedy, Elizabeth Taylor and Mike Todd.

Murrow left the program in 1959 and was succeeded for the duration of its run by Charles Collingwood. John Aaron was executive producer, and other production principals were Fred W. Friendly and Jesse Zoussmer.

PERSONAL ATTACK ▶ the part of the Fairness Doctrine that lays down an affirmative obligation on the part of broadcasters to give persons attacked on the air free access to the airwaves to respond. A personal attack is defined as an attack upon the honesty, character, integrity or like personal qualities of an identified person or group during the presentation of a controversial issue of public importance. The rule was not included in the FCC's 1987 decision repealing most other applications of the Fairness Doctrine.

The concept of "personal attack" was first put forth in 1949 in the Report on Editorializing, in which the commission noted that a personal attack situation might give rise to a more specific obligation on the part of the licensee other than the normal requirements of fairness.

A 1963 Public Notice mailed to licensees advised them that in instances of personal attack on an individual or organization, they had an obligation to transmit a text of the broadcast to the person or group, with a specific offer of time on the facilities.

In 1964, in its Fairness Primer, the commission reiterated this obligation with even more specificity. In 1967, during the middle of the *Red Lion* proceeding, it adopted rules placing an affirmative obligation on licensees when personal attack occurred, or when a licensee broadcast a political editorial.

The rules stated that when a personal attack was made, as defined above, the licensee was obliged, within a reasonable time (but no later than one week) to transmit to the person or group attacked notification of the date, time and identification of the broadcast, a script or tape of the broadcast and an offer of a reasonable opportunity to respond over the licensee's facilities.

When the commission promulgated the rules, it also included some exemptions for certain types of programming. Excluded from the positive obligations of notice and offer of time were attacks on foreign groups and public figures; attacks made by legally qualified candidates and their spokespersons on other candidates and their spokespersons; and attacks that occurred in bona fide newscasts, news interviews and on-the-spot coverage of news events, including commentary or analysis contained in these types of programs. This last provision is sometimes called the Sevareid Ruling, since it seems to be designed to protect commentary such as that given at the time by Eric Sevareid of CBS. Finally, the commission pointed out that while these exemptions may relieve broadcasters of the specific procedural requirements of the Personal Attack Doctrine, they do not relieve them of their general Fairness Doctrine obligations.

The constitutionality of the Personal Attack Doctrine was upheld by the Supreme Court in 1967 (see Red Lion Decision). While the doctrine continues in force, its administration remains difficult and imprecise with respect to definitional problems, particularly with what is a "controversial issue of public importance."

PERSONALITIES ▶ performers with no exceptional musical, acting or comedy talent, and with no valued fund of knowledge, who fill a large, amorphous category in television for their ability to play host, converse with guests and draw affection from viewers. Most TV personalities, though not all, have the gift of glibness and a distinctive manner within the boundaries of conventional behavior; whatever else they may be, TV personalities are not "characters."

The Age of Personalities came in the 1950s and early 1960s, during the years before the networks gave over prime time entirely to film. Often a personality was strong enough to carry a show on the strength of his or her name, and the big ones were among the highest-paid persons in the medium. Arthur Godfrey and Garry Moore had sufficient appeal to spread over several shows. Other big names who "did television," rather than sing or dance, were Ed Sullivan, Dave Garroway, Faye Emerson, Arlene Francis, Art Linkletter, Ted Mack, Robert Q. Lewis, Allen Funt and Dick Clark, among others.

A second group did have the ability to entertain, and occasionally contributed songs or monologues to the proceedings, but nevertheless achieved their prominence through an ability to project a likable personality. They included Jack Paar, Steve Allen, Tennessee Ernie Ford, David Frost, Johnny Carson, Merv Griffin, Mike Douglas, Dick Cavett, Jay Leno, Arsenio Hall, Pat Sajak, Phil Donahue, Geraldo Rivera and Sally Jessy Raphael.

Locally, stations thrived on personalities no less than the networks. Ruth Lyons, in Cincinnati, may have been the biggest local star anywhere in the 1950s; national sponsors waited in line to get on her show. Bob Braun, who followed her, was also popular, as was the late

Paul Dixon with his own show. Chicago had Irv Kupcinet, Studs Terkel, Paul Gibson, Lee Phillip, Jim Conway and a raft of popular "irritable" personalities—Tom Duggan, who went on to greater notoriety on the West Coast, Jack Eigen and Marty Faye. New York had Joe Franklin, Sonny Fox, Carmel Myers and dozens more.

Many of the personalities came to TV from the press or from radio—for many disc jockeys, the transition was natural. While they are far from a dying breed, personalities play a lesser role in TV today because the demand for them is confined to game shows and syndicated talk shows. Locally they have been usurped by newscasters and weathercasters.

PERSUADERS, THE ▶ an attempt by ATV of London to create an action-adventure series that would be both American and British, with Tony Curtis as Danny Wilde and Roger Moore as Lord Brett Sinclair. The comedy-adventure series ran a single season on ABC (1971-72).

PERU ▶ a poor South American country with a mere 1.3 million television homes (against a total population of 22 million) that manages to support eight major channels. Only one of them is state-owned; the others are private. All are based in Lima but achieve national distribution via Panamsat and Intelsat satellites. The state network, Canal 7, devotes 60% of its airtime to indigenous programming and otherwise favors British, German and Argentinean imports. The private stations are more enthusiastic about U.S. programming.

PETE AND GLADYS ▶ domestic situation comedy and one of TV's first spin-offs, the characters having been introduced on the successful *December Bride* series. Produced by CBS (1960-61), it featured Harry Morgan and Cara Williams as Pete and Gladys Porter.

PETER GUNN ▶ stylish private eye series with outstanding jazz theme music by Henry Mancini. It helped launch its creator-producer, Blake Edwards, as a filmmaker. Featuring Craig Stevens as Peter Gunn, Lola Albright as Gunn's girlfriend, Edie Hart, and Herschel Bernardi as Lieutenant Jacoby, it was carried by NBC for two seasons (1958-59) and switched to ABC for one.

Craig Stevens and Diahann Carroll in a scene from *Peter Gunn*

PETER PAN ▶ one of NBC's perennial specials, with Mary Martin and Cyril Ritchard, which had its first telecast March 7, 1955, as a live production and was so popular it was repeated live the following January. After that, video tape made it possible to present a third mounting of the show annually for several years. In December 1976 NBC offered a new version of the James M. Barrie story, with Mia Farrow in the title role and Danny Kaye as Captain Hook; it was presented as a *Hallmark Hall of Fame* special, with a new score, under auspices of Britain's ATV/ITC.

The original production, which aired in the days when specials were called spectaculars, was billed as the first network presentation of a full Broadway production. Martin had created a sensation as Peter Pan, the magical boy who wanted never to grow up. In addition to Ritchard as Captain Hook, Kathy Nolan was featured as Wendy. The producer was Richard Halliday, the musical score was by Moose Charlap and Carolyn Leigh and the special was staged, choreographed and adapted by Jerome Robbins.

The two-hour 1976 production was staged especially for TV by Michael Kidd from a new adaptation by Jack Burns and Andrew Birkin and with an original musical score by Anthony Newley and Leslie Bricusse. The featured cast included Paula Kelly, Virginia McKenna, Briony McRoberts and Tony Sympson. It was produced by Gary Smith and Dwight Hemion, with Hemion directing. Duane Bogie, whose Clarion Productions handled the *Hallmark* series, was executive in charge of production for ATV/ITC.

The original Mary Martin version was aired by NBC in 1990-91 in prime time, to only ordinary ratings.

PETITION FOR RULEMAKING ▶ a formal request to the FCC for changes in existing rules or for the adoption of new rules relating to aspects of broadcasting. The commission requires that the petition set forth arguments and data to support the requested action in order to differentiate a proposal from a casual suggestion.

PETITION TO DENY ▶ a detailed complaint to the FCC asking to deny the renewal of a station's license for having failed to meet its public trust. Petitions to deny are accepted by the FCC at license-renewal time and serve as a means by which citizens groups may act against stations they feel are undeserving of the privilege of broadcasting. A persuasive petition may lead to an investigation by the commission, holding up the license renewal and conceivably resulting in the ultimate removal of the license.

In practice, few licenses have ever been genuinely endangered by these petitions, even before deregulation deprived citizens of most of their leverage. When non-frivolous charges are brought, broadcasters typically enter into a settlement to resolve the challenge.

The petition to deny differs from the license challenge in that the petitioners seek only to cause the operators to lose their license, without bidding to receive the license themselves. Grounds for such competitions range from neglect of significant elements of the community to failure to fulfill the promises of the license application.

PETTICOAT JUNCTION **▶** part of the powerful phalanx of bucolic situation comedies on CBS during the 1960s, concerning three well-endowed girls helping their mother run a small rural hotel. It premiered on CBS in 1963 and still had a sizable audience when CBS canceled it in 1970 in a general housecleaning to change the network's rural image.

Bea Benaderet played the mother, Kate Bradley, for the first five seasons and, after her death in 1968, June Lockhart joined the cast as a country doctor, Janet Craig. The three daughters were represented by Linda Kaye as Betty Jo, Jeannine Riley (later replace by Gunilla Hutton and Meredith MacRae) as Billie Jo and Pat Woodell (replaced by Lori Saunders) as Bobbie Jo. Edgar Buchanan (as Uncle Joe Carson), Mike Minor (Betty Jo's boyfriend, Steve Elliott) and Rufe Davis (train engineer Floyd Smoot) were featured as local color. The series was produced by Filmways.

PETTIT, TOM ▶ ABC news correspondent in London since 1989. Formerly he was executive v.p. of NBC after some 17 years as a correspondent. His appointment came in 1982 when Reuven Frank was named to succeed Bill Small as president of the division. Frank immediately named Pettit his lieutenant. Pettit had been Washington correspondent covering the Senate since 1975, after more than a decade working from the Los Angeles bureau. He was noted for his investigative reports on the NBC newsmagazine *First Tuesday,* such as one on U.S. chemical-biological warfare experiments and another on the country's nuclear establishment. He was also noted for his hard-boiled interviewing style in his stints on *Today.* Pettit has been covering political conventions since 1960.

PEYTON PLACE **▶** successful prime-time soap opera on ABC (1964-69) based on Grace Metalious's best-selling novel about sex in an American small town. The 30-minute episodes initially aired twice weekly; when they were expanded to three a week the series began to falter. *Peyton* was the career springboard for actress Mia Farrow, who played Allison MacKenzie and left the series after two years. Other regulars were Ryan O'Neal as Rodney Harrington, Ed Nelson as Dr. Michael Rossi, Barbara Parkins as Betty Anderson, Dorothy Malone as Constance MacKenzie Carson, Tim O'Connor as Elliott Carson, Frank Ferguson as Eli Carson, Patricia Morrow as Rita Jacks, James Douglas as Steven Cord and Chris Connelly as Norman Harrington. It was by 20th Century-Fox TV.

In 1973 NBC installed a daytime soap opera, *Return to Peyton Place,* with new characters in addition to those created by Metalious and with two actors, Morrow and Ferguson, who had appeared in the ABC nighttime version. The venture was not successful, however.

PFEIFFER, JANE CAHILL ▶ chairperson of the National Broadcasting Company and a director of its parent, RCA Corp. (1978-80). In that post, the highest ever attained by a woman in the broadcast industry, she reported to Fred

Silverman, president and chief executive officer of the company. Pfeiffer had helped recruit Silverman for NBC while she was a consultant to RCA and then was hired by him and RCA president Edgar H. Griffiths to help reorganize and manage the company. While Silverman concentrated on the various broadcast entities, and particularly on rehabilitating the sagging program schedule of NBC-TV, Pfeiffer looked after administration, employee relations, legal affairs and government relations. Her career at NBC ended explosively in 1981 when Silverman, apparently on orders from Griffiths, discharged her. The firing was poorly handled and resulted in Pfeiffer and Silverman exchanging insults and criticisms in the press.

Pfeiffer had become acquainted with Silverman while she was v.p. of communications for IBM, a job that occasionally put her in the role of TV sponsor. Silverman was program chief of CBS-TV at the time. Pfeiffer gave up her job at IBM, which she had held since 1972, after marrying a top IBM executive in 1975.

PHILBIN, JACK ▶ executive producer or producer of virtually all the Jackie Gleason series and specials since the early 1960s.

PHILIPS ▶ Netherlands-based multinational conglomerate that started as a light-bulb manufacturer in 1891 and grew to play a major role in the consumer electronics, broadcast and entertainment fields. In 1962 Philips introduced the Plumbicon TV camera tube. The company's TV cameras acquired a major share of market at U.S. networks and stations, as they did in other countries. Through its purchase of Magnavox in 1974 and GTE Sylvania in 1981, Philips also became a major U.S. marketer of TV. In 1985 Philips merged its TV broadcast products division with that of Germany's Bosch into a jointly owned company named BTS-Broadcast Television Systems.

PHILLIPS, IRNA (d. 1974) ▶ the leading creator and writer of daytime radio and TV serials, for which she earned the title "Queen of the Soaps." Beginning her career as a radio actress in Chicago in 1930, after five years of teaching school in Dayton, she switched to writing with the serial *Today's Children* for WGN. This led to a succession of others: *Women in White, Road of Life, The Guiding Light, The Right to Happiness, Lonely Women, Young Dr. Malone* and *The Brighter Day.* When she began writing for television in 1949, *Guiding Light, Dr. Malone* and *Brighter Day* switched over with her.

She became show doctor for a number of other serials, but her most glorious achievement was to be *As the World Turns,* the first 30-minute soap opera (sharing the distinction with *The Edge of Night,* which started the same day in 1956) and the most successful TV serial ever. For more than a decade it was the number-one daytime show, and Phillips continued to write it until a year before her death.

PHONEVISION ▶ pay-TV system developed by Zenith Radio Corp. in 1947 that endured on an experimental basis until 1969, when the FCC finally authorized it for Los Angeles and Chicago over UHF stations. The system involved the transmission of a scrambled signal which became unscrambled by a device attached to the subscriber's set when activated by the insertion of a ticket. The major experiment with Phonevision took place in Hartford, Conn. (1962-69), on a UHF channel licensed to RKO General. The system offered an average of six new programs a week, with fees ranging from 50 cents for movies to $3.00 for certain sports and cultural events. With access to 500,000 households, the pay programs never achieved a larger audience than 7,000. The typical subscriber spent only $1.20 per week, and the operation was unprofitable.

***PHYLLIS* ▶** CBS situation comedy (1975-77) spinning off the character played by Cloris Leachman on *The Mary Tyler Moore Show;* it had a successful premiere season with buttressing from the network's traditionally strong Monday night lineup. Organic changes were made for the second year, with the essentially unlikable title character made more appealing. The series concerned a newly widowed woman, Phyllis Lindstrom, and her daughter Bess (played by Lisa Gerritsen) relocating from Minneapolis to San Francisco and entering the career world. It was by MTM Enterprises and featured Jane Rose as Phyllis's mother-in-law, Audrey Dexter, and Henry Jones as Audrey's second husband, Judge Jonathan Dexter.

PIERCE, FREDERICK S. ▶ former president of ABC Inc. who left soon after the company was acquired by Capital Cities in 1986 and started the Frederick S. Pierce Co. to produce movies and television programs. He also entered into a production partnership in Hollywood with Fred Silverman, his former program chief at ABC who had left in 1978 to become Pierce's opposite number at NBC.

Pierce was the executive who presided over ABC's surge to prominence during the 1970s.

He became president of ABC Television in November 1974, advancing from senior v.p. to succeed Walter A. Schwartz in a period when ABC's competitive standing in prime time had deteriorated seriously. Almost immediately, after emergency program changes instituted by Pierce, the network began to climb in the ratings. A year later it gained parity with its rivals and in 1976 forged ahead into first place.

In 1979 he was also named executive vice president of ABC Inc., the No. 3 post in the company, behind chairman Leonard Goldenson and president Elton H. Rule, putting him prominently in line of succession. In 1983 he became president and chief operating officer of the corporation and served in that capacity until 1986, when the aging Goldenson felt the necessity to sell the company. When the new owners offered Pierce a lesser position than the one he held, he chose to go off on his own. He left the board of directors in 1988.

While he was president of ABC Inc., Pierce steered the company into several new media ventures, including the cable networks ESPN, Lifetime and Arts & Entertainment.

One of his great coups was to hire away from CBS the leading program expert in network television, Fred Silverman. The combination of Pierce and Silverman became the most formidable in television and resulted in such series hits as *Happy Days, Laverne and Shirley, Charlie's Angels, The Six Million Dollar Man, The Bionic Woman, Starsky & Hutch, Welcome Back, Kotter, Family, Rich Man, Poor Man* and *Barney Miller.* In addition, they brought forth such notable mini-series as *Roots, East of Eden, The Thorn Birds,* and *North and South.* Pierce also had a hand in developing *Good Morning, America, 20/20* and *Nightline,* and he was instrumental in the negotiations for Barbara Walters for the news division, which brought her over from NBC in 1976.

Pierce joined the company in 1956 with a background in accounting. He moved up through the areas of audience research, sales development, sales management and network planning and was recognized as ABC's leading program strategist before his promotion to president of all television operations.

PIERPOINT, ROBERT ▶ veteran CBS News correspondent assigned to *Sunday Morning,* responsible for contributing cover stories and feature pieces. Pierpoint, who has been with CBS News since 1949, is perhaps best known as CBS's longtime White House correspondent; he served 23 years on that watch. He has covered every president since Eisenhower, traveling extensively with all of them. He received his first professional broadcast news experience with the Swedish Broadcasting Corporation, joining CBS News as a Scandinavian correspondent. Soon after he was based in Korea reporting on the Panmunjom peace talks and prisoner-of-war exchanges. In September 1953 Pierpoint was named CBS's Far East bureau chief headquartered in Tokyo, a post he held until being named White House correspondent in 1957.

PIGGY-BACK ▶ a commercial unit purchased by an advertiser who uses it to promote two products, one after the other. In the years when one minute was the shortest commercial unit a network would sell, many companies that manufactured several products divided the minute for two messages, in effect *piggy-backing* the advertisements. The piggy-back proliferated in the late 1960s when advertisers discovered that, through new editing techniques, they could present an effective announcement in half the time they previously consumed.

Variations were the *Split 30* and the *Matched 30.* In the first case, the advertiser agreed to purchase a single minute in a given program if the two 30-second portions could play separately, that is, in separate commercial breaks. the networks permitted the practice as a refinement of the Matched 30 principle, under which two different advertisers agreed to mate halves of their one-minute commercials, so that each had 30 seconds at the start of the show and 30 seconds near the close.

In 1970 the networks and stations yielded to advertiser pressures and made the 30-second spot the standard unit of purchase. The effect was, of course, to increase the number of commercials viewers would be subjected to, without increasing commercial time.

PILOT ▶ a sample program, on film or tape, of a projected TV series, usually created to serve as a first episode but in any case establishing the continuing characters, the character relationships, the essential situation and the style of the proposed series. Pilots are tested by the networks for their appeal to viewers, and the testing scores are important factors in the decision-making process. In most seasons, only one of every four or five pilots produced becomes a series.

The cost of producing a pilot is usually twice that of a series episode because there is no amortization of the sets and props and because of the premiums paid for putting a hold on the services of actors and creative personnel. Rejected pilots recoup a small portion of their costs when they are played off in summertime anthologies, but otherwise they are useless to television.

In recent years, to reduce the financial waste in pilotmaking, pilots have been produced as made-for-TV movies or as episodes in anthology series such as *Police Story.* Pilots for variety shows are usually created as one-hour specials. An attempt was made by ABC in the 1960s to substitute 5-or 10-minute demonstration films for pilots, but the results were highly unsatisfactory. The current pilot preference is the shortflight series of four or six episodes. The theory is that production of actual episodes will show flaws or strengths better than a single pilot would.

PILSON, NEAL ▶ twice president of CBS Sports, from 1981-83 and again since 1986. A lawyer by training, Pilson joined CBS in 1976 as director of business affairs for the sports division. He was spotted as executive timber and before long rose to the presidency and negotiated most of the agreements for CBS Sports's franchise events. In 1983 he was promoted to executive vice president of the Broadcast Group, responsible for sports, the owned-TV stations, radio, and operations & engineering.

Later, when Laurence Tisch took control of CBS, Tisch identified Pilson as one of the aggressive young comers. In a reorganization, Pilson was returned to his previous post apparently to engineer the new Tisch strategy of capturing the major sporting events. The biggest gambles in this deep-pockets approach to securing sports rights came just before the TV advertising market for sports crashed in the mid-1980s. Pilson made an enormous bid of $243 million to win the TV rights to the 1992 Winter Olympics from Albertville, France. Clearly CBS had overbid, reportedly passing second-place bidder NBC by $68 million. Pilson also pitched the network into a $1.1 billion commitment for Major League Baseball, which resulted in significant losses for CBS.

PINKHAM, RICHARD A. R. ▶ one-time program chief for NBC (1955-56) but better known for his subsequent career at Ted Bates & Co., a leading ad agency. As v.p. in charge of TV and radio for Bates, Pinkham exerted a strong influence on TV programming as a major sponsor of shows in the late 1950s and early 1960s. He rose to become vice-chairman of the agency. Pinkham joined NBC in 1951 and became a program executive when the department was under the dynamic leadership of Sylvester Weaver. He became executive producer of the *Today, Home, Tonight* parlay (1952-55), then v.p. in charge of programs and later v.p. in charge of advertising (1956-57), until Bates hired him away.

PITTMAN, ROBERT W. ▶ president and chief executive officer of Time Warner Enterprises, the strategic development unit of Time Warner Inc., overseeing the company's investments in the Court TV cable network, Six Flags amusement parks, Quincy Jones Entertainment and Atari Games, among other ventures. A brash, flamboyant former whiz-kid of radio, Pittman is best known as one of several professed fathers of the MTV cable network, launched in 1981 by Warner Amex Satellite Entertainment, of which Pittman was head of programming. He eventually became president and CEO of the MTV Networks group, including Nickelodeon and VH-1. In 1987 he joined MCA, which agreed to bankroll Pittman in his own company, Quantum Media, formed to produce TV programming and invest in other media properties. The company's most notorious effort was *The Morton Downey, Jr. Show,* a brawling talk show that had a moment of popularity in its brief syndication run. Quantum was absorbed by Warner Communications in September 1989, several months before that company's merger with Time Inc.

Pittman began his career in radio, starting at 15 as a part-time deejay in his native Mississippi. For a time he was program director at WNBC radio in New York, and in 1978 he produced and hosted a weekly video music show for NBC's owned-and-operated TV stations.

***PLANET OF THE APES* ▶** hour-long series on CBS (1974) based on the popular series of motion pictures, which scored powerful ratings when shown on TV. Produced by 20th Century-Fox TV, the video version featured Roddy McDowell as curious ape Galen, Booth Colman as ape leader Zaius, Ron Harper as astronaut Alan Virdon and James Naughton as astronaut Pete Burke. It fizzled and was pulled after 14 weeks.

***PLAY OF THE WEEK, THE* ▶** a series of stage plays mounted for television from 1959 to 1961 by WNTA (Channel 13 in New York City, when it was a commercial station owned by National Telefilm Associates) and syndicated by NTA to a number of commercial stations around the country. Despite critical acclaim and topnotch actors working for scale, the series drew low ratings and had difficulty getting sponsors. When it was canceled, WNTA received thousands of letters from loyal viewers protesting the action. Among the 65 productions were *The World of Sholem Aleichem,* with Gertrude Berg, Sam Levene and Nancy Walker; *The Iceman Cometh,* with Jason Robards, Jr.; and *Medea,* with Judith Anderson.

In 1962, under the sponsorship of the Esso Oil Co. but without commercials, WNEW-TV in New York televised some of the reruns of the plays in prime time.

PLAYING FOR TIME ▶ CBS drama special that raised a controversy in 1980 because of indiscretion in casting. The three-hour drama was based on a memoir by Fania Fenelon, a French Jew who survived Auschwitz, the Nazi concentration camp, by performing in the women's orchestra. Jewish groups assailed the show as an offense to their people, because the role of Fenelon was being played by Vanessa Redgrave, who in private life was an active supporter of the Palestinian cause. Despite an intense campaign to prevent the show from airing, or perhaps because of it, the drama drew an exceptionally large audience for the Sept. 30, 1980 telecast.

The script was adapted for television by Arthur Miller, the novelist and playwright. Daniel Mann directed, and Linda Yellen produced the show for Syzygy Productions Ltd. Jane Alexander co-starred with Redgrave, and the cast included Maud Adams, Marisa Berenson, Verna Bloom, Viveca Lindfors, Melanie Mayron and Shirley Knight.

But what was to have been an artistic triumph that would enhance CBS's prestige had backfired because of the controversy. The CBS executive who approved the casting said it was done without knowledge of Redgrave's political activism for causes inimical to the interests of Israel. The network argued that it could not accede to the demands of the Jewish groups that Redgrave be removed from the cast without establishing a precedent that would allow all pressure groups to exert censorship on programming.

PLEASE DON'T EAT THE DAISIES ▶ situation comedy on NBC (1965-66) based on the Jean Kerr best seller and movie about a happy family coping with a large, run-down house. Produced by MGM-TV, it featured Pat Crowley as Joan Nash, Mark Miller as her husband Jim, Kim Tyler as son Kyle, Brian Nash as son Joel, and Joe and Jeff Fithian as the twins, Trevor and Tracy.

PLIMPTON SPECIALS ▶ series of ABC one-hour nonfiction specials (1970-73) featuring George Plimpton, a writer of derring-do, whose technique is to get on the inside of the activity he writes about. Thus, in *Plimpton! The Great Quarterback Sneak,* he posed as a professional football player for a month in the Baltimore Colts training camp. In *Plimpton! At the Wheel* he entered the world of auto racing. In others, he went on a safari, prepared to do a comedy act at Caesar's Palace, trained for the circus on the flying trapeze, rode in the steeplechase and became a guard at Buckingham Palace. William Kronick produced and directed the documentaries for the Wolper Organization.

David Plowright

PLOWRIGHT, DAVID ▶ chairman since 1987 of Granada Television, the prestigious British broadcasting and production company based in Manchester. Plowright moved up the ranks through journalism and programming, joining in 1957 from a newspaper background to run Granada's regional news service. Later, after editing the *World In Action* documentary series for several years, Plowright was made program controller (head of programming) at Granada in 1968. In 1975 he was named managing director and 12 years later elevated to chairman.

Granada is one of 15 regional stations that comprise the ITV network on Britain's third channel. From 1980-82 Plowright was chairman of the ITV network program committee that selects the programs for the network; from 1984-86 he was chairman of the Independent Television Companies Assn. Plowright has successfully taken Granada through two franchise reviews—the junctures at which licenses can be lost in the U.K.

He is the brother of actress Joan Plowright, who was married to the late Sir Laurence Olivier, arguably the most accomplished actor in the English-speaking world in his time. The family connection was thought to be a reason why Olivier appeared with some frequency in Granada productions.

PLUGOLA ▶ the term for the commercial use (or abuse) of television by means other than advertising, through a prearrangement with producers. Once fairly common in television, the selling of product plugs in programs became illegal after the quiz show and payola scandals late in 1959, when Congress amended the Communications Act to require stations to indicate when money or other consideration was received for broadcast material.

Plugs continue to abound in giveaway shows, but always there is the disclaimer that the prizes are donated. In the years when plugola flourished, companies went openly into business to make contact with producers on behalf of manufacturers. A producer might be paid a set fee for agreeing to use a brand-name product in a scene or might be given the use of an automobile for making it the car driven by the hero in his show. At least one bowling manufacturer created a bowling series that was distributed free to stations, because it showed the company's name every time a ball was lifted or the automatic pin-spotter was lowered.

When cigarette advertising was banned from television, cigarette plugs became a problem. In some cases cigarette companies created sporting events irresistible to television that carried the brand name; in others they purchased billboards at ball parks where they would inevitably fall into camera range.

***PM EAST/PM WEST* ▶** ambitious syndicated series produced by Westinghouse Broadcasting (1961) as competition to NBC's *Tonight,* with talk-variety segments produced on the East and West Coasts. Mike Wallace and Joyce Davidson (wife of David Susskind) were the co-hosts of *PM East,* which was produced in the studios of WNEW-TV New York, and Terrence O'Flaherty was host of *PM West,* produced at Westinghouse station KPIX San Francisco. The five Westinghouse-owned stations formed the nucleus of the lineup, but the program lasted around six months.

POCKETPIECE ▶ the definitive weekly network rating report, which earned its nickname from the fact that it was designed to fit in the inside coat pocket of the network salesmen. Officially the *Nielsen National TV Ratings Report,* it had been issued bi-weekly until the people meter became the major reporting apparatus.

Information in the pocketpiece includes household audience estimates for all sponsored network programs, audience composition estimates by a variety of age groups, season-to-date averages for program performance, program-type averages, overall TV usage compared with the previous year and TV usage by time period.

POD ▶ a grouping of commercials and other announcements in a break during the programming.

***POLICE STORY* ▶** NBC anthology series (1973-77) realistically portraying police work. Joseph Wambaugh, former policeman and author of several best-selling novels about police, created the concept and served also as production consultant. The Columbia TV series, which had no recurring stars, spun off *Police Woman* and *Joe Forrester.* David Gerber was executive producer and Stanley Kallis producer.

***POLICE SURGEON* ▶** one of the first dramatic series produced expressly for the prime time-access rule in 1971 as a barter vehicle for Colgate-Palmolive. Filmed in Canada and featuring Sam Groom as Dr. Simon Locke, under auspices of the Ted Bates advertising agency, the series was intended to look like a network show in competition with lesser syndicated fare. It fooled no one and, although it lasted three seasons, was never a big success.

***POLICE TAPES, THE* ▶** 90-minute documentary by independent producers Alan and Susan Raymond portraying the urban battleground of the South Bronx, New York's highest crime area, as seen during a summer from a police squad car. The program had the distinction of being aired both on public and commercial television. It was originally broadcast on WNET New York, then was acquired by ABC News to air in the *ABC Close-Up* series on Aug. 17, 1978. The documentary won Peabody, DuPont and Emmy awards that year.

***POLICE WOMAN* ▶** successful NBC hour-long series (1974-79) which grew out of an episode of the dramatic anthology *Police Story.* Angie Dickinson as Sergeant Pepper Anderson, Earl

Holliman as Sergeant Bill Crowley, Ed Bernard as Detective Joe Styles and Charlie Dierkop as Detective Pete Royster comprised the regular cast. It was produced by Douglas Benton and was by David Gerber Productions and Columbia Pictures TV.

POLICY STATEMENT ▶ the FCC's interpretation of a rule or law in a given area, or the articulation or the commission's prescription for broadcast performance that stops short of being framed as regulation. Policy statements have been issued on questions concerning UHF, children's programming and programming in general.

POLITICAL ADVERTISING RATES ▶ by law, a station may never sell political time at higher rates than it charges commercial advertisers for comparable time. Moreover, during the 45-day period before a primary election and the 60-day period before a general election, political candidates cannot be charged more than a station's lowest rate in a given time period, provided that the candidate personally appears in the programs or spots. The lowest rate generally is the end rate, the heavily discounted price earned by commercial advertisers for frequency buys; political candidates, however, are not required to buy spots in volume to receive it. Broadcasters may, if they choose, offer special political discounts beyond the requirements of the law.

The law worked reasonably well for the first two decades after its adoption in the Fair Election Campaign Act of 1971. Complications arose, however, as the importance of television advertising in electoral politics magnified and industry practices became increasingly sophisticated. The statutory term, "lowest unit rate," became meaningless as the traditional published rate card was abandoned for a system based on ratings points and targeted demographics. Candidates were forced to pay top dollar to guarantee placement in a particular slot. Massive litigation arose alleging overcharges in hundreds of races during the 1990 election campaigns, after which the FCC and a hardly disinterested Congress struggled to come up with a revised system.

POLITICAL CONVENTIONS ▶ once known as the "Olympics of Television Journalism" for the fact that the quadrennial events of the Democratic and Republican parties were the only predictable times when the network news divisions had the run of the airwaves in prime time and competed with each other head-on in covering the same running story. Journalistic careers often were advanced in these Olympics, and occasionally stars were born—Huntley & Brinkley, a 1956 phenomenon, the notable example. Moreover, the performances of the news divisions at these events sometimes paid dividends in increasing the credibility, stature and popularity of a network's evening newscast when the conventions were over.

With prestige and company pride at stake, the networks invested huge amounts to cover the four-day events, despite the fact that only 30% of the television homes in the U.S. watched the conventions on a typical night. The cost of coverage was so great that the networks rarely recouped more than a third of their expenses from the advertising. Each constructed temporary but elaborate studios, booths and control rooms at the convention site and employed more than 500 news workers and clerical personnel in the coverage. In 1976, CBS and NBC each spent around $10 million to cover the political parleys. But the networks lost their zeal when the political parties began staging their conventions for the cameras so that the conventions ammounted to nothing so much as protracted commercials. In 1980, CBS and NBC began abbreviated coverage—a nightly digest of the day's events—something ABC had begun doing in 1968.

Convention coverage by the networks began in 1952 when the manufacturers of TV sets hitched onto politics for their advertising thrusts. Philco Corp. that year spent $3.8 million for full sponsorship of the campaigns, the conventions and election night on NBC, TV and radio. Admiral then bought similar coverage on ABC, TV and radio, and Westinghouse bought the coverage of CBS and DuMont.

POLITICAL EDITORIALIZING ▶ broadcast activity for which FCC rules were adopted in 1967, concurrent with the rules relating to personal attacks. The rule was not included in the FCC's 1987 decision repealing most other applications of the Fairness Doctrine. Before formulating the rules, the FCC had noted that between 1960 and 1964 the number of radio and TV stations that broadcast political editorials had increased from 53 and 2, respectively, to 103 and 13, and that there was some indication of failure to comply with the obligation to afford time for answer by disfavored candidates.

The 1967 rules state that when a licensee opposes legally qualified candidates in an editorial, the licensee has an obligation within 24 hours to transmit to the other candidates notification of the date and time of the editorial and script or tape of the broadcast, and that it offer a reasonable opportunity to respond. The rule also notes that if an editorial is broadcast 72 hours before the election, the licensee shall comply with the provisions sufficiently far in advance of the broadcast to enable the other candidates to prepare and represent a response.

It should be noted that this provision applies only to licensee endorsements and does not affect the licensee's obligation under the Equal Time provision of Section 315(a) of the Communications Act. While not directly at issue in the *Red Lion* case, it was clearly implied that by upholding the constitutionality of the Personal Attack Doctrine, the court also implicitly passed on the constitutionality of the political advertising rules.

POLITICAL OBITUARY OF RICHARD NIXON ▶ controversial telecast on ABC (Nov. 11, 1962) following Richard M. Nixon's gubernatorial defeat in California and his "final" press conference at which he said "You won't have Dick Nixon to kick around anymore." Conducted by Howard K. Smith, the telecast featured an interview with Alger Hiss, the former government official whose conviction for perjury in 1950—in a famous subversion probe by then Congressman Nixon—served to launch Nixon's national political career.

The reaction to the program was stormy. ABC stations as well as the network were besieged by protests, many of them apparently organized by right-wing groups, and Kemper Insurance retaliated by canceling its sponsorship of ABC's *Evening Report.* James Hagerty, v.p. of news, went on the network Nov. 18 to defend ABC's right to present the news as it saw fit.

The Kemper action was challenged in the courts by ABC, and in 1968 the Supreme Court ruled that the company had no right to cancel sponsorship of its program because it disapproved of another program on the network. The court ordered Kemper to pay ABC $298,800 for sponsorship time it had not used.

POLTRACK, DAVID F. ▶ the audience research and marketing czar at the CBS Broadcast Group, with the title of senior vice president in charge of planning and research. He has considerable influence over all aspects of the network's business, including programming, news and stations. Poltrack joined CBS in 1969 and became senior v.p. in 1988. He is the author of *Television Marketing: Network, Local and Cable,* published in 1983 by McGraw-Hill.

POMPADUR, I. MARTIN ▶ media entrepreneur who in the early 1970s was a top executive and board member of ABC Inc. During the 1980s he put together a number of limited partnerships in the media field and in 1988 organized RP Companies Inc. to centralize his various media holdings. They consist of 11 network-affiliated TV stations, 10 radio stations and MultiVision Cable TV, an MSO with 420,000 subscribers, along with a cellular phone company, a production company, and other properties.

Pompadur was with ABC 17 years and appeared destined for the highest reaches of management when he left suddenly in 1976. He joined Ziff-Davis Publishing as a corporate officer and engineered its acquisition of Rust Craft Broadcasting. He became president of Ziff-Davis but left in 1983 to form a company that acquired the six Ziff stations for $56.2 million. One of the partners in the venture was Ralph E. Becker, the former president of Rust Craft Broadcasting, who continues to oversee the station group.

In 1986 Pompadur joined with Merrill Lynch, the brokerage investment house, in setting up the first publicly held limited partnership to buy media properties via a "blind pool," an entity that raises money without spelling out in advance how it will be invested. Elton H. Rule, the retired chairman of ABC and Pompadur's former boss, was brought into the partnership for the value of his name and reputation. ML Media Partners became a subsidiary of Merrill Lynch in the control of Pompadur. The partnership raised $189 million in equity funds and started off buying cable systems in California and Puerto Rico and later a number of network-affiliated TV stations.

A second blind pool, ML Media Opportunity Partners, made bolder moves into publishing, program production and cellular communications, along with TV, radio and cable. In 1989, through Opportunity Partners, Pompadur and Rule set up a joint venture with veteran producers Bob Banner and Gary L. Pudney to form Paradigm Entertainment to develop and produce TV programs. In the next two years, Paradigm produced two network TV movies and a short-lived syndicated series. In 1990, again through Opportunity

Partners, Pompadur acquired three more TV stations, taking him close to the FCC limit of 12.

Pompadur's appetite for limited partnerships had him involved with seven in 1991, including a joint venture to invest in European media and entertainment businesses. When Rule died in 1990, Pompadur bought out his interest and became sole owner of RP Companies, which sits atop the varied holdings, with headquarters in New York.

PORTER, PAUL A. (d. 1975) ▶ chairman of the FCC from 1944 to 1946 who then became a founding partner with Thurmond Arnold and Abe Fortas in what was to become one of the largest law firms in Washington—Fortas and Porter (now, Arnold and Porter). For a brief period in the late 1930s, he served as Washington counsel for CBS, but his close ties to the Democratic party moved him into a number of high government posts with the Roosevelt and Truman Administrations. An imposing speaker famed for his anecdotes, he was a frequent toastmaster at Washington dinners. His second wife was Kathleen Winsor, author of the successful and spicy 1944 novel, *Forever Amber.*

POSNER, IRINA ▶ executive director of New York's Center for Communication since 1990, after a career as a documentary producer and writer, mainly with CBS News. The Center for Communication, which was founded in 1980 by Frank Stanton, former president of CBS, is a nonprofit organization that provides a link between universities and the professional media world with special seminars for students that involve leading practitioners in broadcasting, publishing and other media fields. Among the companies represented on the Center's board are CapCities/ABC, NBC, CBS, Viacom, Group W, Time Warner, Hearst, Gannett and The Museum of Television and Radio.

Posner, who started with CBS News in 1964, worked variously for *CBS Reports, Sunday Morning, 60 Minutes*, and *Magazine.* On leaving after 19 years, she formed KP Productions, which produced documentaries for Turner Broadcasting and reports for ABC's *20/20,* among other independent projects. She joined the Center for Communication in 1988 as director of its seminar program and was named executive director two years later when Cathy Gay left for another post.

POSTPRODUCTION ▶ everything done to film or video footage after it is shot with a camera but before it airs or screens. More narrowly, postproduction, or "post," applies to such processes as editing, the laying in of dialogue and other audio, and the addition of graphics and effects. Fed in the 1980s by the troika formed of increased viewer sophistication, the demands of ad agencies for trickier effects, and advancing technology, postproduction became an area of high growth, attracting more and more technical-development dollars and spawning an industry formed of more than 1,000 independent postproduction facilities in the U.S. alone.

POTTER, BRIDGET ▶ senior vice president of original programming for HBO, the pay cable service, overseeing all programs produced specifically for the channel, including music, comedy, drama, documentary and series. Under her direction, HBO developed such innovative programming as *Murderers Among Us: The Simon Wiesenthal Story, Dear America: Letters Home From Vietnam, Stories From the Quilt,* and *Tanner '88,* a mock-documentary series that trailed a fictional candidate in his presidential election campaign. Potter joined HBO in 1982 from Lorimar Productions in New York, where she acquired and developed theatrical films and network mini-series. She was previously at ABC as East Coast v.p. in charge of prime-time program development, mini-series, and movies for television. Born in England, Potter came to the U.S. in 1960 and attended the American Theater Wing in New York City. She began her television career with *The Dick Cavett Show,* where she became an associate producer.

***P.O.V.* ▶** PBS series begun in 1988 to provide an outlet for independently produced documentaries with strong social points of view (hence *P.O.V.*). This was a liberating measure, since the public television network, in serving a diverse public, had generally required nonfiction programs to meet journalistic standards of fairness, objectivity and balance. As a result, personal expression in the documentary film form had been effectively squelched.

The series was the brainchild of Marc Weiss, who formerly ran a clearinghouse for independent films of interest to special groups. David Davis, a responsible and highly respected veteran of public television who was the force behind the prestigious *American Playhouse,* was given charge of the project as president of *P.O.V.* The consortium of stations that presented *American Playhouse*—WGBH Boston, WNET New York, KCET Los Angeles and SECA, the South Carolina group—also presented the documentary series. One of the regular sources of funding was the National Endowment for the Arts.

It was clear that by its nature *P.O.V.* would be controversial, but for the first three years it withstood criticism from groups complaining of its essentially liberal tilt, and several of its programs won important national awards. In the summer of 1991, however, two programs scheduled only weeks apart raised such heat within the public TV system that the future of the series was placed in doubt. First there was the controversy in July over *Tongues Untied,* a documentary by Marlon Riggs on black male homosexuality, which contained a scene of men kissing and petting. Around 40% of the stations in the public TV system refused to carry it. The following month PBS itself halted the showing of *Stop the Church,* another film on gay blacks, these AIDS activists protesting at St. Patrick's Cathedral in New York. Several stations aired the film on their own, however.

POWELL, DICK (d. 1963) ▶ screen actor who embraced TV in the early years when other movie stars eschewed it and who flourished in the medium as star, producer and executive. After playing roles in several drama anthologies, Powell joined with three other movie actors—Charles Boyer, Rosalind Russell and Joel McCrea—to form their own program in 1952, *Four Star Playhouse,* which was to involve a rotation. Russell and McCrea withdrew after a time, and David Niven joined as a third partner (there was not to be a fourth again). The venture led to the creation of an independent production company, Four Star Studio, which began producing other shows. The company later passed into other hands but still is active as Four Star Entertainment.

Powell had no idle years in TV and went from one program series to another, with a scattering of guest shots as well. He had a long run with *Dick Powell's Zane Grey Theatre,* a western anthology drawing from the Zane Grey stories, which Powell hosted and occasionally starred in. It ran on CBS from 1956 to 1961. When it ended, Powell began a new series, *The Dick Powell Show* (1961-63), an anthology of action-adventure films.

PRECHT, ROBERT ▶ director and then producer of *The Ed Sullivan Show* until it went off the air in 1970. He remained associated with Sullivan, his father-in-law, in a TV production company until Sullivan's death. Since then Precht has been executive producer of *The Entertainer of the Year Awards,* along with other specials, and of the 1973 situation comedy, *Calucci's Department.*

PREEMPTION ▶ the withdrawal of a scheduled program by a network or station in order to insert another. Often the preemption is for a special news report in a time of crisis or a presidential address; occasionally it is for content that a station has found objectionable. But increasingly preemptions by network affiliates are to replace low-rated prime-time programs with syndicated shows or movies that promise a larger audience. Such preemptions are particularly common during the sweep weeks, and they tend to strain the relationship between the network and the offending station.

PREFREEZE STATIONS ▶ pioneer TV stations, 108 in all, that were either already on the air or had been granted construction permits before Sept. 30, 1948, when the FCC halted all license awards. The prefreeze stations had the TV airways to themselves for four years while the commission developed an orderly table of assignments.

PREMIERE ▶ short-lived pay-cable company formed in April 1980 by Getty Oil, Columbia Pictures, MCA Inc. (Universal Pictures), Paramount Pictures and Twentieth Century-Fox Corp. Its creation shocked other cable entrepreneurs, and especially HBO, since as an alliance of major film studios Premiere would have had a competitive advantage over all other satellite program services for movie titles. A few months later, the Justice Department filed an antitrust suit against Premiere, arguing that the film companies partnered in the new company would control the production, distribution, and exhibition of motion pictures and that a pay-cable network formed of such companies would be anti-competitive.

As a result of the Justice Department action, the companies dissolved Premiere in June 1981. They more than recouped their start-up losses by selling the satellite transponder they had leased for Premiere at a huge profit. Premiere died before it could begin operation.

PRESTEL ▶ British Post Office videotext system that went online in 1979, thus becoming the first publicly available data base on home television sets (with, however, expensive adapters). Prestel did not enjoy the growth expected and soon found that its penetration of the home market was slim: the great majority of subscribers were businesses. Prestel is also the name of the British videotext standard.

PRICE, FRANK ▶ former president of Columbia Pictures from 1978-1991, after having been president of Universal TV from 1974. Price was replaced at Columbia when the studio was purchased by Sony. Under his contract settlement he went into independent production at Columbia Pictures. Earlier he was executive producer or producer of such series as *The Virginian, Ironside* and *It Takes a Thief.* He entered TV in the early 1950s as a story editor for CBS and later for NBC while dramatic anthology series were in vogue. He then became a writer and eventually a producer of series programming.

***PRICE IS RIGHT, THE* ▶** see Game Shows.

PRICE, RICHARD ▶ one of Britain's most successful independent television producers and distributors, whose international credits include *Nicholas Nickleby, Othello* and *Great Expectations,* among many others. As joint head of RPTA/Primetime with his partner Richard Leworthy, Price since the late 1980s has invested in dozens of international productions, mostly with advances in exchange for distribution rights. A Welshman, he had his first significant experience in television as overseas sales director for Granada. He started his own company, RPTA Ltd. (Richard Price Television Associates), in 1968. His major client was London Weekend Television, for whom he served as a sales agent, and he has continued to maintain a relationship with the company. In 1991 Price was elected chairman of the British Academy of Film and Television Arts (BAFTA).

***PRIMAL MAN* ▶** four-part series of specials on ABC (1973-74) dealing with the behavior patterns of prehistoric man to reveal what is atavistic in the human race. The series was produced by Jack Kaufman and directed by Dennis Azzarella for the Wolper Organization.

PRIME NETWORK ▶ national cable sports network formed by linking together 16 regional sports services, six of them owned by the parent company of Prime and 10 by outside affiliates. Together they reach 23.6 million cable subscribers and have the ability to compete for rights to significant events.

Prime Network is owned by Affiliated Regional Communications Ltd. (ARC), a partnership of Daniels & Associates, Tele-Communications Inc. and Group W Services. Ed Frazier is president of Prime Network.

PRIME TIME ▶ the evening hours that, as the period of heaviest viewing, command the highest advertising rates. The FCC defines the prime hours as 7-11 p.m. (6-10 p.m. in the central and mountain time zones). On a typical evening during the main fall-winter season, there are likely to be around 85 million viewers at 8 p.m., close to 100 million at 9 p.m., and around 75 million at 10 p.m.

PRIME TIME-ACCESS RULE ▶ an FCC rule that limited the networks' use of the peak viewing hours to three hours per night. Established in 1970 and put into force in the fall of 1971, it effectively shaved off 30 minutes of prime-time programming from the networks each night and returned it to the local stations in the top 50 markets for their own use. Although the rule permitted the network to use any 3-hour period between 7 and 11 p.m., the FCC informally requested that the networks all use 8 to 11 p.m. to minimize the confusion.

The rule was adopted for a number of reasons: to break the network monopoly over prime time, to open a new market for independent producers who complained of being at the mercy of three customers, to stimulate the creation of new program forms, and to give the stations the opportunity to do their most significant local programming in the choicest viewing hours.

Stations below the top 50 markets had no restrictions on their programming, but since the networks had ceased sending out programs at 7:30 p.m., most chose to use off-network reruns. Network affiliates in the major markets, however, had to use the time for first-run programming, either locally produced or from syndication. Virtually all of it came from syndication, as it proved, and the rule prompted a rebirth of the game show in prime time, chiefly for economic reasons. Game shows could be taped five in a day, making them far cheaper than most filmed series, and they achieved acceptable ratings on the whole.

The rule also fostered a return of bartered programming, shows provided to the stations gratis in return for their carrying several commercials. It also increased the number of commercials, since stations are permitted to use more commercial minutes than networks under the television code. Moreover, around 30 percent of the stations found it easiest to cope with the rule by *stripping* a game show, carrying it five nights a week instead of offering a different program each night.

Several others met the program gap by extending their local newscasts an additional 30 minutes each night.

On weekends, the most popular access rule shows were two of 60-minute length that had been canceled by the networks, *Lawrence Welk* and *Hee Haw.* Weekdays, the programs that succeeded were largely revivals of old game shows, such as *Truth or Consequences, To Tell the Truth* and *Beat the Clock,* or extra editions of such daytime programs as *Masquerade Party, The Hollywood Squares* and *Let's Make a Deal.*

Some of the prime-access programs were imported from abroad, and many of the new programs were made in other countries for economic reasons.

Two of the big access hits in the 1980s were *The Muppet Show,* produced in England, and *PM Magazine,* a series by Group W Productions to which subscribing stations contributed locally produced segments. Although, at first, most stations deplored the rule, fearing it would cut into profits, by the second year a majority wished for its retention because their profits were improved. The rule also benefitted the networks, particularly third-ranked ABC, which was able to discard seven uncompetitive programs in returning time to the stations. This enabled ABC to move closer to its rivals in the rating race.

NBC and CBS gained from the reduction of the program overhead, since it costs as much to produce a program for 7:30 as for 9 o'clock, although the audience is much smaller in the earlier slot. Moreover, the reduction in commercials by 63 minutes a week among the three networks created, for them, a sellers' market which drove prices up for the rest of the schedule.

The rule was cumbersome and caused numerous problems. There were incessant requests for waivers, such as for sports runovers, Olympics coverage and news events, which added to the FCC's work load. Specials for children could not be presented by the networks until 8 p.m., and if they ran longer they interfered with bedtime schedules. Parents who did not understand the rule frequently complained to the networks.

In February 1974 the FCC revised the rule to allow the networks to present children's shows, documentaries and news at 7:30 and to prohibit the use of movies that had already been shown on the networks as prime-access fare. The revision was challenged in court by an ad hoc organization of syndicators, which argued that the agency had suddenly truncated their market after having encouraged them to invest in the development of shows for the fall of 1974. The District Court of Appeals in Washington upheld the syndicators and ruled that the FCC should have allowed more lead time for its revision. The court's ruling forced the networks to juggle the schedules that had already been planned under the FCC's amended rule; each had to drop two half-hour shows because their weekend schedules had shrunk again.

In November 1974 the FCC voted essentially to reinstate the rules that had been knocked down by the court, effective September 1975. The following January, the rules were put into official language. Thus, in the trade, the periods under the rule are classified as PTAR I, PTAR II (which never went into effect) and PTAR III.

To the dismay of much of the industry, the deregulation program of the 1982 FCC under Mark Fowler included the abolishing of PTAR. Stations and syndicators lobbied heavily to retain it.

The original rules grew out of a long-pending proposal by Donald McGannon, head of Westinghouse Broadcasting, which had an interest in syndication, to divide prime time between the networks and stations. This proposal was called the 50-50 rule. Limiting the networks to three hours was a compromise that had its detractors on the commission, notably the then chairman, Dean Burch.

PRIME TIME SUNDAY ▶ NBC's second venture into the weekly newsmagazine field, its first effort, *Weekend,* having attracted scant viewer interest during 1978-79, its first and only season as a prime-time entry. The failure of *Weekend* was a serious embarrassment to NBC News, since CBS was enjoying a huge success with *60 Minutes* and ABC News was having excellent results with its newsmagazine, *20/20.*

Prime Time Sunday, which debuted June 24, 1979, was different from *Weekend* in three conspicuous respects: it had a star TV personality, Tom Snyder, as host-anchor; it concentrated on live television, incorporating elements of *Wide Wide World* and *Person to Person,* and it put the control room on the set, making the television process part of the show. The principal correspondents, Jack Perkins and Chris Wallace (son of Mike Wallace of *60 Minutes* and stepson of Bill Leonard, president of CBS News) each contributed a filmed news piece followed by a live segment in every telecast. Snyder himself conducted a live exploration of a current news story through interviews with various concerned persons, both in the studio and by satellite. The series was given a weekly berth in the NBC fall schedule for 1979-80 but was started during the summer to work out the kinks and, it was hoped, build a following.

Paul Friedman, who conceived the program and had worked with Snyder previously in live situations, such as the local New York newscast, *NewsCenter 4,* was executive producer. Wallace Westfeldt was senior producer and George Paul director.

Jessica Savitch joined the cast in October 1979, but the show continued to flounder in the ratings, and NBC began shunting it around in the schedule to minimize the ratings damage. The next season the series was scrapped in favor of a new version with David Brinkley entitled *NBC Magazine.*

PRIMETIME LIVE ▶ ABC's 1989 entry in the network newsmagazine derby, which after a number of revisions following a bumpy start began developing into a successful prime-time stablemate of *20/20*. The series is co-anchored by Diane Sawyer (hired away from CBS's *60 Minutes*) and veteran correspondent Sam Donaldson, with Chris Wallace (hired from NBC) as chief correspondent.

The weekly series' inauspicious beginnings in August 1989 traced at least partly to excessive hype in what was one of ABC's most unrelenting advance-of-air promotions since Barbara Walters joined Harry Reasoner as co-anchor in 1976. The on-screen chemistry between the *PrimeTime Live* anchors was initially deficient, and the inclusion of a studio audience was pointless. In revamping the program, executive producer Rick Kaplan did away with the studio audience and separated the anchors, having Sawyer in New York and Donaldson in Washington. The alterations worked well, and the series has delivered some first-rate investigative pieces and feature stories, among them a report on the squalid conditions at Veteran Administration hospitals, phony abortion clinics set up by right-to-life advocates, alcohol abuse among pilots, and abuses of power in the Internal Revenue Service.

PRIMO, AL ▶ news executive who is credited with originating the *Eyewitness News* concept, which spread from Philadelphia's KYW-TV to local TV stations across the country in the late 1960s and early 1970s. Hired away from KYW-TV to develop the *Eyewitness* format for WABC-TV New York, Primo scored a success at the station that led to his being named v.p. of news for the ABC-owned stations in 1972. Three years later he shifted to ABC News as executive producer of *The Reasoner Report,* a half-hour weekly series. In 1976 he left ABC News to become a news consultant to local stations.

Patrick McGoohan in the CBS series *The Prisoner*

PRISONER, THE ▶ hour-long adventure series produced by Britain's ATV Ltd., which was carried as a summer replacement by CBS in 1968 and 1969. It featured Patrick McGoohan as prisoner of a mysterious group, struggling for his freedom while trying to learn why he was taken captive and by whom. Though he was known only as Number 6 in *The Prisoner,* his real identity was suggested to be that of John Drake, a character also played by McGoohan in the earlier show *Secret Agent.*

The show has since moved to public television where it developed a kind of cult following. Public television stations often air the series as part of their fundraising drives.

PRIX ITALIA ▶ one of the most prestigious of the international competitions for the recognition of excellence in radio and TV programs. Established in 1948 by RAI, the Italian broadcast system, "The Prix" is held annually in a major city of Italy, with more than 40 broadcast organizations of Europe, Asia and North

America participating. Separate prizes equal to 13,000 Swiss francs are awarded for dramatic programs, documentaries, music programs and ballet, with additional special awards. The Prix is managed by a permanent staff based in Rome.

PRIX JEUNESSE (YOUTH PRIZE) ▶ an international award given every two years by the Prix Jeunesse Foundation for excellence in children's television production. The selection is made at a biennial conference in Munich, held under auspices of the European Broadcasting Union and UNESCO, whose aims are to stimulate competition and improve communication and production standards in children's television. Participants are mainly from European, Canadian, Japanese and Australian television systems, with some attendance by representatives of less developed systems. The U.S. has been an occasional participant.

In 1964, the Free State of Bavaria, the city of Munich and the Bavarian Broadcasting Corporation established the Prix Jeunesse Foundation to promote good programming for the young. Prix Jeunesse is headed by Ursula von Zallinger.

PRODIGY ▶ nationwide videotext system jointly owned by IBM and Sears and reaching nearly one million personal computer-equipped homes via phone line and modem. The system provides such services as encyclopedia text, airline booking, weather forecasts and electronic mail.

PROFESSIONAL BASKETBALL (THE NBA) ▶ a sporting competition of such growing national interest that NBC paid $600 million for the rights in a four-year deal, which began in the 1990-91 season, and Turner Broadcasting's TNT cable channel paid $275 million for a similar period. The Turner contract was nearly triple what it had paid for the cable rights in the previous negotiation, and NBC paid three and a half times what the rights fetched four years earlier. NBC's pact wrested away coverage from CBS, which had carried the National Basketball Association (NBA) for the previous 17 years.

For $600 million NBC bought the privilege of carrying 20 to 26 regular season games on the weekends or in prime time, plus the All Star game and up to 30 playoff games each year. In addition, the contract called for the network to provide $40 million worth of promotion for the game and the league over the course of the contract. Turner's TNT is able to carry 50 regular season games and some 25 playoff games. In the final year of the previous contract, Turner shifted the games from its superstation WTBS to the fledgling TNT network, and the NBA package is deemed a factor in the new network's success.

Each of the 17 NBA teams shares equally in the NBA contract, receiving approximately $5.6 million a year. Of this, some 53% goes directly to players' salaries, increasing the average compensation for an NBA player from $700,000 to nearly $1 million a year. Teams in the NBA are in the best overall financial position of any of the other professional leagues, largely because of the efforts of two men, David Stern and the late Larry Fleisher. Stern was hired as the NBA's first general counsel in 1978, with Fleisher as director of the NBA Players Assn. In 1983, when several of the clubs were close to bankruptcy and others were spending recklessly for stars, Stern and Fleisher between them hatched a collective bargaining agreement that brought stability to the league's finances. Stern guaranteed the players 53% of the league's gross revenues, and Fleisher accepted a ceiling on salaries. The relationship of the NBA teams and their players has been the envy of other professional leagues.

Stern was made commissioner of the league in February 1984. Fleisher left the Players Assn. to join the International Management Group (IMG) in 1988. He died in May 1989 of a heart attack.

PROFESSIONAL FOOTBALL (THE NFL) ▶ television's prime professional sports attraction and one so wedded to the television dollar that it continually revamps its schedule of games to suit each new buyer of rights. The NFL (National Football League) has gone after the television millions for rights like no other institution.

Once a sport played on Sunday afternoons, NFL football started Monday night games to accommodate ABC in 1970, Sunday night games for ESPN in 1987, and nighttime games on Thanksgiving and occasional Thursdays to achieve a larger network contract. The championship Super Bowl also went from daytime to nighttime to reach the maximum audience, of course for a premium in the contract. The four-year television contracts signed by the NFL in 1990 with the three major networks, ESPN, and Turner Broadcasting (for pre-season and early-season games), worked out to a total of $3.6 billion. The total amount for national television rights in 1978 was barely over $200 million.

Professional football and television have been soul mates. They grew up together. Through television football has surpassed baseball as the favorite American sport. The professional football game is the quintessential TV program: fast-moving, melodramatic, frequently violent—a familiar format with an uncertain outcome—and it is surefire with one of the hardest TV audiences to reach, young males.

Television, with its assurance of money, helped create the second professional league, the AFL, which later merged with the NFL to become one of the two conferences that would meet in the Super Bowl. The Super Bowl is a pure television creation, and in rating terms it has become the biggest single television event in almost any year.

Football's relationship with television started quite modestly in the early 1950s. The first network to buy NFL rights was the old Dumont Network, which only wanted the championship games and paid $75,000 for them. In 1955 NBC took over the contract for the same amount of money. The following year CBS became the first network to televise some of the games in selected markets around the country and came to discover it had a hot property.

Pete Rozelle became NFL commissioner in 1960, and in 1961 Congress passed a law allowing sports leagues to enter into single-network sports contracts. CBS made an exclusive deal with NFL, paying $4.65 million for the regular season games, though oddly, NBC, under a previous two-year contract, had the rights to the championship games. In 1964 CBS secured both the regular season and championship games for two years, and NBC countered by entering into a $36 million five-year deal with the new American Football League to begin in 1965. The network money allowed the AFL to secure talented players like Joe Namath and become reasonably competitive with NFL. The merger of the two leagues was announced in June 1966. The winners of each league would compete in a world championship game, and in 1967 the Super Bowl was born. The first game was carried by both CBS and NBC, and it was a matter of some note at the time that CBS won decisively in the common coverage.

Later, when Baltimore, Pittsburgh and Cleveland agreed to join the AFL teams, the NFL was able to divide into two conferences, the AFC and the NFC, each to produce a winner for the Super Bowl. In 1970 ABC became a participant in the NFL action by contracting for a schedule of Monday night games. ABC's gradual emergence from its historical third-place position began with that move.

In 1978 Rozelle expanded the schedule from 13 regular season games to 16, and in addition added four pre-season games. Cable entered the picture in 1987 when ESPN bought a schedule of Sunday night games for three years. Two years later, Rozelle resigned as commissioner and was replaced by Paul Tagliabue, who continued Rozelle's policies.

ESPN, which previously had paid $153 million to televise NFL games in the second half of the season from 1987-89, had to pay $445 million to renew the rights for another three years. Turner weighed in for the first time under the new negotiations and bought three pre-season games and nine early-season Sunday night games for the same amount ESPN was paying.

Under the new TV deal, each NFL team receives approximately $32.5 million a year for national TV rights, almost twice what they received under the previous contract. To help the three major networks cover their new costs, the NFL expanded the duration of its 16 game schedule by giving each team one week off during the season, thereby giving the networks an extra week of coverage. In addition, the playoffs were expanded by two games. Moreover, the provision for commercial time in each game was expanded by a minute in 1992.

With the continuing increase in games and nights of the week, the NFL has run the risk of over-exposure. By 1992 there were three network telecasts on weekends, plus a cable game on Sunday nights, and a network game on Monday nights and sometimes also on Thursday nights. All told, it comes to around 100 nationally televised games in a season, separate from those broadcast locally.

The recession of the 1990s, however, along with the apparent over-saturation of sports on television generally, has resulted in losses for the networks that are bound to reduce demand for NFL football in the 1994 negotiations. It is likely that NFL will look increasingly to pay-per-view to achieve the revenues it needs from television to survive at the money levels at which it has grown accustomed.

See also Appendix.

PROFILES IN COURAGE ▶ series of documentary-dramas of men of courage in American history, many based on episodes in the Pulitzer Prize-winning book of that title by the late President John F. Kennedy. The series of 26 episodes produced by Robert Saudek Associates premiered on NBC in November 1964.

PROMISE ▶ poignant and deeply moving TV drama produced for *Hallmark Hall of Fame* that was televised on CBS Dec. 14, 1986, and won a raft of awards. It starred James Garner as an irresponsible bachelor who, on the death of his mother, is confronted with having to care for his schizophrenic brother, played by James Woods. The 90-minute movie was produced by Peter Duchow and Garner and was directed by Glenn Jordan. It also starred Piper Laurie. Others in the cast were Peter Michael Goetz, Michael Alldredge, Alan Rosenberg, and Mary Marsh.

PROSERV TELEVISION ▶ Dallas-based production company that was formed in 1971 essentially to popularize tennis through television and that has grown to become a leading independent producer and distributor of sports programming. In latter years the company has branched into other kinds of programming, including documentaries and entertainment specials, some for PBS. It is strongly oriented to the international market.

ProServ Television is an arm of ProServ Inc., a sports marketing firm that promotes a range of events and represents a large roster of professional athletes. Its principals, chairman Donald Dell and president Robert Briner, were previously connected with professional tennis organizations. Recognizing that the core tennis enthusiasts at the time were devotees of public TV, they worked with WGBH Boston to provide coverage of various tennis tournaments for PBS stations and secured the backing of corporate underwriters.

Later the company got in on the cable boom as a producer of tennis and other sporting events, along with regular magazine series such as *Sports Probe, SportsWoman, ESPN Outdoors, Tennis Magazine Reports* and *This Week In the NBA*. One of its specials, *A Hard Road to Glory*, won an Emmy in 1986. Its cultural specials have included *Ireland and the Irish, Rubenstein Remembered* and *The Kirov Theater Ballet from Leningrad*.

PROTELE ▶ the American-based program distribution arm of Mexico's dominant broadcast company, Televisa. Some 70% of its programming is in the form of telenovelas—Latin American soap operas that differ from those of the U.S. in that they actually come to an end at some point, which allows them to be marketed as novels for television. In the late 1980s, the telenovela became a hot form in world markets; in 1990, Protele's international sales exceeded $25 million. One of the best-sellers was *Los Ricos Tambien Llaren* (*The Rich Also Cry*).

PSA ▶ widely used abbreviation for public service announcement, a 20-, 30- or 60-second spot carried gratis by a station or network for its informational, moral or social assistance to the viewer, or to help promote a charity or a cause. Most PSA's are produced at the expense of the organizations presenting them—often at commercial production houses under the donated guidance of advertising agencies—and are distributed to stations for use at their discretion. Some are produced by the stations, however, as a service to groups unable to afford the expense of creating a spot.

PTAR ▶ trade shorthand for the Prime Time-Access Rule. It is also represented as PTAR I, PTAR II and PTAR III, to denote the phases of the rule under the FCC's periodic modifications of it.

PUBLIC ACCESS ▶ cable channels reserved for exclusive use of the general public to produce or present uncensored program material on a first-come, first-served basis. The FCC required systems in the top 100 markets to provide such access channels under its 1972 rules, but the Supreme Court struck down the requirement in 1979. However, state authorities through legislation and municipalities through local cable franchises still have the power to require public access channels and facilities.

PUBLIC BROADCASTING LABORATORY ▶ commercial production organization established by the Ford Foundation in 1967 to produce an innovative two-hour Sunday night news program, *PBL*, over the nation's ETV stations. Ford's grant of $10 million a year for the project provided for the interconnection of the stations (most of which had been inactive on Sunday nights at the time) as well as for the production. The program was conceived by Fred W. Friendly, former president of CBS News who had become broadcast consultant to the foundation, and he appointed his CBS protege, Av Westin, to head the project. Although it ran two years, *PBL* was not a success, but it did influence the commercial networks, which borrowed the format for *60 Minutes* and *First Tuesday,* which later became *Chronolog* and then *Weekend.* The Laboratory disbanded when the program ended its run.

PUBLIC HEARINGS ▶ open hearings held by the FCC in the community of any station or stations. The general public is invited to attend, with interested parties acting as witnesses either for or against the licensee. The commission's authority to hold such hearings is stated in Section 403 of the Communications Act.

PUBLIC TELEVISION (PTV) ▶ noncommercial television, whose freedom from the constraints of the marketplace in theory permits it to strive to realize the full humanistic and social potential of the medium. It generally is looked to for a menu of cultural, informational, educational and innovative programming.

In the U.S., public TV is supported by federal and state funds, voluntary contributions from viewers and grants from foundations and corporations. In most other countries, the funds come from an annual tax on television receivers, sometimes supplemented by a limited sale of advertising. The most telling comparison, however, is the per-person spending for public television in America ($6.34) contrasted with the per-person outlay in the United Kingdom ($37.31), Japan ($19.76) and Canada ($48.46).

American public TV has been weaker than most of its foreign counterparts chiefly because it came into being after commercial TV had become firmly rooted as the primary system, the reverse of the pattern in most other countries. Also, PTV's penetration has been hampered by a predominance of UHF stations and its program vistas clouded during the first two decades by the uncertainty and inadequacy of federal funding. Finally, it has suffered from a history of discord within the system itself over the mission of public television.

The disharmony in the system traces to the fact that public television, originally called Educational Television, began in 1952 as a collection of autonomous stations, each serving, in one way or another, the purposes of education. To complicate matters further, they were not all of a kind. At least four distinct types emerged: those licensed to state governments or agencies (117), those licensed to universities and colleges (92), those licensed to local government authority (10), and those licensed to nonprofit community associations (121). The latter type, represented in most of the country's major metropolitan centers, has been dominant by virtue of its audience size and resources. When the system was redefined and redesignated as public television by the Public Broadcasting Act of 1967, the new label did not mean the same thing to all operators, notwithstanding the ideals for noncommercial television put forth in the Carnegie Commission Report that year. Many stations continued to adhere to the original educational mandate, and others were opposed to surrendering any of their sovereignty to the national system.

Regional and political differences among the stations also contributed to factionalism. Many of the larger stations advocated more centralization of the system to strengthen the national impact of PTV and make it a stronger force in American television, while others considered it heresy for PTV to aspire to reach larger audiences. There was also a particular aversion in middle America to public affairs programs emanating from the East Coast.

But despite the internal struggles that have made public television a name without a concept, the noncommercial system has steadily been broadening its audience base and has exerted a positive influence on the commercial system. The networks have borrowed from PTV such program forms as the newsmagazine, the mini-series and the serialized novel.

By 1991 public television had almost 5 million public subscribers voluntarily contributing an average of $56 a year, testifying to the public medium's power to develop a significant constituency. Although audiences for individual shows have been small by commercial television standards, PTV reaches a cumulative audience each week of 90 million viewers, nearly 40% of the nation's population. Nevertheless, only its most popular shows—the *National Geographic Specials, MacNeil/Lehrer NewsHour, This Old House, Nature, The Frugal Gourmet* and the British import *Mystery*—exceed the average rating of less than 3% for its prime-time shows. In the daytime ratings, only *Sesame Street,* among the PBS shows, edges out the commercial competition for its target audience. *The Civil War,* a 1990 series aired on five successive nights, set the all-time rating record for series of limited length with an average rating of 8.8, which translated to 38.9 million viewers. A 1975 *National Geographic Special* on the human body, "The Incredible Machine," set the PBS record for a single show with a rating of 13.9%, higher in some cities than its commercial competition.

Public television's funding is best described as variable, both in source and reliability. Federal funding, which didn't begin until 1967, has risen gradually over the years but still represents only 16.5% of the public television's total annual income of $1.2 billion. The largest single source (21.6%) comes from public TV's audience, viewers who subscribe to their local stations or participate in the station's fund-raising events. Additional income is provided from state governments (18.9%), colleges and universities (8.4%), and foundations (4.8%), with an additional 13.7% from miscellaneous sources. Business, largely through underwriting specific programs or program series, accounts for 16.1% of the total.

In the early 1980s, just when public TV was beginning to show strength as an alternative to commercial television, an economy-minded Reagan Administration cast its future in doubt by severely slashing the public medium's federal appropriations. Forced to look elsewhere, public TV turned to commercials. Congress authorized 10 PTV stations to experiment with paid ads for 18 months, the experiment to be supervised by a Temporary Commission on Alternative Financing charged with exploring financial options for the public medium. The TCAF report, submitted two years later, rejected commercials as a viable option but called on the FCC to relax its rules on the identification of corporate underwriting to permit the use of brand names, trade names, slogans, etc. As a consequence, underwriting credits quickly became almost indistinguishable from the advertising messages on commercial TV.

The Senate Commerce Committee tried in 1988 to return public TV to its goal of long-range federal funding by proposing a public broadcasting trust fund whose revenues would be derived from a 2-5% fee on the transfer of FCC-licensed properties. The measure was effectively defeated by the opposition of commercial broadcasters and jurisdictional disputes within Congress itself.

HISTORY—During the FCC's four-year freeze on station licenses (1948-52), a movement began among educators for channels that would be noncommercial and dedicated to education. Their cause had a champion on the commission in Frieda B. Hennock. When the freeze was lifted and the table of assignments issued in the FCC's historic Sixth Report and Order in 1952, there were 242 channels reserved for noncommercial TV—80 on VHF and 162 on UHF. Those initial allocations were later increased to 116 VHF and 516 UHF. In May 1953 KUHT Houston became the country's first educational TV licensee.

The Ford Foundation, which had been giving financial assistance to the organizations campaigning for the educational reservations, helped get the earliest stations on the air with locally matched equipment grants. To help them with programming, the Foundation created the Educational Television and Radio Center in Ann Arbor, Mich., whose function was not to create programming but to foster the exchange of programming among the stations then on the air. That changed in 1964. The Center, renamed National Educational Television (NET) and with increased Foundation support, moved to New York, hired a production staff, and undertook its own production of documentary, drama and performance programming for its affiliates.

Activation of new channels moved slowly. After a decade of activity only 62 stations had managed to get on the air. But in 1962 Congress enacted the Educational Broadcasting Facilities Act authorizing HEW to disburse $32 million in matching grants over five years to assist in the construction of ETV facilities. In the next four years, the number of stations on the air more than doubled.

But as the system expanded, the funding problem grew more pressing. By 1965 it was clear that long-range funding of a much larger magnitude was needed to replace the Ford Foundation's start-up dollars. The system's call for a study was answered by the Carnegie Corporation, which provided funds for a 15-member committee, the Carnegie Commission on Educational Television, to conduct a study and recommend solutions. The Commission, under the chairmanship of Dr. James R. Killian of MIT, published its report, *Public Television: A Program for Action,* on Jan. 25, 1967. The document was regarded thereafter as Scripture for noncommercial TV.

Predictably, its recommended source of long-range funding was government. However, to insulate the money from the source and prevent the government from assuming any measure of control over the broadcast material, the Commission recommended a dedicated tax whose proceeds would pass automatically, without congressional action, to a nongovernmental Corporation for Public Television. More influential, perhaps, was its recommendation that ETV become *Public* TV, with the aim of addressing "all that is of human interest and public importance." The report emphasized local service and recommended that the system not strive to become a fourth network.

The Carnegie Commission's recommendations formed the basis of the Public Broadcasting Act of 1967. Congress, however, balked at buying the Commission's dedicated tax, favoring instead annual congressional appropriations, the politically sensitive means the Commission had warned against. The legislation created a Corporation for Public Broadcasting (CPB) to receive and disburse federal funds but did not follow the Commission's recommendations for a governing board that could not be controlled from the White House. It also charged the CPB with responsibility for interconnecting the stations but cautioned that it was to be used as a distribution device and not as a network.

After negotiating an interconnection contract with AT&T, CPB created the Public Broadcasting Service to manage the interconnection and guide the flow of programs over the national lines to its member stations, but not to produce or acquire programming on its own. The first programs were fed on the AT&T land lines in October 1970. Eight years later, before any of the three commercial networks had done so, PBS switched its national interconnection to satellites.

Ten years after the first Carnegie Commission, a second Carnegie Commission (Carnegie II), also funded by the Carnegie Corporation, studied the future of public broadcasting in a much altered media environment. The Commission's recommendations–including reorganization of the system to provide more national programming and better insulation from political interference plus greatly increased federal funding—were largely ignored. A supplemental Carnegie-funded study, *Keeping PACE With The New Television,* recommended a new national nonprofit pay cable television network for the Performing Arts, Culture and Education, but it too failed to win the enthusiasm of either the Congress or public broadcasters.

By the 1990s many public broadcasters, faced with increased competition from cable networks that aired similar type programs, called for a return to public television's roots, to the educational purposes on which it was founded. Most large-city stations, however, continued to march to a different drummer, concerned with finding programming that attracted the larger audiences they needed in order to survive.

Q

QB VII ▶ 3 1/2 hour TV adaptation of the Leon Uris novel of that title, presented by ABC as a mini-series in April 1974. The success of both *QB VII* and the adaptation of Joseph Wambaugh's *The Blue Knight* the previous year spurred the networks into the development of short-term series based on novels. Produced by the Douglas S. Cramer Co. and Screen Gems, *QB VII* starred Ben Gazzara, Anthony Hopkins, Leslie Caron, Lee Remick and Jack Hawkins. Tom Gries directed, Edward Anhalt wrote the script and Cramer was producer.

QUADRUPLEX (QUAD) ▶ type of videotape recorder most commonly used for 20 years at television stations and networks, so-called because it has four recording heads. The heads are arranged in a drum that spins at right angles to the tape's motion. The obsolescence of quad recorders was signaled in 1977 with the introduction of one-inch VTRs capable of similar broadcast quality.

QUANTUM LEAP ▶ fantasy action-adventure series that relies more on the solid appeal of its leading man, Scott Bakula, than on its sci-fi plot lines. Bakula, as young scientist Sam Beckett, is sent back in time into the bodies and lives of various 20th century people, male and female, and all relatively ordinary folk (airplane test pilot, baseball player, rock star, prostitute). He is aided in his travels by an observer, Albert, played by noted actor Dean Stockwell, who appears in the form of a hologram visible only to the protagonist. The series, created and produced by Donald Bellisario, debuted on NBC in March 1989.

QUARLES, NORMA ▶ daytime anchor for CNN's New York bureau and co-anchor on *Daybreak* and *Morning News*. She joined CNN after 21 years with the NBC network and its affiliates. From 1982-88, she was New York correspondent for NBC News and a regular anchor of NBC News's *Evening Digest*.

Quarles' broadcast career has included reporting for Chicago's WMAQ and anchoring from WKYC, the NBC-owned Cleveland station.

QUBE ▶ trade name for a dazzlingly futuristic two-way cable system established experimentally in Columbus, Ohio, in December 1977 by Warner Communications. Under the design of the system, one cable line carried TV signals to the customer while the upstream line permitted subscribers to send back responses to a central computer.

The system became reorganized as state-of-the-art technology during the franchising activities of the 1980s, and it—or something comparable—was demanded by every large city. Qube helped Warner Amex cable win the franchises for Pittsburgh, Dallas, Houston, Cincinnati and parts of New York, but the cost of building two-way systems proved unfeasible at the time, and in the mid-1980s Warner folded its Qube operations. Consensus within the television industry was that the system was ahead of its time.

A later-generation Qube console

Subscribers in Columbus received a hand-held console resembling a large pocket calculator on which to make program selections from 30 channels. A row of ten buttons was dedicated to over-the-air television stations and the public-access channel. A second row often was for premium programming—movies, cultural events, games, entertainments, special sports events and self-help courses, each for a specific charge. This group included an optional "adult" channel with soft-core pornography. Rates for the premium programs ranged from seventy-five cents to $9. The third row of ten channels, called the community channels, provided a varied menu of free programming (free, that is, after the $10.95 monthly charge for the basic service), including full-time channels for children's, religious, cultural and sports fare and a nostalgia channel offering old TV series. One channel in this group provided the programs that utilized Qube's unique ability to ask questions of the home viewer and receive answers from the response pad, which it could tabulate and flash on the screen in a matter of moments.

The system lent itself to public-opinion polls and voting on performances in amateur shows, but it also was adaptable to ordering merchandise and for multiple-choice examinations in video college courses. The systems built in Dallas, Pittsburgh and the other major cities were more elaborate than the Columbus installation, involving more than three times the number of channels and a more advanced tuning and response device.

As an interactive system, Qube was also to be used for a variety of home security services, such as burglar-and fire-alarm protection and medical emergency alarms, each for additional monthly fees. Thus, even as the viewer watched television, the television set could watch the home. Warner reportedly invested $20 million in the Columbus experiment. Attracted by Qube and its implications for credit cards, American Express bought a 50% interest in Warner Cable for $175 million in 1980. The company was then renamed Warner Amex Cable.

¿QUE PASA, USA? ▶ bilingual situation comedy on PBS (1978) developed under a regional HEW grant for Cuban-American teenagers in South Florida. The crisply written series, centering on three generations of a Cuban family in Miami, broke new ground in programming for teenagers. Its production values were almost on a par with those of commercial network sitcoms, yet it was produced for approximately $25,000 an episode—about one-tenth the cost of a network show.

The program was produced by WPBT Miami, with Shep Morgan as executive producer and Jose Bahamonde as producer.

QUEEN FOR A DAY ▶ an immensely popular daytime show that, between radio and TV, had a run of nearly 20 years (April 29, 1945, to Oct. 2, 1964), although widely criticized as a vulgar exploitation of human misery in an orgy of commercial plugs. It shifted from NBC radio to television on Jan. 1, 1955, and within months became the number-one daytime show, reaching a daily audience of around 13 million. When it was at the peak of its popularity, NBC increased the show's length from 30 to 45 minutes, in order to gain additional commercial time to sell at the then premium advertising rate of $4,000 per minute. In the fall of 1959 *Queen* moved to ABC, where it spent its final five years.

Five contestants selected from the audience each day competed for the title of "queen" (and for the accompanying raft of prizes) by telling, usually through tears, why they wished for a particular item of merchandise. Always behind the need was a personal story of pathos. The studio audience then was asked to vote, by applause measured by an applause-meter, for the contestant most deserving to be "queen for a day."

Crowned, and decked in a sable-collared velvet robe, the weeping wretch, supported in her emotional state by emcee Jack Bailey, received her gifts from a procession of models as the announcer delivered the plugs for the donated merchandise. The show inspired two successful imitations, *Strike It Rich!* and *It Could Be You.*

Howard Blake, a sometime producer of the show, wrote in an article published in 1966: "Sure, *Queen* was vulgar and sleazy and filled with bathos and bad taste. That was why it was so successful: It was exactly what the general public wanted."

James H. Quello

QUELLO, JAMES H. ▶ FCC commissioner since 1974. He was appointed to a Democratic seat by President Nixon, despite objections by groups in the broadcast reform movement. A chief objection to Quello's appointment was that he had been a broadcaster with the Capital Cities group. He had risen from promotion manager of radio station WJR Detroit in 1947 to v.p. and general manager of that station in 1960. He retired from Capital Cities in 1972, after having simultaneously been a member of the House Housing and Urban Renewal Commission, and two years later was named to the FCC. He was reappointed by President Reagan in 1981 and again in 1984. In 1991 President Bush reappointed him for a fourth term ending in June 1996.

QUEST, THE ▶ hour-long western series introduced by NBC in 1976 in an unsuccessful attempt to revive interest in the genre; it involved the adventures of two brothers in search of their sister, who was captured by Indians. Kurt Russell and Tim Matheson played the leads, Morgan and Quentin Beaudine. The series was by David Gerber Productions in association with Columbia Pictures TV.

QUINCY, M.E. ▶ successful one-hour NBC drama series (1976-83) featuring Jack Klugman as an expert medical examiner for the Los Angeles Coroner's Office with a talent for solving cases through his ability to spot minuscule medical clues. With the series, Klugman overcame strong viewer identification with his previous TV role as the unkempt sportswriter in *The Odd Couple.* The regular supporting cast included Robert Ito as assistant Sam Fujiyama, Val Bisoglio as assistant Danny Tovo, Joseph Roman as Sergeant Brill, Garry Walberg as Lieutenant Frank Monahan and John S. Ragin as coroner Robert J. Asten.

Via Glen A. Larson Productions, the series was created by Larson and Lou Shaw and produced by Peter Thompson.

QUIZ SHOW SCANDAL ▶ a trauma in the television industry that occurred in the fall of 1959 with the revelation that producers of several highly popular giveaway shows had "fixed" them by providing certain contestants with answers in advance. The episode, which ruptured the public's and the government's trust in the integrity of commercial broadcasting, was to have lasting implications on network policies, industry codes and the character of television programming.

Months of rumors, fanned by several magazine articles and fueled by accusations of malpractice by a former contestant on *Twenty One,* Herbert Stempel, led to an investigation early in 1959 by a New York grand jury. The probe of quiz show "rigging" was pursued further in the House of Representatives that fall by the Special Subcommittee on Legislative Oversight, headed by Rep. Oren Harris. On Nov. 2 came the confession from the key witness, Charles Van Doren, who had previously denied having any knowledge of cheating on *Twenty One,* the program on which he became a national celebrity after defeating Stempel. An English instructor at Columbia University, Van Doren became an NBC personality, regularly featured on *Today* with a salary of $1,000 a week, as a result of his popularity on the quiz show, on which over a period of months he had won $129,000.

In his confession, he told of being persuaded by the producer, Albert Freeman, to accept help in the form of a briefing on questions and answers before each program. He said the request was made because Stempel was an unpopular champion, whose weekly successes were hurting the show. He said he was told that quiz shows were only entertainment and that giving help to quiz contestants was a common practice.

The subcommittee was then to learn from other witnesses that two other popular giveaway series, *The $64,000 Question* and *The $64,000 Challenge,* received periodic instructions from the sponsor, Revlon, to eliminate uninteresting contestants or to let attractive ones continue.

Top network executives denied knowing that the programs were manipulated and none was implicated, but quiz shows disappeared from the airways almost at once, and several of the producers were never to work again in the medium. Jack Barry, whose Barry & Enright Productions owned *Twenty One, Tic Tac Dough* and other hit quizzes, was exiled from television for 10 years but made his way back in 1970 as a producer of daytime gameshows for the networks.

The scandal led to widespread self-examination in the industry and to the adoption of policies against even milder forms of deceit. The networks were prompted to assume greater control over their programming, trusting less to the sponsor.

Coupled with the concurrent payola revelations in radio (involving disk jockey payoffs, likened to commercial bribery), the episode led to amendments to the Communications Act in 1960. One amendment made illegal the presentation of programs purporting to be contests of skill or knowledge where the result is in any way prearranged, another made more explicit a station's obligation to make known on the air when money or other consideration is received for broadcast material.

The passing of the quiz programs contributed to the spread of filmed series produced in Hollywood and changed the nature of prime-time competition among the networks. Executives who were adept at live television and the showmanship involved gave way to those astute at selecting and scheduling continuing film series. Thus, Louis Cowan was deposed as president of CBS-TV and replaced by James Aubrey, who was hired away from ABC-TV.

R

RADIO TELEFIS EIREANN (RTE) ▶ the state-run radio and television service in the Republic of Ireland that operates two TV channels transmitting complementary programming for approximately 80 weekly hours each. Until 1990 RTE held a monopoly position in Ireland but now faces competition from the privately owned TV3, which is nationally distributed through existing cable systems and MMDS. RTE, which operates on 625-line PAL standard, is supported with a combination of license fees and advertising and carries a high proportion of domestically produced programming.

RAI (RADIOTELEVISIONE ITALIANA) ▶ Italy's state-operated television network with a mandate to serve the country's educational, social and cultural progress through its three national TV channels. Once largely dedicated to public service and cultural programming, its 61 daily hours of television programming now compete for audience with Silvio Berlusconi's three private networks and manage jointly to capture on average about 50% of the viewers.

In a peculiarly Italian solution to its volatile political situation, each of RAI's channels is effectively controlled by one of its three major political parties. The ruling Social Democrats control the principal channel. RAI is a shareholding corporation in which an agency of the Parliament holds 99.55% of the shares. It is supported by a combination of license fees and limited commercials.

Following a worldwide trend, RAI has become increasingly involved in the coproduction, distribution and marketing of its programs abroad through its subsidiary SACIS. Its New York-based American subsidiary, RAI Corporation, is headed by Renato Pachetti.

RAMAR OF THE JUNGLE **▶** syndicated adventure series (1952-54) featuring Jon Hall as Dr. Tom Reynolds—known as Ramar by the people of Kenya and India, where he works—and Ray Montgomery as Professor Howard Ogden, and produced by Arrow Productions and TPA.

RANCK, JOHN ▶ president of international television for Carolco Pictures, an American executive transplanted to London in 1989. Ranck's career has spanned production and distribution. He began in television in 1969 working on the *Joe Namath Show*. He then ran his own company representing producers and facilities in the U.S. for three years, after which he became involved in the formation of Lexington Broadcasting Services, a syndication company that later became known as LBS. He left in 1977 to form a distribution company, Allied Entertainment, and when it failed he rejoined LBS in 1980. Four years later he left to become one of the four founding partners of Orbis Communications, which in the late 1980s was bought out by Carolco Pictures. Ranck, who had headed international sales for Orbis from New York, moved his base after the sale to London, which is generally considered the capital of international television.

RANDALL, TONY ▶ an enduring TV actor who is best known for his role as the fussy Felix Unger in *The Odd Couple* (1970-75), though his career in TV dates back to *One Man's Family* (1950-52) and *Mr. Peepers* (1952-55), in which he played second banana to Wally Cox. In the 195Os Randall starred in *Philco Playhouse, Kraft Theatre,* and *Studio One.* In the 1960s he concentrated on a film career, returning to TV with *The Odd Couple* in 1970 and, a few years later, the less memorable, *Love, Sidney* (1981-83). Over the years he has been a frequent talk-show guest, and his love of opera has made him a knowledgeable host of PBS's *Live from the Met* telecasts.

RANDOM ACCESS EDITING ▶ electronic system based on a Macintosh or IBM personal computer that digitizes moving images so they can be displayed on the computer screen and then allows the editor to use a keyboard or mouse to select any desired segments of the digitized program and arrange them in any desired sequence.

RANKIN-BASS PRODUCTIONS ▶ independent New York-based company founded by Arthur Rankin, Jr., and Jules Bass, specializing in animation and noted for a number of holiday specials that play perennially on the networks. These include *Rudolph, the Red-Nosed Reindeer, Frosty, the Snowman* and *'Twas the Night Before Christmas,* all on CBS; *The Little Drummer Boy, Santa Claus Is Coming to Town* and *The First Christmas* on NBC; and *A Year Without Santa Claus* and *Rudolph's Shiny New Year* on ABC. Some have been on the air 10 years or more. The firm was acquired by Tomorrow Entertainment in the early 1970s, but Rankin and Bass resumed operations on their own when that company disbanded. They also turned out such Saturday morning children's series as *The Jackson Five, The Osmond Brothers* and *Kid Power.*

RANSOHOFF, MARTIN ▶ founder and chairman of Filmways, highly successful independent production company that had started in 1952 as a producer of commercials and industrial films. On branching into TV series, the company had a string of hits, among them *Mr. Ed, The Beverly Hillbillies, Petticoat Junction* and *The Addams Family.* It also did well in motion pictures, including *The Americanization of Emily* and *Boys' Night Out.* Filmways was sold to Orion Pictures Corp. in 1983.

RAPF, MATTHEW (d. 1991) ▶ producer of numerous TV series, including *The Loretta Young Show* in the 1950s, *Ben Casey* in the 1960s and *Kojak* in the 1970s. His credits include *The Great Gildersleeve, Frontier, The Web, Jefferson Drum, Two Faces West, The Man from Blackhawk, Slattery's People* and *The Young Lawyers.* In the 1970s, he was executive producer of *Switch, Doctor's Hospital* and *The Marcus-Nelson Murders,* a TV movie that was the pilot for *Kojak.*

RAT PATROL **▶** ABC series (1966-67) of fictional adventures in the North African desert during World War II, featuring Christopher George as Sergeant Sam Troy, Gary Raymond as Sergeant Jack Moffitt and Lawrence Casey as Private Mark Hitchcock. It was produced by Mirisch-Rich TV Productions, with Jon Epstein as producer.

RATE CARD ▶ a station's printed price list for commercial spots or program sponsorship.

Dan Rather

RATHER, DAN ▶ anchor of the *CBS Evening News* since March 1981, the successor to Walter Cronkite as the network's premier newsperson. Rather's contract negotiations in 1980 set off a chain of events that led to Cronkite relinquishing the anchor post somewhat earlier than planned and Roger Mudd leaving the network for NBC News after having been passed over. With Rather at the helm, the *Evening News* lost audience share points the first year but began recovering them the second.

Before being elevated to anchor, Rather was a CBS News correspondent who distinguished himself first in covering the assassination of

President John F. Kennedy in 1963, while he was chief of the southwest bureau in Dallas, and later in his coverage of the White House and the Watergate developments during the Nixon Administration. To millions of viewers, Rather came to symbolize the adversary press in his numerous bold news confrontations with the President.

After Watergate, Rather was replaced at the White House and given the new assignment of anchor-correspondent for *CBS Reports* and anchor of the *CBS Weekend News.* At the end of 1975, however, when *60 Minutes* was moved into prime time as a 52-week series, Rather was selected as one of the three editors. In 1977, he doubled as a reporter on the program's spin-off, *Who's Who.*

Rather joined CBS News in 1962 in the Dallas bureau and became White House correspondent in 1964. A year later he went to London as bureau chief, and he returned to his Washington post in 1966, remaining until 1974. Among the CBS special reports on which he served as anchor or reporter were *The White House Tapes: The President's Decision, The Watergate Indictments, The Mysterious Alert* and *Nixon: A Full, Free and Absolute Pardon.* In addition to the *CBS Evening News,* Rather has been anchor for *48 Hours* since its premiere in 1988.

RATING ▶ established unit of audience measurement in TV, carried over from radio, which represents the percentage of households tuned to a given program in a time period from the universe of households equipped to receive television. For a national or network program, the universe is the total number of TV households in the U.S., while for local ratings it is the number of TV households in the station's coverage area, which normally encompasses several counties. Thus, a national rating of 20 means that 20% of all possible TV homes in the country were tuned in, while a local rating of 20 means that 20% of the households with TV receivers were watching in the geographic area to which the station is licensed.

RAWHIDE ▶ action-filled western on CBS that enjoyed a long run (1959-65). Produced by CBS, the series centered on a cattle-drive operation. Its leads were Eric Fleming as Gil Favor, Clint Eastwood as Rowdy Yates, Paul Brinegar as Wishbone and Steve Raines as Quince. The show was a springboard for Eastwood.

RAY BRADBURY THEATRE, THE ▶ science-fiction anthology series that began in 1987 on the USA cable network. It was hosted by famed sci-fi writer Ray Bradbury, and many of the episodes were adaptations of his stories. Bradbury also served as an executive producer, along with Peter Sussman and Larry Wilcox.

RAY MILLAND SHOW, THE **(*MEET MR. McNUTLEY*)** ▶ moderately successful comedy series on CBS (1953-55) that served as a vehicle for the movie star. Milland portrayed Ray McNutley, a professor of dramatics at a women's college. After a season, the setting changed from the women's college to Comstock College, and Ray's surname became McNulty. In both versions, Phyllis Avery portrayed Ray's wife, Peggy. On CBS, the series was first entitled *Meet Mr. McNutley,* but it became better known by its syndication title, *The Ray Milland Show.* It was by Revue Studios.

RAYBURN, GENE ▶ comedian, announcer and television host who was a member of the resident cast of the Steve Allen *Tonight* show on NBC from 1954-59, and then host of several game shows. Those included *Dough-Re-Mi* on NBC (1958-60), *The Match Game* on NBC (1962-69) and two revivals of *Match Game* on CBS, in 1973 and 1978. He came into prominence with a daily radio program on New York's WNEW, *The Rayburn and Finch Show,* a four-hour stint of ad-lib comedy interspersed with records, which ran six years. On splitting with his partner, Dee Finch, in 1953, Rayburn began doing local television in New York until he was tapped for the original *Tonight* show.

RAYE, MARTHA ▶ raucous, slapstick comedienne prominent in TV during the 1950s, rounding out a career that spanned vaudeville, radio, movies and nightclubs. She began on television in 1951 in *All Star Revue* and then launched *The Martha Raye Show* on a monthly basis (1954-56). She was also a frequent guest on *The Steve Allen Show, The Colgate Comedy Hour, The Milton Berle Show* and others. She returned to television in 1976 in a supporting role on *McMillan and Wife.* In the 1980s she had a semi-regular role in the CBS sitcom *Alice,* playing Vic Tayback's mother.

RCA ▶ originally Radio Corporation of America, for decades the largest U.S. television hardware company and a major broadcaster through its ownership of the National Broadcasting Company (NBC). The company lost its way in the 1980s and eventually its existence.

Founded in 1919 at the behest of the U.S. Navy as a U.S.-based wireless communications company that could be of use in the event of a national emergency or war, the company developed under the guidance of its president, David Sarnoff, into a pioneer of the concept of corporate growth through what has since been described as synergy between "hardware" and "software." It manufactured radios (hardware) and created radio programming (software) to encourage sales of its sets. Later applying the same model to television, the company was an early manufacturer of TV sets and established NBC to supply programming to buyers of those sets. In addition to consumer electronics equipment RCA became the leading U.S. manufacturer of broadcast production and transmission equipment. The company owned RCA records as well as the NBC network and its owned stations, developed the RCA Selectavision videodisc system in the mid-1970s, and in 1975 began launching the Satcom series of geostationary satellites for relaying TV signals.

Following a period of investing in such unrelated businesses as Hertz Rent-a-Car and frozen foods, the company underwent several years of internal turmoil from the late 1970s to the mid-1980s that resulted in the closing down of divisions (RCA Broadcast Systems) or the selling of them (RCA Records)—a process that culminated in the sale of the RCA Corporation itself to General Electric in 1986.

In its final years RCA was accused of being too oriented toward short-term profits, closing or selling its units not because they were unprofitable but because they were not profitable enough. To many, RCA ended up epitomizing the short-sightedness of U.S. business competing in a global economy. Ironically, it was RCA's early growth, based on hardware-software synergies, that inspired the strategies of the competitors—many of them Japanese—to which RCA lost its greatest market share.

RCA SATCOM ▶ an RCA 24-channel domestic satellite, launched in December 1975 and followed in March 1976 by Satcom 2. RCA Americom was manufacturer as well as operator of the craft.

Satcom 1 became the primary satellite for cable-TV services, while Satcom 2 was used for commercial television and other communications. In 1978, demand for transponder space on Satcom 1 became so intense that RCA moved up the scheduled launch date for Satcom 3 to the fall of 1979. When launched, however, the satellite failed to go into orbit and became lost in space, creating a crisis for several cable networks. Additional Satcoms followed. After General Electric purchased RCA, the satellite unit was renamed GE Americom.

REAGAN, RONALD ▶ actor-turned-politician whose two-score movies and TV reruns (*Death Valley Days* and *GE Theater*) were barred from the air under the equal time rule during the periods of his various candidacies. He became Governor of California (1966-74), barely missed unseating Gerald Ford as Republican nominee for the presidency in 1976, and won the Presidency in 1980. Under Reagan's free-market policies during his eight years in office, broadcasting was substantially deregulated. The impact of his administration, which fostered the mania for mergers and acquisition, will be felt for a long time.

A radio announcer and sportscaster in the Midwest during the 1930s, using the name "Dutch" Reagan, he broke into films with Warner Bros. in 1937 and played leads in numerous second-line Hollywood movies for the next two decades. For three years he was host-narrator of the syndicated *Death Valley Days* and then host, actor and production supervisor for the CBS anthology *GE Theater.* He was president of Screen Actors Guild from 1947 to 1952 and again in 1959, and it was under his leadership that the union achieved residual payment for actors from the studios as well as a pension and welfare fund.

***REAL McCOYS, THE* ▶** popular countrified situation comedy, starring Walter Brennan as Grandpa Amos McCoy, that originated on ABC (1957-62) and switched to CBS (1963). Featured were Richard Crenna as grandson Luke McCoy and Kathy Nolan as Kate McCoy, Luke's wife. It was via Brennan-Westgate Productions and VT&L Productions.

***REAL WEST, THE* ▶** distinguished NBC documentary (March 1961) presenting, through still photographs and paintings, an unglamorized and historically accurate account of the western movement in the U.S. It exploded many hero-myths and revealed the cruel effects the movement had on the Native American. The film was narrated by Gary Cooper, the noted actor who had appeared in numerous Hollywood westerns and who was dying of cancer at the time; Cooper asked to do the narration "to set the record straight." The documentary was created by the NBC Project 20 unit: Donald Hyatt, producer; Philip Reisman Jr., writer; Daniel Jones, researcher.

REALIDADES ▶ magazine-format public television show by and about the American Latino populations. Largely funded by CPB, it was produced in the mid-1970s by WNET New York at an annual cost of $400,000.

Harry Reasoner

REASONER, HARRY (d. 1991) ▶ longtime CBS News correspondent and a founding co-editor, with Mike Wallace, of *60 Minutes.* He once told an interviewer that he agreed to do the broadcast as a favor to Don Hewitt, the program's executive producer, believing the show would not last. Reasoner was a correspondent on *60 Minutes* from its premiere on September 24, 1968, to the fall of 1970, when he left for ABC News. There, he was teamed for several years with Howard K. Smith anchoring its newscast, before becoming sole anchor in 1975.

His disagreements with ABC began a year later, when in an attempt to bolster the news ratings, the network lured away Barbara Walters from NBC with a reported $1 million dollar-a-year contract to become Reasoner's co-anchor. The chemistry between them was poor, both on and off the screen, and when ABC News president Roone Arledge restyled the newscast in 1978, Reasoner returned to CBS. There, he rejoined *60 Minutes,* where he remained until his final illness.

Reasoner first joined CBS News in July 1956, based in New York. One of his early major assignments was reporting on the racial crisis in Little Rock, Ark., in 1958. In 1959 he covered Nikita Khrushchev's visit to the United States and the following year President Dwight D. Eisenhower's trip to the Far East. Among his other CBS credits: co-hosting the morning television broadcast, reporting on *CBS Reports,* the celebrated documentary series, and narrating "An Essay on Doors," written by Andy Rooney, which became the first of many collaborations between the two over the years.

Reasoner began his journalism career in 1942 on the *Minneapolis Times.* After Army service in World War II, he returned to the *Times* as drama critic from 1946-48. He became a newswriter for WCCO Minneapolis in 1950, spent three years with the U.S. Information Agency in Manila, and returned to Minneapolis as news director of KEYD-TV.

He also wrote three books: *Tell Me About Women,* a novel (1964), *The Reasoner Report,* a collection of essays (1966), and *Before the Colors Fade,* his memoir (1981).

REBEL, THE ▶ post-Civil War adventure series on ABC (1959-60) featuring Nick Adams as Johnny Yuma and produced by Goodson-Todman in association with Celestial Productions and Fen-Ker-Ada Productions. NBC picked up reruns as a summer replacement in 1962.

RED CHANNELS ▶ a paperback book, published in June 1950, that served to destroy, interrupt or retard numerous careers in radio and TV. It was issued at a time when hysteria was mounting over whether communists and communist-sympathizers were working in media and lending themselves to propaganda uses. The book listed the names of performers, writers, composers and producers—with brief dossiers on each—who were alleged to be friendly to communist causes or dupes of the Red conspiracy.

The listings served immediately as a basis for blacklisting: advertisers, networks and program packagers backed away from the names that would create controversy and bring pressure upon them. *Red Channels* also listed organizations cited as subversive or as communist fronts by the House Un-American Activities Committee.

Subtitled "The Report of Communist Influence in Radio and Television," the book carried no author credit beyond that it was published by *Counterattack,* a newsletter dedicated to exposing the communist influence in American corporations. Both publications were products of American Business Consultants, an organization of communist-hunters whose principals were former FBI agents John G. Keenan, Kenneth Bierly and Theodore Kirkpatrick. The unsigned introduction was by Vincent W. Hartnett, a onetime production assistant on *Gangbusters* who, as a solo crusader, kept files on subversive suspects in show business, some of which material was undoubtedly used in *Red Channels.* Hartnett later formed his own organization, Aware Inc., with a Syracuse, N.Y.

owner of supermarkets, Lawrence Johnson. It too was to become effective in blacklisting.

RED LION DECISION ▶ [*Red Lion Broadcasting Co. v. FCC*/359 U.S. 367(1969)] the Supreme Court opinion that upheld the constitutionality of the Fairness Doctrine. The clear implication of the Court's decision was that broadcasters would be held to a different First Amendment standard than newspapers because of the scarcity of broadcast frequencies and because the Government has the right to license these frequencies. In addition, the Court articulated a fiduciary First Amendment obligation on the licensee to present views and voices representative of his community. *Red Lion* carried the implication of a First Amendment right of access by pointing out that the right of viewers and listeners was paramount, and not the right of broadcasters.

From the moment of its issuance, the decision was subjected to relentless criticism from industry and some civil libertarians, and in 1987 the FCC based its repeal of most parts of the Fairness Doctrine on the claim that *Red Lion* lacked continuing constitutional validity because of the proliferation of new media outlets. The U.S. Court of Appeals, however, ruled that the agency had neither the right nor the need to take this stand, but it upheld the repeal on grounds unrelated to *Red Lion.*

Until the retirement of Justice William Brennan, there was great uncertainty as to whether the Supreme Court would overrule *Red Lion,* but as the Court's liberal wing disappeared, opponents began openly predicting ultimate success.

The case derived its name from WGCB in Red Lion, Pa., a fundamentalist radio station which broadcast mainly conservative, anti-communist opinion. In November 1964 WGCB carried a syndicated program, *The Christian Crusade,* which featured an attack by the Reverend Billy James Hargis on a book by journalist Fred J. Cook, entitled *Goldwater: Extremist of the Right.* Hargis alleged that Cook was fired from the *New York World-Telegram* after making false charges, that he worked for a left-wing publication, *The Nation,* and that he had written articles absolving Alger Hiss and attacking J. Edgar Hoover, the FBI and the CIA.

Upon learning of the attack, Cook asked WGCB for an opportunity to reply to Hargis under the personal attack provision of the Fairness Doctrine, and he was denied free reply time.

The personal attack rules were adopted officially by FCC in 1967. They state, essentially, that when an attack is made upon the honesty, character, integrity or other personal qualities of an identified person or group during the presentation of news on a controversial issue of public importance, the person or group attacked must be notified within a week of the broadcast and offered a reasonable opportunity to respond over the licensees facilities.

When WGCB refused time to Cook, he took the matter to the FCC, which ruled that the station was required to give him the air time. WGCB then appealed to the D.C. Court of Appeals claiming that the rules violated the First Amendment rights of the broadcaster. This court held that the Fairness Doctrine and the personal attack rules were constitutional. The station then took the matter to the Supreme Court.

At about the same time, the FCC adopted new rules detailing not only the personal attack doctrine but also the provisions for political advertising. RTNDA (Radio-Television News Director's Association) appealed these rules to the Seventh Circuit Court of Appeals in Chicago, which eventually held that the rules violated the First Amendment. In early 1969, the Supreme Court consolidated the two cases.

To the shock of the broadcast industry, a unanimous Supreme Court (seven judges voting) affirmed the Appeals Court's *Red Lion* decision and reversed the RTNDA decision. The court said that the personal attack rules and the Fairness Doctrine were consistent with the First Amendment.

In his 1975 book *The Good Guys, The Bad Guys and the First Amendment,* former CBS news president Fred W. Friendly charged that the WGCB was a set-up engineered by the Democratic National Committee. Cook, for his part, denied all in his own book, *Maverick: Fifty Years of Investigative Reporting* (1984).

REDMONT, BERNARD ▶ longtime foreign correspondent who left television in the 1980s for academia and is now dean emeritus of the College of Communication at Boston University. After 11 years with Group W (1965-76) as Paris bureau chief he joined CBS News as manager of its Moscow bureau. A native of New York, Redmont had lived in Paris since 1946 working for various English-language news services and news magazines before joining Group W.

REES, MARIAN ▶ producer of quality dramas, most of which have been critically praised. She has served as executive producer for such noted *Hallmark Hall of Fame* presentations as *Decoration Day* (1990), *The Shell Seekers* (1989), *Home Fires Burning* (1989), *Foxfire* (1987), *The Room Upstairs* (1987), *Resting Place* (1986) and *Love is Never Silent* (1985). Her other television film credits include *A Son's Promise* (1990), *Little Girl Lost* (1988), *A Christmas Snow* (1986), *License to Kill* (1984), *Between Friends* (1983) and *Miss All American Beauty* (1982). Rees started her career in the 1950s with live television in New York and later worked with Bud Yorkin and Norman Lear at their Tandem Productions. She has also worked with Tomorrow Entertainment, First Artists Television, EMI Television and the features division of the NRW Company. Before starting her own company, Marian Rees Associates, she produced the TV films, *The Marva Collins Story* and *Angel Dusted* and worked on the series *Sanford and Son* and *All in the Family.*

REID, CHARLOTTE T. ▶ FCC commissioner (1971-76) appointed to a Republican seat by President Nixon after she had completed four terms as a congresswoman from Illinois. She was the first female on the commission in more than two decades and was appointed when the women's movement was in full sail, but she was not an activist commissioner and was a champion of no particular cause. Moreover, she was cited by the press for a poor attendance record. She resigned from the FCC two years before the end of her full term, for marriage. A professional singer early in her career, she performed under the name of Annette King on *Don McNeill's Breakfast Club* on NBC (1936-39).

REINER, CARL ▶ comedian, writer and producer who made his mark in TV as a regular performer on *Your Show of Shows,* with Sid Caesar and Imogene Coca, in the 1950s, and then launched a new career as producer, writer and director of the original *Dick Van Dyke Show* on CBS in the early 1960s. He returned in a similar capacity for the revival of the Van Dyke situation comedy in the early 1970s but resigned when CBS applied a "family" standard to the show's content and would not permit sophisticated subject matter. Specifically at issue was a censored scene in which a child opened the door to his parents bedroom while they were apparently making love.

Reiner, who also made films and recordings (*The 2000 Year Old Man*), returned to TV in 1976 as a comedy actor in *Good Heavens,* a sitcom of brief duration in which he portrayed an angel; he was also executive producer of that ABC series. He also contributed to TV comedy a son, Rob Reiner, who portrayed the son-in-law in *All in the Family,* and is now an accomplished film producer.

REINER, MANNY (d. 1974) ▶ TV film executive prominent in international sales. His last post was executive v.p. of international sales for Paramount TV. Earlier he had been president of Four Star Television and Filmways Intl., foreign manager of Samuel Goldwyn Productions and managing director of the Selznick Organization in Latin America and Australia.

REINER, ROB ▶ film and television director, and son of the noted comedian Carl Reiner, whose career took off as an actor ("Meathead") in the classic sitcom *All In the Family.* His film directing credits include *Stand by Me* and Stephen King's *Misery,* and his television credits include the ground-breaking series *Sessions* for HBO.

REINHARDT, BURT ▶ vice president of Turner Broadcasting System and former president of Cable News Network (1982-1990). He has been with the all-news television channel since its inception in 1979.

Reinhardt began his career in journalism as a World War II combat cameraman, recording MacArthur's return to the Philippines in 1944. Later, as managing editor of Fox Movietone News, one of the major theater newsreel producers, he broke the story of the first major Soviet defector to the West. He designed and supervised the worldwide network operations of UPI Television News, and just prior to joining CNN he served as executive vice president of the non-theatrical and educational division of Paramount Pictures.

REINSCH, J. LEONARD (d. 1991) ▶ long-time president of Cox Broadcasting Co., Atlanta-based station group, who for many years was also active in Democratic politics. He retired as Cox president at the close of 1973 (succeeded by Clifford M. Kirtland, Jr.) but continued as a member of the board and as chairman of Cox Cable Communications, Inc., a subsidiary. In 1978, he served as a member of the Carnegie Commission on the Future of Public Broadcasting.

During the Truman Administration he became radio advisor to the White House and later TV-radio consultant to the Democratic

National Committee. He was executive director of the Democratic national conventions of 1960 and 1964 and arrangements director at the 1968 conventions. Reinsch also was TV-radio director for John F. Kennedy's presidential campaign in 1960. He began his broadcast career with WLS, Chicago, in 1924 and then went on to build the Cox group.

REISS, JEFFREY ▶ former broadcast and cable program executive who created one of the leading national pay-per-view services. He is president and CEO of Reiss Media Enterprises, which operates Request TV and Request 2. The networks, owned by Reiss Media in partnership with Group W, contract with movie studios for the pay-per-view rights to recent theatrical films, then sign on local cable operators to carry the networks and offer the films to their subscribers. Pay-per-view revenues are split between the cable operator and Request.

Reiss previously was president of the Cable Health Network, which was owned by Viacom and is now defunct. Reiss had joined Viacom in 1976 to work on developing the company's pay-TV movie network, which became Showtime. Prior to that he was director of feature films at ABC, where he was involved in developing the two-hour made-for-TV movie concept.

John C. W. Reith

REITH, JOHN C. W. (d. 1968) ▶ first director-general of the British Broadcasting Corp. and the individual who has probably made the greatest impact on broadcasting in the United Kingdom. His paternalistic influence is felt to this day.

Reith regarded broadcasting not simply as a medium of entertainment but as a force that should help to shape the nation's values and aspirations. He believed that radio, and later television, should primarily inform and uplift. A Scotsman and stern Calvinist, he stressed the need for high standards and a strong sense of responsibility at the BBC, and it was under his long reign that the British concept of public service broadcasting developed. He was made a peer of the realm after World War II.

RELIGIOUS TELEVISION ▶ a program area that has taken two forms: paid access, in which evangelists and church-affiliated organizations purchase air time for their broadcasts; and public service, in which networks and stations donate time and production assistance to the major faiths. In the main, public service time has been confined to the marginal hours, usually Sunday mornings, when viewer levels are low and, ironically, when much of the audience is attending church. The swing in recent years has been away from public service time for the established faiths and toward paid time for a new genre known as televangelism—more fundamentalist, more openly proselytizing. But in the late 1980s, televangelism itself fell into sudden decline when scandal and stories of corruption tainted two of its major TV ministries.

Religious television took its first significant turn in the early 1970s with the outcropping of Christian TV stations on the UHF band in various stations in the country. With the advent of satellite distribution in the late 1970s, the station trend led to the creation of three evangelical networks—each of them achieving a more or less national spread through cable TV. The largest of these full-time services was the Christian Broadcasting Network (CBN), later known as the Family Channel, built upon Pat Robertson's talk show, *The 700 Club.*

By 1980, religious evangelists paying for air time on local stations drove out virtually all the long-established programs produced for the networks or syndication by the mainline churches. Many of these television preachers made fantastic amounts of money, not from the sale of advertising but from the solicitation of contributions from viewers. Some of them, on becoming national figures, campaigned for political causes. Jerry Falwell, for example, who was host of *The Oldtime Gospel Hour,* also founded the Moral Majority, an organization with a distinct political point of view that became a leading force in the rise of the New Right. To offset the trend, Norman Lear, a political liberal, created a national organization in 1981, People for the American Way, to fight the repressive influence of TV's religious fundamentalists.

Meanwhile, the television pulpit was producing a raft of new stars, among them Jim Bakker of the PTL Network, who previously had worked for Pat Robertson. One minister of the mainline Protestant churches, Robert Schuller, grew popular by serving psychological as well as spiritual needs (and steering clear of politics) in his syndicated series, *Hour of Power.*

While ABC, CBS, and NBC maintain religious programming departments operating under the wing of the network news divisions, they produce a relatively small amount of the religious programming in television. The vast majority of programs available nationally or regionally are syndicated by religious groups, some with production budgets of more than $1 million a year. A number of programs derive the income for their continuance from on-air solicitations for viewer contributions.

Approximately one-third of the more than 100 religious syndicators place their programs by purchasing air time, while a number of others use both free and paid time. Largely, fundamentalist groups engage in paid broadcasts. Surveys have found that about two-thirds of the TV stations in the U.S—most of them outside the major markets—will accept paid religious broadcasts. The leading carriers in the larger markets are independent stations, those not affiliated with a network. Policies of the networks and their owned stations do not permit the use of "paid religion."

Network policies for religious broadcasting were forged during the radio era and were carried over with some modifications, into television. An early NBC policy was not to sell time for religious broadcasting because "such a course might result in a disproportionate representation of those individual groups who chance to command the largest purse." The basic policy guidelines of all three networks are that they assume the entire cost of production, that they work in program development with "recognized" or "central" religious agencies and that they discourage the treatment of controversial subjects.

The major groups with which the networks regularly have worked are the Broadcasting and Film Commission, National Council of Churches; Department of Film and Broadcasting, Office of Communications, U.S. Catholic Conference; Jewish Theological Seminary in America; New York Board of Rabbis; and the Southern Baptist Convention. Others involved in program development with less frequency are The Greek Orthodox Church in North and South America; the Christian Science Church; the Church of Jesus Christ of Latter Day Saints; Lutheran Church, Missouri Synod; and the American Council of Churches.

Religious broadcasters turned to television early in the medium's development. In 1948 the Protestant Radio Commission founded *Look Up and Live* and *Lamp Unto My Feet* on CBS-TV. *Frontiers of Faith* began as a church service remote on NBC in 1952 and then switched to studio-oriented formats. That same year, *The Eternal Light,* the widely praised half-hour dramatic radio series produced by the Jewish Theological Seminary, was adapted to television as part of NBC's three-faith series.

This Is the Life, a film series by the Lutheran Church, Missouri Synod, began its syndication rounds in 1952 and by 1955 had an annual production budget of $750,000. ABC in 1954 began a studio program with Episcopal Bishop James Pike. The veteran radio preacher Norman Vincent Peale was featured with his wife in an NBC program, *What's Your Trouble?* And on the DuMont Network, Bishop Fulton Sheen began what was to become the most successful of the religious shows, often scoring higher ratings than commercial entertainment programs appearing opposite it in prime time.

As the television audience expanded, the evangelical broadcasters began to use the medium increasingly, purchasing better time periods than other religious broadcasters received gratis. The Rev. Billy Graham, Oral Roberts, Rex Humbard and the Reverend Ike all made highly sophisticated use of the medium with opulently produced prime-time specials featuring name performers. By the 1970s so many paying religious programs were available to broadcasters that the general manager of a TV station in the East claimed to have pulled his station out of the red by accepting "paid religion" almost indiscriminately.

By the late 1980s, however, two of televangelism's most successful ministries were torn apart by charges of corruption and sexual improprieties, scandals ironically generated by their own evangelistic rivalry. Jimmy Swaggart, leader of one of the three wealthiest TV ministries, charged his chief rival, Jim Bakker, leader of the PTL Network (variously said to stand for "Praise The Lord" or "People That Love"), with a lack of spirituality and a taste for materialism. In the ensuing charges and countercharges, both ministries fell. Bakker, already disgraced by revelations of his sexual improprieties with his secretary Jessica Hahn, was later convicted of fraud and sentenced to a long prison term. His original accuser, Jimmy Swaggart, was also forced from his ministry in disgrace when newsmen revealed that he was patronizing a prostitute. On the heels of the two scandals came a lesser but nonetheless significant shock to televangelism with the declaration of Oral Roberts that God would call him "back to Heaven" unless his followers provided $8 million to save his ministry. Robert's plea failed and his audience declined. The combined effect of the scandals has been a loss of confidence in televangelists and a significant shrinkage of their audience and income.

Most stations produce some local religious programming—if only the closing prayer at signoff—or give over time to religious groups in their communities, but almost all rely heavily on syndicated programming to fulfill their obligations to religious service as licensees. Among the leading regularly syndicated programs, paid or unpaid, are *This Is The Life*, *Hour of Power*, *Oral Roberts*, *Insight*, *Christian Lifestyle Magazine*, and *Christopher Close-up*.

REMICK, LEE (d. 1991) ▶ actress of exceptional versatility and charm whose performances in any year ranked among the best in the medium. Though she appeared in numerous motion pictures she never disdained television if the roles were right, and as it proved they were frequent. She became familiar through television during the 1950s in dramas for *Philco Playhouse*, *Hallmark Hall of Fame* and *Playhouse 90*. In latter years she had starring roles in such shows as *Haywire* (1980), *Toughlove* (1985), *Nutcracker: Money, Madness and Murder* (1987), and *Ike* (1989). But probably her most famous TV performance was in the title role of the British mini-series, *Jennie: Lady Randolph Churchill* (1975). Though she lived in England with her British husband, she worked in television, theatre and films on both sides of the Atlantic. Her movies included *A Face In the Crowd*, *The Long Hot Summer*, *Anatomy of a Murder*, *Sometimes a Great Notion*, and *The Europeans*. She died of cancer at the age of 55.

***REMINGTON STEELE* ▶** playful detective drama series that debuted on NBC in October 1982 and ran for five seasons. It starred Stephanie Zimbalist and a then unknown Pierce Brosnan. Michael Gleason and Gareth Davies were executive producers and Glenn Gordon Caron (who went on to create *Moonlighting*) was supervising producer. Zimbalist portrayed Laura Holt, a private eye who opens her own L.A.-based detective agency, has trouble attracting clients because she is a woman, and creates a fictitious boss, Remington Steele. Soon after a mysterious man (Brosnan) appears claiming to be the fictional Remington Steele, and Holt makes him her partner.

***REMOTE CONTROL* ▶** see Game Shows.

REPEATERS ▶ low-powered transmitters set strategically at sites to extend a TV station's signal into farm country and other remote geographical regions. The repeaters automatically amplify and retransmit the signal of the parent station on the same channel.

REPLY COMMENTS ▶ opposing statements or arguments filed by individuals or organizations, on invitation by the FCC, in response to the petitions or filings of others. Reply comments are solicited by the FCC in the interest of examining the various sides of an issue.

REPORT ON EDITORIALIZING BY BROADCAST LICENSEE ▶ [13 FCC 1246 (1949)] first formal articulation of the Fairness Doctrine by the FCC, which also upheld the right of licensees to editorialize on their own airwaves. That right had been in question since 1940, when the commission in the Mayflower decision declared that the broadcaster could not be an advocate. In the Report on Editorializing, which established that there was no prohibition on taking positions, the commission imposed on the licensees an obligation to present all sides of opinion in the discussion of public issues. That was the concept that evolved into the Fairness Doctrine.

Basic to the commission's position was its view that broadcasters operate their facilities as a public trust under the public interest standard of the Communications Act and that the public interest cannot be served by a licensee who did not provide a medium of free speech.

The commission thus articulated the two-step formula of the Fairness Doctrine—the requirement to devote a reasonable amount of time to the presentation of controversial issues of public importance and the obligation to provide time for the expression of contrasting attitudes and viewpoints on those issues. The FCC recognized, however, that the licensee should have general discretion in determining the issues to be covered, the shades of opinion to be presented, the appropriate spokespeople and the amount of time to be offered.

***REPORTER, THE* ▶** hour-long series on CBS (1964) starring Harry Guardino as Danny Taylor, a New York newspaper columnist who becomes involved in the stories he covers. Created by novelist Jerome Weidman, the series was produced by Richelieu Productions in association with CBS and lasted 13 weeks. Others in the cast were Gary Merrill as editor Lou Sheldon, George O'Hanlon as cab driver Artie Burns and Remo Pisani as bartender Ike Dawson.

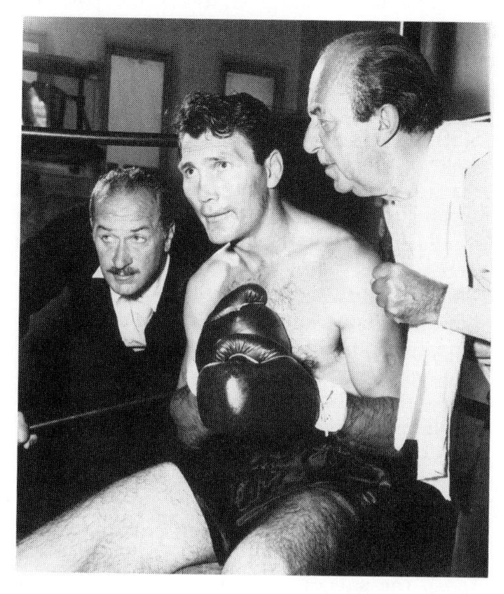

Keenan Wynn, Jack Palance, and Ed Wynn in *Requiem for a Heavyweight*

REQUIEM FOR A HEAVYWEIGHT ▶ a TV drama classic by Rod Serling that aired on CBS's *Playhouse 90* in 1956. A powerful play about a prize-fighter at the end of his career who gets sold out by everyone, including his manager, it was a prize example of the writing, directing and acting that characterized the medium's "golden age." Jack Palance played the washed-up boxer. Others in the cast were Ed Wynn, Keenan Wynn, Kim Hunter, Max Baer and Maxie Rosenbloom. Martin Manulis was the producer and Ralph Nelson the director.

RERUNS ▶ programs repeated some time after their original presentation; in the plural, the reference is usually to entire series.

Networks began using reruns because the producers of filmed shows could not physically operate on continuous 52-week schedules and needed, besides, the supplementary income from repeats. Meanwhile, the reruns served the networks as economical programming during the summer months when viewing levels declined, since the cost of the repeats was only 25% of the firstruns. Programs came to be purchased on a pattern of 39 firstruns and 13 repeats.

But in the mid-1960s the networks dealt with rising production costs by extending the rerun period. When it was perceived that second runs could compete effectively and that most viewers preferred a repeat of a favorite show to other available programming, the networks began to contract for 26 firstruns and 26 reruns. By 1970 the firstrun order was down to 22 episodes, and the time periods were filled out with specials and short-term summer replacements.

Program series that amassed a sufficient library of episodes over four or five years, each having been shown at least twice on the network, were then sold to individual stations in syndication, where they were again replayed, numerous times, in strip form.

Taped shows did not initially lend themselves to the rerun practice because the scale for residuals was prohibitive. Tape was under the jurisdiction of AFTRA, while film contracts for performers were covered by SAG. In time, adjustments were made so that the residual payments required by each union were similar.

Animated cartoons scheduled on Saturday mornings are mostly reruns, since each episode is contracted for six exposures over two years.

Blaming reruns for exacerbating the Hollywood unemployment crisis in the 1970s, representatives of several unions petitioned the FCC to restrict network indulgence in repeats. The FCC, after studying the matter, denied the petition.

RESCUE 911 ▶ one of the more popular reality-based police/crime series, which began on CBS in September 1989. It employs both actual footage and reenactments to portray heroic rescue efforts by police, fire fighters, paramedics and others involved in saving lives. William Shatner is host and narrator. The series is produced by Arnold Shapiro Productions, CBS Entertainment Productions and Katy Film Productions.

RESIDUALS ▶ fees paid to performers and other creative talent for subsequent exposures of their filmed or taped programs and commercials. Under the residuals formula devised by the unions, performers receive 75% of their original compensation for the first and second replays of their work, 50% for the third through fifth replay, 10% for the sixth and 5% for all additional exposures. In addition, there are residuals for home video and foreign use of the materials.

Residual provisions began to appear in motion picture contracts after 1960. Thus performers are compensated for most films made after that year when they are sold to TV but not for movies made before 1960.

RETRANSMISSION CONSENT ▶ controversial and widely debated proposal relating to cable TV's carriage of broadcast signals. The proposal, advanced in 1979 by both NTIA and the House Communications Subcommittee's bill rewriting the Communications Act, would require cable systems to gain the permission of the TV station or the copyright owners of individual programs when they bring in outside signals. The proposal was vigorously supported by the motion picture, TV and sports industries in the belief that cable should bargain for the use of their programming; it was vehemently opposed by cable interests, who contend that they meet their copyright obligations by paying blanket fees to the Copyright Tribunal under an agreement forged after the passage of the new Copyright Act.

The idea was suddenly resurrected by CBS's Larry Tisch in 1990, and by the next year became the centerpiece of the broadcasters' version of a new cable bill.

REVOCATION ▶ an FCC action terminating a licensee's broadcasting privilege. Section 312 of the Communications Act of 1934 grants the commission the power to revoke any station license or construction permit for the following reasons:

• Knowingly making false statements to the FCC, particularly in the license renewal application;

• Repeatedly and willfully failing to operate substantially as promised in the license application;

• Willful or repeated violation of provisions of the Communications Act pertaining to lotteries, wire fraud and obscenity, or of any FCC rule.

• Violating critical sections of the United States Code;

• Failing to observe any cease and desist order issued by the commission.

• Willful or repeated failure to provide candidates for federal office "reasonable access" to the station, or to sell them "reasonable amounts of time."

REWRITE OF THE COMMUNICATIONS ACT ▶ initiatives taken by the House and Senate in 1979 to revise the Communications Act of 1934 so that it might be more relevant to the emerging technologies of the late 20th century. The original Act was deemed inadequate to deal with such breakthroughs as cable, pay TV, microwave and satellite transmissions and laser-based fiber optics.

The prime mover behind the rewrite in Congress was Rep. Lionel Van Deerlin (D-Calif). As chairman of the House Communications Subcommittee, Van Deerlin was the principal architect of Bill H.R. 3333 in 1979, a modified version of the "floor to attic" revision which he unsuccessfully introduced in 1978. In keeping with the "deregulation" mood in Congress and the general public, H.R. 3333 proposed to overhaul the FCC and diminish its regulatory powers, phase out fairness and equal time restrictions on broadcasters and extend license terms indefinitely. In addition, it would lift almost all regulatory barriers on cable TV and establish a spectrum fee for all broadcast and nonbroadcast users. More moderate bills were introduced by Sen. Ernest Hollings (D-S.C.), chairman of the Senate Communications Subcommittee, and by Barry Goldwater (R-Ariz.), the subcommittees ranking member.

The Van Deerlin Bill and its counterparts, in varying degrees, attempted to create an open communications market where the existing and new electronic media could compete relatively free of government regulation. Proponents of the rewrite bills argued that deregulation would result in improved technology, lower operating costs and better service to the public. The chief justification for regulation in the communications field had been that the airwaves constituted a scarce public resource, but the major premise behind the rewrite bills was that the new technologies promised an abundance of communications channels. Specific provisions in the bills tried to negotiate a trade-off between the entrenched commercial broadcasters and the entrepreneurs in the new technologies. In exchange for more broadcasting freedom and security of licensed operations, stations would be required to pay regular fees for operating rights and to compete on a more extensive basis with the cable and pay-television industries.

Although praised in some quarters as a long-overdue attempt at streamlining communications legislation, the House rewrite bill met with stiff resistance from the industries concerned and from public interest groups. Not surprisingly, television industry leaders opposed the imposition of fees and the loosening of restrictions on the cable industry. The cable industry objected to allowing telephone companies to own cable systems. And the media reform groups strongly objected to the absence of any provision requiring broadcasters to serve "the public interest, convenience and necessity." This phrase represented the keystone of communications law since the Radio Act of 1929, and media reformers protested that its omission put the public "at the mercy of unregulated monopolies." Mixed with an apparent indifference toward the rewrite bills in Congress and the public at large, these objections caused the broadcast portion of Rep. Van Deerlin's bill to be scuttled in July 1979.

Van Deerlin lost his bid for reelection in 1980, and, ironically, a Republican-dominated FCC in the Reagan Administration made policies along the lines of his rewrite bill.

REX HUMBARD MINISTRY ▶ one of the longest-running "paid religion" shows, (1952-83) and produced weekly, featuring TV evangelist Humbard and members of his family in an hour format of music and sermons. The series was dubbed in eight languages and carried in 28 countries. Humbard paid each station for carrying his program and financed his broadcast operations on contributions from viewers.

REYNOLDS, FRANK (d. 1983) ▶ twice anchor of the ABC evening newscast, first from 1968-70 and again in 1978 with the restyling of ABC's evening newscast, *World News Tonight.* Although it began as a three-anchor format, Reynolds emerged as the principal newscaster.

As ABC News special correspondent, his assignments included all major political conventions and campaigns since 1965, coverage of the U.S. manned spaceflight program and commentary and analysis of presidential speeches and press conferences. From May 1968 until December 1970 he was co-anchor, with Howard K. Smith, of the *ABC Evening News,* losing that post to Harry Reasoner when he was brought from CBS. He joined the network news division from ABC's Chicago station WBKB (now WLS-TV), where for two years he had anchored two newscasts daily. For 12 years prior to that he was a newsman with WBBM-TV, the CBS station in Chicago.

REYNOLDS, GENE ▶ former child actor in films and then television producer (with Larry Gelbart) of the noted sitcom *M*A*S*H.* He became executive producer of *M*A*S*H* in 1976, and also served in the same capacity for the dramatic series *Room 222* (1969) and *Lou Grant* (1977-82). Reynolds also produced and directed the TV movie *People Like Us* (1976) as well as *In Defense of Kids* (1983) and *Doing Life* (1986).

REYNOLDS, JOHN T. ▶ one-time president of CBS-TV from Feb. 9, 1966, to Dec. 15 of that year, said to have resigned from a preference to reside in Southern California, where he had spent most of his career. He immediately became president of the TV division of Golden West Broadcasters and general manager of its Los Angeles station, KTLA, an independent. He retired when the station was sold to Tribune Broadcasting in 1985.

During his brief presidency at the network, Reynolds authorized the return of *Playhouse 90* in the form of two or three specials a year. Having been for many years in charge of administration of the network's Hollywood operations, and therefore close to the programming function, he had been selected for the post upon John A. Schneider's promotion to head of the CBS Broadcast Group. For 12 years prior to joining CBS in 1959, Reynolds had been a salesman for various stations and an executive with the Don Lee broadcast group.

RHODA ▶ hit CBS situation comedy (1974-78) built upon a character spun off of *The Mary Tyler Moore Show,* the luckless New York oddball Rhoda Morgenstern, played by Valerie Harper. Watched over by the executive producers and creators of *Mary Tyler Moore,* James L. Brooks and Allan Burns, the series was a success from the start. Helping its popularity was a 60-minute special episode several weeks after the premiere, entitled *Rhoda's Wedding,* which scored a healthy rating. The 1976 season brought the new wrinkle of Rhoda's divorce, along with the loss of a key supporting player, Nancy Walker (in the role of Rhoda's mother, Ida Morgenstern), who began a sitcom of her own on ABC. When that series failed, Walker returned to *Rhoda* in the fall of 1977.

Others in support were David Groh as Rhoda's husband Joe Gerard, Julie Kavner as her sister Brenda, Harold Gould as their father Martin and Lorenzo Music, unseen, as the voice of Carlton, the doorman. Music was also co-producer with David Davis. The series was by MTM Enterprises.

RHOMBUS PRODUCTIONS ▶ Canadian independent production company specializing in programs on the performing arts. The company was formed in 1978 when Barbara Willis Sweete and Niv Fichman made the documentary short, *Opus One, Number One.* Larry Weinstein joined soon after, and the trio have produced and directed numerous television programs relating to music and dance, including several international coproductions.

RIBBON ▶ horizontal crawl superimposed on the TV picture, at the bottom of the screen, for news bulletins and special announcements.

RICH, JOHN ▶ director of *All in the Family* during its first four seasons, after which he went into independent production. His first effort was *On the Rocks* (1975-76), an ABC situation comedy drawn from a British show, for which Rich was producer-director. He was director and one of four executive producers on *Benson* from 1980-82 and later, with Henry Winkler, was executive producer of ABC's *MacGyver* series.

RICH, LEE ▶ former chairman and CEO of MGM/UA who had previously been head of Lorimar Productions. Rich left MGM/UA in 1990 when it appeared headed for another change of ownership. He then became an independent producer of TV movies. In the 1989-90 season, Rich produced a sitcom on Fox, *Molloy.*

Under Rich's leadership, Lorimar hit it big with *The Waltons* and went on to produce the series *Doc Elliot, Apple's Way, The Blue Knight* and *Dallas* and a raft of TV movies and dramatic specials, including *Helter Skelter* and *Sybil.*

Rich was an alumnus of Benton & Bowles Advertising, which during the 1960s was an incubator of program executives for the networks. Before organizing Lorimar, he was a partner in Mirisch-Rich Productions, where he produced *Rat Patrol, Hey Landlord* and two Saturday daytime cartoons, *Super Six* and *Super President.*

Partnered in Lorimar with Merv Adelson from 1969-1986, Rich was responsible for such shows as *Eight is Enough, Dallas, Kaz* and *Studs Lonigan. Dallas* yielded him a number of spin-offs and knock-offs of the form, including *Knots Landing, Falcon Crest, King's Crossing,* and *Flamingo Road.*

***RICH MAN, POOR MAN* ▶** 12-hour serialized adaptation of a novel by Irwin Shaw televised by ABC in February and March of 1976; the mini-series was such a smash in the ratings that it was resumed in the fall as a continuing prime-time serial under the title *Rich Man, Poor Man: Book II.* Since one of the brothers dies at the end of the Shaw novel, the continuation invented new stories around the surviving brother Rudy Jordache (played in both versions by Peter Strauss). Both the mini-series and the series were by Universal TV.

Along with Strauss, the original featured Susan Blakely, Nick Nolte, Edward Asner, Fionnuala Flanagan and numerous familiar TV actors in cameo roles. David Greene was director and Alex North composed the score.

With the serialization leading the ratings most of the weeks it was on the air, all three networks were primed for a plunge into short-term series dramatizing popular novels.

***RICHARD BOONE SHOW, THE* ▶** an attempt in 1963 to establish a dramatic repertory company for a weekly anthology series headed by Richard Boone. NBC carried 25 episodes but the project failed. It was produced by Classic Films and Goodson-Todman in association with NBC.

Among those in the repertory company were Harry Morgan, Robert Blake, Jeanette Nolan, Ford Rainey, Lloyd Bochner, Guy Stockwell, and June Harding.

***RICHARD DIAMOND, PRIVATE DETECTIVE* ▶** 30-minute action series (1957-60) that played first on CBS and then on NBC, with David Janssen as a debonair detective. A gimmick character in the series was a telephone answering service girl, named Sam, who was seen on camera only as a pair of legs; the role was played by Mary Tyler Moore. Barbara Bain also appeared as Karen Wells, and Russ Conway played Lieutenant Pete Kile. The series was by Four Star.

RICHARDS CASE ▶ [KMPC (Richards) 14 Fed Reg. 4831 (1949)] early fairness case in which the FCC ruled a misuse of signal against George A. Richards, owner of radio stations in Detroit, Cleveland and Los Angeles. Richards was accused of slanting and distorting the news about President and Mrs. Roosevelt, implying that they were communists; of promoting the candidacy of Gen. Douglas MacArthur for President; and of operating his stations in a manner that totally precluded presentation of views other than his own.

The FCC began an investigation of Richards, and after Richards died in 1951 the commission renewed the three licenses upon a written promise that the stations' deceptive policies would cease. The stations were eventually sold to other parties.

RICHELIEU PRODUCTIONS ▶ independent TV company headed by former actor Keefe Brasselle who sold three programs to CBS in 1964, the failure of which were believed partly responsible for the downfall of then CBS-TV president, James T. Aubrey. The company took its name from the restaurant in New York, Chez Richelieu, where Brasselle and Aubrey had frequently dined. Its ill-fated programs had been *The Cara Williams Show, The Baileys of Balboa* and *The Reporter.*

RIFKIN, MONROE M. ▶ once-prominent figure in the cable industry as a founder of American Television and Communications Corp. (ATC) and its president when the company was formed in 1968. In 1974, he added the title of chairman. Rifkin built it into the second largest of the cable MSOs (behind Teleprompter) and remained its chief executive officer when ATC was acquired by Time Inc. in 1978.

He resigned in 1982 to form a partnership with oilman Marvin Davis, who purchased Twentieth Century-Fox. The new company, Rifkin-Fox Communications, was created to explore the opportunities in the cable industry.

Rifkin was succeeded as chairman and chief executive of ATC by Trygve E. Myhren. At the same time, Joseph J. Collins assumed the post of president.

***RIFLEMAN, THE* ▶** popular western on ABC (1957-62) that featured Chuck Connors as rifleman Lucas McCain, Johnny Crawford as McCain's young son, Mark, and Paul Fix as the town marshal, Micah Torrance, and was produced by Four Star-Sussex Productions.

RINTELS, DAVID W. ▶ screen and TV writer whose TV credits include the acclaimed series *The Defenders* (1961-65) and such TV movies as *Fear on Trial, Clarence Darrow, Gideon's Trumpet, Sakharov, The Last Best Year, Mister Roberts, The Oldest Living Graduate, Member of the Wedding,* and *All the Way Home.* Rintels was president of the Writers Guild of America—West from 1975-77.

RIP-AND-READ NEWSCAST ▶ news roundups that are built entirely on wire service copy, ripped from the teletype machines and read whole or in edited-down form. Such newscasts were prevalent in television until the late 1950s, when viewer interest in local news became manifest and when it became clear that an enterprising news operation was vital to a station's competitive standing in its market. Only the smallest and least affluent TV stations practice rip-and-read news today, although it is still common among radio stations.

RIPPON, ANGELA ▶ first female newscaster on BBC-TV, joining the British network's 9 p.m. newscast in the spring of 1976, replacing one of three anchors. She had first been a newspaper journalist and gained her TV experience on BBC regional programs. She moved to the U.S. in the 1980s to work for a Boston TV station.

RITCHIE, DANIEL L. ▶ former chairman and chief executive officer of Westinghouse Broadcasting (1981-87) named to the post when Donald H. McGannon retired. Ritchie had been president and CEO since early 1979. With expertise in finance and acquisitions, as a former finance executive for MCA Inc. (1960-70) and protege of MCA chairman Jules Stein, Ritchie was a surprise choice to succeed McGannon since his broadcast experience was scant. But it was clear at once that he represented the new generation of management that was to expand Group W, the Westinghouse broadcast company, and chart its course in the changing communications environment of the 1980s. Soon after he was in the post, Ritchie purchased Group W's first UHF station, WRET-TV Charlotte, N.C., for a reported $20 million. He began looking also into the expansion prospects afforded by over-the-air pay-television, cable and FM. After two years with Lehman Bros., as a securities analyst, ten years with MCA and four years in his own health foods business, Ritchie joined Westinghouse in 1974 as head of its Learning and Leisure Time Division. This put him in charge of a miscellany of businesses, ranging from the direct-mail marketing of the Longines Symphonette to Econocar auto rentals. Later he moved up to the parent company, Westinghouse Electric Corp. in Pittsburgh, as executive v.p. In 1978 he returned to Westinghouse Broadcasting as president of the corporate staff and strategic planning. A few months later, he was president and chief operating officer of the company and not long after president and chief executive officer. He retired in 1987 and was succeeded by Burt Staniar.

RITTER, JOHN ▶ actor who became one of TV's familiar faces in the 1970s and 1980s as star of *Three's Company, Three's a Crowd* and

Hooperman. For five years he was also a recurring character on *The Waltons.* In addition, he had lead roles in a number of made-for-TV movies. In latter years his career has tilted to theatrical movies. He is the son of the late country and western singer, Tex Ritter.

RIVERA, GERALDO ▶ storefront lawyer-turned-journalist who early on positioned himself as a kind of ombudsman for the common man and later became a talk-show host and, at times, a practitioner of tabloid journalism.

Since 1987 he has hosted the successful daytime talk show, *Geraldo,* which features a guest or panel with a single topic for discussion, performed before a studio audience. Often the topics are on social or political issues, but more often the shows exploit sex in some fashion. Subjects have included teen-sex, prostitution, cross-dressing, and sexually transmitted diseases. Shortly after the show went on the air, Rivera made the front pages across the country when a studio brawl broke out on the set between black activist Roy Innis and a group of neo-Nazis. Rivera's nose was broken by a chair thrown in the scuffle.

Talk-show host Geraldo Rivera

In 1991 Rivera started hosting a second syndicated series, *Now It Can Be Told,* an investigative news magazine show that has dealt with such topics as airline safety and computer moles. One of his most publicized journalistic ventures was his syndicated special *The Mystery of Al Capone's Vaults* (1986), a show that revealed little when the vaults were opened but became the highest-rated syndicated show of its kind in television history.

Before going off on his own, Rivera was a conspicuous correspondent for ABC News and senior correspondent with *20/20.* He also did a number of latenight specials for the network under the title *Geraldo Rivera: Good Night, America.* Prior to that he was a regular contributor to ABC's *Good Morning America* (1974-78), after he had built a reputation with WABC-TV New York as a member of its *Eyewitness News* team (1970-74). He achieved wide recognition for his local documentary, *Willowbrook: The Last Disgrace,* exposing the horrendous conditions at a state institution for retarded children.

RIVERBOAT **▶** action series set on the Mississippi River in the 1840s, which starred Darren McGavin as Captain Grey Holden and lasted for 44 episodes on NBC, premiering in 1959. Burt Reynolds was also featured as pilot Ben Frazer.

RIVERS, JOAN ▶ comedienne and talk show host who was a regular on variety-talk shows in the 1960s and 1970s. She first appeared on *Tonight* in 1965 and became one of the show's most frequent guests and guest-hosts. In 1983 she became the *only* guest host, replacing Johnny Carson one week each month. When the Fox Network began in 1986, its strategy was to pit Rivers against Carson as its first programming effort. But the ratings failed to materialize, and her show was dropped the following year. She then became a regular on the *New Hollywood Squares.* Her second attempt at a talk show, the syndicated daytime *Joan Rivers Show* (1989—), has been moderately successful.

RKO GENERAL ▶ station group owned by General Tire and Rubber Co., formed in 1950 by the purchase of all stations of the Don Lee Broadcasting System for $12.3 million. In 1952 the group took the name of General Teleradio and changed it in 1955 to General Teleradio Pictures after purchasing RKO Pictures Corp. for $25 million. In 1959, when General Tire bought out the 10% interest in the company held by R.H. Macy & Co., the group was renamed RKO General.

During the 1970s license challenges were directed at several of the RKO stations. In 1976 General Tire proposed a spin-off of the broadcasting subsidiaries because illegal actions by the parent company had put all of the licenses, some $400 million worth, in jeopardy. Shareholders of General Tire were to be apportioned shares in the new separated company, but the FCC rejected the proposal.

The group's TV stations were WOR-TV New York and KHJ-TV Los Angeles, both independents; WNAC-TV Boston, a CBS affiliate; and WHBQ-TV Memphis, an ABC affiliate.

The company's character qualifications were so often called into question that the licenses hung in the balance for more than a decade. In 1982 the company lost its Boston station, WNAC-TV, chiefly on misrepresentations to the FCC. Later in a deal engineered by New Jersey Senator Bill Bradley, the company's New York station, WOR-TV, was saved by moving its transmitter to Secaucus, N.J., giving that state its only commercial VHF station. Eventually RKO sold off all of its stations. WOR-TV went to MCA Inc. and KHJ-TV Los Angeles to Disney (for $324 million). The New York station, now called WWOR-TV, had to be spun-off to a new independent company, Pinelands Broadcasting, when MCA was acquired by the Japanese industrial giant, Matsushita, because of the FCC's restrictions on foreign ownership of stations.

ROADBLOCKING ▶ the technique of force-feeding the audience by arranging for a commercial or a program to play simultaneously on all three networks, and sometimes also on independent stations. The object is to gain maximum exposure for a message or an address.

Since it has been found that most viewers will watch television no matter what is on, the principle of roadblocking is to reduce or eliminate the other program choices on the dial. The concept was adopted for the presidential campaigns of 1972, when television strategists for both political parties bought the same half hour of time on every station in a market to ensure that the presentations reached the uncommitted voter. In large markets like New York, they frequently monopolized only five of the commercial stations, leaving the viewers (children, mainly) the alternative programming on one of the independents. On those occasions, the unbought independent scored extraordinary ratings.

When presidential speeches are televised live by all three networks and PBS they, in effect, roadblock the medium and capture audiences of 70 million or more. Reply time given to the opposition party rarely is in the form of a simultaneous broadcast; carried separately by each of the networks, the televised replies may attract less than half the audience for the President. Equal time thus proves not to be the same as equal audience.

***ROADS TO FREEDOM, THE* ▶** TV adaptation of fiction by Jean-Paul Sartre, produced by the BBC on video tape. The 13 episodes were offered in syndication by Time-Life Films in 1973 and played here on several public TV stations.

ROBBIE, SEYMOUR ▶ veteran director whose credits ranged from *Omnibus, Studio One* and *Play of the Week* to *Kojak, Barnaby Jones* and *Cannon.* He also directed episodes for *Wonderful World of Disney, That Girl* and *Love, American Style,* among other prime time series.

ROBERT WOLD COMPANY, THE ▶ independent company specializing in the temporary interconnection of stations and the distribution logistics for special networks. Wold, a former West Coast ad man, set up the independent networks for such telecasts as the 12-hour Bicentennial Fourth of July extravaganza, the four Nixon-Frost interviews in 1977, Christmas Eve Mass from St. Patrick's in 1978, the annual nationally distributed documentaries of Capital Cities Broadcasting and scores of national and regional sports events. Wold merged with Simmons Satellite in 1989 to form a new company, Keystone Communications, based in Salt Lake City.

ROBERTS, COKIE ▶ special correspondent for ABC News since 1988, appearing regularly on *This Week with David Brinkley* and *World News Tonight with Peter Jennings,* reporting on politics, Congress, and public policy. In addition to her work for ABC, Roberts serves as news analyst for National Public Radio, where she was the congressional correspondent for more than ten years.

Before joining ABC in 1988, Roberts was a contributor to PBS's *MacNeil-Lehrer NewsHour,* a reporter for CBS News in Athens, Greece, and the producer and host of a public affairs program on WRC-TV in Washington, D.C.

ROBINSON, GLEN O. ▶ former FCC commissioner (1974-76) appointed to a Democratic seat by President Nixon. He came to the commission from the faculty of the University of Minnesota Law School (1967-74), where he taught administrative law and regulated industries, and in his brief term was the agency's resident intellectual. Earlier he worked in communications law, serving with the Washington firm of Covington and Burling (1961-62).

Having been appointed to serve out the remaining two years of a seven-year term, Robinson decided early in 1976 not to wait around to learn whether President Ford would reappoint him to a full term and instead returned to academia.

He was named by President Carter to head the U.S. delegation to the 1979 World Administrative Radio Conference, with the title of Ambassador. He also became special advisor to the Aspen Institute and Professor of Law at the University of Virginia School of Law.

ROBINSON, HUBBELL (d. 1974) ▶ head of the CBS program department for 13 years, noted for his ability to provide the network with commercially popular shows as well as prestige dramas and cultural programs. As one of the architects of the schedule that made CBS the leader in audience ratings through two decades, Robinson is credited with developing such series as *Gunsmoke, I Love Lucy, You'll Never Get Rich, Climax* and *Playhouse 90.* He earned a reputation as an innovator.

A newspaper reporter and drama critic during the late 1920s, he later became a radio producer for advertising agencies and, for a brief period, with ABC. CBS hired him away from Foote, Cone & Belding Advertising in 1947, and he remained as its program chief until 1959, when he established his own production company. Robinson returned to CBS in 1962 as senior v.p. for programming but left the following year after a clash with James T. Aubrey, Jr., then network president. On his own, he became executive producer of the short-lived series *Hawk* and then was engaged by ABC to oversee its ambitious experimental series, *Stage 67.*

ROBINSON, MAX (d. 1988) ▶ former national desk anchor of ABC's *World News Tonight.* From 1978-83 Robinson was based in Chicago as one of the multiple anchors of the newscast.

He became a prominent figure in ABC network news coverage not only by his authoritative on-air presence, but also by his on-site coverage of major breaking stories around the country, including 1983's devastating earthquakes in Coalinga, Calif.; reports on the failing steel industry in Pennsylvania; the vanishing Midwest farmlands; the 1981 flight of space shuttle Columbia; and the murders of black children in Atlanta. In 1980 he was floor correspondent for both the Democratic and Republican National Conventions and co-anchored ABC's election night coverage. Robinson became familiar to many viewers immediately after the accident at Three Mile Island, when he headed a team of ABC reporters and anchored *World News Tonight* from the crippled nuclear power plant.

Robinson joined ABC News in 1978 and began anchoring its new evening news broadcast, *World News Tonight,* one month later. He came to ABC News from WTOP-TV in Washington, D.C., where he anchored the station's *Eyewitness News* beginning in 1969. He began his career as a studio director at WTOP-TV in 1965 and became a news reporter shortly thereafter. He helped found the Association of Black Journalists, a group whose efforts are aimed at encouraging blacks in journalism, and started its first internship program in broadcasting with his own funds.

ROBOTIC CAMERA SYSTEMS ▶ computerized camera controls that cause video cameras to tilt, pan and move across the studio without the help of a human operator. Sophisticated robotic systems can be programmed in advance to do all the camerawork required by an entire program like a newscast. Stations in large and medium-sized markets have adopted them as a means to save on camera-operator labor costs.

***ROCK FOLLIES* ▶** Thames Television's 1976 six-part mini-series that chronicled the rise of a female rock group called "The Little Ladies," played by Julie Covington, Charlotte Cornwell and Rula Lenska. Written by Brooklynite Howard Schuman, directed by Brian Farnham and Jon Scoffield, and produced by Andrew Brown, the show had a catchy score by Andy Mackay—a survey of pop styles of the seventies, and earlier. *Rock Follies* dealt with some interesting issues that don't usually get treated on television, and it did it with some wit and good music. It was aired in the U.S. by PBS in 1977. A sequel was less effective.

ROCKEFELLER, SHARON PERCY ▶ president and chief executive officer of Washington's WETA-TV. With considerable political savvy—she is the daughter of a senator and the wife of a governor—Rockefeller has played an important role in shaping the policies of public broadcasting since President Carter appointed her to the Corporation for Public Broadcasting board in 1977. She chaired the board for three years, was unseated by the Reagan-appointed majority in 1984, continued to serve until 1987 and then in 1990 was returned to the board by President Bush. In the interim she served on the board of PBS. In 1990, in an unusual switch, she resigned her position as chair of the WETA board on which she had served for seven years to fill the post of the station's president and CEO.

ROCKFORD FILES, THE ▶ hour-long private-eye series created as a vehicle for James Garner (1974-80), enabling him—as detective Jim Rockford—to resurrect aspects of the character he introduced in *Maverick* 17 years earlier. The series was a Friday night hit on NBC. Featured were Noah Beery as Jim's father, Joe Rockford, Stuart Margolin as Angel Martin, Joe Santos as Sergeant Dennis Becker and Gretchen Corbett as defense attorney Beth Davenport. Production was by Cherokee Productions in association with Universal TV.

ROCKY MOUNTAIN SATELLITE PROJECT ▶ an experiment during 1974-75 with the use of domestic communication satellites to deliver educational materials to remote areas of the Rocky Mountains region. The project, which beamed a series of programs on career education to 56 schools, along with other instructional material, was conducted with NASA's powerful ATS-6 satellite.

RODDENBERRY, GENE (d. 1991) ▶ TV producer-writer best known for creating and producing *Star Trek* and *Star Trek: The Next Generation.* He was also producer of the series *The Lieutenant,* head writer for *Have Gun, Will Travel,* and writer of more than 80 TV scripts for various series. Roddenberry also served as executive producer for the five *Star Trek* motion pictures.

RODGERS, JOHNATHAN ▶ president of the CBS-owned television stations, one of the few blacks among senior level television executives in the U.S. Rodgers came up through the news ranks, having joined the company in 1976 as assistant news director at its Chicago station, WBBM-TV. He moved to KCBS-TV (then KNXT) in Los Angeles as executive producer and later became news director and then station manager. CBS News moved him to New York in 1983 and in time he became executive producer of the *CBS Morning News.* Rodgers went back to the station division in 1986 as general manager of WBBM. On the strength of that performance, he was elevated to president of the CBS TV Stations division in 1990.

ROGERS, EDWARD (TED) ▶ president and CEO of Rogers Communications Inc., Canada's largest cable company and one that, for a time, operated systems in the U.S. Rogers's involvement with cable, which began early in the medium's development, was preceded by an absorption with radio. His father founded CFRB Radio in Toronto, and in his youth Ted Rogers gave up the practice of law to acquire a group of radio stations, starting with one in Toronto. Along the way he acquired a small cable system in North York, Ontario, and then began to expand to other communities in the region. Later he bought Canadian Cablesystems and Premier Cablesystems, which formed the base of his present empire.

Rogers is also the chairman of Unitel Communications and the vice chairman of Rogers Canada Inc., Rogers Cable TV Ltd., Rogers Cablesystems Ltd., Rogers Broadcasting, Rogers Cantel and Rogers Cantel Mobile Inc.

ROGERS, RALPH D. ▶ millionaire Texas businessman who became chairman of the PBS board of governors in the early 1970s and was responsible for settling the wars and skirmishes between factions of the public television industry. It was Rogers who engineered the Partnership Agreement between CPB and PBS on May 31, 1973, resolving, at least for the time, the struggle between those organizations for leadership of the system. Rogers also reorganized PBS, clarifying the roles of lay officials and practitioners.

In 1976 he was the force behind the selection of Lawrence K. Grossman, a New York advertising executive, as president of PBS, a move which gave aggressive national leadership to the public TV system and revived notions of investing PBS with some programming authority. Rogers yielded the PBS chairmanship to Newton Minow in 1978.

ROGERS, THOMAS S. ▶ president of NBC cable and business development, overseeing NBC's cable programming interests. Those include CNBC, SportsChannel America, Arts & Entertainment, American Movie Classics, Court TV and the company's pay-per-view offerings with the 1992 Summer Olympics. As head of business development, he also oversees strategic planning for NBC and the foreign business activities of NBC International.

A Columbia Law School graduate and former Wall Street lawyer, Rogers served for five years (1981-86) as senior counsel to the U.S. House of Representatives Subcommittee on

Telecommunications, Consumer Protection and Finance. He joined NBC as v.p. of policy planning and business development in 1987.

Thomas S. Rogers

ROGUES, THE ▶ sophisticated adventure-comedy concerning well-bred international con men. It drew excellent reviews and poor ratings when it premiered on NBC in 1964. It lasted a single season. Produced by Four Star Television, its cast included two of the company's principals, Charles Boyer and David Niven (as Marcel St. Clair and Alec Fleming), and featured also Gig Young as Tony Fleming, Gladys Cooper as Auntie Margaret and Robert Coote as Timmy Fleming.

ROMPER ROOM ▶ a long-running daily children's series dealing in games, playthings and simple lessons for preschoolers, whose format was widely syndicated by Bert Claster Productions. The program was designed to be presented as a local live show in each market, using children from the community and a resident hostess or "teacher." It premiered on independent stations in 1953 as early morning fare, in studios designed to resemble a classroom. Before long, the format was syndicated to more than 100 markets as well as to numerous countries abroad, and it maintained wide distribution through two decades.

Consumerists called into question some of the practices of the program, such as its persistent featuring of brand-name toys used by the children on the show, its commercials and plugs for so-called "Romper Room Toys" (manufactured by Hasbro) and its use of the "teachers" as commercial announcers. Such criticism, along with a tightening of the NAB code on children's advertising, was effective in somewhat altering the commercialized character of the shows.

ROOKIES, THE ▶ hour-long ABC police series (1972-76) about a trio of youthful officers. It succeeded as a Monday night entry at 8 p.m. but was ousted from the timeslot when family viewing time was adopted in 1975. In its new Tuesday timeslot at 9 p.m., *The Rookies* faltered and was canceled. The police rookies were represented by Georg Stanford Brown as Terry Webster, Sam Melville as Mike Danko and Bruce Fairbairn as Chris Owen (preceded, during the first two seasons, by Michael Ontkean as Willie Gillis). Featured were Gerald S. O'Loughlin as Lieutenant Ed Ryker and Kate Jackson as Danko's wife, Jill. It was an Aaron Spelling-Leonard Goldberg Production.

ROOM 222 ▶ half-hour comedy-drama series on ABC (1969-73) on a racially integrated high school, focusing on a black male teacher, Pete Dixon, portrayed by Lloyd Haynes. The faculty featured Denise Nicholas as guidance counselor Liz McIntyre, Michael Constantine as principal Seymour Kaufman and Karen Valentine as student teacher Alice Johnson; students included Heshimu as Jason Allen, David Jolliffe as Bernie and Judy Strangis as Helen Loomis. The series was by 20th Century-Fox TV.

Andy Rooney

ROONEY, ANDY ▶ CBS news correspondent whose regular commentaries on *60 Minutes* prompted *Time* to dub him "the most felicitous non-fiction writer in television." His sometimes jaundiced, often cantankerous but always literate essays, *A Few Minutes With Any Rooney*, became a regular feature of *60 Minutes* in September 1978. Rooney characteristically chooses subjects that most viewers take for granted. His most famous, *An Essay on Doors*, is typical. In a career generally filled with approbation, Rooney was made to feel the wrath of many viewers when, in a 1989 year-end CBS special, he remarked that some of the ills that kill us are "self-induced" and included among them "homosexual unions." CBS suspended him without pay for 3 months but viewer pressure and a published apology returned him to the show in 3 weeks.

In addition to *60 Minutes,* Rooney has exercised his talent for making the obvious interesting by writing, producing and narrating a series of one-hour specials for CBS, among them *Mr. Rooney Goes to Work, Mr. Rooney Goes to Dinner,* and *Mr. Rooney Goes to Washington.* For 6 years (1962-68) he collaborated with the late CBS News correspondent Harry Reasoner —Rooney writing and producing and Reasoner narrating—on a series of notable CBS specials that included *An Essay on Bridges, An Essay on Hotels, An Essay on Women,* and *An Essay on Chairs.* Another, *An Essay on War,* was turned down by the network and aired in 1971 on PBS's *The Great American Dream Machine,* in which Rooney made his first solo on-camera appearance in connection with his essays.

Rooney began his broadcasting career writing for CBS Radio, first for Arthur Godfrey (1949-55), then for *The Garry Moore Show* (1959-69). He is the author of nine books, including *The Story of Stars and Stripes,* the account of his three years in the European Theater as a correspondent for that publication. He currently writes a two-day-a-week syndicated column that appears in 250 newspapers.

ROOTIE KAZOOTIE ▶ early children's puppet series which began on NBC in 1950. Todd Russel's puppet cast included Rootie Kazootie, El Squeako Mouse and Polka Dottie.

ROOTS ▶ one of TV's milestone programs, an ABC mini-series based on Alex Haley's novel *Roots,* which not only scored the highest ratings in TV history for an entertainment program but was also considered to have marked turning points in the medium, both for its form and for its subject matter. Purchased by ABC two years before the book's publication and aired shortly after the book's release, when it had already reached the top of the best-seller lists, *Roots* emptied theaters, filled bars, caused social events to be canceled and was the talk of the nation during the eight consecutive nights it played on ABC, from Jan. 23 to Jan. 30, 1977—Sunday through Sunday.

The program's popularity was remarkable for the fact that its cast was predominantly black and its villains mostly white, dealing as it did with the history of a black family traced to the capture of a young West African, Kunta Kinte, by American slave traders. Only 10 years before its airing, blacks had been scarce on the TV screens except as entertainers, housekeepers and ball players; according to the industry's conventional wisdom of the 1950s and 1960s, blacks would attract neither a mass audience nor advertisers and would cause Southern stations to defect from the network lineup. The sad experience of Nat (King) Cole on NBC was all the proof that had been needed.

But none of the stations, northern or southern, rejected *Roots,* and the 12-hour mini-series (which contained four two-hour episodes and four one-hour) was a shared experience for most of the country, a book read electronically by everyone at the same time and at the same pace. The mayors of more than 30 cities proclaimed the week "Roots Week," and more than 250 colleges and universities offered, or proposed to offer later, courses based on the film and the book. In the cities that were capitals of the civil rights turmoil of the 1960s, no crosses were burned on station lawns, and disturbances were negligible.

The eight episodes of *Roots* averaged a 44.9 rating and a 66 share of audience, far surpassing any previous series of programs. The seven episodes following the opening show took the top seven spots in the ratings for that week, and the final two-hour telecast notched a 51.1 rating and 71 share—making it the leader in the all-time number of TV homes, with 36.38 million as compared to 33.65 million for *Gone With the Wind: Part I,* aired by NBC earlier that season. According to Nielsen, an average of 80 million viewers watched the final episode of *Roots,* and around 130 million—or 85% of the TV homes—watched all or part of the 12 hours.

Heading the large cast were LeVar Burton as young Kunta Kinte; John Amos as adult Kunta Kinte, renamed Toby; Ben Vereen as Chicken George Moore; Leslie Uggams as Kizzy; Louis Gossett Jr. as Fiddler; Cicely Tyson as Binta; Scatman Crothers as Mingo; Edward Asner as Captain Davies; Lorne Greene as John Reynolds; Lynda Day George as Mrs. Reynolds; Robert Reed as William Reynolds; Chuck Connors as Tom Moore; George Hamilton as Stephen Bennett; Lloyd Bridges as Evan Brent; Lillian Randolph as Sister Sara; Richard Roundtree as Sam Bennett; Georg Stanford Brown as Tom Harvey and Lynne Moody as Irene Harvey.

The series was produced by David L. Wolper Productions, with Wolper as executive producer and Stan Margulies as producer. The scripts were by William Blinn, Ernest Kinoy,

James Lee and Max Cohen, and the original music was by Quincy Jones.

Indicating that ABC had not expected the bonanza that resulted was the fact that the eight episodes were scheduled just before the sweep weeks, a time when the networks tend to play what they believe to be their strongest shows. Meanwhile, the success of *Roots* created a receptive syndication market for a BBC series on a similar subject, *Fight Against Slavery,* distributed by Time-Life Films.

ROOTS: THE NEXT GENERATIONS ▶ 14-hour sequel to the phenomenally popular TV adaptation of Alex Haley's *Roots,* airing two years after the original, for seven nights, Feb. 18-25, 1979. While *Roots II,* as it came to be called, did not rival *Roots I* as an audience draw, it nevertheless did exceedingly well, with a 30.1 rating and 45 share for the entire run, or about two-thirds as well as the original. The total audience, watching all or part of the serial, was estimated at around 110 million. Moreover, the program won every one of its time periods, despite much tougher competition than *Roots I* encountered.

The opening episode was challenged by two big movies, *Marathon Man* on CBS and *American Graffiti* on NBC. During the week, it was up against episodes of *Backstairs at the White House* and *From Here to Eternity.* On the final night—the lowest-rated of the series, even though it featured James Earl Jones as Alex Haley and Marlon Brando as American Nazi leader George Lincoln Rockwell—*Roots II* had to contend with the popular family movie *The Sound of Music. Roots II* was televised during a sweeps period; *Roots I* was not.

Based on unused material from Haley's book, some of the content of a second book, *My Search for Roots,* and additional material supplied by the author, *Roots II* continued the chronicle of Haley's family, from Chicken George to Haley's own emergence, or from Reconstruction to modern times.

The cast included Georg Stanford Brown and Lynne Moody recreating their roles as Tom and Irene Harvey; Beah Richards as the Harveys' daughter, Cynthia; Avon Long (replacing Ben Vereen) as Chicken George; Ruby Dee as Queen Haley; Henry Fonda as Colonel Warner; Olivia de Havilland as Mrs. Warner; Richard Thomas and Marc Singer as the Warners' sons, Jim and Andy; Al Freeman Jr. as Black Muslim spokesperson Malcolm X; Harry Morgan as Bob Campbell; Dorian Harewood and Irene Cara as Simon and Bertha Haley, Alex's parents; Debbie Allen as Nan, Alex's wife; and Christoff St. John, Damon Evans, and James Earl Jones as Alex Haley. Also appearing were Diahann Carroll, Ossie Davis, Ja'net DuBois, Andy Griffith, Rafer Johnson, Claudia McNeill, Carmen McRae, Greg Morris and Della Reese.

David L. Wolper was executive producer, Stan Margulies producer, and John Erman, Charles S. Dubin, Georg Stanford Brown and Lloyd Richards directors. Ernest Kinoy supervised the scripts and wrote the first three episodes. Other writers were Sydney A. Glass, Thad Mumford and Daniel Wilcox, and John McGreevey.

ROSE, CHARLIE ▶ journalist and television interviewer best known for his six years as the anchor of *Nightwatch* for CBS News, where he won a national Emmy for his interview with mass murderer Charles Manson.

A native of South Carolina and a law graduate, Rose came to television in 1974 as managing editor of an early Bill Moyers series for PBS and the following year became executive producer of *Bill Moyers' Journal.* He left public TV to join NBC News as a Washington correspondent, turned full-time interviewer a year later as co-host of *AM/Chicago* on WLS-TV, then joined KXAS-TV in Dallas-Fort Worth as host of his own daily show, later syndicated nationally. In 1981 he moved the *Charlie Rose Show* to Washington, giving it up three years later to anchor *Nightwatch.* He returned to public TV in 1991 as host of his own nightly interview show, *Charlie Rose,* on WNET New York.

ROSE, REGINALD ▶ one of the outstanding playwrights to emerge from TV's drama era of the 1950s, writing for *Studio One, Philco Playhouse* and the other anthology programs. His notable TV plays include *Twelve Angry Men, Thunder on Sycamore Street* and *The Sacco-Vanzetti Story.*

Rose also created and wrote *The Defenders* series (1961) on CBS. His first TV play, *Bus to Nowhere,* aired in 1951.

ROSEANNE ▶ ABC sitcom centering on comedienne Roseanne Barr that was a smash hit from the start and has remained consistently near the top of the Nielsens ever since. Barr later changed her surname to Arnold after her marriage. She and John Goodman portray Roseanne and Dan Connor, a raucous blue-collar couple with three wisecracking kids,

Becky (played by Lecy Goranson), Darlene (Sarah Gilbert), and D. J. (Michael Fishman). Others in the cast include Laurie Metcalf as Jackie and Natalie West as Crystal. Barr was a relatively unknown, overweight stand-up comic with a whiny, understated delivery and an irreverent view of family life before landing the show. Executive producers Marcy Carsey and Tom Werner were also responsible for another hugely successful domestic sitcom, *The Cosby Show.* But where *Cosby* presents an idealized family circle, *Roseanne*'s is imperfect, unglamorous and somewhat vulgar. TV audiences seemed immediately to appreciate the honesty of the show. It debuted on ABC in October 1988.

Roseanne Arnold and John Goodman, stars of the hit series *Roseanne*

ROSEMONT, NORMAN ▶ personal manager turned TV producer and executive in charge of a number of music-variety specials, principally those starring Robert Goulet, his prize client. As his production company grew, it turned out such dramatic specials as *The Man Without a Country, The Count of Monte Cristo, The Man in the Iron Mask, The Hunchback of Notre Dame* and *Ivanhoe.*

ROSEN, KENNETH M. (d. 1976) ▶ writer, producer and director who for a time operated his own company, Profile Productions, in California. As a writer, he collaborated with Marshall Flaum on scripts for several Jacques Cousteau and Jane Goodall nature specials and earlier wrote episodes for such series as *Naked City, Perry Mason* and *Days of Our Lives.* He also wrote the TV adaptation of the book *Future Shock.* As a producer, he was responsible for 23 documentaries, among them a National Geographic special for David Wolper Productions, *Journey to the Outer Limits.*

ROSENBERG, JOHN (d. 1991) ▶ American novelist and story editor who became head of drama programming for Anglia TV in the U.K. He moved to London in 1952 to work as MGM story editor. At Anglia he was responsible for such series as *Roald Dahl's Tales of the Unexpected* and *Devices and Desires.* Other credits include made-for-TV movies such as *The Kingfisher.* He died of cancer at 59.

ROSENBERG, RICK ▶ see Christiansen, Robert W. and Rosenberg, Rick.

James H. Rosenfield

ROSENFIELD, JAMES H. ▶ former high-ranking CBS executive who left in 1985 and organized an investment group that purchased John Blair Communications two years later. As chairman and chief executive of Blair, Rosenfield oversees the company's activities as a national sales rep for TV stations as well as producer and distributor of syndicated TV programs.

Rosenfield joined CBS in 1965 in network sales and moved rapidly up the ladder, becoming president of the TV network in 1977. It was a difficult time for CBS, because ABC had emerged as the prime-time ratings leader and was raiding the other networks for key affiliates. Rosenfield kept the affiliates generally in line and maintained the network's stability.

In 1981 Rosenfield was named executive v.p. of the CBS Broadcast Group in charge of the TV Network, CBS Entertainment and CBS Sports. His title was later upgraded to senior executive vice president.

ROSENZWEIG, BARNEY ▶ executive producer and co-creator (with his then-wife, Barbara Corday, and Barbara Avedon) of the controversial female police series *Cagney and Lacey* (1982-88); he displayed uncommon courage in upholding the integrity of the project in the face of strong resistance by the broadcast establishment. The series was conceived in 1974 and turned down by all three networks as having a too feminist point of view. It finally aired in somewhat diluted form as a TV movie on CBS in 1981 and was picked up as a series by the network the following year. The show ran for one season before being canceled because of the volume of viewer complaints over its handling of hot topical issues. (This was said to have rivalled the number of complaints received by CBS for *Lou Grant.*) Ironically, it was the indignant viewer response to *Cagney*'s cancellation that caused the show to be resurrected. The series ran again from 1984 to 1988. Rosenzweig went on to produce *The Trials of Rosie O'Neill* (1990—) for CBS, starring Sharon Gless (who also played one of the two leads in *Cagney* and whom Rosenzweig married).

ROSS, MICHAEL (d. 1985) ▶ writer-producer who collaborated with Bernie West and Don Nicholl to create and produce *The Jeffersons*, *The Dumplings*, and *Three's Company*, an ABC hit from 1977-83 that was based on the British TV series *Man About the House*. The series spawned two spin-offs for ABC, *The Ropers* (1979-80) and *Three's a Crowd* (1984-1985), for which Ross served as executive producer. Ross, Nicholl and West formed NRW Productions to handle the production of *Three's Company* and its progeny.

ROSS, STEVEN ▶ chairman and co-chief executive officer of the Time Warner media conglomerate since early 1990, when the merger of the two companies was officially consummated. As chairman of Warner Communications before the merger he led the company into some of its boldest ventures.

Ross came to Warner in a 1969 merger. At the time he was head of National Kinney; when the company acquired Warner Bros. Pictures, Ross assumed the chairmanship. Soon after, Warner enjoyed a huge success with its film *Woodstock* and the record album drawn from it and released by Warner-owned Atlantic Records. That encouraged Ross to position the company in the broader media field, prompting Warner's acquisition of its first cable system. By 1971, the company had been renamed Warner Communications Inc. to reflect the new corporate strategy.

Under Ross's leadership, Warner Amex Cable (then in partnership with American Express) launched the futuristic interactive Qube system in Columbus, Ohio, a daring but ultimately unsuccessful experiment that may have been ahead of its time. Ross also had a hand in Warner Communications' creation of several successful cable networks: Nickelodeon, The Movie Channel, and MTV: Music Television, all of which were later sold to Viacom.

After the merger with Time, Ross came under criticism for his immense personal gains from the transaction—estimated at around $70 million—at a time when other stockholders were left to bear the weight of Time Warner's $14 billion debt load.

ROSTEN, IRWIN ▶ producer director-writer of informational nonfiction programs such as those for MGM's *GE Monogram Series,* on which he teamed with Nicolas Noxon in the early 1970s. Those programs included *The Wolf Men, The Man Hunters, Once Before I Die* and *Dear Mr. Gable.* Earlier, while he was with Wolper Productions, Rosten produced and wrote *Grizzly, The World of Jacques Cousteau* and six episodes of *Hollywood and the Stars.* He began as a TV documentary producer in the news division of KNXT Los Angeles.

***ROUTE 66* ▶** popular series on the exploits of two young adventurers traveling across the country, starring Martin Milner as Tod Stiles and George Maharis as Buzz Murdock (Glenn Corbett, playing Lincoln Case, replaced Maharis in the fourth season). Produced by Screen Gems, it ran on CBS from 1960 to 1964.

***ROWAN AND MARTIN'S LAUGH-IN* ▶** a madcap comedy hour, laced with silliness and satire, which gave a new free-wheeling form to TV variety shows and was a prodigious hit and a Monday night fixture for NBC (1967-73). With the nightclub comedy team of Dan Rowan and Dick Martin as hosts, the show featured a "new faces" resident company of skit players and buffoons. A chaotic montage of skits, blackouts, fast-cut inanities, dances, songs, stand-up comedy and recurring routines, it was unlike anything else on television and, with its irreverence and double-entendres, seemed to catch the liberated spirit of the times.

The series poured out one catch-phrase after another—"sock it to me," "verrry interrresting," "here come the judge," "look that up in your Funk & Wagnall's"—and turned up a wealth of new young talent in its revolving repertory company, notably Lily Tomlin, Goldie Hawn, Ruth Buzzi, Teresa Graves and Arte Johnson. Others in the cast, for all or part of the five-year run, were Judy Carne, Joanne Worley, Alan Sues, Dave Madden Strunk, Richard Dawson and Sarah Kennedy.

Laugh-In was produced by Romart Inc., the company owned by Rowan and Martin. George Schlatter and Ed Friendly were the executive producers for the first three seasons, Paul Keyes for the next two. A revival of the series was essayed in 1977 in the form of NBC specials.

ROY ROGERS SHOW, THE ▶ singing-cowboy series on NBC (1955-56), predating the era of the "adult western." It starred Roy Rogers and his wife, Dale Evans, and was produced by their own company, Roy Rogers Productions. Featured were the Sons of the Pioneers, a vocal group; Pat Brady and his jeep, Nellybelle; Trigger, Roy's horse; Buttermilk, Dale's horse; and Bullet, their dog.

ROYAL, JOHN F. (d. 1978) ▶ first v.p. in charge of television at NBC (1940-53) who remained with the network after retirement as a consultant, until his death at 88. A former general manager in vaudeville, and later v.p. in charge of programs for the NBC radio network, Royal was close to performers, and the network benefitted from his relationships with Mary Martin, Bob Hope, Ed Wynn and other stars. As NBC's resident showman, he helped to shape the medium's early programming and to secure the stars for dramas, variety shows and what were then called spectaculars.

RTNDA (RADIO-TELEVISION NEWS DIRECTORS ASSOCIATION) ▶ organization of professional broadcast journalists founded in 1946 to work toward improving the standards of broadcast journalism and to defend the rights of newspeople. It is also concerned with journalism education to meet the specific needs of radio and TV. Members are mainly station news directors, network news executives and academicians.

With a membership of about 1,000, RTNDA conducts an annual conference and periodic regional seminars and workshops. It also confers annual awards for news reporting, editorials and outstanding contributions to broadcast journalism.

RUBEN, AARON (d. 1987) ▶ comedy writer whose career dated to the radio shows of George Burns and Gracie Allen, Fred Allen and Henry Morgan and extended to *Sanford and Son* and *C.P.O. Sharkey.* In the 1950s Ruben wrote for the TV shows of Sam Levenson, Danny Thomas, Milton Berle and Sid Caesar, then became director of Silvers's *You'll Never Get Rich* (*Sgt. Bilko*) and in 1960 produced *The Andy Griffith Show.* He was also creator and producer of *Gomer Pyle* and later producer of *Sanford and Son. Sharkey* was via his own production company.

RUDD, HUGHES ▶ former ABC News correspondent joining in 1979 after a 20-year career with CBS News, during the latter part of which he anchored *The CBS Morning News* (1973-77). Originally teamed with Sally Quinn, he became sole anchor on her departure several months later. A Texan, Rudd retained an appealing countrified style although his journalistic assignments—first for newspapers and then for CBS—took him to many parts of the world. Rudd also was a writer of fiction and just before joining CBS wrote and directed industrial films.

RUDOLPH, THE RED-NOSED REINDEER ▶ perennial children's Christmas special on CBS, playing every year since its premiere in 1964. Based on the song by Johnny Marks and a story by Robert L. May, the hour animated special was produced by Arthur Rankin, Jr., and Jules Bass for Videocraft International Production. Burl Ives is narrator.

Elton H. Rule

RULE, ELTON H. (d. 1990) ▶ onetime president and chief operating officer of the American Broadcasting Companies Inc. (1972-83). Upon retirement from ABC he joined a former colleague, I. Martin Pompadur, in forming RP Companies, which bought TV stations and cable systems and, in association with Merrill

Lynch, managed several successful investment pools in the media field.

Rule was a charismatic and effective leader at ABC, with the aura of a winner and a record of achievement in his various executive positions. His ascent to the corporate tier was rapid after his appointment, in January 1968, as president of the TV network. Sixteen months later he was placed in charge of all broadcast activities for the corporation and in 1970 was elected to the board and given the title of president of the American Broadcasting Co., subsidiary of the parent corporation. In January 1972 he was named president of the corporation. An executive who had developed within the ABC system, Rule had been v.p. and general manager of KABC-TV Los Angeles when he was tapped for the network post. Prior to that he had worked in station sales.

RULEMAKING ▶ the FCC's process for formulating, amending or repealing a rule. The commission, as a government agency, is required to give interested parties an opportunity to participate in rulemaking through submission of written data and arguments. The agency sometimes chooses to hear unsworn oral presentations in "informal" public meetings. The cities of license for new radio and TV stations are determined by means of another form of rulemaking in which Administrative Law Judges hold formal evidentiary hearings. All rulemaking decisions are subject to judicial review in a federal circuit appeals court.

RUMPOLE OF THE BAILEY **▶** British courtroom comedy series televised on PBS's *Mystery!* in the early 1980s and again in 1988. The episodes were based on John Mortimer's books, with Leo McKern portraying the aging barrister, Horace Rumpole, whom his young colleagues think is over the hill but who remains deceptively shrewd. McKern is amusing and endearing in the role. Featured were Marion Mathie, Julian Curry, Jonathan Coy, Maureen Darby Shire and Peter Blythe. Lloyd Shirley of Thames Television was the executive producer.

RUN FOR YOUR LIFE **▶** hour-long adventure series on NBC (1965-67) that starred Ben Gazzara as Paul Bryan, a man determined to squeeze 20 years of living into the few that the doctors tell him remain. It was produced by Roncom Film, with Roy Huggins as executive producer.

RUN OF SCHEDULE ▶ category for ad sales at a local station or cable network. It carries one of the lowest rates because the spots, purchased in quantity, may be placed in any time period at the station's or operator's discretion.

RUNAWAY PRODUCTION ▶ program or films produced abroad or outside the jurisdiction of U.S. unions, usually for reasons of economy. The practice has, of course, been fought and condemned by the unions, which have applied the term to give the programs the stigma of having deprived Americans of work. "Runaways" have exacerbated the decline in film activity in Hollywood—to which the networks' greater use of reruns and growing reliance on video tape have contributed—but the union campaigns against overseas production were not notably successful.

RUSH, ALVIN ▶ head of the MCA Television Group from 1981-91, first as president and for the last five years as chairman. On retiring, he became a consultant for MCA TV.

Previously, he was executive v.p. of NBC-TV and before that senior v.p. of program and sports administration, essentially in charge of talent and program negotiations. Rush came to the network in 1973 after a long career as a talent agent and packager, first with MCA and then with Creative Management Associates.

RUSH, HERMAN ▶ independent producer who was one of the most influential program packagers of the 1960s as head of the television division of a major talent agency, CMA, and earlier as an agent for GAC. In the 1970s, he went out on his own as an independent producer and then joined Marble Arch Productions as president of its TV division. Later he became president of Columbia Pictures Television and then formed his own company.

RUSHNELL, SQUIRE D. ▶ former v.p. of children's and early morning programs for ABC Entertainment; he assumed the first post in 1974 and the second when he was given responsibility also for *Good Morning, America* in April 1978. During his tenure, significant changes were made in children's programming at ABC, notably the addition of the high quality *ABC Afterschool Specials,* the *ABC Weekend Specials, Kids Are People, Too* on Sunday mornings and public service messages on nutrition and health. Previously, Rushnell was with the ABC owned-stations division, where he was responsible for guiding the *Rainbow Sundae* children's series, and before that with WLS-TV

Chicago, where he was assistant program manager.

RUSKIN, COBY ▶ director of *Here's Lucy, Gomer Pyle* and *The Bill Cosby Show.* He also directed episodes for *The Doris Day Show, Julia* and *Love, American Style.*

RUSSERT, TIMOTHY J. ▶ senior vice president and Washington bureau chief of NBC News and in November 1991 named anchor of *Meet the Press.* He had been a regular panelist on the program and appeared bi-weekly on *Today* as a political analyst.

Before joining NBC News as a key executive in the Lawrence Grossman administration, Russert served as counselor to New York State Governor Mario Cuomo (1983-84). Before that he was special counsel and chief-of-staff to New York's Senator Daniel Patrick Moynihan.

RYAN, J. HAROLD (d. 1961) ▶ a co-founder in 1928, with George B. Storer, of the Storer Broadcasting Co., where he spent most of his career as senior v.p. He also served for a time as president of NAB.

RYAN, NIGEL ▶ former v.p. of documentaries and special programs for NBC News (1977-79) after having been editor and chief executive of Britain's Independent Television News. In his post with ITN, which he assumed in 1971, he guided the news organization through a period of innovation, introducing documentary techniques to the U.K., commercial network's popular *News at Ten* and creating a 30-minute lunchtime newscast, *First Report.* He left NBC in the Fred Silverman administration and returned to England as director of programs for Thames Television.

RYAN, TIM ▶ CBS sportscaster since 1977, chiefly covering football, basketball and boxing, after a five-year stint with NBC Sports (1972-77). A Canadian, he broke into broadcasting with CFTO Toronto as a sportscaster, then moved to California to do the play-by-play for the Oakland Seals of the National Hockey League. In 1970 he shifted his base to New York to cover the Rangers hockey games on WOR-TV, serving at the same time as regular sportscaster for WPIX-TV. Two years later he joined NBC when it acquired the rights to televise the NHL and, while there, also covered a variety of other sports. At CBS Sports, Ryan began covering the U.S. Open Tennis Championships in 1987. He has also hosted the CBS Sports weekend anthology series, the World Figure Skating Championships, and NCAA men's basketball.

***RYAN'S HOPE* ▶** see Soap Operas.

S

SABAN, HAIM ▶ a leading international distributor of animated TV programming who has also branched into the production of prime-time network programming. With no previous experience in television but coming off successful ventures in the music business in Paris and Israel, Saban moved to Hollywood in 1980 and burst upon the television scene with sheer ingenuity and derring-do. Four years later he was a force to reckon with in the industry and used every opportunity to promote his name, with lavish trade advertising and giveaways. In a mere two or three years he went from total obscurity to a household name in the international TV field, and he had the programming to back it up.

His initial scheme, which in fact continues, was to buy up animated children's series produced in various European countries and to re-edit them completely—to the point of rewriting the stories, recutting the film, and dubbing them into English—to make them playable in the U.S. They then became saleable abroad, which in original form they were not. Once established, his company became involved also in original animated production and has sold series to NBC, the Fox Children's Network, and Nickelodeon. All together, with international sales, Saban's company claims annual gross revenues of more than $50 million.

Determined to diversify beyond children's programming, Saban established a link with noted Hollywood producer Edgar Scherick in 1989 to produce TV movies, series and motion pictures.

An Egyptian-born Israeli, Saban started in the music business in 1966 and soon became a promoter of rock band concert tours based in Israel. Later he moved to Paris and started his own record label. His introduction to television came with the production of soundtracks for series, including several American shows.

SACKHEIM, WILLIAM ▶ one of TV's more prolific and durable producers whose credits date back to *Goodyear Playhouse* in the late 1950s and extend through *Delvecchio, The Senator,* and *The Law* in the 1970s to the newspaper drama *Hard Copy* and the new *Alfred Hitchcock Presents* mystery anthology series in the 1980s. He has produced over 300 TV movies, including *The Impatient Heart, The Neon Ceiling* and *A Clear and Present Danger.* His feature film credits include co-writing *First Blood* and co-producing *Pacific Heights* and *The Hard Way.* He is the father of Daniel Sackheim, producer-director of the dramatic series *Law and Order.*

SAFER, MORLEY ▶ CBS News correspondent who became one of the principals of *60 Minutes* in 1970 after distinguishing himself in covering the Vietnam war. A Canadian who had been a correspondent and producer with the Canadian Broadcasting Corporation before joining CBS, Safer served as head of the CBS Saigon bureau (1965-67) and then as chief of the London bureau (1967-70). In the fall of 1967 he and cameraman John Peters went into mainland China to film *Morley Safer's Red China Diary.* In 1969 he contributed the special *The Ordeal of Anatoly Kuznetsov,* an exclusive interview with a Soviet writer who had defected to the West. He joined *60 Minutes* as replacement for Harry Reasoner, who quit CBS News for ABC.

Morley Safer

SAGA OF THE WESTERN MAN, THE ▶ an occasional series of 13 specials, each documenting a decisive year in the story of modern human life. Starting on ABC in 1963, the series was produced and written by John Secondari for the ABC News Special Projects Division.

SAGALL, SOLOMON ▶ pioneer promoter of pay TV in its over-the-air form whose first venture was with large screen pay television in two London cinemas in 1938. That company, which he founded, was known as Scophony Ltd. It developed a system of coded television that was proposed for use in military operations during World War II and still is the basis for all pay systems. In 1957 Sagall formed Teleglobe Pay Systems Inc. in the U.S., which had to endure years of FCC delays in permitting over-the-air pay TV to operate. All legal and political barriers were finally removed in 1975.

Sagall envisioned a system that would make every home a private theater and that would, in effect, extend the seating for drama, opera and orchestral performances and for sports and auditorium events. Under his concept, an entire family would be able to watch any program for the price of a single ticket to the event. He developed a decoding unit—a black box to be attached to TV sets—that would perform the dual function of unscrambling the picture and billing the viewer. But by the time the FCC allowed pay TV to proceed, only UHF channels were available for the operations and pay cable had gotten underway.

SAGANSKY, JEFF ▶ president of CBS Entertainment since 1990, when he was brought in to succeed Kim LeMasters in the post. Sagansky had been recruited from Tri-Star Pictures, where he was president, but more important in terms of his qualifications was that he had previously been senior vice president of series programming for NBC and a protege of that network's famed program chief, Brandon Tartikoff. The two were actual competitors for less than a year, however, since Tartikoff left NBC in 1991 to become head of Paramount.

Sagansky's first big programming coup was to commit CBS to an international coproduction of the mini-series *Scarlett,* based on the best-selling novel in 1991 that was created as a sequel to *Gone With the Wind.* Although the book generally received poor reviews, the international partners paid $8 million for the rights in spirited bidding against other producers, by far a record in the television industry for book rights. The production of the series was to require an additional $30 million. Others in the coproduction partnership are U.S. producer Robert Halmi through his RHI Entertainment, Silvio Berlusconi of Italy through his company, Reteitalia, and Leo Kirch of Germany through his BetaFilm.

SAINT, THE ▶ mystery series based on the famed stories of Leslie Charteris, with Roger Moore in the title role of Simon Templar. Produced by ATV/ITC in England, it premiered on NBC in 1967 and returned at intervals in the following two years. Of the 114 episodes, 43 were filmed in color.

The show was revived on CBS in the 1980s with Ian Ogilvy and later Andrew Clarke in the lead role.

ST. ELSEWHERE ▶ realistic hospital drama series that ran on NBC from 1982-1988 as an MTM stablemate of *Hill Street Blues.* Throughout its history the show struggled against low ratings, but its demographics were so good that even when it ranked in the lower quartile of prime-time shows it commanded higher ad rates than many series in the top 40.

St. Elsewhere resembled *Hill Street Blues* in style and pacing, having also a large ensemble cast and intertwined plot lines, but it also had a good deal more humor, much of it anatomical. A dizzying yet digestible mix of social issues and personal problems—all set in fictional St. Eligius, a Boston hospital on the bad side of the tracks—*St. Elsewhere* won several Emmys.

Principal cast members included Ed Flanders, William Daniels, Denzel Washington and Mark Harmon. The latter two went on to pursue successful film careers.

St. Elsewhere's creator and executive producer Bruce Paltrow had previously produced only one other series, *The White Shadow,* a well-liked high school drama that ran on CBS from 1978-81. Following *St. Elsewhere* he developed another series for NBC in 1989, *Tattinger's,* but the show was canceled at the end of the season.

SAJAK, PAT ▶ TV personality who shot into prominence in 1982 as host of the hugely successful syndicated game show, *Wheel of Fortune.* Looking to build on that popularity, CBS created a late night talk show for Sajak in 1988, but it proved no match for Johnny Carson's *Tonight* or Ted Koppel's *Nightline* and was canceled after two seasons.

Sajak got his start as a weatherman at WSM-TV Nashville, then went to KNBC Los Angeles where he received the exposure that landed him a spot on *Wheel.*

SALANT, RICHARD S. ▶ former president of CBS News who in April 1979, immediately on reaching the mandatory retirement age of 65, switched camps and became vice-chairman of the National Broadcasting Co. His new position gave him general supervision over news and responsibility for assessing the role of the new technologies in the future direction of the company. His switch of networks, which startled the industry, raised the issue of company loyalty and pitted it against the issue of the morality of mandatory retirement policies. Energetic and eager to keep working, Salant maintained that he considered himself a broadcast journalist by profession rather than partisan of a network. His role at NBC, however, diminished through the years of the Fred Silverman administration, and by 1982—with Silverman gone—he was little more than a consultant under contract.

He had been twice president of CBS News, the first time 1961 to 1964, the second since February 1966. In the period between, while Fred W. Friendly headed the news division, Salant served as CBS v.p. of corporate affairs and as special assistant to Dr. Frank Stanton, president of CBS. A lawyer, Salant joined the company as a v.p. in 1952. Because he lacked a journalism background, he was at first resented by many within the news division; but he proved knowledgeable and courageous, and he had a distinguished tenure which reached its high point with the bold CBS News coverage of the Watergate events.

SALES, SOUPY ▶ slapstick performer who was popular with children in the 1950s and later gained a following with a somewhat older audience. A comedian of the pie-in-the-face school, he dealt also in puns, corny jokes and communication with animals. His popularity in Detroit won him a network show in the mid-1950s. Later he worked at a New York station, which served as the base for a syndicated show, and in 1976 he began a Saturday morning children's show on ABC, *Junior Almost Anything Goes.*

Lucie Salhany

SALHANY, LUCIE ▶ one of the most influential women in television, who started as a secretary at a local TV station and rose steadily through the programming ranks over a 20-year span to become chairman of Twentieth Television. In this capacity she oversees all of Fox's network, syndication and cable production and distribution.

Salhany began in television in 1967 at WKBF-TV in Cleveland, later moving to WLVI in Boston as program manager. But she established a national reputation at Taft Broadcasting, where she was vice president of television programming (1979-85). She then moved to Paramount Domestic Television, the syndication arm of Paramount Pictures, where her division launched a string of successful projects including *Star Trek: The Next Generation*, the late-night *Arsenio Hall Show* and the off-network syndication of *Cheers* and *Family Ties.* She joined Twentieth Television in July 1991.

SALINGER, PIERRE ▶ senior European editor and chief correspondent since 1983 for ABC News, based in Paris. In that capacity he has reported a number of high-profile stories, including behind-the-scenes efforts to free American hostages in Iran; the investigation of the bombing of Pan Am Flight 103; and the Reagan-Gorbachev summit meeting in Geneva. He played a key role in arranging ABC's coverage of the 27th Communist Party Congress in February 1986.

Salinger first gained national prominence in 1961 as press secretary to President Kennedy and continued in that post under President Johnson until March 1964 when he was appointed to serve out the term of the late Senator Clair Engle of California.

Salinger began his news career as a copy boy on the *San Francisco Chronicle,* returning there as a reporter, and later night city editor, after World War II service as the commander of a Navy subchaser. In 1955, while developing a series of stories for *Collier's* on James Hoffa, the magazine folded, leaving Salinger to continue the Hoffa story as chief investigator for the Senate Labor Rackets Committee, whose counsel was the late Robert Kennedy.

Talk-show host Sally Jessy Raphael

SALLY JESSY RAPHAEL ▶ syndicated daytime talk show that, like others of the genre—*Geraldo, Donahue,* and *Oprah*—often deals in titillating topics, discussed before a studio audience. Sally Jessy Raphael, who honed her interviewing skills on radio, where she had a talk show of her own for years, differs in style from the other talk show hosts in behaving more emotionally and empathizing openly with guests who are distressed. The show began in 1983 with a half hour format and, as its ratings grew, expanded to an hour in 1988. It is produced and distributed by Multimedia. Burt Dubrow is the executive producer.

SALOMON, HENRY, JR. (d. 1957) ▶ distinguished producer and writer of documentaries, whose crowning achievement was probably *Victory at Sea,* an NBC series on the U.S. naval forces in World War II using archive film clips and featuring an original score by Richard Rodgers. Salomon also produced the noted early documentary on the Soviet Union *Nightmare in Red,* and another on Adolph Hitler, *Twisted Cross.* He shared in the credit for a documentary on atomic energy, *Three, Two, One—Zero.*

SAMISH, ADRIAN (d. 1976) ▶ producer associated with Quinn Martin Productions and Spelling-Goldberg Productions, joining the latter in 1975. With QM, where he worked for nine years, he was involved in the creation of such shows as *Cannon, Streets of San Francisco, Barnaby Jones, Dan August* and *Caribe.* He also produced pilots for a number of series, including *Manhunter, Travis Logan, D.A.* and *Crisis Clinic.* Before joining QM in 1966, he was a program v.p. for ABC in Hollywood.

SAMPLING ▶ the industry's perception of how viewers examine the shows. The start of a new season is considered to be a sampling period for three or four weeks, during which viewers try out the new entries before deciding whether to follow them regularly or switch to an established show on a competing channel. Programs which sample favorably—that is, achieve high ratings initially—usually have a good chance of succeeding; those sampling poorly have slim chances because they are destined to go largely undiscovered. Viewing patterns over the years indicate that audiences generally do not return to sampling activities once the season is underway.

Sampling, in another sense, is part of rating methodology. The audience surveys base their viewing estimates on what they hold to be a representative sample of the audience measured. The Nielsen household ratings, for example, are derived from a national sample of 1,200 homes equipped with Audimeters.

SANDBURG'S LINCOLN ▶ four one-hour specials derived from Carl Sandburg's biography of Abraham Lincoln, carried by NBC in 1974-75. Hal Holbrook portrayed Lincoln and Sada Thompson, Mary Todd Lincoln. The series was by David L. Wolper Productions, with Wolper as executive producer and George Schaefer as producer-director.

SANDERS, MARLENE ▶ veteran TV journalist who worked for ABC News and CBS News, and later for public television. Her career in television pre-dated the conscious effort of the networks and stations to hire women for conspicuous roles. She was the first woman to anchor a network evening newscast, which she did for ABC in 1964 as the substitute for the ailing Ron Cochran. She had also delivered a daytime ABC newscast for four years and was a correspondent in Vietnam. Sanders has the distinction also of having been the first network news vice president, receiving the title at ABC in January 1976 at the time she was named head of documentaries. She worked at ABC News from 1964-78, variously as correspondent, producer and executive.

She left in 1978 to become a correspondent for CBS News, working mainly as a producer and reporter for *CBS Reports.* When that unit was disbanded in the 1987 CBS cutbacks, Sanders joined the New York public television station, WNET, as host of several current events series. In 1991 she began working independently, primarily as host-narrator of a documentary series on the Third World, *Profiles in Progress,* for the Discovery channel. In 1988 she was co-author, with Marcia Rock, of the book *Waiting for Primetime: The Women of Television News.*

Sanders joined ABC after working in local New York television as a producer, writer and reporter. Among her early jobs was one with Mike Wallace on his landmark primetime news interview show on the old Dumont Network, *Night Beat.*

SANDO, ARTHUR R. ▶ vice president of corporate affairs for Communications Satellite Corp. (Comsat) since 1991, responsible for Congressional affairs, media, investors and community relations. He had joined Comsat Video Enterprises, a subsidiary, the previous year after a nine-year stint with Turner Broadcasting System, where he headed public relations and promotion. He had followed Robert Wussler, a top executive of the Turner organization, to CVE. Prior to joining Turner, Sando was press secretary to U.S. Rep. James M. Hanley (N.Y.), after having been a news reporter for broadcast stations in Syracuse and Philadelphia.

SANDRICH, JAY ▶ preeminent director of sitcoms, whose credits include *He and She* (1967), *The Mary Tyler Moore Show* (1970-77), *Soap* (1977-79), and *The Cosby Show*'s first two seasons (1984-86). He also directed the pilots of *The Odd Couple, WKRP in Cincinnati, The Golden Girls,* and the first two episodes of *Night Court,* a record of success that is a chief reason for his being Hollywood's most sought-after director of comedy pilots. His first major success was as producer of *Get Smart* (1965), an experience that made him realize he preferred directing.

Sandrich was the first sitcom director to make use of the three-camera film, a production technique now widely utilized, to obtain more intimate close-ups and unusual compositions.

In 1980 he directed the motion picture *Seems Like Old Times.* In 1987, he became the senior v.p. of Grant Tinker's short-lived GTG Productions.

Redd Foxx and Demond Wilson, stars of the NBC series *Sanford and Son*

SANFORD AND SON **▶** hit NBC situation comedy (1972-78) about a querulous old junk dealer and his son, which was adapted with a black cast from the British hit *Steptoe and Son.* Produced by Tandem Productions (Norman Lear and Bud Yorkin), it premiered as a midseason replacement and was instantly popular. Redd Foxx and Demond Wilson were the principals, Fred Sanford and Lamont Sanford. Featured were Whitman Mayo as Grady Wilson, Slappy White as Melvin and LaWanda Page as Aunt Esther. Both *Sanford* and *Steptoe* were created by Ray Galton and Alan Simpson.

When Foxx left the series in 1977 to begin a weekly variety show on ABC, the program was continued under the title *Sanford Arms.* But it foundered and failed to last out the 1977-78 season. Foxx's ABC variety show also failed.

SANTA BARBARA ▶ see Soap Operas.

SAP (SEPARATE AUDIO PROGRAM) ▶ an audio channel that can be received by sets equipped for stereophonic television and used for a separate soundtrack, either for stereo sound or for reception in another language.

SAPAN, JOSHUA ▶ president and chief operating officer of the National Services Division of Rainbow Program Enterprises, the Cablevision Systems subsidiary that operates the Bravo and American Movie Classics (AMC) cable networks. A film buff in college at the University of Wisconsin, Sapan began his career in specialized radio program marketing, then moved to cable marketing at Time Inc.'s Manhattan Cable TV system, before ending up in pay TV marketing at Viacom's Showtime movie service. Rising through marketing and creative services, Sapan joined Rainbow in 1987. His American Movie Classics channel successfully made a move from a pay service to a commercial-free basic-cable network in 1990, a transition that Bravo has been attempting as well.

SARA ▶ one of several unsuccessful attempts to revive the western in the 1970s; this one, introduced by CBS in January 1976, had the special angle of a female lead: Brenda Vaccaro as schoolteacher Sara Yarnell. Featured were Louise Latham as Martha Higgins, Bert Kramer as Emmet Ferguson and Albert Stratton as Martin Pope. It was by Universal TV.

SARNOFF, DAVID (d. 1971) ▶ one of the pioneers in the development of broadcasting who rose from a wireless operator to chairman of the Radio Corporation of America and founder of its subsidiary, the National Broadcasting Co. Advancing through the ranks of RCA in the 1920s after it absorbed his employer, the Marconi Co., Sarnoff, on becoming president, made the company a leader in the manufacture of radio sets (and, later, TV sets as well) and of electronic parts and equipment.

He created the NBC network in 1926 to provide a program service that would stimulate the sale of radios and in the 1940s organized the TV network to build a market for RCA television receivers. At various intervals, he doubled as president of the National Broadcasting Co. Not long after the FCC approved the RCA color system to serve as the basis for color TV in the U.S., Sarnoff had NBC-TV completely in color to help sell RCA's color TV line.

Sarnoff, a Russian immigrant, came into national prominence on the night of April 14, 1912, when, as a wireless operator in Manhattan, he allegedly received the first distress signal from the sinking S.S. Titanic and maintained contact with the ship. Subsequently, he worked for the Marconi Co. and held the title of commercial manager at the time it was taken over by RCA in 1919.

After nearly 20 years in the presidency, he became chairman in 1947. Sarnoff retired in 1970 but was elected honorary chairman, in which capacity he served until his death.

SARNOFF, ROBERT W. ▶ son of General David Sarnoff who, in January 1970, succeeded his father as chairman and chief executive officer of RCA, crowning a career that began in the NBC sales department in 1948 and included tenures as president and chairman of NBC. Sarnoff resigned from RCA in 1975, on pressure from members of the board, after a period of decline for the electronic manufacturing division.

Sarnoff became president of NBC Dec. 7, 1955, when Sylvester L. (Pat) Weaver moved up to board chairman. In 1958 Sarnoff became chairman and Robert E. Kintner president, beginning an era of great profitability for the TV network and stations and of the dramatic rise in the stature of NBC News. In 1965 Sarnoff moved up to RCA as its president. Throughout his 10 years with the parent company, Sarnoff maintained direct supervision of NBC.

Under Sarnoff, RCA kept pace with the exploding electronic technology of the 1970s and moved into the development and production of miniature integrated circuits, weather and communications satellites, control systems, portable moon cameras and the videodisc, among other products. But the company's share of the TV receiver market was seriously eroded by Japanese manufacturers, and RCA was forced to collapse its computer manufacturing operations at a huge loss.

SARNOFF, THOMAS W. ▶ executive v.p. in charge of NBC, West Coast (1962-77), and youngest son of the late *pater familias* of RCA and NBC, Brig. Gen. David Sarnoff. When he resigned in the spring of 1977 to form his own company, Sarnoff International Enterprises, engaged in the production of arena and stage shows, NBC was left for the first time without a Sarnoff in its management echelons.

Tom Sarnoff began his career with ABC as a floor manager in 1949 and two years later went to MGM Studios. In 1952 he joined NBC as assistant to the director of finance and operations and then began to move into executive posts in production and business affairs. He became a v.p. in 1957. As West Coast head of NBC, he was responsible for all functional operations but principally gave his time to administration, business affairs and labor relations.

A Westar Satellite

SATELLITE ▶ also known as communications satellite, orbiting space vehicle used to relay electronically encoded communications services—including television, voice or teletype—over long distances. Synchronous communications satellites, used to relay television signals across oceans and domestically (as a substitute for microwave and coaxial relays), are precisely located at 22,300 miles above the equator, orbiting the earth, but traveling at the same rotation speed as the earth directly below them. Therefore, a synchronous satellite is considered to be in "stationary" orbit, since it always hovers at the same place in the sky.

All communications satellites launched since 1963, except the Soviet Union's Molniya series, are of the synchronous type. Communications satellites receive electromagnetic signals aimed at them from earth stations, then amplify and retransmit them to other earth stations. Because electromagnetic waves of the bandwidth and frequencies used for television generally follow a "line-of-sight" pattern (that is, they do not bend with the curvature of the earth), the satellite must be "visible" from both the transmitting and receiving locations.

The first successful communications satellite, launched by NASA Aug. 12, 1960, was Echo I, a 100-foot balloon, placed in elliptical random orbit. It was a "passive" satellite—that is, it carried no electronic equipment and signals were "bounced" from its surface. The first relay of black-and-white and color television by satellite was accomplished by AT&T's Telstar in 1962. Telstar also followed a random orbit (although it was an "active" satellite) and therefore it could only be used for short and specific periods when both transmitting and receiving locations were in its "line of sight."

Syncom II, launched in 1963, was the first successful synchronous satellite. Commercial satellite communications became a reality with the orbiting of Early Bird (Intelsat I) in 1965, which was the first satellite owned by the International Telecommunications Satellite Consortium. The first domestic synchronous communications satellite was Canada's Anik I, launched in November 1972.

Cable-TV systems make extensive use of domestic satellites for television transmission, and satellite interconnection was the key reason for the medium's surge of growth in the late 1970s. The advent of satellites created the first national networking system for cable TV, stimulating the development of a wide variety of new programs and services that made cable attractive in urban areas, where retransmission of broadcast signals could not provide a sufficient subscriber base. Satellite communications also revolutionized television networking by replacing AT&T's land-line relays with a lower-cost, more efficient system.

SATELLITE STATION ▶ a conventional TV station that receives and rebroadcasts programs from another station, essentially extending the signal of the parent station to communities beyond its reach. Unlike translators, satellites are full-fledged outlets and may operate at maximum powers permitted for TV stations. For many years, the FCC decided each request for satellite status on the basis of detailed presentations designed to prove that a full-service station could not survive in the community of license, and it limited total program origination to 5% of the program schedule. In 1991, the commission substituted a simpler set of presumptions making it easier to obtain satellite status, and it repealed the 5% rule.

Satellite stations maintain the merest facilities and operate with small staffs, chiefly technical. Most of them justify their licenses with local newscasts separate from those of the parent stations.

Recent cast members of *Saturday Night Live*

SATURDAY NIGHT LIVE ▶ successful experiment by NBC (1975—) in creating a showcase for young comedians whose material might be too sophisticated or irreverent to be suitable for prime time. The live 90-minute program, originating from New York, was presented at 11:30 p.m. three Saturdays a month (yielding to the newsmagazine *Weekend* the fourth) and became immediately popular with youthful viewers, thus creating a new profit center for the network. The show premiered Oct. 11, 1975, with George Carlin as guest host (subsequent guests included Candice Bergen, Elliot Gould, Lily Tomlin, Kyle MacLachlan, Andrew Dice Clay and—several times—Buck Henry) and with a resident cast that came to be headed by Chevy Chase. Others were Dan Aykroyd, John Belushi, Jane Curtin, Garrett Morris, Laraine Newman, Gilda Radner and Michael O'Donoghue. Chase developed a following for his satirical newscast and impressions of a clumsy President Ford; he left the show in 1976 to pursue his career independently. He was replaced by Bill Murray.

The show was developed for NBC by Dick Ebersol, programming vice president, and was produced by Lorne Michaels and directed by Dave Wilson.

During the 1979-80 season, Belushi and Aykroyd left the show to work in movies separately and as a team, and Lorne Michaels gave notice of his own departure in 1980. This resulted in the rest of the cast and most of the production staff leaving at the end of the season. Jean Doumanian was chosen to produce the series for the 1980-81 season with an entirely new cast headed by Charles Rocket, Denny Dillon, Eddie Murphy and Joe Piscopo. This new version was a disaster from the start; the critics treated it harshly, and the ratings began declining with the initial show. In danger of losing what had become an extremely valuable attraction, NBC reacted by firing Doumanian and rehiring Ebersol as producer in March 1981. He managed to get one program on the air before it was shut down for a complete overhaul.

By the start of the 1981-82 season, Ebersol had persuaded Michael O'Donoghue to return as head writer, and he also brought back a number of the original writers. He replaced everyone in the cast with the exception of Piscopo and Murphy and added Robin Duke, Mary Gross, Tim Kazurinsky, Christine Ebersole and Tony Rosato. After a wobbly start, *SNL* seemed back on the right track, raised its ratings to a respectable level and won renewal for the 1982-83 season.

Cast changes continued season after season. In the stream of young comedians in the early 1980s were Brian Doyle Murray, brother of Bill Murray, and Jim Belushi, brother of the late John Belushi. Also Julia Louis-Dreyfus, Brad Hall, Gary Kroeger, Harry Shearer, Pamela Stephenson, Christopher Guest, Rick Hall, Billy Crystal and Martin Short.

In 1985 Lorne Michaels returned as producer and the following fall brought in an entirely new cast: Joan Cusack, Robert Downey Jr., Nora Dunn, Anthony Michael Hall, Jon Lovitz, Randy Quaid, Terry Sweeney, Danitra Vance, Don Novello, A. Whitney Brown and Damon Wayans. Subsequent additions included Dana Carvey, Phil Hartman, Jan Hooks, Victoria Jackson, Dennis Miller, Kevin Nealon and Ben Stiller.

In addition to a wide variety of musical guests, *SNL* also features its own band, which has been led by Howard Shore, then Paul Shaffer, then G. E. Smith.

SATURDAY NIGHT LIVE WITH HOWARD COSELL ▶ an attempt by ABC in the fall of 1975 to recapture the essence of the early *Ed Sullivan Show* with a live, topical variety series featuring the acts and celebrities currently in vogue, both in the U.S. and abroad. Scheduled at 8 p.m. on Saturdays—teen time—with Howard Cosell as host (supposedly fueling the debate between his fans and detractors), it originated from the Ed Sullivan Theater in Manhattan and was placed under the supervision of the network's resident expert in live television, Roone Arledge, president of ABC sports. None of those touches, nor the hefty promotional campaign, availed. The program opened to poor ratings and died at mid-season. It was by Jilary Enterprises, with Don Mischer as director, Walter Kempley as head writer and Arledge as executive producer.

SATURDAY NIGHT REVUE ▶ comedy-variety hour of the early 1950s that showcased numerous comedians and was hosted first by Jack Carter and later by Eddie Albert and Hoagy Carmichael.

SAUDEK, ROBERT ▶ producer identified with cultural programming, his credits including *Omnibus, Profiles in Courage* and telecasts of the New York Philharmonic. He had been a v.p. of ABC in 1951 when the Ford Foundation hired him away as director of its TV-Radio Workshop, out of which came *Omnibus,* a show that contained the vision of public television. In 1957 Saudek founded his own company, Robert Saudek Associates. He later became president of New York's Museum of Broadcasting, established in 1976 by CBS chairman William S. Paley. He yielded the post to Robert Batscha in 1982.

SAUTER, VAN GORDON ▶ twice president of CBS News in the years between 1982-86, an inglorious period during which the network lost many of its esteemed journalists, its leadership position, and much of its prestige as well. Sauter was ousted in 1986, leaving behind an organization that scarcely resembled the prideful CBS News of yore. His star having fallen at CBS, Sauter moved back to the West Coast to work at creating shows for syndication.

Sauter was CBS's fastest-rising executive during the 1970s and was clearly destined for a high post in the company. The grooming process was extraordinary; few executives in television had been treated to such varied experience. Sauter was moved back and forth between local and network broadcasting. In a 10-year span, he was news director of WBBM-TV Chicago, Paris bureau chief for CBS News, vice president of program practices for the network, v.p. and general manager of KNXT Los Angeles, and president of CBS Sports. Before all this, he worked in radio news, both network and local, and for a time was a TV anchorman in Chicago.

Van Gordon Sauter

He was named president of CBS News upon Bill Leonard's retirement, and 20 months later was promoted to executive vice president of the CBS Broadcast Group, responsible for overseeing the owned-stations and news divisions. Ed Joyce was named to succeed him at CBS News but, in reporting to Sauter, was required to implement his policies. Another realignment in 1985 sent Sauter back a notch to his previous post as news president, and less than a year later he was replaced by Eric Ober.

Sauter was an anomaly in the CBS executive echelons because he wore a beard and liked to dress somewhat more casually than in dark business suits. He was an anomaly in the news division as well, because he did not hold to its revered traditions—what the veterans called "the Murrow tradition"—but instead seemed to prefer the style and values of local television news, which he had become steeped in. His aim was to modernize the division, to make it more adaptable to the changes that were occurring in television in the 1980s. But he knew the old guard of CBS News would resist the changes he wanted to make, so he systematically removed or shunted aside many of their number. Sauter's vision for a new CBS News did not bear fruit, and meanwhile the old organization was eviscerated.

SAVITCH, JESSICA (d. 1983) ▶ NBC News correspondent who joined the network in 1977 from Group W. She covered the Senate for NBC (1977-79) and then became a general assignment correspondent and principal writer-reporter for the Sunday edition of *Nightly News.* NBC recruited her from its Philadelphia affiliate, KYW-TV, where she had worked seven years on *Eyewitness News,* latterly as co-anchor. Savitch died in a freak auto accident in New Hope, Pennsylvania.

Diane Sawyer

SAWYER, DIANE ▶ co-anchor of ABC News's *PrimeTime Live* since joining the network in February, 1989, after leaving CBS's *60 Minutes,* where she had been co-editor. On *Prime-Time Live* Sawyer has been responsible for a number of investigative reports as well as interviews with frequently inaccessible world leaders. Her probes have included reports on patient neglect in the Veterans Administration health care system nationwide and an investigation of alcohol abuse by commercial and private airline pilots.

On August 20, 1991, she scored an impressive feat by being the first network correspondent to interview then-besieged Soviet leader Boris Yeltsin inside the Russian Parliament at the height of the attempted coup. Other high-profile Sawyer assignments have included co-anchoring a special live broadcast from the White House, where she joined President and Mrs. Bush for a tour of the family's private living quarters.

Prior to joining ABC News, Sawyer spent nine years at CBS News, where she provided reports for *60 Minutes,* CBS *Morning News,* CBS *Early Morning News, Morning with Charles Kuralt,* Walter Cronkite's *Universe* and CBS News specials. She was podium correspondent for the 1988 Democratic and Republican national conventions.

Before coming to CBS News, Sawyer held several administrative press positions in the Nixon administration and was part of the Nixon-Ford transition team from 1974-75. She also assisted former President Nixon in the writing of his memoirs. Sawyer began her broadcasting career in 1967 in Louisville, Kentucky, where she was a reporter for WLKY-TV. She is married to director Mike Nichols.

SAWYER, FORREST ▶ ABC News correspondent who is anchor for *World News Sunday* and who also reports for *Nightline,* often sitting in for Ted Koppel. During the Persian Gulf War, Sawyer was one of the first Western journalists to report from Baghdad after the invasion of Kuwait, filing the first live reports, hostage interviews and video from Iraq. He reported the story of the roundup of Americans in Baghdad to be used as human shields. While he was with Egyptian soldiers at the front, two Iraqi soldiers surrendered to his ABC camera crew.

Sawyer joined ABC News in 1988 as co-anchor of *World News This Morning* and the news segments on *Good Morning America.* From 1985-87 he was co-anchor of *CBS Morning News* after a stint as London correspondent for CBS News in 1986.

Prior to his television work, he was an anchor and reporter in radio news, including Atlanta's WGST Newsradio (1977-80), Gainseville, Florida's WDVH-AM (1975-77), and Boston's WVBF-FM (1974-75).

***SAY GOODBYE* ▶** David L. Wolper documentary on the disappearing animal species, telecast by NBC in 1970; it drew the wrath of the gun lobby for a scene in which a polar bear was shot from a helicopter and apparently killed. As it proved, the animal had only been shot with a drug so that it might be marked for research, and the pro-hunting forces charged that the scene was staged to discredit hunters. Giving credence to their argument was a sympathy-evoking scene of the mother bear's seemingly bereft cubs wandering about the frozen land.

The film and its outtakes were subpoenaed by the House Committee on Interstate and Foreign Commerce and were supplied by Wolper. But although the incident resulted in nothing more than an implicit reprimand, with NBC guiltless since it was not the producer, it nevertheless served to reinforce network policies against accepting nonfiction materials from outside producers because of the network's inability to vouch for their factualness.

Wolper maintained that he was presenting an essay and not a news report and that therefore he was entitled to some dramatic license. Moreover, he noted, the whole one-hour program was unjustly discredited for the five minutes that were devoted to the vanishing of animals by means of hunting.

The program had been narrated by Rod McKuen and was sponsored by Quaker Oats.

SCALE ▶ minimum wage permitted by the unions, AFTRA and SAG, for a TV performance or appearance. The rate varies with the type of performance and with the broadcast's origin—local, regional or network. There is one scale for principal performances, another for actors speaking fewer than five lines and another for extras. The scale is different for voice-over and on-camera work, and there are special minimums for dancers, singing groups and specialty acts.

SCALI, JOHN ▶ diplomatic correspondent during the 1960s and 1970s for ABC News who became a footnote in Cold War history for his role as courier during the Cuban missile crisis in 1962. A few days after President Kennedy threw down the gauntlet to the Soviet Union and raised the possibility of a nuclear war, Scali was contacted by an official of the Soviet embassy in Washington and asked to relay the terms of a possible deal: the U.S.S.R. might pull its missiles out of Cuba for a guarantee that the U.S. would not invade the country. Scali took the message to the State Department and then conveyed to his Soviet contact the response that the U.S. might consider such a resolution to the crisis. A few hours later, Kennedy received a cable from Soviet Premier Khrushchev formalizing the proposal.

While Scali was considered by many to have performed a national service in a time of crisis, the journalism profession was not wholly comfortable with the idea of a newsman acting as an informational go-between in behalf of governments.

Scali was brought into television from the Associated Press by James Hagerty, former press secretary to President Eisenhower, when Hagerty became head of ABC News.

SCAN LINE ▶ one line of the television picture. The NTSC television system in use in the U.S. has 525 lines to complete a picture; the European CCIR system has 625. The picture is scanned from left to right.

SCANAMERICA ▶ a "single-source" service launched in 1987 by Arbitron that combines data on television viewing with consumer purchasing from the same sample households. Arbitron people meters provide tuning and demographic viewing information, while a scanner wand waved over the UPC symbol by a consumer in the same household electronically records food and other purchases.

Arbitron first offered ScanAmerica as a local service in Denver, before moving into Phoenix, St. Louis and Pittsburgh in 1991. Arbitron is also putting together a national "single source" panel of 1,000 households drawn from New York, Los Angeles, Chicago, Atlanta and Dallas.

Nielsen has a similar service called Scantrack, a 15,000-household sample (expanding to 40,000 by 1992) to track consumer purchases of packaged goods. Nielsen combines people meters with Scantrack in a separate sample of 4,500 households. This service, however, is separate from Nielsen's panel of 4,000 people meter households used to report national ratings.

The "single source" concept is highly controversial and expensive. Nielsen, which is on both sides of the issue, is having enough trouble getting people to cooperate just with its people meters. It maintains that using a single-source service as the only currency for program ratings is unreliable. Arbitron, however, maintains that single source represents a significant leap forward in the evolution of market research.

SCANDINAVIA ▶ a region whose countries were long considered by other European broadcasters to have the most boring television on the continent. Sweden, Norway, Denmark and Finland were steadfast in maintaining only state-run networks, with lots of culture and little entertainment, and with hardly any commercial involvement. Sweden, until the 1990s, had allowed no television advertising at all. Because Scandinavian television was so severe, the countries were among the world's hottest markets for home video sales.

But by the late 1980s the Scandinavian group had to concede to the realities of the Satellite Age, and all began loosening their policies for commercial television. The trigger may well have been Kinnevik-owned TV3 (formerly known as Scansat), which in the late 1980s began beaming a network of programming from England to cable households and satellite dishes in Sweden, Norway and Denmark. Cable penetration across the region is high, with all countries at more than 30%. The invasive channel was not only often watched by those who could receive it, but it also carried advertising. The governments of the countries affected began to reason that if anyone was going to be enriched by reaching their citizens with television, it should not be a company outside the country.

Denmark has created a national TV2 network made up of regional commercial stations. Norway has taken the step of licensing a commercial TV network and Sweden intends to, but by the end of 1991 neither country had yet determined how these new commercial systems would be run and what the terms of ownership should be. Finland has started a commercial network, MTV, but it rents broadcasting time from the state network, YLE. Eventually it will move to its own plant and have its own frequency.

One reason for the slowness in building commercial systems in Scandanavia is that the region is not densely populated. The total number of television homes in the four countries is just over 9 million.

SCANSAT ▶ commercial television network beamed from London to three Scandinavian countries by the Astra satellite, penetrating a region that has been slow to adopt advertising-supported television or mass-audience entertainment programming. It is known in Denmark, Sweden and Norway as TV3 and is received by cable systems and satellite dishes in those markets.

Scansat was organized in 1986, a creation of Swedish conglomerate Kinnevik, which owns a 10% share of Astra. It began sending its signal from London in late 1987, initially over one channel to Sweden and Denmark. The following year Norway allowed it to be received on its cable systems. By 1991 it was transmitting on three Astra transponders, one for each country. Although the core program schedule is the same on each transponder, separating them allows for a better targeting of advertising and for the sale of local spots in each territory.

In 1989 Kinnevik launched a companion pay movie channel, TV1000, which is also transmitted to Scandinavia via Astra. In July 1991 TV1000 merged with a satellite pay-TV rival, SF Succe. At the same time, Scansat changed its name to TV3 Broadcasting Group. In 1991 the Kinnevik group entered a bid for the license to operate Sweden's first terrestrial commercial TV station.

SCARED STRAIGHT **▶** powerful hour-long documentary, syndicated in the spring of 1979, on a unique project at New Jersey's Rahway State Prison in which convicts sentenced to life confront juvenile offenders in "shock therapy" sessions to scare the crime out of them. Although it played on TV and not in movie houses, the film won an Oscar that year for short subjects; it also scored tremendous ratings, even on independent stations where it faced prime-time network competition. The Signal Companies, which sponsored the program without commercial interruptions, scheduled a repeat a few months later. The documentary carried an advisory because of the street language used and because of the brutal, searing nature of the confrontations.

Arnold Shapiro was producer and director, and Peter Falk the host and narrator.

SCARLET LETTER, THE **▶** serial adaptation of Nathaniel Hawthorne's 19th-century classic, produced by WGBH Boston and presented on four consecutive nights in April 1979. Conceived and produced by Rick Hauser, it featured Meg Foster as Hester Prynne, Kevin Conway as Roger Chillingworth and John Heard as the Reverend Arthur Dimmesdale.

While it was not generally considered a critical success, the serial enjoyed the highest ratings of any PBS drama series in the 1978-79 season. Several aspects of the production were blamed for the artistic shortcomings of the project, among them the system of "step funding" by which the government underwrites public television programs. This system not only interfered with the creative processes but caused the project to take 4 1/2 years to complete. The rationale for step funding is protection of public funds, but in this instance, as it has in several others, the process turned out to be an outrageously expensive form of insurance.

The four-step process follows this form: a planning grant to investigate the need for the project; then a research and development grant to cover script development costs; then a pilot grant to finance production of a pilot film; and finally a production grant to produce the work. A formal proposal is required at each of these steps, and often the proposals run longer, and are more time-consuming, than the scripts themselves. In the case of *The Scarlet Letter,* the R&D grant proposal alone ran 300 pages.

The National Endowment for the Humanities, a council of 26 Senate appointees, provided the seed money and reviewed the grant proposals for *The Scarlet Letter*. In the spirit of protecting public funds, the Endowment engaged 32 scholar-consultants to review the work from proposal to final script. They also reviewed the contributions of 16 scholar-consultants who were retained by the production team.

The Scarlet Letter went through two writers to qualify for the production grant. Allan Knee, who took the script through two years of proposals and scholar-dictated revisions, was sacrificed when the Endowment held up approval of the production request. Reviewers for the Endowment could not agree on the production's interpretation of the novel. Finally, Alvin Sapinsly was retained as writer, and his scripts were accepted and then produced.

SCATTER BUY ▶ advertising time purchased in a manner that would disperse commercials for a product over several programs on different nights of the week, as opposed to straight sponsorship, wherein the ads are concentrated within a single show.

SCENES FROM A MARRIAGE **▶** Ingmar Bergman's celebrated six-part series for Swedish TV on the disintegration of a once "ideal" marriage, broadcast in Sweden in the spring of 1973 and in the U.S. on public television in 1977. Before it played on PBS—in a dubbed version for the first outing and with subtitles for the repeats later in the week—it had been presented theatrically in America as an abridged two-and-a-half-hour movie.

The leads were played by Liv Ullman and Erland Josephson, with Bibi Andersson and Jan Malmsjo in the supporting cast. Bergman wrote and directed the series, and Lars-Owe Carlberg was executive producer.

SCHAEFER, GEORGE L. ▶ producer-director of quality drama, both for TV and the Broadway stage, who had a long and distinguished association with *Hallmark Hall of Fame* (1955-68) and also produced for *CBS Playhouse*. His dozens of productions for TV, most of them under the aegis of his Compass Productions, included *Little Moon of Alban, Macbeth, Victoria Regina, Do Not Go Gentle Into That Good Night, In This House of Brede* and the series *Sandburg's Lincoln*. He was also executive producer of the short-lived *Love Story* series on NBC in the early 1970s. He continued to be active in the 1990s directing quality made-for-TV movies.

SCHAFFNER, FRANKLIN ▶ producer and director of live TV drama in the "golden age" who went on to direct movies (*Patton, The Best Man, The Stripper*). He was one of the giants of video theater in the 1950s and early 1960s as director for *Studio One* (1948-56), *Ford Theater* (1951-52), *Person to Person* (1956-58) and *Playhouse 90* (1958-60), and producer-director of *The Kaiser Aluminum Hour* (1958) and *DuPont Show of the Week* (1963-65).

SCHENKEL, CHRIS ▶ ABC sports commentator whose wide range of announcing assignments included NCAA football, golf championships, the Professional Bowlers Tour and the summer Olympic Games (since 1968). For nine years prior to his exclusive association with ABC, he regularly reported the Triple Crown events of horse racing on CBS and NBC, in addition to golf tournaments and heavyweight fights. He made his start in network television in 1952 when ABC hired him to replace the ailing Ted Husing for the Monday night boxing shows. That assignment lasted six years.

SCHERER, RAY ▶ NBC correspondent in Washington and London (1947-75) who in 1976 became Washington v.p. for the parent company, RCA.

SCHERICK, EDGAR J. ▶ onetime program chief for ABC-TV who left New York in the late 1960s to become a Hollywood producer. He did well and has been prolific, both in motion pictures and television. Scherick has worked essentially as an independent, though he became engaged in partnerships for periods of time or for individual projects. In the late 1980s he joined with Saban Entertainment to form Saban-Scherick Productions, which has made such one-shot programs as *The Phantom of the Opera* and *The Girl Who Came Between Them*. Previously, Scherick produced the miniseries *Evergreen* and such TV movies as *Unholy Matrimony, The Stepford Children, Hands of a Stranger, Anything to Survive, On Wings of Eagles, Hitler's SS: Portrait of Evil, The Stranger In My Bed,* and *The High Price of Passion.*

SCHIEFFER, BOB ▶ anchor of CBS News's *Face the Nation* and the Saturday Edition of the *CBS Evening News*. He is also the chief Washington correspondent for CBS News. Schieffer has covered Washington for CBS News for 23 years and is one of the few broadcast or print journalists to have covered all four major beats in the capital: the White House, the Pentagon, the State Department, and Capitol Hill.

He has been chief Washington correspondent since 1982 and congressional correspondent since 1989. His anchoring of the Saturday edition of the *CBS Evening News,* which dates back to November 1976, is said to be the longest tenure for an anchor of a regularly scheduled network news broadcast. Schieffer's calm, measured on-camera presence—especially when responding to questions of interpretation or prognosis on major stories posed by such anchors as Walter Cronkite, and later, Dan Rather—has, in the venerable CBS tradition, made him a trusted figure to the viewer.

Before CBS News, Schieffer was with the *Fort Worth Star-Telegram,* reporting in 1965 from Vietnam for that newspaper. Later, he became news anchor at WBAP-TV Fort Worth/Dallas, before eventually joining CBS News.

SCHILDHAUSE, SOL ▶ first chief of the FCC's Cable Television Bureau who resigned early in 1974 after a 25-year career on the commission staff. In the 1960s he headed the cable-TV task force that later became the bureau. His outspoken advocacy of cable was a source of concern to broadcasters and some members of the FCC.

SCHLATTER, GEORGE ▶ variety show producer who made his mark in the late 1960s as executive producer of *Rowan & Martin's Laugh-In.* Then, in the same capacity, he did *The New Bill Cosby Show* and the *Cher* series. He developed and became executive producer of NBC's highly successful *Real People.* Schlatter remained active in the 1980s variously as producer, director, writer and star of variety shows and specials, including *Salute to Lady Liberty* and *Humor and the Presidency,* as well as series, including *George Schlatter's Comedy Club, George Schlatter's Funny People,* and *Real Kids.* His 1989 *Comedy Club Special* is noted for giving rise to Roseanne Barr, now Roseanne Arnold, TV's current outspoken comedy queen.

SCHLIEFF, HENRY ▶ chairman and chief executive of Viacom's Broadcast and Entertainment Groups, overseeing the company's television program production and syndication, its licensing and merchandising, and its group of five TV stations and 14 radio stations. A lawyer who began his career with the New York firm of Davis, Polk and Wardwell, he became Viacom's communications attorney in 1978. In 1981 he left Viacom to become director of business affairs at HBO, having established a friendship with the network's then-director of entertainment programming, Frank Biondi. He returned to Viacom in 1987, after Sumner Redstone purchased the company and recruited Biondi to run it.

SCHLOSSER, HERBERT ▶ former president of NBC (1974-78), after which he became executive v.p. of the parent company, RCA Corporation, responsible for developing the initial line of software for the forthcoming line of video disc playback units. In 1981 he was put in charge of a new RCA group consolidating all entertainment operations—RCA Records; SelectaVision; video discs and cassettes; the partnership with Rockefeller Center in RCTV, the new pay-cable network; and the partnership with Columbia Pictures in international disc and cassette distribution. He left to become an investment banker with Werthheim/Schroeder.

His rise to the top of NBC was steady, ever since his first job with the company, as an attorney for the syndication subsidiary in 1957. Highly competitive and outgoing, and with a background in the program area of television, Schlosser brought to the company an aggressive management style that had been lacking for nearly 10 years. He was named chief executive officer in February 1977.

On graduating from Yale Law School, Schlosser entered a Wall Street law practice and later joined Phillips, Nizer, Benjamin, Krim and Ballon, a New York law firm with a large motion picture and television practice. He left in 1957 to become an attorney for California National Productions, then the syndication arm of NBC.

That led to a position as v.p. of programs on the West Coast for the TV network. In 1973 he was transferred to New York as executive v.p. of NBC-TV and in the summer of the year was named president of the network. Schlosser is credited with authorizing the successful NBC experimental programs *Tomorrow* and *Saturday Night Live.*

SCHMERTZ, HERBERT ▶ possibly the leading TV impresario from the advertising side during the 1970s, as v.p. of public affairs for the Mobil Corporation. He was responsible for creating such PBS series as *Masterpiece Theater, The Nader Report, Mystery* and *The Way It Was* and for the annual ad hoc networks of commercial TV stations for such series as *Ten Who Dared, Between the Wars* and *Edward the King.* These were in addition to network specials and a number of national radio series.

Flamboyant and outspoken, unusual traits for the chief spokesperson of a major corporation, Schmertz mounted his campaign of cultural television at a time in the national energy crisis when the soaring profits of oil companies made them highly suspect to the public at large. That negative image, in Mobil's case, was counterbalanced by the company's new projection as the good provider of such outstanding British series as *Cakes and Ale, Upstairs, Downstairs, Poldark, Lillie* and *I, Claudius.* Other oil companies such as Exxon, Gulf and Arco followed Mobil's lead into public television as program underwriters, which inspired the PBS nickname of the "Petroleum Broadcasting System." Schmertz left Mobil in the 1980s to start his own public relations company.

SCHMIDT, ROBERT ▶ former president of National Cable Television Association (1975-79). Previously, he had been a lawyer in Washington with clients in professional sports and earlier was a public affairs executive for ITT. An accomplished college athlete, he'd had a brief professional football career with the New York Titans, a team that preceded the Jets. From 1961 to 1964 he worked in various staff positions with the Democratic National Committee.

SCHNEIDER, ALAN ▶ one of the leading directors of avant-garde plays who received his grounding in TV in the 1950s. His work for television has included *Pullman Car Hiawatha* in 1951, *Oedipus Rex* in 1958, Samuel Beckett's *Eh, Joe?* in 1966 and Elie Wiesel's *Zalmen, or the Madness of God* in 1976.

SCHNEIDER, ALFRED R. ▶ long time ABC corporate executive who, since 1972, has been v.p. with administrative responsibility for the Standards and Practices department and chairman of the Corporate Contributions Committee of ABC Inc. His title was expanded in 1986 to that of v.p. of Policy and Standards.

For the ten previous years he was v.p. and assistant to the executive vice president of ABC Inc., and before that v.p. in charge of administration for the TV network. A lawyer, he joined ABC in 1952 as a member of the legal department. He was with CBS from 1955 to 1960, first in business affairs and then as executive assistant to the president of the network. He rejoined ABC in a similar capacity.

SCHNEIDER, JOHN A. ▶ former president of the CBS Broadcast Group (1966-77) who was deposed in the management upheaval that made Gene F. Jankowski his successor in October 1977. Schneider, who had been one of the most powerful figures in broadcasting and who for a time was considered heir-apparent to the presidency—if not the chairmanship—of the corporation, left CBS in April 1978 to pursue other ventures. In 1979 he became president of Warner Amex Satellite Entertainment Corp (WASEC), the software subsidiary of Warner Amex Cable. There he had overall responsibility for the Movie Channel, Nickelodeon, Music Television and other cable networks under development by the company. They were subsequently sold to Viacom.

Schneider rose from relative obscurity in 1965 when, as a station manager, he was named to succeed the legendary Jim Aubrey as president of the CBS television network. A low-keyed executive of impeccable reputation, he was at the time the diametrical opposite of Aubrey in the company—businesslike, outgoing and ingratiating. He had been v.p. and general manager of WCBS-TV New York and before that of WCAU-TV Philadelphia. Until then his background had been entirely in broadcast sales, beginning in 1949 in his home town, Chicago, with WGN.

A successful year as network president earned him the promotion as head of the newly created broadcast group. In 1969 he appeared to be the leading candidate to replace Frank Stanton as corporate president when he was appointed executive vice-president of CBS Inc. But when the plans were changed, and the new president brought in from outside the company, Schneider returned to his previous post as president of the broadcast group.

His brush with controversy occurred during 1966 when Fred W. Friendly, then president of CBS News, charged Schneider with denying air time for the coverage of the Senate hearings on the Vietnam war in order to carry the commercially productive reruns of *I Love Lucy.* Friendly's resignation from CBS was tied to that episode. Schneider insisted that he was wronged, and that Friendly's departure was prompted by a change in his relationship with top management rather than by the denial of air time.

SCHOENBRUN, DAVID (d. 1988) ▶ foreign correspondent for CBS News (1945-62), based in France for most of those years, after which he became chief correspondent in the Washington bureau for a year. After that, he became a correspondent and commentator for broadcast groups such as Metromedia, and a freelance journalist.

SCHOLASTIC PRODUCTIONS ▶ television production arm of publishing concern Scholastic Inc. that was organized in 1979 by Martin J. Keltz, a former high school English teacher. In the mid-1970s Keltz became publisher of *Media and Methods* magazine, which promoted the use of audio/visual applications in education. He took this concept to Scholastic in 1978 and began producing and coproducing family-oriented shows for network and syndication. The series *My Secret Identity* won an International Emmy in 1989 as well as an Action for Children's Television award.

SCHONFELD, REESE ▶ founding president and CEO of the Cable News Network (1979-82), hired when he brought an idea for a 24-hour news channel to Ted Turner at the very time the Atlanta magnate was thinking of creating such a channel. Schonfeld chose the anchors and other personnel, created the schedule and designed the presentation. His no-nonsense approach to journalism, which stressed scoring news beats, helped make CNN one of the leading news organizations in the U.S. in a remarkably brief period of time.

Schonfeld left after a dispute with Turner and joined Chuck Dolan's Cablevision Systems Inc., where he developed a program on books with Bill Small and Chris Chase in 1985 that was exploratory to creating a book channel that never came about. Then he founded News 12 for Cablevision's Long Island systems, the first all-news local cable service. In broadcast TV, he produced *People Magazine on TV* for CBS and the syndicated *Crime Watch Tonight* for Orion.

Prior to joining CNN, Schonfeld was managing director of the Independent Television News Association (ITNA), which delivered a satellite news service to subscribing stations. ITNA's original four clients grew to 35 by the time Schonfeld left to join CNN. He had begun his career with UPI, where he rose from copy boy to vice president and managing editor of UPI Television News.

In later years, Schonfeld has been a consultant to such media corporations as Time Warner, the Chicago Tribune Corp. and Whittle Communications. He is chairman of an American company, Sovfoto, which has exclusive rights to market and distribute Tass news photos throughout the world.

***SCHOOLHOUSE ROCK* ▶** umbrella title for five-minute animated series on educational subjects designed for insertion in ABC's Saturday and Sunday morning children's schedules. The series began in 1972 with *Multiplication Rock* and added *Grammar Rock* and *America Rock,* on history, in subsequent seasons. General Foods and Nabisco were sponsors. It was produced by Scholastic Rock Inc., with Tom Yohe as executive producer and Phil Kimmelman and Associates directing the animation.

SCHORR, DANIEL ▶ former CBS newsman known for his investigative skills, whose frequent involvement in journalistic controversies climaxed with one that cost him his job at the network. In February 1976, after reporting on the contents of a secret report by the House Intelligence Committee on improper activities of the CIA and FBI, Schorr passed on the full document to the New York weekly *Village Voice* for publication. Schorr and the *New York Times* had already covered the essentials of the report, but the House nevertheless voted to classify it as secret.

Schorr, who had been with CBS News for 23 years, had advised officials of the company that he meant to find publication somewhere for the copy of the report that had been leaked to him; yet, on the day it appeared in the *Voice,* he denied having been the source. A day later, he did admit to having passed it along. What occurred during the day of denial made it difficult for CBS to retain his services. He was suspended from reporting on Feb. 18, 1976, pending the resolution of a congressional inquiry into the leaking of the secret report.

CBS indicated at the time that it would defend Schorr's right to protect his sources and that it would pay for his defense in the event of a congressional subpoena (which came in August). But there was a strong hint in the terse official statement that he might not be reinstated at the network even if the probe were to end satisfactorily.

In the large sphere, the issue was whether a reporter had the right to override the judgment of Congress and to determine on his own that the people's right to know demanded publication. But at CBS, that issue came down to one of whether the reporter who received the material got it as an independent journalist or as an agent of CBS News; if as the latter, then it should have been up to CBS News and not Schorr to decide whether to preempt the judgment of Congress and have the material published.

While that was a question that haunted the episode, it was not the critical issue in Schorr's relations with the network. On the day of publication, when Schorr denied having had a role in it, suspicion in the Washington bureau fell upon Lesley Stahl, a correspondent who was linked romantically with Aaron Latham, an editor of the *Voice* who had written the preface to the transcript of the House report. It was thought by some that Stahl had taken the document from Schorr's desk and that she made photocopies of it for Latham. Not only had Schorr failed to put that rumor immediately to rest, he was said by some in the bureau to have initiated it.

Schorr later explained that his attorney had advised him to maintain silence that day until he could discuss his action with CBS officials in the presence of company lawyers. But CBS executives found it unforgivable that Schorr would allow a colleague to be unjustly accused of something as serious as stealing the materials.

Schorr's brilliant presentation before the congressional committee was hailed throughout the profession of journalism, and the committee thereupon dropped its investigation into the source of the leak. But just before he was to have entered into discussion with executives of CBS News on his future status, Schorr submitted to an interview on *60 Minutes* with Mike Wallace. Possibly to his surprise, the segment concentrated not on Schorr's great victory for journalism but rather on the tacky episode of his failure to disabuse CBS executives of their momentary suspicions about Stahl. Thus the internal issue at CBS in the Schorr affair was externalized before a national audience.

Soon afterwards Schorr resigned. The arrangement kept his salary in force for the remainder of his three-year contract. He went on to teach, lecture and write a book. In 1979, he signed on as chief anchor of Ted Turner's new Cable News Network. When his contract was not renewed in the mid-1980s, he became a regular commentator for National Public Radio.

SCHOUMACHER, DAVID ▶ news correspondent for CBS and ABC who became anchor for Washington station WMAL-TV in February 1976. A Chicagoan, he worked at TV stations there and in Oklahoma until he was hired to work out of the CBS Washington bureau in 1963. After a nine-year stint, which included a period in Vietnam, he switched to ABC News, again dividing his time between Vietnam and Washington, until WMAL lured him away. He had the reputation of a hard-working and scrupulous reporter and newsfilm producer who, unlike some, always did his own writing.

SCHULBERG, STUART (d. 1979) ▶ executive producer for NBC News who for eight years (1968-76) was producer of the *Today* show, the longest anyone has held that post. His assignment, on leaving *Today,* was to produce documentaries.

Schulberg, brother of novelist Budd Schulberg, joined NBC in 1961 as co-producer with Ted Yates of *David Brinkley's Journal.* In 1965 he became producer of *NBC Sports in Action.* His early documentaries include the *Angry Voices of Watts* (1966), *The Air of Disaster* (1966), *Losers Weepers* (1967), *The New Voices of Watts* (1968) and *Somehow It Works.*

SCHULLER, ROBERT ▶ television preacher in the tradition of Norman Vincent Peale who preaches self-esteem and positive thinking on a weekly syndicated series, *Hour of Power.* The series, which began in 1970, airs on 149 stations and the Armed Forces Network. Like other TV evangelists, Schuller buys the air time on every station that carries the program; unlike the others, he belongs to one of the mainline Protestant churches, the Reformed Church in America, although his denomination does not pay for his telecasts. *Hour of Power* developed a strong following because of Schuller's charismatic personality and his ability to combine psychological with spiritual guidance.

SCHULTZ, BARBARA ▶ executive generally associated with dramas of substance, in both public and commercial TV. In 1974 she became head of the PTV *Visions* project, with the title of artistic director, after grants totaling $6.2 million had been made by the National Endowment of the Arts, the Ford Foundation and CPB for a three-year series of original dramas for TV by American playwrights. The series went on the air in the fall of 1976. Earlier she had been producer of video tape drama for Universal Television. For a number of years she was with CBS, variously as executive producer of *CBS Children's Hour,* executive producer of *CBS Playhouse* and director of program development for the network. She had also been story editor on a number of CBS series, including *The Defenders, Trials of O'Brien* and *Armstrong Circle Theatre.* For a time, she served as consultant to CTW's *Electric Company.*

SCHULZ, CHARLES M. ▶ creator and cartoonist of the *Peanuts* comic strip; he has written all the scripts for the Charlie Brown animated specials derived from that source. He also serves as executive producer with Lee Mendelson and Bill Melendez.

SCHWAB, SHELLY ▶ president of MCA TV, the syndication arm of MCA/Universal. He oversees the division responsible for the station by station sale of off-network MCA series and TV movies, as well as the production of firstrun syndicated programming.

A one-time station manager of WAGA-TV Atlanta, he joined MCA in 1978 as v.p. and director of sales in New York and two years later became responsible also for the development of firstrun programming. He was transferred to MCA TV's Los Angeles office in 1986 and soon after was named president of the division.

SCHWARTZ, SHERWOOD ▶ situation comedy producer who, after a long association as writer for Red Skelton, created and produced such series as *Gilligan's Island, It's About Time* and *Dusty's Trail.* He was also executive producer of *The Brady Bunch* (1969-74), *The Brady Bunch Hour* (1977) and *The Brady Brides* (1981).

SCHWARTZ, WALTER A. ▶ former president of ABC Television (1972-1974); he left ABC in December 1975 to become president of the station division of Blair Television, a rep firm.

First to hold the title of president of ABC Television, a new post that was created in a reorganization, Schwartz had been appointed to it after a successful five-year tenure as president of the four ABC Radio networks. The position put him in charge of all television divisions of the company—network, owned stations and production subsidiaries. Schwartz was relieved of the position and named president of ABC Scenic Attractions, a nonbroadcast unit, when ABC-TV made a poor showing in the ratings in the fall of 1974.

SCHWARTZMAN, ANDREW JAY ▶ communications lawyer who has devoted himself to the public-interest sector since 1971, upon graduation from the U. of Pennsylvania Law School. Where others who were active in the broadcast reform movement of the 1970s moved on to more lucrative law practice in the 1980s, Schwartzman remained as head of the nonprofit Media Access Project (MAP), a Washington public-interest law firm founded in 1972, which Schwartzman joined as executive director in 1978. He is the last of the advocates for citizens' rights on telecommunications issues, and highly respected among his adversaries in the government and media establishment for the sobriety of his approach, as well as for his extensive knowledge.

While in law school, Schwartzman worked as an intern at the Center for Law and Social Policy, another public-interest firm, and found the field to his liking. After graduation, he went to work for one of the leading public-interest activists in the communications field, the Rev. Everett C. Parker, director of the Office of Communication of the United Church of Christ. Some four years later he moved to Washington for a post in the Department of Energy. And when he learned that MAP was looking for an executive director, he applied and has stayed ever since.

SCHWIMMER, WALTER (d. 1989) ▶ Chicago packager and producer of syndicated programs, among them *Championship Bowling, Championship Bridge, All-Star Golf* and *Let's Go to the Races.* He created a sports special event for the networks in *World Series of Golf* (1962) and attempted to make an annual TV series of the Nobel Prize awards, producing the network telecast in 1964 that proved to be the first and last. He sold his company, Walter Schwimmer Inc., to Cox Broadcasting in 1966.

***SCOTLAND YARD* ▶** early British import that played on ABC (1957) for 26 weeks. Edgar Lustgarten hosted the episodes, which were based on cases from the Yard's files. It was by Anglo Amalgamated Film.

SCOTT, WALTER D. ▶ chairman of NBC from April 1, 1966, to April 1, 1974, when he retired. He served briefly as president of the company and as president of the TV network. Scott maintained low visibility outside NBC and was not known for exceptional contributions to television except in the realm of sales. He rose in the company through the sales department, which he had joined in 1938, and became sales v.p. in 1955 and executive v.p. in 1959. He was president of the network for a year in 1965 before moving up to corporate.

SCOTT, WILLARD ▶ jolly weather reporter on NBC's *Today* since 1980, one of that program's most perennially popular personalities, although his segments are brief and his chatter vacuous. For all his depending on cliches and superlatives for everything and everyone, he is immensely likeable for his ebullience, folksiness, and self-effacing humor.

Scott is the personification of the clownish weatherman, the alternative to TV's scholarly meteorologists. He started in show business as a clown and was the original Ronald McDonald, the promotional character for the hamburger chain. He also did a stint in local television as Bozo the Clown.

In 1959 he became the funny-man weatherman on NBC's Washington, D.C., station WRC-TV, and soon was an institution in the capital. On the strength of his popularity there NBC plucked him for *Today*. In traveling about the country to deliver his weather reports from local festivals and country fairs, he has assumed an ambassadorial role for the network. His local appearances have served to strengthen the network's relations with its affiliates.

Scott had a shot at prime-time television during the 1980s with occasional appearances in *The Hogan Family*.

Willard Scott

SCOTTISH TELEVISION ▶ commercial licensee for central Scotland with headquarters in Cowcaddens, Glasgow and other studios in Edinburgh.

SCOURBY, ALEXANDER (d. 1985) ▶ actor considered by many the ideal narrator, and he performed that function hundreds of times on TV for documentaries and cultural and travel programs. He was used frequently by NBC for its *Project 20* specials and by David Wolper for the National Geographic documentaries. He was also one of the most financially successful voice-over actors in commercials in his time. Essentially a stage actor, he had running roles in such daytime soap operas as *The Secret Storm* and *All My Children* and had guest roles in a number of prime-time dramatic series.

SCRAMBLING ▶ altering a TV transmission by encryption so that the signal cannot be received without an operating decoder. Scrambling is vital to pay-television operations in restricting clear pictures to subscribing homes. A number of other satellite-delivered networks scramble their normal transmissions to keep them from being received gratis by satellite dish owners.

SCREEN ACTORS GUILD (SAG) ▶ union for performers in film, powerful in television because a majority of the programs are made on film. Many of the 73,000 members of SAG also belong to AFTRA, the performers union for live or video tape television, and the two have had numerous jurisdictional clashes since 1950. Talk of merging the unions, whose contracts have become fairly similar, has gone on since 1960 but has consistently been rejected by the SAG membership. SAG, which was formed in 1933 to represent performers against the abuses of motion picture studios and producers, has carried out television strikes four times. Its notable innovation has been the residual—the continuing compensation to actors and actresses as their TV films and commercials are reused in reruns. In 1960, after a six-week strike, SAG achieved a formula for payments to actors and actresses when their theatrical movies are sold to TV. A summertime strike in 1980 over the actor's share of home video rights disrupted the fall season and caused programs to premiere on staggered schedules.

The union presidents have included Ronald Reagan, Charlton Heston, Edward Asner, Patty Duke and, since 1987, Barry Gordon.

SCREEN GEMS (now COLUMBIA PICTURES TV) ▶ TV subsidiary of Columbia Pictures Corp. and one of the major program suppliers to the networks from the time the Hollywood film studios entered TV production in the late 1950s. Founded in 1951, Screen Gems was also a pioneer in TV syndication.

The company name was changed in 1976 to Columbia Pictures TV (CPT). John Mitchell, who was one of the fabled "supersalesmen" of the production field during the 1960s, was the executive longest identified with Screen Gems. He resigned as president of CPT in 1977.

***SCTV* (*SECOND CITY TV*) ▶** improvisational comedy show produced out of Toronto, in syndication for several years before NBC acquired it for a Friday late-night spot in the fall of 1981. NBC money bought better production values (including an improved laugh-track) and the network exposure seemed to give the performances a lift. The series was canceled in 1983.

Second City (distantly related to the Chicago improvisational troupe that provided a launching platform for Mike Nichols & Elaine May, Alan Arkin and many others) combined some of the wittiest writing to be seen on TV in years with superb ensemble acting by John Candy, Joe Flaherty, Eugene Levy, Andrea Martin, Rick Moranis, Catherine O'Hara, Dave Thomas and Martin Short. Moranis's and Thomas's extensive catalogue of parodies of comedians (Dick Cavett, Woody Allen, Rodney Dangerfield, Bob Hope and many others) was always a highlight. Moranis and Thomas gained some degree of cult fame in 1981-82 with their beer-swilling Canadian "Great White North" brothers, Bob and Doug McKenzie. Several of the comedians have since launched successful motion picture careers.

SCULLY, VIN ▶ veteran sportscaster who has broadcast the Brooklyn and then Los Angeles Dodgers games since 1950. In addition, as a member of CBS Sports since 1975, he did commentary for the National Football League telecasts and various golf tournaments. He also hosted the network's *Challenge of the Sexes* series and has co-hosted the Tournament of Roses Parade telecasts. In the entertainment sphere, he was the unseen narrator of a 1966 NBC comedy series *Occasional Wife,* the host of an NBC daytime panel show, *It Takes Two* (1969-70) and emcee of a 1973 variety program on CBS, *The Vin Scully Show,* which ran three months. He retired from his network assignments but continues to broadcast the Dodger's games.

SDA PRODUCTIONS ▶ French-Canadian production and facilities company whose origins trace to the early days of television, during the early 1950s. It was the first to offer French-language services and independent production facilities in Montreal. The company was known originally as Phoenix Studios, later took the name Omega and in more recent times changed it to SDA Productions.

As a production company, SDA has been one of Canada's most prolific. In 1990 it produced 350 hours of television and had sales of around $15 million. President of the company is Francois Champagne. He is also a shareholder, along with such other executives as Jacques Blain, Chantel Montgomery-Schell, Daniel and Sylvie Prouix and Louis-George Tetrault.

SEA HUNT **▶** one of the most successful series made expressly for syndication (1957-61), notable also for its excellent underwater photography. The series concerned the adventures of an ex-Navy frogman whose skills are used for underwater searches. Lloyd Bridges starred as Mike Nelson, and Ivan Tors was producer for Ziv-United Artists.

SEARCH FOR TOMORROW **▶** see Soap Operas.

SECA (SOUTHERN EDUCATIONAL COMMUNICATIONS ASSOCIATION) ▶ one of public broadcasting's four regional associations (with EEN, CEN and PMN). SECA, headquartered in Columbia, S.C., serves a membership of TV and radio stations in a 17-state area. Although SECA was the producer of record for William F. Buckley, Jr.'s *Firing Line,* it is not itself a producer of programs. Rather, it satellites programs, primarily instructional, to public TV and radio stations nationwide as well as directly to schools and state education departments. SECA is not to be confused with South Carolina's statewide network SCETV, also headquartered in Columbia.

SECAM ▶ *Sequence á Memoire* color system, developed by French commercial and government interests and first broadcast by France in 1967. It is incompatible with the German-developed PAL system, although they are both a 625-line screen, and the American NTSC, which is a 525-line system. The SECAM system has also been adopted by most middle-eastern and African countries in the French sphere of influence and, in modified form, by the Soviet Union and most Eastern European nations.

SECOND SEASON ▶ the period between late December and late February, when the networks attempt to bolster their schedules by canceling their failures and installing new series that may be contenders for the following fall. The term "second season" was coined by Thomas W. Moore while he was president of ABC-TV to herald extensive program changes his network was forced to make during one of its lesser years in the 1960s. By the early 1970s, revising schedules at mid-season had become common practice for all three networks, with each developing shows expressly for replacement service. Among the big hits that had been second season entries were *Batman, Rowan and Martin's Laugh-In* and *All in the Family.*

SECONDARI, JOHN H. (d. 1975) ▶ news correspondent for CBS and then ABC, who became an independent documentary producer with his wife, Helen Jean Rogers, in 1969. After heading the Rome bureau for CBS, he joined ABC in the late 1950s as Washington bureau chief. In 1961 he organized the network's first documentary unit, serving as executive producer of the *Saga of Western Man* series and as the ABC News liaison with Drew Associates on the *Close-Up* documentary series. At the time of his death he was preparing a Bicentennial series through his own company.

SECRET AGENT ▶ British series carried on CBS here (1965) about a professional spy on dangerous assignments around the world. By ATV, it starred Patrick McGoohan as John Drake.

SECRET STORM ▶ see Soap Operas.

SECTION 315 ▶ see Equal Time Law.

SEE IT NOW ▶ TV's first great documentary series and one that will probably never be exceeded for courage. While Sen. Joseph McCarthy was at the peak of his power, the series dared repeatedly to expose the injustices of McCarthyism and the viciousness of the senator in his zeal to discover communists and sympathizers. Indeed, the CBS series—a collaboration of Edward R. Murrow and Fred W. Friendly—contributed to the downfall of McCarthy, whose demagoguery exposed itself when he went on the program to respond to Murrow's attacks.

See It Now, which made its debut on Nov. 18, 1951, grew out of a radio series, *Hear It Now,* which in turn was inspired by a successful Murrow-Friendly record album, *I Can Hear It Now,* a collection of recorded history. Sponsored by Alcoa, the half-hour prime-time TV program began with fairly standard documentary subjects but drifted gradually to the controversial. In October 1953 the series created a national stir with *The Case Against Milo Radulovich,* pointing up the injustice to an Air Force reservist who was deemed a security risk and asked to resign his commission because his father and sister were suspected by unnamed accusers of having subversive tendencies. This became the first of several programs concerning McCarthyism. On March 9, 1954, *See It Now* offered a report on the senator himself consisting mostly of film clips of McCarthy that revealed his bullying tactics and reckless accusations of disloyalty and subversion. It was followed a week later by a program showing McCarthy badgering Annie Lee Moss, a suspected communist. On April 6 McCarthy went on the program to defend himself and denounce Murrow, and the newsman became a hero to some viewers and a traitor to others. The actual undoing of McCarthy occurred with the televised Army-McCarthy hearings, which began April 22, but the *See It Now* programs opened the way.

The series lost its sponsor, gained another and lost that one in the fall of 1957. It continued to deal with other controversial subjects and was considered by most critics the most distinguished news program of its time. CBS canceled it in 1958, removed Murrow from the forefront and replaced *See It Now* soon afterward with *CBS Reports.* Along with Murrow, who was commentator and writer, and Friendly, executive producer, those connected with *See It Now* included Palmer Williams, producer; Don Hewitt, director; Joe Wershba, producer-reporter; Don Hollenbeck, reporter; and Charlie Mack, cameraman.

SEGAL, ALEX ▶ drama director working between theater and TV, whose prominence in the latter dates to the early 1950s with *Pulitzer Prize Playhouse, Celanese Theater, U.S. Steel Hour* and others. He directed *My Father's House* for *CBS Playhouse* in the 1970s and, in the late 1960s, *Death of a Salesman, The Crucible* and *Diary of Anne Frank,* among others.

SEGELSTEIN, IRWIN B. ▶ former vice chairman of NBC (1981-1990) after having served in a variety of executive capacities from the time he joined the company in 1976. He then entered independent television production. Earlier he had been a high-ranking program executive with CBS (1965-73) and then president of CBS Records (1973-76). Segelstein proceeded up the ladder at both networks without apparent striving for higher office; always he was tapped for the next rung because he had the indicated skills, experience and integrity.

Two years after he joined NBC as executive v.p. of programs, his old friend and colleague Fred Silverman became president of the company; the two had worked together for many years and were neighbors in a Manhattan apartment building. Segelstein at once became Silverman's most trusted captain at NBC and took over large areas of corporate responsibility, including supervision of the radio and owned-stations divisions. It reflects Segelstein's abilities that when Silverman left the company, his successor, Grant Tinker, named Segelstein vice chairman, a higher post than he had held under Silverman.

Segelstein had been head of programming for Benton & Bowles Advertising when CBS recruited him in 1965 in a reorganization of the staff after the departure of James Aubrey as president. Segelstein signed on as v.p. of programs, New York, under Michael H. Dann, and in 1970 he became v.p. of program administration under Fred Silverman. Segelstein had been bypassed for Silverman to succeed Dann as head of programming for CBS.

When a scandal broke at CBS Records (the Columbia label) under the administration of Clive Davis, who subsequently was fired for alleged misuse of company funds, Segelstein was named to succeed him as president. And after NBC endured one of its most embarrassing seasons in the ratings (1975-76), it fired its program chief Marvin Antonowsky, and hired away Segelstein to become the executive in charge, with Paul Klein, reporting to him as head of the department.

SELF, WILLIAM ▸ president of the short-lived CBS Theatrical Films Group in the early 1980s, after having been a leading TV program figure in Hollywood through the 1960s and 1970s.

After working for CBS as an executive producer in the 1950s, Self joined Twentieth Century-Fox in 1959 as head of its television division and continued in that post for 15 years. After leaving Fox, he teamed with Mike Frankovich in producing theatrical movies but rejoined CBS two years later as program v.p. for the West Coast.

Eventually he became v.p. in charge of made-for-TV movies and mini-series for the network, overseeing 40 to 50 titles a season. His adeptness in this field contributed to the revival of CBS in the prime-time ratings and its return to dominance in the 1980s. It also established Self as the logical successor to Michael Levy as head of the theatrical films division.

During his years at Fox, Self was responsible for developing 44 television series that aired on the networks, including *M*A*S*H, Peyton Place, Room 222,* and *Batman.* In his early years with CBS, he was involved in developing *Twilight Zone.*

SELIGMAN, SELIG J. (d. 1969) ▸ a top ABC executive until his death, as head of Selmur Productions, the telefilm production arm of ABC that turned out such series as *Combat, Garrison's Gorillas, Day in Court* and *General Hospital.* Seligman was executive producer of those and other shows and a v.p. of ABC Inc.

With a law and theater administration background, he joined ABC in 1953 as a writer-producer and in 1955 became general manager of KABC-TV Los Angeles. Three years later he became a v.p. and soon afterword headed the network's production subsidiary.

***SELLING OF THE PENTAGON, THE* ▸** CBS News documentary (Feb. 23, 1971) on the Pentagon's promotional activities. It had jarring repercussions and was assailed at high levels of government. An attempt by a House committee to investigate its editing procedures nearly brought a contempt of Congress citation upon the president of CBS Inc., Frank Stanton. In the midst of the furor, however, the film—produced by Peter Davis with Roger Mudd as reporter and narrator—won a special Peabody award; Stanton later received RTNDA's Paul White Memorial Award for his courageous denial of Rep. Harley O. Staggers's subpoena for the outtakes, scripts and other materials used in the preparation of the documentary.

Although the documentary did not deal with the massive defense budget and its implications on the American economy, but concentrated on the use of federal funds to show off American weaponry at state fairs and other civic and social functions, the film was denounced by Vice-President Agnew as "a clever propaganda attempt to discredit the defense establishment" and by Rep. F. Edward Hebert, chairman of the House Armed Services Committee, as "one of the most un-American things I've ever seen on a screen."

The program became vulnerable not for its central argument—that funds were being improperly used to glorify the tools of war at the grassroots and to promote American might in the Cold War—but for a number of liberties taken in the editing process. Those included the discarding of qualifying phrases by some of the persons interviewed and the joining of statements made in a number of contexts as the single answer to a question. This method of excerpting brought complaints from Col. John MacNeil and Daniel Z. Henkin, Assistant Secretary of Defense for public affairs, both of whom claimed to be personally embarrassed by it.

The editing issue prompted Rep. Staggers, chairman of the House Interstate and Foreign Commerce Committee and of its subcommittee on investigations, to subpoena the outtakes and background materials. Stanton insisted that they were equal to a reporter's notes and therefore privileged and said he would turn over only the completed film. Eventually, the House voted down Staggers's proposed citation of Stanton for contempt.

CBS aired *Pentagon* a second time in the *CBS News Hour* less than a month after the original telecast, ostensibly to let viewers see what the controversy was all about. The second broadcast reached a larger audience than the first had.

SELL-THROUGH ▶ term used in the home video business for movies that are sold to consumers rather than rented to them. Direct sales are preferred over rentals by the Hollywood studios because they afford the distributor a substantial share of the customer's dollar, just as at the theater box office. Rentals, on the other hand, represent a single sale to the shopkeeper, who may have scores of customers for a tape without having to share any of the income with the studio. Many movies, *Batman* notably, have been priced low to encourage sell-through.

SENATE COMMUNICATIONS SUBCOMMITTEE (OF THE SENATE COMMERCE, SCIENCE AND TRANSPORTATION COMMITTEE) ▶ the subcommittee most active in broadcast matters, with oversight of the FCC and the communications industries. It is perennially concerned with the possible need for legislation in such areas as cable-TV regulation, FCC regulatory reform, international satellite policy, broadcast license renewals, public broadcasting, UHF, copyright and more. The subcommittee's hearings and investigations, which may lead to amendments to the Communications Act, have reflected its concern with sex and violence on TV, commercial practices in children's television, minority hiring practices in broadcasting and the lack of program diversity.

The subcommittee considers nominations to the FCC, the Corporation for Public Broadcasting and the board of directors of the Communications Satellite Corp.

SGT. BILKO ▶ classic character created by Phil Silvers in the 1955-58 series *You'll Never Get Rich.*

***SERGEANT PRESTON OF THE YUKON* ▶** CBS series (1955-57) on the Royal Canadian Mounted Police, featuring Richard Simmons as Sergeant Frank Preston; Preston's dog, King; and his horse, Rex; and produced by Wrather Corp., the source of *Lassie.*

SERIAL ▶ program form in which a running story line continues from week to week, as opposed to the more common episodic series whose stories are complete in each outing. As with *Dallas, Dynasty* and *Knots Landing,* past events are not forgotten to characters in a serial, while episodic shows usually have no memory and thus little character development.

SERLING, ROD (d. 1975) ▶ TV dramatist, producer and narrator whose credits range from the authorship of such outstanding plays as *Patterns* and *Requiem for a Heavyweight* to commercial spieling. After an apprenticeship as a radio and TV writer for stations in Cincinnati, Serling quickly entered the front rank of playwrights in the medium's "golden age" when *Patterns* was produced on *Kraft Theater* in 1955.

For the various live drama series on the networks, Serling wrote, among other plays, *The Rack, A Town Turned to Dust* and *Requiem for a Heavyweight,* the latter for *Playhouse 90. Patterns* and *Requiem* were made into movies, and both, along with *Dust,* won Emmy Awards.

CBS signed Serling to a contract in 1956. When live dramas began to fade, he created the *Twilight Zone* series of occult tales, which he both wrote and hosted. The series ran from 1959 to 1964 on CBS and afterwards in syndication. A few years later, he created *Rod Serling's Night Gallery,* another—but less successful—anthology of mystery tales, which ran on NBC.

Serling's image on camera was that of a well-educated tough guy, and his earnest delivery was so effective that he was used frequently as a commercial spokesperson in the early 1970s. He also, in his last years, narrated documentaries and nature programs, including the Jacques Cousteau oceanographic specials. Serling had been engaged as host of an ABC summer comedy series, *Keep On Truckin',* in 1975, but he died of complications following open-heart surgery before the series began.

SESAC (SOCIETY OF EUROPEAN STAGE AUTHORS AND COMPOSERS) ▶ smallest of the three music-licensing organizations (the others being ASCAP and BMI) which originally represented European works but now is based in the U.S. and has compiled its own domestic repertory, heavily in the religious music and gospel field. It was established in 1931 and collects music licensing fees from networks and stations.

SESAME STREET ▶ a revolutionary children's program that sought to teach numbers and letters (and, later, social concepts) to preschool children through TV entertainment, chiefly by harnessing the techniques used in commercials.

The brainchild of Joan Ganz Cooney, and the initial production of the Children's Television Workshop (which she headed), it premiered as a daily hour-long show on PBS in November 1969, with an initial budget of $8 million, after two years of research and extensive piloting. The funds were raised from a variety of foundations and from CPB and HEW. The show received enthusiastic reviews, won numerous major awards and drew a regular U.S. audience of some nine million children. Moreover, it gave PTV a show that frequently beat commercial TV competition in the ratings. And in setting a new standard for children's programming, it inspired some commercial imitation of its ability to teach through entertainment.

Characters from the acclaimed children's show *Sesame Street*

Employing a modular format, allowing for a mixture of fresh and repeated sequences in each program, *Sesame Street* adopted the pacing and dazzle of TV spot commercials, making virtuous use of their most arresting devices. Deriving its continuity from a street scene, the series intermingled a regular cast of adults and children with Muppets (Jim Henson's marionette-puppets), animation and live-action film. The episodes cost approximately $50,000 each to produce, and 130 one-hour shows were produced the first year.

Sesame Street's target audience was disadvantaged inner-city children who lacked the language skills of preschoolers of the middle class. Evaluative tests by CTW and Educational Testing Service showed that youngsters who watched the program most learned most. The tests also seemed to validate the three important premises of the series: that children can learn their numbers and letters by film animation, that commercial techniques can be used constructively to gain the attention of four-year-olds and that repetition is effective.

David Connell, formerly with *Captain Kangaroo,* produced the show, and Dr. Gerald Lesser, Harvard psychologist, served as chief adviser. Jeff Moss and Joe Raposo created the music, a vital element of the series.

Original cast members included Loretta Long and Matt Robinson as married couple Susan and Gordon, singer Bob McGrath as a neighbor and Will Lee as candy-store owner Mr. Hooper, along with Henson's Muppets, who, over the years, have included Kermit the Frog, Oscar the Grouch, Big Bird, the Cookie Monster, Grover, Bert and Ernie, Snuffleupagus, Elmo and others.

Over the more than 20 years it has aired, *Sesame Street* has been kept fresh with the addition of newly produced episodes tackling broadened and more complex subjects—the environment, racial understanding, etc.—and by adding new faces and new Muppets. Only Loretta Long and Bob McGrath of the original cast remain. Among those added in more recent years are Alison Bartlett (Gina), Lillias White (Lillian), Linda Bove (Linda), Sonia Manzano (Maria), Bill McCutcheon (Uncle Wally), Emilio Delgado (Luis), David Langston Smyrl (Mr. Handford), Gabriela Rose Reagan (Gabriela), Roscoe Orman (Gordon) and Miles Orman (Miles).

The death of Will Lee (Mr. Hooper) led to a special *Sesame Street* on Thanksgiving Day, 1984, explaining his absence from the cast and treating the delicate subject of dying. It was the 1990 death of Muppet creator Jim Henson, however, that left the largest void in the show. Not only was Henson the creative genius behind the Muppets, but he had also provided the voices for a number of the most popular, including Kermit the Frog.

Sesame Street is funded by the member stations of PBS and by revenues generated by royalties from commercial product licenses and international broadcast sales. The English language version of *Sesame Street* is carried in 85 countries. In addition, there are 13 original international co-productions of the series including an Israeli version produced in Tel Aviv (*Rechov Sumsum*), an Arabic version produced in Kuwait (*Iftah Ya Simsim*) and locally produced versions in France, Mexico, Portugal, Norway, Germany, the Netherlands, Spain and Brazil. Dulcy Singer has been the show's executive producer since 1980.

SETS-IN-USE ▶ in ratings analyses, the total number of television sets in operation at a given time and in a given universe (national or local). Once the term was used interchangeably with HUT (Households Using Television), but the two were separated when households in significant numbers began having more than one television set.

SEVAREID, ERIC ▶ CBS journalist through four decades as a member of the news team assembled by Edward R. Murrow in 1939. In the mid-1960s he became most familiar to viewers as news analyst on the evening newscast and as the network's premier political commentator. Sevareid's long experience as a war correspondent combined with his gifts as an essayist made him one of the unique and most respected figures in all broadcast journalism. During the 1980s, in retirement from CBS, he narrated a number of documentary series for PBS and syndication.

After covering World War II in both the European and China-Burma-India theaters—scoring a major scoop in 1940 on the fall of France—he returned to the United States to report on the founding of the United Nations and then was assigned to the Washington bureau, where he began covering domestic political activities. In 1959, after becoming chief Washington correspondent, he went to London and served two years as roving European correspondent. He then became national correspondent for CBS News, maintaining contact with top government officials and diplomats.

In special broadcasts, he represented CBS News in two televised interviews with President Nixon, participated in the coverage of the resignations of Nixon and Vice-President Agnew, and was one of the correspondents interviewing President Ford in a special "conversation" program in 1975. He also gave his impressions of the Vietnam War in an "illustrated lecture" in 1966.

During his career he was moderator for such broadcasts as *Town Meeting of the World, Years of Crisis, The Great Challenge* and *Where We Stand.* During the summer of 1975 he conducted a series of televised interviews with noted world figures entitled *Conversations with Eric Sevareid.*

A native of North Dakota, he worked on the *Minneapolis Journal* and other newspapers before joining CBS. He reached the mandatory retirement age in November, 1977, but remained active with numerous freelance assignments, including *Between the Wars,* a 1978 documentary series syndicated by Mobil. In 1982 he became the host of a weekly magazine series, *Eric Sevareid's Chronicle.*

Pat Robertson, host of *The 700 Club*

700 CLUB, THE **▶** 90-minute daily talk show that was the keystone of the Christian Broadcasting Network and hosted by its president, Pat Robertson.

The 700 Club remains a daily fixture on The Family Channel, the successor to CBN. The program is named for a fateful fund-raising telethon conducted by Robertson in 1963 to keep his frail, Christian-oriented UHF station, WYAH Virginia Beach, Va., on the air. Robertson's pitch was that the station could meet its monthly operating costs if 700 people would contribute $10 a month. The goal was met and the single station grew to a group of four television and five radio stations, a national satellite network carried mainly on cable systems, with an annual operating budget of $55 million.

The 700 Club began as a local WYAH show in 1966 with Jim Bakker as host. When Bakker left the show after six years to start his own TV ministry and to host, with his wife Tammy Faye, *The PTL Club* (which left the air in 1987 when Bakker was convicted of fraud), Robertson took over as host of *The 700 Club* with Ben Kinchlow, an African-American, as his sidekick and substitute host. Robertson's son, Tim, took over the host's role briefly in 1988 while the elder Robertson campaigned unsuccessfully for the Republican presidential nomination.

SEVEN UP ▶ a series of remarkable sociological documentaries produced at seven-year intervals by Britain's Granada TV, tracing the lives and attitudes of a group of British children as they grow up. The series began in 1956 when Granada's *World in Action* team interviewed a group of 7-year-olds of diverse backgrounds for their views of life, interests and aspirations. The film was widely praised, not only for its excellence in the documentary form, but also for its contribution to anthopology. Seven years later the same children were revisited for a new documentary, *14 Up,* and then again for *21 Up,* examining their development in the intervening years. The latest of the five documentaries, *35 Up,* was made in 1991. All have aired in the U.S. on public television.

The series was swept up by English audiences and has somewhat of a following among viewers internationally. It simply involved turning a camera on the uninhibited conversation of a mixed group of youngsters from the middle-class suburbs of Liverpool, the farms of the Yorkshire dales, London's East End, and the Surrey stockbroker belt. In the sequels their dreams are lived out, frustrated or abandoned: the child who dreamed of becoming a missionary realizes his dream; another, bright and engaging at seven, becomes the lonely vagrant of *28 Up.*

Michael Apted, who has become a noted Hollywood film director, had been a researcher on the original black-and-white film, *7 Up.* He has returned to Granada in the seven-year intervals to direct each of the four subsequent films.

77 SUNSET STRIP ▶ popular, fast-paced private-eye series that had a substantial run on ABC (1958-64) and helped establish an urban action-adventure vogue in the wake of the quiz scandals. By Warner Bros., its regular cast was headed by Efrem Zimbalist Jr. as Stu Bailey, Roger Smith as Jeff Spencer, Edd Byrnes as Gerald Lloyd (Kookie) Kookson III and Jacqueline Beer as Suzanne Fabray.

SEVERINO, JOHN C. ▶ former president of ABC Television, succeeding Frederick S. Pierce, who moved up to executive vice president of ABC Inc. in 1981. Severino had spent the 16 previous years in the company's owned-stations division, where he had been v.p. and general manager of KABC-TV Los Angeles (1974-81) and of WLS-TV Chicago (1970-74).

SFM MEDIA SERVICES CORP. ▶ a leading time-buying service involved also in program packaging and syndication. Thus, in 1976, while one division of the company was engaged in purchasing air time for President Ford's election campaign, another division was mounting a revival of *The Mickey Mouse Club* and repackaging the old *Rin Tin Tin* programs for syndication. SFM also arranged the 50-station lineup for the so-called "Mobil Network" carrying the British series on explorers, *Ten Who Dared,* sponsored by Mobil Oil. On its own, the company mounted an ad hoc network for vintage family movies, which it called the SFM Holiday network. It also bought the air time for Ronald Reagan's successful Presidental campaigns.

The company was founded in 1969 by Walter Staab, Robert Frank and Stanley Moger.

SHAKA ZULU ▶ historical mini-series that was a four-nation coproduction and proved a sleeper in the American syndication market, giving the distributor, Harmony Gold, one of its biggest hits. The series was unusual in centering on black tribal life in Africa during the late-18th century. It was shot on location in South Africa.

The 10-hour, five-part series follows the life story of Shaka (1787-1828) as he grows up to become leader of the powerful Zulu nation and to fulfill an ancient tribal prophecy to unite his people against the encroaching European colonialism of Africa. The mini-series was a coproduction involving companies from the U.S., Germany, Italy and Australia, with an overall budget of $24 million. The large cast was headed by Henry Cele, and featured Robert Powell, Edward Fox, Christopher Lee, Trevor Howard, Duduzile Mkhize, Fiona Fullerton, Roy Dotrice, Kenneth Griffith, Humphrey Makhoba and Gordon Jackson. The executive producer was Leon Rautenbach. It was written by Joshua Sinclair and directed by William Faure.

Henry Cele as the legendary Zulu warrior in *Shaka Zulu*

SHAKESPEARE, FRANK J. ▶ one-time president of RKO General and former director of the USIA during the Nixon Administration (1969-73). During the 1960s, he was a fast-rising executive at CBS, moving from v.p.-g.m. of WCBS-TV in New York to executive v.p. of the TV network under James Aubrey. Later he became president of CBS Television Services, leaving in 1969 for the USIA post. In 1974 Shakespeare became vice-chairman of Westinghouse Broadcasting; the following year he was hired away by RKO General.

SHAKESPEARE PLAYS, THE ▶ a massive coproduction by the BBC and Time-Life Films involving the full 37-play canon of William Shakespeare, that were presented in new productions over a six-year period. Offered during the first season, which began early in 1979, were *Richard II, Romeo and Juliet, Julius Caesar, As You Like It, Measure for Measure* and *Henry VIII.* Cedric Messina, who had been with the BBC since 1958 and was formerly producer of *Play of the Month,* was executive producer for the first two years, with Alan Shallcross as script editor and John Wilders as literary consultant. The directors, varying from play to play, included David Giles, Herbert Wise and Kevin Billington. Jonathan Miller was named producer for years three and four.

A controversy arose in the U.S., while the series was in the planning stages, when the Corporation for Public Broadcasting offered a grant of $1 million to the production to secure the plays for PBS. The CPB drew back when unions and American performers and producers protested the use of Federal funds to finance a foreign public television project. Eventually the necessary funds were raised in grants from Exxon Corp., Metropolitan Life Insurance and the Morgan Guaranty Trust Co. Later talent unions in the U.K. objected to the casting of an American, James Earl Jones, as Othello, but the BBC prevailed in the dispute.

SHALES, TOM ▶ television critic for the *Washington Post* who is widely considered the best in the business and the crown jewel of the *Post*'s Style section. His reputation is said to carry significant weight in the most powerful halls of the TV industry, from news divisions to Hollywood backlots.

Two years before he graduated from American University, Shales got a position as a beat reporter for the *Post* in 1971. He soon shifted to television criticism when he proved not only his dislike for general reportage but also an affinity for witty criticism.

SHALIT, GENE ▶ resident wit and reviewer on NBC's *Today Show,* starting in 1969 with occasional appearances as book and movie reviewer and graduating to a regular role a few years later. With black bushy hair and mustache as distinguishing features, and a staccato, slightly acerbic style, he broke into TV as a film critic for WNBC-TV New York, after having broadcast reviews on NBC Radio's *Monitor.*

SHANE ▶ one of the so-called "adult westerns" of the early 1960s, based on a successful movie and produced by Herbert Brodkin's Titus Productions. It had a brief run on ABC (1960) and featured David Carradine as Shane, a drifter, along with Jill Ireland as the widowed Marian Starrett, Chris Shea as her son Joey, Tom Tully as Tom Starrett, Marian's father-in-law, Bert Freed as Rufe Ryker and Sam Gilman as Grafton.

SHANKS, BOB ▶ former ABC program executive (1972-78) and the initial executive producer of *20/20,* the ABC newsmagazine. When the pilot episode was poorly received and the format and production staff of *20/20* overhauled, Shanks was displaced, and he moved to the West Coast to resume an earlier career as an independent film and TV producer.

At ABC, he served in a variety of programming capacities and became, in 1976, v.p. in charge of all prime-time specials and the early-morning show *Good Morning, America.* He also wrote a nonfiction book on television, *The Cool Fire.* From 1965 to 1970 he was producer of the *Merv Griffin Show* and earlier had worked for Bob Banner, *Candid Camera, Tonight* and *The Great American Dream Machine.*

Not long after leaving ABC, he was plucked by CBS to rebuild its two-hour morning show. When his efforts failed, Shanks moved to Australia and was hired in 1989 as president of the seriously troubled and over-leveraged Ten Network. He put together an American-style prime-time schedule in his first year, but it was a dismal failure and soon Shanks was let go. He remained in Australia and several months later was taken on by the Nine Network as a program consultant.

SHANNON'S DEAL ▶ dramatic series about a reformed gambler who becomes a storefront lawyer in Philadelphia, notable for having been created by movie director and writer John Sayles. After the pilot aired in 1989 as a two-hour movie on NBC, the series began in April 1990. Stan Rogow was executive producer of the one-hour show that starred Jamey Sheridan and featured Elizabeth Pena, Jenny Lewis, Martin Ferrero and Richard Edson. It also featured a memorable score by trumpeter Wynton Marsalis.

SHAPIRO, ARNOLD ▶ producer who made his mark in 1979 with a single syndicated documentary, *Scared Straight*, and in 1990 landed a hit series on CBS, *Rescue 911*. He also produced a limited series for CBS, *True Detectives*. *Scared Straight* won an Oscar for short subjects though it never played theatrically.

SHAPIRO, ESTHER ▶ writer who created *Dynasty* and who with her husband, Richard, shared production credit with Aaron Spelling Productions. The Shapiros' company has also made the prime-time serial *Emerald Point N.A.S.* and the unsuccessful pilot *When We Were Young*, as well as TV movies. One of those, *Blood Ties,* was the pilot for a series for the Fox network.

SHARE (SHARE-OF-AUDIENCE) ▶ a comparative evaluation of the ratings, representing in percentages how programs performed relative to the other programs in direct competition. In figurative terms, the share is the share of the pie. If all television viewing at a given time constitutes the pie, the share denotes the proportion of the pie each program has received.

More than a comparative evaluation, it is a competitive evaluation. In three-network (or three-station) competition, a program that receives approximately one-third of the available audience—or a 33 share—is considered to be competing adequately. Less than a 33 share usually spells trouble for a program because it means too much audience is being lost to the opposition. (Actually, in network competition today, a 20 share is considered the minimum index of success, since some 40% of the prime-time tune-in goes to independent and public TV stations, the Fox Network and the various cable networks.

Among lay persons, there is often confusion about the difference between the rating and the share. A rating is the percentage of households tuned to a program from all the possible TV households in the service area. Since the rating is based on all households it can be directly translated into an absolute number of viewers for a program. The share, on the other hand, is based only on households using television at a specific time and therefore does not lend itself to estimating actual audience size.

Since viewing levels vary by the hour and by the day, the success of a program is told not in the absolute number of people it has reached but rather in its ability to command larger audiences than the programs opposite it. A program with a 20 share in the evening, when viewing levels are high, will normally play to a larger audience than one with a 40 share in the morning, when viewing levels are low. However, the evening program would in all likelihood be canceled for failing to compete adequately while the morning program would almost certainly be renewed.

SHARI LEWIS SHOW, THE ▶ popular NBC children's program in the late 1950s and early 1960s that featured ventriloquist Shari Lewis and her hand puppets, principally Lamb Chop. In January 1992, some 19 years after her final NBC show, she started a daily PBS children's program, *Lamb Chop's Play-Along.*

SHARNIK, JOHN ▶ former veteran executive producer of documentaries and specials for CBS News, who served briefly in the mid-1970s as v.p. of public affairs broadcasts and earlier was senior producer of *CBS Reports.* Sharnik, who joined CBS in 1954 as a writer for Eric Sevareid's *American Week* broadcasts, later coproduced the *Eyewitness* series with Leslie Midgley and worked as a writer-producer for *60 Minutes.* He joined CBS News from the Sunday department of the *New York Times.*

SHATNER, WILLIAM ▶ actor whose substantial career in television since the 1950s has included the lead in four series. His came into prominence in 1966 when he landed the part of Captain James Kirk in *Star Trek,* which led to the six *Star Trek* movies. The other TV series were a latter-day western, *The Barbary Coast* (1975-76), the police drama *T.J. Hooker* (1982-86), and the reality-based show *Rescue 911,* which began in 1989.

William Shatner as Captain James Kirk in *Star Trek*

SHAW, BERNARD ▶ CNN's principal anchor in Washington, who co-anchors *The International Hour* and *The World Today.* Since the network began in 1989, Shaw has anchored CNN's political coverage, including primaries, conventions and elections. In 1988, when he moderated the October presidential debate, he jolted the audience by posing a shocking opening question to democratic candidate Michael Dukakis: Would he drop his opposition to the death penalty if his wife were raped and killed? Caught off-balance, Dukakis gave an insipid and passionless response and never regained strength. Many believed that moment not only won the debate for George Bush but changed the course of the entire election. In an interview that same year with vice presidential nominee Dan Quayle, Shaw visibly enraged the nominee by asking if he (Quayle) had joined the National Guard out of fear of being killed in Vietnam. In 1991, during the first hours of the bombing attack on Baghdad that signaled the start of the Persian Gulf War, Shaw and his CNN colleagues produced a riveting all-night audio account of the beginning of Operation Desert Storm.

Before joining CNN, Shaw did a three-year stint at ABC News, during which time he was a senior Capitol Hill correspondent in Washington; Latin American correspondent and bureau chief (he was one of the first reporters on the scent at the Jonestown, Guyana mass suicides); and he reported from Tehran during the 1979 hostage crisis. In 1971-77 he was at CBS News's Washington bureau, and prior to that at Group W, first in Chicago, and then in Washington as White House correspondent. He began his career in 1964 at WNUS-Chicago, one of the country's first all-news radio stations.

Bernard Shaw

SHEA, JACK ▶ director of the Bob Hope specials and producer-director of such series as *The Glen Campbell Goodtime Hour* and *Hollywood Talent.* His directing credits also include *The Waltons, We'll Get By, Sanford and Son, Calucci's Department* and *Death Valley Days.*

SHEAR, BARRY (d. 1979) ▶ director of TV programs and movies. In the late 1950s, when his specialty was comedy, he directed the Ernie Kovacs specials, the Edie Adams series, *Here's Edie,* occasional outings of *Tonight* and the series *The Lively Ones.* Later he turned to action-adventure and was regular director on *Police Woman* and *Starsky and Hutch,* with directing assignments in a raft of other series such as *Ironside* and *It Takes a Thief.* Before his death from cancer, he completed a four-hour mini-series for NBC, *Power,* for the 1979-80 season. The movies he directed included *Wild in the Streets.*

SHEEHAN, WILLIAM ▶ former president of ABC News (1974-77), demoted to executive v.p. in the reorganization that made Roone Arledge president of ABC News & Sports in June 1977. A year later, he left to become v.p. of public affairs for the Ford Motor Co. in Detroit.

Earlier, Sheehan was London bureau chief for ABC News (1962-66) and co-anchor of the *ABC Evening News* (1961-62). Sheehan came to ABC in 1961 from WJR Radio, Detroit, where he had been news director. He was hired by James Hagerty, then head of the network's news division. Hagerty, who earlier had been press secretary to President Eisenhower, had met Sheehan while he was covering the President's travels in Europe for WJR and was impressed with him. Before becoming president of ABC News, Sheehan had been senior v.p. under Elmer Lower.

SHEEN, FULTON J. (d. 1979) ▶ probably the most popular religious personality to have worked in TV and the only one to receive weekly prime-time exposure in a show of his own. Bishop Sheen's discourses on social and inspirational topics drew substantial ratings in the 1950s against strong entertainment competition, enabling a five-year run. His original weekly program, *Life Is Worth Living,* premiered Feb. 12, 1952 on the DuMont Network in prime time. It moved to ABC on Oct. 13, 1955 and ran until April 8, 1957.

As national director of the Society for Propagation of the Faith (Catholic), Bishop Sheen later resumed the half-hour program in syndication, under auspices of that organization. Two separate series were produced on tape between 1961 and 1968.

SHEPHARD, HARVEY ▶ president of Warner Bros. Television since 1986, having joined from CBS where he was senior vice president of programs and the network's principal scheduling strategist. At Warner, Shephard was responsible for the development of such series as *Murphy Brown, China Beach* and *Life Goes On* and has overseen production of *Growing Pains* and *Night Court,* among other series.

Shephard had spent nearly 20 years at CBS, joining from Lennen & Newell Advertising in 1967 as manager of audience measurement. He became so knowledgeable of audience patterns that he was shifted to the network's program department in 1973. Two years later he was named v.p. of program planning for the network and in 1977 became vice president of programs, New York, for CBS Entertainment. He moved to Los Angeles in 1978 and in 1980, when Bud Grant became president of CBS Entertainment, Shephard was named vice president of the division. Two years later he was given the newly created title of senior vice president of programs, essentially in day-to-day charge of the division. He served as CBS's mastermind of programming until Warner hired him away.

SHERLOCK, MICHAEL ▶ NBC executive responsible for the network's engineering and operations, and an advocate of a "universal" video format to be used throughout network and owned-station operations. In the late 1980s NBC standardized everything from ENG footage acquisition to studio program playback on Panasonic's MII half-inch cassette standard—the only network to do so. Sherlock joined NBC in 1960 and rose through the news and sports divisions before moving into operations. Since 1986 he has been president of operations and technical services.

***SHINDIG* ▶** half-hour rock and roll series on ABC (1964-66) produced in Hollywood and hosted by Jimmy O'Neill, featuring youthful recording artists of the day and a resident chorus line. After one good season it spawned a second edition, and both faltered the next year. It was by Selmur Productions and Circle Seven Productions, with Leon I. Mirell as executive producer and Dean Whitmore as producer.

***SHOGUN* ▶** five-part adaptation of James Clavell's best selling novel of that title set in 17th-century Japan; it aired on NBC in the fall of 1980 and drew a large audience. With Clavell himself as executive producer, the program, which took three years to produce, grew into the most expensive mini-series ever; reportedly, the costs approached $21 million, including $1 million paid to Clavell for the rights. The five parts represented 12 hours of television.

Richard Chamberlain, as English sailor John Blackthorne, headed a cast that otherwise consisted of British and Japanese actors, including the great Japanese star Toshiro Mifune as warlord Toranaga, and Yoko Shimada as interpreter Lady Mariko. The program was made by Paramount Television, with Eric Bercovici as script writer and producer.

SHORE, DINAH ▶ one of TV's most attractive and enduring personalities, who began as a star of music-variety shows in the 1950s and had a second career in the 1970s as a talk-show hostess.

As a well-established recording artist and radio singer, she began working in TV on a full-time basis in 1951 with the *Chevy Show Starring Dinah Shore,* a 15-minute variety series on NBC that aired twice weekly until July 1957. But it was the 15-minute form and not Shore's popularity that had faded, and in October 1957 she began a weekly variety hour in color for NBC, *The Dinah Shore Chevy Show,* that ran five years. That series was produced by Bob Banner, written by Bob Wells and Johnny Bradford and choreographed by Tony Charmoli.

Although she dressed elegantly and stylishly, her warm folksy manner made her somewhat a symbol of grassroots America. Through the latter part of the 1960s she appeared mostly in specials and briefly in a daytime variety show. But in 1972 she began on NBC a women's-oriented talk show, which later grew into a 90-minute daily syndicated series, *Dinah's Place,* carried by most subscribing stations in the afternoon or early evening.

SHORT-SPACING ▶ the concept of lowering the FCC mileage standard between stations using the same channel position so that additional VHF or UHF stations can be added, or "dropped in," in certain markets. The FCC's allocations require stations with the same channel number to be separated by a minimum of 170 miles to avoid signal interference.

SHORT-TERM RENEWAL ▶ a license renewal granted by the FCC for less than the normal five-year term (often for one year or less) in punishment to stations for transgressions of the rules. The FCC began imposing the short-term renewal in the late 1950s, when it felt the need to impose sanctions for certain offenses that in its opinion did not justify the extreme punishment of license revocation.

SHOWTIME/THE MOVIE CHANNEL ▶ principal pay-cable competitor to HBO, founded in 1976 by Viacom and offering recent movies, comedy series, concerts, original movies, championship boxing and classic films. Although HBO has dominated the field from the start, Showtime has made its mark with original programs, among them the sitcoms *Brothers* and *It's Garry Shandling's Show.* At the end of 1991 Showtime had around 7.4 million subscribers.

The Movie Channel, Showtime's sister service, was originally launched in 1973 as The Star Channel, a pay network serving eight Warner Cable systems by videocassette. In 1979, under the joint venture of Warner Communications and American Express, the service went to satellite delivery and a 24-hour schedule, and was renamed The Movie Channel. Viacom acquired it in 1985. The channel has 2.8 million subscribers. Winston (Tony) Cox is chairman and CEO of Showtime Networks.

SHRINER, HERB (d. 1970) ▶ popular TV personality and comedian of the 1950s, with a low-key countrified manner and a harmonica as his trademark. He had his own show on ABC in 1952, *Herb Shriner Time,* then became emcee of the NBC quiz show *Two for the Money.* Later he was signed by CBS, which gave him an evening show in 1957, *The Herb Shriner Show.*

Maria Shriver

SHRIVER, MARIA ▶ NBC News correspondent and anchor of *First Person with Maria Shriver*, a series of prime-time specials profiling newsmakers in the worlds of entertainment, sports, politics and business.

Shriver joined NBC News in 1986 as correspondent for the prime-time series *1986.* Subsequently, she hosted *Main Street*, a monthly newsmagazine for young people. She has been co-anchor of NBC's Sunday morning coverage of the 1988 Summer Olympics from Seoul, Korea, and has hosted a number of NBC News specials, including *The Baby Business*; *Men, Women, Sex and AIDS*; and *Wall Street: Money, Greed and Power*.

Before joining NBC News, Shriver was co-anchor of the *CBS Morning News* and was a national correspondent for Group W's *PM Magazine.* She began her career as a newswriter/producer at KYW-TV Philadelphia in 1977. She is the niece of President John F.

Kennedy and is married to actor Arnold Schwarzenegger.

SIAS, JOHN B. ▶ president of ABC Television since 1986, when Capital Cities acquired ABC Inc. He had previously been head of Cap Cities publishing operations. Sias had had previous television experience but mainly in sales. Before joining Cap Cities in 1971, he had been television group vice president at Metromedia for two years and prior to that had headed Metromedia's sales department for six years. At age 58, with no background in television programming, Sias found himself presiding over such creative legends as Roone Arledge, president of ABC News and Sports, and Brandon Stoddard, president of ABC Entertainment.

John B. Sias

SIDARIS, ANDREW W. ▶ director specializing in sports who was with ABC for 12 years before starting an independent TV and film company in the early 1970s. He directed numerous films for ABC's *Wide World of Sports* and was director in ABC's coverage of the Olympic Games from 1964 to 1972.

SIEGEL, HENRY ▶ chairman and president of LBS Communications, one of the companies that pioneered barter syndication, the distribution to local stations of programs supported by national advertisers. The company fell on hard times in the early 1990s.

LBS originally stood for Lexington Broadcasting Services Co., a wholly owned subsidiary of Grey Advertising and named for Lexington Ave., the Manhattan street on which Grey had its offices. As senior vice president of the agency, Siegel founded LBS in 1976 as an efficient way for national advertisers to reach their target audiences, other than by buying network time. In 1988, he and a group of partners bought LBS from Grey and established it as a company involved also in international distribution and in the sale of programs to cable.

In December 1991 LBS filed for bankruptcy protection under Chapter 11 and soon after began merger negotiations with All American Television.

SIEGEL, SIMON B. (d. 1991) ▶ major figure in ABC Inc. from the time of the merger with United Paramount Theatres in 1953 until his retirement 20 years later. Having been comptroller for Paramount, he initially became treasurer of ABC and, as trusted aide to the president, Leonard Goldenson, was named executive v.p. of the corporation in 1961. Although he maintained low visibility outside the company, he was one of the most powerful figures in all broadcasting during the 1960s as ABC's chief financial officer and overseer of the divisions.

SIEGENTHALER, ROBERT ▶ former ABC News producer who in the fall of 1976 became executive producer of the *Evening News* when Barbara Walters began as co-anchor with Harry Reasoner. Since ABC had a $1 million-a-year investment in Walters and was determined to improve its news ratings, Siegenthaler was chosen to make the news decisions and supervise the production because of his extensive experience in TV news. At the time of his appointment, he was executive producer of special events engaged in overseeing the political conventions of that year.

With the return of Av Westin to ABC News in the summer of 1977, Siegenthaler yielded him the reins of the newscast and received a new assignment. After producing the series of latenight specials on the Iranian crisis in 1980, Siegenthaler was named executive producer of news specials.

In 1985 he was named v.p. of News Practices and in 1989 was appointed president of Broadcast Operations and Engineering for ABC television.

SIE, JOHN ▶ chairman and chief executive of Encore, a pay-TV cable service launched in April 1991 and programmed primarily with theatrical movies from the 1960s, 1970s and 1980s. An electrophysicist by training, Sie worked for a time at equipment manufacturer Jerrold Communications. Later he became an executive at Showtime, the pay-TV service, and then joined Tele-Communications Inc., the largest of the cable operators, in 1984 as senior v.p. for strategic planning. His visibility and clout increased tremendously at TCI, where he engineered the company's rescue of The Discovery Channel in 1986 and consistently urged the cable industry to invest in high-profile, proprietary programming, which he termed "punch through" programming for its ability to break into the American viewer's consciousness.

***SIEMPRE EN DOMINGO* (*ALWAYS ON SUNDAY*)** ▶ for many years, Mexico's most popular program and television's longest format, seven hours of Sunday entertainment, a potpourri of singers, dancers and beauty contests, produced and hosted by Raul Velasco with a mix of Latin polish and down-home sincerity. The program, begun as a local show in Mexico City in 1970, was soon picked up by Televisa and distributed nationwide. The seven-hour show has been trimmed to three-and-half hours in recent years but continues to use material from, and to be distributed to, other Latin American countries. It airs in the U.S. in an edited two-hour version on the Spanish-language stations affiliated with Univision.

Alfred C. Sikes

SIKES, ALFRED C. ▶ chairman of the Federal Communications Commission since his appointment by President Bush in August 1990. Unlike his predecessor, Mark Fowler—whose libertarian principles fostered a hands-off attitude toward government interference, leaving the market forces to self-regulate the industry—Sikes has followed a more traditional pro-business regulatory philosophy in which government becomes the agent for facilitating the goals of the industry. He has not hesitated to drive for government standards in situations where Fowler's hands-off policy would have left it to market forces to decide.

Immediately prior to his appointment to the FCC, he was administrator of the National Telecommunications and Information Administration (NTIA). Although much involved in earlier years with both state government and Republican politics in his native Missouri, he brings to his present post a background in broadcasting, both as president of his own media consulting company and as an officer in several companies owning radio stations in three states.

SILLIPHANT, STIRLING ▶ producer and writer who rose through the TV ranks to top screenwriting assignments (*In the Heat of the Night, Towering Inferno*). He wrote and produced *Naked City,* wrote the *Route 66* pilot in 1960 and created and was executive producer of *Longstreet.* A former New York publicist for 20th Century-Fox and Walt Disney, he broke into TV as a writer on the *Mickey Mouse Club* series (1955). In later years he wrote and produced the mini-series *Pearl* for ABC and the pilot for *Fly Away Home.*

SILVERBACH, ALAN M. ▶ veteran syndication executive who spent much of his career with 20th Century Fox, rising to executive v.p. in charge of worldwide syndication in 1975. He left in 1976 for a private venture, and later became executive v.p. for syndication of Metromedia Producers Corp. After that he teamed with Herb Lazarus to form the Silverbach-Lazarus distribution company.

SILVERMAN, FRED ▶ one of television's greatest programmers, who had been the chief impresario at all three networks before going off on his own in 1981 to become a Hollywood producer. His first producing effort, *Thicke of the Night,* a latenight talk show with Alan Thicke, gave him an inauspicious start. But then he went on to produce a rash of prime-time hits—*Matlock, Father Dowling Mysteries, In the Heat of the Night, Jake and the Fatman,* and a revival of *Perry Mason* in the form of occasional two-hour movies. (All were in association with Dean Hargrove Productions and Viacom, except *In the Heat of the Night,* which was a collaboration with MGM/UA and Juanita Bartlett Productions).

As a producer, Silverman made a stunning comeback from a humiliating three-year experience as president of the National Broadcasting Company, proving that he was indeed television's own child, with an intuitive understanding of the medium that few people have ever possessed. His reputation as a master programmer grew out of his winning streak that carried over from CBS to ABC. In 1970, at a quite young age, he was named to succeed Mike Dann, the legendary head of programming at CBS, and he proved more than equal to the task. He had a string of hit shows that kept coming year after year, among them *Kojak, Cannon, Maude, Rhoda, The Jeffersons, Cher,* and *The Waltons.* Yet the management of CBS took him for granted and often excluded him from strategy sessions and social events.

In 1975 he left CBS to become president of ABC Entertainment, and a year later his old network ended its 20-year dominance of prime time while his new one surged to the top. At ABC Silverman shepherded a string of hits–some of which were on the network or in development before his arrival—including *Happy Days, Laverne and Shirley, Donny and Marie, Family, Rich Man, Poor Man, Starsky and Hutch, Soap,* and *Charlie's Angels.* He was regarded by many Hollywood program suppliers as the most knowledgeable and professional of the program chiefs, and his record of success with new programs was clearly the best for any programmer in many years.

Silverman was considered to have a golden touch, and that prompted a desperate NBC, mired as it was in third place, to go after him. In June 1978, in a blizzard of publicity, Silverman became president of NBC. The price for his programming expertise was making him chief executive of the company under a three-year contract at a reported salary of $1 million a year. That put him, alone among network executives, in television's star class. Indeed, he became better known to the general public than most performers on the screen.

But Silverman's three years at NBC were a fiasco. His program strategies all failed, the ratings continued to decline in daytime as well as nighttime, a number of old-line affiliates switched allegiances to competing networks, and dozens of key executives left the company, some voluntarily. When Silverman was ousted in 1981, the network was a shambles. Grant Tinker was brought in as chairman (eventually turning the network's fortunes around), and Silverman moved west to try his hand at producing.

Silverman's extraordinary failure at NBC—given his history of success dating to 1963, when he started with CBS as director of daytime programming—may be attributed partly to the fact that he was competing with the hit schedule he had left behind at ABC and some of the durable hits he had launched earlier at CBS. But some of his poor showing must be attributed to the Peter Principle. As chief executive responsible for the entire business of NBC—radio, news, sports, the owned stations, the company image and balance sheet, and everything else—the master programmer was out of his water. He probably also tried to accomplish too much too soon.

His three years at NBC are remembered in the industry for the colossal promotion of colossal flops, like *Supertrain;* for frenzied daily revisions of the prime-time schedule in his frantic quest for a hit, and for speech after speech about taking the high road while desperation led him to take the low road.

He came into television as a *wunderkind.* Fresh out of college, as a minor member of the program staff of WGN-TV Chicago, he resourcefully created two successful series from third-rate films languishing in the vaults—*Zim Bomba,* a clever recutting of the old *Bomba, the Jungle Boy* movies, and *Family Classics,* a prime-time anthology series that allowed for the recycling of movies like *Tom Sawyer* and *Son of Fury.* Soon after, he went to WPIX New York and then was hired for the CBS program department in 1963 as head of daytime. He was only 25.

He came to the notice of the networks while at Ohio State University, where he wrote a highly perceptive Master's thesis analyzing 10 years of programming at ABC. When he switched to ABC in 1975, to replace Martin Starger, ABC's stock jumped almost two points the day the announcement was made.

SILVERS, PHIL (d. 1985) ▶ a nightclub and movie comedian who scored on television in a brilliantly funny situation comedy, *You'll Never Get Rich* (soon after retitled *The Phil Silvers Show*), written by Nat Hiken. It made its debut on CBS Sept. 20, 1955 and ran for four seasons, the reruns continuing many years after in syndication.

Silvers portrayed Master Sergeant Ernie Bilko, a lovable promoter and sometime con-man who was incurably occupied with money-making schemes, usually involving his subordinates at an Army camp in Kansas. The series had a rich variety of comic Army characters, but it was Silvers's perfect realization of Bilko that made it one of TV's memorable shows.

Possibly from too strong an identification with Bilko, Silvers did not go on to other series. He starred in several specials and made guest appearances for a few years and then receded from the medium.

SILVERSTEIN, MORTON ▶ producer of investigative news documentaries for both commercial and public TV networks in a career dating back to the 1950s. He joined NBC News in 1979 after having been director of public affairs for WCBS-TV New York and executive producer of its *Eye On ...* series. A few years later he returned to independent production. Among his programs for *NBC Reports* was *The Migrants* (1980), narrated by Chris Wallace. He is perhaps best known for his controversial documentary *Banks and the Poor*, presented on public TV in 1970.

He was producer of *Seasons of Life*, a series of five documentaries on human development hosted by David Hartman, which aired on PBS in 1991, and in the same year he produced *C. Everett Koop, M.D.: Children At Risk*, which aired on NBC.

He began in television during the 1950s working for Mike Wallace's interview series *Nightbeat*, on the DuMont network.

SIMMONS, CHESTER R. (CHET) ▶ veteran network sports executive, who became head of NBC Sports in March 1977 and left the network suddenly, ending a 15-year association, in July 1979 to become president of ESPN, the 24-hour sports cable network.

Simmons had previously been v.p. of NBC sports operations since 1973 and an executive of the network's sports division after leaving ABC in 1964. Simmons had been architect of NBC's weekend sports anthology, *Grandstand*, served as liaison to the various leagues with which NBC was associated and was overseer of the network's sports schedule and its production personnel. On leaving NBC, he became president of a new cable-TV network, backed by Getty Oil, then called the Entertainment and Sports Programming Network.

Bob Simon

SIMON, BOB ▶ chief Middle East correspondent for CBS News. During 1991's Persian Gulf War, Simon himself became news when he, his producer and crew were captured on the Saudi-Kuwaiti border by an Iraqi patrol. They were held, interrogated and beaten during the course of the war until their release 40 days later. Simon had been the first CBS News correspondent allowed into Saudi Arabia after Iraq's invasion of Kuwait in August 1990.

After a career as a State Department foreign service officer, Simon joined CBS News in 1967. He has covered many major breaking international stories since, from Biafra in 1969 to Beirut in the 1980s. He was in Manila for the expulsion of Marcos, in Vietnam for the withdrawal of American forces from Saigon, in the Falklands during the war between Great Britain and Argentina, and in El Salvador, Guatemala and Nicaragua for the conflicts there.

SIMON, NEIL ▶ a former TV gag writer who became the leading comedy playwright on Broadway. Simon started his professional career writing routines and jokes for the television shows of Robert Q. Lewis, Red Buttons, Phil Silvers, Sid Caesar and Garry Moore. Two of his Broadway comedies, *Barefoot in the Park* and *The Odd Couple,* were turned into TV series. In 1975 he wrote one of four playlets for a comedy special, *Happy Endings.*

SIMPSON, JIM ▶ versatile NBC sportscaster who covered NFL games, major league baseball, PGA tournaments, Wimbledon Open tennis and NCAA championships. Simpson holds the distinction of being the first television announcer to broadcast live via satellite from Japan while covering the 1972 Winter Olympics at Sapporo, Japan. He covered nine Olympiads, beginning with the games in Helsinki, Finland in 1952.

O. J. Simpson

SIMPSON, O. J. ▶ a contributing analyst with the NBC Sports pro-football pre-game show *NFL Live* and, as one of the NFL's all-time great running backs, winner of the 1968

Heisman Trophy. Simpson played nine seasons with the Buffalo Bills and two with the San Francisco 49ers, rushing for a total of 11,236 yards to earn induction into the Professional Football Hall of Fame. He began his broadcasting career as a commentator on ABC's *Monday Night Football* from 1983 to 1985. He has also appeared in a leading role in Home Box Office's football series *First and Ten* and has made numerous commercials for Hertz rental cars.

SIMPSONS, THE ▶ animated prime-time comedy series that began in January 1990 and not only became Fox's top-rated series of the season but was critically praised for its brilliant writing. It was a genuine breakthrough show, the first attempt at a prime-time animated series in more than two decades. Its success prompted a revival of the genre.

The show was created by Matt Groening, known for his popular *Life in Hell* comic strip, who serves as executive producer, along with James L. Brooks and Sam Simon. The Simpsons, a typical blue-collar American family, were introduced in brief vignettes on *The Tracey Ullman Show* and then spun out into a separate series. The program features the voices of Julie Kavner as Marge Simpson, Dan Castellaneta as her husband Homer, Nancy Cartwright as son Bart, and Yeardley Smith as daughter Lisa. Penny Marshall, Michael Jackson, Jackie Mason, JoAnn Harris, Pamela Hayden, Russi Taylor, Harry Shearer and Marsha Wallace are among the many actors and celebrities who have provided voices for other characters.

SIMULCAST ▶ joint broadcast by a TV and radio station, most often used today by public television and radio for concerts and operas, with TV providing the visuals and FM the stereophonic sound.

SIN (SPANISH INTERNATIONAL NETWORK) ▶ until 1987 the Spanish-language network serving the Hispanic market in the U.S. through 16 UHF stations and more than 300 cable affiliates. SIN (which adopted Univision as its trade name in 1986) was purchased by Hallmark Cards in 1987.

Forming the nucleus of SIN were six UHF stations licensed to the Spanish International Communications Corp., whose principal owners were Rene Anselmo and Emilio Azcarraga. When Azcarraga's majority ownership—held under a corporate identity—was revealed, the FCC forced SICC to sell its stations under rules barring foreign ownership of broadcast entities. Azcarraga, a citizen of Mexico, is president of that country's broadcasting conglomerate, Televisa. Although he was also the majority stockholder in the SIN network, it was not similarly affected by the FCC rules. Nevertheless, when the stations were sold the network was sold as well. The buyer, Univision Holdings, was in turn bought out a year later by Hallmark Cards.

SIN was one of the first networks in the U.S. to interconnect its affiliates by satellite. The satellite was also used to carry live programming from Televisa, including all 52 games of the 1986 World Cup Soccer Tournament in Mexico City. Rene Anselmo, Azcarraga's partner and the minority stockholder in SIN and SICC, was president of both companies until their sale.

SINATRA, FRANK ▶ one of the great names in popular entertainment who failed to carve out a niche in television. Neither of two attempts at a regular series was successful, the first a half-hour variety series on CBS (October 1950 to April 1952), the second a variety hour alternating with dramatic plays on ABC (October 1957 to June 1958). Both were called *The Frank Sinatra Show*.

More successful were his specials, including one in 1974 that involved live coverage by ABC of his concert at Madison Square Garden. The production was assigned to the sports department because of its experience in covering auditorium events live.

SING ALONG WITH MITCH ▶ musical hour of bouncy tunes on NBC (1961-65) hosted and conducted by Mitch Miller, noted producer for Columbia Records, and growing out of his popular series of *Sing Along* albums. The songs were performed mainly by The Sing Along Gang, a male chorus of 25, and by such resident female vocalists as Leslie Uggams, Diana Trask and Gloria Lambert. Miller wore a beard before beards were fashionable, Uggams was featured before blacks became prominent in TV, and the series itself, for its form, had no precedent for the success it enjoyed. It was produced by All American Features.

SINGING DETECTIVE, THE ▶ controversial and provocative BBC mini-series, which starred Michael Gambon as a writer of detective novels who has been hospitalized in London, incapacitated by a crippling attack of psoriatic arthritis. As the illness rages, he imagines scenes from his first mystery story and from his own life.

Created by British writer Dennis Potter, with Kenith Trodd as executive producer (both of whom were responsible for *Pennies From Heaven,* another surrealistic English mini-series), it was peppered with fantasy scenes, popular songs and sardonic production numbers. Gambon was supported by a huge cast, including Lyndon Davies, Janet Suzman, Patrick Malahide, Joanne Whalley, Bill Paterson, Alison Steadman, David Ryall and Imelda Staunton. The series aired originally on BBC (1986) and was televised on PBS over three Sunday nights in January 1988; each episode was two hours long. Jon Amiel directed; Rick McCallum was also an executive producer.

Michael Gambon in the BBC mini-series *The Singing Detective*

SIPHONING ▶ the drawing off of program fare by one medium from another, as occurred when television "siphoned off" radio's most popular programs. Commercial broadcasters have alerted the FCC to the likelihood of subscription TV and pay cable similarly siphoning its programs. Because this holds the prospect of people being asked to pay for what they now receive free, the FCC adopted anti-siphoning rules for the pay services. The rules were later struck down by the courts as unconstitutional and improper.

SISKEL & EBERT **▶** long-running syndicated movie-review series hosted by two Chicago film critics, Gene Siskel of the *Chicago Tribune* and Roger Ebert of the rival *Chicago Sun-Times.* It is one of the few successful commercially syndicated shows to have sprung from public television.

The show's hosts, known for becoming passionate on air in their disagreements over films, were brought together in 1978 by public TV station WTTW, which produced a series called *Sneak Previews* for PBS. It became so popular that Tribune Entertainment, which is also located in Chicago, spirited the two away for a commercial series in 1982. The show was given a new name, *Siskel & Ebert at the Movies,* and played successfully on commercial TV. The hosts became known for expressing their opinions of films with either a thumbs-up or thumbs-down rating, a practice that has so entered the film review vocabulary that two-thumbs-up has become a standard marketing gambit.

When Tribune dropped the pair for reviewers Rex Reed and Bill Harris, Disney's syndication arm, Buena Vista, picked them up and renamed the show simply *Siskel & Ebert.*

Gene Siskel and Roger Ebert

SIT IN **▶** a historic 1960 documentary on the sit-in movement for civil rights in the South, prepared by Irving Gitlin for NBC News. The 60-minute film concentrated on events in Nashville and covered the issue from both sides of the conflict. Gitlin was executive producer, Al Wasserman producer and Chet Huntley narrator.

SITUATION COMEDY ▶ American television's signature program form, the half-hour story comedy that plays episodically, usually against a laugh track. Sitcoms have evolved over the years from simple domestic contrivances like *Father Knows Best* and *The Life of Riley* to the sophisticated ensemble playlets of *M*A*S*H, Taxi* and *Cheers.*

Hit sitcoms have extraordinary value, both to their networks and their producers. Single 30-minute series like *I Love Lucy, Happy Days, All in the Family* and *The Cosby Show* have had the power to carry an entire evening for their networks, and their reruns seemingly go on forever on independent stations. As generally the most sought-after programs in the syndication market, sitcoms tend to fetch the highest prices; *Cosby,* for example, reaped around $1 million an episode.

The ratings supremacy of CBS through the 1950s, 1960s and most of the 1970s may be traced to a sitcom hit parade that ranged from *I Love Lucy* and *The Honeymooners* to *The Mary Tyler Moore Show, M*A*S*H* and *All in the Family.* In between were some twoscore comedy hits that included *Burns and Allen, Leave It to Beaver, Mr. Ed, The Phil Silvers Show, Our Miss Brooks, Gilligan's Island, My Three Sons, The Andy Griffith Show, The Beverly Hillbillies, Green Acres, Hogan's Heroes, The Dick Van Dyke Show, Maude, Rhoda, Phyllis, The Bob Newhart Show,* and *The Jeffersons.* It would seem that when CBS lost the touch for shows in the form, it also lost the ratings lead.

A form invented by television, the situation comedy derives its name from a dependency on some incident or plot device to activate the comedy talent—Lucille Ball, for example—or the essential comedy premise. Vital to the sitcom is that the characters behave predictably; it is their constancy in each new situation that produces the essential tickle. Sgt. Bilko, Ralph Kramden and Archie Bunker were unfailingly funny whenever they reverted to type.

Not to belittle the form, the closest equivalent to the sitcom in literature is the comic strip—it, too, with characters who never grow or change and always act as expected. It was not surprising, then, that the networks adapted comics to situation comedy. NBC succeeded with *Hazel,* ABC with *The Addams Family* and CBS with *Dennis the Menace.* They also succeeded in turning sitcoms into animated comic strips, as with *The Flintstones, The Jetsons* and *The Simpsons.*

The level of sophistication in situation comedy has changed markedly over the years but not the essential form or formula. Everything before *All in the Family* was wholesome; that program, in 1970, broke new ground for subject matter and made revolutionary changes in how sitcom protagonists address their fellow humans. Bigotry, hysterectomies, homosexuality, menopause and impotency were aspects of life walled out of Lucy's experience; her raciest deed, in 1953, was to have a baby. Yet, although thematically the two shows seem eons apart, they both are at the core comedies about two more or less contrasting couples, and both have a central figure to make the funny faces. The fact that Jackie Gleason's *The Honeymooners* fits the identical pattern, and *The Dick Van Dyke Show* comes close, argues against coincidence.

The sitcom has never been precisely one thing but over the years has branched off into schools. Family comedy was one school, spanning *Mama, Father of the Bride, Trouble with Father, The Life of Riley, Ozzie and Harriet, My Little Margie, The Donna Reed Show, Good Times, Happy Days, The Brady Bunch, The Jeffersons, Cosby, Roseanne* and *The Simpsons.* Related was "heart" comedy, depicting the widows and widowers of the late 1960s and the divorcees of the 1970s—*My Three Sons, Family Affair, Julia, The Doris Day Show, The Courtship of Eddie's Father, Fay* and *One Day at a Time.*

There was also the musical sitcom (*The Partridge Family, The Monkees*); the fantasy sitcom (*I Dream of Jeannie, My Mother the Car, Mr. Ed, Bewitched, Mork and Mindy*); the service sitcom (*McHale's Navy, Hogan's Heroes, F Troop, M*A*S*H*); and the police sitcom (*Barney Miller, The Cop and the Kid*).

But all answer to the basic principle of external circumstances setting in motion a cast of appealing two-dimensional characters and releasing the built-in comedy component. The formula calls for complications in the story but always, always the matter is neatly resolved. And whether it involved the sophisticates of *M*A*S*H* or the witless inhabitants of *Gilligan's Island,* 30 minutes after the start the principals are happy.

SIX MILLION DOLLAR MAN ▶ fantasy adventure series about a former astronaut with a super-human body—the result of its having been rebuilt by futuristic, cybernetic medical science at a cost of $6 million—who is given difficult special assignments by a government agency called the Office of Strategic Information. Lee Majors had the title role of Steve Austin, with Richard Anderson as O.S.I. leader Oscar Goldman and Alan Openheimer (replaced by Martin E. Brooks) as Dr. Rudy Wells, in the series produced by Universal TV. It premiered on ABC in the fall of 1973 as a monthly entry and the following January became a weekly hour series. It was canceled in March 1978.

Based on Martin Caidin's sci-fi novel *Cyborg,* the series became so popular that it spun off a program with a similar premise, *Bionic Woman.* Harve Bennett was executive producer of both series.

SIX WIVES OF HENRY VIII ▶ BBC series of six 90-minute dramas, which found an appreciative audience when CBS offered them in the summer of 1971, two years after they aired in Britain. Anthony Quayle narrated and Keith Mitchell played King Henry. Separately featured in each episode were Annette Crosbie, Dorothy Tutin, Anne Stallybrass, Elvi Hale, Angela Pleasence and Rosalie Crutchley, as the wives.

SIXTH REPORT AND ORDER ▶ momentous document issued by the FCC on April 14, 1952, lifting the four-year freeze on station licenses as of July 1 that year and establishing a permanent table of assignments for TV frequencies in 1,291 cities. The report set off an avalanche of competing applications for the choicest assignments.

The culmination of a long study looking toward an orderly and technically efficient plan for the allocation of TV channels around the country, the Sixth Report and Order provided for 2,053 stations, 617 of them on VHF and 1,463 on UHF. Of that number, 242 were designated noncommercial, 80 of those on VHF. The order also established three broad geographic zones, each with its own mileage separation standards and regulations for antenna height.

The FCC later revised the table, increasing the number of channels for both commercial and educational use.

60 MINUTES ▶ the CBS newsmagazine series, begun on Tuesday, September 24, 1968, that developed into a television institution. Among its other distinctions, the series contributed a new program form to the medium that has been widely adopted, both for serious and tabloid forms of journalism.

Its current correspondents, known as co-editors, are Mike Wallace, who has been with the program since its inception; Morley Safer, who joined in 1970; Ed Bradley, who succeeded Dan Rather in 1981; Steve Kroft, who came on in 1989; and Lesley Stahl, who started in 1991. Essayist Andy Rooney has been a celebrated, and cantankerous, contributor since 1978. Among the originals was Harry Reasoner, who switched networks in 1970 and then rejoined from ABC in 1978. Reasoner died in 1991.

Because of its perennially high viewership, the show's staff changes often generate news, as when Diane Sawyer left in 1989 to join ABC's *Prime-Time Live* as co-anchor.

The hallmarks of *60 Minutes* have been its newsmaking interviews and investigative reports. Over the years, aggressive interviews by Wallace and Safer have included subjects who range alphabetically and philosophically from Spiro Agnew to Deng Xiaoping. With all its critical acclaim, high-ratings (almost invariably in the Nielsen top ten) and awards, *60 Minutes* has also come in for its share of criticism, principally for practicing what has been called "ambush journalism". This involves a reporter, usually Mike Wallace, and a film crew pursuing and surprising the reticent subject of an interview and coming away with either awkward verbal responses or explosive behavior that suggests villainy.

60 Minutes began with anemic ratings, as a Tuesday 10 p.m. show alternating with *CBS Reports* opposite the popular *Marcus Welby, M.D.* on ABC. In the fall of 1971 it was moved to Sundays at 6 p.m. as a weekly series, but because NFL football spilled into that time period the series went off the air until the end of football season. CBS noticed, however, that *60 Minutes* was drawing larger audiences in Sunday fringe time than it had in prime time, partly because it competed only with local or syndicated programs. The breakthrough occurred in 1975 when a change in the FCC's prime time-access rule permitted the networks to claim an extra hour on Sundays, 7-8 p.m., but only for children's programs or news and public affairs. When CBS encountered clearance problems from its affiliates because of its previous hold on the 6 p.m. hour, it freed the earlier hour and took the newly available 7 p.m. prime-time slot. With a loyal following by then, and no competition from popular adult entertainment series, *60 Minutes* began drawing prime-time audiences that ranked with the top entertainment programs. Moreover, it has been an enormously profitable program for CBS.

Its success prompted ABC to create a somewhat similar series with *20/20* and NBC to attempt newsmagazine programs of its own. By the 1990s the cost-conscious networks each had several magazine-style shows in prime time, while the Fox network and the syndication field were flooded with tabloid versions of the newsmagazine form, many of them in the mode dubbed by critics "trash television."

Don Hewitt, who created the series, has remained its executive producer and guiding force. Among the scores of producers (doing most of the actual reporting) who contributed importantly to the program over the years have been Lowell Bergman, David Buksbaum, Joe DeCola, Grace Diekhaus, Holly and Paul Fine, Marion Goldin, Imre Horvath, Jim Jackson, Barry Lando, Jeanne Soloman-Langley, Paul Loewenwarter, William McClure, Harry Moses, Igor Oganesoff, Philip Scheffler, John Tiffin, Al Wasserman and Joe Wershba.

$64,000 QUESTION, THE ▶ see Game Shows.

SKASE, CHRISTOPHER ▶ for a time, as head of the Qintex Group, one of the wealthiest and most flamboyant television executives in Australia. He effectively owned the Seven Network and in the late 1980s moved in on Hollywood, buying the company that owned Hal Roach Studios and Robert Halmi Productions. His Qintex had coproduced an American hit, *Lonesome Dove,* and had the valuable foreign distribution rights. But in 1989, as with Alan Bond and Frank Lowy at the other Australian networks, his bubble burst. By 1990, Qintex was in liquidation and the Seven Network essentially under the control of the banks that had lent money to Skase.

Skase began his rise in 1975 when he left his job as a financial journalist to set up an investment company with a mere $12,000. He had a wave of spectacular successes and parlayed them to head the group that bought the Seven Network in 1988. By then he had already bought a major stake in Hal Roach/Halmi. A sudden steep decline in the Australian economy, coupled with unrealistic program buying by the fiercely competitive television networks under their new owners, brought on his downfall.

SKELTON, RED ▶ a comedian and clown who was the CBS Tuesday night mainstay from 1953 to 1970, having successfully adapted his radio comedy-variety show to a weekly TV hour. His broad, slapstick style and numerous character creations appealed to the unsophisticated, but his artistry as a mime revealed itself in wordless vignettes, often laced with pathos, such as the classic of an old man watching a patriotic parade.

Skelton's most familiar characters were the rustic Clem Kaddidlehopper, the inebriated Willy Lump-Lump, the tophatted Freddie the Freeloader and the Mean Widdle Kid. In 1956 he appeared on *Playhouse 90* in a dramatic role in *The Big Slide.*

CBS canceled Skelton's Tuesday night series in 1970 while it was still high-rated, a move calculated to increase the network's share of the youthful, urban audience. NBC tried Skelton in a half-hour Monday night variety show the following season, but it was unsuccessful.

SKIATRON ▶ an early pay-TV system demonstrated before World War II. A prototype system was tested in the 1950s, but the company faded under the FCC's regulatory delays for pay TV.

SKIPPY, THE BUSH KANGAROO ▶ Australian series for children syndicated in the U.S. (1968-69) under Kellogg Co. sponsorship and produced by Norfolk International. Filmed in Australia's Waratah National Park, the series featured Garry Pankhurst and Ken James as Sonny and Mark, Ed Deveraux as Matt Hammond and Liza Goddard as Clancy.

SKY CABLE ▶ an aborted plan by four substantial partners to launch the first high-power direct broadcast satellite service. The project was especially interesting because of who the partners were: NBC, Cablevision Systems, Rupert Murdoch's News Corp. and Hughes Communications. Hughes's sister company, Hughes Aircraft, was to have built the satellites.

Sky Cable was announced as a venture on Feb. 21, 1991. Though DBS had a modest history of no success in the U.S., the Sky Cable consortium had the financial resources the earlier attempts lacked. Yet in less than a year the venture folded because of the potential difficulty in obtaining existing program services.

Sky Cable's intention to use high-power satellites meant that the consumer could receive the signals by means of small, low-cost antennas. In addition, by employing digital compression on the satellites, each transponder would carry four channels instead of one. The plan envisioned a satellite designed for 27 transponders, which meant that Sky Cable could offer 108 channels of programming, more than any cable system at that time.

Financing plans for this ambitious effort called for $75 million in equity from each partner. Hughes also would commit $325 million itself, money that it could not recover from its partners in the event the venture failed but that would leave the satellite and its attendant hardware in Hughes's hands to market elsewhere. The remainder of the $1 billion expected to be laid out before break-even was to have been secured from banks.

The success of Sky Cable depended on access to existing pay- and basic-cable services, including, for example, CNN, HBO and ESPN. But by mid-1990, some of the partners began to worry that securing these services might not be possible without legislative intervention. NBC and News Corp. were finding the cable networks reluctant to deal with Sky Cable because they did not want to alienate the cable operators on whom they depend for distribution. Cable owners, concerned about being hit with new regulation over the issue, argued that existing anti-trust laws were sufficient to prevent cable from tying up the program services with exclusivity clauses in the contracts for purposes of stifling competition from Sky.

Cable bills introduced in both the House and Senate would have eased Sky's access to the existing cable programming, but a compromise on that issue fell apart, and the lobbying effort of the National Cable Television Association succeeded in scuttling the attempts at cable re-regulation in October 1990. Meanwhile, Murdoch was losing his enthusiasm for Sky Cable as his News Corp. struggled with debt in the billions and with some sectors of his company performing poorly. By early 1991, Hughes was looking for new partners.

SKY KING ▶ a CBS children's series (1953-54) about a cowboy who flies a plane called *The Songbird.* Featuring Kirby Grant and Gloria Winters as Schuyler J. (Sky) King and his niece, Penny, it was produced by Jack Chertok Productions for National Biscuit Co.

SLADE, BERNARD ▶ writer of situation comedies for Screen Gems (Columbia Pictures TV), including the pilot for *The Flying Nun.* He created and wrote *The Partridge Family* and wrote episodes of *Bewitched.* He went on to write a smash hit for Broadway in 1975, *Same Time, Next Year,* and in 1984 wrote the stage play of *Fatal Attraction,* which later became a motion picture.

SLAKOFF, MORT ▶ senior vice president of creative services for MCA TV since 1981, after having served in a similar capacity for Metromedia Television. Previously he worked for Metromedia Producers Corporation, Viacom, Time-Life Films, and NBC Films.

SLATTERY'S PEOPLE ▶ hour-long CBS series (1964) in which Richard Crenna portrayed a state legislator, Jim Slattery, facing modern social and political challenges. Bing Crosby Productions produced 36 episodes.

SLOAN COMMISSION REPORT ON CABLE ▶ major statement on cable TV's potential to benefit society and a powerful endorsement of the medium, issued in 1971 by the Commission on Cable Communications, established by the Alfred P. Sloan Foundation in 1970. The commission's report, entitled *On the Cable,* was published Dec. 8, 1971, by McGraw-Hill. The report portrayed cable TV as "the television of abundance" supplanting the present "television of scarcity," and it noted that the nature of the medium would be transformed when it was no longer based on scarcity. In its conclusions, the commission held it in the public interest to encourage the growth of cable, and it predicted another communications revolution in the 1980s when, as it accurately envisioned, 40 to 60% of U.S. homes would be "on the cable."

SMALL, WILLIAM J. ▶ former president of NBC News (1979-82) who left after management changes in the company made Robert Mulholland, an arch rival, his immediate superior as president of NBC. Small had brought a number of CBS traditions and personnel to NBC, and reportedly these irked Mulholland, a longtime executive of NBC News. After working in cable as host of a book show, Small joined Fordham University in 1986 as a professor of communications and the director of the Center for Communications there.

Before joining NBC, Small was a CBS News executive for 17 years and was Washington v.p. for CBS Inc., serving as the corporation's chief liaison to the government and its agencies.

He had been director of hard news operations for CBS News since 1974, with the title of senior vice-president. During his preceding 12 years as Washington bureau chief for CBS, he established a reputation as a tough-minded and hard-driving news executive.

Before joining CBS in 1962, he had served as a news director of stations in his native Chicago (WLS-AM) and Louisville (WHAS-TV). He was president of RTNDA in 1960 and of Sigma Delta Chi, the professional journalism society, in 1974.

Small's books are *To Kill a Messenger: Television and the Real World* (1970) and *Political Power and the Press* (1972).

SMATV (SATELLITE MASTER ANTENNA SYSTEMS) ▶ miniature cable systems serving housing complexes or hotels that have built-in master antenna systems for closed-circuit television. These are legitimate private cable systems operating within the franchise areas of full-blown cable companies. In buildings and complexes already internally wired, an SMATV entrepreneur need only install a satellite dish to pull down the program services and sell them to the residents. SMATVs flourished in the years before cable penetrated the major cities.

SMITH, "BUFFALO" BOB ▶ creator of *Howdy Doody,* early children's hit on NBC (1947-60). He began in broadcasting as a pianist and vocalist on radio stations WGR and WBEN, Buffalo, from the 1930s through 1946. The following year he started a children's program on WNBC Radio in New York, which blossomed into TV's *Howdy Doody.* After a 16-year retirement from TV, Smith returned with a syndicated revival of the show in 1976, but it was short-lived.

SMITH, HARRY ▶ co-anchor of CBS's *This Morning* since its premiere in November 1987. Smith's daily anchor duties have included a wide range of interviews and breaking-story coverage, both in the studio and on location. During the height of the Persian Gulf War, he reported live from Saudi Arabia. He has also originated *This Morning* broadcasts from Japan, Poland, Hungary, Cuba, France, Italy, Egypt, Israel and Jordan.

Despite its no-frills approach, and with CBS billing it as "breakfast for your head," *This Morning* has perennially finished third in the Nielsens behind ABC's *Good Morning America* and NBC's *Today.*

In addition to his sunrise anchoring, Smith is a frequent contributor to *48 Hours* and has substituted for Charles Kuralt as host of CBS News's *Sunday Morning.* Prior to joining CBS News in 1986, Smith was a reporter and anchor for KMGH-TV, the CBS affiliate in Denver. He began in broadcasting as a radio host and disc jockey in Denver and Cincinnati.

SMITH, HOWARD K. ▶ correspondent and commentator for ABC News (1961-79), after having spent 20 previous years with CBS News, more than half of them as chief European correspondent. Smith became co-anchor of the *ABC Evening News* in May 1969 (teamed initially with Frank Reynolds and in 1970 with Harry Reasoner) and in September 1975 became the program's daily commentator. In a career of many distinctions, Smith had been moderator of the historic first *Great Debate* in 1960 between Kennedy and Nixon.

He resigned from ABC News in April 1979 when he perceived that his role in the newscast was being eliminated. He said that he did not want to be left without a real function.

Recognized by his peers as a political liberal through most of his career, Smith became an outspoken hawk during the Vietnam War and came to be one of the medium's more conservative voices during the Nixon Administration. Indeed, although it was Smith who presented the *Political Obituary of Richard M. Nixon* on ABC in 1962 after Nixon's defeat in the California gubernatorial race (in a program involving an interview with Alger Hiss), he was to become so trusted by President Nixon in the late 1960s that he became the first broadcast newsperson to interview the President in a one-to-one format. The live telecast (March 22, 1971) was entitled *White House Conversation: The President and Howard K. Smith.* Smith also publicly expressed some sympathy with Vice-President Agnew's charge that the broadcast press was politically biased.

A Rhodes Scholar, Smith began his journalism career with the United Press in Europe during World War II. He joined CBS as Berlin correspondent in 1941 and remained in Europe through most of the war. In 1946 he covered the Nuremberg war crimes trials. He became Washington correspondent for CBS News in 1957 and four years later was named chief correspondent and manager of the bureau. After a dispute with management, he switched allegiances to ABC News.

SMITH, KATE (d. 1986) ▶ singer and major radio star who made the transition to TV with two shows in the early 1950s—a daily program in the afternoons and a weekly series at night. They ended midway in the decade, and her work in TV since had largely been confined to guest shots and occasional specials.

SMITH, SIDNEY F. R. ▶ producer-director of TV specials ranging from the Metropolitan Opera *Salute to Rudolf Bing* to the Miss U.S.A. and Miss Universe pageants. His credits include *V.D. Blues* for PBS, *Elizabeth Taylor in London,*

Victor Borge at Lincoln Center, The Bell Telephone Hour and the Emmy Awards telecast.

SMITHSONIAN ▶ series of nonfiction specials on CBS produced during the 1970s by Wolper Productions in cooperation with the Smithsonian Institution. The documentary programs, generally on natural history, followed the tradition of the National Geographic, Jacques Cousteau and Jane Goodall series. George Lefferts was executive producer.

SMOTHERS BROTHERS DISPUTE ▶ an episode in the spring of 1969 in which a pair of star performers, Tom and Dick Smothers, clashed with CBS over the censorial practices of the network's standards and practices department and lost both the battle and their Sunday night program. As grounds for their dismissal, CBS cited their tardiness in delivering tapes of the shows in time for closed-circuit previews for the affiliates, but it was already clear to the network that the comedians would not conform to the CBS acceptance standards and that the conflict would go on indefinitely. The Smothers Brothers had also committed the unforgivable: They spoke abusively of CBS in public and took their case to Washington. It was a classic case of creative expression stifled by the rigid rules of the corporation. But the rules had their origins in the broadcast laws that hold the individual stations, and not the artist, responsible for what goes out over the air.

The Smothers Brothers Comedy Hour on CBS was an unexpected smash when it began early in 1967 as a mid-season replacement to compete with NBC's high-rated *Bonanza.* The youthful comedians took the measure of the established western hit with a style of comedy that inclined to social satire, topical jokes and political shafts. Their brand of humor and their mild identification with the youthful protest movements of the times were largely what brought on their success—*Rowan and Martin's Laugh-In* was a concurrent phenomenon on NBC—but it was also what brought down the censors.

Religious jokes, conversations about dissenters to the Vietnam War and references to the female anatomy (all mild by the liberated standards of the 1970s) were continually cut from the scripts or ordered softened. The comedians took their complaints to the press, and through most of 1968 the CBS deletions were grist for a TV reporter's mill. The brothers also enlisted support from Nicholas Johnson, an FCC commissioner, and visited congressmen with their complaint against the network.

Ironically, less than two years later, CBS brought in another mid-season replacement (*All in the Family*) that not only violated all the rules but forced all the networks to broaden their acceptance standards. Meanwhile, the Smothers Brothers were given a summertime show on ABC, which failed, then had a short-lived syndicated program.

SMPTE (SOCIETY OF MOTION PICTURE AND TELEVISION ENGINEERS) ▶ professional organization of specialists in the closely allied visual arts, which works at establishing technical standards for lighting, equipment and film. Founded in 1916 as The Society of Motion Picture Engineers (SMPE), its original purpose was to disseminate technical information and provide a forum for the standardization of equipment. After the "T" for television was added in 1950, the society became the major U.S. standards-setting organization for TV equipment.

SNG ▶ see ENG (Electronic News Gathering).

SNOOP SISTERS, THE ▶ one of the rotating series in the NBC *Wednesday Mystery Movie* lineup in 1973, which featured Helen Hayes and Mildred Natwick as Ernesta and Gwendolin Snoop, quaint old ladies who write mystery stories and solve crimes. Produced by Talent Associates-Norton Simon Inc., it yielded six films.

SNS (SATELLITE NEWS SERVICE) ▶ a cable channel created in 1982 to compete with Ted Turner's CNN. The partners in the venture were two powerful broadcast organizations, ABC and Group W. Their edge on Turner was that they had long experience in television news and excellent personnel resources, while he was a novice in journalism patching together a news organization. Moreover, SNS was well financed by two prosperous companies, while Turner's finances were shaky and exacerbated by CNN's heavy annual losses.

But Turner had the advantage of a two-year head start on his new competition; more importantly, he had the loyalty and support of the cable industry, since he was one of their number and ABC was not (Group W had owned-cable systems then, as well as broadcast stations). The new channel, which was live 24 hours a day, found CNN too well entrenched, and after 16 months—with less than one-third of Turner's household penetration—it went up for sale. Turner bought his competitor for $25 million and shut it down.

SNYDER, TOM ▶ NBC News personality and host of the *Tomorrow* program (1973-81), who in June 1979 also became anchor of the network's new newsmagazine *Prime Time Sunday,* which lasted one season. Snyder made the leap from local newscaster to the network in the fall of 1973 after his three-year stint as anchor for KNBC, the NBC o&o in Los Angeles, gave the station news leadership in the market. Earlier, he had demonstrated his popular appeal and interviewing abilities at KYW-TV Philadelphia. Snyder began his broadcast news career at a Milwaukee radio station in 1957 and spent the next 16 years working at TV stations around the country until NBC selected him for *Tomorrow.*

For a time, Snyder doubled as anchor of *News Center 4,* the WNBC-TV local newscast in New York, but in 1977 he returned to Los Angeles and made that the originating base for *Tomorrow.* In 1981, he balked at being teamed with Rona Barrett. Soon after, he lost his time period to a new program with David Letterman.

***SOAP* ▶** unusual ABC prime-time series that interpreted daytime soap opera in situation comedy terms; it was launched successfully in September 1977 but only after provoking a storm of protest, while it was still in production, over its heavy concentration on sex and sexuality. The series ended its run in 1981.

Magazine reports on *Soap*'s two-part plot carried the litany of its themes: adultery, transvestism, impotency, frigidity, voyeurism, premarital sex and more. Angered that such a program was being prepared for the prime evening hours when young people would be watching, religious groups organized campaigns to ban the program. Some groups succeeded in driving *Soap*'s charter advertisers out of the series by threatening to boycott their products. The furor subsided with the program's premiere, accompanied by ABC's public statements that subsequent episodes would be toned down and that the series would not, even by implication, condone aberrant behavior.

The show was built around the families of two sisters, one family upper-middle-class, the other distinctly blue-collar. Each member of the families became distinctive through his or her hang-ups. As in soap opera, the various strands of plot continued from week to week, but as in situation comedies the segments managed to stand as episodes in themselves. A new series, *Benson,* was spun off in the 1979-80 season from the character of the butler, played by Robert Guillaume.

Katherine Helmond and Diana Canova—as Jessica Tate and her daughter, Corinne—headed the large cast, which included Robert Mandan as Jessica's husband Chester, Jennifer Salt as Eunice Tate, Jimmy Baio as Rilly Tate, Cathryn Damon as Jessica's sister Mary Campbell, Richard Mulligan as Mary's husband Burt, Billy Crystal as Mary's son Jodie Dallas, Ted Wass as Mary's son Danny, Robert Urich as Peter and Arthur Peterson as Grandpa Tate.

The series was created and written by Susan Harris, who also served as producer. Executive producers were Tony Thomas and Paul Junger Witt, and Jay Sandrich was director. It was via Witt/Thomas/Harris Productions.

SOAP OPERAS ▶ serialized romantic melodramas that have been a mainstay of the network daytime schedules since the glory days of radio. Though they are known formally as daytime dramas or daytime serials, they were long ago dubbed soap operas (or soaps, for short) because, being aimed at housewives, they tended to be sponsored by soap companies, principally Procter & Gamble and Lever Bros. (now Unilever).

Their unique characteristic is that they are conceived with no end in view, meant to run endlessly. *The Guiding Light,* which dates back to radio, is more than half a century old. Each soap is always a complex tapestry of interwoven stories that unfold slowly, and well before any one of the story strands is resolved new strands enter the fabric, usually through the introduction of new characters. The casts are large and ever-changing, but the essential themes and story ingredients are unchanging: everyone's love life is somehow disordered or in crisis, unscrupulous men and despicable "other women" abound, and unhappiness is the prevailing mood. The pot is stirred variously with adultery, nymphomania, drug addiction, untimely pregnancies, racism, homosexuality, insanity, and criminality.

When they are working right, the soaps are addictive; the line, "Tune in tomorrow," was written for them. Traditionally they are scheduled in the span from 11 a.m. to 4:30 p.m., with those in the late afternoon geared to somewhat younger audiences. Unlike Americans, the British schedule their soaps in the early evening, and consistently three of them—

Granada's *Coronation Street*, BBC's *EastEnders* and the Australian import, *Neighbours*—are among the top-rated nighttime programs in any week. *Coronation Street* has been running more than 30 years. Also in marked contrast to the U.S., the successful British soaps are about working-class people, while the American serials all involve middle-class and upper middle-class people, with a strong emphasis on doctors, lawyers, architects and other professionals.

Daytime radio soaps originated in Chicago with *Painted Dreams* in 1930, and for many years afterwards the genre was centered there. In part this was because Irna Phillips, the premier writer and creator of programs in the form, was based in that city. Today, virtually all the daytime serials are produced in New York.

The early soaps ran in 15-minute lengths, which may have been a reason they had difficulty establishing themselves in television. As was discovered later, radio programs needed twice the time when translated to television. The first TV soap to succeed was *Search For Tomorrow*, which began in 1951 and ran until 1986. Mary Stuart, who was in the original cast, remained the star throughout the show's run. *The Guiding Light* switched over from radio in 1952. CBS introduced two new soaps on the same day in 1956, which was news in itself, but the big innovation was that both shows were built on 30-minute episodes. The shows were *As the World Turns*, written by Irna Phillips, and *The Edge of Night. As the World Turns* became a blockbuster hit, the most popular TV soap of all time. Before long, the 30-minute format became standard for all serials. Then in 1975 NBC took the bold step of expanding two of its most successful soaps, *Another World* and *Days of Our Lives*, to daily hour-long episodes, and that ploy also worked.

Because soaps are produced on fairly modest budgets, a fraction of what the big prime-time series cost on a per-episode basis, they can be immensely profitable. But starting a new soap is a hugely expensive commitment because the serials usually require six months to a year to catch on, with no assurances that they will.

On several occasions, new soaps were inspired by what was popular in prime time that season, but that short cut never led to pay-dirt. *Young Dr. Malone* was an attempt in the mid-1960s to get in on the popularity of *Ben Casey* and *Dr. Kildare*. Later, *Texas* hoped to pick up on the popularity of *Dallas*. In 1962, amid the great excitement over space exploration, a soap called *The Clear Horizon* was attempted, supposedly set in Cape Canaveral. As it proved, its only significance was that, as a Hollywood-produced show, it broke the New York lock on the form.

The soaps have been an enormous boon to actors, having employed thousands over the years. For some the daytime serials provided an early career opportunity; for others, whose film careers had faded, soaps offered a chance to work again.

Among the noted actors who paid their dues in the soaps were Eva Marie Saint, Hal Holbrook, Lee Grant, Tony Randall, Ellen Burstyn, Efrem Zimbalist, Jr., Sandy Dennis and Patrick O'Neal. Going back to radio, the list includes Art Carney, Van Heflin, Macdonald Carey, Richard Widmark and Orson Welles, among many others. Following are the notable television soaps:

Larkin Malloy and Susan Lucci in a scene from the ABC serial *All My Children*

ALL MY CHILDREN—(ABC 1970—) dramatic serial surrounding the Martin and Tyler families and other residents of Pine Valley. The show was created by Agnes Nixon and has been lauded for its attention to social issues, along with its heavy doses of romantic fantasy and light satire. The cast has included Ruth Warrick, Mary Fickett, Susan Lucci, Ray MacDonnell, William Mooney, James Mitchell, Harriet Hall, Hugh Franklin, Taylor Miller, Michael Knight, David Canary, Larkin Malloy, and Richard Van Vleet, among many others.

ANOTHER WORLD—(NBC 1964—) ongoing melodrama depicting the travails of a middle-class family living in the midwestern college town of Bay City. The show focuses on the characters' passions and conflicts in their daily lives. Its stars have included Hugh Marlowe, David Canary, Anne Meacham, Paul Stevens, Constance Ford, Irene Dailey, Douglass Watson, Beverly Penberthy, Victoria Wyndham, and Stephen Schnetzer.

AS THE WORLD TURNS—(CBS 1956—) serial revolving on the romantic trials of residents of fictional Oakdale, principally the Hugheses and the Lowells, as they cope with the stresses of love, work and family frictions. The members of the cast have included Helen Wagner, Eileen Fulton, Henderson Forsythe, Don Hastings, Anthony Herrera, Lisa Loring, Elaine Princi, Don MacLaughlin, Larry Bryggman, Kathryn Hays, Lindsay Frost, and Coleen Zenk, among others.

THE BOLD AND THE BEAUTIFUL—(CBS 1987—) daytime serial set in the fashion district of Los Angeles and centering on the Forresters and the Logans. Written by the creators of *The Young and The Restless*, the series also features unusually gorgeous characters as they bravely cope with the vicissitudes of life. Star cast members have included John McCook, Susan Flannery, Clayton Norcross, Jeff Trachta, Ronn Moss, Teri Ann Linn, Colleen Dion, Robert Pine, Judith Baldwin, Katherine Kelly Lang, and others.

THE BRIGHTER DAY—(CBS 1954-62) daily drama revolving around a widowed reverend, his flock, and his family in the town of New Hope. The storylines concentrated on the characters' personal problems, which ranged from alcoholism to psychiatric disorders. William Smith, Blair Davies, Mona Bruns, Maggie O'Neill, Hal Holbrook, Patty Duke, Forrest Compton and Mary Linn Beller made up some of the cast.

CAPITOL—(CBS 1982-87) serial depicting the conflicts and tensions between two feuding Washington, D.C., families, the Cleggs and the McCandlesses. Though the story was set in a city that was more than 70% non-white, not a single black character appeared on the program for the first three years. Some of the cast members were Marj Dusay, Richard Egan, Nicholas Walker, Catherine Hickland, Rory Calhoun, Constance Towers, Dane Witherspoon, Christopher Durham, and Michael Catlin.

DARK SHADOWS—(ABC 1966-71) gothic soap opera dealing with witchcraft, werewolves and vampires, with the story built around a governess in a house of mystery, that of the Collinses. The stories switched between the contemporary family and their ancestors of the 19th century. The serial was revived for NBC prime time in 1991 but was canceled after a few months. The original cast included Alexandra Moltke, Jonathan Frid, Joan Bennett, Mitchell Ryan, Louis Edmonds, Nancy Barrett, Grayson Hall, Lara Parker, and David Henesy, among others.

DAYS OF OUR LIVES—(NBC 1965—) continuing melodrama set in Salem, Mass., dealing with the sexual and psychological ups and downs of the Horton, Martin, Williams, and Craig families. It later became one the first soap operas to incorporate musical numbers. Members of the cast have included Macdonald Carey, Francis Reid, Brenda Benet, Jed Allen, Melinda Fee, Meg Wyllie, John Clark, Robert Clary, Patsy Pease, Michael Sabatino, Lanna Saunders, Peter Reckell, Jane Windsor, Stephen Nichols, and Deidre Hall.

THE DOCTORS—(NBC 1963-82) daytime serial whose stories were built on the personal and professional lives of the medical staff of Hope Memorial Hospital. Members of the cast included Lydia Bruce, Jim Pritchett, Maia Danziger, Larry Riley, Amy Ingersoll, David O'Brien, Meg Mundy, and Elizabeth Hubbard, among others.

THE EDGE OF NIGHT—(CBS 1956-75, ABC 1975-84) mystery serial with an emphasis on crime and intrigue; it was set in the midwestern city of Monticello and centered on the lives of ordinary people in troubling circumstances. Some of the star cast members were Ann Flood, Forrest Compton, Leah Ayers, Frank Gorshin, Lois Kibbee, Joel Cruthers, Sharon Gabet, Joanna Miles, and Larry Hagman.

GENERAL HOSPITAL—(ABC 1963—) daytime serial that began as a medical drama and later evolved into storylines rich in adventure and romance. The soap began to soar in popularity in the 1970s, principally because it achieved something new for the genre, a powerful attraction to teenagers. More than any other daytime program, *General Hospital* is credited with inspiring the remarkable interest in daytime soaps that started in the late 1970s; it was manifested in daily newspaper columns carrying storylines, fan magazines, and scholarly analyses of the soap world. The program began with such cast members as John Beradino, Emily McLaughlin, Denise Alexander, Rachel Ames and Peter Hansen. Its success for drawing in the more youthful audiences is credited to names like rock star Rick Springfield, Leslie Charleson, Robin Mattson, Chris Robinson, and of course Anthony Geary and Genie Francis (Luke and Laura), whose tumultuous romance held viewers enthralled. The contemporary cast has included Finola Hughes, Emma Samms, Tristan Rogers, Kin Shriner, Kristina Malandro, and Jack Wagner, among many others.

THE GUIDING LIGHT—(CBS 1952—) longest running daytime drama, focusing on the Bauers and the Reardons and the other residents of Springfield, U.S.A. It owes its popularity and durability to a strong cast of remarkable characters who are easy to identify with. Leading cast members have included Milette Alexander, Charita Bauer, Christopher Bernau, Jane Elliot, Joseph Campanella, William Roerick, Lisa Brown, Don Stewart, Kim Zimmer, and Robert Milli.

LOVE IS A MANY SPLENDORED THING—(CBS 1967-73) romantic daytime serial based on the hit film of that title. Set in San Francisco, it concerned the star-crossed romance between one of daytime's first interracial couples, an American war correspondent and a Eurasian female doctor. The cast included Nancy Hsueh, Nicholas Pryor, Robert Milli, Ron Hale, Gloria Hoye, Grace Albertson, Tom Fuccello, David Birney, and Bibi Besch, among others.

LOVE OF LIFE—(CBS 1951-80) dramatic story of two sisters, one good, one bad, the storylines contrasting their attitudes and lifestyles. The stars included Audrey Peters, Bonnie Bartlett, and Peggy McKay in the role of Vanessa, the amoral, self-serving one, and Tudi Wiggins and Jean McBride as the selfless, virtuous sister. Other members of the cast included Joanna Roos, Jane Rose, Ron Tomme, Chandler Hill Harben, Christopher Reeve, and Dennis Parnell, among others.

LOVING—(ABC 1983—) initially a domestic drama that centered around familial conflict along with passion and romance, the show has successfully integrated social issues, which it deals with in a thoughtful, forthright manner. The cast has included Peter Brown, Callan White, Perry Stephens, Susan Walters, George Smith, Dorothy Stinnette, Lauren-Marie Taylor, Susan Keith, Christine Tudor Newman, and Noelle Beck.

ONE LIFE TO LIVE—(ABC 1968—) the ongoing melodrama of two feuding families, one upper-class, one from the other side of the tracks, set in the suburban town of Llanview, Pa. A brainchild of Agnes Nixon, it was the first daytime soap to represent a variety of ethnic groups on a regular basis. Social problems are consistently emphasized while the series maintains a sense of humor. The star cast has included Nat Polen, Ellen Holly, Michael Storm, Al Freeman, Jr., Judith Light, Phillip MacHale, Lee Patterson, Anthony Call, Philip Carey, Anthony George, Sally Gracie, Chip Lucia, Clint Ritchie, and Jeremy Slate. The more recent cast includes Robert S. Woods, Andrea Evans, Karen Witter, Ava Haddad, Shelly Burch, Kristen Vigard, Barbara Treutelaar, and Tonja Walker.

RYAN'S HOPE—(ABC 1975-89) daytime drama that centered around an Irish-American family, differing from others of the genre in that it was set in New York City rather than the traditional generic small towns of soapdom. The emphasis was on the clashes between the old values of one generation and the modern ideals of the next, as they struggled against the pressures of urban life. The cast included Bernard Barrow, Helen Gallagher, Ron Hale, Nancy Addison, John Gabriel, Michael Levin, Tom Arledge, Earl Hindman, Peter Haskell, Marg Helgenberger, Jeffrey Pierson, Kate Mulgrew, Malcolm Groome, Robin Mattson, and Yasmine Bleeth.

SANTA BARBARA—(NBC 1984—) daytime serial tracing the lives and loves of two rich and powerful families, the Capwells and the Lockridges, who reside in affluent Santa Barbara. At the start it was considered to be the soap about Beautiful People; most of the female characters had long blonde tresses, and the acting took second place. But the show was rescued when a mass murderer with a weakness for blondes was written in, which proved convenient for eliminating dull characters, while adding adventure and intrigue to the plotlines. Cast members have included Dame Judith Anderson, Nicolas Coster, Louise Sorel, John Allen Nelson, Julie Ronnie, Charles Bateman, Lane Davies, Robin Wright, Marcy Walker, A Martinez, Linda Gibboney, Margaret Michaels, and Nancy Grahn, among others.

SEARCH FOR TOMORROW—(CBS 1951-82, NBC 1982-86) daytime melodrama that, in its beginnings, centered on one principal character, Joanne Gardner Barron—perhaps soap opera's most beloved heroine, played from the start by Mary Stuart. After a quarter century, the storylines shifted to the younger generation's lives and loves. Other leading cast members included Leigh Lassen, Melinda Plank, Melissa Murphey, Gretchen Walther, Trish Van Devere, Patricia Harty, Abigail Kellogg, Lynn Loring, Larry Haines, Rod Arrants,

Nicolette Goulet, Sherry Mathis, Lisa Peluso, Millee Taggart, Marie Cheatham, and Wayne Tippit. Over the years the soap opera featured such marquee names as Don Knotts, Sandy Duncan, Lee Grant, Jill Clayburgh, George Maharis, Roy Scheider, Barbara Baxley, and Hal Linden.

SECRET STORM—(CBS 1954-74) the continuing story of Peter Ames and his troubled family, with highly dramatic storylines rising from family secrets and secret passions. During the serial's 20-year run, the leading cast included Jada Rowland, Beverly Lunsford, Lynne Adams, Lawrence Weber, Ward Costello, Cec Linder, Peter Hobbs, Judy Lewis, Mary McGregor, Frances Helm, Mary Foskett, Norma Moore, Jean Mowry, Stephen Bolster, Wayne Tippit, Ken Gerard, Warren Berlinger, and Robert Morse.

THE YOUNG AND THE RESTLESS—(CBS 1973—) daytime serial dealing most often with the contemporary issues and problems concerning modern youth. The sexy soap has always featured characters who were flawlessly beautiful and started the trend of bare-chested males parading on the screen. Its cast has included Jeanne Cooper, Jamie Lyn Bauer, Victoria Mallory, Janice Lynde, Trish Stewart, Lynne Topping, Pamela Peters, Dorothy Green, Robert Colbert, Julianna McCarthy, Charles Gray, David Hasselhoff, Lauralee Bell, Don Diamont, Peter Barton, Terry Lester, Beth Maitland, Melody Thomas, and Doug Davidson.

SOCCER ▶ the world's most popular sport, whose televised games draw enormous ratings everywhere except in the U.S., where it lacks a tradition. Attempts to popularize soccer through television in America have to date been unsuccessful, but the grassroots approach of organizing soccer leagues among young children, boys and girls alike, could make soccer the major American sport of the future. The organizers of the quadrennial international World Cup competition hope to give that prospect a jump-start by making the U.S. the host country for the 1994 event. Besides being the largest undeveloped market for the soccer movement, the U.S. is also the largest sports advertising market in the world.

Indicative of the sport's popularity around the world, the 1990 World Cup soccer tournament, with 120 countries represented, had an estimated total cumulative audience of 26 billion viewers. The championship finals, beamed around the world by satellite, reached an estimated per-game audience of close to 800 million viewers—a staggering number, made even more so by the omission of the U.S. from the viewing countries.

In hopes that soccer might develop into the third major sport all the networks had been seeking, CBS carried the games of the newly organized professional North American Soccer League in 1967 and 1968, but the ratings were disappointing in the extreme. CBS resumed coverage in 1976 after a concerted effort had been made by the league to popularize the sport. That effort had included the recruiting by the New York Cosmos of the Brazilian soccer superstar Pele, and a six-year, city-by-city campaign by the American Youth Soccer Organizations to establish more than 6,000 teams in boys' leagues around the country.

Still, the 1976 ratings did not reflect a momentous change in U.S. attitudes towards soccer as a spectator sport, and CBS again dropped the coverage. Various television sports packagers offered soccer coverage in syndication for a time, and a number of public TV stations began carrying tapes of British soccer matches. In syndication, soccer did not lend itself nicely to commercial television because the game is played without time-outs. Lacking natural breaks for commercials, the syndicators had to black out the coverage frequently to patch in the commercials, which proved annoying to viewers, especially when the interruptions occurred during important plays.

Promotion of the sport in America is the concern of the U.S. Soccer Federation and its marketing arm, Soccer USA Partners, whose principals include NBC, cable's Sports Channel America, and the Aegus Group. The sport, which already has adherents among immigrant groups in the U.S., is gradually working its way up the generational lines. Soccer leagues for grade school children have become common in small town and suburban communities, high school soccer has grown faster than any other sport since 1980, and colleges now field more soccer teams, male and female, than baseball or football teams. It may yet become TV's third major sport.

SOCOLOW, SANFORD ▶ longtime CBS News executive who in the turmoil of the mid-1980s left to become executive producer of the *Christian Science Monitor*'s new nightly newscast on the Discovery Channel, *World Monitor.* The program began in 1988, and a year later he left to begin working with Walter Cronkite on a huge project, a TV history of the 20th Century. His last assignment for CBS News, begun in 1982, was chief of the London bureau.

Previously he had been executive producer of the *CBS Evening News with Walter Cronkite.* His other positions have included news v.p. for Washington and executive editor in the Washington bureau, assuming the latter post in 1971. In the preceding eight years, he was coproducer of the Cronkite newscast. Socolow joined CBS News in 1956 from INS, where he had served as Far Eastern correspondent.

SOFRONSKI, BERNARD ▶ producer with ABC Productions after having previously been with Warner Bros. Television and executive producer at The Wolper Organization. Previously, Sofronski was v.p. of specials at CBS. He has served as co-executive producer for such TV movies as *Napoleon and Josephine: A Love Story, Dillinger*, and the documentary motion picture *Imagine: John Lennon.*

SOHMER, STEVE ▶ a TV executive and sometime producer who had an extraordinary resume in the 1980s. In the early half of the decade he was the renowned promotion wizard of network television, the master of the "hot sell," whose ads for programs tended to the steamy side. In 1982 NBC hired him away from CBS, where he had helped make *Dallas* the top show in television. A few years later, he was transferred to Hollywood as executive vice president of NBC Entertainment. That somehow led to his becoming president of Columbia Pictures. When that stint ended he became president and CEO in 1989 of a new company, Nelson Entertainment, that sought to become active on the international scene. The company had a short life, however, and Sohmer became an independent producer. Among his credits are *Settle the Score,* a TV movie he produced, and *Favorite Son,* which he wrote and produced.

SOLOMON, MICHAEL JAY ▶ a pioneer of the international television business and probably the best known sales operative, worldwide, in program distribution. As president of Warner Bros. International Television Distribution, he represents the world's largest company in the field.

Solomon began his career in 1958 loading film reels on trucks for United Artists, at the age of 18. Later he traveled around Latin America selling films independently. In 1964 he was hired by MCA to set up a Latin American division for the company, which he operated for a number of years. In 1977 he started his own company, Michael Jay Solomon Films International, and a year later became a co-founder of Telepictures Corp. Solomon was chairman and CEO of Telepictures when it merged with Lorimar to form Lorimar Telepictures in 1985. He remained as head of international even after 1989, when the company was acquired by Warner Communications and when he displaced the veteran Warner chief, Charles MacGregor. When Warner merged with Time Inc. officially at the start of 1990 to form the largest media company in the world, Solomon remained in place. And indeed, Warner's strength in international markets, through executives like Solomon, was thought to be a prime reason for Time's interest in the merger.

***SONNY & CHER HOUR, THE* ▶** see Cher.

SONY CORP. ▶ Japan-based multinational electronics and entertainment company. Consumer products on which the firm has based much of its growth include the Trinitron color TV set and the Walkman personal audio system. In the mid-1970s Sony began steadily to increase its share of the worldwide broadcast equipment marketplace with such products as the U-matic recorder, one-inch Type C recorders, video monitors and video cameras. Throughout the 1980s Sony launched additional broadcast products, including the Betacam system, D-1 and D-2 video recorders, studio CCD cameras, HDTV equipment, the System G real-time video graphics device and the Hi8 8mm high-band video camcorders, solidifying its position as a major world player in the research, development and marketing of video hardware.

As the 1980s drew to a close and many Japanese companies were flush with cash following years of high exports, Sony's management, led by chairman Akio Morita, aggressively sought to support the company's hardware sales through expansion in entertainment "software." The firm bought CBS Records in 1987 and Columbia Pictures Entertainment in 1989 and renamed them Sony Music Entertainment and Sony Pictures Entertainment. To operate the latter it bought Guber-Peters Entertainment for the talent of its principals, the motion picture production team of Peter Guber and Jon Peters, buying out their contract with Warner Bros.

SOUND BITE ▶ a brief statement or excerpt from an interview, recorded on tape for use in a news broadcast or documentary. The operative word is brief; the television sound bite is the equivalent of the one- or two-sentence quote used in newspaper or magazines articles. When politicians caught on to the sound bite, it became an essential mechanism of election campaigns, and candidates were forced to learn how to boil down the essence of a stump speech into 10 or 12 seconds.

SOURCE, THE ▶ online data base, the brainchild of William von Meister, and a precursor of videotext systems. In late 1980, von Meister sold out to Readers Digest. During 1981, The Source lost its early lead to its main competitors, CompuServe and the Dow Jones News Service.

SOUTH AFRICA ▶ a country with a well-developed television system for one that has been isolated from the international community for many years because of its policy of apartheid. Yet even though most countries professed not to be doing business with it, South Africa's television—before its readmittance to the world industry—imported more than 50% of its programming.

The South African Broadcasting Corp. operates two channels that broadcast in English, Afrikaans, Nguni and Sotho. It derives its funding from a combination of receiver license fees and advertising. Competing with the state system is a relatively new pay network, privately owned, called M-Net, around 90% of whose programming is imported. At the end of 1991 it had 530,000 subscribers.

South Africa is a television market that has barely tapped its growth potential. For a country with a total population of 40.5 million, it has only 2.9 million television homes.

***SOUTH AFRICA NOW* ▶** a privately funded half-hour magazine program, which was started in April 1987 to fill the information void resulting from the tough press-censorship regulation imposed in 1986 by the South African government. Produced by Globalvision, a small independent production company, and the Africa Fund, an anti-apartheid organization, the series was carried on some 45 TV stations and local cable channels around the U.S. It operated on a small weekly budget of $10,000 and was put together by Globalvision's principals, Danny Schechter and Rory O'Connor, senior producer Carolyn Craven, a small full- and part-time staff, and a number of volunteers.

SOUTH KOREA ▶ a potential television hot spot as a country with one of the most dynamic economies in Asia and one that ranks as the second largest advertising market, after Japan, in its region. With an estimated 10.6 million TV households, the country has two television operations: the Korean Broadcasting Service, which runs two channels that are funded by receiver license fees, and the Munhwa Broadcasting Corporation, which is run by a group of government departments and funded directly by the government. The government has authorized a new independent television network to be launched in the early 1990s.

North Korea, one of the few remaining Communist states, has one state-run service for an audience of 1 million TV households.

SOVIET UNION ▶ a country whose entire broadcast system is in an uncertain state of flux since the political and economic reorganization began in what had been the U.S.S.R. At the start of the 1990s, the state-operated Central Television, with its two national channels and regional affiliates, remains the Soviet's only TV system. Plans for expansion include the creation of three new national channels, one dedicated to educational and scientific programs, another planned to provide an around-the-clock news service in a format similar to CNN. Intended also is the launch of a group of 10 DBS channels known as Gelikon.

Despite these plans, pressures are building—both inside and outside Central TV—for an alternative national system, either public or private, to offset what had been for almost five decades the Kremlin's official mouthpiece and remains today an unwieldy and inflexible bureaucracy under the control of the Ministry of Television and Radio (Gostelradio). In addition, pressure is building in the constituent republics—including Russia—to separate Moscow from its monolithic control of Central TV.

In the meantime, hope for opening the huge Soviet market to exploitation by commercial television awaits the further resolution of the Soviet's economic and political problems. Advertising has been introduced to Central TV under an agreement signed with Silvio Berlusconi, the Italian TV magnate, but its profitability must await the time when the Soviets succeed in moving to a market economy. Along with Berlusconi, Europe's reigning TV moguls are watching closely for the moment when the Soviet Union is open to and prepared to make deals. However, there is resistance among some in the Soviet Union to any thought of exchanging foreign-owned monopolies for the state monopoly they have lived under so long.

At least one proposal for a privately owned network has been advanced by two Russians, the Americanized Soviet TV star, Vladimir Pozner, and Eduard Sagalayev, head of the Union of Journalists. And NIKA-TV, a Soviet public corporation headed by Nikolai Lutskenko, proposes an alternative system combining broadcasting, cable and satellites. Plans have also been advanced for an increase in the number of local TV stations to nearly 200, and the construction of a cable system in Moscow offering 20 channels of mostly Soviet and Eastern European programming, due for completion in 1992. Despite these plans, however, choice for the Soviet citizen is likely to be limited until the country moves more certainly into a market economy.

SPACE BRIDGE ▶ popular name for a communications satellite link set up to enable two-way videoconference between U.S. students at Tufts University and their Soviet counterparts at Moscow State University.

SPACE FLIGHTS ▶ priority special events for the networks' news divisions, televised since 1961 and reaching a spectacular climax on July 20, 1969, with the live coverage of men setting foot on the moon for the first time. The broadcast of the *Apollo XI* mission was called "the biggest show in history," and it attracted the largest total audience for any single telecast. An estimated 125 million American viewers watched all or part of the 2-hour, 21-minute moon walk by Neil A. Armstrong, commander of *Apollo XI,* and Col. Edwin E. Aldrin, Jr., of the Air Force. Worldwide, the audience was estimated at 723 million in 47 countries, or about one-fifth of the world's population.

The telecast from the moon was in black and white, and the historic walk took place after prime time, facts that make the viewing record all the more impressive. The lunar module had landed on the moon at 4:17 p.m., Eastern daylight time, but Armstrong did not emerge from it to touch the moon's surface until 10:56 p.m.

More than 40 million people in the U.S., in 65% of the households, witnessed the actual moment of Armstrong setting foot on the rock-strewn plain and saying, "That's one small step for man, one giant leap for mankind." But with the innumerable replays in the course of the coverage, the moon walk ultimately was seen by 93.9% of U.S. households.

The networks among them devoted about 150 total hours to coverage of the full *Apollo XI* mission and spent $6.5 million to produce it, using approximately 1,000 personnel.

Not surprisingly, the second moon walk—in November 1969 by astronauts of *Apollo XII*—had less than half the audience of the first. This mission was to have provided color television from the moon, but it lost that novel aspect when the color camera failed to work on the moon's surface.

Apollo XIII, however, was a thriller, a real-life television melodrama that drew 75 million viewers. In the third day of its flight, as it was approaching the moon, the craft was forced to abort its mission by a mysterious blast that caused the command module to lose almost all its oxygen and power supplies and, for a time, its television contact. The return trip by the crippled craft—full of suspense, with three lives in danger—held the nation in thrall.

As space exploration entered the next generation with the development of the space shuttle, television news remained at its side, televising the space shuttle *Columbia*'s historic take-off on April 12, 1981, and its landing three days later.

As shuttle launches became more frequent in the early 1980s, though, they were relegated to a 45-second sound bite on the national news, with the only live coverage provided by Cable News Network. Until, that is, January 28, 1986, when the space shuttle *Challenger*—carrying a crew of six and high-school teacher Christa McAuliffe—exploded 74 seconds into its flight. Only CNN was carrying the take-off live, but within six minutes of the accident the networks broke into regularly scheduled programming and remained at the launch site for five to six hours, following up with prime-time specials. The commercial-free coverage cost the networks about $9 million in lost advertising revenue.

The first launch following the disaster, in 1989, was covered by all the networks, but since then coverage has again been relegated to sound-bite status by all but CNN.

The TV networks had begun covering the manned space missions in earnest with the suborbital flights of astronauts John Glenn and Alan B. Shepard in 1960 and 1961. Initially, the National Aeronautics and Space Administration was reluctant to permit coverage of the flights, but it eventually yielded to the reasoning that the public had a right to know how its tax money was being spent. The telecasts proved to be excellent public relations for NASA.

Each of the networks has developed experts in space coverage—NBC's Roy Neal, for example, has done reporting for every space flight—but those who covered the essential story of each mission were Walter Cronkite at CBS, Frank McGee at NBC (after his death, Jim Hartz had the assignment) and Jules Bergman at ABC.

SPACE: 1999 ▶ syndicated hour-long sci-fi series produced in England by ATV (1975-77) and distributed in the U.S. by its subsidiary, ITC. Produced on a large budget, part of which was justified by its showing on Britain's independent network, *Space* unabashedly sought to cash in on the *Star Trek* rage. Its cast was headed by American actors Martin Landau and Barbara Bain—a husband-wife team that had gained notice in *Mission: Impossible*—who portrayed Commander John Koenig and Dr. Helena Russell. Rejected by the American networks, the show found a receptive market among individual stations, many of which were network affiliates. *Space* made a strong threat in syndication early in the fall of 1975, but the ratings soon flagged. Organic changes were made in the second year to improve its chances.

The changes included the addition of Catherine Schell to the cast as Maya, a nonhuman who could turn herself into any kind of being she wished, and the hiring of Fred Freiberger, who had been associated with *Star Trek,* as producer. The second skein involved more action and greater use of special effects.

SPACE PATROL ▶ futuristic adventure series (1955-56) in which an earth-based patrol group protects the United Planets against the perils of the galaxy. The program featured Ed Kemmer as Commander Buzz Corry, Lyn Osborn as Cadet Happy, Ken Mayer as Major Robbie Robertson, Paul Cavanaugh as Colonel Henderson, Virginia Hewitt as Carol and Nina Bara as Tonga.

SPAIN ▶ Europe's most dynamic television market at the start of the 1990s, reflecting the country's rapid development in the post-Franco era. A country with 11.8 million television households, Spain was served until the mid-1980s by the state-run RTVE on two national channels—TVE 1, offering general programming, and TVE 2, oriented to sports. Then, in response to the regional demands, the government allowed the various autonomous states, as they are called, to build TV stations that would broadcast in the local dialects or native language (TV3 in Barcelona, for example, broadcasts in the Catalan language). In a wave, during the latter half of the 1980s, regional stations went on the air in the Basque country, Galicia, Valencia, Anadalusia and Madrid, in some instances on two channels, and all essentially advertising-supported.

Next, at the end of the decade, the Spanish government granted franchises to three privately owned networks broadcasting nationally: Antenna 3, Tele 5 and Canal Plus Espana, the last a sister channel to the highly successful French pay-television network. By the end of 1990 all three were on the air and received in the major cities but still years away from achieving a national circulation.

The Spanish government has set the stage for competition, which is expected to grow heated in the 1990s as the new channels gain acceptance. For certain big events or ambitious programs, the regional stations have taken to linking up in an ad hoc network. By the end of 1991, the public network, RTVE, still commanded 70% of the national viewing on its two channels, but the process of erosion had begun. The young regional channels collectively averaged a 16 share, while Antenna 3 and Tele 5 claimed 4% and 7%, respectively. The remainder went to Canal Plus and other foreign channels spilling over the country's borders.

Cable may yet add heat to the competition. By the end of 1991 cable penetration in Spain was around 10%.

SPARGER, REX ▶ a former government investigator who was caught trying to rig the Nielsen ratings in 1966 to boost four programs. Sparger, who had worked for the House Investigations Subcommittee during its probe of the ratings services (1961-63), had learned the identity of Nielsen homes and contacted them with promotional matter for the shows. Foiled by the Nielsen security system, Sparger explained that he was just trying to demonstrate that it could be done.

SPECIALS ▶ programs created singly rather than in series form and inserted into a network or station schedule as preemptions of regularly scheduled episodic programs. The increased use of such one-shot programs since the late 1960s has served to expand the range of fare—making feasible the presentation of news, drama and cultural programs in prime time on a limited basis, as well as entertainment extravaganzas—and overall has improved the quality of television. Indeed, the special has generated larger audiences for TV by drawing the selective viewer to the set.

Additionally, the special enabled advertisers to continue the practice of sponsorship when the cost of weekly series became prohibitive for single advertisers, and it has permitted programmers to try out new ideas and formats. Such successful series as *The Waltons, Laugh-In, The Flip Wilson Show, The Untouchables* and *Family* all had their origins as specials.

The special evolved from the *spectacular,* an NBC innovation in the early 1950s and a form to which that network remained devoted for many years before CBS and ABC became active on a comparable scale. An aversion to the special by those networks had grown out of the perception that heavy viewers of TV were creatures of habit who wanted the same shows to occur at the same times each week. Such leading programming figures as James Aubrey, when he was president of CBS, believed that any disruption of the fixed schedule might tend to break the viewer's habit and send him/her to another network.

However, when demographics came to matter more than a head-count of total viewers, in the mid-1960s, the concentration on habit viewers gave way to the quest for an upscale, young adult audience. Research had found that the habit viewer tended to be an older person or a young child and that the audience most drawn to specials was the demographic group advertisers were most eager to reach. By the end of the 1960s, each network was committed to presenting 70 or more specials a season.

Contributing to the rise of the special was the growing disinclination among veteran star performers, such as Bob Hope and Perry Como, to continue the punishing work of providing a weekly series. Such stars might have quit the medium but for the ability to cut back their contributions to four or five specials a season.

Specials gained in importance when the rising costs of producing weekly series brought a steady reduction in the number of first-run episodes a network would buy each year. With series contracts shrinking from 39 original episodes to 22, the networks found that they could fill out the time periods with preemptions for specials before embarking on the rerun cycle.

SPECTACULARS ▶ the original television specials, introduced in 1954 by NBC as one-time-only extravaganzas, usually 90 minutes in length, which preempted regular series. There had been sporadic one-shots previous to 1954—chiefly Christmas programs (*Amahl and the Night Visitors* in 1951) and telethons—but the program that broke the ground for the spectaculars was the two-hour *Ford 50th Anniversary Show,* produced by Leland Hayward and televised simultaneously by CBS and NBC on June 15, 1953. Although it featured a number of stars and celebrities, the program's excitement came from a duet between Ethel Merman and Mary Martin, performing on stools against a bare stage. The pairing of the musical-comedy stars continues to be remembered as one of television's glamorous moments.

On March 29, 1954, NBC's new president, Sylvester L. (Pat) Weaver, noted for his innovations in programming, announced that NBC was developing a number of spectaculars, to be produced by Max Liebman, and that the network was committed to the form. From there, the once-only show achieved a permanent place in the television scheme. Liebman's first spectacular was a 90-minute version of the musical comedy *Satins and Spurs,* starring Betty Hutton, which was telecast Sept. 12, 1954.

Because the term *spectacular* was a hyperbole that verged on the ridiculous as the form proliferated, it gave way to the more modest *special.*

Aaron Spelling

SPELLING, AARON ▶ consistently successful independent producer since 1960 when he launched *Zane Grey Theater.* He followed with *Burke's Law* in 1964, then entered into partnership with Danny Thomas on *Mod Squad* and other series. Later he teamed with Leonard Goldberg, former head of programming for ABC-TV to produce *The Rookies, S.W.A.T,*

Family and *Charlie's Angels,* along with numerous entries for ABC's *Movie of the Week* series. After Goldberg left to go his separate way, Spelling teamed up with Douglas S. Cramer in a production company called Aaron Spelling Productions, now Spelling Entertainment Inc., which has produced *Strike Force, Hotel, Dynasty, The Colbys* (a flop), *Beverly Hills 90210,* and a short-lived but much-criticized series that attempted to portray nurses, *Nightingales* (1989). This series prompted outraged responses from real nurses, because of its unrealistic characterizations of nurses as vacuous and scantily-clad women. The series was canceled very quickly. The company also distributed David Lynch's *Twin Peaks.* Spelling was executive producer of the mini-series *Dynasty: The Reunion,* which aired in 1991.

He had begun his TV career as an actor in 1953, then drifted into writing (including scripts for *Playhouse 90*) and then producing. His early credits include the *Lloyd Bridges Show* and *The June Allyson Show.* In the mid-1960s, he was executive producer of *The Smothers Brothers Comedy Hour.*

SPENSER: FOR HIRE ▶ well-regarded detective series set in Boston and inspired by Robert B. Parker's books about a principled, quotation-spouting private eye with a strong moral code and sense of decency for all people. The show, produced by John Wilder, ran on ABC (1985-1988) and starred Robert Urich in the title role, supported by Barbara Stock, Carolyn McCormick, Richard Jaeckel, Rita Fiore and Ron McLarty. Spenser's street-smart source, played by Avery Brooks, led to a starring role for Brooks in the violent, short-lived spin-off, *A Man Called Hawk* (1989).

SPIDER-MAN ▶ comic book superhero who has inspired an occasional live-action network TV series, a Saturday morning animated series, a syndicated series, and a *Spider-Woman* spin-off. The premise is stock for the genre—a graduate student, bitten by a radioactive spider, becomes a human spider and decides to use his unusual powers to combat evil–but though it was never really a hit, the story has had demonstrable television appeal.

CBS carried a 90-minute pilot film of the prime-time version in 1977, then televised 12 hour-long episodes on an occasional basis over the next two years, with Nicholas Hammond in the title role and Fred Waugh playing the character in the stunt sequences. Charles Fries and Daniel Goodman were the executive producers. After the pilot, the episodes were called *The Amazing Spider-Man. Spider-Woman* actually preceded *Spider-Man* as a Saturday morning animated series for children. It was produced for ABC in the 1979-80 season by DePatie-Freleng, with a somewhat similar premise to that of *Spider-Man. Spider-Man and His Amazing Friends* became a one-hour Saturday morning cartoon series on NBC in 1981-82, produced by David DePatie and Lee Gunther.

SPIELBERG, STEVEN ▶ one of Hollywood's hottest motion picture producer-directors who returns to television from time to time, as with NBC's *Amazing Stories* (1985-87) and the syndicated animated series *Tiny Toons* (1990—) in the 1980s and 1990s.

His career began when, at age 21, he directed the pilot for Rod Serling's *Night Gallery* (1969). His first big TV credit dates back to 1971 with the TV movie *Duel.* Spielberg spent much of the 1970s and 1980s creating fantastical motion picture hits like *Jaws, Close Encounters of the Third Kind, E.T.* and *Raiders of the Lost Ark.* He then went on to produce the fantasy anthology series *Amazing Stories,* which occasionally had the services of such motion picture directors as Martin Scorsese, Clint Eastwood, Paul Bartel and Spielberg himself.

SPIN-OFF ▶ a new program series derived from an existing one, usually through the appropriation of characters. Thus, *Maude* grew out of a single episode of *All in the Family,* while *Good Times* was developed around a regular character in *Maude. The Mary Tyler Moore Show* spun off two characters, resulting in two more popular series for CBS, *Rhoda* and *Phyllis.*

Police Woman had its beginnings in the anthology series *Police Story,* and *Dirty Sally,* which did not last long, was built from characters introduced in a single episode of *Gunsmoke.*

SPONSOR ▶ the advertiser who buys an entire show, rather than participation spots in it, and therefore exercises some control over it in addition to dominating the commercial time.

During the 1950s, when most television programs were sponsored, the advertiser paid the cost of production as well as the network's time charges. It was common for sponsors to own the shows, developing them through their advertising agencies and placing them with a network. The steadiest advertisers were able to reserve the choicest time periods year after year. Programs were scheduled without concern for audience flow or other elements of modern strategy.

Rising program costs led to shared sponsorship, usually by two advertisers, one form of which was alternating sponsorship. This applied mainly in half-hour series, which afforded three commercial minutes. In the alternating arrangement, the advertisers took turns as major and minor advertisers, the major using two of the minutes and the minor the remaining one.

Sponsorship went out of fashion in the mid-1960s, giving way to the less risky and more efficient purchasing of minutes (and later half-minutes) dispersed over a network's schedule. Mainly, sponsorship survives with specials. Some advertisers prefer it to the "scatter plan" because of the benefits inherent in identification with a quality program and/or glamorous star and in the viewer's presumed gratitude.

SPONSOR IDENTIFICATION RULES ▶ FCC requirement that stations and networks reveal, on the air, which announcements are paid for and by whom; also, that they disclose the sources of all gratis program material and details of the acquisition.

SPORTS ▶ considered by many the perfect program form for television, at once topical and entertaining, performed live and suspensefully without a script, peopled with heroes and villains, full of action and human interest and laced with pageantry and ritual. The medium and the events have become so intertwined that playing rules often are altered for the exigencies of TV, contests are created expressly for TV, sports stars graduate from the playing field to the broadcast booth and new stadiums are built with giant screens on their scoreboards to provide paying customers with the instant replay enjoyed by viewers at home. Television is such an integral part of major sports, and so vital to their economics, that many of the professional leagues probably could no longer exist if for some reason they were cast out of the medium.

Sports and television also fit together exceedingly well in business terms. Sports delivers the male audience better than most other forms of programming, and the male audience is sought by a large roster of advertisers: automobiles, beer and soft drinks, shaving equipment and cosmetics, automotive products and fuels, airlines, banks, insurance companies, sneakers, athletic equipment, breakfast cereals, computers, telephone services and movies.

Because sporting events readily find an audience, they were pursued avidly by certain cable networks during the 1980s. ESPN, because of its all-sports format, became the leading basic-cable network, carried on virtually every system in the country, and probably also the most prosperous. MSG and the regional sports networks such as SportsChannel are also devoted to the genre, and USA, WTBS, TNT and HBO include substantial amounts of sports in their schedules. Moreover, sporting events are developing as the staple of cable's pay-per-view operations.

While the three major networks together carry more than 1,000 hours a year of sports programming, they are dwarfed by ESPN, which, with its 24-hour schedule, alone carries 8,760 hours nationally. The numbers become mind-boggling with the inclusion of other cable networks, pay-per-view, local television and syndication.

For virtually every popular sport, each new contract negotiation with the TV networks, cable services or local stations ends with a new record payment for rights, an upward spiral that has continued through four decades. Each new level is reached from confidence by the broadcaster that the increase can be passed on to the advertisers. These increases were reflected during the 1980s in the astonishing salary levels that were being established in professional sports. In baseball, for example, the average player's salary in 1980 was $170,000. In 1985 the average approached $350,000, and by 1990 it reached $600,000. Million-dollar contracts for players with modest credentials became the norm by 1990. Star baseball players were getting as much as $5 million a year. This was television money, and the players, after all, were television stars of sorts.

In an effort to extricate itself from third place, CBS in the late 1980s adopted a strategy of capturing the rights to major sporting events. Its $1.08 billion baseball contract for four years beginning in 1990 represented a 35% increase in the annual average network cost of baseball. The National Football League got increases of 45% to 75% from the three networks in a four-year contract starting in 1991. The four-year National Basketball Association contract with NBC was $424 million more than the previous four-year contract with CBS. Almost every other sport, including the college tournaments, showed steady and sometimes marked increases.

There seemed no end to the spiral, until the sobering developments of 1991. Not only had the general advertising market grown soft in the recession, but the ad market for sports had grown especially weak. This was largely because the explosion in the variety of sports and the number of hours devoted to coverage everywhere on television diluted the audience for all major sports events. Moreover, it spread the available advertising dollars thin, and when supply exceeds demand advertising rates invariably decline.

In November 1991, CBS publicly estimated that its losses from baseball that summer were $600 million. ESPN also lost on baseball in 1991—some $40 million, according to industry estimates. TNT, ABC and NBC all reportedly lost money that year on their NFL contracts. Sports had suddenly begun spilling red ink, which does not bode well for future contract negotiations. Some analysts foresee a crisis when sports leagues discover that conventional television and cable are no longer able to produce the monies they have promised to their stars. Pay-per-view may come to the rescue of the leagues, but viewers may lose the wealth of sports programming they have learned to enjoy from free television.

See also Appendix.

SPORTSCHANNEL AMERICA ▶ an occasional sports network for cable created by linking the various regional SportsChannels, enabling it to provide big-ticket sports programming to some 13 million cable households. The company is co-owned by Chuck Dolan's Cablevision Systems and NBC.

In 1976, Dolan introduced SportsChannel New York, the nation's first pay-cable sports service; it featured New York Islanders hockey games and added Mets and Yankees baseball in 1981. After SportsChannel New England was launched in 1983, The Washington Post Company became a partner in the SportsChannel venture. After regional sports services in Philadelphia and Chicago were acquired, Rainbow bought out the *Washington Post* and became sole owner. The venture was folded into Cablevision's umbrella company for program services, Rainbow Programming Enterprises. After SportsChannel Florida and the national SportsChannel America were launched in 1988, NBC bought in as a 50% partner. In 1989, SportsChannel Ohio (Cleveland-based) was formed, and Rainbow acquired the assets of a Los Angeles-based premium service called Z Channel, turning it into SportsChannel Los Angeles. In 1990 a second sports service was added in Philadelphia, along with SportsChannel Bay Area and SportsChannel Cincinnati.

In 1991, SportsChannel Bay Area merged with its Prime Network competitor to form SportsChannel Pacific, a hybrid pay/basic channel. Most of the regional services and SportsChannel America have not been profitable. Sharon Patrick is president of Rainbow and John Mohr is president of the regional SportsChannels.

SPOT TELEVISION ▶ the field of television advertising concerned with the placement of commercials for national or regional products on a station-by-station basis, rather than by network distribution. Although networks make it possible to achieve national circulation with a single transaction, spot TV thrives because the country is not homogeneous and most advertisers recognize that their products do not sell in a uniform manner across the country.

Some advertisers deal exclusively in spot, placing their business only in markets where there is apt to be greatest need for the product, but most buy a combination of network and spot, using the latter as a way to "heavy up" in cities where greater advertising support is indicated. In spot, it is also possible for commercials to address the rural viewer with a bucolic approach and the city-dweller with an urban approach.

Individual stations engage station representative firms to secure spot advertising for them, while large broadcast groups, like the network o&os, maintain their own spot sales forces in key advertising centers, such as New York, Chicago, Los Angeles, Detroit, Minneapolis, Atlanta, Dallas, St. Louis, Boston, Memphis and Philadelphia.

Spot is classified by stations as national business, as distinct from network and local revenues.

SQUIER, ROBERT ▶ television consultant to Democratic candidates since 1968, and a regular political commentator on NBC's *Today.* In the 1988 Bush-Dukakis campaign, he helped brief the Democratic candidate for the first debate and produced the election eve broadcast. He was more successful in the 1991 campaign of Governor Ann Richards of Texas, overseeing her media efforts. He advises candidates on their commercials as well as their appearances on talk shows. Twenty-one members of the current U.S. Senate are members of Squier's firm, among them Joseph Biden, Bob Byrd, Bob Graham, Al Gore Jr., John D.

Rockefeller IV and Paul Simon. His first television consultancy was for the 1968 Presidential campaign of Hubert Humphrey.

Squier began his television career as a director of cultural and public affairs broadcasts for public television, principally at National Educational Television where he worked on *At Issue* and *The Great American Dream Machine.* Other television credits include such acclaimed works as *William Faulkner: A Life on Paper; Herman Melville: Damned in Paradise; Children of the World, with Danny Kaye; Pablo Casals in Puerto Rico* and *The Family of Man, with Edward Steichen.*

STACK, ROBERT ▶ one of the few actors who's played the lead in four major series, all in the crime idiom. He is best known for his portrayal of Eliot Ness in *The Untouchables* (1959-63), the show that propelled him to stardom after 20 years in "B" movies and defined his image for years. He also starred in *Name of the Game* (1968-71), *Most Wanted* (1976-77) and *Strike Force* (1981-82) and had a part in *Falcon Crest.* Stack has been the host/narrator of the reality-based program *Unsolved Mysteries* since 1989.

Lesley Stahl

STAHL, LESLEY ▶ veteran CBS News correspondent who was named co-editor for *60 Minutes* in 1991. Previously she had been moderator of CBS's *Face the Nation* (1983-90) while serving variously as chief White House correspondent (1989), national affairs correspondent (1986-89) and White House press correspondent (1978-86).

As sole interviewer on *Face the Nation* she probed such world leaders as Margaret Thatcher and Boris Yeltsin, in addition to top U.S. officials, including President Bush.

STANDARDS AND PRACTICES DEPARTMENT ▶ unit at each of the networks responsible for clearing all material to be aired, in accordance with industry codes and the company's own standards of acceptability and good taste; in effect, the network censors. On the station level, such a department may go by the name of Continuity Acceptance. The department's staff reads all scripts, monitors programs in production and screens the completed shows, as well as all commercials, for violations of broadcast policy. Neither programs nor commercials may be aired without the department's approval, which often requires that producers delete scenes or words or even, in the script stage, whole episodes. Although similar sets of standards have been formalized by the three networks, they vary enough so that a commercial rejected by one network is, on occasion, found acceptable by the other two. Similarly, one network may be a trace more permissive with sexual references or political satire than the others.

Burton B. Staniar

STANIAR, BURTON B. ▶ chairman and chief executive officer of Westinghouse Broadcasting Co. (popularly known as Group W) since May 1987. Staniar rose in the company through its cable television subsidiary; he had been president and chief operating officer of Group W Cable until the cable systems were sold in 1986. Staniar was then elevated to senior executive vice president of Group W and was named chairman when Daniel Ritchie elected early retirement.

He heads one of the largest and most respected groups in broadcasting, one whose CEO traditionally has assumed a statesman's role in the industry. Staniar is responsible for the operations of Group W's five TV and 14 radio stations; Group W Productions, a Hollywood-based production and distribution company; and Group W Satellite Communications, which operates a large satellite uplink facility and distributes programming for the broadcast and cable industries. Staniar has worked at building Group W's programming presence both domestically and internationally, and with the acquisition of eight radio stations in 1980 he has made Group W the largest non-network radio operator in the country.

After a background as a marketing specialist in other industries, Staniar joined Group W Cable in 1980 as senior vice president of marketing and programming. Two years later he was named president and chief operating officer.

STANTON, FRANK ▶ famed president of CBS Inc. (1946-72) who not only helped shape that company and raise its prestige, but also became the broadcast industry's leading statesman and its most effective witness before congressional committees. A perfectionist and tireless worker, he formed the perfect complement to the showmanly, socially prominent chairman, William S. Paley, through the decades of the company's critical growth. Stanton received the title of vice-chairman the year before reaching the mandatory retirement age of 65, opening the presidency to his successor. But he remained a director of CBS and a consultant to the corporation, under a long-term contract, on his departure in 1973.

As president, Stanton rarely involved himself with light entertainment programming (an area of Paley's expertise) but concentrated on organizational and policy questions and on the political and cosmic issues growing out of the network's news function. In 1951 he reorganized the company along divisional lines—creating separate administrations for radio, TV and CBS Laboratories—and the plan served as a model for other broadcast companies.

A staunch defender of broadcasting's First Amendment rights, he led campaigns on behalf of the industry for broadcast access to Congress and the courts, equal to that accorded the printed press, and for the elimination of Section 315 of the Communications Act, the Equal Time law. It was through Stanton's efforts that Congress suspended the rule in 1960 to permit the Kennedy-Nixon *Great Debates.*

One of Stanton's greatest contests with the Government in defense of journalistic principles occurred late in his career, in 1971, during a controversy surrounding the CBS News documentary *The Selling of the Pentagon.* Against the threat of being held in contempt of Congress, he steadfastly defied a subpoena from the House Commerce Committee for outtakes, work prints and written scripts for the documentary, arguing that such materials are, as a reporter's notebook, protected as privileged by the freedom of the press guarantees of the First Amendment. Stanton's position found a large body of support in and out of Congress, and the House voted on July 13, 1971, to refuse the Commerce Committee's request for a contempt citation.

Stanton came to CBS as a researcher in 1935, soon after earning a Ph.D. in statistical psychology (the source of his honorific "Dr."); certain officials at the network had been impressed with his doctoral dissertation, a critique of methods for studying radio listening behavior. In 1937, with Dr. Paul Lazarsfeld of Columbia University, he developed the Stanton-Lazarsfeld program analyzer (nicknamed "Little Annie"), a system for testing proposed programs that has remained in use at CBS ever since. Stanton rose to higher positions and was 38 when Paley appointed him president in 1946.

On leaving CBS, Stanton became chairman of the American Red Cross. In 1980, he also founded the Center for Communication, a non-profit organizer of seminars that serve as a bridge between the professional and academic worlds. He had also served as chairman of the U.S. Advisory Commission on Information and of the RAND Corporation and was a trustee of the Rockefeller Foundation and the Carnegie Institution in Washington. He was also a director of the Lincoln Center for the Performing Arts.

STANTON-LAZARSFELD PROGRAM ANALYZER ▶ system used by CBS to test the appeal of programs with a randomly selected audience, which has primary value to the network in determinations made with pilots. The system was devised for radio in 1937 by Dr. Paul Lazarsfeld of Columbia University and Dr. Frank Stanton, a Ph.D. in statistical psychology who later became president of CBS Inc., but it continues to be used for television. Viewers participating in the testing are invited in off the street in New York and Los Angeles to a screening room where they are given seats with knobs on the arms of their chairs. They are asked to press the knob on the left arm when something they dislike appears in the program, and the knob on the right arm when something strongly pleasing to them appears. The buttons are wired to a control room, where a graph records what is liked or disliked from each of around a dozen chairs. The participants are also asked to fill out questionnaires, specifying what they approved or disapproved of in the shows and which characters they especially liked or disliked. Testing results are drawn from several such screenings and have led either to the outright rejection of a pilot or to recommendations for cast changes. CBS maintains that the system, which is nicknamed "Little Annie," has an accuracy rate of 85%.

STAR ▶ billing for a performer, used more loosely in television than in most other forms of show business. In theater tradition, the stars are those whose names appear above the title of the play in letters as large as those for the title, or even larger. All others are considered featured players in their contracts, even if their names are preceded on the programs by the word "starring." Many plays have no actual stars at all. Star billing is more than an honor; it designates performers of great stature or those with such proven popular appeal that their names on the marquee prompt the sale of tickets.

In television, however, star billing is given freely and often indiscriminately, and it has become common to speak of the leads—even if they are relative unknowns—as the stars. Credits in television shows frequently list the principal cast as "starring," the supporting cast as "also starring" and well-known character actors as "guest stars."

The promiscuous use of the word "star" probably made necessary the coinage of "superstar" in later years to assume the original and largely lost meaning of stardom.

***STAR TREK* ▶** TV science-fiction series with an extraordinary history: a failure, in mass audience terms, during three seasons on NBC despite a staunch cultist following, but a bonanza in syndication and merchandise-licensing long after the network run. *Star Trek* premiered on Sept. 8, 1966, was tried in a new timeslot the second season and was saved from cancellation only by a tremendous mail campaign from its fans. After an unimpressive third season, it ended its run in March 1969.

Ten years after its debut, however, it reruns were being carried on more than 140 stations and in 47 other countries, and a *Star Trek* animated cartoon series was running Saturday mornings on NBC (having begun in 1973) with the likenesses and voices of the original cast. Three national *Star Trek* societies drew thousands of "Trekkies"—devoted fans—to their annual conventions; a raft of *Star Trek* products were being marked and a full-length movie, featuring the TV cast and produced by the series creator, Gene Roddenberry, had been ordered by Paramount.

The series concerned the space voyages of the star ship *USS Enterprise* and its crew in reconnaissance missions to other worlds 200 years in the future. Principal characters were William Shatner as Captain James Kirk, Leonard Nimoy as Spock, the half-Vulcan, half-Earthling science officer, and DeForest Kelly as Dr. Leonard (Bones) McCoy. Also featured were Majel Barrett as Christine Chapel, James Doohan as Montgomery (Scotty) Scott, Walter Koenig as Ensign Pavel Chekov, Nichelle Nichols as Lieutenant Uhura, George Takei as Mr. Sulu and Grace Lee Whitney as Yeoman Janice Rand. It was by Norway Productions, in association with Paramount TV and NBC.

A scene from the syndicated series *Star Trek: The Next Generation*

***STAR TREK: THE NEXT GENERATION* ▶** syndicated successor to the original *Star Trek* series that started off on weak legs when it debuted in 1987 but grew to become the most successful weekly show in syndication.

With Gene Roddenberry—the late creator of the Star Trek storyline—serving as executive producer, Paramount Television set about to cash in on the off-network syndicated success of the original series and the four *Star Trek* movies released to that time. The plot is set 85 years after the first series, with a new crew and design for the now-famous *Starship Enterprise.* Special effects have also been vastly improved, with the new starship having undergone a major redesign.

The Next Generation has taken a decidedly more cerebral and less violent tack than the first series, while still reflecting contemporary social problems in its futuristic plots. Starring Shakespearean actor Patrick Stewart, whose Captain Jean-Luc Picard prefers to solve intergalactic disputes with words, not photon torpedoes, the cast also includes Commander William Riker (played by Jonathan Frakes); an empath, Starfleet Counselor Deanna Troi (Marina Sirtis); an android, Lieutenant Commander Data (Brent Spiner), who aspires to be more human; a blind pilot, Lieutenant Geordi LaForge (LeVar Burton), who can see when wearing his high-tech glasses; medical officer Dr. Beverly Crusher (Gates McFadden); Crusher's son, Wesley (Wil Wheaton); lounge hostess Guinan (Whoopi Goldberg); a Klingon officer, Lieutenant Worf (Michael Dorn)—Klingons were fierce enemies in the original series—and medical officer Dr. Kate Pulaski (Diana Muldaur).

STARGER, MARTIN ▶ one-time head of programming for ABC-TV (1969-74) who became an independent producer for the network when Fred Silverman was hired away from CBS to replace him. His term was marked not by successful ratings campaigns but rather by a steady improvement in ABC's credibility with quality specials, particularly in the area of drama. Among his contributions was the introduction of documentary-drama, a form in which real events of recent history were enacted, typified by *Pueblo* and *The Missiles of October.* Starger made several unsuccessful attempts to produce hit shows for the U.S. in Britain, mainly through Lord Lew Grade's company, ATV. As an independent, he produced the widely praised and high-rated drama *Friendly Fire* for ABC in 1979. He became also president of Marble Arch Productions, a motion picture company, in a partnership with Britain's Lew Grade.

He was hired by ABC in 1966, as east coast v.p. of programs, from BBDO, where he had been a v.p. in the television production department. In 1969 he became v.p. in charge of programs for the network and in 1972 became president of ABC Entertainment when the program department was established as a separate division.

***STARSKY AND HUTCH* ▶** successful ABC hour-long detective series (1975-79) about a free-wheeling, wise-cracking two-man team operating in southern California. The leads were Paul Michael Glaser and David Soul as Dave Starsky and Ken Hutchinson, and featured were Bernie Hamilton as Captain Harold Dobey and Antonio Fargas as Huggy Bear. The series was by Spelling-Goldberg Productions, with Aaron Spelling and Leonard Goldberg as executive producers. It grew into one of the more violent series in prime time but was ordered toned down by the network for the 1977-78 season.

***STATE OF THE UNION/'67* ▶** the first nationwide telecasts on educational television, made possible by a $10 million grant to NET by the Ford Foundation in 1966 for an experimental interconnection of the stations. That public affairs series was followed by the regular Sunday night interconnection of the stations in November 1967 for *PBL,* a two-hour newsmagazine produced independently of NET by the Public Broadcasting Laboratory.

***STATE TROOPER* ▶** syndicated fictional series (1957-59) on the Nevada State Police, produced by Revue Studios and starring Rod Cameron as trooper Rod Blake.

STATION ▶ a broadcast entity licensed to a community by the FCC, specifically to serve "the public interest, convenience and necessity in its locale." In theory, a station secures and produces programming that best serves local needs, but in actuality most stations affiliate with networks because it is economically advantageous to do so. Network service covers approximately 60% of the broadcast day. While in the early years of TV the stations produced much of their own programming, now they produce little besides the local newscasts because syndicated programming is cheaper and easier to sell to advertisers. TV station licenses are subject to renewal every five years (seven years for radio).

Key officials at a station are the general manager, the operations or station manager, the sales manager, program director, news director, traffic manager and chief of engineering.

STATION COMPENSATION ▶ monies paid by a network to each affiliated station for carrying its programs. Approximately 10% of a network's advertising revenues for any program is distributed to the stations as compensation. Since each affiliate has its own compensation agreement with the network, the formulas for payment vary. But, as a rule of thumb, the amount a station receives from a network comes to around 25-30% of its rate card price for the time. What is paid in station compensation bears no relation to the rates charged for the advertising by the networks.

STATION IDENTIFICATION ▶ brief advisories, periodically broadcast, giving the call sign of a station and its city of license, either visually (with a slide) or aurally. The FCC requires such IDs at the beginning and ending of each broadcast day and once an hour in between, as close to the hour as feasible.

In practice, station IDs usually precede every program and occur at a greater frequency than is required, because stations consider it valuable for viewers to be reminded of the channel they are watching. While there is no requirement that the ID carry the channel number, most stations give more prominence to the channel position than to the call sign.

The networks usually provide 10- or 12-second station breaks at half-hour intervals. Since the identification can be accomplished in two seconds, many stations share the break with a commercial advertiser, while some tie in public service or self-promotion messages.

STATION PROGRAM COOPERATIVE ▶ a public TV program market, administered by PBS, in which all PTV stations participated in selecting and cooperatively funding about one-third of the programs in the PBS national schedule. The SPC, simple in concept but complex in execution, sprang from an idea by Hartford N. Gunn, then president of PBS, who saw it as a countermove to curtail the Nixon Administration's threat of taking control of programming through its dominance of the board of PTV's principal funding agency, the CPB.

The selection process began with the submission of program proposals and relevant budget data by individual stations and production entities. Several rounds of balloting by the stations reduced the initial catalog of more than 200 proposals to a list of finalists in which a sufficient number of stations were willing to commit production funding, each station's share determined by a complex formula based on audience size, etc. A program was considered "purchased" when the number of stations desiring the show was sufficient to cover the costs of production. Only those who participated in the funding were permitted to air the show.

In 1990 the stations voted to abandon the SPC and to turn over $78 million in local SPC funds to PBS for its discretionary use in funding national programs of its own choosing. The more centralized approach, it was felt, would avoid the major weakness of the SPC balloting: the stations' propensity for returning the same safe, proven programs to the schedule year after year with minimal risk-taking for new and innovative programs.

STATION REPRESENTATIVES ▶ known familiarly as "reps," in effect sales agents for large rosters of local stations that otherwise would have no affordable access to national or regional advertisers. Rep firms are primarily sales organizations that represent client stations in New York, Los Angeles, Chicago, Detroit and wherever else key national advertising agencies are based, leaving the station's own sales staff to concentrate on local advertisers. But these firms also provide their clients with a variety of consultative services, and some have branched into producing and distributing syndicated programs.

The TV rep takes on clients on an exclusive basis, representing only one in a geographic market, a policy originated in radio in the mid-1930s by Edward Petry & Co. (now Petry Television). It is no longer observed in radio, however. A number of the existing TV rep firms began in radio and easily made the transition to television as their radio clients bought or built stations in the new medium. In latter years, however, TV reps have quit radio, and only one—Katz Communications—still maintains a radio division as well as one for television.

Katz actually started in the late 19th Century as a newspaper "agent" (as it was called in that industry) and was still named The Katz Agency well into the television era, even while representing TV and radio as well as newspapers.

As with other facets of the industry, the TV rep firms got caught up in the consolidation mania of the 1980s, and by the end of 1991 there were 11 national companies in all. Three of those are "in-house" reps; that is, units owned by and selling only for a single station group. The three are CC (Capital Cities)/ABC National Television Sales, CBS Television Stations National Sales and Group W Television Sales.

The other eight are the more traditional reps, working with stations from Tacoma to Tampa. They are:

- Katz Television
- Telerep (owned by Cox Enterprises)
- Blair Television
- Petry Television
- Harrington, Righter & Parsons (HRP)
- Seltel (owned by Chase Enterprises)
- MMT Sales
- Adam Young

Until 1991, NBC Spot Television Sales had been the fourth in-house rep operation. But the parent company decided to break up the group, giving over the three biggest stations—in New York, Los Angels and Chicago—to HRP for representation, a big boon to that company, and giving the stations in Washington, Miami and Denver to Petry. NBC's move was a departure from tradition, since the networks nearly always had sales rep organizations for their owned stations in house. ABC had an outside rep once, but when Capital Cities bought the company in 1985 it reinstated the old spot sales division. In early TV days, the network spot sales units also represented other stations, but the FCC banned the practice in the early 1960s on the ground that it contributed to the networks' excessive economic power in the industry.

Rep client lists vary greatly in size. Katz, which has the largest list, serves more than 200 stations. MMT had about 30 in 1991 when its management bought the company from Meredith Corp., whose seven stations it continued to represent.

Given the competition among reps and the difficulty of any single account executive speaking for all the stations in the client list, the rep firms have adopted the structure of sales teams concentrating on a limited station list. Moreover, the reps have increased the number of regional offices in recent years as New York has declined as the primary source of spot business. All the TV rep firms are headquartered in New York, but the three largest firms have 15 or more branch offices.

The reps derive their revenues solely from commissions on the sale of air time. The traditional commission was 15%, but the major stations and groups rarely pay that much today. More typically of late, the commissions have been knocked down to 7.5% or even lower. Some reps, like Telerep and Blair, have derived additional revenues from engaging in program syndication.

Most reps offer their member stations a range of consultative services, free of charge, not only to secure the relationships but also in their own enlightened self-interest. The more successful a station becomes in its market, the easier it gets to sell national spots, and it usually follows that more money flows to the rep. Primarily the reps offer stations marketing advice and services, but probably their most important counsel is in what programs to buy from syndication. The major reps have a staff of experts to evaluate syndicated shows and to track how they perform in other markets. Their recommendations impact sharply on the syndication market; indeed, it was a rep's enthusiastic recommendation of *Wheel of Fortune* that helped make that show a giant hit.

STEINER, GARY A. (d. 1966) ▶ author of a landmark book, *The People Look at Television,* the first major study of the public's attitudes toward television, conducted in 1960. The book was published by Knopf in 1963. Among its findings was that most viewers were satisfied with TV fare, although the average viewer wished TV were more informative; still, when given a choice between informative and escapist fare, most viewers selected the latter. The study, underwritten by CBS, was the first to note the difference between what people said they wanted of television and what they actually watched. Steiner, a University of Chicago psychology professor, died by suicide, apparently as a result of marital problems. Ten years after the publication of his book, CBS brought out another book through its publishing subsidiary, Holt, Rinehart and Winston, which updated Steiner's one-market study in Minneapolis-St. Paul. The sequel, *Television and the Public,* by Robert T. Bower, based on research conducted by the Bureau of Social Science Research in Washington, found that the superfans of TV—the devoted, uncritical viewers—had decreased in number from one-third to about one-quarter of the total audience.

STEP DEAL ▶ the networks' standard arrangement with series producers for the development of new shows, which involves a progression of submissions so that a project may be discarded as impractical at any point, before too much money is invested in it. The process—from the presentation of the idea to its purchase as a series—may span a year.

Program development usually begins in the spring, following the formulation of schedules for the forthcoming season. As a first step, the producer or producing company submits the story idea in the form of a treatment, which is a detailed description of the premise and the characters. The networks pay a sum for an option on the idea, which then proceeds to the next stage, the preparation of a script. The script may undergo several revisions, as the various parties concerned make their recommendations. For his labors, depending on his professional stature, the writer receives up to $50,000 for a situation comedy and twice that for an hour-long series.

The network may quit the project at any one of the steps or stages. Typically, two-thirds of the ideas are eliminated before the script stage and only one-third of those that advance to scripts are made into pilots.

The completed pilots are then studied by network programmers and tested, either on the air or in program testing theaters. In the final step, the network may purchase the series, reject it outright or (rarely) carry it over into further development. Generally, fewer than 25% of the pilots are accepted for TV series. Network programmers estimate that every 100 ideas for which step deals are made ultimately yield only two new TV series.

STEPTOE AND SON ▶ hit British situation comedy about a Cockney London junk dealer and his son, played with great style and charm by Wilfred Brambell and Harry H. Corbett. It led to the American adaptation by Yorkin-Lear for NBC-TV called *Sanford and Son,* with black principals instead of Cockney. It likewise became a ratings winner.

STEREO TV ▶ technology that makes possible stereophonic sound for television. The use of two sound channels on the audio portion of a TV signal provides for reproduction of the acoustic environment in which the sound was recorded. The U.S. standard for such broadcasts, also known as multichannel television sound (MTS), was authorized by the FCC in 1984, and some TV set manufacturers were given approval to make available receivers capable of reproducing transmitted stereo. The two audio channels may also be used to broadcast in two languages simultaneously. Stereo TV has been in use in Japan for several years, but it has been progressing slowly in the U.S.

STERN, CARL ▶ one of broadcasting's lawyer-journalists, assigned by NBC News since 1967 to cover the U.S. Supreme Court, the Federal judiciary and the quasi-judicial proceedings of the Federal agencies. Stern's major assignments included covering the Clarence Thomas and Robert Bork Supreme Court nomination hearings, the court's support of affirmative action and its decisions regarding reproductive freedom. Earlier notable achievements included reporting on Watergate, the Berrigan case and the trials of Sam Sheppard, James Hoffa, Muhammad Ali, Arthur Bremer and Patricia Hearst. In 1973 he won a landmark Freedom of Information lawsuit that required the FBI to reveal the details of its activities in disrupting New Left political organizations, a broadcast which then-Attorney General William Saxbe denounced as "clearly illegal."

STERN, LEONARD B. ▶ producer and creator of TV series. He had been executive producer of *The Governor and J.J., Diana, Faraday & Company, The Snoop Sisters, MacMillan and Wife* and *Holmes and Yo Yo.* He was also creator of *Get Smart.*

STEVENS, GEORGE, JR. ▶ television producer whose credits include coproducing (with Nick Vanoff) the annual *Kennedy Center Honors: A Celebration of the Performing Arts.* He served as executive producer for the NBC mini-series *The Murder of Mary Phagan* and the CBS special *The American Film Institute Salute to James Cagney.* Stevens also wrote and served as executive producer of the ABC mini-series *Separate But Equal.*

STEVENS, LESLIE ▶ prolific writer for the TV drama anthologies that abounded in TV's Golden Age of the 1950s, and later creator and producer-director of the *Stoney Burke* series (1962) and of the science-fiction anthology *Outer Limits* (1963), both on ABC. His plays for *Playhouse 90* included *Invitation to a Gunfighter, Charley's Aunt, Rumors of Evening* and *The Second Man.* In the 1970s he was executive producer of such series as *The Invisible Man* and *Gemini Man.*

STOCKTON, DICK ▶ CBS Sports broadcaster, host from 1978 to 1980 of *CBS Sports Saturday/Sunday* and the network's lead play-by-play announcer for NBA games from 1982 to 1990. Since 1990, Stockton has been teamed with analyst Jim Kaat to cover major league baseball. He got his start in 1964 at KYW News Radio in Philadelphia, moved to KYW-TV a year later, and then to KDKA-TV Pittsburgh in 1967 as sports director. He joined CBS part-time the same year, hosting *The NFL Report* for seven years, adding the NFL play-by-play to his duties in 1974. He moved to WBZ-TV Boston in 1971 as sports director, where he also covered the Boston Celtics, and from 1975 to 1978 was the voice of the Boston Red Sox for WSBK-TV Boston, including a part in NBC's coverage of the 1975 Boston-Cincinnati Reds World Series.

Brandon Stoddard

STODDARD, BRANDON ▶ president of ABC Productions since 1989, when he relinquished his post as president of ABC Entertainment. In his new capacity he in effect heads an in-house production company that may produce programs for any network. Stoddard had been appointed president of ABC Entertainment in 1985 after a decade of developing some of the network's most distinguished dramatic programming. These included such successful mini-series as *Roots, Roots: The Next Generation, Rich Man, Poor Man, The Winds of War, The Thorn Birds,* and the three-hour drama *Friendly Fire.* These triumphs earned him the promotion in June 1979 to president of ABC Motion Pictures, a new unit within ABC Entertainment that proposed to produce theatrical motion pictures (including *Silkwood* and *Prizzi's Honor*), movies for television, dramas for ABC Theater and mini-series to air under the rubric *ABC Novels for Television.* Stoddard was then named senior v.p. of ABC Entertainment in 1979, and president in 1985.

During his tenure as president, ABC's prime-time schedule floundered in the ratings. Also, Stoddard was responsible for the $40 million mini-series flop *Amerika* (1987). But there were a number of acclaimed series, such as *thirtysomething, The Wonder Years,* and *Roseanne.*

Stoddard joined ABC from Grey Advertising in 1970 as director of ABC's daytime programs. He became v.p. two years later and in 1973 added children's programs, such as *ABC Afterschool Specials,* to his bailiwick. In 1974 he became v.p. of motion pictures for television, then added dramatic programs in 1976. In this capacity, he helped develop the series *Vega$, The Love Boat, Fantasy Island, Eight Is Enough,* and *Hart to Hart.* In 1978 he was elevated to senior v.p. of dramatic programs, motion pictures, and novels for television and was on his way to becoming president.

STONE, EZRA ▶ former radio actor (the *Henry Aldrich* series) who became director of TV program development for CBS (1952-54) and then a prolific director of prime time series. He also worked in theater and film. Among the scores of series for which he directed episodes were *Julia, The Debbie Reynolds Show, The Flying Nun, The Sandy Duncan Show* and *Bridget Loves Bernie.*

STONE, SID ▶ a regular on the early Milton Berle series. As the fast-talking pitchman, he contributed to popular speech his familiar line, "Tell ya what I'm gonna do."

STOREFRONT LAWYERS ▶ hour-long series for CBS (1970) in a season when the network was actively seeking "socially relevant" programs. Produced by Leonard Freeman, it concerned three young attorneys of the rock era recruited by a prestigious law firm to operate a storefront law office serving the needs of the underprivileged. It featured Robert Foxworth as David Hanson, Sheila Larken as Deborah Sullivan and David Arkin as Gabe Kaye. After 13 episodes the format, locale and title were changed. As *Men at Law,* Foxworth played the young associate to Devlin McNeil (played by Gerald S. O'Loughlin), senior partner in a large law firm. His former mates had lesser roles. The changes did not avail, and *Men at Law* ran 10 weeks.

STORER, GEORGE B. (d. 1975) ▶ a pioneer broadcaster and founder of the first independent station group, known as Storer Broadcasting Co., which began in Toledo, Ohio, in 1928 and grew to prominence in both radio and TV. One of the first radio broadcasters to enter television, Storer had three stations on the air by 1949: WSPD-TV, Toledo; WJBK-TV, Detroit; and WAGA-TV, Atlanta. Later, he added stations in Cleveland, Milwaukee, Boston and San Diego, the latter two UHFs. As head of a powerful group, Storer exerted an influence on network policies until he went into semi-retirement in the 1960s.

The group was originally known as Fort Industry Broadcasting, taking its name from an oil company owned by the Storer family, of which the stations had been subsidiaries. But it was so widely identified with Storer personally that in 1952—some 20 years after the oil company was sold—the corporate name was changed. Three years later Storer Broadcasting went public, its stock listed on the New York exchange. So that it might be close to his estate, Storer moved the company headquarters to Miami Beach.

In the late 1950s, hospitality that he had accorded FCC chairman John C. Doerfer led to charges against the official of fraternizing with the industry he regulated. When Doerfer resigned, Storer hired him as a vice- president of his company and employed him until his retirement.

In 1985 the Storer group was acquired by Kohlberg, Kravis, Roberts and Co., the leveraged buyout specialists. Later KKR sold a 55% interest in the stations to George Gillett, who by the end of the 1980s was so burdened with debt that he was forced to sell off some of his properties. The Storer group effectively dissolved.

STORY THEATRE ▶ syndicated prime-access series (1970-72) based on the Broadway hit and employing the techniques and cast of the stage production, as well as the direction of Paul Sills. Produced by Winters-Rosen, it was shot in the countryside around Vancouver. It had limited acceptance from stations, however, during the first two years of the prime time-access rule.

STREETS OF SAN FRANCISCO, THE ▶ successful ABC hour-long law-enforcement series (1972-77) featuring Karl Malden as Mike Stone, a veteran police detective, and Michael Douglas as his young partner, Inspector Steve Keller. Douglas was replaced in 1976 by Richard Hatch, who played Inspector Dan Robbins, and Lee Harris also appeared as Lieutenant Lessing. Filmed on location in San Francisco, the series was by QM Productions, with Quinn Martin as executive producer and William R. Yates as producer.

Howard Stringer

STRINGER, HOWARD ▶ president of the CBS/Broadcast Group since 1988, when he was elevated from president of the news division to succeed Gene Jankowski as the executive responsible for all broadcast activities of CBS. This represented the first step in a management reorganization by Laurence Tisch since he took control of the company two years earlier. In leapfrogging over more senior CBS executives with greater experience in entertainment, marketing and sales, Stringer apparently had what the others did not: Tisch's confidence.

Stringer was executive producer of *The CBS Evening News* in 1981 when the network made the difficult transition from Walter Cronkite to Dan Rather. He is credited with conceiving *48 Hours* and then working it into the CBS prime-time schedule.

In 1965, as a 22-year-old Welshman educated at Oxford, he arrived in the U.S. and landed a job as a clerk for WCBS-TV in New York. A few months later he was drafted into the U.S. Army and sent to Vietnam. Three years later he was back at CBS, working first as a researcher in the election unit and then as a documentary producer for *CBS Reports.* He became executive producer of *CBS Reports* in 1976, and during the next five years the unit won 31 Emmys, three Peabody awards, and three duPont-Columbia awards, among a flock of others. Stringer was also executive producer of two acclaimed but controversial documentaries, *The Uncounted Enemy: A Vietnam Deception* and the five-hour series *The Defense of the United States.*

Stringer's rise to the top of CBS was rapid if not meteoric. He shifted from *CBS Reports* to executive producer of *The CBS Evening News with Dan Rather* in 1981, became executive vice president of CBS News in 1984, president of CBS News in 1986, and president of the CBS/Broadcast Group in 1988. He became a U.S. citizen in 1985.

STRIP ▶ a program scheduled in the same time period five or more days a week. Weekly series that have concluded their network runs are frequently resold to individual stations for stripping, as a new means of presenting them. Stations that receive no network service prefer to strip programs, both for their own convenience and for the viewer's easy reference.

STUART, MEL ▶ producer-director associated with Wolper Productions whose TV work included *The Making of the President: 1960* (and the 1964 and 1968 sequels), *China, The Roots of Madness, Way Out Men* and *Love From A to Z.*

STUDS' PLACE ▶ an early TV comedy series from Chicago, which began locally and went on the network in 1950. The episodes took place in a small restaurant, whose proprietor was Studs Terkel. Other regulars were Beverly Younger as Grace, Win Stracke and Chet Roble.

STUNTING ▶ trade term for the employment of inventive programming techniques to win an audience, techniques that do not reflect the true nature of the series or of the program schedule but are momentary stunts.

In its simplest form, stunting involves the presentation of a special two-hour episode of a one-hour series to open the season, the front-loading of movie showcases, and early premieres of shows in weeks before the season officially opens. More complicated stunting involves the interchange of characters between an established series and a new entry, just for the opening weeks; the sharing of storylines, as when a two-part episode begins on *Six Million Dollar Man* and concludes on the next episode of *Bionic Woman;* and the introduction of shows in alien time periods, that is, on nights of the week other than those to which they are normally assigned.

Stunting was heavily practiced by the networks in the mid-1970s and succeeded chiefly in confusing the issue of which network had the most potent schedule of series.

STV (SUBSCRIPTION TELEVISION) ▶ pay television carried on broadcast stations; the scrambled signal is unraveled in subscribing homes equipped with a decoder. In the late 1970s an SRI study predicted that STV would beat out pay cable because as an over-the-air service it could get into the homes more quickly without having to engage in extensive construction. At the time, consumer demand seemed centered on channels such as HBO that provided movies, rather than on all the rest that cable offered. Possibly on the strength of the SRI report, STVs began proliferating in the early 1980s on new UHF channels. Dallas had three such stations and Philadelphia two. The New York metropolitan area was served by WHT, Wometco Home Theatre. But when cable began to spread it swamped the STVs, and now hardly any exist. Many of the stations that began as STVs today are commercial independents or affiliates of Fox or the Home Shopping Network, and some have simply shut down.

SUBLIMINAL ADVERTISING ▶ messages transmitted with great rapidity in single frames with the intention of influencing viewers at levels below normal awareness. Experiments had been conducted with subliminal advertising in the 1950s; industry codes, now repealed, prohibited such practices. Since 1974, the FCC has had a policy prohibiting "Subliminal Perception." Author W.O. Key built a substantial following in the 1970s with a series of books purporting to show that advertisers hide sexual images in pictures of ice cubes, crackers and other objects, but no charge has ever been credible enough to merit serious regulatory attention.

SUBSCRIPTION TELEVISION ▶ company headed by Sylvester L. (Pat) Weaver, former president of NBC. It attempted to establish a major pay-cable operation in Los Angeles and San Francisco in 1962 but was beaten down two years later by a well-financed campaign by theater owners and broadcast interests. STV wired up homes expressly for its service, which largely consisted of baseball games and movies. The threatened interests proposed a state referendum prohibiting pay television that California voters passed in November 1964, largely on the advice of the skillful "Save Free TV" campaign. By the time the state supreme court struck down the proposition as unconstitutional, STV had lost more than $10 million and gone bankrupt.

SUGARFOOT ▶ western about a serious-minded young cowboy that alternated for a time with *Cheyenne* on ABC. Starring Will Hutchins as Tom Brewster and produced by Warner Bros., it played from 1957 to 1961.

SULLIVAN, ED (d. 1974) ▶ Broadway columnist who hosted one of TV's longest-running and most successful variety series. *The Ed Sullivan Show* (originally *The Toast of the Town*) became a Sunday night habit in millions of households and demolished dozens of programs that attempted to compete with it.

Although Sullivan's popularity as a host was puzzling to many—since he was a wooden and unprepossessing performer given to nervous mannerisms and slurred speech—he brought to the medium a newsman's showmanship; the flair for presenting performing acts when they were most topical or when interest in them was high. Typically, Sullivan was first to present The Beatles in the U.S., and he gave Elvis Presley his first network exposure when he became a popular music sensation. His premiere show, on June 20, 1948, marked the TV debut of the comedy team of Dean Martin and Jerry Lewis. The Sullivan show spurred the advancement of scores of show business careers, and relatively obscure performers often parlayed an appearance on the CBS telecast into several months' worth of nightclub bookings.

Sullivan's pronunciation of the word "show" made a national joke of his familiar promise each Sunday of a "really big shew." The program was essentially a vaudeville hour, which used animal acts and circus acts, as well as popular singers and comedians, and the host made a practice of introducing celebrities in the studio audience from the spheres of politics, sports and entertainment. Through all his years on television, Sullivan continued writing his Broadway column for the *New York Daily News.*

Although the program placed in the Nielsen top ten for most of its years, its ratings went into a decline in the late 1960s and the show was canceled in 1971. In part it was a casualty of the diverging entertainment cultures of youth and the older generations, made worse for shows like Sullivan's by the deteriorating patterns of all-family viewing as homes acquired their second or third TV sets. But some have also noted that the program's slip in popularity coincided with the decline of New York City as the nerve center of show business.

When the show ended after more than two decades, Sullivan and his producer (and son-in-law) Bob Precht formed Ed Sullivan Productions, which developed program series and specials with moderate success.

Pat Summerall

SUMMERALL, PAT ▶ lead play-by-play announcer for CBS Sports' NFL coverage. After graduation from the University of Arkansas and a ten-year career as an NFL tight end and placekicker with the Chicago Cardinals and New York Giants, he began broadcasting NFL games part time for CBS in 1961. He was sports director of WCBS Radio, the CBS-owned station in New York City, from 1964 to 1971, during which time he also served as host of the station's four-hour, six-day-a-week morning news program and worked for the CBS Radio Network. Summerall signed a full-time contract with CBS-TV in 1971 and began his partnership with analyst John Madden in 1980. He also anchors golf and tennis coverage.

SUNBOW PRODUCTIONS ▶ independent production company specializing in the production and distribution of TV programming for children. Its properties include the animated series *My Little Pony and Friends, Transformers, JEM* and *G.I. Joe.* Sunbow is a wholly owned subsidiary of Griffin-Bacal, the lead ad agency for Hasbro-Milton Bradley Toys. Hasbro contracts with Sunbow for many of its animated series based on its toy line. The programs are syndicated by Claster TV, the company that owns and distributes *Romper Room.* Claster is owned by Hasbro.

***SUNDAY MORNING* ▶** 90-minute CBS news program that premiered on Jan. 28, 1979, with aspirations of becoming the television equivalent of the Sunday newspaper. To create a spot for the program, CBS canceled three highly respected long-running programs whose station clearances had shrunk to a paltry few: *Lamp Unto My Feet, Look Up and Live* and *Camera Three.*

The show, first produced by Robert (Shad) Northshield, is now produced by Linda Mason. It continues to be anchored by its original host, Charles Kuralt, whose musings on the human condition are still a major feature. Many of its early on-air correspondents and commentators—Richard Threkeld, Leslie Stahl and Jeff Greenfield, among them—have moved to other venues and have beem replaced by a cast that includes reporters Bill Geist, Terrence Smith and Betsy Aaron, and commentators John Leonard and Erika Zuckerman.

***SUNDAY MYSTERY MOVIE* ▶** umbrella title for four 90-minute rotating series (each expanded to two hours in 1975) carried by NBC (1971-77) and produced by Universal TV. Among the original series, which were continued in subsequent seasons, were *Columbo,* with Peter Falk; *MacMillan and Wife,* with Rock Hudson and Susan Saint James (retitled *MacMillan* in 1976, without Saint James); and

McCloud, with Dennis Weaver and J.D. Cannon (*McCloud* actually had begun a year earlier as part of a rotating series called *Four in One.*)

Success eluded the fourth entry, however, and there was an annual turnover in the series. *Hec Ramsey,* with Richard Boone and Rick Lenz, was introduced in the fall of 1972 but was canceled. *Amy Prentiss,* for which its star, Jessica Walter, won an Emmy, replaced *Ramsey* but was also dropped. In the quest for a series that could maintain the rating levels of the other three, *McCoy,* with Tony Curtis, took its place in the rotation in 1975 and gave way the next year to *Quincy* with Jack Klugman. That went on to become a weekly series on its own the following year.

SUNDAY NIGHT AT THE LONDON PALLADIUM ▶ the British equivalent of Ed Sullivan's CBS variety hour, and one of the pioneer rating hits for independent television in the U.K. Starting in September 1955 (the year of independent television's advent in Britain), the show ran live for 12 seasons and was a Sunday night national habit. It ran through a number of hosts, among them Tommy Trinder, Bruce Forsyth, Norman Vaughn and Jimmy Tarbuck.

Associated Television, the show's producer, reactivated the format on a pretaped basis in 1973 with actor Jim Dale as host, but by that time the excitement was gone and it only lasted one season.

SUPER BOWL ▶ showdown game between the two conferences of the National Football League, a championship event literally made for television—indeed created by television—and one of the medium's top attractions since it was initiated in 1967. The game became possible when NBC's huge investment in the TV rights for the fledgling American Football League in 1964 ($42 million for five years) paid off eventually in teams worthy of competing with the long-established National Football League (whose games were carried by CBS). The Super Bowl became the catalyst for the merger of the two leagues, with separate conferences, when an AFL team—the New York Jets—emerged the winner in 1969. But the game was created in the first place because it was bound to be lucrative for both leagues and promised to be a sure-fire spectacle for television.

Under the initial agreement, both CBS and NBC were to carry the first game and then would alternate coverage year by year. With two networks covering, Super Bowl I reached a combined total audience (viewing all or part of the telecast) of more than 77 million. Subsequent games have all had an audience of more than 51 million—larger than the audiences for most prime-time hits—although the Super Bowl was played in the usually low-rated hours of Sunday afternoon. Later that changed and the Super Bowl games were scheduled in the prime viewing hours.

The Super Bowl is the most highly-promoted and anticipated TV event of the year. Not only does it claim the full top ten list for the highest-rated sports events in history, it also takes nine of the top ten places for the all-time most viewed television shows. The only entertainment program to break into this list was the special two-hour final episode of *M*A*S*H* on Feb. 28, 1983. As a result, despite the constant increases in rights costs, it is greatly prized by the television networks and by advertisers, who willingly pay the enormously high rates because the commercials reach the huge audience efficiently. From 1983 to 1991 the cost of a 30-second commercial rose from $400,000 to $800,000.

See also Appendix.

SUPER CHANNEL ▶ one of the first attempts at creating a pan-European general entertainment channel distributed by satellite. It was founded in 1987 by 14 of the 15 regional British commercial TV licensees and Richard Branson's independent Virgin Group, picking up from a defunct satellite channel, Music Box. The channel, broadcasting in English and predicated on the notion that English is the second language for many on the continent, claimed a reach of 22 million homes and hotel rooms across Europe. But proof of audience was hard to establish and large advertising contracts difficult to come by. In November 1988 Italian broadcaster Beta Television, owned by the Marcucci family, bought a controlling 53.5% interest in Super Channel, with Virgin retaining 45%. Led by Marialina Marcucci, Super Channel altered its strategy and aimed for the young adult European audience with music videos and vintage television series. It also has a twice-daily newscast produced by the U.K.'s Financial Times Television, production arm of the newspaper.

SUPER CIRCUS ▶ an early circus-variety show on ABC (1949-56) produced at its Chicago station, WBKB (now WLS-TV). It featured Mary Hartline as band mistress, Claude Kirchner as ringmaster and clowns known as Scampy, Cliffy and Nicky.

SUPERIOR COURT ▶ see Courtroom Shows.

SUPERMAN ▶ syndicated series (1952-57) based on the comic book hero; it featured George Reeves as Superman (a.k.a. Clark Kent, newspaper reporter for the *Daily Planet*), Phyllis Coates and Noel Neill as reporter Lois Lane, Jack Larson as cub Jimmy Olsen, John Hamilton as editor Perry White and Robert Shyne as police inspector William Henderson. It was produced by National Periodical Publications Inc.

SUPERSTATION ▶ the glamor child of satellite technology, an independent TV station that becomes a national station when distributed by satellite to cable systems around the country. Such stations are desired by cable operators because each fills a channel with programming heavily oriented to sports and old movies, and many broadcast around the clock.

The pioneer superstation was WTCG-TV (later changed to WTBS) Atlanta, owned by Turner Broadcasting System, which went on the RCA Satcom satellite in Dec. 1976. But the concept was actually invented by Bob Wormington, president of the Kansas City UHF station, KBMA-TV, in 1973. Cable systems were not equipped to receive satellite transmissions at that time, so Wormington fed out the KBMA signal in a large regional pattern—calling it Target Network Television (TNT)—by microwave relays. Although it had the acceptance of cable systems, TNT was shelved in less than a year for lack of advertiser support.

A few years later, after Home Box Office and other national program services made satellite earth stations standard equipment for modern cable systems, Atlanta's Ted Turner adopted the KBMA idea by arranging for the creation of Southern Satellite Systems as a common carrier to handle the satellite distribution of WTBS. This was necessary because under FCC rules broadcast stations may not lease satellite transponders to extend their signals. Common carriers, however, may lease satellite time and distribute a station nationally with or without its consent.

By mid-1979 there were two other commercial superstations on the RCA satellite—WGN-TV Chicago and KTVU San Francisco, both involuntarily—plus several evangelical religious stations, which were able thereby to call themselves networks. Later, such independents as New York's WWOR and WPIX and Los Angeles' KTLA were enlisted.

Under the WTBS arrangement, Southern Satellite charges the cable systems taking the superstation a monthly fee according to their size, but not exceeding $2,000, while Turner's station makes its money through higher advertising rates reflecting the greater audience reach afforded by cable.

The superstation became a new category of broadcaster, falling between a local station and a network, and it posed a competitive threat to both those entities. It also created confusion in the syndication market. Because the superstation is able to transmit copyrighted programs into cities where the rights to those programs have not yet been sold to a local station, some syndicators have been reluctant to sell to superstations. Others have dealt with the problem by raising the prices of their programs.

SUPERTRAIN ▶ high-budgeted suspense-cum-comedy series that was to have been the centerpiece of NBC's drastically revised mid-season schedule in 1978-79, with which Fred Silverman, as the new president, hoped to reverse the network's prime-time ratings decline. The premiere was preceded by a huge publicity build-up and became the symbol of Silverman's frustrating first year at the NBC helm.

Conceived as a sort of *Love Boat* on rails, with several stories going on at once in each episode, the series starred a huge, futuristic cross-country train whose luxurious appointments included a gymnasium, nightclub and disco. The crew remained constant and included Edward Andrews as conductor Harry Flood, Robert Alda as Dr. Lewis, Patrick Collins as Dave Noonan, Anthony Palmer as chief engineer T.C. and Aarika Wells and William Nuckols as exercise coaches Gilda and Wally, but the key acting parts were played by guest stars.

Set for a mid-winter debut to meet Silverman's timetable for the programming overhaul, *Supertrain* was rushed into production, with crews working around the clock to complete the sets and model train. Reportedly, the costs ran to $12 million for 13 episodes. After scoring a passable rating in its premiere, the series found itself in Nielsen quicksand and was yanked from the schedule for improvements. Dan Curtis was fired as producer during the doctoring period and was replaced by Robert Stambler. The program was brought back in a new time period, but the ratings remained abysmal.

SURFSIDE SIX ▶ hour-long ABC series (1960-61) about a three-man team of detectives based on a houseboat. The Warner Bros. action-adventure series featured Troy Donahue as Sandy Winfield II, Van Williams as Ken Madison, Lee Patterson as Dave Thorne, Diane McBain as Daphne Dutton and Margarita Sierra as Cha Cha O'Brien.

SURGEON GENERAL'S REPORT ON VIOLENCE, THE ▶ an $8 million 1972 study and report commissioned by Surgeon General William H. Stuart's office to determine whether a causal relationship existed between viewing TV violence and subsequent aggressive behavior. In five volumes, and formally titled *Television and Social Behavior,* the report was broken into sections on Media and Content Control, Television and Social Learning, Television and Adolescent Aggressiveness, Television and Day-to-Day Life and Further Explorations.

While the committee was not directly involved in the commissioning of new research, it made available $1 million for support of independent projects through the National Institute of Mental Health (NIMH). More than one hundred published papers representing 50 laboratory studies, correlational field studies, and naturalistic experiments involving 10,000 children and adolescents from every conceivable background all showed that violence-viewing produced increased aggressive behavior in the child and that remedial action in television programming was warranted. Although confused newspaper headlines at first suggested that the commission found no relationship between TV violence and aggressive behavior, each member of the committee acknowledged finding such a correlation. Further discounting of the report occurred when it became known that the committee was selected using a procedure which systematically excluded some of the most distinguished researchers on the subject while including a number of network executives. Forty names had been proposed for the 12-person committee, and the television industry had been given the privilege of reviewing the list to make recommendations. The industry excluded Leo Bogart, of the Bureau of Advertising of the American Newspaper Publishers Association, who had published a book on television; Albert Bandura, a psychology professor at Stanford and an expert on children's imitative learning; Lenard Berkowitz of the University of Wisconsin; and Leon Eisenberg, chairman of the Department of Psychiatry at Harvard University. The television industry was represented, however, by Thomas Coffin, NBC; Joseph T. Klapper, CBS; and Gerhart D. Wiebe, formerly of CBS.

SURVIVORS, THE ▶ an unsuccessful attempt by ABC to create the equivalent of a popular novel on TV, with a concentration on sex, glamour and wealth. Produced by Universal TV for the 1969-70 season, the series was created by novelist Harold Robbins and starred Lana Turner as Tracy Hastings, George Hamilton as Duncan Carlyle, Ralph Bellamy as their father Baylor Carlyle, Kevin McCarthy as Philip Hastings and Rossano Brazzi as Riakos. The episodes were shot in exotic foreign locales, and no expense was spared to establish the show as a Monday night mainstay, in the time period in which *Peyton Place* once flourished. The series was canceled after 15 weeks and gave way to *Paris 7000,* which was devised to honor Hamilton's 25-week contract. It too failed.

SUSSKIND, DAVID (d. 1987) ▶ prolific TV producer usually associated with quality drama, founder of the production company Talent Associates and host of his own syndicated interview program *The David Susskind Show* (originally entitled *Open End*). His Talent Associates produced shows in a range from *Mr. Peepers* and *The Play of the Week* in the 1950s to *Get Smart* and *Supermarket Sweeps* in the 1960s. Susskind also produced the highly praised TV adaptations of *The Glass Menagerie, The Crucible* and *Death of a Salesman* and certain notable dramas for *Kraft Theater, Armstrong Circle Theater, Kaiser Aluminum Hour* and *DuPont Show of the Month.* He was also producer of the excellent CBS series with George C. Scott and Cicely Tyson, *East Side, West Side.*

In the early years, Susskind was an anomaly because he continued to sell programs to television while making newspaper copy around the country for his attacks on the medium and the low quality of its programming. His detractors in turn called him a fast-talking promoter who played it safe in the new medium by sticking to the classics and proven stage plays.

His own syndicated program, *Open End,* created a sensation when it began in 1958, both because it introduced a new form—the open-ended program with no set time limit—and because it featured such guests as Soviet Premier Nikita Khrushchev and then Vice-President Richard M. Nixon. *Open End* gave way in 1967 to *The David Susskind Show,* a discussion program with a finite running time. Susskind took on a partner in Talent Associates in 1967, when Daniel Melnick joined on leaving ABC as program v.p. The company was acquired in 1970 by Norton Simon Inc., with Susskind's services included, and became Talent Associates—Norton Simon. The company has been involved in motion picture as well as TV production.

SUSTAINING SHOWS ▶ programs offered by networks or stations without advertising support or participation, generally in areas of news, public affairs and religion. Certain telecasts are designated sustaining for reasons of taste and propriety, such as presidential speeches, ceremonial events and religious observances; others simply because advertising is not available for them. The rating companies do not measure viewing for sustaining shows in their regular reports.

S-VHS (SUPER VHS) ▶ professional version of the consumer half-inch VHS format that yields image quality similar to that of U-matic.

***S.W.A.T.* ▶** hard-action series on ABC (1974-76) about a special police tactical unit, considered the most violent series in a time when TV violence levels were high. By Spelling-Goldberg Productions, it featured Steve Forrest as unit leader Lieutenant Dan (Hondo) Harrelson, Robert Urich as Officer James Street, Rod Perry as Sergeant David (Deacon) Kay, James Coleman as Officer T.J. McCabe and Mark Shera as Officer Dominic Luca.

John Cameron Swayze

SWAYZE, JOHN CAMERON ▶ one of television's first network newscasters, who began the popular 15-minute *Camel News Caravan* on NBC in 1948 and continued with it in the early evening until 1956. He was noted for his crisp style and distinctive articulation, developed in radio. When *The Huntley-Brinkley Report* replaced Swayze's broadcast, he remained in the medium as an announcer, panel show host and commercial spokesperson.

SWEENEY, BOB ▶ former producer of action-adventure series, although he began in TV as a comedy actor, playing Fibber McGee in the TV version of *Fibber McGee and Molly.* He and Bill Finnegan were coproducers of *Hawaii Five-O* until 1975, when they left to go into independent production. After producing two pilots that weren't sold, Finnegan left to go into motion pictures, and Sweeney remained in TV, producing *The Andros Targets* pilot for CBS and directing episodes of *Fantasy Island, The Love Boat, Trapper John, M.D., Simon & Simon* and the TV movie *If This Is Tuesday, This Must Be Belgium,* which was filmed in Yugoslavia.

SWEEPS ▶ rating surveys conducted three times a year by Nielsen and Arbitron in some 200 individual TV markets. The local viewing data derived from the sweeps serve as the seasonal criteria for national spot advertising. (There is actually a fourth sweep, but since it occurs in midsummer when audiences are small, it has little value.)

Each of the sweeps covers a four-week period, one spanning October-November, another February-March and the third April-May. Since these survey periods provide the only ratings most stations receive for the entire year, and since they directly affect revenues, the sweeps have tempted stations to substitute sure-fire programming, such as movies, for low-appeal normal programming during the sweep weeks. Such deliberate manipulation of the ratings, known as "hypoing," is held illegal by the FCC although the regulations forbidding it have not been aggressively enforced.

Moreover, affiliated stations constantly beseech their networks to schedule their most potent movies, specials and series episodes during the sweep periods, and the networks usually cooperate. This in part explains why the highly appealing programs appear in bunches on television and then give way to arid stretches.

To eliminate the abuses, some network research executives have proposed that the sweep surveys cover eight weeks rather than four, but the idea was rejected by the stations because it would substantially increase the cost of the ratings.

In 1979, with network competition at a high pitch, the sweeps produced the most expensive week and the most expensive single night of programming in television history. The week of Feb. 18 began with the opening episode of ABC's powerhouse mini-series, *Roots II.* In attempting to blunt its impact, NBC countered with the hit movie *American Graffiti* and CBS with another big film, *Marathon Man.* During the week, NBC threw against *Roots* episodes of the high-budgeted mini-series *Backstairs at the White House* and *From Here to Eternity,* and on the final night scheduled the blockbuster *The Sound of Music.*

Feb. 11 was the most expensive single night, with CBS airing *Gone with the Wind,* NBC *One Flew over the Cuckoo's Nest* and ABC a three-hour television movie on the life of Elvis Presley. The total cost of those ventures was estimated at close to $10 million, or about three times the cost of regular programming for a single night.

SWITCH ▶ hour-long CBS private-eye series with comedy touches patterned after the popular movie *The Sting,* and introduced in the fall of 1975. In the leads were Robert Wagner as a reformed convict, Peterson T. (Pete) Ryan, and Eddie Albert as Frank MacBride, a former cop. Featured were Sharon Gless as Maggie, Charlie Callas as Malcolm Argos, James Hong as Wang, and William Bryant as Lieutenant Shilton. The series, by Glen Larson Productions and Universal TV, was moderately successful, ending in 1978. Larson was executive producer.

SYBIL ▶ poignant two-hour drama airing on NBC in 1976 based on the true case of a woman who possessed 16 distinct personalities. Sally Field played the title role and Joanne Woodward that of her psychiatrist. Their brilliant performances, widely praised, were supported by Brad Davis, Martine Bartlett, Jane Hoffman, William Prince and Natasha Ryan. The teleplay was by Stewart Stern, from a book by Flora Rheta Schreiber. Jacqueline Babbin was producer, Daniel Petrie director, and Peter Dunne and Philip Capice executive producers.

SYNDICATED EXCLUSIVITY RULE ("Syndex") ▶ an FCC measure adopted to resolve a complication that arises when a cable system brings in independent stations from other cities (known as distant signals). These imported stations often carry the same syndicated programs as those purchased by local TV stations in the cable system's market. The stations may have paid dearly for the local rights to the reruns of *M*A*S*H* and *The Cosby Show,* for instance, only to find that cable was bringing in the same programs without cost. This hampered the ability of syndicators to sell programs. The FCC ruled that when a cable system carries distant signals it must black out all syndicated programs whose local rights have already been acquired. Rather than simply letting the channel go dark for an hour or two, some cable operators patch in programming from one of the lesser program services, such as the Nostalgia Channel. But the effect of syndex in the main has been to discourage extensive importation of distant signals. Cable networks like American Movie Classics used the effect to their advantage by marketing themselves as an alternative to distant signals.

SYNDICATION ▶ the business of marketing TV programs to local stations. The field is the source of supply of vintage movies, off-network series, talk shows, game shows, children's series, programs from Canada and Britain and a miscellany of low-budget productions, such as exercise shows and country music variety shows.

Syndication dates to the early 1950s, when Frederick Ziv of Cincinnati extended his radio syndication business to TV with popular adventure series like *Highway Patrol* and *Sea Hunt.* Since then hundreds of entrepreneurs in the field have risen and fallen with the trends.

At times, syndication serves as a counterforce to the networks in program production and distribution, as when the studios create original sitcoms and adventure series for the station marketplace. Paramount TV elected to go outside the networks with *Star Trek: The Next Generation* and produced it for first-run syndication, where it was a huge success. Series such as *Fame* and *Too Close for Comfort* were kept in production by the syndication market after being cancelled by the networks. *Entertainment Tonight* has linked stations around the country by satellite for its daily roundup of show-biz news. And occasionally ad hoc networks are created in syndication for fully-sponsored programs and special events.

For many national advertisers, barter syndication presents a desirable alternative to advertising on the networks, since it can offer better economy and also, in some cases, program vehicles that are ideally suited to the advertised product. With barter, the program is generally given free to the station in exchange for carrying built-in national spots. The program's production costs and the syndicator's profit are covered by the national advertising spots; the station derives its profit from the open spots in the program that are the station's to sell.

While for many years the syndication field was largely dependent for its markets on the time periods not used by the networks, principally 4:30-8 p.m., it experienced a boom in the early 1980s with the proliferation of new UHF stations around the country, a phenomenon that accompanied the rapid spread of cable. UHF stations carried on cable did not have the reception problems that impeded the development of the UHF band previously, and new ones came on by the hundreds. Each new station needed a two- or three-year supply of programming to fill its 18-hour a day schedule, and syndicators enjoyed a bonanza for a few years.

Barter came into flower in this period, largely because the new stations would not have been able to afford the huge outlay of cash that would otherwise have been required for their programming needs. Today virtually all syndication involves barter, though many of the more expensive productions and off-network hits are sold marketed for what is known as cash-plus-barter.

The boom of the 1980s ended as suddenly as it began when, in the latter part of the decade, the building of new stations stopped, and the existing UHFs had become amply stocked with programs. The market was further hobbled by the extraordinary success of two game shows, *Wheel of Fortune* and *Jeopardy*, which, while they lifted one small syndicator (King World) to the top of the field, reduced the opportunities for other small syndicators who were trying to market shows that were merely serviceable. Serviceable had previously sufficed with stations for many time periods, but after *Wheel, Jeopardy* and the *Star Trek* sequel the stations began lusting after hits.

Syndicators were dealt yet another blow in the late 1980s with the emergence of the Fox Network, which recruited its affiliates from many of the independent UHFs that previously had been wholly dependent for programming on what the syndication market could supply. But syndication is a field that has always been subjected to the vicissitudes of the television marketplace and one that continually has had to reinvent itself.

With characteristic resiliency, syndicators began selling to cable networks what they could not sell sufficiently at the local station level. When the station market rejected the off-network hour-long action-adventure series, for example, those programs went immediately to cable. While the cable networks do not pay nearly as much as a flourishing syndication market, the sales and distribution costs are considerably lower because they involve a single customer.

The salvation for many American distributors, when the U.S. syndication market began to shrink, was the opening of the European and other foreign markets to commercial television during the latter half of the 1980s. Many program distributors today make more money selling internationally than domestically.

T

TABLOID TELEVISION ▶ a genre of TV that became the program wave of the early 1990s following upon the success of Fox Network's *A Current Affair.* Reality-based, frequently playing upon sensational stories, lurid crimes, sex and celebrities, tabloid TV grew out of the need for low-cost syndicated programming to fill a void in station schedules left by the diminishing use of old movies. By relying on actual situations, and in some cases featuring people who had been involved in those situations rather than actors, the shows manage to avoid the high costs of conventional prime-time entertainment. By some estimates, tabloid shows reduce per-program costs by as much as half.

Tabloid TV's prototype show was *A Current Affair.* The half-hour series hosted initially by Maury Povich was first televised locally on Fox's New York station, WNYW, and went into national distribution in 1988 when its mix of titillation and gruesome detail won a sizeable following. The show's most infamous episode occurred during the trial of "preppie murderer" Robert Chambers, accused, and later convicted, of killing his young woman companion in Central Park in the course of "rough sex." The program secured exclusive home video footage that showed Chambers frolicking with a group of scantily clad young women and apparently performing a parody of the crime with a doll. *A Current Affair*'s successful formula, playing upon the public's baser tastes for the lurid and sensational, spawned a new breed of television with such imitators as Paramount's *Hard Copy* and King-World's *Inside Edition.*

A variation on the genre grew out of another Fox production, *America's Most Wanted,* a breed of reality-based television rooted in the world of cops and crime. The formula, first developed in German and British TV, dramatizes crimes and enlists the audience in the hunt for the perpetrators. NBC produced its own version of the form with *Unsolved Mysteries,* an hour-long show hosted by Robert Stack in which the audience is invited to help unravel the mysteries of missing persons, unsolved murders and unclaimed estates. *Missing/Reward,* a syndicated show, resembles *Unsolved Mysteries* in its dramatized format but differs in offering viewers rewards for solutions to the mysteries of missing persons, unsolved crimes and collectors' quests for hard-to-find items. Two other shows, both drawing upon actual events—though not inviting audience participation—exemplify the new breed of reality-based shows. *Cops,* on the Fox Network since 1989, is a video verite look at the police as they perform their sometimes dangerous tasks. And *Rescue 911,* hosted by William Shatner on CBS, relives actual rescues by emergency services—police, paramedics and firefighters—through dramatic recreations, interviews, and newsreel footage. Other prime-time programs in the genre include *Top Cops, FBI: The Untold Stories* and *American Detective.*

Critics have been hard on tabloid TV, deploring its pandering appeal to voyeurism and downscale tastes. But its relative popularity with audiences has prompted some to try for an upscale version—bearing in mind, perhaps, that the putative father of the form is to be found in CBS's highly successful *60 Minutes.* The syndicated series *Inside Edition* would like to claim the high ground in upscale tabloid TV, but its best exemplar is NBC's *Expose,* a half-hour show hosted by Tom Brokaw, which appeared sporadically before becoming a regular prime-time series in the 1990-91 season.

TAFFNER, DONALD L. ▶ independent program distributor and sometime producer who became involved in international TV commerce in 1963, well ahead of most other U.S. companies. Among other ventures, he served for years from his New York base as American representative for Britain's Thames Television, an association that paid off in the 1980s when he adapted the formats of two Thames series, *Man About the House* and *Keep It in the Family,* for ABC. Those became the hit sitcoms *Three's Company* and *Too Close for Comfort.* When the latter was canceled by the network after a moderately successful run, Taffner undertook to keep it in production as an entry in first-run syndication—something that had not been done before but has been done fairly often since.

Taffner entered the business working in the mailroom at the William Morris talent agency and rose to become co-head of its television department. He left in 1959 to become a TV salesman for Paramount and in 1963 started his own company, known today as DLT Entertainment.

TAISHOFF, SOL J. (d. 1982) ▶ longtime editor of *Broadcasting Magazine,* weekly trade journal for the radio and TV industries, who was such an effective agent for broadcasters in Washington that he was given the NAB's Distinguished Service Award in 1966. Not only was he a staunch defender of commercial broadcast interests in the capital and an influential voice in the Government's communications policies, but he also arranged for individual broadcasters to make personal contact with legislators on their visits to Washington. Although the publication is strongly biased in favor of the industry and frequently attacks its critics, *Broadcasting* is respected for the thoroughness of its coverage of industry news and for its sophistication in examining industry issues. Its editorials are distinctly conservative and generally oppose government regulation.

Taishoff and Martin Codel founded *Broadcasting* in 1931. About 14 years later, after a disagreement between them, Taishoff bought out his partner and became sole owner. The magazine was sold in 1991 to Cahners Publishing Co., which had previously bought *Variety.*

TALBOT, PAUL ▶ a pioneer of international television distribution, who started the Fremantle organization in the early 1950s, a company he continues to head as president and CEO. The organization today has two components: Fremantle Corp., which produces and distributes TV series and specials, and Fremantle International, which specializes in the marketing of U.S. game shows and game show formats abroad. In 1991 the company had placed more than 70 game shows in foreign markets and is easily the world's largest supplier in this category.

Fremantle maintains offices in New York, London, Toronto, Madrid, Athens and Sydney and claims annual revenues of more than $200 million. In the late 1980s, the international advertising conglomerate Interpublic Group bought a majority share of the game show operation.

When Talbot began in the export field there were few countries to deal with because television was still developing around the world. In 1956, when the number of countries with television was becoming significant, Talbot obtained exclusive U.S. and world rights to the Olympics from Melbourne, Australia. Films of the events were delivered to Talbot's TV customers by prop planes and arrived at least two days after the results were known. The enterprise was no great financial success, but the 1956 Olympics established Fremantle worldwide. During the 1960s and 1970s, Fremantle established *Romper Room* programs around the world and, in the U.S., had a successful syndicated series in *The Galloping Gourmet.*

Talbot began his career as a radio actor, appearing in daytime soap operas and such nighttime series as *The Aldrich Family.* He also worked for the CBS television network in its earliest days. He started his company when he acquired the overseas rights to one of the hot TV series of the day, *Hopalong Cassidy.*

TALES FROM THE CRYPT ▶ supernatural anthology series, based on stories that originally appeared in the 1950s magazine of the same name, which premiered on HBO in June 1980. Executive producers Richard Donner, Walter Hill, and Robert Zemeckis also directed several of the early segments, as did Arnold Schwarzenegger. David Giler and Joel Silver were also executive producers.

TALES OF WELLS FARGO ▶ half-hour western series on NBC (1957-60) expanded to an hour in its final season (1961-62). It concerned a troubleshooter for the stage lines, portrayed by Dale Robertson. Overland Productions and Universal produced the half-hour version, Juggernaut Inc. the hour program.

TALK SHOW ▶ possibly the most basic form of television and one that best capitalizes on the fact that television is in essence a personality medium. Talk shows succeed or fail on the ineffable appeal of their hosts, rather than on their subject matter. The audience for a successful host tends to be loyal: Phil Donahue's show has been syndicated successfully since 1973, and Johnny Carson, who retired from *Tonight* in 1992, had a following for 30 years.

There is, however, no norm for a talk show host; the range is from heaven to hell, from the pleasant celebrity flatterers like Mike Douglas, Merv Griffin and Joe Franklin to the coarse, opinionated and verbally violent practitioners of the art like the late Joe Pyne, Howard Stern and Morton Downey, Jr. In the broad area between those extremes are the leading syndicated talk show hosts of the late 1980s and early 1990s: Oprah Winfrey, Sally Jessy Raphael, Geraldo Rivera, Regis Philbin and Kathie Lee Gifford, and the durable Donahue—all different from each other, but all on the air every day, covering or exploiting similar topics.

Because among the popular television forms talk shows are the least expensive to produce, new entrants pepper the syndication market every year. But whether the host is already familiar—like Jesse Jackson, G. Gordon Liddy, Pat Sajak or Ron Reagan (the former President's son)—or a recent discovery, like Wil Shriner, Jenny Jones or Chuck Woolery, the failure rate is extremely high. Experience has found that it is not hype, fame, notoriety, or sex-appeal that make these shows work but some hard-to-discern aspect of personality, with of course intelligence and style.

Because the economics are unbeatable, talk shows will probably always be the bread and butter of daytime television for local stations. Practically every station has at least one from the syndication market, and in addition many produce their own local talk shows. Both *Oprah* and *Donahue,* the two leaders of the field, were local programs in the midwest before they went national in syndication.

TALKING HEADS ▶ pejorative industry term for public affairs and interview programs that only involve people talking to each other, thus making for static visuals. According to the prevailing wisdom among programmers, television, as a visual medium, must feed the eye as well as the ear to satisfy its audience. But when feeding the mind is the issue, talking heads with something to say make for riveting viewing. The Army-McCarthy hearings, the Watergate hearings, and the 1991 Senate hearings on the sexual harassment charges brought against Supreme Court nominee Clarence Thomas, were high drama played before virtually the entire country. All were turning points in American history, all rank among the greatest and most-watched broadcasts in television history, and all involved nothing but talking heads.

TAMMY GRIMES SHOW, THE ▶ a situation comedy in the daffy mode that became legendary as one of the fastest flops in TV history. Premiering on Sept. 18, 1966, it received its cancellation notice from ABC after three weeks. The series was meant to be a vehicle for Grimes (as heiress Tamantha Ward) on the heels of her success on the Broadway stage, but the concept was weak and the program widely ignored by viewers. Dick Sargent and Hiram Sherman were featured as Terence Ward and Uncle Simon; William Dozier was executive producer; and the series was made by Greenway Productions and 20th Century-Fox.

TANNER '88 ▶ HBO's humorous and stingingly satirical look at the American presidential election process, from two unlikely collaborators: Garry Trudeau, creator of the comic strip *Doonesbury,* and filmmaker Robert Altman. Michael Murphy starred as Jack Tanner, Democratic presidential hopeful on the campaign stump. Accompanying him on the trail is his hard-boiled campaign manager, T.J. Cavanaugh (Pamela Reed), the role based directly on one of Trudeau's *Doonesbury* characters. Along the way, all types of political woes plague the candidate: girlfriends, the search for the right sound bite and logistical setbacks. The 12-part series occasionally featured a real-life political figure, with appearances by Bruce Babbitt and Kitty Dukakis. The series aired during the actual presidential primaries from February to August, 1988.

TARSES, JAY ▶ former comedian who got into television as a comedy writer and became a successful producer, director and writer of sitcoms. His producing credits include *The Days and Nights of Molly Dodd* and *The Slap Maxwell Story,* both of which debuted in 1987.

From 1971 to 1983 Tarses worked on all television projects in partnership with Tom Patchett, with whom he had previously developed a stand-up comedy act that had played guest shots on a number of network variety shows. Their first television writing was for *The Carol Burnett Show* and next for *The New Dick Van Dyke Show* in 1971. After that, they gave up performing and went to work as story editors for *The Bob Newhart Show,* which led to a five-year association with MTM Productions. There they produced *The Tony Randall Show, We've Got Each Other* and Mary Tyler Moore's short-lived variety show, *Mary.* Later they teamed with Bernie Brillstein on a number of projects, the last of which was *Buffalo Bill.* After that their partnership dissolved, and Tarses went solo. When his *Molly Dodd* was canceled by NBC, it was picked up by Lifetime, which ordered 13 original episodes in 1989.

Tarses and Patchett met while working at the Armstrong Cork Co. in Lancaster, Pa., during the 1960s. There they created the comedy act that got them into big-time show business. Interestingly, another employee of Armstrong at the time was Hugh Wilson, who later also became a successful Hollywood producer-writer, notably with *WKRP in Cincinnati.*

Brandon Tartikoff

TARTIKOFF, BRANDON ▶ premier TV programmer in the 1980s who jolted the industry in 1991 when he left NBC to become chairman of Paramount Pictures. This immediately gave rise to suspicion that Paramount intended to buy NBC from General Electric. Both NBC Entertainment and Paramount Television underwent a reorganization as a result of his move. Warren Littlefield succeeded him as president of NBC Entertainment.

Tartikoff became the youngest division president in NBC history when he was named to the post in 1980. As a protege of Fred Silverman, Tartikoff held high positions in programming at ABC and NBC while only in his twenties. He caught Silverman's attention through several imaginative on-air promotions he mounted while director of advertising and promotion at Chicago ABC station WLS-TV (1973-76). During that time he was also producing and writing comedy specials. Silverman, then president of ABC Entertainment, recruited Tartikoff for his program staff. A year later Tartikoff was hired away by NBC as director of comedy programs and in July 1978 became v.p. of programs for the West Coast. When Silverman became president of NBC, he made Tartikoff his program chief.

***TARZAN* ▶** hour-long adventure series based on Edgar Rice Burroughs's tales of the jungle man. It premiered on NBC in September 1966 and ran through 1968, with Ron Ely as Tarzan and Manuel Padella as an orphan named Jai. It was produced by Banner Productions.

Danny DeVito and Judd Hirsch in a scene from *Taxi*

***TAXI* ▶** ABC sitcom in the blue-collar genre that was almost instantly successful when introduced in September 1978, partly because it was inserted in the network's powerhouse Tuesday night lineup. The series centered on a group of colorful New York City cabbies, some of whom are only part-time drivers, and was created by the *Mary Tyler Moore Show* team of James L. Brooks, Stan Daniels, David Davis and Ed. Weinberger, who also served as writers and producers. James Burrows directed.

The cast was headed by Judd Hirsch as Alex Reiger and included Marilu Henner as Elaine Nardo, Tony Danza as amateur boxer Tony Banta, Jeff Conaway as struggling actor Bobby Wheeler, Randall Carver as John Burns, Andy Kaufman as mechanic Latka Gravas, Carol Kane as Latka's wife Simka, Christopher Lloyd as "Reverend" Jim Ignatowski and Danny DeVito as dispatcher Louis DiPalma. The show ran until 1983.

TAYLOR, ARTHUR R. ▶ one-time president of CBS Inc. (1972-76); he was forced to resign in October 1976 by chairman William S. Paley, who reportedly decided that, despite his outstanding financial record, Taylor was not the man he wanted as his successor. The action surprised Wall Street and stunned executives of CBS, with whom Taylor had been popular. The quasi-official explanation was that there was a poor "personal chemistry" between Paley and Taylor. John D. Backe, head of the CBS publishing division, was immediately named to succeed Taylor.

In 1980 he began organizing a new pay-cable network in which Rockefeller Center, and later RCA, were principal investors. Taylor, as president of RCTV, secured the American rights to the British Broadcasting Corporation's programming for the new network. This suggested to many that the network would be cultural in orientation, a pay-cable version of PBS. To counter that impression, Taylor called the new program service The Entertainment Network. It made its debut in the spring of 1982, essentially failed, and was merged into what is now the Arts and Entertainment (A&E) network. Taylor went on to become Dean of the Faculty of Business at Fordham University in 1985.

Taylor, who was 37 when he joined CBS in 1972, had been hired away from the International Paper Co., where he had been executive vice-president, chief financial officer, a director and a member of the executive committee. Discovered for CBS by executive headhunters, he was brought in to succeed Dr. Frank Stanton, although the late Charles Ireland had served in the post briefly in between. The selection made Taylor heir-apparent to Paley as chairman.

Having been chosen for his skills in finance and acquisitions, Taylor brought order to a company that had been diversifying haphazardly, maximized the main businesses of CBS and improved the profit performance of the company as a whole. Meanwhile, he acquired a background in broadcasting sufficient to bid for Stanton's mantle as the industry leader.

He led the broadcast industry's campaign against pay cable, became the champion of the "family viewing time" concept in 1975 (and the executive most closely identified with it) and made the most concerted effort in all broadcasting—albeit unsuccessfully—for a suspension of Section 315 of the Communications Act (the equal time law) that would have permitted the networks to mount a set of presidential debates in 1976.

TEBET, DAVID W. ▶ NBC executive in charge of talent relations (1960-79), who, with the title of executive v.p. in the program department, was responsible for maintaining liaison with the network's stars and for acquiring new talent. He resigned early in the Fred Silverman administration and promptly became a consultant to the Lew Grade-Martin Starger company, Marble Arch Productions.

Before joining NBC, Tebet had been a theatrical press agent for a number of Broadway shows and theatrical production companies. Later he formed his own publicity firm, handling, among other clients, Max Liebman Productions, which produced *Your Show of Shows* and numerous TV specials. He joined NBC as a general program executive in 1956 and received the talent post after the death of Manie Sacks.

TEDESCO, LOU ▶ director, principally of game shows and specials. His credits include *Eye Guess, Personality, The Face Is Familiar, Miss Teenage America, Miss U.S.A., Miss America Pageant, Johnny Carson Discovers Cypress Gardens* and *A Salute to Oscar Hammerstein.*

TEENAGE MUTANT NINJA TURTLES ▶ animated cartoon series syndicated by Group W Productions in 1987 that became a national craze among children, and later an international one as well, generating millions of dollars in licensing rights for all manner of products. A live-action movie released in 1990 was a huge box-office success, and that year CBS plucked the series from syndication for its Saturday morning lineup.

The series, which was based on a comic strip, follows the combative adventures of four humanlike turtles who were mutated into that form by exposure to a strange kind of radioactivity. All have developed skill in the martial arts, each is distinguished by his chosen weapon, and each has the name of a famous Italian artist—Leonardo, Michelangelo, Raphael and Donatello.

The Teenage Mutant Ninja Turtles

TELCOS ▶ telephone companies, regulated by the FCC as common carriers and also, to a degree, in their activities with cable TV. Because they own the poles and ducts on or through which the wires would be strung for cable TV, telcos play a critical role in the cable scheme, a role complicated by the fact that the phone companies would find it desirable to control the second wire on the pole since it both affords opportunity for growth and, in certain respects, poses competition to telephone services.

Telcos have in some situations impeded the construction of cable systems by charging excessively high pole or conduit fees, creating delays or even flatly refusing to let their poles be used for cable. AT&T and General Telephone both agreed in 1969 to permit the rental of their poles and ducts by cable entrepreneurs, but disputes have arisen in various localities over attempts to raise the rental rates.

When the FCC adopted a rule barring telcos from owning, directly or through affiliates, cable systems in their operating territories, it was challenged in the Court of Appeals for the Fifth Circuit by General Telephone Co. of the Southwest [449 F2d 846 (Fifth Circuit 1971)].

The court recognized that if phone companies had a proprietary interest in cable systems, competing CATV systems could be excluded from the area by the phone company's refusal to carry their wires or lease its lines. The court specifically rejected General Telephone's claim that it had been unconstitutionally deprived of its right to own a CATV system by pointing out that a phone company was free to do so outside its local service area.

In an earlier case, the D.C. Court of Appeals upheld an FCC rule that required telephone companies, as common carriers in interstate commerce, to apply for special permission to purchase or build CATV systems. General Telephone of California had challenged this ruling [413 F2d 390 (D.C. Cir. 1969)/cert. den. 396 U.S. 888 (1969)] on the ground that cable TV was confined to individual states and was therefore intrastate in nature. It said that certificates of public convenience and necessity, required under Sec. 214 of the Communications Act, concerned interstate matters only and were not applicable here.

The Court of Appeals noted that CATV systems were engaged in interstate communications even when the intercepted signals emanated from stations located in the same state as the subscriber. Additionally, it said, television programming was to a large extent designed for national audiences. The court spoke of an "indivisible stream" of interstate broadcast communication, of which the telephone companies were an "integral part." Since telcos were found to be engaged in interstate communications, they were clearly covered by Sec. 214 of the Act, the court said.

TELE 1ST ▶ an ABC Video Enterprises venture into pay television that had a tryout in Chicago in 1984 and was then abandoned. The idea was intriguing, but the procedures at the consumer end were found to be too complicated for successful marketing. Under the system, ABC affiliates would transmit a movie of recent vintage in the middle of the night to the VCRs in subscribing households. The signal would be unscrambled at the VCR by a special decoder box installed nearby. Subscribers had 30 days to watch the films, all of which were specially coded to break up the picture in that time. Chicago was chosen as the test market because the city had not yet been cabled and had a high penetration of VCRs. Viewers in the test found the guide book difficult and the procedures in setting up the equipment before going to bed bothersome.

TELECINE CHAIN ▶ a film projector and camera combination used to originate filmed material in television.

TELECOMMUNICATIONS ▶ the transmission and reception of signals, sounds, images or written matter by electromagnetic means, whether over radio frequencies or wire. It has become an all-embracing term for television, cable, telephone, computers and satellites.

TELEFILM CANADA ▶ a Crown corporation, through which the government provides support to the private sector to develop and promote Canada's film, television and video industries. In Canada, Telefilm is the primary partner in independent production, with broadcasters second and foreign participants third.

Telefilm injected $265 million into television production between 1986 and 1990, to assist with 2,275 hours of original programming with budgets totaling $800 million. Its goals are to strengthen the competitive position of Canadian works and to raise the export profile of Canadian companies. In addition to providing funding, it assists independents in developing marketing and promotion strategies in Canada and abroad.

Telefilm is responsible for managing coproduction treaty agreements for film or TV programs between Canada and 20 other countries, including Australia, Belgium, Czechoslovakia, Germany, France, Hungary, Ireland, Israel, Italy, Spain, and the United Kingdom. Among other provisions, the agreements stipulate that a coproduction be treated as a domestic program in each of the partner countries for purpose of quotas.

The corporation is based in Montreal and has offices in Toronto, Vancouver, Halifax, Los Angeles, Paris and London. It reports to Parliament through the Minister of Communications.

The chairman of Telefilm Canada is Harvey Corn; Pierre Des Roches is executive director.

TELEMETER (INTERNATIONAL TELEMETER CORP.) ▶ early pay-TV subsidiary of Paramount Pictures active during the 1950s with pay experiments in Palm Springs, Calif., Etobicoke (a suburb of Toronto, Ontario) and London, England. It became dormant when the five-year Etobicoke test ended in 1965, pending a full go-ahead for pay TV by the FCC, and was never reactivated.

TELEMUNDO GROUP ▶ Spanish-language television network covering 84.5% of the growing Hispanic market in the U.S. through 42 outlets, including owned-and-operated stations in six of the seven major Hispanic markets. The stations were acquired as part of a 1986 buyout of Blair Company by Reliance Group Holdings, a financial company whose chairman and CEO is Saul Steinberg. Reliance immediately sold off all the Blair units except the stations, using them as the foundation for a national network which began broadcasting in 1987. Much of its programming is produced in Telemundo's Florida production studios and the rest acquired from suppliers in Mexico, Venezuela, Argentina and Spain. In addition to its stations in Los Angeles, New York, Miami, San Francisco-San Jose, Houston-Galveston and San Antonio, Telemundo also owns WKAQ Puerto Rico.

TELENOVELAS ▶ Latin American version of the soap opera, with the difference that the stories eventually end after a year or more, so that each is a complete video novel. They tend to be programming mainstays in Latin American countries and are scheduled in early evening time periods or prime time. Telenovelas emanate principally from Brazil, Mexico and Venezuela and are among the big sellers in the world market.

TELEPROMPTER CORP. v. CBS **▶** [415 U.S. 394 (1974)] CATV copyright case in which the Supreme Court ruled that a network's copyrights were not violated when its signals were imported by a cable-TV system.

CBS had brought suit against Teleprompter Corp. charging infringement of copyright on the CATV systems that brought in distant signals, as differentiated from those systems that merely amplified the signals of local stations which could be received without cable service. The district court dismissed the suit, but this was, in part, reversed by the Court of Appeals.

The Court of Appeals held that where a CATV system simply transmitted local signals, there was no "performance" within the meaning of copyright laws and thus no violation (*Fortnightly Corp. v. United Artists Television*). The court found, however, that transmission of distant signals amounted to a "performance" because in that case the CATV system was the functional equivalent of a broadcaster.

But the Supreme Court refused to make a distinction between the importation of distant signals and the carriage of local signals, at least for the ambit of copyright laws. The Court specifically rejected the proposition that choosing which distant signal to import was analogous to a broadcaster choosing which program to broadcast in the first instance. Instead, the Court said, the selection of signals by CATV was analogous to a TV viewer deciding which station or program to watch.

Finally, the Court explained that the nature of the broadcaster is to supply the original signal, which can be received as images and sounds. The nature of the viewer is to receive the broadcast signal. Since the CATV service did not alter this relationship, its transmission of the signals did not constitute a "performance" and therefore did not violate the CBS copyright in network TV shows.

TELESAT, CANADA ▶ corporation that owns and operates the Canadian domestic satellite system, used by the CBC for interconnection.

TELETEXT ▶ supplementary home television broadcast service that stores and displays on-screen written and graphic material. Teletext service also includes captions that may be displayed while the picture is on the screen as a service to deaf or foreign-language speaking viewers.

In 1986, the U.S. Court of Appeals reversed an FCC decision that would have left the program matter on teletext services free from all public interest regulation. Over one dissent, appeals court Judge Robert Bork (joined by Judge Antonin Scalia) declined to require application of the Fairness Doctrine to teletext. This decision (*TRAC v. FCC*) became the basis upon which the FCC later repealed most other applications of the Fairness Doctrine.

TELEVANGELISTS ▶ fundamentalist preachers who established television ministries during the 1970s and 1980s by buying air time on local stations and soliciting financial contributions from viewers. Their proliferation drove from the Sunday morning schedules most of the networks' regular religious programs. Stations preferred to sell the airtime to evangelists rather than offer public service time to the mainline religions. Some of the TV ministries grew wealthy, exerted a powerful political influence and came to be known in the political sphere as the Religious Right. But by the end of the 1980s their numbers began to wane, and their political influence as well, weakened by the highly publicized episodes of corruption and improprieties among some of the leading figures in the field.

One of TV's most popular evangelists, Jimmy Swaggart, fell from favor in 1988 after he was dismissed by the Assemblies of God denomination for having sexual relations with a prostitute. The incident cost him 80% of his 2.2 million viewers. In an earlier episode eroding the influence of the televangelists, Jim Bakker's headlined extra-marital affair with Jessica Hahn, including allegations of sexual abuse, led eventually to a 45-year prison term for illegally appropriating $158 million of his followers' contributions.

Stunts such as the Rev. Oral Roberts's 1987 declaration that God would take his life if he didn't raise $4.5 million further weakened the dominance of evangelical programming when Roberts's viewing audience of 1.1 million decreased by half. Overall, Arbitron research indicates that in November 1985 the top 20 religious syndicated programs had over 11 million viewers; five years later, that number had dropped to 7.7 million.

TELEVISA ▶ large privately owned network whose four channels covering 100% of the federal republic of Mexico dominate that country's television viewing. Televisa's principal owner is Emilio Azcarraga Jr., son of the broadcasting pioneer who created Televisa in 1975 by persuading his competitors to join with him to form a single powerful corporation. Although Televisa is commercially operated, it devotes considerable time to educational programming. Its four channels are designed to appeal to different segments of the audience. Thus, while Channel 2, which covers most of Mexico, programs for the middle class (news, soaps and sports), Channel 4 broadcasts films, documentaries and history series to the urban public. Another channel is geared to the youth market and the fourth to the intellectual elite.

Televisa is a major producer of programming for the Spanish-speaking audience in other Latin American countries and in the U.S., where some of its shows are seen on the Univision network.

TELEVISION CODE ▶ a set of "voluntary" standards for proper program and advertising practices outlawed in 1982 by Washington D.C. federal Judge Harold Greene in *United States v. NAB.* Created as a mechanism for industry self-regulation by the National Association of Broadcasters for its member stations, the code enabled lobbyists to deflect efforts to legislate more stringent restrictions. The holding (that the code violated the Sherman Anti-Trust Act by artificially increasing the cost of commercials) and the Justice Department's initiation of the litigation were roundly criticized by the industry and by many consumer and public interest groups.

The NAB's fears were partially realized in 1990, when Congress reimposed limits on the amount of commercialization on children's TV and permitted establishment of guidelines on TV violence.

Code standards for commercials extended to time limits, specific content and techniques. The number of commercial minutes networks and stations could carry in each part of the day was ordained by the Code, and liquor advertising and attempts at subliminal perception were among the items barred by it.

Transgressions by subscribers were punishable only by the loss of the right to display the NAB seal of good practices. The Code was administered by the Code Authority (based in New York), and the industry-appointed Television Code Review Board.

In programming, the Code forbade "profanity, obscenity, smut and vulgarity" and specified that illicit sex relations were not to be treated as commendable. Sex crimes and sex abnormalities were deemed generally unacceptable as TV material. In news presentations, murder could not be represented as justifiable nor suicide as acceptable. Horror for its own sake and the indulgence in morbid detail were to be avoided.

Concerning their special responsibilities toward children, broadcasters were admonished by the Code to treat sex and violence without emphasis and to take "exceptional care" with subjects such as kidnapping or crime episodes involving children.

The industry's adoption of "family viewing time" in 1975, in response to the concern of government officials with excessive violence and mature subject matter to which children were being exposed in prime time, was engineered through the Code by means of an amendment requiring that programs aired between 7 and 9 p.m. (6 to 8 p.m. Central Time) be suitable for all-family viewing.

Amendments to the Code, reflecting either changing mores or pressure from consumer- and special-interest groups, were recommended by the Television Code Review Board to the NAB's Television Board of Directors. The Review Board also considered appeals by the Code Authority and was responsible for preferring formal charges where there were serious violations of the Code.

The NAB Code Authority concerned itself mainly with Code interpretation and the reviewing of commercials for both radio and TV. However, when there was unusual pressure or heightened sensitivity to an issue, other surveillances were initiated. For example, in 1971, when Action for Children's Television exposed unconscionable practices by toy advertisers, all toy commercials were reviewed by the Authority before broadcast. In 1968, after the assassinations of Martin Luther King and Robert F. Kennedy, the Review Board ordered the Code Authority to increase scrutiny of violence in TV programs.

Within the compass of the Code, the networks and station groups maintained their own policies concerning standards. Approximately 70% of TV stations in the U.S. subscribed to the Code.

TELEVISION PROGRAM IMPROVEMENT ACT OF 1990 ▶ law permitting television stations, the National Association of Broadcasters and other trade groups to meet for the purpose of "developing and disseminating voluntary guidelines designed to alleviate the negative impact of violence in telecast material." Passed with muted opposition from the industry, the measure alarmed civil libertarians concerned about the coercive impact of its seemingly bland language.

TELEVISION, TECHNOLOGY OF ▶ transmission and reception of pictures or images and sound electronically, generally by electromagnetic radiation (radio) but also via cable, fiber or on a recording medium. All television systems currently in use (and all of their successfully demonstrated predecessors) utilize the phenomenon of persistence of vision, which makes it possible to break a scene into tiny segments at the origination point and reassemble it in sequence at the receiver.

At the origination point or studio, the pickup tube in the television camera converts an optical image into a corresponding "image" composed of varying electrical charges. This image is scanned by an electron gun, with 525 scanning lines (in the NTSC system) making up a single image. Thirty individual 525-line pictures are scanned each second. The scanning process roughly corresponds to reading a page in a book—each line is read, one at a time, from left to right, from top to bottom. In television scanning using the principle of interlace, alternate lines are scanned in sequence—lines 1, 3, 5, and so forth, until 525 are scanned in 1/60 of a second. Then the electron beam moves to line 2 and scans the even-numbered lines, in effect filling in the spaces between the odd-numbered ones. This interlace system helps reduce flicker and is used in all broadcast television systems. A complete 525-line picture (1/30 of a second) is called a "frame." A half-picture—either odd or even lines (1/60 of a second)—is a "field."

The electrical signal scanned within the camera is amplified and, along with a synchronizing signal and a sound signal, is superimposed on a carrier frequency—the frequency of the channel on which the signal is to be transmitted. The entire carrier and signal is fed to the transmitter, which amplifies it to many times its original power. The broadcast antenna emits the carrier and signal as powerful electromagnetic radiations.

The receiving antenna intercepts the radiations, which are fed to the tuner in the television set. The tuner selects only the desired frequencies (channel). The signal is removed from the carrier, amplified and fed into the picture tube, where the image is reconstructed by reversing the pickup operation. A black-and-white (monochrome) picture tube has a fluorescent face, which glows at the spot where it is struck by an electron beam. An electron gun in the neck of the tube is the source of the beam, which is deflected for scanning by magnetic or electrostatic devices mounted around the tube's neck, while brightness is controlled by the amount of voltage on the gun. The beam then "paints" a recreated 525-line picture, again from left to right, top to bottom, line by line.

In cable television, the cable system's main studio, or "head-end," receives over-the-air signals from stations in its region and delivers them on various channels to subscribers' homes. The cable system can also allocate its channels to signals of TV services it receives off satellites (program services like CNN, MTV, HBO), to live programs originating in its own studios, and to recorded material.

In color television, the camera may have one or more scanning tubes, but in any case the scanned image is, in effect, broken into three individual pictures by means of filters—one containing only red elements of the picture, one only green and the third only blue. These are television's three primary colors, and when the three are combined at the same strength they result in white. The color signals are scanned and combined mathematically into a chrominance signal, which, in effect contains the key to the coloring of the elements of the picture when it is reconstructed at the receiver. Also derived from the camera is the luminance signal, which controls brightness, and is a complete black-and-white picture. These signals, together with a burst signal to keep the colors in phase, are impressed on the carrier frequency.

At the color television receiver, the information in the signal is decoded, and the signals representing each color as the luminance (brightness) signals are amplified separately. The color picture tube contains three guns (or three "barrels" in a single gun) in its neck—one for the electrical impulses representing each of the three primary colors. The phosphor screen contains an array of tiny dots, lines or rectangles (depending on the type of tube) in sets of three, each with a different chemical composition to cause it to glow red, green or blue when excited by the electron beam. Just back of the faceplate, toward the electron guns, is mounted a thin perforated metal mask, known as a shadow mask or aperture grille. The holes, slits or slots in the mask are positioned so that each of the three electron beams can strike only the proper colored phosphor on the screen.

If a black-and-white picture is being transmitted, all three electron guns are activated to the same extent, thereby exciting all three colored phosphors, resulting in a black-and-white picture. When a black-and-white television set is receiving a color picture, it ignores the chrominance signal, using only the luminance, or black-and-white (brightness) information.

This description applies to the American (NTSC) black-and-white and color systems. Other European (CCIR) black-and-white, PAL and SECAM color systems, operate in a similar, but not identical manner.

TELIDON ▶ defunct videotext system developed in the 1970s by the Canadian Department of Communications, which could be transmitted over broadcast, cable or telephone.

TELSTAR I ▶ experimental communication satellite operated by the National Aeronautics and Space Administration that relayed the first live transatlantic transmission on July 10, 1962—a fluttering American flag outside the sending station at Andover, Maine. Two weeks later

Telstar I began carrying more panoramic telecasts exchanged between the U.S. and European countries. Because it had a random elliptical orbit, transmission times were sharply limited.

TENNIS ▶ a sport that knows no season and appears to be growing in popularity with TV viewers, especially when the baseball and football seasons end. As sporting events go, it is one of the easiest to cover technically and comparatively low-budgeted.

Two commercial networks have long had a piece of the tennis Grand Slam action: NBC with Wimbledon since 1969 and the French Open continuously since 1983 (and also 1975-79), and CBS with the U.S. Open since 1967. ABC contents itself with such tournaments as the ATP Tour and the Virginia Slims Championships. Despite the millions of hackers who play the game and the fading of its once-elitist country club image, tennis has rarely achieved extraordinary ratings. Even NBC's Breakfasts at Wimbledon (so named because its live afternoon London coverage begins five hours later than EST) began with a 4.2 rating in 1969 and earned a 4.3 rating in 1991. (By contrast, the Super Bowl on CBS drew a 41.9).

An emerging major TV player on the tennis circuit is the USA Network. In 1991, continuing its production partnership with CBS Sports, it devoted over 90 hours to the U.S. Open, including exclusive full-day coverage on the Sunday of Labor Day weekend. From opening-round action on Aug. 26 until the last handshakes at the net after the women's doubles final on Sept. 8, USA was the channel of choice. Buoyed by a surging national interest in the 11th hour victories of 39-year-old Jimmy Connors, USA Network achieved a Thursday night 5.9 rating with a 10 share, its highest ever for a live sporting event.

Principal commentators for USA have been former player Barry McKay, Vitas Gerulaitus and Tracy Austin; for NBC, Bud Collins, Dick Enberg and Chris Evert; for ABC, Arthur Ashe, Cliff Drysdale and, when not on the court herself, Pam Shriver.

THAMES TELEVISION ▶ a leading British program producer and for many years one of the U.K.'s principal franchise-holders as the weekday commercial broadcaster for the London region (turning over the channel to London Weekend Television on Friday nights for the weekend). But Thames dramatically lost its license in October 1991 in the U.K.'s so-called "franchise auctions" when it was outbid by Carlton Television.

Among the 15 regional ITV companies in Britain, Thames was one of the best known internationally because it produced so many programs for the ITV network that also sold well abroad. The range was from *Benny Hill* to *Jennie: Lady Randolph Churchill, The World at War* and *Rock Follies.* In association with Lorimar, Thames produced the mini-series *Jack the Ripper*, which aired on CBS in the 1989-90 season.

With the loss of its broadcast franchise, Thames becomes an independent producer able to sell its programs to any of the British channels. It is also a shareholder in Astra, the leading European satellite company, opening the possibility of its creating a satellite channel. Thames purchased an American production company, Reeves Entertainment, for $89 million in 1990.

***THAT GIRL* ▶** ABC situation comedy (1966-70) about a hopeful young actress with an apartment of her own. Via Daisy Productions, it starred Marlo Thomas as Ann Marie and featured Ted Bessell as her boyfriend, Don Hollinger, and Rosemary DeCamp and Lew Parker as Ann's parents, Helen and Lew Marie. George Carlin made appearances as Ann's agent, George Lester.

***THAT WAS THE WEEK THAT WAS* ▶** or *TW3*, as it came to be abbreviated, an innovative British sketch series that employed satire and ridicule on current events and personalities. Created and produced by Ned Sherrin (a prolific English producer, air personality and stage dramatist), and with a regular company that numbered among others David Frost, the show was one of a number of "breakthroughs" for the British medium in the 1960s. It enjoyed wide publicity and tall ratings. A year after its debut in 1964, the title, format and Frost transferred to the U.S. airlanes as an ill-fated NBC-TV series produced by Leland Hayward, with actor Elliot Reid as anchor. Also appearing in the American cast were Alan Alda, Buck Henry, Henry Morgan and Phyllis Newman.

***THAT'S MY MAMA* ▶** ABC situation comedy (1974-75) about a black family that runs a barber shop in Washington, D.C. Via Columbia Pictures TV, it featured Theresa Merritt as Eloise (Mama) Curtis and Clifton Davis as her son, Clifton Curtis.

T.H.E. CAT ▶ series about an acrobatic detective on NBC (1966-67) featuring Robert Loggia as reformed catburgler Thomas Hewitt Edward (T.H.E.) Cat, R.G. Armstrong as Captain McCllister and Robert Carricart as Pepe. It was produced by Boris Sagal for NBC Productions.

THEATER IN AMERICA ▶ public TV series, started in 1974, devoted to presenting the work of regional theaters around the country. Among those represented were the Long Wharf Theater in New Haven; the Guthrie Theater, Minneapolis; the Phoenix Theater, New York; and the Arena Stage, Washington, D.C. Most of the productions had dual directors—the original stage director and a co-director for television to restage the work for the cameras. Jac Venza was executive producer for the originating station, WNET New York. The series was funded for PBS chiefly by Exxon.

THEFT OF SERVICE ▶ unauthorized access by consumers to cable installations and pay-cable channels, accomplished by tapping into an apartment building's cable line and using pirated decoders or other devices to receive the pay channels free. These are recognized felonies today, and in recent years numerous perpetrators have been dealt with by the courts as severely as any thief of merchandise or money. Despite the threat of such penalties, the cable industry believes the illegal practices are still widespread and costing the systems millions of dollars in unrealized revenue.

THEN CAME BRONSON ▶ hour-long adventure series on NBC about a free spirit traveling across America on a motorcycle; it premiered in 1969 and lasted one season. It featured Michael Parks as Jim Bronson and was produced by MGM-TV.

THICKE, ALAN ▶ multi-talented Canadian expatriate whose credits in U.S. television run the above-the-line gamut. He scored as a comedy actor in *Growing Pains,* which began in 1985, after having been one of the top comedy writers for TV specials such as those of Flip Wilson, Richard Pryor and Bill Cosby. In the late 1970s he was writer-producer of the zany *Fernwood Tonight* and *America 2-Night* series. He has also appeared as an actor on episodes of *The Love Boat, Masquerade,* and *Scene of the Crime.*

Thicke began as a comedy writer in Canada and later became one of that country's most popular talk show hosts. In 1983 he ventured a syndicated U.S. talk show, *Thicke of the Night,* but it failed to catch on.

A singer and songwriter, Thicke wrote the title songs for such shows as *The Facts of Life* and *Diff'rent Strokes.*

THIN MAN, THE ▶ urbane husband-wife detective series with Peter Lawford and Phyllis Kirk as Nick and Nora Charles, based on the classic movie series that had starred William Powell and Myrna Loy. The television version featured Jack Albertson as Lieutenant Evans, and both versions featured a dog named Asta. Produced by MGM-TV, it played on NBC (1957-59), with the reruns stripped in daytime the following two seasons.

30 MINUTES ▶ junior version of *60 Minutes* for the teenage audience, which aired Saturday afternoons on CBS in the late 1970s. The youth newsmagazine produced by CBS News dealt in topical issues, such as why teenagers run away from home, teenagers with babies and the high accident rate for 16- and 17-year-old drivers. On-camera principals were Christopher Glenn and Betsy Aaron. Joel Heller was executive producer, Allen Ducovny executive editor and Vern Diamond director.

Ken Olin and Mel Harris as Michael and Hope Steadman on *thirtysomething*

THIRTYSOMETHING ▶ an hour-long series on ABC chronicling the day-to-day concerns of a group of upwardly mobile "baby boomers." The series, created by Ed Zwick and Marshall

Herskovitz, attracted an intensely loyal audience of 30-year-olds who readily identified with the seven principals—two married couples and three singles, all in the their thirties. Some critics found *thirtysomething* self- indulgent and tedious, others innovative and topical, but its fans were devoted.

The cast included Mel Harris and Ken Olin as Hope Murdoch and Michael Steadman, introspective spouses and parents; . Timothy Busfield and Patricia Wettig as their friends, Elliot and Nancy Weston; Polly Draper as Hope's long-time friend Ellyn Warren; Melanie Mayron as Michael's cousin Melissa Steadman; and Peter Horton as Michael's friend (and Melissa's sometime lover) Gary Shepherd. Joining the cast later were David Clennon as Michael and Elliot's strange and intimidating boss, advertising executive Miles Drentell; Patricia Kalember as Gary's wife, Susannah, beginning in 1988; Richard Gilliland as Ellyn's lover, Jeffrey Milgrom; and Corey Parker as Melissa's young boyfriend, Lee Owens. The series ran from September 1987 until the end of the 1990-91 season.

THIS HOUR HAS SEVEN DAYS ▶ groundbreaking Canadian series of the 1960s, believed to be the first television news-magazine and the program that inspired *60 Minutes.* In its prime-time Sunday time period on the CBC, the program covered the full spectrum of magazine journalism—current events, international affairs, science, culture, the popular arts, books, law and sports. It ran from 1964-66 and was canceled not from poor ratings but from being often controversial and creating problems for the public television organization. It was, in fact, one of the most popular Canadian programs ever to air.

Its co-hosts, Patrick Watson and Laurier Lapierre, were respected Canadian intellectuals from opposite political poles, whose views on issues often clashed. The producer, Doug Leiterman, had a penchant for muckraking and for dealing with politically explosive issues. CBC management became overwhelmed by the heat generated. Paradoxically, Watson today, after a career as a producer and TV personality, is chairman and CEO of the CBC.

THIS IS THE LIFE ▶ a pioneer (September 1952) entry in religious TV; the Lutheran Church Missouri Synod series consisted of 30-minute dramas dealing with problems of contemporary society—alcoholism, adultery, death, desertion, drugs, gambling and the generation gap—and illuminated the church's position toward them.

THIS IS TOM JONES ▶ music-variety series produced by ATV in London for ABC (1969-71) with a rock singer popular on both sides of the Atlantic. But despite his youthful following in the U.S., and his reputation as a male sex symbol, Tom Jones was not a hit on American TV.

THIS IS YOUR LIFE ▶ one of the big prime-time hits of the 1950s, a sort of TV surprise party in which the honored guest, caught unawares, was subjected repeatedly to voices from the past and in the grand finale encircled by old friends, colleagues, relatives and teachers. Ralph Edwards, host and creator of the series, did his sentimental utmost to induce tears in the subject and presumably also in the viewer, who was made an eavesdropper on the celebrated person's fondest memories. The program premiered in 1952 and later inspired a British version, hosted there by Eammon Andrews.

The series was revived in the U.S. as a syndicated entry for the prime-access time periods, again with Edwards as host and producer. Lever Bros. placed it in 50 markets, but the ratings were disappointing and the series dropped after two seasons.

THIS MORNING ▶ latest CBS entry in the early-morning sweepstakes, an area that has been a source of frustration at the network for decades.

Despite its no-frills approach, with CBS billing it as "breakfast for your head," *This Morning,* like the many attempts before it, has perennially finished behind ABC's *Good Morning America* and NBC's *Today* in the Nielsen ratings. The new version of the two-hour CBS breakfast broadcast premiered in 1987 with Harry Smith and Paula Zahn as co-hosts and a somewhat stronger news orientation than its rivals. Along with covering breaking news, it devotes segments to business, health, life-styles, environment, sports and entertainment.

This Morning had a number of antecedents, dating to 1957 when it was the 15-minute *CBS Morning News.* In 1963 it was expanded to a half-hour and in 1969 to an hour. The program was preceded in all this time by the much-respected children's show *Captain Kangaroo,* which was hardly a compatible companion program. NBC, meanwhile, had established a valuable morning franchise with *Today,* and ABC entered successfully with *Good Morning,*

America. In a highly publicized move in 1973, CBS created an anchor team of Hughes Rudd and Sally Quinn (hired away from *The Washington Post*) in an effort to join the competition. That failed, and in 1979 Robert (Shad) Northshield, who had had great success in producing *CBS Sunday Morning* anchored by Charles Kuralt, was given the weekday assignment as well. With Bob Schieffer as anchor, Northshield revamped the series as *Morning*, giving it some of the style and polish of *Sunday Morning*. In 1981, CBS moved *Captain Kangaroo* to an earlier timeslot and expanded the news program to two hours where it could compete head-to-head with *Today* and *GMA*. That did not avail.

Next CBS News hired away producer George Merlis from *GMA* to revamp the program once again, this time with Diane Sawyer and Bill Kurtis as anchors. Later, for a few years in the 1980s, the program was removed from the domain of the news division and relaunched as a morning entertainment program, with talk-show components and a number of performing guests. Bob Shanks, a former ABC program executive, was brought in to produce it. It proved the most embarrassing flop of all.

Sally Quinn, whose association with the show lasted only a few months in 1973, also suffered embarrassment. Returning to the print world, she wrote about her CBS experience in a 1974 book whose title derived from an executive's quote, *We're Going to Make You a Star*.

THIS OLD HOUSE ▶ popular "how-to" public TV series on the craft of renovating and restoring old houses, produced for PBS by WGBH Boston. In 1989, when the popular host of the series, Bob Vila, came under fire from one of the show's corporate underwriters for his product endorsements on commercial TV, the producers replaced him with Steve Thomas. Russell Morash, executive producer, created the series in 1979 from an idea derived from a similar show on the BBC. Norm Abram has been the carpenter/instructor on the series since its debut.

THOMAS, DANNY (d. 1991) ▶ popular comedian who was also active in TV as actor and producer. In 1953 he began his first situation comedy, *Make Room for Daddy* (later *The Danny Thomas Show*) which ran on CBS until 1965. By then he had his own production company, which also turned out *The Bill Dana Show* and *The Tycoon,* featuring Walter Brennan, and also had a producing partnership with Sheldon Leonard, which had a hand in *The Andy Griffith Show* and its spin-offs.

Thomas soon returned on screen in the 1967 season with *The Danny Thomas Hour* on NBC, a potpourri of one-hour musicals, comedies and dramas; he appeared in all of them either as a performer or storyteller. Meanwhile, he had made a new producing partnership with Thomas-Spelling Productions. They were responsible for such series as *Mod Squad, The Guns of Will Sonnett, Rango, The New People* and *Chopper One.*

After a performing layoff of two years, Thomas was back on air in *Make Room for Grandaddy,* an attempt by ABC in 1970-71 to revive the original sitcom in an updated version. The following season he did a pair of specials for ABC and a new sitcom on NBC, *The Practice,* in which he played an aging doctor. His daughter, Marlo Thomas, was launched on a TV career of her own through *That Girl.*

THOMAS, LOWELL (d. 1981) ▶ legendary journalist, author and broadcaster whose radio career, mostly with CBS, spanned almost half a century and spilled over into TV. During the experimental period with television, his radio newscasts were simulcast in the medium. He also was a key participant in the CBS-TV coverage of the political conventions of 1952, 1956 and 1960. In 1957 Thomas began a TV travel series, *High Adventure,* and even in the 1970s, as an octogenarian, he conducted a syndicated series, *Lowell Thomas Remembers,* and narrated a retrospective television series on the early newsreels of Movietone News.

He was the author of 54 books, a noted world traveler, narrator for innumerable films, a founder of Cinerama and one of the founders of, and principal stockholder in, Capital Cities Broadcasting.

THOMAS, MARLO ▶ actress who as an ingenue did a single successful TV series, *That Girl* (1966-71), then made specials for children, two of which won Emmys—*Free To Be You and Me* (1974) and *The Body Human: Facts for Girls* (1981)—as did a made-for-TV movie, *Nobody's Child* (1986). *That Girl* had the distinction of being the first successful TV series based on the idea of an independent career woman. Prior to that, Thomas had a featured role in the short-lived *The Joey Bishop Show* (1961-62). She is the daughter of the late comedian Danny Thomas and wife of talk-show host Phil Donahue.

Marlo Thomas

THOMAS-HILL HEARINGS ▶ the dramatic televised hearings of charges brought against U.S. Supreme Court nominee Judge Clarence Thomas by a former legal assistant, Anita Hill, which had the country riveted to the screen for entire days on Oct. 11 and 12, 1991. At virtually the end of its protracted confirmation hearings on Thomas, the Senate Judiciary Committee devoted the two extra days to Hill's allegations of sexual harassment while in Thomas's employ. The hearings were prompted by Nina Totenberg's report on National Public Radio that Hill, a University of Oklahoma law professor, had made the charges but had not been taken seriously by the committee. The Senate Judiciary reconvened to hear the allegations and permitted television coverage.

The allegations brought the issue of sexual harassment to the public fore as nothing had before. The candor with which the allegations were discussed was also new to television. The character of the principals involved kept the televised hearings above the level of real-life soap opera, but the event had the intrigue of a melodramatic mini-series, turning on the perplexing question of which of the two highly credible principals was lying.

Hill displayed calm dignity and control as she related incidents in which Judge Thomas allegedly described to her scenes from pornographic films depicting sex with animals, group sex and rape scenes. He also allegedly boasted to her of his sexual prowess. She had, she told the committee, repeatedly told Thomas she did not want to hear such things but sensed that her apparent revulsion only encouraged him. In his appearance the following day, Judge Thomas categorically denied all Hill's allegations, but he turned his anger less upon her than upon the committee, condemning the procedure as "a high-tech lynching."

More than 40 million U.S. households watched the two days of hearings with an emotional intensity that had not been experienced in recent television history. The hearings were discussed everywhere, and the question of who was telling the truth was argued far and wide. The hearings had a positive side: along with raising consciousness of sexual harassment, they punctured the stereotypical image of blacks on the screen, with a steady procession of accomplished and well-spoken black professionals—including the two principals. The testimony, however—at times graphic and sexually explicit in ways that would not otherwise have been permitted on television—raised questions about the propriety of televising hearings that probe into matters of personal privacy. While the public and press debated these matters, the Senate Judiciary Committee voted, by the smallest of majorities, to recommend Judge Thomas's confirmation.

THOMOPOULOS, ANTHONY D. ▶ chairman and CEO of United Artists Pictures since 1985, having previously been president of the ABC Broadcast Group (1983-85). From 1978-83 Thomopoulos was president of ABC Entertainment, the programming arm of ABC-TV, in which position he succeeded Fred Silverman, who resigned to become president of NBC. Prior to that post Thomopoulos was v.p. of ABC-TV and assistant to the president, Frederick S. Pierce, in addition to serving in a number of executive capacities in programming and administration.

Thomopoulos joined ABC in 1973 after two years with Tomorrow Entertainment, where he was involved with the production and marketing of *The Autobiography of Miss Jane Pittman.* Earlier he was with the RCA SelectaVision division as director of programming and before that with Four Star Entertainment Corp. for five years. He began his career in broadcasting with NBC's International Division, working in sales.

THORN BIRDS, THE **▶** highly successful 10-hour mini-series, starring Richard Chamberlain, that was televised by ABC over four consecutive nights in March 1983. Based on a best-selling novel by Colleen McCullough, the story, set in Australia, centers on a torment of a Roman Catholic priest, Ralph de Bricassart, who falls in love with a woman, Meggie Carson. At its conclusion, *The Thorn Birds* ranked as the second highest-rated mini-series of all time, after *Roots.*

It co-starred Rachel Ward. Others in the cast were Barbara Stanwyck as Meggie's grandmother, Mary Carson, Jean Simmons as Fee Cleary, Richard Kiley as Paddy Cleary, Christopher Plummer as Archbishop Contini-Verchese and Bryan Brown as Luke O'Neill.

Richard Chamberlain as Father Ralph de Bricassart in *The Thorn Birds*

THORPE, JERRY ▶ producer-director (son of the late motion picture director Richard Thorpe) who was executive producer of the series *The Untouchables, Kung Fu, The Chicago Teddy Bears* and, with Garry Marshall, co-executive producer of *The Little People.* His more recent credits include producing the series *Fame* (1982-87).

THREE ROCKS, THE ▶ the three TV networks as they were nicknamed in the late 1960s because of their headquarters buildings along the Avenue of the Americas in Manhattan. NBC had long had the nickname "30 Rock," short for its formal address, 30 Rockefeller Plaza. CBS acquired the somewhat derisive name of "Black Rock" (after the movie *Bad Day at Black Rock*) when it moved into its dark granite skyscraper in 1965. To complete the scheme, wags in the trade then dubbed ABC "hard rock" for its trials as the third-ranked network. Today only two "rocks" remain on the Avenue since ABC moved uptown.

Suzanne Somers, John Ritter, and Joyce DeWitt, stars of *Three's Company*

THREE'S COMPANY **▶** situation comedy based on a popular British series *Man about the House,* which turned into a huge hit for ABC after it was introduced in March 1977. During the 1978-79 season it was consistently one of the top three programs in the weekly Nielsen reports and frequently was number one. It ran until 1984.

The series explored the comic possibilities of two women sharing an apartment with a single man, upstairs from the suspicious landlord and his wife. Episodes were fraught with sexual allusions and double entendres. Suzanne Somers, who became an overnight star as ditzy Christmas (Chrissy) Snow, left it after a contract dispute at the end of the 1980-81 season. Somers was replaced first by Jenilee Harrison (as cousin Cindy Snow, who eventually moved out of the apartment) and then by Priscilla Barnes (as Terri Alden). The other roommates were played by Joyce DeWitt as Janet Wood (the sensible one) and John Ritter as Jack Tripper (a caterer who claims to be homosexual to convince the landlords to permit the living arrangement). Norman Fell and Audra Lindley, who played landlords Stanley and Helen Roper, were spun off into their own series, *The Ropers,* in the middle of the 1978-79 season, and replaced by Don Knotts as Ralph Furley. Also appearing were Richard Kline as Jack's friend Larry and Ann Wedgeworth as neighbor Lana Shields. Don Nicholl, Michael Ross and Bernie West developed the series and produced it for the NRW Company, in association with T.T.C. Productions.

THRELKELD, RICHARD ▶ CBS News national correspondent, who has been an anchor and bureau chief at that network during a tenure spanning two decades. Among his many assignments at CBS News was reporting the *Sunday Morning* cover story, covering the combat in Vietnam and working on *CBS Reports.* Threlkeld, one of the most experienced combat correspondents in network television, is known by his colleagues as someone skilled in surviving split infinitives as successfully as incoming artillery. During the Gulf War, he was one of the first broadcast journalists reporting from the front during the ground war along the Kuwait-Iraq border, later filing stories live from Kuwait City immediately after it was liberated. Threlkeld has covered the U.S. invasions of Panama and Grenada and the 1989 student uprisings in Tiananmen Square in Beijing, China. In 1975, reporting on the end of the Vietnam War, Threlkeld was one of the last correspondents evacuated from Saigon. Although most of his career has been spent at CBS News, he was a correspondent for ABC News from 1982-89.

Threlkeld joined CBS News in 1966 as a producer-editor, based in New York. He began his career in 1961 at WHAS-TV, Louisville, Kentucky, and became a reporter for WMT-TV, Cedar Rapids, Iowa.

THRILLER **▶** NBC anthology series (1960-62) of suspense dramas about people caught in unexpected situations, each of which was hosted by Boris Karloff. It was by Hubbell Robinson Productions.

TIANANMEN SQUARE ▶ the site of the historic Chinese student uprisings during May and June, 1989, which became a television landmark in the dramatic intensity of its coverage and its later effect upon the temper of American public opinion toward the Chinese regime. For two weeks during an otherwise balmy Beijing spring, thousands of students camped in Beijing's Tiananmen Square demanding those rights Americans take for granted: free speech and press, and the right to peaceably assemble. The visible symbol of their cause, a papier-maché replica of the Statue of Liberty called the Goddess of Liberty, gave Americans immediate identification with their cause.

The uprising was suddenly and violently crushed on the night of June 4 when various army units shot down and imprisoned hundreds of students and other civilians in Beijing and other parts of China. For television, the story was Tiananmen Square, where all three networks and CNN had their cameras and their network news anchors. CBS's Dan Rather, CNN's Bernard Shaw, NBC's Tom Brokaw and ABC's Ted Koppel (with his *Nightline* crew) were present at the height of the uprising, facing dangers ranging from threats at gunpoint to detention and interrogation for brief periods. The pictures they transmitted were intensely moving, but none more so than the single image of an unwavering student remaining resolutely in front of a moving tank, forcing it and the tank column behind it to come to a halt.

Television's coverage of the Tiananmen Square massacre was remarkable for, among other things, its volume. Rarely, if ever, has American television devoted as much airtime to an event in which we were not directly involved, nor had China ever before been given such high visibility on American screens. It was remarkable also for the effect it had upon both public opinion and political action in the United States. Americans were shocked at the visible evidence of Chinese repression of freedom when it seemed within the students' grasp. Congress reacted with a sense of urgency about a previously bland, hands-off China policy. The Chinese, on the other hand, referring to the students as "counter-revolutionary ruffians," used the American television images to identify some of those involved in the uprising.

TIC TAC DOUGH **▶** see Game Shows.

TIERING ▶ the practice at some cable systems of packaging the basic channels in layers, or tiers, so as to create a price range for subscribers from minimal to maximum service. The first tier of service, for example, might consist of the local television stations and a handful of basic-cable channels for the lowest entry price. An additional $5 a month would get the subscriber the second tier of perhaps 10 additional basic channels. Taking one of the pay services might afford the bonus of a third tier of basic channels, and so on, each tier sweetened by one or more of the most popular channels. Experiments with tiering have been going on since the early 1980s but were accelerated in 1990 when Congress, in response to citizens' complaints over the rising cost of cable service since rate deregulation, threatened to reregulate the industry. Cable operators hope tiering will be seen as a more equitable way to price their service, but many consumers find it confusing and unsatisfying, especially when they've been accustomed to receiving all the basic services for a single price.

TILL DEATH US DO PART ▶ high-rated BBC situation comedy of the late 1960s, written by Johnny Speight, which inspired the American adaptation *All in the Family.* A series about a working-class family whose breadwinner, Alf Garnett, was intended as a satire of mindless bigotry, it was regarded a breakthrough program in that, for the first time in British TV, the storyline comedy form was used to tackle sacred cows and controversy. As *Till Death* rocked Britain, *All in the Family* rocked the U.S. and altered the mores of prime-time television in the 1970s.

Till Death originated as a single program in a BBC summertime anthology and began as a short-term series in June 1966. The series was revived for short runs for several years thereafter, with Speight as its only writer. Warren Mitchell portrayed Alf Garnett, Dandy Nichols his wife, Anthony Booth the son-in-law and Una Stubbs the daughter. Besides the U.S., TV systems in several countries, including Germany and Holland, created series based on *Till Death Us Do Part.*

TIME BANK ▶ system used by many stations to exchange commercial time for programs or other bartered goods. Through time-buying companies, barter houses or other intermediaries, stations are able to purchase office equipment, restaurant charge accounts and even automobiles for air time instead of cash. The time, which is given a price value, then is "banked" on behalf of an advertiser to be used at his discretion. Some syndicated programs are also "sold" to stations in that manner, the advertiser choosing to bank his commercials rather than have them appear in the program he provides free to the station.

TIME TUNNEL ▶ hour-long science fiction series on ABC (1966-67) about three scientists who find themselves transported into the past and future. Produced by Irwin Allen, it featured James Darren as Dr. Tony Newman, Robert Colbert as Dr. Doug Phillips and Lee Meriwether as Dr. Ann MacGregor.

TIME WARNER ▶ the world's largest media conglomerate after the merger between Time Inc. and Warner Communications late in 1989 (officially consummated in early 1990). The company is the largest producer and distributor of movies and television programs in the world, the largest music company, and one of the largest publishers of magazines. It is also one of the biggest players in the American cable industry, owns the most successful pay-cable network, and is involved also in book publishing and distribution. It is, besides, the biggest direct marketer of books in the U.S.

The rationale for the merger was to create an American company that could stand off competition from the great media giants that were developing abroad. Moreover, the synergies implicit in a company that could market a creative property in print, then produce it on film to play on its own cable network and then be distributed internationally, were intoxicating.

On the entertainment side, the merged company consists of Warner Bros., which produces and distributes TV programs and theatrical films and is among the top three Hollywood movie studios; Lorimar, which produces network TV and first-run syndicated programs; two cable companies, American Television & Communications (ATC) and Warner Cable, which together account for about 6.5 million subscribers and rank as the second largest multiple system operator in the U.S.; and Home Box Office and Cinemax, by far the most successful pay-TV operation in the country, with well over 20 million subscribers for the two channels combined. It also has a major interest in two basic-cable networks, Court TV and The Comedy Channel. In addition, Time Warner has a minority but sizeable interest in six TV stations through its ownership of stock in the broadcast subsidiary of Chris-Craft Industries, BHC Inc.

Its properties in the music business include Warner Bros. Records, Atlantic Records, Elektra Entertainment and Warner-Chappell Music Inc., among other units.

In publishing, its magazine company in 1990 accounted for about 40% of industry profits. Its titles include *Time, Life, Fortune, Money, People, Sports Illustrated* and *Entertainment Weekly.* Its book publishing and distribution business includes Book-of-the-Month Club, Time-Life Books, *Mad* magazine and *DC Comics,* among others.

The merger provided for an unusual management structure with co-chairmen/co-chief executive officers. Stephen J. Ross, Warner's CEO, and J. Richard Munro, Time's CEO, shared the power briefly. Munro retired in 1991 and became chairman of the executive committee. Under the merger agreement, Ross would remain co-CEO for five years, to be replaced then (though not as chairman) by N.J. (Nick) Nicholas as sole CEO. Nicholas had been president of Time Inc.

The Time Warner merger had followed by a few months Warner's acquisition of Lorimar Telepictures, a major producer and distributor of both network TV and syndicated programming, with particular strength in foreign sales.

The orginal Time Warner merger plan, announced in March 1989, had called for a tax-free, debt-free stock swap, but two major obstacles emerged. One involved Herbert J. Siegel, chairman of Chris-Craft Industries and the biggest Warner stockholder. (Chris-Craft had exchanged shares with Warner in 1984, when Ross was fighting off a takeover attempt by Australia's Rupert Murdoch. Warner received 42.5% of the Chris-Craft subsidiary, BHC, which owned TV and radio stations, and this effectively blocked Murdoch. Since he was not a U.S. citizen at the time, he could not take over a company that owned broadcast licenses given by the Federal government.) Siegel had sought to scuttle the merger with Time, but his acquiescence was bought with a deal that netted him an enormous profit.

A more serious obstacle was a bid for Time by Martin Davis, CEO of Paramount Communications, who offered $175 a share and later increased that to $200. That would have pleased Time's shareholders, but Time argued in a suit that ended before the Delaware Supreme Court that a stockholder vote was not required. The court agreed. But as a result of the episode, the original stock swap plan was scuttled. Time's board was able to reject Paramount's bid on grounds that Time was acquiring Warner, and in doing so it had to take on a debt load of $12 billion. In addition, it was forced to honor Ross's bonus deal with Warner, which carried over into the new company, and amounted to $193 million.

In an effort to reduce the debt, the company in 1991 was able to raise foreign money by creating a new limited partnership called Time Warner Entertainment. Two Japanese companies, Toshiba and C. Itoh & Co., invested $1 billion for a 12.5% interest in the new venture, which consisted of Warner Bros., all Time Warner cable operations and Home Box Office. Moreover, TWE collateralized $7 billion of the Time Warner debt, reducing much of the pressure.

TIME-BASE CORRECTOR (TBC) ▶ a device that converts the output of a simple videotape recorder/player or other video player to a signal suitable for broadcast or for playing through a standard television receiver or monitor. Using sophisticated techniques, the TBC compensates for the lack of precise timing control in small and low-cost video players. The development of time-base correctors in the early 1970s by several firms made possible electronic newsgathering with portable videotape recorders.

TIME-BUYING SERVICES ▶ companies that sprouted during the early 1970s specializing in purchasing local station time for a variety of advertisers or advertising agencies, whose leverage enabled them to achieve highly favorable rates. Some of them also engage in the placement of programs for advertisers, as Vitt Media International did in 1974 with ITT's children's series, *The Big Blue Marble.*

TIMES-MIRROR CO. ▶ publicly-owned media company based in Los Angeles with substantial interests in broadcast television and cable. Its TV stations are all network affiliates, WVTM Birmingham (NBC), KTVI St. Louis (ABC), KTBC-TV Austin and KDFW-TV Dallas-Fort Worth (CBS). The company once owned Los Angeles independent KTTV (now licensed to Fox). In 1979, Times-Mirror acquired Communications Properties, Inc., now Times-Mirror Cablevision, the nation's seventh largest cable-TV company, adding its 46 systems to 15 already owned by the company. The company publishes, among its many newspapers, the *Los Angeles Times,* the *Hartford Courant,* the *Baltimore Sun Newspapers* and the Long Island and New York *Newsday.*

Otis Chandler is chairman of the executive committee, Robert F. Erburu chairman and chief executive officer, and Philip L. Williams vice chairman. Carl V. Carey is president of Times-Mirror Broadcasting, and Larry W. Wangberg is president of Times-Mirror Cable.

TINKER, GRANT ▶ Hollywood producer who became chairman of the National Broadcasting Company in 1981 and led the television network through one of its most glorious periods. Tinker deftly took the network from last place to first, gave the company the stability it had lacked for years and restored a high morale throughout the ranks. He was the model broadcast leader, liked and respected both inside and outside the company, knowledgeable in the product of television, and a sensible businessman. He chose excellent executives and gave them the latitude to do their best work—Brandon Tartikoff, the prime example as president of NBC Entertainment.

Grant Tinker

Shortly after NBC and its parent, RCA, were acquired by General Electric in 1986, Tinker resigned and returned to Hollywood (he had been commuting coast to coast during his tenure as chairman). He had planned to leave even if the company had not been sold. Soon after he formed a partnership with the Gannett Co. in an independent production company called GTG Productions, which immediately entered into a five-year deal with CBS. But the company's big effort was to be a syndicated television adaptation of Gannett's daily newspaper, *USA Today*. The program, which was launched in September 1988, was initially called *USA Today: The Television Program* and later retitled *USA Today On TV*. The program was a flop, and after its cancellation in January 1990 Gannett withdrew from the partnership, and Tinker became an independent producer.

Prior to joining NBC as chairman, Tinker had been president of MTM Productions, a leading independent TV studio in the 1970s that grew out of the success of *The Mary Tyler Moore Show* on CBS (Tinker and Moore were married at the time). Tinker, who had been a high-ranking executive with Universal and then 20th Century-Fox, became involved with the situation comedy after its first season on the air and proceeded to build the company that was formed to produce it. In a relatively brief time, he placed on the networks *The Bob Newhart Show, Rhoda* and *Phyllis,* among others less successful, and MTM (Moore's initials) began to rival the Norman Lear organization for primacy among Hollywood's independents.

Considered a top-notch program executive throughout his career, Tinker was an NBC programmer from 1961 to 1967, after having spent the 1950s in the TV program departments of such ad agencies as McCann-Erickson and Benton & Bowles. Although he had a promising career with NBC, Tinker chose to join Universal because his wife's work made it difficult for him to live in New York. Tinker and Moore were later divorced.

Laurence A. Tisch

TISCH, LAURENCE A. ▶ CBS chairman (since 1990) and CEO (since 1986) and a billionaire businessman who is also chairman of Loews Corp., which has vast real estate holdings and also owns Bulova Watch Co. and Lorillard Tobacco. He came into the CBS picture by invitation of founding chairman William S. Paley as a "white knight" to fend off a hostile takeover of the company. Tisch bought enough shares to take control but stopped just short of the 25% that would have signified a change of ownership and triggered FCC regulations mandating a sale of the radio stations operating in the same markets as CBS-owned TV stations.

Tisch previously had never been involved in broadcasting or show business, and his style was the very antithesis of the late Bill Paley's, as a result of which the corporation underwent a difficult cultural change. While Paley nurtured the traditions of the company he had built and continually burnished its carefully created image as the "Tiffany Network," Tisch was determined to shape CBS into a prudent business in his fashion, unhindered by sentimentality over company history or by reverence for the company's idols, either in news or entertainment. Paley liked glamour and was himself a bon vivant and prominent figure on the social scene; Tisch is not given or drawn to it. Paley was obsessed with the idea of "classiness" and sought out executives who bespoke "class" in their dress, demeanor and expense accounts; Tisch is a plain sort of fellow whose business is business and whose reputation in the financial world is that of "bottom-feeder," one who buys desperate companies cheaply and makes them profitable through relentless cost-cutting. Paley derived pride from all his network stood for; Tisch derives pride from his companies' balance sheets.

It is paradoxical that everything Paley held sacred and sought to protect from real or imagined bogeymen—the threatened takeovers, for example, engineered by people like Ted Turner and former CBS president Tom Wyman—was undone by his putative white knight.

Tisch's cost-cutting at CBS is now legendary. CBS News, a division that had never shown profits, was hit particularly hard, in part because news was the one program area whose costs a network could actually control. Tisch maintained he was only cutting the fat at CBS News, but many believe he eviscerated the organization. He sold off CBS Records (formerly Columbia Records, a company that preceded the network) to Sony Corp. for $2 billion, something Paley surely would have resisted had he not been aged and near death. Tisch swiftly stripped down the company to its broadcasting essentials—the network, the owned TV stations, the radio division, and almost nothing more. As the other networks ventured into cable program services, foreign partnerships and new technologies, Tisch's CBS held to its core business.

There has been one difference between Tisch's de facto acquisition of CBS and his earlier takeovers: unlike his previous acquisitions through Loews Corp., he has stayed on to run the company. His pattern had been to buy a company, stay on as CEO long enough to trim it down, and then turn it over to some veteran of that industry. Television analysts have interpreted this change in Tisch's behavior as an indication that he has actually become enamored of the TV business over all others.

When Tisch assumed control of CBS Inc. he took the title of president and CEO and allowed Paley to remain as chairman. When Paley died in 1990, Tisch claimed that highest of titles.

TNT (TURNER NETWORK TELEVISION) ▶ Ted Turner's fourth satellite channel, whose launch in 1988 was the most successful ever for a basic-cable network, with an initial reach of 17 million subscribing households. Within three years the number ballooned to 54 million. The network's programming was buttressed from the start by Turner's purchase of the MGM/UA film library for $1.3 billion, enabling TNT to debut with a surefire audience-getter, *Gone With the Wind*. (While providing TNT a solid core of programming, the purchase of the film library severely leveraged Turner Broadcasting System, prompting a consortium of cable investors to bail the company out by buying 36% of TBS).

TNT's programming concept is to deal exclusively in one-shot programs and mini-series rather than weekly episodic series. Along with the classic MGM films, many of which have been colorized by TNT, the network produces TV movies of its own, such as the biographical film, *Margaret Bourke-White*, starring Farrah Fawcett, and *Cold Sassy Tree*, starring Faye Dunaway. TNT has also acquired programs from the international market and involved itself in some ambitious coproductions. In addition, the network has invested heavily in sports with its rights purchases of the National Basketball League, the National Football League and the 1992 and 1994 Winter Olympic Games. Scott Sassa is the president of Turner Entertainment Networks, which includes TNT, and Dennis Miller is TNT executive vice president.

***TO ROME WITH LOVE* ▶** situation comedy about a handsome American widower working in Rome and raising his children there. It ran on ABC (1969-71) and was produced by Don Fedderson Productions. Featured were John Forsythe as Professor Mike Endicott; Joyce Menges, Susan Neher and Melanie Fullerton as daughters Alison, Penny and Pokey; and Kay Medford as Aunt Harriet. Walter Brennan joined the cast in the second season as the girls' grandfather, Andy Pruitt. The series was always only marginally successful.

***TO TELL THE TRUTH* ▶** see Game Shows.

***TODAY* ▶** network television's first and longest-running early-morning show. Since its start on the NBC network on Jan. 14, 1952, the show has filled more than 20,000 hours of air time with its unique melange of news, interviews, features and chitchat. The segmented format, designed to accomodate viewers who are otherwise occupied preparing to leave for work or school, has become the prototype for other early morning shows both here and abroad. The show was the brainchild of then NBC president Sylvester (Pat) Weaver, whose early- morning creation inspired two other Weaver innovations in the NBC schedule,

Tonight and *Home.* In more than 40 years on the air, *Today* has become not only an NBC institution but one of the network's major profit centers.

Begun in a competitive vacuum, the show grew in popularity with no effective rival until the introduction of ABC's early-morning counterpart, *Good Morning, America.* Since then, the race between the rival shows for ratings superiority has see-sawed, prompting periodic changes in the casts—though the pattern of one man, one woman has been immutable—with the outcome dependent on an ineffable force called "chemistry," conveying the sense of the cast as a family.

Today's original host, Dave Garroway—oddly paired with a chimpanzee named J. Fred Muggs—projected a style known then as "the Chicago school of TV," casual, low-key, offhanded, with an emphasis on entertainment. In his nine years as host (1952-61), Garroway was assisted by Betsy Palmer, Jack Lescoulie and newsman Frank Blair. By the time Garroway left the show on June 16, 1961, NBC News had taken production responsibility for *Today* and the entertainment aspects were downplayed for a greater news orientation. The new host (1961-62) was a journalist, John Chancellor. Then on Sept. 10, 1962, the former announcer on the *Tonight* show, Hugh Downs, was installed as the host and held the spot for nine years (1962-71). Downs was succeeded by Frank McGee (1971-74), another newsman, whose term ended with his death in April 1974.

When Barbara Walters, one of the show's featured reporters, was named co-host (1974-76) to succeed McGee she was the first in a series of women to be given a leading role. Among those who preceded her in a variety of lesser duties, mostly to present the lighter features, were Lee Ann Meriwether, Estelle Parsons, Helen O'Connell, Betsy Palmer, Florence Henderson, Louise King, Beryl Pfizer, Robbin Bain and Maureen O'Sullivan. At first paired with a series of guest partners, Walters was finally joined full-time by Jim Hartz. Two years later (June 1976), when Walters left NBC for ABC, she and Hartz were replaced by Tom Brokaw (1976-81), and the protracted search for a female partner ended with the selection of Jane Pauley. The team of Brokaw and Pauley, joined by Gene Shalit,

Floyd Kalber and Bob Ryan (succeeded in 1980 by Willard Scott), managed to turn the show's sinking ratings around.

In February 1982, after Brokaw had been tapped as co-anchor of the *Nightly News,* Bryant Gumbel became Jane Pauley's co-host with Chris Wallace, son of CBS newsman Mike Wallace, reading the news from his base in Washington until he was reassigned and replaced in 1982 with John Palmer. The Gumbel-Pauley-Scott team scored well in the ratings through the latter half of the 1980s until the show's new producer, Dick Ebersol, brought in Deborah Norville, first as the news reader with an expanded role, then as Pauley's replacement when Pauley resigned over the affair (Dec. 28, 1989). The Gumbel-Norville team, however, lacked the requisite chemistry, and the ratings slumped. Ebersol moved back to NBC Sports, and in April 1991 Katie Couric was hired away from *The CBS Early Morning News* to replace Norville as Gumbel's co-host. In the fall of 1991, Jeff Zucker was named executive producer. The appointment was newsworthy because of his age— 26.

TOMA ▶ hour-long series on ABC (1973-74) based on the exploits of a real-life police detective, David Toma, whose reliance on disguises helped him establish an outstanding record of arrests and convictions. The series, produced by Universal TV in association with Public Arts Inc., drew marginally acceptable ratings in its first season (1973) and would have been renewed by ABC for a second year had its star, Tony Musante, not refused to continue. Susan Strasberg and Simon Oakland were featured as Patty Toma and Inspector Spooner. The series was revived a year later under a new title, *Baretta,* with Robert Blake as the lead, and became a hit.

TOMORROW ▶ post-midnight hour-long strip initiated by NBC on Oct. 15, 1973, as a companion to the *Today* and *Tonight* parlay, with Tom Snyder as host. With a 1 a.m. starting time on the east and west coasts, the program explored an uncharted frontier for network television: the middle of the night. The programs consisted mainly of interviews with controversial guests, newsmakers and experts on topical subjects. Originating initially at NBC's Burbank studios, the series moved to New York in 1975 and then back to the Coast in 1977. It was produced and directed by Joel Tator. *Tomorrow* was canceled in 1982 and replaced by *The David Letterman Show.*

TONIGHT ▶ the premier desk-and-sofa show, which started on NBC Sept. 27, 1954, as a 90-minute late-night vehicle for comedian Steve

Allen, growing out of his local New York show, although the ground was broken for it on the network by the earlier *Broadway Open House.* For nearly four decades it has dominated late-night viewing (11:30 p.m. to 1 a.m.) despite periodic changes of host and format and despite imitative competing shows by CBS and ABC. Since the Steve Allen original, the nightly entry has taken such titles over the years as *Tonight, America After Dark, The Jack Paar Tonight Show* and *The Tonight Show Starring Johnny Carson.*

Allen held forth until January 1957. His show was notable for developing a resident company of vocalists and comedians, many of whom went on to become stars themselves. The singers were Andy Williams, Eydie Gorme, Steve Lawrence and Pat Kirby; the comics Don Knotts, Bill Dana, Louis Nye, Pat Harrington Jr., Tom Poston and Gabe Dell. Skitch Henderson was bandleader and Gene Rayburn the announcer.

When Allen left the format was redesigned for an ambitious nightly sweep of the country, with cutaways from anchor Jack Lescoulie in New York to show-business newspaper columnists in various cities—Hy Gardner, Bob Considine, Earl Wilson, Irv Kupcinet, Vernon Scott and Paul Coates, among others. This version fared poorly and lasted only a few months. Jack Paar took over on July 29, 1957, returning *Tonight* to a studio show with informal talk, comedy and musical entertainment.

Paar's forte was the amusing interview, which called for a stream of guests rather than a resident company; but some guests appeared with such frequency as to comprise a regular supporting cast—Genevieve, Dody Goodman, Alexander King, Zsa Zsa Gabor and Cliff Arquette. Hugh Downs was the announcer and Jose Melis the bandleader.

Paar retired from the show in March 1962, and on Oct. 1 (with guest hosts and Paar reruns serving in the interim) Johnny Carson took over, using a similar format but a different school of celebrity guests. Carson's style was cooler and less emotional than Paar's, and his fast quips and schoolboy antics brought *Tonight* to its peak of popularity. In 1971 he moved the show from New York to Hollywood, ostensibly for access to more glamorous guests. To keep the host from tiring of the grind NBC provided him with frequent vacations, filling in with guest hosts. Carson's resident team consisted of announcer Ed McMahon and bandleader Skitch Henderson, later replaced by Doc Severinsen.

In 1991, Carson announced his retirement from the show, after 30 years, effective in the spring of 1992. Comedian Jay Leno, a frequent substitute host, was named to succeed him.

TONY AWARDS TELECAST ▶ annual springtime television event since 1967, the presentation of the Antoinette Perry Awards for excellence in the Broadway Theater. Produced by Alexander H. Cohen, the noted theatrical producer, the two-hour telecasts were true spectaculars, studded with excerpts and big musical numbers from the current shows. But because the Broadway theater is essentially a local industry, albeit a great tourist attraction, Tony telecasts are never ratings blockbusters to compare with the Oscar and Emmy telecasts. The awards were founded in 1947 and administered at first by the American Theater Wing. In 1966, they were taken over by the League of New York Theaters, and Cohen made them a national event the following year with a one-hour telecast on ABC. The event has switched among the networks, but it is always presented on a Sunday night. Joe Cates succeeded Cohen as executive producer in the late 1980s.

***TONY BROWN'S JOURNAL* ▶** television's longest-running and top-ranked series dealing with issues of direct concern to blacks. Host and executive producer Tony Brown steered the series through the TV shoals for more than two decades, first on PBS, then into commercial syndication and later back to public TV, where it has aired on PBS since 1982.

The show began in 1968 as *Black Journal,* NET's response to the Kerner Commission's call for more black participation in the media. Brown, a journalist and former dean of Howard University School of Communications, took over production and hosting chores from Bill Greaves in 1970. In 1978, the show moved from PBS to commercial TV with a new name, *Tony Brown's Journal,* and a sponsor, Pepsi. When it returned to PBS in 1982, Pepsi continued its support as the show's corporate underwriter. Under Brown's aggressive leadership, the program has sometimes been highly confrontational. In recent years it has moved away from a straightforward newsmagazine format toward analysis of contemporary issues with direct community participation. The series is produced by Sheryl Cannady.

***TONY ORLANDO AND DAWN RAINBOW HOUR, THE* ▶** CBS hour-long music-variety series (1974-76) built around a pop recording trio—Tony Orlando and Dawn (Telma Hopkins and Joyce Vincent Wilson)—whose big hit song had been "Tie a Yellow Ribbon 'Round the Old Oak Tree." Originally a summer series, it proved popular enough to be brought back as a mid-season replacement in December 1974. The series was doctored for the 1976 season with a greater emphasis on comedy and the inclusion of a regular segment with George Carlin, but it was canceled at mid-season. It was produced by Ilson-Chambers Productions and Yellow Ribbon Productions, with Saul Ilson and Ernest Chambers as producers and Bill Foster director.

TONY RANDALL SHOW, THE ▶ ABC situation comedy (1976) created as a vehicle for the veteran comedy actor, previously featured in *Mr. Peepers* and *The Odd Couple.* In the series by Mary Tyler Moore's MTM Enterprises, Randall portrayed a widowed municipal judge, Walter Franklin, with two children, a pushy housekeeper and a wise-cracking secretary. Devon Scott (replaced by Penny Peyser) played daughter Roberta (Bobby), Brad Savage played son Oliver, Rachel Roberts was the housekeeper, Bonnie McClellan, and Allyn Ann McLerie portrayed the secretary, Janet Reubner. The program was created by Tom Patchett and Jay Tarses, who also served as producers. It was switched to CBS the following season, but had a brief life there. In 1981 Randall starred in another sitcom, *Love, Sidney,* on NBC, which initially was controversial because he was identified in the pilot as homosexual. This detail was muted in the series as a result of the controversy.

TOOBIN, JEROME (d. 1984) ▶ public-affairs producer and executive working in public television since the mid-1960s, having previously been manager of the *NBC Symphony of the Air* for 10 years. After serving as a producer of *The Great American Dream Machine* and later as executive producer of *Bill Moyers' Journal,* Toobin in 1974 was named director of public affairs for WNET New York, a principal supplier of programs for PBS, a position he held until his death.

Toobin had joined NET in 1964 as exec producer of *The World of Music.* Later he worked for Group W as a producer of public affairs and cultural specials, then returned to the public TV outlet in New York. He was married to TV journalist Marlene Sanders.

TOO CLOSE FOR COMFORT ▶ 1980s sitcom designed as a star vehicle for Ted Knight, who had become known to TV audiences as a featured player on the *Mary Tyler Moore Show.* In a format adapted from a successful British series, *Keep It in the Family,* Knight played a conservative illustrator living in a two-flat townhouse upstairs of his two libidinous daughters—hence the title. The show was produced by D. L. Taffner.

It aired on ABC from 1980-83 and then resumed production for firstrun syndication in 1984. The series was ended by Knight's death in 1986. In its final year it had been renamed *The Ted Knight Show.*

TOPPER ▶ early situation comedy about ghosts based on the Thorne Smith stories, which played one season on each of the three major networks (1953-55). Produced by Loverton-Schubert Productions, it featured Leo G. Carroll and Lee Patrick as new homeowners Cosmo and Henrietta Topper, Anne Jeffreys and Robert Sterling as resident ghosts Marion and George Kirby, and a ghost dog named Neil, played by Buck.

TORS, IVAN (d. 1983) ▶ TV and film producer who specialized in fictional animal adventure series, notably *Flipper* and *Daktari* in the mid-1960s. Earlier his Ivan Tors Productions had been responsible for such shows as *Sea Hunt, Aquanauts, Man and the Challenge* and *Ripcord.* In the 1970s he had a syndicated series about animal life, *Last of the Wild.* Tors began as a playwright in Europe (he was a native of Hungary) and wrote screenplays in the U.S. before forming his company.

TORTORICI, PETER ▶ senior vice president for program planning for CBS Entertainment since January 1990, a post that involves him in all areas of prime-time programming, but with particular emphasis on scheduling and the acquisition of movies. For three years previously, he was v.p. of planning and scheduling, having moved over from CBS Sports, which he'd joined in 1983. He moved to CBS after working in production for ABC Sports in a dramatic career switch. He had previously been a trial attorney for the Appellate Division of the Supreme Court in New York City.

TOUR OF DUTY ▶ dramatic series built on the vicissitudes of an infantry company in the Vietnam War. Bravo Company was seen to fight the enemy within and without in situations in which the tensions of battle gave rise to the dramatic conflicts. The cast included Terence Knox, Stephen Caffrey, Tony Becker, Ramon Franco, Steve Akahoshi, Eric Bruskotter, and Stan Foster. Produced by Zev Braun Productions, the series was the first on network TV to be set in Vietnam. It ran on CBS from September 1987 to August 1990.

Steve Akahoshi and Eric Bruskotter in a scene from *Tour of Duty*

TOUR OF THE WHITE HOUSE WITH MRS. JOHN F. KENNEDY, A ▶ hour-long telecast carried by CBS early on a Sunday evening, Feb. 18, 1962. In the program the President's wife guided the tour through the public rooms of the White House and discussed the efforts she and a committee of citizens were making to restore furnishings that had been purchased by earlier Presidents. It was produced by Perry Wolff and directed by Franklin Schaffner.

TOWNSEND, RONALD ▶ president of the Gannett-owned group of 10 television stations and probably the highest ranking black executive in the business of television broadcasting. A longtime executive at WTOP-TV (now WUSA-TV) in Washington, he was named president and general manager of the station after its purchase by Gannett. In that capacity, he helped bolster the station's reputation as the dominant news outlet in the capital and was a highly involved community leader in Washington. His performance prompted his elevation to head of the entire station group. He was also elected chairman of the National Assn. of Broadcasters' television board.

Townsend began his broadcasting career in 1960 working in various sales, news and finance posts with CBS in New York. He left in 1974 to join WTTG in Washington and later was hired by WTOP.

Tracey Ullman

TRACEY ULLMAN SHOW, THE ▶ one of the earliest series on the Fox network, a half-hour comedy-variety series created and produced by James L. Brooks, which aired from April 1987 to September 1990. Its sketch format was ideal for its brilliantly funny star, Tracey Ullman, the British actress-singer-dancer and master of dialects, who was able to portray an amazingly wide range of characters.

In the regular supporting cast were Julie Kavner, Dan Castellaneta, Joe Malone, and Sam McMurray. Paula Abdul was the choreographer. Inserted between the sketches were short animated pieces created by Matt Groening, author of the *Life in Hell* comics. One of the recurring ones was about an offbeat, middle-American family, which was spun off to become the hit series *The Simpsons.* The other executive producers were Heide Perlman, Ken Estin, Jerry Belson, and Sam Simon.

TRADE PUBLICATIONS ▶ the business press that covers the interior news of the television industry, maps the trends and analyzes the developments on a daily, weekly, bi-monthly and monthly basis. Few industries are covered as extensively, and as well, as television by a highly competitive flock of publications.

Although there are three dailies in the field—*Daily Variety* and *Hollywood Reporter* on the West Coast and *Communications Daily* newsletter in Washington—the leading publications are the weeklies. After decades of dominating the field as the so-termed book of record and apologist for the radio and television industry, *Broadcasting* was overtaken in the 1980s by a spin-off of *Advertising Age,* the lively and glitzy *Electronic Media. EM,* as it is known, had been piloted by Crain Communications as a section in *Ad Age,* then spun out on its own originally as a publication to cover all the new media. Quite soon, however, it homed in on conventional television, and in capitalizing on the graphic shortcomings of the complacent leaders, *Broadcasting* and *Variety,* it took on both and won the day. *EM* is now the best-read publication in the field.

In 1988, *Variety*—a horizontal trade weekly covering all fields of show business and once the most journalistically independent of the trades after the tradition of its founder, Sime Silverman—was sold by Silverman's grandson Syd to Cahners Publications, the U.S. subsidiary of England's Reed International. Two years later, *Variety's* chief competitor in the television field, *Broadcasting,* founded by the late Sol Taishoff, was sold by the Times-Mirror Group to the same Cahners company.

Cahners, determined to run the publications separately, put both through extensive redesign for a more modern look and greater reader accessibility. *Variety*'s new publisher under Cahners, Gerard Byrne, had been the original publisher of *Electronic Media.* For the position of publisher of *Broadcasting* Cahners chose Dave Persson, who had succeeded Byrne as publisher of *EM.* Both Byrne and Persson had summered between those stints as corporate executives of the ill-fated Act III Publishing, Norman Lear's company that had become parent of *Channels, Marketing and Media Decisions, Broadcast Management and Engineering* and *TBI: Television Business International.* All but the latter vanished in the 1990 shakeout of the trades when advertising went into a severe slump. *TBI* was purchased by a small British company, 21st Century Publishing.

The shakeout affected all the bi-weeklies and monthlies. Among the casualties was the venerable bi-weekly *TV/Radio Age,* founded by Sol Paul and edited for many years by Al Jaffe. Another to go down was *View,* a program-oriented monthly that was the chief competitor to *Channels.*

Among the survivors were the various Washington-based trade newletters of Warren Publications, including the weekly the company was founded on, *Television Digest.*

The cable industry is served by such publications as *Multichannel News, Cablevision, Cable World* and *MSO.* The international developments in television are covered principally by *TBI, TV World, Video Age International,* and *Broadcasting Abroad.* On the advertising side, peripheral to television, are *Advertising Age, AdWeek* and *Inside Media.*

TRADE-OUT ▶ a station's acceptance of goods and services in lieu of money for its commercial time. This may involve contest merchandise, furniture and equipment for the station or accumulated credit at hotels and restaurants, the latter useful for entertaining sales clients. Related to the trade-out are reciprocal advertising agreements with other media.

TRAFFICKING ▶ once-outlawed practice of speculating in broadcast licenses. During the 1980s, FCC deregulators determined that the mandatory three-year holding period for licenses, before they could be sold, interfered with free market pricing. Repeal of these trafficking rules in 1984 achieved one of chairman Mark Fowler's top objectives. Reformers and many old line broadcasters were not happy with the idea that station licenses could be traded as freely as commodities. They complained that the new breed of investors who were attracted by the opportunity to speculate on station ownership, buying and selling as they chose, endangered the industry's good will with lawmakers and the public. Legislation to reimpose a holding period received strong support for several years. With the abolition of the anti-trafficking rules, the number of radio and TV station transactions skyrocketed, at soaring prices, and continued lively for several years. But the bubble burst at the end of the 1980s, and trafficking moderated because so many later entrants lost a good deal of money.

TRAMMEL, NILES (d. 1973) ▶ colorful president of NBC (1940-49) and then its chairman (until 1952) whose dynamism in the trial-and-error years of TV resulted in million-dollar advertising deals and program schedules of broad appeal. Trammel was the consummate TV executive who could also devise strategies to outfox the competition, pacify nervous sponsors and soothe temperamental stars.

Trammel spent most of his career with NBC, joining in 1928 as a salesman in Chicago and moving rapidly into executive positions there. In 1939 he was transferred to New York as a v.p. At the radio network he was instrumental in developing such hits as *Amos 'n' Andy* and *Fibber McGee and Molly.*

He resigned as chairman in December 1952, at the age of 58, to become president of Biscayne Television Corp., which won the license to build Channel 7 in Miami.

TRANSLATORS ▶ low-powered relay facilities used by stations to carry their signals beyond the normal coverage area into remote areas. Usually situated in high terrain, the translator receives the over-the-air signal of a station and re-transmits it on another unused channel in a prescribed direction. Unlike a satellite station, a translator maintains no studios, originates no programming of its own and is not required to have an engineer present while it is operating.

Some translator systems are owned by television stations to extend their systems but most are built and supported by rural communities that are otherwise beyond the reach of normal television signals.

TRANSMISSION LINE ▶ a coaxial cable, waveguide or other system used to carry a television or other signal.

TRANSMITTER ▶ the physical facility used by a television station to send the signal out on the air. The transmitter superimposes the signal on the carrier, amplifies it and feeds it into the transmitting antenna.

TRANSMITTER SITE ▶ physical location of the transmitter, tower and sending-antenna of a station. TV station transmitters are often clustered in antenna "farms," so that all stations in the area may be received by orienting reception antennas in one direction.

In TV, the tower acts as a supporting structure for the antenna, which actually transmits the signal (in AM radio, the entire tower radiates). TV towers atop mountains are usually 100-200 feet in height, including the 50-150 feet of the antenna structure itself. Self-supporting towers are rarely more than 700 feet in height, with "guyed" towers usually about 1,000 feet tall but occasionally twice that height. The candelabra tower is one supporting more than one TV antenna at equal heights.

TRANSPONDER ▶ device on a satellite that picks up a signal beamed up from the ground, amplifies it, and returns it to earth where it is received by earth stations.

***TRAPPER JOHN, M.D.* ▶** hour-long medical drama in which Dr. John (Trapper) McIntyre, featured in the popular comedy series *M*A*S*H,* becomes chief of surgery at San Francisco Memorial Hospital 28 years after his discharge from the service. Counterpoint to Trapper John's now-mellowed attitude toward the system is a young doctor, G. Alonzo (Gonzo) Gates, who heard of the legendary Trapper while serving in a Vietnam medical unit. Pernell Roberts and Gregory Harrison played the two leads. Other cast members included Mary McCarty, Christopher Norris, Charles Siebert, and Brian Mitchell. The series ran on CBS from September 1979 to September 1986 and was produced by 20th Century-Fox Television.

TREYZ, OLIVER E. ▶ onetime dynamic president of ABC-TV (1957-62) who took bold and sometimes erratic steps to keep ABC competitive with the larger, better established networks in the "two and a half" network economy that prevailed at the time. Although his background had been in research and advertising, he functioned as a super-salesman, programmer and promoter, the most energetic of the wheeler-dealers in a colorful era. He was fired, sacrificially, not long after the network was censured by the Senate Juvenile Delinquency Subcommittee for carrying a particularly violent episode of the series *Bus Stop.*

As network president, Treyz frequently studied the rating reports for local markets in search of programming leads. Thus, when he found that old Bugs Bunny cartoons were succeeding in prime time on a Chicago independent station, he ordered a new *Bugs Bunny* series created for ABC. Its popularity prompted Treyz to build a stable of animated programs in the early evening: *The Flintstones, The Jetsons, Top Cat* and *Jonny Quest,* among others. Treyz also made heavy use of the top 30-market Nielsen ratings to demonstrate that in the markets where all three networks had full-time outlets, ABC's programs were equal in popularity to those of its rivals.

After leaving ABC Treyz tried to promote a fourth network and became president of the abortive Overmyer Network, which had hoped to link UHF and VHF independents. He later started a consultancy serving TV advertisers.

***TRIALS OF O'BRIEN* ▶** series about Daniel J. O'Brien, a flamboyant lawyer with domestic problems. It was the first regular vehicle for Peter Falk (years before *Columbo*) but failed in the ratings. It was produced by Filmways for CBS in 1965.

TRIBUNE COMPANY ▶ venerable Chicago-based media company that emerged in the 1980s as a powerful force in the television industry. Its flagship station, WGN-TV, became one of the leading superstations on cable in that decade. Its group of six independent television stations, half of them acquired between 1983 and 1985, comprise the largest non-network family of stations in the U.S. As the only company besides ABC, CBS, NBC and Fox owning stations in the three largest markets—New York, Los Angeles and Chicago—it wields extraordinary power with syndicators, who must have those three markets to succeed. And it has its own flourishing production and syndication company, Tribune Entertainment, which—unlike others in the field—has an immediate base of stations for its program products.

In addition to those media properties, the company owns the *Chicago Tribune* and five other daily newspapers, 11 community publications, four radio stations, a radio network program service, marketing and media services and the Chicago Cubs baseball team, whose games receive national exposure via the WGN superstation.

Until they were brought under the umbrella of a group in the 1980s, the influential Chicago station and the New York independent, WPIX, were operated by separate managements and rarely cooperated, although they had common parentage. Tribune's big move was to purchase KTLA Los Angeles in 1985 from Kohlberg Kravis Roberts & Co. for $510 million, the highest price ever for a TV station and a striking departure for Tribune with its reputation for fiscal conservatism. Moreover, the purchase price was $265 million higher than KKR had paid to the original owner, Gene Autry, three years before. Tribune paid the premium for the clout it would gain from a strong presence in the three largest population centers. If there were ever to be a fifth terrestrial television network, it would have to involve Tribune.

Tribune began growing as a group before buying KTLA. In 1983 it bought a New Orleans UHF independent and renamed it WGNO. A year later it acquired an Atlanta UHF station and gave it the call letters WGNX. It had already owned KWGN Denver, a VHF station. All were pulled together as a group under James Dowdle, president of Tribune Broadcasting. Based on total households covered as a percentage of the total national population, the six Tribune stations rank fifth, after the three networks and Fox, with a coverage of 18.7%. In prospect during 1991 was the acquisition of Taft Broadcasting's Philadelphia UHF station, WPHL-TV. If that were to develop, Tribune would be in the four largest markets and reaching well over 20% of the population.

Also reporting to Dowdle, in addition to the TV and radio groups, are Tribune Entertainment, based in Chicago, and Grant Tribune Productions, located in Los Angeles. The latter is a joint venture with Donald (Bud) Grant, former president of CBS Entertainment, which was set up in 1988 with a view to creating programs for the networks. One sitcom for CBS, *Sydney,* was a mid-season replacement during the 1989-90 season, but it was not renewed. Little has come of the venture otherwise beyond some experimentation with offbeat programming.

Far more successful is Tribune Entertainment, which distributes in syndication such talk shows as *Geraldo* and *The Joan Rivers Show,* along with *Soul Train, Tales From the Darkside, Charles in Charge, U.S.Farm Report* and movie packages and other programming. The company also distributes *Now It Can Be Told,* an investigative reporting series fronted by Geraldo Rivera. The president and CEO of Tribune Entertainment is Don Hacker.

The Tribune Company's first broadcast property, WGN radio, went on the air in 1924; the call letters stand for "World's Greatest Newspaper," long the boast on the *Chicago Tribune* masthead. In 1932 the *Tribune*'s owner, Col. Robert R. McCormick, and his cousin, Joseph Medill Patterson, who had founded the tabloid *New York Daily News* in 1919, set up the McCormick-Patterson Trust, which controlled their joint properties and was not dissolved until 1975. In the interim, WGN-TV and WPIX were put on the air in 1948 under the control of the respective cousins, which is why the group was slow to form. WGN acquired the Denver station, KWGN, in 1965.

TROUBLE WITH FATHER ▶ one of the early situation comedies about bumbling fathers. It was introduced in 1953 in syndication, with Stu Erwin playing himself as a high school principal, and his wife, June Collyer, playing his wife. Their TV daughters, Joyce and Jackie, were played by Ann Todd (replaced by Merry Anders) and Sheila James. Later it was retitled *The Stu Erwin Show.* Produced by Hal Roach Jr. and Roland Reed Productions, it ceased after 126 episodes in 1955.

TROUT, ROBERT ▶ broadcast journalist noted for his calm delivery and ability to extemporize during such major events as national political conventions. Throughout most of his career, which began in the early 1930s, he was associated with CBS, but he was with NBC for a period (1958-62) as host of the quiz show *Who*

Said That. Trout reported from Washington until World War II, when he was assigned to London. In 1964 CBS teamed Trout with Roger Mudd to cover the Democratic National Convention in an effort to stem the growing popularity of NBC's Huntley-Brinkley tandem, but without great success. Trout then became anchor for WCBS-TV New York, and during the 1970s went into partial retirement as special roving correspondent for CBS.

TRUMAN TOUR OF THE WHITE HOUSE ▶ first of the First Family tours for television, carried by all three networks in May of 1952. President Truman conducted an informal tour of the renovated White House and played several piano selections. He was accompanied by a news representative of each network: CBS's Walter Cronkite, ABC's Bryson Rash and NBC's Frank Bourgholzer.

TRUNK CABLE ▶ the major distribution coaxial cable used in a cable-television system. Feeder cables branch out from the trunks to the *drop line* cable, which is connected to the subscriber's residence for service.

TRUTH OR CONSEQUENCES ▶ see Game Shows.

TSN ▶ Canada's 24-hour, all-sports cable network, launched in 1984. Five years later when the network shifted from pay TV to a basic tier, it boosted its distribution to over five million cable households. Wholly owned by John Labatt Ltd., a major brewery, it derives its revenue from affiliate fees and advertising sales. The network offers exclusive coverage of top professional and amateur sporting events, including Major League Baseball, CFL and NFL football, NBA basketball, NHL hockey, boxing, wrestling, soccer, tennis, golf, curling and Canadian university sports.

In an effort to respond to the problems created by broadcasting in six different time zones, TSN rebroadcasts its major national and international events so that each airs twice in the 24-hour schedule.

TUNNEL, THE ▶ bold 90-minute NBC News documentary (Dec. 10, 1962) on a tunnel dug beneath the Berlin Wall by a group of European students to help 59 friends trapped in East Berlin to escape. NBC acknowledged that a few parts of the suspenseful program were re-created, but most of the filming was done as the tunnel was being dug. The program was produced by Reuven Frank, who was also co-writer with Piers Anderton. Ray Lockhart was director, and the filming was by Peter and Klaus Dehmel.

TURN ON ▶ shortest-lived TV series in the medium's history, canceled after its first telecast in February 1969 because of complaints from affiliates and the public. The half-hour show was to be ABC's version of the popular *Laugh-In* on NBC, but its playfulness and irreverence overstepped the bounds of good taste.

TURNER BROADCASTING SYSTEM (TBS) ▶ Atlanta-based cable programming company founded by R.E. (Ted) Turner, its high-profile chairman.

Originally the Turner Advertising Company, specializing in outdoor billboards, the company purchased a small Atlanta independent TV station in 1970, which in 1976 was beamed up to a satellite and became the first superstation. Turner enhanced the station's programming by buying the Atlanta Braves baseball team in 1976 and acquiring an interest in the Atlanta Hawks basketball team a year later.

On June 1, 1980, TBS launched CNN, the first live, 24-hour all-news network. Initially dismissed as Ted Turner's folly and derided by broadcast-network journalists as the "Chicken Noodle Network," CNN gained stature through its superior coverage of a number of momentous events, including the explosion of the space shuttle Challenger (the broadcast networks had decided not to cover the launch), the 1989 San Francisco earthquake and the Gulf War. The network's international reach and live coverage have increasingly made it as much a part of the diplomatic process as its chronicler.

In March 1986, in a deal that almost bankrupted the company, TBS acquired the MGM Entertainment Company, later reselling most of its assets but retaining the company's 3,300-title film library. In October 1988 TBS launched TNT, using the MGM library as its programming cornerstone. Struggling under the heavy debt load, Turner was rescued by several of the larger MSOs, which took significant equity positions in the company and seats on the board. In doing so, they curbed Turner's ability to operate as a free-wheeling entrepreneur.

Turner found himself at the center of a controversy for proposing to use a new computer technology to "colorize" some of the classic films he now owned, including *Casablan-*

ca (which he did) and *Citizen Kane* (which he did not). TNT nonetheless quickly became a favorite of classic-film buffs. In addition to vintage films, the channel programs a mix of sports (including NBA and NFL games), children's programs and made-for-TNT movies and mini-series, many of them international coproductions.

Along with the cable networks, TBS also maintains a domestic and international television syndication division, Turner Program Services (TPS).

Since 1985, TBS has carefully nurtured the Goodwill Games, a quadrennial international sports competition organized in partnership with the USSR as an off-year alternative to the Olympics. Held in 1986 in Moscow and 1990 in Seattle, the Games have lost more than $100 million for TBS. That performance, coupled with the political changes in the Soviet Union and a shift in Olympics scheduling that will allow for Summer or Winter Games every two years, has raised doubts about the Goodwill Games' survival.

The company's management team includes Terence McGuirk, executive vice president of TBS; Scott Sassa, president of Turner Entertainment Networks; Tom Johnson, president of CNN; Russ Barry, president of TPS and Howard Karshan, president of Turner International.

TURNER, ED ▶ executive vice president of CNN since 1984, responsible for all newsgathering by the network's 27 domestic and international news bureaus. He supervised the coverage of such events as the Persian Gulf War, the Iran/Contra hearings and the explosion of the space shuttle *Challenger.* He is not related to Ted Turner.

He started at CNN in 1980 as managing editor and executive producer for then-president Reese Schonfeld. He has also served as v.p. in charge of daily operations at CNN's Washington bureau and senior v.p. based in Atlanta. Prior to joining CNN, he was news director at KWTV-TV in Oklahoma City. Before that he held managerial positions with UPITN and Metromedia in New York, where as news director of its WTTG-TV Washington station he had hired such news personalities as Bob Schieffer, Pat Collins, Barbara Howar and Connie Chung. He began his carer as reporter and anchor in Oklahoma City in 1959.

TURNER, TED ▶ arguably the most influential television figure in the 1980s, and certainly the most colorful; with the possible exception of Rupert Murdoch, no one did more to change to change the shape of the industry. Moreover, the cable fraternity has had no better representative before the public than Turner; he is a genuine media star.

Brash, flamboyant and individualistic, he is the antithesis of the corporate television executive. In his heyday, he was a bold entrepreneur who did not think small and who was given to making public announcements of what he planned to do. His record of delivering on his sometimes wild entrepreneurial promises was so remarkable that he was taken seriously by CBS when he threatened a takeover in 1985, though it was well known that he lacked the bankroll to do it. CBS had to sell its St. Louis station to finance its defense against Turner's move.

His yachting skills (he won the 1977 America's Cup with his craft, *Courageous*) earned him the nickname Captain Courageous. But the preferred sobriquet by the industry and press is Captain Outrageous, for Turner's outspokenness, eccentric behavior and derring-do in the business world.

Ted Turner

He created four cable services that have become institutions—WTBS superstation, CNN (Cable News Network), Headline News and TNT (Turner Network Television). CNN has become an international phenomenon, received and respected in every corner of the globe and widely recognized today as one of the world's leading news organizations. At the height of the Cold War, Turner created the Goodwill Games, in cooperation with the Soviet Union, as a kind of off-year Olympics–a startling move for a man who had previously been perceived as politically conservative. And he took the lead in the television industry in creating programs on the environment.

After selling his family's outdoor advertising business, Turner came into television in the early 1970s as owner of an Atlanta UHF station, WTCG-TV (now WTBS). In December 1976 he shook up the television industry's entire sense of order by using an RCA Satcom satellite to distribute the signal of his obscure station to cable systems around the country. In a period of two years, the station gained access to 3 million additional households with 24-hour programming loaded heavily with movies and sports. Turner thus pioneered the superstation, the first of his bold creations. The next, CNN, was launched by Turner in June 1980, despite his total lack of experience with news and with disregard for the feasibility studies conducted by several of the country's largest news organizations, which determined that cable at the time did not reach enough viewers to support a 24-hour news service.

His formal name is Robert Edward Turner.

TURTELTAUB-ORENSTEIN ▶ comedy writing and producing team of Saul Turteltaub and Bernie Orenstein. Their credits include *The New Dick Van Dyke Show*, *Sanford and Son* (from the 1974-75 season until the series was canceled in 1977), *Grady*, *What's Happening*, *Carter's Country*, *One of the Boys*, *Chicken Soup*, and *Baby Talk*.

Turteltaub became a creative consultant with Columbia Pictures from 1979-83 and then with Embassy TV from 1983-85. He joined Taft Entertainment Company as a creative consultant in 1986.

TV GLOBO ▶ most powerful network in Brazil (the most populous country in Latin America), which for its audience delivery claims to be the fourth largest network in the world, after the three major U.S. networks. TV Globo, or Rede Globo in the native Portuguese, is the jewel in the crown of Roberto Marinho's media empire, which includes the leading Brazilian newspaper, *O Globo*. With the two properties alone, Marinho is one of the world's great media barons, who wields extraordinary political influence in his country.

Aside from its clear dominance of the Brazilian television market, TV Globo has two other distinctions: it is the standout network in the world for graphic design and is one of the world's leading exporters of programming. Its stock in trade is the telenovela, the Latino novel for television that resembles the American soap, except that it eventually comes to an end. Typically, Globo realizes some $15 million a year in foreign sales of its telenovelas, ranking it high among the companies involved in international TV program commerce. Marinho also owns Globo Monte Carlo, a network established in Monaco with the nearby Italian market in view. It has been one of Marinho's less successful ventures.

***TV GUIDE* ▶** phenomenally successful weekly magazine devoted to TV listings and feature articles on programs, stars and developments in the industry; its growth has paralleled the growth of the medium itself. Despite the fact that most newspapers provide extensive daily and weekly program listings, *TV Guide* achieved a circulation in 1976 of 20 million copies a week. The magazine, which had been based in Radner, PA since the beginning, moved its headquarters to New York in December 1991.

TV Guide has ruled the program information field since its founding in 1953 by Walter Annenberg. It was sold to Rupert Murdoch along with other Triangle Publications in 1988 for $3 billion.

TV ONTARIO ▶ largest of Canada's provincial educational networks and one that enjoys recognition and respect in the world's community of public broadcasters. Non-commercial and subsidized entirely by the government of the Province of Ontario, the station produces documentaries, performing arts programs and children's programs, in addition to educational works. Many of its programs are sold abroad, and TVO often becomes involved in international coproductions. TVO, which began broadcasting in 1970, also operates a French channel, La Chaine.

Canada has four other provincially funded educational networks: Access, in Alberta, the Knowledge Network in British Columbia, Quebec's Radio-Quebec, and Saskatchewan's Communications Network. The Access network programs in the manner of TVO; the others are strictly educational.

TVB (TELEVISION BUREAU OF ADVERTISING) ▶ organization supported by commercial broadcasters devoted to promoting the advantages of local television advertising over that of other media. It also provides extensive promotional and research tools for its member stations, and holds periodic clinics for sales executives. TVB is based in New York and was headed by Jim Joyella until he resigned in December 1991.

TVN (TELEVISION NEWS INC.) ▶ syndication company formed in 1973 to distribute electronically a daily package of national and international news to subscribing stations. With only 80 stations (many of them Canadian) participating at TVN's peak, the company folded in November 1975 after running up losses of $2 to $3 million a year. A group of independent stations then formed a cooperative, ITNA, using the Westar satellite, to provide a similar news service for member stations.

TVN's principal backing came from Joseph Coors, ultraconservative head of the Adolph Coors Brewing Co., who felt a need (and a desire among stations) for a national news service in TV that would offset the networks. While it was a foregone conclusion that major independent stations would subscribe, TVN was organized in the belief that many affiliated stations would drop their network newscasts if they could receive national and foreign news on the same day from an independent, "unbiased" source. That proved not to be the case. TVN succumbed not to the cost of maintaining news bureaus throughout the U.S. and abroad but to the expense of daily transmission over AT&T lines. A key factor in the resistance of stations to buying the service was the additional cost it would have entailed for them to rent local loops, their own connections to the cross-country lines, likened to cloverleaf exits off super-highways. This was before satellites came to be used for the economical national delivery of programs.

TvQ ▶ periodic studies conducted by Marketing Evaluations Inc. that attempt to define the actual appeal of network and syndicated programs, over and above their rating performance. Sometimes spoken of as qualitative ratings, the TvQ reports are utilized by networks and advertisers as an advance indicator of shifts in program popularity or as evidence that a potentially successful program has been assigned the wrong timeslot.

Questionnaires are mailed to a representative panel, asked to indicate from a list of familiar programs how they would rate them on a scale from "one of my favorites" to "poor." The TvQ score is the percentage of respondents who rated the program a "favorite." The scores are also broken down demographically, to reveal the level of appeal by age or sex. Programs with low ratings but high TvQ scores are occasionally renewed by the networks on the theory that the shows would be favored by viewers who had not yet examined them.

Another TvQ service rates the appeal of TV performers as a guide to casting. This activity has been controversial in the acting community because it was seen as endangering the careers of those who make low scores. Nevertheless, it is widely used in the industry.

TVRO (TV RECEIVE-ONLY) BACKYARD DISHES ▶ private satellite earth stations that began appearing by the thousands after the mid-1970s when broadcast networks, stations and cable began making extensive use of satellite communications to send signals back and forth. The private dishes could "eavesdrop" on these communications until many of the program services decided to scramble their signals. In remote areas unserved by broadcasters and cable, they were the only form of television available. By 1991 more than two million backyard dishes were in use in the U.S.

TVTV (TOP VALUE TELEVISION) ▶ organization of alternative video journalists who produced the first documentaries on portable video equipment ever to be televised. With foundation funding, and using relatively inexpensive cameras, the group produced unorthodox topical documentaries in a "scrapbook" style, as a kind of counterculture answer to conventional network documentaries.

TVTV attracted notice in 1972 for its videotape pieces on the two political conventions of that year. They were purchased by Teleprompter for cable and by Group W for its TV stations. In 1974, with the broadcasting of half-inch tape vastly improved by the development of the time-base corrector, TVTV placed *Lord of the Universe* and *Gerald Ford's America* on public TV, the latter under auspices of WNET. In 1975 public TV also carried the group's documentary on Cajuns, *The Good Times Are Killing Me*. The group was later disbanded, and at least one of its principals, Michael Shamberg, became a producer of commercial movies.

TVX BROADCAST GROUP ▶ UHF station group that under its original owners devised a minimalist approach to station operations that was dubbed in the industry the "cookie-cutter" plan. It prevailed during the 1980s until the company was purchased by Paramount Communications at the end of the decade.

Founded in 1979 by chairman Gene Loving, sales manager John Trinder and president Tim McDonald in Norfolk, Va., TVX primarily reflected McDonald's operating philosophies. He put the station group on an aggressive station acquisition program in the early 1980s. All purchased stations were immediately placed on a rigid formula diet: no station was to have more than 37 employees (one designated as talent) nor lease more than 12,000 square feet of space to operate.

McDonald also purchased the same syndicated programming for the entire group, holding out in the negotiations for the lowest price. Despite all the cost-squeezing, however, TVX never achieved a positive cash flow.

In 1986 TVX added to its burdens by purchasing five under-performing stations from Taft Broadcasting. That acquisition brought about the slow end for the company. Paramount finally acquired the financially strapped group, fulfilling its desire to get into station ownership.

12 O'CLOCK HIGH ▶ World War II series on ABC (1964-67) based on the 20th Century-Fox motion picture of that title about an Air Force bombardment group based in England. Robert Lansing starred in 31 episodes (as Brigadier General Frank Savage) and Paul Burke in the other 47 (as Colonel Joseph Gallagher). Also featured were Andrew Duggan as Brigadier General Edward Britt, Lew Gallo as Major Joe Cobb, Larry Gates as Johnny, John Larkin as Major General Wiley Crowe, Frank Overton as Major Harvey Stoval, Barney Phillips as Major Doc Kaiser and Chris Robinson as Sergeant Komansky. It was produced by Quinn Martin in association with 20th Century-Fox TV.

12-12-12 RULE ▶ the FCC restriction on station ownership, limiting it to no more than 12 AM, 12 FM, and 12 TV stations by an individual or corporation. In addition, licensees may hold partial ownership interests in up to two additional stations in each service if the station is controlled by a person from a racial minority. TV station ownership is further limited by a 25% cap on "audience reach", the percentage of the nation's TV homes within the primary signal area of a single owners' stations (UHF station audiences are halved in making these computations).

The FCC formerly had a seven-station limit, with no more than five of those stations permitted to be in the top 50 markets. In 1984, when the Reagan-era FCC raised the limit to 12, it intended the new standard to last for only five years before "sunsetting" into complete repeal. Congress intervened, and the commission agreed to revise its decision to make the 12-12-12 rule permanent, and adopted the minority ownership and reach provisions. The latter, which in practice restrained only ABC, CBS and NBC, was a nod to the motion picture industry's concern about network power.

In 1991, FCC chairman Alfred C. Sikes began a new "inquiry" which he hoped would create the political and regulatory framework for abolishing the 12-12-12 rule.

20/20 ▶ long-running ABC news-magazine hosted by Hugh Downs and Barbara Walters, with such featured contributors as ABC News correspondents Bob Brown, Tom Jarriel, Stone Phillips, Lynn Sherr and John Stossel. After an inauspicious debut in June 1978, the series was drastically retooled and freshly staffed and hosted. It ultimately became known as ABC's answer to CBS's *60 Minutes,* and although it has never achieved ratings as high as *60 Minutes* it has always played in much more competitive time periods.

Nurtured and protected by ABC News president Roone Arledge, *20/20* has consistently performed well in the Nielsens, even though it has been moved about to different nights. Its format includes investigative pieces, personality profiles and features on science, medicine, consumerism and the arts. Downs and Walters provide facile lead-ins and sometimes seamless, sometimes self-conscious dialogues with the correspondents following their stories. Both often contribute pieces themselves. In one recent *20/20* season, viewers saw reports on the history of exorcism within the Roman-Catholic Church, featuring what was said to be an actual exorcism officially sanctioned by the Church; an investigation of evidence in the Jeffrey MacDonald *Fatal Vision* murder case; and interviews with such newsmakers as Gen. Norman Schwartzkopf, Boris Yeltsin and Margaret Thatcher, as well as pop culture icons Roseanne Barr, Ted Danson, Bo Jackson and Ivana Trump.

TWILIGHT ZONE ▶ dramatic anthology series on CBS (1959-64) concerned with tales of the supernatural; it enjoyed great popularity and turned its creator, Rod Serling, previously a behind-the-scenes playwright, into a TV star. Serling served as host and narrator, providing what programmers call "the glue" for the series, and gave it the serious, mysterious tone that made it a winner. He also wrote several of the playlets. The series originated in half-hour form, expanded to an hour in January 1963 and returned to the half-hour format that fall.

TWIN PEAKS ▶ bizarre and intriguing ABC prime-time serial that opened with a two-hour episode on April 8, 1990, and immediately became something of a nation-wide obsession. The effect was the same in international markets. Nothing like it had ever been mounted for television before, and few TV series have ever stirred so much discussion among viewers.

The series turned on a mystery and was trademarked with the strange cinematographic vision of David Lynch, who directed the first few episodes, including the pilot (which was marketed abroad on video as a complete movie). Created, produced and written by Lynch and Mark Frost, the series started fairly strong in the ratings for one so innovative but began tapering off towards the end of the first season. In its second season, ABC moved the show from Thursday to Saturday night, where it was in danger of losing many of its younger viewers, and in fact did. When the show was canceled by ABC, certain European broadcasters discussed creating a consortium to keep it going, but that failed to develop.

Twin Peaks was the name of the fictive, seemingly peaceful lumber town in the Pacific Northwest where the story was set. Odd and mysterious events began to occur, centering on the mystery of the death of Laura Palmer, that soon exposed undercurrents of greed, adultery, insanity and evil.

The large cast portraying the town's bizarre population featured such established actors as Richard Beymer as Benjamin Horne, Piper Laurie as Catherine Martell, Ray Wise as Leland Palmer, Grace Zabriskie as Leland's wife, Russ Tamblyn as Dr. Jacoby, Peggy Lipton as Norma Jennings, Michael Ontkean as Harry S. Truman, and Kyle MacLachlan (who has starred in two of Lynch's motion pictures) as FBI agent Dale Cooper. The show also introduced a roster of new faces, among them Sherilyn Fenn as Audrey Horne, Dana Ashbrook as Bobby Briggs, Joan Chen as Josie Packard, Michael Horse as "Hawk" Hill, Warren Frost as Dr. Hayward, Lara Flynn Boyle as his daughter Donna, Harry Goaz as Andy Brennan, Madchen Amick as Shelly Johnson, Eric Da Re as her husband Leo, Kimmy Robertson as Lucy Moran, and Sheryl Lee as Laura Palmer. The haunting score was composed by Angelo Badalmenti.

227 ▶ half-hour situation comedy on NBC for five seasons (September 1985-July 1990) built around the lives of a group of residents in a tenement building (No. 227) in a black neighborhood of Washington, D.C. The ensemble cast was headed by Marla Gibbs, familiar to viewers as the wisecracking housekeeper Florence on *The Jeffersons,* and included Hal Williams, Alaina Reed, Jackee, Regina King, Kia Goodwin, Helen Martin and Curtis Baldwin. The popular comedy grew out of a stage play of the same name in which Gibbs starred. The series was produced for television by Lorimar.

TWO-WAY CABLE ▶ an interactive or bidirectional cable system with the ability to carry signals upstream and downstream, so that communication is possible from the subscriber's set to the head-end, usually in a digital mode. This feature enables the subscriber to respond to incoming messages for purposes of polling, at-home shopping and audience-participation entertainment.

In 1978, Warner Communications' Qube system began operation in Columbus, Ohio, as the first fully two-way commercial cable system. The experiment failed to earn a profit and was soon downgraded to a conventional cable system. However, Qube was the breeding ground for general concepts of interactive television that continue to be explored.

TYNE TEES TELEVISION ▶ British commercial licensee for the region in northeast England, with its production centers in Newcastle and Leeds. The company is a subsidiary of Trident Television Ltd., which acts as a station rep in selling air time.

U

UFO ▶ hour-long syndicated science-fiction series (1970) from England, produced by ATV, and featuring Ed Bishop as Commander Edward Straker, George Sewell as Colonel Alec Freeman, Peter Gordono as Captain Peter Carlin and Gabrielle Drake as Lieutenant Gay Ellis. Consisting of 26 episodes, it was found suitable by many U.S. stations for programming under the new prime time-access rule but was not impressive in the ratings.

UHF (ULTRA HIGH FREQUENCY) ▶ the television band in the electronic spectrum from 470 to 890 mHz encompassing channels 14 to 83 (in the U.S., Canada and some other Western countries). In theory, the UHF band could make possible up to 3,000 stations in the U.S. beyond the 650 that can be accommodated by the VHF band. A total of 1,400 UHF channels were allocated by the FCC in its April 1952 Sixth Report and Order, but initially there was no rush to apply for many of the frequencies; the history of UHF has been a struggle for attention against the competition of the easier-to-receive VHF stations. The struggle was effectively ended by the spread of cable, which equalized reception for VHF and UHF. Cable's growth in the 1980s lit up the UHF band around the country.

In retrospect, a glaring omission in the Sixth Report and Order was a requirement that all allocated channels be tuned with equal ease. Most of the early TV sets were not equipped to receive UHF; viewers who wanted to watch those channels had to purchase and attach to their sets special tuners with loop antennas. These proved neither efficient nor reliable. Reception was often marginal.

There was also a manifest need for a much higher power output at the UHF transmitters than the early transmitters were able to attain. UHF requires 5 million watts to cover about the same area that a low-band VHF station (channels 2-6) can cover with only 100,000 watts. The high-band channels, 7-13, are allowed to have 316,000 watts. Even as the technology developed to reach maximum power, cost was a major obstacle to the growth of UHF.

Still, many of the UHF frequencies were claimed when the freeze on allocations ended because those applications were likely to be processed immediately, while bids for VHF channels carried the prospect of long and costly comparative hearings with other applicants. The early UHF operators hoped to become established before the VHF stations could get on the air or, if they did sustain losses, to receive preferential treatment from the FCC for an available VHF channel in return for their pioneering efforts.

The first commercially licensed UHF station was KPTV (Channel 27), Portland, Ore., which began broadcasting Sept. 20, 1952. It went dark on April 17, 1957, after four local VHF stations had been activated.

CBS and NBC both were early UHF operators, bringing their total owned-stations complement up to the maximum seven in 1953-54 with two UHF properties each. Both had stations in Hartford, Conn. NBC's other "U" was in Buffalo and CBS's in Milwaukee. All four of those stations were either abandoned or sold by 1959.

By 1954 approximately 120 UHFs were on the air. Six years later approximately half those stations had ceased operating. After reaching its nadir in 1960, UHF began to grow again in 1961. It took until 1964 for the number of stations to reach 120 again.

The resurgence was, in part, attributable to the growth of educational (now public) television, which had to settle for UHF channels in most markets, including such critical ones as Los Angeles and Washington. Also contributing to growth was the fact that many markets had been allocated only one or two VHF stations, leaving UHF to accommodate the other networks. But the most important impetus was the passage by Congress in 1962 of the All-Channel Law, requiring all sets sold in interstate commerce to have the ability to receive both VHF and UHF by 1964.

The national boom in color TV in 1965 and the demand for portable sets accelerated the sale of new sets and hastened the penetration of UHF. But although close to 90% of the television homes were capable of receiving UHF channels in the 1970s, a "U" in general was considerably inf[illegible] to a "V" in ability to deliver audience.

Gradual technological improvements in UHF have eased the so-called "UHF disadvantage," among them more efficient transmitters and more sophisticated dial tuners. Also, the FCC required set manufacturers to provide "comparable tuning" for UHF and VHF by the 1975 model year, meaning that all stations could be brought in on a "click" (or detent) dial, relieving UHF of the handicap of having to be tuned differently from VHF, in the manner of radio. New tuners feature digital electronic controls similar to hand calculators. These fully equalize UHF and VHF tuning.

Spurs to UHF growth in the 1970s were the emergence of the independent station as an alternative to the three network-affiliated stations in any market and the fact that by 1975 UHF stations as a whole were profitable. Network-affiliated UHF stations had been profitable prior to that year, but 1975 marked a turning of the corner for most of the independent UHFs. The success, in 1978, of several over-the-air pay-television stations put a focus on UHF as a facet of the advancing technologies. In addition, UHF stations were helped by increased cable penetration because cable systems, under the FCC's "must carry" rule, had to allocate each UHF station in their area its own channel. This eliminated UHF stations' over-the-air reception handicap.

The boom in UHF occurred in the 1980s when cable made any UHF as easy to receive as any VHF. As rapidly as cable spread, so did the construction of UHF stations. The promise of STV (over-the-air pay television) fostered some of the growth, although it proved a false promise. Other stations were built on expectations of a huge home-shopping development.

Around 802 UHF stations were operating by mid-1991. Of these, 570 were commercial and 232 public television outlets. The commercial UHFs were divided among network affiliates, independents, and low-power stations. The independents, in turn, were divided between conventional stations and specialty stations. Conventional stations serve predominantly English-speaking general audiences, with program schedules of movies, off-network reruns, sporting events, talk shows and regularly scheduled newscasts. Specialty programs are scheduled primarily in foreign languages to serve Spanish, Japanese, Chinese and other minorities of a community. A few specialize in religious programming, home shopping, or stock market reports.

But for the UHF explosion in the 1980s, there could not have been a fourth TV network. All previous attempts had failed largely because there were not enough stations to pull together for a national network. Fox not only owned the major market VHF stations that had been Metromedia but was able to fill out its coverage with more than 100 UHFs that previously had been struggling independents.

Many of the UHF stations were built by major corporations and established broadcasters with the financial ability to keep the stations going through the difficult years. Among those companies were AVC Corp., Kaiser Industries, Storer, Trans America Corp. (through its subsidiary, United Artists) and Taft Broadcasting. Metromedia had had a UHF station in San Francisco but donated it to the public TV licensee after several years of unprofitable operations. In 1979, Group W began its program of expansion by purchasing a UHF station in Charlotte, N.C.,for $20 million. It was taken as a sign that UHF was finally coming into its own. The station, WPCQ, was subsequently sold.

During the 1950s there had been serious talk at the FCC of moving all television to the UHF band. While the idea was abandoned, most of Western Europe and other countries in the world have concentrated their television on UHF, many of them combining the move to the new band with the inauguration of color. In the U.S., meanwhile, some of the UHF channels have either been reallocated for non-broadcast use or authorized to be "shared" with nonbroadcast services. Channels 70-83 are now allocated to land-mobile, which shares this portion of the band in some parts of the country with TV translators—low-powered repeaters carrying the signal of the nearby TV station to areas where TV service is hard to receive.

Additionally, channels 14-20 are shared with land-mobile in some of the largest urban areas of the country.

U-MATIC ▶ video recording standard based on three-quarter-inch wide tape housed in a cassette; it was launched by Sony in 1971. Originally planned as a possible home video device, U-matic's ease of operation instead established it as the de facto standard for such applications as corporate and industrial video, ENG, and screening reels used in-house by advertising agencies and other organizations. Other manufacturers—notably Panasonic and JVC—also marketed recorders of the U-matic standard, but no one came close to breaking Sony's dominance of the format. So entrenched did U-matic become that Panasonic's more compact S-VHS half-inch standard, launched in 1988 as a potential rival, barely impacted it.

***UNCOUNTED ENEMY: A VIETNAM DECEPTION, THE* ▶** a CBS investigative documentary televised in 1982 that led to a libel suit from Gen. William Westmoreland and a costly trial that many believe chilled all the networks' interest in enterprise documentaries. *The Uncounted Enemy,* produced by George Crile with Mike Wallace as narrator and reporter, attempted to make the case that Westmoreland led a conspiracy to misinform the president on the enemy count in Vietnam to encourage the prosecution of the war. A few months after the show aired *TV Guide* produced an expose of the program's journalistic practices and charged that it went to improper lengths in its determination to prove the premise from which it began. Westmoreland's libel suit for $120 million was filed three months later.

The trial lasted four months and reportedly cost CBS close to $5 million. At the eleventh hour, just as the case was to go before the jury, Westmoreland withdrew his suit, and CBS issued a statement that it never meant to cast doubt on the general's patriotism or loyalty. But while CBS effectively won the libel case, the news division's own in-house inquiry into Crile's journalistic practices found him guilty of most of the charges made by *TV Guide* and in violation of the company's standards.

The episode was laced with paradox. The written document of the in-house investigation, known as the Benjamin Report (for Burton Benjamin, who conducted it), is far more famous than the program that prompted it. And for all the attention *The Uncounted Enemy* received for years after its airing—in the press, in legal circles and in government—the fact is it finished dead last in the network prime-time ratings the week it was broadcast.

UNDA (INTERNATIONAL CATHOLIC ASSOCIATION FOR RADIO, TELEVISION, AND AUDIOVISUALS) ▶ agency based in Brussels, Belgium, representing Catholic radio and TV at the international level and through which its members make contact and share research. Its members consist of autonomous Catholic bodies in more than 100 countries. Founded in 1928 as the International Catholic Bureau for Broadcasting, it took its present name in 1947.

UNDERWRITING ▶ in public television, grants from private corporations or foundations to cover all or part of the cost of producing and/or presenting specific programs or series. When the practice first began in the early 1960s, public TV was barred from using more than the parent corporation's name and a voice announcement. But gradually over the intervening years, and particularly following the Reagan administration's policy of reducing government support in favor of greater private support, the FCC underwriting rules were relaxed to permit corporate logos and slogans, product names, and views of the products themselves. Corporate underwriting credits are now almost indistinguishable from standard commercials.

Notwithstanding the relaxed rules, corporations still view underwriting as institutional advertising, more useful for building image than selling products. Many corporate underwriters further boost their image—and the show's audience—by buying magazine and newspaper space and other promotional gimmicks to promote their affiliation with the show or series. During the energy crisis in the early 1970s, when public opinion had turned harsh toward the major oil companies, Exxon, Mobil, Gulf and Atlantic Richfield became the principal underwriters of cultural programs on PBS.

Although corporate underwriting verges on sponsorship and lends itself to the kind of advertiser control the commercial networks were subject to in the early years, the funding of programs by commercial companies has given the financially starved PTV industry some of its most distinguished and best-watched programs. At the same time, because corporate underwriters customarily avoid what they feel are the negative images of public affairs and controversy, preferring to link their corporate name with the positive images of culture and science, the PBS program schedule is heavily skewed toward the latter.

UNGER, ALVIN E. (d. 1975) ▶ syndication executive who for five years, until his death, was v.p. of domestic sales for Warner Bros. TV. He began in the syndication field in 1939 with the Frederic Ziv organization, becoming v.p. of sales and then v.p. of Chicago for Ziv TV. He moved on to other companies and, before joining Warner, was syndication v.p. for Independent Television Corp.

UNIT MANAGERS SCANDAL ▶ a demoralizing episode at NBC in which several members of the unit managers department were discovered, in the spring of 1979, to have been systematically conducting acts of embezzlement over a period of years. The widespread improprieties, uncovered by the new management of NBC, led to an extensive investigation by federal prosecutors to determine the extent of the white-collar crimes and whether higher officials of the company had collaborated in the schemes. In a matter of weeks, a total of 15 unit managers were fired, including Stephen Weston, who had been v.p. and supervisor of the department.

NBC's unit managers, in a system borrowed from the motion picture industry, travel with news, sports and program production units to handle the living arrangements and financial matters. Because it is sometimes necessary to bribe people—to shoot film on the streets, smooth the way through customs or otherwise expedite the assignment—unit managers frequently carried satchels full of cash with the tacit understanding of their superiors that it might have to be dispensed in ways for which there could be no receipts.

The system invited abuses that extended to falsified expense accounts, fictitious vouchers, kickback schemes and the purchase of airline tickets charged to the network and then returned for cash. The abuses were thought to be flagrant during the coverage of major sports events and political conventions, which involved time pressures and hundreds of personnel.

When the improprieties were uncovered, NBC moved immediately to tighten fiscal controls over the department, which employed about 50 unit managers in New York and Washington. Operating with somewhat different systems, CBS and ABC maintained that they had no comparable problems. Previous top officials of NBC claimed to have been totally unaware of the illegal activities in the company.

UNITED CHURCH OF CHRIST, OFFICE OF COMMUNICATION ▶ a leading organization in the broadcast reform movement, concentrating chiefly on minority rights in the licensed media. While most other religious organizations worked at securing air time to promote their views and their churches, the United Church of Christ chose to work behind the scenes on behalf of the public's rights in radio and TV. The Office of Communication began its work in 1954 under the leadership of the Rev. Dr. Everett C. Parker and has been funded by the Ford and Markle Foundations for some of its programs.

It was notably successful in bringing about the license revocation of WLBT-TV Jackson, Miss., for reasons of race discrimination in programming and employment, and in obtaining rules from the FCC forbidding discriminatory practices. The Office has also helped black groups to purchase stations and assisted racial minorities and women in their negotiations for representation at local stations.

UNITED KINGDOM ▶ a country whose television service is carefully structured by the government, though it is otherwise free from direct government control. The United Kingdom, which embraces Great Britain and Northern Ireland and has 21 million television homes, is served by four national terrestrial channels, each with a clear mandate from the government.

Since 1956, when commercial television began in Britain, the government has attempted to effect a balance of public and commercial television—hence two channels for each. BBC-1 is the primary public channel programmed to appeal to a wide audience, and BBC-2 is a more experimental and elitist channel continuing traditions that earned BBC its good name worldwide. What used to be known as the ITV network, but now is called Channel 3, is the main commercial channel that effectively competes with BBC-1 for the mass audience. Channel 4 Television, which went on the air in 1982, was created essentially to serve minority audiences—minority in both the political and ethnic senses, but also in the artistic. Channel 4's arrival was a great boon to independent producers in Britain.

The careful balance of public and commercial TV was upset in the 1980s by the new technologies of DBS and cable, especially when Rupert Murdoch's Sky Channel entered the market, and it became clear that the old policies would have to adapt to the times. The 1989 Broadcasting Bill forged in the Thatcher era provided for changes that lean to a more market-driven system. Among other things, it calls for the creation of a fifth national channel to start around 1995, and it requires that at least 25% of any network's programming be provided by British independent producers.

But far the most radical change was in abolishing the previous licensing procedures for commercial television and, instead, putting the ITV franchises up for auction. In 1991 the 15 regional franchises that operate on Channel 3 and comprised the ITV network went up for auction on the basis of highest bid and quality criteria. In October, when the results were announced, four companies had lost their franchises to higher bidders, including one of the largest, Thames TV, licensed to the London area. The new tenant was Carlton Communications. Television South, serving perhaps the wealthiest region of England, lost to Meridian Broadcasting; Westward Television in the southwest to West Country Television; and TV-am, the breakfast time contractor with two hours of morning time, lost to Sunrise.

The license periods are all for 10 years, when presumably another auction will be held. In another radical departure from past policy, the government will allow for mergers and takeovers of the licensees. Thus some of the losers may return by buying their way in, and some of the largest franchise holders might move to absorb some of the smaller ones. A number of American companies had held minority stakes in British companies bidding for the franchises, but only Disney, with a 5% interest in Sunrise, had backed a winner.

Channel 4, previously funded by the ITV companies, which sold its advertising and kept the revenues, was turned loose to become self-supporting. The BBC channels escaped change under the new law, but its charter comes up for review in 1996 with the distinct possibility that it might be required to find ways of becoming more self-sufficient, such as in selling advertising or in turning BBC-2 into a pay-TV channel.

The privately-owned regional stations that comprise Channel 3 are these:

Carlton Television (successor to Thames), which operates in the London metropolitan area from Mondays to Fridays at 7 p.m.

London Weekend Television, which takes over on Friday nights for the entire weekend.

Granada Television, which has Lancashire county in northwest England.

Yorkshire Television, the Yorkshire region.

Central Television, the English midlands.

Meridian (successor to Television South), the south England coastal strip.

HTV, which has west England and Wales.

West Country Television (successor to Westward Television), southwest England.

Border Television, the English-Scottish frontier and the Isle of Man in the Irish Sea.

Scottish Television, central Scotland.

Grampian, northeast Scotland.

Anglia Television, east England.

Tyne-Tees Television, northeast England.

Ulster Television, northern Ireland.

Channel Television, the islands in the English channel.

The five largest regional stations, through a committee of executives from each, collaborate in creating the program schedule for all to carry on the national network. They tend also to be the chief producers of indigenous programs for the commercial network. The regionals also share ownership of Independent Television News (ITN), which provides *The News At Ten* for the network.

There is actually a 16th regional station, S4C, which covers much of Wales and often broadcasts in the Welsh language, but it is not part of the Channel 3 membership. Instead it operates on Channel 4 in lieu of the national channel in its region.

All the commercial channels, and the Sunrise morning franchise, are regulated by the

Independent Television Commission (ITC), which prior to the new law was known as the Independent Broadcasting Authority (IBA).

UNITED STATES v. RADIO CORP. OF AMERICA ▶ [358 U.S. 334 (1959)] case in which the Supreme Court held that action which is authorized by the FCC is not exempt from prosecution under the antitrust laws. At issue was an exchange of stations between NBC (a subsidiary of RCA) and Westinghouse Broadcasting Co.

Each of the companies owned five VHF television stations, the maximum number then allowed by the FCC. NBC, with a station in Cleveland, was desirous of trading up for one in Philadelphia, a much larger market. Westinghouse, which had a Philadelphia station, was affiliated with NBC in Boston and Pittsburgh. NBC allegedly threatened to terminate those affiliations if Westinghouse did not agree to swap the Philadelphia station for NBC's Cleveland outlet and $3 million. The FCC approved the transaction without holding a hearing.

Subsequently, the Justice Department filed suit against RCA and NBC for violating the antitrust laws. The defense of RCA and NBC was that approval of transfer by the commission cleared them of any antitrust violation, and the court agreed, dismissing the action. The case was then appealed to the U.S. Supreme Court, which reversed the decision of the trial court.

The Supreme Court held that the statutory grant of power to the FCC in the Communications Act did not give it authority to pass on formal antitrust questions, which were within the province of the courts alone. The FCC only had power to determine if the transfer had been in the "public interest, convenience and necessity." And although the FCC had the authority to find that certain combinations of media control were against the public interest, the Court insisted that this was not the same as a finding that the antitrust laws had been violated. Therefore, the Court remanded the case to the District Court to determine whether the antitrust laws had been violated.

But before the District Court heard the case, Westinghouse and RCA entered into a consent agreement to annul the exchange. The Philadelphia license was returned to Westinghouse, and NBC moved back to Cleveland and was repaid its $3 million.

UNITED STATES v. SOUTHWESTERN CABLE CO. ▶ [392 U.S. 157 (1968)] case in which the Supreme Court upheld the FCC's jurisdiction over cable TV's impact on broadcasting.

When Southwestern Cable, operating in San Diego, began importing signals from Los Angeles to attract additional subscribers, a local TV station (KFMB-TV) operated by Midwest Television Inc. complained to the FCC that the importations were adversely affecting San Diego broadcasters and that they were contrary to the public interest.

After considering both sides of the argument, the FCC ordered Southwestern, pending a decision on the merits, to restrict its services to areas it had operated in prior to Feb. 15, 1966. Southwestern appealed, and the Court of Appeals for the Ninth Circuit reversed. The court held that the FCC had no jurisdiction over CATV systems and that it therefore could not require Southwestern to restrict its services. The case was then appealed to the Supreme Court, which reinstated the commission's initial order.

The Court found substance to the commission's argument that regulation of cable TV was necessary to regulate its broadcast licensees effectively. The Court noted that the Communications Act of 1934 was explicitly applicable to "all interstate and foreign communication by wire or radio" and that since CATV systems were interstate communications by wire, the FCC had the power to regulate cable systems generally.

Further, it reasoned, since the commission has the power to issue "such orders, not inconsistent with (the Act), as may be necessary in the execution of its functions," the order limiting Southwestern's services pending a full hearing on the merits was proper.

UNITED STATES v. STORER BROADCASTING CO. ▶ [351 U.S. 192 (1956)] case that affirmed the right of the FCC to limit the number of licenses any one person or firm could have. It also gave the FCC the power to summarily dismiss any application that was, on its face, in violation of the commission rules.

In 1953 the commission promulgated rules which placed maximum limits on the number of television, AM and FM licenses any one person or company could control. The rule also stated that no future licenses would be granted if an applicant already held the maximum number of licenses. Storer Broadcasting Co., which held the maximum complement of licenses in each category, challenged the rules because it felt there might be situations in which the public interest dictated an extra station.

The Court of Appeals vacated the rules insofar as they placed absolute limits on the number of stations a licensee could control. The FCC then appealed the case to the Supreme Court, which reversed the judgment of the Court of Appeals.

The Supreme Court noted that an applicant always had right to apply for a waiver of the rules if it could demonstrate that the public interest would be served. Thus, broadcasters still had the ability to seek and obtain a full hearing for an additional license, despite the rules, even if it already had the maximum number of licenses.

UNIVERSITY OF MID-AMERICA ▶ a four-state project developed by the University of Nebraska and the Nebraska Educational Telecommunications Center that represented the first attempt in the U.S. to establish an open learning system offering a four-year college degree program via public television. Formed in the early 1970s, the system expanded when it received major federal funding in 1974. In addition to TV, the system involved the use of radio, telephone and books and provided for personal consultation.

UNIVISION ▶ Spanish-language network serving an estimated 22 million viewers in the United States and audiences in 18 Latin American countries with a wide range of family-oriented programming. Formerly SIN (Spanish International Network), it was founded in 1961 and became a wholly owned subsidiary of Hallmark Cards in February 1988. Univision owns and operates nine UHF stations: KMEX Los Angeles, WXTV New York, WLTV Miami, KDTV San Francisco, KWEX San Antonio, KLUZ Albuquerque, KUVN Dallas, KFTV Fresno and KTVW Phoenix. In addition, its programs are distributed by satellite to seven major-market affiliates, 16 low-power stations and 546 cable systems.

From its Miami network headquarters and production studios, completed in 1991, Univision originates a nightly news program, *Noticiero Univision;* a weekday talk show, *Cristina;* and a popular Saturday night game show, *Sabado Gigante.* Joaquin Blaya is president of the network.

UNSOLVED MYSTERIES **▶** one of the more successful of the reality-based series that peppered the networks in the early 1990s, which with reenactments and interviews with law enforcement officials examines actual unsolved mysteries. It began as a series of irregular specials that ran on NBC during the 1987-88 season and then earned a weekly slot as an hour-long show in October 1988. Hosted and narrated by Robert Stack, the episodes focus on such topics as missing persons, unsolved murders and unclaimed estates. In the manner of *America's Most Wanted*, it encourages viewers with information on any of the cases to help authorities by calling a toll-free number. The specials that preceded the series were hosted variously by Raymond Burr and Karl Malden. Executive producers John Cosgrove and Terry Dunn Meurer created the series.

UNTOUCHABLES, THE **▶** landmark police series on ABC (1959-63) that became notorious for its escalation of violence in prime time and its association of Italian names with the gangland crime of the Prohibition Era. On the positive side were its quasi-documentary style, with Walter Winchell narrating in the staccato idiom of headlines, and the careful attention to authentic detail in depicting the period. Robert Stack played Eliot Ness, head of the "untouchable" government agents cracking down on the mobs. Also featured were Abel Fernandez as Youngfellow, Nicholas Georgiade as Rossi, Steve London as Rossman, Jerry Paris as Marvin Flaherty and Paul Picerni as Hobson.

Although it was highly popular, the series was attacked by Italian-American groups for ethnic defamation and by others for the sensationalism of machine-gun murders and acts of brutality. It was produced by Quinn Martin for Desilu, in association with Langford Productions.

UPFRONT MARKET ▶ the first selling wave for the networks; it occurs in the spring when they present their newly minted fall schedules to major advertisers. This is when TV's big spenders stake out the choice programs and positions for the next season, paying top dollar for the spots but with guarantees from the networks that they will get all the audience paid for, if necessary through bonus spots and make-goods. Upfront is the barometer for the year's business; when it is strong, the spots remaining for late-arriving scatter buyers tend to sell at higher rates than when the upfront market is weak and the leftover spots answer to the law of supply and demand.

UPLINK ▶ a satellite dish capable of relaying television signals from earth to the appropriate transponders in space. Signals from abroad, such as news dispatches or the coverage of live events, often require multiple transfers of satellites and thus must be downlinked at various uplinking points until they reach their destination. Though the logistics may seem complex, such signals barely lose time in travel and are generally considered to be received instantaneously.

The cast of the British series *Upstairs, Downstairs*

UPSTAIRS, DOWNSTAIRS ▶ taped British series, via London Weekend Television, about the intrigues of the wealthy and the servant classes living under the same elegant roof in Edwardian England at the turn of the century. The series was a great success in the U.K. and also developed a staunch following in the U.S. on PBS, where it played as a subseries of *Masterpiece Theatre.* It featured Jean Marsh (who became well known in the U.S. through the series and was winner of a 1974 Emmy) as Rose, David Langton as Richard Bellamy, Meg Wynn Owen as Hazel Bellamy, Rachel Gurney as Lady Marjorie, Gordon Jackson as Hudson and Angela Baddely as Mrs. Bridges, among others. In 1975, CBS attempted an American version, *Beacon Hill,* which had a brief run. The Robert Stigwood Organisation produced both the original and the imitation.

Upstairs, Downstairs ended its firstrun episodes on PBS in April 1977.

UPSTREAM/DOWNSTREAM ▶ designating the directions traveled by TV signals on two-way cable systems. Upstream signals are those transmitted by the subscriber to the head-end, usually in digital form; downstream signals are those traveling from the head-end to the receiver, generally in picture form.

URICH, ROBERT ▶ actor who has appeared on eight series, mostly action adventure, including *S.W.A.T.* (1975-76), *Vega$* (1978-81), and *Spenser: For Hire* (1985-88). However, it was the part of the sexy tennis pro on *Soap* in 1977 that gave his career the boost it needed. He has also appeared in a number of TV movies and miniseries, including *Fighting Back, Princess Daisy,* and *Invitation to Hell.*

USA NETWORK ▶ one of the more successful basic-cable networks, programmed for mass-audience appeal in the manner of commercial TV stations. The channel originated in 1977 as the Madison Square Garden Network (MSG), carrying events from the New York sports arena and others around the U.S. USA Network was spun out of MSG in 1980, when UA-Columbia Cable entered into a partnership with MSG Sports in the channel, and its programming was made more general. In 1981 the network was acquired by Paramount Pictures Corp. and MCA Inc.

USA is one of the more pervasive basic-cable networks, reaching 54.5 million TV households. Its prime-time lineup regularly leads other basic networks in the ratings with its concentration on off-network series and movies. In latter years USA has commissioned around 30 original movies a year, mostly in the thriller genre. USA's sports programming, which includes boxing, wrestling and U.S. Open Tennis, also gets high viewership. In particular, the network's coverage of the 1991 U.S. Open drew exceptional notice as aging former champ Jimmy Connors fought his way into the final rounds. Kay Koplovitz is USA's president and CEO.

UTLEY, GARRICK ▶ co-anchor of NBC News' *Sunday Today* and the weekend editon of *NBC Nightly News.* He was also moderator of *Meet the Press* from 1989-91. During some 30 years with NBC News, Ultey has been one of the network's most durable and dependable correspondents. While covering foreign affairs, he reported from more than 70 countries, starting with Belgium in 1963. A year later he went to Saigon, where he filed extensive reports on the Vietnam War. He has also reported from bureaus in Berlin, Paris, Africa and Asia. He has been a correspondent for *NBC Magazine* (1980-82), and has hosted another NBC monthly magazine, *First Tuesday* (later renamed *Chronolog*).

His father, Clifton Utley, was a noted NBC correspondent and local anchor in Chicago during the 1950s, and his mother, Frayn, was an NBC reporter.

V

VALENTI, JACK ▶ former special assistant to President Lyndon Johnson who became, in 1966, president of the Motion Picture Association of America and its related agencies, the Association of Motion Picture and Television Producers and the Motion Picture Export Association. As the film industry's representative in Washington, he became one of the leaders of the campaign to persuade the FCC to loosen or discard the rules restricting pay cable. In the 1990s he led the campaign to preserve the Financial Interest and Syndication ("Fin-Syn") Rules. Before joining the White House, he headed a Houston ad agency, Weekly & Valenti.

VAN DEERLIN, LIONEL ▶ chairman of the House Communications Subcommittee (1976-80), succeeding the late Rep. Torbert Macdonald. A nine-term Democratic congressman from San Diego, Van Deerlin, a cable TV advocate and former broadcast journalist, proposed to rewrite the Communications Act of 1934, making it more applicable to the television era and the emerging technologies.

Van Deerlin's proposals, first issued in 1978 and revised in 1979, created a storm of controversy in the communications industry and among public interest groups. He advocated a free-marketplace approach to Federal communications policy, eliminating most government regulation of radio, television and cable TV. He proposed an easing of broadcast licensing requirements and a virtual elimination of the public interest standard by which the FCC regulates stations, but in exchange for that he proposed that broadcasters pay a fee for their use of the public airwaves. For lack of support, either on his subcommittee or in the concerned industries, Van Deerlin was forced in July 1979 to scrap the rewrite provisions for broadcasting, although he proceeded with a bill for changes in the communications laws affecting common carriers. He was defeated in his bid for reelection in 1980, but many of his proposals were adopted in the Reagan administration. Upon leaving office, he became a newspaper columnist and also taught at San Diego State University, where a chair in Communications Policy was named for him.

In the 1950s, before he was elected to Congress, Van Deerlin had been a newscaster in San Diego and news director for stations KOGO and XETV.

VAN DYKE, DICK ▶ one of the big, appealing television stars who curiously was unable to translate his success to the big screen. In 1966 he voluntarily ended his extremely popular, multi-Emmy Award winning series *The Dick Van Dyke Show,* which began in 1961. After starring in a few films (*Mary Poppins, Chitty Chitty Bang Bang, Bye Bye Birdie*), he came back to TV in 1971 with *The New Dick Van Dyke*

Show, a moderately successful series that managed to stay on the air for three years. In the late 1970s he attempted a variety show that lasted only one season and he briefly appeared as co-star to Carol Burnett on her show. He also made a couple of television movies, *Dropout Dad* and *Found Money*. After several years off the air, he reappeared with two made-for-TV-movies under the title *The Dick Van Dyke Mystery Movies*. Produced by Viacom and intended as pilots, the first of the movies aired on CBS in the fall of 1991.

VAN VOLKENBURG, J. L. ("JACK") (d. 1963) ▶ first president of the CBS television network, appointed July 16, 1951, and credited with lining up many of the most desirable early stations as CBS affiliates and many of the early advertisers. A tough and shrewd executive, he lasted four years in the post, to cap a CBS career of 23 years.

Van Volkenburg joined the company as sales manager of KMOX St. Louis in 1932 and a year later became president and general manager of the radio station. In 1945, he moved to New York as general sales manager of CBS Radio Sales, later becoming director of sales administration for all the owned stations. In 1948 he was made v.p. of CBS television operations and two years later v.p. in charge of CBS-TV sales. Before taking his first job in broadcasting, he had worked in a Chicago advertising agency and rose to head of its radio department in 1928.

VANE, EDWIN T. ▶ former president of Group W Productions Inc. (1979-89) and previously a senior program executive with ABC for 15 years. With the network he was instrumental in introducing such programs as *Good Morning America, Family Feud, The Dating Game, The Newlywed Game, Dark Shadows, Concentration, Jeopardy* and many of the notable dramas in the *ABC Theater* series.

Starting as director of daytime programs he rose to a number of higher posts through several network administrations and in 1976 was named v.p. and national program director for ABC Entertainment, the network's programming arm. Vane began his broadcasting career with NBC as a page while still at Fordham University. He later advanced through several departments and became manager of daytime programming in 1961. In heading Group W Productions, Vane changed his base from New York to Los Angeles.

VANOCUR, SANDER ▶ ABC News senior correspondent and anchor of *Business World*, which premiered October 1986. For this series, Vanocur has covered international economic summits and conducted live interviews with such high-profile financial leaders as Carl Icahn and Paul Volcker.

A veteran reporter, Vanocur has been covering national and international beats since 1958. He gained national prominence during his 14 years with NBC News as a national political correspondent and was known as one of the journalists close to President Kennedy and his family. He left NBC in 1971 to become senior correspondent for the PBS National Public Affairs Center for Television (NPACT), but it was not a satisfying stint. The Nixon Administration charged NPACT with having a liberal bias, singling out Vanocur and Robert MacNeil; and various government officials, including Democrats, were critical of the anchor salary levels, which they believed were too high for public television. Vanocur's was $85,000 annually.

Vanocur left to teach at Duke for two years, then joined the *Washington Post* as its television critic. In 1977, ABC's Roone Arledge brought him back to broadcasting to head up a special unit for investigative and political reporting. For a time he was chief diplomatic correspondent and contributed to the evening newscast's *Special Assignment* series. He was ABC News' chief "overview" correspondent covering the Democratic and Republican candidates in the 1980 and 1984 presidential elections.

Vanocur began his journalism career as a reporter in London for the *Manchester Guardian*. Before joining NBC News in 1957, he was a general assignment reporter for the *New York Times*.

VANOFF, NICK (d. 1991) ▶ producer-director of variety shows whose credits included the second *Sonny and Cher Show* and the *Perry Como Kraft Music Hall*. He was also a partner in Yongestreet Productions, packagers of *Hee Haw* and other TV series and specials.

Beginning his career as a principal dancer with the New York City Opera and as a musical performer in *Kiss Me, Kate* on Broadway, Vanoff entered television as a co-producer of the Steve Allen *Tonight* show and added to his credits *The King Family* series and *Hollywood Palace*. In 1978 Vanoff became producer of the annual *Kennedy Center Honors* show, and in 1990 he won a Tony award for producing the stage musical *City of Angels*. Vanoff died of a heart attack in March 1991 at the age of 61.

VAST WASTELAND ▶ phrase that rocked the broadcast industry when it was used by a new FCC chairman, Newton N. Minow, in 1961 to describe the state of TV programming. Minow coined the phrase in his first speech to the industry, at the NAB convention in May, five months after becoming FCC chairman in the Kennedy administration. To broadcasters, a regulator passing judgment on the quality of programming suggested government interference with their right of free speech. But the press gave prominent coverage to Minow's assessment of television, and the "vast wasteland" speech reverberated throughout his productive two-year tenure as chairman and inspired broadcasters to increase and improve their public affairs programming. The famous phrase was used in the following context: "I invite you to sit down in front of your television set when your station goes on the air and stay there without a book, magazine, profit and loss sheet or rating book to distract you—and keep your eyes glued to the set until the station signs off. I assure you that you will observe a vast wasteland."

***VD BLUES* ▶** a PBS special (Oct. 1972) that attempted with a fair degree of success to convey information on venereal disease to the young through the light entertainment devices of songs and sketches. Produced by WNET New York, the program was hosted by Dick Cavett, produced by Don Fouser, directed by Sidney Smith and written by Fouser and Gary Belkin. Special material and skits were by Jules Feiffer, Israel Horovitz and Clayton Riley. The underwriter was 3M. Some public TV stations refused to carry the telecast because of strong language used and because of the open discussion about sex as the medium for transmitting VD, but WNET alone received 15,000 calls from viewers asking for the guidance promised by the program.

VECCHIONE, AL ▶ veteran journalist who became president of MacNeil-Lehrer Productions in 1983, after having been executive producer of *The MacNeil-Lehrer Report*. After 20 years with NBC, he joined public television's NPACT in Washington in the early 1970s. He served variously as exec producer, director of production operations and general manager. In 1975 he was named executive director of public affairs programming for NPACT and WETA Washington but left the following year to serve as broadcast advisor to the Democratic National Committee. He returned to public television after the elections as executive producer of *The MacNeil-Lehrer Report*. When MacNeil and Lehrer decided to form a production company for documentaries and documentary series, Vecchione became responsible for running it, and Les Crystal became executive producer.

***VEGA$* ▶** hour-long ABC detective series (1978-81) whose action took place against the background of Las Vegas hotels and casinos. Robert Urich starred as Dan Tanna in the Spelling-Goldberg Production. Featured were Bart Braverman as Binzer, Tony Curtis as Roth, Phyllis Davis as Beatrice Travis, Judy Landers as Angie Turner and Naomi Stevens as police sergeant Bella Archer.

VENZA, JAC ▶ a leading producer of performing arts programs for public TV since 1966, including the much-honored PBS series of *Great Performances*, which Venza created by combining two of his earlier performance series, *Theater in America* and *Dance in America*.

As WNET's director of performance programming since the early 1970s, Venza has been executive producer not only of *Great Performances* but also of such series as *The Adams Chronicles* and *Biography*, and he played key roles in the creation of *American Playhouse* and *American Masters*. Earlier, as director of drama for National Educational Television, Venza created the system's first weekly drama series, *NET Playhouse*, in 1966.

Venza began his television career in 1949 as a scenic designer for CBS. He moved into the production of public affairs programs, was associate producer of the *Adventure* series in 1953, and later worked on the *Roots of Freedom*. In addition to his TV work, he has been a scenic designer for theater, opera and ballet.

VERTICAL BLANKING INTERVAL ▶ a series of 20 or 21 horizontal lines transmitted between pictures. These lines normally carry no video information but have recently been used to convey test and monitoring data for automatic monitoring of start and end of commercials, or for color reference signals (vertical interval reference or VIR). More recently the vertical interval has been used to transmit teletext data. In the U.S., line 21 of the vertical interval is used for carriage of closed captioning information for the hearing impaired, and all TV sets sold after 1992 will be required to be able to decode it.

VERTUE, BERYL ▶ British producer who worked in American TV as co-deputy chairman of the Robert Stigwood Group and head of its television operations. Her U.S. credits included *Beacon Hill,* the mini-series *Charleston* and the special *The Entertainer,* which starred Jack Lemmon. In association with Bob Banner, she produced the series *Almost Anything Goes,* and she was executive producer of the movie *Tommy.* She made her entry in American TV handling the rights arrangements for the British shows on which *All in the Family* and *Sanford and Son* were based.

VHF (VERY HIGH FREQUENCY) ▶ the FCC's designation for the radio spectrum band 30 to 300 megahertz. The original 12 television channels in the United States extend from 54 to 72 MHz (Channels 2-4), to 76 to 88 MHz (Channels 5 and 6) and 174 to 216 MHz (Channels 7-13).

VH-1 ▶ see MTV/VH-1.

VHS ▶ home video format based on half-inch-wide tape housed in cassettes that since it was launched in 1976 has become the de facto worldwide home video standard. Developed in Japan by JVC and marketed aggressively by Matsushita, VHS became locked in a battle for dominance with Sony's rival half-inch format, the Betamax, launched a year earlier. While many technicians claimed that Betamax produced a superior image, VHS eventually prevailed in the marketplace because its cassettes could record and play back for a longer time and because—in the U.S.—it enlisted then-giant RCA as its marketing partner, under whose label many of the recorders were sold.

VIACOM INTERNATIONAL ▶ a diversified entertainment and communications company based in New York. Its holdings include basic-cable networks MTV, VH-1 and Nickelodeon, plus part-ownership of Lifetime and Comedy Central; pay networks Showtime and The Movie Channel; cable systems serving more than one million subscribers; five TV and 14 radio stations; and a TV production and distribution company that produces shows such as *Matlock* and *Jake and the Fatman* and distributes in syndication such series as *The Cosby Show* and *Roseanne.*

The company is owned by Sumner Redstone's National Amusements Inc., which acquired it in 1987 following a failed leveraged buyout attempt by Viacom's top management.

Viacom was formed in June 1971 as a spin-off of CBS following an FCC order requiring the networks to divest themselves of their program syndication and cable-TV divisions. The spin-off included executives as well as properties, and the company's first president was Clark B. George, former president of CBS Radio. Later he was replaced by Ralph Baruch. Since the acquisition by National Amusements, Viacom has been headed by Frank Biondi.

VICTOR, DAVID (d. 1989) ▶ veteran executive producer associated with Universal TV, whose credits included *Marcus Welby, M.D., Owen Marshall, The Man and the City, Griff, Lucas Tanner* and *Kingston.* During the 1960s he was producer of several series, among them *Dr. Kildare.*

***VICTORY AT SEA* ▶** a classic documentary series of 26 half-hour episodes on the exploits of the U.S. Navy during World War II, utilizing combat footage and a stirring musical score by Richard Rodgers. It had its first presentation in 1952, was aired numerous times afterwards and remains a model for the form of historical documentary. Produced by Henry Salomon and narrated by Leonard Graves, it won dozens of awards.

VIDEO COMPRESSION ▶ technology that allows for the multifold expansion of cable channels and satellite capacity. Some available compression systems make possible the multiplying of every existing satellite transponder and cable channel by five or even more, so that a 30-channel cable system may be increased to 150 channels without rebuilding the basic plant.

The technology works by reducing the amount of data required in the recording or transmission of a TV image while attempting to retain as much detail as possible visible to the human eye. NTSC color was an early compression technique. Newer video compression technologies are expected to allow the development of several applications, including the "squeezing" of data-intensive high-definition television signals into normal 6-MHZ broadcast or cable channels. The new video digital compression systems are being used initially in the satellite field.

VIDEO FEEDBACK ▶ the optical effect produced by aiming a television camera at a television monitor, so that it simultaneously sees and displays its own electronic image. Since the movement of the camera's position in relation to the monitor alters the imagery, kaleidoscopic effects are possible. Video feedback has been basic to the development of electronic television art. In the 1980s, however, the advent of new digital video effects and image manipulation systems provided artists and experimenters with more interesting imagery.

VIDEO FORMAT ▶ a system of video recording in which all recorders and tapes are compatible with each other and interchangeable with all other recorders and tapes of the same format. Popular video formats have included quadruplex, one-inch Type C, U-matic, Betacam, S-VHS, D-1 and D-2. A format is not to be confused with a video standard such as NTSC, PAL or SECAM, each of which can include any number of formats.

VIDEOCASSETTE ▶ a cartridge containing videotape, generally on two reels, designed for simple operation in video recording and playback units. The earliest widely used videocassette system in broadcast and closed-circuit TV was Sony's U-Matic (with 3/4-inch tape). Videocassette systems have been widely adapted at TV stations for electronic newsgathering operations.

Other systems followed. Sony's Betacam, which uses 1/2-inch tape, achieved dominance in the broadcast world in the late 1980s. Future professional videocassette systems will include 1/2-inch digital recording as well as 8mm tape.

In home video recording, Sony's Betamax system, launched in 1975, lost out after a long marketing struggle with Matsushita's VHS system, first introduced in the U.S. by RCA in 1976. Both use 1/2-inch tape. Sony's 8mm home system has carved out a niche market in camcorder use.

VIDEOCONFERENCING ▶ use of satellite technology to allow live face-to-face meetings over great distances. Videoconferences with one-way video and two-way audio allow an audience to see a speaker or group, while that speaker or group can only hear the audience. Videoconferences with two-way video allow both parties to see each other as they interact.

VIDEODISC, VIDEO DISC ▶ a disc with the general appearance of a phonograph record, on which video and audio information is stored for playback through a home television receiver in the same way a phonograph plays back an audio signal.

The first videodisc was demonstrated in 1927 in Great Britain by John Logie Baird, using a waxed phonograph record, but the signals were of such low resolution that the project was abandoned.

The first videodisc system actually placed on the marker was the TeD system developed by Telefunken of Germany, Decca of the United Kingdom and Teldec, a joint subsidiary of the two companies. TeD, a mechanical system, played pre-recorded material in color when attached to the antenna terminals of a color television receiver.

Other videodisc systems using a variety of technologies were shown by RCA Selectavision, Philips, Hitachi and Thomson-CSF. The only one actively marketed in the U.S., however, was the system from MCA, called MCA Discovision, launched in 1977.

Videodiscs fell victim to videocassette recorders, also launched in the mid-1970s. VCRs had two major advantages: a much longer playing time (two to four hours per tape, versus 30 minutes on one side of a disc) and the ability to record.

MCA Discovision's technology was adopted by Japan's Pioneer Electronics, which continues to market discs and players of that format to a niche group of consumers who enjoy its quality.

VIDEOTAPE RECORDING ▶ the recording of television signals on magnetic tape for later replay. The videotape recorder (VTR) is the principal device used for storing television programs.

The first VTRs were of the longitudinal-scan type; on these, the tape passes at high speed before fixed recording and playback heads, in a manner similar to an audio recorder. The first VTR to be publicly demonstrated was built by Bing Crosby Laboratories in 1951. The tape ran at 100 inches per second, with a total of 16 minutes recording time per reel. The picture had poor resolution, flickered and displayed a diagonal pattern. RCA displayed longitudinal-scan monochrome and color VTRs in 1953; they had similar deficiencies.

The type of VTR that revolutionized television—and is in use at virtually all television stations today—was demonstrated for the first time by Ampex Corporation in 1956, where it created a sensation at the annual convention of the National Association of Broadcasters in Chicago. The quadruplex (quad) VTR, rather than recording information longitudinally, records it transversely, with four heads rotating at high speed at right angles to a two-inch-wide tape moving at 15 inches per second, depositing a diagonal track. The quad VTR could accommodate about 90 minutes of programming on a 14.5-inch reel. Slowed down to 7.5 inches per second, it could record for three hours on a reel.

Color versions of the quad VTR were developed in 1958. Ampex and RCA were the only American producers of this standard VTR.

The helical-scan, or slant-track, VTR was introduced in the early 1960s, providing significant cost reductions as compared to quad units, although for many years it did not compare in picture quality.

In the helical VTR, the tape is wrapped in a spiral (or helix) around a drum containing one or more rotating heads. The heads produce a diagonal track on the tape. Helical-scan VTRs were popularized by Sony Corporation of Japan for closed-circuit use, but in 1973 and later International Video Corp., Ampex, Bosch-Fernseh, Sony and others were to introduce helical recorders of broadcast quality. By 1977 this simpler and more economical format using one-inch-wide reel-to-reel tape was starting to replace quad. One-inch systems dominated broadcast operations for more than a decade. Through the 1980s, their dominance was gradually whittled away by cassette based systems like the half-inch Betacom and MII, and the new cassette-based digital D-2 format.

VIDEOTEXT ▶ generic for the various electronic text systems that allow printed information to be called up on a television screen or a separate computer terminal.

Teletext is the form that operates on broadcast frequencies, specifically the vertical blanking interval of television transmissions. It is a one-way service, flashing pages of text in a prearranged order and in a cycle that is repeated continuously. The information travels at the rate of four pages a second, which means that the consumer may have to wait half a minute or more for the information requested. Teletext may be called up on a blank screen or can be superimposed on a program in progress. Closed captioning is a form of teletext.

Videotext, also known as "Videotex" without the "t," refers to two-way on-line text systems delivered either through telephone or cable. Major videotext systems used in the U.S. are CompuServe and Prodigy. British systems are known as Prestel, Ceefax and Oracle. The French have developed Minitel.

VIERA, MEREDITH ▶ CBS News correspondent whose assignments have included the prime-time series *Verdict,* which reports on and shows excerpts of actual courtroom trials.

From 1989-91 Viera was co-editor of *60 Minutes.* But in 1991, saying she wanted to cut down her schedule because she was pregnant, executive producer Don Hewitt simply released her, contending that *60 Minutes* needed full-time correspondents and that granting her a lighter schedule would be an unfair burden on the other correspondents, all of whom happened to be male. Viera's dismissal created a flap, with charges of sexism and counter-charges by Hewitt that her work was not memorable, keeping the tabloids perking for weeks.

Prior to joining *60 Minutes,* Viera was a principal correspondent for CBS News' *West 57th* since its 1985 premiere. She began at CBS News as a reporter in its Chicago bureau in January 1983 and was named a correspondent in 1984. Before that she had been a reporter at New York's WCBS-TV. She began her career as a news announcer for WORC Radio in Worcester, Mass., in 1975, and as a reporter and anchor at WJAR-TV Providence, R.I.

VIETNAM: A TELEVISION HISTORY **▶** acclaimed 13-part documentary series and the most comprehensive review of the U.S. experience in the Vietnam War; it aired on PBS in 1983. Six years in production at a cost of $4.5 million, it was a coproduction of WGBH Boston, the U.K.'s Central Independent Television, and France's Antenne-2. Richard Ellison was executive producer and Stanley Karnow, who had reported on the war for the *Washington Post,* was chief correspondent. Will Lyman was narrator, and the National Endowment for the Humanities contributed to the funding.

The series contained hundreds of interviews and drew footage from archives in 11 countries. But though it was scholarly and painstakingly researched and the recipient of numerous awards, the series was assailed by Accuracy in Media, a right-wing organization that watches over the press. The organization requested and received an hour of rebuttal time on public TV.

VIEWDATA ▶ British term for videotext.

VILLA ALEGRE **▶** bilingual (English and Spanish) PBS series for children produced on grants from HEW, Exxon Corp. and the U.S.A. and Ford Foundations. It premiered in 1974 as a daily half-hour series, with Mario Guzman as producer for BC/TV, Oakland, Calif. The program's prime purpose was to ease the transition from home to school for millions of Spanish-speaking children.

VIOLENCE HEARINGS ▶ formal inquiries by congressional bodies and commissions into the question of whether the viewing of violence on television contributes to actual violent behavior and to the increase of crime in the U.S.

In chronological order, the principal hearings were the following:

• In 1954, the Kefauver hearings, prompted by the view of Sen. Estes Kefauver that television was a contributor to the growing crime rate. He was chairman of the Senate Subcommittee on Juvenile Delinquency at the time.

• In 1961 and 1964, the Dodd hearings, in which Sen. Thomas Dodd of Connecticut reacted to what he felt was the industry's rampant and opportunistic use of violence.

• In 1968, hearings by the National Commission on the Causes and Prevention of Violence, led by Milton Eisenhower, on the role of the mass media. Network executives were questioned about research that they had promised, which was not forthcoming.

• In 1969, the Surgeon General's Inquiry on Violence with the National Institute of Mental Health, was ordered to establish what harmful effects, if any, televised crime, violence and antisocial behavior have on children. The study resulted in a five-volume report, *Television and Social Behavior: A Technical Report to the Surgeon General's Scientific Advisory Committee on Television and Social Behavior.*

• In 1972, shortly after publication of the Surgeon General's report, the Pastore Hearings sorted out some confused statements and compromise language that had made the summary of the report indecisive concerning the relationship of TV violence to subsequent violent behavior. In these sessions Sen. John Pastore questioned all 12 members of the Surgeon General's Committee, and all of them—with varying views and backgrounds—agreed that the scientific evidence indicated that viewing of television violence by young people causes them to behave more aggressively.

After these hearings, the networks made some attempt to reduce the violence quotient, but the problem persisted. Pastore's and other committees continued to pressure the networks, and they expanded the issue to sex and violence. The networks responded to the concern by removing the more violent cartoons from the Saturday morning children's block and later by adopting, with the NAB, the concept of "family viewing time," designating the period from 7 to 9 p.m. for programming suitable for all age groups.

VIP (VIEWERS IN PROFILE) ▶ title of the periodic Nielsen reports containing, for each local market, audience data (size and composition) to assist the buyers and sellers of national spot and local TV advertising. The NSI equivalent of the NTI "pocketpiece," the VIP reports are issued from a minimum of three times a year to a maximum of eight times, depending on the size of the market.

Nielsen measures the audiences for individual stations in most markets through the use of diaries. These are placed in sample homes by telephone contact and remain in each home for one week. What is reported in the VIP is audience data for the average week, measured over four weeks.

The first of three sections in the VIP report is the Day Part Audience Summary, which breaks down audience estimates by day parts (e.g., 7:30-11 p.m., Sunday through Saturday; 9 a.m.-Noon, Monday through Friday, etc.) and includes age and sex demographics and each station's average weekly cumulative audience.

Another section, the Program Audience Averages, reports audience data for individual programs. The third section, Time Period Audiences, reports audience data by half-hour or quarter-hour segments.

***VIRGINIAN, THE* ▶** popular Western based on Owen Wister's classic novel, which was one of the first TV series in the 90-minute form. Produced by Universal for NBC, it ran for eight seasons (1962-70) and featured James Drury as the Virginian, Doug McClure as Trampas, Lee J. Cobb as Judge Henry Garth (who owned the Shiloh Ranch, where the action took place) and Pippa Scott as Molly Wood. Cobb was replaced by Charles Bickford (as John Grainger, new owner of the Shiloh Ranch) and then by John McIntire (as Clay Grainger, the ranch's third owner). In its final season, the series took the title of *The Men from Shiloh* and added Stewart Granger (as yet another Shiloh owner, Colonel Alan MacKenzie) and Lee Majors (as Roy Tate) to the principal cast.

VISION ON ▶ pantomime series produced by BBC-TV in the early 1970s, which was developed with the hearing-impaired child as its prime target, although it proved popular with children of normal hearing as well. Three sets of the half-hour series were produced, totaling 74 episodes, which were syndicated to commercial stations in the U.S. by Time-Life Films. *Vision On* won a Prix Jeunesse as "best children's program in the world." The series, which combined live performances with animation sequences by Tony Hart, was carried by the ABC-owned stations and other groups, such as Post-Newsweek, Capital Cities, Cox and Storer.

VISIONS ▶ series of original TV dramas by new American playwrights introduced by PBS in the fall of 1976 on grants totaling $7 million from the Ford Foundation, the National Endowment for the Arts and the Corporation for Public Broadcasting. The two-year series was created in hopes of revitalizing TV playwrighting, with the additional purpose of bringing new ideas and new creative talent into the medium. With Barbara Schultz (former executive producer of *CBS Playhouse*) as artistic director, the 14 plays for the first season—each running about 90 minutes—were produced on budgets averaging $210,000 per show at the studios of KCET Los Angeles.

VISNEWS ▶ London-based supplier of international news footage to the television industry, founded in 1957 as an internationally held trust and now owned by a consortium of the BBC, Reuters and NBC. Visnews has a permanent satellite link using a Eutelsat transponder and a dedicated earth station at its London headquarters. It also has permanent uplink facilities in Paris, Rome and Berlin. Visnews claims to have more than 400 broadcasters as clients, each of which has access to about 50 news stories daily, each averaging about 90 seconds in length. Visnews has offices, journalists and camera crews throughout the world to carry out the news gathering. The managing director is Julian Kerr.

VOICE OF FIRESTONE ▶ long-running classical music series in prime time (1949-63) sponsored by Firestone Tire and Rubber Co. after 21 years on radio, with Howard Barlow as conductor of the orchestra. Regular vocalists over the years included Thomas L. Thomas and Vivienne della Chiesa, with John Daly as host. The weekly hour began on NBC and in 1954 switched to ABC. Although the size of the TV audience satisfied the sponsor, the program was dropped from the schedule because its comparatively low ratings were felt to have diminished the audience for adjacent shows.

VON ZERNECK-SERTNER FILMS ▶ production company very active on the TV movie front. Its credits include the four-hour *The Big One: The Great Los Angeles Earthquake* as well as *Opposites Attract, Gore Vidal's "Billy the Kid," Hostage Flight, Final Jeopardy, Too Young to Die, Lady Mobster* and *Menu for Murder.* Frank Von Zerneck and Robert Sertner are the partners.

VOYAGE TO THE BOTTOM OF THE SEA ▶ hour-long science fiction series based on the hit motion picture. It had a moderately successful run on ABC (1964-68). Richard Basehart and David Hedison were the leads, portraying Admiral Harriman Nelson and Captain Lee Crane, and Terry Becker portrayed CPO Sharkey, Bob Dowdell played Lieutenant Commander Chip Morrow, Henry Kulky was CPO Curley Jones, Del Monroe portrayed Kowalski and Paul Trinka was Patterson. It was produced by 20th Century-Fox in association with Irwin Allen Productions.

W

WACKIEST SHIP IN THE ARMY, THE ▶ comedy series in the World War II motif that was based on a popular 1960 motion picture of that title. Premiering on NBC in the fall of 1965, it lasted 29 weeks. Heading the cast of the Screen Gems series were Jack Warden as Major Simon Butcher, Gary Collins as Lieutenant Rip Riddle and Mike Kellin as Chief Miller.

WADSWORTH, JAMES T. ▶ FCC commissioner (1965-69), a New York Republican who considered himself moderate-to-liberal and who voted against the Boston *Herald-Traveler* in the WHDH license case but for the renewal of WLBT in Jackson, Miss., a vote later overturned by the D.C. Court of Appeals. Prior to joining the commission he was a member of the New York state legislature and worked in the Federal Government for agencies concerned with international relations.

WAGNER, ALAN ▶ independent producer who in December 1990 formed Boardwalk Entertainment with Fred Tarter. Wagner had been a New York-based program executive with CBS for 21 years, then became the first president and CEO of The Disney Channel, and in 1985 became executive vice president of Grosso-Jacobson Entertainment. There he became involved with such international coproductions as *Diamonds, Counterstrike* and *The Gunfighters,* and with the network series *Top Cops,* on which Wagner continues to serve as supervising producer. Tarter, an enterpreneur in the film business, is chairman of Boardwalk Entertainment, and Wagner is president.

Wagner started with CBS in 1961 after four years in the network program department of Benton & Bowles Advertising. Earlier, he had a brief career as a standup comedian, the highlight of which was a performance on *The Ed Sullivan Show* in 1956. At CBS he held a variety of programming positions, the last of them v.p. for entertainment programs from New York and Europe. He left in 1982 to work on the start-up of the Disney Channel, and while he helped launch it successfully his tenure as president of the venture was fairly brief. He started his own company, which later became associated with Grosso-Jacobson.

WAGNER, LINDSAY ▶ actress best known as the star of *The Bionic Woman* (1976-78), a role inspired by a guest shot on *The Six Million Dollar Man* in 1975. Since the early 1970s she has appeared on television frequently in a wide range of series, made-for-TV movies and miniseries, including *Scruples* (1980) and *Princess Daisy* (1983). Her other regular series—*Jessie* (1984), in which she played a police psychiatrist, and *A Peaceable Kingdom* (1989), in which she portrayed a zoo manager—survived only one season.

WAGNER, ROBERT ▶ former movie actor frequently cast in dramatic TV series calling for a suave and sophisticated lead. From the late 1960s, when he starred with Fred Astaire in *It Takes a Thief,* he has had starring roles in five series. His biggest success was *Hart to Hart* (1979-84). The others were *Switch* (1975-78), *Pearl* (1978) and *Lime Street* (1985).

A scene from the popular western series *Wagon Train*

***WAGON TRAIN* ▶** successful dramatic western series about families moving to settle the new frontier. It began on NBC in one-hour form (1957-61) and switched to ABC in a 90-minute format (1962). The following year it returned to the hour format, and its reruns were stripped during the daytime by ABC. Produced by Universal TV, it originally had starred Ward Bond and Robert Horton as the wagon train scouts, Major Seth Adams and Flint McCullough. They were replaced in the later version by John McIntire and Robert Fuller, as Chris Hale and Cooper.

***WAIT TILL YOUR FATHER GETS HOME* ▶** animated comedy series produced by Hanna-Barbera for prime-access syndication (1972-74) with characters suggestive of *All in the Family* and dealing primarily with the generation gap. It drew moderate ratings. The voices were by Tom Bosley (as Harry Boyle), Joan Gerber (Harry's wife, Irma), Tina Holland (their daughter, Alice), David Hayward (their son, Chet), Jackie Haley (their son, Jamie) and Jack Burns (their neighbor, Ralph).

Richard C. Wald

WALD, RICHARD C. ▶ a key ABC News executive since 1978 who has held high positions in both print and broadcast journalism. A former president of NBC News, he was hired by Roone Arledge, president of ABC News, as senior vice president over all hard-news operations. His position has since expanded to supervision of all news programming.

Wald started his journalism career in 1951 with the *New York Herald-Tribune,* where he rose through the editorial ranks to become managing editor and then executive vice president of the parent Whitney Communications. When the *Herald-Tribune* folded, Wald was hired by NBC News and was named president of the divison in 1973. He left four years later after a clash with NBC president Herb Schlosser and joined Times Mirror Corp. as assistant to the chairman. Then he was hired by Arledge, a former classmate at the Columbia Graduate School of Journalism, and was instrumental in stabilizing what had been a somewhat unruly organization and in establishing ABC's credibility in news.

WALKER, NANCY ▶ during 1976 and 1977, a popular TV comedienne in search of a vehicle. Under contract to ABC, she opened the fall season in 1976 in *The Nancy Walker Show,* a situation comedy produced by Norman Lear's T.A.T. Productions, in which she portrayed a Hollywood talent agent. When that series showed scant promise, ABC scuttled it and immediately found a new vehicle for her, *Blansky's Beauties,* via Garry Marshall's production organization at Paramount TV. In this, she played house mother to a group of Las Vegas chorines and was teamed with Roz Kelly, the young actress who had scored a hit in a guest role on *Happy Days* as Pinky Tuscadero, a momentary sweetheart of the Fonz.

Blansky's entered the ABC schedule as a January replacement. Thus, Walker, who had never before starred in a TV series, became one of few performers to venture two series in a single season.

Although she had extensive stage and screen credits, the diminutive actress came into prominence on TV late in her career, first in commercials for Bounty Towels and then as the mother in the *Rhoda* series and concurrently in a regular featured role in *MacMillan and Wife.* She returned to *Rhoda* when both her ABC series failed. Walker became a regular on the sitcom *True Colors* in 1990.

WALKER, PAUL A. (d. 1965) ▶ one of the most distinguished members of the FCC who served 19 years (1934-53), the last 14 months of that long term as chairman. A lawyer who had a brief fling with politics in his native Oklahoma and then became a member of the state utilities commission, he was appointed to the FCC by President Roosevelt just after the agency was formed. Walker worked toward regulating monopolistic practices in broadcasting and network control over station programming, and he led the hearings on the FCC proposals for a new table of allocations during the license freeze. He also supported the adoption of the 1946 Blue Book, which attempted to set minimum public interest standards for broadcast licensees.

In February 1952, at the age of 71, he was finally appointed chairman by President Truman and presided over the commission during the frenetic period when the freeze was lifted and applications had to be processed. Walker lost the chairmanship to Rosel Hyde after the election of President Eisenhower, and he retired in 1953 to Oklahoma.

WALL, CAROLYN ▶ vice president and general manager of Fox-owned WNYW-TV in New York since 1987, one of the few women to hold the top position at a television station. She came to the job from a post at the Murdoch magazine group without any previous television experience, but she proved herself an able TV executive. She organized a strong local news staff, improved local sales and also helped develop *Good Day New York,* a morning program that frequently outperforms its network station competitors in the ratings.

WALL STREET WEEK ▶ weekly 30-minute series on PBS concerned with issues and trends in business and finance and featuring interviews with stock market experts. The series, created by Anne Truex Darlington, began in January 1972 and has been hosted by Louis Rukeyser, former financial correspondent for ABC News. It originates in Owings Mills, Maryland, and is produced by Maryland Public Television with John Davis as executive producer.

WALLACE, CHRIS ▶ chief correspondent for ABC News' *PrimeTime Live* since the series premiered in August 1989. With an aggressive on-camera style suggesting the influence of his famous father, *60 Minutes* co-editor Mike Wallace, the younger Wallace has contributed important investigative reports to the ABC news magazine. Among them: a report on phony abortion clinics run by anti-abortion forces, the Defense Department's public auction of toxic waste, corruption and abuse of power in the Internal Revenue Service, and the intolerable conditions uncovered in homes for the elderly and disabled in Texas.

Wallace came to ABC News from NBC News, where he served as the network's chief White House correspondent from 1982, anchor of *Meet the Press* from 1987, anchor of the Sunday edition of *NBC Nightly News,* and briefly, in 1982, co-anchor of the *Today* show. He covered the presidential campaigns in 1980, 1984, and 1988 and was floor correspondent for NBC News' coverage of the Republican and Democratic national conventions in those years. He joined NBC as a reporter for WNBC-TV New York and later headed its investigative unit.

Mike Wallace

WALLACE, MIKE ▶ co-editor of CBS News's *60 Minutes* since its premiere on September 24, 1968. His no-holds-barred interviewing technique and scrappy, enterprising reporting are personal hallmarks. His often timely, and frequently irreverent, interviews have been with subjects who comprise a virtual *Who's Who* of newsmakers: every American President from

John F. Kennedy to George Bush; world leaders for better or worse, including the Ayatollah Khomeini, Deng Xiaoping, Manuel Noriega, Menachem Begin, Anwar el-Sadat, Yasir Arafat, the Shah of Iran, King Hussein, Muammar Qaddafi, Hafez Assad; and, closer to home, such artists as Vladimir Horowitz, Itzhak Perlman, Mikhail Baryshnikov and Leonard Bernstein.

Wallace joined CBS in 1951, leaving the network in 1955 and returning in 1963, when he was named a CBS News correspondent. He reported from Vietnam several times between 1967-71.

Wallace's experience as a journalist dates back to the 1940s, when he worked for the old *Chicago Sun*. After serving as a naval communications officer during World War II, he became a news reporter for Chicago station WMAQ. He became prominent in television initially as a quiz-show host (*The $100,000 Big Surprise*) and game-show panelist (*Who Pays?*).

He returned to journalism as the persistent, hard-boiled interviewer on *Night Beat*, produced by Ted Yates for the old DuMont Television Network, based in New York during 1956-57, and *The Mike Wallace Interview* on ABC, 1957-60. His probing style—a marked departure from the blandly cordial TV interviewers of that era—became widely imitated and has had a lasting influence on TV journalism.

Three books bear his name as author: *Mike Wallace Asks*, a compilation of interviews from *Night Beat;The Mike Wallace Interview* in 1958; and his memoir *Close Encounter*, written with Gary Paul Gates.

WALLIS, W. ALLEN ▶ chancellor of the University of Rochester who became chairman of the Corporation for Public Broadcasting in March 1977 and quit abruptly, without explanation, in July 1978. He had been appointed to the CPB board, as a political independent, by President Ford in 1975. Wallis served on numerous boards and government commissions and for a time had been a special assistant to President Eisenhower.

WALSH, BILL (d. 1975) ▶ producer for Walt Disney. In TV he was co-producer of Disney's first Christmas special in 1950 and producer of *The Mickey Mouse Club* and the *Davy Crockett* series in the Disney anthology.

WALT DISNEY CO. ▶ multi-faceted entertainment company which, after a long period of doldrums, was revitalized in the 1980s to attain the stature of a major Hollywood studio. The company had flourished during the lifetime of its founder, the famed animator, but hit the doldrums after his death. Its fortunes changed with the arrival of Michael Eisner, former head of Paramount Studios, as new chairman in 1984. Recognizing that the Disney name was not to be associated with anything but family entertainment, but aware too that the modern market has a limited appetite for G-rated fare, Eisner created two other brand names within the company, Touchstone Pictures and Hollywood Pictures, under which somewhat racier movies and TV programs could be released.

Disney went from last place in theatrical box-office receipts in 1984 to first place in 1988 and 1989 with such hit films as *Down and Out in Beverly Hills* and *Who Framed Roger Rabbit*. Before Eisner's arrival, the company in 1983 had entered the pay-cable field with The Disney Channel, an enterprise whose success, along with that of the Disney theme parks, added to the company's momentum. Under Eisner the company resumed production of full-length animated features and enjoyed enormous revenues from strategic re-releases of the Disney motion picture classics and the release of certain lesser titles to the retail market through its Buena Vista Home Video subsidiary.

The Disney company in the late 1980s became an active supplier to television again, an area in which it had faltered when the long-running *Wonderful World of Disney* came to an end. Under its adult Touchstone label, it had one of the big prime-time hits of the 1980s with *The Golden Girls* on NBC. It was followed by *Empty Nest*, *Nurses* and *Pacific Station*, all on NBC. Disney's syndication company, Buena Vista TV, has had success with a two-hour block of animated children's shows, *DuckTales*, *Gummy Bears*, *Tailspin* and *Chip 'n Dale's Rescue Rangers*. It also syndicates *Siskel and Ebert* and reruns of *The Wonderful World of Disney*. An attempt to revive that series on the networks brought forth *The Disney Sunday Movie* on ABC in 1986. In 1988 it switched to NBC as *The Magical World of Disney*, but it failed to catch on.

In 1987 Disney made its first acquisition of a TV station, purchasing the Los Angeles independent KHJ from RKO General for $324 million. The company has an equity stake in Sunrise, the British company that won the U.K.'s breakfast television franchise in 1991. It was the only American company to emerge with a winner in the British franchise auctions.

WALTERS, BARBARA ▶ first female anchor on a network newscast and, at the time, the highest-paid news performer in television, achieving both distinctions in 1976 when ABC wooed her away from NBC with a five-year contract guaranteeing $1 million a year. After a controversial and generally unsuccessful stint as co-anchor with Harry Reasoner on *The ABC Evening News,* Walters moved to ABC's *20/20,* first as a correspondent, then in 1984 as co-host with Hugh Downs. Her occasional *Barbara Walters Specials* for ABC have established her reputation as one of television's most skillful interviewers. Her subjects, ranging from heads of state to Hollywood stars, have included every U.S. president since Richard Nixon and such world leaders as the Shah of Iran, Fidel Castro, Margaret Thatcher, Muommar Qadaffi, Boris Yeltsin and Menachem Begin.

Barbara Walters

Walters began her broadcasting career with NBC as a staff writer on the early-morning *Today* show. In 1964, while *Today* was in search of a regular female cast member, she was given the assignment on a trial basis and won the spot permanently with an aggressive, intelligent performance. She was elevated to co-host with Jim Hartz in April 1974. With the death of Aline Saarinen in 1971, Walters took over the syndicated program *For Women Only* (later retitled *Not for Women Only*), and continued as daily host until the fall of 1975 when, to reduce her workload, she alternated weeks on the show with Hugh Downs. She also did reporting assignments for NBC News and hosted several prime-time specials.

Walters became a star in the medium despite a speech fault that turned "r" into "w" and despite the relatively low visibility of early-morning broadcasts. She did, however, gain more prominent exposure in covering certain major events, such as President Nixon's first visit to the People's Republic of China, and in substituting occasionally for Johnny Carson on *Tonight.*

ABC's offer of $1 million a year, and NBC's counter-offer at a similar fee, was front-page news around the country in the spring of 1976. Walters accepted the ABC offer because it involved the co-anchoring with Harry Reasoner of the evening newscast; NBC was not prepared to give her such an assignment. Although she accepted the offer in April, her contract with NBC did not permit her to join ABC until September. The contract also called for a number of prime-time interview specials for ABC. On the first of them, Walters interviewed President and Mrs. Carter.

Walters is the daughter of the late Lou Walters, a show-business impresario who for many years operated the Latin Quarter in New York.

***WALTONS, THE* ▶** highly popular CBS dramatic series concerning the struggles of a large, close-knit family in Appalachia during the Depression. Drawn from an autobiographical TV special, *The Homecoming,* by Earl Hamner Jr., the series premiered in 1972 in a time period considered hopeless—that opposite *The Flip Wilson Show* on NBC, then one of the medium's big hits. After a slow start, *The Waltons* eventually conquered Wilson and ruled the time period for several years.

The series featured Richard Thomas as the oldest child, John (John-Boy) Walton Jr. (he left the cast in 1977, four years before the series ended), and Michael Learned and Ralph Waite as the parents, Olivia and John Walton. Will Geer played the grandfather, Zeb Walton, until his death in 1978, and Ellen Corby played the grandmother, Esther Walton. The children were played by Jon Walmsley as Jason, Judy Norton as Mary Ellen, Eric Scott as Ben, Mary Elizabeth McDonough as Erin, David S. Harper as James Robert (Jim-Bob) and Kami Cotler as Elizabeth. Featured were Helen Kleeb and Mary Jackson as moonshine-brewing spinsters Mamie and Emily Baldwin, Joe Conley and Ronnie Claire Edwards as storeowners Ike and Cora Beth Godsey, Rachel Longaker as the Godsey's adopted daughter Aimee, John Crawford as Sheriff Ep Bridges, Mariclare Costello as schoolteacher Emily Hunter and John Ritter as the Reverend Fordwick, who married Emily. It was via Lee Rich's Lorimar Productions.

WANTED: DEAD OR ALIVE ▶ western series that propelled Steve McQueen to stardom, playing bounty hunter Josh Randall. It played on CBS (1958-61) via Four Star-Malcolm Productions.

WAR AND REMEMBRANCE ▶ hugely expensive ABC mini-series, a 29-hour sequel to *Winds of War*, based on a novel by Herman Wouk. It was televised over six nights in November 1988 and three in May 1989. Like its predecessor, it was produced and directed by Dan Curtis. Reportedly it cost $100 million.

The 12-part mini-series picks up the story of a fictional Navy family one week after Pearl Harbor and follows the various members through such events as the Battle of Midway, Guadalcanal, Yalta, the assassination attempt on Hitler by his senior officers, the D-Day invasion at Normandy, the Battle of the Bulge, Leyte Gulf, Iwo Jima, and the explosion of the first atomic bomb. The historical drama was shot on location in 11 countries. It starred Robert Mitchum and Jane Seymour, with a supporting cast of Hart Bochner, Victoria Tennant, Polly Bergen, David Dukes, Michael Woods, Sharon Stone, Robert Morley, Barry Bostwick, Ralph Bellamy, Sir John Gielgud, Peter Graves, Barry Morse and Howard Duff, among others. Curtis, Wouk and Earl Wallace wrote the screenplay.

WARD, JAY (d. 1989) ▶ an early producer of animation expressly for television and creator of *Crusader Rabbit* for ABC in 1949 and *Rocky and His Friends* (later called *The Bullwinkle Show*) for ABC in 1959. Ward had a penchant for puns and word play, but also for political and social satire. *Rocky and His Friends,* which featured Rocky (a flying squirrel, more properly known as Rocket J. Squirrel) and Bullwinkle (his friend, a moose), while ostensibly aimed at children, was laced with political references and on another level could be watched as well by adults. Indeed, when the program's original child generation grew up, many of its members took such delight in the throwaway lines they had missed as kids that they followed the old reruns of the cartoons in cult fashion.

Ward became a creator of TV cartoons literally by accident. He was a graduate of Harvard Business School with a real estate company of his own when he was injured by a truck that had lost its brakes and crashed into his office. While recuperating, he created the character Crusader Rabbit with a friend and decided to try selling it to television. Its acceptance led to the founding of Jay Ward Productions in Los Angeles. *Rocky and His Friends* started on ABC in 1959 and two years later moved to NBC, where it played through 1964. It then returned to ABC and ran until 1973. NBC revived it in the 1981-82 season.

WAREHOUSING ▶ the networks' tactic of purchasing movies from studios with exclusivity provisions in the contracts that effectively barred the films from pay cable, or that diminished the period of time they were available to pay cable under the FCC's original rules. (Those rules had permitted pay cable to use a movie only within the first two years of its theatrical release; later that was increased to three years.) The rules and the practice of warehousing were knocked out by a D.C. Court of Appeals ruling in 1977 that held the restrictions on pay cable to be unconstitutional.

WARREN, ALBERT ▶ owner of Warren Publishing Co., the respected Washington-based publisher of leading industry newsletters, among them *Communications Daily, Television Digest, Public Broadcasting Report, Satellite Week* and *Video Week.* In addition, the company publishes the annual *Television and Cable Factbook.* Since the newsletters are supported by subscriptions alone, they tend not to be compromised in the way of other trades by concessions to advertisers.

Warren has covered television from its very beginnings as a commercial, mass-audience medium. After serving in the Navy in World War II, he joined *Television Digest* as a reporter in December 1945 and rose to top editorial posts. In 1961 he acquired the newsletter and has served as its editor and publisher since. From it he spun off the other publications, taking a big risk in the early 1980s by creating a daily covering all aspects of television, telecommunications and space, with a particular focus on matters affecting those industries in Washington. His timing was right, and *Communications Daily* caught on.

WASHBURN, ABBOTT M. ▶ former FCC commissioner appointed by President Nixon in 1974 for a two-year term in a Republican seat. After establishing a special concern about television for children, Washburn was reappointed to a seven-year term in 1976. Prior to joining the commission, Washburn had headed the department of public services for General Mills. Earlier he was deputy director of the United States Information Agency (USIA; 1953-61) and had served with Radio Free Europe (1950-51).

After leaving the commission in 1982, Washburn became the ambassador to the International Telecommunications Union Radio Conference. In 1984 he became a consultant for the State Department.

WASHINGTON: BEHIND CLOSED DOORS ▶ 12-hour serialized drama, based in part on John Erlichman's novel *The Company,* presented on ABC-TV on six consecutive nights, Sept. 6-11, to open the 1977-78 season. The program, about corruption spawned in the pursuit of political power, was fiction with thinly disguised characters from the Nixon Administration. The fictive president, Richard Monckton, was played by Jason Robards. Other principals in the cast were John Houseman, Cliff Robertson, Harold Gould, Robert Vaughn, Andy Griffith and Stefanie Powers.

David W. Rintels was the creator, and also cowriter with Eric Bercovici, of the opening and closing episodes. Bercovici wrote the episodes between. Stanley Kallis was executive producer for Paramount Television, Norman Powell was producer and Gary Nelson director.

WASHINGTON WEEK IN REVIEW ▶ long-running PBS series (since February 1967) on which a panel of journalists examine and comment upon recent developments in the capital. Produced by WETA Washington, the half-hour series has regularly featured such print media correspondents as Peter Lisagor (d. 1977), Elizabeth Drew, Hedrick Smith, Charles Corddry, Neil McNeil, Jack Nelson, Haynes Johnson and George Anne Geyer, with Paul Duke as moderator.

WASILEWSKI, VINCENT T. ▶ former president of the National Association of Broadcasters (1965-83), succeeding Gov. Leroy Collins, and in that capacity the leading spokesperson for the interests of the industry. Unlike Collins, whose attempts to inspire broadcasters to greater achievement were controversial with station operators, Wasilewski, as a veteran of the NAB staff, understood the broadcast industry and how it wished to be represented in the capital.

He joined NAB in 1949 after receiving his law degree from the University of Illinois, became chief attorney in 1953, manager of government relations in 1955 and v.p. for government affairs in 1960. Wasilewski was serving as executive vice-president of the association when he was selected to be president. He was succeeded by Edward O. Fritts.

WASSERMAN, AL ▶ veteran independent documentary producer-director who worked for both CBS and NBC News. At CBS News, in his second stint there, he worked mainly on *60 Minutes,* contributing a number of investigative pieces and penetrating reports. Previously, at NBC News, he wrote and produced many of its *White Paper* documentaries, including the series' premiere broadcast, *The U-2 Affair.* Others included *Sit-In* and *Battle of Newburgh* (with Arthur Zegart).

Wasserman followed Irving Gitlin, who had been head of public affairs for CBS News, to NBC News in 1960. At NBC Gitlin developed the *White Paper* series and Wasserman figured importantly in that series. Earlier, at CBS, Wasserman produced such documentaries as *Out of Darkness, Hoffa and the Teamsters* and *Biography of a Cancer.*

WASSERMAN, DALE ▶ dramatist active in TV during the 1950s. His TV play *I, Don Quixote,* for the *DuPont Show of the Month* in 1959, led to the script for his best-known work, the stage musical *Man of La Mancha.* Among his other TV credits were *The Fog, The Power and the Glory* (starring Sir Laurence Olivier), *The Lincoln Murder Case, The Eichmann Story* and *The Stranger.*

WATERGATE ▶ a squalid episode in American history whose chapters unfolded for the entire nation on network television and whose developments dominated network news from early 1973 until President Nixon's resignation in August 1974. Although the heroic work in uncovering the story and bringing the scandal to light was done by the *Washington Post*'s Bob Woodward and Carl Bernstein, it was television—entering somewhat late, to be sure—that disseminated it nationally and illuminated the issues and the new disclosures for the citizenry.

Television itself became part of the fabric of the story as the medium for the President's speeches and news conferences, and as carrier of two extraordinary Congressional proceedings: the Senate Select Committee's inquiry into the role of the Nixon Administration in the Watergate break-in and subsequent cover-up (begun in the spring of 1973 and concluded in the fall) and the House Judiciary Committee's climactic debate on the impeachment of President Nixon (televised July 24-30, 1974).

If TV had a hero in the Watergate affair to compare with the *Washington Post* it was easily CBS News, which offered the most intrepid and intensive coverage, often to the despair of its affiliates who were either sympathetic to the President or still responsive to the Administration's admonitions that local broadcasters would be held responsible for what they carried of biased or nonobjective reporting by the networks. Indeed, it was CBS News that gave the *Post* the validating support it needed, at a critical time, when it devoted 23 minutes to a two-part report on *The CBS Evening News with Walter Cronkite* in October 1972 laying out, for the first time to a national audience, the Woodward and Bernstein disclosures. After this, CBS made its own contributions to the story through distinguished reporting by Dan Rather, Daniel Schorr, Fred Graham, Roger Mudd and others.

As to the fears of local stations, they were heightened by the license challenges against two Florida TV stations—WJXT Jacksonville and WPLG Miami—in 1973. The challenging groups were identified as Nixon loyalists, in the main, and the stations in jeopardy were owned by Post-Newsweek, parent company of the *Washington Post.*

By far, the biggest television event of the period was the coverage by all three networks and PBS of the Senate Watergate Hearings, which introduced Americans to the full cast of characters in the running story and produced the bombshell, from Alexander Butterfield, that Nixon had made audio tape recordings of all conversations in the Oval Office. The tapes, when they were eventually surrendered by Nixon, paved the way for the impeachment proceedings.

For a total of 11 weeks during the spring, summer and fall of 1973 the Senate Watergate Hearings were a huge attraction on daytime TV and also reached large audiences at night in taped replays on PBS. Because of the length of hearings and the expense involved in presenting them, the coverage was rotated daily among the commercial networks.

The hearings began on May 17 and ran for 37 weekdays. They recessed for seven weeks and were resumed in the fall for 16 more days, ending on November 15. Another round was set for the following January, but it was canceled.

The almost 300 hours of rotated coverage by the three networks was estimated to have cost them a combined total of $10 million in lost advertising revenues and air time. Audience surveys found that 85% of the nation's households watched all or part of at least one of the sessions. CBS estimated that viewers spent 1.6 billion total home-hours watching the daytime coverage on the three networks and an additional 400 million home-hours watching at night on PBS. Public television stations, meanwhile, enjoyed a financial windfall from their twice-a-day coverage. Viewers responding to the PTV appeals for new subscribers made contributions of more than $1.5 million, which was taken as a show of appreciation for the nighttime repeats.

While normally the preemption of daytime soap operas and game shows produces a flood of angry mail from viewers, in the case of Watergate the mail to the networks was overwhelmingly in favor of the preemptions.

On May 9, 1974, the House Judiciary Committee began its debate on the possible impeachment of President Nixon. Only 18 minutes of the opening session was allowed to be televised. For the next 11 weeks the meetings were closed to all outsiders, but after numerous disturbing leaks they were opened to broadcast on July 24. The networks again covered on a rotating basis, and PBS again carried nighttime repeats as well as the live daytime coverage. The committee's deliberations were on the air for six days—a total of 46 hours of coverage.

When the hearings ended on July 30, three articles of impeachment had been voted against the President. They were to be presented before the full House on August 19. The House voted to permit TV coverage of the floor debate, and the Senate was expected to do the same, but it was all academic. On August 8, Nixon went on the air to announce his resignation. That speech, running 16 minutes, was watched by 110 million people, more than had watched any Presidential speech in history and was exceeded only by the TV audience for the first walk on the moon.

Watergate served to raise the prestige of television and, more importantly, restored the credibility of American journalism, which had been under severe attack by the Nixon Administration even before the scandal developed. The ratings for network news grew steadily as the Watergate story unfolded, the evening newscasts gaining more than two million additional viewers a night during the first year. Watergate also stimulated a new interest in investigative reporting at broadcast stations and was the spur for the reentry of ABC News in the field of investigative documentaries with the monthly series *ABC Close-Up.*

WATSON, ARTHUR (d. 1991) ▶ former president of NBC Sports (1979-89) who distinguished himself as a negotiator for sports rights. Watson also knew when to say no, as in the 1989 Major League Baseball negotiations. Although NBC had carried baseball for 40 years, Watson refused to top the CBS bid of $1.06 billion, which he considered excessive and impractical. As it turns out, CBS has been losing significant amounts of money on its baseball coverage.

Watson was known as a crafty bargainer. For instance, he entered negotiations for the 1992 Olympic summer games indicating that NBC would not be a major contender, yet he walked out with rights for $401 million.

Watson joined NBC as an operations analyst in 1956 and served as general manager of NBC stations in New York, Philadelphia and Cleveland before being named executive vice president of the NBC-TV network in 1979, only five months before being appointed head of sports. He gave up that post in 1989 to become executive vice president in charge of sports rights negotiations. He is also credited with having brought Wimbledon and the French Open tennis tournaments as well as soccer's World Cup to NBC.

WATSON, GEORGE ▶ vice president and Washington bureau chief of ABC News, where he has worked since 1962, starting as an assignment editor. In 1965 he became a television correspondent and soon after was sent to Moscow as bureau chief. He then went to Southeast Asia, where he covered some of the heaviest fighting of the Vietnam War. Following this, he was made London bureau chief (1970-75) and then White House correspondent (1975-80) and Washington bureau chief (1985).

Beginning in 1981, he was responsible for the policies, standards and practices that apply to all news programs. During this period he developed and produced *Viewpoint,* an ombudsman-like program that was a forum for viewer criticism.

In 1980, Watson left ABC for a one-year stint at CNN, where he helped founding president Reese Schonfeld develop the network. Watson began his journalism career as a reporter for the *Washington Post* and the *Detroit News.*

WATSON, PATRICK ▶ noted Canadian journalist and filmmaker who, in a surprising move by the Canadian Broadcasting Corp. board, was named chairman of the CBC in 1989. His selection was widely applauded. Previously he was associated with the famed current affairs series *This Hour Has Seven Days* (1964-66), which many believe was the prototype for CBS's *60 Minutes.* In 1989 he produced the celebrated documentary series, *The Struggle for Democracy,* based on his own book of that title. He also wrote a number of other journalistic books and in 1983 adapted *The Book of Job* for the stage as a one-person play. He formed his own TV production company in 1984, Democracy Films, which he operated until his appointment to the CBC. In 1981 he was made an Officer of the Order of Canada, the highest honor Canada can bestow upon a citizen.

WAY IT WAS, THE ▶ sports retrospective series on PBS (1974-76) involving film of memorable sports events followed by a studio discussion with athletes who took part in those events. Curt Gowdy was host. The series was underwritten by Mobil Oil and produced by Gerry Gross Productions at KCET Los Angeles, in association with Syndicast Services.

WBBM "POT PARTY" INCIDENT ▶ a 1967 controversy focusing on the issues of "news staging" and deception of the public, growing out of a two-part documentary by WBBM-TV Chicago entitled *Pot Party at a University* (Nov. 1 and 2, 1967). Presented as an investigative report on the pervasiveness of marijuana use on college campuses, the film covered an actual marijuana party of Northwestern University students at a campus rooming house. Northwestern filed a complaint with the FCC, charging news staging, on the ground that a reporter for the station had arranged for the party to be held so that he could film it.

The FCC ruled that it was an authentic party, not one staged by actors but involving regular marijuana smokers gathered in an apartment where similar pot parties had been given. However, the FCC reprimanded WBBM-TV on two counts: first for representing itself to the public as having been invited to the party when in fact it had induced the party, therefore misleading its audience; and second for having induced the commission of a crime, the smoking of marijuana. "The licensee has to be law-abiding," the commission said.

WEATHER CHANNEL, THE ▶ basic-cable network devoted to weather reports that received a gloomy forecast from cable industry leaders when it launched in 1982 but has proved a surprising success. The channel is widely accepted by cable systems and reaches 49 million households. It claims a cumulative weekly audience of 25 million viewers for its single-topic programming. The creation of Landmark Communications based in Norfolk, Virginia, the network has carved out a unique service niche as television's 24-hour local and national weather forecaster. Its viewership runs especially high in times of hurricanes, blizzards and national meteorological disasters. Michael J. Eckert is CEO and Paul A. FitzPatrick president and chief operating officer.

WEAVER, SYLVESTER L. (PAT), JR. ▶ one of television's most creative executives, whose relatively brief term as president of the National Broadcasting Co. (Dec. 4, 1953-Dec. 7, 1955) was marked by innovation and a profound understanding of the new medium's natural program forms. He is the acknowledged father of the TV talk show—the desk-and-sofa format represented by the programs he created, *Today, Home* and *Tonight*—and of the "spectacular," now more modestly called the special. Weaver was also responsible for the *Wide Wide World* concept. Dave Garroway, Steve Allen and Arlene Francis were among those caught by Weaver's keen eye for talent.

Weaver was elevated to chairman of NBC in 1955, but he resigned a year later in a dispute with management of the parent company, RCA. Meanwhile, he developed program executives such as Richard A.R. Pinkham, Mort Werner and Michael H. Dann, who were later to become the program chiefs of NBC and CBS. On leaving NBC, Weaver formed his own broadcast company and then became an advertising executive with McCann-Erickson.

From 1963-1966, he headed Subscription Television Inc., the company that attempted to wire Los Angeles and San Francisco for pay TV but was demolished by a well-organized campaign of theater owners and commercial broadcasters. Although STV finally established in the courts its right to promote pay TV, its funds were dissipated by the time the court handed down its decision. After a brief fling with drawing program proposals for a proposed fourth network that never came to pass, Weaver returned to the advertising field as consultant to the Wells, Rich, Greene agency.

He had joined NBC in 1949 as head of its new television operations after two decades in broadcasting and advertising. He had been a writer-producer for CBS and the Don Lee radio network in the 1930s, and in the 1940s he was advertising manager for American Tobacco and v.p. of radio-TV for Young & Rubicam Advertising. His daughter is the actress Sigourney Weaver.

WEBB, JACK (d. 1982) ▶ enormously successful TV producer, after a career as a popular actor (in the 1952 *Dragnet,* which he also directed). He formed an independent production company, Mark VII Ltd., and had a string of hits, including *Dragnet* (a revival), *Adam-12* and *Emergency.* Other series by Webb were *The D.A., The Rangers, O'Hara, U.S. Treasury, Hec Ramsey* and *Mobile One.*

Webb's patented style, carried over from *Dragnet* (which began on radio), was to play down the melodramatic glamour of the perilous assignments of his protagonists and to give their execution an all-in-a-day's-work flavor. The shows seemed more realistic and authentic than most others of the genre, but the heroes were no less heroic.

WEBSTER ▶ successful ABC half-hour sitcom (1983-87) built upon the appeal of black child actor Emmanuel Lewis. In the title role, Lewis played an orphan who moves in with his white godfather (ex-football star Alex Karras) and his wife (Susan Clark). Lewis was discovered in a Burger King ad by a network executive, who then had a show built around him. It was produced by Paramount TV.

WEBSTER, EDWARD MOUNT, COMMODORE (d. 1976) ▶ FCC commissioner (1947-56). He had joined in 1934 as assistant chief engineer and remained on staff until his appointment as commissioner by President Truman. He received his military title with the U.S. Coast Guard, serving as chief communications officer.

WEBSTER, NICHOLAS ▶ director active in documentaries and prime-time entertainment series. With the Wolper organization he directed *Showdown at O.K. Corral* and *The Last Days of John Dillinger* in docu-drama form for the CBS *Appointment with Destiny* series. His documentaries included *The Long Childhood of Timmy, Walk in My Shoes* and *The Violent World of Sam Huff.* He also directed episodes of *The Waltons, The FBI, Big Valley, Dan August, Get Smart* and *East Side, West Side.*

WEEKEND ▶ monthly 90-minute latenight news magazine introduced by NBC in 1974 to alternate with rock concerts and the then-experimental comedy series *Saturday Night Live* at 11:30 p.m. on Saturdays. As an attempt by NBC to stay even with CBS News with its popular *60 Minutes* news magazine, *Weekend* adapted to its inferior time period by putting its accent on nonfiction of particular interest to youth. *Weekend,* whose progenitors were *First Tuesday* and *Chronolog,* was developed by Reuven Frank, senior producer for NBC News, shortly after he stepped down as president of the division. Producers of the program's segments included Bill Brown, William B. Hill, Peter Jeffries, Clare Crawford, James Gannon, Karen Lerner, Sy Pearlman, Anthony Potter and Craig Leake. Gerald Polikoff was the director.

WEINBERGER-DANIELS ▶ writing-producing team of Ed. Weinberger and Stan Daniels, whose credits include producing *The Mary Tyler Moore Show* and *Phyllis.* Weinberger alone went on to become executive producer of *Dear John* and co-writer of the pilot for *The Cosby Show.*

WEINRIB, LEONARD ▶ writer and director who wrote all the scripts for NBC's children's shows *H.R. Pufnstuf* and *Dr. Doolittle.* He also wrote episodes of *All in the Family; Love, American Style* and other prime-time series.

WEISWASSER, STEPHEN ▶ executive vice president of ABC News, appointed in October 1991 although he had had no previous experience in journalism. He was highly regarded by the top management of Capital Cities/ABC Inc. from the time he served as general counsel to the corporation, and he was known to be groomed for a key position in the company. He moved to the news division from the ABC television network, where he held the same title, executive vice president—in both situations, second in command.

At ABC News, Weiswasser is in charge of managing the day-to-day operations of the division and administering its budget, under the leadership of Roone Arledge. The post was previously held by David Burke, before he was hired away in 1988 to head CBS News. In the interval, those managerial duties were added responsibilities for two vice presidents, Richard Wald and Joanna Bistany.

Weiswasser is by no means the first to hold so high a position in network news without a practical background in the field. His predecessor, Burke, came from a position in state government, by way of Wall Street. His boss, Arledge, came from production and ABC Sports. Lawrence Grossman became president of NBC News after having been president of PBS, with a background in advertising. But Weiswasser's credentials most resemble those of Richard Salant, who, like himself, had been a lawyer and had been picked as a comer by corporate management when he was named president of CBS News.

***WELCOME BACK, KOTTER* ▶** successful ABC situation comedy (1975-79) that sprang John Travolta to stardom, although it was created as a vehicle for comedian Gabriel Kaplan. Kaplan played a young teacher, Gabe Kotter, assigned to the Brooklyn high school from which he had graduated, but the series derived much of its appeal from the group of obstreperous misfits in the class, who called themselves The Sweathogs. Travolta played one of them, Vinnie Barbarino, along with Ron Palillo as Arnold Horshack, Lawrence Hilton-Jacobs as Freddie (Boom-Boom) Washington, Robert Hegyes as Juan Epstein, Melonie Haller as Angie Globagoski and Stephen Shortridge as Beau De Labarre. Also featured were John Sylvester White as vice principal Michael Woodman and Marcia Strassman as Kotter's wife, Julie. Created by Kaplan and Alan Sacks, the series was produced by The Komack Co. and Wolper Productions.

WELLS, ROBERT ▶ FCC commissioner (1969-71) whose appointment had been controversial because he was, at the time, an active broadcaster in Kansas. Wells was at the center of an even stormier controversy in 1975 when President Ford had planned to nominate him as director of the Office of Telecommunications Policy. That prospect raised a furor among citizens groups, the cable industry and certain influential members of Congress because, on leaving the FCC, Wells had returned to his broadcast post and reacquired his minority interest in four radio stations owned by Harris Enterprises. Those who opposed his appointment argued that a commercial broadcaster could not be objective in assessing the country's communications priorities. Their efforts ended his candidacy for OTP. He became chairman of Broadcast Music Inc. in 1979.

WELPOTT, RAYMOND W. (d. 1973) ▶ president of the NBC-owned TV stations from 1965 until his retirement in 1971. He had been general manager of the NBC Philadelphia stations, WRCV-AM-TV, until they were moved to Cleveland in 1962. He then became v.p. of the stations division and spot sales, and three years later he was named president.

WENDKOS, PAUL ▶ director of such TV movies as *A Death of Innocence, The Woman I Love, Haunts of the Very Rich, Brotherhood of the Bell, The Family Rico* and *The Mephisto Waltz.*

WERNER, MORT ▶ program chief for NBC from 1961 to 1972. Earlier he had helped to develop *Today, Home* and *Tonight* for the network and became executive producer of all three. Werner joined NBC in 1951 after a varied show business career in which he had been a radio actor, band leader, singer and summer stock manager. In 1957 he left the network to become an executive of Kaiser Industries and later went with Young & Rubicam Advertising as director of radio and TV. NBC rehired him in 1961, and as head of programs he was responsible for such innovations as rotating series, 90-minute series and made-for-TV movies. In retirement, he moved to Mexico.

WERSHBA, JOSEPH ▶ former CBS News producer and reporter whose career spanned the noted *See It Now* documentaries of the early 1950s and the popular news-magazine of the mid-1970s, *60 Minutes.* He worked with Edward R. Murrow and Fred W. Friendly on such famed *See It Now* broadcasts as the expose on Sen. Joseph McCarthy, *Desegregation in North Carolina* and *The Milo Radulovich Story.* During the 1960s he became a producer of *CBS Reports.* Wershba joined CBS News in 1944 as a writer and later became news director of WCBS-TV and then a Washington correspondent. He was co-editor, with Don Hollenbeck, of the original *CBS Views the Press* and was also a reporter-director on the *Hear It Now* radio series that later became *See It Now.*

WESH-TV LICENSE RENEWAL CASE ▶ a precedent-setting case concerning the license renewal of a Daytona Beach, Fla., television station in a comparative proceeding with a challenging applicant. In the early 1970s, the FCC ruled, in the face of the challenge, that WESH-TV had provided sufficient service to the community, and it renewed the operating license of the station's owner, Cowles Communications Inc. But in September 1978, a three-judge panel of the Court of Appeals in Washington sent the case back to the FCC for further consideration, declaring that the incumbent operator would have to demonstrate a record of performance indicating its clear superiority to the competing applicant, Central Florida Enterprises Inc.

The full Court of Appeals subsequently denied the FCC's request for a review of the panel's decision but did eliminate the explicit requirement that the record of the station must be superior to assure renewal. Although the court clearly indicated that it objected to the "renewal expectancy" of most licensees, station operators were somewhat relieved that the language referring to superior performance was dropped.

The court had previously overruled the FCC in a landmark case when it denied the license renewal of WLBT Jackson, Miss., after various citizen groups appealed the case. The WESH-TV case, however, marked the first time that the court rejected the FCC's judgment in a license renewal proceeding involving a competing applicant.

When the case was reheard at the FCC, the commission came up with a new formulation designed to meet the court's objections. Under it, incumbents earn a renewal expectancy by demonstrating that their past records have been "substantial"—that is, "sound, favorable and substantially above a level of mediocre service which might just warrant renewal." The industry's fears were allayed in 1982 when the Court of Appeals upheld the revised standard, since it was recognized that it gave the FCC ample room to renew almost any license. This proved to be the case; and challenges ceased to be a serious threat.

In the decade that followed, the industry continued to lobby Congress for a more protective law, but these calls were increasingly ritualistic as it became clear that the WESH test was adequate, except for broadcasters already in regulatory hot water for other reasons.

WESTAR ▶ first domestic satellite in the U.S., launched by Western Union in April 1974, with a second craft, Westar 2, sent aloft in October of that year. Both were manufactured by Hughes Aircraft.

WESTERN ▶ a program type that for a decade had such a grip on the medium that no American would have predicted its virtual disappearance from the airwaves by 1975. The western in fact had been a TV staple from the earliest days of the medium. In the first wave were the horse operas of the movie matinee genre, low-budget formula fare aimed largely at the juvenile audience: Hopalong Cassidy, Gene Autry, Roy Rogers, The Lone Ranger and others. 1955 brought the second wave, the so-termed "adult western," typified by *Cheyenne, Gunsmoke, The Life and Times of Wyatt Earp* and *Tales of the Texas Rangers.* These not only dealt with hard-riding cowboys but also with social and philosophical themes, relatively complex characters and offbeat heroes. Frequently in the adult western, the demarcation between good and evil was blurred.

Nevertheless, they were essentially "action" shows, and they served to introduce violence to television on a grand scale. Because there were so many westerns on TV in a concentrated period—a total of 32 in the 1959 season, for example—each strived to succeed against the field by doubling the gunplay and driving up the body count. Teasers featured the most violent scenes to lure the viewer—for example, an outlaw using his foot to push a man's head into the campfire. The heightened violence quotient was inherited by the next action-adventure trend, the private-eye series, and subsequent ones, the spy and then the police series.

Of the adult westerns that rode into prime time in the 1955-56 season, *Cheyenne* was probably the most significant since it played in the *Warner Bros. Presents* showcase, which represented a breakthrough in the production of TV series by the major Hollywood film studios. Its profitability to WB prompted 20th, Paramount, MGM and Universal to get in on the television action, and they too broke in with westerns. The form was appealing because it enabled the studios to use stock footage for many scenes.

Some believe the Eisenhower Presidency contributed to the rash of oaters, the former war hero fanning a hero-consciousness in the land. Eisenhower made it known that he fancied the western story and legend. At any rate, the time was apparently right, and season after season the westerns came thick and fast to television.

Every producer looked for a new wrinkle—the cowardly hero, *Maverick;* the fancy-dan with a cane, *Bat Masterson;* the ingenue, *Sugarfoot;* the knife-slinger, *Adventures of Jim Bowie;* the frontier newspaperman, *Jefferson Drum.* Some worked, some didn't. *The Virginian*'s game was to run 90 minutes, and with it NBC stole half an evening on its rivals who tried but couldn't match it for success. *Frontier* attempted to outclass the field by pressing into the service of westerns Worthington Miner, one of the big names of the "golden age" of TV drama.

A lot of nobodies were pitched into starring roles—Will Hutchins, Scott Forbes, Wayde Preston, Jeff Richards, Tony Young and Don Durant, among scores of others—but quite a few of the nobodies made it to actual stardom. Steve McQueen sprang from *Wanted: Dead or Alive;* Clint Walker from *Cheyenne;* Lorne Greene, *Bonanza;* James Garner, *Maverick;* Gene Barry, *Bat Masterson;* Chuck Connors, *Rifleman;* Jim Arness and Dennis Weaver, *Gunsmoke;* Richard Boone, *Have Gun, Will Travel;* Hugh O'Brian, *Wyatt Earp;* Clint Eastwood, *Rawhide.*

Others who rose from obscurity were Ty Hardin, Nick Adams, Dale Robertson, the late Dan Blocker, the late Michael Landon, Robert Horton, Robert Culp, Neville Brand, Robert Conrad, Ryan O'Neal and James Drury. They mingled among established stars who went western, such as the late Henry Fonda, Joel McCrea, William Bendix, Dick Powell, Ward Bond, George Montgomery, Preston Foster and Ronald Reagan.

The titles smacked of machismo and action: *Rawhide, Broken Arrow, Death Valley Days, Lawman, Colt .45, Wagon Train, Johnny Ringo, Shotgun Slade, Cimarron City, Restless Gun, Wells Fargo, Wild Wild West.*

Wild Wild West was cut down in its prime by congressional hearings on violence, and in the early 1970s all that remained were *Gunsmoke* and *Bonanza.* They too disappeared by 1975 and, ironically, the networks tried sporadically to revive an interest in the western in order to find a way to cut back on the violence of police shows. *Barbary Coast, Dirty Sally, Sara* and *The Quest* all were tried, and all failed, but the networks were not deterred. There were more than half a dozen attempts to revive the western during the 1980s. All failed until ABC scored with *The Young Riders* in 1989.

WESTFELDT, WALLACE ▶ former producer for ABC News. Previously he was executive producer of public affairs for WETA, the Washington public TV station, and for 15 years before that a producer and reporter for NBC News. With WETA, Westfeldt was executive producer for numerous special events carried by PBS and of the 1976 series, *USA: People and Politics.*

At NBC News, which he had joined in 1961 as a writer, he served variously as reporter, producer, exec producer of the *Nightly News* (1969-73) and exec producer for documentaries (1973-76). His documentaries included *How Watergate Changed Government, The Meaning of Watergate, The Nuclear Threat to You, The Man Who Changed the Navy* and *1975: The World Turned Upside Down.* Before joining NBC, he was a reporter for *The Nashville Tennessean* and a correspondent for *Time* and *Life.* Since 1991 Westfeldt has been producing *Talking With David Frost* for PBS.

WESTIN, AV ▶ news executive prominent at ABC during the 1970s and previously in public

TV and at CBS News. He left ABC in a dispute with management in 1976 and became an independent producer and news consultant. But he returned to the network in summer of 1977 as a key figure in the rebuilding of the division by Roone Arledge, president of ABC News and Sports. Westin was put in charge of the evening newscast with the title of v.p.

During his previous hitch with ABC, he redesigned the evening newscast and organized the *ABC Close-Up* documentary operation; in February 1975 both vital areas of the news division were put in his charge.

Westin began in broadcast journalism with CBS News in the 1950s and rose rapidly from newswriter to editor, director and producer of news programs as a protege of Fred W. Friendly, then president of the division. In 1967 Westin left to join the newly formed Public Broadcasting Laboratory as producer of *PBL,* the experimental Sunday night newsmagazine. Two years later he signed on with ABC News.

In the 1986-87 season, Westin create *Our World,* a nostalgia series built on footage from the news division's vaults. It was a clever and well-executed series, reputed to be the least-expensive on the networks, but it was scheduled against *The Cosby Show* in that show's prime, and was no match.

Westin joined King World in 1989 as senior v.p. of reality-based programming and is executive producer of *Inside Edition.* He was also the creator of the nostalgia show *Instant Recall,* which premiered in 1990 and was canceled in 1991.

WESTMORELAND LIBEL CASE ▶ lawsuit brought against CBS News in 1982 by Gen. William C. Westmoreland alleging that he had been libeled by a documentary aired earlier that year, *The Uncounted Enemy: A Vietnam Deception.* The documentary, produced by George Crile and narrated by Mike Wallace, accused Westmoreland and his staff of having purposely deceived President Lyndon Johnson on the enemy's troop strength to encourage a continuation of the war. Gen. Westmoreland had been commander of U.S. forces in Vietnam during the LBJ era.

The libel suit was filed after the publication in May 1982 of a *TV Guide* cover story, *Anatomy of a Smear: How CBS News Broke the Rules and 'Got' General Westmoreland,* by Don Kowet and Sally Bedell Smith. The article charged that the documentary broke many of CBS News's journalistic rules, including interviewing one person twice to get a more punchy response, failing to mention that one interviewee was a paid consultant to the program, and shortening or disregarding certain interviews that might have diluted or flatly refuted the program's conclusions.

CBS News met the charges by conducting an internal investigation headed by the highly respected veteran journalist Burton (Bud) Benjamin. The report, which came after months of study, concluded that a number of the CBS News standards had been violated but that CBS should stand by the broadcast nonetheless.

Eventually Westmoreland dropped the suit, and CBS issued a statement that it never meant to defame or demean the general's patriotism. The producer, Crile, was briefly suspended.

The institution of the television documentary suffered most. It is probably no coincidence that the production of news documentaries went into decline, almost to the vanishing point, after the Westmoreland episode.

WGBH ▶ Boston public TV station and one of the leading production centers for PBS. The station is the source of such innovative and respected programming as *Frontline, Nova, Evening at Pops, The American Experience, Vietnam: A Television History, Mystery!, Zoom,* and *Where In The World Is Carmen Sandiego?*

Its prestige in the public system was established in the early 1970s when it acquired and assembled for PBS the *Masterpiece Theater* series of dramatic productions from Britain. The success of the British anthology followed closely on the heels of another WGBH success, *The French Chef,* which featured one of public TV's most popular performers, Julia Child.

Blessed with a Channel 2 position, WGBH was one of the first PTV stations to establish a substantial following in its community. This, together with the cultural resources at hand in the Boston/Cambridge area, contributed in large measure to the Boston station's vitality from public TV's earliest days as a producer of national programming. Known for being innovative and resourceful, WGBH has regularly produced a number of fringe-time, skill programs, including *Crockett's Victory Garden, Erica* (needlework), *Joyce Chen Cooks,* and *Maggie and the Beautiful Machine.* The most popular with PBS viewers in recent years is the series *This Old House.*

The station, licensed to the WGBH Educational Foundation, was the first to use closed-captioning for the deaf. In addition to WGBH-TV, the foundation operates a second channel in Boston (Channel 44), an FM radio station, and a TV station in Springfield (Channel 57) serving western Massachusetts.

WHAT'S HAPPENING! ▶ ABC sitcom (1976-79) about three black high school students who live in a middle-class neighborhood. Originally presented as a four-week summer replacement, the series returned on a regular basis in November of the same year and scored excellent ratings. The leads were Ernest Thomas as Roger (Raj) Thomas, Haywood Nelson Jr. as Dwayne, Fred Berry as Freddie (Rerun) Stubbs, Mabel King as Roger's Mama, Danielle Spencer as Roger's sister Dee and Shirley Hemphill as the waitress, Shirley.

WHAT'S MY LINE? ▶ see Game Shows.

WHDH CASE ▶ first in which a competing applicant was awarded a broadcast license over an incumbent with no substantial negative record. The decision by the FCC in January 1969 to award Channel 5 in Boston to a group known as Boston Broadcasters Inc., after the Boston Herald-Traveler Corp. had operated the station for more than a decade, sent shockwaves through the industry and spurred a drive for legislation that would protect broadcasters from license challenges.

The WHDH case was a unique one since the Herald-Traveler Corp. had been operating the station only on a temporary authorization from the FCC, except for a brief period when it was awarded a license for four months. Herald-Traveler, which had been one of four mutually exclusive applicants for Channel 5 in 1954, had been granted a construction permit for the station in April 1957. The award was challenged by two of the other applicants in federal courts.

A new issue of improper *ex parte* contacts entered the case when Robert Choate, president of the corporation, was charged with entertaining FCC chairman George C. McConnaughey at several social luncheons. The meetings were assumed to be attempts by Choate to influence the commission outside the normal adjudicatory processes. In July 1958 the U.S. Court of Appeals remanded the case to the FCC to investigate the *ex parte* question.

The commission found that although the president of WHDH had demonstrated an attempted pattern of influence, this did not disqualify WHDH but warranted setting aside the construction permit and holding new comparative hearings with the four original applicants. WHDH, meanwhile, was permitted to continue broadcasting under a special temporary authorization. In September 1962, the FCC determined that WHDH was the most desirable applicant and awarded it a short-term license. On its expiration, three applicants (only one of them one of the original applicants in 1954) challenged the license with competing bids.

During the long comparative hearings that followed, the FCC applied its own 1965 policy statement on Comparative Broadcast Hearings, which ruled out the broadcaster's past performance from consideration unless it had been exceptional. With this concept eliminated, the commission in January 1969 voted three to one to award the license to Boston Broadcasters Inc.

A chief reason for denying the station to Herald-Traveler was its ownership of a Boston newspaper (albeit a financially ailing one) and an FM station in the market. The FCC, concerned about media concentration in general and having adopted a policy supporting diversity of ownership, favored BBI for its lack of other media properties and for the greater integration between ownership and management that it promised to provide. BBI renamed the station WCVB-TV.

In its appeals, Herald-Traveler noted that the newspaper was being kept alive only by the profits from the TV station and that if it were to lose the station it would be forced to cease publication of the *Boston Herald-Traveler*. When the appeals failed, the newspaper did collapse.

To calm an industry fearful of the precedents that might be set by the WHDH case, the FCC issued a policy statement early in 1970 saying that, in license challenges, it would give preference to the incumbent licensee if the licensee could demonstrate that the programming had substantially served the community needs and interests. But the D.C. Court of Appeals struck down the policy statement as overly protective of the incumbent broadcaster.

WHEEL OF FORTUNE ▶ phenomenally successful game show in the syndicated version that was mounted by Merv Griffin Productions in 1983 as a strip for the prime-access time periods. The show, hosted by Pat Sajak and featuring Vanna White, became the highest-rated syndicated series in TV history and has dominated the syndication charts every year since. At times its ratings have been equal to a Top 20 network show. Moreover, the garish game show has enjoyed similar popularity in France in a direct adaptation of the format.

American stations that had bought *Wheel* and its stablemate *Password* and scheduled them back-to-back, proved unbeatable in their markets in the critical early-evening time periods five nights a week. As a lead-in they gave a powerful boost to a station's prime-time schedule. But if the shows were a boon to stations, they were a klondike for the distributor, King World, elevating the relatively small syndicator to a position of wealth and power in the industry.

Wheel, whose format is based on the parlor game "Hangman" while employing the device of a large wheel for contestants to spin, started in 1975 in NBC's daytime lineup with Chuck Woolery as host. Woolery held that role for six years and was replaced by Sajak 1981. Two years later Sajak was assigned to the new syndicated version, along with White, who had joined the daytimer in 1982. The daytime version has continued into the 1990s, and the daily double exposure seems not to have diluted the show's popularity.

The program's extraordinary success earned Sajak a late-night talk show on CBS in 1988, but it never caught on in its two-year trial. Vanna White became a major celebrity through *Wheel*, even though she performed as a letter-turner on the show and never spoke a word.

See also Game Shows.

Vanna White and Pat Sajak of *Wheel of Fortune*

WHELDON, HUW (d. 1986) ▶ Welsh careerist with the British Broadcasting Corp. who started as an air personality and producer, and who did a great deal to popularize programming that covered the arts. He later became a program executive and then managing director of BBC-TV, retiring on Dec. 31, 1975, at the mandatory age of 60. Shortly thereafter he was knighted by Queen Elizabeth II. His retirement as an executive allowed him to pick up, from time to time, his earlier career as a performer. He served as host and narrator for a number of BBC documentaries, including those on the U.S. Library of Congress and Britain's royal family.

WHEN THINGS WERE ROTTEN ▶ situation comedy created and produced by Mel Brooks that failed to survive its first season on ABC (1975). A spoof of the Robin Hood fable, it drew encouraging ratings initially and then faded. Featured were Dick Gautier as Robin Hood, Dick Van Patten as Friar Tuck, David Sabin as Little John, Misty Rowe as Maid Marian, Richard Dimitri as twins Bertram and Renaldo, Bernie Kopell as Alan-A-Dale and Henry Polic II as the Sheriff of Nottingham. It was by Paramount TV.

WHIRLYBIRDS ▶ syndicated adventure series concerning helicopter heroics, produced by Desilu (1957-59) and featuring Kenneth Tobey as Chuck Martin, Craig Hill as P.T. Moore, and Nancy Hale.

WHITAKER, JACK ▶ senior sports commentator for ABC Sports since 1982. He joined that network after a 20-year career with CBS Sports, coming from the Philadelphia o&o, WCAU-TV, in 1961. Initially hosting the *CBS Sports-Spectacular,* he later did play-by-play for NFL football and then became host of the pregame, postgame and half-time shows. He was also a principal commentator for CBS on golf events.

WHITE, BETTY ▶ actress whose comedy career dates to the 1950s and extends to the 1990s with *The Golden Girls.* In 1953 she starred in *Life With Elizabeth* and in 1958 *A Date With the Angels,* then in panel shows (*Make the Connection*). She was also regularly a commentator on the Rose Bowl Parade on New Year's Day. Her acting career caught fire again in the mid-1970s when she became a featured player in *The Mary Tyler Moore Show.* When that show folded she became star of a new series, *The Betty White Show,* on CBS (1977-78). She hit it big again as one of the four leads in *The Golden Girls* (1985—).

WHITE, FRANK ▶ one-time president of NBC from January to August 1953, succeeding Joseph H. McConnell who left to become president of Colgate-Palmolive-Peet Co. He resigned after seven months because of ill health, and in December Sylvester L. (Pat) Weaver was named president.

White entered broadcasting in 1937 as treasurer of CBS, later became president of Columbia Records and then of the Mutual Broadcasting System. He joined NBC in 1952 and soon became v.p. and general manager of the network.

WHITE, JOHN F. ▶ first president of National Educational Television (1958-69) through the period when it served as the network for educational television. He left to become president of Cooper Union in New York, thus resuming an academic career that had begun in 1941. Before joining NET, he had been general manager of WQED, the educational station in Pittsburgh.

WHITE, LAWRENCE R. ▶ program chief for NBC (1972-75) who later became executive v.p. of production for Columbia Pictures Television. In the brief period between he had formed Larry White Productions, which developed the ABC series *Feather and Father.*

White began his broadcast career as a producer-director for the DuMont Network in 1948. Three years later he became director of programming for Benton and Bowles Advertising, from which post he served as executive producer of the soap opera *The Edge of Night.* He left the agency to join CBS in 1959 as v.p. of daytime programming, then moved to Goodson-Todman Productions and then back to CBS as director of program development. He joined NBC in 1965 as v.p. of daytime programs and after several promotions became v.p. in charge of programs.

WHITE, MARGARETA (MARGITA) ▶ FCC commissioner from 1976 to 1978, appointed by President Ford for two years to complete the term of Charlotte Reid. White, a Republican, had previously been assistant press secretary and director of the Office of Communication at the White House. After leaving the commission she became president of the Association of Maximum Service Telecasters.

WHITE, PAUL (d. 1955) ▶ newsman who made his mark principally in radio, building the CBS News bureau into the most prestigious of the network news organizations. He founded the bureau in 1933 when he was named v.p. and general manager of Columbia Broadcasting News. During his 13-year administration, White directed a staff that included Edward R. Murrow, William Shirer, Robert Trout, Elmer Davis, Cecil Brown, H.V. Kaltenborn, Quincy Howe and other prominent newscasters.

In 1945 White won a Peabody Award for outstanding news coverage, then left CBS to write a book, *News on the Air.* He became associate editor of the *San Diego Journal* (1948-50) and then joined KFMB and KFMB-TV in San Diego as news director.

***WHITE SHADOW, THE* ▶** CBS dramatic series (1978-81) concerning the white coach of a basketball team at a racially mixed school. Ken Howard starred as coach Ken Reeves, and the featured cast included Jason Bernard (replaced by Ed Bernard) as principal Jim Willis, Joan Pringle as vice principal Sybil Buchanon, Kevin Hooks as Morris Thorpe, Eric Kilpatrick as Curtis Jackson, Nathan Cook as Milton Reese, Robin Rose as Katie Donahue and Jerry Fogel as Bill Donahue. The series was via MTM Productions, with Bruce Paltrow as executive producer and Mark C. Tinker as producer.

WHITE, VANNA ▶ model and fashionplate who, in assisting host Pat Sajak on the syndicated game show *Wheel of Fortune,* became something of a television phenomenon—a full-blown national celebrity who achieved fame without ever having spoken a word on camera. White was required only to be a well-dressed, attractive presence while performing the simple task of flipping letter cards. Her celebrity and its importance to the show, however, earned her a promotion in the early 1990s to co-host.

WHITEHEAD, CLAY T. ▶ first director of the White House Office of Telecommunications Policy (1970-74) who helped both to establish the agency and almost to destroy it by using it politically. The OTP under Whitehead became a base for attacks on network news, one of President Nixon's favorite targets.

The post, created in September 1970, made Whitehead the ranking White House advisor in the field of broadcasting, responsible for developing policy on present and emerging communications technologies and for regulating the federal government's own communications system. As a brilliant young management specialist and electrical engineer, with three degrees from M.I.T., he was eminently qualified for the office. But he began from the first to rail against network journalism, calling it "ideological plugola" and "elitist gossip" for its alleged liberal slant. His cautionary speeches to commercial and public broadcasters—made while Administration-sponsored legislation hung in the balance—were widely interpreted as bold moves by the White House to bring broadcasters ideologically in line and to win sympathetic treatment on the air for the President's policies.

Indeed, Whitehead's speeches carried the strong suggestion that legislation desired by the broadcasters could be traded off for their compliance with the Administration's view of good journalism. The tactic backfired, however, as Congress and the press read sinister motives into the bills drafted by the OTP—principally the one in 1972 that would have extended the broadcast license period from three years to five.

Only when Watergate destroyed the credibility of the White House media campaign did Whitehead and the OTP function as they were supposed to. Whitehead was responsible for an admirable cabinet committee report on cable TV in January 1974, which received a great deal of praise, although Dean Burch of the FCC noted that it came two years too late to be useful. Whitehead also produced a long-range funding bill for public TV. His last act in government service, before leaving to return to academia (as a fellow at Harvard's Institute of Politics), was to join a small team in preparing the transition from the Nixon to the Ford Administration when it became apparent that Nixon would have to resign. He later became president of Hughes Satellite Corporation which owns the Galaxy Satellite system.

Although valuable studies and reports began to come from OTP, Whitehead will undoubtedly be better remembered for his attempts to shape broadcast news policy than for forging the more cosmic telecommunications policy.

In his "ideological plugola" speech, delivered at a Sigma Delta Chi luncheon in Indianapolis on Dec. 18, 1972, Whitehead said that stations that tolerate bias by the networks can only be considered willing participants in the bias. Not only did the speech seem designed to drive a wedge between the networks and their affiliated stations, it also suggested a carrot-and-stick ploy, since it was coupled with his announcement that OTP had drafted a bill to safeguard and extend broadcast licenses. The speech created such a furor over attempted government censorship that the bill was never introduced.

At an NAEB convention in Miami in the fall of 1971, Whitehead criticized the growth of PBS in the direction of a "fourth network," expressed the Administration's displeasure with PTV's liberal leanings, and called for the system to deemphasize national programming and to embrace "grassroots localism."

As if to punctuate that speech, President Nixon in 1972 vetoed a two-year funding bill for PTV that called for $165 million, on the ground that the industry's power was too centralized. Hungry for federal funding, public broadcasters promptly dissolved PBS as a network and adopted a plan of overproducing national shows, to allow stations to select what they wished, following Whitehead's suggestion. "Localism" became the PTV byword.

Whitehead's use, or abuse, of the office gave it a low priority in the executive branch, and when the Ford Administration tried to reduce the executive budget early in 1975 the OTP was one of the agencies ticketed for extinction. The office was saved when John Eger, Whitehead's successor as acting director, alerted Congress to the plan. However, the office was dismantled in 1977 by the Carter Administration.

WHITTLE COMMUNICATIONS ▶ entrepreneurial "new media" company founded and run by Christopher Whittle out of Knoxville, Tenn., and 50% owned by Time Warner. The company specializes in creating unusual editorial products as conveyances for advertising. In television it is best known for its Channel One service—now called The Whittle Educational Network—an ad-supported newscast satellite-delivered to high schools throughout the country. The schools receive support equipment from Whittle, such as satellite dishes and TV sets, in return for requiring students to view each morning's program. The service became immediately controversial, with parent and teacher groups objecting to the inclusion of commercials in the programming and arguing that schools should not be used for selling goods and services.

The company also runs Special Reports TV, which delivers television programming to doctors' waiting rooms and publishes special-interest magazines for the same market. Its earliest efforts were a series of sponsored wall posters for schools and health clubs, and its projects have included a quarterly business magazine underwritten by IBM and a series of original hardcover nonfiction books that include ads for Federal Express within their pages.

Christopher Whittle formerly founded the 1330 Corp. with partner Philip Moffit. 1330 was best known for buying and retooling *Esquire* magazine and then selling it to Hearst Corp.

WHO'S THE BOSS ▶ popular sitcom that reverses stereotypical sex roles. The story centers on a single father, Tony Micelli, who goes to work as a live-in housekeeper for a divorced woman, Angela Bower, who is an advertising executive living with her mother and young son in suburban Connecticut. The show began in 1984, and over the course of time the relationship of the two principals, played by Tony Danza and Judith Light, has gradually progressed towards love. The cast also features Katherine Helmond as Angela's mother Mona, Alyssa Milano as Tony's daughter Samantha, and Danny Pintauro as Angela's son Jonathan. Televised on ABC, the series is produced by Martin Cohan and Blake Hunter. Hunter also created the series, writes many of the episodes and composed its theme song, *Brand New Life*.

WHO'S WHO ▶ nonfiction magazine series devoted to featurettes on newsmakers, celebrities and interesting obscure persons essayed by CBS as a prime-time entry in 1977. The series was a spin-off of *60 Minutes* in a year when that program achieved Top-20 popularity, and it was signaled by the trend to "people" magazines on the newsstands and the resurgence of gossip columns in the press.

Don Hewitt, executive producer of *60 Minutes,* and Dan Rather, a key correspondent on that show, both doubled on *Who's Who.* Along with Rather, the regular *Who's Who* correspondents were Barbara Howar and Charles Kuralt.

The ratings for the series were generally unimpressive its first months on the air, but that was largely a function of its having to compete with *Happy Days* and *Laverne and Shirley,* the top-rated series in TV at the time. *Who's Who* was given another test in a new period during June 1977 but failed to win a renewal for the fall.

WIC (WESTERN INTERNATIONAL COMMUNICATIONS) ▶ one of Canada's largest broadcast group owners. By virtue of its stations affiliated with CTV, WIC has a 17.5% equity stake in the national private network. WIC also owns the Allarcom Studio in Edmonton, a major production facility, and Allarcom Pay Television, which operates Superchannel, the pay movie service with an exclusive license for Western Canada. The company is also 50% owner of the Family Channel in Canada. WIC's president and CEO is Doug Holtby.

WIDE WIDE WORLD ▶ novel and much-praised Sunday afternoon series on NBC (1955-58) that traveled about the country electronically (and also to Canada and Mexico) to develop a subject—aging, holiday preparations, etc. Dave Garroway was host of the 90-minute program, which also occasionally used film from abroad. The title had such an attractive ring that ABC later borrowed it for *Wide World of Sports* and *Wide World of Entertainment.*

WIDE WORLD OF ENTERTAINMENT ▶ umbrella title for the potpourri of latenight shows instituted by ABC-TV in the fall of 1972 as a new attempt to compete with NBC's *Tonight* and CBS's movies, following three years of third-place standing with *The Dick Cavett Show.*

Initially, *Wide World* rotated a week of Cavett, a week of original TV movies, a week of Jack Paar in his television return and a week of music-variety shows from 11:30 p.m. to 1 a.m. (EST). Within a year Paar was dropped and Cavett cut back to one program a month, as the format loosened to accommodate a diversity of comedy, variety, dramatic, news and event programs—in effect, a special every night, providing an opportunity to test new formats and talent. When Cavett left ABC in December 1974 for opportunities that CBS might afford, *Wide World*'s only regular commitment was to a bimonthly rock concert on Friday nights, entitled *In Concert.*

Among the special programs offered on *Wide World of Entertainment* were Alan King at Las Vegas (Jan. 1973), *David Frost Presents the Guinness Book of World Records* (Nov. 1973), *Dick Clark Presents the Rock of the 60s* (Jan. 1974), *Geraldo Rivera's Good Night America* (five programs, 1973-74), *Marilyn Remembered* (Dec. 1974) and a variety of testimonials, salutes and celebrity tours. The concept was abandoned in 1976 as ABC gave over the latenight hours increasingly to reruns of primetime action-adventure shows. These proved more effective in the ratings than the *Wide World* originals.

WIDE WORLD OF SPORTS ▶ ABC sports anthology on Saturday afternoons, begun in 1961, which has become the keystone of the network's sports programming. With a kind of magazine format, *WWS* covers a wide range of fringe competitive sports that would not otherwise receive network exposure, events involving figure skating, barrel jumping, Ping Pong, motorcycle feats, auto racing, gymnastics and a variety of track and field competitions. During ABC's leanest years, *WWS* was one of the network's most consistently popular programs and always heavily sponsored.

The series was started on ABC by Edgar Scherick, then head of sports for the network, who had to build a series quickly when Gillette quit NBC for dropping Friday night boxing and was prepared to give ABC $9 million in billings for a suitable sports showcase. *Wide World* was threatened with cancellation after 13 weeks but won a reprieve from Tom Moore, then program chief, and established itself soon afterwards. Scherick hired away a young producer from NBC to take charge of the series, and it became the career springboard for Roone Arledge.

Arledge, who was executive producer of *Wide World of Sports,* rose swiftly to become president of ABC Sports and the most dynamic and successful sports executive in television. Geoffrey Mason has been the executive producer since 1988. The series was also springboard for Jim McKay, its host, and has been a prime showcase for all of ABC's sports commentators.

WILD BILL HICKOK ▶ early syndicated western series (1952) about the adventures of U.S. Marshal James Butler (Wild Bill) Hickok and his sidekick, Jingles B. Jones, in the Old West. The program featured Guy Madison and Andy Devine. It was revived by ABC (1957-58) when TV's western cycle was in flower.

WILD KINGDOM ▶ natural history series actually billed as *Mutual of Omaha's Wild Kingdom,* which began on NBC in January 1963 and ran through the 1970 season when the network dropped it in program cutbacks under the prime time-access rule. After that, with the same host, Marlin Perkins; the same producer, Don Meier Productions; and the same sponsor, Mutual of Omaha, the series continued for a time in syndication as a prime-access entry.

WILD, WILD WEST, THE ▶ hour-long series about special government agents in the Old West, one of whom specialized in disguises. Produced by Bruce Lansbury Productions for CBS (1965-70), the series featured Robert Conrad as James West and the late Ross Martin as Artemus Gordon. It was canceled not for declining ratings but because government officials were voicing concern about television violence. Having pledged to Congress that CBS would reduce violence, Dr. Frank Stanton, then president of CBS Inc., ordered the program off the schedule.

WILD, WILD WORLD OF ANIMALS ▶ half-hour nature series on patterns of animal survival, produced by the BBC in association with Windrose-Dumont-Time, and distributed here for prime time-access syndication in 1973. William Conrad did the narration.

WILDMON, DONALD ▶ United Methodist Church minister who gave up his parish ministry in 1977 to organize the National Federation for Decency and its companion, the Christian Leaders for Responsible Television. Under their banner, he has waged a vigorous campaign in recent years to rid television—and other media as well—of what he sees as harmful and gratuitous sex, violence and profanity. From his base in Tupelo, Mississippi, Wildmon has organized his nationwide constituency for mail-in campaigns, product boycotts and picketing, cagily directed at the offending show's most vulnerable pressure point, the advertiser. His efforts have produced results: Procter & Gamble, General Foods and Bristol-Myers, among TV's major advertisers, have called for less sex and violence in the shows in which their ads appear. Wildmon's shots at specific shows have been less effective, particularly his campaign against such popular shows as *Hill Street Blues* and *Saturday Night Live.* The conservative minister's critics, including the targeted TV industry, charge him with trying to force his rigid minority standards upon widely accepted majority tastes. His organizations, once largely financed by the Rev. Jerry Falwell's Moral Majority, gained some strength in the 1980s with the election of Ronald Reagan and the country's subsequent swing to the right.

WILEY, RICHARD E. ▶ chairman of the FCC (1974-77) noted for his efficiency, intelligence and pragmatic approach to regulation. Although the commission acted on dozens of controversial and politically sensitive issues during his administration, none of those matters was ever resolved in a way that created drastic changes in conventional broadcasting.

A possible exception was "family viewing time" as an answer to the sex and violence question, but technically this was adopted voluntarily by the industry and was not an official FCC action. On leaving the FCC, he joined the Washington law firm of Kirkland and Ellis.

A conservative Republican from Illinois who came to the FCC in 1970 as general counsel, Wiley was named commissioner in 1972 and chairman in March 1974. He maintained an unshakable aversion to government intervention in business and believed that most broadcast problems were best dealt with through industry self-regulation. In his first speech to the industry as chairman, he called for a "new ethic," urging broadcasters to dedicate themselves voluntarily to excellence and public service and to resist the temptation of fraudulent practices. And he immediately took steps to "re-regulate" the industry, doing away with regulations found to be obsolete.

His sympathy toward business and his philosophy of nonintervention permeated his commission, which was made up entirely of Nixon appointees (Robert E. Lee, the sole holdover, having been reappointed to a fourth term by Nixon). Thus, a set of FCC rules sought by ACT to govern children's programming resulted only in a policy statement offering guidelines; the Justice Department push for an FCC policy on media cross-ownership yielded a mild rule that essentially prohibited the creation of new newspaper-broadcast combinations and did not break up most existing ones; and a plea by the cable industry for more liberal pay-cable rules brought only a slight relaxation of the rules. The courts rebuffed Wiley's commission both on the cross-ownership and cable rules.

Wiley's commission declined to impose limits on network reruns, to bar the use of strip programming in prime time-access slots or to juggle station assignments to satisfy New Jersey's plea for a VHF station of its own. Perhaps its most radical action was a reinterpretation of the equal time rule, permitting TV to cover debates between major party candidates if they are bona fide news events—that is, organized by nonbroadcast organizations and presented outside the studios.

But if he was not a reformer as a regulator, he brought reforms on the commission itself altering the bureaucratic process to permit greater efficiency and to handle more work. A prodigious worker himself, he set a timetable on all matters before the commission and pushed the staff and other commissioners to meet the deadlines. He is believed to have called more *en banc* sessions of the commission than any chairman before him.

Wiley was also adept at bargaining and jawboning, using those skills frequently to achieve consensus votes from the commissioners. He believed near-unanimous votes to carry greater force than the decisions reached by the narrowest 4-3 margin. His jawboning talent, however, involved him in a lawsuit by Hollywood producers in 1976 who charged him with forcing "family viewing time" upon the industry while he was under pressure from three congressional committees to do something to control sex and violence on TV. Wiley maintained that he and his staff merely visited with the heads of the networks, made suggestions on how they might deal with the problem and left the rest to industry self-regulation.

WILLIAM MORRIS AGENCY ▶ third-largest of the talent agencies, behind CAA and ICM, engaged in motion picture and television program packaging and in the representation of performers, writers, directors and producers. Founded in 1898 by William Morris, the agency originally represented talent working in vaudeville and theater. Progressively it included other forms of show business—motion pictures, radio, records, concerts, fairs, night clubs and television. The agency at present operates with 30 agents and receives 10% of the fees for the individuals it represents or 10% of the package (producer, writer, director, stars) it may place with a network.

The agency assists the film studios in selling to the networks shows in which it has an interest.

WILLIAMS, MARY ALICE ▶ co-anchor for NBC News' *Sunday Today* since 1990, while working on special assignments and serving as substitute anchor on *NBC News at Sunrise, Today, NBC Nightly News with Tom Brokaw* and weekend editions of *NBC Nightly News.* She co-anchored the four editions of *Yesterday, Today* and *Tomorrow,* telecast during summer 1989.

Williams returned to NBC News in 1989 from CNN, where she was prime-time anchor and vice president in charge of the New York bureau. During her 10-year CNN stint she was the New York anchor for *Newswatch* and *PrimeNews* and a member of the political anchor team during the Presidential election year. She joined CNN in 1979, where she helped to develop its news operation.

Before joining CNN, she was a reporter and anchor at NBC's New York station, WNBC-TV (1974-78). Prior to that, she was at New York's WPIX-TV, where, at 23, she became an executive producer and news manager. She began her career at KSTP-TV in Minneapolis.

WILLIAMS, MATT ▶ writer-producer who created *Roseanne* (1988—) for ABC and who was co-executive producer until Roseanne Barr fired him. His company, Wind Dancer Productions, was then signed to a multi-million dollar contract with Touchstone TV. Williams served as executive producer for NBC's *Carol and Company* (1990-91) and created ABC's *Home Improvement* (1991—). He also wrote episodes for NBC's *The Cosby Show* (1984—).

WILLIAMS, PALMER ▶ legendary veteran of CBS News, who began in 1951 as a key member of the Edward R. Murrow-Fred W. Friendly *See It Now* team and remained to become a producer of the popular *60 Minutes,* a post he has held since the premiere in September 1968. He joined Murrow and Friendly as a newsreel photographer and was credited by them with guiding their transition from radio to the visual medium. Later he became director of operations for *CBS Reports* and then executive producer. He worked on numerous CBS documentaries, including Jay McMullen's famed *Biography of a Bookie Joint.*

WILLIAMS, ROBIN ▶ one of America's most inventive comedians who, like many masters of comedy, is also a gifted actor. And like many of today's film stars, he went from unknown to a household name because he caught the public's fancy in a TV series. The show, *Mork and Mindy* (1978-82), grew out of a single guest shot on *Happy Days,* in which he played an amiable extraterrestrial, Mork from Ork.

Although Williams has since worked mainly in movies (*Good Morning, Vietnam, Dead Poets Society, Awakenings* and *The Fisher King*), he continues to do TV guest shots and comedy concerts on cable. Before *Mork and Mindy* he was a regular on *The Richard Pryor Show* in the late 1970s and also appeared in the ill-fated revival of *Laugh-In.*

WILLIS, JACK ▶ program producer and broadcast executive who since 1990 has been president of the Twin Cities Public Television stations, KTCA-TV and KTCI. Willis spent his early years producing, directing and writing programs for Talent Associates, the CBC and NET (*Great American Dream Machine, Hard Times in the Country, Every Seventh Child*). Later, as vice president of programming for WNET, he created the acclaimed newsmagazine *The 51st State.*

In 1980, after five years as an independent producer of drama and documentaries (*Paul Jacobs and the Nuclear Gang*), he became vice president of programming and production for CBS Cable. Before shifting from programming to the executive suite in the Twin Cities, Willis spent six years producing shows for Metromedia, Multimedia and his own company.

WILSON, HUGH ▶ creator and producer of *WKRP In Cincinnati, Frank's Place, The Last Resort* and *The Famous Teddy Z.*

WINANT, ETHEL ▶ casting director for CBS through most of two decades, regarded the most powerful in her field, until she left in July 1975 to join the Children's Television Workshop as executive producer of a new history series designed for adult viewers, *The Best of Families.* Later she joined NBC as head of casting, resigning in 1981 to join Metromedia Producers Corp. as an independent producer.

After nine years as director of casting for CBS Hollywood, she became in 1973 vice-president of talent and casting for the network, responsible for casting all network pilots, series and specials and for maintaining the personal relationship between the network and its stars, producers and directors.

With a background in various production jobs in Broadway theater, she entered television in the mid-1950s to work on *Studio One;* then became head of casting for Talent Associates, which produced *Armstrong Circle Theater* and *Philco Playhouse;* then casting director of *Playhouse 90* for CBS. She served as associate producer of various TV shows and of four movies produced by John Houseman. In the early 1960s, she produced *The Great Adventure,* an American history series, for CBS.

WINCHELL, WALTER (d. 1972) ▶ newspaper gossip columnist and radio personality who probably realized his greatest TV success, after a number of tries, as off-camera narrator of the hit crime series *The Untouchables.* His first effort in television, on ABC in 1952, was a personalized news program in his inimitable clipped style. It lasted three years. In 1956 he essayed a variety series and the following year hosted a dramatic series, *The Walter Winchell File.* But the reportorial antics that suggested deadline pressure in print and on the radio were betrayed as affectation on camera.

WINDOW ▶ in programming transactions, the period during which a network or station has contractual rights to a show, after which the show may be playable elsewhere. Windows vary with each deal, but they impose deadlines for scheduling. When the network window closes, a series may pass directly to its cable window even while being sold for the next window, syndication. Motion picture studios are obsessed with windows of release—first theatrical, then pay-per-view, then pay cable, next home video, then network, then syndication—each strategically timed to maximize revenues. A movie may pass through all the windows in a period of four or five years, though the big hits take much longer.

A scene from the ABC mini-series *The Winds of War*

WINDS OF WAR, THE **▶** ambitious and sprawling adaptation of Herman Wouk's best-selling novel of that title, whose story takes place during World War II and spans a number of countries. Produced and directed by Dan Curtis for ABC, the 1983 epic mini-series ran for 18 hours over seven nights. At $40-million, it was the single most expensive television production to that time and was filmed in more than 400 different locations. The huge cast, headed by Robert Mitchum as the patriarch of a Navy family, also starred Ali MacGraw (in her first TV role), Jan-Michael Vincent, Polly Bergen, Lisa Eilbacher, David Dukes, Topol, Ben Murphy, Peter Graves, Ralph Bellamy, Victoria Tennant and John Houseman. Wouk wrote the screenplay. Its 29-hour sequel, *War and Remembrance,* aired on ABC in 1988-89.

WINFREY, OPRAH ▶ television's premier talk show host who became a national figure almost overnight in 1986 when her local Chicago program, *A.M. Chicago,* was repackaged for syndication by King World as *The Oprah Winfrey Show.* Though an unknown at the time, and a black person in a field that had always been predominantly white, she won a strong following in short order, and stations around the country began clamoring for the program, whose appeal centered almost entirely on the warm and refreshingly unaffected personality of the host. The show eventually overtook *Donahue* in the national ratings, and with ownership of the program and of a Chicago production company, Harpo Productions, Winfrey became the highest-paid woman in show business. Her 1991 earnings reportedly exceeded $40 million.

While *Oprah,* like the other talk shows, focuses on a single topic daily, Winfrey's approach is not as clinically probing as the others or as given to sensationalism. Winfrey frequently displays emotion when interviewing guests and on occasion discusses her own life and personal concerns, such as her struggle with being overweight. Her spartan diet, under which she acquired a svelte figure for a brief time, became a matter of national interest.

Winfrey began in television as a newscaster in Nashville, Tenn., and after a talk show stint in Baltimore she moved to WLS-TV Chicago in 1984 to take over the morning talk show that became her springboard. She has also proved an able actress, making her movie debut in a supporting role in *The Color Purple.* She also produced and starred in *The Women of Brewster Place,* a TV movie on ABC that in 1990 became the short-lived series *Brewster Place.*

WINKY DINK AND YOU **▶** a CBS children's series (1953-57) that encouraged viewer participation. It featured Jack Barry and youngster Harlan Barnard. Winky Dink, an elfin character, was a drawing.

"WINNER TAKE ALL" TENNIS SCANDAL ▶ situation that developed after CBS Sports promoted a series of four tennis specials in the late 1970s as "winner take all" competitions when in fact the participants were all guaranteed substantial fees, whether they won or not. The FCC determined in 1978, after a ten-month inquiry, that CBS deliberately attempted to deceive its viewers for the sake of ratings. It also found the network in violation of its sponsor identification rules for giving plugs to the luxury hotels hosting the matches without noting on the air that these were in exchange for a variety of special considerations by the hotels.

The matches were presented on television under the umbrella title of *The World Heavyweight Championship of Tennis,* and all four featured Jimmy Connors.

The scandal apparently precipitated the departures of Robert Wussler and Barry Frank, who were president and v.p. of CBS Sports, respectively. Meanwhile, CBS was censured by the FCC and punished with a short-term (one year) license renewal for its Los Angeles o&o, KNXT.

WIRELESS CABLE ASSOCIATION ▶ trade group representing interests of MMDS (multichannel multipoint distribution service) operators.

***WISEGUY* ▶** sophisticated crime series on CBS from Stephen J. Cannell Productions, with multi-layered plots and story arcs of five to 10 episodes, which ran from 1987-90. In it Ken Wahl played a street-smart federal agent, Vinnie Terranova, who has joined the FBI's Organized Crime Bureau and works undercover as a trusted member of the Mob's inner-circle in an Atlantic City crime syndicate. The hour-long series featured, at one time or another, such actors as Patti D'Arbanville, Jonathan Banks, Kevin Spacey, Jerry Lewis, Ron Silver, Joan Severance, William Russ, Ray Sharkey, and David Strathairn. When Wahl left the series in 1990, the action focused on the character played by Steven Bauer, as Cuban-American federal agent Michael Santana. Cannell and Frank Lupo created the show and wrote the first episodes.

WISEMAN, FREDERICK ▶ filmmaker specializing in *cinema verite* documentaries on American institutions, virtually all of which were made for public TV. During the 1970s and 1980s, the presentation of the latest Wiseman work conventionally marked the opening of the new PBS season.

A lawyer who became a filmmaker in 1967, Wiseman, working only with a cameraman, produces, directs and edits all his own documentaries. His works, which often run two hours or longer, depict the daily routines of the institutions being examined and employ no narration to explain or interpret the events. His social analysis is therefore implicit.

Titicut Follies, a controversial film shot at the Massachusetts State Hospital for the Criminally Insane, was his first effort. It was followed by such documentaries as *Welfare* (1975), *Canal Zone* (1977), *Sinai Field Mission* (1978), *Multi-handicapped* (1986), *Missile* (1987), *Near Death* (1989), *Central Park* (1989), and *Aspen* (1991).

WITT, PAUL JUNGER ▶ producer whose credits include *The Partridge Family, The Rookies* and the TV movie *Brian's Song.* As head of production for Danny Thomas Productions, he was also executive producer of the situation comedies *Fay* and *The Practice.* As partner with Thomas's son Tony, in Witt-Thomas Productions, he coproduced *Soap* (created by his wife, Susan Harris) and its spin-off, *Benson.* Since then, sitcoms written by his wife have been produced by Witt-Thomas-Harris Productions (*The Golden Girls, Empty Nest, Nurses,* and *Good and Evil*), with all three as executive producers. Witt and Thomas, without Harris, have produced *Beauty and the Beast* and *Blossom.* Both production companies are usually aligned with Touchstone TV of the Disney Co.

WITTING, CHRIS J. ▶ a leading figure in television in the early years as managing director of the DuMont Network (1950-53) when it owned three stations and had 65 affiliates. Witting is credited with having brought Sid Caesar, Imogene Coca, Jackie Gleason, Dennis James and Bishop Sheen to network TV. He joined DuMont in 1947 and left to become president of Westinghouse Broadcasting Co. In 1955, he became v.p. and general manager of the Westinghouse consumer products division, later went on to ITT and in 1965 became president and chief executive officer of the Crouse-Hinds Co., an electrical equipment manufacturer.

***WIZARD OF OZ, THE* ▶** in certain respects, the most successful single program in TV history, a 1939 historical movie that was presented 18 times between 1956 and 1976 and never received a rating lower than 20.2. The MGM film, based on L. Frank Baum's book and starring Judy Garland, has passed between CBS and NBC, earning millions with each transaction for long-term licensing permitting one play a year. There being no reason to assume after more than three decades of exposure that *Oz* will be any less an attraction in the future, the film bids fair to become the first on TV to amass an accumulated U.S. audience of one billion.

The film made its TV debut Nov. 3, 1956, on CBS's *Ford Star Jubilee,* airing 9-11 p.m., too late for very young children. Yet it scored a 33.9 rating and 53 share. CBS offered it again three years later, after which it has had an unbroken string of annual showings. The second outing, at 6 p.m. on a Sunday, garnered a 36.5 rating and 58 share. For the initial nine telecasts on CBS—from 1956 to 1967—*The Wizard of Oz* averaged an incredible 53 share.

NBC then acquired the film, and for the next eight years it averaged a 40 share. CBS regained *Oz* in 1976, scoring a 42 share with a showing in March. On all but three occasions, the movie was scheduled on a Sunday evening, either at 6 or at 7 p.m.

In the initial sale of the film to television, MGM was paid $250,000 a showing. The value of the rights has increased steadily, and CBS's five-year purchase in 1976 was at the rate of $800,000 a showing.

After reaching its 50th anniversary in 1989, *The Wizard of Oz* was released to home video, which diminished its potency on television, though it continues to be shown annually.

WKRP IN CINCINNATI ▶ CBS sitcom introduced twice during the 1978-79 season, the second time successfully. The program, about the people working in a small Top-40 radio station, opened the season as a companion to another new series, *People.* After a few weeks, CBS canceled *People* and put *WKRP* on the shelf, having decided that the program needed a stronger lead-in to succeed. It was returned at mid-season in the hammock slot between *M*A*S*H* and *Lou Grant* and began to flourish. During the summer of 1979, the *WKRP* reruns went to the top of the Nielsen ratings.

Produced by MTM Enterprises, and resembling in style and concept MTM's *Mary Tyler Moore Show,* it featured Gordon Jump as station manager Arthur Carlson, Gary Sandy as program director Andy Travis, Howard Hesseman as disc jockey Johnny Caravella (better known as Dr. Johnny Fever), Tim Reid as deejay Gordon Sims (known as Venus Flytrap), Richard Sanders as news reporter Les Nesman, Jan Smithers as program assistant Bailey Quarters, Frank Bonner as sales manager Herb Tarlek, Loni Anderson as secretary Jennifer Marlowe and Sylvia Sydney (replaced by Carol Bruce) as Mama Carlson.

WLAF (WORLD LEAGUE OF AMERICAN FOOTBALL) ▶ a new football league formed in 1989 to extend the sport on television after the National Football League season ends. The new league was in fact created by the NFL (with two teams, Chicago and Phoenix, demurring) for a 12-week season starting in March and ending in June. ABC bought the rights for the first two years for an estimated $20 million; cable's USA Network, carrying part of the schedule, paid about the same for four years. Ratings were poor the first year, and the networks and the league all took a loss.

The World League has 10 franchises, which includes three European teams and one Canadian, and it hopes to capitalize on the growing interest in American football abroad. If it should fare modestly in the U.S. but do well internationally, it could be a bonanza. That's what 26 of the 28 NFL teams envisioned when each ponied up $50,000 to help get the league started.

Player salaries have been kept low, with a base of $15,000 to $25,000 for the 10-game regular season and incentive bonuses with a cap of $100,000. The league represents a farm system for the NFL and a way to develop players who do not go to college. In addition, the WLAF gives the NFL almost year-round control over televised professional football.

The World League emerged in the wake of the United States Football League, which was originally formed to play in the post-NFL months of February to June. But when the teams began bidding up huge salaries for collegiate prospects like Herschel Walker, the owners felt the answer to higher ratings and fatter TV contracts was to move the schedule to the fall, where it would compete against the NFL. That plan did not excite the networks or the viewers, and the league failed.

WLBT LOSS OF LICENSE ▶ [*United Church of Christ v. FCC/* 359 F2d 994 (D.C. Cir. 1966)/425 F2d 543 (D.C. Cir. 1969)] case in which Lamar Life Insurance Co. was denied license renewal for WLBT Jackson, Miss., in 1969 when citizens groups proved that the station used its air time to promote a segregationist philosophy and in general denied the use of its airwaves to blacks and proponents of the civil rights cause.

Apart from the Fairness Doctrine considerations, the station was in violation of its license pledge to serve the needs, interests and convenience of its community, since around 40% of the Jackson population was black. This was the first time a TV license was lost on substantive grounds, but it was brought about by an action of the court rather than by the FCC.

The FCC had repeatedly warned the station during the 1960s that it was required under the Fairness Doctrine to inform black leaders when they or their causes were attacked. Eventually, the Office of Communication of the United Church of Christ decided to bring a test case that would force access to broadcasting for blacks in the South.

After monitoring the station to accumulate evidence, the UCC, along with some local residents, filed a petition in 1964 to deny renewal of the WLBT license. The petition claimed that WLBT discriminated against blacks in its commercials and entertainment programming and was unfair in its presentation of controversial issues. The commission held, in 1965, that the UCC and other petitioners had no legal standing to intervene. While recognizing the seriousness of the allegations, the FCC, with two members dissenting, concluded that WLBT was entitled to a one-year renewal on the condition that the station comply strictly with the established requirements of the Fairness Doctrine.

The UCC then appealed to the Court of Appeals for the District of Columbia. In 1966 a three-judge panel unanimously ruled that the UCC and citizens groups did have standing because they were consumers with a genuine and legitimate interest. This proved a landmark decision, making it possible for private groups around the country to file petitions to deny against local stations.

The Court of Appeals also held that the grant of a one-year renewal to WLBT was in error, and it directed the FCC to conduct hearings on the station's renewal application. During the next two years, while the FCC was investigating WLBT, the station tried to improve its record. In June 1968, the FCC granted WLBT a full three-year renewal (again, two members dissented).

Again the UCC appealed to the court, and again the court reversed the FCC, vacating the grant of the license and directing the commission to invite applications for the license. The court held that the commission's conclusion had not been supported by substantial evidence. Lamar Life then asked the Supreme Court to grant certiorari, and the request was denied.

WLBT did not go off the air when the license was lost in 1969 but continued to operate under supervision of a biracial, nonprofit caretaker group, Communications Improvements Inc., while the FCC considered five new applicants for the license, one of which was the original owner, Lamar Life. Lamar meanwhile, was paid a monthly fee of $35,000 by the operating group for the use of its facilities and equipment.

The case had the effect of propelling the broadcast reform movement by establishing the right of citizens' groups to have their views made part of the official license-renewal proceedings. It also proved the effectiveness of the petition to deny as an instrument for change.

WNTA ▶ the commercial station which preceded WNET, the public TV station, on Channel 13 in New York. Assigned in 1952 to Newark, N.J., it was originally operated by a TV syndication concern, National Telefilm Associates, and was noted for the *Play of the Week* series it produced, which its parent company sold nationally. Having run up losses of $3 million, it was sold in 1961 to Educational Broadcasting Corp. to become the New York metropolitan area's first educational TV station, WNDT. In 1970, when WNDT merged with National Educational Television, the station became WNET. In the transaction, however, New Jersey was left without a single commercial VHF station licensee. In latter years WNET has been required to recognize its obligations to New Jersey with some programming tailored expressly to the needs of the state.

WOLF, DICK ▶ writer-producer associated with Universal TV who was responsible for the *Law & Order* series (1990—) on NBC and *The Human Factor*, a mid-season back-up series for CBS in the 1991-92 season. He was executive producer of the "Christine Cromwell" elements of ABC's *Saturday Night Mystery Wheel* and of two short-lived series, *H.E.L.P.* on ABC and *The Nasty Boys* on NBC.

WOLFE, JAMES D. ▶ head writer for *That Was the Week That Was* and *The Bill Cosby Show* and comedy consultant for *Laugh-In*. He was also producer-director and writer of *Opryland, USA* and served in a creative capacity on numerous specials.

WOLFF, PERRY (SKEE) ▶ veteran writer and producer of documentaries for CBS News, who, in a career that began in 1947, produced more than 200 hours of documentaries for the network. He was named executive producer of CBS News specials in 1976.

Wolff's credits as producer include *The Selling of the Pentagon, Voices from the Russian Underground, You and the Commercial, The Italians, The Japanese* and *The Israelis.* He also wrote and produced a 1961 news special on the building of the Berlin Wall and in 1962 *A Tour of the White House with Mrs. John F. Kennedy.*

He came to CBS from its Chicago o&o, WBBM Radio, in 1947, where he worked in the dual capacity of music director and investigative reporter. He transferred to the network in the early 1950s and created the public affairs series *Adventure* with the American Museum of Natural History. In 1956 he took over the documentary series *Air Power.*

WOLPER, DAVID L. ▶ independent producer whose company, Wolper Productions, specialized in documentaries and other nonfiction programs and launched the careers of numerous young film directors and producers. Wolper succeeded better than any other independent at getting around network policies requiring documentaries to be produced by their own news divisions.

But in the 1970s, frustrated by the resistance of the networks to outside documentaries, he switched fields and began producing entertainment programs. With James Komack, he produced the situation comedies *Welcome Back Kotter* and *Chico and the Man,* both successful. He hit the jackpot, however, when he purchased the rights to Alex Haley's *Roots,* reportedly for $250,000, and produced the 12-hour mini-series that became, in January 1977, the highest-rated program in TV history. He also produced the sequel *Roots: The Next Generations,* a big rating hit in 1979.

In the documentary field, Wolper broke the network barrier initially with *Race for Space* (1958) and followed with numerous others: *The Rafer Johnson Story* (1962), *The Story of Hollywood and the Stars* (1963), *Escape to Freedom* (1963), *The Rise and Fall of American Communism* (1963) and *The Legend of Marilyn Monroe* (1964).

One of Wolper's tactics was to secure sponsorship before taking a program to the networks. With two sponsors in tow, he placed the *National Geographic* specials—four a year—with CBS in 1964. He also produced the quadrennial series *The Making of a President,* based on the Theodore H. White books; *The Undersea World of Jacques Cousteau;* the *Smithsonian* series; and a number of theatrical movies.

WONDER WOMAN ▶ a "floating" series while on ABC (1974-77) but given a regular berth by CBS, which acquired it for the fall of 1977. The series was piloted for ABC in 1974 and then was re-cast and piloted again in 90-minute form. Although it drew encouraging ratings wherever ABC chose to play it, the series continued to hold bench-warmer status with the network, which ordered only a limited number of episodes each season. CBS won it with an offer of a weekly slot.

Based on the comic book super-heroine (whose undercover name was Diana Prince), the series featured Lynda Carter, glamorous and shapely, in the title role. Featured were Lyle Waggoner as Major Steve Trevor, Richard Eastham as General Blankenship and Beatrice Colen as Corporal Etta Candy, and Debra Winger appeared as Wonder Girl—Diana's sister, Drusilla. *Wonder Woman* was produced by Warner Bros. TV and the Douglas S. Cramer Co., with Cramer as executive producer and W.L. Baumes as producer.

WONDER YEARS, THE ▶ praised and often-poignant comedy-drama series, set in the late 1960s, which looks back through the eyes of Kevin, the youngest of three children in the Arnold family, on the joys and tribulations of growing up in a typical suburban household. Created, produced, written and sometimes directed by the husband-and-wife team of Neal Marlens and Carol Black, the series had a limited run in the spring of 1988 and went into the ABC fall schedule that year, and has continued since. Fred Savage plays the lead and Daniel Stern provides the narration in the voice of the adult Kevin. Also featured are Dan Lauria as Kevin's father Jack, Alley Mills as Kevin's mother Norma, Jason Hervey as his brother Wayne, Olivia D'Abo as his sister Karen, Danica McKellar as Winnie Cooper, and Josh Saviano as Paul Pfeiffer. In 1989, Bob Brush became the executive producer.

WONDERFUL WORLD OF DISNEY, THE ▶ sturdy Sunday evening family series on NBC (since 1961), unlike any other series on TV in that it offered a varied menu of nature films, animated cartoons, dramas, comedies, serials and movies, making it almost a network unto itself. Virtually all the Disney forms succeeded, and the series—which had gone by other titles, such as *Walt Disney's Wonderful World of Color* and, while it was on ABC (1954-61), *Disneyland*—was never seriously threatened by competing programs on the other networks. Meanwhile, it spawned such successful subseries as *Davy Crockett, Elfego Baca* and *Zorro.* It was also an expandable series, lending itself to two-hour presentations when that served NBC's purposes.

The historical significance of the series is that, under its original title, *Disneyland,* it provided the opening wedge in 1954 for the entry of the major Hollywood studios into TV production.

After the 1980-81 season, NBC dropped the long-running series, which had been having trouble competing with CBS's *60 Minutes* on Sunday nights at 7, but CBS immediately signed the Disney Studio to supply it with specials during 1981-82. This deal soon turned into the Walt Disney series on Saturdays at 8 p.m., which did quite well in the ratings even though the programming mix was not that different from the mix used on *Disney's Wonderful World,* which had been its title during the last two years on NBC.

CBS dropped the show in late 1983, and when it reappeared on ABC in 1986, it had again been given a new title, *The Disney Sunday Movie.* It also had a new executive producer and host, Michael Eisner, the head of the studio. But the show never again found a strong audience on Sunday nights, where it was again forced to compete with *60 Minutes.* It was retired finally in 1989.

WONDERWORKS FAMILY MOVIE ▶ public TV's prime-time anthology series of dramatic works with particular appeal to children and to family audiences. Begun in 1984, the series frequently bases its movies on the best in young people's literature. The series has dramatized for television such children's literary classics as Frances Hodgson Burnett's *Little Princess*, C. S. Lewis's *Chronicles of Narnia,* and Lucy Maud Montgomery's *Anne of Green Gables.* Jay Rayvid is the executive producer for WQED Pittsburgh, lead station in a five-station public TV consortium.

WOOD, ROBERT D. (d. 1986) ▶ president of CBS-TV (1969-76), the executive chiefly responsible for the bolder direction taken by television during the 1970s. He resigned early in 1976, saying he could no longer endure the pressures of the job, and moved to Hollywood as an independent producer in a new company financed by CBS. In 1979, he was named president of Metromedia Producers Corp.

Wood was an effective network president, noted for his candor and his willingness to take chances. His first significant action, a year after he took office, was to rebuild the prime-time schedule even though CBS was first in the ratings—with entertainment programs keyed to the times and capable of dealing with mature themes. He startled the industry by discarding a number of programs that were still popular—those of Jackie Gleason, Red Skelton, Ed Sullivan and Andy Griffith, along with *Beverly Hillbillies, Petticoat Junction, Green Acres* and *Hee-Haw*—and replaced those programs, all of distinct rural appeal, with new urban-oriented shows.

Although most of the new 1970 series that purported to what Wood termed "contemporary relevance" were failures, CBS managed to hold onto its ratings leadership. And, as Wood had intended, the network improved its audience profile with respect to age levels, attracting more viewers in the 18-49 year age range than it had previously. Those were the young adults advertisers were most eager to reach.

Wood's most courageous—and, as it proved, most significant—decision was made at mid-season in 1970-71, when he purchased for the schedule *All in the Family,* after ABC had twice rejected its pilots. The series, whose central character was a bigot, opened the way to the new era of outspokenness and permissiveness in prime-time programming. It was, of course, a prodigious hit and led to other programs that quickly put many of the long-standing taboos of broadcasting to rest.

Until he became president of the network, where he displayed a knack for programming, Wood had spent his entire career at CBS in station management and sales. He joined KNX, the CBS radio station in Los Angeles, following graduation from USC in 1949, and shortly afterwards moved to the TV station there in a sales capacity. In 1955 he became general sales manager of KNXT (TV) and five years later v.p. and general manager of the station. He moved to New York in 1966 as executive v.p. of the CBS Television Stations and the following year became president of that division. Two years later he became head of the network. Wood held the office longer than any previous president.

WOODS, MARK ▶ early president of ABC after it was formed from NBC's Blue Network. He was elected chairman in 1950, when Robert E. Kintner became president, and became vice-chairman in 1953 in the merger with United Paramount Theatres. He resigned soon afterwards.

WORLD AT WAR, THE ▶ series of 26 documentary films produced by Thames TV of Britain and narrated by Sir Laurence Olivier, covering critical episodes of World War II. It was syndicated in the U.S. in 1973.

WORLD INTERNATIONAL NETWORK (WIN) ▶ a Hollywood-based company that has aligned 16 television operators in various territories of the world into a consortium to produce mini-series and made-for-TV movies. The ingenious financing scheme was devised by Lawrence Gershman, who previously had held high executive posts at MGM, Viacom and NBC. He founded WIN in 1988 and has since produced several original films per year.

The members of the consortium comprise the WIN board. Periodically Gershman presents the members with a project and gives them a deadline of about two weeks to decide whether they want to invest in it or not. Gershman prices each board member's involvement according to the size of the represented market, and he decides to go ahead with the project if the commitments suffice to cover the costs. In addition to the 16 television companies, five other members are video companies. The investors not only get the rights to their own territories for each project but a share of the sales to all other territories once all the production and distribution costs are covered.

The arrangement is not unlike one that was devised for U.S. independents stations in the 1970s, known as Operation Prime Time.

WORLD NEWS TONIGHT ▶ ABC evening newscast anchored by Peter Jennings that in the late 1980s established itself as number one among the three networks. The newscast made its debut in July 1978 and after a number of permutations caught fire when Jennings became anchor in 1983.

The ABC evening newscast was developed in the Roone Arledge administration, under Av Westin's supervision, and made its debut in July 1978. As the successor to the floundering *ABC Evening News* with Harry Reasoner and Barbara Walters, a program whose problems included a widely publicized feud between the two anchors, the new entry had as its distinguishing feature a three-anchor format that involved switching among three cities—Washington, Chicago and London. The anchors were Frank Reynolds in the capital, Max Robinson in the heartland and Jennings in Europe.

With Reasoner gone back to CBS, Walters represented the New York contingent as a contributor of special reports and interviews. Howard K. Smith was also part of the regular cast as commentator, although he resigned in the spring of 1979 on learning that his segment was being eliminated.

The "whiparound" system, with its electronic gimmickry and profusion of introductions that consumed precious news time, was jeered at by critics and other broadcast journalists. But after less than a year, the newscast settled into a more orthodox mold with Reynolds emerging as the dominant figure and principal anchorman. By spring of 1979, the ratings began to inch upwards to where they eventually challenged NBC's and, on occasion, even pulled ahead. In part, the gains were a reflection of ABC's growing popularity in entertainment programming and its improved affiliate lineup, resulting from the spiriting away of major affiliates from the other networks. But it was clear also that ABC News had gained credibility with viewers and that the changes in the newscast were effective.

WORLD OF SURVIVAL, THE ▶ syndicated animal documentary series produced in England by Survival-Anglia Ltd. in association with the World Wildlife Fund. With John Forsythe hosting the American version, the series was bartered for prime-access time periods by the J. Walter Thompson agency. It began in 1971 and the reruns continue in syndication.

WORLD PREMIERE MOVIES ▶ NBC's umbrella title for two-hour features made expressly for television by Universal TV during the late 1960s when theatrical motion pictures suitable for television were in short supply. The films, most of which were produced for $800,000, were essentially standard TV entertainment but were introduced—successfully at first—as movie premieres. ABC later was to beat NBC at this game by scheduling 90-minute TV movies called *The Movie of the Week,* produced by a variety of companies for half the price of the NBC films. In 1974 NBC made *The World Premiere Movie* a weekly 90-minute series, like ABC's, but returned the following year to the occasional two-hour type, shuffled in with theatrical movies.

WORLDVISION ENTERPRISES ▶ domestic and international distribution company, a unit of Spelling Entertainment Inc., whose programming has included such off-network series as

Beverly Hills 90210, Twin Peaks, Love Boat and *Streets of San Francisco.*

The company was formed in 1972 from what had been ABC Films, when the networks were forced to divest themselves of their syndication operations under the FCC's newly adopted Financial Interest and Syndication Rule. ABC sold the division, reportedly for $10 million, to a group formed by its own syndication executives, Kevin O'Sullivan, Jerry Smith, Neil Delman, Colin Campbell and Howard Lloyd. O'Sullivan, who had been president of ABC Films, became president of the new company, which the group named Worldvision.

In 1979 the company was acquired by Taft Broadcasting. In 1987 Great American Broadcasting did a buyout of Taft, and in 1989 Aaron Spelling Productions merged with Worldvision.

WPIX LICENSE CHALLENGE ▶ stormy ten-year contest for the license to operate Channel 11 in New York; it was resolved finally in May 1979 in an out-of-court settlement that secured the license for the incumbent, WPIX Inc., owned by the *New York Daily News.* The settlement involved the purchase by WPIX of all the shares in Forum Inc., the company formed expressly to file for the license, for approximately $10 million.

The proceeding, which took a number of twists and turns in its course, was begun in May 1969 after reports appeared in the press that WPIX-TV had engaged in a number of news deceptions, such as superimposing the words "via satellite" over stock military training footage and mislabeling the origins of other news reports to suggest that they were eyewitness accounts. These abuses seemed serious enough to make the license vulnerable to a challenge, and Forum was created with a widely representative group from the locale, including singer Harry Belafonte. The president of Forum was Lawrence K. Grossman, a former NBC v.p. who headed his own advertising agency, but he withdrew from Forum when he was named president of PBS.

At various points, each side scored victories that were subsequently overturned. In 1975, the competing parties worked out a settlement, but the FCC disallowed it on the ground that the public benefits to be derived from it were vague. In June 1978, the FCC voted 4-3 to renew the WPIX license, but the three who voted nay—FCC chairman Charles W. Ferris and commissioners Joseph Fogarty and Tyrone Brown, all lawyers—filed a stinging 83-page dissent that formed the basis for a court appeal by Forum. The dissenters argued that offenses that occur during a three-year license period cannot be forgiven by the positive record of a station before or after that period. Legally, they said, everything was extraneous but the station's performance during the license period in question.

Eleven months later Forum's appeal was withdrawn and the case closed by the settlement. The FCC could not oppose the payment of cash to be rid of a challenger because the matter was no longer in its jurisdiction.

The entire proceeding involved hundreds of hours of hearings and millions of dollars in legal fees, and early on it cost Fred Thrower his job as president of the station.

WRATHER, JACK (d. 1984) ▶ president of Wrather TV Productions (*Lassie, The Lone Ranger, Sgt. Preston of the Yukon*) and of Wrather-Alvarez Broadcasting Co., a station group (KFMB-TV San Diego, and others). In the late 1960s he was appointed to the board of the Corporation for Public Broadcasting by President Nixon. Wrather was also one of the founders in the 1950s of two prominent syndication companies, Television Programs of America and Independent Television Corp. (ITC), the latter now owned by Britain's ATV as its American arm.

An oil producer before he entered movie and TV production, Wrather's many interests included several hotels in the West, including the Disneyland Hotel, and he was chairman of Muzak Inc. His wife, the actress Bonita Granville, served as producer of the *Lassie* series through its long run on CBS and later in syndication.

***WRATHER-ALVAREZ BROADCASTING v. FCC* ▶** [248 F2d 646 (D.C. Cir. 1957)] case in which the Court of Appeals held that a U.S. network may affiliate with a foreign television station but that the FCC must first consider whether the station's locally originated programming merits such affiliation.

ABC had petitioned the FCC for permission to supply its programs to XETV in Tijuana, Mexico, a station that transmits a city-grade signal to San Diego, Calif. Since San Diego had only two local stations, and they carried CBS and NBC, the commission deemed it in the public interest for residents of San Diego to receive the third network. Over the objections of the two San Diego stations, the commission granted ABC's petition.

Wrather-Alvarez Broadcasting, licensee of one of the San Diego stations, appealed the case. The D.C. Court of Appeals held that there was nothing inherently wrong in permitting a foreign station transmitting into the U.S. to affiliate with an American network. The fact that this foreign station might have an advantage over nearby American stations because of its freedom from American taxes and regulatory schemes was not significant.

However, the court said, since network affiliation would immediately make XETV's programming more prominent, the FCC should have determined whether the added exposure of the local programming was in the public interest. The court remanded the case to the commission for a determination of the local program issue but held that until decided otherwise ABC could feed its programs to the Mexican station.

Robert C. Wright

WRIGHT, ROBERT C. ▶ president of NBC, succeeding Grant Tinker after 1986 and the purchase of RCA and its network by General Electric. A law graduate, Wright entered the General Electric corporate ladder as a staff attorney but quickly showed a talent for strategic planning, moving into GE management, first through plastic sales, then into housewares and audio, and by 1984 into the presidency of GE Financial Services. Before heading NBC, his experience in television was limited to a three-year break from GE to be executive v.p. of Cox Communications and president of its cable operations.

In appointing him to the NBC post, GE's chairman, Jack Welch, looked to Wright for management skills that would strengthen NBC's financial position. Wright did not disappoint, cutting the budget by $200 million and the staff by 25%, at the same time increasing NBC's revenues, particularly from sources outside the network itself.

WRITERS GUILD OF AMERICA (EAST, WEST) ▶ union formed in 1954 to represent writers in TV, radio and movies as a synthesis of the old Screen Writers, Radio Writers and Dramatists guilds, which had operated as branches of the Authors League. With a total membership of more than 10,000, the guild is made up of two units, Writers Guild of America West (WGAW) and Writers Guild of America East (WGAE), divided geographically by the Mississippi River. Each has its own council and its own branches for TV- radio and screen, but the two cooperate closely.

Writers Guild broadcast contracts cover staff writers, news writers and freelancers. They do not prohibit nonmembers from selling a first script, but those new writers are required to apply for membership within 30 days of script acceptance. In addition to establishing minimum fees and residual payments for writing, the guild specifies how writers' credits must appear on the screen and provides for their artistic rights.

The Writers Guild staged a fairly successful 13-week strike against the networks in the spring of 1981 to gain residual concessions for disc and cassette uses of television material.

WTBS SUPERSTATION ▶ the first local independent satellite to be beamed nationally by satellite, making it what came to be called a superstation. On Dec. 17, 1976, the Ted Turner-owned Atlanta station WTBS made its debut as a national station (although only 700,000 households were able to receive it) and added a new dimension to cable. The event was significant, too, in that it launched the Turner Broadcasting System, which became one of the most important forces in television during the 1980s. In also opened the way to a raft of other superstations, such as WGN-TV Chicago and WWOR-TV New York.

WTBS's broad-based entertainment service, now with a reach of more than 57 million homes, made it the first program service on basic cable to qualify for metered research by the A.C. Nielsen rating service. That was in 1981. The superstation airs some 35 movies a week along with off-network sitcoms and sports events—including the games of the teams Turner owns, the Atlanta Braves for baseball and the Atlanta Hawks for basketball. TBS also carries the Turner-created Goodwill Games, an international multi-sport summer event, held every four years since 1986. Terry Segal is TBS's executive vice president and general manager.

WTN (WORLD TELEVISION NEWS) ▶ an international news agency that, from its London base, distributes breaking news and news features to subscribing broadcasters around the world. Built on the foundation of UPITN—the erstwhile international partnership of United Press Intl. in the U.S. and ITN, the news operation of Britain's commercial ITV stations—it is owned today by America's ABC News, Britain's ITN and Australia's Nine Network. In conjunction with British Aerospace, WTN launched Starbird, Europe's first company to offer SNG (satellite newsgathering) vehicles and crews for hire.

Robert Wussler

WUSSLER, ROBERT ▶ veteran television executive who has held high posts at CBS and Turner Broadcasting, and who in September 1989 became president and CEO of Comsat Video Enterprises (CVE), a subsidiary of Communications Satellite Corp. Along with its primary business of delivering programming to hotels and motels by satellite, CVE is involved in acquiring sports and entertainment programming and in joint ventures in Eastern Europe.

Wussler joined Comsat from Turner Broadcasting System, where he was senior executive v.p. and member of the board and its executive committee. He had joined TBS in 1980 and was a key figure in the company's remarkable rise to international prominence in the span of a decade. Among his other activities, Wussler served as general manager of TBS's 129-hour telecast of the 1986 Goodwill Games from Moscow and was involved in organizing the 1990 edition from Seattle.

Earlier he was president of CBS-TV (1976-77) and twice head of CBS Sports, resigning in March 1978 to become an independent producer. Wussler's rapid rise in the executive echelons of the network, after 15 years with CBS News, came to an abrupt end with the massive reorganization of CBS in November, 1977, prompted by the network's decline in the ratings. In the reorganization, Wussler was downgraded to president of CBS Sports, and he left several months later in the wake of the "winner take all" tennis scandal, for which CBS was reprimanded by the FCC.

On his own, Wussler created ad hoc networks for several major events, including the live telecast by satellite of the Cannes Film Festival and the 1979 pre-Olympics summer series from Moscow, *Spartacade.*

In a 20-year period at CBS, Wussler rose from mailroom clerk to president of the network. He was groomed for the presidency by John A. Schneider, then president of the CBS Broadcast Group, who was impressed with the executive abilities and production savvy Wussler displayed at CBS News as director of special events (space flights, political conventions, state funerals, the coverage of assassinations, etc.). Schneider lifted him from the news division and assigned him to WBBM-TV Chicago as v.p. and general manager, at a time when the station was at a low point with the audience. After two years, the station was back on the upswing, and Wussler was rewarded with a promotion as v.p. in charge of CBS Sports, although he had little background in that field. Less than two years later, he was named president of CBS-TV when Robert D. Wood resigned.

WXUR CASE ▶ [*Brandywine-Main Line Radio Inc. v. FCC*/473 F2d 16 (D.C. Cir. 1972)] case notable for the fact that the FCC revoked a license for the first time because of Fairness Doctrine implications. The station involved was WXUR in Media, Pa. (a small town near Philadelphia), owned by Dr. Carl McIntire, head of the Faith Theological Seminary, a fundamentalist religious organization.

McIntire purchased the radio station in 1964, promising to operate in accordance with the NAB code and to comply with the Fairness Doctrine. Eighteen organizations opposed the purchase because of alleged attacks by McIntire on other religious organizations, governmental agencies and political figures. In 1965 the FCC, with one dissent, permitted the transfer of license on the ground that Faith Theological Seminary guaranteed it would provide reasonable opportunity for presentation of contrasting viewpoints on controversial issues.

A year later McIntire filed for a normal three-year license. The groups that had opposed the transfer filed against the renewal, charging that WXUR had been one-sided, unbalanced and weighted on the side of extreme right-wing radicalism. Various other religious and civic organizations attacked McIntire, and the Pennsylvania House of Representatives passed a resolution calling for an FCC investigation into its extremist views.

The FCC ordered that the renewal application be denied because the licensee had not afforded reasonable time for presentation of contrasting views on controversial issues of public importance, that it ignored the personal attack rule and that the licensee misrepresented the manner in which the station would be operated.

A petition for reconsideration was filed, which claimed that the FCC had applied the Fairness Doctrine in a manner that violated the constitutional protections of the First Amendment. When this petition was denied by the FCC, McIntire appealed to the D.C. Court of Appeals.

In the fall of 1972 the Court of Appeals affirmed the FCC's right to terminate WXUR's permit on the general ground that WXUR knowingly misrepresented itself in its transfer application and deliberately deceived the commission and the people of the Philadelphia area by not adhering to the promise of fairness.

An important aspect of the case was the dissent by Chief Judge David L. Bazelon, who wrote that this application of the Fairness Doctrine did infringe on the First Amendment rights of broadcasters. Bazelon argued that the decision imposed a double standard on broadcasters and print journalism, and he stated that the "democratic reliance on a truly informed American public is threatened if the overall effect of the Fairness Doctrine is the very censorship of controversy which it was promulgated to overcome."

After a refusal by the Supreme Court to hear McIntire's appeal, WXUR ceased operation in July 1973. When it went off the air, McIntire transferred broadcast operations to a "pirate ship" off the New Jersey coast. This operation was stopped by an order from a federal court.

WYLIE, MAX (d. 1975) ▶ writer who created the situation comedy *The Flying Nun,* and earlier wrote and produced shows for *Omnibus, The March of Time* and *Wide, Wide World,* among others. In radio days (1933-40) he worked for CBS as script director, producer and writer, then worked for Lennen & Newell Advertising in TV programming.

Thomas H. Wyman

WYMAN, THOMAS H. ▶ former chairman, president, and chief executive officer of CBS Inc. who joined in 1980 and, in boardroom melodrama, was ousted in 1986 by Laurence A. Tisch, who immediately assumed charge of the company.

During the preceding months, with Tisch gaining power through his purchase of CBS stock and asserting himself on the board, Wyman, feeling threatened, sought out Coca-Cola as a possible buyer of CBS. When Coca-Cola evinced interest, Wyman initially advised only the CBS directors he considered friendly to him, and thus outraged the others. His attempt on his own to find a buyer for the company was not only considered devious and insubordinate, but it contravened the board's determination to keep CBS independent. At any rate, it provided grounds for Wyman's dismissal.

Wyman's six-year tenure as head of the corporation was generally undistinguished. The network sank in the ratings, and the news division, disarrayed by internal changes, suffered a decline in stature and lost much of its prestige. In the Wyman years, founder William S. Paley's vaunted "Tiffany Network" became tarnished silver. Wyman's most conspicuous achievement was foiling Ted Turner's almost laughable takeover attempt in 1985, which Wyman accomplished by loading the company with so much debt that Turner, even with his junk bond offer, could not possibly afford it. The debt, however, was so heavy that CBS was forced to sell off its St. Louis station, KMOX-TV, to pay it down. While other broadcast groups were growing, CBS was down to four o&os.

Wyman was recruited by Paley from the Pillsbury Co., where he had been vice chairman, to succeed John D. Backe, the latest in a nine-year parade of presidents and heirs-apparent to be dismissed by the aging founder. Wyman was a surprising choice, because his background was in packaged foods (Nestle, Green Giant, Pillsbury) and not in media or entertainment. Within two years of his arrival, Wyman maneuvered Paley's semi-retirement as a board decision and took his title, becoming only the second chairman in the company's history.

WYNN, ED (d. 1966) ▶ venerable vaudevillian who was prominent on TV in the 1950s, first as star of a variety show and later as a lead in a family situation comedy. He also played serious dramatic roles, notably on *Playhouse 90* in *Requiem for a Heavyweight,* and made guest appearances on scores of shows.

Billed in vaudeville as "The Perfect Fool," he was a visual comedian who served the new medium well in his initial series on CBS, *The Ed Wynn Show* (1949-50). When that concluded, he appeared on a rotating basis in NBC's *Four Star Revue* (1950-51). He also starred in *The Pet Milk All Star Revue* and appeared on *Shower of Stars* and *Hallmark Hall of Fame.*

The Ed Wynn Show, produced by Screen Gems in 1958, was a family situation comedy in which Wynn portrayed the grandfather. It had a brief run. In September 1957 *Texaco Command Performance* on NBC saluted Wynn for 55 years in show business.

WYNN, TRACY KEENAN ▶ TV writer (son of actor Keenan Wynn) whose credits include *The Autobiography of Miss Jane Pittman, Tribes* and *The Glass House*—all powerful and widely praised TV dramas on film. He also wrote the pilot for the 1976 western series *The Quest* and made his directing debut with a 1975 TV movie, *Hit Lady.*

Y

YALE BROADCASTING CO. v. FCC ▶ [478 F2d 594 (D.C. Cir. 1973)/cert. den. 414 U.S. 914 (1973)] case in which the Court of Appeals upheld the right of the FCC to require management-level personnel of radio stations to be aware of the meanings of drug-related recorded music.

Having become aware in the early 1970s that numerous popular songs glorified or promoted the use of drugs, couching their messages in the esoteric language of the drug culture, the FCC issued a Notice advising management level personnel to make "reasonable efforts" to determine the meaning of the lyrics of popular recordings. The commission subsequently clarified the Notice by issuing a Memorandum stating that it was not prohibiting the playing of any records and that no reprisals would be taken against stations that played "drug-oriented" music but that it was still necessary for a station to know the content of the records played and make a judgment regarding the wisdom of playing such records.

The Yale Broadcasting Co. brought suit to challenge the Notice and Memorandum as an unconstitutional infringement upon free speech. The D.C. Court of Appeals rejected the argument, noting that to require a licensee to have knowledge of its program content was merely a form of reminder to act within the public interest standard. There was no burden upon free speech, the court said, because licensees were not required to pre-screen all programming material, and even if they were, such a burden would not be overwhelming.

Chief Judge Bazelon, who had not heard the case, proposed that the entire Circuit hear the case *en banc;* when the other judges rejected his proposal, Judge Bazelon wrote a dissent. He argued that the record clearly indicated that broadcasters had every reason to interpret the Notice as a prohibition of certain types of songs, and this, he said, amounted to an unconstitutional censorship. He cited also congressional testimony given by the chairman of the FCC in which he explicitly stated that he would vote to deny the renewal application of any licensee who played songs containing lyrics that promoted drug use.

YANKI NO! ▶ a notable hour news documentary of the *Bell and Howell Close-Up* series on ABC which aired in 1960. Produced for ABC News by an outside company, Robert Drew Associates, it examined anti-American sentiment in Cuba and other Latin American countries and revealed the widening gulf in relations between the U.S. and its neighbors. Joseph Julian narrated and William Worthy and Quinera King were reporters. Drew was executive producer and the filmmakers were Richard Leacock, Albert Maysles and Donn Pennebaker.

YATES, TED (d. 1967) ▶ producer and correspondent for NBC News who died of gunshot wounds while covering the Six Day War in the Middle East. For the DuMont Network in 1956, he helped create the Mike Wallace interview show *Nightbeat.* Later he was co-producer of *David Brinkley's Journal* (1961) for NBC News.

YES, MINISTER ▶ British comedy series satirizing government bureaucracy, which developed a strong but small following in the U.S. The series was one of the first from the BBC to bypass PBS; instead it was televised in 1982 on The Entertainment Channel, an early pay-cable service that had made a large exclusive deal with the BBC for its programming. (The channel has evolved into Arts & Entertainment, a basic service).

The foibles of British bureaucracy are amusingly illuminated through events involving the central character, an idealistic, newly elected Member of Parliament who finds many of his ideas for reform openly opposed by the civil servants whose job it is to carry them out. Produced by Sydney Lotterby, it starred Paul Eddington and featured Diane Hoddinott, Nigel Hawthorne, Derek Fowlds, and Neal Fitzwilliams.

YOGI BEAR ▶ popular cartoon character created for TV by Hanna-Barbera in 1958. Initially, the series of 30-minute cartoons was sold to Kellogg's, which placed them in markets of its choosing in early evening time. The series went to ABC in 1961 for several seasons and has been in syndication ever since. In 1973 ABC began a new series on Saturday mornings, *Yogi's Gang.*

YORKIN, BUD ▶ partner with Norman Lear in Tandem Productions, the company that broke new ground in TV in the early 1970s with such explosive hits as *All in the Family, Sanford and Son, Maude* and their several spin-offs. Yorkin was the executive producer of *Sanford* from its inception and also of the short-lived spin-off, *Grady.* He was also executive creative consultant to the *What's Happening!* series.

Before teaming with Lear to concentrate on making movies in the mid-1960s, Yorkin had made his reputation in TV as a producer-director of variety specials, such as *Another Evening with Fred Astaire,* and of the Tony Martin and Tennessee Ernie Ford weekly series. He and Lear returned to TV after securing the rights to produce American versions of the controversial but popular British series *Till Death Us Do Part* and *Steptoe and Son;* they yielded *All in the Family* and *Sanford and Son,* respectively.

YORKSHIRE TELEVISION ▶ one of Britain's 15 regional commercial television companies, serving Yorkshire in northeastern England from production studios in Leeds. As one of the "big five" of the UK's Independent TV—those regional companies that supply the bulk of programming seen nationally—Yorkshire TV is a major producer of drama, cultural programs and documentaries, some of which have been aired in the U.S., including *Sorrel and Son, Old Man and the Sea, Whicker's World on the Orient Express, Royal Family, K2: Triumph and Tragedy* and *Only When I Laugh.*

YOU ARE THERE ▶ CBS public affairs series (1954-57) and revived (1971-72) which presented dramatic re-creations of history as news events, using contemporary TV reporting techniques upon such episodes as the final hours of Joan of Arc, the death of John Dillinger and the Boston Tea Party. Walter Cronkite served as anchor, cutting away to various correspondents on the scene, as it were. Burton Benjamin was executive producer and Vera Diamond producer of the second series of half-hours.

YOU ASKED FOR IT ▶ half-hour novelty series (1955-59) that involved unusual people performing unusual stunts, with Smiling Jack Smith and Art Baker as emcees. It was revived in syndication (1971-73) by Markedon Production, with Smith hosting 56 new episodes.

It was revived again in the 1981-82 season as *The New You Asked for It,* hosted by Rich Little and syndicated by Sandy Frank.

YOU BET YOUR LIFE ▶ see Game Shows.

YOUNG AND THE RESTLESS, THE ▶ see Soap Operas.

YOUNG, COLLIER (d. 1980) ▶ a creative force in the early years of TV as producer of the *Alcoa Presents* drama series. Later, in the 1960s, he produced the series *The Rogues,* whose ratings did not reflect its critical acclaim.

YOUNG PEOPLE'S ASSOCIATION FOR THE PROPAGATION OF THE GOSPEL ▶ [6 FCC 178 (1938)] instance in which the FCC denied an application for a construction permit primarily because of the applicant's policy of refusing to allow its broadcast facilities to be used by persons or organizations wishing to present any viewpoints different from its own.

YOUNG PEOPLE'S CONCERTS ▶ CBS series of music education programs with the New York Philharmonic, which began in 1958 while Leonard Bernstein was conductor of the orchestra. Bernstein's exceptional ability to explain the intricacies of music and the purposes of the composers gave *Concerts* wide appeal and helped make it a long-running series. Michael Tilson Thomas succeeded Bernstein in the early 1970s. Roger Englander was producer-director.

YOUNG RIDERS, THE ▶ western series set in the 1860s and based on the real-life experiences of a group of frontier teenagers who risked their lives as workers for the Pony Express. It premiered on ABC in September 1989. The beautifully photographed hour-long ABC series, which was created by Ed Spielman, proved one of the most successful attempts in the western genre in recent times. The cast includes Ty Miller as The Kid, Josh Brolin as Jimmy Hickok, Anthony Zerbe as Teaspoon Hunter, and Stephen Baldwin as Billy Cody, along with Travis Fine as Ike McSwain, Gregg Rainwater as Buck Cross, Yvonne Suhor as Lou McCloud, Melissa Leo as Emma Shannon, Clare Wren as Rachel, Brett Cullen as Marshal Cain, and Don Franklin as Noah Dixon. Michael Ogiens and Josh Kane were executive producers for the first two seasons, followed by Jonas McCord and Scott Shepherd.

In August 1989, the cast members, along with members of the National Pony Express Assn., took part in a ride across eight states—a re-creation of the historic Pony Express ride—as part of a campaign to collect signatures supporting an effort to make the Pony Express Route and Historic Trail part of the National Trails System.

YOUNG, ROBERT ▶ former movie star who entered TV with a continuation of his radio situation comedy *Father Knows Best* (1954-63), and began a second career in the medium as *Marcus Welby, M.D.* (1969-76), an hour-long medical melodrama. For one season, in between, he starred in *Window on Main Street* and then did guest shots in other dramatic series.

YOUR HIT PARADE ▶ weekly series carried over from network radio spotlighting the seven most popular songs of the week, according to trade surveys, with a buildup to the song that was number one. Sponsored by Lucky Strike cigarettes, it ran nine seasons on TV, starting in 1950. Along with the top tunes, the shows featured "extras," which usually were production numbers initially staged by Tony Charmoli, and then by Ernie Flatt and Peter Gennaro.

For the first two seasons, the cast consisted of Eileen Wilson, Dorothy Collins and Snooky Lanson. Two years later, Lanson and Collins were joined by June Valli and Russell Arms, with Raymond Scott as music director. Gisele MacKenzie joined in 1953, replacing Valli. In 1957 there was a complete change of cast: Jill Corey, Virginia Gibson, Tommy Leonetti and Alan Copeland. The show was canceled in 1958 but was mounted again the following year with Dorothy Collins and Johnny Desmond, running only a few months. It was considered to be a victim of the new trend in pop music, rock.

YOUR SHOW OF SHOWS ▶ historic and remarkable 90-minute live Saturday night comedy series on NBC (1949-54) that starred Sid Caesar and Imogene Coca, featured numerous others who went on to stardom and hatched from its writing stable such talents as Neil Simon, Mel Brooks, Woody Allen, Mel Tolkin and Larry Gelbart.

Originally called *Admiral Broadway Revue,* the series took its new title soon afterwards and developed a large following for the brilliant pantomimes, satirical sketches and burlesques that became hallmarks of the Caesar-Coca artistry. Regularly featured were Carl Reiner, Howard Morris, Marguerite Piazza, the Hamilton Trio, the Billy Williams Quartet and dancers Bambi Linn and Rod Alexander. Max Liebman was the producer-director.

In 1975, kinescopes of the skits were fashioned into a theatrical movie, *Ten From Your Show of Shows,* and in 1976 Liebman compiled eight 90-minute specials from other kinescopes to offer in syndication.

Z

ZAHN, PAULA ▶ co-anchor with Harry Smith of CBS's *This Morning*, succeeding Kathleen Sullivan in February 1990. Zahn returned to CBS in 1990 after on-air assignments at ABC News, where she co-anchored *World News This Morning* and broadcast the news segments of *Good Morning America*.

In 1986-87 she was an anchor and reporter at KCBS-TV, the CBS-owned television station in Los Angeles, where she received an Emmy for her reporting on the mid-air collision of an Aeromexico jet and a private plane over Cerritos, California. Zahn began her career at WFAA-TV Dallas in 1978.

ZAMORA TRIAL ▶ a widely publicized Florida murder case in 1977 in which television was named "an accomplice" by the defense. Ronald Zamora, the 15-year-old defendant, pleaded that heavy viewing of television violence had incited him to kill an 82-year-old woman neighbor. During the week-and-a-half-long trial in Miami during October 1977, Zamora's lawyers argued persistently that television had "intoxicated" him to the point of causing him to lose his ability to distinguish right from wrong. The judge, however, refused to hear the opinions solicited by the defense from social scientists concerning the general behavioral effects of television violence. Zamora was found guilty of first-degree murder and sentenced to 25 years. After his conviction, Zamora filed a multimillion-dollar damage suit against the three networks.

Another notable aspect of the trial was the ironic presence of a television camera in the courtroom. Courts in some other states had allowed television coverage of trials, but the precedent in the Zamora case was the most far-reaching because the State Supreme Court ruled that cameras could be placed in the courtroom regardless of the desires of the prosecution or the defense.

***ZANE GREY THEATRE* ▶** successful "adult western" anthology on CBS (1956-60), hosted by and occasionally starring Dick Powell. The episodes used more than 154 guest stars, including Hedy Lamarr, Ginger Rogers and Esther Williams. It was by Four Star, Zane Grey and Pamric Productions.

ZAPPING ▶ the practice by viewers with remote-control tuners of switching channels when the commercials come on; the commercials are considered zapped like insects, in effect killed where that viewer is concerned. Advertisers and broadcasters are well aware of the dangers of zapping becoming epidemic. Meanwhile, this weapon against irritating commercials has challenged the ad industry to create more appealing spots. Ad agencies appear for the most part to have succeeded; zapping has been held reasonably in check, though it remains a potential menace to the economic system of television.

See also Grazing and Zipping.

ZAPPLE RULE ▶ the FCC's 1970 extension of the Fairness Doctrine as it applies to political campaigns, which resulted from a series of hypothetical questions posed by Nicholas Zapple, then staff counsel to the Senate Commerce Committee. In a letter to Zapple, the commission established that broadcasting's equal time obligations would apply to supporters of legally qualified candidates as well as to the candidates themselves. Thus, a broadcaster who sells air time to any person or organization supporting a candidate in an election period cannot deny the sale of comparable time to supporters of the opponents.

ZAPRUDER, ABRAHAM (d. 1970) ▶ an ordinary citizen in the wholesale clothing business who established a place in television history by filming the Kennedy motorcade in Dallas on Nov. 22, 1963, at the instant the president was shot. His 22 seconds of film, made on amateur 8mm equipment, has been replayed on television more often by far than any other newsfilm, and as a unique record of history it will continue to be televised ages hence. The TV networks were not able to show the Zapruder film until well after the assassination, however, because a lawyer representing Zapruder had accepted *Life* magazine's bid for first exclusive rights.

***ZIM BOMBA* ▶** a 13-episode syndicated TV series created by editing down to hour-long episodes old *Bomba, the Jungle Boy* (Allied Artists) theatrical movies, which had starred Johnny Sheffield. Syndication in that form began in the early 1960s, but the series' unique success was limited by the availability of only 13 films.

ZIMMERMAN, DERK ▶ veteran broadcaster who became president and CEO of Group W Productions in May 1988. Previously he was president and chief operating officer of the Fox Television Stations, and for seven years before that vice president and general manager of WFLD-TV Chicago, which became one of the Fox stations when Rupert Murdoch bought the Metromedia group.

Zimmerman's extensive background in local station operations and his programming skills figured importantly in his selection as Ed Vane's successor at Group W Productions, which produces and distributes syndicated programs to stations. He was also a known quantity at Group W, having worked there previously as senior vice president of Group W Satellite Communications and in the programming department of the company's Pittsburgh station, KDKA. Earlier in his career, he had held a range of programming and management positions with the now-defunct Kaiser Broadcasting and Field Communications station groups.

With Group W Productions, Zimmerman immediately established a working relationship with the five Group W stations, using them to test new projects intended for national syndication.

Derk Zimmerman

ZINBERG, MICHAEL ▶ producer-director for MTM Productions who, in June 1979, joined NBC-TV as v.p. of comedy development on the West Coast. In his eight years with MTM, Zinberg was executive producer of *The Bob Newhart Show,* and at various times a director and writer of episodes for *The Mary Tyler Moore Show, Rhoda, The Tony Randall Show* and *Phyllis.* Before MTM, he worked for a time with Talent Associates and with James Garner's company, Cherokee Productions.

ZIPPING ▶ companion to zapping, practiced by VCR viewers who tape shows off the air and, with the remote-control tuner, zip past the commercials on fast-forward. See also Grazing and Zapping.

ZIV, FREDERICK W. ▶ founder of the largest and most potent syndication company in the history of television, Ziv Television Programs, the leading programming force outside the networks during the 1950s. Ziv-TV produced and distributed telefilms for local station use—chiefly for 7:30 and 10:30 p.m., before those half-hours were claimed by the networks—releasing them at the rate of one every two or three months. Among its big hits were *Highway Patrol, Sea Hunt* and *Whirlybirds,* shows that eventually brought the networks into the action-adventure field. Employing scores of salesmen around the country, Ziv-TV turned out to be the Harvard Business School of television syndication, since most of its staff went on to form companies of their own or to take executive positions with a host of syndication companies that sprang up in the late 1950s and 1960s.

Ziv built his colossus from what had been a transcription company, World Broadcasting System, which he acquired from Decca Records in August 1948 for $1.5 million. Before long, he split the company into two divisions, one selling first-run programs, the other off-network reruns. In 1959 Ziv sold 80% of the company to Wall Street investment firms for $14 million. A year later the entire company went to United Artists for approximately $20 million and took the new name of Ziv-UA Television. John L. Sinn, who had been president of Ziv-TV, became president of United Artists TV. But as the conditions of the market changed, the company in 1962 gave up first run production and concentrated on selling movies and reruns. With the sale to UA, Ziv retired to reside in his native Cincinnati.

ZNAIMER, MOSES ▶ founder and president of CITY-TV, the popular youth-oriented station in Toronto. He also heads MuchMusic, a music video cable network, and its French-Canadian counterpart, MusicPlus. A sometime actor, he occasionally hosts programs his station presents, as for example a biographical series, *The Originals.*

ZONES ▶ three geographical areas designated by the FCC in its 1952 frequency allocation plan, each with a separate set of requirements for mileage separation and antenna height.

Zone I embraces Massachusetts, Rhode Island, Connecticut, New Jersey, Maryland, Pennsylvania, Delaware, District of Columbia, Ohio, Indiana, Illinois and parts of New Hampshire, Vermont, New York, Virginia, W. Virginia, Michigan, Wisconsin and Maine. In this zone, the minimum co-channel separation is 170 miles for VHF and 135 miles for UHF stations.

Zone II has a minimum co-channel separation of 190 miles for VHF and 175 for UHF. It covers Kentucky, Tennessee, N. Carolina, S. Carolina, Missouri, Iowa, Minnesota, Arkansas, Kansas, Nebraska, Oklahoma, N. Dakota, S. Dakota, Utah, Idaho, Arizona, New Mexico, Montana, Wyoming, Nevada, Colorado, Oregon, Washington, California, Alaska, Hawaii and parts of Maine, New Hampshire, Vermont, New York, Virginia, W. Virginia, Georgia, Alabama, Mississippi, Louisiana, Michigan, Wisconsin and Texas.

In Zone III, the separation is 220 miles for stations on the same VHF channel and 205 for those on UHF. This zone includes Florida and parts of Georgia, Alabama, Louisiana, Mississippi and Texas.

***ZOO GANG, THE* ▶** mini-series by ATV of London, based on Paul Gallico's best-selling book about members of a Resistance group who worked underground against the Nazis in France and meet 30 years later. Stars were Brian Keith as the Fox (Stephen Halliday), John Mills as the Elephant (Captain Tommy Devon), Lilli Palmer as the Leopard (Manouche Roget), Barry Morse as the Tiger (Alec Marlow), and Michael Petrovitch and Seretta Wilson, with music by Paul McCartney. NBC carried the six-part series during the summer of 1975.

***ZOO PARADE* ▶** early children's series on NBC (1950-57) involving visits with animals behind the scenes at Chicago's Lincoln Park Zoo. The long-running show featured Marlin Perkins, the zoo's director, and news reporter Jim Hurlbut, who asked the layperson's questions. The shows included travel films to Amazon jungles and snake farms. The series began as a local Chicago program in 1949 and went on the network the following year.

***ZOOM* ▶** public TV series of weekly half-hour programs designed to capture the whimsy and humor of children in the 6-12 age group and to encourage the active participation of young viewers. A magazine of skits, songs, dances, jokes and puzzles was presented by a resident cast of seven non-professional children from material submitted by viewers. The cast was changed every 26 weeks.

Originating on WGBH Boston, and produced initially by Christopher Sarson, the show premiered on PBS in January 1972, went off for lack of funding after three years and was revived from 1976 to 1979.

***ZORRO* ▶** briefly popular ABC adventure series (1957-59) featuring a mysterious masked rider who defends the weak and oppressed and signs his work with the initial "Z," usually carved out by sword. Set in California in 1820, the series was a Walt Disney Production. It starred Guy Williams as Zorro (whose real name was Don Diego de la Vega) and featured Gene Sheldon as Zorro's servant Bernardo, Britt Lomond as Captain Monastario, Henry Calvin as Sergeant Garcia and George J. Lewis as Zorro's father, Don Alejandro de la Vega.

The character inspired a new series in the late 1980s, an international coproduction titled *The New Zorro,* starring Duncan Regehr. It aired in the U.S. on the Family Channel, which participated in the production with New World International and France's Canal Plus for its pay channel in Spain.

ZOUSMER, JESSE (d. 1966) ▶ news executive with all three networks but usually associated with the Edward R. Murrow unit at CBS as co-producer, with John A. Aaron, of *Person to Person* and editor and writer for *Edward R. Murrow and the News.* In his 19 years with CBS, he had also been associated with Murrow's *See It Now* and its radio precursor, *Hear It Now.* In 1959 he and Aaron resigned from CBS in a dispute over the adoption of a network policy, after the quiz show scandals, requiring an advisory that the shows were rehearsed. He then joined NBC as a producer and in 1963 went to ABC as director of television news. He and his wife died in the crash of a commercial plane near Mt. Fuji in Japan.

ZWICK, EDWARD ▶ see Herskovitz, Marshall and Zwick, Edward.

ZWORYKIN, VLADIMIR K. (d. 1982) ▶ U.S. electronics engineer and inventor considered the father of modern television for inventing the iconoscope (electronic camera) and the kinescope (picture tube). Although the iconoscope was eventually replaced by the orthicon and image orthicon tubes, Zworykin's invention was the basis for further developments in television cameras. The modern TV picture tube, however, is essentially Zworykin's kinescope.

A radio expert in the Russian Army Signal Corps during World War I, Zworykin worked on X-rays and electrical and gaseous discharges and was associated with the Russian Society of Wireless Telephone and Telegraph. He immigrated to the U.S. in 1919 and a year later joined the Westinghouse Electric Corporation. It was there, while working with the cathode-tube principle he had developed in 1907, that Zworykin invented the first practical television transmission tube, his iconoscope. The device used photoelectric effects (i.e., the ejection of electrons from metals by the action of light) as the basis for scanning and converting images into electric currents.

In 1924, a year after filing a patent application for the iconoscope, he filed another for the kinescope, his TV receiver. While the older systems were electromechanical, usually involving a rapidly rotating perforated disc, Zworykin's inventions formed an all-electronic television system. Westinghouse officials were unconvinced by Zworykin's early demonstrations of his system, but in 1929 they impressed an RCA official, and the inventor accepted a position as director of electronic research at RCA. Zworykin's system became the basis for the electronic system developed by RCA.

Zworykin was named honorary vice president of RCA when he retired in 1954 and continued to remain active as a consultant. From then until 1962, he served also as director of the medical electronics center of the Rockefeller Institute for Medical Research (now Rockefeller University) in New York City. In 1967, the National Academy of Sciences awarded him the National Medal of Science for his contributions to science, engineering and television.

Vladimir K. Zworykin, the father of modern television, with a kinescope

COMING UP NEXT

BIBLIOGRAPHY

Adler, Richard and Baer, Walter S., *The Electronic Box Office: Humanities and Arts on the Cable,* Praeger, 1974.

Auletta, Ken, *Three Blind Mice,* Random House, 1991.

Barnouw, Erik, *The Image Empire,* Vol. 3: *History of Broadcast in America,* Oxford University Press, 1971.

Barnouw, Erik, *Documentary,* Oxford University Press, 1983.

Barrett, Marvin, *The Politics of Broadcasting,* Thomas Y. Crowell, 1973.

Blackwell, Earl, *Earl Blackwell's Entertainment Celebrity Register,* Visible Ink Press, 1991.

Bliss, Ed, *And Now the News,* Columbia University Press, 1991.

Bluem, A. William, *Documentary in American Television,* Hastings House, 1965.

Bluem, A. William, *Religious Television Programs,* Television Information Office and the National Assn. of Broadcasters, 1969.

Boyer, Peter J., *Who Killed CBS?,* St. Martin's Press, 1988.

Brooks, Tim and Marsh, Earle, *The Complete Directory to Prime Time Network Television Shows,* Ballantine, 1988.

Brown, Les, *Televi$ion: The Business Behind the Box,* Harcourt Brace Jovanovich, 1971.

Brown, Les, *Keeping Your Eye on Television,* Pilgrim Press, 1979.

Campbell, Robert, *The Golden Years of Broadcasting: A Celebration of the First 50 Years of Radio and TV on NBC,* Charles Scribner's Sons, 1976.

Cater, Douglass and Strickland, Stephen, *TV Violence and the Child: Evolution and Fate of the Surgeon General's Report,* Russell Sage Foundation, 1975.

Diamond, Edwin, *The Tin Kazoo,* The MIT Press, 1975.

Emery, Walter B., *Broadcasting and Government,* Michigan State University Press, 1971.

Frank, Reuven, *Out of Thin Air,* Simon & Schuster, 1991.

Friendly, Fred W., *Due to Circumstances Beyond Our Control,* Random House, 1967.

Green, Timothy, *The Universal Eye,* Stein & Day, 1972.

Jennings, Ralph and Richards, Pamela, *How to Protect Your Rights in Radio and Television,* Office of Communication, United Church of Christ, 1974.

Kanfer, Stefan, *A Journal of the Plague Years,* Atheneum, 1973.

Lesser, Gerald S., *Children and Television: Lessons from Sesame Street,* Random House, 1974.

Lichty, Lawrence W. and Topping, Malachi C., *A Source Book on the History of Radio and Television,* Hastings House, 1975.

Mayer, Martin, *About Television,* Harper & Row, 1972.

McNeil, Alex, *Total Television,* Penguin, 1991.

Metz, Robert, *CBS: Reflections in a Bloodshot Eye,* Playboy Press, 1975.

Mitchell, Curtis, *Cavalcade of Broadcasting,* Follett, 1969.

National Association of Broadcasters, *Political Broadcast Catechism,* NAB, 1976.

Quaal, Ward L. and Martin, Leo A., *Broadcast Management,* Hastings House, 1968.

Ray, Verne M., ed., *Interpreting Broadcast Rules and Regulations,* TAB, 1966 and 1972.

Rivers, William L. and Nyhan, Michael J., eds., *Aspen Notebook on Government and the Media,* Praeger, 1973.

Rivers, William L. and Slater, William T., *Aspen Handbook on the Media,* Aspen Institute Program on Communications and Society, 1975.

Rosenthal, Alan, *The Documentary Conscience,* University of California Press, 1980.

Scheuer, Steven H., ed., *Who's Who in Television and Cable,* Facts on File, 1983.

Schneider, Cy, *Children's Television,* NTC, 1989.

Schwartz, David, and Ryan, Steve and Westbrook, Fred *The Encyclopedia of TV Game Shows,* Zoetrope, 1987.

Shanks, Bob, *The Cool Fire,* W.W. Norton, 1976.

Shulman, Arthur and Youman, Roger, *How Sweet It Was,* Shorecrest, 1966.

Sloan Commission on Cable Communications, *On the Cable: The Television of Abundance,* McGraw-Hill, 1971.

Smith, Anthony, *The Shadow in the Cave: The Broadcaster, His Audience, and the State,* University of Illinois Press, 1973.

Stanley, Robert H. and Steinberg, Charles S., *The Media Environment,* Hastings House, 1976.

Stetler, Susan, ed., *Actors, Artists, Authors, and Attempted Assassins,* Visible Ink Press, 1991.

Terrace, Vincent, *The Complete Encyclopedia of Television Programs 1947-1976* (Vols. 1 and 2), A.S. Barnes, 1976.

Whitmore, Hank, *CNN: The Inside Story,* Little, Brown and Company, 1990.

Who's Who in America, Marquis.

Wilk, Max, *The Golden Age of Television,* Delacorte, 1976.

BIB Channels TV Programming Source Book

Broadcasting

Broadcasting Yearbook

Cablevision

Channels Magazine

Columbia Journalism Review

Communications Daily

Currents

Electronic Media

Entertainment Weekly

Forbes

Hollywood Creative Directory

Hollywood Reporter Blu-Book

Multichannel News

New York Times

TBI (Television Business International) Magazine

TBI's World Guide '90

Television Critics Association's National Cable Forum Guide

Television Digest Fact Book

Time Magazine

TV Guide

Variety

Wall St. Journal

APPENDIX

TOP-RATED NETWORK PRIME-TIME FEATURE FILMS

Rank	Program	Type	Date	Net	Rating	Share
1	Gone With The Wind (Part I)	T	11/7/76	NBC	47.7	65
2	Gone With The Wind (Part II)	T	11/8/76	NBC	47.4	64
3	Day After, The	M	11/20/83	ABC	46.0	62
4	Love Story	T	10/1/72	ABC	42.3	62
4	Airport	T	11/11/73	ABC	42.3	63
6	Godfather, The (Part II)	T	11/18/74	NBC	39.4	57
7	Jaws	T	11/4/79	ABC	39.1	57
8	Poseidon Adventure, The	T	10/27/74	ABC	39.0	62
9	True Grit	T	11/12/72	ABC	38.9	63
9	Birds, The	T	1/6/68	NBC	38.9	59
11	Patton	T	11/19/72	ABC	38.5	65
12	Bridge On The River Kwai	T	9/25/66	ABC	38.3	61
13	Jeremiah Johnson	T	1/18/76	ABC	37.5	56
13	Helter Skelter (Part II)	M	4/2/76	CBS	37.5	60
15	Rocky	T	2/4/79	CBS	37.1	53
15	Ben Hur	T	2/14/71	CBS	37.1	56
17	Godfather, The (Part I)	T	11/16/74	NBC	37.0	61
18	Little Ladies of The Night	M	1/16/77	ABC	36.9	53
19	Wizard Of Oz, The	T	12/13/59	CBS	36.5	58
20	Burning Bed, The	M	10/8/84	NBC	36.2	52
21	Wizard Of Oz, The	T	1/26/64	CBS	35.9	59
22	Planet Of The Apes	T	9/14/73	CBS	35.2	60
22	Helter Skelter (Part I)	M	4/1/76	CBS	35.2	57
24	Wizard Of Oz, The	T	1/17/65	CBS	34.7	49
25	Born Free	T	2/22/70	CBS	34:2	53
26	Wizard Of Oz, The	T	11/3/56	CBS	33.9	53
27	Sound Of Music, The	T	2/29/76	ABC	33.6	49
28	Bonnie & Clyde	T	9/20/73	CBS	33.4	48
29	Ten Commandments, The	T	2/18/73	ABC	33.2	54
29	Night Stalker, The	M	1/11/72	ABC	33.2	48
31	Case Of Rape, A	M	2/20/74	NBC	33.1	49
31	Longest Yard, The	T	9/25/77	ABC	33.1	53
33	Wizard Of Oz, The	T	12/9/62	CBS	33.0	55
33	Return To Mayberry	M	4/13/86	NBC	33.0	49
33	Dallas Cowboys Cheerleaders, The	M	1/14/79	ABC	33.0	48
36	Brian's Song	M	11/30/71	ABC	32.9	48
37	King Of The Grizzlies (Part II)	T	11/4/73	NBC	32.8	51
38	Fatal Vision (Part II)	M	11/19/84	NBC	32.7	49
38	Wizard Of Oz, The	T	12/11/60	CBS	32.7	52
40	Beneath The Planet Of The Apes	T	10/26/73	CBS	32.6	54
41	Wizard Of Oz, The	T	12/10/61	CBS	32.5	53

T-theatrical M-made for TV

TOP-RATED NETWORK SPORTS EVENTS

	Program	Date	Net.	H'sehold Rat.	Share
1.	Super Bowl XVI (San Francisco vs. Cincinnati)	1/24/82	CBS	49.1	73
2.	Super Bowl XVII (Washington vs. Miami)	1/30/83	NBC	48.6	69
3.	Super Bowl XX (Chicago vs. New England)	1/26/86	NBC	48.3	70
4.	Super Bowl XII (Dallas vs. Denver)	1/15/78	CBS	47.2	67
5.	Super Bowl XIII (Dallas vs. Pittsburgh)	1/21/79	NBC	47.1	74
6.	Super Bowl XVIII (L.A. Raiders vs. Washington)	1/22/84	CBS	46.4	71
6.	Super Bowl XIX (San Francisco vs. Miami)	1/20/85	ABC	46.4	63
8.	Super Bowl XIV (L.A. Rams vs. Pittsburgh)	1/20/80	CBS	46.3	67
9.	Super Bowl XXI (N.Y. Giants vs. Denver)	1/25/87	CBS	45.8	66
10.	Super Bowl XI (Minnesota vs. Oakland Raiders)	1/9/77	NBC	44.4	73
10.	Super Bowl XV (Philadelphia vs. Oakland Raiders)	1/25/81	NBC	44.4	63
12.	Super Bowl VI (Dallas vs. Miami)	1/16/72	CBS	44.2	74
13.	Super Bowl XXIII (Cincinnati vs. San Francisco)	1/22/89	NBC	43.5	68
14.	NFC Championship Game (Dallas vs. San Francisco)	1/10/82	CBS	42.9	62
15.	Super Bowl VII (Washington vs. Miami)	1/14/73	NBC	42.7	72
16.	Super Bowl IX (Minnesota vs. Pittsburgh)	1/12/75	NBC	42.4	72
17.	Super Bowl X (Dallas vs. Pittsburgh)	1/8/76	CBS	42.3	78
18.	Super Bowl XXV (Buffalo vs. N.Y. Giants)	1/27/91	ABC	41.9	63
18.	Super Bowl XXII (Washington vs. Denver)	1/31/88	ABC	41.9	62
20.	Super Bowl VIII (Minnesota vs. Miami)	1/13/74	CBS	41.6	73
21.	World Series Game #6 (Kansas City vs. Philadelphia)	10/21/80	NBC	40.0	60
22.	Super Bowl V (Dallas vs. Baltimore)	1/17/71	NBC	39.9	75
23.	World Series Game #7 (Boston vs. Cincinnati)	10/22/75	NBC	39.6	60
24.	World Series Game #4 (Yankees vs. Dodgers)	10/6/63	NBC	39.5	87
25.	Super Bowl IV (Minnesota vs. Kansas City)	1/11/70	CBS	39.4	69

* includes preliminary bouts

SUPER BOWL RATING HISTORY

Year	Game	Network	Total Rating	Audience Share
1967	Green Bay-Kansas City	CBS	33.1	43
1968	Green Bay-Oakland	CBS	48.3	68
1969	N.Y. Jets-Baltimore	NBC	47.1	71
1970	Kansas City-Minnesota	CBS	52.7	69
1971	Baltimore-Dallas	NBC	50.7	75
1972	Dallas-Miami	CBS	55.0	74
1973	Miami-Washington	NBC	54.1	72
1974	Miami-Minnesota	CBS	51.9	73
1975	Minnesota-Pittsburgh	NBC	53.9	72
1976	Dallas-Pittsburgh	CBS	53.7	78
1977	Oakland-Minnesota	NBC	44.4	73
1978	Dallas-Denver	CBS	47.2	67
1979	Dallas-Pittsburgh	NBC	47.1	74
1980	Los Angeles-Pittsburgh	CBS	46.3	67
1981	Oakland-Philadelphia	NBC	44.4	63
1982	Cincinnati-San Francisco	CBS	49.1	73
1983	Washington-Miami	NBC	48.6	69
1984	Washington-L.A. Raiders	CBS	46.4	71
1985	San Francisco-Miami	ABC	46.4	63
1986	Chicago-New England	NBC	48.3	70
1987	Denver-N.Y. Giants	CBS	45.8	66
1988	Washington-Denver	ABC	41.9	62
1989	San Francisco-Cincinnati	NBC	43.5	68
1990	San Francisco-Denver	CBS	39.0	63
1991	N.Y. Giants-Buffalo	ABC	41.9	63

TOP-RATED NETWORK PROGRAMS

Rank	Program	Telecast Date	Net.	Dur. Min.	Avg. Aud. %	Share	Avg. Aud.‡
1	M*A*S*H Special	Feb. 28, 1983	CBS	150	60.2	77	50,150
2	Dallas	Nov. 21, 1980	CBS	60	53.3	76	41,470
3	Roots Pt. VIII	Jan. 30, 1977	ABC	115	51.1	71	36,380
4	Super Bowl XVI Game	Jan. 24, 1982	CBS	213	49.1	73	40,020
5	Super Bowl XVII Game	Jan. 30, 1983	NBC	204	48.6	69	40,480
6	Super Bowl XX Game	Jan. 26, 1986	NBC	231	48.3	70	41,490
7	Gone With the Wind Pt. 1*	Nov. 7, 1976	NBC	179	47.7	65	33,960
8	Gone With the Wind Pt. 2†	Nov. 8, 1976	NBC	119	47.4	64	33,750
9	Super Bowl XII Game	Jan. 15, 1978	CBS	218	47.2	67	34,410
10	Super Bowl XIII Game	Jan. 21, 1979	NBC	230	47.1	74	35,090
11	Bob Hope Christmas Show	Jan. 15, 1970	NBC	90	46.6	64	27,260
12	Super Bowl XVIII Game	Jan. 22, 1984	CBS	218	46.4	71	38,800
12	Super Bowl XIX Game	Jan. 20, 1985	ABC	218	46.4	63	39,390
14	Super Bowl XIV Game	Jan. 20, 1980	CBS	178	46.3	67	35,330
15	ABC Theater (The Day After)	Nov. 20, 1983	ABC	144	46.0	62	38,550
16	Roots Pt. VI	Jan. 28, 1977	ABC	120	45.9	66	32,680
16	The Fugitive	Aug. 29, 1967	ABC	60	45.9	72	25,700
18	Super Bowl XXI Game	Jan. 25, 1987	CBS	206	45.8	66	40,030
19	Roots Pt. V	Jan. 27, 1977	ABC	60	45.7	71	32,540
20	Ed Sullivan	Feb. 9, 1964	CBS	60	45.3	60	23,240
21	Bob Hope Christmas Show	Jan. 14, 1971	NBC	90	45.0	61	27,050
22	Roots Pt. III	Jan. 25, 1977	ABC	60	44.8	68	31,900
23	Super Bowl XI Game	Jan. 9, 1977	NBC	204	44.4	73	31,610
23	Super Bowl XV Game	Jan. 25, 1981	NBC	220	44.4	63	34,540
25	Super Bowl VI Game	Jan. 16, 1972	CBS	170	44.2	74	27,450
26	Roots Pt. II	Jan. 24, 1977	ABC	120	44.1	62	31,400
27	Beverly Hillbillies	Jan. 8, 1964	CBS	30	44.0	65	22,570
28	Roots Pt. IV	Jan. 26, 1977	ABC	60	43.8	66	31,190
28	Ed Sullivan	Feb. 16, 1964	CBS	60	43.8	60	22,445
30	Super Bowl XXIII Game	Jan. 22, 1989	NBC	213	43.5	68	39,320
31	Academy Awards	Apr. 7, 1970	ABC	145	43.4	78	25,390
32	Thorn Birds Pt. III	Mar. 29, 1983	ABC	120	43.2	62	35,990
33	Thorn Birds Pt. IV	Mar. 30, 1983	ABC	180	43.1	62	35,900
34	CBS NFC Champ. Game	Jan. 10, 1982	CBS	195	42.9	62	34,960
35	Beverly Hillbillies	Jan. 15, 1964	CBS	30	42.8	62	21,960

*Big Event Part 1 †NBC Monday Movie ‡ in thousands

continued

TOP-RATED NETWORK PROGRAMS (cont'd)

Rank	Program	Telecast Date	Net.	Dur. Min.	Avg. Aud. %	Share	Avg. Aud.‡
36	Super Bowl VII Game	Jan. 14, 1973	NBC	185	42.7	72	27,670
37	Thorn Birds Pt. II	Mar. 28, 1983	ABC	120	42.5	59	35,400
38	Super Bowl IX Game	Jan. 12, 1975	NBC	190	42.4	72	29,040
38	Beverly Hillbillies	Feb. 26, 1964	CBS	30	42.4	60	21,750
40	Super Bowl X Game	Jan. 18, 1976	CBS	200	42.3	78	29,440
40	Airport (Movie Specials)	Nov. 11, 1973	ABC	170	42.3	63	28,000
40	Love Story (Sun. Night Mov.)	Oct. 1, 1972	ABC	120	42.3	62	27,410
40	Cinderella	Feb. 22, 1965	CBS	90	42.3	59	22,250
40	Roots Pt. VII	Jan. 29, 1977	ABC	60	42.3	65	30,120
45	Beverly Hillbillies	Mar. 25, 1964	CBS	30	42.2	59	21,650
46	Beverly Hillbillies	Feb. 6, 1964	CBS	30	42.0	61	21,550
47	Super Bowl XXV Game	Jan. 27, 1991	ABC	208	41.9	63	39,010
47	Beverly Hillbillies	Jan. 29, 1964	CBS	30	41.9	62	21,490
47	Super Bowl XXII Game	Jan. 31, 1988	ABC	229	41.9	62	37,120
50	Miss America Pageant	Sept. 9, 1961	CBS	150	41.8	75	19,600
50	Beverly Hillbillies	Jan. 1, 1964	CBS	30	41.8	59	21,440

‡ in thousands

Note: Average audience % rankings based on reports made July 1960 through January 31, 1991. Above data represent sponsored programs telecast on individual networks; i.e., no unsponsored or joint network telecasts are reflected. Programs under 30 minutes scheduled duration are excluded.

NFL INCOME FROM NATIONAL TV IN COMPARATIVE PERIODS

Network	1990-93 Contract	Avg./season	1987-89 Avg./season	% Gain
CBS	$1.06 billion	$265 million	$150 million	76.7%
ABC	$900 million	$225 million	$155 million	45.2%
NBC	$752 million	$188 million	$120 million	56.7%
Cable	$900 million	$225 million	$51 million	341.2%
Total	$3.65 billion	$913 million	$476 million	91.8%

TELEVISION HOUSEHOLDS IN U.S.

Year	Total Households*	Total TV Households*	% With TV
1949-1950	43,000	3,880	9.0
1950-1951	43,890	10,320	23.5
1951-1952	44,760	15,300	34.2
1952-1953	45,640	20,400	44.7
1953-1954	46,660	26,000	55.7
1954-1955	47,620	30,700	64.5
1955-1956	48,600	34,900	71.8
1956-1957	49,500	38,900	78.6
1957-1958	50,370	41,920	83.2
1958-1959	51,150	43,950	85.9
1959-1960	52,500	45,750	87.1
1960-1961	53,170	47,200	88.8
1961-1962	54,300	48,855	90.0
1962-1963	55,100	50,300	91.3
1963-1964	55,900	51,600	92.3
1964-1965	56,900	52,700	92.6
1965-1966	57,900	53,850	93.0
1966-1967	58,900	55,130	93.6
1967-1968	59,900	56,670	94.6
1968-1969	61,300	58,250	95.0
1969-1970	61,410	58,500	95.3
1970-1971	62,910	60,100	95.5
1971-1972	64,850	62,100	95.8
1972-1973	67,210	64,800	96.4
1973-1974	68,310	66,200	96.9
1974-1975	70,520	68,500	97.1
1975-1976	71,460	69,600	97.4
1976-1977	73,100	71,200	97.4
1977-1978	74,700	72,900	97.6
1978-1979	76,240	74,500	97.7
1979-1980	77,900	76,300	97.9
1980-1981	81,480	79,900	98.1
1981-1982	83,120	81,500	98.1

* in thousands

continued

TELEVISION HOUSEHOLDS IN U.S. (cont'd)

Year	Total Households*	Total TV Households*	% With TV
1982-1983	84,940	83,300	98.1
1983-1984	85,430	83,800	98.1
1984-1985	86,530	84,900	98.1
1985-1986	87,590	85,900	98.1
1986-1987	89,125	87,400	98.1
1987-1988	90,270	88,600	98.1
1988-1989	92,030	90,400	98.1
1989-1990	93,760	92,100	98.1
1990-1991	94,800	93,100	98.2
1991-1992	93,680	92,100	98.2

* in thousands

Source: NBC 1950-1969 (Jan. each year), Nielsen 1970-90 (Sep. each year); all years prior to 1988-89 excluded Alaska and Hawaii.

NETWORK SUBSCRIBER COUNTS

Basic Services	Affiliates	Subscribers
American Movie Classics	2,828	35,000,000
Arts & Entertainment Network	7,000	51,000,000
Black Entertainment Television	2,407	31,371,550
Bravo	455	6,000,000
C-SPAN	4,055	54,000,000
C-SPAN II	800	24,500,000
Cable News Network	10,877	56,892,000
Channel America	13	429,300
CNBC	3,000	43,000,000
Comedy Central	1,282	18,250,000
Country Music Television	1,974	13,700,000
Courtroom Television Network	N/A	4,800,000
Discovery Channel, The	9,397	56,000,000

continued

NETWORK SUBSCRIBER COUNTS (cont'd)

Basic Services	Affiliates	Subscribers
E! Entertainment Television	777	18,750,000
ESPN*	23,300	59,195,000
EWTN	774	23,300,000
Family Channel, The	9,500	53,500,000
Fox Net	275	1,000,000
Galavision	249	1,750,000
Headline News	5,506	46,856,000
Home Shopping Network	1,502	18,000,000
Home Shopping Network II	400	7,000,000
HSN Infomercial Channel	N/A	N/A
Inspirational Network, The	850	6,500,000
International Channel	35	2,200,000
KTLA	292	4,800,000
KTVT	481	2,200,000
Learning Channel, The	1,196	15,600,000
Lifetime	5,400	53,000,000
Mind Extension University	402	15,000,000
Monitor Channel, The	340	3,500,000
MTV	7,430	56,600,000
Nashville Network, The	12,259	53,900,000
Nick At Nite	3,837	50,250,000
Nickelodeon	8,635	55,400,000
Nostalgia Television	640	12,300,000
Prevue Guide	835	24,526,075
QVC Fashion Channel	380	6,000,000
QVC Network	3,900	41,000,000
SportsChannel America†	58	2,320,000
TBS Superstation	11,105	57,207,000
Telemundo	36	1,362,036
TNT	6,958	54,190,000
Travel Channel, The	735	17,500,000
Trinity Broadcasting Network	1,015	13,300,000
Univision	814	11,062,692
USA Network	10,100	58,000,000
VH-1	3,985	41,800,000
Video Jukebox Network	96	9,050,000
VISN	670	10,200,000
Weather Channel, The	4,500	49,063,000
WGN	13,969	34,900,000
WPIX	641	9,200,000
WSBK	73	2,000,000
WWOR	3,013	13,500,000

N/A-information not available   * includes MMDS/SMATV systems

continued

† count represents stand-alone affiliates/subscribers; portions are carried on various regional sports networks

NETWORK SUBSCRIBER COUNTS (cont'd)

Pay Services	Affiliates	Subscribers
Cinemax	5,458	6,400,000
Disney Channel, The	7,000	5,665,000
Encore	854	25,000
Home Box Office	8,833	17,300,000
Movie Channel, The	3,250	2,800,000
Showtime	6,000	7,400,000
TV-Japan	5	N/A

NETWORK SUBSCRIBER COUNTS
(Regional)

Basic Services	Affiliates	Subscribers
Arizona Sports	1	310,000
Atlanta Interfaith	3	225,000
Bay Area Religious Channel	6	113,000
Cable TV Network of New Jersey	34	1,500,000
CAL-SPAN	42	2,100,000
The Ecumenical Channel	9	170,000
Empire Sports Network	15	316,000
Florida Tourism Channel	20	754,000
Home Sports Entertainment	475	2,400,000
KBL Sports Network	67	1,200,000
Madison Square Garden Network	16	4,500,000
Meadows Racing Network	17	700,000
Midwest Sports Channel	90	610,000
NewsChannel 8	8	650,000
News 12 Long Island	4	601,000
Northwest Cable Sports Network	3	700,000
Orange County Cable News	8	350,000
Pennsylvania Cable Network‡	28	750,000
Prime Sports/Intermountain West	30	328,000
Prime Sports/Midwest	6	182,000
Prime Sports/Northwest	65	1,100,000
Prime Sports/Rocky Mountain	110	935,000
Prime Sports/Upper Midwest	4	185,000
Prime Ticket	128	4,200,000
SportsChannel Bay Area	35	300,000
SportsChannel Chicago	75	1,980,000
SportsChannel Cincinnati	14	300,541

N/A-information not available ‡ formerly Pennarama

continued

NETWORK SUBSCRIBER COUNTS (cont'd)
(Regional)

Basic Services	Affiliates	Subscribers
SportsChannel Florida	74	1,100,000
SportsChannel Ohio	33	904,000
SportsChannel Philadelphia	41	1,300,000
SportSouth	70	1,000,000
Sunshine Network	189	3,078,542

Pay Services	Affiliates	Subscribers
Home Team Sports	205	2,200,000
New England Sports Network	171	380,000
Prism	87	470,000
Pro-Am Sports	240	750,000
SportsChannel Los Angeles	76	125,000
SportsChannel New England	164	1,300,000
SportsChannel New York	117	1,400,000
SportsChannel Pacific	65	1,700,000

N/A-information not available

Source: *Cablevision* magazine

HISTORICAL U.S. CABLE PENETRATION

Measurement Period		Total Est. Households	% Cable Penetration
1981	Jul	21,930,490	27.3
	Nov	23,219,200	28.3
1982	Feb	23,726,220	29.0
	May	27,362,000	33.4
	Jul	27,884,000	34.0
	Nov	29,340,570	35.0
1983	Feb	31,124,450	37.2

continued

HISTORICAL U.S. CABLE PENETRATION (cont'd)

Measurement Period		Total Est. Households	% Cable Penetration
1983	May	31,766,500	37.9
	Jul	32,930,140	39.3
	Nov	34,113,790	40.5
1984	Feb	34,740,330	41.2
	May	35,783,000	42.5
	Jul	36,105,500	42.9
	Nov	37,290,870	43.7
1985	Feb	38,018,100	44.6
	May	38,673,270	45.3
	Jul	38,955,150	45.7
	Nov	39,872,520	46.2
1986	Feb	40,389,760	46.8
	May	40,921,970	47.4
	Jul	41,248,380	47.8
	Nov	42,237,140	48.1
1987	Feb	42,820,780	48.7
	May	43,279,980	49.2
	Jul	43,490,700	49.5
	Nov	44,970,880	50.5
1988	Feb	45,480,100	51.1
	May	46,296,010	52.0
	Jul	47,042,470	52.8
	Nov	48,636,520	53.8
1989	Feb	49,537,730	54.8
	May	50,241,840	55.6
	Jul	50,897,080	56.4
	Nov	52,564,470	57.1
1990	Feb	53,238,990	57.8
	May	53,903,630	58.6
	Jul	54,235,200	58.9
	Nov	54,871,330	59.0
1991	Feb	55,561,780	59.7
	May	56,072,270	60.3
	Jul	56,072,840	60.3

HISTORICAL U.S. VCR AND PAY CABLE PENETRATION

Measurement Period		% VCR Penetration	% Pay Cable Penetration
1983	Nov	9.0%	24.2%
1984	Feb	10.7%	24.8%
	May	12.4%	25.5%
	Jul	13.7%	25.8%
	Nov	15.8%	25.9%
1985	Feb	20.8%	26.3%
	May	23.2%	26.4%
	Jul	25.3%	N/A
	Nov	29.1%	26.8%
1986	Feb	36.0%	26.7%
	May	39.0%	26.5%
	Jul	39.9%	26.1%
	Nov	43.5%	26.2%
1987	Feb	48.7%	26.6%
	May	49.7%	26.8%
	Jul	50.9%	27.4%
	Nov	53.3%	28.6%
1988	Feb	58.1%	28.3%
	May	59.0%	28.3%
	Jul	60.0%	28.8%
	Nov	62.2%	29.1%
1989	Feb	64.6%	29.2%
	May	65.5%	29.4%
	Jul	65.8%	29.4%
	Nov	66.9%	29.4%
1990	Feb	68.6%	29.7%
	May	69.4%	29.2%
	Jul	69.8%	29.0%
	Nov	70.2%	28.6%
1991	Feb	71.9%	28.5%
	May	72.5%	28.2%
	Jul	72.5%	28.0%

FCC COMMISSIONERS

Name	Party	State	Term From	Term To
Eugene O. Sykes (d)	Democrat	Mississippi	Jul 11, 1934	Apr 5, 1939
			*Jul 11, 1934	Mar 8, 1935
Thad H. Brown (d)	Republican	Ohio	Jul 11, 1934	Jun 30, 1940
Paul A. Walker (d)	Democrat	Oklahoma	Jul 11, 1934	Jun 30, 1953
			†Nov 3, 1947	Dec 28, 1947
			*Feb 28, 1952	Apr 17, 1953
Norman Case (d)	Republican	Rhode Island	Jul 11, 1934	Jun 30, 1945
Irvin Stewart	Democrat	Texas	Jul 11, 1934	Jun 30, 1937
George Henry Payne (d)	Republican	New York	Jul 11, 1934	Jun 30, 1943
Hampson Gary (d)	Democrat	Texas	Jul 11, 1934	Jan 1, 1935
Anning S. Prall (d)	Democrat	New York	Jan 17,1935	Jul 23, 1937
			*Mar 9, 1935	Jul 23, 1937
T.A.M. Craven (d)	Democrat	Dist. of Col.	Aug 25, 1937	Jun 30, 1944
		Virginia	Jul 2, 1956	Mar 25, 1963
Frank McNinch (d)	Democrat	N. Carolina	Oct 1, 1937	Aug 31, 1939
			*Oct 1, 1937	Aug 31, 1939
Frederick I. Thompson (d)	Democrat	Alabama	Apr 13, 1939	Jun 30, 1941
James Lawrence Fly (d)	Democrat	Texas	Sep 1, 1939	Nov 13, 1944
			*Sep 1, 1939	Nov 13, 1944
Ray C. Wakefield	Republican	California	Mar 22, 1941	Jun 30, 1947
Clifford J. Durr (d)	Democrat	Alabama	Nov 1, 1941	Jun 30, 1948
Ewell K. Jett (d)	Independent	Maryland	Feb 15, 1944	Dec 31, 1947
			‡Nov 16, 1944	Dec 20, 1944
Paul A. Porter (d)	Democrat	Kentucky	Dec 21, 1944	Feb 25, 1946
			*Dec 21, 1944	Feb 25, 1946
Charles R. Denny	Democrat	Dist. of Col.	Mar 30, 1945	Oct 31, 1947
			†Feb 26, 1946	Dec 3, 1946
			*Dec 4, 1946	Oct 31, 1947

(d) deceased *Chairman †Acting Chair ‡Interim Chair

continued

FCC COMMISSIONERS (cont'd)

Name	Party	State	Term From	Term To
William H. Willis (d)	Republican	Vermont	Jul 23, 1945	Mar 6, 1946
Rosel H. Hyde	Republican	Idaho	Apr 17, 1946	Oct 31, 1969
			*Apr 18, 1953	Apr 18, 1954
			†Apr 19, 1954	Oct 3, 1954
			†May 1, 1966	Jun 26, 1966
			*Jun 27, 1966	Oct 31, 1969
Edward M. Webster (d)	Independent	Dist.of Col.	Apr 10, 1947	Jun 30, 1956
Robert F. Jones (d)	Republican	Ohio	Sep 5, 1947	Sep 19, 1952
Wayne Coy (d)	Democrat	Indiana	Dec 29, 1947	Feb 21, 1952
			*Dec 29, 1947	Feb 21, 1952
George E. Sterling	Republican	Maine	Jan 2, 1948	Sep 30, 1954
Frieda B. Hennock (d)	Democrat	New York	Jul 6, 1948	Jun 30, 1955
Robert T. Bartley (d)	Democrat	Texas	Mar 6, 1952	Jun 30, 1972
Eugene H. Merrill (d)	Democrat	Utah	Oct 6, 1952	Apr 15, 1953
John C. Doerfer	Republican	Wisconsin	Apr 15, 1953	Mar 10, 1960
			*Jul 1, 1957	Mar 10, 1960
Robert E. Lee	Republican	Illinois	Oct 6, 1953	Jun 30, 1981
			‡Feb 5, 1981	Apr 12, 1981
			*Apr 13, 1981	May 18, 1981
Geo. C. McConnaughey (d)	Republican	Ohio	Oct 4, 1954	Jun 30, 1957
			*Oct 4, 1954	Jun 30, 1957
Richard A. Mack (d)	Democrat	Florida	Jul 7, 1955	Mar 3, 1958
Frederick W. Ford (d)	Republican	W. Virginia	Aug 29, 1957	Dec 31, 1964
			*Mar 15, 1960	Mar 1, 1961
John S. Cross (d)	Democrat	Arkansas	May 23, 1958	Sep 30, 1962
Charles H. King	Republican	Michigan	July 19, 1960	Mar 2, 1961
Newton N. Minow	Democrat	Illinois	Mar 2, 1961	Jun 1, 1963
			*Mar 2, 1961	Jun 1, 1963

(d) deceased *Chairman †Acting Chair ‡Interim Chair

continued

FCC COMMISSIONERS (cont'd)

Name	Party	State	Term From	To
E. William Henry	Democrat	Tennessee	Oct 2, 1962 *Jun 2, 1963	May 1, 1966 May 1, 1966
Kenneth A. Cox	Democrat	Washington	Mar 26, 1963	Aug 31, 1970
Lee Loevinger	Democrat	Minnesota	Jun 11, 1963	Jun 30, 1968
James J. Wadsworth (d)	Republican	New York	May 5, 1965	Oct 31, 1969
Nicholas Johnson	Democrat	Iowa	July 1, 1966	Dec 5, 1973
H. Rex Lee	Democrat	Dist. of Col.	Oct 28, 1968	Dec 31, 1973
Dean Burch	Republican	Arizona	Oct 31, 1969 *Oct 31, 1969	Mar 8, 1974 Mar 8, 1974
Robert Wells	Republican	Kansas	Nov 6, 1969	Nov 1, 1971
Thomas J. Houser	Republican	Illinois	Jan 6, 1971	Oct 5, 1971
Charlotte T. Reid	Republican	Illinois	Oct 8, 1971	Jul 1, 1976
Richard E. Wiley	Republican	Illinois	Jan 5, 1972 *Mar 8, 1974	Oct 13, 1977 Oct 13, 1977
Benjamin L. Hooks	Democrat	Tennessee	Jul 5, 1972	Jul 25, 1977
James H. Quello	Democrat	Michigan	Apr 30, 1974--	
Glen O. Robinson	Democrat	Minnesota	July 10, 1974	Aug 30, 1976
Abbott M. Washburn	Republican	Minnesota	July 10, 1974	Oct 1, 1982
Joseph R. Fogarty	Democrat	Rhode Island	Sep 17, 1976	Jun 30, 1983
Margita E. White	Republican	Sweden	Sep 23, 1976	Feb 28, 1979
Charles D. Ferris	Democrat	Massachusetts	Oct 17, 1977 *Oct 17, 1977	Apr 10, 1981 Feb 4, 1981
Tyrone Brown	Democrat	Virginia	Nov 15, 1977	Jan 31, 1981
Anne P. Jones	Republican	Massachusetts	Apr 7, 1979	May 31, 1983
Mark S. Fowler	Republican	Canada	May 18, 1981	Apr 17, 1987

(d) deceased *Chairman †Acting Chair ‡Interim Chair

continued

FCC COMMISSIONERS (cont'd)

Name	Party	State	Term From	To
Mark S. Fowler (cont'd)			*May 18, 1981	Apr 17, 1987
Mimi Weyforth Dawson	Republican	Missouri	Jul 6, 1981	Dec 3, 1987
Henry M. Rivera	Democrat	New Mexico	Aug 10, 1981	Sep 15, 1985
Stephen A. Sharp	Republican	Ohio	Oct 4, 1982	Jun 30, 1983
Dennis R. Patrick	Republican	California	Dec 2, 1983 *Apr 18, 1987	Apr 17, 1987 Aug 7, 1989
Patricia Diaz Dennis	Democrat	New Mexico	Jun 25, 1986	Sep 29, 1989
Alfred C. Sikes	Republican	Missouri	Aug 8, 1989-- *Aug 8, 1989--	
Sherrie P. Marshall	Republican	Florida	Aug 21, 1989--	
Andrew C. Barrett	Republican	Georgia	Sep 8, 1989--	
Ervin S. Duggan	Democrat	Georgia	Feb 28, 1990--	

(d) deceased *Chairman †Acting Chair ‡Interim Chair

WORLDWIDE TV ADVERTISING EXPENDITURES

Africa

Country	Pop.‡	1990 Adv. Exp.†	Adv. Exp. Per Cap.*	1991 Forecast†	Adv. Exp. % '91 vs. '90
Egypt	(51.4)	(34)	(0.7)		
Kenya	(23.3)	(2)	(0.1)		
South Africa	35.5	237	6.7	247	4.3
Zambia	(7.8)	(1)	(0.1)		
Zimbabwe	(9.6)	(4)	(0.5)		
Total	35.3	237	6.7	247	4.3

‡ in millions * in U.S. $ † in millions U.S.

continued

WORLDWIDE TV ADVERTISING EXPENDITURES (cont'd)

Europe

Country	Pop.‡	1990 Adv. Exp.†	Adv. Exp. Per Cap.*	1991 Forecast†	Adv. Exp. % '91 vs. '90
Austria	7.6	265	34.9	274	3.5
Belgium	9.9	394	39.8	409	3.9
Cyprus	(0.7)	(9)	(13.2)		
Denmark	5.1	97	19	141	45.3
Finland	5.0	169	33.8	167	-1.3
France	56.4	2,314	41	2,365	2.2
Germany (W)	62.3	1,711	27.5	1,904	11.3
Greece	10	221	22.1	288	30.4
Ireland	3.5	85	24.3	84	-0.6
Italy	57.6	3,364	58.4	3,451	2.6
Malta	(0.4)	(3)	(9.4)		
Netherlands	14.9	343	23	400	16.7
Norway	4.3	18	4.2	22	24
Portugal	10.5	182	17.3	188	3.1
Spain	38.9	2,460	63.2	2,713	10.3
Sweden	8.5	46	5.4	84	83.5
Switzerland	6.7	158	23.6	159	0.9
Turkey	58.8	280	4.8	311	11
United Kingdom	57.4	4,150	72.3	3,893	-6.2
Total	417.4	16,257	38.9	16,853	3.7

North America

Country	Pop.‡	1990 Adv. Exp.†	Adv. Exp. Per Cap.*	1991 Forecast†	Adv. Exp. % '91 vs. '90
Canada	26.5	1,345	50.8	1,272	-5.4
United States	251.3	29,410	117	28,969	-1.5
Total	277.8	30,755	110.7	30,241	-1.7

‡ in millions   * in U.S. $ † in millions U.S.

continued

WORLDWIDE TV ADVERTISING EXPENDITURES (cont'd)

Asia/Pacific

Country	Pop.‡	1990 Adv. Exp.†	Adv. Exp. Per Cap.*	1991 Forecast†	Adv. Exp. % '91 vs. '90
Australia	17	1,338	78.7	1,307	-2.3
China	1,135	85	0.1	56	-34.7
Hong Kong	5.8	422	72.8	439	4
India	827	145	0.2	168	15.6
Indonesia	182.6	28	0.2	168	15.6
Japan	123.7	11,082	89.6	11,570	4.4
Malaysia	17.1	125	7.3	154	23.3
New Zealand	3.3	210	63.6	213	1.4
Pakistan	(110)	(30)	(0.3)		
Philippines	61.5	128	2.1	143	11.4
Singapore	2.7	96	35.6	111	15.4
South Korea	42.8	845	19.7	1,040	23.1
Sri Lanka	(16.8)	(3)	(0.2)		
Taiwan	20.2	596	29.5	676	13.5
Thailand	56.4	254	4.5	282	11.1
Total	2,495.1	15,354	6.2	16,275	6.0

Latin America/Caribbean

Country	Pop.‡	1990 Adv. Exp.†	Adv. Exp. Per Cap.*	1991 Forecast†	Adv. Exp. % '91 vs. '90
Argentina	(31.9)	(104)	(3.3)		
Bolivia	(7.1)	(46)	(6.5)		
Brazil	(147.3)	(967)	(6.7)		
Chile	13.3	106	8.0	118	10.9
Colombia	31.9	282	8.8	298	5.7
Costa Rica	(2.7)	(34)	(12.5)		
Dominican Republic	(7.0)	(26)	(3.7)		
Ecuador	(10.3)	(19)	(1.9)		
Guatemala	(9.0)	(9.0)	(1.0)		
Mexico	86	526	6.1	536	1.9
Panama	(2.4)	(17)	(7.2)		
Puerto Rico	3.5	315	90	291	-7.6

‡ in millions   * in U.S. $ † in millions U.S.

continued

WORLDWIDE TV ADVERTISING EXPENDITURES (cont'd)

Country	Pop.‡	1990 Adv. Exp.†	Adv. Exp. Per Cap.*	1991 Forecast†	Adv. Exp. % '91 vs. '90
Trinidad & Tobago	(1.3)	(6.0)	(4.5)		
Venezuela	19.8	275	13.9	264	-4.1
Total	154.5	1,504	9.7	1,507	0.2
Middle East					
Israel	(4.5)	(18)	(4.0)		
Jordan	(4.0)	(1.0)	(0.3)		
Kuwait	(2.0)	(18)	(8.9)		
Lebanon	(1.7)	(15)	(8.8)		
Oman	(1.5)	(2.0)	(1.5)		
Qatar	(0.4)	(1.0)	(0.3)		
Saudi Arabia	(13.6)	(45)	(3.3)		
Un. Arab Emirates	(1.5)	(20)	(13.1)		
Yemen	(11.2)	(1.0)	(0.1)		
Total					

‡ in millions * in U.S. $ † in millions U.S. $

Notes:

1) The figures are mostly taken from industry sources as published by two organizations: (i) Zenith Media Worldwide, the media independent representing the Saatchi and Saatchi Advertising group, and (ii) Starch INRA Hooper, on whose behalf the data were gathered by NTC Publications, based in the United Kingdom.

2) The Zenith figures cover 1990 expenditure for 38 countries. Published in July 1991, their end of year forecasts take into account 1991 first quarter measured expenditures. They have converted all their figures into US$ at the average rates of exchange for 1990. The Zenith figures are without brackets.

3) The Starch INRA Hooper figures cover a wider range of 72 countries, but only go as far as 1989 and are in brackets to differentiate them from the Zenith figures. They have been included in the table in order to fill some of the gaps, albeit with 1989 data. Like Zenith Media Worldwide they have converted their data into US$ at the prevailing annual rates of exchange.

4) The projected 1991 television expenditures for Zenith have been obtained by multiplying their 1990 figures by their forecasts of real growth for 1991. The figures are expressed in terms of 1990 constant prices using the 1990 average rates of exchange.

Source: *TBI 1992 Yearbook*

EUROPEAN SATELLITE BROADCASTERS

Channel	Satellite	Loc. (Deg.)	Tr.	Pol.	Freq. (GHz)	Hrs.	Aud. Freq. (MHz)	Video	Scramble
AFRTS Germany	Intelsat VB F15	60.0 E	79	V	11.495	24	(d)	B-MAC	B-MAC
AFRTS Turkey	Intelsat VB F15	60.0 E	69A	V	11.472	24	(d)	B-MAC	B-MAC
Antena Tres	Eutelsat I F4	7.0 E	7Eu	V	11.012	18	6.60	PAL	Nagravision
Antenne 2	TDF 1/2	19.0 W	17	R	12.034	18	(d)	D2-MAC	Clear
Antenne 2 (France)	Telecom 1C	5.0 W	R2	V	12.564	18	5.80	SECAM	Clear
BBC Wld. Serv. TV	Intelsat VI F4	27.5 W	71	V	10.995	17	6.65	PAL	SAVE
BFS3	DFS1 Kopern.	23.5 E	E7	V	12.725	10	6.65	PAL	Clear
Bravo	Intelsat VI F4	27.5 W	62A	H	11.055	12	6.65	PAL	SAVE
Canal Courses	Eutelsat II F2	10.0 E	46S	V	12.583	6	(d)	B-MAC	B-MAC
Canal J	Telecom 1C	5.0 W	R6	V	12.732	10	5.80	SECAM	Clr/Discret
Canal Jimmy	Telecom 1C	5.0 W	R6	V	12.732	5	5.80	SECAM	Clear
Canal Plus	Telecom 1C	5.0 W	R4	V	12.648	22	5.80	SECAM	Clr/Discret
Canal Plus	TDF 1/2	19.0 W	1	R	11.727	22	(d)	D2-MAC	Eurocrypt
Canal Plus (Espana)	Eutelsat I F4	7.0 E	11A	V	12.573	8	6.60	PAL	Nagravision
Canal Sante	Eutelsat II F1	13.0 E	47	V	12.625	2	5.80	SECAM	Clear
Children's Channel	Intelsat VI F4	27.5 W	61B	H	11.015	12	6.60	PAL	Clear
Children's Channel	Astra 1A	19.2 E	5	H	11.273	4	6.50	PAL	Clear
CNN International	Intelsat VI F4	27.5 W	73	V	11.155	24	6.65	PAL	Clear
Discovery Channel	Intelsat VI F4	27.5 W	63B	H	11.175	8	6.65	PAL	Clear
3SAT	Astra 1A	19.2 E	10	V	11.347	10	6.50	PAL	Clear
3SAT	DFS1 Kopern.	23.5 E	A2	H	11.526	10	6.65	PAL	Clear
3SAT	TV Sat 2	19.2 W	10	L	11.900	10	(d)	D2-MAC	Clear
Eins Plus	Astra 1B	19.2 E	19	H	11.494	4	6.50	PAL	Clear
Eins Plus	DFS1 Kopern.	23.5 E	C1	H	11.625	4	6.65	PAL	Clear
Eins Plus	TV Sat 2	19.2 W	18	L	12.054	4	(d)	D2-MAC	Clear
ET 1	Eutelsat I F4	7.0 E	5E	H	11.555	10	6.60	PAL	Clear
Euromusique/MCM	TDF 1/2	19.0 W	5	R	11.804	24	(d)	D2-MAC	Clear
EuroPACE	Eutelsat I F4	7.0 E	4W	H	11.510	2	6.60	PAL	Clear
Eurosport	Astra 1B	19.2 E	22	V	11.538	12	6.60	PAL	Clear
Eurosport	Eutelsat II F1	13.0 E	20S	H	10.971	12	6.65	PAL	Clear
Eurosport	DFS1 Kopern.	23.5 E	B1	V	11.550	12	6.65	PAL	Clear
FilmNet 24 (Scand.)	Astra 1A	19.2 E	11	H	11.362	24	(d)	PAL	Satbox
FilmNet 24 (Benelux)	Eutelsat II F1	13.0 E	34S	H	11.678	24	(d)	PAL	Satbox
Galavision	Eutelsat II F1	13.0 E	33S	H	11.59Hz	24	6.65	PAL	Clear
Galavision	PAS 1	45.0 W	19B	H	11.515	24	6.80	PAL	Clear
IRIB-1	Intelsat VA F11	63.0 E	73	V	11.155	8	6.80	SECAM	Clear
IRIB-2	Intelsat VA F11	63.0 E	71	V	10.992	6	6.80	SECAM	Clear
JSTV	Astra 1B	19.2 E	24	V	11.568	11	6.50	PAL	Clear
KinderNet	Intelsat VI F4	27.5 W	63B	H	11.175	3	6.65	PAL	Clear
La Cinq	Telecom 1C	5.0 W	R3	V	12.606	24	5.80	SECAM	Clear
La Sept	TDF 1/2	19.0 W	9	R	11.881	12	(d)	D2-MAC	Clear
Lifestyle	Astra 1A	19.2 E	5	H	11.273	15	6.50	PAL	Clear
M6	Telecom IC	5.0 W	R1	V	12.522	10	5.80	SECAM	Clear
Movie Channel, The	Astra 1B	19.2 E	18	V	11.479	24	6.60	PAL	VideoCrypt
Movie Channel, The	Marcopolo 1/2	31.0 W	20	R	12.092	24	(d)	D-MAC	Eurocypher

(d) digital

continued

EUROPEAN SATELLITE BROADCASTERS (cont'd)

Channel	Satellite	Loc. (Deg.)	Tr.	Pol.	Freq. (GHz)	Hrs.	Aud. Freq. (MHz)	Video	Scramble
MTV Europe	Astra 1A	19.2 E	15	H	11.421	24	6.50	PAL	Clear
Nordic Channel	Eutelsat II F1	13.0 E	34S	H	11.638	5	6.60	PAL	Clear
Norges Nettet	Intelsat VA F1	1.0 W	61A	H	10.969	2	(d)	D-MAC	Clear
NRK	Tele-X	5.0 E	32	L	12.322	9	(d)	D-MAC	Clear
Premiere	Astra 1B	19.2 E	17	H	11.464	15	6.50	PAL	Nagravision
Premiere	DFS Kopern.	23.5 E	E3	V	12.591	15	6.65	PAL	Nagravision
Pro 7	Astra 1A	19.2 E	17	V	11.406	24	6.50	PAL	Clear
Pro 7	DFS1 Kopern.	23.5 E	E2	H	12.558	24	6.65	PAL	Clear
Rai Due	Eutelsat II F2	10.0 E	26W	V	11.095	16	6.60	PAL	Clr/Discret
Rai Uno	Eutelsat II F2	10.0 E	25W	V	10.972	18	6.60	PAL	Clr/Discret
RIK	Eutelsat I F4	7.0 E	5E	H	11.595	4	6.60	PAL	Clear
RTL-4	Astra 1A	19.2 E	13	H	11.391	18	6.50	PAL	Clr/L'crypt
RTL Plus	Astra 1A	19.2 E	2	V	11.229	20	6.50	PAL	Clear
RTL Plus	DFS1 Kopern.	23.5 E	C2	H	11.675	20	6.65	PAL	Clear
RTL Plus	TV Sat 2	19.2 W	2	L	11.747	20	(d)	D2-MAC	Clear
Sat1	Astra 1A	19.2 E	6	V	11.288	19	6.50	PAL	Clear
Sat1	DFS1 Kopern.	23.5 E	A1	H	11.475	19	6.65	PAL	Clear
Sat1	TV Sat 2	19.2 W	6	L	11.823	19	(d)	D2-MAC	Clear
Screensport	Astra 1A	19.2 E	1	H	11.214	18	6.50	PAL	Clear
SF Succe	Intelsat VI F4	27.5 W	61A	H	10.975*	8	(d)	D-MAC	Eurocrypt S
SIP Canal Courses	Eutelsat II F2	10.0 E	46	V	12.584	6	(d)	B-MAC	B-MAC
SIS Satellite Racing	Intelsat VI F4	27.5 W	69	H	11.591	6	(d)	B-MAC	B-MAC
Sky Movies +	Astra 1A	19.2 E	16	V	11.436	24	6.50	PAL	VideoCrypt
Sky Movies +	Marcopolo 1/2	31.0 W	16	R	12.015	24	(d)	D-MAC	Eurocypher
Sky News	Astra 1A	19.2 E	12	V	11.377	24	6.50	PAL	Clear
Sky News	Marcopolo 1/2	31.0 W	4	R	11.785	24	(d)	D-MAC	Eurocypher
Sky One	Astra 1A	19.2 E	8	V	11.318	17	6.50	PAL	Clear
Sky One	Marcopolo 1/2	31.0 W	8	R	11.862	21	(d)	D-MAC	Eurocypher
Sky Sports	Astra 1B	19.2 E	20	V	11.509	11	6.50	PAL	VideoCrypt
Sky Sports	Marcopolo 1/2	31.0 W	12	R	11.938	11	(d)	D-MAC	Eurocypher
Star 1	Eutelsat II F2	10.0 E	38W	V	11.617	14	6.65	PAL	Clear
Star 1	Eutelsat II F1	13.0 E	27W	V	11.163	14	6.65	PAL	Clear
Super Channel	Eutelsat II F1	13.0 E	25W	V	10.987	20	6.65	PAL	Clear
SVT1	Intelsat VA F12	1.0 W	69B	H	11.683	6-7	(d)	D-MAC	Eurocrypt
SVT2	Intelsat VA F12	1.0 W	63B	H	11.177	6-7	(d)	D-MAC	Eurocrypt
Tele-5 (Germany)	Astra 1B	19.2 E	21	H	11.523	24	6.50	PAL	Clear
Tele-5 (Germany)	DFS1 Kopern.	23.5 E	E6	H	12.692	24	6.65	PAL	Clear
Tele-5 (Spain)	Eutelsat I F	7.0 E	1Eu	H	10.974	11	6.60	PAL	Nagravision
Teleclub	Astra 1A	19.2 E	9	H	11.332	15	6.50	PAL	Clr/Payview 3
TF1	Telecom I	5.0 W	R5	V	12.690	18	5.80	SECAM	Clear
TRT TV1	Intelsat VB F15	60.0 E	69B	H	11.647	12	6.80	PAL	Clear
TRT TV2/TV Gap	Intelsat VB F15	60.0 E	69C	H	11.683	10	6.80	PAL	Clear
TRT TV3	Intelsat VB F15	60.0 E	63A	H	11.138	8	6.80	PAL	Clear
TRT TV4	Intelsat VB F15	60.0 E	61A	H	10.974	9	6.80	PAL	Clear
TRT TV5	Eutelsat II F1	13.0 E	22S	H	11.181	7	6.60	PAL	Clear
TV 1000	Astra 1A	19.2 E	7	H	11.303	7	(d)	D2-MAC	D2-MAC

(d) digital * MHz

continued

EUROPEAN SATELLITE BROADCASTERS (cont'd)

Channel	Satellite	Loc. (Deg.)	Tr.	Pol.	Freq. (GHz)	Hrs.	Aud. Freq. (MHz)	Video	Scramble
TV3 Swed./Norway	Astra 1A	19.2 E	3	H	11.244	8	(d)	D2-MAC	Clear
TV3 Danmark	Astra 1B	19.2 E	29	H	11.641	8	(d)	D2-MAC	Eurocrypt
TV3 Norge	Astra 1B	19.2 E	31	H	11.671	8	(d)	D2-MAC	Clear
TV3 Sverige	Astra 1A	19.2 E	3	H	11.244	8	(d)	D2-MAC	Clear
TV4 Norge	Intelsat VA F12	1.0 W	63A	H	11.133	5	6.60	PAL	Clear
TV4	Tele-X	5.0 E	26	L	12.207	5	6.50	PAL	Clear
TV5 Europe	Eutelsat II F1	13.0 E	26W	V	11.080	8	6.65	PAL	Clear
TVB Beograd	Eutelsat I F4	7.0 E	3W	H	11.178	6	6.60	PAL	Clear
TVE Internacional	Eutelsat II F2	10.0 E	22S	H	11.149	14	6.60	PAL	Clear
TVN	Intelsat VA F12	1.0 W	61B	H	11.016	5	6.60	PAL	Clear
West 3	DFS1 Kopern.	23.5 E	E5	V	12.658	10	6.65	PAL	Clear
WorldNet	Eutelsat II F1	13.0 E	26W	H	11.080	4	6.60	PAL	Clear
Yest. in Commons	Intelsat VI F4	27.5 W	63B	H	11.175	6	6.65	PAL	Clear

(d) digital

TV VIEWING PER HOUSEHOLD

Year*	Hours Per Day
1949-1950	4:35
1950-1951	4:43
1951-1952	4:49
1952-1953	4:40
1953-1954	4:46
1954-1955	4:51
1955-1956	5:01
1956-1957	5:09
1957-1958	5:05
1958-1959	5:02
1959-1960	5:06
1960-1961	5:07

* broadcast year (Sep.-Aug.)

continued

TV VIEWING PER HOUSEHOLD (cont'd)

Year*	Hours Per Day
1961-1962	5:06
1962-1963	5:11
1963-1964	5:25
1964-1965	5:29
1965-1966	5:32
1966-1967	5:42
1967-1968	5:46
1968-1969	5:50
1969-1970	5:56
1970-1971	6:02
1971-1972	6:12
1972-1973	6:15
1973-1974	6:14
1974-1975	6:07
1975-1976	6:18
1976-1977	6:10
1977-1978	6:17
1978-1979	6:28
1979-1980	6:36
1980-1981	6:45
1981-1982	6:48
1982-1983	6:55
1983-1984	7:08
1984-1985	7:07
1985-1986	7:10
1986-1987	7:05
1987-1988	6:59
1988-1989	7:02
1989-1990	6:55
1990-1991	6:56

* broadcast year (Sep.-Aug.)

TOP-RATED SATURDAY MORNING CHILDREN'S PROGRAMS
(Based on Children 2-11 Rating)

Season	Rank	Network	Program	Rating %
1990-91	1	CBS	Mutant Ninja Turtles II	12.9
	2	CBS	Mutant Ninja Turtles I	11.9
	3	CBS	Garfield & Friends II	9.6
	4	ABC	Bugs Bunny/Tweety Show II	8.9
	5	ABC	Slimer! And Real Ghostbusters II	7.9
1989-90	1	ABC	Slimer! And Real Ghostbusters II	12.3
	2	ABC	Beetlejuice	11.1
	3	ABC	Slimer! And Real Ghostbusters I	10.3
	4	CBS	Muppet Babies II	10.2
	5	ABC	Bugs Bunny/Tweety Show II	10.1
1988-89	1	ABC	Bugs Bunny/Tweety Show II	12.2
	2	CBS	Garfield & Friends	12.2
	3	CBS	Pee Wee's Playhouse	11.8
	4	CBS	Muppet Babies II	11.5
	5	ABC	Slimer! And Real Ghostbusters II	11.2
1987-88	1	CBS	Pee Wee's Playhouse	13.9
	2	CBS	Muppet Babies III	12.0
	3	NBC	Alvin & Chipmunks	11.3
	4	NBC	Smurfs III	10.7
	5	NBC	Alf-Sat. Morning	10.6

Source: Nielsen Media Research - People Meter Sample

TOP MULTIPLE SYSTEM OPERATORS (MSOs)

	Company	Basic subscribers
1	Tele-Communications Inc. (TCI)*	9,475,000
2	American Television & Communications (ATC)†	4,700,000
3	UA Entertainment	2,773,000
4	Continental Cablevision	2,710,000
5	Warner Cable†	1,919,000
6	Comcast	1,661,000
7	Cox Cable	1,644,000
8	Jones Intercable	1,611,000
9	Cablevision Systems	1,611,000
10	Storer Cable	1,597,000
11	Newhouse Broadcasting	1,258,000
12	Times Mirror Cable TV	1,135,000
13	Cablevision Industries	1,121,000
14	Viacom Cable	1,069,000
15	Adelphia Communications	1,033,000
16	Sammons Communications	919,000
17	Century Communications	890,000
18	Falcon Cable	874,000
19	Paragon Communications	829,000
20	Prime Cable	695,000

* Count includes only those systems wholly owned by TCI.

† ATC and Warner Cable are both owned by Time Warner Inc., but are operated as separate divisions.

Source: *Cablevision* magazine; MSOs

I N D E X

Numbers in bold refer to main entries